Companion Dictionaries

English – Español
Spanish – Inglés

Arthur Swift Butterfield

Pan Books London and Sydney

Trademarks

The symbol ® designates entered words that we have reason to believe constitute

Trademarks

The symbol ® designates entered words that we have reason to believe constitute trademarks. However, neither the presence nor absence of such designation should be regarded as affecting the legal status of any trademark.

Marcas registradas

Hay ciertas palabras apuntadas que tenemos motivo para creer ue forman marcas registradas, y que se senalan por el simbolo ® . Sin embargo, la personalidad juridica de cualquier marca registrada no se afecta ni por la presencia ni por la ausencia de tal simbolo.

First published 1982 by Pan Books Ltd
This revised edition first published 1986
by Pan Books Ltd,
Cavaye Place, London SW10 9PG
9 8 7 6 5 4 3
© Laurence Urdang Associates 1982
ISBN 0 330 29347 8
Printed and bound in Great Britain by Hunt Barnard Printing Ltd., Aylesbury, Bucks.

Abbreviations/Abreviaciones

adj adjective, adjetivo
adv adverb, adverbio
aero aeronautics, aeronáutica
agr agriculture, agricultura
anat anatomy, anatomía
arch architecture
arq arquitectura
art article, artículo
astrol astrology, astrología
astron astronomy, astronomía
auto automobile, automóvil
bot botany, botánica
chem chemistry
coll colloquial
com comercio
comm commerce
conj conjunction, conjunción
culin culinario
derog derogatory
econ economics, economía
elec electricity, electricidad
f feminine, femenino
fam familiar, colloquial
ferr ferrocarril
fig figurative, figurativo
foto fotografía
geog geography, geografía
geol geology, geología
gram gramática
gramm grammar
impol impolite

interj interjection, interjección
interrog interrogative, interrogativo
invar invariable
jur jurisprudencia
m masculine, masculino
mar marítimo
mat matemáticas
math mathematics
mec mecánica
mech mechanics
med medicine, medicina
mil military, militar
mot motoring
n noun
naut nautical
phone telephone
phot photography
pl plural
pol politics, política
prep preposition, preposición
pron pronoun, pronombre
psych psychology
quím química
rail railways
rel religion, religión
s sustantivo
sing singular
tech technology, technical
tecn tecnología
v verb, verbo
V vide (see, vea)
zool zoology, zoología

Spanish pronunciation

a cada ['kaða]
e entre ['entre]
i libro ['liβro]
o loco ['loko]
u lunes ['lunes]
j nieve ['njeβe]
b bueno ['bweno]
d desde ['desðe]
f fácil ['faθil]
g grande ['grande]
k poco ['poko]
l salud [sa'luð]

m hombre ['ombre]
n noche ['notʃe]
p lápiz ['lapiθ]
r cerca ['θerka]
rr perro ['perro]
s servir [ser'βir]
t todo ['toðo]
w luego ['lwego]
θ cerveza [θer'βeθa]
β hábil ['aβil]
tʃ muchacho [mu'tʃatʃo]
ð ciudad [θju'ðað]
ʎ calle ['kaʎe]
ɲ señor [se'ɲor]
x ojo, ágil ['oxo], ['axil]

The symbol ' indicates that the following syllable should be stressed.

Pronunciación del inglés

a hat [hat]
e bell [bel]
i big [big]
o dot [dot]
ʌ bun [bʌn]
u book [buk]
ə alone [ə'loun]
a: card [ka:d]
ə: word [wə:d]
i: team [ti:m]
o: torn [to:n]
u: spoon [spu:n]
ai die [dai]
ei ray [rei]
oi toy [toi]
au how [hau]
ou road [roud]
eə lair [leə]
iə fear [fiə]
uə poor [puə]
b back [bak]
d dull [dʌl]
f find [faind]

g gaze [geiz]
h hop [hop]
j yell [jel]
k cat [kat]
l life [laif]
m mouse [maus]
n night [nait]
p pick [pik]
r rose [rouz]
s sit [sit]
t toe [tou]
v vest [vest]
w week [wi:k]
z zoo [zu:]
ө think [өiŋk]
ð those [ðouz]
ʃ shoe [ʃu:]
ʒ treasure ['treʒə]
tʃ chalk [tʃo:k]
dʒ jump [dʒʌmp]
ŋ sing [siŋ]

El signo de acentuación ' se coloca directamente delante de la sílaba aguda.
El signo , se coloca delante de la sílaba aguda secundaria.

Guide to the dictionary

The infinitives of all irregular verbs appearing in the headword list are marked with an asterisk. These and examples of Spanish stem-changing verbs, and the tenses in which such changes occur, can be found in the following verb tables. Composite verbs, such as *deshacer* from *hacer*, are also included under the parent verb.

The Spanish alphabet includes three symbols or combinations of letters that are not found in the English alphabet. These are **ch, ll,** and **ñ,** which are treated as individual letters and follow **c, l,** and **n** respectively in the alphabetical order.

The plurals of almost all Spanish nouns are formed regularly by the addition of *s* or *es* to the singular form. Occasional irregular plural forms are shown immediately after the part of speech referring to the headword. Some nouns do not change in the plural and these are marked *invar* (invariable).

Adverbs are regularly formed by adding *-mente* to the feminine (or occasionally masculine) form of the adjective, and are not normally shown unless a different translation is called for.

Guía al diccionario

Los plurales irregulares de los sustantivos se hallen junto al encabezamiento. Las categorías siguientes de los plurales se consideran regulares en inglés:

cat   cats
glass   glasses
fly   flies
half   halves
wife   wives

Los verbos irregulares en la lista de encabezamientos se señalan por medio de un asterisco y se hallen en las tablas de los verbos.

Los adverbios regulares no se indican. Los adverbios ingleses que se forman añadiendo -*(al)ly* al adjetivo, se consideran regulares. Los adverbios españoles que se forman añadiendo -*mente* al adjetivo femenino (de vez en cuando masculino), se consideran regulares y no se indican sino exigiendo una traducción diferente.

Spanish verb tables

1. The final consonants preceding the infinitive endings (**-ar**, **-er**, and **-(u)ir**) change, for reasons of euphony, when they occur before certain vowels.

Infinitives	Change	Before
-car	the c to qu	e
-cer	the c to z	a or o
-cir	the c to z	a or o
-gir	the g to j	a or o
-guir	the gu to g	a or o
-quir	the qu to c	a or o
-gar	the ga to gu	e
-zar	the z to c	e

2. Verbs adding **z**. There are numerous verbs ending in **-ecer** (*e.g.* **parecer**) and other verbs ending in a vowel + **-cer** (*e.g.* **conocer**). When the ending of these verbs is **a** or **o** (specifically, present indicative 1 *sing*, and present subjunctive, all persons), a **z** is added before the **c** (*e.g.* **parezco**, **conozco**).

3. Verbs in the following tables change the vowels in their stems in certain persons and tenses. The sections below are arranged according to the vowel change involved and are followed by a selection of verbs exemplifying the change. Note that composite verbs (*e.g.* **desplegar**) are conjugated in the same way as their base forms (*e.g.* **plegar**).

    (i) Stem changes **e** to **ie** in present indicative and present subjunctive 1, 2, 3 *sing* and 3 *pl*, and in imperative *sing*.

acertar	aterrar	comenzar	dentar	entender
acrecentar	aventar	concertar	desalentar	entesar
aferrar	calentar	confesar	descender	fregar
apretar	cegar	contender	desempedrar	gobernar
arrendar	cerner	decentar	despernar	hacendar
ascender	cerrar	defender	despertar	heder

helar	merendar	recentar	sembrar	tentar
hender	negar	recomendar	sentar	trascender
herrar	nevar	regar	serrar	trasegar
incensar	pensar	remendar	sosegar	trasverter
invernar	perder	restregar	soterrar	tropezar
manifestar	plegar	reventar	temblar	verter
mentar	quebrar	segar	tender	

(ii) Stem changes o to **ue** in present indicative and present subjunctive 1, 2, 3 *sing* and 3 *pl*, and in imperative *sing*.

acordar	colar	jugar	resollar	soñar
acostar	colgar	moler	rodar	torcer
aforar	contar	mostrar	rogar	tostar
almorzar	costar	mover	solar	trocar
apostar	doler	poblar	soldar	tronar
aprobar	encontrar	probar	soler	voler
avergonzar	forzar	recordar	soltar	volcar
azolar	holgar	renovar	sonar	volver

(iii) Stem changes from e to **i** in present indicative 1, 2, 3 *sing* and 3 *pl*; preterite 3 *sing* and *pl*; present, imperfect, and future subjunctives, all persons; imperative *sing* and present participle.

colegir	derretir	henchir	regir	seguir
concebir	elegir	medir	rendir	servir
corregir	gemir	pedir	repetir	vestir

(iv) Stem changes e to **ie** in present indicative and present subjunctive 1, 2, 3 *sing* and 3 *pl*; imperative *sing*.
Stem changes e to **i** in preterite 3 *sing* and *pl*; present subjunctive 1, 2 *pl*; imperfect and future subjunctives, all persons; present participle.

advertir	digerir	hervir	preferir
cernir	divertir	inferir	requerir
convertir	hendir	ingerir	sentir
diferir	herir	mentir	sugerir

4. The verbs shown below change in various ways. In the table, 1 and 3 *sing* are shown under the present indicative and 1 *sing* under the preterite and future.

Infinitive	Present Indicative	Preterite	Future	Past Participle
andar	ando, anda	anduve	andaré	andado
caber	quepo, cabe	cupe	cabré	cabido
caer	caigo, cae	caí	caeré	caido
dar	doy, da	di	daré	dado
decir	digo, dice	dije	diré	dicho
dormir	duermo, duerme	dormí	dormiré	dormido
erguir	yergo, yergue	erguí	erguiré	erguido
errar	yerro, yerra	erré	erraré	errado
estar	estoy, está	estuve	estaré	estado
haber	he, ha	hube	habré	habido
hacer	hago, hace	hice	haré	hecho
huir	huyo, huye	huí	huiré	huido
ir	voy, va	fui	iré	ido
oir	oigo, oye	oí	oiré	oido
oler	huelo, huele	olí	oleré	olido
poder	puedo, puede	pude	podré	podido
poner	pongo, pone	puse	pondré	puesto
querer	quiero, quiere	quise	querré	querido
reducir	reduzco, reduce	reduje	reduciré	reducido
reír	río, ríe	reí	reiré	reido
saber	sé, sabe	supe	sabré	sabido
ser	soy, es	fui	seré	sido
tener	tengo, tiene	tuve	tendré	tenido
traer	traigo, trae	traje	traeré	traído
valer	valgo, vale	valí	valdré	valido
venir	vengo, viene	vine	vendré	venido
ver	veo, ve	vi	veré	visto

Verbos irregulares ingleses

Infinitivo	Pretérito	Participo Pasado	Infinitive	Pretérito	Participo Pasado
abide	abode	abode	**deal**	dealt	dealt
arise	arose	arisen	**dig**	dug	dug
awake	awoke	awoken	**do**	did	done
be	was	been	**draw**	drew	drawn
bear	bore	borne *or* born	**dream**	dreamed *or* dreamt	dreamed *or* dreamt
beat	beat	beaten	**drink**	drank	drunk
become	became	become	**drive**	drove	driven
begin	began	begun	**dwell**	dwelt	dwelt
behold	beheld	beheld	**eat**	ate	eaten
bend	bent	bent	**fall**	fell	fallen
bet	bet	bet	**feed**	fed	fed
beware			**feel**	felt	felt
bid	bid	bidden *or* bid	**fight**	fought	fought
			find	found	found
bind	bound	bound	**flee**	fled	fled
bite	bit	bitten	**fling**	flung	flung
bleed	bled	bled	**fly**	flew	flown
blow	blew	blown	**forbid**	forbade	forbidden
break	broke	broken	**forget**	forgot	forgotten
breed	bred	bred	**forgive**	forgave	forgiven
bring	brought	brought	**forsake**	forsook	forsaken
build	built	built	**freeze**	froze	frozen
burn	burnt *or* burned	burnt *or* burned	**get**	got	got
			give	gave	given
burst	burst	burst	**go**	went	gone
buy	bought	bought	**grind**	ground	ground
can	could		**grow**	grew	grown
cast	cast	cast	**hang**	hung *or* hanged	hung *or* hanged
catch	caught	caught			
choose	chose	chosen	**have**	had	had
cling	clung	clung	**hear**	heard	heard
come	came	come	**hide**	hid	hidden
cost	cost	cost	**hit**	hit	hit
creep	crept	crept	**hold**	held	held
cut	cut	cut	**hurt**	hurt	hurt

Infinitivo	Pretérito	Participo Pasado	Infinitivo	Pretérito	Participo Pasado
keep	kept	kept	say	said	said
kneel	knelt	knelt	see	saw	seen
knit	knitted	knitted	seek	sought	sought
	or knit	or knit	sell	sold	sold
know	knew	known	send	sent	sent
lay	laid	laid	set	set	set
lead	led	led	sew	sewed	sewn
lean	leant	leant			or sewed
	or leaned	or leaned	shake	shook	shaken
leap	leapt	leapt	shear	sheared	sheared
	or leaped	or leaped			or shorn
learn	learnt	learnt	shed	shed	shed
	or learned	or learned	shine	shone	shone
leave	left	left	shoe	shod	shod
lend	lent	lent	shoot	shot	shot
let	let	let	show	showed	shown
lie	lay	lain	shrink	shrank	shrunk
light	lit	lit	shut	shut	shut
	or lighted	or lighted	sing	sang	sung
lose	lost	lost	sink	sank	sunk
make	made	made	sit	sat	sat
may	might		sleep	slept	slept
mean	meant	meant	slide	slid	slid
meet	met	met	sling	slung	slung
mow	mowed	mown	slink	slunk	slunk
must			slit	slit	slit
ought			smell	smelt	smelt
pay	paid	paid		or smelled	or smelled
put	put	put	sow	sowed	sown
quit	quitted	quitted			or sowed
	or quit	or quit	speak	spoke	spoken
read	read	read	speed	sped	sped
rid	rid	rid			or speeded or speeded
ride	rode	ridden	spell	spelt	spelt
ring	rang	rung		or spelled	or spelled
rise	rose	risen	spend	spent	spent
run	ran	run	spill	spilt	spilt
saw	sawed	sawn		or spilled	or spilled
		or sawed	spin	spun	spun

Infinitivo	Pretérito	Participo Pasado	Infinitivo	Pretérito	Participo Pasado
spit	spat	spat	**swim**	swam	swum
split	split	split	**swing**	swung	swung
spread	spread	spread	**take**	took	taken
spring	sprang	sprung	**teach**	taught	taught
stand	stood	stood	**tear**	tore	torn
steal	stole	stolen	**tell**	told	told
stick	stuck	stuck	**think**	thought	thought
sting	stung	stung	**throw**	threw	thrown
stink	stank	stunk	**thrust**	thrust	thrust
	or stunk		**tread**	trod	trodden
stride	strode	stridden	**wake**	woke	woken
strike	struck	struck	**wear**	wore	worn
string	strung	strung	**weave**	wove	woven
strive	strove	striven	**weep**	wept	wept
swear	swore	sworn	**win**	won	won
sweep	swept	swept	**wind**	wound	wound
swell	swelled	swollen	**wring**	wrung	wrung
	or swelled		**write**	wrote	written

English—Español

A

a, an [ə, ən] *art* un, -a.
aback [ə'bak] *adv* be taken aback quedar desconcertado.
abandon [ə'bandən] *v* abandonar. *n* abandono *m*.
abashed [ə'baʃt] *adj* avergonzado, confundido.
abate [ə'beit] *v* disminuir. abatement *n* disminución *f*.
abattoir ['abətwaː] *n* matadero *m*.
abbey ['abi] *n* abadía *f*. abbess *n* abadesa *f*. abbot *n* abad *m*.
abbreviate [ə'briːvieit] *v* abreviar. abbreviation *n* abreviación *f*.
abdicate ['abdikeit] *v* abdicar. abdication *n* abdicación *f*.
abdomen ['abdəmən] *n* abdomen *m*. abdominal *adj* abdominal.
abduct [əb'dʌkt] *v* raptar. abduction *n* rapto *m*.
aberration [abə'reiʃən] *n* extravío *m*, engaño *m*. abberant *adj* extraviado.
abet [ə'bet] *v* instigar, inducir.
abeyance [ə'beiəns] *n* in abeyance en suspenso.
abhor [əb'hoː] *v* aborrecer, odiar. abhorrence *n* aborrecimiento *m*, odio *m*. abhorrent *adj* aborrecible.
*abide [ə'baid] *v* residir, habitar; (*tolerate*) aguantar, sufrir. abide by atenerse a, cumplir con.
ability [ə'biləti] *n* habilidad *f*, capacidad *f*. to the best of one's ability lo mejor que pueda.
abject [,abdʒekt] *adj* abyecto.
ablaze [ə'bleiz] *adj* en llamas.
able ['eibl] *adj* capaz; (*talented*) hábil.

able-bodied *adj* entero. able-bodied seaman marinero de primera *m*. be able poder. ably *adv* hábilmente.
abnormal [ab'noːml] *adj* anormal. abnormality *n* anormalidad *f*.
aboard [ə'boːd] *adv*, *prep* a bordo (de). all aboard! ¡viajeros a bordo! go aboard embarcarse.
abode [ə'boud] *n* domicilio *m*.
abolish [ə'boliʃ] *v* abolir. abolition *n* abolición *f*.
abominable [ə'bominəbl] *adj* abominable. abominate *v* abominar (de). abomination *n* abominación *f*.
Aborigine [abə'ridʒini] *n* aborigen *m*.
abortion [ə'boːʃən] *n* aborto *m*. abort *v* abortar.
abound [ə'baund] *v* abundar.
about [ə'baut] *adv* (*approximately*) casi, alrededor de, más o menos. all about por todas partes. *prep* (*place*) alrededor de; (*near*) cerca de; (*concerning*) de, acerca de.
above [ə'bʌv] *adv* encima, arriba. *prep* (*place*) encima de, sobre; (*number*) más de; (*rank*) superior a. above-mentioned *adj* susodicho, citado.
abrasion [ə'breiʒən] *n* raspadura *f*. abrasive *adj* raspante.
abreast [ə'brest] *adv* de frente. keep abreast of or with ir al paso de.
abridge [ə'bridʒ] *v* abreviar, resumir. abridgement *n* abreviación *f*, resumen *m*.
abroad [ə'broːd] *adv* en el extranjero.
abrupt [ə'brʌpt] *adj* abrupto, brusco.
abscess ['abses] *n* absceso *m*.
abscond [əb'skond] *v* fugarse.
absent ['absənt] *adj* ausente. absent-minded *adj* distraído. absent onself ausentarse. absence *n* ausencia *f*. absentee *n* ausente *m*, *f*. absenteeism *n* absentismo *m*.

absolute ['absəluɪt] *adj* absoluto. **absolutely** *adv* absolutamente; (*interj*) categóricamente. **absolutism** *n* absolutismo *m*.

absolve [əb'zɔlv] *v* absolver. **absolution** *n* absolución *f*.

absorb [əb'zɔɪb] *v* absorber. **be absorbed in** enfrascarse en. **absorbent** *adj* absorbente. **absorbing** *adj* (*coll*) sumamente interesante.

abstain [əb'stein] *v* abstenerse (de). **abstention** *n* abstención *f*. **abstinence** *n* abstinencia *f*.

abstemious [əb'stiːmiəs] *adj* abstemio.

abstract ['abstrakt; *v* ab'strakt] *adj* abstracto. *n* resumen *m*. *v* extractar. **abstractedly** *adv* distraidamente. **abstraction** *n* abstracción *f*.

absurd [əb'səɪd] *adj* absurdo. **absurdity** *n* absurdidad *f*.

abundance [ə'bʌndəns] *n* abundancia *f*. **abundant** *adj* abundante.

abuse [ə'bjuːz; *n* ə'bjuːs] *v* abusar (de). *n* abuso *m*; injuria *f*. **abusive** *adj* abusivo; injurioso.

abyss [ə'bis] *n* abismo *m*. **abysmal** *adj* abismal; profundo.

academy [ə'kadəmi] *n* academia *f*. **academic** *adj* académico.

accede [ak'siːd] *v* acceder.

accelerate [ək'seləreit] *v* acelerar. **acceleration** *n* aceleración *f*. **accelerator** *n* acelerador *m*.

accent ['aksənt] *n* acento *m*. *v* acentuar.

accept [ək'sept] *v* aceptar. **acceptable** *adj* aceptable. **acceptance** *n* aceptación *f*.

access ['akses] *n* acceso *m*. **accessible** *adj* asequible.

accessory [ək'sesəri] *nm, adj* accessorio. *n* (*law*) cómplice *m, f*. **accessories** *pl n*, (*mot, etc.*) complementos *m pl*.

accident ['aksidənt] *n* accidente *m*. **by accident** sin querer, por casualidad. **accidental** *adj* accidental.

acclaim [ə'kleim] *v* aclamar, aplaudir. *n* also **acclamation** aclamación *f*, aplauso *m*.

acclimatize [ə'klaimətaiz] *v* aclimatar.

accolade ['akəleid] *n* acolada *f*.

accommodate [ə'kɔmədeit] *v* acomodar; (*lodge*) alojar, hospedar; adaptar; (*provide*) proveer (de). **accommodating** *adj* complaciente. **accommodation** *n* alojamiento *m*.

accompany [ə'kʌmpəni] *v* acompañar. **accompaniment** *n* acompañamiento *m*. **accompanist** *n* acompañante, -a *m, f*.

accomplice [ə'kʌmplis] *n* cómplice *m, f*.

accomplish [ə'kʌmpliʃ] *v* cumplir. **accomplished** *adj* (*talented*) talentoso. **accomplishment** *n* efectuación *f*; talentos *m pl*.

accord [ə'kɔːd] *v* conceder; concordar. *n* acuerdo *m*. **of one's own accord** espontáneamente. **in accordance with** conforme a. **accordingly** *adv* en consecuencia. **according to** según.

accordion [ə'kɔːdiən] *n* acordeón *m*.

accost [ə'kɔst] *v* abordar.

account [ə'kaunt] *n* (*bank, etc.*) cuenta *f*; (*narrative*) relato *m*; (*status*) importancia *f*. **on account of** a causa de. **on no account** de ninguna manera. **take into account** tener en cuenta. **account for** dar una explicación de. **accountant** *n* contador *m*; (*chartered*) contador colegiado.

accrue [ə'kruː] *v* crecer.

accumulate [ə'kjuːmjuleit] *v* acumular. **accumulation** *n* acumulación *f*.

accurate ['akjurət] *adj* exacto. **accuracy** *n* precisión *f*.

accuse [ə'kjuːz] *v* acusar. **accusation** *n* acusación *f*. **the accused** acusado, -a *m, f*.

accustom [ə'kʌstəm] *v* acostumbrar.

ace [eis] *n* as *m*. **within an ace of** de dos dedos de.

ache [eik] *n* dolor *m*. *v* doler.

achieve [ə'tʃiːv] *v* ejecutar. **achievement** *n* ejecución *f*; (*feat*) hazaña *f*.

acid ['asid] *nm, adj* ácido. **acidity** *n* acidez *f*.

acknowledge [ək'nɔlidʒ] *v* reconocer, aceptar. **acknowledge receipt of** acusar recibo de. **acknowledgement** *n* reconocimiento *m*; acuse de recibo *m*.

acne ['akni] *n* acné *m*.

acorn ['eikɔɪn] *n* bellota *f*.

acoustic [ə'kuːstik] *adj* acústico. **acoustics** *pl n* acústica *f sing*.

acquaint [ə'kweint] *v* informar, avisar. **acquaintance** *n* (*knowledge*) conocimiento *m*; (*person*) conocido, -a *m, f*. **be acquainted with** conocer(a).

acquiesce [akwi'es] *v* consentir, conformarse. **acquiescence** *n* conformidad *f*. **acquiescent** *adj* sumiso.

acquire [ə'kwaiə] *v* adquirir. **acquisition** *n* adquisición *f*. **acquisitive** *adj* adquisitivo; (*derog*) ahorrativo.

acquit [ə'kwit] v absolver. **acquit oneself** portarse. **acquittal** (*law*) absolución *f*.

acrid ['akrid] *adj* acre.

acrimonious ['akriməni] *n* acrimonia *f*. **acrimonious** *adj* áspero.

acrobat ['akrəbat] *n* acróbata *m*, *f*. **acrobatic** *adj* acrobático. **acrobatics** *pl n* acrobacia *f sing*.

across [ə'kros] *adv* a través, al través. *prep* a través de, al través de, de través de; al otro lado de, del otro lado de.

acrylic [ə'krilik] *adj* acrílico.

act [akt] v (*theatre*) representar; (*function*) funcionar, marchar; (*behave*) comportarse; (*take action*) obrar, tomar medidas; (*affect*) afectar. *n* acto *m*, acción *f*; obra *f*; (*law*) decreto; (theatre) acto *m*. **actor** *n* actor *m*. **actress** *n* actriz *f*.

action ['akʃən] *n* acción *f*, hecho *m*; (*mil*) acción *f*, batalla *f*; (*mech*) mecanismo *m*. **bring an action against** entablar demanda contra. **put out of action** inutilizar.

active ['aktiv] *adj* activo. **activate** v activar. **activist** *n* activista *m*, *f*. **activity** *n* actividad *f*; movimiento *m*.

actual ['aktʃuəl] *adj* verdadero, efectivo. **actually** *adv* en realidad.

actuate ['aktjueit] v mover; accionar.

acupuncture ['akjupʌŋktʃə] *n* acupuntura *f*.

acute [ə'kjuːt] *adj* agudo.

adamant ['adəmənt] *adj* firme, seguro.

Adam's apple [adəm'zapl] *n* nuez de la garganta *f*.

adapt [ə'dapt] v adaptar; ajustar; (*play, book*) refundir; (*music*) arreglar. **adaptable** *adj* adaptable. **adaptation** *n* adaptación *f*; refundición *f*; arreglo *m*. **adapter** *n* (*theatre*) refundidor *m*; (*elec*) enchufe de reducción *m*.

add [ad] v añadir; (*increase*) aumentar. **add up** sumar. **add up to** subir a. **addition** *n* el añadir *m*; (*math*) suma *f*, adición *f*. **additional** *adj* adicional.

addendum [ə'dendəm] *n invar* adenda *f*.

adder ['adə] *n* víbora *f*.

addict ['adikt] *n* partidario, -a *m*, *f*; (*drugs*) toxicómano, -a *m*, *f*. **addiction** *n* adicción *f*; propensión *f* **be addicted to** ser adicto a.

additive ['aditiv] *n* aditivo *m*.

address [ə'dres] v (*letter*) dirigir; (*meeting*, *etc.*) pronunciar un discurso ante. **address oneself to** dirigirse. *n* (*postal*) dirección *f*; (*speech*) discurso *m*; (*envelope*) sobrescrito *m*. **addressee** *n* destinatario, -a *m*, *f*.

adenoids ['adənoidz] *pl n* amígdalas vegetaciones *f pl*.

adept [ə'dept] *nm*, *adj* experto.

adequate ['adikwət] *adj* adecuado, suficiente.

adhere [əd'hiə] v pegarse; (*to a policy*) adherirse a. **adhesion** *n* adhesión *f*. **adhesive** *adj* adhesivo. **adhesive tape** esparadrapo *m*.

adherent [əd'hiərənt] *n* partidario, -a *m*, *f*.

adjacent [ə'dʒeisənt] *adj* próximo, contiguo.

adjective ['adʒiktiv] *n* adjetivo *m*.

adjoin [ə'dʒoin] v lindar (con). **adjoining** *adj* contiguo.

adjourn [ə'dʒəːn] v aplazar; (*session*) levantar la sesión. **adjournment** *n* aplazamiento *m*; (*of a session*) suspensión *f*.

adjudicate [ə'dʒuːdikeit] v adjudicar; (*law*) juzgar. **adjudication** *n* adjudicación *f*; (*law*) fallo *m*. **adjudicator** *n* árbitro *m*.

adjust [ə'dʒʌst] v arreglar; (*tech*) ajustar. **adjustment** *n* arreglo *m*; ajuste *m*.

ad-lib ['ad'lib] *adv* a voluntad, a discreción. v improvisar.

administer [əd'ministə] v administrar; (*law*) aplicar; (*med*) suministrar. **administration** *n* administración *f*; (*ministry*) gobierno *m*. **administrative** *adj* administrativo. **administrator** *n* administrador *m*.

admiral ['admərəl] *n* almirante *m*.

admire [əd'maiə] v admirar. **admirable** *adj* admirable. **admiration** *n* admiración *f*.

admit [əd'mit] v dar entrada a; (*concede*) conceder; (*acknowledge*) reconocer. **admission** *n* entrada *f*; (*acknowledgement*) confesión *f*.

adolescence [adə'lesns] *n* adolescencia *f*. **adolescent** *n(m + f)*, *adj* adolescente.

adopt [ə'dopt] v adoptar; (*report*) aprobar. **adopted** *adj* (*child*) adoptivo. **adoption** *n* adopción *f*.

adore [ə'doː] v adorar. **adoration** *n* adoración *f*.

adorn [ə'doːn] v adornar, embellecer. **adornment** *n* adorno *m*.

adrenaline [ə'drenəlin] *n* adrenalina *f*.

adrift [ə'drift] *adv* a la deriva.

adroit [ə'droit] *adj* diestro, hábil.

adulation [adju'leiʃən] *n* adulación *f*.

adult ['adʌlt] *n*, *adj* adulto, -a.

adulterate [ə'dʌltəreit] *v* adulterar.

adultery [ə'dʌltəri] *n* adulterio *m*. **adulter-er** *n* adúltero, -a *m*, *f*.

advance [əd'vɑːns] *v* adelantar; avanzar. *n* progreso *m*, avance *m*, adelanto *m*; (*cash*) anticipo *m*.

advantage [əd'vɑntidʒ] *n* ventaja *f*. **take advantage of** aprovecharse de. **advantageous** *adj* ventajoso.

advent ['advənt] *n* advenimiento *m*. **Advent** *n* Adviento *m*.

adventure [əd'ventʃə] *n* aventura *f*; (*comm*) especulación *f*. **adventurer** *n* aventurero *m*. **adventurous** *adj* aventurero.

adverb ['advəːb] *n* adverbio *m*.

adversary ['advəsəri] *n* adversario, -a *m*, *f*.

adverse ['advəːs] *adj* adverso. **adversity** *n* adversidad *f*.

advertise ['advətaiz] *v* anunciar; publicar. **advertisement** *n* anuncio *m*. **advertising** *n* publicidad *f*.

advise [əd'vaiz] *v* aconsejar; avisar. **advisable** *adj* conveniente. **advisedly** *adv* con intención. **adviser** *n* consejero *m*. **advice** *n* consejo *m*.

advocate ['advəkeit] *v* recomendar.

aerial ['eəriəl] *adj* aéreo. *n* antena *f*.

aerodynamics [eərədai'namiks] *n* aerodinámica *f sing*.

aeronautics [eərə'nɔːtiks] *n* aeronáutica *f sing*.

aeroplane ['eərəplein] *n* avión *m*.

aerosol ['eərəsol] *n* aerosol *m*.

aesthetic [iːs'θetik] *adj* estético. **aesthetics** *n* estética *f sing*.

affair [ə'feə] *n* asunto *m*; episodio *m*; (*love*) aventura amorosa *f*. **affairs** (*business*) negocios *m pl*.

affect¹ [ə'fekt] *v* (*influence*) influir en; (*move*) conmover.

affect² [ə'fekt] *v* (*pretend*) afectar.

affection [ə'fekʃən] *n* cariño *m*.

affiliate [ə'filieit] *v* afiliarse (a). **affiliation** *n* afiliación *f*.

affinity [ə'finəti] *n* afinidad *f*.

affirm [ə'fəːm] *v* afirmar. **affirmation** *n* afirmación *f*. **affirmative** *adj* afirmativo.

affix [ə'fiks] *v* fijar; añadir; pegar; poner.

afflict [ə'flikt] *v* aflijir, aquejar. **affliction** *n* aflicción *f*, dolor *m*.

affluent ['afluənt] *adj* afluente, opulento. **affluence** *n* afluencia *f*, opulencia *f*.

afford [ə'fɔːd] *v* tener medios; (*produce*) dar; ofrecer.

affront [ə'frʌnt] *v* afrentar. *n* afrenta *f*, ofensa *f*.

afloat [ə'flout] *adv* a flote.

afoot [ə'fut] *adv* a pie; (*fig*) en proyecto.

aforesaid [ə'fɔːsed] *adj* susodicho, mencionado.

afraid [ə'freid] *adj* temeroso, espantado. **be afraid** tener miedo (a *or* de).

afresh [ə'freʃ] *adv* de nuevo.

Africa ['afrikə] *n* África *f*. **African** *n*, *adj* africano, -a.

aft [ɑːft] *adv* a popa.

after ['ɑːftə] *prep* (*time*) después de; (*place*) detrás de; tras. *adv* (*time*) después; (*place*) detrás. *conj* después (de) que. **after all** con todo. **afterwards** *adv* después. **after-effect** *n* consecuencia *f*. **aftershave** *n* loción de afeitar *f*.

afternoon [ɑːftə'nuːn] *n* tarde *f*. **good afternoon!** ¡buenas tardes!

again [ə'gen] *adv* de nuevo, otra vez; además. **again and again** aún una y otra vez. **now and again** de vez en cuando.

against [ə'genst] *prep* contra; (*touching*) tocante.

age [eidʒ] *n* edad *f*; (*era*) época *f*. **of age** mayor de edad. **under age** menor de edad. *v* envejecer. **aged** *adj* de la edad de; (*old*) viejo.

agency ['eidʒənsi] *n* agencia *f*; mediación *f*.

agenda [ə'dʒendə] *n* agenda *f*.

agent ['eidʒənt] *n* agente *m*, *f*; (*comm*) representante *m*, *f*.

aggravate ['agrəveit] *v* agravar; (*coll*) exasperar. **aggravation** *n* agravamiento *m*; (*coll*) irritación *f*.

aggregate ['agrigət] *m*, *adj* agregado. *v* agregar, juntar.

aggression [ə'greʃən] *n* agresión *f*. **aggressive** *adj* agresivo. **aggressiveness** *n* belicosidad *f*. **agressor** *n* agresor, -a *m*, *f*.

aghast [ə'gɑːst] *adj* horrorizado.

agile ['adʒail] *adj* ágil, ligero. **agility** *n* agilidad *f*.

agitate ['adʒiteit] *v* agitar, excitar. **agitate for** luchar por. **agitation** *n* agitación *f*; perturbación *f*.

agnostic [ag'nostik] *n*, *adj* agnóstico, -a. **agnosticism** *n* agnosticismo *m*.

ago [ə'gou] *adv* hace, ha. **long ago** hace mucho tiempo. **a short time ago** hace poco.

agog [ə'gog] *adj* ansioso.

agony ['agəni] *n* agonía *f*, angustia *f*. **agonize** *v* atormentar.

agree [ə'griː] *v* estar de acuerdo, convenir (en); (*consent*) consentir (en); (*gram*) concordar; (*correspond*) estar conforme (con). **agreeable** *adj* agradable. **agreement** *n* (*pact*) pacto *m*; (*comm*) contrato *m*.

agriculture ['agrikʌltʃə] *n* agricultura *f*. **agricultural** *adj* agrícola.

aground [ə'graund] *adv* encallado. **run aground** encallar, varar.

ahead [ə'hed] *adv* delante, al frente. **be ahead** estar adelante. **go ahead!** ¡adelante!

aid [eid] *v* ayudar, socorrer. *n* ayuda *f*. **in aid of** en beneficio de. **first aid** primera cura. **go to the aid of** acudir en defensa de.

aim [eim] *v* (*weapon*) apuntar (a); (*remark*) dirigir (a). *n* (*weapon*) puntería *f*; (*fig*) propósito *m*, meta *f*, blanco *m*. **aimless** *adj* sin objeto. **aimlessly** *adv* a la ventura.

air [eə] *n* aire *m*; (*music*) aire *m*, tonada *f*; (*aspect*) aspecto *m*. *v* airear, ventilar. **airbed** ['eəbed] *n* colchón de viento *m*.

airborne ['eəbɔin] *adj* en el aire.

aircraft ['eəkraift] *n* avión *m*. **aircraft-carrier** *n* portaaviones *m invar*.

airfield ['eəfiild] *n* campo de aviación *m*.

air force *n* fuerza *or* flota aérea *f*.

air-hostess *n* azafata *f*.

air lift *n* puente aéreo *m*.

airline ['eəlain] *n* línea aérea *f*.

airmail ['eəmeil] *n* correo aéreo *m*.

airport ['eəpɔit] *n* aeropuerto *m*.

air-raid *n* bombardeo aéreo *m*.

airtight ['eətait] *adj* hermético, herméticamente cerrado.

airy ['eəri] *adj* aéreo; (*flippant*) frívolo.

aisle [ail] *n* nave lateral *f*.

ajar [ə'dʒaɪ] *adv* entreabierto, entornado.

alabaster ['aləbaistə] *n* alabastro *m*. *adj* alabastrino.

alarm [ə'laɪm] *n* alarma *f*. *v* alarmar. **alarm clock** *n* despertador *m*.

alas [ə'las] *interj* ¡ay!

Albania [al'beinjə] *n* Albania *f*. **Albanian** *n*, *adj* albanés, -esa.

albatross ['albətros] *n* albatros *m*.

albino [al'biɪnou] *n*, *adj* albino, -a.

album ['albəm] *n* álbum *m*.

alchemy ['alkəmi] *n* alquimia *f*. **alchemist** *n* alquimista *m*.

alcohol ['alkəhol] *n* alcohol *m*. **alcoholic** *n*, *adj* alcohólico, -a. **alcoholism** *n* alcoholismo *m*.

alcove ['alkouv] *n* nicho *m*, hueco *m*.

alderman ['oildəmən] *n* teniente de alcalde *m*, concejal *m*.

ale [eil] *n* cerveza *f*.

alert [ə'ləit] *adj* alerto, vivo, despierto. *v* poner sobre aviso, alertar.

algebra ['aldʒibrə] *n* álgebra *f*.

Algeria [al'dʒiəriə] *n* Argelia *f*. **Algerian** *n*, *adj* argelino, -a.

alias ['eiliəs] *nm*, *adv* alias.

alibi ['alibai] *n* coartada *f*.

alien ['eiliən] *n*, *adj* extranjero, -a. **alienate** *v* enajenar, alejar. **alienation** *n* alienación *f*.

alight¹ [ə'lait] *v* desmontar, bajar, apearse.

alight² [ə'lait] *adj* encendido, iluminado, en llamas.

align [ə'lain] *v* alinear. **alignment** *n* alineación *f*.

alike [ə'laik] *adj* igual, parecido, semejante. *adv* igualmente, del mismo modo.

alimentary canal [ali'mentəri] *n* tubo digestivo *m*.

alimony ['aliməni] *n* alimentos *m pl*.

alive [ə'laiv] *adj* vivo, activo. **alive to** sensible de. **alive with** rebosante de.

alkali ['alkəlai] *n* álcali *m*.

all [oil] *adj* todo. *pron* todo el mundo. *n* todo *m*, totalidad *f*. *adv* todo, enteramente. **all but** casi. **all right** está bien. **all the more** cuanto más. **all the same** sin embargo.

allay [ə'lei] *v* aliviar, calmar.

allege [ə'ledʒ] *v* alegar, afirmar.

allegiance [ə'liidʒəns] *n* fidelidad *f*, lealtad *f*.

allegory ['aligəri] *n* alegoría *f*.

allergy ['alədʒi] *n* alergia *f*. **allergic** *adj* alérgico.

alleviate [ə'liivieit] *v* aliviar. **alleviation** *n* alivio *m*.

alley ['ali] *n* callejuela *f*, paseo *m*. **blind alley** callejón sin salida *m*.

alliance [ə'laiəns] *n* alianza *f*.

allied ['alaid] *adj* aliado.

alligator ['aligeitə] *n* caimán *m*.

alliteration [əlitə'reiʃən] *n* aliteración *f*.

allocate ['aləkeit] *v* asignar, distribuir. **allocation** *n* asignación *f*, repartimiento *m*.

allot [ə'lot] *v* asignar. **allotment** *n* lote *m*.

allow [ə'lau] *v* permitir, admitir. **allow for** tener en cuenta. **allowable** *adj* permisible, legítimo. **allowance** *n* ración *f*; pensión *f*. **monthly allowance** mesada *f*.

alloy ['aloi; *v* ə'loi] *n* aleación *f*; (*fig*) mezcla *f*. *v* alear, ligar.

allude [ə'luːd] *v* aludir. **allusion** *n* alusión *f*. **allusive** *adj* alusivo.

allure [ə'ljuə] *v* seducir, fascinar. **allurement** *n* incentivo *m*, anzuelo *m*. **alluring** *adj* halagüeño, tentador.

ally ['alai; *v* ə'lai] *n* aliado, -a *m*, *f*, asociado, -a *m*, *f*. *v* unir.

almanac ['ɔːlmənak] *n* almanaque *m*.

almighty [ɔːl'maiti] *adj* omnipotente, todopoderoso.

almond ['aːmənd] *n* (*nut*) almendra *f*; (*tree*) almendro *m*.

almost ['ɔːlmoust] *adv* casi.

alms [aːmz] *n* limosna *f*. **almsgiving** *n* caridad *f*. **almshouse** *n* hospicio *m*.

aloft [ə'loft] *adv* en alto, arriba.

alone [ə'loun] *adj* solo, único. *adv* solamente, a solas. **leave alone** dejar en paz.

along [ə'lon] *prep* a lo largo de. **along with** en compañía de, junto con. **come along!** ¡ven! **alongside** *adv* al lado, (*naut*) al costado de.

aloof [ə'luːf] *adv* a distancia. *adj* altanero, reservado. **keep aloof** mantenerse alejado. **aloofness** *n* alejamiento *m*.

aloud [ə'laud] *adv* en voz alta, recio, alto.

alphabet ['alfəbit] *n* alfabeto *m*.

Alps [alps] *n* Alpes *m pl*.

already [ɔːl'redi] *adv* ya.

also ['ɔːlsou] *adv* también, además.

altar ['ɔːltə] *n* altar *m*. **high altar** altar mayor. **altar boy** monaguillo *m*. **altarpiece** retablo *m*.

alter ['ɔːltə] *v* cambiar, modificar, corregir, transformar; (*clothes*) arreglar. **alteration** *n* cambio *m*, modificación *f*; (*building*) reforma *f*.

alternate [ɔːl'təːnət; *v* 'ɔːltəneit] *adj* alterno. *v* alternar. **alternating current** corriente alterna.

alternative [ɔːl'təːnətiv] *n* alternativa *f*.

adj alternativo. **have no alternative but** . . . no poder menos de . . . .

although [ɔːl'ðou] *conj* aunque.

altitude ['altitjuːd] *n* altura *f*, altitud *f*.

altogether [ɔːltə'geðə] *adv* en total, en conjunto, del todo.

altruistic [altru'istik] *adj* altruista. **altruism** *n* altruismo. **altruist** *n* altruista *m*, *f*.

aluminium [alju'miniəm] *n* aluminio *m*.

always ['ɔːlweiz] *adv* siempre.

am [am] *V* be.

amalgamate [ə'malgəmeit] *v* amalgamar, combinar, unir; combinarse, unirse. **amalgamation** *n* amalgamación *f*; mezcla *f*.

amass [ə'mas] *v* acumular, amontonar.

amateur ['amətə] *n*, *adj* aficionado, -a. **amateurish** *adj* de aficionado, superficial.

amaze [ə'meiz] *v* asombrar, sorprender, confundir. **amazement** *n* asombro *m*. **amazing** *adj* asombroso.

ambassador [am'basədə] *n* embajador *m*.

amber ['ambə] *n* ámbar *m*. *adj* ambarino.

ambidextrous [ambi'dekstrəs] *adj* ambidextro.

ambiguous [am'bigjuəs] *adj* ambiguo. **ambiguity** *n* ambigüedad *f*.

ambition [am'biʃən] *n* ambición *f*. **ambitious** *adj* ambicioso.

ambivalent [am'bivələnt] *adj* ambivalente.

amble ['ambl] *v* amblar, andar lentamente. *n* paso de andadura *m*.

ambulance ['ambjuləns] *n* ambulancia *f*.

ambush ['ambuʃ] *n* emboscada *f*, asechanza *f*. *v* emboscar, asechar.

ameliorate [ə'miːliəreit] *v* mejorar. **amelioration** *n* mejora *f*.

amenable [ə'miːnəbl] *adj* tratable, dócil, sujeto.

amend [ə'mend] *v* enmendar, modificar, rectificar. **amendment** *n* enmienda *f*. **make amends** dar satisfacción, indemnizar.

amenity [ə'miːnəti] *n* amenidad *f*, comodidad *f*.

America [ə'merikə] *n* América *f*. **American** *n*, *adj* americano, -a *m*, *f*.

amethyst ['aməθist] *n* amatista *f*.

amiable ['eimiəbl] *adj* amistoso, afable.

amicable ['amikəbl] *adj* amigable.

amid [ə'mid] *prep* entre, rodeado por, en medio de.

amiss [ə'mis] *adv* mal, de más, impropiamente. **take amiss** llevar a mal.

ammonia [ə'mouniə] n amoníaco m.

ammunition [amju'niʃən] n municiones f pl.

amnesia [am'niːziə] n amnesia f.

amnesty ['amnəsti] n amnistía f.

amoeba [ə'miːbə] n ameba f.

among [ə'mʌŋ] prep entre, en medio de.

amoral [ei'morəl] adj amoral.

amorous ['amərəs] adj amoroso.

amorphous [ə'mɔːfəs] adj amorfo.

amount [ə'maunt] n cantidad f, importe m, suma f. v llegar a, subir a, valer. gross amount importe bruto m. net amount importe neto m. it amounts to this se reduce a esto.

ampere ['ampeə] n amperio m.

amphetamine [am'fetəmiːn] n anfetamina f.

amphibian [am'fibiən] nm, adj anfibio.

amphitheatre ['amfiθiətə] n anfiteatro m.

ample ['ampl] adj amplio, abundante; (enough) bastante, suficiente.

amplify ['amplifai] v ampliar, amplificar, aumentar. amplifier n amplificador m.

amputate ['ampjuteit] v amputar. amputation n amputación f.

amuse [ə'mjuːz] v divertir, distraer, entretener. amuse oneself divertirse.

amusement n diversión f, entretenimiento m, recreo m; (hobby) pasatiempo m. amusement park parque de atracciones m. amusing adj divertido, gracioso.

anachronism [ə'nakrənizəm] n anacronismo m. anachronistic adj anacrónico.

anaemia [ə'niːmiə] n anemia f. anaemic adj anémico.

anaesthetic [anəs'θetik] nm, adj anestésico.

anagram ['anəgram] n anagrama m.

analogy [ə'nalədʒi] n analogía f. analogous adj análogo.

analysis [ən'aləsis] n, pl -ses análisis m. analyst n analista m, f. analytic(al) adj analítico.

anarchy ['anəki] n anarquía f. anarchic adj anárquico. anarchist n anarquista m, f.

anathema [ə'naθəmə] n anatema m, f.

anatomy [ə'natəmi] n anatomía f. anatomical adj anatómico.

ancestor ['ansestə] n antepasado m.

ancestral adj ancestral, hereditario. ancestry n linaje m.

anchor ['aŋkə] n ancla f; (fig) áncora f. v anclar, fijar, fondear.

anchovy ['antʃəvi] n anchoa f.

ancient ['einʃənt] adj anciano, antiguo. ancients pl n los antiguos m pl. from ancient times de antiguo.

ancillary [an'siləri] adj auxiliar.

and [and] conj y, e.

anecdote ['anikdout] n anécdota f.

anemone [ə'neməni] n anémona f.

anew [ə'njuː] adv de nuevo, otra vez.

angel ['eindʒəl] n ángel m. angelic adj angélico.

anger ['aŋgə] n cólera f, ira f, enojo m. v enojar, enfadar, encolerizar. angry adj enojado, enfadado.

angina [an'dʒainə] n angina f. angina pectoris angina de pecho.

angle ['aŋgl] n ángulo m, rincón m; (viewpoint) punto de vista m.

angling ['aŋgliŋ] n pesca con caña f. angler n pescador, -a m, f.

anguish ['aŋgwiʃ] n angustia f, agonía f, dolor m.

animal ['animəl] n animal m, bestia f. adj animal. animal kingdom reino animal m. animal spirits brío m, energía f, exuberancia vital f.

animate ['animeit; adj 'animət] v animar, alentar, vivificar. adj viviente, animado. animated adj animado, vivo. animated cartoon dibujo animado.

animosity [ani'mosəti] n animosidad f, hostilidad f.

aniseed ['anisiːd] n grano de anís m.

ankle ['aŋkl] n tobillo m.

annals ['anlz] pl n anales m pl.

annex ['aneks; v ə'neks] n anexo m. v anexar, anexionar; unir, juntar. annexation n anexión f.

annihilate [ə'naiəleit] v aniquilar. annihilation n aniquilación f.

anniversary [ani'vɔːsəri] n aniversario m.

annotate ['anəteit] v anotar, acotar, glosar. annotation n anotación f, nota f.

announce [ə'nauns] v anunciar, publicar, proclamar. announcement n anuncio m, aviso m, publicación f; (of engagement) participación f. announcer n annuncidor, -a m, f; (radio) locutor, -a m, f.

annoy [ə'noi] v molestar, irritar, fastidiar. annoyance n molestia f, disgusto m. annoyed adj enojado. annoying adj fastidioso, enojoso, molesto.

annual ['anjuəl] *adj* anual. *n* (*book*) anuario *m*; (*plant*) planta anual *f*.
annul [ə'nʌl] *v* anular; (*law*) abrogar. **annulment** *n* anulación *f*.
Annunciation [ə,nʌnsi'eiʃən] *n* (*rel*) Anunciación *f*.
anode ['anoud] *n* ánodo *m*.
anomaly [ə'noməli] *n* anomalía *f*. **anomalous** *adj* anómalo.
anonymous [ə'noniməs] *adj* anónimo.
anorak ['anərak] *n* anorak *m*.
another [ə'nʌðə] *adj* otro. *pron* otro, -a *m*, *f*. **one after another** uno después de otro.
answer ['aːnsə] *n* contestación *f*, respuesta *f*; (*solution*) solución *f*; (*math*) resultado *m*. *v* contestar, responder; (*a bell*) acudir; (*door*) abrir. **answer back** replicar. **answer by return** contestar a vuelta de correo. **answerable** *adj* responsable.
ant [ant] *n* hormiga *f*.
antagonize [an'tagənaiz] *v* antagonizar, contender. **antagonism** *n* antagonismo *m*, oposición *f*. **antagonist** *n* antagonista *m*, *f*. **antagonistic** *adj* antagónico.
antecedent [anti'siːdənt] *nm*, *adj* antecedente.
antelope ['antəloup] *n* antílope *m*.
antenatal [anti'neitl] *adj* antenatal.
antenna [an'tenə] *n* antena *f*.
anthem ['anθəm] *n* motete *m*. **national anthem** himno nacional *m*.
anthology [an'θolədʒi] *n* antología *f*.
anthropology [anθrə'polədʒi] *n* antropología *f*.
anti-aircraft [anti'eəkraːft] *adj* anti-aéreo.
antibiotic [antibai'otik] *nm*, *adj* antibiótico.
antibody ['anti,bodi] *n* anticuerpo *m*.
anticipate [an'tisipeit] *v* prever, esperar; anticiparse a. **anticipation** *n* anticipación *f*, esperanza *f*, adelantamiento *m*. **in anticipation of** en espera de.
anticlimax [anti'klaimaks] *n* anticlímax *m*.
anticlockwise [anti'klokwaiz] *adj* en dirección contraria a las agujas del reloj.
antics ['antiks] *pl n* cabriola *f sing*, travesura *f sing*, payasadas *f pl*.
anticyclone [anti'saikloun] *n* anticiclón *m*.
antidote ['antidout] *n* antídoto *m*, contraveneno *m*.
antifreeze ['antifriːz] *n* anticongelante *m*.
antipathy [an'tipəθi] *n* antipatía *f*, aversión *f*.

antique [an'tiːk] *n* antigualla *f*, antigüedad *f*. *adj* antiguo. **antique dealer** anticuario *m*. **antique shop** tienda de antigüedades. **antiquity** *n* antigüedad *f*.
anti-Semitic [antisə'mitik] *adj* antisemítico. **anti-Semitism** *n* antisemitismo *m*.
antiseptic [anti'septik] *nm*, *adj* antiséptico.
antisocial [anti'souʃəl] *adj* antisocial.
anti-tank [anti'taŋk] *adj* antitanque.
antithesis [an'tiθəsis] *n*, *pl* -ses antítesis *f*.
antler ['antlə] *n* asta *f*, cuerno *m*.
antonym ['antənim] *n* antónimo *m*.
anus ['einəs] *n* ano *m*. **anal** *adj* anal.
anvil ['anvil] *n* yunque *m*.
anxious ['aŋkʃəs] *adj* ancioso, preocupado, inquieto. **anxiety** *n* inquietud *f*, ansiedad *f*, intranquilidad *f*.
any ['eni] *adv* cualquier; (*some*) algún, ningún; (*every*) todo. *pron* alguno, -a *m*, *f*; cualquiera *m*, *f*; ninguno, -a *m*, *f*. *adv* algo. **anybody** *or* **anyone** *pron* cualquiera, alguien, nadie. **anyhow** *adv* de cualquier modo. **anything** *n* algo *m*; (*negative*) nada *f*. **anywhere** *adv* dondequiera.
apart [ə'paːt] *adv* aparte.
apartment [ə'paːtmənt] *n* apartamento *m*, cuarto *m*, habitación *f*; (*flat*) piso *m*.
apathy ['apəθi] *n* apatía *f*, indiferencia *f*. **apathetic** *adj* apático.
ape [eip] *n* simio *m*, mono, -a *m*, *f*. *v* imitar.
aperitive [ə'peritiv] *nm*, *adj* aperitivo.
aperture ['apətjuə] *n* abertura *f*, orificio *m*, agujero *m*.
apex ['eipeks] *n* ápice *m*.
aphrodisiac [afrə'diziak] *n* afrodisíaco *m*.
apiece [ə'piːs] *adv* por persona, por cabeza, cada uno.
apology [ə'polədʒi] *n* disculpa *f*, apología *f*, excusa *f*. **apologize** *v* disculparse, pedir perdón; (*regret*) sentir.
apoplexy ['apəpleksi] *n* apoplejía *f*. **apoplectic** *adj* apopléctico.
apostle [ə'posl] *n* apóstol *m*.
apostrophe [ə'postrəfi] *n* (*punctuation*) apóstrofo *m*; (*speech*) apóstrofe *m*, *f*.
appal [ə'poːl] *v* espantar, aterrar. **appalling** *adj* espantoso, horrible.
apparatus [apə'reitəs] *n* aparato *m*, máquina *f*.
apparent [ə'parənt] *adj* aparente; notable, obvio, evidente, claro. **apparently** *adv* al parecer.

apparition [apə'riʃən] *n* aparición *f*, fantasma *m*.

appeal [ə'piːl] *v* (*law*) apelar; (*attract*) atraer. *n* (*law*) apelación *f*; atractivo *m*. **appeal against** suplicar de.

appear [ə'piə] *v* aparecer; (*seem*) parecer; (*in court*) comparecer. **appearance** *n* aparición *f*; (*aspect*) apariencia *f*, aspecto *m*; (*arrival*) llegada *f*.

appease [ə'piːz] *v* aplacar, apaciguar. **appeasement** *n* aplacamiento *m*, apaciguamiento *m*.

appendix [ə'pendiks] *n* apéndice *m*. **appendicitis** *n* apendicitis *f*.

appetite ['apitait] *n* apetito *m*. **have an appetite** tener ganas. **appetizing** *adj* apetitoso.

applaud [ə'plɔid] *v* aplaudir. **applause** *n* aplauso *m*.

apple ['apl] *n* (*fruit*) manzana *f*; (*tree*) manzano *m*. **apple sauce** compota de manzanes *f*.

apply [ə'plai] *v* dirigirse a, recurrir; aplicar; (*use*) emplear; (*for a job*) proponerse a. **apply oneself** to dedicarse a. **appliance** *n* aparato *m*. **applicable** *adj* aplicable. **applicant** *n* aspirante *m*, *f*. **application** *n* aplicación *f*.

appoint [ə'point] *v* nombrar, designar. **be appointed to** colocarse a. **be appointed as** ser nombrado. **appointment** *n* puesto *m*, empleo *m*; (*assignation*) cita *f*. **make an appointment with** citar.

apportion [ə'pɔiʃən] *v* distribuir, repartir.

appraisal [ə'preizl] *n* valoración *f*, estimación *f*. **appraise** *v* valorizar, tasar.

appreciate [ə'priːʃieit] *v* apreciar, darse cuenta de; (*affection*) encarecer; (*in value*) tener en alza. **appreciation** *n* apreciaciún *f*, aprecio *m*; (*understanding*) percepción *f*; (*of shares, etc.*) aumento de valor *m*.

apprehend [apri'hend] *v* (*arrest*) prender, capturar; (*understand*) aprehender, percibir; (*fear*) temer. **apprehension** *n* (*arrest*) aprehensión *f*; (*understanding*) comprensión *f*; (*fear*) aprensión *f*. **apprehensive** *adj* aprensivo.

apprentice [ə'prentis] *n* aprendiz *m*. **apprenticeship** *n* aprendizaje *m*.

approach [ə'proutʃ] *v* acercarse a, aproximar; (*speak to*) hablar con. *n* acercamiento *m*, aproximación *f*; (*arrival*) llegada *f*; (*entrance*) entrada *f*.

appropriate [ə'prouprieit; *adj* ə'proupriət] *v* tomar posesión de, apropiar; (*assign*) asignar, destinar. *adj* propio, pertinente, correspondiente. **appropriateness** *n* conveniencia *f*.

approve [ə'pruːv] *v* aprobar. **approval** *n* aprobación *f*. **on approval** a prueba. **approved** *adj* bien visto.

approximate [ə'proksimeit; *adj* ə'proksimət] *v* aproximar, aproximarse. *adj* aproximado. **approximately** *adv* poco más o menos.

apricot ['eiprikot] *n* (*fruit*) albaricoque *m*; (*tree*) albaricoquero *m*.

April ['eiprəl] *n* abril *m*.

apron ['eiprən] *n* delantal *m*; (*stage*) proscenio *m*.

apt [apt] *adj* apto; propenso; (*suitable*) apropiado.

aptitude ['aptitjuːd] *n* aptitud *f*.

aqualung ['akwəlʌŋ] *n* aparato de aire comprimido *m*.

aquarium [ə'kweəriəm] *n* acuario *m*.

Aquarius [ə'kweəriəs] *n* Acuario *m*.

aquatic [ə'kwatik] *adj* acuático.

aqueduct ['akwidʌkt] *n* acueducto *m*.

Arab ['arəb] *m*(*m+f*), *adj* árabe. **Arabia** *n* Arabia *f*. **Arabic** *adj* arábigo.

arable ['arəbl] *adj* arable.

arbitrary ['aibitrəri] *adj* arbitrario.

arbitrate ['aibitreit] *v* arbitrar. **arbitration** *n* arbitraje *m*. **arbiter** *or* **arbitrator** *n* árbitro *m*.

arc [aik] *n* arco *m*. **arc lamp** lámpara de arco *f*.

arcade [ai'keid] *n* arcada *f*, galería *f*.

arch[1] [aitʃ] *n* arco *m*. *v* arquear.

arch[2] [aitʃ] *adj* (*chief*) principal; archi-.

archaeology [aiki'olədʒi] *n* arqueología *f*. **archaeologist** *n* arqueólogo *m*.

archaic [ai'keiik] *adj* arcaico, arcaizante.

archbishop [aitʃ'biʃəp] *n* arzobispo *m*.

archduke [aitʃ'djuːk] *n* archiduque *m*.

archery ['aitʃəri] *n* tiro con arco *m*. **archer** *n* arquero, -a *m*, *f*.

archetype ['aikitaip] *n* arquetipo *m*.

archipelago [aiki'peləgou] *n* archipiélago *m*.

architect ['aikitekt] *n* arquitecto *m*. **architecture** *n* arquitectura *f*.

archives ['aikaivz] *n pl* archivo *m sing*.

arctic ['aiktik] *adj* ártico. **the Arctic** el Ártico.

ardent ['aidənt] *adj* ardiente, apasionado.

ardour ['ɑːdə] *n* ardor *m*.

arduous ['ɑːdjuəs] *adj* arduo.

are [ɑː] *V* be.

area ['eəriə] *n* área *f*, superficie *f*; extensión *f*.

arena [ə'riːnə] *n* arena *f*, liza *f*.

Argentina [ɑːdʒən'tiːnə] *n* Argentina *f*. **Argentinian** *n*, *adj* argentino, -a.

argue ['ɑːgjuː] *v* debatir, disputar, discutir. **argue against** oponer. **arguable** *adj* discutible. **argument** *n* argumento *m*. **argumentative** *adj* contencioso.

arid ['arid] *adj* árido, seco.

Aries ['eəriːz] *n* (*astrol*) Aries *m*.

***arise** [ə'raiz] *v* elevarse, subir; (*revolt*) sublevarse; (*from bed*) levantarse.

aristocracy [ari'stokrəsi] *n* aristocracia *f*. **aristocrat** *n* aristócrata *m*, *f*. **aristocratic** *adj* aristocrático.

arithmetic [ə'riθmətik] *n* aritmética *f*.

ark [ɑːk] *n* arca *f*. **Noah's Ark** arca de Noé *f*.

arm¹ [ɑːm] *n* (*limb*) brazo *m*. **armchair** *n* sillón *m*, **arm in arm** de bracete, de bracero. **armpit** *n* sobaco *m*. **within arm's reach** al alcance del brazo.

arm² [ɑːm] *n* arma *f*. *v* armar. **to arms!** ¡a las armas! **take up arms** alzarse en armas. **under arms** sobre las armas.

armistice ['ɑːmistis] *n* armisticio *m*.

armour ['ɑːmə] *n* armadura *f*, arnés *m*; (*ships, vehicles*) blindaje *m*. *v* blindar, acorazar. **armour-plate** *n* coraza *f*. **armoury** *n* armería *f*.

army ['ɑːmi] *n* ejército *m*.

aroma [ə'roumə] *n* aroma *m*, fragancia *f*. **aromatic** *adj* aromático.

around [ə'raund] *prep* alrededor de, cerca de; a la vuelta de. *adv* alrededor, en torno, por todas partes.

arouse [ə'rauz] *v* despertar, excitar.

arrange [ə'reindʒ] *v* arreglar, disponer; organizar; (*music*) adaptar; concertarse. **arrangement** *n* arreglo *m*; (*agreement*) acuerdo *m*; (*music*) adaptación *f*. **arrangements** *pl n* preparativos *m pl*.

array [ə'rei] *v* ataviar, poner en orden de batalla. *n* (*dress*) atavío *m*; (*troops*) formación *f*.

arrears [ə'riəz] *pl n* atrasos *m pl*. **in arrears** atrasado en pagos.

arrest [ə'rest] *v* arrestar, detener. *n* (*stop*) parada *f*; (*detention*) detención *f*. **under arrest** bajo arresto.

arrive [ə'raiv] *v* llegar. **arrival** *n* llegada *f*, venida *f*. **on arrival** al llegar.

arrogant ['arəgənt] *adj* arrogante, altanero. **arrogance** *n* arrogancia *f*.

arrow ['arou] *n* flecha *f*, saeta *f*.

arse [ɑːs] *n* (*vulgar*) culo *m*, ojete *m*.

arsenal ['ɑːsənl] *n* arsenal *m*.

arsenic ['ɑːsnik] *n* arsénico *m*.

arson ['ɑːsn] *n* incendiarismo *m*, incendio premeditado *m*.

art [ɑːt] *n* arte *m*; (*cunning*) artificio *m*. **art gallery** museo de pinturas *m*. **artful** *adj* artero, mañoso.

artery ['ɑːtəri] *n* arteria *f*.

arthritis [ɑː'θraitis] *n* artritis *f*.

artichoke ['ɑːtitʃouk] *n* alcachofa *f*.

article ['ɑːtikl] *n* articulo *m*; (*object*) objeto *m*.

articulate [ɑː'tikjuleit; *adj* ɑː'tikjulət] *v* articular. *adj* claro, distinto.

artifice ['ɑːtifis] *n* artificio *m*.

artificial [ɑːti'fiʃəl] *adj* artificial, falso. **artificiality** *n* lo artificial. **artificial respiration** respiración artificial *f*.

artillery [ɑː'tiləri] *n* artillería *f*.

artisan [ɑːti'zan] *n* artesano, -a *m*, *f*.

artist ['ɑːtist] *n* artista *m*, *f*. **artistic** *adj* artístico.

as [az] *adv* tan. *prep*, *conj* como, ya que, según, a medida que; (*when*) cuando; (*since*) puesto que; (*because*) porque; (*although*) aunque. **as a rule** por regla general. **as far as** en cuanto a. **as from** desde. **as good as** tan bueno como. **as if** como si. **as it were** en cierto modo. **as soon as** en cuanto. **as soon as possible** cuanto antes. **as usual** como de costumbre. **as well** también. **as well as** además de.

asbestos [az'bestos] *n* asbesto *m*.

ascend [ə'send] *v* subir. **ascendancy** *n* ascendiente *m*. **be in the ascendant** ir en aumento. **ascension** *n* subida *f*. **ascent** *n* subida *f*; (*slope*) cuesta *f*.

ascetic [ə'setik] *adj* ascético. *n* asceta *m*, *f*.

ash¹ [aʃ] *n* (*cinder*) ceniza *f*, cenizas *f pl*. **ashtray** *n* cenicero *m*.

ash² [aʃ] *n* (*tree*) fresno *m*.

ashamed [ə'ʃeimd] *adj* avergonzado.

ashore [ə'ʃɔː] *adv* a tierra. **go ashore** desembarcar.

Ash Wednesday *n* miércoles de ceniza *m*.

Asia ['eiʃə] n Asia f. **Asian** n, adj asiático, -a.

aside [ə'said] adv aparte, a un lado. n (theatre) aparte m.

ask [a:sk] v preguntar, pedir, invitar. **ask for trouble** buscársela. **for the asking** sin más que pedirlo.

askew [ə'skju:] adj oblicuamente, a un lado.

asleep [ə'sli:p] adj, adv dormido. **fall asleep** dormirse.

asparagus [ə'spærəgəs] n espárrago m.

aspect ['aspekt] n aspecto m, vista f.

asphalt ['asfalt] n asfalto m.

asphyxiate [əs'fiksieit] v asfixiar.

aspire [ə'spaiə] v aspirar. **aspiration** n aspiración f.

aspirin ['aspərin] n aspirina f.

ass [as] n asno m. **asinine** adj asnal.

assail [ə'seil] v atacar. **assailant** n asaltador, -a m, f.

assassinate [ə'sasineit] v asesinar. **assassin** n asesino m, f. **assassination** n asesinato m.

assault [ə'sɔːlt] n asalto m. v asaltar.

assemble [ə'sembl] v (people) convocar; (things) juntar; (machines) armar. **assemblage** n reunión f. **assembly** n asamblea f. **assembly line** línea de montaje f.

assent [ə'sent] v asentir. n asentimiento m.

assert [ə'səːt] v afirmar, declarar. **assertion** n afirmación f, aserción f.

assess [ə'ses] v evaluar, asesorar. **assessment** n valoración f.

asset ['aset] n ventaja f. **assets** pl n activo m sing, haber m sing, bienes m pl.

assiduous [ə'sidjuəs] adj asiduo, aplicado.

assign [ə'sain] v asignar, señalar; (law) consignar; (goods) traspasar. **assignment** n asignación f.

assimilate [ə'simileit] v asimilar, incorporarse. **assimilation** n asimilación f.

assist [ə'sist] v asistir, ayudar. **assistance** n ayuda f. **assistant** n ayudante m, colaborador m.

associate [ə'sousiət; v ə'sousieit] n socio, -a m, f, compañero, -a m, f, cómplice m, f. v asociar, juntar. **associate with** ir con con. **association** n asociación f, sociedad f.

assorted [ə'sɔːtid] adj surtido, mezclado. **assortment** n clasificación f, mezcla f.

assume [ə'sjuːm] v asumir, tomar; (suppose) suponer. **assumed** adj fingido.

assuming that dado que. **assumption** n asunción f.

assure [ə'ʃuə] v asegurar, garantizar. **assurance** n seguridad f, certeza f; (comm) seguro m. **assuredly** adv seguramente.

asterisk ['astərisk] n asterisco m.

asthma ['asmə] n asma f.

astonish [ə'stoniʃ] v asombrar. **astonishment** n asombro m.

astound [ə'staund] v aturdir. **be astounded** quedarse muerto.

astray [ə'strei] adv desviado. **go astray** perderse.

astride [ə'straid] adv a horcajadas. prep a horcajadas sobre.

astringent [ə'strindʒənt] adj astringente.

astrology [ə'strolədʒi] n astrología f. **astrologer** n astrólogo, -a m, f.

astronaut ['astrənɔːt] n astronauta m, f.

astronomy [ə'stronəmi] n astronomía f. **astronomer** n astrónomo m. **astronomical** adj astronómico.

astute [ə'stjuːt] adj astuto, agudo. **astuteness** n astucia f, sagacidad f.

asunder [ə'sʌndə] adv separadamente, en dos.

asylum [ə'sailəm] n (refuge) asilo m; (for the insane) manicomio m.

at [at] prep a, en.

ate [et] V eat.

atheism ['eiθiizəm] n ateísmo m. **atheist** n ateo, -a m, f.

Athens ['aθinz] n Atenas f. **Athenian** n(m+f), adj ateniense.

athlete ['aθliːt] n atleta m, f. **athletic** adj atlético. **athletics** n atletismo m.

Atlantic [ət'lantik] n Atlántico m. adj atlántico.

atlas ['atləs] n atlas m.

atmosphere ['atməsfiə] n atmósfera f, aire m; (feeling) ambiente m. **atmospheric** adj atmosférico. **atmospherics** pl n perturbaciones atmosféricas f pl.

atom ['atəm] n átomo m. **atomic** adj atómico.

atone [ə'toun] v expiar. **atonement** n expiación f.

atrocious [ə'trouʃəs] adj atroz. **atrocity** n atrocidad f.

attach [ə'tatʃ] v atar, adherir, pegar. **attach oneself to** asociarse con. **attachment** n unión f; (hook) enganche m; (friendship) amistad f.

attaché [ə'taʃei] n agregado m. attaché case maletín m.

attack [ə'tak] v atacar. n ataque m; (mil) ofensiva f. attacker n atacador, -a m, f.

attain [ə'tein] v lograr, alcanzar. attainable adj asequible, realizable. attainment n logro m. attainments pl n prendas f pl.

attempt [ə'tempt] n tentativa f. v procurar, tratar de.

attend [ə'tend] v atender, servir; concurrir; (the sick) asistir; (listen) escuchar. attendance n servicio m, asistencia f; (audience) auditorio m. attendant n criado, -a m, f, servidor, -a m, f.

attention [ə'tenʃən] n atención f. call attention to destacar, hacer presente. pay attention prestar atención. attentive adj atento, cortés. attentiveness n cuidado m.

attic ['atik] n desván m, sotabanco m.

attire [ə'taiə] n atavío m, ropaje m, traje m, adorno m. v ataviar, vestir.

attitude ['atitjuːd] n actitud f, postura f, ademán m.

attorney [ə'təːni] n (agent) apoderado, -a m, f; (solicitor) abogado, -a m, f. power of attorney poderes m pl.

attract [ə'trakt] v atraer, llamar. attraction n atracción f, imán m. attractive adj atractivo, atrayente.

attribute ['atribjuːt; v ə'tribjuːt] n atributo m. v atribuir. attributable adj atribuible. attribution n atributo m.

attrition [ə'triʃən] n atrición f.

atypical [ei'tipikl] adj atípico.

aubergine ['oubəʒiːn] n berenjena f.

auburn ['ɔːbən] adj castaño rojizo.

auction ['ɔːkʃən] n remate m, almoneda f, subasta f. v rematar, subastar. auctioneer n subastador m.

audacious [ɔː'deiʃəs] adj audaz, arrojado. audacity n audacia f, arrojo m, atrevimiento m.

audible ['ɔːdəbl] adj audible. audibility n audibilidad f.

audience ['ɔːdjəns] n audiencia f; oyentes m pl.

audiovisual [ɔːdiou'viʒuəl] adj audiovisual.

audit ['ɔːdit] v intervenir. n intervención f, ajuste (de cuentas) m. auditor n inteventor m, contador m.

audition [ɔː'diʃən] n audición f. v dar audición.

auditorium [ɔːdi'tɔːriəm] n auditorio m, sala de espectáculos f.

augment [ɔːg'ment] v aumentar, engrosar; acrecentarse. .

august [ɔː'gʌst] adj augusto.

August ['ɔːgəst] n agosto m.

aunt [aːnt] n tía f. great-aunt n tía abuela f.

aura ['ɔːrə] n aura f; exhalación f.

auspicious [ɔː'spiʃəs] adj propicio.

austere [ɔː'stiə] adj austero, severo. austerity n austeridad f, severidad f.

Australia [o'streiljə] n Australia f. Australian n, adj australiano, -a.

Austria ['ostriə] n Austria f. Austrian n, adj austriaco, -a.

authentic [ɔː'θentik] adj auténtico

author ['ɔːθə] n autor, -a m, f.

authority [ɔː'θorəti] n autoridad f. on good authority de buena fuente. authoritarian adj autoritario.

authorize ['ɔːθəraiz] v autorizar. authorization n autorización f.

autobiography [ɔːtoubai'ogrəfi] n autobiografía f. autobiographical adj autobiográfico.

autocratic [ɔːtou'kratik] adj autocrático. autocrat n autócrata m, f.

autograph ['ɔːtəgraːf] n autógrafo m. v firmar, dedicar.

automatic [ɔːtə'matik] adj automático. automation n automatización f.

automobile ['ɔːtəməbiːl] n automóvil m.

autonomous [ɔː'tonəməs] adj autónomo.

autopsy ['ɔːtopsi] n autopsia f.

autumn ['ɔːtəm] n otoño m. autumnal adj otoñal.

auxiliary [ɔːg'ziljəri] adj auxiliar. n auxiliador m.

avail [ə'veil] v servir, valer, importar; aprovechar. avail oneself of aprovecharse de. to no avail en balde.

available [ə'veiləbl] adj útil, disponible. availability n utilidad f, disponibilidad f.

avalanche ['avəlaːnʃ] n avalancha f, alud m.

avarice ['avəris] n avaricia f, codicia f. avaricious adj avariento.

avenge [ə'vendʒ] v vengar, vindicar. avenge oneself vengarse de. avenger n vengador, -a m, f.

avenue ['avinjuː] n avenida f.

average ['avəridʒ] n promedio m, término medio m. adj de promedio, corriente. v hallar el término medio. on average por regla general.

aversion [ə'vəːʃən] *n* aversión *f.* **averse**
adj opuesto. **be averse to** ser enemigo de.
avert [ə'vəːt] *v* apartar; (*avoid*) evitar.
aviary ['eiviəri] *n* avería *f.*
aviation [eivi'eiʃən] *n* aviación *f.* **aviator** *n*
aviador, -a *m, f.*
avid ['avid] *adj* ávido, codicioso, voraz.
avidity *n* avidez *f.* codicia *f.*
avocado [avə'kaːdou] *n* aguacate *m.*
avoid [ə'void] *v* evitar, eludir, evadir.
avoidance *n* evitación *f.*
await [ə'weit] *v* esperar, aguardar.
*awake [ə'weik] *v* despertar; despertarse.
adj despierto, atento (a). **awakening** *n*
despertamiento *m.*
award [ə'woːd] *n* fallo *m,* premio *m,*
recompensa *f. v* otorgar, conceder, conferir.
aware [ə'weə] *adj* enterado, vigilante,
consciente. **become aware of** darse
cuenta de. **make aware of** hacer saber.
awareness *n* conocimiento *m.*
away [ə'wei] *adv* a lo lejos, ausente, fuera,
en otro lugar.
awe [oː] *n* temor *m,* pasmo *m*; reverencia
f. v intimidar, atemorizar. **awesome** *adj*
pavoroso, imponente.
awful ['oːful] *adj* tremendo, atroz, terrible,
espantoso. **how awful!** ¡i qué barbaridad!
awfully *adv* (*coll*) muy.
awkward ['oːkwəd] *adj* difícil; (*clumsy*)
desmañado; (*ungraceful*) sin gracia.
awl [oːl] *n* punzón *m,* lezna *f.*
awning ['oːniŋ] *n* toldo *m.*
axe [aks] *n* hacha *f.*
axiom ['aksiəm] *n* axioma *m.*
axis ['aksis] *n* eje *m.*
axle ['aksl] *n* eje *m,* peón *m,* árbol *m.*

B

babble ['babl] *v* balbucear; garlar. *n*
murmullo *m,* cháchara *f.*
baboon [bə'buːn] *n* babuino *m.*
baby ['beibi] *n* bebé *m,* criatura *f,* nene
m; (*animals*) crío *m.* **babyhood** *n* niñez *f.*
babyish *adj* infantil.
bachelor ['batʃələ] *n* soltero *m*; (*of Arts
or Science*) licenciado *m,* bachiller *m.*
back [bak] *n* (*anat*) espalda *f*; dorso *m*;

(*sport*) defensa *f. adj* trasero, posterior,
de atrás; (*of pay, etc.*) atrasado. *adv*
atrás; detrás; otra vez, de nuevo. *v*
retroceder; (*support*) apoyar; (*bet on*)
apostar a. **back down** abandonar. **back
out** echarse atrás; (*retract*) desdecirse.
backache ['bakeik] *n* dolor de espaldas
m.
backbone ['bakboun] *n* espinazo *m.*
backdate [bak'deit] *v* poner fecha
atrasada.
backfire [bak'faiə] *n* petardeo *m. v*
petardear.
backgammon ['bak,gamən] *n* chaquete *m.*
backhand ['bakhand] *n* (*sport*) revés *m.*
back-handed *adj* de revés; (*fig*) ambiguo.
backing ['bakiŋ] *n* forro *m*; (*support*) apoyo
m; (*lining*) refuerzo *m*; (*betting*) el apostar
(a) *m.*
backlash ['baklaʃ] *n* reacción *f.*
backlog ['baklog] *n* atrasos *m pl.*
backside ['baksaid] *n* trasero *m,* parte
trasera *f.*
backward ['bakwəd] *adj* atrasado, vuelto
hacia atrás. **backwardness** *n* atraso *m,*
torpeza *f.* **backward and forward** de acá
para allá.
backwards ['bakwədz] *adv* hacia atrás, al
revés.
backwater ['bakwoːtə] *n* (*pool*) remanso
m.
bacon ['beikən] *n* tocino *m.*
bacteria [bak'tiəriə] *n pl* bacteria *f pl.*
bad [bad] *adj* malo; (*ill*) enfermo; (*rotten*)
podrido; (*debt*) incobrable; (*dangerous*)
peligroso; (*coin*) falso; (*pain*) fuerte;
(*unlucky*) desgraciado. **bad-tempered** *adj*
de mal genio. **from bad to worse** de mal
en peor. **badly** *adv* mal; (*seriously*) gravemente.
badge [badʒ] *n* insignia *f,* marca *f,* divisa
f.
badger ['badʒə] *n* tejón *m. v* molestar.
badminton ['badmintən] *n* volante *m,*
badminton *m.*
baffle ['bafl] *v* frustrar, desconcertar, confundir. **baffling** *adj* desconcertante,
difícil; (*person*) enigmático.
bag [bag] *n* bolsa *f,* saco *m,* valija *f*; (*sewing*) costurera *f*; (*suitcase*) maleta *f. v*
ensacar; (*coll, esp. game*) matar, tomar.
pack one's bags liar el petate. **baggage** *m*
equipaje *m.*
baggy ['bagi] *adj* holgado.

bagpipes ['bagpaips] *n pl* gaita *f*.

bail[1] [beil] *n* (*law*) fianza *f*, caución *f*. *v* poner bajo fianza.

bail[2] *or* **bale** [beil] *v* **bail out** (*flooded boat*) achicar, baldear; (*from aircraft*) lanzarse en paracaídas.

bailiff ['beilif] *n* (*law*) alguacil *m*; (*of estate*) capataz *m*.

bait [beit] *n* (*fishing*) cebo *m*, anzuelo *m*; (*lure*) añagaza *f*. *v* cebar, azuzar; (*annoy*) molestar.

bake [beik] *v* cocer al horno. **baker's dozen** la docena del fraile *f*. **baker** *m* panadero *m*. **bakery** *n* panadería *f*. **baking powder** levadura en polvo *f*.

balance ['baləns] *n* equilibrio *m*; (*scales*) balanza *f*; (*comm*) balance *m*. *v* equilibrar; (*comm*) saldar.

balcony ['balkəni] *n* balcón *m*, galería *f*; (*theatre*) anfiteatro *m*.

bald [boːld] *adj* calvo, pelado; (*tyre*) desgastado. **baldness** *n* calvicie *f*.

bale[1] [beil] *n* fardo *m*, bala *f*. *v* embalar.

bale[2] *V* **bail**[2].

ball[1] [boːl] *n* pelota *f*; globo *m*, bola *f*; (*shot*) bala *f*; (*of wool*) ovillo *m*; (*of the foot*) planta del pie *f*. **ball-and-socket joint** articulación esférica *f*. **ball bearings** cojinete de bolas *m sing*. **ball-point pen** bolígrafo *m*.

ball[2] [boːl] *n* (*dance*) baile *m*. **fancy-dress ball** baile de disfraces. **ballroom** *n* salón de baile *m*.

ballad ['baləd] *n* balada *f*, romance *m*, trova *f*; (*music*) canción *f*.

ballast ['baləst] *n* lastre. *v* lastrar.

ballet ['balei] *n* ballet *m*, danza *f*. **ballet dancer** bailarín, bailarina *m*, *f*.

ballistic [bə'listik] *adj* balístico. **ballistic missile** proyectil balístico *m*.

balloon [bə'luːn] *n* globo *m*. **balloonist** *n* aeronauta *m*, *f*.

ballot ['balət] *n* votación *f*, sufragio *m*. *v* votar, balotar. **ballot-box** *n* urna electoral *f*.

bamboo [bam'buː] *n* bambú *m*.

ban [ban] *n* prohibición *f*, interdicción *f*. *v* prohibir, proscribir.

banal [bə'naːl] *adj* trivial, trillado.

banana [bə'naːnə] *n* (*fruit and tree*) plátano *m*; (*S. Am.*) (*fruit*) banana, (*tree*) banano *m*.

band[1] [band] *n* (*troop*) grupo *m*, banda *f*; (*music*) orquesta *f*, banda *f*. *v* congregar, unir, asociar.

band[2] [band] *n* (*strip*) lista *f*, tira *f*, banda *f*.

bandage ['bandidʒ] *n* venda *f*. *v* vendar.

bandit ['bandit] *n* bandido *m*.

bandy ['bandi] *adj also* **bandy-legged** estevado. *v* trocar.

bang [baŋ] *n* golpazo *m*, detonación *f*, golpe *m*. *v* golpear, estallar.

bangle ['baŋgl] *n* ajorca *f*, pulseta *f*, brazalete *m*.

banish ['baniʃ] *v* desterrar, despedir, exilar, deportar. **banishment** *n* destierro *m*.

banister ['banistə] *n* baranda *f*, pasamano *m*.

banjo ['bandʒou] *n* banjo *m*.

bank[1] [baŋk] *n* (*of river, etc.*) ribera *f*, orilla *f*, margen *m*.

bank[2] [baŋk] *n* banco *m*. **bank account** cuenta bancaria *f*. **bank holiday** día festivo *m*. *v* depositar en el banco. **banker** *n* banquero *m*.

bankrupt ['baŋkrʌpt] *n* quebrado, -a *m*, *f*. *adj* insolvente, quebrado. **go bankrupt** hacer bancarrota, declararse en quiebra. **bankruptcy** *n* bancarrota *f*, quiebra *f*.

banner ['banə] *n* bandera *f*, estandarte *m*.

banns [banz] *n pl* amonestaciones *f pl*. **publish the banns** decir las amonestaciones.

banquet ['baŋkwit] *m* banquete *m*. *v* banquetear.

bantam ['bantəm] *n* gallina enana *f*. **bantamweight** *n* peso gallo *m*.

banter ['bantə] *n* burla *f*, chanza *f*. *v* burlarse, tomar el pelo a.

baptize [bap'taiz] *v* bautizar. **baptism** *n* bautismo *m*. **baptist** *n* bautista *m*. **baptistry** *n* baptisterio *m*, bautisterio *m*.

bar [baː] *n* barra *f*; (*soap, chocolate, etc.*) pastilla *f*; (*music*) barra *f*, compás *m*; (*barrier*) barrera *f*; (*refreshments*) bar *m*; (*law*) foro *m*, curia *f*; *v* atrancar, obstruir, impedir. **barman** *n* mozo de bar *m*. **barmaid** *n* camarera *f*.

barb [baːb] *n* púa *f*; (*fish-hook*) lengüeta *f*.

barbarian [baːˈbeəriən] *n, adj* bárbaro, -a *m*, *f*. **barbaric** *adj* barbárico. **barbarity** *n* barbaridad *f*.

barbecue ['baːbikjuː] *n* barbacoa *f*.

barber ['baːbə] *n* barbero *m*, peluquero *m*. **barber's shop** barbería *f*, peluquería *f*.

barbiturate [baːˈbitjurət] *n* barbitúrico *m*.

bare [beə] *adj* desnudo, descubierto. *v* desnudar, descubrir. **barefaced** *adj*

descarado. **barefoot** *adj* descalzo. **bare-
headed** *adj* sin sombrero. **barely** *adv*
apenas.
bargain ['baɪgin] *n* (*cheap*) ganga *f*;
(*agreement*) pacto *m*, ajuste *m*, convenio
m. *v* negociar, regatear. **bargain sale**
saldo *m*. **into the bargain** por más señas.
barge [baɪdʒ] *n* barca *f*, bote *m*, barcaza
f. **barge in** irrumpir. **barge into** entrometerse.
baritone ['baritoun] *n* baritono *m*.
bark¹ [baɪk] *n* (*dog*) ladrido *m*. *v* ladrar.
bark² [baɪk] *n* (*tree*) corteza *f*.
barley ['baɪli] *n* cebada *f*. **barley water** *n*
hordiate *m*.
barn [baɪn] *n* granero *m*, pajar *m*.
barometer [bə'romitə] *n* barómetro *m*.
baron ['barən] *n* barón *m*. **baroness** *n*
baronesa *f*. **baronet** *n* baronet *m*.
baroque [bə'rok] *adj* barroco.
barracks ['barəks] *pl n* cuartel *m*, barraca
f.
barrage ['baraɪʒ] *n* presa *f*; (*mil*)
bombardeo *m*, cortina de fuego *f*.
barrel ['barəl] *n* (*cask*) barril *m*; (*gun,
etc.*) cañón *m*. **barrel organ** organillo *m*.
barren ['barən] *adj* (*land*) yermo, árido;
estéril. **barrenness** *n* aridez *f*; esterilidad
f.
barricade [bari'keid] *n* barrera *f*, barricada *f*, empalizada *f*. *v* barrear, obstruir.
barrier ['bariə] *n* barrera *f*; impedimento
m; valla *f*.
barrister ['baristə] *n* abogado, -a *m*, *f*.
barrow ['barou] *n* carretilla *f*.
barter ['baɪtə] *v* cambiar, trocar. *n*
trueque *m*, cambio *m*, tráfico *m*.
base¹ [beis] *n* base *f*, fundamento *m*, pie
m. *v* fundar, apoyarse, basar. **baseless**
adj sin base.
base² [beis] *adj* bajo, vil, impuro. **base-
ness** *n* bajeza *f*, vileza *f*.
baseball ['beisbɔil] *n* béisbol *m*.
basement ['beismənt] *n* sótano *m*.
bash [baʃ] *n* golpe *m*. *v* golpear.
bashful ['baʃful] *adj* vergonzoso, tímido,
encogido. **bashfulness** *n* vergüenza *f*,
encogimiento *m*.
basic ['beisik] *adj* fundamental; (*chem*)
básico.
basil ['bazl] *n* albahaca *f*.
basilica [bə'zilikə] *n* basílica *f*.
basin ['beisin] *n* bacia *f*, jofaina *f*; (*wash-
basin*) palangana *f*; (*dock*) dársena *f*;
(*river*) cuenca *f*.

basis ['beisis] *n* base *f*, fundamento *m*.
bask [bask] *v* calentarse.
basket ['baskit] *n* cesta *f*, canasta *f*. **basketball** *n* baloncesto *m*.
Basque [bask] *n*, *adj* vasco, -a *m*, *f*; (*language*) vascuence *m*.
bas-relief ['basri,liɪf] *n* bajorrelieve *m*.
bass¹ [beis] *n* (*voice*) bajo *m*. **bass clef** *n*
clave de fa *f*.
bass² [bas] *n* (*freshwater*) róbalo *m*; (*sea*)
lobina *f*.
bassoon [bə'suɪn] *n* bajón *m*.
bastard ['baɪstəd] *n* bastardo, -a *m*, *f*.
baste [beist] *v* (*cookery*) enlardar, pringar; (*sewing*) bastear, hilvanar.
bastion ['bastjən] *n* bastión *m*, baluarte
m.
bat¹ [bat] *n* maza *f*, palo *m*; (*cricket*)
paleta *f*; (*table tennis*) pala *f*. *v* golpear
con le paleta.
bat² [bat] *n* (*zool*) murciélago *m*.
batch [batʃ] *n* grupo *m*; (*loaves*) hornada
f.
bath [baɪθ] *n* baño *m*. *v* bañar, lavar,
tomar un baño. **bath-chair** *n* cochecillo
de inválido *m*. **bathrobe** *n* albornoz *m*.
bathroom *n* cuarto de baño *m*. **bathtowel**
n toalla de baño *f*. **swimming baths** *n* *pl*
piscina *f* *sing*.
bathe [beið] *v* bañar, bañarse. **bathing cap**
gorra de baño *f*. **bathing costume** traje de
baño *m*. **bathing pool** piscina *f*. **bathing
trunks** pantalones de baño *m* *pl*.
baton ['batn] *n* (*mil*) bastón de mando *m*;
(*police*) porra *f*; (*music*) batuta *f*.
battalion [bə'taljən] *n* batallón *m*.
batter¹ ['batə] *v* apalear, golpear, derribar.
batter² ['batə] *n* (*cookery*) batido *m*, pasta
f.
battery ['batəri] *n* (*elec*) pila *f*, batería *f*;
(*mil*) batería; (*law*) agresión *f*. **storage
battery** acumulador *m*. **battery cell** pila
de batería eléctrica *f*.
battle ['batl] *n* batalla *f*, combate *m*. *v*
batallar, luchar. **battlefield** *n* campo de
batalla *m*. **battlement** *n* almenaje *m*. **bat-
tleship** *n* buque de guerra *m*.
bawdy ['bɔidi] *adj* obsceno, escabroso.
bawl [bɔil] *v* vocear.
bay¹ [bei] *n* (*geog*) bahía *f*.
bay² [bei] *v* (*cry*) aullar. **at bay** acor-
ralado.
bay³ [bei] *n* (*tree*) laurel *m*.

bayonet ['beiənit] *n* bayoneta *f*. *v* dar un bayonetazo.

bay window *n* mirador *m*.

bazaar [bə'zaɪ] *n* bazar *m*.

***be** [biː] *v* ser, existir; estar; (*place*) encontrarse, quedar.

beach [biːtʃ] *n* playa *f*; costa *f*. *v* varar, encallar en la costa.

beacon ['biːkən] *n* fanal *m*, faro *m*; (*naut*) boya *f*.

bead [biːd] *n* cuenta *f*, perla *f*, gota *f*. **beads** *n pl* rosario *m sing*.

beagle ['biːgl] *n* sabueso *m*.

beak [biːk] *n* pico *m*; punta *f*. **beaked** *adj* picudo.

beaker ['biːkə] *n* vaso *m*, copa *f*.

beam [biːm] *n* (*light*) rayo *m*, destello *m*; (*arch*) madero *m*; (*width of a ship*) manga *f*; (*smile*) sonrisa brillante *f*. *v* irradiar; (*smile*) sonreír radiantemente.

bean [biːn] *n* (*broad*) haba *f*; (*black*) fréjol *m*; (*kidney*) habichuela *f*, alubia *f*, judía *f*.

***bear**[1] [beə] *v* soportar, aguantar, sufrir; (*carry*) llevar; (*have*) tener, (*fruit*) dar; (*give birth to*) parir; (*a strain*) resistir. **bear in mind** tener presente. **bearing** *n* porte *m*, aspecto *m*; relación *f*.

bear[2] [beə] *n* oso *m*.

beard [biəd] *n* barba *f*. *v* enfrentarse con, mesar la barba a. **bearded** *adj* barbudo. **beardless** *adj* imberbe.

bearings ['beəriŋz] *n pl* situación *f sing*, relación *f sing*, camino *m sing*. **lose one's bearings** desorientarse, desatinar. **take one's bearings** orientarse.

beast [biːst] *n* bestia *f*; res *f*; (*wild*) fiera *f*. **beastly** *adj* bestial; desagradable.

***beat** [biːt] *v* batir; (*games*) derrotar, vencer; (*with weapon*) golpear; (*carpet*) sacudir. **beat down** atropellar. *n* (*med*) latido *m*, pulsación *f*; golpe *m*; (*music*) compás *m*.

beauty ['bjuːti] *n* hermosura *f*, belleza *f*; (*coll*) lo mejor. **beauty spot** lunar *m*. **beautiful** *adj* bello, hermoso; guapo. **beautify** *v* embellecer.

beaver ['biːvə] *n* castor *m*.

because [bi'koz] *conj* porque. **because of** a causa de.

beckon ['bekən] *v* llamar con señas, atraer, invitar.

***become** [bi'kʌm] *v* convenir; llegar a ser, ponerse; hacerse. **becoming** *adj* que sienta bien, propio, decoroso. **becomingly** *adv* con gracia.

bed [bed] *n* cama *f*, lecho *m*; (*coal, etc.*) yacimiento *m*; (*flowers*) macizo *m*. **bedding** *n* ropa de cama *f*. **bedroom** *n* dormitorio *m*. **bedsitter** *n* salón con cama *m*. **bedspread** *n* colcha *f*.

bedbug ['bedbʌg] *n* chinche *f*.

bedraggled [bi'dragld] *adj* mojado y sucio, enlodado.

bee [biː] *n* abeja *f*. **bee line** línea recta *f*. **beehive** *n* colmena *f*. **bumble-bee** *n* abejorro *m*.

beech [biːtʃ] *n* (*tree*) haya *f*; (*nut*) hayuco *m*.

beef [biːf] *n* carne de vaca *f*. **roast beef** rosbif *m*.

been [biːn] *V* be.

beer [biə] *n* cerveza *f*.

beetle ['biːtl] *n* (*zool*) escarabajo *m*; (*tech*) pisón *m*. **death-watch beetle** carcoma *f*. **beetle-browed** *adj* cejijunto.

beetroot ['biːtruːt] *n* remolacha *f*.

before [bi'foɪ] *adv* delante; al frente; (*time*) antes; (*already*) ya. *prep* delante de; frente de; (*time*) ante; (*rather than*) antes de. *conj* antes (que). **beforehand** *adv* de antemano.

befriend [bi'frend] *v* favorecer, amistar, proteger, ayudar.

beg [beg] *v* pedir, suplicar; mendigar. **I beg your pardon?** ¿cómo dice? **I beg your pardon!** ¡Vd dispense! **beg the question** dejar a un lado. **beggar** *n* mendigo *m*.

***begin** [bi'gin] *v* comenzar, empezar, iniciar. **to begin with** en primer lugar. **beginner** *n* principiante, -a *m*, *f*. **beginning** *n* principio *m*.

begrudge [bi'grʌdʒ] *v* envidiar; conceder de mala gana.

beguile [bi'gail] *v* engañar; (*charm*) encantar.

behalf [bi'haɪf] *n* provecho *m*. **on behalf of** en nombre de, a favor de.

behave [bi'heiv] *v* comportarse, manejarse, portarse; funcionar, obrar. **behaviour** *n* comportamiento *m*, conducta *f*; funcionamiento *m*.

behead [bi'hed] *v* decapitar.

behind [bi'haind] *adv* atrás, detrás, hacia atrás; (*time*) después; (*late*) con retraso. *prep* detrás de, por detrás de. *n* (*coll*) trasero *m*. **fall behind** retrasarse. **behind the times** pasado de moda.

*behold [bi'hould] *v* mirar, contemplar. *interj* ¡aqui está!, ¡he aquí!

belge [beiʒ] *adj* beige.

being ['biiŋ] *n* ser *m*, existencia *f*, estado *m*. **human being** ser humano *m*. **well-being** *n* bienestar *m*.

belated [bi'leitid] *adj* tardío.

belch [beltʃ] *n* eructo *m*. *v* eructar, arrojar.

belfry ['belfri] *n* campanario *m*.

Belgium ['beldʒəm] *m* Bélgica *f*. **Belgian** *n(m+f)*, *adj* belga.

believe [bi'liːv] *v* creer, pensar; opinar. **believer** *n* creyente *m*, *f*, fiel *m*. **belief** *n*, *pl* -s creencia *f*; opinión *f*.

bell [bel] *n* campana *f*, campanilla *f*; (*electric*) timbre *m*; (*hand*) esquila *f*.

belligerent [bi'lidʒərənt] *n*, *adj* beligerante, -a *m*, *f*.

bellow ['belou] *v* bramar, rugir. *n* bramido *m*.

bellows ['belouz] *n pl* fuelle *m sing*.

belly ['beli] *n* barriga *f*, panza *f*, vientre *m*. **bellyful** *n* hartón *m*.

belong [bi'loŋ] *v* pertenecer, tocar a. **belong to** ser de. **belongings** *n pl* bienes *m pl*.

beloved [bi'lʌvid] *n* amado, -a *m*, *f*, querido, -a *m*, *f*. favorito, -a *m*, *f*.

below [bi'lou] *adv* abajo, debajo. *prep* (por) debajo de.

belt [belt] *n* cinturón *m*, cinto *m*, faja *f*; (*tech*) correa *f*; (*geog*) zona *f*. *v* ceñir, rodear, fajar.

bench [bentʃ] *n* banco *m*, banca *f*, escaño *m*, (*law*) tribunal *m*.

*bend [bend] *v* torcer, doblar; inclinar, encorvar. *n* recodo *m*, curva *f*.

beneath [bi'niːθ] *adv* abajo, debajo. (*prep*) bajo, debajo de. **beneath regard** indigno de consideración.

benefactor ['benəfaktə] *n* bienhechor *m*, patrono *m*.

benefit ['benəfit] *n* beneficio *m*, provecho *m*. *v* beneficiar. **beneficial** *adj* ventajoso. **beneficiary** *n* beneficiario *m*.

benevolent [bi'nevələnt] *adj* benévolo; caritativo. **benevolence** *n* benevolencia *f*, caridad *f*.

benign [bi'nain] *adj* benigno.

bent [bent] *adj* torcido, encorvado; (*on a course of action*) resuelto (a); (*fam*) invertido. *n* talento *m*, inclinación *f*.

bequeath [bi'kwiːð] *v* legar; transmitir. **bequest** *n* legado *m*.

bereaved [bi'riːvd] *adj* afligido. **bereave** *v* quitar; afligir. **bereavement** *n* pérdida *f*, aflicción *f*.

beret ['berei] *n* boina *f*.

berry ['beri] *n* baya *f*, grano *m*.

berserk [bə'səːk] *adj* demente.

berth [bəːθ] *n* camarote *m*; (*dock*) fondeadero *m*. *v* fondear. **give a wide berth to** apartarse de.

beside [bi'said] *prep* junto a, cerca de. **beside oneself** fuera de sí. **beside the point** no venir al caso. **besides** *adv* (*as well*) también; (*moreover*) además.

besiege [bi'siːdʒ] *v* asediar, sitiar.

bespoke [bi'spouk] *adj* hecho a medida. **bespeak** *v* reservar.

best [best] *adj*, *adv* mejor. **at best** a lo mejor. **do one's best** hacer todo lo posible. **make the best of** sacar el mayor provecho de. **best man** padrino de boda *m*. **best-seller** *n* éxito de librería *m*.

bestow [bi'stou] *v* conferir, otorgar.

*bet [bet] *v* apostar; jugar. *n* apuesta *f*, postura *f*. **better, bettor** *n* apostador, -a *m*, *f*. **betting shop** establecimiento de apuesta *m*.

betray [bi'trei] *v* traicionar; engañar; revelar. **betrayal** *n* traición *f*.

better ['betə] *adj*, *adv* mejor. **get better** mejorarse. **better half** (*coll*) media naranja *f*. **better off** mejor situado. **so much the better** tanto mejor. *v* mejorarse.

between [bi'twiin] *prep* entre. *adv* entre los dos. **far between** a grandes intervalos. **between ourselves** entre nosotros.

beverage ['bevəridʒ] *n* bebida *f*, brebaje *m*.

*beware [bi'weə] *v* tener cuidado de. *interj* ¡atención!

bewilder [bi'wildə] *v* desconcertar, aturrullar, aturdir. **bewilderment** *n* aturdimiento *m*, anonadamiento *m*.

beyond [bi'jond] *adv* más allá, más lejos. *prep* superior a, fuera de. **beyond doubt** fuera de duda. **beyond measure** sobremanera. **beyond question** indiscutible.

bias ['baiəs] *n* sesgo *m*, través *m*; propensión *f*, prejuicio *m*. *v* sesgar; influir, predisponer. **biased** *adj* predispuesto. **cut on the bias** contar al sesgo.

bib [bib] *n* babero *m*, pechera *f*.

Bible ['baibl] *n* Biblia *f.* **biblical** *adj* bíblico.

bibliography [bibli'ogrəfi] *n* bibliografía *f.* **bibliographer** *n* bibliógrafo *m.* **bibliographical** *adj* bibliográfico.

biceps ['baiseps] *n* biceps *m.*

bicker ['bikə] *v* disputar, reñir, altercar. **bickering** *n* altercado *m.*

bicycle ['baisikl] *n* bicicleta *f.*

*bid [bid] *v* ofrecer, pujar; (*command*) mandar; rogar. *n* oferta *f*; (*attempt*) tentativa *f.* **make a bid for** procurar. **no bid** (*cards*) paso. **bidder** *n* postor *m.*

bidet ['biːdei] *n* bidé *m.*

biennial [bai'eniəl] *adj* bienal, bianual.

bifocals [bai'foukəlz] *pl n* lentes bifocales *m pl.*

big [big] *adj* grande; grueso; abultado; importante.

bigamy ['bigəmi] *n* bigamia *f.* **bigamist** *n* bígamo, -a *m, f.* **bigamous** *adj* bígamo.

bigot ['bigət] *n* beatón, -ona *m, f*, fanático, -a *m, f.* **bigoted** *adj* fanático, intolerante. **bigotry** *n* fanatismo *m*, intolerancia *f.*

bikini [bi'kiːni] *n* bikini *m.*

bilingual [bai'lingwəl] *adj* bilingüe.

bilious ['biljəs] *adj* bilioso. **bile** *n* bilis *f.*

bill¹ [bil] *n* (*comm*) cuenta *f*, factura *f*; (*poster*) cartel *m*; (*pol*) proyecto de ley *m*; anuncio *m.* **billboard** *n* cartelera *f.* **bill of lading** conocimiento de embarque *m.* **bill of sale** escritura de venta *f.* *v* enviar una cuenta; anunciar. **bill and coo** arrullar; (*coll*) besuquearse.

bill² [bil] *n* (*beak*) pico *m.*

billiards ['biljədz] *n* billar *m.*

billion ['biljən] *n* (*10¹²*) billón *m*; (*10⁹*) mil millones *m pl.*

bin [bin] *n* arcón *m*, hucha *f*; papelera *f*; (*wine*) estante *m.*

binary ['bainəri] *adj* binario.

*bind [baind] *v* atar; ligar, unir; (*bandage*) vendar; (*sheaves*) agavillar, (*books*) encuadernar; (*captive*) aprisionar; (*sewing*) ribetear; (*oblige*) comprometer.

binding ['baindiŋ] *n* (*books*) encuadernación *f*; atadura *f. adj* válido; obligatorio.

binge [bindʒ] *n* (*coll*) parranda *f.* **go on the binge** ir de parranda.

binoculars [bi'nokjuləz] *n pl* binóculos *m pl*, prismáticos *m pl*, gemelos *m pl.*

biography [bai'ogrəfi] *n* biografía *f.* **biographer** *n* biógrafo, -a *m, f.* **biographical** *adj* biográfico.

biology [bai'olədʒi] *n* biología *f.* **biological** *adj* biológico. **biologist** *n* biólogo *m.*

birch [bəːtʃ] *n* abedul *m.* *v* varear.

bird [bəːd] *n* pájaro *m*, ave *f*; (*slang*) chica *f.* **bird's eye view** vista de pájaro *f.* **birdcage** *n* jaula *f.* **birdseed** *n* alpiste *m.*

birth [bəːθ] *n* nacimiento *m*, parto *m*; linaje *m*; comienzo *m.* **give birth to** dar a luz; parir. **birth certificate** partida de nacimiento *f.* **birth control** anticoncepcionismo *m.* **birthday** *n* cumpleaños *m.* **birthplace** *n* lugar de nacimiento *m.* **birthrate** *n* natalidad *f.* **birthright** *n* herencia *f.*

biscuit ['biskit] *n* bizcocho *m*, galleta *f.*

bishop ['biʃəp] *n* obispo *m*; (*chess*) alfil *m.*

bison ['baisən] *n* bisonte *m.*

bit¹ [bit] *n* (*drill*) barrena *f*, taladro *m*; (*horse*) bocado *m.* **take the bit between one's teeth** desbocarse.

bit² [bit] *n* pedazo *m*, poco *m*, trocito *m*; (*time*) ratito *m*; (*jot*) jota *f.* **bit by bit** poco a poco. **not a bit** nada de eso.

bitch [bitʃ] *n* (*dog*) perra *f*; (*slang*) zorra *f.*

*bite [bait] *v* morder; (*insect, etc.*) picar. *n* mordedura *f*; picadura *f.* **biting** *adj* (*remark, etc.*) mordaz.

bitter ['bitə] *adj* amargo, áspero. **to the bitter end** hasta la muerte. **bitterness** *n* amargura *f.*

bizarre [bi'zaː] *adj* extravagante, grotesco.

black ['blak] *n, adj* negro, -a *m, f.* **blacken** *v* ennegrecer; (*character*) denigrar.

blackberry ['blakbəri] *n* (*bush*) zarza *f*; (*fruit*) zarzamora *f.*

blackbird ['blakbəːd] *n* mirlo *m.*

blackboard ['blakbɔːd] *n* pizarra *f.*

blackcurrant [ˌblak'kʌrənt] *n* grosella negra *f.*

black eye *n* ojo a la funerala *m.*

blackhead ['blakhed] *n* espinilla *f.*

blackleg ['blakleg] *n* esquirol *m.*

blackmail ['blakmeil] *n* chantaje *m.* *v* hacer chantaje. **blackmailer** *n* chantajista *m, f.*

black market *n* mercado negro *m.*

blackout ['blakaut] *n* apagón *m*, apagamiento *m*; (*fainting*) desmayo *m.*

black pudding *n* morcilla *f.*

blacksmith ['blaksmiθ] *n* herrero *m.*

bladder ['bladə] *n* vejiga *f.*

blade [bleid] *n* (*grass*) brizna *f*; (*razor*) hoja *f*; (*propeller*) paleta *f*; (*oar*) pala *f.*

blame [bleim] n culpa f. v culpar. **blame-less** adj inculpable. **blameworthy** adj culpable.

bland [bland] adj afable; dulce.

blank [blaŋk] adj en blanco; (empty) vacío; confuso. n blanco m, hueco m; vacío m. **blank cartridge** cartucho para salvas m. **blank verse** verso libre m, verso suelto m.

blanket ['blaŋkit] n manta f, frazada f; (of dust) capa f. v cubrir con manta. adj comprensivo.

blare [bleə] v vociferar, rugir. n trompetazo m, fragor m; estrépito m.

blaspheme [blas'fiːm] v blasfema. **blas-phemer** n blasfemador, -a m, f. **blasphe-mous** adj blasfemo. **blasphemy** n blas-femia f.

blast [blaːst] n explosión f; (trumpet) trompetazo m; (wind) ráfaga f. v (rocks) barrenar; (wither) marchitar; (curse) maldecir. **full blast** en plena marcha. **blast furnace** alto horno m.

blatant ['bleitənt] adj discarado, vocinglero, llamativo.

blaze [bleiz] n incendio m, llamarada f, conflagración f. v llamear, flamear; arder. **blaze a trail** abrir un camino. **blaze of colour** masa de color f. **blazer** n chaqueta deportiva f.

bleach [bliːtʃ] v blanquear, descolorar. n lejía f.

bleak [bliːk] adj desabrido, desierto, crudo; (prospect) sombrío.

bleat [bliːt] v balar. n balido m.

***bleed** [bliːd] v sangrar. **bleed to death** morir desangrado. **bleeding** n hemorragia f.

blemish ['blemiʃ] n mácula f, defecto m, mancha f. v empañar, manchar.

blend [blend] v mezclar, combinar, fundir; (colour) matizar. n mezcla f, combinación f.

bless [bles] v bendecir; consagrar; favorecer. **blessedness** n felicidad f. **blessing** n bendición f; merced f; favor m.

blew [bluː] V **blow**².

blight [blait] n (plants) tizne m; (fig) influencia maligna f. v atizonar; (fig) malograr.

blind [blaind] adj ciego. n pretexto m; (window) persiana f. v cegar. **blindness** n ceguera f. **turn a blind eye** hacer la vista gorda.

blindfold ['blaindfould] n venda f. v vendar los ojos de.

blink [bliŋk] v parpadear, pestañear, guiñar. n parpadeo m, guiño m; (of light) destello m. **blinkers** pl n anteojeras f pl.

bliss [blis] n bienaventuranza f, felicidad f. **blissful** adj bienaventurado, feliz.

blister ['blistə] n vesícula f, ampolla f. v ampollar.

blizzard ['blizəd] n ventisca f.

bloated ['bloutid] adj abotagado.

blob [blob] n gota f, goterón m; borrón m.

bloc [blok] n (pol) bloque m.

block [blok] n bloque m; (butcher's) tajo m; (houses) manzana f; (obstruction) atasco m. v bloquear, obstruir, cerrar el paso. **block and tackle** polea con aparejo f.

blockade [blo'keid] n bloqueo m. v bloquear.

bloke [blouk] n (coll) tío m, fulano m.

blond [blond] adj rubio. **blonde** n rubia f.

blood [blʌd] n sangre f; (lineage) parentesco m. **bloodless** adj exangüe. **blood donor** donante de sangre m, f. **blood group** grupo sanguíneo m. **blood poisoning** envenenamiento de la sangre m. **blood pressure** n presión arterial f. **bloodshed** n matanza f. **bloodshot** adj inyectado de sangre. **bloodstream** n corriente sanguínea f. **bloodthirsty** adj sanguinario. **bloody** adj sangriento; (slang) maldito.

bloom [bluːm] n flor f; florecimiento m; (prime) lozanía f. v florecer. **in bloom** en flor. **blooming** adj floreciente.

blossom ['blosəm] n flor f. v florecer.

blot [blot] n borrón m; mancha f. v manchar, tachar; (dry) secar. **blot out** borrar. **blotter** n libro borrador m. **blotting paper** papel secante m.

blotch [blotʃ] n mancha f; (med) erupción f. v manchar, ennegrecer.

blouse [blauz] n blusa f.

blow¹ [blou] n (hit) golpe m, bofetada f; (shock) choque m; (misfortune) revés m. **come to blows** venir a las manos.

***blow**² [blou] n soplido m. v soplar, hacer viento; (pant) jadear; (fuse) fundirse; (music) tocar. **blow away** disipar. **blow one's nose** sonarse las narices. **blow out** (a light) apagar soplando. **blow up** (explode) volar; (inflate) inflar.

blubber ['blʌbə] n grasa de ballena f. v gimotear.

blue [bluː] adj azul; (mournful) deprimido; (obscene) verde. **bluebell** n campanilla f. **bluebottle** n moscón m. **blueprint** n fotocopia f, plan m.

bluff [blʌf] v fanfarronear. n fanfarronada f; (cliff) morro m, tisco m, peñasco. adj campechano, brusco.

blunder [blʌndə] n desatino m, yerro m. v desatinar; tropezar (con); (coll) meter la pata. **blunderer** n desatinado m.

blunt [blʌnt] adj desafilado, embotado; (abrupt) franco, descortés; (plain) claro. v despuntar, desafilar, embotar; (pain) mitigar. **bluntness** n embotamiento m.

blur [bləː] v empañar; emborronar. n borrón m. **blurred** adj borroso.

blush [blʌʃ] v ruborizarse, enrojecerse. n rubor m, sonrojo m; (of shame) bochorno m.

boar [boː] n jabalí m.

board [boːd] n tabla f; (chess, draughts) tablero m; (for notices) tablón m; (table) mesa f; (food) comida f; (committee) junta f, tribunal m; (naut) bordo m. v (carpentry) enmaderar, entablar; (embark) embarcarse en.

boast [boust] n jactancia f, alarde m, baladronada f. v jactarse, presumir. **boastful** adj jactancioso.

boat [bout] n bote m, lancha f, barca f; buque m, barco m. v navegar, ir en bote. **boatman** n barquero m. **boatswain** n contramaestre m. **lifeboat** n lancha de socorro f.

boater ['boutə] n (hat) canotié m, canotier m.

bob [bob] v bambolean, menear. n balanceo m; borla f.

bobbin ['bobin] n (sewing-machine, loom) bobina f.

bobsleigh ['bobslei] n trineo doble m. v ir en trineo.

bodice ['bodis] n corpiño m.

body ['bodi] n cuerpo m, masa f, entidad f; (corpse) cadáver m; (mot) carrocería f. **bodyguard** n guardia de corps f.

bog [bog] n pantano m.

bogus ['bougəs] adj espurio, fingido, falso.

bohemian [bə'hiːmiən] adj bohemio.

boil[1] [boil] v hervir. n hervor m. **boil over** irse. **boiler** n caldera f. **boiling point** punto de ebullición m.

boil[2] [boil] n divieso m, grano m, furúnculo m.

boisterous ['boistərəs] adj borrascoso, bullicioso. **boisterousness** n bullicio m.

bold [bould] adj osado, arrojado, atrevido; resuelto; (showy) llamativo. **bold-faced** adj descarado. **bold-faced type** letra negra f. **boldness** n temeridad f, intrepidez f.

Bolivia [bə'liviə] n Bolivia f. **Bolivian** adj, n boliviano, -a m, f.

bolster ['boulstə] n travesaño m; almohada f. v estribar, levantar, apoyar.

bolt [boult] n (door) cerraja f, cerrojo m; (for nut) perno m; rayo m. v (run) huir; (secure) empernar; (food) zampar. **bolt upright** enhiesto. **thunderbolt** n rayo m.

bomb [bom] n bomba f. v bombardear. **bombard** [bəm'baːd] v bombardear. **bombardment** n bombardeo m.

bonafide [bounə'faidi] adj fidedigno.

bond [bond] n lazo m, unión f, vínculo m; (comm) obligación f; (security) fianza f; (customs) depósito m. v unir, ligar; dar fianza. **bonds** n pl cadenas f pl. **bondage** n esclavitud f.

bone [boun] n hueso m; (fish) espina f. v desosar. **bony** adj huesudo. **all skin and bones estar en los huesos. pick a bone with** arreglar las cuentas con.

bonfire ['bonfaiə] n hoguera f.

bonnet ['bonit] n capota f, gorra f; (mot) capó m.

bonus ['bounəs] n extra m, prima f.

booby trap ['buːbi] n trampa f; (mil) mina f.

book [buk] n libro m; tomo m. v (a seat) tomar; (reserve) reservar; (engage) contratar. **bookcase** ['bukkeis] n librería f. **book-ends** ['bukendz] n pl sujetalibros m pl.

booking ['bukiŋ] n taquilla f.

book-keeper ['buk,kiːpə] n tenedor de libros m.

booklet ['buklit] n folleto m.

bookmark ['bukmaːk] n marcador m.

bookseller ['bukselə] n librero m.

bookshop ['bukʃop] n librería f.

boom [buːm] n (noise) ruido m; (econ) auge repentino m. v (comm) prosperar, estar en bonanza; sonar, bramar.

boost [buːst] v (advertise) dar bombo (a); (coll) empujar. n (coll) empujón m.

boot [buɪt] n (shoe) bota f; (mot) maleta f. **get the boot** ser despedido.

booth [buːð] n cabina f, quiosco m.

booze [buɪz] n (coll) bebida alcohólica f. v (coll) emborracharse, coger una turca.

border ['bɔɪdə] n confín m; frontera f; margen m; (sewing) ribete m; (garden) arriate m. v lindar con. **borderline** n límite m.

bore[1] [bɔɪ] v (hole, etc.) perforar, horadar, taladrar. n taladro m, barreno m; (gun) calibre m.

bore[2] [bɔɪ] v aburrir, fastidiar. n aburrimiento m; (person) pelmazo m. **boredom** n tedio m, hastío m. **boring** adj aburrido, tedioso.

bore[3] [bɔɪ] V bear[1].

born [bɔɪn] adj nacido, nato. **be born** nacer.

borne [bɔɪn] V bear[1].

borough ['bʌrə] n municipio m.

borrow ['borou] v tomar prestado, pedir prestado. **borrower** n prestatario m.

bosom ['buzəm] n seno m; pecho m.

boss [bos] n amo m, jefe m, patrón m; (political) cacique m. v dominar, dirigir.

botany ['botəni] n botánica f. **botanical** adj botánico. **botanist** n botánico, -a m, f.

both [bouθ] adj, pron ambos, los dos.

bother ['boðə] v molestar; (worry) preocuparse. n molestia f; preocupación f.

bottle ['botl] n botella f, frasco m; (water) cantimplora f; (wine) porrón m. v embotellar.

bottom ['botəm] n fondo m; casco m; (anat) trasero m, (vulgar) culo m; (river) lecho m; (page) pie m; (chair) asiento m. adj más bajo. **bottomless** adj sin fondo.

boudoir ['buɪdwaɪ] n tocador m, gabinete m.

bough [bau] n rama f.

bought [bɔɪt] V buy.

boulder ['bouldə] n peñasco m, pedrusco m.

bounce [bauns] v rebotar, botar, saltar; (cheque) ser rechazado. n rebote m, respingo m.

bound[1] [baund] v (leap) saltar, brincar. n salto m, brinco m.

bound[2] [baund] n límite m. **within bounds** dentro del límite.

bound[3] [baund] V bind.

bound[4] [baund] adj bound for destinado a, con rumbo a.

boundary ['baundəri] n lindero m, término m.

bouquet [buːkei] n ramo m, ramillete m; perfume m; (wine) nariz f.

bourgeois ['buəʒwaɪ] adj burgués.

bout [baut] n turno m; (illness) ataque m.

bow[1] [bau] v (bend) inclinarse, saludar; (submit) someterse (a). n inclinación f; reverencia f.

bow[2] [bou] n (music, weapon) arco m; (ribbon) lazo m. **bow-legged** adj patiestevado. **bow window** ventana f arqueada.

bow[3] [bau] n (naut) proa f.

bowels ['bauəlz] n pl intestinos m pl, entrañas f pl.

bowl[1] [boul] n receptáculo m; (soup) escudilla f; (washing) jofaina f.

bowl[2] [boul] v tirar; (cricket) sacar. **bowl over** (fig) desconcertar. **bowls** pl n juego de bolos m sing.

bowler hat n hongo m.

box[1] [boks] n caja f, cajón m; (luggage) baúl m; (theatre) palco m; (sentry) garita f, casilla f. v encajonar. **box office** taquilla f. **post-office box** apartado de correos m.

box[2] [boks] v (sport) boxear. **boxer** n boxeador m, puglista m. **boxing** n boxeo m, pugilato m.

Boxing Day n Día de San Esteban m.

boy [boi] n muchacho m, niño m, chico m. **boyfriend** n novio m. **boy scout** muchacho explorador m. **boyhood** niñez f.

boycott ['boikot] n boicot m. v boicotear.

bra [braɪ] n (coll) sostén m.

brace [breis] n refuerzo m; (tech) abrazadera f; (pair) par m. v reforzar; refrescar. **braces** n pl tirantes m pl. **bracing** adj tónico.

bracelet ['breislit] n pulsera f; brazalete m.

bracken ['brakən] n helecho m.

bracket ['brakit] n soporte m; (writing) paréntesis m, corchete m.

brag [brag] v jactarse. n jactancia f.

Braille [breil] n Braille m, alfabeto para los ciegos m.

brain [brein] n cerebro m, sesos m pl. v romper la crisma. **brains** n pl talento m sing. **brainwash** v lavar el cerebro. **brainwave** n idea luminosa f. **brainy** adj sesudo. **rack one's brains** devanarse los sesos.

braise [breiz] v estofar.
brake [breik] n freno m. v frenar.
bramble ['brambl] n zarza f, maleza f. bramble patch breña f, matorral m.
bran [bran] n salvado m.
branch [braintʃ] n rama f; (of learning) ramo m; (river) tributario m; (road, rail) ramal m; (company) dependencia f. v echar ramas, dividirse.
brand [brand] n (manufacture) marca f; (animals) hierro m; (fire) tizón m; (stigma) estigma m. v marcar; tildar. brand-new adj enteramente nuevo.
brandish ['brandiʃ] v blandir.
brandy ['brandi] n coñac m.
brass [brais] n latón m; (music) cobre m, metal m; (coll) pasta f. brassy adj de latón; (coll) presuntuoso.
brassière ['brasiə] V bra.
brave [breiv] adj valiente, intrépido. v desafiar. bravery n valentía f.
brawl [broːl] n alboroto m, riña f. v alborotar.
brawn [broin] n carnosidad f, músculo m; (food) carne de cerdo adobada f. brawny adj musculoso.
brazen ['breizn] adj (metal) de latón; (fig) desahogado.
Brazil [brə'zil] n (el) Brasil m. Brazilian n, adj brasileño, -a m, f. Brazil nut nuez del Brasil f.
breach [briːtʃ] n brecha f. v abrir brecha; romper. breach of promise infracción f. breach of the peace alteración de orden público f.
bread [bred] n pan m. breadcrumb n migaja f. breadcrumbs n pl pan rallado m sing. slice of bread rebanada f.
breadth [bredθ] n anchura f.
*break [breik] v romper; quebrar; quebrantar; (burst) reventar; (violate) infringir. break away desprenderse. break down (mech) averiarse; (cry) deshacerse en lágrimas. break in forzar la entrada. break out estallar. break up desmenuzar. n ruptura f, rotura f; (opening) abertura f; (interruption) interrupción f. breakdown n colapso m. breakthrough n avance m.
breakfast ['brekfəst] n desayuno m. v desayuner.
breast [brest] n pecho m; (female) mama f, teta f. breastbone n esternón m. breast pocket bolsillo de pecho m. breaststroke n brazada de pecho f.

breath [breθ] n respiración f, aliento m; (breeze) soplo m. breathless adj sin aliento. under one's breath en voz baja.
breathalyser ['breθəlaizə] n alcohómetro m.
breathe [briːð] v respirar, exhalar, inspirar. breathing n respiración f.
*breed [briːd] v criar, engendrar. n raza f, casta f. breeding n cría f, reproducción f; (upbringing) crianza f, educación f.
breeze [briːz] n brisa f. breezy adj fresco; (of manner) animado.
brew [bruː] v (infuse) infusionar; (beer) fabricar. n poción f. brewery n fábrica de cerveza f.
bribe [braib] n soborno m. v sobornar. bribery n soborno m.
brick [brik] n ladrillo m. v enladrillar. bricklayer n albañil m. brickyard n ladrillar m.
bride [braid] n novia f, desposada f. bridal adj nupcial. bridegroom m novio m, desposado m. bridesmaid n dama de honor f, madrina de boda f.
bridge[1] [bridʒ] n puente m. drawbridge n puente levadizo m. suspension bridge puente colgante m. v pontear.
bridge[2] [bridʒ] n (cards) bridge m.
bridle ['braidl] n brida f, freno m. v enfrenar; picarse.
brief [briːf] adj breve. n resumen m; (law) escrito m, relación f. v (law) instruir. briefcase n cartera f. briefly adv brevemente.
brigade [bri'geid] n brigada f.
bright [brait] adj brillante; (intelligent) inteligente. brighten v hacer brillar; (make happy) alegrar; (polish) pulir; (weather) aclarar. brightness n brillantez f; (intelligence) talento m.
brilliant ['briljənt] adj brillante. brilliance n brillo m, fulgor m.
brim [brim] n (of a container) borde m; (hat) ala f.
brine [brain] n salmuera f.
*bring [briŋ] v traer, llevar, conducir. bring about causar, ocasionar. bring down rebajar. bring in introducir. bring off lograr, conseguir. bring out sacar; publicar. bring together reunir. bring to light descubrir. bring up criar, educar.
brink [briŋk] n borde m. on the brink of a dos dedos de.

brisk [brisk] *adj* animado, vivo.
bristle ['brisl] *n* cerda *f*. *v* erizarse. **bristly** *adj* erizado.
Britain ['britn] *n* Gran Bretaña *f*. **British** *adj* británico. **Briton** *n* britano, -a *m, f*, británico, -a *m, f*.
brittle ['britl] *adj* quebradizo.
broad [broid] *adj* ancho; *(fig)* lato, amplio; *(accent)* fuerte. **broad-minded** *adj* tolerante. **broaden** *v* ensanchar. **broadly** *adv* en general. **broadness** *n* anchura *f*.
broadcast ['broidkaist] *n* emisión *f*, radiodifusión *f*; *v* emitir, radiar. **broadcasting station** *n* emisora *f*.
broccoli ['brokəli] *n* bróculi *m*, brécol *m*.
brochure ['brouʃuə] *n* folleto *m*.
broke [brouk] *V* break. *adj (coll)* pelado, sin blanca.
broken ['broukn] *V* break.
broker ['broukə] *n* corredor de bolsa *m*.
bronchitis [broŋ'kaitis] *m* bronquitis *f*.
bronze [bronz] *n* bronce *m*.
brooch [broutʃ] *n* broche *m*.
brood [bruid] *n (chickens)* pollada *f*; *(birds)* nidada *f*; *(other animals)* cria *f*. *v* empollar. **brood over** ruminar.
brook [bruk] *n* arroyo *m*.
broom [bruim] *n* escoba *f*; *(bot)* retama *f*.
broth [broθ] *n* caldo *m*.
brothel ['broθl] *n* burdel *m*, lupanar *m*.
brother ['brʌðə] *n* hermano *m*. **brother-in-law** *n* cuñado *m*. **brotherhood** *n* fraternidad *f*. **brotherly** *adv* fraternal.
brow [brau] *n* frente *f*; *(hill)* cumbre *f*. **browbeat** *v* intimidar verbalmente.
brown [braun] *adj* castaño, moreno. *v (cookery)* dorar; *(tan)* tostar. **brown paper** papel de estraza *m*. **brownish** *adj* pardusco.
browse [brauz] *v* pacer.
bruise [bruiz] *n* contusión *f*, magulladura *f*. *v* magullar.
brunette [brui'net] *n* morena *f*.
brush [brʌʃ] *n* cepillo *m*; *(broom)* escoba *f*; *(for painting)* pincel *m*; *(undergrowth)* matorral *m*. *v* cepillar; *(sweep)* barrer; *(touch)* rozar. **brush aside** echar a un lado. **brush off** sacudir(se).
brusque [brusk] *adj* brusco, rudo.
Brussels ['brʌsəlz] *n* Bruselas. **Brussels sprouts** coles de Bruselas *f pl*.
brute [bruit] *n* bruto *m*, bestia *m, f*. **brutal** *adj* brutal, bestial. **brutality** *n* brutalidad *f*.

bubble ['bʌbl] *n* burbuja *f*; borbollón *m*. *v* burbujear, borbollar.
buck [bʌk] *n* gamo *m*. *v* encorvarse. **buck up** animarse.
bucket ['bʌkit] *n* cubo *m*, balde *m*.
buckle ['bʌkl] *n* hebilla *f*. *v* enhebillar; doblarse.
buck-tooth *n* diente saliente *m*.
bud [bʌd] *n* brote *m*. *v* brotar, germinar.
budge [bʌdʒ] *v* mover, moverse, menearse.
budgerigar ['bʌdʒərigai] *n* periquito *m*.
budget ['bʌdʒit] *n* presupuesto *m*. *v* presupuestar.
buffalo ['bʌfəlou] *n* búfalo *m*.
buffer ['bʌfə] *n* parachoque *m*.
buffet[1] ['bʌfit] *n (blow)* bofetón *m*, bofetada *f*. *v* abofetear, golpear.
buffet[2] ['bufei] *n* fonda *f*, bar *m*.
bug [bʌg] *n* chinche *m*. *v (coll)* ocultar un micrófono en.
bugger ['bʌgə] *n* sodomita *m*. *v* cometer sodomía. *interj* ¡joder! **bugger off!** ¡vete a la mierda! **buggery** *m* sodomía *f*.
bugle ['bjuigl] *n* corneta *f*. **bugler** *n* trompetero *m*.
*build [bild] *v* const. ir; edificar; fundar. **building** *n* edificio *m*. **building site** *n* solar *m*. **built-up area** *n* zona urbana *f*.
bulb [bʌlb] *n (elec)* bombilla *f*; *(bot)* bulbo *m*.
Bulgaria [bʌl'geəriə] *n* Bulgaria *f*. **Bulgarian** *n, adj* búlgaro, -a *m, f*.
bulge [bʌldʒ] *n* hinchazón *f*, bulto *m*. *v* hincharse. **bulging** *adj* hinchado (de).
bulk [bʌlk] *n* bulto *m*; masa *f*; *(larger part)* grueso *m*. **in bulk** *(comm)* en bruto. **bulky** *adj* voluminoso.
bull [bul] *n* toro *m*. **bullfight** *n* corrida de toros *f*. **bullfighter** *n* torero *m*. **bull in a china shop** un caballo loco en una cacharrería *m*. **bullring** *n* plaza de toros *f*. **bull's-eye** *n* centro del blanco *m*.
bulldozer ['buldouzə] *n* bulldozer *m*, excavadora *f*.
bullet ['bulit] *n* bala *f*. **bullet-proof** *adj* a prueba de balas.
bulletin ['bulətin] *n* boletín *m*.
bullion ['buliən] *n (gold)* oro en barras *m*; *(silver)* plata en barras *f*.
bully ['buli] *n* valentón *m*, rufián *m*. *v* intimidar.
bum [bʌm] *n (coll)* posaderas *f pl*. *v* holgazanear.

bump [bʌmp] *n (swelling)* hinchazón *f*; *(blow)* golpe *m*. *v* chocar, golpear.

bumper ['bʌmpə] *n (mot)* parachoques *m invar*. *adj* abundante.

bun [bʌn] *n* buñuelo *m*; *(hair)* moño *m*.

bunch [bʌntʃ] *n (flowers)* ramo *m*; *(fruit)* racimo *m*; *(coll: gang)* pandilla *f*. *v* agruparse.

bundle ['bʌndl] *n* fardo *m*, bulto *m*. *v* enfardar, liar.

bungalow ['bʌŋgəlou] *n* chalet *m*, casa de un solo piso *f*.

bungle ['bʌŋgl] *v* estropear, chapucear. *n* chapucería *f*. **do a bunk** pirarse. **bunker** ['bʌŋkə] *n chapucero, -a *m*, *f*. **bungling** *adj* chapucero.

bunion ['bʌnjən] *n* juanete *m*.

bunk [bʌŋk] *n* litera *f*; *(coll: nonsense)* palabrería *f*. **do a bunk** pirarse.

bunker ['bʌŋkə] *n (refuge)* refugio *m*; *(coal)* carbonera *f*; *(golf)* bunker *m*, hoya de arena *f*.

buoy [boi] *n* boya *f*. **buoyancy** *n* fluctuación *f*. **buoyant** *adj* boyante.

burden ['bəːdn] *n* carga *f*. *v* cargar.

bureau ['bjuərou] *n (desk)* escritorio *m*; *(office)* oficina *f*; departmento *m*.

bureaucracy [bju'rɔkrəsi] *n* burocracia *f*. **bureaucrat** *n* burócrata *m*, *f*. **bureaucratic** *adj* burocrático.

burglar ['bəːglə] *n* ladrón *m*. **burglar alarm** alarma contra ladrones *f*. **burglary** *n* robo *m*. **burgle** *v* robar.

*** burn** [bəːn] *v* quemar, incendiar. *n* quemadura *f*. **burner** *n* quemador *m*. **burning** *adj* ardiente.

burrow ['bʌrou] *n* madriguera *f*. *v* amadrigar, minar.

*** burst** [bəːst] *n* estallido *m*, explosión *f*. *v* reventar, estallar. **burst into tears** romper a llorar. **burst open** forzar.

bury ['beri] *v* enterrar, sepultar. **burial** *n* entierro *m*.

bus [bʌs] *n* autobús *m*, ómnibus *m*. **double-decker bus** ómnibus de dos pisos *m*. **bus station** término *m*. **bus-stop** *n* parada de autobús or ómnibus.

bush [buʃ] *n* arbusto *m*; *(undergrowth)* maleza *f*. **bushy** *adj* denso, espeso, matoso.

business ['biznis] *n* negocio *m*, comercio *m*; ocupación *f*. **business hours** horas de trabajo *f pl*. **businesslike** *adj* práctico,

sistemático. **businessman** *n* hombre de negocios *m*. **mean business** estar resuelto. **mind one's own business** no meterse donde no le llaman.

bust[1] [bʌst] *n (anat)* pecho *m*; *(art)* busto *m*.

bust[2] [bʌst] *adj (fam)* quebrado, reventado. **go bust** quebrar.

bustle ['bʌsl] *n* animación *f*. *v* menearse, dar prisa (a).

busy ['bizi] *adj* ocupado; activo, diligente. **busybody** *n* entrometido *m*.

but [bʌt] *conj* pero, sino. *prep* excepto. *adv* solamente. **but for** a no ser por. **nothing but** nada más que.

butane ['bjutein] *n* butano *m*.

butcher [butʃə] *n* carnicero *m*. **butcher's shop** carnicería *f*. *v* matar, destrozar.

butler ['bʌtlə] *n* mayordomo *m*.

butt[1] [bʌt] *n (gun)* culata *f*; *(cigarette, etc.)* colilla *f*.

butt[2] [bʌt] *n (of jokes, etc.)* objeto *m*.

butt[3] [bʌt] *v* topar, acornear. **butt in** entrometerse.

butter ['bʌtə] *n* mantequilla *f*; *v* untar con mantequilla.

buttercup ['bʌtəkʌp] *n* ranúnculo *m*.

butterfly ['bʌtəflai] *n* mariposa *f*.

butterscotch ['bʌtəskotʃ] *n* dulce de azúcar y mantequilla *m*.

buttocks ['bʌtəks] *n pl* nalgas *f pl*.

button ['bʌtn] *n* botón *m*. *v* abotonear. **buttonhole** *n* ojal *m*. *v (coll)* importunar.

buttress ['bʌtris] *n* estribo *m*, contrafuerte *m*; *(fig)* apoyo *m*. *v* estribar.

*** buy** [bai] *v* comprar. *n* compra *f*. **buy up** acaparar. **buyer** *n* comprador, -a *m*, *f*.

buzz [bʌz] *v* zumbar. *n* zumbido *m*. **buzzer** *n* zumbador *m*; *(bell)* timbre *m*.

by [bai] *prep* por, de, a; *(near)* cerca de. *adv* al lado, cerca; aparte. **by all means** naturalmente. **by and large** en general. **by the way** de paso.

bye-law ['bailɔː] *n* reglamento *m*.

by-election ['baiiˌlekʃən] *n* elección parcial *f*.

bypass ['baipaːs] *n* desviación *f*. *v* desviar.

by-product ['baiprodəkt] *n* subproducto *m*.

bystander ['baiˌstandə] *n* espectador, -a *m*, *f*.

C

cab [kab] *n* taxi *m*; (*lorry*) cabina *f*.
cabaret ['kabərei] *n* cabaret *m*; (*show*) attracciones *f pl*.
cabbage ['kabidʒ] *n* col *f*, repollo *m*.
cabin ['kabin] *n* cabaña *f*; (*naut*) camarote *m*; (*aircraft, etc.*) cabina *f*. **cabin cruiser** *n* motonave *f*.
cabinet ['kabinit] *n* (*cupboard*) armario *m*; (*display*) vitrina *f*; (*pol*) gabinete *m*, consejo de ministros *m*. **medicine cabinet** botiquín *m*. **cabinet-maker** *n* ebanista *m*.
cable ['keibl] *n* (*rope, wire*) cable *m*; (*message*) cablegrama *m*. **cable address** dirección telegráfica *f*. **cable car** funicular *m*. *v* cablegrafiar.
cackle ['kakl] *v* carcarear. *n* carcareo *m*.
cactus ['kaktəs] *n pl* -i *or* -uses cacto *m*.
caddie ['kadi] *n* caddy *m*; (*trolley*) carrito *m*.
cadence ['keidəns] *n* cadencia *f*.
cadet [kə'det] *n* cadete *m*.
café ['kafei] *n* café *m*, restaurante *m*.
cafeteria [kafə'tiəriə] *n* cafetería *f*, restaurante de autoservicio *m*.
caffeine ['kafiːn] *n* cafeína *f*.
cage [keidʒ] *n* jaula *f*. *v* enjaular.
cake [keik] *n* pastel *m*; (*soap*) pastilla *f*. **Christmas cake** tarta de Navidad *f*. **a piece of cake** (*coll*) ser pan comido. **sell like hot cakes** (*coll*) venderse como rosquillas. **take the cake** (*coll*) llevarse la palma. *v* endurecerse.
calamine ['kaləmain] *n* calamina *f*.
calamity [kə'laməti] *n* calamidad *f*.
calcium ['kalsiəm] *n* calcio *m*.
calculate ['kalkjuleit] *v* calcular; (*guess, suppose*) confiar en. **calculated** *adj* intencional, deliberado. **calculating** *adj* calculador. **calculation** *n* cálculo *m*. **calculator** *n* calculador *m*.
calendar ['kaləndə] *n* calendario *m*. **calendar month** mes civil *m*.
calf[1] [kaːf] *n* (*zool*) becerro *m*, ternero *m*.
calf[2] [kaːf] *n* (*anat*) pantorrilla *f*.
calibre ['kalibə] *n* (*measurement*) calibre *m*; (*talent*) capacidad *f*, talento *m*.
call [koːl] *n* llamada *f*, llamamiento *m*; (*cry*) grito *m*; (*visit*) visita *f*. **on call** de guardia. **trunk call** conferencia *f*. *v* llamar. **call for** pedir. **call off** cancelar. **call on** visitar. **call up** evocar; convocar.

callous ['kaləs] *adj* insensible, duro.
calm [kaːm] *adj* calmoso, sosegado, tranquilo. *n* calma *f*, tranquilidad *f*. *v* calmar, sosegar.
calorie ['kaləri] *n* caloría *f*.
came [keim] *V* come.
camel ['kaməl] *n* camello *m*.
camera ['kamərə] *n* máquina fotográfica *f*. **in camera** a puerta cerrada. **cameraman** *n* cameraman *m*.
camouflage ['kaməflaʒ] *n* camuflaje *m*. *v* camuflar.
camp[1] [kamp] *n* (*site*) campamento *m*. **camp-bed** *n* cama plegable *f*. **holiday camp** campamento de vacaciones *m*. *v* acampar.
camp[2] [kamp] *adj* (*coll*) afeminado; afectado; homosexual.
campaign [kam'pein] *n* campaña *f*. **advertising campaign** campaña publicitaria *f*. **election campaign** campaña electoral *f*. *v* hacer (una) campaña.
campus ['kampəs] *n* recinto universitario *m*, campus *m*, ciudad universitaria *f*.
*can[1] [kan] *v* (*be able*) poder; (*know how to*) saber.
can[2] [kan] *n* (*container*) lata *f*. **can-opener** *n* abrelatas *m invar*. *v* enlatar, conservar en lata. **canned** *adj* enlatado.
Canada ['kanədə] *n* Canadá *m*. **Canadian** *n*(*m*+*f*), *adj* canadiense.
canal [kə'nal] *n* canal *m*.
canary [kə'neəri] *n* canario *m*.
Canary Islands *n pl* (*islas*) Canarias *f pl*.
cancel ['kansəl] *v* (*contract, decree, etc.*) cancelar; (*cheque, order, invitation*) anular; (*delete*) tachar; (*maths*) eliminar. **cancel out** anularse. **cancellation** *n* cancelación *f*; anulación *f*.
cancer ['kansə] *n* cáncer *m*. **cancerous** *adj* canceroso.
Cancer ['kansə] *n* Cáncer *m*.
candid ['kandid] *adj* franco, sincero.
candidate ['kandidət] *n* candidato *m*. **candidacy** *n* candidatura *f*.
candle ['kandl] *n* vela *f*; (*in a church*) cirio *m*. **burn the candle at both ends** hacer de la noche día. **candlestick** *n* candelero *m*.
candour ['kandə] *n* franqueza *f*, sinceridad *f*.
candy ['kandi] *n* caramelo *m*. *v* escarchar, cristalizar.

cane [kein] *n* caña *f*; (*walking stick*) bastón *m*; (*school*) palmeta *f*, vara *f*. **sugar cane** caña de azúcar *f*. **cane furniture** muebles de mimbre *m pl*. *v* castigar con la palmeta *or* vara.

canine ['keinain] *adj* canino. **canine tooth** diente canino *m*.

cannabis ['kanəbis] *n* marijuana *f*.

cannibal ['kanibəl] *n*(*m*+*f*), *adj* caníbal. **cannibalism** *n* canibalismó *m*.

cannon ['kanən] *n* cañón *m*. **cannonball** *n* bala de cañón *f*.

canoe [kə'nuː] *n* canoa *f*. *v* ir en canoa.

canon ['kanən] *n* canónigo *m*. **canonical** *adj* canónico. **canonize** *v* canonizar. **canonization** *n* canonización *f*.

canopy ['kanəpi] *n* (*awning*) toldo *m*; (*over a bed*) dosel *m*, baldaquín *m*.

canteen [kan'tiːn] *n* (*restaurant*) cantina *f*; (*flask*) cantimplora *f*; (*cutlery*) juego de cubiertos *m*.

canter ['kantə] *n* medio galope *m*. *v* ir a medio galope.

canton ['kantən] *n* cantón *m*.

canvas ['kanvəs] *n* (*fabric*) lona *f*; (*art*) lienzo.

canvass ['kanvəs] *v* solicitar votos de; (*comm*) buscar clientes; (*public opinion*) sondear.

canyon ['kanjən] *n* cañón *m*.

cap [kap] *n* gorra *f*; (*military or bathing*) gorro *m*; (*cover*) tapa *f*; (*bottle*) chapa *f*; (*pen*) capuchón *m*. *v* (*fig: crown*) coronar; (*do better than*) superar.

capable ['keipəbl] *adj* capaz, hábil. **capability** *n* capacidad *f*, habilidad *f*.

capacity [kə'pasəti] *n* capacidad *f*; (*mot*) cilindrada *f*.

cape[1] [keip] *n* (*cloak*) capa *f*; (*cycling*) impermeable de hule *m*.

cape[2] [keip] *n* (*geog*) cabo *m*.

caper ['keipə] *n* (*jump*) cabriola *f*; (*prank*) travesura *f*; (*cookery*) alcaparra *f*.

capillary [kə'piləri] *n* capilar *m*.

capital ['kapitl] *adj* capital. **capital punishment** pena capital *f*. *n* (*letter*) mayúscula *f*; (*city*) capital *f*; (*money*) fondo de operaciones *m*. **capitalism** *n* capitalismo *m*. **capitalist** *n* capitalista *m*, *f*. **capitalistic** *adj* capitalista. **capitalize** *v* capitalizar. **capitalization** *n* capitalización *f*.

capitulate [kə'pitjuleit] *v* capitular. **capitulation** *n* capitulación *f*.

capricious [kə'prifəs] *adj* caprichoso. **caprice**, **capriciousness** *n* capricho *m*.

Capricorn ['kaprikoɪn] *n* Capricornio *m*.

capsicum ['kapsikəm] *n* pimiento *m*, chile *m*.

capsize [kap'saiz] *v* volcar, zozobrar.

capsule ['kapsjuːl] *n* cápsula *f*.

captain ['kaptin] *n* capitán *m*. *v* capitanear. **captaincy** *n* capitanía *f*.

caption ['kapfən] *n* encabezamiento *m*, pie *m*. *v* poner pie a.

captive ['kaptiv] *n*, *adj* cautivo, -a. **captivate** *v* cautivar. **captivity** *n* cautividad *f*.

capture ['kaptfə] *v* capturar; (*place*) tomar; (*market*) acaparar; (*fig*) atraer. *n* captura *f*, apresamiento *m*; (*place*) toma *f*.

car [kaɪ] *n* coche *m*, automóvil *m*; (*rail*) vagón *m*; (*cable*) cabina *f*. **car park** aparcamiento *m*. **car wash** lavado de coches *m*. **dining car** coche comedor *m*. **racing car** coche de carreras *m*. **sleeping car** coche cama *m*.

caramel ['karəmel] *n* caramelo *m*, azúcar quemado *m*.

carat ['karət] *n* quilate *m*.

caravan ['karəvan] *n* (*mot*) remolque *m*; (*travellers*) caravana *f*; (*gipsy*) carromato *m*.

caraway ['karəwei] *n* (*seed*) carvi *m*; (*plant*) alcaravea *f*.

carbohydrate ['kaɪbə'haidreit] *n* carbohidrato *m*.

carbon ['kaɪbən] *n* (*chem*) carbono *m*; carbón *m*. **carbon dioxide** bióxido de carbono *m*. **carbon paper** papel carbón *m*.

carbuncle ['kaɪbʌŋkl] *n* (*med*) carbunco *m*, carbunclo *m*.

carburettor ['kaɪbjuretə] *n* carburador *m*.

carcass ['kaɪkəs] *n* (*animal*) res muerta *f*.

card [kaɪd] *n* tarjeta *f*; (*visiting*) tarjeta de visita *f*; (*postcard*) tarjeta postal *f*; (*playing card*) carta *f*, naipe *m*; (*membership*) carnet *m*; (*thin cardboard*) cartulina *f*; (*coll*) gracioso, -a *m*, *f*. **cardboard** *n* cartón *m*. **card index** fichero *m*.

cardiac ['kaɪdiak] *adj* cardiaco.

cardigan ['kaɪdigən] *n* rebeca *f*.

cardinal ['kaɪdənl] *n* (*church*, *bird*) cardenal *m*. *adj* cardinal, esencial. **cardinal number** número cardinal *m*.

care [keə] *n* cuidado *m*, atención *f*; (*worry*) inquietud *f*; (*responsibility*) cargo *m*. **medical care** asistencia médica *f*. **care of** para entregar a. **handle with care** frágil. **take care!** ¡ojo! *v* importar, preocuparse por. **take care of** guardar, tener cuidado de. **careful** *adj* cuidadoso. **carefulness** *n* cuidado *m*, esmero *m*. **careless** *adj* descuidado, desatento.

career [kə'riə] *n* carrera *f*, curso *m*. *v* correr a toda velocidad.

caress [kə'res] *n* caricia *f*. *v* acariciar.

cargo ['kaɪgou] *n* carga *f*, cargamento *m*.

caricature ['karikətjuə] *n* caricatura *f*. *v* caricaturizar.

carnage ['kaɪnidʒ] *n* carnicería *f*.

carnal ['kaɪnl] *adj* carnal. **carnality** *n* carnalidad *f*.

carnation [kaɪ'neiʃən] *n* clavel *m*.

carnival ['kaɪnivəl] *n* carnaval *m*.

carnivorous [kaɪ'nivərəs] *adj* carnívoro. **carnivore** *n* carnívoro, -a *m, f*.

carol ['karəl] *n* villancico *m*.

carpenter ['kaɪpəntə] *n* carpintero *m*. **carpentry** *n* carpintería *f*.

carpet ['kaɪpit] *n* alfombra *f*; (*fitted*) moqueta *f*. **carpet-sweeper** escoba mecánica *f*. *v* alfombrar.

carriage ['karidʒ] *n* carruaje *m*, carro *m*; vagón *m*; (*posture*) manera de andar *f*; (*comm*) porte *m*. **carriageway** *n* calzada *f*. **dual carriageway** carretera de doble calzada *f*.

carrier ['kariə] *n* portador *m*; (*comm*) empresa de transportes *f*; (*med*) portador, -a *m, f*.

carrot ['karət] *n* zanahoria *f*.

carry ['kari] *v* llevar; (*bring*) traer; (*a load*) transportar; (*by pipes*) conducir; (*sustain*) sostener. **carry forward** (*comm*) pasar. **carry out** realizar. **carrycot** *n* cuna portátil *f*.

cart [kaɪt] *n* carro *m*; (*handcart*) carro de mano *m*; (*trolley*) carrito *m*. *v* carretear. **cart horse** caballo de tiro *m*.

cartilage ['kaɪtilidʒ] *n* cartílago *m*.

cartography [kaɪ'togrəfi] *n* cartografía *f*.

carton ['kaɪtən] *n* cartón *m*, caja de cartón *f*.

cartoon [kaɪ'tuɪn] *n* caricatura *f*, chiste *m*; (*art*) cartón *m*; (*film*) dibujos animados *m pl*. **cartoonist** *n* caricaturista *m, f*, humorista *m, f*.

cartridge ['kaɪtridʒ] *n* cartucho *m*; (*blank*) cartucho sin bala *m*.

carve [kaɪv] *v* (*meat*) trinchar; (*cut*) cortar; (*sculpture*) tallar. **carve up** (*divide*) dividir; (*stab*) acuchillar. **carving knife** cuchillo de trinchar *m*.

cascade [kas'keid] *n* cascada *f*, salto de agua *m*. *v* caer en cascada.

case[1] [keis] *n* caso *m*; (*affair*) asunto *m*. **in any case** en todo caso. **in case** en caso. **in no case** de ningún modo. **in the case of** en cuanto a. **it's not a case of ...** no se trata de .... **just in case** por si acaso. **state the case** exponer los hechos.

case[2] [keis] *n* (*box*) caja *f*; (*rigid*) estuche *m*; (*soft*) funda. **suitcase** *n* maleta *f*. *v* encajonar, embalar.

cash [kaʃ] *n* dinero al constante *m*; (*comm*) pago al contado *m*. **cash account** cuenta de caja *f*. **cash book** libro de caja *m*. **cash discount** descuento por pago al contado *m*. **cash on delivery** envío contra reembolso *m*. **cash register** caja registradora *f*. **petty cash** dinero para gastos menores *m*.

cashier[1] [ka'ʃiə] *n* (*bank*) cajero, -a *m, f*.

cashier[2] [ka'ʃiə] *v* (*mil*) dar de baja.

cashmere [kaʃ'miə] *n* cachemira *f*.

casing ['keisiŋ] *n* cubierta *f*; (*wrapping*) envoltura *f*; (*cylinder*) camisa *f*.

casino [kə'siɪnou] *n* casino *m*.

cask [kaɪsk] *n* barril *m*.

casket ['kaɪskit] *n* joyero *m*, cofre *m*.

casserole ['kasəroul] *n* (*dish*) cacerola *f*; (*food*) cazuela *f*.

cassette [kə'set] *n* (*tape*) cassette *m*; (*phot*) cartucho *m*.

cassock ['kasək] *n* sotana *f*.

*cast ['kaɪst] *n* (*acting*) reparto *m*; (*throw*) lanzamiento *m*; (*appearance*) aspecto *m*; (*tech*) molde *m*; (*squint*) estrabismo *m*; (*plaster*) escayola *f*. *v* echar, arrojar; (*tech*) moldear, fundir. **castaway** *n* náufrago *m*. **cast aside** desechar. **cast down** bajar. **cast iron** hierro colado *m*. **cast off** abandonar; (*naut*) desamarrar.

castanets [kastə'nets] *pl n* castañuelas *f pl*.

caste [kaɪst] *n* casta *f*.

castle ['kaɪsl] *n* castillo *m*.

castor ['kaɪstə] *n* (*wheel*) ruedecilla *f*.

castor oil *n* aceite de ricino *m*.

castrate [kə'streit] *v* castrar. **castration** *n* castración *f*.

casual ['kaʒuəl] *adj* casual, informal; (*carefree*) despreocupado. **casual clothes** ropa de sport *f sing*. **casually** *adv* de paso.

casualty ['kaʒuəlti] *n* accidente *m*; víctima *f*; (*mil*) baja *f*.

cat [kat] n gato, -a m, f. l-t the cat out of the bag descubrir el pastel.

catalogue ['katəlog] n catálogo m. v catalogar.

catalyst ['katəlist] n catalizador m.

catapult ['katəpʌlt] n catapulta f. honda f. v catapultar.

cataract ['katərakt] n catarata f.

catarrh [kə'taː] n catarro m.

catastrophe [kə'tastrəfi] n catástrofe f. catastrophic adj catastrófico.

*catch [katʃ] v (seize) agarrar, cojer; (capture) prender, atrapar; (disease) contraer; (hook) engancharse. catch on (coll) comprender. catch out sorprender. catch up alcanzar. n (act of catching) cogida f; (prey) presa f; (bolt) pestillo m; (buckle) hebijón m; (drawback) trampa f; (trick) truco m. safety catch fiador m. catching adj contagioso. catchy adj pegadizo.

category ['katəgəri] n categoría f. categorical adj categórico, rotundo. categorize v clasificar.

cater ['keitə] v proveer de comida. cater for atender a. caterer n proveedor, -a m, f. catering n abastecimiento m.

caterpillar ['katəpilə] n oruga f.

cathedral [kə'θiːdrəl] n catedral f.

cathode ['kaθoud] n cátodo m. cathode-ray tube tubo de rayos catódicos m.

catholic ['kaθəlik] n, adj católico, -a. adj universal; ortodoxo. catholicism n catolicismo m. catholicity n catolicidad f.

catkin ['katkin] n candelilla f.

cattle ['katl] n ganado m.

catty ['kati] adj malicioso.

caught [koɪt] V catch.

cauliflower ['koliflauə] n coliflor m.

cause [koɪz] n causa f, motivo m. v causar, provocar. in the cause of por.

causeway ['koɪzwei] n terraplén m.

caustic ['koɪstik] adj cáustico, mordaz.

caution ['koɪʃən] n cautela f, cuidado m; (warning) advertencia f. v (reprimand) amonestar; (warn) advertir. cautionary adj amonestador. cautious adj cauteloso, precavido.

cavalry ['kavəlri] n caballería f.

cave [keiv] n cueva f, caverna f. cave in derrumbarse. cavernous adj cavernoso.

caviar ['kaviaɪ] n caviar m.

cavity ['kavəti] n cavidad f; (dental) cavies f invar.

cayenne [kei'en] n pimentón m.

cease [siːs] v cesar. cease-fire n alto el fuego. ceaseless adj incesante.

cedar ['siːdə] n cedro m.

cedilla [si'dilə] n cedilla f.

ceiling ['siːliŋ] n techo m; (aero) altura f; (fig) tope m, límite m. hit the ceiling subirse por las paredes.

celebrate ['seləbreit] v celebrar, festejar. celebrated adj célebre. celebration n celebración f. celebrant n celebrante m.

celery ['seləri] n apio m.

celestial [sə'lestiəl] adj celestial; (astron) celeste.

celibate ['selibət] n(m+f), adj célibe. celibacy n celibato m.

cell [sel] n celda f; (biol) célula f; (elec) pila f.

cellar ['selə] n sótano m; (wine) bodega f.

cello ['tʃelou] n violoncelo m. cellist n violoncelista m, f.

cellular ['seljulə] adj celular.

cement [sə'ment] n cemento. v (tech) cementar; (fig) cimentar.

cemetery ['semətri] n cementerio m.

cenotaph ['senətaɪf] n cenotafio m.

censor ['sensə] n censor m. v censurar; (delete) tachar. censorious adj censorador. censorship n censura f.

censure ['senʃə] n censura f. v censurar. censurable adv censurable.

census ['sensəs] n censo m. take a census of empadronar.

cent [sent] n centavo m.

centenary [sen'tiːnəri] nm, adj centenario. centenarian n, adj centenario, -a. centennial adj centenario.

centigrade ['sentigreid] adj centígrado.

centimetre ['sentimiːtə] n centímetro m.

centipede ['sentipiːd] n ciempiés m invar.

centre ['sentə] n centro m. community centre centro social m. v centrar. central adj central, céntrico. central heating calefacción central f. centralize v centralizar. centralization n centralización f.

centrifugal [sen'trifjugəl] adj centrífugo.

century ['sentʃuri] n siglo m.

ceramic [sə'ramik] adj cerámico. ceramics n cerámica f sing.

cereal ['siəriəl] nm, adj cereal.

ceremony ['serəməni] n ceremonia f. stand on ceremony andarse con ceremonias. ceremonial nm, adj ceremonial. ceremonious adj ceremonioso.

certain ['səɪtn] adj cierto, seguro. make certain asegurarse. certainly adv desde luego, naturalmente. **certainly not** de ninguna manera. **certainty** n certeza f, certidumbre f; seguridad f.

certificate [sə'tifikət] n certificado m; (*academic*) título m, diploma f. **birth certificate** partida de nascimiento f. **death certificate** partida de defunción f. **marriage certificate** partida de matrimonio f. **certify** v certificar; garantizar.

cesspool ['sespuɪl] n pozo negro m.

chafe [tʃeif] v (*rub*) rozar; (*irritate*) irritar; (*for warmth*) frotar; (*fig*) enfadar. n rozadura f; irritación f.

chaffinch ['tʃafintʃ] n pinzón m.

chain [tʃein] n cadena f. **chain store** sucursal m. v encadenar.

chair [tʃeə] n silla f; (*university*) cátedra f; (*meeting*) presidencia f. **folding chair** silla plegable f. **take the chair** tomar la presidencia. **chairman** n presidente m. v presidir.

chalet ['ʃalei] n chalet m.

chalk [tʃɔɪk] n (*geol*) creta f; (*for writing*) tiza f. **not by a long chalk** ni mucho menos. v marcar con tiza. **chalk up** apuntarse. **chalky** adj cretáceo, yesoso.

challenge ['tʃalindʒ] n reto m, desafío m; (*sentry*) alto m; (*incentive*) estimulo m; (*law*) recusación f. v desafiar, retar. **challenger** n desafiador m, retador m.

chamber ['tʃeimbə] n (*room, legislative body*) cámara f; (*tech*) recámara f. **chambermaid** n doncella f, camarera f. **chamber music** música de cámara f. **chamber pot** orinal m.

chameleon [kəmiːliən] n camaleón m.

chamois ['ʃamwaɪ] n gamuza f.

champagne [ʃam'pein] n champaña f.

champion ['tʃampiən] n, adj campeón, -ona. v defender, hacerse el campeón de. **championship** n campeonato m.

chance [tʃains] n casualidad f, suerte f, azar m; oportunidad f, ocasión f; posibilidad f; riesgo m. adj casual, fortuito. v arriesgar; probar; (*happen*) acaecer. **chance upon** tropezarse con.

chancellor [tʃainsələ] n canciller m. **chancellery** n cancillería f.

chandelier [ʃandə'liə] n araña f.

change [tʃeindʒ] n cambio m; (*money*) suelto m; (*clothes*) muda f. **for a change** para variar. v cambiar; mudar. **changeable** adj (*character, weather*) variable; (*inconsistent*) cambiadizo; (*able to be*

changed) cambiable. **changing room** vestuario m.

channel ['tʃanl] n canal m; (*of a river*) cauce m; (*fig*) vía f; (*groove*) ranura f. **English Channel** Canal de la Mancha m.

chant [tʃaɪnt] n canción f, canto m. v cantar; entonar.

chaos ['keios] n caos m. **chaotic** adj caótico.

chap¹ [tʃap] v (*skin*) agrietar. n grieta f.

chap² [tʃap] n (*coll*) tipo m, sujeto m.

chapel ['tʃapəl] n capilla f.

chaperon ['ʃapəroun] n carabina f. v acompañar.

chaplain ['tʃaplin] n capellán m.

chapter ['tʃaptə] n capítulo m; (*rel*) cabildo m. **quote chapter and verse** citar literalmente.

char¹ [tʃaɪ] v (*burn*) carbonizar.

char² [tʃaɪ] n (*charwoman*) asistenta f.

character ['karəktə] n carácter m; (*person*) personaje m; (*role*) papel m; (*coll*) tipo m. **character reference** informe m. **characterize** v caracterizar. **characterization** n caracterización f.

characteristic [karəktə'ristik] adj característico. n característica f.

charcoal ['tʃaɪkoul] n carbón de leña m.

charge [tʃaɪdʒ] n (*responsibility*) cargo m; (*task*) tarea f; (*battery, explosive, attack*) carga f. **charge account** cuenta a cargo f. **in charge of** encargado de. **take charge of** hacerse cargo de. v (*accuse*) acusar; (*bill*) cobrar; (*mil*) atacar.

chariot ['tʃariət] n carro m.

charity ['tʃarəti] n caridad f; (*alms*) limosna f; (*society*) sociedad benéfica f. **charitable** adj caritativo.

charm [tʃaɪm] n encanto m; (*spell*) hechizo m. v encantar; hechizar. **charming** adj encantador, simpático.

chart [tʃaɪt] n (*naut*) carta marina f; (*map*) mapa m; (*table*) tabla f; (*graph*) gráfico m. v tabular; trazar.

charter ['tʃaɪtə] n (*law*) carta f; (*comm*) flete m, fletamento m, fletamiento m; (*transport*) alquiler m. v fletar; alquilar; (*grant a charter*) conceder carta a. **charter flight** vuelo charter' m. **charter member** socio fundador m.

chase [tʃeis] v perseguir; (*hunt*) cazar. **chase after** ir detrás de. **chase away/off** ahuyentar. n persecución f; caza f.

chasm ['kazəm] n sima f, abismo m.

chassis ['ʃasi] n (mech) chasis m.

chaste [tʃeist] adj casto; (style) sobrio. chastity n castidad f.

chastise [tʃas'taiz] v castigar.

chat [tʃat] n charla f. v charlar. chatty adj charlador.

chatter ['tʃatə] v chacharear, parlotear; (teeth) castañetear. n cháchara f, parloteo m; (in exams) copiar. n timador, m; castañeteo m. chatterbox n charlatán, -ana m, f.

chauffeur ['ʃoufə] n chófer m, conductor, -a m, f.

chauvinism ['ʃouvinizəm] n chauvinismo m. chauvinist n(m+f), adj chauvinista.

cheap [tʃiːp] adj barato. dirt cheap baratísimo adj, adv. cheapen v abaratar.

cheat [tʃiːt] v (swindle) timar, estafar; (deceive) engañar; (at games) hacer trampas; (in exams) copiar. n timador, -a m, f, estafador, -a m, f; tramposo, -a m, f; (trick) trampa f.

check [tʃek] v parar, detener; (restrain) reprimir, refrenar; (inspect) inspeccionar; (facts) comprobar; (mark) poner contraseña a; (chess) dar jaque a. check in registrarse. check on averiguar. check with cotejar con. n parada f, detención f; (restraint) restricción f; (control) inspección f; (pattern) cuadro m; (chess) jaque m. checkmate v dar el mate; n jaque mate m. checkpoint n control m. check-up n (med) reconocimiento general m.

cheek [tʃiːk] n carrillo m, mejilla f; (coll) caradura f. turn the other cheek poner la otra mejilla. cheekbone n pómulo m. cheeky adj descarado.

cheer [tʃiə] v (shout) vitorear, aclamar; (gladden) alegrar. cheer on animar. cheer up alentar. n (shout) viva m; (comfort) consuelo m; (joy) ánimo m. cheers! interj ¡a su salud! cheerful adj alegre, animado. cheerfulness n alegría f. cheerio! interj ¡hasta luego! cheerless adj triste.

cheese [tʃiːz] n queso m. cheesecake n pastel de queso m. cheesecloth n estopilla f.

cheetah ['tʃiːtə] n leopardo cazador m.

chef [ʃef] n jefe de cocina m.

chemistry ['kemistri] n química f. chemical adj químico. chemist n químico m; farmacéutico m. chemist's shop farmacia f.

cheque [tʃek] n cheque m. chequebook n talonario de cheques m. cheque card

tarjeta de crédito f. traveller's cheque cheque de viaje m.

cherish ['tʃeriʃ] v (love) querer; (nourish) abrigar; (take care of) cuidar.

cherry ['tʃeri] n (fruit) cereza f; (tree) cerezo m.

chess [tʃes] n ajedrez m. chessboard n tablero de ajedrez m. chessman n pieza de ajedrez f.

chest [tʃest] n (anat) pecho m; (box) caja f. chest of drawers n cómoda f. chesty adj (cough) delicado de los broncios.

chestnut ['tʃesnʌt] n (fruit) castaña f; (tree) castaño m. adj (hair) castaño.

chew [tʃuː] v masticar. chewing gum chicle m. chew the cud rumiar. chew up estropear.

chick pea ['tʃik,piː] n garbanzo m.

chicken ['tʃikin] n pollo m. chickenpox n varicela f. chicken out (slang) ser una gallina.

chicory ['tʃikəri] n (coffee) achicoria f; (salad) escarola f.

chief [tʃiːf] n pl -s jefe m, f. adj principal. chiefly adv principalmente; sobre todo.

chilblain ['tʃilblein] n sabañón m.

child [tʃaild] n pl -ren niño, -a m, f. childbirth n parto m. childhood n niñez f. childish adj infantil, pueril. childless adj sin hijos.

Chile ['tʃili] n Chile m. Chilean n, adj chileno, -a.

chill [tʃil] n frio m; (med) tiritona f; (shiver) escalofrío m; (fig) frialdad f. v enfriar. chilled to the bone enfriado hasta los huesos. chilly adj fresco.

chilli ['tʃili] n chile m.

chime [tʃaim] v sonar, repicar. chime in intervenir. n carillón m.

chimney ['tʃimni] n chimenea f. chimney pot cañón de chimenea m. chimney sweep deshollinador m.

chimpanzee [tʃimpən'ziː] n chimpancé m.

chin [tʃin] n barbilla f, mentón m.

china ['tʃainə] n porcelana f.

China ['tʃainə] n China f. Chinese n, adj chino, -a. the Chinese los chinos.

chink¹ [tʃiŋk] n (fissure) raja f, grieta m.

chink² [tʃiŋk] n (sound) sonido metálico m. v hacer tintinear.

chip [tʃip] n (fragment) pedacito m; (in cup, etc.) desportilladura f; (gambling) ficha f. chipboard n madera aglomerada f. chips pl n (cookery) patata frita f. v astillar. **chip in** (*interrupt*) interrumpir; (*contribute money*) poner.

chiropodist [ki'rɔpədist] *n* pedicuro, -a *m*, *f*. **chiropody** *n* quiropodia *f*.

chirp [tʃəɪp] *v* (*birds*) gorjear; (*crickets*) chirriar. *n* gorjeo *m*; chirrido *m*. **chirpy** *adj* animado.

chisel ['tʃizl] *n* cincel *m*. *v* cincelar.

chivalry ['ʃivəlri] *n* caballerosidad *f*. **chivalrous** *adj* caballeroso.

chive [tʃaiv] *n* cebolleta *f*.

chlorine ['klɔtriɪn] *n* cloro *m*. **chlorinate** *v* tratar con cloro.

chloroform ['klɔrəfɔɪm] *n* cloroformo *m*. *v* cloroformizar.

chlorophyll ['klɔrəfil] *n* clorofila *f*.

chocolate ['tʃɔkələt] *n* chocolate *m*. **drinking chocolate** chocolate a la taza *m*.

choice [tʃois] *n* elección *f*, selección *f*; preferencia *f*. *adj* (*best*) flor y nata.

choir ['kwaiə] *n* coro *m*, coral *f*. **choirboy** *n* niño de coro *m*. **choirmaster** *n* director de coro *m*.

choke [tʃouk] *v* (*strangle*) estrangular; (*block*) obstruir. *n* (*mot*) estrangulador *m*.

cholera ['kɔlərə] *n* cólera *m*.

***choose** [tʃuɪz] *v* escoger, elegir.

chop¹ [tʃɔp] *n* (*meat*) chuleta *f*; (*blow*) golpe *m*. *v* (*cut*) cortar; (*mince*) picar; (*lop*) tronchar. **chop down** talar. **chopper** *n* hacha *f*; (*slang*) helicóptero *m*.

chop² [tʃɔp] *v* **chop and change** cambiar de opinión. **choppy** *adj* (*sea*) picado.

chops [tʃɔps] *pl n* (*jaws*) morros *m pl*. **lick one's chops** relamerse.

chopstick ['tʃɔpstik] *n* palillo *m*.

chord [kɔɪd] *n* (*music*) acorde *m*; (*anat*) cuerda *f*.

chore [tʃɔɪ] *n* (*unpleasant*) tarea penosa *f*. **chores** *pl n* (*household*) faenas de la casa *f pl*.

choreography [kɔri'ɔgrəfi] *n* coreografía *f*. **choreographer** *n* coreógrafo *m*.

chorus ['kɔɪrəs] *n* (*refrain*) estribillo *m*; (*singers*) coro *m*. **chorus girl** corista *f*. **choral** *adj* coral. **choral society** orfeón *m*.

chose [tʃouz] *V* **choose**.

christen ['krisn] *v* bautizar; (*nickname*) llamar. **christening** *n* bautismo *m*.

Christian ['kristʃən] *n, adj* cristiano, -a *m*, *f*. **Christian name** nombre de pila *m*. **Christianity** *n* cristianismo *m*.

Christmas ['krisməs] *n* Navidad *f*. **Christmas Day** día de Navidad *m*. **Christmas Eve** Nochebuena *f*.

chromatic [krə'matik] *adj* cromático.

chrome [kroum] *n* cromo *m*.

chromium ['kroumiəm] *n* cromo *m*. **chromium-plated** *adj* cromado.

chronic ['kronik] *adj* crónico; (*coll*: *dreadful*) terrible.

chronicle ['kronikl] *n* crónica *f*.

chronological [kronə'lɔdʒikəl] *adj* cronológico.

chrysalis ['krisəlis] *n* crisálida *f*.

chrysanthemum [kri'sanθəməm] *n* crisantemo *m*.

chubby ['tʃʌbi] *adj* gordinflón.

chuck [tʃʌk] *v* (*coll*: *throw*) tirar; (*give up*) abandonar.

chuckle ['tʃʌkl] *v* reir entre de dientes. *n* risa *f*.

chunk [tʃʌŋk] *n* pedazo *m*; (*large amount*) cantidad grande *f*.

church [tʃəɪtʃ] *n* iglesia *f*. **church service** oficio religioso *m*. **churchyard** *n* cementerio *m*.

churn [tʃəɪn] *n* mantequera *f*. *v* batir. **churn out** producir en profusión.

chute [ʃuɪt] *n* tolva *f*.

cider ['saidə] *n* sidra *f*.

cigar [si'gaɪ] *n* cigarro puro *m*.

cigarette [sigə'ret] *n* cigarillo *m*. **cigarette case** pitillera *f*. **cigarette holder** boquilla *f*. **cigarette lighter** encendedor *m*, mechero *m*. **cigarette paper** papel de fumar *m*.

cinder ['sində] *n* carbonilla *f*, ceniza *f*.

cinema ['sinəmə] *n* cine *m*. **cinematography** *n* cinematografía *f*.

cinnamon ['sinəmən] *n* canela *f*.

circle ['səɪkl] *n* círculo *m*; (*theatre*) piso principal *m*. **go round in circles** dar vueltas. *v* rodear; (*surround*) circundar. **circular** *adj*. *n* circular *f*.

circuit ['səɪkit] *n* (*route*) circuito *m*; (*perimeter*) perímetro *m*; (*law*) distrito *m*; (*cinemas, theatres*) cadena *f*. **short circuit** cortocircuito *m*. **circuitous** *adj* indirecto.

circulate ['səɪkjuleit] *v* circular. **circulation** *n* circulación *f*.

circumcise ['səɪkəmsaiz] *v* circuncidar. **circumcision** *n* circuncisión *f*.

circumference [sərˈkʌmfərəns] *n* circunferencia *f*.

circumflex ['səɪkəmfleks] *n* circunflejo *m*.

circumscribe ['sɔɪkəmskraib] v circunscribir. circumscription n circunscripción
f.

circumstance ['sɔɪkəmstəns] n circunstancia f. extenuating circumstances cir-
cunstancias atenuantes f pl. under no circumstances de ninguna manera. under
the circumstances en estas circun-
stancias. circumstantial adj (incidental)
circunstancial; (detailed) circun-
stanciado. circumstantial evidence testimonio indirecto m.

circus ['sɔɪkəs] n circo m.

cistern ['sistən] n cisterna f. aljibe m.

cite [sait] v citar. citation n citación f;
(mil) mención f.

citizen ['sitizn] n ciudadano, -a m. f. citizenship n ciudadanía f.

citrus ['sitrəs] n cidro m. citrus fruit n
agrios m pl. citric acid ácido cítrico m.

city ['siti] n ciudad f.

civic ['sivik] adj cívico.

civil ['sivl] adj civil; (polite) cortés. civil
engineering ingeniería civil f. civil rights
derechos civiles m pl. civil servant funcionario, -a m. f. civil service administración pública f. civil war guerra civil f.

civilian [sə'viljən] adj civil, de paisano. n
paisano, -a m, f.

civilization [,sivilai'zeiʃən] n civilización f.
civilize v civilizar.

clad [klad] adj vestido (de).

claim [kleim] v (damages) exigir; (a right)
reclamar; (assert) declarar; (need)
requerir. n (right) derecho m; (demand)
demanda f, reclamación f; (statement)
declaración f; (land) propiedad f. claimant (law) n demandante m, f; (pretender)
pretendiente m, f.

clairvoyant [kleə'voiənt] n(m+f), adj
clarividente. clairvoyance n clarividencia.
f.

clam [klam] n almeja f.

clamber ['klambə] v trepar.

clammy ['klami] adj pegajoso.

clamour ['klamə] n clamor m. v clamar,
vociferar.

clamp [klamp] n abrazadera f. v sujetar
con abrazadera. clamp down on suprimir.

clan [klan] n clan m. clannish adj
exclusivista.

clandestine [klan'destin] adj clandestino.

clang [klaŋ] v sonar estripitosamente. n
sonido metálico m.

clap [klap] v aplaudir, dar palmadas. n
(with hands) palmada f; (noise) ruido
seco m. clap of thunder trueno m.

claret ['klarət] n clarete m.

clarify ['klarəfai] v aclarar; (liquid) clarificar. clarification n aclaración f; clarificación f.

clarinet [klarə'net] n clarinete m.

clarity ['klarəti] n claridad f.

clash [klaʃ] v (collide) chocar; (cymbals)
golpear; (interests) estar en desacuerdo;
(dates) coincidir; (colours) matarse., n
ruido metálico m; (encounter) choque m;
(interests) conflicto m; coincidencia f;
disparidad f.

clasp [klɑɪsp] v (grasp) agarrar; (fasten)
abrochar. n (hands) apretón m; (fastening) cierre m; (belt) broche m.

class [klɑɪs] n clase f.

classic ['klasik] adj clásico. classical adj
clásico. classics n pl clásicas f pl.

classify ['klasifai] v clasificar. classification n clasificación f. classified advertisement anuncio por palabras m.

clatter ['klatə] n estruendo m; (hooves)
chacoloteo m. v sonar con estrépito;
chacolotear.

clause [klorz] n (law) cláusula f; (gramm)
oración f.

claustrophobia [kloɪstrə'foubiə] n claustrofobia f.

claw [kloɪ] n (talon) garra f; (cat) uña f;
(crab) pinza f; (tech) garfio m. v agarrar;
arañar; (tear) desgarrar.

clay [klei] n arcilla f, barro m.

clean [kliɪn] adj limpio; (irreproachable)
sin tocha. v limpiar. clean out (empty)
vaciar. clean up (tidy) ordenar; (win)
ganarse. clean-cut adj bien hecho, perfi-
lado. cleaner (person) n asistenta f. cleanliness n limpieza f. clean-shaven adj bien
afeitado.

cleanse [klenz] v limpiar, purificar.

clear [kliə] adj claro, transparente; (conscience) tranquilo; evidente; (free) libre;
(unobstructed) despejado; (profit) neto.
adv claramente. v aclarar; despejar; (law)
absolver. clearance n espacio m, altura
libre f. margen m; despeje m; acredita-
ción f. clearance sale liquidación f.

clef [klef] n clave f.

clench [klentʃ] v apretar, sujetar.

clergy ['klɔɪdʒi] n clero m. clergyman n
clérigo m.

clerical ['klerikəl] *adj* (*clerk*) de oficina; (*rel*) clerical. **clerical error** error de copia *m*.

clerk [klaɪk] *n* oficinista *m*, *f*; (*law*) escribano *m*.

clever ['klevə] *adj* listo; inteligente; (*skilful*) hábil; (*cunning*) astuto. **cleverness** *n* habilidad *f*; ingenio *m*.

cliché ['kliːʃei] *n* cliché *m*, clisé *m*.

click [klik] *n* chasquido *m*; taconeo *m*. *v* chascar, chasquear; taconear.

client ['klaiənt] *n* cliente *m*, *f*.

cliff [klif] *n* (*coast*) acantilado *m*; (*crag*) risco *m*.

climate ['klaimət] *n* clima *m*; (*atmosphere*) ambiente *m*. **climatic** *adj* climático.

climax ['klaimaks] *n* punto culminante *m*; clímax *m*. *v* llevar al punto culminante.

climb [klaim] *v* subir, escalar; (*plants*) trepar. *n* subida *f*, escalada *f*. **climber** *n* escalador, -a *m*, *f*; (*mountaineer*) alpinista *m*, *f*; (*plant*) planta trepadora *f*.

***cling** [kliŋ] *v* agarrarse; (*stick to*) adherirse a, pegarse a. **clinging** *adj* ceñido; pegajoso.

clinic ['klinik] *n* dispensario *m*; clínica *f*. **clinical** *adj* clínico.

clip¹ [klip] *v* (*trim*) recortar; (*animals*) esquilar; (*ticket*) picar; (*coll*: *cuff*) abofetear. *n* (*film*) fragmento; (*cuff*) bofetada *f*.

clip² [klip] *v* (*fasten*) sujetar. *n* grapa *f*; sujetapapeles *m invar*; (*hair*) horquilla *f*; (*pen, pencil*) prendedor *m*.

cloak [klouk] *n* capa *f*; (*fig*) manto *m*; (*mil*) capote. **cloak-and-dagger** *adj* de capa y espada. **cloakroom** *n* guardarropa *m*; (*toilet*) servicios *m pl*. *v* encubrir, cubrir, encapotar.

clock [klok] *n* reloj *m*. **against the clock** contra reloj. **alarm clock** despertador *m*. **around the clock** durante 24 horas. **clockwise** *adj* en el sentido de las agujas del reloj. **clockwork** *n* aparato de relojería *m*. *v* registrar.

clog [klog] *n* zueco *m*. *v* atascar, obstruir.

cloister ['kloistə] *n* claustro *m*. *v* enclaustrar.

close [klouz; *adj, adv* klous] *v* cerrar; (*block*) tapar; (*end*) acabar; (*account*) saldar; (*distance*) acortar. **close in** acercarse. *n* conclusión *f*; final *m*. *adj* cercano; íntimo; (*air*) cargado; (*game*) reñido. *adv* cerca. **close-up** *n* primer plano *m*.

closet ['klozit] *n* (*WC*) retrete *m*, water *m*; armario *m*.

clot [klot] *n* (*blood*) coágulo *m*; (*liquid*) grumo *m*. *v* coagular, cuajar.

cloth [kloθ] *n* (*rag*) trapo *m*; (*fabric*) paño *m*; (*tablecloth*) mantel *m*.

clothe [klouð] *v* vestir; (*cover*) cubrir.

clothes [klouðz] *pl n also* **clothing** ropa *f sing*; vestidos *m pl*. **clothes basket** cesta de la ropa sucia *f*. **clothes brush** cepillo de la ropa *m*. **clothes line** tendedero *m*. **clothes peg** pinza *f*.

cloud [klaud] *n* nube *f*; (*gas*) capa *f*. *v* nublar; (*darken*) ensombrecer, oscurecer. **cloudburst** *n* chaparrón *m*. **cloudiness** *n* nubosidad *f*. **cloudless** *adj* despejado. **cloudy** *adj* nuboso; nublado.

clove¹ [klouv] *n* (*spice*) clavo *m*.

clove² [klouv] *n* (*of garlic, etc.*) diente *m*.

clover ['klouvə] *n* trébol *m*.

clown [klaun] *n* payaso *m*. *v* hacer el payaso.

club [klʌb] *n* (*association*) club *m*; (*stick*) porra *f*, garrote *m*; (*golf*) palo *m*. *v* (*beat*) aporrear. **clubfoot** *n* pie zopo *m*.

clue [kluː] *n* (*police lead*) pista *f*; (*piece of evidence*) indicio *m*.

clump [klʌmp] *n* (*trees*) grupo *m*; (*flowers*) matar *f*; (*earth*) terrón *m*; (*noise*) pisada fuerte *f*. *v* agrupar; andar con pisadas fuertes.

clumsy ['klʌmzi] *adj* (*awkward*) torpe; (*unskilful*) desmañado; (*tactless*) sin tacto. **clumsiness** *n* torpeza *f*; desmaña *f*.

cluster ['klʌstə] *n* grupo *m*; (*fruits*) racimo *m*. *v* agruparse, arracimarse.

clutch [klʌtʃ] *v* agarrar, apretar. *n* (*grip*) agarrón *m*; (*mot*) embrague *m*. **engage the clutch** embragar.

clutter ['klʌtə] *n* desorden *m*, confusión *f*. *v* desordenar, atentar.

coach [koutʃ] *n* (*carriage*) coche *m*; (*ceremonial carriage*) carroza *f*; (*mot*) autocar *m*; (*tutor*) profesor particular *m*; (*trainer*) entrenador *m*. *v* dar clases particulares; entrenar.

coagulate [kou'agjuleit] *v* coagular. **coagulation** *n* coagulación *f*.

coal [koul] *n* carbón *m*, hulla *f*. **coal cellar** carbonera *f*. **coalman** *n* carbonero *m*. **coalmine** *n* mina de carbón *f*. **coalminer** *n* minero de carbón *m*. **coal scuttle** cubo para el carbón *m*.

coalesce [kouə'les] v (*unite*) unirse; (*merge*) fundirse.

coalition [kouə'liʃən] n coalición f.

coarse [kots] adj (*gross*) grosero; (*ill-made*) basto. coarse-grained adj de grano grueso. coarseness n grosería f; basteza f.

coast [koust] n costa f. the coast is clear no hay moros en la costa. v (*freewheel*) deslizarse cuesta abajo. coastguard n guardacostas m invar. coastline n litoral m.

coat [kout] n chaqueta f; (*overcoat*) abrigo m; (*animal*) pelo m. coat-hanger percha f. coat of arms escudo de armas m. coat of paint mano de pintura f. v cubrir; dar una mano de pintura; (*cookery*) rebozar. coating n capa f; mano f; rebozo m.

coax [kouks] v engatusar.

cobbler ['koblə] n zapatero m.

cobra ['koubrə] n cobra f.

cobweb ['kobweb] n telaraña f.

cocaine [kə'kein] n cocaína f.

cock¹ [kok] n (*male fowl*) gallo m; (*male bird*) macho m; (*impol: penis*) polla f. cocky adj engreído.

cock² [kok] v (*gun*) amartillar; (*ears*) aguzar el oído.

cockle ['kokl] n berberecho m.

cockpit ['kokpit] n (*aero*) cabina del piloto f; (*cockfighting*) reñidero m.

cockroach ['kokroutʃ] n cucaracha f.

cocktail ['kokteil] n cóctel m. cocktail shaker coctelera f.

cocoa ['koukou] n cacao m.

coconut ['koukənʌt] n coco m. coconut palm cocotero m.

cocoon [kə'kum] n capullo m.

cod [kod] n bacalao m.

code [koud] n código m; (*signals*) cifra f, clave f; (*area code*) prefijo m. highway code codigo de la circulación m. Morse code alfabeto Morse m. v cifrar.

codeine ['koudiin] n codeína f.

coeducation [kouedju'keiʃən] n coeducación f.

coerce [kou'əis] v forzar, obligar.

coexist [kouig'zist] v coexistir. coexistence n coexistencia f.

coffee ['kofi] n café m. black/white coffee café solo/con leche m. coffee bean grano de café m. coffee pot cafetera f. coffee table mesita de café f.

coffin ['kofin] n ataúd m.

cog [kog] n diente m; (*wheel*) rueda dentada f.

cognac ['konjak] n coñac m.

cohabit [kou'habit] v cohabitar, vivir juntos. cohabitation n cohabitación f.

cohere [kə'hiə] v adherirse, pegarse. coherence n coherencia f. coherent adj coherente.

coil [koil] n (*rope*) rollo m; (*smoke*) espiral m; (*elec*) carrete m. coil spring muelle en espiral m. v enrollar, arrollar.

coin [koin] n moneda f. toss a coin echar a cara o cruz. v acuñar; inventar. coinage n moneda f.

coincide [kouin'said] v coincidir. coincidence n coincidencia f. coincidental adj coincidente.

colander ['koləndə] n escurridor m.

cold [kould] adj frío. be cold (*person*) tener frío; (*weather*) hacer frío. cold front frente frío m. cold storage conservación f. cold war guerra fría f. catch a cold resfriarse. cold-blooded adj (*biol*) de sangre fría; (*fig*) insensible.

colic ['kolik] n cólico m.

collaborate [kə'labəreit] v colaborar. collaboration n colaboración f. collaborator n (*colleague*) colaborador, -a m, f; (*pol*) colaboracionista m, f.

collapse [ke'laps] v derrumbar; (*med*) sufrir un colapso. n derrumbamiento m; colapso; (*failure*) fracaso m. collapsible adj plegable.

collar ['kolə] n cuello m; (*dog, etc.*) collar m. collarbone n clavícula f. v (*seize*) agarrar por el cuello; (*put a collar on*) acollarar.

collate [ko'leit] v cotejar. collation n (*food*) colación f; (*texts*) cotejo m.

colleague ['kolig] n colega m, f.

collect [kə'lekt] v (*bring together*) juntar, reunir; (*hobby*) coleccionar; (*funds*) allegar; (*taxes*) recaudar; (*bills*) cobrar; (*gather*) recoger. collected works obras completas f pl. collection (*hobby*) colección f; (*charity*) colecta f; (*people*) grupo m; (*things*) reunión f; (*rent, bills*) cobro m; (*taxes*) recaudación f; (*postal*) recogida f. collective adj colectivo. collector n (*tax*) recaudador, -a m, f; (*bills, rent*) cobrador m; (*hobbies*) coleccionista m, f.

college ['kolidʒ] n colegio m. collegiate adj colegiado.

collide [kə'laid] *v* chocar. **collision** *n* choque *m*.

colloquial [kə'loukwiəl] *adj* familiar, popular. **colloquialism** *n* expresión familiar *f*.

Colombia [kə'lombiə] *n* Colombia *f*. **Colombian** *n, adj* colombiano, -a.

colon ['koulon] *n* dos puntos *m pl*; (*anat*) colon *m*.

colonel ['kə:nl] *n* coronel *m*.

colony ['koləni] *n* colonia *f*. **colonial** *adj* colonial. **colonialist** *n(m+f)*, *adj* colonialista. **colonist** *n* colono *m*. **colonization** *n* colonización *f*. **colonize** *v* colonizar.

colossal [kə'losəl] *adj* colosal.

colour ['kʌlə] *n* color *m*. **colour bar** barrera racial *f*. **colour-blind** *adj* daltoniano. **colourful** *adj* animado. **fast colour** color sólido *m*. **in colour** en colores. *v* colorear; (*dye*) teñir.

colt [koult] *n* potro *m*.

column ['koləm] *n* columna *f*. **columnist** *n* columnista *m, f*.

coma ['koumə] *n* coma *m*.

comb [koum] *n* peine *m*; (*honey*) panal *m*. *v* peinar.

combat ['kombat] *n* combate *m*. *v* combatir, luchar contra. **combatant** *n(m+f)*, *adj* combatiente.

combine [kəm'bain; *n* 'kombain] *v* combinar, reunir. *n* (*comm*) cártel *m*. **combination** *n* combinación *f*, asociación *f*.

combustion [kəm'bʌstʃən] *n* combustión *f*. **combustible** *adj* combustible.

***come** [kʌm] *v* venir, llegar; proceder; salir. **come about** ocurrir. **come across** dar con. **come along!** ¡vamos! **come back** volver. **comeback** *n* restablecimiento *m*. **come off** desprender; (*succeed*) tener éxito. **come out** salir. **come to** (*from faint*) volver ensí; (*total*) ascender a.

comedy ['komədi] *n* comedia *f*. **comedian** *n* cómico *m*.

comet ['komit] *n* cometa *m*.

comfort ['kʌmfət] *n* (*relief*) alivio *m*; (*consolation*) consuelo *m*; (*well-being*) bienestar *m*; (*convenience*) comodidad *f*. *v* aliviar; consolar; animar. **comfortable** *adj* cómodo; agradable. **comfortably** *adv* cómodamente; confortablemente.

comic ['komik] *adj* cómico, divertido. *n* (*magazine*) tebeo *m*. **comical** *adj* cómico.

comma ['komə] *n* coma *f*. **inverted commas** comillas *f pl*.

command [kə'maind] *n* (*order*) orden *f*; (*authority*) mando *m*; (*mastery*) dominio

m. *v* mandar, ordenar; dominar. **commandant** *n* comandante *m*. **commander** *n* comandante *m*; (*leader*) jefe *m*. **commander-in-chief** *n* comandante-en-jefe *m*. **commandment** *n* mandamiento *m*.

commandeer [komən'diə] *v* expropiar.

commando [kə'maindou] *n* comando *m*.

commemorate [kə'meməreit] *v* conmemorar. **commemoration** *n* conmemoración *f*. **commemorative** *adj* conmemorativo.

commence [kə'mens] *v* empezar, comenzar. **commencement** *n* comienzo *m*.

commend [kə'mend] *v* (*recommend*) recomendar; (*entrust*) encomendar; (*praise*) alabar. **commendable** *adj* recomendable. **commendation** *n* alabanza *f*, elogio *m*, encomio *m*.

comment ['koment] *n* observación *f*; (*explanation*) comentario. **no comment** sin comentarios. *v* comentar, hacer observaciones. **commentary** *n* comentario *m*, observación *f*. **running commentary** reportaje en directo *m*.

commerce ['komə:s] *n* comercio *m*. **commercial** *adj* comercial. **commercial traveller** agente comercial *m*. **commercialism** *n* mercantilismo *m*. **commercialize** *v* comercializar.

commiserate [kə'mizəreit] *v* compadecerse. **commiseration** *n* conmiseración *f*.

commission [kə'miʃən] *n* (*profit*) comisión *f*; (*to a post, etc.*) nombramiento *m*; (*assignment*) cometido *m*; (*charge*) encargo; (*crime*) ejecución *f*; (*mil*) grado de oficial *m*. *v* comisionar; encargar; (*mil*) nombrar. **commissionaire** *n* portero *m*. **commissioner** *n* comisionado *m*. **High Commissioner** alto comisario *m*.

commit [kə'mit] *v* (*crime*) cometer; (*entrust*) confiar; (*imprison*) encarcelar. **commit oneself** comprometerse. **commitment** *n* (*assignment*) cometido *m*; (*pledge*) compromiso *m*.

committee [kə'miti] *n* comité *m*, comisión *f*.

commodity [kə'modəti] *n* mercancía *f*, producto *m*, artículo *m*.

common ['komən] *adj* común; público; ordinario; frecuente. **commoner** *n* plebeyo, -a *m, f*. **Common Market** Mercado Común *m*. **commonness** *n* frecuencia *f*; vulgaridad *f*. **commonplace**

adj común, trivial. **commonsense** *adj* lógico. **commonwealth** *n* república *f*.

commotion [kə'mouʃən] *n* disturbio *m*; tumulto *m*.

commune[1] [kə'mjuːn] *v* (*communicate*) comunicarse; (*meditate*) meditar. **communion** *n* comunión *f*.

commune[2] ['komjuːn] *n* comuna *f*. **communal** *adj* comunal.

communicate [kə'mjuːnikeit] *v* comunicar. **communication** *n* comunicación *f*. **communicative** *adj* comunicativo.

communism ['komjunizəm] *n* comunismo *m*. **communist** *n*(*m*+*f*), *adj* comunista.

community [kə'mjuːnəti] *n* comunidad *f*. **community centre** centro social *m*.

commute [kə'mjuːt] *v* (*travel*) viajar; (*law*) conmutar. **commuter** *n*, *adj* viajero, -a.

compact[1] [kəm'pakt] *adj* compacto; recogido; conciso; denso. *v* condensar; comprimir.

compact[2] ['kompakt] *n* pacto *m*; (*powder*) polvera *f*.

companion [kəm'panjən] *n* compañero, -a *m*, *f*; (*professional*) acompañante *m*, *f*. **companionship** *n* compañerismo *m*.

company ['kʌmpəni] *n* (*comm*) compañiá *f*, empresa *f*; (*companionship*) compañerismo *m*, sociedad *f*.

compare [kəm'peə] *v* comparar. **comparable** *adj* comparable. **comparative** *adj* relativo; (*gram*) comparativo. **comparison** *n* comparación *f*.

compartment [kəm'paitmənt] *n* compartimiento *m*, departamento *n*.

compass ['kʌmpəs] *n* (*naut*) brújula *f*; (*extent*) extensión *f*. **compasses** *n pl* (*maths*) compás *m*.

compassion [kəm'paʃən] *n* compasión *f*. **compassionate** *adj* compasivo.

compatible [kəm'patəbl] *adj* compatible. **compatibility** *n* compatibilidad *f*.

compel [kəm'pel] *v* compeler, obligar. **compelling** *adj* convincente.

compensate ['kompənseit] *v* (*make up for*) compensar; (*repay*) indemnizar. **compensation** *n* compensación *f*; indemnización *f*; (*reward*) recompensa *f*.

compete [kəm'piːt] *v* competir. **competition** *n* competición *f*; (*contest*) concurso *m*; (*comm*) competencia *f*. **competitive** *adj* competitivo; (*spirit*) de competencia. **competitor** *n* competidor, -a *m*, *f*. (*contestant*) concursante *m*, *f*.

competent ['kompətənt] *adj* competente; (*suitable*) adecuado. **competence** *n* competencia *f*, aptitud *f*.

compile [kəm'pail] *v* compilar. **compilation** *n* compilación *f*. **compiler** *n* compilador, -a *m*, *f*.

complacent [kəm'pleisnt] *adj* complaciente. **complacence**, **complacency** *n* satisfacción de si mismo *f*.

complain [kəm'plein] *v* quejarse. **complaint** *n* queja *f*; (*med*) enfermedad *f*; (*law*) demanda *f*.

complement ['kompləmənt] *n* complemento *m*. *v* complementar. **complementary** *adj* complementario.

complete [kəm'pliːt] *adj* completo; (*finished*) acabado, concluido, terminado; (*entire*) entero. *v* completar; terminar; (*fill in*) llenar. **completion** *n* cumplimiento *m*; terminación *f*.

complex ['kompleks] *adj* complejo, complicado. *n* complejo *m*. **complexity** *n* complejidad *f*.

complexion [kəm'plekʃən] *n* tez *f*, cutis *m*; aspecto *m*.

complicate ['komplikeit] *v* complicar. **complicated** *adj* complicado. **complication** *n* complicación *f*.

complicity [kəm'plisəti] *n* complicidad *f*.

compliment ['kompləmənt] *n* cumplido *m*. **compliments** *n pl* saludos *m pl*. **complimentary** *adj* elogioso; (*gratis*) de favor.

comply [kəm'plai] *v* conformarse; (*obey*) obedecer.

component [kəm'pounənt] *nm*, *adj* componente.

compose [kəm'pouz] *v* componer; calmar. **composed** *adj* sereno. **be composed of** constar de. **composer** *n* compositor, -a *m*, *f*. **composite** *adj* compuesto. **composition** *n* composición *f*.

compost ['kompost] *n* abono *m*.

composure [kəm'pouʒə] *n* calma *f*, serenidad *f*.

compound[1] [kəm'paund; *n*, *adj* 'kompaund] *v* componer; mezclar. *nm*, *adj* compuesto. **compound fracture** fractura complicada *f*.

compound[2] ['kompaund] *n* (*enclosure*) recinto cercado *m*.

comprehend [kompri'hend] *v* comprender. **comprehensible** *adj* comprensible. **comprehension** *n* comprensión *f*.

comprehensive *adj* extenso, amplio. **comprehensive insurance** seguro a todo riesgo *m*. **comprehensive school** colegio integrado *m*.

compress ['kompres; *v* kəm'pres] *n* (*med*) compresa *f*. *v* comprimir; (*condense*) condensar. **compression** *n* compresión *f*.

comprise [kəm'praiz] *v* comprender.

compromise ['komprəmaiz] *n* compromiso *m*, arreglo *m*. *v* (*agree*) llegar a un arreglo; (*yield*) transigir; (*endanger*) comprometer. **compromising** *adj* comprometedor.

compulsion [kəm'pʌlʃən] *n* obligación *f*; (*coercion*) coacción *f*; (*impulse*) impulso *m*. **compulsive** *adj* compulsivo. **compulsory** *adj*

computer [kəm'pjuːtə] *n* computador *m*, computadora *f*, ordenador *m*. **compute** *v* computar, calcular. **computerize** *v* tratar.

comrade ['komrid] *n* camarada *m*, *f* compañero, -a *m*, *f*. **comradeship** *n* camaradería *f*.

concave [kon'keiv] *adj* cóncavo. **concavity** *n* concavidad *f*.

conceal [kən'siːl] *v* ocultar. **concealed** *adj* oculto. **concealment** *n* encubrimiento *m*.

concede [kən'siːd] *v* conceder; (*admit*) reconocer. **concede victory** darse por vencido.

conceit [kən'siːt] *n* presunción *f*, vanidad *f*. **conceited** *adj* engreído, vanidoso.

conceive [kən'siːv] *v* concebir. **conceive of** imaginarse. **conceivable** *adj* concebible.

concentrate ['konsəntreit] *v* concentrar. *n* concentrado. **concentration** *n* concentración *f*. **concentration camp** campo de concentración *m*.

concentric [kən'sentrik] *adj* concéntrico.

concept ['konsept] *n* concepto *m*. **conception** *n* concepción *f*; idea *f*.

concern [kən'səːn] *n* asunto *m*; (*interest*) interés *m*; (*business*) empresa *f* (*worry*) preocupación *f*: *v* (*have as a subject*) tratar de; (*affect*) afectar; (*be related to*) referirse a. **concerned** *adj* preocupado. **concerning** *prep* con respecto a.

concert ['konsət; *v* kən'səːt] *n* concierto *m*. *v* concertar.

concertina [konsə'tiːnə] *n* concertina *f*.

concerto [kən'tʃəːtou] *n* concierto *m*.

concession [kən'seʃən] *n* concesión *f*.

conciliate [kən'silieit] *v* conciliar. **conciliation** *n* conciliación *f*. **conciliator** *n* conciliador, -a *m*, *f*. **conciliatory** *adj* conciliatorio.

concise [kən'sais] *adj* conciso.

conclude [kən'kluːd] *v* acabar, terminar; (*treaty*) concertar; (*deduce*) concluir. **conclusion** *n* conclusión *f*. **conclusive** *adj* conclusivo; concluyente.

concoct [kən'kokt] *v* (*mix*) confeccionar; (*plot*) urdir; inventar. **concoction** *n* (*mixture*) mezcla *f*; (*lies*) fabricación *f*.

concrete ['konkriːt] *n* hormigón *m*. **concrete mixer** hormigonera *f*. **reinforced concrete** hormigón armado *m*. *adj* concreto; (*tech*) de hormigón.

concussion [kən'kʌʃən] *n* conmoción cerebral *f*. **concuss** *v* conmocionar.

condemn [kən'dem] *v* condenar; (*building*) declarar en ruina. **condemnation** *n* condenación *f*. **condemnatory** *adj* condenatorio. **condemned** *adj* condenado.

condense [kən'dens] *v* (*cut*) abreviar, resumir; (*physics*) condensar. **condensation** *n* condensación *f*; (*vapour*) vaho *m*; (*abbreviation*) resumen *m*. **condenser** *n* condensador *m*.

condescend [kondi'send] *v* condescender, dignarse. **condescending** *adj* condescendiente, superior. **condescension** *n* condescendencia *f*.

condition [kən'diʃən] *n* condición *f*, estado *m*. *v* condicionar, determinar. **conditional** *adj* condicional. **conditionally** *adv* con reservas. **conditioning** *n* condicionamiento *m*.

condolence [kən'douləns] *n* condolencia *f*, pésame *m*. **condole** *v* condolerse, dar el pésame.

condom ['kondom] *n* condón *m*.

condone [kən'doun] *v* condonar, perdonar.

conducive [kən'djuːsiv] *adj* conducivo; (*helpful*) propicio.

conduct ['kondʌkt; *v* kən'dʌkt] *n* conducta *f*, comportamiento *m*. *v* (*lead*) conducir; (*music, business*) dirigir; (*behave*) comportarse. **conductance** *n* conductancia *f*. **conduction** *n* conducción *f*. **conductivity** *n* conductividad *f*.

conductor [kən'dʌktə] *n* (*music*) director, -a *m*, *f*; (*guide*) guía *m*; (*bus*) cobrador *m*; (*physics*) conductor *m*. **lightning conductor** pararrayos *m sing*.

cone [koun] *n* cono *m*; (*bot*) piña *f*; (*ice*

cream) cucurucho de helado *m*. **cone-shaped** *adj* cónico.

confectioner [kən'fekʃənə] *n* confitero, -a *m, f.* **confection** *n* dulce *m*. **confectionery** *n* (*sweets*) dulces *m pl*; (*shop*) confitería *f*; (*cake shop*) repostería *f*.

confederate [kən'fedərət] *nm, adj* confederado. *v* confederar. **confederation** *n* confederación *f*.

confer [kən'fəː] *v* consultar, conferir; (*hold a conference*) conferenciar. **conference** *n* consulta *f*; (*meeting*) conferencia *f*; (*talks*) entrevista *f*.

confess [kən'fes] *v* confesar. **confession** *n* confesión *f*. **confessional** *n* (*rel*) confesionario *m*. **confessor** *n* confesor *m*; (*priest*) director espiritual *m*.

confetti [kən'feti] *n* confeti *m*.

confide [kən'faid] *v* confiar. **confidence** *n* (*trust*) confianza *f*; (*secret*) confidencia *f*; (*self-reliance*) seguridad en sí mismo *f*. **confidence trick** estafa *f*. **confident** *adj* lleno de confianza. **confidential** *adj* confidencial. **confidentially** *adv* en confianza.

confine [kən'fain] *n* confín *m*; límite *m*. *v* confinar; limitar; (*med*) estar de parto. **confined** *adj* reducido. **confinement** *n* encierro *m*; (*med*) parto *m*.

confirm [kən'fəːm] *v* confirmar; (*treaty*) ratificar. **confirmation** *n* confirmación *f*; ratificación *f*. **confirmed** *adj* confirmado; (*inveterate*) empedernido.

confiscate ['konfiskeit] *v* confiscar. **confiscation** *n* confiscación *f*.

conflict ['konflikt; *v* kən'flikt] *n* conflicto *m*. *v* luchar; (*clash*) chocar. **conflicting** *adj* contrapuesto.

conform [kən'fɔːm] *v* conformarse. **conformist** *n*(*m*+*f*), *adj* conformista. **conformity** *n* conformidad *f*.

confound [kən'faund] *v* confundir; (*foil*) frustrar; (*disconcert*) desconcertar.

confront [kən'frʌnt] *v* hacer frente a; (*present with*) presentarse; (*bring face to face*) enfrentar, confrontar. **confrontation** *n* confrontación *f*.

confuse [kən'fjuːz] *v* confundir; desconcertar; complicar. **confused** *adj* confuso; perplejo. **confusing** *adj* confuso; desconcertante. **confusion** *n* confusión *f*, desorden *m*.

congeal [kən'dʒiːl] *v* congelar; coagular.

congenial [kən'dʒiːniəl] *adj* (*pleasant*) agradable; (*suitable*) conveniente; (*similar*) compatible.

congenital [kən'dʒenitl] *adj* congénito.

congested [kən'dʒestid] *adj* congestionado; (*crowded*) superpoblado. **congestion** *n* congestión *f*; superpoblación *f*.

conglomeration [kəngloməˈreiʃən] *n* conglomeración *f*. **conglomerate** *v* conglomerar.

congratulate [kən'gratjuleit] *v* felicitar, dar la enhorabuena. **congratulations** *pl n* felicitaciones *f pl*; *interj* ¡felicidades!

congregate ['kongrigeit] *v* congregarse. **congregation** *n* congregación *f*, asamblea *f*; (*rel*) feligreses *m pl*.

congress ['kongres] *n* congreso *m*.

conical ['konikəl] *adj* cónico.

conifer ['konifə] *n* conífera *f*. **coniferous** *adj* conífero.

conjecture [kən'dʒektʃə] *n* conjetura *f*. *v* conjeturar. **conjectural** *adj* conjetural.

conjugal ['kondʒugəl] *adj* conyugal.

conjugate ['kondʒugeit] *v* conjugar. **conjugation** *n* conjugación *f*.

conjunction [kən'dʒʌŋkʃən] *n* (*gramm*) conjunción *f*. **conjunctive** *adj* conjuntivo.

conjunctivitis [kəndʒʌŋkti'vaitis] *n* conjuntivitis *f*.

conjure ['kʌndʒə; (*appeal to*) kən'dʒuə] *v* (*magic*) hacer juegos de manos; (*appeal to*) conjurar. **conjurer** *n* ilusionista *m*, prestidigitador *m*. **conjuring trick** juego de manos *m*.

connect [kə'nekt] *v* (*join*) unir, juntar; (*relate*) relacionar; (*elec*) conectar. **connected** *adj* (*joined*) conectado, unido; (*related*) emparentado; (*associated*) relacionado; coherente. **connection** *n* relación *f*; (*transport*) empalme *m*; (*elec*) conexión *f*; (*joint*) unión *f*; (*relative*) pariente *m*. **in connection with** con respecto a.

connoisseur [konə'səː] *n* experto, -a *m, f*, conocedor, -a *m, f*.

connotation [konə'teiʃən] *n* connotación *f*.

conquer ['koŋkə] *v* vencer, triunfar. **conquering** *adj* victorioso. **conqueror** *n* conquistador *m*, vencedor, -a *m, f*. **conquest** *n* conquista *f*.

conscience ['konʃəns] *n* conciencia *f*.

conscientious [konʃi'enʃəs] *adj* concienzudo. **conscientious objector** objetor de conciencia *m*. **conscientiousness** *n* escrupulosidad *f*.

conscious ['kɒnʃəs] *adj* (*aware*) consciente; (*deliberate*) intencional. **be conscious** tener conocimiento. **be conscious of** tener conciencia de. **become conscious** volver en sí. **become conscious of** darse cuenta de. **consciousness** *n* conocimiento *m*.

conscript ['kɒnskript] *n* recluta *m*.

consecrate ['kɒnsikreit] *v* consagrar. **consecration** *n* consagración *f*.

consecutive [kən'sekjutiv] *adj* consecutivo.

consensus [kən'sensəs] *n* consenso *m*.

consent [kən'sent] *n* consentimiento *m*. **by common consent** de acuerdo mutuo. *v* consentir (en).

consequence ['kɒnsikwəns] *n* consecuencia *f*, resultado *m*. **consequent** *adj* consiguiente. **consequently** *adv* consecuentemente, por lo tanto.

conserve [kən'sɜːv] *v* conservar. *n* conserva *f*. **conservation** *n* conservación *f*. **conservative** *adj* conservador, moderado. **conservatory** *n* (*plants*) invernadero *m*; (*music*) conservatorio *m*.

consider [kən'sidə] *v* considerar; (*think*) pensar (en); (*study*) examinar; (*realize*) darse cuenta de; (*take into account*) tener en cuenta. **considerable** *adj* considerable. **considerably** *adv* considerablemente. **consideration** *n* consideración *f*; (*payment*) retribución *f*. **considerate** *adj* considerado.

consign [kən'sain] *v* consignar; (*send*) enviar; (*entrust*) confiar. **consignee** *n* consignatorio *m*. **consignment** *n* consignación *f*; envío *m*.

consist [kən'sist] *v* consistir; (*made up of*) constar, componerse. **consistency** *n* (*density*) consistencia *f*; (*agreement*) conformidad *f*. **consistent** *adj* de acuerdo; firme. **consistently** *adv* constantemente; consecuentemente.

console[1] ['kɒnsoul] *n* (*table, organ*) consola *f*; (*support*) ménsula *f*; mesa de control *f*; pupitre *m*.

console[2] [kən'soul] *v* consolar. **consolation** *n* consuelo *m*. **consolation prize** premio de consolación *m*.

consolidate [kən'sɒlideit] *v* consolidar. **consolidation** *n* consolidación *f*.

consommé [kən'sɒmei] *n* consomé *m*, caldo *m*.

consonant ['kɒnsənənt] *n* consonante *f*. *adj* conforme.

consortium [kən'sɔːtiəm] *n* consorcio *m*.

conspicuous [kən'spikjuəs] *adj* visible; (*remarkable*) notable; (*attracting attention*) llamativo.

conspire [kən'spaiə] *v* conspirar. **conspiracy** *n* conspiración *f*. **conspirator** *n* conspirador, -a *m*, *f*.

constable ['kʌnstəbl] *n* policía *m*, guardia *m*. **constabulary** *n* policía *f*.

constant ['kɒnstənt] *adj* (*continuous*) constante; (*faithful*) fiel, leal. **constancy** *n* constancia *f*; fidelidad *f*, lealdad *f*.

constellation [kɒnstə'leiʃən] *n* constelación *f*.

constipation [kɒnsti'peiʃən] *n* estreñimiento *m*. **constipated** *adj* estreñido.

constitute ['kɒnstitjuːt] *v* constituir. **constituency** *n* distrito electoral *m*. **constituent** *n* (*component*) componente *m*; (*pol*) votante *m*. *adj* (*component*) constitutivo, constituyente; electoral. **constitution** *n* constitución *f*. **constitutional** *adj* constitucional. *n* (*coll*) paseo *m*.

constraint [kən'streint] *n* (*restriction*) encierro *m*; (*compulsion*) coacción *f*; (*inhibition*) turbación *f*. **constrain** *v* encerrar; (*compel*) constreñir; (*inhibit*) incomodar.

constrict [kən'strikt] *v* (*narrow*) estrechar; (*compress*) oprimir. **constricted** *adj* estrecho. **constriction** *n* constricción *f*.

construct [kən'strʌkt] *v* construir. **construction** *n* construcción *f*; (*structure*) estructura *f*; (*meaning*) interpretación *f*. **constructive** *adj* constructivo. **constructor** *n* constructor *m*.

consul ['kɒnsəl] *n* cónsul *m*. **consular** *adj* consular. **consulate** *n* consulado *m*.

consult [kən'sʌlt] *v* consultar. **consultant** *n* (*adviser*) asesor *m*; (*med*) especialista *m*; (*tech*) consejero técnico *m*. **consultation** *n* consulta *f*. **consulting room** consultorio *m*.

consume [kən'sjuːm] *v* consumir; (*time*) tomar; (*food*) comerse; (*drink*) beberse. **consumer** *n* consumidor, -a *m*, *f*. **consumer goods** bienes de consumo *m pl*. **consumption** *n* consumo *m*; (*med: tuberculosis*) tisis *f*. **consumptive** *n*, *adj* (*med*) tísico, -a.

contact ['kɒntakt] *n* contacto *m*. **contact lens** lente de contacto *f*. *v* ponerse en contacto con.

contagious [kən'teidʒəs] *adj* contagioso. contagion *n* contagio *m*.

contain [kən'tein] *v* contener. container *n* (*package*) envase *m*; (*receptacle*) recipiente *m*. (*transport*) contenedor *m*. containment *n* contención *f*.

contaminate [kən'tamɔneit] *v* contaminar. contamination *n* contaminación *f*.

contemplate ['kontɔmpleit] *v* contemplar; (*expect*) contar con; (*consider*) considerar. contemplation *n* contemplación *f*, meditación *f*; consideración *f*. contemplative *adj* contemplativo.

contemporary [kən'tempɔrɔri] *nm, adj* contemporáneo.

contempt [kən'tempt] *n* desprecio *m*, desdén *m*. contempt of court desacato a los tribunales *m*. hold in contempt despreciar. contemptible *adj* despreciable, desdeñable. contemptuous *adj* despreciativo, desdeñoso.

contend [kən'tend] *v* (*struggle*) contender; (*compete*) competir; (*dispute*) disputir; (*affirm*) afirmar. contender *n* competidor, -a *m, f*. contention *n* contienda *f*; (*argument*) discusión *f*; (*opinion*) opinión *f*. contentious *adj* (*person*) pendenciero; (*issue*) discutible. contentiousness *n* carácter pendenciero *m*.

content¹ ['kontent] *n* contenido *m*.

content² [kən'tent] *adj* also contented contento, satisfecho. be contented with contentarse con. contentment *n* contento *m*.

contest [kən'test; *n* 'kontest] *v* (*dispute*) disputar; (*question*) impugnar. *n* (*struggle*) contienda *f*; (*competition*) competición *f*; (*controversy*) controversia *f*. contestant *n* contrincante *m*; (*election*) candidato, -a *m, f*.

context ['kontekst] *n* contexto *m*.

continent ['kontinɔnt] *n* continente *m*. the Continent el continente europeo *m*. continental *adj* continental.

contingency [kən'tindʒɔnsi] *n* (*possibility*) contingencia *f*, eventualidad *f*; (*event*) acontecimiento fortuito *m*. contingent *adj* (*accidental*) fortuito; (*probable*) contingente; (*incidental*) derivado; (*dependent*) subordinado; (*dependent on chance*) aleatorio.

continue [kən'tinjut] *v* continuar, seguir; (*extend*) prolongar. continual *adj* continuo. continually *adv* constantemente.

continuation *n* continuación *f*. continuity *n* continuidad *f*; (*cinema, radio*) guión *m*. continuous *adj* continuo.

contort [kən'tott] *v* retorcer, torcer. contortion *n* contorsión *f*; deformación *f*. contortionist *n* contorsionista *m, f*.

contour ['kontuə] *n* (*map*) curva de nivel *f*; (*outline*) contorno *m*.

contraband ['kontrɔband] *n* contrabando *m*. *adj* de contrabando.

contraception [kontrɔ'sepʃɔn] *n* contracepción *f*. contraceptive *nm, adj* contraceptivo. contraceptive pill píldora contraceptiva *f*.

contract ['kontrakt; *v* kən'trakt] *n* contrato *m*. *v* (*shrink*) contraer; (*make a contract*) contratar; (*ailment*) coger. contraction *n* contracción *f*. contractor *n* contratista *m*. contractual *adj* contractual.

contradict [kontrɔ'dikt] *v* contradecir. contradiction *n* contradicción *f*. contradictory *adj* contradictorio.

contralto [kən'traltou] *n* contralto *m, f*.

contraption [kən'trapʃɔn] *n* (*coll*) chisme *m*.

contrary ['kontrɔri] *adj* contrario. on the contrary al contrario.

contrast [kən'traist; *n* 'kontraist] *v* contrastar. *n* contraste *m*. in contrast por contraste. in contrast to a diferencia de. contrasting *adj* contrastante.

contravene [kontrɔ'viin] *v* contravenir. contravention *n* contravención *f*.

contribute [kən'tribjut] *v* contribuir (con); (*write*) escribir; (*give information*) aportar. contribution *n* contribución *f*; artículo *m*; aportación *f*; (*to conversation*) intervención *f*. contributive *adj* contributivo. contributor *n* contribuyente *m, f*; (*writer*) colaborador, -a *m, f*. contributory *adj* contribuyente.

contrive [kən'traiv] *v* idear, inventar; (*manage*) conseguir. contrived *adj* artificial. contrivable *adj* realizable; imaginable. contrivance *n* aparato *m*; invención *f*; (*resourcefulness*) ingenio *m*.

control [kən'troul] *n* control *m*; autoridad *f*; dominación *f*; (*standard of comparison*) testigo *m*. remote control mando a distancia *m*. controls *pl n* mandos *m pl*. *v* controlar; tener autoridad sobre; (*direct*) dirigir; (*regulate*) regular; (*vehicle*)

cordial

manejar. **controller** *n* director *m*. **air traffic controller** controlador del tráfico aéreo *m*. **controlling** *adj* predominante; *(decisive)* determinante.

controversy [kən'trovəsi] *n* controversia *f*. **controversial** *adj* discutible.

convalesce [konvə'les] *v* convalecer. **convalescence** *n* convalecencia *f*.

convector [kən'vektə] *n* estufa de convección *f*. **convection** *n* convección *f*.

convenience [kən'viːnjəns] *n* conveniencia *f*; *(comfort)* comodidad *f*; *(advantage)* ventaja *f*; *(useful object)* dispositivo útil *m*. **at your convenience** cuando le sea posible. **public convenience** servicios *m pl*. **convenient** *adj (handy)* cómodo; *(suitable)* conveniente; *(place)* bien situado; *(time)* oportuno.

convent ['konvənt] *n* convento *m*.

convention [kən'venʃən] *n (usage)* convención *f*; *(assembly)* asamblea *f*; *(international agreement)* convenio *m*. **conventions** *n pl* conveniencias *f pl*. **conventional** *adj (not original)* convencional; *(traditional)* clásico.

converge [kən'vɜːdʒ] *v* convergir, converger. **convergence** *n* convergencia *f*. **converging** *adj* convergente.

converse[1] [kən'vɜːs] *v* conversar, hablar. **conversant** *adj* versado, familiarizado. **conversation** *n* conversación *f*.

converse[2] [kən'vɜːs] *n* lo opuesto *m*. *adj* opuesto, contrario.

convert ['konvɜːt; *v* kən'vɜːt] *n* converso, -a *m, f. v* convertir. **conversion** *n* conversión *f*; transformación *f*.

convertible [kən'vɜːtəbl] *adj* convertible; transformable. *n (mot)* descapotable *m*.

convex ['konveks] *adj* convexo.

convey [kən'vei] *v (carry)* llevar, transportar; *(suggest)* sugerir, dar a entender; *(transmit)* transmitir; *(meaning)* expresar. **conveyance** *n* transporte *m*; transmisión *f*; *(deed)* escritura de traspaso *f*. **conveyancer** *n* notario que hace escritura de traspaso *m*. **conveyancing** *n* redacción de una escritura de traspaso *f*.

convict ['konvikt; *v* kən'vikt] *n* presidiario, -a *m, f. v (prove guilty)* condenar; *(betray)* traicionar.

conviction [kən'vikʃən] *n* condena *f*; *(belief)* convicción *f*.

convince [kən'vins] *v* convencer. **convincing** *adj* convincente.

convivial [kən'viviəl] *adj* alegre, sociable, festivo.

convoy ['konvoi] *n* convoy *m. v* convoyar.

convulsion [kən'vʌlʃən] *n (med)* convulsión *f*; *(laughter)* carcajadas *f pl*. **convulse** *v* convulsionar.

cook [kuk] *v* cocinar; *(coll: the books)* falsificar. *n* cocinero, -a *m, f.* **cooker** *n* cocina *f*; olla *f*. **pressure cooker** olla de presión *f*. **cookery** *n* arte de cocina *m*; cocción *f*; cocina *f*. **cookery book** libro de cocina *m*. **do the cooking** guisar.

cool [kuːl] *adj* fresco; *(calm)* tranquilo; *(unenthusiastic)* frío. *v* enfriar; calmar. **cooler** *n* enfriador *m*. **cooling** *adj* refrescante. **cooling system** *n* sistema de refrigeración *m*. **coolish** *adj* fresquito. **coolly** *adv* fríamente; tranquilamente. **coolness** *n* frescor *m*; frialdad *f*; serenidad *f*; sangre fría *f*.

coop [kuːp] *n (poultry)* gallinero *m*. **coop up** encerrar.

cooperate [kou'opəreit] *v* cooperar. **cooperation** *n* cooperación *f*. **cooperative** *adj* cooperativo.

coordinate [kou'ɔːdineit] *n* coordenada *f*. *adj* igual. *v* coordinar. **coordination** *n* coordinación *f*.

cope[1] [koup] *v* arreglárselas; dar abasto; poder con.

cope[2] [koup] *n (rel)* capa pluvial *f*.

Copenhagen [koupən'heigən] *n* Copenhague.

copious ['koupiəs] *adj* copioso, abundante.

copper[1] ['kopə] *n (metal)* cobre *m. adj* de cobre; *(colour)* cobrizo. **copper plate** plancha de cobre *f*.

copper[2] ['kopə] *n also* cop *(slang)* poli *m*.

copulate ['kopjuleit] *v* copular. **copulation** *n* cópula *f*.

copy ['kopi] *n* copia *f*; *(book)* ejemplar *m*; *(pattern)* modelo *m*; *(reportage)* asunto *m*. **carbon copy** papel carbón *m*. **fair copy** copia en limpio *f*. **rough copy** borrador *m. v* copiar; imitar. **copyright** *n* propiedad literaria.

coral ['korəl] *n* coral *m. adj* coralino.

cord [kɔːd] *n (string, rope)* cuerda *f*; *(insulated wire)* cordón *m*. **spinal cord** médula espinal *f*. **umbilical cord** cordón umbilical *m*. **vocal cords** cuerdas vocales *f pl*.

cordial ['kɔːdiəl] *adj, nm* cordial. **cordiality** *n* cordialidad *f*.

cordon ['kɔɪdn] n cordón m. **cordon off** acordonar.

corduroy ['kɔɪdəroi] n pana f.

core [kɔɪ] n (fruit) corazón m; (geol) núcleo; (fig) centro m, esencia f. v quitar el corazón de.

cork [kɔɪk] n (bot) corcho m; (stopper) tapón m. **cork tree** alcornoque m. **cork-tipped** adj con boquilla de corcho. v taponar. **uncork** v (bottle) descorchar. **corked** adj (bottle) taponado; (wine) que sabe a corcho. **corkscrew** n sacacorchos m invar.

corn[1] [kɔɪn] n (wheat) trigo m; (maize) maíz m; (cereals) granos cereales m pl. **corn on the cob** maíz en la mazorca m.

corn[2] [kɔɪn] n (med) callo m.

corner ['kɔɪnə] n (inside angle) rincón m; (outside angle) esquina f; (of an object) pico m. **cut corners** tomar atajos. v poner en un aprieto; (accost) abordar; (mot) tomar una curva; (comm) monopolizar.

cornet ['kɔɪnit] n corneta f; (ice cream) cucurucho m.

coronary ['kɔrənəri] adj coronario. **coronary thrombosis** trombosis coronaria f.

coronation [kɔrə'neiʃən] n coronación f.

corporal[1] ['kɔɪpərəl] adj corporal. **corporal punishment** castigo corporal m.

corporal[2] ['kɔɪpərəl] n (mil) cabo m.

corporation [kɔɪpə'reiʃən] n corporación f; sociedad anónima f. **municipal corporation** ayuntamiento m. **corporate** adj colectivo, corporativo.

corps [kɔɪ] n cuerpo m. **corps de ballet** cuerpo de ballet. **diplomatic corps** cuerpo diplomático.

corpse [kɔɪps] n cadáver m.

correct ['kə'rekt] adj (accurate) exacto; (behaviour) correcto; (right) justo. v corregir. **correction** n corrección f. **corrective** adj correctivo. **correctness** n corrección f; exactitud f; (judgment) rectitud f.

correlate ['kɔrəleit] v correlacionar. **correlation** n correlación f.

correspond [kɔrə'spond] v corresponder; (write) escribirse. **correspondence** n correspondencia f. **correspondent** n corresponsal m, f; (newspaper) corresponsal m, f.

corridor ['kɔridɔɪ] n pasillo m, corredor m.

corroborate [kə'robəreit] v corroborar. **corroboration** n corroboración f.

corrode [kə'roud] v corroer. **corrosion** n corrosión f. **corrosive** adj corrosivo.

corrugated ['kɔrəgeitid] adj ondulado.

corrupt [kə'rʌpt] adj corrupto; corrompido; (rotten) estragado; (perverted) pervertido; (bribable) venal. v corromper; (bribe) sobornar. **corruptible** adj corruptible. **corruption** n corrupción f.

corset ['kɔɪset] n faja f.

Corsica ['kɔɪsikə] n Córcega f. **Corsican** n, adj corso, -a m, f.

cosmetic [koz'metik] nm, adj cosmético.

cosmic ['kozmik] adj cósmico.

cosmopolitan [kozmə'politən] n(m+f), adj cosmopolita.

*****cost** [kost] n costo m, coste m; (price) precio m; (expenses) gastos m pl. **costs** pl n (law) costas f pl. **at all costs** cueste lo que cueste. **cost of living** coste de vida m. **to one's cost** a expensas de uno. v costar; valer. **costly** adj caro.

Costa Rica [kostə'riːkə] n Costa Rica. **Costa Rican** n(m+f), adj costarriquense; n, adj costarriqueño, -a m, f.

costume ['kostjuːm] n traje m. **bathing costume** traje de baño. **costume jewellery** bisutería f.

cosy ['kouzi] adj confortable; (place) acogedor.

cot [kot] n cuna f.

cottage ['kotidʒ] n casa de campo f; chalet m. **cottage cheese** requesón m.

cotton ['kotn] n algodón m. adj de algodón. **cotton-wool** n algodón hidrófilo m.

couch [kautʃ] n sofá m; (bed) lecho m. v (express) expresar.

cough [kof] n tos f. v toser. **cough up** (coll) cascar.

could [kud] V **can**[1].

council ['kaunsəl] n consejo m; (assembly) ayuntamiento m. **council house** vivienda protegida f. **town council** concejo municipal m. **councillor** n concejal m.

counsel ['kaunsəl] n consejo m; (lawyer) abogado m; (legal adviser) asesor jurídico m. v aconsejar; pedir consejo.

count[1] [kaunt] v contar, calcular; (consider) considerar. **count against** ir en contra de. **count for** valer por. **countable** adj contable. **countdown** n cuenta atrás f. **countless** adj incontable. n cuenta f, cálculo m; (sum) total m; (votes) escrutinio m.

count² [kaunt] n (noble) conde m. **countess** n condesa f.

countenance ['kauntinəns] n semblante m, cara f. v (approve) aprobar; (support) apoyar.

counter¹ ['kauntə] n (disc) ficha f; (table top) mostrador m, contador m. **Geiger counter** contador Geiger m. **under the counter** bajo mano.

counter² ['kauntə] adj (opposed) contrario, opuesto. v contraatacar; oponerse. **go counter to** ir en contra de.

counterattack ['kauntərə,tak] n contraataque m. v contraatacar.

counterfeit ['kauntəfit] adj falso, falsificado. v falsificar. n falsificación f.

counterfoil ['kauntə,foil] n talón m.

counterpart ['kauntə,part] n contraparte f.

country ['kʌntri] n (state) pais m; (out of town) campo. **country estate** finca f. **country house** casa de campo f. **countryman** n campesino m; compatriota m. **countryside** n campo m; (landscape) paisaje m.

county ['kaunti] n condado m. **county council** diputación provincial f.

coup [kuː] n golpe m. **coup d'état** golpe de estado m.

couple ['kʌpl] n par m; (married, engaged, etc.) pareja f. v emparejar; (associate) asociar; (vehicles) enganchar; (elec) conectar; (copulate) copular.

coupon ['kuːpon] n cupón m; (pools) boleto m.

courage ['kʌridʒ] n valor m, valentía f. **pluck up courage** armarse de valor. **take courage** cobrar ánimo. **courageous** adj valiente.

courgette [kuə'ʒet] n calabacín m.

courier ['kuriə] n guía m, f; agente de turismo m, f; mensajero, -a m, f.

course [kɔːs] n (direction) dirección f, rumbo m; (progress) curso m; (way, means) camino m; (action, conduct) linea f; (meal) plato m; (track) pista f; (golf) campo m. **in due course** a su debido tiempo. **main course** plato fuerte m. **of course** claro, por supuesto. **set course for** hacer rumbo a. v (hunt) cazar; (run: liquid) correr.

court [kɔːt] n (royalty) corte f; (alley) callejón sin salida m; (law) audiencia f, tribunal m; (sport) cancha f. **court order** orden judicial f. **go to court** acudir a los tribunales. **courtyard** n patio m. v (woo)

cortejar, hacer la corte a; buscar; pedir, solicitar. **courtier** n cortesano m. **courtly** adj cortés. **court-martial** n consejo de guerra m. **courtship** n noviazgo m.

courteous ['kɜːtiəs] adj cortés. **courtesy** n cortesía f.

cousin ['kʌzn] n primo, -a m, f. **first cousin** primo, -a carnal m, f.

cove [kouv] n cala f; (slang) tio m.

cover ['kʌvə] n cubierta f; (lid) tapa f; (bed) colcha f; (table) tapete m; (refuge) refugio m; (parcel) envoltura f; (envelope) sobre m; (pretence) excusa f; (protection) amparo m. **cover charge** precio del cubierto m. **take cover** ponerse a cubierto. v cubrir, tapar. **coverage** n alcance m.

cow [kau] n vaca f; (female animal) hembra f. v intimidar. **cowboy** n vaquero m, (Amer) gaucho m. **cowshed** n establo m. **cowslip** n prímula f.

coward ['kauəd] n cobarde m, f. **cowardice** n cobardía f. **cowardly** adj cobarde.

cower ['kauə] v encogerse; agacharse.

coy [koi] adj (shy) tímido; (demure) remilgado.

crab [krab] n cangrejo m. **crab apple** manzana silvestre f. **crabbed** adj (bad-tempered) malhumorado; (writing) indecifrable.

crack [krak] n (noise) restallido m, chasquido m; (opening) abertura f; (split) raja f; (in walls, etc.) hendidura f; (slit) rendija f; (blow) golpe m; (coll: joke) chiste m. **crack of dawn** al amenecer. **have a crack at** intentar. v restallar, chasquear; golpear; (break) romper; (a nut) cascar; hender, rajar; (burst) reventar; (give in) ceder; (break down) hundirse; (coll: joke) bromear; (coll: safe) forzar. **get cracking** darse prisa. **crackpot** n, adj (coll) chiflado, -a m, f.

cracker ['krakə] n (Christmas) sorpresa f; (firework) buscapiés m invar; (biscuit) galleta f.

crackle ['krakl] n crepitación f, crujido m. v crepitar, crujir. **crackling** n (cookery) chicharrón m.

cradle ['kreidl] n cuna f; soporte m. v acunar; (in one's arms) mecer; soportar.

craft [krɑːft] n (trade) trabajo manual m; (skill) arte m; (guild) gremio m; (cunning) astucia f, maña f; (ship) embarcación f; (aircraft) avión m. **craftily** adv astutamente. **craftsman** n artesano m.

craftsmanship *n* artesanía *f.* crafty *adj* astuto, socarrón.

cram [kram] *v* (*fill up*) aborratar; (*force in*) meter a la fuerza; (*for exam*) empollar.

cramp [kramp] *n* (*med*) calambre *m.* *v* dar calambre a. cramped *adj* (*crowded*) apiñado; (*writing*) apretado.

cranberry ['kranbəri] *n* arándano *m.*

crane [krein] *n* (*hoist*) grúa *f;* (*bird*) grulla *f. v* (*neck*) estirar.

crank [kraŋk] *n* (*tech*) manivela *f;* (*fool*) chiflado, -a *m, f. v* arrancar con la manivela. crankcase *n* cárter *m.* crankiness *n* irritabilidad *f;* excentricidad *f;* chifladura *f.* crankshaft *n* cigüeñal *m.*

crap [krap] *n* (*slang: nonsense*) disparate; (*impol*) mierda *f. v* (*impol*) cagar.

crash [kraʃ] *n* accidente *m,* choque *m;* (*noise*) estrépito *m;* (*aircraft*) caída *f;* (*business*) quiebra *f.* crash course curso intensivo *m.* crash helmet casco protector *m. v* chocar; caer; quebrar; (*make a loud noise*) retumbar. crash-land hacer un aterrizaje de emergencia.

crate [kreit] *n* cajón de embalaje *m. v* embalar.

crater ['kreitə] *n* cráter *m.*

crave [kreiv] *v* (*desire*) ansiar; (*beg*) suplicar; (*attention*) reclamar. craving *n* ansia *f.*

crawl [krɔːl] *v* arrastrarse, andar a gatas; (*move slowly*) andar lentamente. *n* arrastramiento *m;* marcha lenta *f.*

crayfish ['kreifiʃ] *n* ástaco *m,* cangrejo de río *m.*

crayon ['kreiən] *n* lápiz de tiza *m. v* dibujar al pastel.

craze [kreiz] *n* (*wild enthusiasm*) locura *f;* (*fad*) manía *f;* (*fashion*) moda *f. v* enloquecer. craziness *n* locura *f.* crazy *adj* loco.

creak [kriːk] *n* crujido *m. v* crujir. creaky *adj* que cruje.

cream [kriːm] *n* nata *f,* crema *f.* whipped cream nata batida. *adj* color crema. *v* (*beat*) batir; (*skim*) desnatar. cream cheese queso de nata *m.*

crease [kriːs] *n* (*fold*) pliegue *m;* (*wrinkle*) arruga *f;* (*trousers*) raya *f.* crease-resistant *adj* inarrugable. *v* plegar; arrugar; hacer la raya de.

create [kriˈeit] *v* crear. creation *n* creación *f.* creator *n* creador, -a *m, f.*

credentials [kriˈdenʃəlz] *pl n* credenciales *f pl.*

credible ['kredəbl] *adj* creíble. credibility *n* credibilidad *f.*

credit¹ ['kredit] *n* crédito *m;* (*comm*) haber *m;* (*prestige*) honor *m.* credits *pl n* (*film*) ficha técnica *f sing.* credit balance saldo acreedor *m.* credit card tarjeta de crédito *f.* credit rating solvabilidad *f.* on credit a plazos. we do not give credit no se fía.

credit² ['kredit] *v* (*believe*) creer; (*fig*) atribuir; (*an account*) abonar en cuenta. creditable *adj* (*believable*) digno de crédito; (*praiseworthy*) encomiable; (*well spoken of*) de buena reputación. creditably *adv* honrosamente. creditor *n* acreedor, -a *m, f.*

credulous ['kredjuləs] *adj* crédulo.

creed [kriːd] *n* credo *m.*

*creep [kriːp] *v* deslizarse, arrastrarse; (*flesh*) ponerse a uno la carne de gallina. *n* (*coll*) pelotillero, -a *m, f.* creepy *adj* horripilante.

cremate [kriˈmeit] *v* incinerar. cremation *n* incineración *f.* crematorium *n* horno crematorio *m.*

crescent ['kresnt] *n* medialuna *f,* luna creciente *f. adj* creciente.

cress [kres] *n* berro *m.*

crest [krest] *n* (*on animal's head, wave*) cresta *f;* (*hill*) cima *f,* cumbre *f;* (*heraldry*) timbre *m.* crested *adj* crestado. crestfallen *adj* alicaído.

crevice ['krevis] *n* grieta *f;* hendedura *f.*

crew [kruː] *n* (*body of workers*) equipo *m;* (*ship, aircraft*) tripulación *f;* (*mob*) banda *f.* ground crew personal de tierra *m.*

crib [krib] *n* (*rack*) pesebre *m;* (*small cot*) cuna *f;* (*coll: exam*) chuleta *f. v* plagiar.

cricket¹ ['krikit] *n* (*insect*) grillo *m.*

cricket² ['krikit] *n* (*sport*) criquet *m.*

crime [kraim] *n* crimen *m;* criminalidad *f.* criminal *nm, adj* criminal.

crimson ['krimzn] *nm, adj* carmesí.

cringe [krindʒ] *v* agacharse, encogerse. cringing *adj* servil.

crinkle ['kriŋkl] *n* arruga *f. v* arrugarse.

cripple ['kripl] *n, adj* tullido, -a *m, f. v* (*person*) tullir; (*object*) estropear; (*fig*) paralizar.

crisis ['kraisis] *n pl* -ses crisis *f invar.*

crisp [krisp] *adj* fresco; (*bread*) crurruscante; (*style*) crespo; (*snow*) crujiente; (*talk*) animado. *v* encrespar, rizar. potato

crisp patata frita a la inglesa *f*. **crispness** *n* encrespado *m*.

criterion [krai'tiəriən] *n pl* -a criterio *m*.

criticize ['kriti,saiz] *v* criticar. **critic** (*fault-finder*) criticón, -ona *m*, *f*; (*reviewer*) crítico *m*. **critical** *adj* crítico. **criticism** *n* crítica *f*.

crochet ['krouʃei] *n* croché *m*, ganchillo *m*. *v* hacer a ganchillo.

crockery ['krokəri] *n* loza *f*, vajilla *f*.

crocodile ['krokə,dail] *n* cocodrilo *m*.

crocus ['kroukəs] *n* azafrán *m*.

crook [kruk] *n* (*shepherd's*) cayado *m*; (*bishop's*) báculo *m*; (*coll*) ladrón *m*, timador *m*.

crooked ['krukid] *adj* (*bent*) curvado; (*twisted*) torcido; (*path*) sinuoso; (*nose*) ganchudo; (*coll*) poco limpio. **crookedness** *n* sinuosidad *f*; (*coll*) falta de honradez *f*.

crop [krop] *n* (*harvest*) cosecha *f*; (*cultivated produce*) cultiva *f*; (*whip*) fusta *f*; (*bird*) buche *m*; (*haircut*) corte de pelo *m*. **crop rotation** rotación de cultivos *f*. *v* (*graze*) pacer; (*ears*) desorejar; (*tail*) cortar la cola de; (*hair*) cortar muy corto. **come a cropper** darse un batacazo.

croquet ['kroukei] *n* croquet *m*.

cross [kros] *n* cruz *f*; (*breeding*) cruce *f*. **make the sign of the cross** santiguarse. *adj* cruzado; (*angry*) enfadado. *v* (*move*) atravesar; (*limbs*) cruzar; (*oppose*) contrariar; (*mark*) marcar con una cruz. **cross out** tachar. **cross one's mind** ocurrírsele a uno.

cross-country *adj* a campo traviesa.

cross-current *n* contracorriente *f*.

cross-examination *n* repregunta *f*.

cross-eyed *adj* bizco.

crossfire ['kros,faiə] *n* fuego cruzado *m*.

crossing ['krosiŋ] *n* (*intersection*) cruce *f*; (*voyage*) travesía *f*; (*pedestrian*) paso de peatones *m*.

cross-purposes *pl n* fines opuestos *m pl*.

cross-reference *n* remisión *f*.

crossroads ['kros,roudz] *pl n* cruce *f sing*; (*fig*) encrucijada *f sing*.

cross section *n* sección transversal *f*.

crossword ['kros,wəːd] *n* crucigrama *m*.

crotchet ['krotʃit] *n* (*music*) negra *f*. **crotchety** *adj* de mal genio.

crouch [krautʃ] *v* agacharse, encogerse.

crow¹ [krou] *n* (*bird*) cuervo *m*. **as the crow flies** en línea recta. **crowbar** *n* palanca *f*.

crow² [krou] *v* cantar; cacarear. *n* cacareo *m*.

crowd [kraud] *n* muchedumbre *f*, multitud *f*. *v* amontonar; congregarse. **crowded** *adj* lleno.

crown [kraun] *n* corona *f*; (*hat*) copa *f*; (*hill*) cumbre *f*; (*head*) coronilla *f*. **crown jewels** joyas reales *f pl*. **crown prince** príncipe heredero *m*. *v* coronar. **to crown it all** para rematarlo todo. **crowning** *adj* supremo.

crucial ['kruːʃəl] *adj* crucial, decisivo.

crucify ['kruːsi,fai] *v* crucificar. **crucifix** *n* crucifijo *m*. **crucifixion** *n* crucifixión *f*.

crude [kruːd] *adj* (*raw*) crudo; (*steel*) bruto; (*oil*) sin refinar; (*vulgar*) basto; (*ill-made*) tosco. **crudeness, crudity** *n* crudeza *f*; tosquedad *f*.

cruel ['kruːəl] *adj* cruel. **cruelty** *n* crueldad *f*.

cruise [kruːz] *n* crucero *m*. *v* hacer un crucero; (*patrol*) patrullar; (*at cruising speed*) ir a una velocidad de crucero. **cruiser** *n* (*naut*) crucero *m*.

crumb [krʌm] *n* migaja *f*, miga *f*.

crumble ['krʌmbl] *v* desmenuzar; desmigar. **crumbly** *adj* desmenuzable.

crumple ['krʌmpl] *v* arrugar, ajar. **crumple up** desplomarse.

crunch [krʌntʃ] *n* crujido *m*; (*coll*) punto decisivo *m*. *v* crujir; mascar. **crunchy** *adj* crujiente.

crusade [kruː'seid] *n* cruzada *f*; (*fig*) campaña *f*. *v* hacer una cruzada. **crusader** *n* cruzado *m*.

crush [krʌʃ] *n* aplastamiento *m*; (*crowd*) aglomeración *f*; (*squeeze*) apretón *m*. **have a crush on** (*coll*) estar loco perdido por. *v* aplastar; apretar; (*pulverize*) machacar; (*overwhelm*) abrumar. **crushing** *adj* aplastante.

crust [krʌst] *n* (*of a loaf*) corteza *f*. **upper crust** la flor y nata *f*. **crusty** *adj* de corteza dura; (*coll*) brusco.

crutch [krʌtʃ] *n* (*support*) muleta *f*; (*fig*) apoyo *m*.

crux [krʌks] *n* quid *m*.

cry [krai] *n* grito *m*. *v* (*call*) gritar; (*weep*) llorar. **cry out** clamar.

crypt [kript] *n* cripta *f*. **cryptic** *adj* secreto; enigmático.

crystal ['kristl] *n* cristal *m*. *adj* de cristal. **crystal clear** cristalino. **crystallize** *v* cristalizar.

cub [kʌb] *n (bear, lion, tiger, wolf)* cachorro *m; (other animals)* cría *f.* **cub scout** niño explorador *m.*

Cuba ['kjuːbə] *n* Cuba *f.* **Cuban** *n, adj* cubano, -a.

cube [kjuːb] *n (math)* cubo *m; (sugar, etc.)* terrón *m. v (math)* cubicar. **cube root** raíz cúbica *f.* **cubic** *adj* cúbico.

cubicle ['kjuːbikl] *n* cubículo *m; (for sleeping)* cubilla *f; (for changing)* caseta *f.*

cuckoo ['kukuː] *n* cuco *m,* cuclillo *m.*

cucumber [kjuˈkʌmbə] *n* pepino *m.*

cuddle ['kʌdl] *n* abrazo *m. v* abrazar. **cuddly** *adj* mimoso.

cue[1] [kjuː] *n (theatre)* señal *f;* entrada *f. v* indicar.

cue[2] [kjuː] *n (billiards)* taco *m.*

cuff[1] [kʌf] *n (shirt)* puño *m.* **cufflinks** *pl n* gemelos *m pl.* **off the cuff** de improviso.

cuff[2] [kʌf] *n (hit)* bofetada *f. v* abofetear.

culinary ['kʌlinəri] *adj* culinario.

culminate ['kʌlmiˌneit] *v* culminar. **culmination** *n* culminación *f.*

culprit ['kʌlprit] *n* culpado, -a *m, f;* culpable *m, f.*

cult [kʌlt] *n* culto *m.*

cultivate ['kʌltiˌveit] *v* cultivar. **cultivated** *adj (land)* cultivado; *(person)* culto. **cultivation** *n* cultivo *m.*

culture ['kʌltʃə] *n* cultura *f;* cultivo *m.* **cultured** *adj* culto.

cumbersome ['kʌmbəsəm] *adj* molesto; *(annoying)* incómodo.

cunning ['kʌniŋ] *adj (sly)* taimado; *(clever)* astuto; *(skilful)* mañoso. *n* astucia *f;* maña *f.*

cup [kʌp] *n* taza *f; (prize)* copa *f.*

cupboard ['kʌbəd] *n* armario *m.*

curate ['kjuərət] *n* cura *m.*

curator [kjuəˈreitə] *n* conservador, -a *m, f.*

curb [kəːb] *v* contener, refrenar. *n (obstacle)* estorbo *m; (fig)* freno *m.*

curdle ['kəːdl] *v* cuajar, cuajarse. **curd** cuajada *f.*

cure [kjuə] *n (course of treatment; smoking food)* cura *f; (remedy)* remedio *m; (of leather)* curtido *m; (salting)* salazón *m. v* curar; remediar; salar; curtir. **cure-all** *n* curalotodo *m.*

curfew ['kəːfjuː] *n* toque de queda *m.*

curious ['kjuəriəs] *adj* curioso. **curiosity** *n* curiosidad *f.*

curl [kəːl] *n (hair)* bucle *m; (smoke)* voluta *f; (twist)* torcedura *f;* serpenteo *m.*

v (hair) rizar. **curl oneself up** hacerse un ovillo. **curler** *n* rulo *m.* **curly** *adj* rizado; sinuoso; en espiral.

currant ['kʌrənt] *n (dried grape)* pasa *f; (berry)* grosella *f; (bush)* grosellero *m.*

currency ['kʌrənsi] *n* moneda *f; (general use)* uso corriente *m.*

current ['kʌrənt] *n* corriente *f;* curso *m.* **alternating/direct current** corriente alterna/continua *f. adj (general)* corriente, prevalente; *(now)* actual; *(accepted)* admitido. **current account** cuenta corriente *f.* **current affairs** actualidades *f pl.* **current rate of exchange** cambio del día *m.* **current year** año en curso. **currently** *adv* corrientemente; actualmente.

curry ['kʌri] *n* cari *m,* curry. *m. v* preparar con cari. **curry powder** especias en polvo *f pl.*

curse [kəːs] *n* maldición *f. v* maldecir; *(swear)* decir palabrotas; *(blaspheme)* blasfemar.

curt [kəːt] *adj* brusco. **curtness** *n* brusquedad *f.*

curtail [kəːˈteil] *v (cut short)* abreviar; *(expenses)* reducir. **curtailment** *n* abreviación *f;* reducción *f.*

curtain ['kəːtn] *n* cortina *f; (theatre)* telón *m.* **curtain call** llamada a escena *f.* **draw the curtain** correr la cortina. *v* poner cortinas en; encubrir.

curtsy ['kəːtsi] *n* reverencia *f. v* hacer una reverencia.

curve [kəːv] *n* curva *f;* vuelta *f. v* doblar; encorvar. **curvature** *n* curvatura *f; (earth)* esfericidad *f; (spine)* encorvamiento *m.* **curved** *adj* curvo; doblado.

cushion ['kuʃən] *n* cojín *m,* almohadón *m. v* amortiguar, acolchar.

custard ['kʌstəd] *n* natillas *f pl.*

custody ['kʌstədi] *n* custodia *f,* guardia *f;* prisión *f.* **in custody** bajo custodia. **take into custody** detener. **custodian** *n* custodio *m;* guardián, -ana *m, f.*

custom ['kʌstəm] *n (habit)* costumbre *f; (customers)* clientela *f sing.* **customs** *n* derechos de aduana *m pl.* **customary** *adj* de costumbre. **custom-built** *adj* hecho de encargo. **customer** *n* cliente *m, f.*

*cut [kʌt] *n* corte *m; (wound)* herida *f; (notch)* muesca *f; (reduction)* reducción *f; (med)* incisión *f.* **short cut** atajo *m.* **cut-and-dried** previsto. **cut and thrust** la lucha *f. v* cortar; reducir; *(reap)* segar; *(shorten)* acortar. **cut short** cortar en

seco. *adj* cortado; reducido. **cut-price** *adj*
a precio reducido.
cute [kjutt] *adj* (*attractive*) mono, lindo;
(*clever*) astuto. **cuteness** *n* monería *f*;
astucia *f*.
cuticle ['kjutikl] *n* cutícula *f*.
cutlery ['kʌtləri] *n* cubiertos *m pl*.
cutlet ['kʌtlit] *n* chuleta *f*.
cycle [saikl] *n* ciclo *m*; bicicleta *f*. *v* pasar
por un ciclo; ir en bicicleta. **cyclical** *adj*
cíclico. **cycling** *n* ciclismo *m*. **cyclist** *n*
ciclista *m*, *f*.
cyclone ['saikloun] *n* ciclón *m*.
cylinder ['silində] *n* cilindro *m*. **cylinder
block** bloque de cilindros *m*. **cylindrical**
adj cilíndrico.
cymbal ['simbəl] *n* címbalo *m*, platillo *m*.
cynic ['sinik] *n*, *adj* cínico, -a *m*, *f*. **cynical**
adj cínico. **cynicism** *n* cinicismo *m*.
cypress ['saiprəs] *n* ciprés *m*.
Cyprus ['saiprəs] *n* Chipre. **Cypriot**
n(*m*+*f*), *adj* chipriota.
cyst [sist] *n* quiste *m*. **cystitis** *n* cistitis *f*.
Czechoslovakia [ˌtʃekəsləˈvakiə]
Checoslovaquia *f*. **Czechoslovakian,
Czechoslovak, Czech** *n*, *adj* checoslovaco, -a.

D

dab [dab] *n* (*light blow*) golpe ligero *m*;
(*touch*) toque *m*; (*bit*) pizca *f*. *v* golpear
ligeramente; dar unos toques de. *adj* **be
a dab hand at** ser un hacha en.
dabble ['dabl] *v* (*splash*) salpicar; (*wet*)
mojar. **dabble in** (*water*) chapotear; (*participation*) meterse en.
dad [dad] *n* (*coll*) papá *m*.
daffodil ['dafədil] *n* narciso *m*.
daft [dɑːft] *adj* (*coll*) tonto.
dagger ['dagə] *n* daga *f*; puñal *m*.
daily ['deili] *adj* diario, cotidiano. *adv*
diariamente, cada día. *n* (*coll: newspaper*)
diario *m*.
dainty ['deinti] *adj* (*taste*) delicado, fino;
(*fussy*) difícil. **daintiness** *n* delicadeza *f*;
elegancia *f*.
dairy ['deəri] *n* lechería *f*. **dairy cattle**
vacas lecheras *f pl*. **dairy farm** granja de
vacas *f*. **dairy products** productos lácteos
m pl.

daisy ['deizi] *n* margarita *f*.
dam [dam] *n* (*barrier*) dique *m*; (*reservoir*)
embalse *m*; (*zool*) madre *f*. *v* construir un
dique; embalsar.
damage ['damidʒ] *n* daño *m*; (*fig*)
perjuicio *m*. **damages** *pl n* (*law*) daños y
perjuicios *m pl*. *v* dañar; perjudicar;
(*spoil*) estropear.
damn [dam] *v* (*condemn*) condenar;
(*curse*) maldecir. **damn!** (*interj*)
¡mechacis! **damnable** *adj* condenable;
detestable. **damnation** *n* condenación *f*;
(*interj*) ¡maldición! **damned** *adj* condenado; (*coll*) maldito; tremendo. *adv*
sumamente.
damp [damp] *adj* húmedo. *n* humedad *f*.
damp course aislante hidráfugo *m*. *v* (*also
dampen*) humedecer; (*extinguish*) apagar,
sofocar; (*discourage*) desanimar; (*sound*)
amortiguar. **damper** *n* humedecedor *m*;
(*chimney*) regulador *m*. **put a damper on**
caer como un jarro de agua fría en.
damson ['damzən] *n* (*fruit*) ciruela damas-
cena *f*; (*tree*) ciruelo damsceno *m*.
dance [dɑːns] *n* baile *m*; (*ritual*) danza *f*.
dance band orquesta de baile *f*. **dance
floor** pista de baile *f*. **dance hall** sala de
baile *f*. *v* bailar. **dancer** *n* bailarín, -ina
m, *f*.
dandelion ['dandiˌlaiən] *n* diente de león
m.
dandruff ['dandrəf] *n* caspa *f*.
Dane [dein] *n* danés, -esa *m*, *f*. **Danish**
nm, *adj* danés. **Great Dane** perro danés
m.
danger ['deindʒə] *n* peligro *m*. **danger
zone** área de peligro. **dangerous** *adj*
peligroso.
dangle ['dangl] *v* (*hang*) colgar, dejar col-
gado; (*swing*) balancear en el aire.
dare [deə] *v* (*challenge*) desafiar; (*have the
impudence to*) atreverse a. **I dare say**
quizás. *n* desafío *m*, reto *m*. **daredevil** *n*
temerario, -a *m*, *f*. **daring** *adj* atrevido;
osado. *n* osadía *f*.
dark [dɑːk] *adj* oscuro; (*hair, complexion*)
moreno; (*sombre*) triste; (*menacing*)
amenazador; (*mysterious*) misterioso.
Dark Ages edad de las tinieblas *f*. **dark
room** cámara oscura *f*. **grow dark**
anochecer. *n* oscuridad *f*. **after dark**
después del anochecer. **be in the dark**
estar a oscuras. **darken** *v* oscurecer;
entristecer. **darkness** *n* oscuridad *f*.

darling ['dɑːlɪŋ] *n, adj* querido, -a *m, f.*

darn [dɑːn] *v* zurcir. *n* zurcido *m.* **darning needle** aguja de zurcir *f.*

dart [dɑːt] *n* (*missile*) dardo *m;* (*movement*) movimiento rápido *m. v* lanzar. **dartboard** *n* blanco *m.* **darts** *pl n* (*sport*) dardos *m pl.*

dash [daʃ] *n* (*rush*) carrera *f;* (*printing*) guión *m;* (*cookery*) poco *m,* gotas *f pl;* (*verve*) brío *m. v* (*rush*) precipitarse, ir de prisa; (*hopes*) defraudar. **dash off** (*letter, etc.*) escribir deprisa. **dashboard** *n* salpicadero *m.* **dashing** *adj* gallardo.

data ['deitə] *pl n* datos *m pl.* **data processing** proceso de datos *m.*

date[1] [deit] *n* (*calendar*) fecha *f;* época *f.* **be up to date** estar al día. **out of date** anticuado. **to date** hasta la fecha. **date line** meridiano de cambio de fecha *m. v* fechar.

date[2] [deit] *n* (*fruit*) dátil *m.* **date palm** palmera datilera *f.*

dative ['deitiv] *nm, adj* dativo.

daughter ['dɔːtə] *n* hija *f.* **daughter-in-law** *n* nuera *f,* hija política *f.*

daunt [dɔːnt] *v* (*dishearten*) desanimar; (*intimidate*) intimidar. **dauntless** *adj* intrépido.

dawdle ['dɔːdl] *v* (*loiter*) holgazanear; (*waste time*) malgastar; (*walk slowly*) andar despacio.

dawn [dɔːn] *n* alba *m,* amanecer *m;* (*fig*) alborear *m.* **from dawn to dusk** de sol a sol. *v* alborear, amanecer.

day [dei] *n* día *m;* (*of work*) jornada *f.* **all day** todo el día. **every day** todos los días. **the day after tomorrow** pasado mañana. **the day before yesterday** anteayer. **from day to day** de día en día. **daybreak** *n* amanecer *m.* **daydream** *n* ensueño *m; v* soñar despierto. **daylight** *n* luz del día *f.* **in broad daylight** en pleno día. **good day!** ¡buenos días!

daze [deiz] *n* aturdimiento *m. v* aturdir. **be in a daze** estar aturdido.

dazzle ['dazl] *n* brillo *m. v* deslumbrar. **dazzling** *adj* deslumbrante, deslumbrador.

dead [ded] *adj* muerto; (*absolute*) absoluto; (*insensible*) insensible; (*battery*) descargado; (*extinguished*) apagado. **deadline** *n* fecha *f.* **deadly** *adj* mortal; (*unerring*) absoluto; (*habit*) pernicioso.

deaden ['dedn] *v* (*sound, etc.*) amortiguar; (*pain*) calmar; (*feeling*) embotar. **deadening** *adj* (*tech*) aislante.

deaf [def] *adj* sordo. **turn a deaf ear** hacerse el sordo. **deaf-and-dumb** *adj* sordomudo. **deafen** *v* ensordecer. **deafening** *adj* ensordecedor. **deafness** *n* sordera *f.*

*deal [diːl] *v* repartir, distribuir. **deal in** comercir en. *n* transacción *f,* negocio *m;* (*treatment*) trato *m;* (*agreement*) convenio *m;* (*amount*) cantidad *f;* (*cards*) reparto *m;* (*wood*) abeto *m.* **it's a deal!** ¡trato hecho! **your deal** te toca. **dealer** *m* comerciante *m, f;* (*cards*) mano *f.* **dealing** *n* trato *m;* (*behaviour*) conducta *f.* **dealings** *pl n* relaciones *f pl.*

dean [diːn] *n* (*rel*) deán *m;* (*academic*) decano *m.*

dear [diə] *adj* querido; (*costly*) caro, costoso. **dear me!** ¡Dios mío! **dear sir** estimado señor. **dearly** *adv* (*affectionately*) cariñosamente; (*costly*) caro.

death [deθ] *n* muerte *f;* (*formal*) fallecimiento *m.* **death certificate** certificado de defunción *m.* **death duty** derechos de sucesión *m pl.* **deathless** *adj* inmortal. **deathly** *adj* (*appearance*) cadavérico; (*silence*) sepulcral. **death penalty** pena de muerte *f.* **death rate** mortalidad *f.*

debase [di'beis] *v* degradar; (*coins*) alterar. **debasement** *n* degradación *f;* alteración *f.*

debate [di'beit] *n* debate *m,* discusión *f;* controversia *f. v* discutir; controvertir; considerar. **debatable** *adj* discutible. **debating society** asociación que organiza debates *f.*

debit ['debit] *n* (*entry of debt*) débito *m;* (*left-hand side of account*) debe *m. v* cargar en cuenta.

debris ['deibriː] *n* escombros *m pl.*

debt [det] *n* deuda *f.* **run into debt** contraer deudas. **debtor** *n* deudor, -a *m, f.*

decade ['dekeid] *n* decenio *m.*

decadent ['dekədənt] *n(m+f), adj* decadente. **decadence** decadencia *f.*

decant [di'kant] *v* decantar. **decanter** *n* garrafa *f,* jarra *f.*

decapitate [di'kapiˌteit] *v* decapitar. **decapitation** *n* decapitación *f.*

decay [di'kei] *n* descomposición *f;* (*teeth*) caries *f invar;* decadencia *f;* (*physics*) desintegración progresiva *f. v* descomponerse; cariarse; decaer.

decease [di'siːs] *n* fallecimiento *m*. *v* fallecer. **deceased** *n*, *adj* difunto, -a.

deceit [di'siːt] *n* (*cheating*) engaño *m*; fraude *m*; decepción; (*lying*) mentira *f*. **deceitful** *adj* engañoso; fraudulento; mentiroso. **deceitfulness** *n* lo engañoso *m*; falsedad *f*.

deceive [di'siːv] *v* engañar; defraudar. **deceiver** *n* embustero, -a *m*, *f*.

December [di'sembə] *n* diciembre *m*.

decent ['diːsənt] *adj* decente; (*satisfactory*) razonable; (*coll*) bueno, simpático. **decency** *n* decencia *f*, decoro *m*.

deceptive [di'septiv] *adj* engañoso. **deceptiveness** *n* apariencia engañosa *f*.

decibel ['desi,bel] *n* decibel *m*, decibelio *m*.

decide [di'said] *v* decidir; (*line of action*) determinar; (*conflict*) resolver; (*choose*) optar por. **decided** *adj* decidido; determinado; resuelto; (*difference*) marcado.

deciduous [di'sidjuəs] *adj* de hoja caduca.

decimal ['desiməl] *nf*, *adj* decimal. **decimal point** coma de decimales *f*.

decipher [di'saifə] *v* descifrar.

decision [di'siʒən] *n* decisión *f*. **decisive** *adj* decisivo; concluyente; (*manner*) decidido; (*tone*) tajante. **decisively** *adv* con decisión.

deck [dek] *n* (*ship*) cubierta *f*; (*bus*) piso *m*. **deck chair** tumbona *f*.

declare [di'kleə] *v* declarar; proclamar. **declaration** *n* declaración *f*; proclamación *f*. **declaratory** *adj* declaratorio.

decline [di'klain] *n* (*decrease*) disminución *f*; (*life*) ocaso *m*; (*decay*) decaimiento; (*number*) baja *f*. *v* (*to act*) negarse (a); (*an offer*) rehusar; (*gramm*) declinar; bajar; (*med*) debilitarse. **declining** *adj* declinante.

decompose [,diːkəm'pouz] *v* (*break up*) descomponer; (*rot*) pudrir. **decomposition** *n* descomposición *f*; putrefacción *f*.

decorate ['dekə,reit] *v* decorar, adornar; (*medal*) condecorar; (*paint*) pintar. **decoration** *n* (*medal*) condecoración *f*; (*ornament*) adorno *m*; (*décor*) decoración *f*. **decorative** *adj* decorativo. **decorator** *n* decorador, -a *m*, *f*.

decoy ['diːkoi] *n* señuelo *m*.

decrease [di'kriːs] *v* disminuir, reducir. *n* disminución *f*, reducción *f*. **decreasing** *adj* decresciente.

decree [di'kriː] *n* decreto *m*. *v* decretar; pronunciar.

decrepit [di'krepit] *adj* decrépito.

dedicate ['dedi,keit] *v* (*book*, *life*, *etc.*) dedicar; (*church*) consagrar. **dedication** *n* (*devotion*) dedicación *f*; (*inscription*) dedicatoria *f*. **dedicatory** *adj* dedicatorio.

deduce [di'djuːs] *v* deducir.

deduct [di'dʌkt] *v* descontar. **deductible** *adj* deducible. **deduction** *n* (*discount*) deducción *f*, rebaja *f*, descuento *m*; (*conclusion*) conclusión *f*, deducción *f*.

deed [diːd] *n* acto *m*, acción *f*; (*something done*) hecho *m*; (*feat*) hazaña *f*; (*law*) escritura *f*.

deep [diːp] *adj* profundo, hondo. **a hole a metre deep** un pozo de un metro de hondo. **deep in debt** cargado de deudas. **go off the deep end** perder los estribos. *n* (*sea*) piélago *m*. **deepfreeze** *n* congelador *m*.

deer [diə] *n* ciervo *m*.

deface [di'feis] *v* desfigurar; mutilar. **defacement** *n* desfiguración *f*; mutilación *f*.

default [di'fɔːlt] *n* (*debt*) falta de pago; (*absence*) falta *f*; (*law*) contumacia *f*, rebeldía *f*. **judgment by default** sentencia en rebeldía *f*. **win by default** ganar por incomparecencia del adversario. *v* dejar de pagar; condenar en rebeldía; (*a contest*) perder por incomparecencia.

defeat [di'fiːt] *n* derrota *f*. *v* derrotar, vencer. **defeatism** *n* derrotismo *m*. **defeatist** *n*(*m*+*f*). *adj* derrotista.

defect ['diːfekt; *v* di'fekt] *n* defecto *m*. *v* desertar. **defection** *n* deserción *f*. **defective** *adj* defectuoso; incompleto; (*gramm*) defectivo. **defectiveness** *n* imperfección *f*.

defend [di'fend] *v* defender. **defence** *n* defensa *f*. **self-defence** *n* autodefensa *f*. **defenceless** *adj* indefenso. **defendant** *n* (*civil*) demandado, -a *m*, *f*; (*criminal*) acusado, -a *m*, *f*. **defender** *n* defensor, -a *m*, *f*. **defensible** *adj* defensible; justificable. **defensive** *adj* defensivo. **on the defensive** a la defensiva.

defer [di'fəː] *v* (*postpone*) diferir; (*submit*) someter; (*delay*) tardar. **deference** *n* deferencia *f*. **in deference to** por respeto a. **deferential** *adj* deferente, respetuoso. **deferment** *n* aplazamiento *m*; (*mil*) prórroga *f*. **deferrable** *adj* diferible. **deferred** *adj* diferido; aplazado.

defiant [di'faiənt] *adj* provocativo; (*challenging*) desafiante. **defiance** *n* desafío *m*. **in defiance of** con desprecio de.

deficient [di'fiʃənt] *adj* deficiente; (*med*) atrasado.

deficit ['defisit] *n* déficit. *adj* deficitario.

define [di'fain] *v* definir; caracterizar; formular; determinar. **definition** *n* definición *f*; (*phot*) claridad *f*.

definite ['definit] *adj* definido; determinado; claro; definitivo; seguro. **definitely** *adv* claramente; categóricamente; (*without doubt*) seguramente.

deflate [di'fleit] *v* desinflar; (*comm*) provocar la deflación de; (*hopes*) reducir. **deflation** *n* desinflado *m*; (*comm*) deflación *f*.

deform [di'fɔːm] *v* deformar, desfigurar. **deformation** *n* deformación *f*.

defraud [di'frɔːd] *v* defraudar, estafar.

defrost [diː'frɔst] *v* deshelar.

deft [deft] *adj* hábil, diestro. **deftness** *n* habilidad *f*, destreza *f*.

defunct [di'fʌŋkt] *adj* difunto.

defy [di'fai] *v* (*challenge*) desafiar, retar; (*resist*) resistir a.

degenerate [di'dʒenə,reit; *n*, *adj* di'dʒenərit] *v* degenerar. *n*, *adj* degenerado, -a. **degeneration** *n* degeneración *f*. **degenerative** *adj* degenerativo.

degrade [di'greid] *v* (*humiliate, reduce in rank*) degradar; (*quality*) rebajar; (*morals*) envilecer. **degradation** *n* degradación *f*. **degrading** *adj* degradante.

degree [di'griː] *v* (*stop*) grado *m*; categoría *f*; (*university*) título *m*. **bachelor's degree** licenciatura *f*. **by degrees** poco a poco. **doctor's degree** doctorado *m*. **to some degree** hasta cierto punto.

dehydrate [diː'haidreit] *v* deshidratar. **dehydration** *n* deshidratación *f*.

de-icer [diː'aisə] *n* descongelador *m*.

deity ['diːiti] *n* deidad *f*.

dejected [di'dʒektid] *adj* descorazonado, desanimado. **dejection** *n* desaliento *m*, abatimiento *m*.

delay [di'lei] *n* dilación *f*, retraso *m*; (*wait*) demora *f*. *v* retrasar; (*postpone*) aplazar. **delaying** *adj* dilatorio.

delegate ['deləgit; *v* 'deləgeit] *n* delegado, -a *m*, *f*. *v* delegar. **delegation** *n* delegación *f*.

delete [di'liːt] *v* tachar, borrar. **deletion** *n* supresión *f*.

deliberate [di'libərət; *v* di'libəreit] *adj* (*intentional*) deliberado; (*unhurried*) lento; (*premeditated*) premeditado; (*cautious*) prudente. *v* deliberar; (*ponder*) reflexionar. **deliberately** *adv* (*on purpose*) a propósito; prudentemente; lentamente. **deliberation** *n* deliberación *f*; lentitud *f*; reflexión *f*.

delicate ['delikət] *adj* delicado; (*food*) exquisito; refinado; escrupuloso; (*touch*) ligero; (*health*) frágile. **delicacy** *n* delicadeza *f*, fragilidad *f*.

delicious [di'liʃəs] *adj* delicioso.

delight [di'lait] *n* deleite *m*; encanto *m*. *v* deleitar; encantar. **delightful** *adj* delicioso; encantador.

delinquency [di'liŋkwənsi] *n* delincuencia *f*. **delinquent** *n*(*m*+*f*). *adj* delincuente.

delirious [di'liriəs] *adj* delirante. **be delirious** delirar. **delirium** *n* delirio *m*.

deliver [di'livə] *v* (*hand over*) entregar; (*goods, post*) repartir; (*message*) dar; (*opinion*) expresar; (*speech*) pronunciar; (*baby*) asistir para dar a luz; (*free*) liberar. **deliverance** *n* liberación *f*. **delivery** *n* entrega *f*; reparto *m*; pronunciación *f*; lanzamiento *m*; (*med*) parto *m*; manera de expresarse *f*. **delivery service** servicio a domicilio *m*. **delivery van** furgoneta de reparto *f*. **take delivery of** recibir.

delta ['deltə] *n* delta *m*.

delude [di'luːd] *v* engañar. **delusion** *n* engaño, *m*, error *m*, ilusión *f*.

deluge ['deljuːdʒ] *n* diluvio *m*. *v* inundar; (*fig*) abrumar.

delve [delv] *v* cavar. **delve into** ahondar.

demand [di'maind] *n* (*comm*) demanda *f*; (*request*) petición *f*; (*for payment*) reclamación *f*. *v* (*require*) requerir; (*ask urgently*) exigir; reclamar. **demanding** *adj* (*tiring*) agotador; (*absorbing*) aborbente; (*person*) exigente.

demented [di'mentid] *adj* demente, loco. **dementia** *n* demencia *f*.

democracy [di'mokrəsi] *n* democracia *f*. **democrat** *n* demócrata *m*, *f*. **democratic** *adj* democrático.

demolish [di'moliʃ] *v* (*building*) demoler, derribar; (*fig*) destruir. **demolition** *n* demolición *f*, derribo *m*; destrucción *f*.

demon ['diːmən] *n* demonio *m*, diablo *m*.

demonstrate ['demən,streit] *v* demostrar, probar; (*show how something operates*) mostrar; (*pol*) hacer la manifestación. **demonstration** *n* demostración *f*, prueba *f*; manifestación *f*. **demonstrative** *adj* demostrativo. **demonstrator** *n* ayudante *m*, *f*; (*protester*) manifestante *m*, *f*.

demoralize [di'morə,laiz] *v* desmoralizar. **demoralization** *n* desmoralización *f*. **demoralizing** *adj* desmoralizador, desmoralizante.

demure [di'mjuə] *adj* recatado.

den [den] *n* (*of animals, etc.*) guardia *f*; (*study*) estudio *m*.

denial [di'naiəl] *n* (*refusal*) negativa *f*; (*disavowal*) negación *f*; (*rejection*) rechazamiento *m*. **self-denial** abnegación *f*.

denim ['denim] *n* mahón *m*.

Denmark ['denmaik] *n* Dinamarca *f*.

denomination [di,nomi'neiʃən] *n* (*measure*) denominación *f*; (*rel*) secta *f*, confesión *f*; (*coins*) valor *m*; (*type*) clase *f*, tipo *m*. **denominational** *adj* sectario. **denominator** *n* (*math*) denominador *m*.

denote [di'nout] *v* denotar.

denounce [di'nauns] *v* denunciar.

dense [dens] *adj* (*thick*) denso; (*coll: person*) torpe. **densely** *adv* densamente. **density** *n* densidad *f*; torpeza *f*.

dent [dent] *n* abolladura *f*. *v* abollar.

dental ['dentl] *adj* dental.

dentist ['dentist] *n* dentista *m*, *f*. **dentistry** *n* odolontogía *f*.

denture ['dentʃə] *n* dentadura *f*, postiza *f*.

denude [di'njuːd] *v* desnudar.

denunciation [dinʌnsi'eiʃən] *n* denuncia *f*; (*condemnation*) condena *f*; (*criticism*) censura *f*.

deny [di'nai] *v* (*refuse, dispute*) negar; (*request*) denegar; (*give the lie to*) desmentir; (*repudiate*) repudiar.

deodorant [diː'oudərənt] *n* desodorante *m*.

depart [di'paːt] *v* (*go away*) marcharse; (*set off*) salir; (*deviate*) apartarse. **departed** *adj* pasado; (*dead*) difunto. **departure** *n* marcha *f*; salida *f*; desviación *f*.

department [di'paːtmənt] *n* (*in a shop*) departamento *m*; (*in a business*) servicio *m*; (*college, university*) sección *f*; (*ministry*) negociado *m*; (*branch*) ramo *m*; (*fig: sphere*) esfera *f*. **department store** gran almacén *m*. **departmental** *adj* departamental.

depend [di'pend] *v* depender. **dependence** *n* dependencia *f*. **dependent** *adj* dependiente; subordinado.

depict [di'pikt] *v* (*art*) pintar; (*fig*)

describir. **depiction** *n* pintura *f*; descripción *f*.

deplete [di'pliːt] *v* vaciar, agotar. **depletion** *n* agotamiento *m*.

deplore [di'ploː] *v* deplorar, lamentar. **deplorable** *adj* deplorable, lamentable.

deport [di'poːt] *v* expulsar. **deport oneself** comportarse. **deportation** *n* expulsión *f*. **deportment** *n* porte *m*; conducta *f*.

depose [di'pouz] *v* deponer.

deposit [di'pozit] *n* (*bank*) depósito *m*; (*substance*) sedimento *m*, poso *m*; (*pledge*) señal *f*; (*on accommodation*) entrada *f*. *v* depositar; (*money in account*) ingresar; dar de señal. **deposit account** cuenta de depósitos a plazo *f*.

depot ['depou] *n* (*store*) almacén *m*; (*buses*) cochera *f*; (*mil*) depósito *m*.

deprave [di'preiv] *v* depravar. **depravity** *n* depravación *f*.

depreciate [di'priːʃi,eit] *v* (*belittle, money*) despreciar; (*goods*) abaratar; (*price*) bajar. **depreciation** *n* depreciación *f*; abaratamiento *m*; (*fig*) desprecio *m*.

depress [di'pres] *v* (*dishearten*) deprimir; (*weaken*) debilitar; (*lessen*) disminuir; (*lower*) bajar; (*push down*) presionar; (*pedal*) pisar. **depressed** *adj* deprimido; (*indigent*) necesitado; (*comm*) de depresión. **depressing** *adj* deprimente. **depression** *n* (*dejection*) abatimiento *m*; (*geog, med, comm*) depresión *f*.

deprive [di'praiv] *v* privar, desposeer. **deprivation** *n* privación *f*; (*loss*) pérdida *f*.

depth [depθ] *n* profundidad *f*; (*colour*) intensidad *f*; (*sound*) gravedad *f*. **out of one's depth** perder pie; (*fig*) no entender nada.

deputy ['depjuti] *n* delegado *m*; (*substitute*) suplente *m*; (*politician*) diputado *m*. **deputation** *n* delegación *f*. **deputize** *v* diputar; delegar; sustituir.

derail [di'reil] *v* hacer descarrilar. **derailment** *n* descarrilamiento *m*.

derelict ['derilikt] *adj* abandonado. *n* (*neut*) derrelicto *m*; (*person*) deshecho *m*. **dereliction** *n* abandono *m*; (*negligence*) negligencia *f*.

deride [di'raid] *v* ridicular. **derision** *n* mofas *f pl*. **derisive** *or* **derisory** *adj* (*mocking*) mofador; (*petty*) irrisorio.

derive [di'raiv] *v* derivar; (*profit*) sacar. **derivation** *n* derivación *f*. **derivative** *nm*, *adj* derivado.

derogatory [di'rogətəri] *adj* despectivo, rebajante.

descend [di'send] *v* descender, bajar. **descendant** *n(m+f)*, *adj* descendiente. **descent** *n* descenso *m*, bajada *f*; (*slope*) declive *m*; (*lineage*) descendencia *f*.

describe [di'skraib] *v* describir; (*draw*) trazar. **describe oneself as** presentarse como. **description** *n* descripción *f*; (*sort*) clase *f*. **descriptive** *adj* descriptivo.

desert[1] ['dezət] *n* (*land*) desierto *m*.

desert[2] [di'zəːt] *v* abandonar; (*mil*) desertar de. **deserter** *n* desertor *m*. **desertion** *n* (*mil*) deserción *f*; abandono *m*.

deserts [di'zəːts] *pl n* **get one's deserts** llevarse su merecido.

deserve [di'zəːv] *v* merecer; ser digno de. **deserving** *adj* digno; (*deed*) meritorio.

design [di'zain] *n* (*intention*) propósito *m*; (*plan*) proyecto *m*; (*drawing*) dibujo *m*; (*style*) estilo *m*. **have designs on** haber puesto sus miras en. *v* (*prepare plans for*) diseñar; dibujar; proyectar; inventar; (*create*) crear; imaginar. **designer** *n* diseñador, -a *m*, *f*. (*draughtsman*) delineante *m*. **dress designer** modista *m*. **designing** *adj* intrigante.

designate ['dezigneit] *v* (*name for a duty*) designar; (*name*) denominar; (*appoint*) nombrar; (*point out*) señalar. *adj* designado; nombrado. **designation** *n* designación *f*; denominación *f*; nombramiento *m*.

desire [di'zaiə] *n* deseo *m*; (*request*) petición *f*. *v* desear; pedir; (*want*) querer. **desirable** *adj* deseable; atractivo. **desirability** *n* lo atractivo; conveniencia *f*. **desirous** *adj* deseoso.

desk [desk] *n* (*office*) escritorio *m*; (*school*) pupitre *m*.

desolate ['desələt] *adj* (*waste*) desolado; solitario; desierto; disconsolado. *v* (*lay waste*) asolar; abandonar; desconsolar. **desolating** *adj* desolador. **desolation** *n* desolación *f*; soledad *f*.

despair [di'speə] *n* desesperación *f*, desesperanza *f*. *v* desesperar.

desperate ['despərət] *adj* desesperado; (*resistance*) enérgico; (*urgent*) apremiante. **desperation** *n* desesperación *f*.

despise [di'spaiz] *v* despreciar. **despicable** *adj* despreciable. **despicableness** *n* bajeza *f*.

despite [di'spait] *prep* a pesar de.

despondent [di'spondənt] *adj* desanimado, desalentado. **despondency** *n* desánimo *m*, desaliento *m*.

despot ['despot] *n* déspota *m*. **despotic** *adj* despótico. **despotism** *n* despotismo *m*.

dessert [di'zəːt] *n* postre *m*. **dessertspoon** *n* cuchara de postre *f*.

destine ['destin] *v* destinar. **destination** *n* destinación *f*. **destiny** *n* destino *m*.

destitute ['destitjuːt] *adj* indigente, menesteroso. **be destitute** estar en la miseria. **destitution** *n* indigencia *f*, miseria *f*.

destroy [di'stroi] *v* destruir, destrozar. **destroyer** *n* (*naut*) destructor *m*. **destruction** *n* destrucción *f*; ruina *f*. **destructive** *adj* destructivo.

detach [di'tatʃ] *v* despegar; separar. **detachable** *adj* separable; (*collar*) postizo. **detached** *adj* independiente; (*untroubled*) indiferente. **detachment** *n* separación *f*; indiferencia *f*; (*mil*) destacamento *m*.

detail ['diːteil] *n* detalle *m*. *v* detallar; (*itemize*) enumerar; (*mil*) destacar.

detain [di'tein] *v* retener; (*law*) detener. **detention** *n* detención *f*, arresto *m*.

detect [di'tekt] *v* (*discover*) descubrir; (*perceive*) percibir; (*note*) advertir; (*tech*) detectar. **detection** *n* descubrimiento *m*; detección *f*. **detective** *n* detective *m*. **detective story** novela policíaca *f*. **detector** *n* detector *m*. **lie detector** detector de mentiras *m*.

deter [di'təː] *v* desuadir. **deterrent** *adj* disuasivo. *n* fuerza de disuasión *f*.

detergent [di'təːdʒənt] *nm*, *adj* detergente.

deteriorate [di'tiəriə,reit] *v* (*wear out*) deteriorar; (*become worse*) empeorar; (*in value*) depreciar. **deterioration** *n* deterioro *m*; empeoramiento *m*; (*decline*) decadencia *f*.

determine [di'təːmin] *v* (*fix*) determinar; (*cause*) provocar; (*limits*) definir; (*decide*) decidir; resolver. **determination** *n* determinación *f*; resolución *f*; decisión *f*. **determined** *adj* resuelto; decidido; determinado.

detest [di'test] *v* destestar, odiar. **detestable** *adj* detestable, odioso. **detestation** *n* odio *m*.

detonate ['detə,neit] *v* detonar. **detonating** *adj* detonante. **detonation** *n* detonación *f*.

detour ['diːtuə] *n* desvío *m*, desviación *f*; vuelta *f*. **make a detour** dar un rodeo.

detract [di'trakt] v (*take away*) quitar, reducir; (*denigrate*) denigrar. **detraction** n denigración f.

detriment ['detrimənt] n detrimento m, perjuicio m. **detrimental** adj perjudicial.

devalue [di:'valju:] v devaluar, desvalorizar. **devaluation** n devaluación f.

devastate ['devəsteit] v devastar. **devastating** adj devastador. **devastation** n devastación f.

develop [di'veləp] v (*expand*) desarrollar; (*business*) explotar; (*land*) urbanizar; (*resources*) aprovechar; (*promote*) fomentar; (*taste*) adquirir; (*ailment*) contraer; (*tendency*) manifestar; (*talent*) mostrar; (*phot*) revelar. **developer** n (*phot*) revelador m. **development** n desarrollo m; evolución f; progreso m.

deviate ['di:vieit] v desviarse. **deviation** n desviación f; (*from truth*) alejamiento m; (*sexual*) inversión f. **deviationism** n desviacionismo m. **deviationist** n desviacionista m, f.

device [di'vais] n (*tech*) mecanismo; ingenio; (*scheme*) ardid m; estratagema f.

devil ['devl] n diablo. **devilish** adj diabólico. **devil's advocate** abogado del diablo m.

devise [di'vaiz] v inventar; (*plan*) concebir; (*plot*) tramar.

devoid [di'void] adj desprovisto.

devolution [,di:və'lu:ʃən] n (*powers*) delegación f. **devolve** v delegar; transmitir.

devote [di'vout] v dedicar. **devoted** adj dedicado; (*loyal*) leal; (*devout*) devoto. **devotion** n dedicación f; lealtad f; devoción f. **devotional** adj piadoso.

devour [di'vauə] v devorar. **devouring** adj devorador.

devout [di'vaut] adj devoto; sincero. **devoutness** n devoción f.

dew [dju:] n rocío m.

dexterous ['dekstrəs] adj diestro, hábil. **dexterity** n destreza f, habilidad f.

diabetes [,diə'bi:ti:z] n diabetes f. **diabetic** n, adj diabético, -a.

diagnose [,diəg'nouz] v diagnosticar. **diagnosis** n diagnóstico m.

diagonal [dai'agənəl] nf, adj diagonal. **diagonally** adv diagonalmente.

diagram ['daiəgram] n (*math*) figura; (*chart*) gráfico m; (*sketch*) esquema; (*explanatory*) diagrama m. **diagrammatic** adj esquemático.

dial ['daiəl] n (*clock*) esfera f; (*selector*) botón m; (*telephone*) disco m. v marcar. **dialling tone** señal para marcar f.

dialect ['diəlekt] n dialecto m.

dialogue ['daiəlog] n diálogo m.

diameter [dai'amitə] n diámetro m. **diametrically** adv diametralmente.

diamond ['daiəmənd] n diamante m. **diamond-shaped** adj romboidal.

diaper ['daiəpə] n (*US*) pañal m.

diaphragm ['daiəfram] n diafragma m.

diarrhoea [,daiə'riə] n diarrea f.

diary ['daiəri] n diario m; (*for appointments*) agenda f.

dice [dais] n pl dados m pl. v jugar a los dados. **dice with death** jugar con la muerte.

dictate [dik'teit] v dictar; (*order*) mandar; (*impose*) imponer. n mandato m. **dictation** n dictado m. **dictator** n dictador m. **dictatorial** adj dictatorial. **dictatorship** n dictadura f.

dictionary ['dikʃənəri] n diccionario m.

did [did] V do.

die [dai] v morir, fallecer. **die away** (*sound*) desvanecer. **die down** (*fire*) apagarse; (*wind*) amainar; (*conversation*) decaer. **die out** desaparecer.

diesel ['di:zəl] nm, adj diesel. **diesel engine** motor diesel m. **diesel oil** gasoil m.

diet ['daiət] n dieta f, régimen m. v poner a dieta or régimen. **dietary** adj dietético. **dietetics** n dietética f. **dietician** n dietético m.

differ ['difə] v ser diferente, ser distinto. **difference** n diferencia f; (*disagreement*) desacuerdo m. **different** adj diferente, distinto. **differential** nf, adj diferencial. **differentiate** v diferenciar, distinguir.

difficult ['difikəlt] adj difícil. **difficulty** n dificultad f.

*****dig** [dig] v cavar; excavar; (*coal, etc.*) extraer. **dig in** enterrar. **dig into** clavar. **dig up** desenterrar. n (*in the ribs*) golpe m; excavación arqueológica f; (*fig*) pinchazo m.

digest [dai'dʒest] n resumen m. v digerir; (*summarize*) resumir; (*fig*) asimilar. **digestible** adj digerible. **digestion** n digestión f. **digestive** adj digestivo. **digestive system** aparato digestivo m.

digit ['didʒit] n (*finger, toe*) dedo m; (*math*) dígito m. **digital** adj digital.

dignified ['digniˌfaid] *adj* digno; solemne.
dignify *v* dignificar.
dignity ['digniti] *n* dignidad *f*. **dignitary** *n* dignatorio *m*.
digress [dai'gres] *v* desviarse, apartarse. **digression** *n* digresión *f*.
digs [digz] *n pl* (*coll*) pensión *f sing*.
dilapidated [di'lapiˌdeitid] *adj* (*building*) ruinoso; (*clothes*) muy estropeado. **dilapidate** *v* deteriorar; estropear. **dilapidation** *n* estado ruinoso *m*.
dilate [dai'leit] *v* dilatar.
dilemma [di'lemə] *n* dilema *m*.
diligent ['dilidʒent] *adj* diligente. **diligence** *n* diligencia *f*.
dilute [dai'luːt] *v* diluir, aguar; (*fig*) atenuar. *adj* diluido; atenuado. **dilution** *n* dilución *f*.
dim [dim] *adj* oscuro; (*memory*) lejano; (*sound*) sordo; (*sight*) turbio; (*light*) débil; (*vague*) borroso; (*colour*) apagado; (*slang*) tonto. **take a dim view of** ver con malos ojos. *v* (*light*) bajar; (*sight*) nublar. **dimly** *adv* vagamente; poco iluminado.
dimension [di'menʃən] *n* dimensión *f*.
diminish [di'miniʃ] *v* disminuir.
diminutive [di'minjutiv] *adj* diminuto. *nm*, *adj* (*gramm*) diminutivo.
dimple ['dimpl] *n* hoyuelo *m*. *v* formar hoyuelos en.
din [din] *n* estrépito *m*, alboroto *m*.
dine [dain] *v* cenar. **dining car** coche restaurante *m*. **diningroom** *n* comedor *m*.
dinghy ['diŋgi] *n* bote *m*.
dingy ['dindʒi] *adj* sucio, sórdido.
dinner ['dinə] *n* (*evening*) cena *f*; (*midday*) comida *f*. **dinner jacket** esmoquin *m*. **dinner party** cena *f*. **dinner table** mesa de comedor *f*.
dinosaur ['dainəˌsoː] *n* dinosaurio *m*.
diocese ['daiəsis] *n* diócesis *f*. **diocesan** *n*, *adj* diocesano, -a.
dip [dip] *v* (*wet*) mojar; (*immerse*) sumergir; (*someone*) zambullir; (*scoop*) sacar; (*put a hand in*) meter; (*flag*) inclinar; (*headlights*) poner luz de cruce; (*road*) bajar; *n* baño *m*; (*slope*) declive *m*.
diphthong ['difθoŋ] *n* diptongo *m*.
diploma [di'ploumə] *n* diploma *m*.
diplomacy [di'plouməsi] *n* diplomacia *f*. **diplomat** *n* diplomático *m*. **diplomatic** *adj* diplomático. **diplomatic corps** cuerpo diplomático *m*. **diplomatic immunity** inmunidad diplomática *f*.

dipstick ['dipstik] *n* varilla graduada *f*.
dire [daiə] *adj* extremo; terrible.
direct [di'rekt] *adj* (*straight*) directo; (*blunt*) tajante; (*frank*) franco. **direct current** corriente continua *f*. *v* dirigir; (*order*) mandar; (*show the way*) indicar; (*gaze, attention*) señalar. **direction** *n* dirección *f*. **directions** *n pl* instrucciones *f pl*. **directive** *n* instrucción *f*. **directly** *adv* directamente; (*at once*) en seguida. **directness** *n* franqueza *f*. **director** *m* director *m*. **board of directors** consejo de administración *n*. **managing director** director gerente *m*.
dirt [dəːt] *n* suciedad *f*; (*filth*) mugre *f*; (*rubbish*) basura *f*. **dirt-cheap** *adj* baratísimo. **dirty** *adj* sucio; (*obscene: person*) verde; (*language*) grosero. **dirty trick** mala pasada *f*.
disability [disə'biləti] *n* incapacidad *f*. **disable** *v* incapacitar; (*cripple*) lisiar. **disabled** *adj* inválido. **disablement** *n* incapacidad *f*.
disadvantage [ˌdisəd'vaːntidʒ] *n* desventaja *f*. **be at a disadvantage** estar en situación desventajosa.
disagree [ˌdisə'griː] *v* discrepar; no estar de acuerdo. **disagreeable** *adj* desagradable. **disagreement** *n* desacuerdo *m*.
disappear [ˌdisə'piə] *v* desaparecer. **disappearance** *n* desaparición *f*.
disappoint [ˌdisə'point] *v* decepcionar; defraudar. **disappointing** *adj* decepcionante. **disappointment** *n* decepción *f*; disgusto *m*.
disapprove [ˌdisə'pruːv] *v* desaprobar; estar en contra. **disapproval** *n* desaprobación *f*. **disapproving** *adj* desaprobador. **disapprovingly** *adv* con desaprobación.
disarm [dis'aːm] *v* desarmar. **disarmament** *n* desarme *m*.
disaster [di'zaːstə] *n* desastre *m*. **disastrous** *adj* desastroso.
disband [dis'band] *v* disolver; (*mil*) licenciar.
disc *or US* **disk** [disk] *n* disco *m*. **disc jockey** presentador de discos *m*.
discard [dis'kaːd; *n* 'diskaːd] *v* (*cast away*) desechar; (*cards*) descartar; (*fig*) renunciar. *n* descarte *m*.
discern [di'səːn] *v* discernir. **discernible** *adj* perceptible. **discerning** *adj* perspicaz.
discharge [dis'tʃaːdʒ] *v* descargar; (*debt*) saldar; (*gun*) disparar; (*sack*) despedir;

(law) absolver; *(duty)* desempeñar; *(prisoner)* liberar; *(patient)* dar de alta; *(bankrupt)* rehabilitar. *n* descarga *f*; *(debt)* descargo; *(gas)* escape *m*; liberación *f*; rehabilitación *f*; absolución *f*; desempeño *m*; alta *f*; disparo *m*.

disciple [di'saipl] *n* discípulo, -a *m*, *f*.

discipline ['disiplin] *n* disciplina *f*. *v* castigar. **disciplinarian** *n* disciplinario, -a *m*, *f*. **disciplinary** *adj* disciplinario.

disclaim [dis'kleim] *v* rechazar; *(law)* renunciar. **disclaimer** *n* *(denial)* denegación *f*; *(law)* renuncia *f*.

disclose [dis'klouz] *v* revelar. **disclosure** *n* revelación *f*; descubrimiento *m*.

discolour [dis'kʌlə] *v* descolorar; *(stain)* manchar. **discolouration** *n* descoloración *f*.

discomfort [dis'kʌmfət] *n* molestia *f*; incomodidad *f*; malestar. *v* molestar.

disconcert [diskən'səːt] *v* desconcertar, perturbar. **disconcerting** *adj* desconcertante.

disconnect [diskə'nekt] *v* *(elec)* desconectar; *(separate)* separar. **disconnection** *n* desconexión *f*; separación *f*.

disconsolate [dis'kɔnsələt] *adj* desconsolado. **disconsolateness** *n* desconsuelo *m*.

discontinue [diskən'tinjuː] *v* discontinuar, interrumpir; suspender. **discontinuance** *or* **discontinuation** *n* cesación *f*; suspensión *f*. **discontinuity** *n* discontinuidad *f*; interrupción *f*. **discontinuous** *adj* discontinuo.

discord ['diskɔːd] *n* discordia *f*; *(music)* disonancia *f*. **discordant** *adj* discordante; *(music)* discorde.

discotheque ['diskətek] *n* discoteca *f*.

discount ['diskaunt] *n* descuento *m*; *(reduction)* rebaja *f*. *v* descontar; rebajar; *(disregard)* no hacer caso de.

discourage [dis'kʌridʒ] *v* desanimar. **discourage from** recomendar que no. **discouragement** *n* desánimo *m*. **discouraging** *adj* desalentador.

discover [dis'kʌvə] *v* descubrir; *(realize)* darse cuenta de. **discoverer** *n* descubridor, -a *m*, *f*. **discovery** *n* descubrimiento *m*.

discredit [dis'kredit] *v* desacreditar; *(disbelieve)* dudar de; *(dishonour)* deshonrar. *n* descrédito *m*; duda *f*. **discreditable** *adj* indigno; vergonzoso.

discreet [dis'kriːt] *adj* discreto; prudente.

discretion *n* discreción; circunspección *f*. **at your discretion** a su gusto. **discretionary** *adj* discrecional.

discrepancy [di'skrepənsi] *n* discrepancia *f*; diferencia *f*. **discrepant** *adj* discrepante; diferente.

discrete [di'skriːt] *adj* discreto.

discriminate [di'skrimi,neit] *v* distinguir. **discriminate against** discriminar contra. **discriminating** *adj* *(law)* discriminatorio; *(taste)* muy bueno. **discrimination** *n* discriminación *f*; discernimiento *m*; buen gusto *m*. **discriminatory** *adj* discriminatorio.

discus ['diskəs] *n* disco *m*.

discuss [di'skʌs] *v* discutir; hablar de. **discussion** *n* discusión *f*.

disease [di'ziːz] *n* enfermedad *f*. **diseased** *adj* enfermo.

disembark [disim'baːk] *v* desembarcar. **disembarkation** *n* *(people)* desembarco *m*; *(cargo)* desembarque *m*.

disengage [disin'geidʒ] *v* *(detach)* soltar; *(unhook)* desenganchar; *(free)* liberar; *(mil)* retirar; *(gears)* desengranar; *(clutch)* desembragar. **disengagement** *n* liberación *f*; retirada *f*; desembrague *m*.

disfigure [dis'figə] *v* desfigurar; *(spoil)* afear. **disfigurement** *n* desfiguración *f*; afeamiento *m*.

disgrace [dis'greis] *n* *(disfavour)* desgracia *f*; *(cause of shame)* vergüenza *f*; deshonra *f*; ignominia *f*. *v* deshonrar. **disgraceful** *adj* deshonroso; vergonzoso.

disgruntled [dis'grʌntld] *adj* malhumorado.

disguise [dis'gaiz] *v* disfrazar. *n* disfraz *m*.

disgust [dis'gʌst] *n* repugnancia *f*. *v* repugnar.

dish [diʃ] *n* plato *m*; *(serving vessel)* fuente *f*. *v* servir. **dish out** dar. **dishwasher** *n* lavaplatos *m*.

dishearten [dis'haːtn] *v* descorazonar, desanimar. **disheartening** *adj* descorazonador.

dishevelled [di'ʃevəld] *adj* despeinado; desarreglado.

dishonest [dis'ɔnist] *adj* fraudulento.

dishonour [dis'ɔnə] *n* deshonra *f*, deshonor *m*. *v* deshonrar.

disillusion [disi'luːʒən] *v* desilusionar. *n* desilusión *f*.

disinfect [disin'fekt] *v* desinfectar. **disinfectant** *nm, adj* desinfectante.

disinherit [disin'herit] v desheredar. **disinheritance** n desheradamiento m.

disintegrate [dis'inti.greit] v desintegrar. **disintegration** n desintegración f.

disinterested [dis'intristid] adj desinteresado; imparcial. **disinterest** n desinterés m.

disjointed [dis'dʒointid] adj desarticulado; (incoherent) inconexo.

disk V **disc**.

dislike [dis'laik] v aborrecer, tener aversión a. n aversión f, antipatía f.

dislocate ['disləkeit] v (joint) dislocar; (plans) desarreglar. **dislocation** n dislocación f; desarreglo m.

dislodge [dis'lodʒ] v desalojar. **dislodgement** n desalojamiento.

disloyal [dis'loiəl] adj desleal. **disloyalty** n deslealtad f.

dismal ['dizməl] adj triste; (face) sombrío; (voice) lúgubre.

dismantle [dis'mantl] v desmantelar; desmontar.

dismay [dis'mei] n consternación f; (fright) espanto m. v consternar; espantar; (discourage) desalentar.

dismiss [dis'mis] v despedir; (discharge) licenciar; (assembly) disolver; (mil) romper filas; (idea) descartar. **dismissal** n (employee) despido m; abandono m.

dismount [dis'maunt] v desmontar.

disobey [disə'bei] v desobedecer. **disobedience** n desobediencia f. **disobedient** adj desobediente.

disorder [dis'oɪdə] n desorden m; (riot) disturbio m; (illness) trastorno m. v desordenar. **disorderliness** n desorden m.

disorderly adj (person) desordenado; (place) desarreglado; (meeting) alborotado.

disorganize [dis'oɪgənaiz] v desorganizar. **disorganization** n desorganización f.

disown [dis'oun] v repudiar; (deny) negar; no reconocer.

disparage [di'sparidʒ] v desacreditar; (belittle) menospreciar; (denigrate) denigrar. **disparagement** n descrédito m; menosprecio m; denigración f. adj despectivo; menospreciativo; denigrante. **disparagingly** adv con desprecio.

disparity [dis'pariti] n disparidad f. **disparate** adj dispar.

dispassionate [dis'paʃənit] adj desapasionado; imparcial.

dispatch [di'spatʃ] n (message) despacho

m, expedición f; (messenger, parcels) envío m; (promptness) diligencia f. v despachar; enviar; matar.

dispel [di'spel] v disipar.

dispense [di'spens] v (drugs) preparar; (justice) administrar; (distribute) distribuir; (laws) aplicar. **dispense with** prescindir de. **dispensable** adj prescindible. **dispensary** n dispensario m; farmacia f. **dispensation** n distribución f; administración f; (exemption) dispensa f.

disperse [di'spəɪs] v dispersar. **dispersal** n dispersión f.

displace [dis'pleis] v desplazar; (oust) quitar el puesto; (remove from office) destituir. **displacement** n desplazamiento m; destituición f; reemplazo m.

display [di'splei] v exhibir; demostrar. n exhibición f; demostración f; despliegue m; (emotion) alarde m; (show) exposición f; (parade) desfile m; (tech) representación visual f.

displease [dis'pliz] v desagradar, disgustar. **displeasing** adj desagradable. **displeasure** n desagrado m, disgusto m.

dispose [di'spouz] v (arrange) disponer; determinar; inclinar; mover. **dispose of** tirar; (transfer) traspasar; (argument) echar por tierra; (kill) liquidar; (sell) vender; (consume) consumir. **disposable** adj disponible; (to be thrown away) para tirar. **disposal** (arrangement) desposición f; eliminación f; resolución f; traspaso m; venta f. **disposition** n disposición f; traspaso m; predisposición f.

disprove [dis'pruːv] v refutar.

dispute [di'spjuːt] n disputa f; discusión f; controversia f; (law) litigio m. v disputar; discutir; (question) poner en duda. **disputation** n discusión f; controversia f.

disqualify [dis'kwolifai] v (render unfit) incapacitar; (competitor) descalificar. **disqualification** n incapacidad f; descalificación f.

disregard [disrə'gaɪd] v (neglect) descuidar; desatender. n descuido m; indiferencia f.

disreputable [dis'repjutəbl] adj (shabby) lamentable; (not respectable) de mala fama. **disrepute** n descrédito m.

disrespect [disrə'spekt] n falta de respeto f. **disrespectful** adj irrespetuoso.

disrupt [dis'rʌpt] v (upset) trastornar; (interrupt) interrumpir; (break up) romper; desorganizar. **disruption** n trastorno *m*; ruptura *f*; interrupción *f*; desorganización *f*. **disruptive** *adj* perjudicial.

dissatisfy [di'satisfai] *v* no satisfacer. **dissatisfaction** *n* descontento *m*.

dissect [di'sekt] *v* disecar. **dissection** *n* disección *f*.

dissent [di'sent] *n* disensión *f*; (*disagreement*) disentimiento *m*. *v* (*disagree*) disentir. **dissension** *n* disensión *f*.

dissident ['disidənt] *n(m+f)*, *adj* disidente. **dissidence** *n* disidencia *f*.

dissimilar [di'similə] *adj* desigual; distinto. **dissimilarity** *n* desigualdad *f*.

dissociate [di'sousieit] *v* disociar. **dissociation** *n* disociación *f*.

dissolute ['disəluːt] *adj* disoluto. **dissolution** *n* (*society, marriage, melting*) disolución *f*.

dissolve [di'zolv] *v* disolver; (*disintegrate*) descomponer; disipar; (*law, contract*) rescindir.

dissuade [di'sweid] *v* disuadir. **dissuasion** *n* disuasión *f*. **dissuasive** *adj* disuasivo.

distance ['distəns] *n* distancia *f*. *v* distanciar. **distant** *adj* distante, lejano.

distaste [dis'teist] *n* disgusto *m*, aversión *f*. **distasteful** *adj* desagradable.

distemper [di'stempə] *n* (*dogs*) moquillo *m*; (*paint*) temple *m*.

distend [di'stend] *v* distender. **distension** *n* distensión *f*.

distil [di'stil] *v* destilar. **distillation** *n* destilación *f*. **distillery** *n* destilería *f*.

distinct [di'stiŋkt] *adj* (*clear*) claro; (*different*) distinto; (*definite*) bien determinado. **distinction** *n* distinción *f*. **distinctive** *adj* distintivo. **distinctness** *n* claridad *f*; diferencia *f*.

distinguish [di'stiŋwiʃ] *v* distinguir. **distinguishable** *adj* distinguible. **distinguished** *adj* (*elegant*) distinguido; (*eminent*) eminente.

distort [di'stoːt] *v* torcer; (*fig*) desvirtuar. **distortion** *n* torcimiento *m*; desvirtuación *f*.

distract [di'strakt] *v* (*divert attention*) distraer; (*confuse*) aturdir; (*madden*) enloquecer. **distraction** *n* distracción *f*; aturdimiento *m*; locura *f*.

distraught [di'stroːt] *adj* distraido; enloquecido.

distress [di'stres] *n* aflicción *f*; (*poverty*) miseria *f*; (*danger*) peligro *m*. *v* afligir; angustiar. **distressed** *adj* afligido; en la miseria; en peligro. **distressing** *adj* angustioso.

distribute [di'stribjut] *v* distribuir, repartir. **distribution** *n* distribución *f*; reparto *m*. **distributor** *n* distribuidor, -a *m, f*; (*mot*) distribuidor *m*.

district ['distrikt] *n* (*pol*) distrito *m*; (*town*) barrio *m*; (*region*) región *f*. **district manager** representante regional *m*.

distrust [dis'trʌst] *n* desconfianza *f*. *v* desconfiar. **distrustful** *adj* desconfiado.

disturb [di'stəːb] *v* molestar; perturbar; agitar; preocupar. **disturbance** *n* molestia *f*; perturbación *f*; agitación *f*; preocupación *f*; (*row*) alboroto *m*; (*public disorder*) disturbio *m*. **disturbing** *adv* molesto; perturbador; preocupante.

disuse [dis'juːs] *n* desuso *m*; abandono *m*.

ditch [ditʃ] *n* (*trench*) zanja *f*; (*roadside*) cuneta *f*; (*irrigation*) acequia *f*; (*drainage*) canal *m*. *v* (*coll: get rid of*) tirar; (*coll: abandon*) abandonar.

ditto ['ditou] *n* idem *m*.

divan [di'van] *n* diván *m*.

dive [daiv] *n* zambullida *f*. *v* zambullirse; saltar; bajar en picado; sumergirse. **diver** *n* buzo *m*; saltador, -a *m, f*.

diverge [dai'vəːdʒ] *v* divergir; desviar. **divergence** *n* divergencia *f*. **divergent** *adj* divergente.

diverse [dai'vəːs] *adj* diverso; distinto; diferente; variado. **diversity** *n* diversidad *f*.

divert [dai'vəːt] *v* (*reroute*) desviar; (*distract*) distraer; (*amuse*) divertir. **diversion** *n* desviación *f*; diversión *f*.

divide [di'vaid] *v* dividir. **division** *n* división *f*; separación *f*; distribución *f*; sección *f*; (*fig: opinions*) discrepancia *f*; (*fig: discord*) desunión *f*.

dividend ['dividend] *n* dividendo *m*.

divine [di'vain] *adj* divino. *v* adivinar. **divinity** *n* divinidad *f*; teología *f*.

divorce [di'voːs] *n* divorcio *m*. **sue for a divorce** pedir el divorcio. *v* divorciar; divorciarse de. **divorcee** *n* divorciado, -a *m, f*.

divulge [dai'vʌldʒ] *v* divulgar.

dizzy ['dizi] *adj* mareado; (*height, speed*) vertiginoso. **dizziness** *n* mareo *m*, vértigo *m*.

*do [duː] *v* (*act*) hacer; (*deal with*) ocuparse de; (*fulfil*) cumplir con; (*serve*) venir bien; (*feel*) estar, sentirse; (*be suitable*) valer; (*work*) trabajar; **do away with**

suprimir. do for llevar la casa a; do up
(buttons, belt, etc.) abrocharse; (laces)
atarse; (renovate) renovar. do well ir
bien, salir bien; recuperarse. do without
prescindir de. doesn't do to no conviene.
how do you do? (after being introduced)
encantado; (how are you?) ¿cómo está
usted? make do with arreglárselas con.
please do por supuesto, por favor.

docile ['dousail] adj dócil. **docility** n
docilidad f.

dock¹ [dok] n (wharf) dársena f; v (ship)
atracar al muelle; (arrive) llegar.

dock² [dok] n (law) banquillo de los
acusados m.

dock³ [dok] v (cut, shorten) cortar;
reducir; (coll: deduct) descontar; (coll:
fine) multar.

doctor ['doktə] n médico, -a m, f; (university title) doctor, -a m, f. v atender;
adulterar; falsificar. **doctorate** n
doctorado m.

doctrine ['doktrin] n doctrina f. **doctri-
naire** doctrinario. **doctrinal** adj doctrinal.

document ['dokjumənt] n documento m.
v documentar. **documentary** nm, adj doc-
umental.

dodge [dodʒ] v esquivarse; eludir; (bide)
echarse; (avoid) evitar. n (manoeuvre)
regate m; (trick) truco m. **dodgy** (coll) adj
astuto; (unreliable) incierto.

dog [dog] n perro m. **beware of the dog**
cuidado con el perro. v seguir; perseguir.

dog biscuit n galleta de perro f.

dog days n pl canícula f sing.

dog-eared adj sobado.

dogged ['dogid] adj tenaz. **doggedness** n
tenacidad f.

doggerel ['dogərəl] n aleluyas f pl.

dogma ['dogmə] n dogma m. **dogmatic** adj
dogmático.

do-it-yourself [,duːitjɔː'self] adj hágalo
usted mismo.

dole [doul] n (alms) limosna f; (unemployment pay) subsidio de paro m. **be on the
dole** estar parado. **dole out** repartir.

doleful ['doulful] adj triste. **dolefulness** n
tristeza f.

doll [dol] n muñeca f.

dollar ['dolə] n dólar m.

dolphin ['dolfin] n delfín m.

domain [də'mein] n dominio m; (fig)
campo m.

dome [doum] n (arch) cúpula f, domo m.

domestic [də'mestik] adj doméstico;
(home-loving) hogareño; (market)
nacional. **domestic animal** animal doméstico m. **domestic help** doméstico, -a m, f.
domesticate domesticar. **domestication** n
domesticación f. **domesticity** n domesticidad f.

dominate ['domi,neit] v dominar. **dominant** adj dominante. **domineering** adj
dominante.

dominion [də'minjən] n dominio m.

domino ['dominou] n dominó m. **play
dominoes** jugar al dominó.

don [don] v ponerse. n catedrático m.

donate [də'neit] v donar. **donation** n
donativo m.

done [dʌn] V do.

donkey ['doŋki] n burro m.

donor ['dounə] n donante m, f.

doom [duːm] n perdición f. v condenar.
doomsday n día del juicio final m.

door [dɔː] n puerta f. **next door** en la casa
de al lado.

doorbell ['dɔːbel] n timbre m.

door-keeper n portero m; conserje m.

door-handle n mano de la puerta f.

doorknob ['dɔːnob] n tirador de puerta
m.

door-knocker n llamador m.

doormat ['dɔːmat] n felpudo m.

doorstep ['dɔːstep] n peldaño m; (threshold) umbral m.

doorway ['dɔːwei] n portal m.

dope [doup] n (coll: drug) droga f; (coll:
varnish) barniz m; (coll: information)
informes m pl. v drogar.

dormant ['dɔːmənt] adj letárgico; inactivo; latente.

dormitory ['dɔːmitəri] n dormitorio m.

dormouse ['dɔːmaus] n lirón m.

dose [dous] n dosis f invar. v dar la dosis.
dosage n dosis f invar.

dot [dot] n punto m. **on the dot** puntuai-
mente. v poner el punto a; (scatter)
salpicar.

dote [dout] v chochear. **dote on** estar
chocho por. **dotage** n chochez f. **doting**
adj chocho.

double ['dʌbl] nm, adj, adv doble. v
doblar.

double bass n contrabajo m.

double bed n cama de matrimonio f.

double-breasted [,dʌbl'brestid] adj cruzado.

double-cross [,dʌbl'kros] n traición f. v traicionar.

double-edged [,dʌbl'edʒd] adj de dos filos.

double-entendre [duːblā'tādr] n expresión con doble sentido f.

double entry n (comm) partida doble f.

doubt [daut] n duda f. **no doubt** sin duda. v dudar. **doubtful** adj dudozo; sospechoso. **doubtless** adv indudablemente.

dough [dou] n masa f. **doughnut** n buñuelo m.

dove [dʌv] n paloma f.

dowdy ['daudi] adj desaliñado. **dowdiness** n desaliño m.

down¹ [daun] adv hacia abajo. prep abajo. adj descendente, bajo. **down payment** al contado. v derribar; tirar al suelo; (food) tragar; (drink) vaciar de un trago.

down² [daun] n plumón m; (fine hair) vello m; (upland) loma f.

downcast ['daun,kaɪst] adj (sad) abatido; (in a downward direction) bajo.

downfall ['daun,fotl] n ruina f; perdición f; caída f; (rain) chaparrón m.

downhearted [,daun'haɪtid] adj descorazonado.

downhill [,daun'hil] adj en pendiente. adv cuesta abajo.

downpour ['daun,poɪ] n aguacero m, chaparrón m.

downright ['daun,rait] adj categórico; sincero; evidente; verdadero. adv categóricamente; verdaderamente; completamente.

downstairs ['daun,steəz] adv ,daun'steəz] adj de abajo. adv abajo.

downstream [,daun'striːm] adj, adv río abajo.

downtrodden ['daun,trodn] adj (fig) oprimido.

downward ['daunwəd] adj descendente. adv hacia abajo.

downwards ['daunwədz] adv hacia abajo.

dowry ['dauəri] n dote f.

doze [douz] v dormitar. n cabezada f.

dozen ['dʌzn] n docena f. **baker's dozen** docena del fraile f.

drab [drab] adj pardo; monótono.

draft [draɪft] n (version) redacción f; (drawing) esbozo m; (plan) bosquejo m; (payment) libramiento m; (bill) letra de cambio f; (naut) calado m; (conscription) quinta f. v hacer un proyecto; (draw up) redactar; esbozar; (conscript) reclutar.

drag [drag] v arrastrar; (river, etc.) dragar. **drag down** hundir. n (tow) arrastre m; (that which hinders) estorbo m; (device for dragging rivers, etc.) rastra f; (theatre) disfraz de mujer m; (aero) resistencia aerodinámica; (tech: brake) galga f. **what a drag!** ¡qué lata!

dragon ['dragən] n dragón m. **dragonfly** n libélula f.

drain [drein] n desaguadero m; (sewer inlet) sumidero m; (strength) pérdida f. v desaguar; (drink empty) vaciar; (marshes) desecar; (strength) agotar. **drainage** n desagüe m; desecación f. **drawing board** escurridero m. **drainpipe** n tubo de desagüe m.

drama ['draɪmə] n drama m. **dramatic** adj dramático. **dramatics** n pl teatro m. **dramatist** n dramaturgo, -a m, f. **dramatize** v adaptar al teatro.

drape [dreip] v cubrir con ropa, adornar con colgaduras. n colgadura f. **draper** n pañero, -a m, f. **drapery** n telas f pl.

drastic ['drastik] adj drástico.

draught [draɪft] n (air) corriente de aire f; (plan) bosquejo m; (drink) trago m. adj (animals) de tiro. **draughtboard** n tablero de damas m. **draughtsman** n delineante m. **draughtsmanship** n dibujo lineal m.

*draw [drot] n (sport) empate m; (lots) sorteo m; (lottery) lotería f. v (pull) tirar de; (extract) extraer; (attract) atraer; (art) dibujar; (a line) trazar; (nail, water, confession, profits, etc.) sacar; (comparisons) hacer; (breath) tomar; (earn) cobrar; (cheque) librar; (prize) ganar; sortear; (close curtains) descorrer; (blinds) bajar; (cards) robar. **draw attention** llamar la atención. **draw up** (document) redactar a.

drawback ['drotbak] n (disadvantage) desventaja f; (shortcoming) inconveniente m.

drawer ['drotə] n (container) cajón m; (art) dibujante m, f.

drawing ['drotiŋ] n (art) dibujo m; (extraction) extracción f. **drawing board** tablero de dibujo m. **drawing pin** chincheta f. **drawing room** salón m.

drawl [drotl] n voz lenta f. v arrastrar las palabras.

drawn [drotn] adj (weary) cansado. **drawn to** atraído por.

dread [dred] *n* miedo; terror. *v* temer.
dreadful *adj* terrible; espantoso.
*dream [driːm] *v* soñar; imaginarse. *n* sueño *m*. **bad dream** pesadilla *f*. **daydream** *n* ensueño *m*. **dream up** inventar.
dreary ['driəri] *adj* triote; monótono; (*boring*) aburrido. **dreariness** *n* tristeza *f*; monotonía *f*.
dredge [dredʒ] *v* dragar. *n* draga *f*.
dregs [dregz] *n pl* heces *f pl*.
drench [drentʃ] *v* empapar, mojar. **drenched to the skin** estar mojada hasta los huesos.
dress [dres] *n* (*frock*) vestido *m*; (*clothing*) ropa; (*evening dress: men*) traje de etiqueta *m*, (*women*) traje de noche *m*; (*wedding*) traje de novia *m*. *v* vestir. **dress up** poner de tiros largos. **dress up as** disfrazarse de.
dress circle *n* piso principal *m*.
dress coat *n* frac *m*.
dress designer *n* modelista *m*, *f*.
dresser ['dresə] *n* aparador *m*.
dressing ['dresiŋ] *n* (*act*) vestir *m*; (*clothes*) ropa *f*; (*med*) vendaje *m*; (*cookery*) aliño *m*; (*agriculture*) abono *m*. **dressing gown** bata *f*.
dressmaker ['dresmeikə] *n* modista *m*, *f*. **dressmaking** *n* costura *f*.
dress rehearsal *n* ensayo general *m*.
dress shirt *n* camisa de frac *f*.
dressy ['dresi] *adj* elegante.
dribble ['dribl] *n* goteo *m*. *v* gotear.
drier ['draiə] *n* secador *m*; (*for clothes*) secadora *f*.
drift [drift] *n* arrastramiento *m*; (*snow*) ventisquero *m*; (*sand*) montón *m*; (*naut*, *aero*) deriva *f*. *v* ser arrastrado; amontonarse; derivar; (*fig*) vivir sin rumbo. **drift along** vagar. **drifter** *n* (*vagrant*) vagabundo *m*; (*boat*) trainera *f*.
drill [dril] *n* (*tech*) taladro *m*; (*dental*) fresa *f*; (*mil*) instrucción *f*. *v* (*mil*) ejercitar; (*bore*) taladrar, perforar. **drilling** *n* instruccion *f*; perforación *f*.
*drink [driŋk] *v* beber, tomar; (*toast*) brindar por. **drink down** beber de un trago. **drink in** beberse. **drink up** bebérselo todo. *n* bebida *f*; (*alcoholic*) copa; (*water, milk*) vaso *m*; algo de beber. **soft drink** bebida no alcohólica *f*. **have a drink** tomar algo.
drinkable ['driŋkəbl] *adj* potable.
drinker ['driŋkə] *n* bebedor, -a *m*, *f*.

drinking ['driŋkiŋ] *n* beber *m*; bebida *f*. **drinking fountain** fuente de agua potable *f*. **drinking water** agua potable *f*.
drip [drip] *n* goteo *m*; (*drop*) gota *f*. *v* gotear. **drip-dry** *adj* de lava y pon.
*drive [draiv] *v* (*push onwards*) empujar; (*control a vehicle*) conducir; (*carry in a vehicle*) llevar; (*some distance*) recorrer; (*force someone out*) echar; (*compel*) obligar. **drive at** (*physically*) dirigirse hacia; (*fig*) insinuar. **drive away** irse; alejar. **drive by** passar (por). **drive in** entrar; clavar. **drive into** chocar contra. **drive on** seguir su camino. **drive up** llegar. *n* paseo *m*; excursión *f*; (*journey*) viaje *m*; (*fig*) vigor *m*; (*mil*) ofensiva *f*; (*tennis*, *golf*) drive *m*; (*mot*) tracción *f*; transmisión *f*; propulsión *f*; (*instinct*) instinto *m*. **driver** *n* conductor, -a *m*, *f*; chófer *m*; (*taxi*) taxista *m*, *f*; (*train*) maquinista *m*. **driveway** *n* camino de entrada *m*.
drivel ['drivl] *n* tonterías *f pl*. *v* decir tonterías.
driving ['draiviŋ] *n* conducción *f*. **driving licence** carnet de conducir *m*. **driving school** autoescuela *f*. **driving test** examen para sacar el carnet de conducir *m*.
drizzle ['drizl] *n* llovizna *f*. *v* lloviznar.
drone [droun] *n* (*noise*) zumbido *m*; (*voices*) murmullo *m*; (*bee*) zángano *m*; (*aero*) teledirigido *m*. *v* zumbar; murmurar.
droop [druːp] *n* (*shoulders*) encorvamiento *m*; (*head*) inclinación *f*. *v* estar encorvado; inclinarse; (*flowers*) marchitarse; (*eyelids*) caerse; (*fig*) desanimarse; debilitarse.
drop [drop] *n* gota *f*; (*sweet*) pastilla *f*; (*bit*) pizca *f*; (*fall*) caída *f*; (*in value*) disminución *f*; (*in prices*) baja *f*; (*in temperature*) descenso *m*. *v* (*release*) soltar; (*let fall*) dejar caer; (*tears*) derramar; (*a friend*) dejar; (*prices, eyes, voice*) bajar; (*give up a habit*) dejar de; (*leave behind*) despegarse de. **drop behind** quedarse atrás. **drop dead** caerse muerto. **drop in on** pasar por casa de. **drop off** dormirse.
dropout ['dropaut] *n* abandono *m*; marginado, -a *m*, *f*.
dropsy ['dropsi] *n* hidropesía *f*.
drought [draut] *n* sequía *f*.
drown [draun] *v* ahogar.
drowsy ['drauzi] *adj* soñoliento. **be drowsy** tener sueño. **drowse** *v* dormitar.

drudge [drʌdʒ] *n* esclavo *m*. *v* currelar.
drudgery *n* trabajo penoso *m*.
drug [drʌg] *n* droga *f*; medicamento *m*. *v* drogar. **drug addict** drogadicto, -a *m*, *f*. **drug addiction** toxicomanía *f*.
drum [drʌm] *n* (*music*) tambor *m*; (*container*) bidón *m*; (*ear*) tímpano *m*. *v* tocar el tambor; (*fingers*) tamborilear. **drummer** *n* tambor *m*; batería *f*. **drumstick** *n* palillo de tambor *m*.
drunk [drʌŋk] *adj* borracho; (*fig*) ebrio. **get drunk** emborracharse. **drunkard** *n* borracho, -a *m*, *f*. **drunkenness** *n* embriaguez *f*.
dry [drai] *adj* seco; (*measure*) para áridos; (*boring*) aburrido; (*thirsty*) sediento; (*wit*) agudo; (*subject*) árido. *v* secar. **dry-clean** *v* limpiar en seco. **dry cleaner** tintorero, -a *m*, *f*.
dual ['djuəl] *adj* doble. **dual carriageway** pista doble *f*. **dual-purpose** *adj* de dos usos.
dubbed ['dʌbd] *adj* (*named*) apodado; (*knighted*) armado; (*film*) doblado. *v* apodar; armar; doblar.
dubious ['djubiəs] *adj* dudoso; ambiguo; indeciso; discutible; sospechoso.
duchess ['dʌtʃis] *n* duquesa *f*.
duck¹ [dʌk] *n* (*bird*) pata *f*; (*drake*) pato *m*; (*dodging*) esquiva *f*; (*in water*) zambullida *f*.
duck² [dʌk] *v* (*crouch*) agachar; zambullir.
duckling ['dʌkliŋ] *n* patito *m*.
duct [dʌkt] *n* (*anat*) canal *m*; (*gas*) conducto *m*; (*elec*) tubo *m*.
dud [dʌd] *n* (*coll*) desastre *m*; (*mil*) projectil fallido *m*. *adj* falso; inútil; defectuoso; (*cheque*) sin fondos.
due [djuə] *adj* (*care, time*) debido; (*payable*) pagadero. **due date** vencimiento *m*. **be due to** deberse a. *n* merecido *m*. *adv* derecho hacia. **dues** *pl n* derechos *m pl*. **duly** *adv* debidamente; a su debido tiempo.
duel ['djuəl] *n* duelo *m*. *v* batirse en duelo. **duellist** *n* duelista *m*.
duet [dju'et] *n* dúo *m*.
duke [djuk] *n* duque *m*.
dull [dʌl] *adj* monótono; (*obtuse*) torpe; (*slow*) tardo; (*tedious*) pesado; (*colour*) apagado; (*surface*) mate; (*weather*) gris; (*sullen*) sombrío; (*blunt*) embotado. *v* (*emotions*) enfriarse; (*pain*) aliviar; (*sound*) apagar. **dullness** *n* monotonía *f*;

torpeza *f*; pesadez *f*. **dully** *adv* torpemente; lentamente.
dumb [dʌm] *adj* mudo; (*coll*) estúpido. **dumbbell** *n* pesa *f*. **dumbfound** *v* dejar sin habla. **dumbfounded** *adj* confuso, atónito. **dumbwaiter** *n* carrito *m*.
dummy ['dʌmi] *n* (*teat*) chupete *m*; (*tailor's*) maniquí *m*; (*puppet*) muñeco *m*; (*cards*) muerto *m*; (*coll*) lobo, -a *m*, *f*. *adj* ficticio, falso. *v* (*sport*) fintar.
dump [dʌmp] *n* (*rubbish dump*) depósito de basura *m*; (*heap*) montón *m*; (*scrapheap*) vertedero *m*; (*coll: wretched place*) tugurio *m*. *v* (*throw away*) tirar; (*get rid of*) deshacerse de; (*unload*) descargar. **dumping** *n* descarga *f*. **dumpy** *adj* regordete.
dumpling ['dʌmpliŋ] *n* masa hervida *f*.
dunce [dʌns] *n* tonto *m*, burro *m*.
dune [djun] *n* duna *f*.
dung [dʌŋ] *n* excrementos *m pl*; (*manure*) estiércol *m*.
dungarees [dʌŋgə'riz] *n pl* mono *m sing*.
dungeon ['dʌndʒən] *n* calabozo *m*, mazmorra *f*.
duplicate ['djuplikət; *v* 'djuplikeit] *n* copia *f*, doble *m*, duplicado *m*. *adj* duplicado. *v* duplicar; multicopiar. **duplicating machine** multicopista *f*. **duplication** *n* duplicación *f*; copia *f*.
durable ['djuərəbl] *adj* duradero. **durability** *n* durabilidad *f*.
duration [dju'reifən] *n* duración *f*.
during ['djuriŋ] *prep* durante.
dusk [dʌsk] *n* crepúsculo *m*. **dusky** *adj* oscuro; (*complexion*) moreno.
dust [dʌst] *n* polvo *m*. *v* (*clean*) limpiar el polvo; (*powder*) espolvorear. **dustbin** *n* cajón de basura *m*. **duster** (*cloth*) trapo *m*; (*feather*) plumero *m*. **dustman** *n* basurero *m*. **dustpan** *n* recogedor *m*. **dusty** *adj* polvoriento; cubierto de polvo.
duty ['djuti] *n* deber *m*, obligación *f*; (*tax*) impuesto *m*. (*at customs*) derechos de aduana *m pl*. **off duty** estar libre. **on duty** de servicio. **dutiful** *adj* obediente; deferente. **duty-free** *adj* libre de derechos de aduana.
duvet ['duvei] *n* colcha de plumón *f*.
dwarf [dwotf] *n*, *adj* enano, -a. *v* achicar.
***dwell** [dwel] *v* vivir. **dwell on** (*emphasize*) insistir en; (*a subject*) extenderse en. **dwelling** *n* vivienda *f*.
dwindle ['dwindl] *v* disminuir, menguar.

dye [dai] *n* (*colouring substance*) tinte *m*; (*colour*) fast dye color sólido *m*. *v* teñir.

dyke [daik] *n* (*ditch*) zanja *f*; (*bank*) dique *m*.

dynamic [dai'namik] *adj* dinámico.

dynamite ['dainə,mait] *n* dinamita *f*. *v* dinamitar.

dynamo ['dainə,mou] *n* dínamo *f*.

dynasty ['dinəsti] *n* dinastía *f*. **dynastic** *adj* dinástico.

dysentery ['disəntri] *n* disentería *f*.

dyslexia [dis'leksiə] *n* dislexia *f*.

dyspepsia [dis'pepsiə] *n* dispepsia *f*. **dyspeptic** *adj* dispéptico.

E

each [iːtʃ] *adj* cada. *pron* cada uno, cada una. **each other** el uno al otro.

eager ['iːgə] *adj* ávido; ansioso; impaciente. **eagerness** *n* ansia *f*; impaciencia *f*.

eagle ['iːgl] *n* águila *f*. **eagle-eyed** *adj* tener ojos de lince.

ear[1] [iə] *n* oreja *f*; (*fig*) oído *m*. **earache** dolor de oído *m*. **eardrum** *n* tímpano *m*. **earmark** *v* reservar; destinar. **earring** *n* pendiente *m*; **earshot** *n* alcance del oído *m*.

ear[2] [iə] *n* (*grain*) espiga *f*.

earl [əːl] *n* conde *m*.

early ['əːli] *adv* temprano; pronto; al principio. *adj* temprano; próximo; pronto.

earn [əːn] *v* ganar; merecer. **earnings** *pl n* (*income*) ingresos *m pl*; (*salary*) sueldo *m sing*.

earnest ['əːnist] *adj* sincero; aplicado; serio. **in earnest** en serio.

earth [əːθ] *n* tierra *f*. **earthenware** *n* alfarería *f*.

earwig ['iəwig] *n* tijereta *f*.

ease [iːz] *n* facilidad *f*; naturalidad *f*; (*comfort*) comodidad *f*; (*from pain*) alivio *m*. *v* facilitar; aliviar; tranquilizar; (*tension*) relajar.

easel ['iːzl] *n* caballete *m*.

east [iːst] *n* este *m*. *adj also* **easterly**, **eastern** oriental; del este; *adv* al este, hacia el este. **eastward** *adj*, *adv* hacia el este.

Easter ['iːstə] *n* Pascua de Resurrección *f*. **Easter egg** huevo de Pascua *m*.

easy ['iːzi] *adj* fácil. **easy chair** sillón *m*. **easy-going** *adj* acomodadizo; indolente. **take it easy!** ¡tómatelo con calma! **easiness** *n* facilidad *f*.

*eat [iːt] *v* comer. **eat up** comerse. **eatable** *adj also* **edible** comestible.

eavesdrop ['iːvzdrop] *v* fisgonear. **eavesdropper** *n* fisgón, -era *m*, *f*.

ebb [eb] *n* reflujo *m*, menguante *m*. *v* menguar; decaer. **ebb tide** marea menguante *f*.

ebony ['ebəni] *n* ébano *m*.

eccentric [ik'sentrik] *n*, *adj* excéntrico, -a. **eccentricity** *n* excentricidad *f*.

ecclesiastical [ikliːzi'astikl] *adj also* **ecclesiastic** eclesiástico.

echo ['ekou] *n* eco *m*; resonancia *f*; repetición *f*. *v* resonar; repetir; imitar.

eclair [ei'kleə] *n* relámpago *m*.

eclipse [i'klips] *n* eclipse *m*. *v* eclipsar.

ecology [i'kolədʒi] *n* ecología *f*. **ecological** *adj* ecológico. **ecologist** *n* ecólogo *m*.

economy [i'konəmi] *n* economía *f*. **economic** *adj also* **economical** económico. **economics** *n* economía *f*. **economist** *n* economista *m*, *f*. **economize** *v* economizar.

ecstasy ['ekstəsi] *n* éxtasis *m*. **ecstatic** *adj* extático. **go into ecstasies over** extasiarse ante.

Ecuador ['ekwədoɪ] *n* Ecuador *m*. **Ecuadoran**, **Ecuadorean**, *or* **Ecuadorian** *n*, *adj* ecuatoriano, -a.

eczema ['eksimə] *n* eczema *m*.

edge [edʒ] *n* borde *m*; (*blade*) filo *m*, corte *m*. **have the edge on** llevar ventaja a. **be on edge** tener los nervios de punta. *v* bordear; mover poco a poco. **edging** *n* (*sewing*) orla *f*; (*path*) borde *m*. **edgy** *adj* nervioso.

edible ['edəbl] *adj* comestible.

Edinburgh ['edinbərə] *n* Edimburgo *m*.

edit ['edit] *v* (*text*) redactar; (*film*) montar; (*direct a paper*, *magazine*) dirigir. **editor** *n* radactor *m*; director *m*. **editorial** *n* editorial *m*; artículo de fondo *m*. **editorial staff** redacción *f*.

edition [i'diʃən] *n* edición *f*; tirada *f*.

educate ['edju,keit] *v* educar. **educated** *adj* culto. **education** *n* educación *f*; (*teaching*) enseñanza *f*; (*specific*) instrucción *f*. **educational** *adj* educativo; (*teaching*) docente.

eel [iːl] *n* anguila *f.*

eerie ['iəri] *adj* misterioso; espantoso.

effect [i'fekt] *n* efecto *m*; resultado *m*; impresión *f*; (*meaning*) significado *m*. **side effect** efecto secundario. **take effect** (*drúgs, etc.*) surtir efecto; (*law, etc.*) tener efecto. **v** efectuar. **effective** *adj* (*efficient*) eficaz; (*real*) efectivo; (*in force*) vigente. **effectiveness** *n* eficacia *f*; efecto *m*; vigencia *f.*

effeminate [i'feminət] *adj* afeminado.

effervescent [,efə'vesənt] *adj* efervescente. **effervesce** *v* estar en efervescencia.

efficient [i'fiʃənt] *adj* eficaz, eficiente. **efficiency** *n* eficacia *f*, eficiencia *f.*

effigy ['efidʒi] *n* efigie *f.*

effort ['efət] *n* esfuenzo *m*. **effortless** *adj* sin esfuerzo.

egg [eg] *n* huevo *m*. **bad egg** huevo podrido. **boiled egg** huevo pasado por agua. **hard-boiled egg** huevo duro. **new-laid egg** huevo fresco. **poached egg** huevo escalfado. **scrambled eggs** huevos revueltos *m pl*. **eggcup** *n* huevera *f.* **egg-shaped** *adj* oviforme. **eggshell** *n* cascarón de huevo *m*. **egg on** incitar.

egotism ['egətizm] *n* egotismo *m*. **egotist** *n* (*self-important person*) egotista *m, f*; (*selfish person*) egoísta *m, f.*

Egypt ['iːdʒipt] *n* Egipto *m*. **Egyptian** *n, adj* egipcio, -a.

eiderdown ['aidədaun] *n* edredón *m.*

eight [eit] *nm, adj* ocho. **eighth** *n, adj* octavo, -a.

eighteen [ei'tiːn] *nm, adj* dieciocho. **eighteenth** *n, adj* decimoctavo, -a.

eighty ['eiti] *nm, adj* ochenta. **eightieth** *n, adj* octogésimo, -a.

either ['aiðə] *adj* cada, ambos. *pron* uno u otro; cualquiera de los dos. *adv* tampoco. *conj* o. **either ... or ...** o ... o ... .

ejaculate [i'dʒakjuleit] *v* exclamar; (*med*) eyacular. **ejaculation** *n* exclamación *f*; eyaculación *f.*

eject [i'dʒekt] *v* expulsar; echar; (*tenant*) desahuciar. **ejection** *n* expulsión *f*; desahucio *m*. **ejector seat** asiento eyectable *m.*

eke [iːk] *v* **eke out** (*add to*) complementar; (*make last*) escatimar.

elaborate [i'labərət; *v* i'labəreit] *adj* complicado; detallado. *v* elaborar. **elaborate** on ampliar. **elaborately** *adv* cuidadosamente; complicadamente; detalladamente. **elaboration** *n* elaboración *f*; explicación *f*; complicación *f.*

elapse [i'laps] *v* transcurrir.

elastic [i'lastik] *nm, adj* elástico. **elastic band** goma elástica *f*. **elasticity** *n* elasticidad *f.*

elated [i'leitid] *adj* jubiloso; exaltado. **elation** *n* júbilo *m*; exaltación *f.*

elbow ['elbou] *n* codo *m*. **elbow grease** fuerza de puños *f*. **elbow room** espacio suficiente *m.*

elder[1] ['eldə] *nm, adj* mayor. **elderly** *adj* mayor de edad. **eldest** *adj* mayor.

elder[2] ['eldə] *n* (*bot*) saúco *m*. **elderberry** *n* baya del saúco.

elect [i'lekt] *v* elegir. *adj* elegido. **election** *n* elección *f*. **electoral** *adj* electoral. **electorate** *n* electorado *m.*

electric [ə'lektrik] *adj also* **electrical** eléctrico. **electric blanket** manta eléctrica *f.* **electric fire** estufa eléctrica *f*. **electric shock** electrochoque *m*. **electrician** *n* electricista *m, f*. **electricity** *n* electricidad *f*. **electrify** *v* (*rail, industry*) electrificar; (*produce electricity*) electrizar; (*fig*) entusiasmar.

electrocute [i'lektrəkjuːt] *v* electrocutar. **electrocution** *n* electrocución *f.*

electrode [i'lektroud] *n* electrodo *m.*

electronic [elək'tronik] *adj* electrónico. **electronics** *n* electrónica *f.*

elegant ['elɪgənt] *adj* elegante; bello. **elegance** *n* elegancia *f.*

elegy ['elidʒi] *n* elegía *f.*

element ['elɪmənt] *n* elemento *m*; factor *m*. **elementary** *adj* elemental; fundamental.

elephant ['elifənt] *n* elefante *m.*

elevate ['eliveit] *v* elevar; (*voice, eyes*) levantar; (*honour*) enaltecer. **elevation** *n* elevación *f*; (*hill*) altura *f*; (*thought*) nobleza *f.*

eleven [i'levn] *nm, adj* once. **eleventh** *n* undécimo, -a *m, f*; *adj* onceavo.

elf [elf] *n* duende *m*. **elfin** *adj* de los duendes.

eligible ['elidʒəbl] *adj* elegible; atractivo.

eliminate [i'limineit] *v* eliminar. **elimination** *n* eliminación *f.*

elite [ei'liːt] *n* élite *f.*

ellipse [i'lips] *n* elipse *f*. **elliptical** *adj* elíptico.

elm [elm] *n* olmo *m.*

elocution [elə'kjuːʃən] *n* elocución *f*; declamación *f*.

elope [i'loup] *v* fugarse. **elopement** *n* fuga *f*.

eloquent ['eləkwənt] *adj* elocuente. **eloquence** *n* elocuencia *f*.

else [els] *adv* más, de otra manera. **or else** si no. **elsewhere** *adv* otro sitio.

elude [i'luːd] *v* eludir, escapar; (*a blow*) evitar. **elusive** *adj* escurridizo.

emaciated [i'meisieitid] *adj* demacrado. **emaciation** *n* demacración *f*.

emanate ['eməneit] *v* emanar. **emanation** *n* emanación *f*.

emancipate [i'mansipeit] *v* emancipar. **emancipation** *n* emancipación *f*.

embalm [im'baːm] *v* embalsamar.

embankment [im'baŋkmənt] *n* (*road, rail*) terraplén *m*; (*river*) dique *m*.

embargo [im'baːgou] *n* prohibición *f*.

embark [im'baːk] *v* embarcar. **embark on** emprender. **embarkation** *n* (*people*) embarco *m*; (*cargo*) embarque *m*.

embarrass [im'barəs] *v* desconcertar; molestar. **embarrassment** *n* desconcierto *m*; molestia *f*. **financial embarrassment** apuros de dinero *m pl*.

embassy ['embəsi] *n* embajada *f*.

embellish [im'beliʃ] *v* embellecer; adornar. **embellishment** *n* embellicimiento *m*; adorno *m*.

ember ['embə] *n* ascua *f*.

embezzle [im'bezl] *v* malversar. **embezzlement** *n* malversación *f*. **embezzler** *n* malversador, -a *m, f*.

embitter [im'bitə] *v* (*person*) amargar. **embittered** *adj* amargado; rencoroso.

emblem ['embləm] *n* emblema *m*. **emblematic** *adj* emblemático.

embody [im'bodi] *v* personificar; materializar; incluir. **embodiment** *n* personificación *f*; incorporación *f*.

emboss [im'bos] *v* grabar en relieve; (*paper*) gofrar; (*leather, silver*) repujar. **embossed** *adj* (*letterhead*) gofrado.

embrace [im'breis] *v* abrazar; (*encompass*) abarcar; (*opportunity*) aprovecharse de. *n* abrazo *m*.

embroider [im'broidə] *v* bordar; (*fig*) adornar. **embroidery** *n* bordado *m*; adorno *m*.

embryo ['embriou] *n* embrión *m*. **in embryo** en embrión. **embryonic** *adj* embrionario.

emerald ['emərəld] *n* esmeralda *f*.

emerge [i'məːdʒ] *v* salir; sacarse. **emergence** *n* salida *f*.

emergency [i'məːdʒənsi] *n* emergencia *f*; (*med*) urgencia *f*. **emergency exit** salida de emergencia *f*. **emergency landing** aterrizaje forzoso *m*. **in case of emergency** en caso de emergencia.

emigrate ['emigreit] *v* emigrar. **emigrant** (*m+f*), *adj* emigrante. **emigration** *n* emigración *f*.

eminent ['eminənt] *adj* eminente. **eminence** *n* eminencia *f*.

emit [i'mit] *v* (*light, sound*) emitir; (*cry*) dar; (*heat*) desprender; (*smoke*) echar; (*smell*) despedir. **emission** *n* emisión *f*.

emotion [i'mouʃən] *n* emoción *f*. **emotional** *adj* (*concerning the emotions*) emocional; (*occasion, person*) emotivo. **emotionally** *adv* con emoción.

empathy ['empəθi] *n* empatía *f*.

emperor ['empərə] *n* emperador *m*. **empress** *n* emperatriz *f*.

emphasis ['emfəsis] *n, pl* -ses (*fig*) énfasis *m*; importancia *f*; (*stress*) acento *m*. **emphasize** *v* subrayar; (*stress*) acentuar. **emphatic** *adj* enfático; enérgico; categórico.

empire ['empaiə] *n* imperio *m*.

empirical [im'pirikəl] *adj* empírico. **empiricism** *n* empirismo *m*.

employ [im'ploi] *v* emplear. *n also* employment empleo *m*. **employee** *n* empleado, -a *m, f*. **employer** *n* empresario, -a *m, f*; empleador, -a *m, f*. **employment agency** agencia de colocaciones *f*.

empower [im'pauə] *v* autorizar, habilitar.

empty ['empti] *adj* vacío; vacante; desocupado; desierto. **empty-handed** *adj* con las manos vacías. **empty-headed** *adj* casquivano. *v* vaciar; (*river*) desaguar. **emptiness** *n* vacío *m*; vacuidad *f*.

emu ['iːmjuː] *n* emú *m*.

emulate ['emjuːleit] *v* emular. **emulation** *n* emulación *f*.

emulsion [i'mʌlʃən] *n* emulsión *f*. **emulsify** *v* emulsionar.

enable [i'neibl] *v* permitir; capacitar.

enact [i'nakt] *v* (*represent*) representar; (*a law*) promulgar; (*decree*) decretar; (*do*) hacer. **enactment** *n* promulgación *f*; decreto *m*.

enamel [i'naməl] *n* esmalte *m*. *v* esmaltar.

enamour [i'namə] v enamorar. **be enamoured of** estar enamorado de.

encase [in'keis] v (*enclose*) encerrar; (*box*) encajonar.

enchant [in'tʃaint] v encantar. **enchanter** n (*magician*) hechicero m; encanto m. **enchanting** adj encantador. **enchantment** n (*charm*) encanto m; (*magic*) hechizo m. **enchantress** n hechicera f; encanto m.

encircle [in'səikl] v cercar, rodear.

enclose [in'klouz] v (*shut in*) encerrar; (*surround*) rodear; (*in a letter*) adjuntar. **enclosed** adj adjunto. **enclosure** n encierro m; carta adjunta f.

encore ['oŋkoi] interj ¡bis! ¡otra vez! n repetición f. v pedir la repetición; repetir.

encounter [in'kauntə] v encontrarse con; enfrentarse a. n encuentro m.

encourage [in'kʌridʒ] v animar, alentar; estimular; incitar. **encouragement** n ánimo m, aliento m; estimulación f; incitación f. **encouraging** adj alentador; prometedor.

encroach [in'kroutʃ] v invadir; usurpar. **encroachment** n invasión f; usurpación f.

encumber [in'kʌmbə] v (*hamper*) estorbar; (*load*) cargar; (*block*) obstruir. **encumbrance** n estorbo m; obstáculo m.

encyclopaedia [insaiklə'piːdiə] n enciclopedia f.

end [end] n (*tip*) punta f; (*tail end*) cabo m; (*finish*) fin m, final m. **end product** (*comm*) producto final m; (*result*) resultado m. **make ends meet** pasar con lo que se tiene. v acabar, terminar. **ending** n fin m, final m. **endless** adj interminable.

endanger [in'deindʒə] v arriesgar, poner en peligro.

endeavour [in'devə] n esfuerzo m, empeño m. v esforzarse, procurar.

endemic [en'demik] adj endémico.

endive ['endiv] n escarola f, endibia f.

endorse [in'dois] v (*cheque, etc.*) endosar; (*approve*) aprobar. **endorsement** n endoso m; aprobación f; (*mot*) nota de inhabilitación f.

endow [in'dau] v dotar; (*prize, etc.*) fundar. **endowment** n dotación f; fundación f.

endure [in'djuə] v (*support*) aguantar; (*last*) durar. **endurable** adj soportable. **endurance** n aguante m; resistencia f. **enduring** adj resistente; duradero.

enemy ['enəmi] n enemigo, -a m, f.

energy ['enədʒi] n energía f. **energetic** adj enérgico.

enfold [in'fould] v envolver; abrazar.

enforce [in'fois] v (*discipline*) imponer; (*law*) hacer cumplir.

engage [in'geidʒ] v (*employ*) ajustar; (*pledge*) comprometer; (*attention*) llamar; (*keep busy*) ocupar; (*clutch*) embragar. **engaged** adj prometido; ocupado. **get engaged** comprometerse. **engagement** n compromiso m; (*appointment*) cita f; (*encounter*) encuentro m. **engagement ring** sortija de pedida f.

engine ['endʒin] n motor m; máquina f. **engine driver** maquinista m. **engine room** sala de máquinas f.

engineer [endʒi'niə] n ingeniero m; (*workman*) mecánico m. **engineering** n ingeniería f.

England ['iŋglənd] n Inglaterra f. **English** nm, adj inglés. **the English** los ingleses. **English Channel** n Canal de la Mancha m.

engrave [in'greiv] v grabar. **engraver** n grabador, -a m, f. **engraving** n grabado m.

engross [in'grous] v absorber. **engrossing** adj absorbente.

engulf [in'gʌlf] v tragarse; (*sink*) hundir.

enhance [in'hains] v (*prices, etc.*) aumentar; (*beauty*) realzar. **enhancement** n aumento m; realce m.

enigma [i'nigmə] n enigma m. **enigmatic** adj enigmático.

enjoy [in'dʒɔi] v (*like*) gustar; (*delight in, have the use of*) gozar de, disfrutar de; (*party*) divertirse en. **enjoyable** adj agradable; divertido. **enjoyment** n placer m; diversión f.

enlarge [in'laidʒ] v ampliar, agrandar; (*expand*) extender. **enlargement** n aumento m; extensión f; (*phot*) ampliación f. **enlarger** n (*phot*) ampliadora f.

enlighten [in'laitn] v iluminar; (*inform*) informar; aclarar. **enlightenment** n aclaración f.

enlist [in'list] v alistar; alistarse; (*obtain support*) conseguir. **enlistment** n alistamiento m.

enmity ['enmɪti] n enemistad f.

enormous [i'nɔiməs] adj enorme. **enormity** n enormidad f. **enormously** adv enormemente.

enough [i'nʌf] *adj, adv* bastante. *n* lo bastante. enough is enough basta y sobra. curiously enough por extraño que parezca. sure enough más que seguro. that's enough con eso basta.

enquire [in'kwaiə] *V* inquire.

enrage [in'reidʒ] *v* enfurecer.

enrich [in'ritʃ] *v* enriquecer; (*soil*) fertilizar. enrichment *n* enriquecimiento *m*; fertilización *f*.

enrol [in'roul] *v* inscribir; registrar; matricular; (*mil*) alistar. enrolment *n* inscripción *f*; registro *m*; matriculación *f*; alistamiento *m*.

ensign [in'ensain] *n* (*flag*) enseña *f*; (*badge*) insignia *f*; (*naut*) bandera de popa *f*.

enslave [in'sleiv] *v* esclavizar. enslavement *n* esclavitud *f*.

ensue [in'sjuː] *v* seguir; resultar. ensuing *adj* siguiente; resultante.

ensure [in'ʃuə] *v* asegurar.

entail [in'teil] *v* (*involve*) suponer; (*follow as a result of*) acarrear; (*law*) vincular. entailment *n* vinculación *f*.

entangle [in'tangl] *v* enredar; complicar. entanglement *n* enredo *m*; (*fig*) lío *m*.

enter ['entə] *v* entrar en; penetrar; meterse en; registrar; matricular; presentar. enter for tomar parte en. enter into empezar; establecer; comprender.

enterprise ['entəpraiz] *n* empresa *f*; iniciativa *f*. enterprising *adj* emprendedor.

entertain [,entə'tein] *v* (*host*) recibir; (*amuse*) divertir; (*ideas*) abrigar. entertainer *n* artista *m, f*. entertaining *adj* divertido, entretenido. entertainment *n* entretenimiento *m*.

enthral [in'θroil] *v* encantar. enthralling *adj* cautivador.

enthusiasm [in'θuːziˌazəm] *n* entusiasmo *m*. enthusiast *n* entusiasta *m, f*. enthusiastic *adj* (*person*) entusiasta; (*praise, etc.*) entusiástico.

entice [in'tais] *v* tentar, seducir. enticing *adj* tentador; atractivo. enticement *n* atracción *f*; seducción *f*.

entire [in'taiə] *adj* entero, completo. entirety *n* totalidad *f*.

entitle [in'taitl] *v* (*authorize*) dar derecho a; (*written work*) titular. be entitled tener derecho.

entity ['entəti] *n* entidad *f*, ente *m*.

entrails ['entreilz] *pl n* entrañas *f pl*.

entrance[1] ['entrəns] *n* entrada *f*; ingreso *m*. entrance examination examen de ingreso *m*. entrance hall vestíbulo *m*. tradesmen's entrance entrada de servicio *f*.

entrance[2] [in'trains] *v* arrebatar. entrancing *adj* encantador.

entrant ['entrənt] *n* participante *m, f*.

entreat [in'triːt] *v* suplicar, implorar. entreaty *n* súplica *f*, imploración *f*.

entrée ['ontrei] *n* entrada *f*.

entrench [in'trentʃ] *v* atrincherar. entrenchment *n* atrincheramiento *m*; (*encroachment*) invasión *f*.

entrepreneur [,ontrəprə'nəi] *n* empresario *m*; intermediario *m*.

entrust [in'trʌst] *v* (*commit*) confiar; (*someone*) encargar.

entry ['entri] *n* (*entrance*) entrada *f*; (*into profession*) ingreso *m*; (*in a book*) anotación *f*; (*book-keeping*) asiento *m*. no entry dirección prohibida *f*.

entwine [in'twain] *v* entrelazar.

enunciate [i'nʌnsiˌeit] *v* enunciar. enunciation *n* enunciación *f*.

envelop [in'veləp] *v* envolver. enveloping *adj* envolvente.

envelope ['envəˌloup] *n* sobre *m*.

environment [in'vaiərənmənt] *n* ambiente *m*. environmental *adj* ambiental.

envisage [in'vizidʒ] *v* (*imagine*) imaginarse; (*foresee*) prever.

envoy ['envoi] *n* enviado *m*.

envy ['envi] *n* envidia *f*. *v* envidiar. enviable *adj* envidiable. envious *adj* envidioso. enviously *adv* con envidia.

enzyme ['enzaim] *n* enzima *f*.

epaulet ['epəlet] *n* charretera *f*.

ephemeral [i'femərəl] *adj* efímero.

epic ['epik] *n* poema épica *f*. *adj* épico.

epidemic [epi'demik] *n* epidemia. *adj* epidémico.

epilepsy ['epilepsi] *n* epilepsia *f*. epileptic *n, adj* epiléptico, -a. epileptic fit ataque epiléptico *m*.

Epiphany [i'pifəni] *n* Epifanía *f*.

episcopal [i'piskəpəl] *adj* episcopal.

episode ['episoud] *n* episodio *m*. episodic *adj* episódico.

epitaph ['epiˌtaif] *n* epitafio *m*.

epitome [i'pitəmi] *n* epitome *m*; (*fig*) personificación *f*. epitomize *v* compendiar; ser la personificación de.

epoch ['iːpok] *n* época *f*.

equable ['ekwəbl] *adj* uniforme; *(calm)* tranquilo.

equal ['iːkwəl] *n* (*m+f*), *adj* igual. *v* igualar. **equality** *n* igualdad *f*. **equalize** *v* igualar; *(draw)* empatar.

equanimity [ekwə'niməti] *n* ecuanimidad *f*.

equate [i'kweit] *v* igualar; comparar; poner en ecuación. **equation** *n* ecuación *f*.

equator [i'kweitə] *n* ecuador *m*. **equatorial** *adj* ecuatorial.

equestrian [i'kwestriən] *adj* ecuestre. *n* caballista *m*.

equilateral [iːkwi'latərəl] *n* figura equilátera *f*. *adj* equilátero.

equilibrium [iːkwi'libriəm] *n* equilibrio *m*.

equinox ['ekwinoks] *n* equinoccio *m*. **equinoctial** *adj* equinoccial.

equip [i'kwip] *v* equipar. **equipment** *n* equipo *m*; *(tools)* herramientas *f pl*.

equity ['ekwəti] *n* equidad *f*, justicia *f*.

equivalent [i'kwivələnt] *nm*, *adj* equivalente.

era ['iərə] *n* era *f*.

eradicate [i'radiˌkeit] *v* erradicar. **eradication** *n* erradicación *f*.

erase [i'reiz] *v* borrar. **eraser** *n* goma de borrar. **erasure** *n* borradura *f*.

erect [i'rekt] *adj* erguido. *v* erigir; *(assemble)* montar. **erection** *n* erección *f*; *(building)* construcción *f*; montaje *m*.

ermine ['əːmin] *n* ermiño *m*.

erode [i'roud] *v* corroer; *(wear away)* erosionar. **erosion** *n* corrosión *f*; erosión *f*. **erosive** *adj* erosivo.

erotic [i'rotik] *adj* erótico. **eroticism** *n* erotismo *m*.

err [əː] *v* errar, desviarse; *(sin)* pecar. **erring** *adj* extraviado; pecaminoso.

errand ['erənd] *n* recado *m*. **run an errand** hacer un recado. **errand boy** recadero *m*.

erratic [i'ratik] *adj* desigual; errático.

error ['erə] *n* (*mistake*) error *m*; *(wrongdoing)* extravío *m*.

erudite ['erudait] *adj* erudito. **erudition** *n* erudición *f*.

erupt [i'rupt] *v* estar en erupción, salir con fuerza. **eruption** *n* erupción *f*. **eruptive** *adj* eruptivo.

escalate ['eskəˌleit] *v* intensificar, agravar. **escalation** *n* intensificación *f*. **escalator** *n* escalera mecánica *f*.

escalope ['eskəˌlop] *n* escalope *m*.

escape [is'keip] *n* (*flight*) fuga *f*; *(liquid)* salida *f*; *(gas)* escape *m*; *(responsibilities, etc.)* evasión *f*. **escape hatch** escotilla de salvamento *f*. **fire escape** escalera de incendios *f*. *v* escapar de; evadir; eludir. **escape notice** pasar inadvertido. **escapism** *n* evasión *f*.

escort ['eskoːt; *v* i'skoːt] *n* acompañante *m*; *(mil)* escolta *f*. *v* acompañar; *(mil)* escoltar.

esoteric [esə'terik] *adj* esotérico.

especial [i'speʃəl] *adj* especial, particular; excepcional. **especially** *adv* especialmente, sobre todo.

espionage ['espiəˌnaːʒ] *n* espionaje *m*.

esplanade [ˌesplə'neid] *n* explanada *f*, bulevar *m*, paseo *m*.

essay ['esei] *n* ensayo *m*; composición *f*; *(attempt)* intento *m*. *v* probar; intentar. **essayist** *n* ensayista *m*, *f*.

essence ['esns] *n* esencia *f*. **essential** *adj* esencial, imprescindible; fundamental. *n* lo esencial. **essentials** *pl n* elementos esenciales *m pl*.

establish [i'stabliʃ] *v* establecer. **establishment** *n* establecimiento *m*. **The Establishment** clase dirigente *f*.

estate [i'steit] *n* (*property*) propiedad *f*; *(land)* finca *f*, *(S. Am.)* hacienda *f*, estancia *f*; *(inheritance)* herencia *f*; *(fortune)* fortuna *f*; *(social class)* estado *m*; *(of the deceased)* testamentaria *f*. **estate agency** agencia inmobiliaria *f*. **estate agent** agente inmobiliario *m*. **estate car** furgoneta *f*.

esteem [i'stiːm] *v* estimar, apreciar. *n* estima *f*, aprecio *m*.

estimate ['estimət; *v* 'estiˌmeit] *n* (*valuation*) estimación *f*; *(statement of cost)* presupuesto *m*. *v* estimar; hacer un presupuesto de. **estimation** *n* juicio *m*; *(esteem)* aprecio *m*.

estuary ['estjuəri] *n* estuario *m*.

eternal [i'təːnl] *adj* eterno. **eternity** *n* eternidad *f*.

ether ['iːθə] *n* éter *m*. **ethereal** *adj* etéreo.

ethical ['eθikl] *adj* ético. **ethics** *pl n* ética *f sing*.

ethnic ['eθnik] *adj* étnico.

etiquette ['etiˌket] *n* etiqueta *f*.

etymology [ˌeti'molədʒi] *n* etimología *f*. **etymologist** *n* etimólogo, -a *m*, *f*.

Eucharist ['juːkərist] *n* Eucaristía *f*.

eunuch ['juːnək] *n* eunuco *m*.

euphemism ['juːfəˌmizəm] *n* eufemismo *m*. **euphemistic** *adj* eufemístico.

euphoria [juːˈfɔːriə] *n* euforia *f*. **euphoric** *adj* eufórico.

Europe ['juərəp] *n* Europa *f*. **European** *n, adj* europeo, -a.

European Economic Community (EEC) *n* Comunidad Económica Europea (CEE) *f*.

euthanasia [juːθəˈneiziə] *n* eutanasia *f*.

evacuate [iˈvakjuˌeit] *v* evacuar. **evacuation** *n* evacuación *f*. **evacuee** *n* evacuado, -a *m, f*.

evade [iˈveid] *v* evadir, eludir. **evasion** *n* evasión *f*. **evasive** evasivo.

evaluate [iˈvaljuˌeit] *v* evaluar. **evaluation** *n* evaluación *f*.

evangelical [ˌiːvanˈdʒelikəl] *adj* evangélico. **evangelist** *n* evangelizador, -a *m, f*.

evaporate [iˈvapəˌreit] *v* evaporar; deshidratar. **evaporated milk** leche evaporada *f*. **evaporation** *n* evaporación *f*; deshidratación *f*.

eve [iːv] *n* víspera *f*. **Christmas Eve** Nochebuena *f*. **New Year's Eve** Noche Vieja *f*. **on the eve of** en vísperas de.

even ['iːvən] *adj* (*surface*) uniforme; (*smooth*) suave; (*calm*) ecuánime; (*fair*) justo; (*same level*) a nivel; (*equal*) igual; (*number*) par. **break even** quedar igual. **get even** desquitarse. *adv* siquiera; incluso, even **if** incluso si, even **so** aun así. **even though** aunque. **even-tempered** *adj* sereno. *v* nivelar; igualar. **evenly** *adv* uniformemente; imparcialmente.

evening ['iːvniŋ] *n* tarde *f*; anochecer *m*. **evening class** clase nocturna *f*. **evening dress** (*man*) traje de etiqueta *m*; (*woman*) traje de noche *m*. **good evening!** (*early*) ¡buenas tardes! (*late*) ¡buenas noches!

event [iˈvent] *n* (*occurrence*) acontecimiento *m*; (*case*) caso *m*; (*outcome*) consecuencia *f*; (*in a programme*) número *m*; (*sport*) prueba *f*. **in the event of** en caso de. **eventful** *adj* agitado; memorable. **eventual** *adj* final; consiguiente. **eventuality** *n* eventualidad *f*. **eventually** *adv* finalmente; con el tiempo.

ever ['evə] *adv* (*always*) siempre; nunca, jamás. **we hardly ever go out** casi nunca salimos. **not ever** nunca jamás. **ever after** desde (que).

evergreen ['evəˌgriːn] *adj* de hoja perenne.

everlasting [ˌevəˈlaːstiŋ] *adj* eterno; perpetuo.

every ['evri] *adj* (*all*) todo; (*each*) cada. **everybody** *also* **everyone** *pron* todo el mundo. **everyday** *adj* diario. **every other day** cada dos días. **everything** *pron* todo. **everywhere** *adv* por *also* en todas partes.

evict [iˈvikt] *v* desahuciar. **eviction** *n* desahucio *m*.

evidence ['evidəns] *n* evidencia *f*; (*sign*) indicio *m*; (*law: proof*) prueba *f*; (*law: testimony*) testimonio *m*. *v* evidenciar. **give evidence** declarar como testigo. **evident** *adj* evidente, patente.

evil ['iːvl] *adj* malo; perverso; maligno. *n* mal *m*; desgracia *f*. **evildoer** *n* malhechor, -a *m, f*. **evil-minded** *adj* malpensado.

evoke [iˈvouk] *v* evocar. **evocation** *n* evocación *f*. **evocative** *adj* evocador.

evolve [iˈvolv] *v* evolucionar; (*develop*) desarrollarse. **evolution** *n* evolución *f*; desarrollo *m*. **evolutionary** *adj* evolutivo.

ewe [juː] *n* oveja *f*.

exacerbate [igˈzasəˌbeit] *v* exacerbar. **exacerbation** *n* exacerbación *f*.

exact [igˈzakt] *adj* exacto. *v* exigir. **exacting** *adj* (*person*) exigente; (*condition*) severo; (*work*) duro. **exactly** *adv* exactamente; precisamente.

exaggerate [igˈzadʒəˌreit] *v* exagerar; acentuar. **exaggerated** *adj* exagerado. **exaggeration** *n* exageración *f*.

exalt [igˈzolt] *v* exaltar, elevar; (*praise*) glorificar. **exaltation** *n* exaltación *f*; (*ecstasy*) arrobamiento. **exalted** *adj* exaltado, eminente.

examine [igˈzamin] *v* examinar; (*search*) reconocer; (*by touch*) analizar; (*law*) interrogar. **examination** examen *m*; (*law*) interrogatorio *m*. **sit an exam** examinarse. **written exam** prueba escrita *f*. **examiner** *n* examinador, -a *m, f*; inspector, -a *m, f*.

example [igˈzaːmpl] *n* ejemplo *m*. **follow someone's example** tomar ejemplo de uno. **for example** por ejemplo. **set an example** dar ejemplo.

exasperate [igˈzaːspəˌreit] *v* exasperar. **exasperation** *n* exasperación *f*.

excavate ['ekskəˌveit] *v* excavar. **excavation** *n* excavación *f*. **excavator** (*person*) excavador *m*; (*tech*) excavadora *f*.

exceed [ikˈsiːd] *v* exceder. **exceedingly** *adv* sumamente.

excel [ik'sel] *v* superar, sobresalir. **excellence** *n* excelencia *f*. His Excellency su Excelencia *m*. **excellent** *adj* excelente.

except [ik'sept] *prep* excepto, salvo, con excepción de. **except for** excepto. *v* excluir, exceptuar. **exception** *n* exclusión *f*; excepción *f*. **take exception to** ofenderse por. **exceptional** *adj* excepcional.

excerpt ['eksəɪpt] *n* extracto *m*. *v* extractar.

excess [ik'ses] *n* exceso *m*. *adj* excedente. **excess fare** suplemento *m*. **excess luggage** exceso de equipaje *also* peso *m*. **excessive** *adj* excesivo. **excessively** *adv* excesivamente.

exchange [iks'tʃeindʒ] *v* (*change*) cambiar; (*interchange*) intercambiar; (*courtesies*) hacerse; (*prisoners*) canjear; (*blows*) darse. *n* cambio *m*; intercambio *m*. **exchange control** control de divisas. **exchange rate** tipo de cambio *m*. **Stock Exchange** bolsa de valores *f*. **telephone exchange** central telefónica *f*.

exchequer [iks'tʃekə] *n* (*finances*) hacienda *f*; tesoro público *m*. **Chancellor of the Exchequer** Ministro de Hacienda *m*.

excise ['eksaiz] *n* impuestos sobre el consumo *m pl*.

excite [ik'sait] *v* (*stimulate*) excitar; emocionar; entusiasmar; (*irritate*) poner nervioso; (*urge*) incitar; (*imagination*) despertar; (*admiration*, *etc.*) provocar. **get excited** emocionarse; entusiasmarse. **excitement** *n* excitación *f*; emoción *f*; entusiasmo *m*; agitación *f*. **exciting** *adj* excitante; emocionante; apasionante.

exclaim [ik'skleim] *v* exclamar. **exclamation** *n* exclamación *f*. **exclamation mark** punto de admiración *m*.

exclude [ik'skluɪd] *v* excluir. **exclusion** *n* exclusión *f*. **exclusive** *adj* (*policy*) exclusivista; (*sole*) exclusivo; (*select*) selecto.

excommunicate [ekskə'mjuɪni,keit] *v* excomulgar. **excommunication** *n* excomunión *f*.

excrete [ik'skriɪt] *v* excretar. **excrement** *n* excremento *m*. **excretion** *n* excreción *f*.

excruciating [ik'skruʃieitiŋ] *adj* (*noise*) intolerable; (*pain*) atroz.

excursion [ik'skəɪʃən] *n* excursión *f*.

excuse [ik'skjuɪz] *n* excusa *f*, disculpa *f*. *v*

excusar, disculpar, perdonar; (*duty*) dispensar de. **excuse me!** ¡perdón! ¡discúlpeme! **excusable** *adj* excusable, disculpable, perdonable.

execute ['eksi,kjuɪt] *v* (*order*, *will*, *criminal*) ejecutar; (*carry out*) llevar a cabo. **execution** *n* ejecución *f*; (*of order*) cumplimiento *m*. **executioner** *n* verdugo *m*.

executive [ig'zekjutiv] *adj* (*power*) ejecutivo; (*function*) dirigente; (*ability*) de ejecución. *n* (*government branch*) poder ejecutivo *m*; (*person*) ejecutivo *m*.

exemplify [ig'zempli,fai] *v* ilustrar con ejemplos. **exemplification** *n* ejemplificación *f*.

exempt [ig'zempt] *adj* exento. *v* exentar, dispensar. **exemption** *n* exención *f*.

exercise ['eksə,saiz] *n* ejercicio *m*; gimnasia *f*. **exercise book** *n* cuaderno *m*. **take exercise** hacer ejercicio. *v* (*rights*, *etc.*) ejercer; (*physically*) ejercitarse; (*patience*) usar de.

exert [ig'zəɪt] *v* ejercer. **exert oneself** esforzarse. **exertion** *n* esfuerzo *m*; (*of strength*) empleo *m*.

exhale [eks'heil] *v* exhalar; (*breathe out*) espirar. **exhalation** *n* exhalación *f*; espiración *f*.

exhaust [ig'zoɪst] *v* agotar. *n* (*system*) escape *m*. **exhaust pipe** tubo de escape *m*. **exhausting** *adj* agotador. **exhaustion** *n* agotamiento *m*. **exhaustive** *adj* exhaustivo. **exhaustively** *adv* exhaustivamente.

exhibit [ig'zibit] *v* (*display*) mostrar; (*paintings*, *etc.*) exponer; (*documents*) presentar. *n* objeto expuesto *m*. **exhibition** *n* exposición *f*. **make an exhibition of oneself** ponerse en ridículo. **exhibitor** *n* expositor *m*.

exhilarate [ig'zilə,reit] *v* alegrar, animar. **exhilarating** *adj* estimulante. **exhilaration** *n* alegría *f*, regocijo *m*.

exile ['eksail] *n* exilio *m*, destierro *m*; (*person*) exiliado, -a *m*, *f*; desterrado, -a *m*, *f*. **go into exile** exiliarse, exilarse. *v* exiliar, exilar, desterrar.

exist [ig'zist] *v* existir; (*live*) vivir. **existence** *n* existencia *f*. **existent** *also* existing *adj* existente; (*present*) actual. **existentialism** *n* existencialismo *m*. **existentialist** *n* (*m + f*). *adj* existencialista.

exit ['egzit] *n* salida *f*; (*theatre*) mutis *m*. *v* (*theatre*) hacer mutio.

exonerate [ig'zonə,reit] *v* (*from blame*)

disculpar; *(from obligation)* dispensar de.
exoneration *n* disculpa *f*; dispensa *f*.
exorbitant [ig'zɔːbitənt] *adj* exorbitante.
exorcize ['eksɔːsaiz] *v* exorcizar. **exorcism** *n* exorcismo *m*. **exorcist** *n* exorcista *m, f*.
exotic [ig'zotik] *adj* exótico. **exoticism** *n* exotismo *m*.
expand [ik'spænd] *v (cause to increase)* desarrollar; *(make larger)* dilatar; *(add to)* ampliar. **expansion** *n* expansión *f*; desarollo *m*; dilatación *f*; ampliación *f*. **expansive** *adj (person)* expansivo; *(wide)* extenso. **expansiveness** *n* expansibilidad *f*.
expanse [ik'spæns] *n* extensión *f*; *(wings)* envergadura *f*.
expatriate [eks'peitriət; *v* eks'peitrieit] *n, adj* expatriado, -a. *v* desterrar. **expatriation** *n* expatriación *f*.
expect [ik'spekt] *v (anticipate, hope for, require)* esperar; *(suppose)* suponer. **expectant** *adj* expectante. **expectant mother** futura madre *f*. **expectation** *n* expectación *f*; *(hope)* esperanza *f*; *(anticipation)* previsión *f*.
expedient [ik'spiːdiənt] *adj* expeditivo, oportuno. *n* expediente. **expedience** *also* **expediency** *n* conveniencia *f*.
expedition [,ekspi'diʃən] *n* expedición *f*.
expel [ik'spel] *v* expulsar.
expenditure [ik'spenditʃə] *n* gasto *m*. **expend** *v* gastar; *(effort)* dedicar. **expendable** *adj (objects)* gastable; *(people)* prescindible.
expense [ik'spens] *n* gasto *m*. **at the expense of** a costa de. **expense account** cuenta de gastos de representación *f*. **expensive** *adj* caro, costoso.
experience [ik'spiəriəns] *n* experiencia *f*. *v* experimentar; *(difficulty)* tener. **experienced** *adj* experimentado; experto.
experiment [ik'sperimənt] *n* experimento *m*. *v* hacer experimentos, experimentar. **experimental** *adj* experimental.
expert ['ekspɔːt] *n, adj* experto, -a.
expertise [,ekspɔː'tiːz] *n* pericia *f*.
expire [ik'spaiə] *v (finish, die)* expirar; *(become void)* caducar; *(expel air)* espirar. **expiration** *also* **expiry** *n* expiración *f*; *(comm)* vencimiento *m*.
explain [ik'splein] *v* explicar. **explanation** *n* explicación *f*. **explanatory** *adj* explicativo.
expletive [ek'spliːtiv] *n (gramm)* expletiva *f*; *(oath)* taco *m*.

explicit [ik'splisit] *adj* explícito.
explode [ik'sploud] *v* estallar, hacer explotar; *(myth)* refutar; *(rumour)* desmentir. **explosion** *n* explosión *f*. **explosive** *nm, adj* explosivo.
exploit[1] ['eksploit] *n* hazaña *f*.
exploit[2] [ik'sploit] *v* explotar. **exploitation** *n* explotación *f*.
explore [ik'sploɪ] *v* explorar. **exploration** *n* exploración *f*. **exploratory** *adj* exploratorio. **explorer** *n* explorador, -a *m, f*.
exponent [ik'spounənt] *n* exponente *m, f*.
export ['ekspoɪt; *v* ik'spoɪt] *n* exportación *f*. *v* exportar. **exporter** *n* exportador, -a *m, f*.
expose [ik'spouz] *v (leave uncovered)* exponer; *(reveal)* revelar; *(plot, etc.)* descubrir; *(phot)* exponer. **exposure** *n* exposición *f*; revelación *f*; descubrimiento *m*; *(denunciation)* denuncia *f*; *(phot)* fotografía *f*. **exposure meter** exposímetro *m*. **indecent exposure** exhibicionismo *m*.
expound [ik'spaund] *v* exponer; comentar.
express [ik'spres] *v* expresar; *(press)* exprimir. *n (train)* rápido *m*; *(mail)* correo urgente *m. adj, adv* expreso; rápido. **expression** *n* expresión *f*. **expressive** *adj* expresivo.
expulsion [ik'spʌlʃən] *n* expulsión *f*.
exquisite ['ekswizit] *adj* exquisito; intenso.
extend [ik'stend] *v* extender, aumentar; *(widen)* ampliar; *(lengthen)* prolongar; *(stretch)* estirar; *(invitation)* enviar; *(aid)* ofrecer; *(hand)* tender; *(time-limit)* prorogar. **extension** *n* extensión *f*; prolongación *f*; aumento *m*; prórroga *f*. **telephone extension** extensión *f*. **extensive** *adj* extenso.
extent [ik'stent] *n (length)* extensión *f*; *(degree)* punto *m*; *(scope)* alcance *m*.
exterior [ik'stiəriə] *nm, adj* exterior.
exterminate [ik'stɔːmiˌneit] *v* exterminar. **extermination** *n* exterminio *m*.
external [ik'stɔːnl] *adj* externo. **for external use only** sólo para uso externo.
extinct [ik'stiŋkt] *adj* extinto; *(fire, volcano)* extinguido. **extinction** *n* extinción *f*.
extinguish [ik'stiŋgwiʃ] *v* extinguir; apagar; *(hope)* destruir. **extinguisher** *n (fire)* extintor.

extort [ik'stɔɪt] v arrancar, sacar por fuerza. **extortion** n extorsión f. **extortionate** adj exorbitante.

extra ['ekstrə] adj extra; de más; adicional; extraordinario; no incluido. n (extra charge) recargo m; (actor) extra m, f. adv extraordinariamente.

extract [ik'strakt; n 'ekstrakt] v extraer; (obtain, parts of books, etc.) sacar. n extracto m. **extraction** n extracción f; (descent) origen m.

extradite ['ekstrə,dait] v conceder la extradición de; obtener la extradición de. **extradition** n extradición f.

extramural [,ekstrə'mjuərəl] adj para estudiantes libres.

extraordinary [ik'strɔɪdənəri] adj extraordinario; raro.

extravagant [ik'stravəgənt] adj (lavish) pródigo; (wasteful) despilfarrador; (taste) dispendioso; (language, ideas) extravagante. **extravagance** n prodigalidad f; despilfarro m; extravagancia f.

extreme [ik'striɪm] nm, adj extremo. **go to extremes** llegar a extremos. **extremist** n (m+f), adj extremista. **extremity** n (end) extremidad f; (necessity) apuro m.

extrovert ['ekstrəvɔɪt] n, adj extrovertido, -a.

exuberant [ig'zjuːbərənt] adj exuberante; enfórico. **exuberance** n exuberancia f; enforia f.

exude [ig'zjuɪd] v exudar.

exult [ig'zʌlt] v exultar. **exult over** triunfar sobre. **exultant** adj exultante. **exultation** n exultación f.

eye [ai] n ojo m. **an eye for an eye** ojo por ojo. **private eye** detective m. **make eyes at** echar miradas a. **see eye to eye with** ver con los mismos ojos que. **turn a blind eye** cerrar los ojos. **up to one's eyes in work** estar hasta aquí en trabajo. **with an eye to** con miras a. **with the naked eye** a simple vista. v mirar.

eyeball ['aibɔɪl] n globo del ojo m.

eyebrow ['aibrau] n ceja f.

eye-catching ['aikatʃiŋ] adj llamativo.

eyelash ['ailaʃ] n pestaña f.

eyelid ['ailid] n párpado m.

eye shadow n sombreador de ojos m.

eyesight ['aisait] n vista f.

eyesore ['aisɔɪ] n algo que ofende la vista.

eyewitness ['ai,witnis] n testigo ocular m.

F

fable ['feibl] n fábula f.

fabric ['fabrik] n (cloth) tejido m; estructura f, construcción f. **fabricate** v (invent) fingir. **fabrication** n fabricación f; invención f.

fabulous ['fabjuləs] adj fabuloso; (coll) macanudo.

façade [fə'saɪd] n fachada f.

face [feis] n cara f, rostro m; (side) lado m; (aspect) aspecto m; (grimace) mueca f; (surface) superficie f; (clock) esfera f. **face down** boca abajo. **face up** boca arriba. **face to face** cara a cara. **on the face of it** a primera vista. **fly in the face of** burlarse de. **in the face of** frente a. **keep a straight face** mantenerse impávido. **lose face** quedar mal. **pull faces** hacer muecas. **save face** salvar las apariencias. v mirar hacia, dar a; estar en frente de; enfrentarse con; presentarse ante; (consequences) arrostrar; (stand) aguantar; (resurface) revestir.

face cloth n paño m.

facelift ['feislift] n (coll) lavado m.

face pack n mascarilla de belleza f.

face powder n polvos para la cara m pl.

facet ['fasit] n faceta f.

facetious [fə'siɪʃəs] adj chistoso; gracioso.

face value n (bill) valor nominal m; (stamps) valor facial. **take something at face value** creer algo a pie juntillas.

facing ['feisiŋ] n (sewing) guarnición f; (building) revestimiento m. adj de enfrente.

facsimile [fak'siməli] nm, adj facsímil.

fact [fakt] n hecho m; realidad f. **as a matter of fact** en realidad. **in fact** en verdad. **factual** adj objetivo.

faction ['fakʃən] n facción f. **factious** adj faccioso.

factor ['faktə] n factor m, elemento m; (comm) agente m.

factory ['faktəri] n fábrica f.

faculty ['fakəlti] n (university) facultad f; (gift) facilidad f.

fad [fad] n manía f; novedad f. **faddish** adj maniático.

fade [feid] v (colour) descolorarse; (light) apagarse; (sound) desvanecerse; (interest) decaer. **faded** adj descolorido; marchito.

fag [fag] n (coll: cigarette) pitillo m. fag end sobras f pl; (cigarette) colilla f. fagged out rendido.

fail [feil] v fallar; (not succeed) fracasar, no lograr; (hopes) frustrarse; (run out) acabarse; (weaken) decaer; (exams) ser suspendido; (neglect) dejar (de). without fail sin falta. failing n defecto m. failure n fracaso m; fallo m; suspenso m; (breakdown) avería f.

faint [feint] adj (near collapse) mareado; (weak) débil; (colour) pálido; (timid) timorato; (slight) ligero; vago; indistinto. v desmayarse. n desmayo m.

fair¹ [feə] adj bello; hermoso; (skin) blanco; (hair) rubio; (just) justo; (reputation, weather) bueno; (prospects) favorable; (play) limpio; (price) razonable; (comment) acertado; (average) mediano. by fair means or foul por las buenas o por las malas. fairly adv con justicia; (reasonably) bastante. fairness n belleza f; justicia f.

fair² [feə] n (amusements) verbena f; (market) feria f. fun fair parque de atracciones m. fairground n real m.

fairy ['feəri] n hada f. adj de hada. fairy lights bombillas de colores f pl.

faith [feiθ] n confianza f. have faith in fiarse de. religious faith fe religiosa f. faithful adj fiel; exacto. faithfulness n fidelidad f; exactitud f. faithless adj desleal; infiel.

fake [feik] n falsificación f; impostor m. adj falso; falsificado; (feigned) fingido. v falsificar; fingir.

falcon ['fɔːlkən] n halcón m.

*fall [fɔːl] v caer; (prices, temperature, water) bajar; (wind) amainar; (decay) decaer; (task, duty, privilege) tocar; (accent) recaer. fall apart caerse a pedazos. fall back on echar mano a. fall behind retrasarse. fall in love enamorarse. fall out (quarrel) reñir. fall through venirse abajo. n (body, earth, leaves) caída f; (prices) baja f; (slope) declive m; (US: season) otoño m.

fallacy ['faləsi] n falacia f; (deception) engaño m. fallacious adj erróneo.

fallible ['faləbl] adj falible. fallibility n falibilidad f.

fallow ['falou] adj (land) en barbecho; inculto.

false [fɔːls] adj falso; erróneo. false alarm falsa alarma f. false pretences estafa f.

false teeth dientes postizas m pl. falsehood n falsedad f; mentira f. falseness n falsedad f; inexactitud f; perfidia f. falsify v falsificar; desvirtuar. falsification n falsificación f.

falsetto [fɔːl'setou] n falsete m. adj de falsete.

falter ['fɔːltə] v (action) vacilar; (voice) titubear. faltering adj vacilante; titubeante. falteringly adv con paso vacilante; con voz titubeante.

fame [feim] n fama f.

familiar [fə'miljə] adj familiar, conocido. be familiar with estar familiarizado con. familiarity n familiaridad f. familiarize v familiarizar.

family ['faməli] n familia f. family allowance subsidio familiar m. family doctor médico de cabecera m. family planning planificación familiar f. family tree árbol genealógico m.

famine ['famin] n (general scarcity) escasez f; (food) hambre f. famished ['famiʃt] adj famélico. be famished estar muerto de hambre.

famous ['feiməs] adj famoso, célebre.

fan¹ [fan] n (hand) abanico m; (tech) ventilador m. fan belt correa del ventilador f. v abanicar; agitar.

fan² [fan] n aficionado, -a m, f; admirador, -a m, f. fan club club de admiradores m. fan mail correspondencia de los admiradores f.

fanatic [fə'natik] n, adj fanático, -a. fanaticism n fanatismo m.

fancy ['fansi] adj de adorno; de fantasía. n fantasía f; (whim) capricho m; (desire) afición f; (delusion) ilusión f; (taste) gusto m. v imaginarse; suponer; gustar; (suspect) parecerle(a); (desire) apetecer. fancy oneself ser un creído. fancy that! ¡imagínate! fancy dress disfraz m. fancied adj favorito; imaginario. fanciful adj imaginario; caprichoso.

fanfare ['fanfeə] n fanfarria f.

fang [faŋ] n colmillo m; (snake) diente m.

fantastic [fan'tastik] adj fantástico.

fantasy ['fantəsi] n fantasía f; capricho m.

far [faː] adv lejos; (much) mucho; muy. adj lejano; distante. as far as hasta; por lo que. far and wide por todas partes. far away lejos. far-away adj remoto. Far East Extremo Oriente m. far-fetched adj inverosímil. far-reaching adj de mucho alcance. **so far so good** hasta ahora todo va bien.

farce [faɪs] n farsa f. **farcical** adj ridículo; absurdo.

fare [feə] n precio del billete m, tarifa f; (boat) pasaje m; (passenger) pasajero, -a; (in a taxi) cliente m, f; (in a bus) viajero, -a m, f; (food) comida f. v (get on) irle bien (a uno).

farewell [feə'wel] (interj) ¡adiós! **say farewell** decir adiós, despedirse de. adj de despedida.

farm [faɪm] n also **farmhouse** granja f, finca f; (S. Am.) estancia f, hacienda f. **farmhand** n peón m. **farmland** n tierras de labrantío f pl. **farmyard** n corral m. v cultivar. **farm out** mandar hacer fuera. **farmer** n agricultor m; granjero m. **farming** n labranza f; agricultura f.

fart [faɪt] (impol) n pedo m. v peerse.

farther ['faɪðə] adv (space) más lejos; (time) más adelante. adj (space, time) más lejano.

farthest ['faɪðist] adv más lejos. adj (most distant) más lejano; (longest) más largo.

fascinate ['fasineit] v fascinar. **fascinating** adj fascinador. **fascination** n fascinación f.

fascism ['faʃizəm] n fascismo m. **fascist** n(m+f), adj fascista.

fashion ['faʃən] n manera f, modo m; moda f. **after a fashion** en cierto modo. **fashion show** desfile de modas m. **in fashion** de modo. **out of fashion** pasado de moda. v hacer, formar; (mould) moldear.

fast¹ [faɪst] adj rápido, veloz; (colour) sólido; (clock, etc.) adelantado; (secure) seguro; firme. **fast asleep** profundamente dormido. **make fast** sujetar, atar. **pull a fast one** jugar una mala jugada. **stuck fast** (in mud) completamente atascado.

fast² [faɪst] n ayuno m. v ayunar.

fasten ['faɪsn] v (fix) fijar; (attach) sujetar; (dress) abrochar; (close) cerrar. **fastener** or **fastening** n corchete m; fijación f.

fastidious [fa'stidiəs] adj quisquilloso; (demanding) exigente. **fastidiousness** n melindre m.

fat [fat] n grasa f; (on meat) gordo m. adj grueso; gordo. **fatten** v (person) engordar; (animal) cebar. **fattening** adj que engorda.

fatal ['feitl] adj fatal, mortal. **fatality** n fatalidad f.

fate [feit] n destino m; suerte f. **fated** adj

predestinado; condenado. **fateful** adj profético; fatal.

father ['faɪðə] n padre m. **Father Christmas** Papá Noel m. **father-in-law** n suegro m. **fatherland** n patria f. **fatherless** adj huérfano de padre m. **fatherly** adj paternal.

fathom ['faðəm] n braza f. v (water depth) sondar, sondear; (unravel) desentrañar. **fathomless** adj insondable.

fatigue [fə'tiɪg] n fatiga f. v fatigar.

fatuous ['fatjuəs] adj fatuo; necio. **fatuity** or **fatuousness** n fatuidad f; necedad f.

fault [foɪlt] n culpa f; defecto m; error m; falta f; (geol) falla f. **be at fault** tener la culpa. **faultiness** n imperfección f. **faultless** adj perfecto. **faulty** adj malo; erróneo; defectuoso.

fauna ['foɪnə] n fauna f.

favour ['feivə] n favor m; favoritismo m; (gift) obsequio m; (comm) carta f, atenta f. **be in favour of** estar a favor de. v favorecer. **favourable** adj favorable. **favourite** n, adj favorito, -a.

fawn [foɪn] n cervato m. adj color de gamuza m. **fawn on** or **upon** adular.

fear [fiə] n miedo m; temor m. v temer; tener miedo de or a. **fearful** adj (frightening) espantoso; (frightened) temeroso. **fearless** adj intrépido, audaz.

feasible ['fiɪzəbl] adj factible. **feasibility** n viabilidad f.

feast [fiɪst] n fiesta f; banqueta m. **feast day** día festivo m.

feat [fiɪt] n hazaña f.

feather ['feðə] n pluma f. **feather bed** colchón de plumas m.

feature ['fiɪtʃə] n característica f; (shape) figura f; (face) rasgo m; (written article) artículo principal m. **feature film** película principal f. v presentar; representar; (emphasize) destacar.

February ['februəri] n febrero m.

fed [fed] V **feed**.

federal ['fedərəl] adj federal.

federate ['fedəreit] v federar. **federation** n federación f.

fee [fiɪ] n (professional) honorarios m pl; (club) cuota f. **entrance fee** entrada f.

feeble ['fiɪbl] adj débil; (unconvincing) de poco peso. **feebleness** n debilidad f.

***feed** [fiɪd] v alimentar; dar de comer; (eat) comer. **be fed up with** (coll) estar harto de. **feed on** alimentarse con. n (for babies) comida f; (fodder) forraje m;

(*tech*) alimentación *f*. **feedback** *n* reaprovechamiento *m*; (*tech*) realimentación *f*.

*feel [fiːl] *v* tocar; mirar; sentir; (*realize*) darse cuenta de; (*caress*) sobar; (*think*) pensar. *n* tacto *m*; sensación *f*; atmósfera *f*; sentido *m*. **feeler** *n* antena *f*; tentáculo *m*. **feeling** *n* sentimiento *m*; sentido *m*; sensación *f*; opinión *f*; impresión *f*.

feet [fiːt] *V* foot.

feign [fein] *v* fingir; inventar.

feline ['fiːlain] *nm, adj* felino.

fell¹ [fel] *V* fall.

fell² [fel] *v* derribar; (*trees*) talar.

fellow ['felou] *n* hombre *m*; compañero; (*coll*) tipo *m*; (*of a society*) miembro *m*. **fellowship** *n* comunidad *f*; asociación *f*.

felony ['feləni] *n* delito grave *m*. **felon** *n* criminal *m*.

felt¹ [felt] *V* feel.

felt² [felt] *n* fieltro *m*. **felt-tip pen** rotulador *m*.

female ['fiːmeil] *adj* hembra; femenino. *n* (*animal*) hembra *f*; (*person*) mujer *f*.

feminine ['feminin] *nm, adj* femenino. **femininity** *n* feminidad *f*. **feminism** *n* feminismo *m*. **feminist** *n*(*m*+*f*), *adj* feminista.

fence [fens] *n* cerca *f*, valla *f*. *v* cercar, vallar; (*sport*) practicar la esgrima. **fencing** *n* (*sport*) esgrima *f*.

fend [fend] *v* **fend for oneself** arreglárselas. **fend off** desviar.

fender ['fendə] *n* guardafuegos *m invar*; (*US: car*) guardabarros *m invar*.

fennel ['fenl] *n* hinojo *m*.

ferment [fə'ment; *n* 'fəment] *v* fermentar. *n* fermento *m*; agitación *f*. **fermentation** *n* fermentación *f*.

fern [fəːn] *n* helecho *m*.

ferocious [fə'rouʃəs] *adj* feroz. **ferocity** *n* ferocidad *f*.

ferret ['ferit] *n* hurón *m*. **ferret out** conseguir, descubrir.

ferry ['feri] *n* transbordador *m*. *v* transportar.

fertile ['fəːtail] *adj* fértil; (*person*) fecundo. **fertility** *n* fertilidad *f*; fecundidad *f*. **fertilization** *n* fertilización *f*; fecundación *f*. **fertilize** *v* abonar; fecundar. **fertilizer** *n* abono *m*.

fervent ['fəːvənt] *adj* ferviente. **fervour** *n* fervor *m*.

fester ['festə] *v* supurar; (*fig*) enconarse.

festival ['festəvəl] *n* fiesta *f*.

festoon [fə'stuːn] *v* festonear. *n* guirnalda *f*.

fetch [fetʃ] *v* (*bring*) traer; (*procure*) buscar; (*reach*) alcanzar. **fetching** *adj* atractivo.

fête [feit] *n* fiesta *f*. *v* festejar.

fetid ['fiːtid] *adj* fétido.

fetish ['fetiʃ] *n* fetiche *m*.

fetter ['fetə] *v* encadenar. **fetters** *pl n* grilletes *m pl*; (*fig*) trabas *f pl*.

feud [fjuːd] *n* enemistad hereditaria *f*. *v* pelear, reñir.

feudal ['fjuːdl] *adj* feudal. **feudalism** *n* feudalismo *m*.

fever ['fiːvə] *n* fiebre *f*. **feverish** *adj* febril.

few [fjuː] *adj* poco. *n* pocos, -as *pl*. **a few** algunos, unos, unos pocos. **quite a few** bastante. **fewer** *adj* menos. **the fewer the better** cuantos menos mejor. **fewest** *adj* menos.

fiancé [fi'onsei] *n* novio *m*. **fiancée** *n* novia *f*.

fiasco [fi'askou] *n* fiasco *m*.

fib [fib] *n* mentirijilla *f*. *v* decir una mentirijilla.

fibre ['faibə] *n* fibra *f*. **fibreglass** *n* fibra de vidrio *f*.

fickle ['fikl] *adj* inconstante, veleidoso.

fiction ['fikʃən] *n* (*stories*) novela *f*; (*invention*) ficción *f*. **fictional** *or* **fictitious** *adj* novelesco; ficticio.

fiddle ['fidl] *n* violín *m*; (*coll: trick*) trampa *f*. *v* tocar el violín; (*coll: cheat*) camelar; (*coll: falsify*) amañar. **fiddle with** juguetear con. **fiddling** *adj* trivial; fútil.

fidelity [fi'deləti] *n* fidelidad *f*.

fidget ['fidʒit] *v* agitar nerviosamente. **fidgety** *adj* nervioso, agitado.

field [fiːld] *n* campo *m*; (*fig*) esfera *f*. **field glasses** gemelos *m pl*. **field marshal** mariscal de campo *m*. **fieldwork** *n* trabajo en el terreno *m*.

fiend [fiːnd] *n* demonio *m*, diablo *m*; (*coll*) fanático, -a *m, f*. **fiendish** *adj* diabólico.

fierce [fiəs] *adj* feroz, fiero; (*person*) violento; (*heat*) intenso; (*battle*) encarnizado. **fierceness** *or* **ferocity** *n* ferocidad *f*; violencia *f*; furia *f*; intensidad *f*.

fiery ['faiəri] *adj* (*burning*) ardiente; (*flaming*) llameante; (*passionate*) apasionado; (*temper*) fogoso.

fifteen [fif'tim] *nm, adj* quince. **fifteenth** *n, adj* decimoquinto, -a.

fifth [fifθ] *n, adj* quinto, -a.

fifty ['fifti] *nm, adj* cincuenta. **go fifty-fifty** ir a medias. **fiftieth** *n, adj* quincuagésimo, -a. **fiftyish** *adj* cincuentón.

fig [fig] *n (fruit)* higo *m*; *(tree)* higuera *f*.

***fight** [fait] *v* luchar contra, combatir. *n* lucha *f*, pelea *f*.

figment ['figmənt] *n* invención *f*.

figure ['figə] *n (number)* número *m*, cifra *f*; *(price)* precio *m*; *(statue, design, personage)* figura *f*; *(human)* línea *f*. **figurehead** *n* mascarón de proa *m*; *(fig)* testaferro *m*. **figure skating** patinaje artístico *m*. *v (math)* poner en cifras; *(calculate)* calcular. **figure out** comprender; resolver.

filament ['filəmənt] *n* filamento *m*.

file¹ [fail] *n (folder)* carpeta *f*; *(card index)* fichero *m*; *(document holder)* archivador *m*; *(dossier)* expediente *m*. *v* archivar; *(a claim)* presentar. **file in/out** entrar/salir en fila. **file past** desfilar ante. **in single file** en fila de a uno. **filing** *n* clasificación *f*. **filing cabinet** archivo *m*. **filing clerk** archivero, -a *m, f*, archivista *m, f*.

file² [fail] *n (tool)* lima *f*. *v* limar. **filings** *pl n* limaduras *f pl*.

filial ['filiəl] *adj* filial.

fill [fil] *v* llenar; *(space, time)* ocupar; *(vacancy)* cubrir; *(tooth)* empastar; *(hole)* tapar; *(cookery)* rellenar; *(requirements)* satisfacer. **fill in** *(form)* rellenar. **fill up** llenar. **filling** *n* relleno *m*; empaste *m*. **filling station** estación de servicio *f*.

fillet ['filit] *n* filete *m*. *v* cortar en filetes.

film [film] *n (phot, cinema)* película *f*; *(layer)* capa *f*; *(eye)* nube *f*; *(mist, etc.)* velo *m*. **roll of film** rollo de película *m*. **filmgoer** *n* aficionado al cine *m*. **film star** astro de cine *m*, estrella de cine *f*.

filter ['filtə] *n* filtro *m*. *v* filtrar. **filtering** *n* filtración *f*. **filter-tipped** *adj* con filtro, emboquillado.

filth [filθ] *n* inmundicia *f*, suciedad *f*; *(fig)* obscenidades *f pl*. **filthy** *adj* asqueroso, inmundo; obsceno.

fin [fin] *n* aleta *f*.

final ['fainl] *adj (last)* último; decisivo; definitivo. *n* final *f*. **finalist** *n* finalista *m, f*. **finalize** *v* finalizar. **finally** *adv* finalmente.

finance [fai'nans] *n* finanzas *f pl*. *v*

finanzar. **financial** *adj* financiero. **financial year** año económico *m*. **financier** *n* financiero *m*.

finch [fintʃ] *n* pinzón *m*.

***find** [faind] *v* encontrar, hallar. **find out** averiguar; descubrir. *n* hallazgo *m*. **findings** *pl n* hallazgos *m pl*; resultados *m pl*.

fine¹ [fain] *adj* excelente; elegante; *(pleasant)* agradable; bueno; fino; delicado. **that's fine!** ¡muy bien! *adv* en trozos pequeños; fino; muy bien. **fine arts** bellas artes *f pl*. **finely** *adv (small)* finamente; *(well)* primorosamente. **finery** *n* galas *f pl*.

fine² [fain] *n* multa *f*. *v* multar.

finesse [fi'nes] *n* fineza *f*, delicadeza *f*; tacto *m*; *(bridge)* impás *m*.

finger ['fiŋgə] *n* dedo *m*. **little finger** meñique *m*. *v* tocar. **fingernail** *n* uña *f*. **fingerprint** *n* huella dactilar *f*. **fingertip** *n* punta del dedo *f*. **have at one's fingertips** saberse al dedillo.

finish ['finiʃ] *v* terminar, acabar; *(sport)* llegar. **finish off** rematar. *n* fin *m*, conclusión *f*; *(surface)* acabado *m*; *(sport)* llegada. **finishing line** meta *f*. **finishing touch** última mano *f*.

finite ['fainait] *adj* finito.

Finland ['finlənd] *n* Finlandia *f*. **Finn** *n* finlandés, -esa *m, f*. **Finnish** *nm, adj* finlandés.

fir [fəː] *n* abeto *m*. **fir cone** piña *f*.

fire ['faiə] *n* fuego *m*; *(uncontrolled)* incendio *m*; *(electric or gas)* estufa *f*. **be on fire** estar ardiendo. **catch fire** encenderse. **set on fire, set fire to** pegar fuego, incendiar. *v (with enthusiasm, etc.)* infundir (a); *(gun)* disparar; *(salute)* tirar; *(missile)* lanzar; *(sack)* echar. **fire on** hacer fuego sobre.

fire alarm *n* alarma de incendios *f*.

firearm ['faiəˌaːm] *n* arma de fuego *f*.

fire brigade *n* cuerpo de bomberos *m*.

fire door *n* puerta incombustible *f*.

fire drill *n* ejercicios para casos de incendio *m pl*.

fire engine *n* bomba de incendios *f*.

fire-escape *n* escalera de incendios *f*.

fire-extinguisher *n* extintor *m*.

firefly ['faiəflai] *n* luciérnaga *f*.

fire-guard *n* guardafuego *m*.

firelight ['faiəˌlait] *n* lumbre *f*.

fireman ['faiəmən] *n* bombero *m*.

fireplace ['faiə‚pleis] n chimenea f.
fireproof ['faiə‚pruːf] adj ininflamable, incombustible.
fireside ['faiə‚said] n hogar m.
fire station n parque de bomberos m.
firewood ['faiə‚wud] n leña f.
firework ['faiə‚wəːk] n fuego de artificio m.
firing squad n pelotón de ejecución m.
firm¹ [fəːm] adj firme, sólido; estable. **firmness** n firmeza f.
firm² [fəːm] n empresa f, firma f.
first¹ [fəːst] adj primero; básico; elemental. **first aid** primeros auxilios m pl. **first-class** adj de primera clase. **first cousin** primo hermano m. **first edition** edición príncipe m. **first floor** primer piso m. **first name** nombre de pila m. **first-rate** adj de primera calidad. **in the first place** en primer lugar.
first² [fəːst] adv antes, primero. **first and foremost** antes que nada. **first and last** en todos los aspectos. **travel first** viajar en primera. **you go first** usted primero.
first³ [fəːst] n primero, -a m, f; sobresaliente m. **at first** al principio. **be the first to** ser el primero en. **get a first** sacar sobresaliente.
fiscal ['fiskəl] adj fiscal.
fish [fiʃ] n (food) pescado m; (in water) pez m. **fish and chips** pescado frito con patatas fritas. v pescar. **fishy** adj (coll) sospechoso.
fishbone ['fiʃ‚boun] n espina f.
fish-bowl n pecera f.
fisherman ['fiʃəmən] n pescador m.
fish fingers n filete de pescado empanado m.
fish hook n anzuelo m.
fishing ['fiʃiŋ] n pesca f. **fishing line** sedal m. **fishing net** red de pesca f. **fishing rod** caña de pescar f. **fishing tackle** aparejo de pescar m. **go fishing** ir de pesca.
fish market n mercado de pescado.
fishmonger ['fiʃ‚mʌŋgə] n pescadero m. **fishmonger's** n pescadería f.
fission ['fiʃən] n fisión f, escisión f.
fissure ['fiʃə] n grieta f.
fist [fist] n puño m. **fistful** n puñado m.
fit¹ [fit] adj conveniente; apto; adecuado; (qualified) capacitado; (competent) capaz; (worthy) digno; (healthy) sano. **not fit to eat** no se puede comer. **see fit** juzgar conveniente. v (try on) probar; (qualify) capacitar; (tally with) cuadrar

con; adaptar; preparar; unir; (supply with) equipar con; (clothes) sentar bien a; (tailor) entallar. **fitness** n conveniencia f; salud f; aptitud f. **fitter** n (tailor) probador, -a m, f; (tech) ajustador m. **fitting** adj oportuno; digno; apropiado; propio. **fitting room** cuarto de pruebas m. **fittings** pl n muebles m pl; accesorios m pl.
fit² [fit] n (med) ataque m.
five [faiv] nm, adj cinco.
fix [fiks] v fijar; sujetar; (decide) establecer; (date) señalar; (hopes) poner; (coll: put right) arreglar. n aprieto m; (coll) una dosis de froga f. **fixation** n obsesión f. **fixed** adj fijo; (coll: rigged) amañado. **fixture** n instalación f; (sport) partido m; (coll) permanencia f.
fizz [fiz] n burbujeo m; (coll) gaseosa f. v burbujear.
flabbergasted ['flabə‚gaːstid] adj pasmado.
flabby ['flabi] adj fláccido; (spineless) blandengue. **flabbiness** n flaccidez f; blandura f.
flag¹ [flag] n bandera f; (stone) baldosa f. **flag down** detener haciendo señales. **flagpole** n asta de bandera f. **flagship** n buque insignia m.
flag² [flag] v (weaken) flaquear; (interest) decaer. **flagging** adj flojo; desmadejado.
flagon ['flagən] n (jug) jarra f; (bottle) botella (de dos litros) f.
flagrant ['fleigrənt] adj flagrante; escandaloso.
flair [fleə] n don m; instinto m; talento m.
flake [fleik] n (snow) copo m; (soap) escama f; (paint) desconchón m. v caer en copos; desconchar. **flaky** adj escamoso. **flaky pastry** hojaldre m.
flamboyant [flam‚bɔiənt] adj llamativo. **flamboyance** n extravagancia f.
flame [fleim] n llama f. **burst into flames** incendiarse. v llamear. **flammable** adj inflamable.
flamingo [flə'miŋgou] n flamenco m.
flan [flan] n flan m.
flank [flaŋk] n (animal) ijada f; (person) costado m; (mil) flanco m. v bordear.
flannel ['flanl] n (fabric) franela f; (face cloth) pañito para lavarse la cara m. **flannels** pl n pantalones de franela m pl.
flap [flap] v (shake) sacudir; (arms) agitar; (wings) batir. n (pocket) carterita f; (envelope, etc.) solapa f; (table) ala

abatible *f*; (*coat*) faldón *m*; (*aero*) alerón *m*; (*coll*) crisis *f*.

flare [fleə] *n* (*blaze*) llamarada *f*; (*signal*) cohete de señales *m*; (*widening*) ensanchamiento *m*. *v* llamear; ensanchar; (*clothes*) acampanar. **flare up** (*anger*) ponerse furioso.

flash [flaʃ] *n* destello *m*; (*sparkle*) centelleo *m*; (*phot*) flash *m*; (*moment*) instante *m*; (*inspiration*) ráfaga *f*; (*genius*) rasgo *m*; (*hope*) resquicio *m*. **flashback** *n* escena retrospectiva *f*. **flash bulb** bombilla de magnesio *f*. **flashlight** *n* linterna *f*. *v* despedir; lanzar; encender; destellar; centellear. **flashing** *adj* intermitente.

flask [flɑɪsk] *n* frasco *m*; (*vacuum*) termo *m*.

flat[1] [flat] *adj* plano, llano, chato; horizontal; (*fig*) categórico; monótono; (*boring*) pesado; (*rate*) fijo; (*below pitch*) desafinado; (*tyre*) desinflado; (*battery*) descargado; (*horse racing*) sin obstáculos. **flat beer** cerveza muerta *f*. **flat-footed** *adj* de pies planos. **be flat broke** estar sin blanca. **go flat out** ir a todo gas. **flatly** *adv* categóricamente; completamente. *n* (*music*) bemol *m*; (*land*) llano *m*; (*tyre*) pinchazo *m*. **flatten** *v* (*make flat*) aplanar; (*crush*) aplastar; (*smooth*) alisar.

flat[2] [flat] *n* apartamento *m*. **flatlet** *n* piso pequeño *m*.

flatter ['flatə] *v* adular, halagar; favorecer. **flatterer** *n* adulador, -a *m*, *f*. **flattering** *adj* (*words*) halagüeño; (*person*) halagador; (*clothes*) favorecedor. **flattery** *n* halago *m*, adulación *f*.

flatulence ['flatjuləns] *n* flatulencia *f*.

flaunt [flɔɪnt] *v* ostentar. **flaunt oneself** pavonearse.

flautist ['flɔɪtist] *n* flautista *m*, *f*.

flavour ['fleivə] *n* sabor *m*, gusto *m*; (*cookery*) sazón *m*, sainete *m*. *v* saborear; condimentar. **flavouring** *n* condimento *m*, sainete *m*.

flaw [flɔɪ] *n* defecto *m*; (*error*) fallo *m*. *v* (*crack*) agrietar; (*spoil*) estropear. **flawed** *adj* falto; imperfecto. **flawless** *adj* sin tacha; perfecto.

flax [flaks] *n* lino *m*. **flaxen** *adj* de lino; (*hair*) rubio.

flea [fliː] *n* pulga *f*. **fleabite** *n* picadura de pulga *f*.

fleck [flek] *n* (*speck*) mota *f*; (*colour*) mancha *f*; (*dust*) partícula *f*. *v* motear; (*paint*) salpicar.

fled [fled] *V* **flee**.

***flee** [fliː] *v* evitar; escapar de.

fleece [fliːs] *n* (*wool*) lana *f*; (*sheared wool*) velón *m*. *v* (*coll*) pelar. **fleecy** *adj* (*woolly*) lanoso.

fleet [fliːt] *n* flota *f*; (*navy*) armada *f*. *adj* veloz. **fleeting** *adj* fugaz, breve.

Flemish ['flemiʃ] *nm*, *adj* flamenco. **Fleming** *n* flamenco, -a *m*, *f*.

flesh [fleʃ] *n* carne *f*. **flesh-coloured** *adj* de color carne. **flesh-eating** *adj* carnívoro. **flesh wound** herida superficial *f*. **in the flesh** en carne y hueso. **fleshy** *adj* gordo.

flew [fluː] *V* **fly**.

flex [fleks] *n* flexible *m*. *v* doblar. **flexibility** *n* flexibilidad *f*. **flexible** *adj* (*pliable*) flexible; (*fig*) elástico.

flick [flik] *v* dar un golpecito a. **flick through** (*book*) hojear. *n* (*whip*) latigazo suave *m*; (*light stroke*) golpecito *m*; (*duster*) pasada *f*; (*wrist*) movimiento rápido *m*. **the flicks** (*coll*) el cine *m*.

flicker ['flikə] *v* (*light*) parpadear; (*flames*) vacilar. *n* parpadeo *m*; (*flame*) llama vacilante *f*; (*hope, etc.*) requicio *m*.

flight[1] [flait] *n* (*birds*) bandada *f*; (*aircraft*) escuadrilla *f*; (*act of flying*) vuelo *m*; (*distance flown*) recorrido *m*. **flight crew** tripulación *f*. **flight deck** cubierta de aterrizaje *f*. **flight of stairs** tramo de escalera *m*. **flight path** trayectoria de vuelo *f*. **in flight** en vuelo. **flightiness** *n* ligereza *f*. **flightless** *adj* incapacitado para volar. **flighty** *adj* volátil; caprichoso.

flight[2] [flait] *n* (*escape*) huida *f*, fuga *f*.

flimsy ['flimzi] *adj* (*lacking substance*) poco sólido; (*fragile*) frágil; (*weak*) débil; (*paper*) fino; (*cloth*) ligero; (*excuse*) flojo. **flimsiness** *n* fragilidad *f*; debilidad *f*; finura *f*; ligereza *f*.

flinch [flintʃ] *v* (*draw back*) retroceder; (*hesitate*) vacilar; (*muscular movement*) encogerse.

***fling** [fliŋ] *v* arrojar, tirar; (*dash*) precipitarse. **fling aside** dejar de lado. *n* (*throw*) lanzamiento *m*; (*wild tune*) juerga *f*.

flint [flint] *n* pedernal *m*; (*of lighter*) piedra de mechero *f*.

flip [flip] *v* (*flick*) dar un capirotazo. (*coin*) echar a cara o cruz. *n* capirotazo *m*. **flipper** *n* aleta *f*.

flippant ['flipənt] *adj* frívolo. **flippancy** *n* ligereza *f*.

flirt [fləːt] *n* (*female*) coqueta *f*; (*male*) mariposón *m*. *v* flirtear, coquetear. **flirtation** *n* coqueteo *m*.

flit [flit] *v* revolotear.

float [flout] *v* flotar; (*support*) hacer flotar. *n* flotador *m*; (*angling*) corcho *m*; (*carnival*) carroza *f*.

flock[1] [flok] *n* (*sheep, goats*) rebaño *m*; (*birds*) bandada *f*; (*people*) muchedumbre *f*. *v* congregarse.

flock[2] [flok] *n* (*filling*) borra *f*.

flog [flog] *v* (*beat*) azotar; (*coll: sell*) vender. **flogging** *n* paliza *f*; flagelación *f*.

flood [flʌd] *v* inundar; irrigar; (*overflow*) desbordar. *n* inundación *f*; flujo *m*; diluvio *m*. **in flood** crecido.

***floodlight** ['flʌdlait] *n* foco *m*. *v* iluminar con focos. **floodlighting** *n* iluminación con focos *f*.

floor [floː] *n* suelo *m*, piso *m*; (*ocean*) fondo *m*; (*dance*) pista *f*. **first floor** primer piso *m*. **ground floor** planta baja *f*. **take the floor** (*speak*) tomar la palabra. *v* (*knock down*) echar al suelo. **floorboard** *n* tabla del suelo *f*. **floorcloth** *n* trapo *m*. **flooring** *n* solado *m*. **floor polish** cera para el suelo *f*. **floor show** espectáculo de cabaret *m*. **floorwalker** *n* supervisor de división *m*.

flop [flop] *v* desplomarse; (*fail*) fracasar. *n* (*coll*) fracaso *m*. **floppy** *adj* flojo; colgante.

flora ['floːrə] *n* flora *f*.

florist ['florist] *n* florista *m*, *f*. **florist's shop** florería *f*.

flounce[1] [flauns] *v* **flounce in/out** entrar/salir enfadado. *n* movimiento brusco *m*.

flounce[2] [flauns] *n* (*of dress*) volante *m*.

flounder ['flaundə] *v* forcejear; confundirse.

flour ['flauə] *n* harina *f*. *v* enharinar. **flour mill** molino harinero *m*. **floury** *adj* (*covered with flour*) enharinado; (*like flour*) harinoso.

flourish ['flʌriʃ] *v* (*prosper*) florecer; (*wave*) agitar; (*brandish*) esgrimir. *n* ostentación *f*; (*gesture*) ademán *m*; (*writing*) rasgo *m*. **flourishing** *adj* floreciente.

flout [flaut] *v* burlarse de.

flow [flou] *v* (*liquid*) fluir; (*tears*) correr; (*blood in the body*) circular; (*blood from the body*) derramarse; (*tide*) subir. **flow away** irse. **flow from** salir de. **flow in/out** entrar/salir a raudales. **flow into**

desembocar. *n* circulación *f*; movimiento *m*. **flow chart** organigrama *m*. **flowing** *adj* (*river*) fluente; (*style*) fluido; (*hair*) suelto; (*beard*) largo.

flower ['flauə] *n* flor *f*. **flower arrangement** ramillete *m*. **flower bed** arriate *m*. **flowerpot** *n* maceta *f*. **flower shop** florería *f*. **flower show** exposición de flores *f*. *v* florecer. **flowering** *adj* floreciente; *n* florecimiento *m*. **flowery** *adj* florido.

flown [floun] *V* **fly**.

flu [fluː] *n* gripe *f*.

fluctuate ['flʌktjueit] *v* fluctuar; vacilar. **fluctuation** *n* fluctuación *f*.

flue [fluː] *n* chimenea *f*; conducto de humo *m*.

fluent ['fluənt] *adj* (*language*) bueno; (*writing*) fluido. **fluency** *n* facilidad *f*; dominio *m*. **fluently** *adv* (*speech*) con soltura; (*writing*) con fluidez.

fluff [flʌf] *n* pelusa *f*; mota *f*; masa esponjosa *f*. **fluffy** *adj* (*pillow, cushion*) mullido; (*downy*) velloso; (*cloth*) que tiene pelusa.

fluid ['fluid] *nm, adj* fluido.

fluke [fluːk] *n* chiripa *f*. **fluky** *adj* de suerte.

flung [flʌŋ] *V* **fling**.

fluorescent [fluə'resnt] *adj* fluorescente. **fluorescence** *n* fluorescencia *f*.

fluoride ['fluəraid] *n* fluoruro *m*. **fluoridation** *n* fluoración *f*.

flurry ['flʌri] *n* (*excitement*) agitación *f*; (*snow*) borrasca *f*; (*rain*) chaparrón *m*; (*wind*) ráfaga *f*.

flush[1] [flʌʃ] *n* (*blush*) rubor *m*; (*fever*) sofoco *m*; (*lavatory*) cisterna *f*. *v* ruborizarse; tener sofocos; (*light*) resplandecer. **flush the toilet** tirar de la cadena. **flushed** *adj* rebosante.

flush[2] [flʌʃ] *adj* (*abundant*) copioso; (*lavish*) liberal; (*coll: well off*) adinerado. **flush with** (*level*) a nivel con.

fluster ['flʌstə] *v* poner nervioso. *n* agitación *f*.

flute [fluːt] *n* flauta *f*.

flutter ['flʌtə] *v* (*leaves, etc.*) revolotear; (*wings*) batir; (*curtains, flags*) ondular; (*heart*) palpitar; (*flap*) agitar. *n* ondulación *f*; (*wings*) aleteo *m*; agitación *f*; (*eyelids*) parpadeo *m*; palpitación *f*.

flux [flʌks] *n* (*flow*) flujo *m*; (*changes*) cambios frecuentes *m pl*. **be in a state of flux** estar siempre cambiando.

fly¹ [flai] v volar; (*escape*) huir; (*time*) pasar volando; (*kite*) echar a volar; (*aircraft*) pilotar; (*flag*) izar, enarbolar; (*go across*) atravesar; (*mileage*) recorrer. **fly away** emprender el vuelo. **fly over** sobrevolar. **fly past** desfilar. **flies** pl n (*trousers*) bragueta f.

fly² [flai] n mosca f.

fly-blown adj cochambroso.

fly-fishing n pesca con moscas f.

flying ['flaiiŋ] adj volador; volante. n aviación f.

flying colours pl n éxito rotundo m.

flying field n campo de aviación m.

flying fish n pez volador m.

flying saucer n platillo volante m.

flying squirrel n ardilla volante f.

flying start n salida lanzada f; (*fig*) principio feliz m.

flyleaf ['flailiːf] n guarda f.

flyover ['flai,ouvə] n paso elevado m.

fly-paper n papel matamoscas m.

fly swatter n matamoscas m invar.

flyweight ['flaiweit] n peso mosca m.

flywheel ['flaiwiːl] n volante m.

foal [foul] n potro, -a m, f. v parir.

foam [foum] n espuma f. v espumar; (*animal*) espumajear. **foam rubber** gomespuma f. **foaming** adj espumoso.

focal ['foukəl] adj focal. **focal point** punto focal.

focus ['foukəs] n foco m. **in focus** enfocado. **out of focus** fuera de foco. v enfocar; concentrar.

fodder ['fodə] n forraje m.

foe [fou] n enemigo, -a m, f.

foetus ['fiːtəs] n feto m. **foetal** adj fetal.

fog [fog] n niebla f, bruma f. **fogbound** adj (*foggy*) cubierto de niebla; (*immobilized*) detenido por la niebla. **foghorn** n sirena de niebla f. **foglamp** or **foglight** (*mot*) faro antiniebla m. **fogginess** n nebulosidad f. **foggy** adj nebuloso, brumoso.

foible ['foibl] n extravagancia f; (*fad*) manía f.

foil¹ [foil] v frustrar.

foil² [foil] n hoja fina de metal f; (*fig*) contraste m.

foil³ [foil] n (*fencing*) florete m.

foist [foist] v colar; meter.

fold¹ [fould] n (*crease*) pliegue m; (*wrinkle*) arruga f. v doblar, plegar; (*surround*) envolver; (*coll: close down*) liquidarse. **fold one's arms** cruzar los brazos. **folder**

n carpeta f. **folding** adj plegable. **folding door** puerta de fuelle f.

fold² [fould] n (*sheep*) redil m; (*religion*) grey f.

foliage ['fouliidʒ] n follaje m.

folk [fouk] pl n gente f sing; pueblo m. **folks** pl n (*coll*) familia f sing. **folk art** arte popular. **folk dance** baile folklórico m. **folklore** n folklore m. **folk music** música popular f. **folk singer** cantante de canciones populares. **folk song** canción popular f.

follicle ['folikl] n folículo m.

follow ['folou] v seguir; (*pursue*) perseguir; (*practise*) ejercer; (*ensue*) resultar. **follow up** investigar sobre; reforzar. **follower** n seguidor, -a m, f; discípulo m; aficionado, -a m, f. **following** adj siguiente. n partidarios m pl.

folly ['foli] n locura f.

fond [fond] adj cariñoso; indulgente. **be fond of** tenerle cariño a. **fondly** adj cariñosamente. **fondness** n cariño m.

fondle ['fondl] v acariciar; mimar.

font [font] n (*baptismal*) pila f; (*printing*) fundición f.

food [fuːd] n comida f, alimento m; comestibles m pl. **food and drink** comida y bebida f. **food poisoning** intoxicación alimenticia f. **food shop** tienda de comestibles f. **foodstuff** n producto alimenticio m.

fool [fuːl] n tonto, -a m, f; bobo, -a m, f; idiota m, f; (*jester*) bufón m. **foolproof** adj infalible. v (*deceive*) engañar; (*joke*) bromear. **fool about** or **around** juguetear. **foolhardy** adj temerario. **foolhardiness** n temeridad f. **foolish** adj insensato; tonto. **foolishly** adv neciamente. **foolishness** n insensatez f; tontería f.

foolscap ['fuːlskap] n papel de barba m.

foot [fut] n, pl feet pie m; (*animal*) pata f. **from head to foot** de pies a cabeza. **on foot** a pie. **get cold feet** tener miedo.

football ['fut,boːl] n fútbol m; (*ball*) pelota f. **football pools** pl n quinielas f pl.

foot brake n freno de pedal m.

footbridge ['fut,bridʒ] n pasarela f.

foothills ['futhilz] pl n estribaciones f pl.

foothold ['fut,hould] n punto de apoyo para el pie m; (*fig*) posición f.

footing ['futiŋ] n pie m, equilibrio m; condición f; posición f. **on an equal footing** en un pie de igual.

footlights ['fut,laits] pl n candilejas f pl.

footloose ['futluːs] adj libre.

footnote ['fut,nout] n nota f.

footpath ['fut,paːθ] n senda f; (pavement) acera f.

footprint ['fut,print] n pisada f.

footstep ['fut,step] n paso m.

for [foː] prep para; por; de; (time) desde; durante; (in favour of) en favor de; (in honour of) en honor de; (in place of) en lugar de; (as regards) en cuanto a; (against) contra; (in order that) para que. conj pues, puesto que, ya que.

forage ['foridʒ] v forrajear; (fig: seek) buscar. n forraje m.

*****forbear** [fəˈbeə] v contenerse; abstenerse. **forbearance** n abstención f; indulgencia f; paciencia f.

*****forbid** [fəˈbid] v prohibir; (prevent) impedir. **forbidding** adj impresionante; inhóspito; severo; (threatening) amenazador.

force [foːs] n fuerza f; (mil) cuerpo m. in force en vigor. **sales force** vendedores m pl. **join forces** unirse. v forzar; obligar; (tech) inyectar. **be forced to** verse obligado a. **forceful** adj fuerte; contundente.

forceps ['foːseps] pl n fórceps m sing.

ford [foːd] n vado m. v vadear.

fore [foː] adj delantero; anterior. adv delante. n (naut) proa f. **come to the fore** empezar a destacar. interj (golf) ¡cuidado!

forearm ['foːraim] n antebrazo m. v prevenir.

forebears ['foːbeəz] pl n antepasados m pl.

foreboding [foːˈboudiŋ] n presentimiento m.

*****forecast** ['foːkaist] n previsión f; pronóstico m; plan m. v pronosticar. **weather forecast** pronóstico meteorológico m.

forecourt ['foːkoit] n antepatio m.

forefather ['foːfaiðə] n antepasado m.

forefinger ['foːfiŋgə] n dedo índice m.

forefront ['foːfrʌnt] n delantera f; sitio de mayor importancia m.

foregone ['foːgon] adj conocido de antemano. **foregone conclusion** conclusión inevitable f.

foreground ['foːgraund] n primer plano m; primer término m.

forehand ['foːhand] n (tennis) golpe derecho m.

forehead ['forid] n frente f.

foreign ['forən] adj extranjero; ajeno. **foreign affairs** asuntos exteriores m pl. **foreign trade** comercio exterior m. **foreign exchange** cambio exterior m. **foreign legion** legión extranjera f. **foreigner** n extranjero, -a m, f.

foreleg ['foːleg] n pata delantera f.

foreman ['foːmən] n capataz m.

foremost ['foːmoust] adj delantero; principal. **first and foremost** ante todo.

forename ['foːneim] n nombre de pila m.

forensic [fəˈrensik] adj forense. **forensic medicine** medicina legal f.

forerunner ['foːrʌnə] n precursor, -a m, f; (herald) anunciador, -a m, f.

*****foresee** [foːˈsiː] v prever. **foreseeable** adj previsible.

foreshadow [foːˈʃadou] v presagiar; prefigurar.

foresight ['foːsait] n previsión f.

foreskin ['foːskin] n prepucio m.

forest ['forist] n selva f; bosque m. **forester** n guardabosque m. **forestry** n silvicultura f. **Forestry Commission** administración de montes f.

forestall [foːˈstoil] v prevenir; impedir; anticiparse a.

foretaste ['foːteist] n anticipación f.

*****foretell** [foːˈtel] v predecir; presagiar.

forethought ['foːθoit] n premeditación f.

forever [foːˈevə] adv siempre, para siempre. **forever more** por siempre jamás.

forewarn [foːˈwoin] v avisar, advertir. **forewarning** n aviso m, advertencia f.

foreword ['foːwoid] n prefacio m; prólogo m.

forfeit ['foːfit] v (right) perder; (property) comisar.

forge¹ [foːdʒ] v (counterfeit) falsificar; (metal) fraguar. n fragua f. **forger** n falsificador m; (metal) herrero m. **forgery** n falsificación f; (things forged) documento falsificado m; moneda falsificada f.

forge² [foːdʒ] v **forge ahead** hacer grandes progresos.

*****forget** [fəˈget] v olvidar, olvidarse de. **forget-me-not** n nomeolvides f. **forgetful** adj olvidadizo; descuidado. **forgetfulness** n olvido m; descuido m.

*****forgive** [fəˈgiv] v perdonar; dispensar. **forgiveness** n perdón m; remisión f. **forgiving** adj indulgente; clemente.

*****forgo** [foːˈgou] v abstenerse; renunciar.

fork [fɔːk] n (*cutlery*) tenedor m; (*gardening*) horca f; (*tree*) horcadura f; (*road*) bifurcación f; (*river*) horcajo m. **tuning fork** diapasón m. v bifurcarse. **forked** adj bifurcado.

forlorn [fə'lɔːn] adj desamparado; triste.

form [fɔːm] n (*shape*) forma f; (*figure*) figura f; (*type*) tipo m; (*document*) formulario m; (*school year*) curso m. v (*make*) hacer; (*model*) modelar; (*habit*) crear; (*constitute*) constituir; (*put together*) formar. **form a queue** ponerse en cola. **formation** n formación f. **formative** adj de formación, formativo.

formal ['fɔːməl] adj formal; solemne; (*person*) formalista; ceremonioso; de cortesía; en debida forma. **formality** n (*requirement*) formalidad f; ceremonia f; rigidez f.

format ['fɔːmat] n formato m.

former ['fɔːmə] adj (*previous*) anterior; (*ex-*) antiguo, pasado. pron ése, ésa, aquél, equélla, el primero, la primera. **formerly** adv anteriormente; antiguamente.

formidable ['fɔːmidəbl] adj formidable.

formula ['fɔːmjulə] n, pl -ae fórmula f.

formulate ['fɔːmjuleit] v formular. **formulation** n formulación f.

***forsake** [fə'seik] v abandonar.

fort [fɔːt] n fuerte m, fortaleza f.

forte ['fɔːtei] n fuerte m.

forth [fɔːθ] adv en adelante. **and so forth** y así sucesivamente. **forthcoming** adj próximo; (*approaching*) venidero; (*person*) abierto. **forthright** adj franco. **forthwith** adv en seguida; en el acto.

fortify ['fɔːtifai] v (*health, moral strength*) fortalecer; (*town*) fortificar; (*wine*) encabezar; (*argument*) reforzar. **fortification** n fortalecimiento m; fortificación f; reforzamiento m.

fortitude ['fɔːtitjuːd] n fortaleza f; firmeza f.

fortnight ['fɔːtnait] n quincena f. **fortnightly** adj quincenal. adv quincenalmente.

fortress ['fɔːtris] n fortaleza f.

fortuitous [fə'tjuːitəs] adj, adv casual.

fortunate ['fɔːtʃənət] adj afortunado; oportuno. **fortunately** adv afortunadamente.

fortune ['fɔːtʃən] n (*fate*) fortuna f; (*luck*) suerte f. **cost a fortune** costar un dineral. **stroke of fortune** golpe de suerte m. **fortune-teller** n adivino, -a m, f.

forty ['fɔːti] nm, adj cuarenta. **fortieth** nm, adj cuarentavo.

forum ['fɔːrəm] n foro m; (*meeting*) tribuna f.

forward ['fɔːwəd] adj (*front*) delantero; (*movement*) hacia adelante; (*progressive*) avanzado; (*impertinent*) impertinente. v (*send*) expedir; (*promote*) promover. **please forward** remítase al destinario. n (*football*) delantero m. **forwards** adv adelante.

fossil ['fɒsl] nm, adj fósil. **fossilized** adj fosilizado.

foster ['fɒstə] v (*child*) criar; (*idea*) abrigar; (*project*) patrocinar; (*favour*) favorecer. adj adoptivo.

fought [fɔːt] V **fight**.

foul [faul] adj asqueroso; (*dirty*) sucio; (*air*) viciado; (*language*) grosero; (*smell*) fétido. **foul play** jugada sucia f. n falta f. v ensuciar; (*reputation*) manchar; (*sport*) cometer una falta.

found[1] [faund] V **find**.

found[2] [faund] v fundar; construir; (*opinion*) fundamentar. **foundation** n (*establishment*) fundación f; (*building*) cimientos m pl; (*fig*) fundamento m. **founder** n fundador, -a m, f.

founder ['faundə] v (*ship*) hundirse; (*fall*) derrumbarse.

foundry ['faundri] n fundición f.

fountain ['fauntin] n fuente f. **fountainhead** n manantial m. **fountain pen** pluma estilográfica f.

four [fɔː] nm, adj cuatro. **fourth** m, adj cuarto, -a m, f.

fourteen [fɔː'tiːn] nm, adj catorce. **fourteenth** n, adj decimocuarto, -a m, f.

fowl [faul] n aves de corral f pl; (*cock*) gallo m; (*hen*) gallina f; (*chicken*) pollo m.

fox [fɒks] n zorro, -a m, f. v (*baffle*) desconcertar; (*trick*) engañar. **foxglove** n digital f. **foxhound** n perro raposero m. **foxhunting** n caza de zorros f.

foyer ['fɔiei] n foyer m.

fraction ['frakʃən] n fracción f; pequeña parte f. **fractional** adj fraccionario.

fracture ['fraktʃə] n fractura f. v fracturarse.

fragile ['fradʒail] adj frágil. **fragility** n fragilidad f.

fragment ['fragmənt] n fragmento m. v fragmentar.

fragrant ['freigrənt] adj fragante. fragrance n fragancia f.

frail [freil] adj frágil; débil; delicado. frailty n fragilidad f; debilidad f; delicadez f.

frame [freim] n (building) armazón f; (picture) marco m; (bicycle) cuadro m; (spectacles) montura f; (film) imagen f. frame of mind estado de ánimo m. v (enclose) enmarcar; (devise) elaborar; (shape) formar; hacer la armazón de.

France [frains] n Francia f.

franchise ['frantʃaiz] n derecho de voto m.

frank [frank] adj franco; abierto. frankness n franqueza f.

frankfurter ['frankfəːtə] n salchicha alemana f.

frantic ['frantik] adj frenético; loco.

fraternal [frə'təːnl] adj fraternal. fraternity n (brotherhood) fraternidad f; (association) asociación f; (religious) hermandad f. fraternize v fraternizar.

fraud [froːd] n (law) fraude m; (deception) engaño m; (person) impostor m. fraudulent adj fraudulento.

fraught [froːt] adj fraught with cargado de.

fray¹ [frei] v raer, desgastar.

fray² [frei] n (brawl) riña f; (fight) combate m.

freak [friːk] n capricho m; fantasía f; monstruosidad f. adj imprevisto; extraño.

freckle ['frekl] n peca f. freckled adj pecoso.

free [friː] adj libre; gratis; (loose) suelto; generoso; sincero; (manner) desenvuelto. free and easy adj poco ceremonioso.

freedom ['friːdəm] n libertad f; soltura f.

free-for-all n refriega f.

freehand ['friːhand] adj a pulso.

freehold ['friːhould] n propiedad absoluta f.

freelance ['friːlains] n persona que trabaja independientemente f.

freely ['friːli] adj libremente; voluntariamente; gratuitamente.

freemason ['friːmeisn] n francmasón. freemasonry n francmasonería f.

freesia ['friːziə] n fresia f.

freestyle ['friːstail] n estilo libre m.

free trade n librecambio m.

free will n libre albedrío m.

*****freeze** [friːz] v (preserve) congelar; (chill) refrigerar; (from cold) helarse; (prices, etc.) bloquear; (turn to ice) helar; (stand still) quedarse inmóvil. n helada f; bloqueo m. freezer n congelador m. freezing adj glacial. freezing point punto de congelación.

freight [freit] n (load) carga f; (transportation) transporte m; (by ship, plane) flete m; (other) mercancías f pl. freight train tren de mercancías m. freighter n (ship) buque de carga m; (aircraft) avión de carga m.

French [frentʃ] nm, adj francés. the French los franceses. French bean judía verde f. French horn trompa de llaves f. French polish barniz de muebles m. French window puerta ventana f.

frenzy ['frenzi] n frenesí m, delirio m. frenzied adj frenético.

frequent ['friːkwənt; v fri'kwent] adj frecuente; (usual) común. v frecuentar. frequency n frecuencia f. frequently adv frecuentemente.

fresco ['freskou] n fresco m.

fresh [freʃ] adj fresco; (bread) tierno; (water) dulce; (air) puro; (complexion) de buen color; (new) nuevo. adv recientemente. freshwater adj (fish) de aqua dulce. freshen up refrescarse. freshness n frescura f; novedad f.

fret¹ [fret] v irritar; (complain) quejarse. fretful adj mal humorado; (upset) apenado.

fret² [fret] n (music) traste m. v adornar con calados. fretsaw n sierra de calar f. fretwork n calado m.

friar ['fraiə] n fraile m, monje m. friary n monasterio m.

friction ['frikʃən] n fricción f.

Friday ['fraidei] n viernes m. Good Friday Viernes Santo m.

fridge [fridʒ] n (coll) nevera f.

fried [fraid] adj frito.

friend [frend] n amigo, -a m, f. make friends with hacerse amigo de. the best of friends muy amigos. friendliness n simpatía f. friendly adj simpático; amistoso. friendship n amistad f.

frieze [friːz] n friso m.

frigate ['frigit] n fragata f.

fright [frait] n susto m; miedo m; terror m. frighten v asustar. be frightened tener

miedo. **frightening** *adj* espantoso. **frightful** *adj* horrible; (*fig*) tremendo.

frigid ['fridʒid] *adj* glacial; (*manner*) frío;
(*med*) frígido. **frigidity** *n* frialdad *f*; (*med*)
frigidez *f*.

frill [fril] *n* (*shirt*) pechera *f*; (*fluting*)
encañonado *m*; (*flared edge*) volante *m*;
(*ruff*) gorguera *f*. **frilly** *adj* con volantes.

fringe [frindʒ] *n* franja *f*; (*edge*) borde *m*.
fringe benefits beneficios complementa-
rios *m pl*. *v* franjar.

frisk [frisk] *v* brincar; (*coll: search*)
cachear. **friskiness** *n* viveza *f*. **frisky** *adj*
juguetón.

fritter[1] ['fritə] *v* **fritter away** malgastar.
fritter[2] ['fritə] *n* (*cookery*) buñuelo *m*.

frivolity [fri'voliti] *n* frivolidad *f*. **frivolous**
adj frívolo; trivial.

frizz [friz] *v* (*hair*) rizar. **frizzy** *adj* crespo.

fro [frou] *adv* **to and fro** de un lado a
otro. **go to and fro** ir y venir.

frock [frok] *n* vestido *m*.

frog [frog] *n* rana *f*. **frogman** *n* hombre
rana *m*. **frogs' legs** ancas de rana *f pl*.
have a frog in one's throat tener carras-
pera.

frolic ['frolik] *n* juego *m*; diversión *f*. *v*
juguetar; divertirse. **frolicsome** *adj*
juguetón.

from [from] *prep* de; desde; (*made from*)
con; (*steal, buy, take, etc.*) a; (*drink,
learn*) en; (*speak, act*) por; (*according to*)
según.

front [frʌnt] *n* (*building*) fachada *f*; (*shop*)
escaparate *m*; parte delantera *f*;
principio *m*; (*face*) cara *f*; (*weather*)
frente *m*. **in front of** delante de. *adj*
delantero; principal; primero.

frontier ['frʌntiə] *n* frontera *f*. *adj* fronter-
izo.

frost [frost] *n* escarcha *f*; helada *f*. **frost-
bite** *n* congelación *f*. **frostbitten** *adj* congelado. *v* cubrir de escarcha. **frosted
glass** vidrio deslustrado *m*. **frosty** *adj*
escarchado; helado.

froth [froθ] *n* espuma *f*; (*fig*) frivolidad *f*.
v espumar. **frothy** *adj* espumoso; frívolo.

frown [fraun] *n* ceño *m*. *v* fruncir el
entrecejo. **frown on** *or* **upon** desaprobar.
frowning *adj* severo; amenazador.

froze [frouz] *V* **freeze**.

frozen ['frouzn] *adj* congelado, helado.
frozen food comestibles congelados *m pl*.

frugal ['fruːgəl] *adj* frugal; sobrio. **frugality** *n* frugalidad *f*; sobriedad *f*.

fruit [fruːt] *n* (*on tree*) fruto *m*, (*as food*)
fruta *f*. **fruit cake** pastel de fruta *m*. **fruit
machine** máquina tragaperras *f*. **fruit salad** ensalada de frutas *f*. *v* dar fruto. **fruitful** *adj* fructífero; (*fig*) fructuoso. **fruition**
n fruición *f*; realización *f*; (*bot*) fructifi-
cación *f*.

frustrate [frʌ'streit] *v* (*plans, etc.*) frustrar;
impedir.

***fry** [frai] *v* freír. **frying pan** sartén *f*.

fuchsia ['fjuːʃə] *n* fucsia *f*.

fuck [fʌk] *v* (*impol*) joder.

fudge [fʌdʒ] *v* fallar; inventar.

fuel ['fjuəl] *n* combustible *m*; gasolina *f*;
(*mot*) carburante *f*. **fuel gauge** indicador
del nivel de gasolina *m*. **fuel pump**
gasolinera *f*. *v* (*mot*) echar gasolina a;
(*furnace*) alimentar; (*ship*) abastecer de
combustible.

fugitive ['fjuːdʒitiv] *n, adj* fugativo, -a.

fulcrum ['fulkrəm] *n* fulcro *m*.

fulfil [ful'fil] *v* (*promise, obligation*) cumplir; (*ambition*) realizar; (*purpose*) servir;
(*wishes*) satisfacer; (*function*)
desempeñar; (*plan*) llevar a cabo. **fulfilment** *n* cumplimiento *m*; realización *f*;
satisfacción *f*; (*instructions*) ejecución *f*.

full [ful] *adj* lleno; completo; (*text*)
íntegro; (*whole*) entero; (*price*) sin
descuento; (*extensive*) extenso; (*daylight,
development*) pleno; (*speed*) todo; (*capacity*) máximo; (*measure, weight*) exacto;
(*flavour*) mucho. **full employment** pleno
empleo *m*. **full up** completamente lleno.
I'm full no puedo más. **in full colour** a
todo color.

full-blooded *adj* (*thoroughbred*) de pura
sangre; (*robust*) vigoroso; (*true blue*)
verdadero.

full-bodied *adj* (*wine*) de mucho cuerpo.

full-dress *adj* de etiqueta; de gala.

full-grown *adj* crecido; adulto.

full-hearted *adj* completo.

full house *n* (*theatre or cinema notice*) no
hay localidades.

full-length *adj* de cuerpo entero.

full-scale *adj* de tamaño natural.

full stop *n* punto *m*.

full-time *adj* de jornada completa.

fumble ['fʌmbl] *v* tojetear; (*drop*) dejar
caer; (*feel*) hurgar; (*search*) buscar.

fume [fjuːm] *v* (*fig*) bufar de cólera. **fumes**
pl n numo *m*.

fun [fʌn] n alegría f; gracia f; diversión f.
for fun en broma. funfair n parque de
atracciones m. have fun divertirse. make
fun of reirse de. what fun! ¡qué divertido!

function ['fʌŋkʃən] n función f; acto m;
recepción f. v funcionar. functional adj
funcional.

fund [fʌnd] n fondo m; (source) fuente f.

fundamental [fʌndə'mentl] adj fundamental.

funeral ['fjuɪnərəl] n funeral m; (state)
exequias nacionales f pl. funeral parlour
funeraria f. funeral procession cortejo
fúnebre m. funeral service misa de cuerpo presente f.

fungus ['fʌŋgəs] n, pl -i (bot) hongo m;
(med) fungo m.

funnel ['fʌnl] n (pourer) embudo m; (smoke-
stack) chimenea f. v verter por un
embudo; (direct) encauzar.

funny ['fʌni] adj divertido; gracioso;
(curious) extraño. taste funny tener un
sabor extraño. funny business cosas
varas f pl. funny-bone hueso de la alegría
m. funnily adv graciosamente.

fur [fəɪ] n pelo m; (pelt) piel f; (kettle)
sarro m; (tongue) saburra f. fur coat
abrigo de pieles m. v forrar con pieles;
incrustar; cubrir de sarro. furrier n
peletero m; (shop) peletería f. furry adj
peludo; sarroso.

furious ['fjuəriəs] adj furioso; violento.

furnace ['fəɪnis] n horno m; (domestic)
estufa f; (boiler) hogar m.

furnish ['fəɪniʃ] v (house) amueblar; (supply) suministrar; (give) facilitar; (opportunity) dar; (proof) aducir. furnishings pl
n muebles m pl; mobiliario m.

furniture ['fəɪnitʃə] n muebles m pl. furniture van camión de mudanzas m.

furrow ['fʌrou] n (ploughing) surco m;
(forehead) arruga f; (groove) ranura f. v
surcar; arrugar.

further ['fəɪðə] adj (distant, additional)
otro; (another) nuevo; (later) posterior;
(education) superior. adv más; más lejos,
más allá; (moreover) además. v favorecer.
furtherance n adelantamiento m; for-
mento m. furthermore adv además. fur-
thermost adj más lejano. furthest adj más
lejano; extremo.

furtive ['fəɪtiv] adj furtivo.

fury ['fjuəri] n furia f, furor m.

fuse¹ [fjuɪz] n (elec) fusible m. fuse box

caja de fusibles f. v (join) fusionar; (melt)
fundir.

fuse² [fjuɪz] n (explosives) mecha f; (deto-
nator) espoleta f.

fuselage ['fjuɪzəˌlaɪʒ] n fuselaje m.

fusion ['fjuɪʒən] n fusión f.

fuss [fʌs] n (trouble) lío m; (commotion)
alboroto m; (complaints) quejas f pl. a lot
of fuss about nothing mucho ruido y
pocas nueces. v agitarse; quejarse; preocuparse; molestar. fussiness n agitación
f. fussy adj escrupuloso; exigente; melindroso.

futile ['fjuɪtail] adj vano; frívolo.

future ['fjuɪtʃə] n futuro m; porvenir m.
adj futuro; venidero.

fuzz [fʌz] n (on face) vello m; (fluff)
pelusa f. fuzzy adj velloso; (blurred) borroso.

G

gabble ['gabl] v chacharear. n cháchara f.
gabbler n chacharero, -a m, f.

gable ['geibl] n gablete m.

gadget ['gadʒit] n aparato m; accesorio
m.

gag¹ [gag] v amordazar. n mordaza f.

gag² [gag] n (joke) broma f; chiste m.

gaiety ['geiəti] n alegría f; jovialidad f.

gain [gein] n ganancia f; provecho m;
aumento m. v ganar; avanzar.

gait [geit] n modo de andar m.

gala ['gaɪlə] n fiesta f, gala f.

galaxy ['galəksi] n galaxia f.

gale [geil] n vendaval m.

gallant ['galənt] adj (to women) galante;
(brave) valiente; (stately) elegante. gallantry n galantería f; valor m; (courtesy)
cortesía f.

gall-bladder ['gɔɪlˌbladə] n vesícula biliar
f.

galleon ['galiən] n galeón m.

gallery ['galəri] n galería f; (spectators)
tribuna f; (theatre) gallinero m.

galley ['gali] n (ship) galera f; (kitchen)
cocina f.

gallon ['galən] n galón m.

gallop ['galəp] n galope m. v galopar.

gallows ['galouz] pl n cadalso m sing.

gallstone ['gɔːlstoun] n cálculo biliar m.

galore [gə'lɔː] adj, adv en cantidad.

galvanize ['gælvənaiz] v galvanizar.

gamble ['gæmbl] v (bet) apostar; (risk) arriesgar. **gamble on** contar con. n (risky enterprise) empresa arriesgada f; (game) jugada f. **gambler** n jugador, -a m, f. **gambling** n juego m. **gambling den** garito m.

game [geim] n juego m; (sport) deporte m; (of football, tennis, etc.) partido m; (cards, chess, etc.) partida f; (hunting) caza f. **game bird** ave de caza f. **gamekeeper** n guardabosque m. **play the game** jugar limpio. adj (coll) valiente.

gammon ['gæmən] n jamón ahumado m.

gang [gæŋ] n (band) cuadrilla f; (of gangsters) banda f. v **gang up on** conspirar contra. **gangster** n gángster m.

gangrene ['gæŋgriːn] n gangrena f. **gangrenous** adj gangrenoso.

gangway ['gæŋwei] n (passage) pasillo m; (naut) pasarela f.

gaol V **jail**.

gap [gæp] n (empty space) vacío m; (breach) brecha f; (cavity) hueco m; (in a wall) portillo m; (between hills) quebrada f; (in education) laguna f; (crack) resquicio m; (in a wood) claro m.

gape [geip] v (stare) quedarse boquiabierto; (open wide) abrirse mucho.

garage ['gæraidʒ] n garaje m.

garbage ['gɑːbidʒ] n basura f. **garbage can** cubo de la basura m. **garbage disposal** vertedero de basuras m. **garbage man** basurero m.

garble ['gɑːbl] v amañar; mutilar. **garbled** adj amañado; mutilado.

garden ['gɑːdn] n jardín m; huerto m. v cultivar un huerto. **garden city** ciudad jardín f. **garden party** recepción al aire libre f. **garden produce** hortalizas f pl. **gardener** n jardinero, -a m, f. **gardening** n jardinería f.

gargle ['gɑːgl] v hacer gárgaras. n gárgaras f pl.

garland ['gɑːlənd] n guirnalda f. v enguirnaldar.

garlic ['gɑːlik] n ajo m.

garment ['gɑːmənt] n prenda f, traje m, vestido m.

garnish ['gɑːniʃ] v adornar, embellecer; (cookery) aderezar. n adorno m; aderezo m.

garrison ['gærisn] n guarnición f. v guarnecer.

garter ['gɑːtə] n liga f. **Order of the Garter** orden de la jarretera f.

gas [gæs] n gas m; (petrol) gasolina f, bencina f. **step on the gas** (coll) acelerar. v asfixiar con gas. **gaseous** adj gaseoso. **gas burner** n mechero de gas m. **gas fire** n estufa de gas f. **gas main** n cañería maestra de gas f. **gasmask** n máscara para gases f. **gas meter** n contador de gas m. **gaspipe** n cañería de gas f. **gas-ring** n fogón de gas m. **gas stove** n cocina de gas f. **gasworks** n fábrica de gas f.

gash [gæʃ] n herida f; cuchillada f. v acuchillar.

gasket ['gæskit] n junta de culata f.

gasoline ['gæsəliːn] n gasolina f.

gasp [gɑːsp] n (breathing difficulty) jadeo m; (surprise) boqueada f. v jadear; boquear.

gastric ['gæstrik] adj gástrico. **gastric fever** fiebre gástrica f. **gastric juice** jugo gástrico. **gastric ulcer** ulcera gástrica f. **gastritis** n gastritis f. **gastroenteritis** n gastroenteritis f.

gastronomic [gæstrə'nomik] adj gastronómico. **gastronomy** n gastronomía f.

gate [geit] n puerta f, entrada f; (metal) verja f; (level-crossing) barrera f. **gatecrash** v asistir sin invitación. **gatekeeper** n portero, -a m, f. **gatepost** n soporte de la puerta m. **gateway** n entrada f, paso m.

gateau ['gætou] n tarta f.

gather ['gæðə] v coger, amontonar; (strength) cobrar; (harvest) cosechar; (understand) colegir; (money) recaudar; (sewing) fruncir. **gather together** reunirse, congregarse. **gathering** n reunión f, afluencia f.

gaudy ['gɔːdi] adj chillón, cursi.

gauge [geidʒ] n (rail) entrevía f; (gun) calibre m; (measure) indicador m; (fig) medida f. v medir, juzgar; calibrar. **broad/narrow gauge railway** ferrocarril de vía ancha/estrecha m. **pressure gauge** manómetro m.

gaunt [gɔːnt] adj demacrado; (grim) feroz; (fig) lúgubre.

gauze [gɔːz] n gasa f.

gave [geiv] V **give**.

gay [gei] adj alegre; gozoso; (dress) guapo; (event) festivo; (coll) homosexual. n (coll: homosexual) maricón m.

gaze [geiz] v mirar fijamente. n mirada fija f.

gazelle [gə'zel] n gacela f.

gazetteer [gazə'tiə] n gacetero m.

gear [giə] n (mech) engranaje m, juego m, marcha f; (dress) traje m; (tackle) utensilios m pl; (naut) aparejo m. **gearbox** caja de velocidades f. **gear lever** palanca de cambio de velocidad. **in gear** engranado. v aparejar; engranar; adaptar.

geese [giːs] V goose.

gelatine ['dʒelə,tiːn] n gelatina f.

gelignite ['dʒelignait] n gelignita f.

gem [dʒem] n joya f, gema f; (delight) preciosidad f.

Gemini ['dʒemini] pl n Géminis m.

gender ['dʒendə] n género m; sexo m.

gene [dʒiːn] n gene m.

genealogy [dʒiːni,alədʒi] n genealogía f. **genealogical** adj genealógico.

general ['dʒenərəl] nm, adj general. **general election** elección general f. **general opinion** voz común f. **general practitioner** médico, -a general m, f. **in general** generalmente. **generalization** n generalización f. **generalize** v generalizar.

generate ['dʒenəreit] v producir; (elec) generar. **generation** n generación f. **generator** n generador m; dínamo m.

generic [dʒi'nerik] adj genérico.

generous ['dʒenərəs] adj generoso; magnánimo. **generosity** n generosidad f; liberalidad f.

genetic [dʒi'netik] adj genético. **genetics** n genética f.

Geneva [dʒi'niːvə] n Ginebra. **Lake Geneva** Lago de Ginebra.

genial ['dʒiːmiəl] adj genial, cordial.

genital ['dʒenitl] adj genital. **genitals** pl n genitales m pl.

genitive ['dʒenitiv] nm, adj genitivo.

genius ['dʒiːnjəs] n genio m.

genteel [dʒen'tiːl] adj fino; melindroso.

gentle ['dʒentl] adj (light) lijero; (mild) suave; (slow) lento; (tame) manso; (moderate) moderado; (friendly) amable; (kind) bondadoso. **gentleman** n caballero m, señor m. **gentlemen** pl n (in correspondence) muy señores míos, muy señores nuestros m pl. **gentleness** n amabilidad f; bondad f; suavidad f.

gentry ['dʒentri] n pequeña nobleza f.

gents [dʒents] n (sign) caballeros m pl.

genuine ['dʒenjuin] adj puro; genuino; verdadero; auténtico.

genus ['dʒiːnəs] n género m.

geography [dʒi'ogrəfi] n geografía f. **geographer** n geógrafo m. **geographic** adj also **geographical** geográfico.

geology [dʒi'olədʒi] n geología f. **geological** adj geológico. **geologist** n geólogo m.

geometry [dʒi'omətri] n geometría f. **geometrical** adj geométrico.

geranium [dʒə'reiniəm] n geranio m.

geriatric [dʒeri'atrik] adj geriátrico. **geriatrics** n geriatría f.

germ [dʒəːm] n (med) bacilo m; microbio m; (fig) germen m.

Germany ['dʒəːməni] n Alemania f. **German** n, adj alemán, -ana m, f. **German measles** rubéola f. **Germanic** adj germánico.

germinate ['dʒəːmineit] v germinar, brotar. **germination** n germinación f.

gerund ['dʒerənd] n gerundio m.

gesticulate [dʒe'stikju,leit] v gesticular. **gesticulation** n gesticulación f.

gesture ['dʒestʃə] v gesticular. n gesto m.

*get [get] v obtener; tener; recibir; (fetch) buscar; (buy) comprar; (call) llamar; (find) encontrar; (catch, reproduce) coger; (bring) llevar; (extract) sacar; (succeed) conseguir; (coll: understand) llegar a comprender; (coll: kill) matar. **get about** desplazarse. **get across** (cross) atravesar; hacer comprender. **getaway** n huida f. **get at** (reach) alcanzar; (tease) meterse con. **get back** (return) volver; (recover) recobrar. **get by** (manage) arreglárselas. **get down** (descend) bajar; (write) poner por escrito. **get down to** ponerse a. **get off** bajarse de; escapar. **get on** (mount) subir a; (progress) progresar; (agree) llevarse bien; (grow old) envejecer. **get out** salir; (fig) sacar. **get up** (arise) levantarse; (climb) subirse.

geyser ['giːzə] n (hot spring) géiser m; (water-heater) calentador de agua m.

ghastly ['gaːstli] adj horroroso; (pale) de una palidez mortal.

gherkin ['gəːkin] n cohombrillo m.

ghetto ['getou] n judería f.

ghost [goust] n fantasma m; espectro; (spirit) alma f. **ghost writer** escritor fantasma m. **Holy Ghost** Espíritu Santo m. **give up the ghost** entregar el alma. **ghostly** adj espectral. **ghostliness** n espiritualidad f.

giant ['dʒaiənt] *nm, adj* gigante.

gibberish ['dʒibəriʃ] *n* galimatías *m invar*.

gibe [dʒaib] *n* mofa *f*. *v* jibe at mofarse de.

giblets ['dʒiblits] *pl n* menudillos *m pl*.

giddy ['gidi] *adj* (*dizzy*) mareado; (*height*) vertiginoso; (*scatter-brained*) frívolo. **giddiness** *n* mareo *m*, vértigo *m*.

gift [gift] *n* regalo *m*; (*talent*) don *m*; (*offering*) ofrenda *f*. **gift-token** vale para comprar un regalo *m*. **gifted** *adj* dotado; talentoso.

gigantic [dʒai'gantik] *adj* gigantesco.

giggle ['gigl] *v* reírse tontamente. *n* risita *f*. **the giggles** la risa tonta *f sing*.

gill [gil] *n* (*fish*) branquia *f*; (*plant*) laminilla *f*; (*measure*) medida de líquidos *f*.

gilt [gilt] *nm, adj* dorado. **gilt-edged** (*book*) con cantos dorados. **gilt-edged securities** valores de máxima garantía *m pl*.

gimmick ['gimik] *n* (*coll: gadget*) artefact *m*; (*coll: trick*) truco *m*.

gin [dʒin] *n* ginebra *f*.

ginger ['dʒindʒə] *n* jengibre *m*. **ginger beer** gaseosa *f*. **gingerbread** *n* pan de jengibre *m*. *adj* (*hair*) rojizo. *v* (*coll*) animar.

gingerly ['dʒindʒəli] *adv* delicadamente.

gipsy ['dʒipsi] *n* gitano, -a *m, f*.

giraffe [dʒi'raif] *n* jirafa *f*.

girder ['gəidə] *n* viga *f*.

girdle ['gəidl] *n* (*belt*) cinturón *m*; (*corset*) faja *f*. *v* ceñir; (*fig*) rodear.

girl [gəil] *n* niña *f*, chica *f*; muchacha *f*; señorita. **girlfriend** *n* amiguita *f*, novia *f*. **girlhood** *n* niñez *f*; juventud *f*. **girlish** *adj* de niña; (*of boys*) afeminado.

girth [gəiθ] *n* circumferencia *f*; (*waist, etc.*) gordura *f*; (*saddle*) cincha *f*.

gist [dʒist] *n* esencia *f*, importe *m*.

*give [giv] *v* dar; (*offer as a present*) regalar; (*deliver*) entregar; (*hand over*) pasar; (*provide with*) proveer de; (*grant*) conceder; (*infect*) contagiar; (*communicate*) comunicar; (*a speech*) pronunciar; (*med: administer*) poner; (*telephone: connect with*) poner con. **give-and-take** *n* toma y daca *m*. **give away** distribuir; regalar; revelar. **giveaway** *n* revelación *f*. **give back** devolver. **give in** darse por vencido; ceder; (*hand in*) entregar. **give off** despedir. **give out** distribuir; emitir; anunciar; divulgar; (*run out*) agotarse.

give up abandonar; renunciar a; rendirse; entregar; ceder. **give way to** retirarse ante; abandonarse a.

glacier ['glasiə] *n* glaciar *m*. **glaciation** *n* glaciación *f*.

glad [glad] *adj* feliz, alegre. **be glad** alegrarse. **gladden** *v* regocijar. **gladly** *adv* alegremente.

glamour [glamə] *n* encanto *m*. **glamorous** *adj* encantador.

glance [glains] *n* (*look*) vistazo *m*, ojeada *f*; (*light*) vislumbre *f*; (*projectile*) desviación *f*. *v* echar un vistazo, ojear; relumbrar; desviarse.

gland [gland] *n* glándula *f*. **glandular** *adj* glandular. **glandular fever** fiebre glandular *f*.

glare [gleə] *n* (*look*) mirada feroz *f*; (*dazzle*) deslumbramiento *m*. *v* mirar con ferocidad; deslumbrar. **glaring** *adj* feroz; deslumbrante; (*conspicuous*) manifiesto.

glass [glais] *n* vidrio *m*; cristal *m*; (*for drinking*) vaso *m*; (*mirror*) espejo *m*; (*lens*) lente *f*. **glasses** *pl n* gafas *f pl*. **glassware** *n* cristalería *f*. **glassworks** *n* fábrica de cristal y vidrio *f*. **glassy** *adj* vítreo; (*eyes*) vidrioso; (*smooth*) liso.

glaze [gleiz] *v* (*pottery*) vidriar; (*window*) poner cristales a; (*cookery*) glasear. *n* vidriado *m*; brillo *m*. **glazier** *n* vidriero *m*.

gleam [gliim] *n* rayo *m*. *v* relucir. **gleaming** reluciente.

glean [gliin] *v* espigar.

glee [glii] *n* alegría *f*. **gleeful** *adj* alegre.

glib [glib] *adj* locuaz; fácil. **glibly** *adv* con labia.

glide [glaid] *v* (*aero*) planear; (*slide*) resbalar. **glide away** escurrirse. *n* planeo *m*; (*slide*) deslizamiento *m*. **glider** *n* planeador *m*.

glimmer ['glimə] *n* luz trémula *f*; (*fig*) vislumbre *m*. *v* brillar con luz trémula.

glimpse [glimps] *v* entrever. *n* vistazo *m*. **catch a glimpse of** vislumbrar.

glint [glint] *n* destello *m*. *v* destellar.

glisten ['glisn] *v* relucir. **glistening** *adj* reluciente.

glitter ['glitə] *v* brillar. *n* brillo *m*. **glittering** *adj* brillante.

gloat [glout] *v* recrearse con.

globe [gloub] *n* globo *m*. **globe artichoke** alcachofa *f*. **globe-trotter** *n* trotamundos *m invar*. **global** *adj* global; mundial.

gloom [gluːm] *n* obscuridad *f*; (*fig*) melancolía *f*. **gloomy** *adj* obscuro; melancólico.

glory ['glɔːri] *n* gloria *f*; esplendor. **glorify** *v* glorificar. **glorious** *adj* glorioso; espléndido.

gloss [glos] *n* brillo *m*; lustre *m*; (*fig*) apariencia *f*. *v* **gloss over** disculpar.

glossary ['glosəri] *n* glosario *m*.

glove [glʌv] *n* guante *m*. **boxing gloves** *pl n* guantes de boxeo *m pl*. **glovecompartment** guantera *f*. **fit like a glove** sentar como anillo al dedo. **hand in glove with** juntar diestra con diestra. *v* enguantar.

glow [glou] *v* (*shine*) brillar.

glucose ['gluːkous] *n* glucosa *f*.

glue [gluː] *n* cola *f*. *v* pegar.

glum [glʌm] *adj* deprimido, sombrío.

glut [glʌt] *n* exceso *m*. *v* hartar.

glutton ['glʌtən] *n* glotón, -ona *m, f*. **gluttonous** *adj* glotón. **gluttony** *n* glotonería *f*.

gnarled [naːld] *adj* nudoso; (*persons*) curtido.

gnash [naʃ] *v* **gnash one's teeth** crujir los dientes.

gnat [nat] *n* mosquito *m*.

gnaw [nɔː] *v* roer. **gnawing** *adj* roedor.

gnome [noum] *n* gnomo *m*.

*go [gou] *v* irr; (*depart*) irse; (*lead to*) conducir a; (*go towards*) dirigirse a; (*leave*) dejar; (*vanish*) desaparecer; (*be removed*) quitarse; (*turn, become*) ponerse; (*function*) funcionar. **go off** (*leave*) marcharse; (*rot*) estropearse; (*gun*) dispararse. **go out** salir; (*lights, fire, etc.*) apagarse. **go round** dar la vuelta. **go with** acompañar; (*harmonize*) hacer juego con. **go without** (*manage*) arreglárselas. *n* (*coll*) energía *f*. **it's your go** te toca a ti. **on the go** ocupado. **go-between** *n* intermediario, -a *m, f*.

goad [goud] *v* aguijar; (*fig*) incitar; *n* garrocha *f*; (*fig*) estímulo *m*.

goal [goul] *n* (*structure*) meta *f*; (*score*) gol *m*; (*destination*) destinación *f*; (*purpose*) objeto *m*. **goalkeeper** *n* portero *m*; **goalpost** *n* poste *m*.

goat [gout] *n* (*nanny*) cabra *f*; (*billy*) cabrón *m*.

gobble ['gobl] *v* engullir.

goblin ['goblin] *n* trasgo *m*, duende *m*.

god [god] *n* dios *m*. **by God!** ¡vive Dios! **for God's sake** por el amor de dios. **goddaughter** *n* ahijada *f*. **godfather** padrino

m. **godmother** *n* madrina *f*. **godsend** *n* don del cielo *m*. **godson** *n* ahijado *m*. **goddess** *n* diosa *f*.

goggles ['goglz] *pl n* anteojos *m pl*.

goings-on [ˌgouiŋz'on] *pl n* (*coll*) tejemanejes *m pl*.

gold [gould] *n* oro *m*. **golden** *adj* dorado; de oro.

goldfinch ['gouldfintʃ] *n* jilguero *m*.

goldfish ['gouldfiʃ] *n* pez de colores *m*. **goldfish bowl** pecera *f*.

goldsmith ['gouldsmiθ] *n* orfebre *m*.

golf [golf] *n* golf *m*. **golf course** campo de golf *m*. **golfer** *n* golfista *m, f*.

gondola ['gondələ] *n* góndola *f*. **gondolier** *n* gondolero *m*.

gone [gon] *V* go.

gong [goŋ] *n* gong *m*.

gonorrhoea [ˌgonə'riə] *n* gonorrea *f*.

good [gud] *adj* bueno; (*before m sing nouns*) buen; (*wholesome*) sano; (*pleasant*) amable; (*genuine*) legítimo; (*virtuous*) virtuoso. *n* bien *m*. **no good** inútil. **for good** para siempre. **goodness** *n* bondad *f*. **good-looking** *adj* guapo.

good afternoon *interj* buenas tardes *f pl*.

goodbye [gud'bai] *interj* ¡adiós!

good evening *interj* buenas tardes *f pl*.

good-for-nothing *n*(*m+f*), *adj* inútil.

Good Friday *n* Viernes Santo *m*.

good morning *interj* buenos días *m pl*.

good night *interj* buenas noches *f pl*.

goods [gudz] *pl n* (*comm*) artículos *m pl*; (*possessions*) bienes *m pl*. **goods and chattels** muebles y enseres *m pl*. **goods train** tren de mercancías *m*.

goose [guːs] *n*, *pl* **geese** ganso *m*, oca *f*.

gooseberry ['guzbəri] *n* (*fruit*) grosella espinosa *f*; (*bush*) grosellero espinoso *m*.

gore¹ [gɔː] *v* cornear.

gore² [gɔː] *n* sangre *f*.

gorge [gɔːdʒ] *n* cañón *m*. *v* hartarse.

gorgeous ['gɔːdʒəs] *adj* magnífico.

gorilla [gə'rilə] *n* gorila *m*.

gorse [gɔːs] *n* tojo *m*.

gory [gɔːri] *adj* ensangrentado.

gospel ['gospəl] *n* evangelio *m*.

gossip ['gosip] *n* (*chat*) charla *f*; (*unkind*) chisme; (*person*) murmurador, -a *m, f*; chismoso, -a *m, f*. **gossip column** ecos de sociedad *m pl*. *v* (*talk scandal*) cotillear; (*chatter*) charlar.

got [got] *V* get.
Gothic ['goθik] *adj* gótico.
goulash ['guːlaʃ] *n* estofado húngaro *m*.
gourd [guəd] *n* calabaza *f*.
gourmet ['guəmei] *n* gastrónomo *m*.
gout [gaut] *n* gota *f*.
govern ['gʌvən] *v* (*rule*) gobernar; (*administer*) dirigir; (*determine*) guiar; (*restrain*) dominar; (*prevail*) prevalecer. **governess** *n* aya *f*. **government** *n* gobierno *m*. **governor** *n* gobernador *m*; administrador *m*; (*coll: boss*) jefe *m*.
gown [gaun] *n* traje largo *m*; (*law, university*) toga *f*. **dressing gown** bata *f*.
grab [grab] *v* agarrar, arrebatar. *n* asimiento *m*, presa *f*; (*mech*) gancho *m*.
grace [greis] *n* gracia *f*, elegancia; (*courtesy*) cortesía *f*; (*kindness*) bondad *f*; (*forgiveness*) perdón *m*; (*before meals*) bendición mesa *f*; (*favour*) favor; (*delay*) plazo *m*. **graceful** *adj* elegante; gracioso; cortés. **gracious** *adj* gracioso; grato.
grade [greid] *n* grado *m*; (*persons, things*) clase *f*; (*mark*) nota *f*; (*gradient*) pendiente *f*. *v* graduar; (*goods*) clasificar.
gradient ['greidiənt] *n* (*declivity*) decline *m*; (*slope*) cuesta *f*.
gradual ['gradjuəl] *adj* gradual.
graduate ['gradjuət]; *v* 'gradjueit] *n*, *adj* graduado, -a. *v* graduarse; diplomarse.
graft [graːft] *n* injerto *m*. *v* injertarse.
grain [grein] *n* grano *m*; (*wood*) fibra *f*.
gram [gram] *n* gramo *m*.
grammar ['gramə] *n* gramática *f*. **grammar school** instituto de segunda enseñanza *m*. **grammatical** *adj* gramático.
gramophone ['graməfoun] *n* gramófono *m*; tocadiscos *m invar*.
granary ['granəri] *n* granero *m*.
grand [grand] *adj* magnífico; grande; importante; espléndido. **grandiose** *adj* grandioso.
grand-dad *n also* **grandpa** (*coll*) abuelito *m*.
grandchild ['grantʃaild] *n* nieto, -a *m*, *f*.
grandfather ['gran,faːðə] *n* abuelo *m*.
grandma ['granmaː] *n also* **granny** (*coll*) abuelita *f*.
grandmother ['gran,mʌðə] *n* abuela *f*.
grandparent ['gran,peərənt] *n* abuelo, -a *m*, *f*.
grand piano *n* piano de cola *m*.
grandstand ['granstand] *n* tribuna *f*.
granite ['granit] *n* granito *m*. *adj* granítico.

grant [graɪnt] *v* conceder; (*agree to*) acceder; (*bestow*) otorgar; (*assume*) suponer. *n* concesión *f*; otorgamiento *m*; (*student*) beca *f*.
granule ['granjuɪl] *n* gránulo *m*. **granulated sugar** azúcar en polvo *m*.
grape [greip] *n* uva *f*. **grapevine** *n* vid *f*; (*coll*) rumores *m pl*.
grapefruit ['greipfruɪt] *n* pomelo *m*.
graph [graf] *n* gráfica *f*. **graph paper** papel cuadriculado *m*. **graphic** *adj* gráfico.
grapple ['grapl] *v* **grapple with** (*fight*) luchar cuerpo a cuerpo; (*fig*) intentar a resolver.
grasp [graɪsp] *v* agarrar; (*fig*) comprender. *n* agarro *m*; (*reach*) alcance *m*. **grasping** *adj* avaro.
grass [graɪs] *n* hierba *f*; (*pasture*) pasto *m*; (*lawn*) césped *m*. **grasshopper** *n* saltamontes *m*. **grass snake** culebra *f*. **grassy** *adj* cubierto de hierba; (*like grass*) herbáceo.
grate[1] [greit] *n* parrilla *f*. **grating** *n* rejilla *f*.
grate[2] [greit] *v* rallar; (*teeth*) hacer rechinar. **grater** *n* rallador *m*.
grateful ['greitful] *adj* agradecido.
gratify ['gratifai] *v* satisfacer; (*please*) agradar. **gratifying** *adj* satisfactorio; agradable.
gratitude ['gratitjuɪd] *n* agradecimiento *m*.
gratuity [grə'tjuəti] *n* propina *f*.
grave[1] [greiv] *n* sepultura *f*; (*monument*) tumba *f*. **gravedigger** *n* sepulturero *m*. **gravestone** *n* lápida sepulcral. **graveyard** *n* cementerio *m*.
grave[2] [greiv] *adj* grave, serio.
gravel ['gravəl] *n* grava *f*.
gravity ['gravəti] *n* (*force*) gravedad *f*; (*seriousness*) solemnidad *f*.
gravy ['greivi] *n* salsa *f*.
graze[1] [greiz] *v* (*scrape*) raspar; (*rub*) rozar. *n* rozadura *f*.
graze[2] [greiz] *v* pastar.
grease [griːs] *n* grasa *f*. **greasepaint** *n* maquillaje *m*. **greaseproof paper** papel vegetal *m*. *v* engrasar. **greasy** *adj* grasiento; (*slippery*) resbaladizo.
great [greit] *adj* gran, grande; famoso; poderoso. **greatly** *adv* grandemente, enormemente. **greatness** *n* grandeza *f*.
great-aunt *n* tía abuela *f*.

Great Britain n Gran Bretaña f.
Great Dane n perro danés m.
great-grandchild n biznieto, -a m, f.
great-grandfather n bisabuelo m.
great-grandmother n bisabuela f.
great-uncle n tío abuelo m.
Greece [griːs] n Grecia f. **Greek** n, adj griego, -a m, f.
greed [griːd] n avaricia f; (for food) glotonería f. adj avaro; glotón.
green [griːn] adj verde; (inexperienced) novato; (fresh) fresco; (recent) nuevo. n (colour) verde m; (meadow) prado m; (lawn) césped m. **greens** pl n verduras f pl. **greenery** n verdor m.
greenfly ['griːnflai] n pulgón m.
greengage ['griːngeidʒ] n ciruela claudia f.
greengrocer ['griːngrousə] n verdulero m. **greengrocery** n verdulería f.
greenhouse ['griːnhaus] n invernadero m.
Greenland ['griːnlənd] n Groenlandia f. **Greenlander** n groenlandés, -esa m, f.
greet [griːt] v saludar. **greeting** n salutación f. **greetings** pl n recuerdos m pl.
gregarious [gri'geəˌriəs] adj gregario.
grew [gruː] V grow.
grey [grei] nm, adj gris; (hair) cano. **grey-haired** adj canoso. **greyhound** n galgo m. **go grey** (hair) encanecer.
grid [grid] n rejilla f; (elec) red f.
grief [griːf] n pena f, dolor m. **grief-stricken** adj desconsolado.
grieve [griːv] v afligir; lamentar. **grieve for** echar de menos. **grievous** adj doloroso; grave; apenado; lamentable. **grievous bodily harm** daños corporales m pl.
grill [gril] v (cook) asar a la parrilla; (interrogate) interrogar. n arrilla f; (meal) asado a la parrilla m. **grillroom** n parrilla f.
grille [gril] n reja f; rejilla f.
grim [grim] adj feroz; severo; horrible; (coll) desagradable. **grimly** adv severamente; horriblemente.
grimace [gri'meis] n mueca f. v hacer muecas.
grime [graim] n mugre f. **grimy** adj mugriento.
*****grind** [graind] v (coffee, etc.) moler; (sharpen) afilar; (teeth) crujir. n (coll) trabajo pesado m. **grinder** n afilador m. **grindstone** n muela f. **keep one's nose to the grindstone** batir al yunque.

grip [grip] n (of hand) mano f; (hold) agarro m; (bag) maleta f; (understanding) comprensión f. v **asir;** (wheels) agarrarse; (press) apretar; (the attention) atraer. **gripping** adj impresionante.
gripe [graip] v retortijón m. v (coll) quejarse.
grisly ['grizli] adj espantoso; horroroso; repugnante.
gristle ['grisl] n cartílago m.
grit [grit] n cascajo m; polvo m; (coll: courage) valor m. v (teeth) rechinar.
groan [groun] n gemido m; (dismay) gruñido m. v gemir; gruñir.
grocer ['grousə] n tendero, -a m, f. **groceries** pl n comestibles m pl. **grocery** n tienda de comestibles f.
groin [groin] n ingle f.
groom [gruːm] n (horse) mozo de caballos m; (of bride) novio m. v (horse) almohazar; (smarten) arreglar.
groove [gruːv] n ranura f, muesca f; (record) surco m; (fig) rutina f. v hacer ranuras en; estriar. **grooved** adj acanalado; estriado. **groovy** adj (coll) fenómeno.
grope [group] v andar a tientas. **grope for** buscar a tientas. **gropingly** adv a tientas.
gross [grous] adj (not net) bruto; (coarse) grosero; grueso, denso. n gruesa f.
grotesque [grə'tesk] nm, adj grotesco.
grotto ['grotou] n gruta f.
ground¹ [graund] V grind.
ground² [graund] n suelo m; (earth) tierra f; (sport) campo m; (basis) base f; (background) fondo m; (fig) terreno m. v poner en tierra; (teach) enseñar los rudimentos de. **grounds** pl n jardines m pl; (sediment) sedimento m sing; (reason) causa f sing.
ground control n control desde tierra m.
ground floor n planta baja f.
grounding ['graundiŋ] n **have a good grounding in** tener una buena base en.
groundless ['graundlis] adj sin fundamento.
ground level n nivel del suelo m.
ground rent n alquiler del terreno m.
groundsheet ['graundʃit] n tela impermeable f.
groundwork ['graundwəːk] n base f.
group [gruːp] n grupo m. v agrupar.
grouse¹ [graus] n ortega f.
grouse² [graus] v (coll) quejarse.

grove [grouv] n boscaje m.

grovel ['grovl] v arrastrarse; (fig) humillarse.

*grow [grou] v crecer; (increase) aumentar; (become) hacerse; (turn) ponerse; (develop) desarrollarse; (cultivate) cultivar. grown-up n adulto, -a m, f. growth n crecimiento m; aumento m; desarrollo m; (med) bulto m; vegetación f.

growl [graul] v gruñir. n gruñido m.

grub [grʌb] n larva f; (coll: food) comida f. v cavar. grubby adj sucio.

grudge [grʌdʒ] v envidiar. n rencor m. bear a grudge tener ojeriza. grudging adj mezquino. grudgingly adv de mala gana.

gruelling ['gruəliŋ] adj penoso; agotador.

gruesome ['gruːsəm] adj pavoroso, macabro.

gruff [grʌf] adj (manner) brusco; (voice) bronco. gruffness n brusquedad f; bronquedad f.

grumble ['grʌmbl] v quejarse. n queja f.

grumpy ['grʌmpi] adj malhumorado. grumpiness n malhumor m.

grunt [grʌnt] v gruñir. n gruñido m.

guarantee [garən'tiː] n garantía f. v garantizar. guarantor n garante m, f.

guard [gaːd] n (soldier) guardia m; (sentry) centinela m; (escort) escolta f; (keeper) guardián m; (train) jefe de tren m; (protection) defensa f; (watchfulness) vigilancia f. be on guard estar de guardia. guard dog perro de guardia m. guard's van furgón de equipajes m. v guardar; proteger. guarded adj (cautious) cauteloso. guardian n (custodian) guardián m; (of an orphan) tutor, -a m, f. guardian angel ángel de la Guardia m.

guerrilla [gə'rilə] n guerrillero m. guerrilla warfare guerrilla f.

guess [ges] n cálculo m; conjetura f; suposición f. at a guess a primera vista. guesswork n conjetura f. v adivinar; suponer; acertar.

guest [gest] n invitado, -a m, f; (hotel) huésped, -a m, f. be my guest yo invito. guest of honour invitado de honor m. guest-house n casa de huéspedes f. guestroom cuarto de huéspedes m.

guide [gaid] n guía m, f; (counsellor) consejero, -a m, f. girl guide exploradora f. guidebook n guía turística f. v guiar; conducir; dirigir. guidance n consejo m.

guided missile projectil teledirigido m. guided tour visita acompañada f.

guild [gild] v (association) gremio m; (craftsmen, etc.) guilda f.

guillotine ['gilətiːn] n guillotina f. v guillotinar.

guilt [gilt] n culpabilidad f. guilty adj culpable. plead guilty confesarse culpable.

guinea pig ['ginipig] n conejillo de Indias m.

guitar [gi'taː] n guitarra f. guitarist n guitarrista m, f.

gulf [gʌlf] n golfo m; (abyss) abismo m.

gull [gʌl] n gaviota f.

gullet ['gʌlit] n esófago m; (throat) garganta f.

gullible ['gʌləbl] adj crédulo. gullibility n credulidad f.

gully ['gʌli] n hondonada f.

gulp [gʌlp] v tragar. n (drink) trago m; (food) bocado m.

gum¹ [gʌm] n goma f. v engomar.

gum² [gʌm] n (mouth) encía f.

gun [gʌn] n (weapon) arma f; revólver m; pistola f; (hunting) escopeta f; rifle m; cañón m. gunfire n cañonazos m pl. gunman n pistolero m. gunpowder pólvora f. gun-running n contrabanda de armas f. gunshot n disparo m.

gurgle ['gɔːgl] n (water) borboteo m; (child) gorjeo m. v borbotear; gorjear.

gush [gʌʃ] v derramar. n chorro m; (fig) efusión f. gushing adj (person) efusivo.

gust [gʌst] n (wind) ráfaga f; (smoke) bocanada f; (rain) aguacero m; (laughter, anger) accesión f. gusty adj borrascoso.

gusto ['gʌstou] n placer m; brío m; entusiasmo m.

gut [gʌt] n (anat) intestino m, tripa f. guts pl n (coll) agallas f pl. v destripar; vaciar.

gutter ['gʌtə] n (roof) canal m; (street) arroyo m.

guy¹ [gai] n (coll) tipo m.

guy² [gai] n (rope) tirante m.

gymnasium [dʒim'neiziəm] n gimnasio m.

gymnast n gimnasta m, f. gymnastic adj gimnástico. gymnastics n gimnasia f.

gynaecology [gainə'kolədʒi] n ginecología f. gynaecological adj ginecológico. gynaecologist n ginecólogo, -a m, f.

gypsum ['dʒipsəm] n yeso m.

gyrate [ˌdʒai'reit] v girar. gyration n giro m.

gyroscope ['dʒairə,skoup] giroscopio m.

H

haberdasher ['habədaʃə] n mercero, -a m, f. haberdashery n mercería f.

habit ['habit] n costumbre f; (clothes) traje m. habitual adj acostumbrado.

habitable ['habitəbl] adj habitable.

habitat ['habitat] n medio m, habitación f.

hack¹ [hak] v acuchillar, cortar; (kick) dar un puntapié. n corte m; puntapié m. hacking adj (cough) seco.

hack² [hak] n (horse) rocín m; (writer) escritorzuelo m.

hackneyed ['haknid] adj usado, trillado.

had [had] V have.

haddock ['hadək] n eglefino m.

haemorrhage ['heməridʒ] n hemorragia f.

haemorrhoids ['heməroidz] pl n hemorroides f pl.

hag [hag] n (coll) bruja f.

haggard ['hagəd] adj ojeroso; extraviado.

haggle ['hagl] v regatear. n regateo m.

Hague, The [heig] n La Haya.

hail¹ [heil] n granizo m. hailstone n granizo m, piedra f. hailstorm n granizada f.

hail² [heil] v (salute) saludar; (coll) llamar. hail from proceder de.

hair [heə] n pelo m; (human head) cabello m. comb one's hair peinarse. have one's hair done ir a la peluquería. let one's hair down (coll) soltarse el pelo. split hairs hilar muy fino. tear one's hair out tirarse de los pelos. hairy adj peludo.

hairbrush ['heəbrʌʃ] n cepillo (para el pelo) m.

haircut ['heəkʌt] n corte de pelo m. have a haircut cortarse el pelo.

hairdresser ['heə,dresə] n peluquero, -a m, f. hairdresser's n peluquería f. hairdressing n peluquería f.

hair dryer n secador (para el pelo) m.

hairnet ['heənet] n redecilla f.

hairpiece ['heəpiis] n postizo m.

hairpin ['heəpin] n horquilla f.

hair-remover n depilatorio m.

hairspray ['heəsprei] n fijador (para el pelo) m.

hairstyle ['heəstail] n peinado m.

Haiti ['heiti] n Haití m. Haitian n, adj haitiano, -a.

half [haif] n mitad f; medio m; (division of a match) tiempo m. by half con mucho. half-and-half mitad y mitad. in half por la mitad. go halves with ir a medias con. adj medio. half an hour media hora. half a dozen media docena. adv a medias; media. half as many or much la mitad. half as much again la mitad más. not half! (coll) ¡no poco!

half-baked [,haif'beikt] adj (coll: idea) mal concebido; (coll: person) disparatado.

half-breed ['haifbrid] n mestizo, -a m, f.

half-brother ['haif,brʌðə] n hermanastro m.

half-hearted [,haif'haitid] adj poco entusiasta.

half-mast [,haif'maist] n at half-mast a media asta.

half-price [,haif'prais] adj, adv a mitad de precio.

half-sister ['haif,sistə] n hermanastra f.

half-time [,haif'taim] n (sport) descanso m. adj (work) de media jornada.

halfway [,haif'wei] adv a medio camino. meet halfway (compromise) partir la diferencia (con). adj medio.

half-wit ['haifwit] n tonto, -a m, f.

halibut ['halibət] n halibut m.

hall [hoil] n (entrance) vestíbulo m; (room) sala f. hall porter conserje m. hallstand n perchero m.

hallmark ['hoilmaik] n contraste m; (fig) sello m. v contrastar.

hallowed ['haloud] adj santo. hallow santificar.

Hallowe'en [halou'iin] n víspera del Día de todos los Santos f.

hallucination [hə,luisi'neiʃən] n alucinación f.

halo ['heilou] n halo m; (rel) aureola f.

halt [hoilt] n alto m, parada f. v parar; interrumpir.

halter ['hoiltə] n cabestro m.

halve [haiv] v compartir; partir en dos; reducir a la mitad.

ham [ham] n jamón m.

hamburger ['hambəigə] n hamburguesa f.

hammer ['hamə] n martillo m; (firearm) percursor m. come under the hammer salir a subasta. v martillar, martillear; (nail) clavar; (iron) batir. hammer out (disputes, etc.) elaborar.

hammock ['hamək] *n* hamaca *f.*
hamper¹ ['hampə] *v* impedir; embarazar.
hamper² ['hampə] *n* canasta *f.*
hamster ['hamstə] *n* hámster *m.*
hamstring ['hamstriŋ] *v* (*coll*) paralizar.
hand [hand] *n* mano *f*; (*watch, etc.*) aguja *f*; (*worker*) trabajador *m*; (*writing*) escritura *f*; (*applause*) ovación *f*; (*measure*) palmo *m*; (*naut*) marinero *m.* **at first hand** de primera mano. **at hand** a mano. **by hand** en mano. **hand and foot** de pies y manos. **hand in hand** de la mano. **hands up!** ¡arriba las manos! **hand to hand** cuerpo a cuerpo. **keep one's hand in** no perder la práctica. **on the other hand** por otra parte. *v* dar. **hand down** transmitir. **hand in** entregar. **hand over** ceder. **handful** *n* puñado *m.*
handbag ['handbag] *n* bolso *m.*
handbook ['handbuk] *n* manual *m*; guía *f.*
handbrake ['handbreik] *n* freno de mano *m.*
handcuff ['handkʌf] *v* poner las esposas a. **handcuffs** *pl n* esposas *f pl.*
handicap ['handikap] *n* desventaja *f*; (*sport*) handicap *m. v* perjudicar.
handicraft ['handikrɑːft] *n* mano de obra *f.*
handiwork ['handiwɔːk] *n* obra *f.*
handkerchief ['haŋkətʃif] *n* pañuelo *m.*
handle ['handl] *n* (*cup, bag, etc.*) asa *f*; (*grip of a tool*) mango *m*; (*stick, door knob*) pomo *m*; (*door lever*) tirador *m*; (*lever*) brazo *m. v* tocar; (*naut*) dirigir; (*mot*) conducir; (*tool*) manejar; (*lift, shift*) manipular; (*cope*) poder con; (*deal with*) ocuparse de. **handle with care** frágil. **handlebars** *pl n* manillar *m sing.*
handmade [ˌhand'meid] *adj* hecho a mano.
hand-out ['handaut] *n* (*leaflet*) prospecto *m*; (*charity*) limosna *f.* **hand out** dar; distribuir.
hand-pick [hand'pik] *v* (*people*) escoger a dedo; (*objects*) escoger con sumo cuidado.
handrail ['handreil] *n* pasamano *m.*
handshake ['handʃeik] *n* apretón de manos *m.*
handsome ['hansəm] *adj* hermoso, bello; guapo.
handstand ['handˌstand] *n* pino *m.*
handwriting ['handˌraitiŋ] *n* escritura *f.* **handwritten** *adj* escrito a mano.

handy ['handi] *adj* (*near*) a mano; (*skilful*) mañoso; diestro; (*convenient*) cómodo; (*manageable*) manejable; (*useful*) útil. **come in handy** venir bien.
*hang [haŋ] *v* colgar, suspender; (*execute*) ahorcar; (*head*) bajar; (*wallpaper*) empapelar; (*of clothes*) caer. **hang about** *or* **around** vagar. **hang fire** estar en suspenso. **hang-gliding** *n* vuelo libre *m.* **hangman** *n* verdugo *m.* **hang on** mantenerse firme; (*remain*) quedarse; (*hold on*) agarrarse; (*depend upon*) depender de. **hangover** *n* (*slang*) resaca *f.* **hang-up** *n* (*coll*) complejo *m.*
hangar ['haŋə] *n* hangar *m.*
hanker ['haŋkə] *v* **hanker for** *or* **after** anhelar. **hankering** *n* anhelo *m.*
haphazard [ˌhap'hazəd] *adj* fortuito.
happen ['hapən] *v* acontecer, suceder; (*take place*) tener lugar; (*arise*) sobrevenir. **happening** *n* suceso *m*, ocurrencia *f.*
happy ['hapiː] *adj* feliz, alegre. **happy birthday!** ¡feliz cumpleaños! **happy Christmas!** ¡felices Pascuas! **happy-go-lucky** *adj* descuidado. **happiness** *n* alegría *f.* **happily** *adv* felizmente.
harass ['harəs] *v* hostigar. **harassment** *n* hostigamiento *m.*
harbour ['hɑːbə] *n* puerto *m*; (*haven*) asilo *m. v* dar refugio a; (*cherish*) abrigar.
hard [hɑːd] *adj* duro; firme; violento; inflexible; cruel; (*unjust*) opresivo; (*weather*) severo; (*stiff*) tieso. *adv* duro; de firme; vigorosamente; (*raining*) a cántaros; (*closely*) de cerca; (*badly*) mal; (*heavily*) pesadamente. **hard-and-fast** *adj* (*rule*) inalterable. **hard-bitten** *adj* also **hard-boiled** (*fig*) duro, tenaz. **hard-hearted** *adj* insensible. **hard labour** trabajos forzados *m pl.* **hard up** (*coll*) apurado. **hardware** *n* ferretería *n.* **harden** *v* endurecer; (*make callous*) hacer insensible. **hardness** *n* dureza *f*; inhumanidad *f*; tiesura *f*; dificultad *f.* **hardship** *n* penas *f pl*; sufrimiento *m*; privación *f.*
hardy ['hɑːdi] *adj* audaz; fuerte; (*bot*) resistente.
hare [heə] *n* liebre *f.* **hare-brained** *adj* casquivano. **hare-lip** *n* labio leporino *m.*
haricot ['harikou] *n* judía *f.*
harm [hɑːm] *n* mal *m*; daño *m.* **harmful** *adj* malo; dañino. **harmless** *adj* inofensivo; inocuo.

harmonic [haɪ'monik] *nm, adj* armónico.
harmonica [haɪ'monikə] *n* armónica *f.*
harmonize ['haɪmənaiz] *v* armonizar.
harmony ['haɪməni] *n* armonía *f.* harmonious *adj* armonioso.
harness ['haɪnis] *n* guarniciones *f pl. v* enjaezar; (*power, etc.*) represar.
harp [haɪp] *n* arpa *f. v* harp on volver a repetir. harpist *n* arpista *m, f.*
harpoon [haɪ'puɪn] *n* arpón *m. v* arponear.
harpsichord ['haɪpsi̩kɔɪd] *n* arpicordio *m,* clavicémbalo *m.*
harrowing ['harouiŋ] *adj* atormentador, patibulario.
harsh [haɪʃ] *adj* (*features*) duro; (*voice*) ronco; (*sound*) discordante; (*texture*) áspero.
harvest ['haɪvist] *n* cosecha *f. v* cosechar.
has [haz] *V* have.
hash [haʃ] *n* (*food*) picadillo *m;* (*coll*) lío *m.* make a hash of estropear por completo. *v* (*food*) picar.
hashish ['haʃiːʃ] *n* hachís *m invar.*
haste [heist] *n* prisa *f.* hasten *v* dar prisa a; apresurar. hastily *adv* de prisa; (*rashly*) a la ligera. hasty *adj* precipitado; (*rash*) apresurado.
hat [hat] *n* sombrero *m.* bowler hat sombrero hongo *m.* Panama hat jipijapa *m.* top hat sombrero de copa *m.* take one's hat off to descubrirse ante.
hatch[1] [hatʃ] *v* hacer salir del cascarón; (*coll: plot*) maquinar.
hatch[2] [hatʃ] *n* (*serving*) ventanilla *f;* (*naut*) escotilla *f;* (*trapdoor*) trampa *f.*
hatchet ['hatʃit] *n* hacha *f.*
hate [heit] *v* odiar, aborrecer. *n* also hatred odio *m.* pet hate pesadilla *f.* hateful *adj* odioso.
haughty ['hɔːti] *adj* altanero. haughtiness *n* altanería *f.*
haul [hɔːl] *v* (*drag*) arrastrar; (*transport*) acarrear. *n* (*pull*) tirón *m;* (*journey*) recorrido *m;* (*fish*) redada *f;* (*loot*) botín *m.* haulage *n* acarreo *m,* transporte *m.*
haunt [hɔːnt] *v* (*ghost*) aparecer en; (*follow*) perseguir; (*frequent*) frecuentar; (*memories*) obsesionar. *n* lugar predilecto *m.* haunting *adj* obsesionante.
*have [hav] *v* tener; (*receive*) recibir; (*drink, food*) tomar; (*get*) conseguir; (*coll: deceive*) engañar. have on (*wear*) llevar; (*coll: tease*) tomar el pelo a. have to tener que.

haven ['heivn] *n* abrigo *m;* (*fig*) refugio *m.*
haversack ['havəsak] *n* mochila *f.*
havoc ['havək] *n* estragos *m pl.* play havoc with hacer estragos en.
hawk [hɔːk] *n* halcón *m.*
hawthorn ['hɔːθɔːn] *n* espino *m.*
hay [hei] *n* heno *m.* make hay while the sun shines hacer su agosto. hay fever fiebre del heno *f.* haystack *n* almiar *m.* go haywire (*machine*) estropearse; (*plans*) desorganizarse.
hazard ['hazəd] *n* peligro *m;* (*chance*) azar *m. v* arriesgar; (*guess*) aventurar. hazardous *adj* arriesgado, peligroso.
haze [heiz] *n* neblina *f;* (*fig*) confusión *f.* hazy *adj* nebuloso; (*fig*) confuso.
hazel ['heizl] *n* avellano *m.* hazel-nut *n* avellana *f. adj* de avellano.
he [hiː] *pron* él.
head [hed] *n* cabeza *f;* (*chief*) jefe *m;* (*school*) director, -a *m, f;* (*bed, table, river*) cabecera *f;* (*coin*) cara *f;* (*spear, arrows*) punta *f;* (*steam*) presión *f;* (*hammer*) cotillo *m. v* (*demonstration, list, etc.*) encabezar; (*lead*) estar a la cabeza de; dirigir; conducir; (*goal*) meter de cabeza. head off cortar el paso a. head for dirigirse hacia. headed *adj* (*notepaper*) con membrete. heading *n* título *m.* heady *adj* embriagador.
headache ['hedeik] *n* dolor de cabeza *m.*
headfirst [,hed'fɜːst] *adv* de cabeza.
headlamp ['hedlamp] *or* headlight *n* (*mot*) faro *m.*
headland ['hedlənd] *n* punta *f,* promontorio *m.*
headline ['hedlain] *n* (*book*) título *m;* (*newspaper*) titular *m.* make the headlines estar en primera plana.
headlong ['hedloŋ] *adv* (*headfirst*) de cabeza; (*rush*) precipitado.
headmaster [,hed'maistə] *n* director *m.* headmistress *n* directora *f.*
head-on [,hed'on] *adj, adv* de frente.
headphones ['hedfounz] *pl n* auriculares *m pl.*
headquarters [,hed'kwɔːtəz] *n* (*mil*) cuartel general *m;* (*firm*) domicilio social *m;* (*organization*) sede *f.*
headrest ['hedrest] *n* cabecero *m,* cabezal *m.*
headscarf ['hedskaɪf] *n* pañuelo *m.*
headstrong ['hedstroŋ] *adj* testarudo.

headway ['hedwei] n progreso m.

heal [hiːl] v (disease) curar, sanar; (wound) cicatrizar.

health [helθ] n salud f. **health certificate** certificado médico m. **health food** alimentos naturales m pl. **health officer** inspector de sanidad m. **health resort** balneario m. **Ministry of Health** Dirección General de Sanidad f. **public health** sanidad pública f. **your health!** ¡a su salud! **healthy** adj sano, saludable; salubre. **healthy appetite** buen apetito m.

heap [hiːp] n montón m, pila f; (people) muchedumbre f. v amontonar, apilar.

*****hear** [hiə] v oír; (listen) escuchar; (attend) asistir a; (give audience) dar audiencia; (news) enterarse de. **hear from** enterarse de. **hear hear!** ¡¡ muy bien! **hear about** or **of** oír hablar de. **hearing** n (sense) oído m; (act of hearing) audición f. **hearing aid** aparato para sordos m. **hearsay** n rumor m.

hearse [həːs] n coche fúnebre m.

heart [haːt] n (anat) corazón m; (feelings) entrañas f pl; (courage) ánimo m; (soul) alma f; (cards) copas f pl; (lettuce) repollo m. **by heart** de memoria. **set one's heart on** poner el corazón en. **to one's heart's content** hasta quedarse satisfecho. **a man after my own heart** un hombre de los que me gustan. **hearten** v animar. **heartless** adj cruel. **hearty** adj (welcome) cordial; (meal) abundante.

heart attack n ataque cardíaco m.

heartbeat ['haːtbiːt] n latido del corazón m.

heart-breaking ['haːtbreikiŋ] adj desgarrador. **heart-broken** adj acongojado.

heartburn ['haːtbəːn] n acedía f.

heart failure n colapso cardíaco m.

heartfelt ['haːtfelt] adj de todo corazón.

hearth [haːθ] n hogar m. **hearthrug** n alfombra f.

heart-throb ['haːtθrob] n ídolo m.

heart-to-heart adj franco, sincero. **have a heart-to-heart talk** tener una conversación íntima.

heartwarming ['haːtwoːmiŋ] adj caluroso.

heat [hiːt] n calor m; (animals) celo m; (fig) vehemencia f; (passion) ardor m; (of a race) carrera eliminatoria f. v calentar; excitar; (annoy) irritar. **heatstroke** n insolación f. **heatwave** n onda de calor f. **in the heat of the moment** en el calor del momento. **heated** adj calentado; (argument) apasionado. **heater** n calentador m. **heating** n calefacción f. **central heating** calefacción central f.

heath [hiːθ] n (plant) brezo m; (land) brezal m.

heathen ['hiːðn] n, adj pagano, -a.

heather ['heðə] n brezo m.

heave [hiːv] n (lift) gran esfuerzo m; (pull) tirón m; (sea) movimiento m; (breast) palpitación f; (retching) náusea f. v (pull) tirar de; (lift) levantar; (sigh) exhalar; (waves) subir y bajar; (retch) tener náusea; (breast) palpitar. **heave to** ponerse al pairo.

heaven ['hevn] n cielo m, paraíso m. **heavenly** adj celeste; (fig) delicioso.

heavy ['hevi] adj pesado, torpe; (slow) lento; (thick) grueso; (hard) duro; (strong) fuerte; (oppressive) opresivo; (cold) malo; (sky) anublado; (meal) abundante; (food) indigesto; (soil) recio. **heavyweight** nm, adj peso pesado. **heaviness** n peso m; torpor m; tristeza f; ponderosidad f.

Hebrew ['hiːbruː] n (people) hebreo, -a m, f; (language) hebreo m. adj hebreo.

heckle ['hekl] v interrumpir. **heckler** n perturbador, -a m, f. **heckling** n interrupción f.

hectare ['hektaɪ] n hectárea f.

hectic ['hektik] adj agitado.

hedge [hedʒ] n seto m. v cercar con un seto; (fig) vacilar; (a bet) compensar.

hedgehog ['hedʒhog] n erizo m.

heed [hiːd] v atender. n atención f, cuidado m. **heedless** adj desatento; negligente.

heel [hiːl] n (anat) talón m; (shoe) tacón m. v poner tacón a.

hefty ['hefti] adj (heavy) pesado; (robust) robusto.

heifer ['hefə] n novilla f.

height [hait] n altura f; (people) estatura f; (hill) colina f; (fig) colmo m; cumbre f. **heighten** v elevar; (fig) aumentar.

heir [eə] n heredero m; **heiress** n heredera f. **heirloom** n reliquia de familia f.

held [held] V hold.

helicopter ['helikoptə] n helicóptero m.

hell [hel] n infierno m. **go to hell!** (impol) ¡vete al infierno! **go hell for leather** ir como si se llevara el diablo. **to hell with it!** ¡qué diablos! **hellish** adj infernal; (fig) horrible.

hello [hə'lou] *interj* (*greeting*) ¡hola!; (*attract attention*) ¡oye!; (*phone*) ¡oiga!; (*answering the phone*) ¡diga!

helm [helm] *n* caña del timón *f*. **be at the helm** empuñar el timón.

helmet ['helmit] *n* casco *m*; (*of motorcyclist, labourer, etc.*) careta *f*.

help [help] *n* ayuda *f*; socorro *m*; auxilio *m*; remedio *m*; (*employee*) empleado *m*; (*servant*) criado, -a *m, f*. *interj* ¡socorro! *v* ayudar; auxiliar; socorrer; (*relieve*) aliviar; (*serve*) servir; (*avoid*) evitar; (*facilitate*) facilitar; (*prevent oneself from*) no poder menos que. **help yourself!** ¡sírvese! **it can't be helped!** ¡no hay más remedio! **helper** *n* ayudante *m*. **helpful** *adj* útil; provechoso; amable. **helping** *n* porción *f*. **helpless** *adj* desamparado.

hem [hem] *n* dobladillo *m*. *v* hacer un dobladillo en. **hem in** (*fig*) rodear. **hemline** *n* bajo *m*.

hemisphere ['hemi,sfiə] *n* hemisferio *m*.

hemp [hemp] *n* cáñamo *m*.

hen [hen] *n* (*chicken*) gallina *f*; (*female of other birds*) hembra *f*. **henhouse** *n* gallinero *m*. **hen party** (*coll*) reunión de mujeres *f*. **henpecked** *adj* dominado por su mujer.

hence [hens] *adv* por eso, por lo consiguiente; (*time*) de ahora; (*place*) de aqui. **henceforth** *adv* desde aquí en adelante.

henna ['henə] *n* alheña *f*.

her [həɪ] *pron* ella; (*direct object*) la; (*indirect object*) le, a ella. *adj* su (*pl* sus).

herald ['herəld] *n* heraldo *m*. *v* proclamar. **heraldic** *adj* heráldico. **heraldry** *n* heráldica *f*.

herb [həɪb] *n* hierba *f*. **herbal** *adj* herbario.

herd [həɪd] *n* rebaño *m*, manada *f*. *v* (*round up*) reunir en manada; (*drive*) conducir; (*fig*) agrupar.

here [hiə] *adv* aquí. **hereafter** *adv* en lo futuro; en adelante. **here and now** ahora mismo. **here and there** aquí y allá. **here goes!** ¡vamos a ver! **here is/are** aquí está/están.

hereditary [hi'redətəri] *adj* hereditario.

heredity [hi'redəti] *n* herencia *f*.

heresy ['herəsi] *n* herejía *f*. **heretic** *n* hereje *m, f*. **heretical** *adj* herético.

heritage ['heritidʒ] *n* herencia *f*.

hermit ['həɪmit] *n* ermitaño *m*.

hernia ['həɪniə] *n* hernia *f*.

hero ['hiərou] *n* héroe *m*. **heroine** *n* heroína *f*. **hero-worship** *n* culto a los héroes *m*. **heroic** *adj* heroico. **heroism** *n* heroísmo *m*.

heroin ['herouin] *n* heroína *f*.

heron ['herən] *n* garza *f*.

herring ['heriŋ] *n* arenque *m*. **red herring** (*coll*) pista falsa *f*.

hers [həɪz] *pron* suyo, suya.

herself [həɪ'self] *pron* (*reflexive*) se; (*emphatic*) ella misma. **by herself** a solas.

hesitate ['heziteit] *v* vacilar. **hesitant** *adj* vacilante. **hesitation** *n* vacilación *f*.

heterosexual [hetərə'sekʃuəl] *n(m+f)*, *adj* heterosexual.

hexagon ['heksəgən] *n* hexágono *m*. **hexagonal** *adj* hexagonal.

heyday ['heidei] *n* auge *m*, apogeo *m*.

hiatus [hai'eitəs] *n* laguna *f*.

hibernate ['haibəneit] *v* hibernar. **hibernation** *n* hibernación *f*.

hiccup ['hikʌp] *n* hipo *m*. **have the hiccups** tener hipo. *v* hipar.

***hide*[1]** [haid] *v* esconder. **hide something from someone** ocultar algo a alguien. **hide-and-seek** *n* escondite *m*. **hide-out** *n* escondrijo *m*.

hide[2] [haid] *n* piel *f*; (*leather*) cuero *m*.

hideous ['hidiəs] *adj* horroroso.

hiding[1] ['haidiŋ] *n* **be in hiding** estar escondido. **go into hiding** esconderse. **hiding place** escondite *m*.

hiding[2] ['haidiŋ] *n* (*beating*) paliza *f*.

hierarchy ['haiərɑːki] *n* jerarquía *f*. **hierarchical** *adj* jerárquico.

hi-fi ['hai,fai] *n* alta fidelidad *f*.

high [hai] *adj* alto; de alto; (*speed, hopes, number*) grande; (*post*) importante; (*wind*) fuerte; (*altar, Mass*) mayor; (*voice*) agudo; (*quality*) superior; (*river*) crecido; (*noon*) pleno; (*game*) manido; (*shine, polish*) brillante; (*colour*) subido. **highbrow** ['haibrau] *n(m+f)*, *adj* intelectual.

high chair *n* silla alta para niño *f*.

high frequency *adj* de alta frecuencia.

high-heeled *adj* de tacón alto.

high jump *n* salto de altura *m*.

highland ['hailənd] *n* tierras altas *f pl*. *adj* montañoso.

highlight ['hailait] *v* destacar. *n* (*art*) toque de luz *m*; (*fig*) atracción principal *f*.

Highness ['hainis] *n* Alteza *f*.
high-pitched *adj* de tono alto.
high-rise block *n* torre *f*.
high-speed *adj* de gran velocidad.
high-spirited *adj* brioso.
high street *n* calle principal *f*.
highway ['haiwei] *n* camino real *m*, carretera *f*. **highway code** código de la circulación *m*. **highwayman** *n* salteador de caminos *m*.
hijack ['haidʒak] *v* (*aircraft*) secuestrar; (*people*) asaltar; (*goods*) robar. *n* secuestro *m*; asalto *m*.
hike [haik] *n* excursión a pie *f*. *v* ir de excursión. **hiker** *n* excursionista *m*, *f*. **hiking** *n* excursionismo *m*.
hilarious [hi'leəriəs] *adj* (*funny*) hilarante; (*merry*) alegre. **hilarity** *n* hilaridad *f*.
hill [hil] *n* colina *f*, cerro *m*; (*slope*) cuesta *f*. **hillside** *n* ladera *f*. **hilly** *adj* montañoso.
him [him] *pron* él; (*direct object*) le, lo.
himself [him'self] *pron* (*reflexive*) se; sí, sí mismo; (*emphatic*) él mismo. **by himself** a solas.
hind [haind] *adj* trasero, posterior. **hindquarters** *pl n* cuarto trasero *m sing*. **hindsight** *n* percepción retrospectiva *f*.
hinder ['hində] *v* impedir; interrumpir. **hindrance** *n* impedimento *m*; obstáculo *m*.
Hindu [hin'duː] *n*(*m+f*), *adj* hindú. **Hinduism** *n* hinduismo *m*.
hinge [hindʒ] *n* bisagra *f*; (*stamps*) fijasellos *m invar*. *v* **hinge on** depender de.
hint [hint] *n* indirecta *f*; (*tip*) consejo *m*; (*clue*) pista *f*; indicación *f*; (*trace*) pizca *f*. **broad hint** una insinuación muy clara. **take the hint** (*pejorative*) darse por aludido; (*follow advice*) aprovechar el consejo. *v* insinuar; soltar indirectas.
hip [hip] *n* cadera *f*.
hippopotamus [hipə'potəməs] *n* hipopótamo *m*.
hire [haiə] *v* alquilar; (*person*) contratar. **hire out** alquilar. *n* (*house, etc.*) alquiler *m*; (*engagement*) contratación *f*; (*wages*) sueldo *m*. **for hire** de alquiler; (*taxi*) libre. **hire purchase** compra a plazos *f*.
his [hiz] *adj* su (*pl* sus); de él. *pron* suyo, suya.
hiss [his] *n* silbido *m*. *v* silbar.
history ['histəri] *n* historia *f*. **historian** *n* historiador, -a *m*, *f*. **historic** *adj* histórico.
*hit [hit] *v* golpear, pegar a; (*target*) dar

en; (*wound*) herir; (*collide*) chocar con. **hit home** dar en el blanco. **hit it off with** hacer buenas migas con. *n* golpe *m*; (*mil*) impacto *m*; (*success*) exito *m*. **hit-or-miss** *adv* a la buena de Dios.
hitch [hitʃ] *n* obstáculo *m*; problema *m*; (*knot*) vuelta de cabo *m*. *v* (*travel*) hacerse llevar en coche; (*tie*) atar; (*link*) enganchar. **hitch-hike** *v* hacer autostop. **hitch-hiker** *n* autostopista *m*, *f*. **hitch-hiking** *n* autostop *m*.
hitherto [hiðə'tuː] *adv* hasta ahora.
hive [haiv] *n* colmena *f*.
hoard [hoːd] *n* acumulación *f*; tesoro *m*. *v* acumular, amasar.
hoarding ['hoːdiŋ] *n* (*fence*) valla *f*; (*advertising*) cartelera *f*.
hoarse [hoːs] *adj* ronco. **hoarsely** *adv* roncamente. **hoarseness** *n* ronquera *f*.
hoax [houks] *n* estafa *f*; engaño *m*; burla *f*. *v* estafar; engañar; burlar.
hobble ['hobl] *v* cojear. *n* (*gait*) cojera *f*.
hobby ['hobi] *n* pasatiempo *m*.
hock¹ [hok] *n* (*pork, etc.*) pernil *m*.
hock² [hok] *n* vino del Rin *m*.
hockey ['hoki] *n* hockey *m*. **hockey stick** bastón de hockey *m*.
hoe [hou] *n* azadón *m*. *v* azadonar.
hog [hog] *n* cerdo *m*, puerco *m*. *v* (*coll*) acaparar.
hoist [hoist] *v* (*heavy objects*) levantar; (*sails, flag*) izar. *n* (*lifting*) levantamiento *m*; (*crane*) grúa *f*; (*lift*) montacargas *m invar*; (*lifting mechanism*) cabria *f*.
*hold¹ [hould] *v* tener; mantener; agarrar; (*believe*) creer; (*keep*) guardar; (*sustain*) sostener; (*opinion*) defender. **hold back** reprimir. **hold forth** perorar. **hold on** sujetar; (*wait*) aguantar; (*grip*) agarrarse. **hold out** (*hand*) tender, ofrecer; (*last*) durar; (*resist*) resistir. **hold up** (*raise*) levantar; (*support*) sostener; (*delay*) retrasar. *n* (*grip*) asimiento *m*, agarro *m*; (*handhold*) asidero *m*; (*control*) autoridad *f*. dominio *m*. **get hold of** coger, agarrar. **hold-up** *n* interrupción *f*; (*robbery*) atraco a mano armada *m*; (*traffic jam*) embotellamiento *m*. **holder** *n* (*person*) poseedor, -a *m*, *f*; (*object*) receptáculo *m*.
hold² [hould] *n* (*naut*) bodega *f*.
hole [houl] *n* agujero *m*; (*from digging*) hoyo *m*; (*in garments*) boquete *m*; (*mouse*) ratonera *f*; (*rabbit*) madriguera *f*.

holiday ['holədi] n (day) fiesta f; (several days) vacaciones f pl. **holiday resort** centro de turismo m.

Holland ['holənd] n Holanda f.

hollow ['holou] n hueco m; (in ground) hondonada f. adj, adv hueco. v ahuecar.

holly ['holi] n acebo m.

hollyhock ['holihok] n malva loca f.

holster ['houlstə] n pistolera f.

holy ['houli] adj santo; sacro; sagrado; (bread, water) bendito. **holiness** n santidad f.

homage ['homidʒ] n homenaje m. **pay homage** rendir homenaje.

home [houm] n casa f; hogar m; domicilio m; (fig) morada f. **at home** en casa. **make yourself at home** está usted en su casa. adv a casa. **go home** volver a casa. **homeless** adj sin casa ni hogar. **home address** dirección privada f. **homesick** adj nostálgico.

homicide ['homisaid] n (act) homicidio m; (person) homicida m, f. **homicidal** adj homicida.

homogeneous [homə'dʒiːniəs] adj homogéneo.

homosexual [homə'sekʃuəl] n(m+f). adj homosexual. **homosexuality** n homosexualidad f.

honest ['onist] adj honrado; sincero; franco. **honesty** n honradez f; sinceridad f; rectitud f.

honey ['hʌni] n miel f. **honeycomb** n panal m. **honeymoon** n luna de miel f. **honeysuckle** n madreselva f.

honour ['onə] n honor m; rectitud f. v honrar. **honorary** adj honorario. **honourable** adj honorable.

hood [hud] n capucha f; (car, pram) capota f.

hoof [huːf] n casco m; (cloven) pezuña f.

hook [huk] n gancho m; (fish) anzuelo m; (dress) corchete m; (hanger) colgadero m. v enganchar; (fish) pescar; (dress) abrochar; colgar. **hooked** adj (shaped) ganchudo. **get hooked on** (coll) enviciarse en.

hooligan ['huːligən] n rufián m. **hooliganism** n rufianería f.

hoop [huːp] n (toy) aro m; (barrel) fleje m.

hoot [huːt] n (owl) ululato m; (person) silbato m; (shout) grito m; (boat, factory) toque de sirena m. v ulular; silbar; dar un bocinazo; gritar; dar un toque de sirena; (boo) abuchear.

hop¹ [hop] v saltar; brincar; saltar con un pie. n salto m; brinco m; (coll: dance) baile m; (coll: stage in a journey) etapa f.

hop² [hop] n (bot) lúpulo m.

hope [houp] n esperanza f. v esperar. **hopeful** adj lleno de esperanzas; confiado. **hopeless** adj desesperado; (coll) inútil.

horde [hoːd] n horda f.

horizon [hə'raizn] n horizonte m.

horizontal [hori'zontl] adj horizontal.

hormone ['hoːmoun] n hormona f.

horn [hoːn] n cuerno m; (mot) bocina f.

hornet ['hoːnit] n avispón m.

horoscope ['horəskoup] n horóscopo m.

horrible ['horibl] adj horrible, espantoso.

horrid ['horid] adj horroroso, odioso.

horrify ['horifai] v horrorizar. **horrific** adj horrífico, horrendo.

horror ['horə] n horror m. adj (film, story, etc.) de miedo.

hors d'œuvres [oː'dəivr] pl n entremeses m pl.

horse [hoːs] n caballo m. **on horseback** a caballo. **horsepower** n caballo de vapor m. **horseradish** n rábano picante m. **horse show** concurso hípico m.

horticulture ['hoːtikʌltʃə] n horticultura f. **horticultural** adj horticultural.

hose [houz] n manga f; manguera f; (stockings) medias f pl. v regar con una manga.

hosiery ['houziəri] n medias f pl; (business) calcetería f.

hospitable [ho'spitəbl] adj hospitalario.

hospital ['hospitl] n hospital m. **hospitalize** v hospitalizar.

hospitality [hospi'taliti] n hospitalidad f.

host¹ [houst] n huésped m. **hostess** n huéspeda f.

host² [houst] n (crowd) muchedumbre f.

hostage ['hostidʒ] n rehén m.

hostel ['hostəl] n hostería f; residencia f. **youth hostel** albergue juvenil m.

hostile ['hostail] adj hostil; enemigo. **hostility** n hostilidad f; enemistad f.

hot [hot] adj caliente; (climate) cálido; (sun) abrasador; (day) caluroso; (spicy) picante; (temper) vivo; (issue) controvertido; (pursuit) porfiado. **be hot** (person) tener calor; (weather) hacer calor. **hot dog** perro caliente m. **hot-house** invernadero m. **hotplate** n calientaplato

m invar. **hot-tempered** *adj* enfadadizo.
hot-water bottle bolsa de agua caliente *f.*
hotel [hou'tel] *n* hotel *m.*
hound [haund] *n* perro de caza *m.* *v* (*fig*) perseguir.
hour ['auə] *n* hora *f.* **after hours** fuera de horas. **by the hour** por horas. **hour by hour** de hora en hora. **peak hours** horas de mayor consumo. **rush hour** hora punta. **small hours** altas horas. **zero hour** hora H. **hourly** *adv* de cada hora.
house [haus; *v* hauz] *n* casa *f*; (*theatre*) sala *f*; (*audience*) público *m.* *v* (*hold*) alojar; (*put up*) albergar.
houseboat ['hausbout] *n* casa flotante *f.*
housecoat ['hauskout] *n* bata *f.*
household ['haushould] *n* casa *f*, familia *f.* *adj* casero.
housekeeper ['haus,kipə] *n* (*paid*) ama de llaves *f*; (*housewife*) ama de casa *f.* **housekeeping** *n* (*work*) quehaceres domésticos *m pl*; (*money*) dinero para gastos domésticos *m.*
housemaid ['hausmeid] *n* criada *f.*
house-to-house *adj, adv* de casa en casa.
house-trained ['haustreind] *adj* enseñado.
house-warming ['haus,woːmiŋ] *n* **have a house-warming party** inaugurar la casa.
housewife ['hauswaif] *n* ama de casa *f.*
housing ['hauziŋ] *n* alojamiento *m.* **housing estate** urbanización *f.*
hovel ['hovəl] *n* casucha *f.*
hover ['hovə] *v* cernerse; (*fig*) rondar. **hovercraft** *n* aerodeslizador *m.*
how [hau] *adv* (*as*) como; (*in what way*) cómo; (*in exclamation before adv or adj*) qué. **how are you?** *or* **how do you do?** ¿cómo está usted? **how much?** ¿cuánto?
however [hau'evə] *conj* sin embargo. *adv* de cualquier manera que.
howl [haul] *v* (*dog, wolf*) aullar; (*wind*) bramar; (*pain*) dar alaridos; (*child*) berrear. *n* aullido *m*; bramido *m*; alarido *m*; grito *m*; berrido *m.*
hub [hʌb] *n* (*wheel*) cubo *m*; (*fig*) centro *m.* **hubcap** *n* (*mot*) tapacubos *m invar.*
huddle ['hʌdl] *v* amontonar. *n* grupo *m.*
hue [hjuː] *n* color *m.*
huff [hʌf] *n* **in a huff** enojado.
hug [hʌg] *v* abrazar. *n* abrazo *m.*
huge [hjuːdʒ] *adj* enorme.
hulk [hʌlk] *n* (*ship*) carraca *f*; (*derog: person*) armatoste *m.* **hulking** *adj* voluminoso.
hull [hʌl] *n* (*naut*) casco *m.*

hum [hʌm] *n* (*bees, engines*) zumbido *m*; (*a tune*) canturreo *m.* *v* zumbar; canturrear; (*fig: with activity*) hervir. **humming-bird** *n* colibrí *m.*
human ['hjuːmən] *nm, adj* humano. **human being** ser humano *m.* **human nature** naturaleza humana *f.*
humane [hjuː'mein] *adj* humano.
humanity [hjuː'manəti] *n* humanidad *f.* **humanitarian** *adj* humanitario.
humble ['hʌmbl] *adj* humilde. *v* humillar.
humdrum ['hʌmdrʌm] *adj* monótono.
humid ['hjuːmid] *adj* húmedo. **humidity** *n* humedad *f.*
humiliate [hjuː'milieit] *v* humillar. **humiliation** *n* humillación *f.*
humility [hjuː'miləti] *n* humildad *f.*
humour ['hjuːmə] *n* humor *m*; (*temperament*) disposición *f.* *v* complacer. **humorist** *n* humorista *m, f.* **humorous** *adj* humorístico.
hump [hʌmp] *n* horoba *f.* *v* (*coll: carry*) cargar con.
hunch [hʌntʃ] *v* encorvarse. *n* (*coll*) presentimiento *m.* **hunchback** *n* jorobado, -a *m, f.*
hundred ['hʌndrəd] *n* ciento *m*; centenar *m*; centena *f.* *adj* cien, ciento. **hundredth** *nm, adj* centésimo.
hung [hʌŋ] *V* **hang.**
Hungary ['hʌŋgəri] *n* Hungría *f.* **Hungarian** *n, adj* húngaro, -a.
hunger ['hʌŋgə] *n* hambre *f.* *v also* **be hungry** tener hambre, estar hambriento. **hunger for** desear. **hungrily** *adv* hambrientamente.
hunt [hʌnt] *n* caza *f*; (*search*) busca *f.* *v* cazar; buscar. **hunting** *n* caza *f.* **huntsman** *n* cazador *m.*
hurdle ['həːdl] *n* (*sport*) valla *f*; (*fig*) obstáculo *m.* *v* vallar.
hurl [həːl] *v* lanzar, arrojar; (*abuse*) soltar.
hurricane ['hʌrikən] *n* huracán *m.*
hurry ['hʌri] *n* prisa *f.* **be in a hurry** llevar prisa. *v* dar prisa (a), apresurar. **hurried** *adj* apresurado. **hurriedly** *adj* apresuradamente.
***hurt** [həːt] *v* (*cause pain*) doler; (*wound*) herir; (*damage*) hacer daño (a); ofender; (*feelings*) mortificar. *n* herida *f*; daño *m*; mal *m.* *adj* lastimado; herido. **hurtful** *adj* dañoso; perjudicial; (*words*) hiriente.
husband ['hʌzbənd] *n* marido *m*, esposo *m.*

hush [hʌʃ] *n* silencio *m*. *interj* ¡calla! *v* silenciar. **hush up** echar tierra a. **hushed** *adj* callado.

husk [hʌsk] *n* (*cereals*) cáscara *f*; (*peas and beans*) vaina *f*; (*chestnut*) erizo *m*. *v* descascarar; desvainar; pelar.

husky [ˈhʌski] *n* (*dog*) perro esquimal *m*. *adj* (*hoarse*) ronco; (*strong*) fuerte. **huskily** *adv* con voz ronca. **huskiness** *n* ronquera *f*.

hussar [həˈzaː] *n* húsar *m*.

hustle [ˈhʌsl] *v* empujar; (*fig*) precipitar. *n* (*energy*) empuje *m*; (*hurry*) prisa *f*; (*push*) empujón *m*. **hustle and bustle** vaivén *m*.

hut [hʌt] *n* choza *f*, cabaña *f*.

hutch [hʌtʃ] *n* (*rabbit*) conejera *f*.

hyacinth [ˈhaiəsinθ] *n* jacinto *m*.

hybrid [ˈhaibrid] *nm*, *adj* híbrido. **hybridization** *n* hibridación *f*.

hydraulic [haiˈdrɔːlik] *adj* hidráulico.

hydrocarbon [ˌhaidrəˈkaːbən] *n* hidrocarburo *m*.

hydro-electric *adj* hidroeléctrico.

hydrofoil [ˈhaidrəfoil] *n* aerodeslizador *m*.

hydrogen [ˈhaidrədʒən] *n* hidrógeno *m*.

hyena [haiˈiːnə] *n* hiena *f*.

hygiene [ˈhaidʒiːn] *n* higiene *f*. **hygienic** *adj* higiénico.

hymn [him] *n* himno *m*. **hymn-book** *or* **hymnal** *n* himnario *m*.

hyphen [ˈhaifən] *n* guión *m*.

hypnosis [hipˈnousis] *n* hipnosis *f*. **hypnotic** *adj* hipnótico. **hynotism** *n* hipnotismo *m*. **hypnotist** *n* hipnotizador, -a *m*, *f*. **hypnotize** *v* hipnotizar.

hypochondria [ˌhaipəˈkondriə] *n* hipocondría *f*. **hypochondriac** *n*, *adj* hipocondriaco, -a *m*, *f*.

hypocrisy [hiˈpokrəsi] *n* hipocresía *f*. **hypocrite** *n* hipócrita *m*, *f*. **hypocritical** *adj* hipócrita.

hypodermic [ˌhaipəˈdəːmik] *adj* hipodérmico. *n* jeringa hipodérmica *f*.

hypothesis [haiˈpoθəsis] *n*, *pl* **-ses** hipótesis *f*. **hypothetical** *adj* hipotético.

hysterectomy [ˌhistəˈrektəmi] *n* histerectomía *f*.

hysteria [hiˈstiəriə] *n* histeria *f*. **hysterical** *adj* histérico. **hysterics** *n* histerismo *m*; ataque histérico *m*.

I

I [ai] *pron* yo.

Iberian [aiˈbiəriən] *adj* ibérico. *n* ibero, -a *m*, *f*.

ice [ais] *n* hielo *m*. **iceberg** *n* iceberg *m*. **icebreaker** *n* rompehielos *m invar*. **ice-cold** *adj* helado. **ice cream** helado *m*. **ice-skate** *n* patín de cuchilla *m*. *v* (*turn into ice*) helar; (*chill*) enfriar. **icing** *n* escarchado *m*. **icing sugar** azúcar en polvo *m*, *f*. **icy** *adj* (*wind*, *place*) glacial; (*hand*, *foot*) helado.

Iceland [ˈaislənd] *n* Islandia *f*. **Icelander** *n* islandés, -esa *m*, *f*. **Icelandic** *adj* islandés.

icicle [ˈaisikl] *n* carámbano *m*.

icon [ˈaikon] *n* icono *m*.

idea [aiˈdiə] *n* idea *f*.

ideal [aiˈdiəl] *nm*, *adj* ideal. **idealist** *n* idealista *m*, *f*. **idealistic** *adj* idealista.

identical [aiˈdentikəl] *adj* idéntico. **identical twins** gemelos homólogos *m pl*.

identify [aiˈdentifai] *v* identificar. **identify with** identificarse con. **identification** *n* identificación *f*; (*papers*) documentos de identidad *m pl*.

identity [aiˈdentiti] *n* identidad *f*. **identity card** carnet de identidad *m*.

ideology [ˌaidiˈolədʒi] *n* ideología *f*.

idiom [ˈidiəm] *n* (*expression*) idiotismo *m*; (*language*) idioma *m*. **idiomatic** *adj* idiomático.

idiosyncrasy [ˌidiəˈsiŋkrəsi] *n* idiosincrasia *f*.

idiot [ˈidiət] *n* imbécil *m*, *f*, idiota *m*, *f*. **idiotic** *adj* idiota.

idle [ˈaidl] *adj* (*lazy*) perezoso; (*at leisure*) ocioso; (*unemployed*) desocupado; (*machine*) parado; (*talk*) frívolo; (*fears*) infundado. *v* (*waste time*) perder el tiempo; (*be lazy*) holgazanear; (*mechanism*) girar loco. **idleness** *n* (*laziness*) holgazanería *f*; (*leisure*) ociosidad *f*; (*unemployment*) paro *m*.

idol [ˈaidl] *n* ídolo *m*. **idolatry** *n* idolatría *f*. **idolize** *v* idolatrar.

idyllic [iˈdilik] *adj* idílico.

if [if] *conj* si. **as if** como si. **if not** si no. **if only** ¡ojalá que! **if so** si es así.

ignite [igˈnait] *v* encender, prender fuego a.

ignition [igˈniʃən] *n* ignición *f*; (*mot*)

encendido *m*. **ignition key** llave de contacto *f*. **ignition switch** interruptor del encendido *m*.

ignorant ['ignərənt] *adj* ignorante. **ignorance** *n* ignorancia *f*.

ignore [ig'nɔɪ] *v* (*warning*) no hacer caso de; (*person*) no hacer caso a; (*leave out*) pasar por alto.

ill [il] *adj* (*sick*) enfermo; (*bad*) malo. *nm*. *adv* mal. **ill-advised** *adj* malaconsejado. **ill-at-ease** *adj* molesto. **ill-mannered** *adj* mal educado. **ill health** mala salud *f*. **ill-treat** *v* maltratar. **ill will** mala voluntad *f*. **illness** *n* enfermedad *f*.

illegal [i'liːgəl] *adj* ilegal.

illegible [i'ledʒəbl] *adj* ilegible.

illegitimate [ˌiliˈdʒitimit] *adj* ilegítimo. **illegitimacy** *n* ilegitimidad *f*.

illicit [i'lisit] *adj* ilícito.

illiterate [i'litərit] *n*, *adj* analfabeto, -a. **illiteracy** *n* analfabetismo *m*.

illogical [i'lodʒikəl] *adj* ilógico.

illuminate [i'luːmiˌneit] *v* (*light up*) iluminar; (*clear*) aclarar. **illumination** *n* iluminación *f*; aclaración *f*.

illusion [i'luːʒən] *n* ilusión *f*.

illustrate ['iləstreit] *v* ilustrar; (*demonstrate*) demostrar. **illustration** *n* ilustración *f*; ejemplo *m*. **illustrator** *n* ilustrador, -a *m*, *f*.

illustrious [i'lʌstriəs] *adj* ilustre.

image ['imidʒ] *n* imagen *f*; (*fig*) reputación *f*. **be the image of** ser el retrato de. **imagery** *n* imágenes *f pl*.

imagine [i'madʒin] *v* imaginar. **imaginary** *adj* imaginario. **imagination** *n* imaginación *f*. **imaginative** *adj* imaginativo.

imbalance [im'baləns] *n* desequilibrio *m*.

imbecile ['imbəsiːl] *n* imbécil *m*, *f*.

imitate ['imiˌteit] *v* imitar. **imitation** *n* imitación *f*.

immaculate [i'makjulit] *adj* inmaculado.

immaterial [ˌiməˈtiəriəl] *adj* indiferente; no importa.

immature [ˌiməˈtjuə] *adj* inmaduro. **immaturity** *n* inmadurez *f*.

immediate [i'miːdiət] *adj* inmediato; (*near*) cercano. **immediately** *adv* inmediatamente; directamente.

immense [i'mens] *adj* inmenso, enorme.

immerse [i'məɪs] *v* sumergir. **immersion** *n* sumersión *f*. **immersion heater** calentador de inmersión *m*.

immigrate ['imiˌgreit] *v* inmigrar. **immigrant** *n*(*m*+*f*), *adj* inmigrante. **immigration** *n* inmigración *f*.

imminent ['iminənt] *adj* inminente.

immobile [i'moubail] *adj* inmóvil. **immobilize** *v* inmovilizar.

immoral [i'morəl] *adj* inmoral. **immorality** *n* inmoralidad *f*.

immortal [i'moːtl] *adj* inmortal. **immortality** *n* inmortalidad *f*. **immortalize** *v* inmortalizar.

immovable [i'muːvəbl] *adj* inmóvil; (*steadfast*) inflexible.

immune [i'mjuːn] *adj* inmune. **immunity** *n* inmunidad *f*. **immunization** *n* inmunización *f*. **immunize** *v* inmunizar.

imp [imp] *n* diablillo *m*.

impact ['impakt] *n* impacto *m*.

impair [im'peə] *v* dañar. **impairment** *n* daño *m*.

impale [im'peil] *v* atravesar.

impart [im'paɪt] *v* (*give*) impartir; (*grant*) conceder; (*make known*) comunicar.

impartial [im'paɪʃəl] *adj* imparcial. **impartiality** *n* imparcialidad *f*.

impasse [am'paɪs] *n* callejón *m*.

impassive [im'pasiv] *adj* impasible.

impatient [im'peiʃənt] *adj* impaciente. **become impatient** perder la paciencia. **impatience** *n* impaciencia *f*.

impeach [im'piːtʃ] *v* acusar; (*prosecute*) encausar; (*a witness*) recusar. **impeachment** *n* acusación *f*; (*prosecution*) enjuiciamiento *m*; recusación *f*.

impeccable [im'pekəbl] *adj* impecable.

impede [im'piːd] *v* estorbar; impedir.

impediment [im'pedimənt] *n* estorbo *m*; obstáculo *m*; defecto *m*.

impel [im'pel] *v* impeler; mover; (*push*) empujar; obligar.

impending [im'pendiŋ] *adj* inminente; próximo.

imperative [im'perativ] *adj* (*peremptory*) perentorio; (*urgent*) imperioso; (*necessary*) indispensable.

imperfect [im'pəɪfikt] *adj* imperfecto; incompleto. *n* (*gramm*) imperfecto *m*.

imperial [im'piəriəl] *adj* imperial; (*fig*) señorial. **imperialism** *n* imperialismo *m*.

impersonal [im'pəɪsənl] *adj* impersonal.

impersonate [im'pəɪsəˌneit] *v* hacerse pasar por; (*theatre*) imitar. **impersonation** *n* imitación *f*.

impertinent [im'pəɪtinənt] *adj* impertinente. **impertinence** *n* impertinencia *f*.

impervious [im'pɜːviəs] *adj* impenetrable;
(*to criticism, pain, etc.*) insensible.

impetuous [im'petjuəs] *adj* impetuoso.

impetus ['impətəs] *n* (*force*) ímpetu *m*;
(*fig*) impulso *m*; estímulo *m*.

impinge [im'pindʒ] *v* **impinge on** tropezar
con; usurpar.

implement ['implimənt; *v* 'impliment] *n*
(*tool*) herramienta *f*; (*utensil*) utensilio;
implements *pl n* (*writing*) artículos *m pl*;
(*agr*) aperos *m pl*. *v* llevar a cabo; (*law*)
aplicar.

implication [impli'keiʃən] *n* implicación *f*;
complicidad *f*; consecuencia *f*. **implicate**
v implicar; comprometer.

implicit [im'plisit] *adj* implícito; absoluto.

implore [im'plɔː] *v* suplicar. **imploring** *adj*
suplicante.

imply [im'plai] *v* implicar; presuponer;
significar; dar a entender. **implied** *adj*
implícito.

impolite [impə'lait] *adj* descortés.

import [im'pɔːt] *n* (*comm*) artículo
importado *m*; (*meaning*) sentido *m*;
importancia *f*. *v* (*comm*) importar;
significar.

importance [im'pɔːtəns] *n* importancia *f*.
important *adj* importante.

impose [im'pouz] *v* imponer; (*tax*) gravar
con. **impose on** abusar de. **imposing** *adj*
imponente. **imposition** *n* imposición *f*;
abuso *m*; (*tax*) impuesto *m*.

impossible [im'posəbl] *adj* imposible.

impostor [im'postə] *n* impostor, -a *m*, *f*.

impotent ['impətənt] *adj* impotente.
impotence *n* impotencia *f*.

impound [im'paund] *v* confiscar.

impoverish [im'povəriʃ] *v* (*people*)
empobrecer; (*land*) agotar.

impregnate ['impreg,neit] ˜*v* fecundar;
(*saturate*) empapar. **impregnable** *adj*
inexpugnable. **impregnation** *n* fecundación *f*; impregnación *f*.

impress [im'pres] *v* impresionar; (*print*)
imprimir. **impression** *n* impresión *f*.
impressive *adj* impresionante.

imprint ['imprint; *v* im'print] *n* impresión
f. *v* imprimir.

imprison [im'prizn] *v* encarcelar. **imprisonment** *n* encarcelamiento *m*.

improbable [im'probabl] *adj* improbable;
(*story, etc.*) inverosímil.

impromptu [im'promptjuː] *adv*
improvisadamente. *adj* improvisado.

improper [im'propə] *adj* indecente;
indecoroso; incorrecto.

improve [im'pruːv] *v* mejorar; favorecer;
perfeccionar. **improvement** *n* mejora *f*;
progreso *m*; reforma *f*.

improvise ['imprə,vaiz] *v* improvisar.
improvisation *n* improvisación *f*.

impudent ['impjudənt] *adj* impudente.
impudence *n* impudencia *f*.

impulse ['impʌls] *n* impulso *m*. **impulsive**
adj impulsivo.

impure [im'pjuə] *adj* impuro. **impurity** *n*
impureza *f*.

in [in] *prep* en; de; durante; a. *adv* dentro. **be in** (*at home*) estar en casa. **be in**
on estar enterado de.

inability [,inə'biləti] *n* incapacidad *f*.

inaccessible [,inak'sesəbl] *adj* inaccesible.
inaccessibility *n* inaccesibilidad *f*.

inaccurate [in'akjurit] *adj* inexacto. **inaccuracy** *n* inexactitud *f*.

inactive [in'aktiv] *adj* inactivo. **inaction** *n*
inacción *f*. **inactivity** *n* inactividad *f*.

inadequate [in'adikwit] *adj* insuficiente.
inadequacy *n* insuficiencia *f*.

inadvertent [,inəd'vəːtənt] *adj* inadvertido; descuidado. **inadvertently** *adv* por
inadvertencia.

inane [in'ein] *adj* (*futile*) inane; (*silly*)
necio. **inanity** *n* inanidad *f*; necedad *f*.

inanimate [in'animit] *adj* inanimado.

inarticulate [,inaː'tikjulit] *adj* (*sound*) inar-
ticulado; (*person*) incapaz de expresarse.

inasmuch [,inaz'mʌtʃ] *adv* **inasmuch as**
puesto que, visto que.

inaudible [in'ɔːdəbl] *adj* inaudible.

inaugurate [in'nɔːgju,reit] *v* inaugurar.
inaugural *adj* inaugural. **inauguration** *n*
inauguración *f*.

inborn [,in'bɔːn] *adj* innato; (*med*) congénito.

incapable [in'keipəbl] *adj* incapaz.

incendiary [in'sendiəri] *adj* incendiario.
incendiary bomb bomba incendiaria *f*.

incense¹ ['insens] *n* incienso *m*.

incense² [in'sens] *v* encolerizar.

incentive [in'sentiv] *n* incentivo *m*.
estímulo *m*.

incessant [in'sesənt] *adj* incesante, continuo.

incest ['insest] *n* incesto *m*. **incestuous** *adj*
incestuoso.

inch [intʃ] *n* pulgada *f*. **inch by inch** poco
a poco. **within an inch of** a dos pasos de.
v **inch forward** avanzar poco a poco.

incident ['insidənt] *n* incidente *m*; (*in a story*) episodio *m*. **incidental** *adj* incidente; incidental; imprevisto; (*expense*) accesorio *m*; (*music*) de fondo; (*secondary*) secundario; (*casual*) fortuito. **incidentally** *adv* (*by the way*) a propósito.
incinerator [in'sinə‚reitə] *n* quemador de basuras *m*. **incinerate** *v* quemar. **incineration** *n* incineración *f*.
incite [in'sait] *v* incitar; provocar. **incitement** *n* incitamiento *m*; estímulo *m*.
incline [in'klain] *v* inclinar. **be inclined to** inclinarse a. *n* pendiente *f*. **inclination** *n* (*tilt*) inclinación *f*; (*slope*) pendiente *f*; (*leaning*) tendencia *f*.
include [in'kluːd] *v* incluir; (*enclose in a letter*) adjuntar. **including** *adj* incluso. **inclusion** *n* inclusión *f*. **inclusive** *adj* inclusivo.
incognito [‚inkog'niːtou] *adv* de incógnito.
incoherent [‚inkə'hiərənt] *adj* incoherente. **incoherence** *n* incoherencia *f*. **incoherently** *adv* de modo incoherente.
income ['inkʌm] *n* ingresos *m pl*. **income tax** impuesto de utilidades *m*.
incomparable [in'kompərəbl] *adj* incomparable. **incomparably** *adv* incomparablemente.
incompatible [inkəm'patəbl] *adj* incompatible. **incompatibility** *n* incompatibilidad *f*.
incompetent [in'kompitənt] *adj* incompetente. **incompetence** *n* incompetencia *f*.
incomplete [‚inkəm'pliːt] *adj* incompleto; sin terminar.
incomprehensible [in‚kompri'hensəbl] *adj* incomprensible.
inconceivable [inkən'siːvəbl] *adj* inconcebible.
incongruous [in'koŋgruəs] *adj* incongruo; incompatible. **incongruity** *n* incongruidad *f*.
inconsiderate [‚inkən'sidərit] *adj* (*thoughtless*) inconsiderado; (*lacking consideration for others*) desconsiderado.
inconsistent [‚inkən'sistənt] *adj* (*substance*) inconsistente; (*actions, thoughts*) inconsecuente. **inconsistency** *n* inconsistencia *f*; inconsecuencia *f*.
incontinence [in'kontinəns] *n* incontinencia *f*. **incontinent** *adj* incontinente.
inconvenient [inkən'viːnjənt] *adj* (*place*) incómodo; (*time*) inoportuno. **inconvenience** *n* inconvenientes *m pl*, molestia *f*. *v* incomodar, molestar.

incorporate [in'koːpə‚reit] *v* incorporar, incluir; (*contain*) contenir; (*comm*) constituir en sociedad.
incorrect [inkə'rekt] *adj* incorrecto; erróneo.
increase [in'kriːs] *v* aumentar. *n* aumento *m*. **increasing** *adj* creciente. **increasingly** *adv* cada vez más.
incredible [in'kredəbl] *adj* increíble.
incredulous [in'kredjuləs] *adj* incrédulo. **incredulity** *n* incredulidad *f*.
increment ['iŋkrəmənt] *n* aumento *m*.
incriminate [in'krimineit] *v* incriminar. **incriminating** *adj* acriminador.
incubate ['iŋkju‚beit] *v* incubar. **incubation** *n* incubación *f*. **incubator** *n* incubadora *f*.
incur [in'kəː] *v* incurrir; (*debt*) contraer; (*loss*) sufrir.
incurable [in'kjuərəbl] *adj* incurable.
indebted [in'detid] *adj* (*owing money*) endeudado (con); (*fig*) agradecido. **indebtedness** *n* deuda *f*; agradecimiento *m*.
indecent [in'diːsnt] *adj* indecente. **indecency** *n* indecencia *f*.
indeed [in'diːd] *adv* en efecto; realmente. **yes indeed!** ¡ya lo creo!
indefinite [in'definit] *adj* indefinido; impreciso.
indelible [in'deləbl] *adj* indeleble.
indemnity [in'demnəti] *n* (*security*) indemnidad *f*; reparación *f*.
indent [in'dent] *v* (*dent*) abollar; (*notch*) dentar; (*comm*) pedir; (*print*) sangrar. **indentation** *n* (*notch*) muesca *f*; (*print*) sangría *f*.
independent [‚indi'pendənt] *adj* independiente. **independence** *n* independencia *f*.
index ['indeks] *n* índice *m*; (*math*) exponente *m*. **index finger** dedo índice *m*. **cost-of-living index** el índice del coste de la vida. *v* (*file*) clasificar; (*a book*) poner un índice a.
India ['indjə] *n* India *f*. **Indian** *n* indio, -a *m, f*; (*language*) indio *m. adj* indio. **Indian ink** tinta china *f*. **Indian summer** veranillo de San Martín *m*. **india paper** papel de China *m*. **india rubber** goma de borrar *f*.
indicate ['indikeit] *v* indicar, señalar. **indication** *n* indicación *f*, señal *f*. **indicative** *nm, adj* indicativo. **indicator** *n* indicador *m*.

indict [in'dait] v acusar. indictment n acusación f.

indifferent [in'difrənt] adj indiferente; insignificante; (mediocre) regular. indifference n indiferencia f.

indigenous [in'didʒinəs] adj indígena.

indigestion [,indi'dʒestʃən] n indigestión f. indigestible adj indigesto.

indignant [in'dignənt] adj indignado. get indignant indignarse. indignantly adv con indignación. indignation n indignación f.

indignity [in'dignəti] n (lack of dignity) indignidad f; (outrage) afrenta f.

indirect [,indi'rekt] adj indirecto.

indiscreet [,indi'skri:t] adj indiscreto. indiscretion n indiscreción f.

indiscriminate [,indi'skriminit] adj indistinto; universal; (person) sin criterio.

indispensable [,indi'spensəbl] adj indispensable.

indisposed [,indi'spouzd] adj (ill) indispuesto, enfermo; (reluctant) maldispuesto. indisposition n indisposición f; aversión f.

individual [,indi'vidjuəl] adj individual; personal. n individuo m. individuality n individualidad f.

indoctrinate [in'doktri,neit] v adoctrinar. indoctrination n adoctrinamiento m.

indolent ['indələnt] adj indolente. indolence n indolencia f.

indoor ['indɔ:] adj interior. indoor pool piscina cubierta f. indoors adv dentro; en casa.

induce [in'dju:s] v (convince) inducir, persuadir; (cause) causar, provocar. inducement n incentivo m; (motive) móvil m.

indulge [in'dʌldʒ] v (pamper) mimar; (give way to) ceder a. indulge in entregarse a. indulgence n indulgencia f; satisfacción f; tolerancia f; (self-indulgence) desenfreno m. indulgent adj indulgente.

industry ['indəstri] n industria f; diligencia f. industrial adj industrial. industrial relations relaciones profesionales f pl. industrialist n industrial m. industrialize v industrializar. industrious adj trabajador.

inebriated [in'i:brieitid] adj ebrio.

inedible [in'edibl] adj incomible.

inefficient [,ini'fiʃnt] adj ineficaz; incompetente. inefficiency n ineficacia f; incompetencia f.

inept [i'nept] adj inepto.

inequality [,ini'kwoləti] n desigualdad f; injusticia f.

inert [i'nɔ:t] adj inerte. inertia n inercia f.

inevitable [in'evitəbl] adj inevitable. inevitability n inevitabilidad f.

inexpensive [,inik'spensiv] adj poco costoso, barato.

inexperienced [,inik'spiəriənst] adj inexperto.

infallible [in'faləbl] adj infalible.

infamous ['infəməs] adj de mala fama; odioso. infamy n infamia f.

infancy ['infənsi] n infancia f; niñez f.

infant ['infənt] n niño, -a m, f. adj naciente. infantile adj infantil.

infantry ['infəntri] n infantería f.

infatuate [in'fatjueit] v be infatuated with (person) estar chiflado por; (idea) estar encaprichado por. infatuation n enamoramiento m.

infect [in'fekt] v infectar; contaminar. infection n infección f; contaminación f. infectious adj infeccioso; contagioso.

infer [in'fə:] v deducir. inference n deducción f.

inferior [in'fiəriə] nm, adj inferior. inferiority n inferioridad f. inferiority complex complejo de inferioridad m.

infernal [in'fə:nl] adj infernal; (coll) maldito.

infest [in'fest] v infestar. infestation n infestación f.

infidelity [,infi'deliti] n infidelidad f.

infiltrate [in'fil,treit] v infiltrarse. infiltration n infiltración f.

infinite ['infinit] nm, adj infinito. infinity n infinidad f; (math) infinito m.

infinitive [in'finitiv] nm, adj infinitivo.

infirm [in'fə:m] adj débil. infirmity n debilidad f; (illness) enfermedad f.

infirmary [in'fə:məri] n enfermería f; hospital m.

inflame [in'fleim] v (set on fire) inflamar; (passion) avivar; (anger) encender. inflammable adj inflamable. inflammation n inflamación f. inflammatory adj incendiario.

inflate [in'fleit] v hinchar; (prices) provocar la inflación de. inflation n (air) inflado m; (comm) inflación f. inflationary adj inflacionista.

inflection [in'flekʃən] n inflexión f.

inflict [in'flikt] v infligir, imponer. infliction n (punishment) castigo m.

influence ['influəns] *n* influencia *f*. **under the influence of** bajo los efectos de. *v* (*person*) influenciar; (*decision*) influir en. **influential** *adj* influyente.

influenza [ˌinflu'enzə] *n* gripe *f*.

influx ['inflʌks] *n* (*gas, etc.*) entrada *f*; (*people*) afluencia *f*.

inform [in'foːm] *v* informar. **informative** *adj* informativo. **informer** *n* denunciante *m, f*.

informal [in'foːml] *adj* sin ceremonia; (*person*) sencillo; (*tone*) familiar; (*unofficial*) no oficial. **informality** *n* ausencia de ceremonia *f*; sencillez *f*.

information [ˌinfə'meiʃən] *n* información *f*. **information bureau** centro de informaciones *m*. **information desk** informaciones *f pl*.

infra-red [ˌinfrə'red] *adj* infrarrojo.

infringe [in'frindʒ] *v* infringir, violar. **infringe on** usurpar. **infringement** *n* infracción *f*; usurpación *f*.

infuriate [in'fjuəriˌeit] *v* enfurecer; exasperar. **infuriating** *adj* exasperante.

ingenious [in'dʒiːniəs] *adj* ingenioso. **ingenuity** *n* ingeniosidad *f*.

ingot ['ingət] *n* lingote *m*.

ingredient [in'griːdjənt] *n* ingrediente *m*.

inhabit [in'habit] *v* (*occupy*) habitar; (*live in*) vivir en. **inhabitant** *n* habitante *m*.

inhale [in'heil] *v* inhalar; (*smoke*) tragar.

inherent [in'hiərənt] *adj* inherente.

inherit [in'herit] *v* heredar. **inheritance** *n* herencia *f*; sucesión *f*.

inhibit [in'hibit] *v* (*restrain*) inhibir; (*prevent*) impedir. **inhibition** *n* inhibición *f*.

inhuman [in'hjuːmən] *adj* inhumano; insensible. **inhumanity** *n* inhumanidad *f*.

iniquity [i'nikwəti] *n* iniquidad *f*. **iniquitous** *adj* inicuo.

initial [i'niʃl] *adj* inicial, primero. *n* inicial *f*; (*used as abbreviation*) siglas *f pl*. *v* poner iniciales a. **initially** *adv* al principio.

initiate [i'niʃiˌeit] *v* iniciar; (*proceedings*) entablar; (*membership*) admitir. **initiation** *n* iniciación *f*.

initiative [i'niʃiətiv] *n* iniciativa *f*.

inject [in'dʒekt] *v* inyectar. **injection** *n* inyección *f*.

injure ['indʒə] *v* herir; lastimar; ofender. **injury** *n* herida *f*; daño *m*; ofensa *f*. **injurious** *adj* injurioso; ofensivo.

injustice [in'dʒʌstis] *n* injusticia *f*.

ink [iŋk] *n* tinta *f*. **ink-well** *n* tintero *m*. *v* entintar.

inkling ['iŋkliŋ] *n* idea *f*; algo *m*; sospecha *f*; indicio *m*.

inland ['inlənd; *adv* in'land] *adj* interior. **Inland Revenue** fisco *m*. *adv* hacia el interior.

in-laws ['inˌloːs] *pl n* (*coll*) familia política *f sing*.

***inlay** [in'lei; *n* 'inlei] *v* incrustar; adornar con marquetería. *n* incrustación *f*; (*with coloured woods*) taracea *f*.

inlet ['inlet] *n* cala *f*; brazo de mar *m*; (*tech*) entrada *f*.

inmate ['inmeit] *n* (*prison*) preso *m*; (*asylum*) internado, -a *m, f*; (*hospital*) enfermo, -a *m, f*.

inn [in] *n* posada *f*; taberna *f*. **innkeeper** *n* posadero, -a *m, f*; tabernero, -a *m, f*.

innate [ˌi'neit] *adj* innato.

inner ['inə] *adj* interior; íntimo. **inner tube** cámara de neumático *f*.

innocent ['inəsnt] *adj* inocente. **innocence** *n* inocencia *f*.

innocuous [i'nokjuəs] *adj* inocuo; inofensivo.

innovation [inə'veiʃən] *n* innovación *f*.

innuendo [ˌinju'endou] *n* insinuación *f*.

innumerable [i'njuːmərəbl] *adj* innumerable.

inoculate [i'nokjuˌleit] *v* inocular. **inoculation** *n* inoculación *f*.

inorganic [ˌinoː'ganik] *adj* inorgánico.

input ['input] *n* entrada *f*; (*computer*) input *m*.

inquest ['inkwest] *n* encuesta *f*.

inquire [in'kwaiə] *v* informarse de; preguntar. **inquire into** investigar. **inquiring** *adj* (*mind*) curioso; (*look*) inquisidor. **inquiry** *n* pregunta *f*; (*official*) investigación *f*; (*request for information*) petición de información *f*. **inquiry office** oficina de informaciones *f*. **inquiries** *pl n* (*sign*) información *f sing*.

inquisition [ˌinkwi'ziʃən] *n* investigación *f*. **the Inquisition** la Inquisición *f*.

inquisitive [in'kwizitiv] *adj* preguntón; curioso. **inquisitiveness** *n* curiosidad *f*.

insane [in'sein] *adj* loco. **insane asylum** manicomio *m*. **insanity** *n* locura *f*.

insatiable [in'seiʃəbl] *adj* insaciable.

inscribe [in'skraib] *v* inscribir; (*engrave*) grabar. **inscription** *n* inscripción *f*.

insect ['insekt] *n* insecto *m*; (*coll*) bicho *m*. **insecticide** *n* insecticida *f*.

insecure [,insi'kjuə] *adj* inseguro; (*unstable*) inestable. **insecurity** *n* inseguridad *f*.
inseminate [in'semineit] *v* inseminar. insemination *n* inseminación *f*.
insensitive [in'sensətiv] *adj* insensible. insensitivity *n* insensibilidad *f*.
inseparable [in'sepərəbl] *adj* inseparable.
insert [in'səːt; *n* 'insəːt] *v* introducir; (*advert*) insertar; (*between pages*) intercalar. *n* (*in a book*) encarte *m*. **insertion** *n* inserción *f*; encarte *m*; (*advert*) anuncio *m*.
inshore [,in'ʃoː] *adj* cercano a la orilla.
inside [,in'said] *adv* dentro, adentro. *prep* dentro de. *adj* interior; confidencial. *n* interior *m*; parte de adentro *f*. **inside out** al revés.
insidious [in'sidiəs] *adj* insidioso. insidiousness *n* insidia *f*.
insight ['insait] *n* perspicacia *f*.
insignificant [,insig'nifikənt] *adj* insignificante. insignificance *n* insignificancia *f*.
insincere [,insin'siə] *adj* insincero; hipócrita. insincerity *n* insinceridad *f*; hipocresía *f*.
insinuate [in'sinjueit] *v* insinuar. insinuation *n* insinuación *f*.
insipid [in'sipid] *adj* insípido, soso.
insist [in'sist] *v* insistir, empeñarse. insistence *n* insistencia *f*, empeño *m*. insistent *adj* insistente. insistently *adv* insistentemente.
insolent ['insələnt] *adj* insolente. insolence *n* insolencia *f*.
insoluble [in'soljubl] *adj* insoluble.
insomnia [in'somniə] *n* insomnio *m*. insomniac *n*(*m*+*f*). *adj* insomne.
inspect [in'spekt] *v* inspeccionar, examinar. inspection *n* inspección *f*, examen *m*. inspector *n* inspector *m*, *f*.
inspire [in'spaiə] *v* inspirar. inspiration *n* inspiración *f*. inspirational *adj* inspirador.
instability [,instə'biləti] *n* inestabilidad *f*, instabilidad *f*.
install [in'stoːl] *v* instalar. installation *n* instalación *f*.
instalment [in'stoːlmənt] *n* (*payment*) plazo *m*; (*serial*) fascículo *m*. **monthly instalment** mensualidad *f*.
instance ['instəns] *n* ejemplo *m*. **for instance** por ejemplo.
instant ['instənt] *n* instante *m*, momento *m*. *adj* (*coffee, soup, etc.*) instantáneo; urgente; inmediato; inminente; (*this*

month) corriente. **instantaneous** *adj* instantáneo. **instantly** *adv* al instante.
instead [in'sted] *adv* en su lugar. **instead of** en vez de.
instep ['instep] *n* empeine *m*.
instigate ['instigeit] *v* instigar, incitar; fomentar. instigation *n* instigación *f*. instigator *n* instigador, -a *m*, *f*.
instil [in'stil] *v* instilar; inculcar.
instinct ['instiŋkt] *n* instinto *m*. **instinctive** *adj* instintivo.
institute ['institjuːt] *n* instituto *m*. *v* instituir, establecer; (*start*) empezar. institution *n* institución *f*; establecimiento *m*.
instruct [in'strʌkt] *v* (*teach*) instruir; (*order*) mandar. instruction *n* instrucción *f*. instructive *adj* instructivo. instructor *n* instructor *m*; profesor *m*; maestro *m*.
instrument ['instrəmənt] *n* instrumento *m*. instrumental *adj* instrumental. **be instrumental in** contribuir a.
insubordinate [,insə'boːdənət] *adj* insubordinado. **insubordination** *n* insubordinación *f*.
insufficient [,insə'fiʃənt] *adj* insuficiente. insufficiency *n* insuficiencia *f*.
insular ['insjulə] *adj* insular; (*outlook*) estrecho de miras.
insulate ['insjuleit] *v* aislar. insulation *n* aislamiento *m*; (*material*) aislador *m*.
insulin ['insjulin] *n* insulina *f*.
insult [in'sʌlt; *n* 'insʌlt] *v* insultar. *n* insulto *m*.
insure [in'ʃuə] *v* asegurar. insurance *n* seguro *m*. **insurance broker** corredor de seguros *m*. **insurance policy** póliza de seguro *f*. **fully comprehensive insurance** seguro a todo riesgo *m*. **third party insurance** seguro contra terceros *m*. **national insurance** seguros sociales *m pl*. **take out insurance** hacerse un seguro.
intact [in'takt] *adj* intacto.
intake ['inteik] *n* (*air, water*) toma *f*; (*mot*) entrada *f*; (*fuel, steam*) válvula de admisión *f*; (*food*) ración *f*; (*school*) número de personas admitidas *m*; (*thing taken in*) consumo *m*.
intangible [in'tandʒəbl] *adj* intangible. intangibility *n* intangibilidad *f*.
integral ['intigrəl] *adj* (*part*) integrante; (*complete*) integral. *n* integral *f*.
integrate ['intigreit] *v* integrar. **integration** *n* integración *f*.

integrity [in'tegrəti] *n* integridad *f*.
intellect ['intilekt] *n* intelecto *m*, inteligencia *f*. **intellectual** *n*(*m*+*f*), *adj* intelectual.
intelligent [in'telidʒənt] *adj* inteligente.
intelligence *n* inteligencia *f*; (*information*) noticia *f*; (*secret information*) información *f*.
intelligible [in'telidʒəbl] *adj* inteligible.
intend [in'tend] *v* proponerse.
intense [in'tens] *adj* intenso; fuerte; profundo; ardiente; enorme. **intensify** *v* intensificar; aumentar. **intensity** *n* intensidad *f*. **intensive** *adj* intensivo. **intensive care** asistencia intensiva *f*.
intent¹ [in'tent] *n* intención *f*, propósito *m*.
intent² [in'tent] *adj* atento; profundo; constante.
intention [in'tenʃən] *n* intención *f*. **intentional** *adj* intencional.
inter [in'tɜː] *v* enterrar. **interment** *n* entierro *m*.
interact [,intər'akt] *v* actuar recíprocamente. **interaction** *n* interacción *f*.
intercede [,intə'siːd] *v* interceder. **intercession** *n* intercesión *f*.
intercept [,intə'sept] *v* (*message*) interceptar; (*stop someone*) parar. **interception** *n* intercepción *f*, interceptación *f*.
interchange [,intə'tʃeindʒ] *n* intercambio *m*; cambio *m*. **interchangeable** *adj* intercambiable.
intercom ['intəkɒm] *n* interfono *m*.
intercourse ['intəkɔːs] *n* (*social*) trato *m*; (*pol, comm*) relaciones *f pl*; (*sexual*) contacto sexual *m*.
interest ['intrist] *n* interés *m*; (*advantage*) beneficio *m*. **business interests** negocios *m pl*. *v* interesar. **be interested** interesarse en.
interfere [,intə'fiə] *v* entrometerse. **interfere with** (*hinder*) estorbar; (*touch*) tocar; (*interests*) oponerse a. **interference** *n* intromisión *f*; obstrucción *f*; (*radio*) parásitos *m pl*. **interfering** *adj* (*person*) entrometido; interferente.
interim ['intərim] *n* interin *m*. *adj* provisional.
interior [in'tiəriə] *nm, adj* interior.
interjection [,intə'dʒekʃən] *n* interjección *f*.
interlude ['intəluːd] *n* intervalo *m*; (*theatre*) entremés *m*; (*music*) interludio *m*.

intermediate [,intə'miːdiət] *adj* intermedio. **intermediary** *n* intermediario, -a *m, f*.
interminable [in'tɜːminəbl] *adj* interminable.
intermission [,intə'miʃən] *n* (*interruption*) intermisión *f*; (*theatre*) entreacto *m*; (*cinema*) descanso *m*.
intermittent [,intə'mitənt] *adj* intermitente. **intermittently** *adv* a intervalos.
intern [in'tɜːn] *n* interno *m*. *v* internar. **internment** *n* internamiento *m*.
internal [in'tɜːnl] *adj* interno. **internal combustion engine** motor de combustión interna *m*.
international [,intə'naʃənl] *adj* internacional. **international date line** línea de cambio de fecha *f*.
interpose [,intə'pəuz] *v* interponer; intervenir. **interposition** *n* interposición *f*.
interpret [in'tɜːprit] *v* interpretar. **interpretation** *n* interpretación *f*. **interpreter** *n* intérprete *m, f*.
interrogate [in'terəgeit] *v* interrogar. **interrogation** *n* interrogatorio *m*. **interrogator** *n* interrogador, -a *m, f*.
interrogative [,intə'rogətiv] *adj* (*sentence*) interrogativo; (*look*) interrogador. *n* palabra interrogativa *f*.
interrupt [,intə'rʌpt] *v* interrumpir. **interruption** *n* interrupción *f*.
intersect [,intə'sekt] *v* cruzar; (*math*) cortar. **intersection** *n* (*mot*) cruce *m*; (*math*) intersección *f*.
intersperse [,intə'spɜːs] *v* esparcir.
interval ['intəvl] *n* (*time, space, music*) intervalo *m*; (*theatre*) entreacto *m*; (*cinema*) descanso *m*.
intervene [,intə'viːn] *v* intervenir; (*happen*) ocurrir; (*time*) transcurrir; (*distance*) mediar. **intervention** *n* intervención *f*.
interview ['intəvjuː] *n* entrevista *f*, interviú *f*. *v* entrevistar. **interviewer** *n* entrevistador, -a *m, f*.
intestine [in'testin] *n* intestino *m*. **intestinal** *adj* intestinal.
intimate¹ ['intimət] *adj* íntimo; (*individual*) personal; (*loving*) amoroso; (*detailed*) profundo. **intimacy** *n* relaciones íntimas *f pl*.
intimate² ['intimeit] *v* insinuar; anunciar. **intimation** *n* insinuación *f*; indicación *f*; indicio *m*.

intimidate [in'timideit] v intimidar. **intim-idation** n intimidación f.

into ['intu] prep en; a; hacia; contra; dentro.

intolerable [in'tolərəbl] adj intolerable.

intolerant [in'tolərənt] adj intolerante. **intolerance** n intolerancia f.

intonation [,intə'neifən] n entonación f. **intone** v entonar.

intoxicate [in'toksikeit] v embriagar, emborrachar. **intoxicated** adj borracho, ebrio. **intoxication** n embriaguez f, borrachera f.

intransitive [in'transitiv] nm, adj intransitivo.

intravenous [,intrə'vinəs] adj intravenoso.

intrepid [in'trepid] adj intrépido.

intricate ['intriket] adj intrincado; complejo. **intricacy** n intrincamiento m; complejidad f.

intrigue ['intriːg; v in'triːg] n intriga f. v intrigar.

intrinsic [in'trinsik] adj intrínseco.

introduce [,intrə'djuːs] v presentar; introducir; (acquaint) iniciar. **introduction** n presentación f; introducción f. **introductory** adj introductorio.

introspective [,intrə'spektiv] adj introspectivo. **introspection** n introspección f.

introvert ['intrə,vəːt] n introvertido, -a m, f. **introverted** adj introvertido.

intrude [in'truːd] v imponer; meter por fuerza. **intruder** n intruso, -a m, f. **intrusion** n entremetimiento m.

intuition [,intjuː'ifən] n intuición f. **intuitive** adj intuitivo.

inundate ['inʌndeit] v inundar. **inundation** n inundación f.

invade [in'veid] v invadir. **invader** n invasor, -a m, f. **invasion** n invasión f.

invalid¹ ['invəlid] nm, adj (disabled) inválido; (sick) enfermo.

invalid² [in'valid] adj (not valid) nulo.

invaluable [in'valjuəbl] adj inestimable.

invariable [in'veəriəbl] adj invariable. **invariably** adv invariablemente; constantemente.

invective [in'vektiv] n invectiva f.

invent [in'vent] v inventar. **invention** n invención f. **inventive** adj inventivo. **inventor** n inventor, -a m, f.

inventory ['invəntri] n inventario m.

invert [in'vəːt] v invertir. **inverted commas** comillas f pl. **inversion** n inversión f.

invertebrate [in'vəːtibrət] nm, adj invertebrado.

invest [in'vest] v invertir; (install) investir. **invest in** (fig) comprarse. **invest with** (fig) envolver en. **investment** n inversión f. **investor** n inversionista m, f.

investigate [in'vestigeit] v investigar, examinar; estudiar. **investigation** n investigación f; estudio m.

invigorating [in'vigəreitiŋ] adj tónico, estimulante. **invigorate** v vigorizar, estimular.

invincible [in'vinsəbl] adj invencible.

invisible [in'vizəbl] adj invisible. **invisibility** n invisibilidad f.

invite [in'vait] v invitar, convidar; (questions) solicitar; (ask for) pedir; (cause) provocar. **invitation** n invitación f. **inviting** adj atractivo; seductor; tentador; apetitoso.

invoice ['invois] n factura f. v facturar.

invoke [in'vouk] v invocar; (ask for) pedir; (fall back on) recurrir. **Invocation** n invocación f.

involuntary [in'voləntəri] adj involuntario. **involuntarily** adv sin querer.

involve [in'volv] v (concern) concernir; (imply) suponer; (affect) afectar; (entail) ocasionar; (draw somebody in) comprometer; mezclar; (require) exigir; (complicate) complicar. **involved** adj complicado. **involvement** n envolvimiento m; participación f; compromiso m.

inward ['inwəd] adj interior, interno; (thoughts) íntimo. **inwardly** adv interiormente. **inwards** adv hacia dentro.

iodine ['aiədiːn] n yodo m.

ion ['aiən] n ion m.

irate [ai'reit] adj furioso.

Ireland ['aiələnd] n Irlanda f. **Irish** nm, adj irlandés. **the Irish** los irlandeses m pl.

iris ['aiəris] n lirio m.

irk [əːk] v molestar. **irksome** adj molesto.

iron ['aiən] n (metal) hierro m; (for pressing) plancha f; (golf) palo de golf m. **cast iron** hierro colado m. **Iron Curtain** telón de acero m. **wrought iron** hierro forjado m. **ironmonger's** n quincallería f. v planchar. **iron out** (fig) allanar. **ironing** n planchado m. **ironing board** tabla de planchar.

irony ['aiərəni] n ironía f. **ironic** adj irónico.

irrational [i'rafənl] adj irracional. n (math) número irracional m.

irregular [i'regjulə] *adj* irregular. **irregularity** *n* irregularidad *f*.

irrelevant [i'reləvənt] *adj* (*remark*) fuera de propósito; (*beside the point*) no pertinente.

irreparable [i'repərəbl] *adj* irreparable.

irresistible [,iri'zistəbl] *adj* irresistible.

irrespective [,iri'spektiv] *adj* **irrespective of** sin tener en cuenta.

irresponsible [,iri'sponsəbl] *adj* irresponsable; irreflexivo.

irrevocable [i'revəkəbl] *adj* irrevocable.

irrigate ['irigeit] *v* irrigar. **irrigation** *n* irrigación *f*.

irritate ['iriteit] *v* irritar. **irritable** *adj* irritable. **irritation** *n* irritación *f*.

is [iz] *V* be.

island ['ailənd] *n* isla; (*traffic*) refugio *m*.

isolate ['aisəleit] *v* aislar. **isolation** *n* aislamiento *m*.

issue ['iʃuː] *n* (*stamps, shares, etc.*) emisión *f*; (*publication*) publicación *f*; (*edition*) tirada *f*; (*copy*) número *m*; (*passport*) expedición *f*; (*distribution*) reparto *m*; (*outcome*) resultado *m*; (*question*) cuestión *f*; (*affair*) asunto *m*; (*offspring*) progenie *f*. **take issue with** estar en desacuerdo con. *v* salir; resultar; publicar; distribuir; (*give*) dar; emitir; (*decree*) promulgar; (*warrant, cheque*) extender; (*tickets*) expender; (*licence*) facilitar.

isthmus ['isməs] *n* istmo *m*.

it [it] *pron* él, ella ello; (*direct object*) lo, la; (*indirect object*) le.

italic [i'talik] *adj* itálico. **italics** *pl n* bastardilla *f sing*.

Italy ['itəli] *n* Italia *f*. **Italian** *n, adj* italiano, -a.

itch [itʃ] *n* picazón *f*; (*desire*) ganas *f pl*. *v* picar.

item ['aitəm] *n* artículo *m*; noticia *f*; detalle *m*; punto *m*. **itemize** *v* detallar.

itinerary [ai'tinərəri] *n* itinerario *m*.

its [its] *adj* su (*pl* sus).

itself [it'self] *pron* se; él/ello mismo, ella misma; (*after prep*) sí mismo, -a. **by itself** aislado; (*alone*) solo.

ivory ['aivəri] *n* marfil *m*.

ivy ['aivi] *n* hiedra *f*, yedra *f*.

J

jab [dʒab] *v* (*stab*) pinchar; (*elbow*) dar un codazo a. *n* pinchazo *m*; codazo *m*; (*blow*) golpe seco *m*; (*coll: injection*) injección *f*.

jack [dʒak] *n* (*mot*) gato *m*; (*cards*) valet *m*, jota *f*; (*Spanish cards*) sota *f*. *v* **jack up** levantar con el gato.

jackal ['dʒakoːl] *n* chacal *m*.

jackdaw ['dʒakdoː] *n* grajilla *f*.

jacket ['dʒakit] *n* chaqueta *f*; (*book*) sobrecubierta *f*; (*tech: cylinder, pipe, etc.*) camisa *f*.

jackpot ['dʒakpot] *n* premio gordo *m*.

jade [dʒeid] *nm, adj* jade *m*.

jaded ['dʒeidid] *adj* cansado.

jagged ['dʒagid] *adj* dentado.

jaguar ['dʒagjuə] *n* jaguar *m*.

jail [dʒeil] *n* cárcel *f*. *v* encarcelar. **jailer** *n* carcelero *m*.

jam¹ [dʒam] *v* (*force in*) meter a la fuerza; (*squash*) apretar; (*catch*) pillar; (*pack*) atestar; (*clog*) atorar; (*block*) bloquear; (*moving part*) atascar; (*radio*) interferir; (*become wedged*) atrancarse. *n* atasco *m*; (*people*) agolpamiento *m*; (*traffic*) embotellamiento *m*. **be in a jam** (*coll*) estar en un apuro.

jam² [dʒam] *n* mermelada *f*.

janitor ['dʒanitə] *n* portero *m*.

January ['dʒanjuəri] *n* enero *m*.

Japan [dʒə'pan] *n* Japón *m*. **Japanese** *nm, adj* japonés.

jar¹ [dʒaɪ] *n* (*vessel*) vasija *f*; (*jam pot*) tarro *m*; (*large pot*) tinaja *f*.

jar² [dʒaɪ] *v* (*sound*) chirriar; (*shake*) sacudir; (*colours*) chocar; (*music*) sonar mal; (*nerves*) irritar.

jargon ['dʒaɪgən] *n* jerga *f*.

jasmine ['dʒazmin] *n* jazmín *m*.

jaundice ['dʒoɪndis] *n* ictericia *f*; (*fig*) celos *m pl*.

jaunt [dʒoɪnt] *n* paseo *m*.

jaunty ['dʒoɪnti] *adj* vivaz; desenvuelto.

javelin ['dʒavəlin] *n* jabalina *f*.

jaw [dʒoɪ] *n* (*person*) mandíbula *f*; (*animal*) quijada *f*. **jawbone** *n* mandíbula *f*; quijada *f*.

jazz [dʒaz] *n* jazz *m*. **jazz band** orquesta de jazz *f*.

jealous ['dʒeləs] *adj* celoso; envidioso. **jealousy** *n* celos *m pl*; envidia *f*.

jeans [dʒiːns] *pl n* pantalones vaqueros *m pl.*

jeep [dʒiːp] *n* jeep *m.*

jeer [dʒiə] *v* (*boo*) abuchear; (*mock*) mofarse de. *n* abucheo *m*; mofa *f.*

jelly ['dʒeli] *n* jalea *f.* **jellyfish** *n* medusa *f.*

jeopardize ['dʒepədaiz] *v* arriesgar. **jeopardy** *n* riesgo *m*, peligro *m.*

jerk [dʒəːk] *n* sacudida *f*; (*shove*) empujón *m*; (*pull*) tirón. *v* sacudir; mover a tirones. **jerkily** *adv* con sacudidas. **jerky** *adj* espasmódico.

jersey ['dʒəːzi] *n* jersey *m.*

jest [dʒest] *v* bromear. *n* broma *f.* **jester** *n* bromista *m, f.*

jet [dʒet] *n* (*liquid*) chorro *m*; (*flame*) llama *f*; (*plane*) avión de reactor *m.* **jet-propelled** *adj* de reacción.

jetty ['dʒeti] *n* muelle *m.*

Jew [dʒuː] *n* judío, -a *m, f.* **Jewish** *adj* judío.

jewel ['dʒuːəl] *n* joya *f*, piedra preciosa *f*; (*in a watch*) rubí *m.* **jeweller** *n* joyero *m.* **jeweller's** *n* joyería *f.* **jewellery** *n* joyería *f.*

jig [dʒig] *n* giga *f.* *v* bailar la giga; dar saltitos.

jigsaw ['dʒigsɔː] *n* (*puzzle*) rompecabezas *m invar*; (*saw*) sierra de vaivén *f.*

jilt [dʒilt] *v* dejar plantado a.

jingle ['dʒiŋgl] *n* tintineo *m*; (*verse*) copla *f.* *v* tintinear.

jinx [dʒiŋks] *n* (*coll*) maleficio *m.* **put a jinx on** echar mal de ojo a.

job [dʒob] *n* trabajo *m*, empleo *m.* **job lot** colección miscelánea *f.* **make a good job of (something)** hacer (algo) bien. **odd-job man** factótum *m.*

jockey ['dʒoki] *n* jinete *m*; jockey *m.*

jocular ['dʒokjulə] *adj* jocoso; bromista.

jodhpurs ['dʒodpəz] *pl n* pantalones de montar *m pl.*

jog [dʒog] *n* sacudida *f*; (*with elbow*) codazo *m.* **jogtrot** *n* trote corto *m.* *v* sacudir; (*memory*) refrescar. **jog someone's elbow** darle en el codo a uno. **jogging** *n* jogging *m.*

join [dʒoin] *v* juntar, unir; (*roads*) ir a dar a; (*friends*) reunirse con; (*a company*) ingresar en; (*a club*) hacerse socio de; (*a political party*) afiliarse a; (*hands*) darse la mano; (*two pieces*) ensamblar; (*rivers*) confluir. **join in** participar en. **join up** (*mil*) alistarse. **joiner** carpintero *m.*

joint [dʒoint] *n* juntura *f*, unión *f*; (*anat*) articulación *f*; (*meat*) corte para asar; (*slang: place*) antro *m.* *adj* unido; colectivo; conjunto; mutuo. **jointly** *adv* en común.

joist [dʒoist] *n* vigueta *f.*

joke [dʒouk] *n* chiste *m*; (*prank*) broma *f.* *v* contar chistes; bromear. **joker** *n* chistoso, -a *m, f*; bromista *m, f*; (*fool*) payaso, -a *m, f*; (*cards*) comodín *m.*

jolly ['dʒoli] *adj* alegre, jovial; divertido. *adv* (*coll: emphatic*) muy. **jollity** *n* alegría *f*, jovialidad *f.*

jolt [dʒoult] *v* sacudir; (*vehicle*) traquetear. *n* sacudida *f*; choque *m*; (*fig: shock*) susto *m.*

jostle ['dʒosl] *v* (*push*) empujar; (*elbow*) codear. *n* empujones *m pl.*

jot [dʒot] *n* jota *f.* *v* **jot down** apuntar.

journal ['dʒəːnl] *n* (*newspaper*) periódico *m*; (*magazine*) revista *f*; (*diary*) diario *m*; (*of a learned society*) boletín *m.* **journalism** *n* periodismo *m.* **journalist** *n* periodista *m, f.*

journey ['dʒəːni] *n* viaje *m.* *v* viajar.

jovial ['dʒouviəl] *adj* jovial. **joviality** *n* jovialidad *f.*

joy [dʒoi] *n* alegría *f*; placer *m.* **joyful** *or* **joyous** *adj* alegre, gozoso.

jubilant ['dʒuːbilənt] *adj* jubiloso. **jubilation** *n* júbilo *m.*

jubilee ['dʒuːbiliː] *n* jubileo *m.*

Judaism ['dʒuːdei,izəm] *n* judaísmo *m.*

judge [dʒʌdʒ] *n* juez *m*; árbitro *m.* *v* juzgar; arbitrar. **judging by** a juzgar por. **judgement** *n* (*trial*) juicio; (*legal sentence*) sentencia *f*; apreciación *f.*

judicial [dʒuːˈdiʃəl] *adj* judicial.

judicious [dʒuːˈdiʃəs] *adj* juicioso.

judo ['dʒuːdou] *n* judo *m.*

jug [dʒʌg] *n* jarra *f*; (*slang: prison*) chirona *f.*

juggernaut ['dʒʌgənɔːt] *n* camión grande *m.*

juggle ['dʒʌgl] *v* hacer juegos malabares. **juggler** *n* malabarista *m, f.* **juggling** *n* juegos malabares *m pl.*

jugular ['dʒʌgjulə] *nf, adj* yugular.

juice [dʒuːs] *n* jugo *m.* **juicy** *adj* jugoso.

jukebox ['dʒuːkbɔks] *n* máquina de discos *f.*

July [dʒuˈlai] *n* julio *m.*

jumble ['dʒʌmbl] *v* embrollar; mezclar. *n* embrollo *m*; mezcolanza *f.* **jumble sale** venta de caridad *f.*

jump [dʒʌmp] *n* salto *m*. *v* saltar. **jump at** (*offer*, *etc*.) aprovechar. **make someone jump** sobresaltar a uno. **jumpy** *adj* (*coll*) nervioso.

jumper ['dʒʌmpə] *n* (*garment*) jersey *m*.

junction ['dʒʌŋkʃən] *n* (*join*) unión *f*; (*rail*) empalme *m*; (*road*) cruce *f*.

juncture ['dʒʌŋkʃə] *n* coyuntura *f*. **at this juncture** en esta coyuntura.

June [dʒuːn] *n* junio *m*.

jungle ['dʒʌŋgl] *n* selva *f*.

junior ['dʒuːnjə] *adj* (*younger*) hijo; (*lower rank*) subalterno. *n* menor *m, f*; subalterno, -a *m, f*; (*in school*) pequeño, -a *m, f*.

juniper ['dʒuːnipə] *n* enebro *m*. **juniper berry** enebrina *f*.

junk[1] [dʒʌŋk] *n* trastos viejos *m pl*; (*coll*: *rubbish*) porquería *f*. **junk-shop** *n* baratillo *m*.

junk[2] [dʒʌŋk] *n* (*naut*) junco *m*.

jurisdiction [dʒuəris'dikʃən] *n* jurisdicción *f*.

jury ['dʒuəri] *n* jurado *m*. **juror** *n* jurado, -a *m, f*.

just [dʒʌst] *adv* justo; justamente; precisamente. **have just** acabar de. *adj* justo; exacto.

justice ['dʒʌstis] *n* justicia *f*. **Justice of the Peace** juez de paz *m*.

justify ['dʒʌstifai] *v* justificar. **justifiable** *adj* justificable. **justification** *n* justificación *f*.

jut [dʒʌt] *v* **jut out** sobresalir.

jute [dʒuːt] *n* yute *m*.

juvenile ['dʒuːvənail] *n* joven *m, f*, adolescente *m, f*, menor *m, f*. *adj* juvenil; infantil. **juvenile delinquent** delincuente juvenil *m, f*.

juxtapose [,dʒʌkstə'pouz] *v* yuxtaponer. **juxtaposition** *n* yuxtaposición *f*.

K

kaftan ['kaftan] *n* caftán *m*.

kaleidoscope [kə'laidəskoup] *n* calidoscopio *m*.

kangaroo [kaŋgə'ruː] *n* canguro *m*.

karate [kə'raːti] *n* karate *m*.

kebab [ki'bab] *n* pincho *m*.

keel [kiːl] *n* quilla *f*. **keel over** (*naut*) zozobrar; (*coll*: *faint*) desplomarse.

keen [kiːn] *adj* entusiasta; fuerte, vivo; penetrante; (*prices*) competitivo; (*mind*) agudo; (*sharp*) afilado. **keenly** *adv* con entusiasmo; profundamente. **keenness** *n* entusiasmo *m*; deseo *m*; profundidad *f*; agudeza *f*; finura *f*.

*****keep** [kiːp] *v* guardar; tener. (*promise*) cumplir; (*appointment*) acudir a; (*hang on to*) quedarse; (*support*) mantener; (*hold*) reservar; (*detain*) detener; (*look after*) cuidar; (*continue*) seguir. **keep up** seguir con. **keep away** mantener a distancia. **keep down** contener. **keep fit** mantenerse en forma. **keep out!** ¡prohibida la entrada! **keep up with** seguir. **keeper** *n* guarda *m*.

keg [keg] *n* barril *m*.

kennel ['kenl] *n* perrera *f*.

kerb [kəːb] *n* bordillo *m*.

kernel ['kəːnl] *n* (*nut*) pepita *f*; (*seed*) grano.

kerosene ['kerəsiːn] *n* queroseno *m*.

ketchup ['ketʃəp] *n* salsa de tomate *f*.

kettle ['ketl] *n* hervidor *m*. **kettledrum** *n* timbal *m*.

key [kiː] *n* llave *f*; (*for a code*) clave *f*; (*music*) tono *m*; (*piano*, *typewriter*) tecla *f*. **keyboard** *n* teclado *m*. **keyhole** *n* ojo de la cerradura *m*. **key-ring** *n* llavero *m*. *adj* clave.

khaki ['kaːki] *nm*, *adj* caqui.

kick [kik] *n* patada *f*, puntapié *m*; (*animal*) coz *f*; (*recoil*) culatazo *m*; (*fig*: *energy*) fuerza *f*. *v* dar una patada a; dar una coz. **kick off** (*football*) hacer el saque del centro; (*fig*) comenzar. **kick-off** *n* saque del centro *m*; (*coll*) comienzo *m*. **kick out** (*coll*) poner de patitas en la calle.

kid[1] [kid] *n* (*goat*) cabrito *m*; (*leather*) cabritilla *f*; (*coll*: *child*) niño, -a *m, f*.

kid[2] [kid] *v* (*coll*) tomar el pelo.

kidnap ['kidnap] *v* secuestrar, raptar. **kidnapper** *n* secuestrador, -a *m, f*, raptor, -ora *m, f*. **kidnapping** *n* secuestro *m*, rapto *m*.

kidney ['kidni] *n* riñón *m*.

kill [kil] *v* matar; (*fig*: *hopes*) arruinar. *n* muerte *f*; caza *f*. **killjoy** *n* aguafiestas *m, f invar*. **killer** *n* asesino, -a *m, f*. **killing** *n* (*murder*) asesinato *m*; (*slaughter*) matanza *f*.

kiln [kiln] *n* horno *m*.
kilo ['kiːlou] *n* kilo *m*.
kilogram ['kiləgram] *n* kilogramo *m*.
kilometre ['kiləmiːtə] *n* kilómetro *m*.
kin [kin] *n* parientes *m pl*. **kinship** *n* parentesco *m*.
kind¹ [kaind] *adj* amable; bueno. **kind-hearted** *adj* bondadoso. **kindness** *n* amabilidad *f*; bondad *f*.
kind² [kaind] *n* clase *f*, tipo *m*; género *m*; especie *f*. **in kind** en especie.
kindergarten ['kindəgaitn] *n* jardín de la infancia *m*.
kindle ['kindl] *v* encender; despertar.
kindred ['kindrid] *n* parientes *m pl*. *adj* (*related*) emparentado; (*similar*) semejante. **kindred spirits** almas gemelas *f pl*.
kinetic [kin'etik] *adj* cinético.
king [kiŋ] *n* rey *m*; (*draughts*) dama *f*. **kingfisher** *n* martín pescador *m*. **kingdom** *n* reino *m*. **king-size** *adj* enorme, gigante.
kink [kiŋk] *n* (*rope*) retorcimiento *m*; (*hair*) rizo *m*. *v* retorcer. **kinky** *adj* retorcido; (*coll*) extraño.
kiosk ['kiɔsk] *n* quiosco *m*, kiosko *m*.
kipper ['kipə] *n* arenque ahumado *m*.
kiss [kis] *v* besar. *n* beso *m*. **kiss of life** respiración boca a boca *f*.
kit [kit] *n* (*tools*) herramientas *f pl*; (*sport*) equipo *m*; (*first aid*) botiquín *m*; (*model for assembling*) maqueta *f*. **kit out** equipar.
kitchen ['kitʃin] *n* cocina *f*. **kitchen sink** fregadero *m*.
kite [kait] *n* cometa *f*; (*bird*) milano *m*.
kitten ['kitn] *n* gatito *m*.
kitty ['kiti] *n* plato *m*, platillo *m*.
kleptomania [kleptə'meiniə] *n* cleptomanía *f*. **kleptomaniac** *n*(*m*+*f*), *adj* cleptómano.
knack [nak] *n* facilidad *f*; tino *m*; habilidad *f*. **get the knack of** coger el tino de.
knapsack ['napsak] *n* mochila *f*.
knead [niːd] *v* amasar.
knee [niː] *n* rodilla *f*. **kneecap** *n* rótula *f*.
*kneel [niːl] *v* arrodillarse.
knew [njuː] *V* **know**.
knickers ['nikəz] *pl n* bragas *f pl*.
knife [naif] *n* cuchillo *m*. *v* (*stab*) apuñalar.
knight [nait] *n* caballero *m*. *v* armar caballero. **knighthood** *n* título/de caballero *m*.
knit [nit] *v* tejer. **knit together** juntar;

(*bones*) soldarse. **knitting** *n* tejido de punto *m*. **knitting machine** máquina de hacer punto *f*. **knitting needle** aguja de hacer punto *f*.
knob [nob] *n* bulto *m*; (*door*) pomo *m*; (*radio, etc.*) botón *m*; (*drawer*) tirador *m*; (*butter*) pedazo *m*.
knobbly ['nobli] *adj* nudoso.
knock [nok] *n* golpe *m*, toque *m*. *v* golpear, pegar; (*fig: criticize*) meterse con. **knock down** (*price*) rebajar; (*person*) atropellar; (*object*) derribar. **knock-kneed** *adj* patizambo. **knock out** (*stun*) dejar K.O.; (*from contest*) eliminar. **knockout** *n* (*boxing*) knock out *m*, K.O. *m*. **knock over** tirar. **knocker** *n* aldaba *f*, aldabón *m*.
knot [not] *n* nudo *m*. *v* anudar. **knotty** (*problem*) espinoso.
*know [nou] *v* (*facts*) saber; (*people, places*) conocer; (*recognize*) reconocer; (*distinguish*) distinguir. **know-all** *n* (*coll*) sabelotodo *m*, *f*. **know-how** *n* (*coll*) habilidad *f*; conocimientos *m pl*. **knowing** *adj* astuto; (*look*) de entendimiento.
knowledge ['nolidʒ] *n* conocimiento *m*. **knowledgeable** *adj* informado; erudito.
knuckle ['nʌkl] *n* nudillo *m*. **knuckle down to** ponerse seriamente a. **knuckle under** someterse.

L

label ['leibl] *n* etiqueta *f*. *v* poner etiqueta a.
laboratory [lə'borətəri] *n* laboratorio *m*.
labour ['leibə] *n* (*work*) trabajo *m*; (*task*) tarea *f*; (*effort*) esfuerzo *m*; (*childbirth*) parto *m*; (*manpower*) trabajadores *m pl*. **labour-saving** *adj* que ahorra trabajo. *v* trabajar; esforzarse. **laborious** *adj* laborioso. **labourer** *n* obrero *m*; peón *m*.
labyrinth ['labərinθ] *n* laberinto *m*.
lace [leis] *n* (*fabric*) encaje *m*. (*shoe*) cordón *m*. *v* atar; (*drink*) rociar.
lacerate ['lasəreit] *v* lacerar. **laceration** *n* laceración *f*.
lack [lak] *n* falta *f*, carencia *f*. **for lack of** por falta de. *v* carecer de, faltar a; necesitar.

lackadaisical [ˌlakə'deizikəl] *adj* apático; descuidado; tardo.

lacquer ['lakə] *n* (*hair*) laca *f*; (*paint*) pintura al duco *f*. *v* echar laca a; pintar al duco.

lad [lad] *n* (*coll*) chico *m*, muchacho *m*.

ladder ['ladə] *n* escalera de mano *f*; (*stocking*) carrera *f*. **ladderproof** *adj* indesmallable.

laden ['leidn] *adj* cargado.

ladle ['leidl] *n* cucharón *m*.

lady ['leidi] *n* señora *f*. **ladies** (*sign*) servicios de señoras *m pl*. **ladies and gentlemen!** ¡señoras y señores! **ladybird** *n* mariquita *f*. **lady-in-waiting** *n* dama de honor *f*. **ladylike** *adj* distinguida.

lag¹ [lag] *v* (*be behind time*) retrasarse; (*trail*) quedarse atrás. *n* intervalo *m*; (*delay*) retraso *m*.

lag² [lag] *v* poner un revestimiento calorífugo a. **lagging** *n* revestimiento calorífugo *m*.

lager ['laːgə] *n* cerveza dorada *f*.

lagoon [lə'guːn] *n* laguna *f*.

laid [leid] *V* lay¹.

lain [lein] *V* lie¹.

lair [leə] *n* guarida *f*.

laity ['leiəti] *n* laicado *m*.

lake [leik] *n* lago *m*.

lamb [lam] *n* cordero *m*. **lamb chop** chuleta de cordero *f*.

lame [leim] *adj* cojo; (*excuse, etc.*) malo. **lame duck** incapaz *m*, *f*. *v* dejar cojo. **lamely** *adv* cojeando. **lameness** *n* cojera *f*; debilidad *f*.

lament [lə'ment] *n* lamento *m*. *v* lamentar, llorar. **lamentable** *adj* lamentable. **lamentation** *n* lamentación *f*.

laminate ['lamineit] *v* laminar. **laminated** *adj* laminado.

lamp [lamp] *n* lámpara *f*; (*street*) farol *m*; (*mot*) faro *m*. **lamppost** *n* poste de alumbrado *m*. **lampshade** *n* pantalla *f*.

lance [laːns] *n* lanza *f*. *v* (*med*) abrir.

land [land] *n* tierra *f*; (*country*) país *m*. **landlady** *n* patrona *f*, dueña *f*. **landlord** *n* patrón *m*, dueño *m*. **landmark** *n* señal *f*. **landscape** *n* paisaje *m*. *v* desembarcar; (*aircraft*) aterrizar; (*fall*) caer; (*arrive*) llegar. **landing** *n* (*passengers*) desembarco *m*; (*cargo*) desembarque *m*; aterrizaje *m*. (*staircase*) rellano *m*. **landing stage** desembarcadero *m*.

lane [lein] *n* camino *m*; (*motorway*) banda *f*; (*running, swimming*) calle *f*.

language ['laŋgwidʒ] *n* (*means of expression*) lenguaje *m*; (*of a nation*) lengua *f*. **bad** *or* **foul language** palabrotas *f pl*.

languish ['laŋgwiʃ] *v* languidecer.

lanky ['laŋki] *adj* larguirucho.

lantern ['lantən] *n* farol *m*, linterna *f*.

lap¹ [lap] *n* (*sport*) vuelta *f*. *v* dar una vuelta; (*fold*) doblar; (*wrap*) envolver.

lap² [lap] *v* (*drink*) chapotear; beber a lengüetadas.

lap³ [lap] *n* rodillas *f pl*.

lapel [lə'pel] *n* solapa *f*.

lapse [laps] *n* (*time*) lapso *m*; (*failure*) fallo *m*; (*moral error*) desliz *m*; (*fall*) caída *f*. *v* (*time*) transcurrir; cometer un desliz; caer.

larceny ['laːsəni] *n* ratería *f*.

larch [laːtʃ] *n* alerce *m*.

lard [laːd] *n* manteca de cerdo *f*.

larder ['laːdə] *n* despensa *f*.

large [laːdʒ] *adj* grande, amplio. **at large** libre. **large-scale** *adj* en gran escala. **largely** *adv* en gran parte.

lark¹ [laːk] *n* (*zool*) alondra *f*.

lark² [laːk] *n* (*coll*) *n* juerga *f*; (*joke*) broma *f*. **lark about** hacer el tonto.

larva ['laːvə] *n*, *pl* **larvae** larva *f*.

larynx ['lariŋks] *n* laringe *f*. **laryngitis** *n* laringitis *f*.

laser ['leizə] *n* laser *m*.

lash [laʃ] *n* (*whip*) azote *m*; (*tail*) coletazo *m*; (*waves*) embate *m*; (*eyelash*) pestaña *f*. *v* azotar; (*wind*) sacudir; (*bind*) atar. **lash out** repartir golpes a diestro y siniestro; (*coll: money*) gastar. **lashing** *n* flagelación *f*; **lashings** *pl n* (*coll*) montones *m pl*.

lass [las] *n* chica *f*, muchacha *f*.

lassitude ['lasitjuːd] *n* lasitud *f*.

lasso [la'suː] *n* lazo *m*. *v* coger con el lazo.

last [laːst] *adj* último. **last-minute** *adj* de última hora. **last night** anoche. *adv* el último, la última, lo último; por última vez; finalmente. *n* último, -a *m*, *f*; final *m*. **at least** por fin. **lastly** *adv* por último. *v* durar; permanecer; aguantar. **last out** resistir. **lasting** *adj* duradero.

latch [latʃ] *n* picaporte *m*. *v* cerrar.

late [leit] *adj* tardío; (*recent*) reciente; (*last*) último; (*delayed*) retrasado; (*former*) antiguo; (*dead*) fallecid. *adv* (*not on time*) tarde; (*after the appointed time*) con retraso; recientemente; anteriormente. **lately** *adv* hace poco. **lateness** *n* retraso *m*. **later** *adj* más tarde. **see you**

later! ¡hasta luego! latest adj (most recent) último. at the latest a más tardar.

latent ['leitənt] adj latente.

lateral ['latərəl] adj lateral.

lathe [leið] n torno m.

lather ['laiðə] n (soup) espuma f; (horse) sudor m. v enjabonar.

Latin ['latin] n, adj latino, -a. n (language) latín m.

Latin America n América Latina f. Latin American n, adj latinoamericano, -a m, f.

latitude ['latitjuid] n latitud f.

latrine [lə'triːn] n letrina f. retrete m.

latter ['latə] adj último. the latter éste, ésta.

lattice ['latis] n celosía f; enrejado m.

laugh [lɑːf] v reír, reírse. laugh at reírse de. n risa f. laughable adj ridículo. it's no laughing matter no es cosa de risa. laughing-stock n hazmerreír m invar. laughter n risa f. risas f pl.

launch¹ ['lɔintʃ] v (ship) botar; (lifeboat) echar al mar; (missile) lanzar; (issue) emitir; (an attack) emprender; (a company) fundar; (film, play) estrenar. launching n botadura f; lanzamiento m; fundación f; iniciación f.

launch² ['lɔintʃ] n lancha f. motor launch lancha motora f.

launder ['lɔində] v lavar. launderette n lavandería automática f. laundry n (place) lavandería f.

laurel ['lɔrəl] n laurel m.

lava ['lɑːvə] n lava f.

lavatory ['lavətəri] n retrete m; servicios m pl.

lavender ['lavində] n espliego m.

lavish ['laviʃ] adj pródigo; generoso; abundante; lujoso. v prodigar.

law [lɔː] n ley f; (profession) derecho m. leyes f pl. law-abiding adj respetuoso de las leyes. lawsuit n proceso m. lawful adj legal; lícito. lawyer n jurista m, f; abogado m.

lawn [lɔin] n césped m. lawn-mower n cortacéspedes m invar.

lax [laks] adj flojo; elástico; negligente. laxity n laxitud f; elasticidad f; negligencia f; flojedad f.

laxative ['laksətiv] nm, adj laxante.

*lay¹ [lei] v (place) poner; (table) cubrir. layabout n holgazán, -ana m, f. lay-by n área de aparcamiento f. lay off (workers) despedir. lay on (provide) proveer de. lay-out n (arrangement) disposición f; (printing) composición f; (money) gasto m.

lay² [lei] adj laico. layman n seglar m.

lay³ [lei] V lie.

layer ['leiə] n capa f.

lazy ['leizi] adj perezoso. laze around holgazanear. laziness n pereza f.

*lead¹ [liːd] v llevar, conducir; remitir; (orchestra) dirigir; ir a la cabeza. lead on (encourage) animar; (seduce) seducir a. lead up to conducir a; preparar el terreno para. n (role) primer papel m; supremacía f; (clue) pista f; ejemplo; primer lugar; (advantage) ventaja f; (elec) cable m; (newspaper) noticia más importante f. leader n guía m, f; jefe m, f; caudillo m; editorial m. leadership n dirección f; mando m; jefatura f. leading adj primero principal; que encabeza.

lead² [led] n plomo m; (pencil) mina f.

leaf [liːf] n hoja f; página f; (table) hoja abatible f. v leaf through hojear. leaflet n (pamphlet) folleto m.

league [liːg] n liga f; in league with asociado con.

leak [liːk] n gotera f; (hole) agujero m; (gas, liquid) fuga f, salida f; (information) filtración f. v gotear; salirse; (boat) hacer agua; salirse; perder; filtrarse.

*lean¹ [liːn] v inclinarse. lean back reclinarse. lean on apoyarse. lean over backwards to (coll) no escatinar esfuerzos para. leaning (liking) predilección f; (tendency) tendencia f.

lean² [liːn] adj magro, sin grasa; (person) flaco. n carne magra f. leanness n magrez f; flaqueza f.

*leap [liːp] v saltar; lanzarse. n salto m, brinco m. by leaps and bounds a pasos agigantados. leapfrog n pídola f. leap year año bisiesto m.

*learn [ləm] v aprender. learn of enterarse de. learned adj instruido; erudito. learner n principiante m, f; (driver) aprendiz, -a m, f. learning n erudición f, saber m.

lease [liːs] n arrendamiento m. v arrendar. leasehold adj arrendado.

leash [liːʃ] n correa f.

least [liːst] adj menor. pron lo menos. adv menos. at least por lo menos.

leather ['leðə] n cuero m, piel f. patent leather charol m. leathery adj (meat) correoso; (skin) curtido.

*leave¹ [liːv] v irse, marcharse; (*abandon*) dejar; (*go out of*) salir de. **be left** quedar. **leave off** dejar de. **leave out** omitir. **left-luggage office** consigna *f*. **left-overs** pl n sobras *f* pl.

leave² [liːv] n permiso m. **be on leave** estar de permiso. **take leave of** despedirse de.

lecherous ['letʃərəs] adj lascivo. **lecher** n lascivo, -a m, *f*. **lechery** n lascivia *f*.

lectern ['lektən] n atril m.

lecture ['lektʃə] n conferencia *f*. **lecture hall** sala de conferencias *f*. v dar una conferencia; dar clase. **lecturer** n conferenciante m, *f*; (*university*) profesor, -a m, *f*.

led [led] V **lead¹**.

ledge [ledʒ] n saliente m; (*window*) antepecho m; (*shelf*) repisa *f*.

ledger ['ledʒə] n libro mayor m.

lee [liː] n (*shelter*) abrigo m; (*naut*) sotavento m. **leeward** adj, adv a sotavento.

leech [liːtʃ] n sanguijuela *f*; (*person*) lapa *f*.

leek [liːk] n puerro m.

leer [liə] v mirar de soslayo. n mirada de soslayo *f*. **leering** adj de soslayo.

leeway ['liːwei] n (*naut*) deriva *f*; (*fig*) campo m.

left¹ [left] V **leave¹**.

left² [left] adj izquierdo. n izquierda *f*. adv a or hacia la izquierda. **left-handed** adj zurdo. **left-wing** adj izquierdista.

leg [leg] n (*person*) pierna *f*; (*animal*) pata *f*; (*furniture*) pie; (*trousers*) pernera *f*; (*cookery: lamb*) pierna *f*; (*chicken*) muslo m; (*pork, venison*) pernil m; (*sport, journey*) etapa *f*.

legacy ['legəsi] n legado m, herencia *f*.

legal ['liːgəl] adj jurídico; legal; legítimo; lícito. **legality** n legalidad *f*. **legalize** v legalizar.

legend ['ledʒənd] n leyenda *f*. **legendary** adj legendario.

legible ['ledʒəbl] adj legible. **legibility** n legibilidad *f*.

legion ['liːdʒən] n legión *f*.

legislate ['ledʒisleit] v legislar; establecer por ley. **legislation** n legislación *f*. **legislature** n legislatura *f*.

legitimate [lə'dʒitimət] adj legítimo; válido; auténtico. **legitimacy** n legitimidad *f*.

leisure ['leʒə] n ocio n; tiempo libre m.

lemon ['lemən] n (*fruit*) limón m; (*tree*) limonero m; (*colour*) amarillo limón m. **lemonade** n limonada *f*. **lemon squeezer** exprimelimones m invar.

*lend [lend] v prestar. **lending library** biblioteca de préstamo *f*.

length [leŋθ] n longitud *f*, largo m; (*distance*) distancia *f*; (*space*) espacio m; (*piece*) pedazo m; **lengthen** v alargar; prolongar. **lengthy** adj largo; prolongado.

lenient ['liːniənt] adj indulgente, clemente. **leniency** n indulgencia *f*, clemencia *f*.

lens [lenz] n lente *f*; (*magnifying glass*) lupa *f*; (*photo*) objetivo m; (*eye*) cristalino m. **contact-lens** lente de contacto *f*.

lent [lent] V **lend**.

Lent [lent] n Cuaresma *f*.

lentil ['lentil] n lenteja *f*.

Leo ['liːou] n (*astrol*) León m.

leopard ['lepəd] n leopardo m.

leotard ['liːətaːd] n leotardo m.

leper ['lepə] n leproso, -a m, *f*. **leprosy** n lepra *f*. **leprous** adj leproso.

lesbian ['lezbiən] n*f*, adj lesbiana. **lesbianism** n lesbianismo m.

less [les] adj menos; menor; inferior. adv, prep menos. n menor m, *f*. **less and less** cada vez menos. **lessen** v disminuir, reducir. **lesser** adj menor.

lesson ['lesn] n lección *f*; clase *f*.

lest [lest] conj de miedo que; para no.

*let [let] v permitir, dejar; (*rent*) alquilar. **let down** (*lower*) bajar, descender; (*disappoint*) fallar. **let-down** n decepción *f*. **let in** dejar entrar; hacer entrar. **let out** dejar salir; (*clothes*) ensanchar;

lethal ['liːθəl] adj mortífero.

lethargy ['leθədʒi] n letargo m. **lethargic** adj letárgico.

letter ['letə] n (*character*) letra *f*; (*message*) carta *f*. **letter-box** n buzón m.

lettuce ['letis] n lechuga *f*.

leukaemia [luːˈkiːmiə] n leucemia *f*.

level ['levl] adj horizontal; (*flat*) llano; (*even*) a nivel; (*equal*) igual; (*spoonful*) raso; uniforme. **be level with** al nivel de. **level crossing** paso a nivel m. **level-headed** adj juicioso. n nivel m. **on the level** (*coll*) honrado. v nivelar, allanar.

lever ['liːvə] n palanca *f*. **leverage** n apalancamiento m.

levy ['levi] n exacción *f*; impuesto m. v exigir; imponer.

lewd [luːd] adj lascivo.
liable ['laiəbl] adj sujeto; (law) responsable. liable to capaz de. liability n responsabilidad f; inconveniente m; (nuisance) estorbo m.
liaison [liˈeizon] n enlace m.
liar ['laiə] n mentiroso, -a m, f.
libel ['laibəl] n (act) difamación f; (writing) escrito difanatorio m. v difamar. libellous adj disfamatorio.
liberal ['libərəl] adj liberal; libre; generoso.
liberate ['libəreit] v liberar. liberation n liberación f.
liberty ['libəti] n libertad f. at liberty libre.
Libra ['liːbrə] n Libra f.
library ['laibrəri] n biblioteca f. librarian n bibliotecario, -a m, f.
libretto [liˈbretou] n libreto m.
lice [lais] V louse.
licence ['laisəns] n licencia f, permiso m, autorización f; (driving) carnet de conducir m. licence number matrícula f. v conceder una licencia; autorizar. licensed adj autorizado. licensee n concesionario m.
lichen ['laikən] n liquen m.
lick [lik] v lamer. n lamedura f, lamido m.
lid [lid] n tapa f, tapadera f.
*lie¹ [lai] v acostarse; echarse. lie around estar tirado. lie down acostarse. lie in quedarse en la cama.
lie² [lai] n mentira f. v mentir.
lieutenant [ləfˈtenənt] n (mil) teniente m; (deputy) lugarteniente m.
life [laif] n vida f. lifeless adj sin vida, muerto.
lifebelt ['laifbelt] n cinturón salvavidas m.
lifeboat ['laifbout] n bote salvavidas m.
lifebuoy ['laifboi] n boya salvavidas f.
lifeguard ['laifgaːd] n vigilante m.
life insurance n seguro de vida m.
life-jacket n chaleco salvavidas m.
lifelike ['laiflaik] adj natural; parecido.
lifeline ['laiflain] n (diver's) cordel de señales m; (fig) cordón umbilical m.
lifelong ['laiflon] adj de toda la vida.
life-size adj de tamaño natural.
lifetime ['laiftaim] n vida f.
lift [lift] n ascensor m; (act of lifting) levantamiento m; (upward support) empuje m. give someone a lift llevar en coche. v levantar; alzar; coger; elevar.
ligament ['ligəmənt] n ligamento m.

*light¹ [lait] v (set fire to) encender; (room, etc.) iluminar. n luz f; lámpara f; (mot) faro m. adj claro; luminoso. light bulb bombilla f. lighthouse n faro m. light meter fotómetro m. light-year n año luz m. lighten v aclarar. lighter (cigarette) n mechero m. lighting n alumbrado m; iluminación f.
light² [lait] adj liviano; ligero. light-headed adj mareado; delirante. light-hearted adj alegre. lightweight adj ligero, de poco peso. lighten v alijerar; aliviar. lightness n ligereza f.
*light³ [lait] v light upon posarse.
lightning ['laitnin] n relámpago m. lightning conductor pararrayos m invar.
like¹ [laik] adj parecido; semejante; igual; mismo. prep como, igual que. be or look like parecerse a. liken v comparar. likeness n semejanza f; forma f; retrato m. likewise adv del mismo modo.
like² [laik] v gustarle (a uno); querer a; (want) querer. likeable adj amable, simpático. liking n cariño m; simpatía f; gusto m.
likely ['laikli] adj probable; posible; plausible. be likely to ser probable que. adv probablemente. likelihood n probabilidad f.
lilac ['lailək] n lila f; (colour) lila m. adj de color lila.
lily ['lili] n azucena f. lily-of-the-valley n lirio de los valles m.
limb [lim] n miembro m.
limbo ['limbou] n (rel) limbo m; (fig) olvido m.
lime¹ [laim] n cal f. limestone n piedra caliza f.
lime² [laim] n (fruit) lima f; (tree) limero m. lime juice jugo de lima m.
limelight ['laim,lait] n in the limelight en el candelero.
limerick ['limərik] n quintilla humorística f.
limit ['limit] n límite m. v limitar. limitation n limitación f. limitless adj ilimitado.
limousine ['liməziːn] n limusina f.
limp¹ [limp] v cojear.
limp² [limp] adj flácido. limpness n flojedad f.
limpet ['limpit] n lapa f.
line [lain] n línea f, rayo m, trazo m; (wrinkle) arruga f; (row) fila f; (wire) cable m; (people) cola f; (of poem) verso

m; (*rope*) cuerda *f*; (*flex*) cordón *m*; (*of communication*) vía *f*; (*shipping*) compañía *f*. *v* rayar; arrugar; alinearse por; bordear; (*provide an inner layer*) forrar; (*brakes*) guarnecer. **line up** poner en fila. **linear** *adj* lineal.

linen ['linin] *n* hilo *m*, lino *m*; (*sheets, etc.*) ropa blanca *f*. **linen basket** canasta de la ropa *f*.

liner ['lainə] *n* transatlántico *m*.

linger ['liŋgə] *v* (*person*) quedarse; (*memory, etc.*) persistir; (*dawdle*) rezagarse; (*loiter*) callejear.

lingerie ['lãʒəriː] *n* ropa interior *f*.

linguist ['liŋgwist] *n* lingüista *m*, *f*. **linguistic** *adj* lingüístico. **linguistics** *n* lingüística *f*.

lining ['lainiŋ] *n* (*clothes*) forro *m*; (*brakes*) guarnición *f*.

link [liŋk] *n* (*chain*) eslabón *m*; (*cuff*) gemelos *m pl*; (*fig*) vínculo *m*. *v* unir; acoplar; conectar.

linoleum [li'nouliəm] *n also* **lino** linóleo *m*.

linseed ['linˌsiːd] *n* linaza *f*. **linseed oil** aceite de linaza *m*.

lint [lint] *n* hilas *f pl*.

lion ['laiən] *n* león *m*. **lioness** *n* leona *f*.

lip [lip] *n* labio *m*; (*jug*) pico *m*; (*cup*) borde *m*. **lip-read** *v* leer en los labios. **lipstick** *n* barra de labios *f*.

liqueur [li'kjuə] *n* licor *m*.

liquid ['likwid] *nm, adj* líquido. **liquidate** *v* liquidar. **liquidation** *n* liquidación *f*.

liquor ['likə] *n* bebida alcohólica *f*.

liquorice ['likəris] *n* regaliz *m*.

Lisbon ['lizbən] *n* Lisboa.

lisp [lisp] *n* ceceo *m*. *v* decir ceceando.

list¹ [list] *v* hacer una lista de; enumerar. *n* lista *f*; catálogo *m*.

list² [list] *v* (*naut*) escorar. *n* escora *f*.

listen ['lisn] *v* escuchar, oír. **listener** *n* oyente *m*, *f*.

listless ['listlis] *adj* decaído, apático.

lit [lit] *V* **light**.

litany ['litəni] *n* letanía *f*.

literacy ['litərəsi] *n* capacidad de leer y escribir *f*. **be literate** saber leer y escribir.

literal ['litərəl] *adj* literal.

literary ['litərəri] *adj* literario.

literature ['litrətʃə] *n* literatura *f*; (*advertising matter*) folletos publicitarios *m pl*.

litigation [liti'geiʃən] *n* litigio *m*.

litre ['liːtə] *n* litro *m*.

litter ['litə] *n* basura *f*; desorden *m*; (*zool*)

camada *f*; (*bedding for animals*) pajaza *f*; (*stretcher*) camilla *f*. **litter-bin** *n* papelera *f*. *v* ensuciar; cubrir; desordenar.

little ['litl] *adj* (*small*) pequeño; (*quantity*) poco. *nm, adv* poco. **little by little** poco a poco.

liturgy ['litədʒi] *n* liturgia *f*. **liturgical** *adj* litúrgico.

live¹ [liv] *v* vivir. **live down** conseguir que se olvide. **live up to** cumplir con.

live² [laiv] *adj* vivo; (*broadcast*) en directo; (*coal*) en ascuas; (*elec*) cargado. *adv* en directo.

livelihood ['laivlihud] *n* sustento *m*.

lively ['laivli] *adj* vivo; enérgico; activo. **liveliness** *n* viveza *f*; animación *f*.

liven ['laivn] *v* **liven up** animar.

liver ['livə] *n* hígado *m*.

livestock ['laivstok] *n* ganado *m*.

livid ['livid] *adj* lívido; (*coll*) furioso.

living ['liviŋ] *adj* vivo, viviente. *n* vida *f*; vivos *m pl*. **living room** sala de estar *f*.

lizard ['lizəd] *n* lagarto *m*.

load [loud] *n* (*burden*) carga *f*; (*animals, vehicles*) cargamento *m*; (*fig*) peso *m*. *v* cargar. **loaded** *adj* cargado; (*coll: rich*) podrido de dinero.

loaf¹ [louf] *n* pan *m*.

loaf² [louf] *v* **loaf around** callejear. **loafer** *n* (*coll*) holgazán, -ana *m*, *f*.

loan [loun] *n* préstamo *m*. *v* prestar.

loathe [louð] *v* aborrecer. **loathing** *n* aborrecimiento *m*. **loathsome** *adj* asqueroso.

lob [lob] *v* volear. *n* volea alta *f*. **lob** *m*.

lobby ['lobi] *n* pasillo *m*; vestíbulo *m*; grupo de presión *m*. *v* ejercer presiones sobre.

lobe [loub] *n* lóbulo *m*.

lobster ['lobstə] *n* langosta *f*.

local ['loukəl] *adj* local; vecinal. *n* (*coll: pub*) bar del barrio *m*. **the locals** (*coll: people*) la gente del lugar *f*. **locality** *n* (*neighbourhood*) localidad *f*; (*place*) lugar *m*. **localize** *v* localizar. **locally** *adv* localmente; en el sitio.

locate [lə'keit] *v* (*find*) encontrar; (*look for and discover*) localizar; situar. **location** *n* localización *f*; colocación *f*; situación *f*; (*cinema*) exteriores *m pl*. **film on location** *v* rodar.

lock¹ [lok] *n* (*on door, box, etc.*) cerradura *f*; (*canal*) esclusa *f*. *v* cerrarse con llave; (*mech*) bloquearse. **lock away** guardar bajo llave. **lock in** encerrar. **lock out** cerrar la puerta a. **lock up** (*house*) cerrar;

(*money*) dejar bajo llave; (*imprison*) encarcelar.

lock² [lok] *n* (*of hair*) mecha *f*, mechón *m*.

locker ['lokə] *n* (*shelf*) casillero *m*, (*cup-board*) armario *m*.

locket ['lokit] *n* relicario *m*.

locomotive [,loukə'moutiv] *n* locomotiva *f*. *adj* locomotor. **locomotion** *n* locomoción *f*.

locust ['loukəst] *n* langosta *f*.

lodge [lodʒ] *n* (*porter's*) portería *f*; (*care-taker's*) casa del guarda *f*; (*hunting*) pabellón *m*. *v* alojar; (*place*) colocar; presentar; (*appeal*) interponer. **lodger** *n* huésped, -a *m, f*. **lodgings** *pl n* habitación *f*. **board and lodging** pensión completa *f*.

loft [loft] *n* (*for hay*) pajar *m*; (*attic*) desván *m*. **lofty** *adj* (*high*) alto; (*principles*) elevado; (*haughty*) arrogante.

log [log] *n* tronco *m*. **logbook** *n* (*naut*) cuaderno de bitácora *m*; (*aero*) diario de vuelo *m*. *v* anotar, apuntar.

logarithm ['logəriðəm] *n* logaritmo *m*.

loggerheads ['logəhedz] *pl n* be at logger-heads estar a mal.

logic ['lodʒik] *n* lógica *f*. **logical** *adj* lógico.

loins [loins] *pl n* lomos *m pl*.

loiter ['loitə] *v* callejear.

lollipop ['loli,pop] *n* chupón *m*.

London ['lʌndən] *n* Londres.

lonely ['lounli] *adj* solo; aislado; solitario. **loneliness** *n* soledad *f*.

long¹ [loŋ] *adj* (*length*) largo; (*memory*) bueno; (*time*) mucho; (*long-lasting*) viejo. **as long as** mientras. **long-range** *adj* de larga distancia. **long-sighted** *adj* hipermétrope; (*having foresight*) previsor. **long-sleeved** *adj* de mangas largas. **long-standing** *adj* de muchos años. **long-term** *adj* a largo plazo. **long-winded** *adj* (*per-son*) prolijo; (*speech*) interminable.

long² [loŋ] *v* **long for** desear con ansia. **long to** tener muchas ganas de. **longing** *n* anhelo *m*.

longevity [lon'dʒevəti] *n* longevidad *f*.

longitude ['londʒitjuːd] *n* longitud *f*. **lon-gitudinal** *adj* longitudinal.

loo [luː] *n* (*coll*) retrete *m*.

look [luk] *n* (*glance*) mirada *f*; (*inspection*) ojeada *f*; aspecto *m*. *v* mirar; parecer; representar. **look after** cuidar a, cuidar de; (*watch over*) vigilar. **look at** mirar. **look down on** mirar despectivamente.

look for buscar. **look forward to** esperar. **look out** tener cuidado. **look up** levantar los ojos; (*improve*) ponerse mejor; (*research*) consultar, buscar. **look up to** apreciar.

loom¹ [luːm] *v* perfilarse; surgir.

loom² [luːm] *n* telar *m*.

loop [luːp] *n* lazo *m*; (*belt*) presilla *f*. *v* hacer un lazo en.

loophole ['luːphoul] *v* (*fig*) escapatoria *f*.

loose [luːs] *adj* suelto; (*fitting*) holgado; (*knot*) flojo; (*translation*) libre; (*tooth*) que se mueve; **get loose** escaparse. **let loose** soltar. **loose change** dinero suelto *m*. **loose-leaf** *adj* de hojas sueltas. *v* (*free*) soltar; (*untie*) desatar. **loosely** *adv* sin apretar; aproximadamente; vagamente. **loosen** *v* aflojar, soltar.

loot [luːt] *n* botín *m*. **looter** *n* saqueador, -a *m, f*. **looting** saqueo *m*.

lop [lop] *v* cortar.

lopsided [,lop'saidid] *adj* ladeado; dese-quilibrado.

lord [loːd] *n* señor *m*.

lorry ['lori] *n* camión *m*. **lorry-driver** *n* camionero *m*.

*****lose** [luːz] *v* perder; (*watch, clock*) atrasar. **loser** *n* perdedor, -a *m, f*. **lost property** objetos perdidos *m pl*.

loss [los] *n* pérdida *f*; (*damage*) daño *m*, (*defeat*) derrota *f*. **be at a loss** estar perdido. **sell at a loss** vender con pérdida.

lost [lost] *V* lose.

lot [lot] *n* destino *m*; porción *f*; (*auction*) lote *m*; (*ground*) parcela *f*. **a lot** mucho. **lots of** cantidades de. **quite a lot of** bas-tante.

lotion ['louʃən] *n* loción *f*.

lottery ['lotəri] *n* lotería *f*.

lotus ['loutəs] *n* loto *m*.

loud [laud] *adj* fuerte; alto; ruidoso; sonoro; (*colours*) chillón; vulgar. *adv* (*laugh*) estrepitosamente. **loud-hailer** *n* megáfono *m*. **loud-mouthed** *adj* fanfar-rón, -ona *m, f*. **loudspeaker** *n* altavoz *m*. **loudly** *adv* en voz alta. **loudness** *n* fuerza *f*.

lounge [laundʒ] *n* salón *m*. **lounge suit** traje de calle *m*. *v* (*lazy posture*) repanti-garse; (*idle*) gandulear. **lounger** *n* tumbona *f*.

louse [laus] *n, pl* **lice** piojo *m*. **lousy** *adj* piojoso; (*slang*) malísimo.

lout [laut] *n* bruto *m*. **loutish** *adj* bruto.

love [lʌv] *n* amor *m*; cariño *m*; pasión *f*; (*tennis*) cero *m*. **fall in love with** enamorarse de. **love affair** amorío *m*. **make love** hacer el amor con. **with love from** (*in letter*) abrazos *m pl*. *v* amar, querer. **lovable** *adj* adorable. **lover** *n* amante *m, f*; (*enthusiast*) aficionado, -a *m, f*. **loving** *adj* cariñoso; amoroso.

lovely ['lʌvli] *adj* encantador; delicioso; precioso.

low [lou] *adj* bajo; pequeño; (*scarce*) escaso; (*weak*) débil; (*downhearted*) desanimado. **lowland** *n* tierra baja *f*. **low-lying** *adj* bajo. **low-paid** *adj* mal pagado. **low-priced** *adj* barato. **lowly** *adj* humilde.

lower ['louə] *adj* inferior; más bajo. *v* bajar. **lower oneself** rebajarse.

loyal ['lɔiəl] *adj* leal; fiel. **loyalty** *n* lealtad *f*; fidelidad *f*.

lozenge ['lozindʒ] *n* pastilla *f*.

lubricate ['luːbrikeit] *v* lubrificar, lubricar. **lubricant** *n* lubrificante *m*, lubricante *m*. **lubrication** *n* lubrificación *f*, lubricación *f*, engrase *m*.

lucid ['luːsid] *adj* lúcido; claro. **lucidity** *n* lucidez *f*; claridad *f*.

luck [lʌk] *n* suerte *f*; destino *m*. **bad luck** mala suerte *f*. **good luck** buena suerte *f*. **lucky** *adj* afortunado; oportuno. **be lucky** tener mucha suerte.

lucrative ['luːkrətiv] *adj* lucrativo.

ludicrous ['luːdikrəs] *adj* ridículo, absurdo.

lug [lʌg] *v* arrastrar.

luggage ['lʌgidʒ] *n* equipaje *m*; maletas *f pl*. **luggage label** etiqueta *f*. **luggage rack** portaequipajes *m invar*. **luggage van** furgón de equipajes *m*.

lukewarm ['luːkwɔːm] *adj* tibio.

lull [lʌl] *n* (*in storm*) calma *f*; (*fig*) tregua *f*. *v* sosegar.

lullaby ['lʌlə,bai] *n* canción de cuna *f*.

lumbago [lʌm'beigou] *n* lumbago *m*.

lumber[1] ['lʌmbə] *n* (*wood*) maderos *m pl*; (*junk*) trastos viejos *m pl*. **lumberjack** *n* leñador *m*. **lumber yard** depósito de madera *m*. *v*. **lumber with** (*coll*) hacer que cargue con.

lumber[2] ['lʌmbə] *v* moverse pesadamente.

luminous ['luːminəs] *adj* luminoso.

lump [lʌmp] *n* pedazo *m*, trozo *m*; (*mass*) masa *f*; (*clay*) pella *f*; (*stone*) bloque *m*; (*earth, sugar*) terrón *m*; (*med*) chichón.

lump sum cantidad total *f*. **lumpy** *adj* lleno de bultos.

lunar ['luːnə] *adj* lunar.

lunatic ['luːnətik] *n, adj* loco, -a *m, f*. **lunacy** *n* locura *f*.

lunch [lʌntʃ] *n* almuerzo *m*. *v* almorzar. **lunchtime** *n* hora de comer *f*.

lung [lʌŋ] *n* pulmón *m*.

lunge [lʌndʒ] *v* embestir, lanzarse. *n* embestida *f*.

lurch[1] [ləːtʃ] *v* dar bandazos. **lurch along** ir dando bandazos. *n* bandazo *m*.

lurch[2] [ləːtʃ] *n* **leave in the lurch** dejar en la estacada.

lure [luə] *v* atraer. *n* aliciente *m*; encanto *m*; (*decoy*) cebo *m*.

lurid ['luərid] *adj* espeluznante; sensacional.

lurk [ləːk] *v* (*lie in wait*) estar al acecho; (*be hidden*) esconderse; (*fig: be always around*) rondar. **lurking** *adj* vago; oculto.

luscious ['lʌʃəs] *adj* exquisito; apetitoso; voluptuoso.

lush [lʌʃ] *adj* lozano, exuberante.

lust [lʌst] *n* (*sexual*) lascivia *f*; (*for power, etc.*) anhelo *m*. *v* **lust after** (*object*) codiciar; (*person*) desear. **lusty** *adj* robusto, fuerte.

lustre ['lʌstə] *n* lustre *m*.

lute [luːt] *n* laúd *m*.

Luxembourg ['lʌksəm,bəːg] *n* Luxemburgo *m*.

luxury ['lʌkʃəri] *n* lujo *m*. **luxuriant** *adj* exuberante. **luxurious** *adj* lujoso.

lynch [lintʃ] *v* linchar.

lynx [links] *n* lince *m*.

lyre [laiə] *n* lira *f*.

lyrical ['lirikəl] *adj* lírico.

lyrics ['liriks] *pl n* letra *f sing*. **lyricist** *n* autor de la letra de una canción *m*.

M

mac [mak] *n* (*coll*) impermeable *m*.

macabre [mə'kaːbr] *adj* macabro.

macaroni [makə'rouni] *n* macarrones *m pl*.

mace[1] [meis] *n* (*staff*) maza *f*.

mace[2] [meis] *n* (*spice*) macis *f*.

machine [mə'ʃiːn] *n* máquina *f*. **machine-**

gun *n* ametralladora *f*. **machinery** *n* maquinaria *f*; mecanismo *m*.

mackerel ['makrəl] *n* caballa *f*.

mackintosh ['makin,toʃ] *n* impermeable *m*.

mad [mad] *adj* loco, demente; rabioso; *(angry)* furioso. **madden** *v* enloquecer; enfurecer. **maddening** *adj* desesperante. **madly** *adv* locamente; furiosamente. **madness** *n* locura *f*; rabia *f*; furia *f*.

madam ['madəm] *n* señora *f*.

made [meid] *V* make.

Madeira [mə'diərə] *n* (*island*) Madera *f*; (*wine*) madera *m*.

magazine [,magə'ziːn] *n* (*publication*) revista *f*; (*warehouse*) almacén *m*; (*explosives store*) polvorín *m*; (*rifle*) recámara *f*.

maggot ['magət] *n* gusano *m*, cresa *f*. **maggoty** *adj* gusanoso.

magic ['madʒik] *n* magia *f*. *adj also* **magical** mágico. **magician** *n* ilusionista *m*, *f*.

magistrate ['madʒistreit] *n* magistrado *m*; juez municipal *m*.

magnanimous [mag'naniməs] *adj* magnánimo. **magnanimity** *n* magnanimidad *f*.

magnate ['magneit] *n* magnate *m*.

magnet ['magnət] *n* imán *m*. **magnetic** magnético; atractivo. **magnetism** *n* magnetismo *m*. **magnetize** *v* magnetizar; atraer.

magnificent [mag'nifisnt] *adj* magnífico. **magnificence** *n* magnificencia *f*.

magnify ['magnifai] *v* magnificar; aumentar; exagerar. **magnifying glass** lupa *f*. **magnification** *n* aumento *m*; exageración *f*.

magnitude ['magnitjuːd] *n* magnitud *f*.

magnolia [mag'nouliə] *n* magnolia *f*.

magpie ['magpai] *n* urraca *f*.

mahogany [mə'hogəni] *n* caoba *f*.

maid [meid] *n* (*servant*) criada *f*; muchacha *f*. **old maid** solterona *f*.

maiden ['meidən] *n* doncella *f*. *adj* virgen; soltera; inaugural. **maiden name** apellido de soltera *m*.

mail [meil] *n* (*letters*) correspondencia *f*; (*service*) correo *m*. **mailbag** *n* saca de correspondencia *f*. **mail order** pedido hecho por correo *m*.

maim [meim] *v* mutilar.

main [mein] *adj* principal. **main course** plato principal *m*. **mainland** *n* continente *m*. **main line** línea principal *f*. **main road** carretera general *f*. **mainstay** *n* estay

mayor *m*. *n* (*gas, water*) cañería principal *f*. **in the main** por lo general. **mains** *n* (*elec*) la red eléctrica *f*.

maintain [mein'tein] *v* mantener; conservar. **maintenance** *n* mantenimiento *m*; conservación *f*. **maintenance allowance** pensión alimenticia *f*.

maisonette [meizə'net] *n* casita *f*.

maize [meiz] *n* maíz *m*.

majesty ['madʒəsti] *n* majestad *f*. **majestic** *adj* majestuoso.

major ['meidʒə] *adj* mayor; principal. *n* (*mil*) comandante *m*.

majority [mə'dʒoriti] *n* mayoría *f*. **overwhelming majority** mayoría abrumadora *f*.

***make** [meik] *v* hacer, efectuar; servir de; llegar a. *n* marca *f*; hechura *f*. **make-believe** *n* simulación *f*. **make out** (*draw up*) hacer; (*cheque*) extender. **make do with** arreglárselas con. **makeshift** *adj* improvisado. **make up** inventar; completar; recuperar; (*face*) maquillarse. **make-up** *n* maquillaje *m*; carácter *m*. **make up for** compensar. **maker** *n* fabricante *m*. **making** *n* fabricación *f*.

maladjusted [malə'dʒʌstid] *adj* inadaptado. **maladjustment** *n* inadaptación *f*.

malaria [mə'leəriə] *n* malaria *f*, paludismo *m*.

male [meil] *nm, adj* macho.

malevolent [mə'levələnt] *adj* malévolo. **malevolence** *n* malevolencia *f*.

malfunction [mal'fʌŋkʃən] *n* funcionamiento defectuoso *m*. *v* funcionar defectuosamente.

malice ['malis] *n* malicia *f*. **malicious** *adj* malicioso.

malignant [mə'lignənt] *adj* malvado; malo; (*med*) maligno. **malignancy** *n* maldad *f*; malignidad *f*.

malinger [mə'liŋgə] *v* fingirse enfermo.

mallet ['malit] *n* mazo *m*.

malnutrition [malnju'triʃən] *n* desnutrición *f*.

malt [moːlt] *n* malta *f*.

Malta ['moːltə] *n* Malta. **Maltese** *n*, *adj* maltés, -esa.

maltreat [mal'triːt] *v* maltratar. **maltreatment** *n* maltrato *m*.

mammal ['maməl] *n* mamífero *m*.

mammoth ['maməθ] *n* mamut *m*. *adj* gigantesco.

man [man] *n, pl* **men** hombre *m*. *v* armar; ocupar. **manhood** *n* virilidad *f*. **manly** *adj* masculino.

manage ['manidʒ] *v* (*business, affairs, etc.*) dirigir; (*instrument*) manejar; (*property*) administrar. **manage to** conseguir, arreglárselas. **manageable** *adj* manejable; (*undertaking*) factible; (*animal, person*) dócil. **management** *n* gestión *f*, administración *f*, dirección *f*; (*board of directors*) junta directiva *f*. **manager** *n* gerente *m*, director *m*. **managerial** *adj* directorial. **managing director** director gerente *m*.

mandarin ['mandərin] *n* mandarín *m*. *adj* mandarino. **mandarin orange** mandarina *f*; (*tree*) mandarino *m*.

mandate ['mandeit] *n* mandato *m*. **mandatory** *adj* obligatorio.

mandolin ['mandəlin] *n* mandolina *f*.

mane [mein] *n* crin *f*, crines *f pl*.

mange [meindʒ] *n* sarna *f*. **mangy** *adj* sarnoso; (*coll*) asqueroso.

manger ['meindʒə] *n* pesebre *m*.

mangle¹ ['maŋgl] *n* (*wringer*) escurridor *m*. *v* pasar por el escurridor.

mangle² ['maŋgl] *v* despedazar; (*fig*) deformar.

mango ['maŋgou] *n* mango *m*.

manhandle [man'handl] *v* (*person*) maltratar; (*goods*) manipular.

manhole ['manhoul] *n* registro *m*.

mania ['meiniə] *n* mania *f*. **maniac** *n* maníaco, -a *m, f*; (*fig*) fanático, -a *m, f*.

manicure ['manikjuə] *n* manicura *f*. *v* hacer la manicura a. **manicurist** *n* manicuro, -a *m, f*.

manifest ['manifest] *adj* manifiesto, evidente. *v* mostrar, manifestarse. **manifestation** *n* manifestación *f*.

manifesto [mani'festou] *n* manifiesto *m*.

manifold ['manifould] *adj* múltiple; diverso. *n* **exhaust manifold** (*mot*) colector de escape *m*.

manipulate [mə'nipjuleit] *v* manipular. **manipulation** *n* manipulación *f*.

mankind [man'kaind] *n* raza humana *f*, humanidad *f*.

man-made [man'meid] *adj* sintético, artificial.

manner ['manə] *n* manera *f*, modo *m*; clase *f*; aire *m*. **manners** *pl n* modales *m pl*.

mannerism ['manərizəm] *n* amaneramiento *m*.

manoeuvre [mə'nuıvə] *n* maniobra *f*. *v* maniobrar.

manor ['manə] *n* señorío *m*. **manor house** casa solariega *f*.

manpower ['man,pauə] *n* mano de obra *f*.

mansion ['manʃən] *n* (*country*) gran casa de campo *f*; (*town*) palacete *m*.

manslaughter ['man,slɔıtə] *n* homicidio sin premeditación *m*.

mantelpiece ['mantlpiis] *n* repisa de chimenea *f*.

mantle ['mantl] *n* (*cloak*) capa *f*; (*gaslamp*) manguito *m*.

manual ['manjuəl] *nm, adj* manual. **manually** *adv* a mano.

manufacture [manju'faktʃə] *n* (*product*) producto manufacturado; (*act*) fabricación *f*. *v* manufacturar, fabricar. **manufacturer** *n* fabricante *m*.

manure [mə'njuə] *n* estiércol *m*, abono. *v* estercolar, abonar.

manuscript ['manjuskript] *nm* manuscrito.

many ['meni] *adj* muchos, mucho, un gran número de. *pron* muchos. **as many** as tantos. **how many?** ¿cuántos? ¿cuántas? **so many** tantos, tantas. **too many** demasiado.

map [map] *n* mapa *m*; (*town*) plano *m*. *v* levantar un mapa de. **map out** proyectar.

maple ['meipl] *n* arce *m*.

mar [maı] *v* estropear; frustrar.

marathon ['marəθən] *nm, adj* maratón *f*.

marble ['maıbl] *n* mármol *m*; (*toy*) bola *f*. *v* jaspear.

march [maıtʃ] *v* marchar. *n* marcha *f*.

March [maıtʃ] *n* marzo *m*.

marchioness [,maıʃə'nes] *n* marquesa *f*.

mare [meə] *n* yegua *f*.

margarine [,maıdʒə'riın] *n* margarina *f*.

margin ['maıdʒin] *n* borde *m*; lado *m*; orilla *f*; margen *m*. **marginal** *adj* marginal. **marginally** *adv* por muy poco.

marguerite [,maıgə'riıt] *n* margarita *f*.

marigold ['marigould] *n* caléndula *f*.

marijuana [mari'waınə] *n* marijuana *f*, marihuana *f*.

marina [mə'riınə] *n* puerto deportivo *m*.

marinade [,mari'neid] *n* adobo *m*. *v* adobar.

marine [mə'riın] *adj* marino. *n* (*mil*) soldado de infantería de marina. **merchant marine** marina mercante *f*.

marital ['maritl] *adj* marital, matrimonial.

maritime ['maritaim] *adj* marítimo.
marjoram ['maɪdʒərəm] *n* mejorana *f.*
mark¹ [maɪk] *n* marca *f.* señal *f.* mancha *f*; (*school*) nota *f*; calificación *f*; (*trace*) huella *f.* **marksman** *n* tirador *m. v* marcar, señalar; calificar. **marked** *adj* marcado; pronunciado; sensible.
mark² [maɪk] *n* (*currency*) marco *m.*
market ['maɪkit] *n* mercado *m*; (*demand*) salida *f.* **market day** día de mercado *m.* **market place** plaza de mercado *f.* **market research** estudio de mercados *m.* **market value** valor corriente *m. v* poner en venta, vender. **marketing** *n* comercialización.
marmalade ['maɪməleid] *n* mermelada de naranja *f.*
maroon¹ [mə'ruɪn] *adj* castaño.
maroon² [mə'ruɪn] *v* abandonar.
marquee [maɪ'kiɪ] *n* gran tienda de campaña *f.*
marquess ['maɪkwis] *n* marqués *m.*
marquetry ['maɪkətri] *n* marquetería *f.*
marriage ['maridʒ] *n* · matrimonio *m*; (*wedding*) boda *f.* **marriage certificate** partida de casamiento *f.*
marrow ['marou] *n* (*bone*) médula *f.* **vegetable marrow** calabacín *m.*
marry ['mari] *v* casar; (*get married*) casarse. **married** *adj* casado. **married couple** matrimonio *m.* **married name** apellido de casada *m.*
Mars [maɪz] *n* Marte *m.* **Martian** *n, adj* marciano, -a.
marsh [maɪʃ] *n* pantano *m.* **marshmallow** *n* (*bot*) malvavisco *m*; (*cookery*) melcocha *f.* **marshy** *adj* pantanoso.
marshal ['maɪʃəl] *n* (*mil*) mariscal *m*; (*organizer*) maestro de ceremonias *m. v* poner en orden; (*mil*) formar.
martial ['maɪʃəl] *adj* marcial.
martin ['maɪtin] *n* avión *m.*
martyr ['maɪtə] *n* mártir *m, f. v* martinizar. **martyrdom** *n* martirio *m.*
marvel ['maɪvəl] *n* maravilla *f. v* maravillarse. **marvellous** *adj* maravilloso.
marzipan [maɪzi'pan] *n* mazapán *m.*
mascara [ma'skaɪrə] *n* rímel *m.*
mascot ['maskət] *n* mascota *f.*
masculine ['maskjulin] *adj* masculino. **masculinity** *n* masculinidad *f.*
mash [maʃ] *v* machacar. *n* (*animal feed*) afrecho remojado *m.*
mask [maɪsk] *n* máscara *f.* careta *f. v* enmascarar.

masochist ['masəkist] *n* masoquista *m, f.* **masochism** *n* masoquismo *m.* **masochistic** *adj* masoquista.
mason ['meisn] *n* albañil *m.* **masonry** *n* albañilería.
masquerade [maskə'reid] *n* (*pretence*) mascarada *f. v* **masquerade as** hacerse pasar por.
mass¹ [mas] *n* masa *f.* **mass media** medios informativos *m pl.* **mass meeting** mitin popular *m.* **mass-produce** *v* fabricar en serie. **mass production** fabricación en serie *f. v* agrupar.
mass² [mas] *n* (*rel*) misa *f.*
massacre ['masəkə] *n* matanza *f. v* matar en masa.
massage ['masaɪʒ] *n* masaje *m. v* dar un masaje. **masseur, masseuse** *n* masajista *m, f.*
massive ['masiv] *adj* sólido; masivo.
mast [maɪst] *n* (*naut*) palo *m*, mástil *m*; (*radio, etc.*) poste *m.*
master ['maɪstə] *n* (*owner*) dueño *m*; (*college*) director *m*; (*secondary school*) profesor *m*; (*primary school*) maestro; (*graduate*) licenciado, -a *m, f*; (*household*) señor *m*; (*work force*) patrón *m*; (*ship*) capitán *m.* **master copy** original *m.* **master key** llave maestra *f.* **master of ceremonies** maestro de ceremonias *m.* **masterpiece** *n* obra maestra *f. v* (*passions, language*) dominar; (*an animal*) domar; (*difficulties*) vencer. **mastery** *n* dominio *m*; maestría *f.*
masturbate ['mastəbeit] *v* masturbarse. **masturbation** *n* masturbación *f.*
mat [mat] *n* (*floor*) estera *f*; (*door*) esterilla *f*; (*table*) salvamanteles *m invar*; (*doily*) tapete *m.* **matted** *adj* (*hair*) enmarañado.
match¹ [matʃ] *n* fósforo *m*, cerilla *f.* **matchbox** *n* caja de fósforos *or* cerillas *f.*
match² [matʃ] *n* (*sport*) partido *m*; (*equal*) igual *m*; (*pair*) pareja *f. v* igualar; (*colours*) casar; (*gloves, etc.*) parear; (*clothes, furnishings*) hacer juego con; (*fit*) encajar; corresponder. **matchless** *adj* sin igual.
mate [meit] *n* (*animals*) macho, hembra *m, f*; amigo, -a *m, f*; camarada *m, f*; (*spouse*) compañero, -a *m, f. v* acoplar; casar; (*chess*) dar jaque mate a.
material [mə'tiəriəl] *n* material *m*; (*cloth*) tela *f.* **materials** *pl n* (*building*) materiales *m pl*; (*teaching*) material *m*; artículos *m*

pl. adj material; esencial. **materialist** *n(m+f)*, *adj* materialista. **materialize** *v* materializar; realizar.

maternal [mə'tɜɪnl] *adj* maternal; (*relation*) materno.

maternity [mə'tɜɪnəti] *n* maternidad *f*. **maternity hospital** casa de maternidad *f*.

mathematics [maθə'matiks] *n* matemáticas *f pl*. **mathematical** *adj* matemático. **mathematician** *n* matemático, -a *m, f*.

matinée ['matinei] *n* (*cinema*) primera sesión *f*; (*theatre*) función de la tarde *f*. **matinée idol** ídolo del público *m*.

matins ['matinz] *n* maitines *m pl*.

matriarch ['meitriaɪk] *n* mujer que manda *f*. **matriarchal** *adj* matriarcal.

matrimony ['matriməni] *n* matrimonio *m*. **matrimonial** *adj* matrimonial.

matrix ['meitriks] *n* matriz *f*.

matron ['meitrən] *n* matrona *f*; (*hospital*) enfermera jefe *f*; (*school*) ama de llaves *f*.

matt [mat] *adj* mate.

matter ['matə] *n* materia *f*; material *m*; asunto *m*; cuestión *f*; tema *m*. **as a matter of fact** en realidad. **matter-of-fact** *adj* prosaico. **what's the matter?** ¿qué pasa? *v* importar. **it doesn't matter** no importa.

mattress ['matris] *n* colchón *m*. **spring-mattress** *n* colchón de muelles *m*.

mature [mə'tjuə] *adj* maduro. *v* madurar. **maturity** *n* madurez *f*.

maudlin ['mɔɪdlin] *adj* sensiblero.

maul [mɔɪl] *v* maltratar; herir gravemente.

mausoleum [mɔɪsə'liəm] *n* mausoleo *m*.

mauve [mouv] *nm, adj* malva.

maxim ['maksim] *n* máxima *f*.

maximum ['maksiməm] *nm, adj* máximo.

*may [mei] *v* poder.

May [mei] *n* mayo *m*. **May Day** primero de mayo *m*.

maybe ['meibi] *adv* quizás, quizá.

mayday ['meidei] *n* señal de socorro *f*.

mayonnaise [,meiə'neiz] *n* mayonesa *f*.

mayor [meə] *n* alcalde *m*. **mayoress** *n* alcaldesa *f*.

maze [meiz] *n* laberinto *m*.

me [miɪ] *pron* me; (*after prep*) mí.

mead [miɪd] *n* (*drink*) aguamiel *f*.

meadow ['medou] *n* prado *m*.

meagre ['miɪgə] *adj* escaso, pobre.

meal¹ [miɪl] *n* (*food*) comida *f*.

meal² [miɪl] *n* (*flour*) harina *f*.

*mean¹ [miɪn] *v* (*signify*) tener la intención de, querer decir.

mean² [miɪn] *adj* (*humble*) humilde; (*petty*) mezquino; (*stingy*) agarrado; (*character*) vil; (*unkind*) malo. **meanness** *n* humildad *f*; mezquindad *f*; (*stinginess*) tacañería *f*; vileza *f*; maldad *f*.

mean³ [miɪn] *n* (*average*) promedio; (*math*) media *f*. *adj* medio; mediano.

meander [mi'andə] *v* (*river*) serpentear; (*person*) vagar. *n* meandro *m*.

meaning ['miɪniŋ] *n* significación *f*; sentido *m*; pensamiento *m*. **meaningful** *adj* significativo. **meaningless** *adj* sin sentido; insignificante.

means [miɪnz] *n* (*way*) medio *m*, manera *f*; (*wealth*) fondos *m pl*. **by all means!** ¡por supuesto! **by means of** por medio de. **by no means** de ningún modo.

meanwhile ['miɪnwail] *adv* mientras tanto.

measles ['miɪzlz] *n* sarampión *m*.

measure ['meʒə] *v* medir. *n* medida *f*. **made to measure** hecho a medida. **measurement** *n* medida *f*.

meat [miɪt] *v* carne *f*. **cold meat** fiambre *m*. **meatball** *n* albóndiga *f*. **meat pie** empanada *f*.

mechanic [mi'kanik] *n* mecánico *m*. **mechanical** *adj* mecánico. **mechanics** *n* mecánica *f sing*. **mechanism** *n* mecanismo *m*. **mechanize** *v* mecanizar.

medal ['medl] *n* medalla *f*. **medallion** *n* medallón *m*. **medallist** *n* condecorado con una medalla.

meddle ['medl] *v* **meddle in** meterse en; **meddle with** toquetear. **meddlesome** *adj* entremetido.

media ['miɪdiə] *pl n* medios *m pl*.

mediate ['miɪdieit] *v* ser mediador en; mediar. **mediation** *n* mediación *f*. **mediator** *n* mediador, -a *m, f*.

medical ['medikəl] *adj* médico; de medicina. **medical consultant** médico consultor *m*. **medical school** facultad de medicina *f*. **medicate** *v* medicinar. **medicated** *adj* medicinal.

medicine ['medsən] *n* (*art and drug*) medicina *f*; (*coll*) purga *f*. **medicine cabinet** botiquín *m*. **medicinal** *adj* medicinal.

medieval [medi'iɪvəl] *adj* medieval.

mediocre [miɪdi'oukə] *adj* mediocre. **mediocrity** *n* mediocridad *f*.

meditate ['mediteit] *v* meditar. **meditation** *n* meditación *f*. **meditative** *adj* meditativo.

Mediterranean [,meditə'reiniən] *adj* mediterráneo. *n* Mediterráneo *m*.

medium ['miːdiəm] *n* (*environment*) medio ambiente *m*; (*means*) medio *m*; (*spiritualism*) médium *m*, *f*. **happy medium** justo medio *m*. *adj* mediano. **medium wave** (*radio*) onda media *f*.

medley ['medli] *n* mezcla *f*; (*music*) popurrí *m*.

meek [miːk] *adj* dócil, manso; humilde. **meekness** *n* docilidad *f*, mansedumbre *f*.

***meet** [miːt] *v* (*encounter*) encontrar. encontrarse a; (*come together*) entrevistarse con; (*come across*) cruzarse con; (*roads*) desembocar en; (*correspond to*) empalmar con; satisfacer; (*requirement, engagement*) cumplir con; (*expenses*) costear; (*claims*) acceder a. **meet someone half-way** llegar a un arreglo con alguien. **pleased to meet you!** ¡mucho gusto! **meeting** *n* encuentro *m*; reunión *f*; sesión *f*; (*interview*) cita *f*; (*official*) entrevista *f*.

megaphone ['megəfoun] *n* megáfono *m*.

melancholy ['melənkəli] *n* melancolía *f*. *adj also* **melancholic** melancólico.

mellow ['melou] *adj* (*ripe*) maduro; (*wine*) añejo; (*voice*) suave. *v* madurar; suavizar.

melodrama ['melədraːmə] *n* melodrama *m*. **melodramatic** *adj* melodramático.

melody ['melədi] *n* melodía *f*. **melodious** *adj* melodioso.

melon ['melən] *n* melón *m*.

melt [melt] *v* fundir; derretir; (*fig*) ablandar. **melting** *n* fusión *f*, fundición *f*.

member ['membə] *n* miembro *m*. **membership** *n* calidad de miembro *f*. **membership fee** cuota de socio *f*.

membrane ['membrein] *n* membrana *f*. **membranous** *adj* membranoso.

memento [mə'mentou] *n* recuerdo *m*.

memo ['memou] *n* (*coll*) memorándum *m*.

memoirs ['memwaːz] *pl n* memorias *f pl*.

memorable ['memərəbl] *adj* memorable.

memorandum [memə'randəm] *n* memorándum *m*.

memory ['meməri] *n* memoria *f*; (*thing remembered*) recuerdo *m*. **memorize** *v* memorizar, aprender de memoria.

men [men] *V* **man**.

menace ['menis] *n* amenaza *f*. *v* amenazar.

menagerie [mi'nadʒəri] *n* casa de fieras *f*.

mend [mend] *v* remendar; reparar; (*improve*) mejorar. **be on the mend** (*coll*) estar mejorando.

menial ['miːniəl] *adj* (*of a servant*) doméstico; (*mean*) bajo. *n* (*servant*) criado, -a *m*, *f*.

meningitis [,menin'dʒaitis] *n* meningitis *f*.

menopause ['menəpɔːz] *n* menopausia *f*.

menstrual ['menstruəl] *adj* menstrual. **menstruate** *v* menstruar. **menstruation** *n* menstruación *f*.

mental ['mentl] *adj* mental; (*coll*: *mad*) chiflado. **mental arithmetic** cálculo mental *m*. **mental deficiency** deficiencia mental *f*. **mental home** *or* **hospital** manicomio *m*. **mentality** *n* mentalidad *f*. **mentally** *adj* mentalmente. **mentally handicapped** anormal.

menthol ['menθəl] *n* mentol *m*.

mention ['menʃən] *v* mencionar, hablar de. **don't mention it!** ¡de nada! ¡no hay de qué! **not to mention** por no decir nada de. *n* mención *f*.

menu ['menjuː] *n* carta *f*, lista de platos *f*.

mercantile ['məːkənˌtail] *adj* mercantil; mercante.

mercenary ['məːsinəri] *nm*, *adj* mercenario.

merchandise ['məːtʃəndaiz] *n* mercancías *f pl*. **merchandizing** *n* comercio mercantil *m*.

merchant ['məːtʃənt] *n* comerciante *m*, *f*, negociante *m*, *f*; (*shopkeeper*) tendero, -a *m*, *f*. **merchant navy** marina mercante *f*.

mercury ['məːkjuri] *n* mercurio *m*.

mercy ['məːsi] *n* misericordia *f*, merced *f*. **at the mercy of** a merced de. **merciful** *adj* clemente; misericordioso. **merciless** *adj* despiadado.

mere [miə] *adj* mero.

merge [məːdʒ] *v* (*parties, companies*) fusionar; (*join*) unir; (*colours*) fundir. **merger** *n* fusión *f*; unión *f*.

meridian [mə'ridiən] *nm*, *adj* meridiano.

meringue [mə'raŋ] *n* merengue *m*.

merit ['merit] *n* mérito *m*. *v* merecer.

mermaid ['məːmeid] *n* sirena *f*.

merry ['meri] *adj* alegre; divertido; (*coll*: *slightly drunk*) achispado. **merry-go-round** *n* tiovivo *m*. **merriment** *n* alegría *f*; diversión *f*.

mesh [meʃ] *n* mella *f*; (*gears*) engranaje *m*. *v* engranar (con).

mesmerize ['mezməraiz] *v* hipnotizar.

mess [mes] *n* confusión *f*, desorden *m*; (*dirt*) porquería *f*, suciedad *f*; (*awkward situation*) lío *m*; (*mil*) comedor de la tropa *m*. **make a mess of** desordenar;

ensuciar. **what a mess!** ¡qué asco! ¡qué porquería! ¡qué lío! **mess up** desordenar; ensuciar. **messy** adj confuso; desordenado; sucio.

message ['mesidʒ] n recado m; (official communication) mensaje m; (errand) encargo m. **messenger** n mensajero, -a m, f.

met [met] V meet.

metal ['metl] n metal m. adj de metal. **metallic** adj metálico. **metallurgist** n metalúrgico m. **metallurgy** n metalurgia f.

metamorphosis [metə'mɔːfəsis] n metamorfosis f.

metaphor ['metəfə] n metáfora f. **metaphorical** adj metafórico.

metaphysics [metə'fiziks] n metafísica f. **metaphysical** adj metafísico. **metaphysician** n metafísico m.

meteor ['miːtiə] n meteoro. **meteoric** adj meteórico. **meteorite** n meteorito m.

meteorology [miːtiə'rolədʒi] n meteorología f. **meteorological** adj meteorológico. **meteorologist** n meteorologista m, f.

meter ['miːtə] n contador m.

methane ['miːθein] n metano m.

method ['meθəd] n método m; técnica f. **methodical** adj metódico.

Methodist ['meθədist] n metodista m, f. **Methodism** n metodismo m.

methylated spirits ['meθileitid] pl n alcohol desnaturalizado m.

meticulous [mi'tikjuləs] adj meticuloso.

mètre ['miːtə] n metro m. **metric** adj métrico.

metronome ['metrənoum] n metrónomo m.

metropolis [mə'tropəlis] n metrópoli f. **metropolitan** adj metropolitano.

Mexico ['meksikou] n Méjico, México. **Mexican** n, adj mejicano, -a, mexicano, -a.

mice [mais] V mouse.

microbe ['maikroub] n microbio m.

microfilm ['maikrəfilm] n microfilm m.

microphone ['maikrəfoun] n micrófono m.

microscope ['maikrəskoup] n microscopio m. **microscopic** adj microscópico.

microwave ['maikrəweiv] n microonda f.

mid [mid] adj medio; mediados.

mid-air [mid'eə] n **in mid-air** entre cielo y tierra.

midday [mid'dei] n mediodía m.

middle ['midl] n medio m, centro m; mitad f. **in the middle** en el centro. adj central; mediano; de en medio; medio; intermedio. **middle-aged** adj de mediano edad. **the Middle Ages** Edad Media f sing. **middle-class** adj de la clase media; burgués. **Middle East** Oriente Medio m. **middleman** n intermediario m. **middle-of-the-road** adj centrista, moderado. **middleweight** n peso medio m. **middling** adj regular, mediano.

midge [midʒ] n mosca enana f.

midget ['midʒit] n enano, -a m, f.

midnight ['midnait] n medianoche f.

midriff ['midrif] n diafragua m.

midst [midst] n **in our midst** entre nosotros. **in the midst of** en medio de.

midstream [mid'striːm] n **in midstream** en medio del río.

midsummer ['midsʌmə] n pleno verano m. **Midsummer Day** el día de San Juan m.

midway [mid'wei] adv, adj a medio camino.

midweek [mid'wiːk] n medio de la semana m.

midwife ['midwaif] n comadrona f, partera f. **midwifery** n obstetricia f.

midwinter [mid'wintə] n pleno invierno m.

might[1] [mait] V may.

might[2] [mait] n poder m; fuerza f.

mighty ['maiti] adj poderoso; fuerte; enorme. adv (coll) muy.

migraine ['miːgrein] n migraña f.

migrate [mai'greit] v emigrar. **migration** n migración. adj migratoria.

mike [maik] n (coll: microphone) micro m.

mild [maild] adj (person) dulce, apacible; (weather) templado; (wind) suave; (disease) benigno. **mildness** n dulzura f; suavidad f; benignidad f.

mildew ['mildjuː] n moho m; (vine) mildeu m; (plants) tizón m.

mile [mail] n milla f. **mileage** recorrido en millas m. **milestone** n mojón m; (fig) jalón m.

militant ['militənt] adj belicoso; (pol) militante. n militante m, f.

military ['militəri] adj militar.

milk [milk] n leche f. **milk chocolate** n chocolate con leche m. **milkman** n lechero m. **milk of magnesia** n leche de magnesia f. v ordeñar; (fig) exprimir.

milkiness *n* aspecto lechoso *m*. **milking** *n* ordeño *m*. **milky** *adj* lechoso.
Milky Way *n* Vía Láctea *f*.
mill [mil] *n* molino *m*; (*grinder*) molinillo *m*; (*factory*) fábrica *f*. **millstone** *n* muela *f*; (*burden*) cruz *f*. *v* moler. **miller** *n* molinero, -a *m*, *f*.
millennium [mi'leniəm] *n* milenario *m*.
millet ['milit] *n* mijo *m*.
milligram ['miliₐgram] *n* miligramo *m*.
millimetre ['miliₐmitə] *n* milímetro *m*.
milliner ['milinə] *n* sombrerero, -a *m*, *f*. **milliner's** *n* sombrerería *f*. **millinery** *n* sombreros de señora *m pl*.
million ['miljən] *n* millón *m*. **millionaire** *n* millonario, -a *m*, *f*. **millionth** *n*, *adj* millonésimo, -a *m*, *f*.
mime [maim] *n* mimo *m*, pantomima *f*. *v* actuar de mimo.
mimic ['mimik] *adj* mímico; imitativo. *n* mimo *m*; imitador, -a *m*, *f*. *v* imitar, remedar. **mimicry** *n* mímica *f*; (*zool*) mimetismo *m*.
minaret [minə'ret] *n* minarete *m*.
mince [mins] *n* (*meat*) carne picada *f*. **mincemeat** *n* conserva de fruta picada y especias *f*. **mince pie** pastel con frutas picadas *m*. *v* picar; (*walk*) andar con pasos menuditos. **mince words** tener pelos en la lengua. **mincer** *n* máquina de picar carne *f*. **mincing** *adj* afectado.
mind [maind] *n* mente *f*. **bear in mind** tener en cuenta. **go out of one's mind** perder el juicio. **have a good mind to** tener ganas de. **keep in mind** acordarse de. **make up one's mind** decidirse. **read someone's mind** adivinar el pensamiento de alguien. **to my mind** a mi parecer. *v* (*look out*) tener cuidado; (*guard*) cuidar; (*rules*) cumplir; (*pay attention*) prestar atención. **do you mind?** ¿le importa? **I don't mind** a mí no me importa. **never mind** no se precocupe.
mine¹ [main] *pron* (el) mío, (la) mía, (lo) mío.
mine² [main] *n* mina *f*. **minefield** *n* campo de minas *m*. **mineshaft** *n* pozo de extracción *m*. **minesweeper** *n* dragaminas *m invar*. *v* minar; (*mil*) sembrar minas en. **miner** *n* minero *m*. **mining** *n* minería *f*. **mining engineer** ingeniero de minas *m*.
mineral ['minərəl] *nm*, *adj* mineral. **minerals** (*coll: drinks*) *pl n* gaseosas *f pl*.
mingle ['mingl] *v* mezclar.
miniature ['minitʃə] *nf*, *adj* miniatura.

minim ['minim] *n* mínima *f*, blanca *f*.
minimum ['miniməm] *nm*, *adj* mínimo. **minimal** *adj* mínimo. **minimize** *v* minimizar.
minister ['ministə] *n* ministro *m*. *v* **minister to** atender a. **ministerial** *adj* ministerial. **ministry** *n* ministerio *m*.
mink [miŋk] *n* visón *m*.
minor ['mainə] *adj* menor, más pequeño; secundario; de poca importancia. *n* menor de edad *m*, *f*.
minority [mai'noriti] *n* minoría *f*. **in the minority** en la minoría. *adj* minoritario.
minstrel ['minstrəl] *n* trovador *m*.
mint¹ [mint] *n* (*bot*) menta *f*.
mint² [mint] *n* casa de la moneda *f*. *adj* nuevo. *v* acuñar.
minuet [minju'et] *n* minué *m*.
minus ['mainəs] *prep* menos. *adj* negativo. **minus sign** signo menos *m*.
minute¹ ['minit] *n* minuto *m*. **minutes** *pl n* actas *f pl*.
minute² [mai'njuːt] *adj* (*tiny*) diminuto; (*detailed*) minucioso.
miracle ['mirəkl] *n* milagro *m*. **miraculous** *adj* milagroso.
mirage ['miraːʒ] *n* espejismo *m*.
mirror ['mirə] *n* espejo *m*; (*mot*) retrovisor *m*. *v* reflejar.
mirth [məːθ] *n* alegría *f*; hilaridad *f*.
misadventure [misəd'ventʃə] *n* desgracia *f*.
misanthropist [miz'anθrəpist] *n* misántropo *m*. **misanthropic** *adj* misantrópico. **misanthropy** *n* misantropía *f*.
misapprehension [misapri'henʃən] *n* malentendido *m*.
misbehave [misbi'heiv] *v* portarse mal. **misbehaviour** *n* mala conducta *f*.
miscalculate [mis'kalkjuleit] *v* calcular mal. **miscalculation** *n* cálculo erróneo *m*.
miscarriage [mis'karidʒ] *n* (*med*) aborto *m*; (*plans, etc.*) fracaso *m*. **miscarriage of justice** error judicial *m*.
miscellaneous [misə'leiniəs] *adj* diverso.
mischief ['mistʃif] *n* (*evil*) maldad *f*; (*of child*) travesura *f*; (*damage*) daño *m*. **get into mischief** hacer tonterías. **make mischief** sembrar la discordia. **mischievous** *adj* malo; travieso; dañino.
misconception [miskən'sepʃən] *n* concepto falso *m*.
misconduct [mis'kondʌkt] *n* (*misbehaviour*) mala conducta *f*; (*mismanagement*) mala administración *f*.

misconstrue [miskən'struː] v interpretar mal.

misdeed [mis'diːd] n delito m.

misdemeanour [misdi'miːnə] n (law) infracción f; (misbehaviour) mala conducta f.

miser ['maizə] n avaro, -a m, f. **miserly** adj mezquino.

miserable ['mizərəbl] adj (sad) triste; (sick) mal; (unfortunate) desgraciado; (wretched) miserable; (distressing) de pena.

misery ['mizəri] n tristeza f; (pain) dolor m; desgracia f; miseria f; (coll: person) aguafiestas m, f.

misfire [mis'faiə] v fallar; (mot) tener fallos. n fallo m.

misfit ['misfit] n inadaptado, -a m, f.

misfortune [mis'fɔːtʃən] n desgracia f.

misgiving [mis'giviŋ] n recelo m; inquietud f.

misguided [mis'gaidid] adj descaminado; poco afortunado.

mishap ['mishap] n contratiempo m.

misinterpret [misin'tɔːprit] v interpretar mal. **misinterpretation** n interpretación errónea f.

misjudge [mis'dʒʌdʒ] v juzgar mal. **misjudgment** n estimación errónea f.

***mislay** [mis'lei] v extraviar.

***mislead** [mis'liːd] v engañar; equivocar. **misleading** adj engañoso.

misnomer [mis'noumə] n nombre inapropiado m.

misogynist [mi'sodʒənist] n misógino m.

misplace [mis'pleis] v colocar mal; (lose) extraviar.

misprint ['misprint] n errata f.

miss[1] [mis] v fallar; no dar en; (train, bus, etc.) perder; (a meeting) no asistir a; (long for) echar de menos. **miss out** omitir. n tiro errado m; (failure) fracaso m. **missing** adj (lacking) que falta; perdido; ausente; desaparecido.

miss[2] [mis] n señorita.

misshapen [miʃ'ʃeipən] adj (object) deformado; (person) deforme.

missile ['misail] n proyectil m. **guided missile** proyectil teledirigido m.

mission ['miʃən] n misión f. **missionary** n, adj misionero, -a.

mist [mist] n (haze) calina f; (fog) neblina f; (at sea) bruma f; (on glasses) vaho m. **mist over** or **up** empañar. **misty** adj de niebla; brumoso; vago; empañado.

***mistake** [mi'steik] v (be wrong) equivocarse en; (the way) equivocarse de; (misunderstand) entender mal. n error m; equivocación f; falta f. **by mistake** sin querer. **make a mistake** equivocarse. **mistaken** adj equivocado; erróneo; mal comprendido. **be mistaken** estar equivocado.

mistletoe ['misltou] n muérdago m.

mistress ['mistris] n (of the house) señora f; (owner) dueña f; (lover) amante f; (teacher) profesora f.

mistrust [mis'trʌst] n desconfianza f; (suspicion) recelo m. v desconfiar de; recelar de. **mistrustful** adj desconfiado; receloso.

***misunderstand** [misʌndə'stand] v entender mal. **misunderstanding** n malentendido m.

misuse [mis'juːs; v mis'juːz] n mal uso m; abuso m; maltrato m; mal empleo m. v abusar de; maltratar; emplear mal.

mitigate ['mitigeit] v mitigar; aliviar; atemar. **mitigation** n mitigación f; alivio m; atenuación f.

mitre ['maitə] n (rel) mitra f; (carpentry) inglete m. v unir con ingletes.

mitten ['mitn] n mitón m.

mix [miks] v mezclar; (drinks) preparar; (salad) aliñar; (flour, cement, etc.) amasar. **mix up** mezclar; confundir. **mix-up** n lío m; confusión f. **mixed feelings** sentimientos contradictorios m pl. **mixed grill** plato combinado m. **mixer** n (elec) mezclador m; (cement) mezcladora f. **mixture** n mezcla f; (med) mixtura f.

moan [moun] v gemir; (coll: complain) quejarse. n gemido m; queja f.

moat [mout] n foso m.

mob [mob] n multitud f; (rabble) chusma f. v acosar.

mobile ['moubail] nm, adj móvil. **mobility** n movilidad f. **mobilize** v movilizar.

moccasin ['mokəsin] n mocasín m.

mock [mok] v burlarse de; ridiculizar. adj simulado; falso; imitado. **mockery** n burla f; simulacro m; imitación f. **mocking** adj burlón.

mode [moud] n modo m, manera f; (fashion) moda f.

model ['modl] n modelo m; (of a statue) maqueta f; (fashion) maniquí m; (dressmaking pattern) patrón m. v modelar; (dress) presentar.

moderate ['modərət; *v* 'modəreit] *n, adj* moderado, -a. *v* moderar; aplacar. **moderately** *adv* moderadamente; (*fairly*) mediocremente. **in moderation** con moderación.

modern ['modən] *adj* moderno. **modern languages** lenguas vivas *f pl*. **modernization** *n* modernisación *f*. **modernize** *v* modernizar.

modest ['modist] *adj* modesto; discreto. **modesty** *n* modestia *f*.

modify ['modifai] *v* modificar. **modification** *n* modificación *f*.

modulate ['modjuleit] *v* modular. **modulation** *n* modulación *f*.

module ['modjuːl] *n* módulo *m*.

mohair ['mouheə] *n* moer *m*.

moist [moist] *adj* húmedo. **moisten** *v* numedecer. mojar. **moisture** *n* humedad *f*. **moisturize** *v* humedecer. **moisturizing cream** crema hidratante *f*.

molasses [mə'lasiz] *n* melaza *f*.

mole[1] [moul] *n* (*on skin*) lunar *m*.

mole[2] [moul] *n* (*zool*) topo *m*. **molehill** *n* topera *f*.

molecule ['molikjuːl] *n* molécula *f*. **molecular** *adj* molecular.

molest [mə'lest] *v* molestar, importunar.

mollusc ['moləsk] *n* molusco *m*.

molten ['moultən] *adj* fundido.

moment ['moumənt] *n* momento *m*. **at the moment** de momento. **momentary** *adj* momentáneo. **momentarily** *adv* momentáneamente. **momentous** *adj* de gran importancia.

momentum [mə'mentəm] *n* momento *m*; ímpetu *m*; impulso *m*.

monarch ['monək] *n* monarca *m*. **monarchist** *n, adj* monárquico, -a. **monarchy** *n* monarquía *f*.

monastery ['monəstəri] *n* monasterio *m*. **monastic** *adj* monacal.

Monday ['mʌndi] *n* lunes *m*.

money ['mʌni] *n* dinero *m*. **get one's money's worth** sacar jugo al dinero. **moneylender** *n* prestamista *m, f*.

mongol ['mongəl] *n, adj* (*med*) mongol, -a. **mongolism** *n* mongolismo *m*.

mongrel ['mʌngrəl] *n* (*dog*) perro mestizo *m*.

monitor ['monitə] *n* monitor *m*; instructor *m*; (*tech*) radioescucha *m*. *v* controlar.

monk [mʌnk] *n* monje *m*.

monkey ['mʌnki] *n* mono *m*. **monkey around** entretenerse, perder el tiempo.

monogamy [mə'nogəmi] *n* monogamia *f*. **monogamous** *adj* monógamo.

monogram ['monəgram] *n* monograma *m*.

monologue ['monəlog] *n* monólogo *m*.

monopolize [mə'nopəlaiz] *v* monopolizar. **monopoly** *n* monopolio *m*.

monosyllable ['monəsiləbl] *n* monosílabo *m*. **monosyllabic** *adj* (*word*) monosílabo; (*statement*) monosilábico.

monotone ['monətoun] *n* monotonía *f*. **monotonous** *adj* monótono. **monotony** *n* monotonía *f*.

monsoon [mon'suːn] *n* monzón *m*.

monster ['monstə] *n* monstruo *m*. **monstrosity** *n* monstruosidad *f*. **monstrous** *adj* monstruoso.

month [mʌnθ] *n* mes *m*. **calendar month** mes civil *m*. **monthly** *n, adj* mensual. *adv* mensualmente.

monument ['monjumənt] *n* monumento *m*. **monumental** *adj* monumental; enorme.

mood[1] [muːd] *n* humor *m*. **moody** *adj* malhumorado; caprichoso.

mood[2] [muːd] *n* (*gramm*) modo *m*.

moon [muːn] *n* luna *f*. **crescent moon** media luna *f*. **full moon** luna llena *f*. **new moon** luna nueva *f*. **moonbeam** *n* rayo de luna *m*. **moonlight** *n* claro de luna *m*. **moonlighting** *n* (*coll*) pluriempleo *m*.

moor[1] [muə] *n* páramo *m*.

moor[2] [muə] *v* marrrar.

mop [mop] *n* (*floor*) fregona *f*; (*hair*) pelambrera *f*. *v* fregar. **mop up** limpiar.

mope [moup] *v* tener ideas negras.

moped ['mouped] *n* ciclomotor *m*.

moral ['morəl] *adj* moral; virtuoso. **moral support** apoyo moral *m*. *n* (*fable*) moraleja *f*. **morals** *pl n* moralidad *f sing*. **moralist** *n* moralista *m, f*. **moralize** *v* moralizar.

morale [mə'raɪl] *n* moral *f*.

morbid ['moːbid] *adj* mórbido.

more [moː] *adj* más; superior; mayor. *pron, adv* más. **all the more** aún más. **and what's more** y lo que es más. **even more** más aún. **more and more** cada vez más. **more than ever** más que nunca. **once more** una vez más.

moreover [moː'rouvə] *adv* además, también; por otra parte.

morgue [moːg] *n* depósito de cadáveres *m*.

morning ['mɔːnɪŋ] *n* mañana *f. adj* de la mañana. **morning coat** chaqué *m*. **morning sickness** náuseas *f pl.*

moron ['mɔːron] *n* retrasado mental *m*; (*coll*) imbécil *m, f*. **moronic** *adj* retrasado mental; (*coll*) idiota.

morose [mə'rous] *adj* malhumorado.

morphine ['mɔːfiːn] *n* morfina *f.*

Morse code [mɔːs] *n* morse *m.*

morsel ['mɔːsəl] *n* bocado *m.*

mortal ['mɔːtl] *nm, adj* mortal. **mortality** *n* mortalidad *f.*

mortar ['mɔːtə] *n* mortero *m.*

mortgage ['mɔːgɪdʒ] *n* hipoteca *f.*

mortify ['mɔːtɪfai] *v* mortificar. **mortification** *n* mortificación *f.*

mortuary ['mɔːtʃuəri] *n* depósito de cadáveres *m.*

mosaic [mə'zeiik] *n* mosaico *m. adj* de mosaico.

Moscow ['moskou] *n* Moscú.

mosque [mosk] *n* mezquita *f.*

mosquito [mə'skiːtou] *n* mosquito *m*. **mosquito bite** picadura de mosquito *f.* **mosquito net** mosquitero *m.*

moss [mos] *n* musgo *m*. **mossy** *adj* musgoso.

most [moust] *adj* más; la mayoría de. *pron* la mayoría; la mayor parte; lo máximo. *adv* más; (*very*) de lo más. at most a lo sumo. **make the most of** sacar el mayor provecho de. **mostly** *adv* principalmente, sobre todo; en general.

motel [mou'tel] *n* motel *m.*

moth [moθ] *n* mariposa nocturna *f*. **clothes moth** polilla *f*. **mothball** bola de naftalina *f*. **moth-eaten** *adj* apolillado; (*fig*) anticuado.

mother ['mʌθə] *n* madre *f*. **mother-in-law** *n* suegra *f*. **mother-of-pearl** *n* madreperla *f*. **Mothers' Day** día de la Madre *m*. **mother-to-be** futura madre *f*. **motherhood** *n* maternidad *f*. **motherly** *adj* maternal.

motion ['mouʃən] *n* movimiento *m*; (*signal*) señas *f pl*; (*indication*) ademán *m*; (*of a machine*) mecanismo *m*; (*med*) deposición *f*; (*at a meeting*) moción *f*. **set in motion** poner en marcha. *v* indicar con la mano; hacer señas. **motionless** *adj* inmóvil.

motivate ['moutiveit] *v* motivar. **motivation** *n* motivo *m.*

motive ['moutiv] *n* (*reason*) motivo *m*; (*law*) móvil *m. adj* motor, motriz.

motor ['moutə] *n* motor *m*. **motorbike** *n*

(*coll*) moto *f*. **motorboat** *n* lancha motora *f*. **motorcar** *n* automóvil *m*, coche *m*. **motorcyclist** *n* motociclista *m, f*. **motoring** *n* automovilismo *m*. **motorist** *n* automovilista *m, f*. **motorway** *n* autopista *f.*

mottled ['motld] *adj* abigarrado.

motto ['motou] *n* lema *m.*

mould[1] [mould] *n* (*container*) molde *m*; (*shape*) forma *f*; (*pattern*) modelo *m. v* moldear; formar.

mould[2] [mould] *n* (*fungus*) moho *m*. **mouldy** *adj* mohoso. **go mouldy** enmohecerse.

moult [moult] *v* mudar. *n* muda *f.*

mound [maund] *n* (*natural*) montículo *m*; (*artificial*) terraplén *m*; (*heap*) montón *m*; (*burial*) túmulo *m.*

mount[1] [maunt] *v* subir; montar a caballo. **mount up** aumentar. *n* (*horse*) montura *f*; (*base*) soporte *m*; (*phot*) borde *m*; (*drawing*) fondo *m.*

mount[2] [maunt] *n* monte *m.*

mountain ['mauntən] *n* montaña *f*. **mountaineer** *n* montañero, -a *m, f*. **mountaineering** *n* montañismo *m*. **mountainous** *adj* montañoso.

mourn [mɔːn] *v* lamentar. **mournful** *adj* triste; afligido. **mourning** *n* luto *m*, duelo *m.*

mouse [maus] *n, pl* **mice** ratón *m*. **mousetrap** *n* ratonera *f*. **mousy** *adj* (*coll: hair*) pardusco; (*coll: shy*) tímido.

mousse [muːs] *n* crema batida *f.*

moustache [mə'staːʃ] *n* bigote *m.*

mouth [mauθ] *n* boca *f*; (*opening*) abertura *f*; (*entrance*) entrada *f*; (*bottle*) gollete *m*; (*river*) desembocadura *f*. **mouthpiece** *n* (*music*) boquita *f*; (*phone*) micrófono *m*; (*spokesman*) portavoz *m*. **mouthwash** *n* enjuague *m*. **mouth-watering** *adj* muy apetitoso. *v* articular.

move [muːv] *v* cambiar de; mudarse de; mover; transportar; (*from one place to another*) trasladar; poner en marcha; (*emotionally*) emocionar; (*in debate*) proponer. *n* (*fig*) paso *m*; marcha *f*; medida *f*; (*house*) mudanza *f*; (*turn*) turno *m*; (*chess, etc.*) jugada *f*. **movable** *adj* movible, móvil. **movement** *n* movimiento *m*; (*gesture*) ademán *m*; acto *m*; tendencia *f*; transporte *m*; traslado *m*; (*vehicles*) tráfico *m*; (*tech*) mecanismo *m*; (*mil*) maniobra *f*. **moving** *adj* móvil; en movimiento; (*emotional*) conmovedor.

movie ['muːvɪ] n (US) película f. go to the movies ir al cine.

*mow [mou] v (lawn) cortar, segar. mow down barrer.

Mr ['mɪstə] n señor m; Sr.

Mrs ['mɪsɪz] n señora f; Sra.

much [mʌtʃ] adj, adv, pron mucho. as much tanto (como). how much? ¿cuánto? much as por mucho que. so much tanto. too much demasiado.

muck [mʌk] n (manure) estiércol m; (dirt) suciedad f. v muck about (coll) perder el tiempo. mucky adj asqueroso.

mucus ['mjuːkəs] n mucosidad f. mucous adj mucoso.

mud [mʌd] n barro m; (thick mud) fango m. mudguard n guardabarros m invar. muddy adj fangoso.

muddle ['mʌdl] n desorden m; confusión f. v confundir, embrollar. muddle through salir del paso. muddleheaded adj atontado.

muff [mʌf] n manguito m.

muffle ['mʌfl] v amortiguar. muffle up embozar. muffler n bufanda f.

mug [mʌg] n tazón m; (slang: face) jeta f; (slang: fool) primo, -a m, f. v asaltar. mugging n asalto m.

muggy ['mʌgi] adj bochornoso.

mulberry ['mʌlbəri] n (fruit) mora f; (tree) morera f, moral m.

mule¹ [mjuːl] n (animal) mulo, -a m, f. mulish adj testarudo.

mule² [mjuːl] n (slipper) babucha f.

multicoloured [,mʌltɪ'kʌləd] adj multicolor.

multilingual [,mʌltɪ'lɪŋgwəl] adj poligloto.

multiple ['mʌltɪpl] adj múltiple. n múltiplo m. multiple sclerosis esclerosis en placas f.

multiply ['mʌltɪplaɪ] v multiplicar. multiplication n multiplicación f. multiplication table tabla de multiplicar f.

multiracial [,mʌltɪ'reɪʃəl] adj multiracial.

multitude ['mʌltɪtjuːd] n multitud f, muchedumbre f.

mumble ['mʌmbl] v mascullar. n refunfuño m.

mummy¹ ['mʌmi] n momia f. mummification n momificación f. mummify v momificar.

mummy² ['mʌmi] n (coll: mother) mamá f.

mumps [mʌmps] n paperas f pl.

munch [mʌntʃ] v mascar.

mundane [mʌn'deɪn] adj mundano.

municipal [mju'nɪsɪpəl] adj municipal. municipality n municipio m.

mural ['mjuərəl] nm, adj mural.

murder ['məːdə] n homicidio m, asesinato m. murderer n asesino m. murderess n asesina f. murderous adj homicida, asesino.

murky ['məːki] adj oscuro; lóbrego.

murmur ['məːmə] v murmurar. n murmullo m.

muscle ['mʌsl] n músculo m. v muscle in (coll) meterse por fuerza en. muscular adj muscular; (person) musculoso.

muse [mjuːz] n musa f. v meditar, contemplar.

museum [mju'zɪəm] n museo m.

mushroom ['mʌʃrum] n hongo m, seta f; (food) champiñón m. v crecer como hongos.

music ['mjuːzik] n música f. music hall music-hall m. music stand atril m. musical adj de música; (ear) musical; (person) aficionado a la música. musical (comedy) n comedia musical f. musical instrument instrumento de música m. musician n músico, -a m, f.

musk [mʌsk] n almizcle m.

musket ['mʌskit] n mosquete m. musketeer n mosquetero m.

Muslim ['mʌzlim] n, adj musulmán, -ana.

muslin ['mʌzlin] n muselina f.

mussel ['mʌsl] n mejillón m.

*must [mʌst] v deber; tener que.

mustard ['mʌstəd] n mostaza f. mustard pot mostacera f.

muster ['mʌstə] v reunir; (mil) formar. n reunión f; asamblea f; (mil) revista f. pass muster ser aceptable.

musty ['mʌsti] adj mohoso. smell musty oler a cerrado.

mute [mjuːt] n, adj mudo, -a; (music) sordina f. v apagar; poner sordina a. muted adj sordo.

mutilate ['mjuːtileit] v mutilar. mutilation n mutilación f.

mutiny ['mjuːtini] n motín m, rebelión f. v amotinarse, rebelarse. mutinous adj amotinado; (fig) rebelde.

mutter ['mʌtə] v murmurar. n murmullo m. muttering n refunfuño m.

mutton ['mʌtn] n cordero m.

mutual ['mjuːtʃuəl] adj mutuo; común.

muzzle ['mʌzl] n (nose) hocico m; (device) bozal m; (gun) boca f. v abozalar.

my [mai] *adj* mi (*pl* mis), mío, mía (*pl* míos, mías).
myself [mai'self] *pron* (*reflexive*) me; (*emphatic*) yo mismo, -a; (*after prep*) mí. **by myself** (completamente) solo, -a.
mystery ['misteri] *n* misterio *m*. **mysterious** *adj* misterioso.
mystic ['mistik] *n* iniciado, -a *m, f*; místico, -a *m, f*. *adj also* **mystical** místico; esotérico; oculto; sobrenatural.
mystify ['mistifai] *v* oscurecer; desconcertar; desorientar; (*deceive*) engañar. **mystification** *n* mistificación *f*; complejidad *f*; confusión *f*.
mystique [mi'stik] *n* mística *f*.
myth [miθ] *n* mito *m*. **mythical** *adj* mítico. **mythological** *adj* mitológico. **mythology** *n* mitología *f*.

N

nag [nag] *v* regañar. *n* (*horse*) rocín *m*.
nail [neil] *n* (*metal*) clavo *m*; (*anat*) uña *f*; (*claw*) garra *f*. **nailbrush** *n* cepillo de uñas *m*. **nail-file** *n* lima de uñas *f*. **nail polish** esmalte de uñas *m*. **nail-scissors** *n* tijeras para las uñas *f pl*. *v* clavar.
naive [nai'iːv] *adj* ingenuo. **naivety** *n* ingenuidad *f*.
naked ['neikid] *adj* desnudo. **nakedness** *n* desnudez *f*.
name [neim] *n* nombre *m*; (*surname*) apellido *m*; fama *f*; título *m*. **my name is . . .** me llamo . . . . **namesake** *n* tocayo, -a *m, f*. **what's your name?** ¿cómo se llama? *v* llamar; nombrar. **nameless** *adj* sin nombre; anónimo. **namely** *adv* a saber.
nanny ['nani] *n* niñera *f*.
nap¹ [nap] *n* sueño ligero *m*. *v* dormitar. **be caught napping** estar desprevenido.
nap² [nap] *n* (*of cloth*) lanilla *f*.
nape [neip] *n* nuca *f*.
napkin ['napkin] *n* servilleta *f*.
nappy ['napi] *n* pañal *m*.
narcotic [naɪ'kotik] *nm, adj* narcótico.
narrate [nə'reit] *v* contar. **narration** *n* narración *f*. **narrator** *n* narrador, -a *m, f*.
narrative ['narətiv] *n* narrativa *f*. *adj* narrativo.
narrow ['narou] *adj* estrecho. **narrow-gauge** *adj* de vía estrecha. **narrow-minded** *adj* de miras estrechas. *v* estrechar. **narrow down** reducir. **narrowly** *adv* (*only just*) por muy poco; estrechamente. **narrowness** *n* estrechez *f*.
nasal ['neizəl] *adj* nasal. **nasalize** *v* nasalizar.
nasturtium [nə'stəɪfəm] *n* capuchina *f*.
nasty ['naɪsti] *adj* sucio; repugnante; (*unfriendly*) antipático; grosero; desagradable.
nation ['neiʃən] *n* nación *f*. **national** *nm, adj* nacional. **national anthem** himno nacional *m*. **nationalism** *n* nacionalismo *m*. **nationalist** *n*(*m+f*), *adj* nacionalista. **nationality** *n* nacionalidad *f*. **nationalization** *n* nacionalización *f*. **nationalize** *v* nacionalizar.
native ['neitiv] *adj* (*country, town*) natal; (*inhabitant*) nativo; (*language*) materno; (*product*) del país. *n* natural *m, f*; nativo, -a *m, f*.
nativity [nə'tivəti] *n* nacimiento *m*.
natural ['natʃərəl] *adj* natural. **naturalism** *n* naturalismo *m*. **naturalist** *n* naturalista *m, f*. **naturally** *adv* naturalmente; por naturaleza.
nature ['neitʃə] *n* naturaleza *f*; (*character*) natural *m*; esencia *f*.
naughty ['noɪti] *adj* travieso; malvado. **naughtiness** *n* travesura *f*.
nausea ['noɪziə] *n* náusea *f*. **nauseate** *v* dar asco.
nautical ['noɪtikəl] *adj* marítimo, náutico.
naval ['neivəl] *adj* naval; de marina. **naval officer** oficial de marina *m*.
navel ['neivəl] *n* ombligo *m*. **navel orange** naranja navel *f*.
navigate ['navigeit] *v* navegar; (*steer*) gobernar. **navigable** *adj* navegable. **navigation** *n* navegación *f*. **navigator** *n* navegante *m*.
navy ['neivi] *n* marina *f*. **navy blue** azul marino *m*.
near [niə] *adv* cerca. *prep* cerca de. *adj* cercano. *v* acercarse a; aproximarse a. **the near future** el futuro próximo. **nearby** *adv* cerca. **nearly** *adv* casi. **not nearly** ni con mucho. **very nearly** casi casi.
neat [niɪt] *adj* limpio; bien cuidado; ordenado; (*drink*) solo. **neaten** *v* limpiar; ordenar. **neatly** *adv* con cuidado; (*dress*) con gusto; (*skilfully*) hábilmente. **neatness** *n* limpieza *f*; orden *m*; gusto *m*.

necessary ['nesisəri] *adj* necesario. **if nec-essary** si es preciso. **it is necessary** es preciso. **necessitate** *v* necesitar. **necessity** *n* necesidad *f*.

neck [nek] *n (human, garment)* cuello *m*; *(animal)* pescuezo *m*; *(bottle)* gollete *m*. **neck and neck** parejos. **necklace** *n* collar *m*.

nectar ['nektə] *n* néctar *m*.

need [niːd] *n* necesidad *f*; *(lack)* carencia *f*. *v* necesitar; hacer falta a uno. **needless** *adj* innecesario; inútil. **needy** *adj* necesitado. *n* **the needy** los necesitados *m pl*.

needle ['niːdl] *n* aguja *f*. **darning needle** aguja de zurcir. **knitting needle** aguja de hacer punto. **needlework** *n* costura *f*. *v (coll)* pinchar.

negative ['negətiv] *adj* negativo. *n (gramm)* negación *f*; *(phot)* negativo *m*; *(reply)* contestación negativa *f*.

neglect [ni'glekt] *v* no cumplir con; dejar de; no observar; descuidar; abandonar. *n* negligencia *f*; abandono *m*; inob-servancia *f*; dejadez *f*. **neglected** *adj* descuidado; abandonado.

negligée ['negliʒei] *n* negligé *m*.

negligence ['neglidʒəns] *n* negligencia *f*; descuido *m*. **negligent** *adj* negligente; descuidado.

negotiate [ni'goufieit] *v* negociar; *(obsta-cle)* franquear; *(hill)* subir; *(bend)* tomar. **negotiable** *adj* negociable; franqueable. **negotiation** *n* negociación *f*.

Negro ['niːgrou] *nm, adj* negro.

neigh [nei] *v* relinchar. *n* relincho *m*.

neighbour ['neibə] *n* vecino, -a *m, f*. **neighbourhood** *n* vecindad *f*; *(district)* barrio *m*. **neighbouring** *adj* vecino; *(near)* cercano. **neighbourly** *adj* de buena vecindad.

neither ['naiðə] *adv* tampoco. **neither ... nor ...** ni ... ni .... *conj* ni, tampoco. *pron* ninguno, -a *m, f*. *adj* ninguno de los dos.

neon ['niːon] *n* neón *m*.

nephew ['nefjuː] *n* sobrino *m*.

nepotism ['nepətizəm] *n* nepotismo *m*.

nerve [nəːv] *n* nervio *m*; valor *m*; *(coll: cheek)* cara *f*. **get on someone's nerves** crisparle los nervios a uno. **lose one's nerve** *(coll)* rajarse. **nerve-wracking** *adj* crispante; horribilante. **nerves** *pl (coll)* nerviosismo *m*. **nervous** *adj* nervioso;

(apprehensive) miedoso. **nervous break-down** depresión nerviosa *f*.

nest [nest] *n* nido *m*. *v* anidar.

nestle ['nesl] *v* arrellanarse; acurrucarse.

net¹ [net] *n* red *f*. **net curtains** visillo *m sing*. **network** *n* red *f*. *v* coger.

net² [net] *adj* neto. **net weight** peso neto *m*.

Netherlands ['neðələndz] *pl n* Países Bajos *m pl*.

nettle ['netl] *n* ortiga *f*. **nettle rash** urti-caria *f*. *v* irritar.

neuralgia [nju'raldʒə] *n* neuralgia *f*. **neu-ralgic** *adj* neurálgico.

neurosis [nju'rousis] *n* neurosis *f*. **neurotic** *n, adj* neurótico, -a.

neuter ['njuːtə] *nm, adj* neutro.

neutral ['njuːtrəl] *adj* neutro. *n (mot)* pun-to muerto *m*. **neutrality** *n* neutralidad *f*. **neutralize** *v* neutralizar.

never ['nevə] *adv* nunca, jamás. **never-ending** *adj* sin fin. **nevermore** *adv* nunca más.

nevertheless [nevəðə'les] *adv* sin embar-go, no obstante.

new [njuː] *adj* nuevo; fresco.

newcomer ['njuːkʌmə] *n* recién llegado, -a *m, f*.

new-born ['njuːbɔːn] *adj* recién nacido, -a *m, f*.

new-fangled ['njuːfaŋgəld] *adj* recién inventado.

new-laid [njuː'leid] *adj (egg)* recién pues-to.

newly-wed ['njuːli,wed] *adj* recién casado, -a *m, f*.

news [njuːz] *n* noticias *f pl*; actualidad *f*; *(radio)* diario hablado *m*; *(TV)* telediario *m*; *(film)* noticiario *m*. **news agency** agencia de información *f*. **newsagent** *n* vendedor de periódicos *m*. **news flash** noticia de última hora *f*. **news item** noticia *f*. **newsletter** *n* boletín *m*. **newspa-per** *n* periódico *m*, diario *m*. **newsstand** *n* quiosco de periódicos *m*.

newt [njuːt] *n* tritón *m*.

New Testament *n* Nuevo Testamento *m*.

New Year *n* Año Nuevo *m*. **Happy New Year!** ¡feliz Año Nuevo! **New Year's Eve** nochevieja *f*.

New Zealand [njuː'ziːlənd] *n* Nueva Zelanda *f*, Nueva Zelandia *f*. **New Zea-lander** neocelandés, -esa *m, f*, neoze-landés, -esa *m, f*.

next [nekst] *adj* próximo; siguiente; que viene; (*adjoining*) vecino. *adv* luego, después; la proxima vez; ahora. *prep* junto a, cerca de. **the next day** el día siguiente *m*. **next-door** *adj* de al lado. **next to** al lado de. **next-of-kin** *n* pariente más cercano *m*. **who's next?** ¿a quién le toca?

nib [nib] *n* plumilla *f*.

nibble ['nibl] *v* mordiscar, mordisquear. *n* mordisqueo *m*.

nice [nais] *adj* (*kind*) amable; (*agreeable*) agradable; (*likeable*) simpático; (*pretty*) bonito; (*pleasant*) ameno; precioso; escrupuloso; (*weather*) bueno; (*point*) delicado. **nicely** *adv* amablemente; agradablemente; bien. **nicety** *n* precisión *f*; delicadeza *f*.

niche [nitʃ] *n* nicho *m*, hornacina *f*.

nick [nik] *n* (*notch*) muesca *f*. (*cut*) rasguño *m*. **in the nick of time** justo a tiempo. *v* hacer muescas; cortar; (*slang: steal*) birlar; (*slang: arrest*) pescar.

nickel ['nikl] *n* níquel *m*.

nickname ['nikneim] *n* apodo *m*. *v* apodar.

nicotine ['nikətiɪn] *n* nicotina *f*.

niece [niɪs] *n* sobrina *f*.

niggle ['nigl] *v* ocuparse de menudencias. **niggling** *adj* de poca monta; molesto.

night [nait] *n* noche *f*. **good night!** ¡buenas noches! **last night** anoche *f*. **tomorrow night** mañana por la noche *f*. **night cap** *n* (*garment*) gorro de dormir; (*coll: drink*) bebida tomada antes de acostarse *f*.

nightclub ['naitklʌb] *n* night club *m*.

nightdress ['naitdres] *n* camisón *m*, camisa de dormir *f*.

nightfall ['naitfoɪl] *n* anochecer *m*.

nightingale ['naitiŋgeil] *n* ruiseñor *m*.

night-life ['naitlaif] *n* vida nocturna *f*.

night-light ['naitlait] *n* lamparilla *f*.

nightly ['naitli] *adj* nocturno. *adv* por las noches; todas las noches.

nightmare ['naitmeə] *n* pesadilla *f*.

night-school ['nait.skuɪl] *n* escuela nocturna *f*.

nightshade ['naitʃeid] *n* **deadly nightshade** belladona *f*.

night shift *n* turno de noche *m*.

night-watchman [.nait'wotʃmən] *n* guarda nocturno *m*; sereno *m*.

nil [nil] *n* nada *f*; ninguno, -a *m*, *f*; (*sport*) cero *m*.

nimble ['nimbl] *adj* ágil; (*mind*) vivo. **nimbleness** *n* agilidad *f*; vivacidad *f*.

nine [nain] *nm, adj* nueve. **dressed up to the nines** de punta en blanco. **ninth** *n, adj* noveno, -a.

nineteen [nain'tiɪn] *nm, adj* diecinueve. **nineteenth** *n, adj* decimonoveno, -a.

ninety ['nainti] *nm, adj* noventa. **ninetieth** *n, adj* nonagésimo, -a.

nip¹ [nip] *v* (*pinch*) pellizcar; (*bite*) morder; (*coll: go quickly*) pegar un salto. **nip in the bud** cortar de raíz. *n* pellizco *m*; mordisco *m*. **nippy** *adj* rápido; (*chilly*) fresquito.

nip² [nip] *n* (*drop*) gota *f*; (*drink*) trago *m*.

nipple ['nipl] *n* (*female*) pezón *m*; (*male*) tetilla *f*; (*bottle*) tetina *f*.

nit [nit] *n* liendre *f*; (*coll*) papanatas *m invar*.

nitrogen ['naitrədʒən] *n* nitrógeno *m*.

no [nou] *adv* no. *adj* ninguno. **no longer or more** ya no. **no parking** prohibido aparcar. **no smoking** prohibido fumar. **no thoroughfare** calle sin salida.

noble ['noubl] *n(m+f), adj* noble. **nobility** *n* nobleza *f*.

nobody ['noubodi] *pron* nadie.

nocturnal [nok'təɪnəl] *adj* nocturno.

nod [nod] *v* inclinar; asentir con la cabeza; saludar con la cabeza; (*sleepily*) dar cabezadas. *n* inclinación de cabeza *f*; saludo con, la cabeza *m*; cabezada *f*.

noise [noiz] *n* ruido *m*. **noiseless** *adj* silencioso. **noisy** *adj* ruidoso.

nomad ['noumad] *n* nómada *m, f*. **nomadic** *adj* nómada.

nominal ['nominl] *adj* nominal.

nominate ['nomineit] *v* (*appoint*) nombrar; (*propose*) designar. **nomination** *n* nombramiento *m*, designación *f*.

nonchalant ['nonʃələnt] *adj* imperturbable; indiferente. **nonchalance** *n* imperturbabilidad *f*; indiferencia *f*.

nonconformist [nonkən'foɪmist] *n(m+f), adj* disidente.

nondescript ['nondiskript] *adj* indescriptible.

none [nʌn] *pron* nadie; ninguno, -a. *adv* de ningún modo, de ninguna manera.

nonentity [non'entəti] *n* nulidad *f*.

nonetheless [.nʌnðə'les] *adv* sin embargo, no obstante.

non-existent [nonig'zistənt] *adj* inexistente.

non-fiction [non'fikʃən] *n* literatura no novelesca *f*.

non-resident [non'rezidənt] *n(m+f)*, *adj* no residente.

nonsense ['nonsəns] *n* tonterias *f pl*. **nonsensical** *adj* disparatado.

non-stop [non'stop] *adj* directo; continuo; sin escalas. *adv* sin parar; directamente.

noodles ['nuːdlz] *pl n* fideos *m pl*.

noon [nuːn] *n* mediodía *m*.

no-one ['nouwʌn] *pron* nadie.

noose [nuːs] *n* nudo corredizo *m*; lazo *m*; (*hangman's*) soga *f*.

nor [noɪ] *conj* ni; tampoco.

norm [noɪm] *n* norma *f*.

normal ['noɪməl] *adj* normal. *n* lo normal *m*.

north [noɪθ] *n* norte *m*. *adj also* **northerly**, **northern** del norte, norteño; (*facing north*) que da al norte. *adv* hacia el norte. **northbound** *adj* de dirección norte. **north-east** *nm*, *adj* nordeste. **north-west** *nm*, *adj* noroeste.

Norway ['noɪwei] *n* Noruega *f*. **Norwegian** *n*, *adj* noruego, -a.

nose [nouz] *n* nariz *f*; (*sense of smell*) olfato *m*; (*aircraft*, *car*) morro *m*. **blow one's nose** sonarse. **have a nosebleed** sangrar por la nariz. **nosey** *adj* (*coll*) entremetido.

nostalgia [no'staldʒə] *n* nostalgia *f*. **nostalgic** *adj* nostálgico.

nostril ['nostrəl] *n* ventanilla de la nariz *f*; (*horse*) ollar *m*. **nostrils** *pl n* narices *f pl*.

not [not] *adv* no; ni; como no; sin. **certainly not!** ¡de ninguna manera! **not at all** (*acknowledging thanks*) no hay de qué.

notable ['noutəbl] *adj* notable. **notably** *adv* notablemente, señaladamente.

notary ['noutəri] *n* notario *m*.

notch [notʃ] *n* (*cut*) muesca *f*; (*degree*) grado *m*. *v* hacer una muesca en.

note [nout] *n* nota *f*; (*key of piano*, *organ*) tecla *f*; (*sound*) sonido *m*; (*money*) billete *m*; (*music*) tono *m*; (*renown*) renombre *m*; marca. **notebook** *n* cuaderno *m*. **notepaper** papel de escribir *m*. **noteworthy** *adj* notable. *v* tomar nota de; darse cuenta de; anotar, apuntar. **noted** *adj* notable; célebre.

nothing ['nʌθiŋ] *pron* nada; no ... nada. *n* cero *m*. **nothing but** sólo.

notice ['noutis] *n* (*advert*) anuncio *m*; (*poster*) cartel *m*; (*sign*) letrero *m*; atención *f*; (*warning*) aviso *m*; (*dismissal*) despido *m*; (*resignation*) dimisión *f*. **notice-board** *n* tablón de anuncios *m*. **at short notice** a corto plazo. **notice to quit** desahucio *m*. *v* darse cuenta de; fijarse en; observar; ver; prestar atención. **noticeable** *adj* notable; evidente.

notify ['noutifai] *v* avisar, notificar.

notion ['nouʃən] *n* idea *f*, concepto *m*.

notorious [nou'toɪriəs] *adj* notorio. **notoriety** *n* notoriedad *f*.

notwithstanding [notwið'standiŋ] *prep* a pesar de. *adv* sin embargo. *conj* por más que.

nougat ['nuːgaɪ] *n* turrón de almendras *m*.

nought [noɪt] *n* cero *m*.

noun [naun] *n* nombre *m*, sustantivo *m*.

nourish ['nʌriʃ] *v* alimentar. **nourishing** *adj* alimenticio. **nourishment** *n* alimento *m*.

novel[1] ['novəl] *n* novela *f*. **novelist** *n* novelista *m*, *f*.

novel[2] ['novəl] *adj* nuevo; original. **novelty** *n* novedad *f*.

November [nə'vembə] *n* noviembre *m*.

novice ['novis] *n* novicio, -a *m*, *f*.

now [nau] *adv* ahora; ya; ya ahora; actualmente; inmediatamente. **from now on** de ahora en adelante. **nowadays** *adv* hoy día. **now and again** de vez en cuando. **up to now** hasta ahora.

nowhere ['nouweə] *adv* por ninguna parte; en ninguna parte; a ninguna parte.

noxious ['nokʃəs] *adj* nocivo.

nozzle ['nozl] *n* boca *f*, boquilla *f*.

nuance ['njuːãs] *n* matiz *m*.

nuclear ['njuːkliə] *adj* nuclear.

nucleus ['njuːkliəs] *n* núcleo *m*.

nude ['njuːd] *nm*, *adj* desnudo. **nudism** *n* nudismo *m*. **nudist** *n(m+f)*, *adj* nudista. **nudity** *n* desnudez *f*.

nudge [nʌdʒ] *v* dar un codazo a. *n* codazo *m*.

nugget ['nʌgit] *n* pepita *f*.

nuisance ['njuːsns] *n* (*thing*) molestia *f*; (*person*) molesta *f*. **be a nuisance** ponerse pesado. **what a nuisance!** (*coll*) ¡qué pesadez!

null [nʌl] *adj* nulo. **null and void** nulo y sin valor.

numb [nʌm] *adj* entumecido; (*with fear*) petrificado. *v* entumecer; dejar helado.

numbness *n* entumecimiento *m*; parálisis *f*.

number ['nʌmbə] *n* número *m*. **number plate** (*mot*) matrícula *f*. *v* numerar; contar.

numeral ['njuːmərəl] *n* número *m*, cifra *f*.

numeration [,njuːmə'reiʃn] *n* numeración *f*. **numerator** *n* numerador *m*.

numerical [njuːˈmerikl] *adj* numérico.

numerous ['njuːmərəs] *adj* numeroso.

nun [nʌn] *n* monja *f*.

nurse [nəːs] *n* enfermera *f*; (*nanny*) niñera *f*. *v* (*the sick*) cuidar; (*suckle*) criar; (*cradle*) mecer; (*hopes*) abrigar; (*plans*) acariciar. **nursing home** clínica *f*.

nursery ['nəːsəri] *n* (*room*) habitación de los niños *f*; (*day nursery*) guardería infantil *f*; (*plants*) vivero *m*. **nursery rhyme** poesía infantil *f*. **nursery school** escuela de párvulos *f*.

nurture ['nəːtʃə] *v* nutrir, alimentar; (*rear*) criar.

nut [nʌt] *n* (*bot*) nuez *f*; (*tech*) tuerca *f*; (*person*) loco, -a *m*, *f*. **in a nutshell** en pocas palabras. **nutcracker** *n* cascanueces *m invar*. **nutmeg** *n* nuez moscada *f*.

nutrient ['njuːtriənt] *n* alimento nutritivo *m*.

nutrition [njuˈtriʃən] *n* nutrición *f*. **nutritious** *adj* nutritivo.

nuzzle ['nʌzl] *v* hocicar.

nylon ['nailon] *n* nilón *m*.

nymph [nimf] *n* ninfa *f*.

O

oak [ouk] *n* roble *m*.

oar [oː] *n* remo *m*. **oarsman** *n* remero *m*.

oasis [ou'eisis] *n* oasis *m invar*.

oath [ouθ] *n* (*law*) juramento *m*; (*expletive*) blasfemia *f*. **take the oath** prestar juramento.

oats [outs] *pl n* avena *f sing*. **oatmeal** *n* harina de avena *f*.

obedient [ə'biːdiənt] *adj* obediente. **obedience** *n* obediencia *f*.

obese [ə'biːs] *adj* obeso. **obesity** *n* obesidad *f*.

obey [ə'bei] *v* obedecer.

obituary [ə'bitjuəri] *n* necrología *f*.

object ['obʒikt; *v* əb'ʒekt] *n* objeto *m*; (*gramm*) complemento *m*; (*aim*) meta *f*. *v* oponerse; objetar; protestar. **objection** *n* objeción *m*; reparo *m*. **objectionable** *adj* censurable; desagradable. **objective** *nm*, *adj* objetivo.

oblige [ə'blaidʒ] *v* (*compel*) obligar; (*please*) complacer; (*assist*) hacer un favor. **be obliged to** (*have to*) verse obligado a; (*be grateful*) estar agradecido a. **obligation** *n* obligación *f*; (*comm*) compromiso *m*. **obligatory** *adj* obligatorio.

oblique [ə'bliːk] *adj* sesgado; indirecto.

obliterate [ə'blitəreit] *v* borrar; cancelar. **obliteration** *n* borrado *m*; cancelación *f*.

oblivion [ə'bliviən] *n* olvido *m*. **oblivious** *adj* olvidadizo; ignorante.

oblong ['obloŋ] *adj* oblongo. *n* cuadrilongo *m*.

obnoxious [əb'nokʃəs] *adj* ofensivo; execrable.

oboe ['oubou] *n* oboe *m*. **oboist** *n* oboe *m*, oboísta *m*, *f*.

obscene [əb'siːn] *adj* obsceno. **obscenity** *n* obscenidad *f*.

obscure [əb'skjuə] *adj* oscuro; confuso. *v* oscurecer; (*hide*) esconder. **obscurity** *n* oscuridad *f*.

observe [əb'zəːv] *v* observar; ver; decir. **observant** *adj* observador; atento. **observation** *n* (*remark*) observación *f*; (*of rules*) observancia *f*. **observatory** *n* observatorio *m*.

obsess [əb'ses] *v* obsesionar. **obsession** *n* obsesión *f*.

obsolescent [obsə'lesnt] *adj* que cae en desuso. **obsolescence** *n* caída en desuso *f*.

obsolete ['obsəliːt] *adj* anticuado.

obstacle ['obstəkl] *n* obstáculo *m*.

obstetrics [ob'stetriks] *n* obstetricia *f*. **obstetrician** *n* tocólogo *m*.

obstinate ['obstinət] *adj* obstinado; terco; rebelde. **obstinacy** *n* obstinación *f*; terquedad *f*.

obstruct [əb'strʌkt] *v* obstruir; (*hinder*) estorbar. **obstruction** *n* obstrucción *f*; estorbo *m*.

obtain [əb'tein] *v* obtener; lograr; (*acquire*) adquirir; (*extract*) sacar.

obtrusive [əb'truːsiv] *adj* importuno, molesto; (*meddlesome*) entrometido. **obtrusion** *n* intrusión *f*.

obtuse [əb'tjuːs] *adj* obtuso.

obverse ['obvəːs] *n* anverso *m*. *adj* del anverso.

obvious ['obviəs] *adj* obvio.
occasion [ə'keiʒən] *n* ocasión *f*, oportunidad *f*; (*cause*) motivo *m*; circunstancia *f*. *v* ocasionar; incitar. occasional *adj* ocasional. occasionally *adv* de vez en cuando.
occult ['okʌlt] *adj* oculto. *n* the occult ciencias ocultas *f pl*.
occupy ['okjupai] *v* ocupar; emplear. occupant *n* (*place*) ocupante *m*, *f*; (*position*) posesor, -a *m*, *f*. occupation *n* ocupación *f*; profesión *f*; trabajo *m*. occupational *adj* profesional. occupational hazard gajes del oficio *m pl*.
occur [ə'kəː] *v* (*happen*) ocurrir, acontecer; producirse; (*opportunity*) presentarse; (*take place*) tener lugar. occurrence *n* acontecimiento *m*; caso *m*.
ocean ['ouʃən] *n* océano *m*. oceanic *adj* oceánico.
ochre ['oukə] *n* ocre *m*.
o'clock [ə'klok] *adv* one o'clock la una. two/three/etc. o'clock las dos/tres/etc.
octagon ['oktəgən] *n* octágono *m*. octagonal *adj* octagonal.
octane ['oktein] *n* octano *m*.
octave ['oktiv] *n* octava *f*.
October [ok'toubə] *n* octubre *m*.
octopus ['oktəpəs] *n* pulpo *m*.
oculist ['okjulist] *n* oculista *m, f*.
odd [od] *adj* extraño, raro; (number) impar; (*left over*) sobrante; (*occasional*) alguno. odd jobs pequeños arreglos *m pl*. oddity *n* (*thing*) curiosidad *f*; (*quality*) singularidad *f*. oddment *n* saldo *m*. odds *pl n* (*betting*) apuesta *f sing*; (*chances*) posibilidades *f pl*. be at odds with estar peleado con uno. it makes no odds no importa. odds and ends pedazos *m pl*.
ode [oud] *n* oda *f*.
odious ['oudiəs] *adj* odioso.
odour ['oudə] *n* olor *m*; perfume *m*. odourless *adj* inodoro.
oesophagus [iː'sofəgəs] *n* esófago *m*.
of [ov] *prep* de.
off [of] *adj* (*substandard*) malo; (*fruit, vegetables, meat, fish*) pasado; (*wine*) agriado; (*cancelled*) suspendido; (*elec*) apagado; (*water*) cortado; (*brake*) suelto. *prep* de; fuera de; a . . . de; desde; en. offal ['ofəl] *n* asadura *f*.
off-chance [,of'tʃains] *n* on the off-chance (*coll*) por si acaso.
off-colour [of'kʌlə] *adj* be off-colour (*coll*) encontrarse indispuesto.

offend [ə'fend] *v* ofender; escandalizar; (*eyes, ears*) herir. offence *n* ofensa *f*; escándalo *m*; (*law*) delito *m*. take offence ofenderse por. offender *n* ofensor, -a *m, f*; delincuente *m, f*. offensive *adj* ofensivo; chocante; insultante.
offer ['ofə] *v* ofrecer; (*proposal*) proponer; presentarse. *n* oferta *f*; propuesta *f*. offering *n* (*action*) oferta *f*; (*gift*) regalo *m*.
offhand [of'hand] *adj* improvisado; brusco. *adv* sin pensarlo; bruscamente.
office ['ofis] *n* (*place*) oficina *f*; (*service*) oficio *m*; (*public office*) cargo *m*; (*function*) funciones *f pl*. take office entrar en funciones. officer *n* (*mil*) oficial *m*; (*public appointee*) funcionario, -a *m, f*; (*police*) policía *f*.
official [ə'fiʃəl] *adj* oficial. *n* funcionario, -a *m, f*.
officious [ə'fiʃəs] *adj* oficioso.
offing ['ofiŋ] *n* in the offing en perspectiva.
off-licence ['oflaisns] *n* bodega *f*.
off-peak [of'piːk] *adj, adv* de menos tráfico; (*elec*) de menor consumo.
off-season [of'sizn] *n* estación muerta *f*. *adv, adj* fuera de temporada.
offset [of'set; *n* 'ofset] *v* compensar; desviar. *n* (*printing*) offset *m*.
offshore ['offoː] *adj* de la costa.
offside [of'said] *n* (*mot: right*) lado derecho *m*; (*mot: left*) lado izquierdo *m*; (*sport*) fuera de juego *m*.
offspring ['ofspriŋ] *n* progenitura *f*; (*fig*) fruto *m*.
offstage ['ofsteidʒ] *adv, adj* entre bastidores.
off-the-cuff [ofðə'kʌf] *adj* espontáneo. *adv* de proviso.
off-white [of'wait] *adj* blancuzco.
often ['ofn] *adv* a menudo. as often as not la mitad de las veces. every so often alguna que otra vez.
ogre ['ougə] *n* ogro *m*.
oil [oil] *n* aceite *m*; petróleo *m*; (*painting*) óleo *m*; fuel *m*. oily *adj* (*tech*) grasiento; (*food*) aceitoso; (*skin*) graso; (*fig: manner*) zalamero.
oilcan ['oilkan] *n* aceitera *f*; (*for storage*) bidón de aceite *m*.
oilcloth ['oilkloθ] *n* hule *m*.
oil colour *n* óleo *m*.

oilfield ['oilfiːld] *n* yacimiento perrtrolífero *m*.

oil-fired [oil'faiəd] *adj* alimentado con mazut.

oilskin ['oil,skin] *n* impermeable de hule *m*.

oil stove *n* estufa de mazut *f*.

oil tanker *n* petrolero *m*.

oil well *n* pozo de petróleo *m*.

ointment ['ointmənt] *n* ungüento *m*.

O.K. [ou'kei] *interj* ¡de acuerdo!

old [ould] *adj* viejo; antiguo; (*adult*) mayor; (*clothes*) usado; (*wine*) añejo; (*other food*) pasado; (*familiar*) conocido. **I am six years old** tengo seis años. **how old is he?** ¿cuántos años tiene? **old age** vejez *f*. **old-age pensioner** pensionista *m, f*. **old-fashioned** *adj* chapado a la antigua; pasado de moda. **old maid** solterona *f*.

olive ['oliv] *n* (*fruit*) aceituna *f*, oliva *f*; (*tree*) olivo *m*. **olive green** *nm, adj* verde oliva *m*. **olive oil** aceite de oliva *m*.

Olympic [ə'limpik] *adj* olímpico. **Olympic Games** juegos olímpicos *m pl*.

omelette ['omlit] *n* tortilla *f*.

omen ['oumən] *n* presagio *m*, augurio *m*.

ominous ['ominəs] *adj* amenazador.

omit [ou'mit] *v* omitir; suprimir. **omission** *n* omisión *f*; olvido *m*.

omnipotent [om'nipətənt] *adj* omnipotente. **omnipotence** *n* omnipotencia *f*.

on [on] *pron* en, sobre; a. **oncoming** *adj* venidero. **onlooker** *n* espectador, -a *m, f*. **onset** *n* principio *m*; ataque *m*. **onshore** *adj* hacia la tierra. **onslaught** *n* ataque violento *m*. **onward(s)** *adj, adv* hacia adelante. **from now onwards** de ahora en adelante.

once [wʌns] *adv* una vez; (*formerly*) antes, hace tiempo. *conj* una vez que. **at once** en seguida. **once again** una vez más. **once and for all** de una vez para siempre.

one [wʌn] *n, pron, adj* uno, -a *m, f*. **be one up** on marcar un tanto a costa de. **one by one** uno por uno. **one-sided** *adj* parcial; desigual. **one-way** *adj* de dirección única. **that one** ése or aquél, ésa or aquélla. **this one** éste, ésta. **which one?** ¿cuál?

oneself [wʌn'self] *pron* se; si; sí mismo, -a; (*emphatic*) uno mismo, una misma. **by oneself** solo, -a.

onion ['ʌnjən] *n* cebolla *f*.

only ['ounli] *adj* solo; único. *adv* sólo, solamente. *conj* pero, sólo que.

onus ['ounəs] *n* responsabilidad *f*.

onyx ['oniks] *n* ónice *m, f*.

ooze [uːz] *v* rezumar; exudar.

opal ['oupəl] *n* ópalo *m*.

opaque [ə'paik] *adj* opaco; oscuro. **opacity** *n* opacidad *f*; oscuridad *f*.

open ['oupən] *v* abrir; (*exhibition*) inaugurar; iniciar. *adj* abierto; (*unfolded*) desplegado; (*frank*) franco; (*meeting*) público; (*unsolved*) pendiente; (*post*) vacante; (*free*) libre; (*sea*) alta. **open-air** *adj* al aire libre. **open-handed** *adj* generoso. **open-minded** *adj* imparcial. **open-mouthed** *adj, adv* boquiabierto.

opening ['oupəniŋ] *n* abertura *f*; inauguración *f*; oportunidad *f*; vacante *f*; principio *m*; (*act of opening*) apertura *f*; (*breach*) brecha *f*. *adj* inaugural. **opening night** noche de estreno *f*.

opera ['opərə] *n* ópera *f*. **opera glasses** prismáticos *m pl*. **opera house** ópera *f*. **opera singer** cantante de ópera *m, f*. **operatic** *adj* operístico. **operetta** *n* opereta *f*, zarzuela *f*.

operate ['opəreit] *v* (*machine*) manjar; (hacer) funcionar; (*direct*) dirigir; (*med*) operar. **operable** *adj* operable. **operating table** quirófano *m*. **operation** *n* funcionamiento *m*; manejo *m*; maniobra *f*; aplicación *f*; actividad *f*. **in operation** en vigor; en funcionamiento. **operational** *adj* operacional. **operative** *adj* en vigor; operativo; eficaz. **operator** *n* operario, -a *m, f*; maquinista *m, f*; telefonista *m, f*; (*tour*) agente de viajes; (*wireless*) radiotelegrafista *m*.

ophthalmic [of'θalmik] *adj* oftálmico.

opinion [ə'pinjən] *n* opinión *f*. **in my opinion** a mi parecer. **public opinion poll** sondeo de la opinión pública *m*.

opium ['oupiəm] *n* opio *m*.

opponent [ə'pounənt] *n* adversario, -a *m, f*; contrario, -a *m, f*.

opportune [opə'tjuːn] *adj* oportuno. **opportunism** *n* oportunismo *m*. **opportunist** *n(m+f)*, *adj* oportunista.

opportunity [opə'tjuːnəti] *n* oportunidad *f*.

oppose [ə'pouz] *v* oponerse a. **opposed** *adj* opuesto. **be opposed to** oponerse a. **opposition** *n* oposición *f*; resistencia *f*.

opposite ['opəzit] *adj* opuesto; contrario. **the opposite sex** el otro sexo. *prep* enfrente de, frente a. *n* lo opuesto, lo contrario.

oppress [ə'pres] *v* oprimir. **oppression** *n* opresión *f*. **oppressive** *adj* opresor, opresivo; (*heat*) sofocante; (*mentally*) agobiante. **oppressor** *n* opresor, -a *m, f*.

opt [opt] *v* **opt out** of no meterse. **opt to** optar por.

optical ['optikl] *adj* óptico. **optical illusion** ilusión óptica *f*. **optician** *n* óptico *m*.

optimism ['optimizəm] *n* optimismo *m*. **optimist** *n* optimista *m, f*. **optimistic** *adj* optimista.

optimum ['optiməm] *adj* óptimo. *n* lo óptimo.

option ['opʃən] *n* opción *f*; posibilidad *f*; elección *f*. **optional** *adj* facultativo.

opulent ['opjulənt] *adj* opulento; abundante. **opulence** *n* opulencia *f*.

or [oɪ] *conj* o; (*negative*) ni. **or else** si no. **or not** o no.

oracle ['orəkl] *n* oráculo *m*.

oral ['oɪrəl] *nm, adj* oral.

orange ['orindʒ] *n* (*fruit*) naranja *f*; (*tree*) naranjo *m*; (*colour*) naranja *m*. *adj* naranja. **orangeade** *n* naranjada *f*.

orator ['orətə] *n* orador, -a *m, f*. **orate** *v* perorar. **oration** *n* oración *f*. **oratory** *n* oratoria *f*.

orbit ['oɪbit] *n* órbita *f*. *v* estar en órbita; dar vueltas.

orchard ['oɪtʃəd] *n* huerto *m*; (*apple*) manzanal *m*; (*pear*) peral *m*.

orchestra ['oɪkəstrə] *n* orquesta *f*. **orchestral** *adj* orquestal. **orchestrate** *v* orquestar. **orchestration** *n* orquestación *f*.

orchid ['oɪkid] *n* orquídea *f*.

ordain [oɪ'dein] *v* (*rel*) ordenar; (*fate*) destinar. **ordination** *n* ordenación *f*.

ordeal [oɪ'diːl] *n* sufrimiento *m*.

order ['oɪdə] *n* orden *m*; (*rel*) orden *f*; (*comm*) pedido *m*; (*medal*) condecoración *f*. **in order** (*correct*) en regla. **in order to** para. **out of order** no funcionar. *v* ordenar; organizar; clasificar; pedir; mandar.

orderly ['oɪdəli] *adj* ordenado; metódico; disciplinado. *n* (*mil*) ordenanza *m*.

ordinal ['oɪdinl] *adj* ordinal.

ordinary ['oɪdənəri] *adj* corriente, usual; (*mediocre*) ordinario; simple; (*average*) medio. *n* lo corriente, lo ordinario. **out of the ordinary** extraordinario, excepcional.

ore [oɪ] *n* mineral *m*.

oregano [ori'gainou] *n* orégano *m*.

organ ['oɪgən] *n* órgano *m*. **organist** *n* organista *m, f*.

organic [oɪ'ganik] *adj* orgánico.

organism ['oɪgənizəm] *n* organismo *m*.

organize ['oɪgənaiz] *v* organizar. **organization** *n* organización *f*. **organizer** *n* organizador, -a *m, f*.

orgasm ['oɪgazəm] *n* orgasmo *m*.

orgy ['oɪdʒi] *n* orgia *f*.

oriental [oɪri'entl] *n*(*m+f*), *adj* oriental.

orientate ['oɪriənteit] *v* orientar. **orientation** *n* orientación *f*.

orifice ['orifis] *n* orificio *m*.

origin ['oridʒin] *n* origen *m*. **originate** *v* originar, provocar; comenzar. **originate from** ser descendiente de. **originator** *n* autor, -a *m, f*; creador, -a *m, f*.

original [ə'ridʒinl] *adj* original; (*first*) primero. *n* original *m*. **originally** *adv* al principio; con originalidad.

ornament ['oɪnəmənt] *n* ornamento *m*, adorno *m*. *v* ornamentar, adornar. **ornamental** *adj* ornamental, de adorno.

ornate [oɪ'neit] *adj* recargado.

ornithology [oɪni'θolədʒi] *n* ornitología *f*. **ornithological** *adj* ornitológico. **ornithologist** *n* ornitólogo *m*.

orphan ['oɪfən] *n, adj* huérfano, -a. *v* dejar huérfano. **orphanage** *n* orfanato *m*.

orthodox ['oɪθədoks] *adj* ortodoxo. **orthodoxy** *n* ortodoxia *f*.

orthopaedic [oɪθə'piɪdik] *adj* ortopédico.

oscillate ['osileit] *v* oscilar; fluctuar. **oscillation** *n* oscilación *f*; fluctuación *f*.

ostensible [o'stensəbl] *adj* aparente. **ostensibly** *adv* aparentemente.

ostentatious, [osten'teifəs] *adj* ostentoso. **ostentation** *n* ostentación *f*.

osteopath ['ostiəpaθ] *n* osteópata *m, f*.

ostracize ['ostrəsaiz] *v* condenar al ostracismo. **ostracism** *n* ostracismo *m*.

ostrich ['ostritʃ] *n* avestruz *m*.

other ['ʌðə] *pron, adj* otro, -a. **other than** de otra manera que.

otherwise ['ʌðəwaiz] *adj* distinto. *adv* de otra manera; a parte de eso.

otter ['otə] *n* nutria *f*.

*ought [oɪt] *v* deber; tener que.

our [auə] *pron* nuestro, -a; el nuestro, la nuestra. *adj* nuestro.

ours [auəz] *pron* nuestro, -a; el nuestro, la nuestra.

ourselves [auə'selvz] *pron* nos; nosotros, nosotras; (*emphatic*) nosotros mismos, nosotras mismas. **by ourselves** solos, solas.

oust [aust] *v* expulsar. echar.

out [aut] *adj* fuera; (*light, fire, etc.*) apagado; (*games*) eliminado. **out loud** en voz alta. **out of** fuera de; (*through*) por; (*from*) de; (*without*) no tener, sin.

outboard ['autbɔɪd] *adj* fuera borda, fuera bordo.

outbreak ['autbreik] *n* (*start*) comienzo *m*; (*disease*) epidemia *f*; (*spots*) erupción *f*; (*violence, crime*) ola *f*; (*revolution*) motín *m*; (*temper*) arrebato *m*.

outbuilding ['autbildiŋ] *n* dependencia *f*.

outburst ['autbɜɪst] *n* explosión *f*; (*applause*) salvo *m*; (*temper*) arrebato *m*.

outcast ['autkaɪst] *n* proscrito, -a *m, f*; paria *m, f*.

outcome ['autkʌm] *n* resultado *m*; consecuencias *f pl*.

outcry ['autkrai] *n* (*noise*) alboroto *m*; protesta *f*.

*outdo [aut'duɪ] *v* superar.

outdoor ['autdɔɪ] *adj* al aire libre; (*clothes*) de calle. **outdoors** *adv* fuera; al aire libre.

outer ['autə] *adj* externo, exterior. **outer space** espacio exterior *m*.

outfit ['autfit] *n* (*gear*) equipo *m*; (*clothes*) ropa *f*; (*lady's costume*) conjunto *m*.

outgoing ['autgouiŋ] *adj* saliente; (*manner*) sociable. **outgoings** *pl n* gastos *m pl*.

*outgrow [aut'grou] *v* crecer más que; (*lose*) perder con la edad. **outgrowth** *n* excrecencia *f*.

outing ['autiŋ] *n* excursión *f*; paseo *m*.

outlandish [aut'landiʃ] *adj* extraño; apartado.

outlaw ['autlɔɪ] *n* proscrito, -a *m, f*. *v* proscribir; declarar ilegal.

outlay ['autlei] *n* gastos *m pl*.

outlet ['autlit] *n* salida *f*; (*drain*) desaguadero *m*; (*elec*) toma *f*; (*comm*) mercado *m*.

outline ['autlain] *n* contorno *m*; perfil *m*; silueta *f*; (*draft*) bosquejo *m*; (*summary*) resumen *m*; (*map*) trazado *m*; (*sketch*) esbozo *m*. *v* perfilar; bosquejar; resumir; trazar.

outlive [aut'liv] *v* sobrevivir.

outlook ['autluk] *n* vista *f*; punto de vista *m*.

outlying ['autlaiiŋ] *adj* exterior; remoto.

outnumber [aut'nʌmbə] *v* exceder en número.

out-of-date [autəv'deit] *adj* anticuado; pasado de moda.

outpatient ['autpeiʃənt] *n* paciente no internado *m*.

outpost ['autpoust] *n* puesto avanzado *m*.

output ['autput] *n* producción *f*; (*tech*) rendimiento *m*; (*power*) potencia *f*.

outrage ['autreidʒ] *n* ultraje *m*; desafuero *m*. *v* ultrajar.

outrageous [aut'reiʤəs] *adj* ultrajante; escandaloso.

outright [aut'rait; *adj* 'autrait] *adv* francamente; (*entirely*) en su totalidad; (*at once*) en el acto. *adj* completo; absoluto; categórico; franco.

outset ['autset] *n* principio *m*. **at the outset** al principio.

outside [aut'said; *adj* 'autsaid] *adv* fuera. afuera. *prep* fuera de; más allá de. *n* exterior *m*. *adj* exterior, externo; al aire libre; remoto; independiente. **outsider** *n* (*to a group*) intruso, -a *m, f*; (*to a place*) forastero, -a *m, f*; (*horse racing*) caballo no favorito *m*.

outsize ['autsaiz] *adj* de talla muy grande.

outskirts ['autskɜɪtz] *pl n* afueras *f pl*; cercanías *f pl*.

outspoken [aut'spoukən] *adj* franco. **outspokenness** *n* franqueza *f*.

outstanding [aut'standiŋ] *adj* destacado, notable; (*features*) sobresaliente; (*success*) excepcional; (*debt*) pendiente; (*still to be done*) por hacer.

outstrip [aut'strip] *v* dejar atrás.

outward ['autwəd] *adj* exterior; (*journey*) de ida. **outward bound** que sale. **outwardly** *adv* exteriormente; aparentemente. **outwards** *adv* hacia fuera.

outweigh [aut'wei] *v* pesar más que; (*value*) valer más que.

outwit [aut'wit] *v* burlar.

oval ['ouvəl] *adj* oval, ovalado. *n* óvalo *m*.

ovary ['ouvəri] *n* ovario *m*.

ovation [ou'veiʃən] *n* ovación *f*.

oven [ʌvn] *n* horno *m*. **ovenproof** *adj* de horno.

over ['ouvə] *adv* encima, por encima; (*too much*) demasiado; al otro lado. *adj* (*finished*) terminado. *prep* sobre, encima de; al otro lado de; superior a; durante.

overall ['ouvərɔɪl] *adj* de conjunto; total. *adv* en conjunto; por todas partes. **overalls** *pl n* guardapolvo *m sing*.

overbalance [ouvə'baləns] v (hacer)
perder el equilibrio.

overbearing [ouvə'beəriŋ] adj dominante,
autoritario.

overboard ['ouvəbɔid] adv (fall) por la
borda. go overboard (coll) pasarse de la
raya. man overboard! ¡hombre al agua!

overcast [ouvə'kaist] adj nublado.

overcharge [ouvə'tʃaidʒ] v cobrar un
precio excesivo; (overload) sobrecargar.

overcoat ['ouvəkout] n abrigo m.
sobretodo m.

*overcome [ouvə'kʌm] v vencer; triunfar.
be overcome by estar muerto de.

overcrowded [ouvə'kraudid] adj atestado;
superpoblado. overcrowding n ates-
tamiento m; superpoblación f.

*overdo [ouvə'dui] v exagerar; (exhaust)
fatigarse demasiado.

overdose ['ouvədous] n dosis excesiva f.

overdraft ['ouvədraift] n giro en
descubierto m.

*overdraw [ouvə'drɔi] v girar en
descubierto. be overdrawn adj tener un
descubierto en su cuenta.

overdue [ouvə'djui] adj (train, etc.)
atrasado; (comm) vencido y sin pagar.

overestimate [ouvə'estimeit] v sobrees-
timar.

overexpose [ouvəik'spouz] v (phot)
sobreexponer.

overflow [ouvə'flou; n 'ouvəflou] v (flow
over) derramarse; (flood) inundar. n
desbordamiento m; derrame m; inundación f; (pipe) cañería de desagüe f.

overgrown [ouvə'groun] adj cubierto de
hierba; (too big) demasiado crecido para
su edad.

*overhang [ouvə'haŋ; n 'ouvəhaŋ] v
sobresalir. n saliente m. overhanging adj
saliente, sobresaliente.

overhaul [ouvə'hɔil] v investigar; revisar.
n examen m, revisión f; arreglo m.

overhead [ouvə'hed] adv arriba. adj de
arriba. overheads pl n gastos generales m
pl.

*overhear [ouvə'hiə] v oír (por casu-
alidad); sorprender.

overheat [ouvə'hiit] v recalorar; (fig)
acalorar.

overjoyed [ouvə'dʒoid] adj contentísimo.

overland [ouvə'land] adv por vía terrestre.
adj terrestre.

overlap [ouvə'lap; n 'ouvəlap] v traslapar.
n traslapo m.

*overlay [ouvə'lei; n 'ouvəlei] v revestir. n
revestimiento m; cubierta f.

overleaf [ouvə'liif] adv a la vuelta.

overload [ouvə'loud; n 'ouvəloud] v
sobrecargar. n sobrecarga f.

overlook [ouvə'luk] v (miss) no notar;
(ignore) no darse cuenta de; (excuse)
perdonar; (command a view) dar a:
dominar.

overnight [ouvə'nait] adv (during the
night) por la `noche; (suddenly) de la
noche a la mañana. stay overnight pasar
la noche. adj (journey) de noche; (stay)
por una noche.

overpower [ouvə'pauə] v subyugar;
(smell, etc.) trastornar; dominar. over-
powering adj (desire) irresistible;
abrumador.

overrated [ouvə'reitid] adj sobreestimado.

*override [ouvə'raid] v (ride over) pasar
por encima de; dominar; (fig) anular,
rechazar. overriding adj principal.

overrule [ouvə'ruil] v denegar, no admitir.

*overrun [ouvə'rʌn] v (exceed) rebasar;
(overflow) derramarse; (invade) invadir;
(flood) inundar; (infest) plagar.

overseas [ouvə'siiz] adv en ultramar. adj
de ultramar; (foreign) extranjero;
(comm) exterior.

overseer [ouvə'siə] n capataz m; inspector, -a m, f.

overshadow [ouvə'ʃadou] v sombrear;
(fig) eclipsar.

*overshoot [ouvə'ʃuit] v ir más allá de.

oversight ['ouvəsait] n descuido m; omisión f. through an oversight por descuido.

*oversleep [ouvə'sliip] v dormir dema-
siado.

overspill ['ouvəspil] n exceso m.

overt [ou'vəit] adj abierto; manifiesto.
overtly adv evidentemente.

*overtake [ouvə'teik] v (pass) adelantar;
(catch up) alcanzar.

*overthrow [ouvə'θrou; n 'ouvəθrou] v
(overturn) volcar; (plans) desbaratar;
(government) derrocar; (empire) derrumbar. n desbaratamiento m; derro-
camiento m; derrumbamiento m.

overtime ['ouvətaim] n horas
extraordinarias f pl.

overtone ['ouvətoun] n (music) armónico
m; (fig) alusión f.

overture ['ouvətjuə] n (music) obertura f;
(proposal) propuesta f.

overturn [ouvə'tɔɪn] v (car) volcar; (government, etc.) derrocar.

overweight [ouvə'weit] adj be overweight pesar demasiado.

overwhelm [ouvə'welm] v (conquer) vencer; (with grief) postrar; (work) inundar; (in argument) confundir; (joy) rebosar. **overwhelming** adj (desire) irresistible; (defeat) aplastante; (work) abrumador.

overwork [ouvə'wɔɪk] v usar demasiado; hacer trabajar demasiado. n exceso de trabajo m.

overwrought [ouvə'rɔɪt] adj sobreexcitado, nerviosísimo.

ovulation [ovju'leiʃn] n ovulación f.

owe [ou] v deber; tener deudas. **owing** adj que se debe. **owing to** debido a.

owl [aul] n lechuza f.

own [oun] v tener, poseer; (acknowledge) reconocer. **own up** confesar. adj propio. **get one's own back** desquitarse. **on one's own** solo, sola. **owner** n dueño, -a m, f; poseedor, -a m, f. **ownership** n propiedad f; posesión f.

ox [oks] n, pl **oxen** buey m. **oxtail** n rabo de buey m.

oxygen ['oksidʒən] n oxígeno m. **oxygen tent** cámara de oxígeno f.

oyster ['oistə] n ostra f.

P

pace [peis] n paso m; (gait) andar m; (horse) andadura f; (speed) velocidad f. **keep pace with** ajustarse al paso de; (events) mantenerse al corriente de. v andar; recorrer. **pace up and down** dar vueltas.

pacific [pə'sifik] adj pacífico.

Pacific Ocean n Océano Pacífico m.

pacifism ['pasifizəm] n pacifismo m. **pacifist** n(m+f), adj pacifista.

pacify ['pasifai] v pacificar; calmar.

pack [pak] n (gang) partida f; (hounds) jauría f; (cards) baraja f; (bundle) bulto m; (med) paño m, compresa f. **packhorse** n caballo de carga m. v embalar; envasar; (suitcase) hacer; (cram) apretar. **pack it in** (coll) dejarlo. **packing** n embalaje m; envase m.

package ['pakidʒ] n paquete m; (bundle) fardo m. adj (deal) acuerdo global m; (holiday, tour) viaje todo comprendido m. v embalar; envasar.

packet ['pakit] n paquete m; (tea, etc.) sobre m; (cigarettes) cajetilla f.

pact [pakt] n pacto m.

pad[1] [pad] n (paper) bloc m; (blotting) carpeta f; (ink) tampón m; (cushion) almohadilla f; (launching) plataforma de lanzamiento f. v acolchar; rellenar. **pad out** (coll) meter paja en. **padding** n acolchado m; relleno m; (fig) paja f.

pad[2] [pad] v andar a pasos quedos.

paddle[1] ['padl] n (oar) canalete m; (waterwheel) álabe m. **paddle boat** or **steamer** vapor de ruedas m. v remar con canalete.

paddle[2] ['padl] n (wade) chapotear.

paddock ['padək] n paddock m.

padlock ['padlok] n candado m. v cerrar con candado.

paediatric [piːdi'atrik] adj pediátrico. **paediatrician** n pediatra m, pediatra m. **paediatrics** n pediatría f.

pagan ['peigən] n, adj pagano, -a.

page[1] [peidʒ] n (book) página f.

page[2] [peidʒ] n also **page-boy** (hotel) botones m invar; (court, wedding) paje m. v (person) hacer llamar por un paje.

pageant ['padʒənt] n desfile histórico m. **pageantry** n aparato m, pompa f.

paid [peid] V pay.

pail [peil] n cubo m.

pain [pein] n dolor m. **painkiller** n calmante m. **pains** pl n (effort) esfuerzo m. **painstaking** adj concienzudo; cuidadoso. v doler; afligir. **painful** adj doloroso; (embarrassing) difícil. **painless** adj sin dolor; (easy) fácil.

paint [peint] n pintura f. **paintbox** n caja de pinturas f. **paintbrush** (artist) pincel m; (house painter) brocha f. **paint roller** rodillo m. v pintar; (fig) describir. **painter** n pintor, -a m, f. **painting** n pintura f; (picture) cuadro m.

pair [peə] n (objects) par m; (people, animals) pareja f; (oxen) yunta f; (horses) tronco m. v (socks, etc.) emparejar; (mate) aparearse. **pair off** (people) formar pareja.

pal [pal] n (coll) amigote m; camarada m, f.

palace ['paləs] n palacio m. **palatial** adj magnífico; suntuoso.

palate ['palit] n paladar m. **palatable** adj
sabroso; (fig) agradable.
pale [peil] adj pálido. v palidecer. **paleness** n palidez f.
palette ['palit] n paleta f.
pall¹ [pɔil] v perder el sabor; aburrirse
(de).
pall² [pɔil] n paño mortuorio m; (smoke)
cortina f; (snow) capa f.
pallid ['palid] adj pálido.
palm¹ [paim] n (hand) palma f. **palm off**
(coll) colar. **palmist** n quiromántico, -a
m, f. **palmistry** n quiromancia f.
palm² [paim] n (tree) palma f. palmera f.
palpitate ['palpiteit] v palpitar. **palpitation**
n palpitación f.
paltry ['pɔiltri] adj miserable.
pamper ['pampə] v mimar.
pamphlet ['pamflit] n folleto m.
pan [pan] n cacerola f.
Panama [panə'mai] n Panamá m. **Panama City** n Panamá.
pancake ['pankeik] n pancake m. **Pancake
Tuesday** martes de carnaval.
pancreas ['paŋkriəs] n páncreas m. **pan-
creatic** adj pancreático.
panda ['pandə] n panda m.
pandemonium [pandi'mouniəm] n
pandemonio m.
pander ['pandə] v **pander to** complacer.
pane [pein] n vidrio m, cristal m.
panel ['panl] n (door) panel m; (wall)
lienzo m; (dress) paño m; (control)
tablero m; (experts) grupo m; (judges)
jurado m. v revestir con paneles;
artesonar. **panelist** n miembro del jurado
m. **panelling** n revestimiento de madera
m; artesonado m.
pang [paŋ] n (pain, hunger) punzada f;
(jealousy) angustia f; (love) herida f;
(conscience) remordimiento m.
panic ['panik] n pánico m. **panic-stricken**
adj preso de pánico. v asustarse.
panorama [panə'raimə] n panorama m.
panoramic adj panorámico.
pansy ['panzi] n pensamiento m.
pant [pant] v jadear. n jadeo m.
panther ['panθə] n pantera f.
pantomime ['pantəmaim] n (mime)
pantomima f.
pantry ['pantri] n despensa f.
pants [pants] pl n (underpants) calzoncillos m pl; (coll: trousers) pantalones m pl.
papal ['peipl] adj papal.

paper ['peipə] n papel m; (news) periódico m, diario m; (blotting) papel
secante m; (brown) papel de estraza m;
(carbon) papel carbón m; (drawing)
papel de dibujo m; (greaseproof) papel
vegetal m; (tissue) papel de seda m; (toilet) papel higiénico m; (writing) papel de
escribir m; (identity) documentación f. v
(walls) empapelar.
paperback ['peipəbak] n libro en rústica
m.
paper bag n saco de papel m.
paper-boy n repartidor de periódicos m.
paper-clip n sujetapapeles m invar.
paper-knife n cortapapeles m invar.
paper-mill n fábrica de papel f.
paper shop n (coll) vendedor de periódicos m.
paperweight ['peipəweit] n pisapapeles m
invar.
paperwork ['peipəwəik] n papeleo m.
paprika ['paprikə] n paprika f.
par [pai] n igualdad f; (comm) par f;
(golf) recorrido normal m. **be on a par
with** correr parejas con. **feel below par**
(coll) no sentirse bien.
parable ['parəbl] n parábola f.
parachute ['parəʃuit] n paracaídas m
invar. v saltar con paracaídas. **parachutist**
n paracaidista m, f.
parade [pə'reid] n alarde m; (mil) desfile
m; (promenade) paseo público m. v (display) hacer alarde de; hacer desfilar;
(placard) pasear.
paradise ['parədais] n paraíso m.
paradox ['parədoks] n paradoja f. **paradoxical** adj paradójico.
paraffin ['parəfin] n (solid) parafina f;
(fuel) petróleo m.
paragraph ['parəgraif] m párrafo m. **new
paragraph** punto y aparte.
parallel ['parəlel] adj paralelo. n paralela
f. **parallelogram** n paralelogramo m.
paralyse ['parəlaiz] v paralizar. **paralysis** n
parálisis f. **paralytic** n, adj paralítico, -a.
adj (coll: drunk) como una cuba.
paramilitary [parə'militəri] adj
paramilitar.
paramount ['parəmaunt] adj supremo.
paranoia [parə'nɔiə] n paranoia f. **para-
noid** n, adj paranoico, -a.
parapet ['parəpit] n parapeto m.
paraphernalia [parəfə'neiliə] n avíos m
pl.

paraphrase ['parəfreiz] n paráfrasis f. v parafrasear.
paraplegic [,parə'pliːdʒik] n, adj parapléjico, -a.
parasite ['parəsait] n parásito m. **parasitic** adj parasito.
parasol ['parəsol] n parasol m.
paratrooper ['parə,truːpə] n soldado paracaidista m.
parcel ['paːsəl] n paquete m; (portion) parcela f. **parcel office** despacho de paquetes m. **parcel post** servicio de paquetes m. v also parcel up empaquetar.
parch [paːtʃ] v (land) resecar; (person) abrasar; **be parched with thirst** abrasarse de sed.
parchment ['paːtʃmənt] n pergamino m.
pardon ['paːdn] n perdón m; (law) indulto m; (rel) indulgencia f. v perdonar; disculpar; indultar. **pardon?** ¿cómo? **I beg your pardon** dispénseme.
pare [peə] v reducir; (vegetables) pelar; (fruit) mondar.
parent ['peərənt] n padre, madre m, f. **parents** pl n padres m pl. **parental** adj de los padres. **parenthood** n paternidad f, maternidad f.
parenthesis [pə'renθəsis] n paréntesis m invar. **in parentheses** entre paréntesis.
Paris ['paris] n París.
parish ['pariʃ] n parroquia f; (civil) municipio m. **parish church** iglesia parroquial f. **parishioner** n parroquiano, -a m, f.
parity ['pariti] n paridad f.
park [paːk] n parque (público) m. **car park** aparcamiento de coches m. v aparcar. **parking** n estacionamiento m. **parking meter** parcómetro m. **parking ticket** multa por aparcamiento indebido f.
parliament ['paːləmənt] n parlamento m. **parliamentary** adj parlamentario.
parlour ['paːlə] n salón m; sala de recibir f.
parochial [pə'roukiəl] adj parroquial; (derog) pueblerino.
parody ['parədi] n parodia f. v parodiar.
parole [pə'roul] n libertad bajo palabra f.
paroxysm ['parəksizəm] n paroxismo m; (joy, anger, etc.) ataque m.
parrot ['parət] n loro m. **parrot fashion** como un loro.
parsley ['paːsli] n perejil m.
parsnip ['paːsnip] n pastinaca f.

parson ['paːsn] n (priest) cura m; (Protestant) pastor m. **parsonage** n casa del cura f.
part [paːt] n parte f; (role) papel m; (tech) pieza f. **on my part** di mi parte. **part exchange** cambio de un objeto por otro pagando la diferencia. **part-time** adv a media jornada; adj de media jornada. v dividir; separar; (leave) despedirse. **part one's hair** hacerse la raya. **part with** tener que separarse de. **parting** n separación f; despedida f; (hair) raya f. **partly** adv en parte.
*****partake** [paːteik] v **partake of** compartir.
partial ['paːʃəl] adj parcial. **be partial to** ser aficionado a. **partiality** n parcialidad f; inclinación f.
participate [paː'tisipeit] v participar. **participant** n partícipe m, f. **participation** n participación f.
participle ['paːtisipl] n participio m.
particle ['paːtikl] n partícula f; (dust, etc.) grano m; (fig) pizca f.
particular [pə'tikjulə] adj particular; detallado; exigente. n detalle m. **in particular** particularmente. **I'm not particular** me da igual. **full particulars** información completa f.
partisan [paːti'zan] n partidario, -a m, f; (mil) guerrillero m. **partisanship** n partidismo m.
partition [paː'tiʃən] n división f; (section) parte f. v dividir; repartir.
partner ['paːtnə] n (comm) asociado, -a m, f, socio, -a m, f; (dancing) pareja f; (cards, etc.) compañero, -a m, f; (marriage) cónyuge m, f. v asociarse con; ser pareja de. **partnership** n asociación f; (firm) sociedad f. **go into partnership with** asociarse con.
partridge ['paːtridʒ] n perdiz f.
party ['paːti] n (pol) partido m; (law) parte f; (reception) fiesta f; (gathering) reunión f. **party line** (phone) línea telefónica compartida entre abonados f; (pol) línea política del partido f.
pass [paːs] v pasar; (exam) aprobar; (be acceptable) aceptarse; **pass away** or **on** (die) pasar a mejor vida. **pass out** (faint) desmayarse. **pass round** (detour) dar la vuelta a; (distribute) pasar de mano en mano. **pass up** (decline) rechazar. n (permit) pase m; (exam) aprobado m; (mountain) desfiladero m; (sport) pase m.

passage ['pasɪdʒ] n (way) pasaje m, (alley) callejón m; (house) corredor m, (time) paso m, (literature) trozo m; (bill) aprobación f; (sea voyage) travesía f.

passenger ['pasɪndʒə] n pasajero, -a m, f.

passer-by [,pasə'baɪ] n transeúnte m, f.

passion ['paʃən] n pasión f; (anger) cólera f. passionate adj apasionado; colérico.

passive ['pasɪv] adj pasivo. n (gramm) voz pasiva f. passiveness also passivity n pasividad f.

Passover ['paɪsouvə] n pascua (de los Judíos) f.

passport ['paɪsport] n pasaporte m.

password ['paɪswəɪd] n contraseña f.

past [paɪst] nm, adj pasado. prep por delante de; (beyond) más allá de; (time) más de. twenty past nine las nueve y veinte. go past pasar.

pasta ['pastə] n pastas f pl.

paste [peɪst] n (meat) pasta f; (glue) engrudo m; (jewellery) estrás m. v pegar.

pastel ['pastəl] n pastel m.

pasteurize ['pastʃəraɪz] v pasteurizar. pasteurization n pasteurización f.

pastime ['paɪstaɪm] n pasatiempo m.

pastoral ['paɪstərəl] adj pastoril; (rel) pastoral.

pastry ['peɪstri] n (dough) pasta f; (cakes) pasteles m pl. puff pastry hojaldre m. pastry-cook n pastelero m.

pasture ['paɪstʃə] n (grass) pasto m; (field) prado m. v apacentar.

pasty¹ ['peɪsti] adj pastoso; (face) pálido.

pasty² ['pasti] n empanada f.

pat [pat] v dar palmaditas; (a pet) acariciar. n palmadita f; caricia f; (of butter) porción f. adj adecuado. adv oportunamente.

patch [patʃ] n (clothes) pieza f, remiendo m; (for puncture, wound, etc.) parche m; (land) parcela f. patchwork n labor de retazos m. v remendar; poner un parche. patchy adj desigual.

patent ['peɪtənt] adj patente, evidente; patentado. patent leather charol m. v patentar. n patente f. patently adv evidentemente.

paternal [pə'təɪnl] adj paterno, paternal. paternity n paternidad f.

path [paɪθ] n (way) camino m, sendero m; (star, sun) curso m.

pathetic [pə'θetik] adj patético.

pathology [pə'θolədʒi] n patología f. pathological adj patológico. pathologist n patólogo m.

patient ['peɪʃənt] adj paciente. n enfermo, -a m, f. patience n paciencia f; (game) solitario m.

patio ['patiou] n patio m.

patriarchal ['peɪtriaɪkəl] adj patriarcal.

patriot ['patriət] n patriota m, f. patriotic adj patriótico. patriotism n patriotismo m.

patrol [pə'troul] n patrulla f. patrol car coche patrulla m. v patrullar.

patron ['peɪtrən] n patrocinador, -a m, f; (saint) patrón, -ona m, f, patrono m; (arts) mecenas m; (customer) cliente m, f. patronage n (sponsorship) patrocinio m; (royal) patronato m. patronize v (comm) patrocinar; (arts) fomentar; (artist) proteger; (be condescending) tratar con condescencia. patronizing adj de superioridad.

patter¹ ['patə] v (rain) repiquetear; (footsteps) corretear. n golpecitos m pl; repiqueteo m.

patter² ['patə] n (salesman) charlatanería f. v chapurrear.

pattern ['patən] n (design) dibujo m; (needlework) patrón m; (sample) muestra f; (example) ejemplo m. v diseñar; (cloth) estampar. patterned adj adornado con dibujos.

paunch [pɔɪntʃ] n panza f, barriga f.

pauper ['pɔɪpə] n pobre m, f.

pause [pɔɪz] n pausa f; silencio m. v hacer una pausa; descansar; vacilar; pararse.

pave [peɪv] v empedrar, enlosar. pave the way for facilitar el paso de. pavement n acera f. paving n pavimento m. paving stone adoquín m.

pavilion [pə'vɪljən] n pabellón m.

paw [pɔɪ] n pata f; (cat) garra f. v tocar con la pata; (coll) manosear.

pawn¹ [pɔɪn] v empeñar. n prenda f. pawnbroker n prestamista m, f. pawnshop n casa de empeños f.

pawn² [pɔɪn] n peón m.

*pay [peɪ] v pagar; dar; (compliment, visit) hacer; (attention) prestar. pay back (money) reembolsar; (avenge) devolver. pay in ingresar. pay off (debt) saldar; (creditor) reembolsar; (mortgage) redimir; (be worthwhile) merecer la pena; (be fruitful) dar resultado. n paga f;

salario *m*. **pay-as-you-earn** *n* deducción del sueldo para los impuestos *f*. **payday** *n* día de paga *m*. **pay rise** aumento de sueldo *m*. **pay-roll** *n* nómina *f*. **pay-slip** *n* hoja de paga *f*. **payable** *adj* pagadero. **payee** *n* beneficiario, -a *m*, *f*. **payment** *n* pago *m*; recompensa *f*.

pea [piː] *n* guisante *m*.

peace [piːs] *n* paz *f*. **peacemaker** *n* pacificador, -a *m*, *f*. **peace offering** sacrificio propiciatorio *m*. **peaceful** *adj* pacífico.

peach [piːtʃ] *n* (*fruit*) melocotón *m*; (*tree*) melocotonero *m*.

peacock ['piːkok] *n* pavo real *m*.

peak [piːk] *n* punta *f*; peñasco *m*; (*cap*) visera *f*. **peak hours** horas punta *f pl*.

peal [piːl] *n* (*bells*) ripiqueteo *m*; (*laughter*) carcajada *f*; (*thunder*) trueno *m*. *v* repiquetear; (*thunder*) retumbar; (*laugh*) resonar.

peanut ['piːnʌt] *n* cacahuete *m*.

pear [peə] *n* (*fruit*) pera *f*; (*tree*) peral *m*.

pearl [pəːl] *n* perla *f*. **pearly** *adj* nacarado.

peasant ['peznt] *n*, *adj* campesino, -a.

peat [piːt] *n* turba *f*.

pebble ['pebl] *n* guijarro *m*. **pebbly** *adj* guijarroso.

peck [pek] *v* picotear; picar. *n* picotazo *m*; (*coll: kiss*) besito *m*.

peckish ['pekiʃ] *adj* **feel peckish** (*coll*) tener gazuza.

peculiar [pi'kjuːljə] *adj* raro; extraño; característico; propio; especial. **peculiarity** *n* particularidad *f*; rareza *f*; característica *f*.

pedal ['pedl] *n* pedal *m*. *v* pedalear.

pedantic [pi'dantik] *adj* pedante.

peddle ['pedl] *v* vender de puerta en puerta.

pedestal ['pedistl] *n* pedestal *m*.

pedestrian [pi'destriən] *n* peatón *m*. **pedestrian crossing** paso de peatones. **pedestrian precinct** zona reservada para peatones *f*. *adj* (*style*) prosaico.

pedigree ['pedigriː] *n* (*ancestry*) linaje *m*; (*animals*) pedigrí *m*. **pedigree animal** animal de raza *m*.

pedlar ['pedlə] *n* vendedor ambulante *m*.

peel [piːl] *v* pelar. **peel off** quitar, despegar. *n* (*potatoes, oranges*) monda *f*, cáscara *f*; (*candied*) piel confitada *f*. **potato-peeler** *n* pelapatatas *m invar*. **peelings** *pl n* peladuras *f pl*.

peep [piːp] *n* ojeada *f*. *v* echar una ojeada

(a). **peeping Tom** mirón *m*. **peep out** asomar.

peer[1] [piə] *v* entornar los ojos. **peer into** mirar dentro de.

peer[2] [piə] *n* (*nobility*) par *m*; (*equal*) igual *m*. **peerage** *n* pares *m pl*. **peerless** *adj* sin par.

peevish ['piːviʃ] *adj* displicente; enojadizo.

peg [peg] *n* (*hats, coats*) percha *f*; (*clothes*) pinza *f*; (*tent*) estaca *f*. **off the peg** *adj* de confección. *v* enclavijar; (*prices*) estabilizar.

pejorative [pə'dʒorətiv] *adj* pejorativo.

Peking [ˌpiːˈkiŋ] *n* Pekín, Pequín.

pelican ['pelikən] *n* pelicano *m*.

pellet ['pelit] *n* bolita *f*; (*gun*) perdigón *m*; (*med*) píldora *f*.

pelmet ['pelmit] *n* galería *f*.

pelt[1] [pelt] *v* tirar, arrojar; (*with questions*) acribillar; (*rain*) llover a cántaros; (*coll: run*) ir a todo correr. **at full pelt** a toda mecha.

pelt[2] [pelt] *n* pellejo *m*, piel *f*.

pelvis ['pelvis] *n* pelvis *f*. **pelvic** *adj* pélvico.

pen[1] [pen] *n* pluma *f*. **penknife** *n* cortaplumas *m invar*. **pen-name** *n* seudónimo *m*.

pen[2] [pen] *n* (*farm animals*) corral *m*; (*sheep*) redil *m*; (*pigs*) pocilga *f*. *v* scorralar.

penal ['piːnl] *adj* penal. **penal colony** penal *m*. **penalize** *v* penar, castigar. **penalty** *n* pena *f*; (*football*) penalty *m*; (*fig*) castigo *m*.

penance ['penəns] *n* penitencia *f*.

pencil ['pensl] *n* lápiz *m*. **pencil-sharpener** *n* sacapuntas *m invar*. *v* escribir con lápiz.

pendant ['pendənt] *n* colgante *m*.

pending ['pendiŋ] *adj* pendiente. *prep* hasta; durante.

pendulum ['pendjuləm] *n* péndulo *m*.

penetrate ['penitreit] *v* penetrar. **penetrable** *adj* penetrable. **penetration** *n* penetración *f*.

penguin ['peŋgwin] *n* pingüino *m*.

penicillin [peni'silin] *n* penicilina *f*.

peninsula [pə'ninsjulə] *n* península *f*. **peninsular** *adj* peninsular.

penis ['piːnis] *n* pene *m*.

penitent ['penitənt] *n(m+f)*, *adj* penitente. **penitence** *n* penitencia *f*.

pennant ['penənt] *n (small flag)* band-
erin *m*; *(naut)* gallardete *m*.
penniless ['penilis] *adj* sin dinero.
pension ['penʃən] *n (old age, retirement)*
jubilación *f*; *(allowance)* pensión *f*. pension fund caja de jubilaciones *f. v* pensionar. **pension off** jubilar. **pensioner** *n*
pensionista *m, f*.
pensive ['pensiv] *adj* pensativo.
pentagon ['pentəgən] *n* pentágono *m*.
pentagonal *adj* pentagonal.
penthouse ['penthaus] *n* ático *m*.
pent-up [pent'ʌp] *adj* reprimido.
penultimate [pi'nʌltimət] *adj* penúltimo.
people ['piːpl] *n* personas *f pl*; gente *f*
sing; *(nation)* nación *f sing*; pueblo *m*
sing; habitantes *m pl*; *(coll)* familia *f*
sing. v poblar.
pepper ['pepə] *n (spice)* pimienta *f*; *(vegetable)* pimiento *m*. **peppercorn** *n* grano
de pimiento *m*. **peppermint** *n (plant)*
hierbabuena *f*; *(flavour)* menta *f*; *(sweet)*
pastilla de menta *f*. **pepper-pot** *n*
pimentero *m. v* sazonar con pimienta.
peppery *adj* picante.
per [pəːr] *prep* por. **per cent** por ciento.
percentage *n* porcentaje *m*.
perceive [pə'siːv] *v* percibir; *(notice)*
notar.
perceptible [pə'septibl] *adj* perceptible;
sensible. **perceptibly** *adv* sensiblemente.
perception [pə'sepʃən] *n* percepción *f*;
sensibilidad *f*. **perceptive** *adj* perceptivo;
perspicaz.
perch [pəːtʃ] *n* percha *f. v (bird)*
posarse; encaramar.
percolate ['pəːkəleit] *v* filtrar. **percolator** *n*
cafetera de filtro *f*.
percussion [pə'kʌʃən] *n* percusión *f*.
perennial [pə'reniəl] *adj* perenne. *n*
planta perenne.
perfect ['pəːfikt; *v* pə'fekt] *adj* perfecto;
absoluto. *n (gramm)* pretérito perfecto
m. v perfeccionar. **perfection** *n* perfección *f*; *(perfecting)* perfeccionamiento *m*.
perfectionist *n(m+f)*, *adj* perfeccionista.
perforate ['pəːfəreit] *v* perforar. **perforation** *n* perforación *f*.
perform [pə'fɔːm] *v* llevar a cabo,
ejecutar; *(duty)* cumplir; *(functions)*
desempeñar; *(act)* representar. **performance** *n* ejecución *f*; cumplimiento *m*;
desempeño *m*; representación *f*;
(machine) funcionamiento *m*; *m*;
celebración *f*; *(sport)* actuación *f*.

perfume ['pəːfjuːm] *n* perfume *m. v*
perfumar.
perhaps [pə'haps] *adv* quizá, quizás, tal
vez.
peril ['peril] *n* peligro *m*. **perilous** *adj*
peligroso.
perimeter [pə'rimitə] *n* perímetro *m*.
period ['piəriəd] *n* periodo *m*; época *f*;
edad *f*; tiempo *m*; *(school)* clase *f*; *(menstrual)* regla *f*. **periodic** *adj* periódico.
periodical *nm, adj* periódico.
peripheral [pə'rifərəl] *adj* periférico.
periphery *n* periferia *f*.
periscope ['periskoup] *n* periscopio *m*.
perish ['periʃ] *v* perecer. **perishable** *adj*
perecedero.
perjure ['pəːdʒə] *v* **perjure oneself**
perjurarse. **perjurer** *n* perjuro, -a *m, f*.
perjury *n* perjurio *m*. **commit perjury**
jurar en falso.
perk [pəːk] *v* **perk up** animarse. **perky** *adj*
descarado; fresco.
perm [pəːm] *n (coll)* permanente *f*. **have a
perm** hacerse la permanente.
permanent ['pəːmənənt] *adj* permanente.
permanence *n* permanencia *f*. **permanent-
ly** *adv* permanentemente, para siempre.
permeate ['pəːmieit] *v* penetrar; *(soak)*
impregnar. **permeable** *adj* permeable.
permit [pə'mit; *n* 'pəːmit] *v* permitir; dar
permiso; tolerar. *n* permiso *m*; licencia *f*;
pase *m*. **permissible** *adj* permisible. **permission** *n* permiso *m*; licencia *f*. **permissive** *adj* permisivo; tolerante.
permutation [pəːmju'teiʃən] *n* permutación *f*.
pernicious [pə'niʃəs] *adj (med)* pernicioso; *(evil)* funesto.
perpendicular [pəːpen'dikjulə] *nf, adj*
perpendicular.
perpetrate ['pəːpitreit] *v* perpetrar; cometer. **perpetration** *n* perpetración *f*; comisión *f*. **perpetrator** *n (law)* perpetrador, -a
m, f; *(author)* autor, -a *m, f*.
perpetual [pə'petʃuəl] *adj* perpetuo.
perpetuate [pə'petʃueit] *v* perpetuar. **perpetuation** *n* perpetuación *f*.
perplex [pə'pleks] *v* dejar perplejo, confundir. **perplexed** *adj* perplejo; confuso.
perplexing *adj* confuso; complicado;
difícil. **perplexity** *n* perplejidad *f*; confusión *f*.
persecute ['pəːsikjuːt] *v* perseguir; molestar. **persecution** *n* persecución *f*.

persevere [,pəɪsi'viə] v perseverar. **perseverance** n perseverancia f. **persevering** adj perseverante.

persist [pə'sist] v persistir. **persistence** n persistencia f. **persistent** adj persistente; continuo.

person ['pəɪsn] n persona f. **personal** adj personal; en persona. **personality** n personalidad f. **personally** adv personalmente.

personify [pə'sonifai] v personificar. **personification** n personificación f.

personnel [pəɪsə'nel] n personal m.

perspective [pə'spektiv] n perspectiva f.

perspire [pə'spaiə] v transpirar, sudar. **perspiration** n transpiración f. sudor m.

persuade [pə'sweid] v persuadir. **persuasion** n persuasión f. **persuasive** adj persuasivo; convincente.

pert [pəɪt] adj impertinente; alegre; animado.

pertain [pə'tein] v pertenecer; ser propio de. **pertinent** adj pertinente. **pertinent to** relacionado con.

perturb [pə'təɪb] v perturbar. **perturbation** perturbación f.

Peru [pə'ruɪ] n Perú m.

peruse [pə'ruɪz] v leer atentamente; examinar. **perusal** n lectura atenta f; examen m.

pervade [pə'veid] v penetrar; saturar.

perverse [pə'vəɪs] adj obstinado; contrario; (wicked) perverso. **perversity** n obstinación f; perversidad f.

pervert [pə'vəɪt; n 'pəɪvəɪt] v (person) pervertir; (facts) desnaturalizar. n pervertido (-a) sexual m, f. **perversion** n perversión f; desnaturalización f.

pessimism ['pesimizəm] n pesimismo m. **pessimist** n pesimista m, f. **pessimistic** adj pesimista.

pest [pest] n animal or insecto mocivo m; (coll: person) lata f. **pesticide** n pesticida m.

pester ['pestə] v importunar, molestar.

pet [pet] n animal doméstico m; (person) preferido, -a m, f. **my pet!** ¡mi cielo! adj mimado. **pet hate** pesadilla f. **pet name** nombre cariñoso m. **pet subject** tema preferido m. v minar; (caress) acariciar.

petal ['petl] n pétalo m.

petition [pə'tiʃən] n petición f. v suplicar; pedir.

petrify ['petrifai] v petrificarse; quedarse seco.

petrol ['petrəl] n gasolina f; (S.Am.) nafta f. **petrol pump** surtidor de gasolina m. **petrol station** gasolinera f. **petrol tank** depósito de gasolina m.

petroleum [pə'trouliəm] n petróleo m.

petticoat ['petikout] n enaguas f pl, enagua f.

petty ['peti] adj pequeño; insignificante. **petty cash** dinero suelto m. **petty-minded** mezquino. **petty officer** contramaestre m.

pettiness n pequeñez f; insignificancia f.

petulant ['petjulənt] adj malhumorado, irritable. **petulance** n mal humor m, irritabilidad f.

pew [pjuɪ] n banco de iglesia m.

pewter ['pjuɪtə] n estaño m, peltre m.

phantom ['fantəm] n fantasma m.

pharmacy ['faɪməsi] n farmacia f. **pharmaceutical** adj farmacéutico. **pharmacist** n farmacéutico, -a m, f.

pharynx ['fariŋks] n faringe f. **pharyngitis** n faringitis f.

phase [feiz] n fase f. **phase in** introducir progresivamente. **phase out** reducir progresivamente.

pheasant ['feznt] n faisán m.

phenomenon [fə'nomənən] n, pl -ena fenómeno m. **phenomenal** adj fenomenal.

phial ['faiəl] n frasco m.

philanthropy [fi'lanθrəpi] n filantropía f. **philanthropic** adj filantrópico. **philanthropist** n filántropo, -a m, f.

philately [fi'latəli] n filatelia f. **philatelic** adj filatélico. **philatelist** n filatelista m, f.

philosophy [fi'losəfi] n filosofía f. **philosopher** n filósofo, -a m, f. **philosophical** adj filosófico. **philosophize** v filosofar.

phlegm [flem] n flema f. **phlegmatic** adj flemático.

phobia ['foubiə] n fobia f.

phone [foun] n (coll) teléfono m. v telefonear.

phonetic [fə'netik] adj fonético. **phonetics** n fonética f.

phoney ['founi] adj (coll) falso, espurio.

phosphate ['fosfeit] n fosfato m.

phosphorescence [fosfə'resəns] n fosforescencia f. **phosphorescent** adj fosforescente.

phosphorus ['fosfərəs] n fósforo m. **phosphorous** adj fosforoso.

photo ['foutou] n (coll) foto f.

photocopy ['foutou,kopi] n fotocopia f. v fotocopiar. **photocopier** n fotocopiadora f. **photocopying** n fotocopiaje m.

photogenic [ˌfoutou'dʒenik] *adj* fotogénico.

photograph ['foutəgraɪf] *n* fotografía *f*. **photograph album** álbum de fotografías *m*. *v* fotografiar. **photographer** *n* fotógrafo, -a *m,f*. **photographic** *adj* fotográfico. **photography** *n* fotografía *f*.

phrase [freiz] *n* frase *f*, expresión *f*; (*gramm*) locución *f*. **phrase-book** *n* repertorio de expresiones *m*. *v* expresar.

physical ['fizikəl] *adj* físico; *n* (*coll*) reconocimiento médico *m*.

physician [fi'ziʃən] *n* médico *m*.

physics ['fiziks] *n* física *f*. **physicist** *n* físico *m*.

physiology [ˌfizi'olədʒi] *n* fisiología *f*. **physiological** *adj* fisiológico. **physiologist** *n* fisiólogo, -a *m, f*.

physiotherapy [ˌfiziou'θerəpi] *n* fisioterapia *f*. **physiotherapist** *n* fisioterapeuta *m, f*.

physique [fi'ziːk] *n* constitución *f*; (*appearance*) físico *m*.

piano [pi'anou] *n* piano *m*. **pianist** *n* pianista *m, f*.

pick¹ [pik] *n* elección *f*, selección *f*. **take one's pick** elegir a su gusto. *v* escoger; seleccionar; (*fruit*) recoger; (*flowers*) coger; (*lock*) abrir con ganzúa. **pick at** (*food*) picar (la comida). **pick-me-up** *n* (*coll*) tónico. *m*. **pick out** escoger; distinguir; (*highlight*) hacer resaltar. **pickpocket** *n* ratero, -a *m, f*. **pick up** levantar; recoger; (*improve*) mejorarse; (*learn*) aprender; (*arrest*) detener.

pick² [pik] *n* (*tool*) piqueta *f*; (*music*) plectro *m*.

picket ['pikit] *n* piquete *m*; (*person*) huelguista *m, f*. *v* estar de guardia.

pickle ['pikl] *v* conservar en vinagre. *n* encurtido *m*.

picnic ['piknik] *n* merienda campestre *f*. *v* merendar en el campo.

pictorial [pik'toːriəl] *adj* pictórico, ilustrado.

picture ['piktʃə] *n* ilustración *f*; (*portrait*) retrato *m*; (*painting*) cuadro *m*; (*film*) película *f*. **picture frame** marco *m*. **picture gallery** museo de pintura *m*. **pictures** *n* (*coll*) cine *m*. *v* describir; imaginarse.

picturesque [piktʃə'resk] *adj* pintoresco.

pidgin ['pidʒən] *n* lengua macarrónica *f*.

pie [pai] *n* (*fruit*) pastel *m*; (*meat*) pastel de carne *m*.

piece [piːs] *n* pedazo *m*, trozo *m*; parte *f*; (*material*) pieza *f*. **piecemeal** *adv* hecho por partes. **piecework** *n* trabajo a destajo *m*. *v* **piece together** juntar.

pier [piə] *n* malecón *m*; (*landing-stage*) muelle *m*.

pierce [piəs] *v* penetrar; perforar; (*go through*) traspasar. **piercing** *adj* penetrante; (*wind*) cortante.

piety ['paiəti] *n* piedad *f*.

pig [pig] *n* puerco *m*, cerdo *m*. **pigskin** *n* piel de cerdo *f*. **pigsty** *n* pocilga *f*. **pigtail** *n* coleta *f*.

pigeon ['pidʒən] *n* paloma *f*. **pigeonhole** *n* casilla *f*.

pigment ['pigmənt] *n* pigmento *m*.

pike [paik] *n* (*fish*) lucio *m*.

pilchard ['piltʃəd] *n* sardina arenque *f*.

pile¹ [pail] *n* (*heap*) pila *f*, montón *m*. *v* amontonar. **pile up** acumular. **pile-up** *n* accidente múltiple *m*.

pile² [pail] *n* (*post*) poste *m*.

pile³ [pail] *n* (*of carpet, etc.*) pelo *m*.

piles [pailz] *pl n* (*med*) hemorroides *f pl*.

pilfer ['pilfə] *v* (*coll*) sisar. **pilferage** *n* sisa *f*.

pilgrim ['pilgrim] *n* peregrino, -a *m, f*. **pilgrimage** *n* peregrinación *f*.

pill [pil] *n* píldora *f*.

pillage ['pilidʒ] *n* saqueo *m*. *v* saquear.

pillar ['pilə] *n* pilar *m*, columna *f*. **pillarbox** *n* buzón *m*.

pillion ['piljən] *n* grupa *f*. **ride pillion** ir a la grupa.

pillow ['pilou] *n* almohada *f*. **pillowcase** *n* funda de almohada *f*.

pilot ['pailət] *n* piloto *m*. **pilot-light** *n* piloto *m*. *v* guiar; conducir.

pimento [pi'mentou] *n* pimienta de Jamaica *f*.

pimp [pimp] *n* chulo *m*.

pimple ['pimpl] *n* espinilla *f*. **pimply** *adj* espinilloso.

pin [pin] *n* alfiler *m*; (*hairpin*) horquilla *f*; (*safety pin*) imperdible *m*; (*tech*) pezonera *f*; (*bolt*) perno *m*. **pincushion** *n* almohadilla *f*. **pin-money** *n* alfileres *m pl*; **pinpoint** *v* localizar con toda precisión. **pins and needles** hormigueo *m*. **pinstripe** *n* raya muy fina *f*. *v* prender con alfileres. **pin down** (*fix*) sujetar; (*find*) encontrar; (*enemy*) inmovilizar. **pin up** (*notice*) fijar.

pinafore ['pinəfoɪ] *n* (*apron*) delantal *m*. **pinafore dress** falda con peto *f*.

pincers ['pinsəz] *pl n* (*tool*) tenazas *f pl*; (*zool*) pinzas *f pl*.

pinch [pintʃ] *n* pellizco *m*; (*salt*, *etc.*) pizca *f*. **at a pinch** en caso de necesidad. **feel the pinch** empezar a pasar apuros. *v* pellizcar; (*shoes*, *etc.*) apretar; (*coll*: *steal*) mangar.

pine[1] [pain] *n* pino. *m*. **pine-cone** *n* piña *f*.

pine[2] [pain] *v* languidecer. **pine for** anhelar.

pineapple ['painapl] *n* ananás *m*, piña *f*.

ping-pong ['piŋpoŋ] *n* ping-pong *m*, tenis de mesa *m*.

pinion ['pinjən] *n* ala *f*. *v* maniatar.

pink [piŋk] *n* (*colour*) rosa *m*; (*flower*) clavel *m*. *adj* rosa.

pinnacle ['pinəkl] *n* pináculo *m*.

pioneer [,paiə'niə] *n* pionero *m*, iniciador *m*.

pious ['paiəs] *adj* pío, devoto.

pip[1] [pip] *n* (*seed*) pepita *f*.

pip[2] [pip] *n* (*phone*, *etc.*) señal *f*.

pipe [paip] *n* (*gas*, *water*, *etc.*) tubo *m*, tubería *f*, cañería *f*; (*tobacco*) pipa *f*; (*music*) caramillo *m*. **pipe-cleaner** limpiapipas *m invar*. **pipeline** *n* (*oil*) oleoducto *m*; (*gas*) gasoducto *m*; (*water*) tubería *f*. *v* conducir por tubería; transportar por oleoducto. **pipe down** (*coll*) callarse. **piping** *n* (*music*) sonido de la gaite *m*; (*sewing*) ribete; tubería *f*.

piquant ['piːkənt] *adj* picante. **piquancy** *n* picante.

pique [piːk] *n* pique *m*. *v* picar; herir.

pirate ['paiərət] *n* pirata *m*. *v* piratear. **piracy** *n* piratería *f*.

pirouette [piru'et] *n* pirueta *f*. *v* hacer piruetas.

Pisces ['paisiːz] *n* Piscis *m*.

piss [pis] *n* (*impol*) meada *f*. *v* mear. **piss off!** ¡vete al cuerno! **pissed** *adj* (*drunk*) trompa. **be pissed off** estar furioso (con).

pistachio [pi'staʃiou] *n* pistacho *m*.

pistol ['pistl] *n* pistola *f*.

piston ['pistən] *n* émbolo *m*, pistón *m*.

pit [pit] *n* (*hole*) pozo *m*, hoyo; mina; (*orchestra*) foso de la orquesta *m*; (*of the stomach*) boca *f*; *v* llenar de agujeros; (*oppose*) oponer. **pit oneself against** medirse con.

pitch[1] [pitʃ] *n* (*throw*) lanzamiento *m*; (*sport*) campo *m*; (*music*) tono *m*; (*gradient*) grado de inclinación *m*; (*of a ship*) cabezada *f*. *v* lanzar, echar; entonar; (*of a ship*) cabecear; (*tent*) armar; (*fall*) caerse. **pitchfork** *n* horca *f*. *v* (*fig*) catapultar.

pitch[2] [pitʃ] *n* pez *f*, brea *f*. **pitch-black** *adj* negro como el carbón.

pitfall ['pitfɔːl] *n* escollo *m*; trampa *f*.

pith [piθ] *n* médula *f*; (*fig*) meollo *m*. **pithy** *adj* conciso, expresivo.

pittance ['pitəns] *n* miseria *f*.

pituitary [pi'tjuitəri] *n* glándula pituitaria *f*.

pity ['piti] *n* compasión *f*; lástima *f*. **take pity on** tener lástima de. **what a pity!** ¡qué lástima! *v* compadecese de. **pitiful** *adj* lastimoso; (*bad*) lamentable. **pitiless** *adj* despiadado.

pivot ['pivət] *n* pivote *m*; eje *m*. *v* girar sobre su eje.

placard ['plakaːd] *n* cartel *m*. *v* fijar carteles.

placate [plə'keit] *v* aplacar. **placatory** *adj* placativo.

place [pleis] *n* sitio *m*, lugar *m*; (*post*) puesto *m*; local *m*; posición *f*. **all over the place** por todas partes. **in place** en su sitio. **in place of** en lugar de. **out of place** fuera de lugar. **take place** suceder, ocurrir. **take the place of** sustituir a. *v* colocar; poner; situar; (*an order*) hacer. **be well placed** estar en buena posición.

placenta [plə'sentə] *n* placenta *f*.

placid ['plasid] *adj* plácido. **placidity** *n* placidez *f*.

plagiarize ['pleidʒəraiz] *v* plagiar. **plagiarism** *n* plagio *m*. **plagiarist** *n* plagiario, -a *m*, *f*.

plague [pleig] *n* (*disease*) peste *f*; (*social scourge*) plaga *f*; (*nuisance*) molestia *f*. *v* importunar.

plaice [pleis] *n* platija *f*.

plaid [plad] *n* tartán *m*. *adj* escocés.

plain [plein] *adj* (*clear*) claro; simple; puro; completo; (*frank*) franco; natural; (*unattractive*) sin atractivo. **plain-clothes** *adj* en traje de calle. **make plain** poner de manifiesto. *n* llanura *f*.

plaintiff ['pleintif] *n* demandante *m*, *f*.

plaintive ['pleintiv] *adj* quejumbroso.

plait [plat] *n* (*fold*) pliegue *m*; (*hair*) trenza *f*. *v* plisar; trenzar.

plan [plan] *n* (*map*) plano *m*; (*scheme*) plan *m*, proyecto *m*. *v* (*for the future*) hacer planes para; (*holidays*) hacer el plan de; (*design*) hacer el plano de; (*action*) planear; (*production*) planificar. **planning** *n* planificación *f*.

plane¹ [plein] *n* plano *m*; (*coll: aeroplane*) avión *m. adj* plano.

plane² [plein] *n* (*tool*) cepillo *m. v* cepillar.

plank [plaŋk] *n* tabla *m*.

plankton ['plaŋktən] *n* plancton *m*.

plant [plɑːnt] *n* (*bot*) planta *f*; (*tech*) maquinaria *f*; (*factory*) fábrica *f*; (*installation*) instalación *f. v* plantar. **plantation** *n* plantación *f*; hacienda *f*.

plaque [plɑːk] *n* placa *f*.

plasma ['plazmə] *n* plasma *m*.

plaster ['plɑːstə] *n* (*walls*) yeso *m*; (*for wounds*) emplasto *m*. **plaster of Paris** yeso blanco *m. v* enyesar; cubrir. **plasterer** yesero *m*.

plastic ['plastik] *nm, adj* plástico. **plastic surgery** cirugía plástica *f*.

plate [pleit] *n* (*dish*) plato *m*; (*of metal*) chapa *f*; (*tableware*) vajilla *f*; (*in book*) lámina *f. v* chapar; (*silver*) platear; (*gold*) dorar. **plateful** *n* plato *m*.

plateau ['platou] *n* meseta *f*.

platform ['platfɔːm] *n* plataforma *f*; (*rail*) andén *m*; (*stage*) estrado *m*; (*builders*) andamio *m*; (*pol*) programa *m*. **platform ticket** billete de andén *m*.

platinum ['platinəm] *n* platino *m*.

platonic [plə'tonik] *adj* platónico.

platoon [plə'tuːn] *n* (*mil*) pelotón *m*.

plausible ['plɔːzəbl] *adj* plausible; (*person*) convincente. **plausibility** *n* plausibilidad *f*.

play [plei] *n* juego *m*, diversión *f*. (*theatre*) obra de teatro *f*; (*manoeuvre*) jugada *f. v* jugar. **player** *n* jugador, -a *m, f*; (*music*) intérprete *m, f*; (*theatre*) actor, actriz *m, f*. **playful** *adj* juguetón. **playfulness** *n* carácter juguetón *m*.

playback ['pleibak] *n* reproducción *f*. **play back** *v* volver a poner.

playground ['pleigraund] *n* campo de juegos *m*.

playhouse ['pleihaus] *n* teatro *m*.

playing card *n* carta *f*, naipe *m*.

playing field *n* campo de deportes *m*.

plaything ['pleiθiŋ] *n* juguete *m*.

playwright ['pleirait] *n* autor de teatro *m*.

plea [pliː] *n* súplica *f*; petición *f*; (*law*) alegato *m*.

plead [pliːd] *v* suplicar; implorar; intervenir; hacer un alegato.

pleasant ['pleznt] *adj* agradable.

please [pliːz] *v* gustar, agradar. **if you please** por favor. **pleased** *adj* contento. **pleasing** *adj* agradable.

pleasure ['pleʒə] *n* placer *m*, gusto *m*. **pleasurable** *adj* grato.

pleat [pliːt] *n* pliegue *m. v* plisar.

plectrum ['plektrəm] *n* plectro *m*.

pledge [pledʒ] *n* prenda *f*; promesa *f. v* dar en prenda; prometer.

plenty ['plenti] *n* abundancia *f*; cantidad *f*. **plenty of** bastante. **plentiful** *adj* abundante, copioso.

pleurisy ['pluərisi] *n* pleuresía *f*.

pliable ['plaiəbl] *adj* flexible; (*person*) dócil. **pliability** *n* flexibilidad *f*; docilidad *f*.

pliers ['plaiəz] *pl n* alicates *m pl*.

plight [plait] *n* aprieto *m*; crisis *f*.

plimsolls ['plimsəlz] *pl n* zapatos de tenis *m pl*.

plod [plod] *v* andar con paso pesado; (*coll: work*) trabajar con ahínco. **plodder** *n* empollón, -ona *m, f*.

plonk [ploŋk] *n* (*coll*) pirriaque *m*.

plop [plop] *n* plaf *m. v* hacer plaf.

plot¹ [plot] *n* (*story, etc.*) argumento *m*; (*conspiracy*) conspiración *f*; *v* tramar, maquinar; (*route*) trazar.

plot² [plot] *n* (*land*) terreno *m*; (*garden*) cuadro *m*.

plough [plau] *n* arado *m. v* arar. **plough one's way through** abrirse paso. **ploughman** *n* arador.

pluck [plʌk] *n* valor *m*; (*music*) plectro *m*; (*pull*) tirón *m. v* (*pull*) arrancar; (*music*) puntear; (*fruit*) coger; (*fowl*) desplumar; (*eyebrows*) despilarse. **pluck out** arrancar. **pluck up courage** armarse de valor. **plucky** *adj* valiente.

plug [plʌg] *n* (*stopper*) taco *m*; (*sink, bath*) tapón *m*; (*elec*) enchufe *m*; (*mot*) bujía *f. v* taponar; tapar; enchufar; (*block up*) atascar; (*coll: advertise*) dar publicidad a. **plug away at** perseverar en. **plug in** enchufar.

plum [plʌm] *n* (*fruit*) ciruela *f*; (*tree*) ciruelo *m*.

plumage ['pluːmidʒ] *n* plumaje *m*.

plumb [plʌm] *n* plomada *f*, plomo *m*. **plumbline** *n* cuerda de plomada *f*; (*in water*) sonda *f. adj* vertical. *adv* a plomo. *v* aplomar; sondar. **plumber** *n* fontanero *m*. **plumbing** *n* fontanería *f*; instalación de cañerías *f*.

plume [pluːm] *n* (*feather*) pluma *f*; (*smoke*) penacho *m. v* emplumar.

plummet ['plʌmit] *n* plomo *m*. *v* (*bird, aircraft*) caer en picado; (*person, thing*) caer a plomo; (*prices*) caer verticalmente.

plump¹ [plʌmp] *adj* (*person*) rellenito; (*animal*) gordo. **plumpness** *n* gordura *f*.

plump² [plʌmp] *v* caer de golpe. **plump for** decidirse por.

plunder ['plʌndə] *v* saquear; robar. *n* saqueo *m*; (*loot*) botín *m*. **plunderer** *n* saqueador *m*. **plundering** *n* saqueo *m*.

plunge [plʌndʒ] *n* (*fall*) caída *f*; (*short dive*) zambullida *f*; (*high dive*) salto *m*. **take the plunge** aventurarse. *v* (*knife, etc.*) meter; sumergir; (*into despair*) hundirse; (*launch oneself*) lanzarse; (*fall*) caer.

pluperfect [plu'pəfikt] *n* pluscuamperfecto *m*.

plural ['pluərəl] *nm, adj* plural.

plus [plʌs] *prep* más. *n* cantidad positiva *f*; (*sign*) signo más *m*. *adj* positivo.

ply¹ [plai] *v* (*tool*) manejar; (*trade*) ejercer; (*questions*) acosar; (*ship, etc.*) hacer el trayecto de. **ply between** hacer el servicio entre.

ply² [plai] *n* (*wood*) chapa *f*; (*wool*) cabo *m*; (*fabric*) capa *f*. **plywood** *n* contrapachado *m*.

pneumatic [nju'matik] *adj* neumático. **pneumatic drill** barreno neumático *m*.

pneumonia [nju'mouniə] *n* pulmonía *f*.

poach¹ [poutʃ] *v* cazar *or* pescar en vedado. **poacher** *n* cazador *or* pescador furtivo *m*. **poaching** *n* caza *or* pesca furtiva *f*.

poach² [poutʃ] *v* (*egg*) escalfar.

pocket ['pokit] *n* bolsillo *m*. **pocket-money** *n* dinero de bolsillo *m*. *v* embolsarse.

pod [pod] *n* vaina *f*.

podgy ['podʒi] *adj* (*coll*) gordo.

poem ['pouim] *n* poema *m*.

poet ['pouit] *n* poeta *m*. **poetess** *n* poetisa *f*. **poetic** *adj* poético. **poetry** *n* poesía *f*.

poignant ['poinjənt] *adj* conmovedor.

point [point] *n* punto *m*; (*sharp end*) punta *f*; (*decimal*) coma *f*; (*elec*) contacto *m*; (*meaning*) sentido *m*; motivo; (*headland*) cabo *m*. **points** *pl n* (*railway*) agujas *f pl*. **beside the point** que no viene al caso. **come** *or* **get to the point** ir al grano. **make a point of** insistir en. **point-blank** *adv* (*shoot*) a quema ropa;

(*demand*) sin rodeos; (*refuse*) categóricamente. **what's the point?** ¿para qué sirve? *v* señalar; (*a weapon*) apuntar. **point out** señalar; advertir. **pointed** *adj* (*sharpened*) afilado; (*shape*) puntiagudo; (*remark*) directo. **pointless** *adj* inútil.

poise [poiz] *n* equilibrio *m*; (*bearing*) porte *m*; elegancia *f*; serenidad *f*. *v* poner en equilibrio; preparar. **be poised** estar en equilibrio; estar preparado.

poison ['poizən] *n* veneno *m*. *v* envenenar. **poisoning** *n* envenenamiento *m*. **poisonous** *adj* venenoso; tóxico.

poke [pouk] *n* empujón con el dedo; (*with elbow*) codazo *m*; (*fig*) hurgonada *f*. *v* dar con la punta del dedo; dar un codazo; hurgar. **poker** *n* hurgón *m*.

poker ['poukə] *n* (*cards*) póker *m*. **poker-faced** *adj* de cara inmutable.

Poland ['poulənd] *n* Polonia *f*. **Pole** *n* polaco, -a *m*, *f*. **Polish** *nm, adj* polaco.

polar ['poulə] *adj* polar. **polar bear** oso blanco. **polarize** *v* polarizar.

pole¹ [poul] *n* (*wood*) palo *m*; (*metal*) barra *f*; (*telegraphs*) poste *m*; (*flag*) asta *f*. **pole-vault** *n* salto de pértiga *m*.

pole² [poul] *n* (*geog, elec*) polo *m*. **pole star** estrella polar *f*.

police [pə'liːs] *n* policía *f*. **the police force** el cuerpo de policía *m*. **policeman** *n* policía *m*, guardia *m*. **police station** comisaría de policía *f*. **policewoman** *n* mujer policía *f*.

policy¹ ['poləsi] *n* (*government*) política *f*; principio *m*; táctica *f*.

policy² ['poləsi] *n* (*insurance*) póliza *f*.

polio ['pouliou] *n* polio *f*.

polish ['poliʃ] *n* (*shine*) brillo *m*; (*act*) pulimento *m*; (*furniture*) cera *f*; (*shoes*) betún *m*; (*nails*) esmalte *m*; (*fig*) elegancia *f*. *v* (*shoes*) limpiar; (*metal*) pulir; (*floors*) encerar. **polish off** zampar. **polish up** dar brillo a; (*improve*) perfeccionar.

polite [pə'lait] *adj* cortés. **politeness** *n* cortesía *f*.

politics ['politiks] *n* política *f*. **political** *adj* político. **politician** *n* político.

polka ['polkə] *n* polca *f*.

poll [poul] *n* votación *f*; elecciones *f pl*; (*survey*) sondeo *m*. *v* obtener; sondear. **polling booth** cabina electoral *f*; **polling day** día de elecciones *m*. **polling station** central electoral *m*.

pollen ['polən] *n* polen *m*. **pollen count**

indice de polen *m*. **pollinate** *v* polinizar.
pollination *n* polinización *f*.
pollute [pə'luːt] *v* contaminar. **pollution** *n*
contaminación *f*.
polo ['poulou] *n* polo *m*. **water polo** polo
acuático *m*. **polo-neck** *n* cuello vuelto *m*.
polyester [,poli'estə] *n* poliéster *m*.
polygamy [pə'ligəmi] *n* poligamia *f*.
polygon ['poligən] *n* polígono *m*.
polystyrene [,poli'staiəriːn] *n* poliestireno
m.
polytechnic [,poli'teknik] *n* escuela
politécnica *f*.
polythene ['poliθiːn] *n* polietileno *m*.
pomegranate ['pomigranit] *n* (*fruit*) granada *f*; (*tree*) granado *m*.
pomp [pomp] *n* pompa *f*. **pompous** *adj*
pomposo.
pond [pond] *n* charca *f*; (*artificial*) estanque *m*.
ponder ['pondə] *v* considerar; meditar.
pony ['pouni] *n* poney *m*. **pony-tail** *n* cola
de caballo *f*.
poodle ['puːdl] *n* perro de lanas *m*.
poof [puːf] *n* (*derog*) marica *m*.
pool¹ [puːl] *n* (*liquid*) charco *m*; (*swimming*) piscina *f*.
pool² [puːl] *n* (*money*) banca *f*; (*things*)
recursos comunes *m pl*; (*reserve*) reserva
f; (*comm*) fondos comunes *m pl*; (*typing*)
servicio de mecanografía *m*. **pools** *pl n*
(*football*) quinielas *f pl*. *v* aunar; reunir;
poner en un fondo común.
poor [puə] *adj* pobre; mediocre.
poorly ['puəli] *adj* pobremente; mal. **be
poorly** estar malo.
pop¹ [pop] *n* taponazo *m*; (*drink*) gaseosa
f. **popcorn** *n* rosetas de maíz *f pl*. *v*
pinchar; (*cork*) hacer saltar; (*put*) meter.
pop in entrar un momento.
pop² [pop] *adj* popular. **pop music** música
pop *f*.
pope [poup] *n* papa *m*.
poplar ['poplə] *n* álamo *m*.
poplin ['poplin] *n* popelina *f*.
poppy ['popi] *n* amapola *f*.
popular ['popjulə] *adj* popular. **popularity**
n popularidad *f*. **popularize** *v* popularizar.
population [,popju'leifən] *n* población *f*.
populate *v* poblar.
porcelain ['poːslin] *n* porcelana *f*.
porch [poːtf] *n* pórtico *m*.
porcupine ['poːkjupain] *n* puerco espú *m*.

pore¹ [poː] *n* (*anat*) poro *m*.
pore² [poː] *v* **pore over** estar absorto en.
pork [poːk] *n* cerdo *m*.
pornography [poː'nogrəfi] *n* pornografía
f. **pornographic** *adj* pornográfico.
porous ['poːrəs] *adj* poroso.
porpoise ['poːpəs] *n* marsopa *f*.
porridge ['poridʒ] *n* gachas de avena *f pl*.
port¹ [poːt] *n* (*harbour*) puerto *m*.
port² [poːt] *n* (*naut: left*) babor *m*.
port³ [poːt] *n* (*wine*) oporto *m*.
portable ['poːtəbl] *adj* portátil.
portent ['poːtent] *n* presagio *m*.
porter ['poːtə] *n* (*attendant*) mozo *m*;
(*doorman*) portero; (*in government build-
ings*) conserje *m*.
portfolio [poːt'fouliou] *n* (*folder*) carpeta
f; (*pol*) cartera *f*.
porthole ['poːthoul] *n* portilla *f*.
portion ['poːfən] *n* porción *f*; parte *f*.
portrait ['poːtrət] *n* retrato *m*.
portray [poː'trei] *v* retratar; representar.
portrayal *n* retrato *m*; representación *f*.
Portugal ['poːtjugl] *n* Portugal *m*. **Portuguese** *nm, adj* portugués. **the Portuguese**
los portugueses.
pose [pouz] *n* postura *f*; afectación *f*. *v*
colocar; (*question*) formular; (*problem*)
plantear. **pose as** dárselas de.
posh [pof] *adj* elegante, de lujo; afectado.
position [pə'zifən] *n* posición *f*; sitio *m*;
situación *f*; opinión *f*; (*job*) empleo *m*. *v*
situar, disponer.
positive ['pozətiv] *adj* seguro; categórico;
verdadero; afirmativo; positivo.
possess [pə'zes] *v* poseer. **possession** *n*
posesión *f*. **possessive** *nm, adj* posesivo.
possible ['posəbl] *adj* posible. **possibility** *n*
posibilidad *f*. **possibly** *adv* (*perhaps*) tal
vez.
post¹ [poust] *n* (*pole*) poste *m*. *v* pegar.
post² [poust] *n* (*sentry, job*) puesto *m*. *v* (*a
sentry*) apostar; (*mil: send*) destinar.
post³ [poust] *n* (*mail*) correo *m*; (*letters*)
cartas *f pl*. *v* mandar, enviar; echar. **postage** *n* franqueo *m*. **postage stamp** sello *m*.
postal *adj* postal. **postal order** giro postal
m.
postbox ['pousboks] *n* buzón *m*.
postcard ['pouskaːd] *n* tarjeta postal *f*.
post-code *n* código postal *m*.
poster ['poustə] *n* cartel *m*.
poste restante [poust'restãt] *n* lista de
correos *f*.

posterior [po'stiəriə] *adj* posterior. *n* (*coll*) trasero *m*.

posterity [po'sterəti] *n* posteridad *f*.

postgraduate [poust'gradjuit] *n, adj* postgraduado, -a.

post-haste *adv* a toda prisa.

posthumous ['postjuməs] *adj* póstumo.

postman ['pousmən] *n* cartero *m*.

postmark ['pousmaɪk] *n* matasellos *m invar. v* matasellar.

postmaster ['pousmaɪstə] *n* administrador de correos *m*. **postmistress** *n* administradora de correos *f*.

post-mortem *n* autopsia *f*.

post office *n* correos *m pl*.

postpone [pous'poun] *v* aplazar. **postponement** *n* aplazamiento *m*.

postscript ['poussskript] *n* posdata *f*.

postulate ['postjuleit; *n* 'postjulət] *v* postular. *n* postulado *m*.

posture ['postʃə] *n* postura *f*, actitud *f*.

pot [pot] *n* (*cooking*) olla *f*; (*flowers*) tiesto *m*; (*preserves*) tarro *m*. **pot roast** carne asada *f*. **pots and pans** batería de cocina *f*. *v* (*plant*) poner en tiesto.

potassium [pə'tasjəm] *n* potasio *m*.

potato [pə'teitou] *n* patata *f*.

potent ['poutənt] *adj* poderoso; (*drink*) fuerte.

potential [pə'tenʃəl] *adj* posible; (*phys*) potencial. *n* posibilidad *f*; (*phys*) potencial *m*; (*elec*) voltaje *m*.

pot-hole ['pothoul] *n* (*in road*) bache *m*; (*underground*) cueva *f*. **pot-holer** *n* espeleólogo *m*. **pot-holing** *n* espeleología *f*.

potion ['pouʃən] *n* dosis *f*, poción *f*.

potter[1] ['potə] *v* (*coll*) **potter about** *or* **around** no hacer nada de particular.

potter[2] ['potə] *n* alfarero *m*. **potter's wheel** torno de alfarero *m*.

pottery ['potəri] *n* (*shop, craft*) alfarería *f*; (*pots*) cacharros de barro *m pl*.

potty ['poti] *n* (*coll*: *baby's*) orinal *m*. *adj* (*coll*: *crazy*) chiflado.

pouch [pautʃ] *n* bolsa *f*; (*tobacco*) petaca *f*.

poultice ['poultis] *n* cataplasma *f*.

poultry ['poultri] *n* aves de corral *f pl*.

pounce [pauns] *v* saltar. *n* salto *m*, ataque *m*.

pound[1] [paund] *v* aporrear; martillear; azotar.

pound[2] [paund] *n* libra *f*.

pour [poɪ] *v* verter; echar; servir; (*rain*)

diluviar; (*flow*) fluir; (*people*) salir en tropel.

pout [paut] *n* mala cara *f*. *v* poner mala cara.

poverty ['povəti] *n* pobreza *f*.

powder ['paudə] *n* polvo *m*; (*cosmetic*) polvos *m pl*; (*gun*) pólvora *f*. **powder puff** borla *f*. **powder room** cuarto tocador *m*. *v* pulverizar. **powdery** *adj* en polvo; pulverizado.

power ['pauə] *n* poder *m*; (*elec*) potencia *f*; (*tech*) fuerza *f*; (*energy*) energía *f*. **power station** central eléctrica *f*. *v* accionar, impulsar. **powerful** *adj* poderoso; potente. **powerless** *adj* impotente; sin autoridad.

practicable ['praktikəbl] *adj* practicable; utilizable; realizable. **practicability** *n* practicabilidad *f*.

practical ['praktikəl] *adj* práctico. **practical joke** broma pesada *f*.

practice ['praktis] *n* práctica *f*; (*music*) ejercicios *m pl*; (*training*) entrenamiento *m*; (*profession*) ejercicio *m*.

practise ['praktis] *v* practicar; (*professionally*) ejercer; (*exercise*) ejercitarse; (*patience, etc.*) tener; (*music*) hacer ejercicios en.

practitioner [prak'tiʃənə] *n* (*med*) médico *m*. **general practitioner** internista *m*.

pragmatic [prag'matik] *adj* pragmático; dogmático.

Prague [praɪg] *n* Praga.

prairie ['preəri] *n* llanura *f*, pradera *f*.

praise [preiz] *n* alabanza *f*, elogio *m*. *v* alabar, elogiar. **praiseworthy** *adj* laudable.

pram [pram] *n* cochecito de niño *m*.

prance [prains] *v* caracolear, encabritarse.

prank [praŋk] *n* (*joke*) broma *f*; (*mischief*) travesura *f*.

prattle ['pratl] *v* (*chatter*) charlar; (*of a child*) balbucear. *n* chácara *f*; balbuceo *m*.

prawn [proɪn] *n* gamba *f*.

pray [prei] *v* orar, rezar. **prayer** *n* oración *f*, rezo *m*. **prayer book** devocionario *m*.

preach [priɪtʃ] *v* predicar. **preacher** *n* predicador, -a *m, f*. **preaching** *n* predicación *f*.

precarious [pri'keəriəs] *adj* precario.

precaution [pri'kotʃən] *n* precaución *f*. **take precautions** tomar precauciones.

precede [pri'siɪd] *v* preceder, anteceder.

precedence *n* precedencia *f*; prioridad *f*.
precedent *n* precedente *m*.
precinct ['priːsiŋkt] *n* recinto *m*; frontera *f*; zona *f*. **shopping precinct** zona comercial *f*.
precious ['preʃəs] *adj* precioso.
precipice ['presipis] *n* precipicio *m*.
precipitate [pri'sipiteit; *adj* pri'sipitət] *v* (*throw*) precipitar, arrojar; (*hasten*) acelerar; (*cause*) causar. *adj* precipitado.
precipitation *n* precipitación *f*.
précis ['preisi] *n* resumen *m*.
precise [pri'sais] *adj* preciso; exacto. **precision** *n* precisión *f*; exactitud *f*.
preclude [pri'kluːd] *v* excluir; evitar; impedir.
precocious [pri'kouʃəs] *adj* precoz. **precociousness** *or* **precocity** *n* precocidad *f*.
preconceive [ˌpriːkən'siːv] *v* preconcebir. **preconception** *n* preconcepción *f*.
precursor [ˌpriːˈkəːsə] *n* precursor, -a *m*, *f*.
predator ['predətə] *n* animal de rapiña *m*; (*person*) depredador, -a *m*, *f*.
predecessor ['priːdisesə] *n* predecesor, -a *m*, *f*.
predestine [pri'destin] *v* predestinar. **predestination** *n* predestinación *f*.
predicament [pri'dikəmənt] *n* situación difícil *f*.
predicate ['predikət] *n* predicado *m*. *v* afirmar; implicar.
predict [pri'dikt] *v* predecir. **predictable** *adj* previsible. **prediction** *n* predicción *f*.
predominate [pri'domineit] *v* predominar. **predominance** *n* predominio *m*. **predominant** *adj* predominante.
pre-eminent [pri'eminənt] *adj* preeminente. **pre-eminence** *n* preeminencia *f*.
preen [priːn] *v* limpiar. **preen oneself** pavonearse.
prefabricate [priːˈfabrikeit] *v* prefabricar. **prefabrication** *n* prefabricación *f*. **prefab** *n* (*coll*) casa prefabricada *f*.
preface ['prefis] *n* prólogo *m*. *v* (*introduce*) introducir.
prefect ['priːfekt] *n* (*school*) alumno/alumna responsable de disciplina *m*, *f*.
prefer [pri'fəː] *v* preferir. **preferable** *adj* preferible. **preference** *n* preferencia *f*. **preferential** *adj* preferente.
prefix ['priːfiks] *n* prefijo *m*. *v* poner un prefijo; anteponer.
pregnant ['pregnənt] *adj* (*woman*)

embarazada, encinta; (*animal*) preñada. **pregnancy** *n* embarazo *m*.
prehistoric [ˌpriːhi'storik] *adj* prehistórico.
prejudice ['predʒədis] *n* prejuicio *m*; parcialidad *f*. *v* predisponer; (*damage*) perjudicar. **prejudiced** *adj* predispuesto; parcial. **prejudicial** *adj* perjudicial.
preliminary [pri'liminəri] *adj* preliminar. **preliminaries** *pl n* preliminares *m pl*.
prelude ['preljuːd] *n* preludio *m*.
premarital [priːˈmaritl] *adj* premarital.
premature [premə'tʃuə] *adj* prematuro.
premeditate [priːˈmediteit] *v* premeditar. **premeditation** *n* premeditación *f*.
premier ['premiə] *adj* primero. *n* primer ministro *m*.
première ['premiə] *n* estreno *m*.
premise ['premis] *n* premisa *f*. **premises** *pl n* local *m sing*; edificio *m sing*.
premium ['priːmiəm] *n* (*comm*) prima *f*; (*award*) premio *m*. **at a premium** a premio.
premonition [ˌpremə'niʃən] *n* premonición *f*.
preoccupied [priːˈokjupaid] *adj* preocupado. **preoccupation** *n* preocupación *f*.
prepare [pri'peə] *v* preparar, disponer. **preparation** *n* preparación *f*. **preparations** *pl n* preparativos *m pl*. **preparatory** *adj* preparatorio; preliminar. **preparatory school** escuela preparatoria *f*.
preposition [ˌprepə'ziʃən] *n* preposición *f*.
preposterous [pri'postərəs] *adj* ridículo, absurdo.
prerogative [pri'rogətiv] *n* prerrogativa *f*.
prescribe [pri'skraib] *v* prescribir; (*med*) recetar. **prescription** *n* (*med*) receta *f*, prescripción *f*.
presence ['prezns] *n* presencia *f*.
present¹ ['preznt] *adj* presente. *n* presente *m*, actualidad *f*. **at present** ahora, en la actualidad. **those present** los presentes. **presently** *adv* luego.
present² [pri'zent; *n* 'preznt] *v* presentar; regalar; (*a problem*) plantear; (*an argument*) exponer. *n* regalo *m*. **presentable** *adj* presentable. **presentation** *n* presentación *f*; (*gift*) regalo *m*; (*ceremony*) entrega *f*.
preserve [pri'zəːv] *v* (*food*) conservar; (*protect*) preservar. **preserved** *adj* en conserva. **preserves** *pl n* conservas *f pl*; (*jam*) confitura *f*. **preservation** *n* conservación

f; (*protection*) preservación *f*. **preservative** *n* producto de conservación *m*.

preside [pri'zaid] *v* presidir.

president ['prezidənt] *n* presidente. -a *m*, *f*. **presidency** *n* presidencia *f*. **presidential** *adj* presidencial.

press [pres] *n* (*newspapers*) prensa *f*; (*printing*) imprenta *f*. **press conference** rueda de prensa *f*. **press cutting** recorte de periódico *m*. *v* (*mechanical*) prensar; (*push*) apretar; (*iron*) planchar; (*button*) dar a; (*squeeze*) estrucar; (*urge*) urgir. **press for** pedir con insistencia. **pressing** *adj* urgente.

pressure ['preʃə] *n* presión *f*; (*weight*) peso *m*; (*strength*) fuerza *f*; (*elec, med*) tensión *f*. **pressure cooker** olla de presión *f*. **pressure gauge** manómetro *m*. **pressurize** *v* (*cabin, etc.*) presurizar; (*coll: force*) acozar.

prestige [pre'stirʒ] *n* prestigio *m*.

presume [pri'zjuːm] *v* suponer; permitirse. **presumption** *n* presunción *f*; (*daring*) atrevimiento *m*. **presumptuous** *adj* presuntuoso; atrevido.

pretend [pri'tend] *v* fingir; (*claim*) pretender; (*imagine*) suponer. **pretence** *n* fingimiento *m*; pretensión *f*; pretexto *m*; apariencia *f*. **pretension** *n* pretensión *f*. **pretentious** *adj* pretencioso; (*showy*) presumido.

pretext ['priːtekst] *n* pretexto *m*.

pretty ['priti] *adj* bonito, lindo. *adv* bastante.

prevail [pri'veil] *v* prevalecer, triunfar; predominar. **prevail upon** convencer. **prevailing** *adj* (*wind*) predominante, reinante; (*present*) actual. **prevalent** *adj* predominante; (*present-day*) actual; (*common*) común; extendido.

prevent [pri'vent] *v* impedir; (*avoid*) evitar. **prevention** prevención *f*; impedimento *m*. **preventive** *adj* preventivo.

preview ['priːvjuː] *n* preestreno *m*. *v* ver antes que los demás.

previous ['priːviəs] *adj* anterior. **previously** *adv* antes.

prey [prei] *n* presa *f*; víctima *f*. **be a prey to** ser víctima de. *v* **prey on** (*animals*) alimentarse de. **prey on one's mind** preocupar mucho.

price [prais] *n* precio *m*. **fixed price** precio fijo *m*. **full price** precio fuerte *m*. **price list** tarifa *f*. **sale price** precio de venta *m*.

v poner precio a; valorar. **priceless** *adj* inestimable.

prick [prik] *n* pinchazo *m*. *v* pinchar. **prick up one's ears** aguzar el oído.

prickle ['prikl] *n* espina. *v* picar. **prickly** *adj* espinoso.

pride [praid] *n* orgullo *m*; dignidad *f*. **pride oneself on** enorgullecerse de.

priest [priːst] *n* sacerdote *m*. **priesthood** *n* (*office*) sacerdocio *m*; (*clergy*) clero *m*.

prim [prim] *adj* (*fussy*) remilgado; (*demure*) recatado.

primary ['praiməri] *adj* primario; básico; primero.

primate ['praimət] *n* (*zool*) primate *m*; (*rel*) primado *m*.

prime [praim] *adj* primero; principal; original; selecto; (*math*) primo. **prime minister** primer ministro *m*. *v* preparar; (*person*) informar. **primer** *n* (*book*) cartilla *f*. **prime coat** primera mano *f*.

primitive ['primitiv] *adj* primitivo.

primrose ['primrouz] *n* primavera *f*.

prince [prins] *n* príncipe *m*. **princely** *adj* principesco. **princess** *n* princesa *f*.

principal ['prinsəpəl] *adj* principal. *n* (*school*) director, -a *m*, *f*.

principle ['prinsəpəl] *n* principio *m*. **on principle** por principio.

print [print] *n* (*finger*) huella *f*; (*impression*) marca *f*; (*phot*) prueba *f*; (*edition*) tirada *f*; (*type*) tipo *m*; (*picture*) grabado *m*. **out of print** agotado. *v* imprimir; (*phot*) sacar. **printed matter** impresos *m pl*. **printer** *n* impresor *m*. **printing** *n* impresión *f*; (*phot*) tiraje *m*. **printing press** prensa *f*.

prior ['praiə] *adj* anterior; preferente. **prior to** antes de. **priority** *n* prioridad *f*.

prise [praiz] *v* **prise off/open** abrir; levantar por fuerza.

prism ['prizm] *n* prisma *m*.

prison ['prizn] *n* cárcel *f*. **prisoner** *n* preso, -a *m*, *f*.

private ['praivət] *adj* privado; personal; reservado; (*house, car, lessons, etc.*) particular; confidencial. *n* soldado raso *m*. **privacy** *n* intimidad *f*; aislamiento *m*. **privately** *adv* en privado; personalmente.

privet ['privət] *n* alheña *f*.

privilege ['privəlidʒ] *n* privilegio *m*. **privileged** *adj* privilegiado.

privy ['privi] *n* letrina *f*.

prize [praiz] *n* premio *m*. **prizewinner** *n*

premiado, -a *n*, *f*. *adj* premiado. *v* estimar.

probable ['probəbl] *adj* probable; (*credible*) verosímil. **probability** *n* probabilidad *f*. **probably** *adv* probablemente.

probation [prə'beiʃən] *n* (*law*) libertad vigilada *f*; (*trial period*) período de prueba *m*. **on probation** a prueba. **probationary** *adj* de prueba.

probe [proub] *n* (*act*) sondeo *m*; (*med*) sonda *f*. *v* sondear; explorar.

problem ['probləm] *n* problema *m*. **problematic** *adj* problemático.

proceed [prə'siːd] *v* seguir; proceder; avanzar. **proceed to** ponerse a. **procedure** *n* procedimiento *m*. **proceedings** *pl n* debates *m pl*; (*law*) proceso *m sing*.

process ['prouses] *n* proceso *m*; procedimiento *m*; método *m*. **in the process of** en curso de. *v* tratar; (*phot*) revelar.

procession [prə'seʃən] *n* procesión *f*, desfile *m*.

proclaim [prə'kleim] *v* proclamar; declarar. **proclamation** *n* proclamación *f*; declaración *f*.

procreate ['proukrieit] *v* procrear. **procreation** *n* procreación *f*.

procure [prə'kjuə] *v* conseguir.

prod [prod] *n* golpecito *m*. *v* punzar; (*urge*) estimular.

prodigal ['prodigəl] *adj* pródigo.

prodigy ['prodidʒi] *n* prodigio *m*. **prodigious** *adj* prodigioso.

produce [prə'djuːs; *n* 'prodjuːs] *v* producir; (*manufacture*) fabricar; causar. *n* productos *m pl*. **producer** *n* productor, -a *m*, *f*; (*theatre*) escenógrafo *m*. **product** *m* producto *m*. **production** *n* producción *f*; fabricación *f*; presentación *f*; (*theatre*) dirección *f*. **productive** *adj* productivo; fecundo. **productivity** *n* productividad *f*.

profane [prə'fein] *adj* profano. *v* profanar. **profanity** *n* lo profano; impiedad *f*.

profess [prə'fes] *v* (*state*) declarar; (*claim*) pretender; (*affirm*) afirmar.

profession [prə'feʃən] *n* profesión *f*. **professional** *n(m+f)*, *adj* profesional.

professor [prə'fesə] *n* catedrático, -a *m*, *f*. **professorship** *n* cátedra *f*.

proficient [prə'fiʃənt] *adj* competente; experto. **proficiency** *n* competencia *f*; pericia *f*.

profile ['proufail] *n* perfil *m*; (*biography*) reseña *f*.

profit ['profit] *n* (*financial*) ganancia *f*; (*fig*) provecho *m*. **profit-making** *adj* productivo. *v* **profit by** *or* **from** beneficiarse de. **profitable** *adj* provechoso.

profound [prə'faund] *adj* profundo. **profoundly** *adv* profundamente.

profuse [prə'fjuːs] *adj* profuso; abundante. **profusely** *adv* profusamente. **profusion** *n* profusión *f*; abundancia *f*.

programme ['prougram] *n* programa *m*. *v* programar. **programmer** *n* programador, -a *m*, *f*. **programming** *n* programación *f*.

progress ['prougres] *n* progreso *m*. **in progress** en curso. **make progress** hacer progresos. *v* progresar, avanzar, hacer progresos. **progression** *n* progresión *f*. **progressive** *adj* progresivo; (*political, social*) progresista.

prohibit [prə'hibit] *v* prohibir; impedir. **prohibition** *n* prohibición *f*.

project ['prodʒekt] *v* prə'dʒekt] *n* proyecto *m*. *v* proyectar; (*protrude*) hacer resaltar. **projectile** *n* proyectil *m*. **projecting** *adj* saliente. **projection** *n* proyección *f*; saliente *m*. **projector** *n* proyector *m*; (*planner*) proyectista *m*, *f*.

proletarian [proulə'teəriən] *n*, *adj* proletario, -a. **proletariat** *n* proletariado *m*.

proliferate [prə'lifəreit] *v* proliferar. **proliferation** *n* proliferación *f*.

prolific [prə'lifik] *adj* prolífico.

prologue ['proulog] *n* prólogo *m*.

prolong [prə'loŋ] *v* prolongar. **prolongation** *n* prolongación *f*.

promenade [promə'naːd] *n* paseo *m*. *v* pasear, pasearse.

prominent ['prominənt] *adj* prominente; saliente; preeminente. **prominence** *n* prominencia *f*; importancia *f*.

promiscuous [prə'miskjuəs] *adj* promiscuo; (*person*) libertino. **promiscuity** *n* promiscuidad *f*.

promise ['promis] *n* promesa *f*. *v* prometer. **promising** *adj* que promete.

promontory ['proməntəri] *n* promontorio *m*.

promote [prə'mout] *v* promover, ascender; (*comm*) promocionar; (*encourage, stir up*) fomentar; financiar. **promotion** *n* ascenso *m*; promoción *f*; fomento *m*.

prompt [prompt] *adj* pronto; rápido; inmediato; puntual. *v* incitar; inspirar;

sugerir; (*theatre*) apuntar. **prompter** *n*
apuntador, -a *m, f.*
prone [proun] *adj* propenso; (*lying*) boca
abajo.
prong [proŋ] *n* diente *m*, púa *f.*
pronoun ['prounaun] *n* pronombre *m.*
pronounce [prə'nauns] *v* pronunciar;
declarar. **pronouncement** *n* declaración *f.*
pronunciation *n* pronunciación *f.*
proof [pruːf] *n* prueba *f*; (*alcohol*) graduación normal *f.* *adj* resistente (a); al
abrigo de. **proof-read** *v* corregir pruebas.
proof-reading *n* corrección de pruebas *f.*
prop[1] [prop] *n* puntal *m*; (*fig*) sostén *m*,
apoyo *m.* *v* (*lean*) apoyar; (*support*)
mantener.
prop[2] [prop] *n* (*coll: theatre*) accesorio *m.*
propaganda [propə'gandə] *n* propaganda
f.
propagate ['propəgeit] *v* propagar. **propagation** *n* propagación *f.*
propel [prə'pel] *v* propulsar, impulsar.
propeller *n* propulsor *m*; (*aircraft, ship*)
hélice *f.* **propelling pencil** portaminas *m*
invar.
proper ['propə] *adj* propio; correcto;
decente; formal; justo; (*suitable*) apto;
(*true*) verdadero; (*characteristic*) peculiar. **proper noun** nombre propio *m.*
properly *adv* propiamente; bien;
decentemente; correctamente.
property ['propəti] *n* (*estate*) hacienda *f*;
(*possessions*) bienes *m pl*, propiedad *f.*
(*quality*) cualidad *f.*
prophecy ['profəsi] *n* profecía *f.* **prophesy**
v profetizar. **prophet** *n* profeta *m.* **prophetic** *adj* profético.
proportion [prə'poːʃən] *n* proporción *f*;
parte *f.* **out of proportion** desproporcionado. *v* proporcionar; distribuir. **proportional** *adj* proporcional, en proporción.
propose [prə'pouz] *v* proponer; (*marriage*) declararse; (*toast*) brindar;
(*intend*) intentar. **proposal** *n* proposición
f; (*marriage*) oferta de matrimonio *f*;
(*plan*) proyecto *m.* **proposition** *n* proposición *f*; proyecto *m.*
proprietor [prə'praiətə] *n* propietario, -a
m, f; dueño *m, f.*
propriety [prə'praiəti] *n* decoro *m*; conveniencia *f*; oportunidad *f*; corrección *f.*
propulsion [prə'pʌlʃən] *n* propulsión *f.*
prose [prouz] *n* prosa *f.*
prosecute ['prosikjuːt] *v* proseguir; (*law*)

procesar. **prosecution** *n* (*of duty*) cumplimiento *m*; (*continuation*) continuación
f; (*action of prosecuting*) procesamiento
m; (*trial*) proceso *m*; (*party*) parte
acusadora *f.*
prospect ['prospekt; *v* prə'spekt] *n* perspectiva *f*; vista *f.* **prospects** *pl n* (*of a
job, etc.*) perspectivas *f pl.* *v* prospectar.
prospective *adj* eventual; futuro.
prospectus [prə'spektəs] *n* prospecto *m.*
prosper ['prospə] *v* prosperar. **prosperity**
n prosperidad *f.* **prosperous** *adj* próspero.
prostitute ['prostitjuːt] *n* prostituta *f.* *v*
prostituir. **prostitution** *n* prostitución *f.*
prostrate ['prostreit; *v* pro'streit] *adj*
(*lying down*) boca abajo; (*exhausted*)
postrado. *v* postrar. **prostrate oneself**
postrarse. **prostration** *n* prostración *f*;
prosternación *f.*
protagonist [prou'tagənist] *n* protagonista
m, f.
protect [prə'tekt] *v* proteger. **protection** *n*
protección *f.* **protective** *adj* protector.
protégé ['protəʒei] *n* protegido *m.* **protégée** *n* protegida *f.*
protein ['proutiin] *n* proteína *f.*
protest ['proutest; *v* prə'test] *n* protesta *f.*
v protestar. **protester** *n* (*on march*)
manifestador, -a *m, f.*
Protestant ['protistənt] *n(m+f)*, *adj*
protestante.
protocol ['proutəkol] *n* protocolo *m.*
prototype ['proutətaip] *n* prototipo *m.*
protractor [prə'traktə] *n* transportador *m.*
protrude [prə'truːd] *v* sacar; sobresalir.
protruding *adj* saliente, sobresaliente.
proud [praud] *adj* orgulloso; soberbio.
prove [pruːv] *v* probar; demostrar; (*show*)
mostrar.
proverb ['provəːb] *n* proverbio *m.* **proverbial** *adj* proverbial.
provide [prə'vaid] *v* proveer; dar;
preparar (por); proporcionar medios de
vida (a). **provided that** si siempre que.
provident ['providənt] *adj* próvido. **providence** *n* providencia *f.* **providential** providencial.
province ['provins] *n* provincia *f*; esfera *f.*
the provinces la provincia *f.* **provincial**
adj provincial.
provision [prə'viʒən] *n* (*supply*) suministro *m*; (*providing*) provisión *f*; (*of treaty,
law, etc.*) disposición *f.* **make provision
for** prever. **provisions** *pl n* provisiones *f*
pl. **provisional** *adj* provisional.

proviso [prə'vaizou] *n* condición *f*; estipulación *f*.

provoke [prə'vouk] *v* provocar. **provocation** *n* provocación *f*. **provocative** *adj* provocador.

prow [prau] *n* proa *f*.

prowess ['prauis] *n* valor *m*; proeza *f*.

prowl [praul] *v* rondar. **prowler** *n* rondador, -a *m*, *f*.

proximity [prok'siməti] *n* proximidad *f*.

proxy ['proksi] *n* poder *m*, procuración *f*. **by proxy** por poderes.

prude [pruːd] *n* mojigato, -a *m*, *f*. **prudish** *adj* mojigato.

prudent ['pruːdənt] *adj* prudente. **prudence** *n* prudencia *f*.

prune¹ [pruːn] *n* (*fruit*) ciruela pasa *f*.

prune² [pruːn] *v* podar; cortar; reducir.

pry [prai] *v* fisgar, fisgonear. **pry into** entrometerse en. **prying** *adj* fisgón.

psalm [saːm] *n* salmo *m*.

pseudonym ['sjuːdənim] *n* pseudónimo *m*.

psychedelic [,saikə'delik] *adj* psiquedélico.

psychiatry [sai'kaiətri] *n* psiquiatría *f*.

psychic ['saikik] *adj* psíquico. *n* medium *m*.

psychoanalysis [,saikouə'naləsis] *n* psicoanálisis *m*. **psychoanalyse** *v* psicoanalizar. **psychoanalyst** *n* psicoanalista *m*, *f*.

psychology [sai'kolədʒi] *n* psicología *f*. **psychological** *adj* psicológico. **psychologist** *n* psicólogo, -a *m*, *f*.

psychopath ['saikəpaθ] *n* psicópata *m*, *f*. **psychopathic** *adj* psicopático.

psychosis [sai'kousis] *n* psicosis *f*. **psychotic** *adj* psicopático. *n* psicópata *m*, *f*.

psychosomatic [,saikəsə'matik] *adj* psicosomático.

psychotherapy [,saikə'θerəpi] *n* psicoterapia *f*.

pub [pʌb] *n* taberna *f*. **pub crawl** chateo *m*.

puberty ['pjuːbəti] *n* pubertad *f*.

pubic ['pjuːbik] *adj* púbico.

public ['pʌblik] *nm*, *adj* público.

publication [,pʌbli'keiʃən] *n* publicación *f*.

publicity [pʌb'lisəti] *n* publicidad *f*.

publicize ['pʌblisaiz] *v* publicar.

public library *n* biblioteca de préstamo *f*.

public relations *n* colegio privado de enseñanza media *m*.

public-spirited *adj* de espíritu cívico.

public transport *n* servicio de transportes *m*.

publish ['pʌbliʃ] *v* publicar. **publisher** *n* editor, -a *m*, *f*. **publishing** *n* publicación *f*. **publishing house** casa editora *f*.

pucker ['pʌkə] *v* (*wrinkle*) arrugar; (*pleat*) fruncir. *n* (*pleat*) frunce *m*.

pudding ['pudiŋ] *n* pudín *m*, budín *m*.

puddle ['pʌdl] *n* charco *m*.

puerile ['pjuərail] *adj* pueril.

Puerto Rico [,pwəitou'riːkou] *n* Puerto Rico.

puff [pʌf] *n* (*breath*) resoplido *m*; (*air*) soplo *m*; (*wind*) ráfaga *f*; (*smoke*) bocanada *f*; *v* (*blow*) soplar; (*pant*) jadear; (*smoke*) echar bocanadas. **puff out** *or* **up** hinchar. **puffy** *adj* hinchado.

pull [pul] *n* tracción *f*; (*tide*) arrastre *m*; esfuerzo *m*; (*influence*) enchufe *m*; atracción *f*. *v* (*open*) tirar de; (*drag*) arrastrar; (*uproot*) arrancar; (*tooth*) sacar; (*trigger*) apretar; (*attract*) atraer. **pull ahead** destacarse. **pull away** separar, apartar. **pull down** bajar; echar abajo. **pull in** entrar; llegar. **pull oneself together** serenarse. **pull out** (*mot*) salirse; sacar; arrancar; (*mil*) retirarse. **pull through** sacar de un apuro. **pull together** aunar sus esfuerzos. **pull up** (*mot*) parar; (*socks*) subirse; (*a chair*) acercar.

pulley ['puli] *n* polea *f*.

pullover ['pul,ouvə] *n* jersey *m*.

pulp [pʌlp] *n* pulpa *f*. *v* reducir a pulpa.

pulpit ['pulpit] *n* púlpito *m*.

pulsate [pʌl'seit] *v* palpitar; vibrar; brillar. **pulsation** *n* pulsación *f*; vibración *f*.

pulse [pʌls] *n* (*med*) pulso *m*; (*phys*) pulsación *f*. *v* latir; vibrar.

pulverize ['pʌlvəraiz] *v* pulverizar. **pulverization** *n* pulverización *f*.

pump [pʌmp] *n* bomba *f*; (*petrol*) surtidor *m*; (*plimsoll*) zapato de lona *m*. *v* bombear; sacar. **pump up** inflar.

pumpkin ['pʌmpkin] *n* calabaza *f*.

pun [pʌn] *n* retruécano *m*.

punch¹ [pʌntʃ] *n* puñetazo *m*; golpe *m*. *v* dar um puñetazo.

punch² [pʌntʃ] *n* (*drink*) ponche *m*.

punch³ [pʌntʃ] *n* (*tool*) sacabocados *m* invar; perforadora *f*. *v* taladrar; perforar; picar.

punctual ['pʌŋktʃuəl] *adj* puntual. **punctuality** *n* puntualidad *f*.

punctuate ['pʌŋktʃueit] v puntuar. **punctuation** n puntuación f.

puncture ['pʌŋktʃə] n (tyre) pinchazo m; (leather, skin) perforación f. **have a puncture** tener un pinchazo. v pinchar; perforar.

pungent ['pʌndʒənt] adj (smell) acre; (taste) picante. **pungency** n acritud f; lo picante; mordazidad f.

punish ['pʌniʃ] v castigar. **punishment** n castigo m.

punt¹ [pʌnt] n (boat) batea f.

punt² [pʌnt] v. (bet) apostar. **punter** n jugador m.

puny ['pjuːni] adj escuchimizado.

pupil¹ ['pjuːpl] n alumno, -a m, f.

pupil² ['pjuːpl] n (eye) pupila f.

puppet ['pʌpit] n títere m; marioneta f.

puppy ['pʌpi] n cachorro m.

purchase ['pəɪtʃəs] n compra f. **purchase tax** impuesto sobre la venta m. v comprar.

pure ['pjuə] adj puro. **purify** v purificar. **purist** n purista m, f. **purity** n pureza f.

purée ['pjuərei] n puré m.

purgatory ['pəɪgətəri] n purgatorio m.

purge [pəɪdʒ] v purgar; purificar. n purga f. **purgative** nm, adj purgante.

puritan ['pjuəritən] n, adj puritano, -a. **puritanical** adj puritano.

purl [pəɪl] v ribetear; hacer al revés. n (on lace) puntilla f; (thread) hilo de oro o de plata m.

purple ['pəɪpl] nm, adj morado.

purpose ['pəɪpəs] n propósito m, objetivo m; destino m; determinación f; uso m; utilidad f. **on purpose** a propósito. **purposeful** adj decidido; (person) resuelto; útil.

purr [pəɪ] v ronronear. n ronroneo m.

purse [pəɪs] n monedero m, portamonedas m invar; (prize) premio m. v **purse one's lips** apretar los labios.

purser ['pəɪsə] n contador m.

pursue [pə'sjuɪ] v perseguir. **pursuer** n perseguidor, -a m, f. **pursuit** n persecución f; profesión f; ocupación f; pasatiempo m.

pus [pʌs] n pus m.

push [puʃ] n empujón m; (force) empuje m. v empujar; presionar; (notice on doors) empujen. **be pushed for time** tener prisa. **pushing** adj ambicioso.

*****put** [put] v poner; meter; echar; (question) hacer; (state) decir. **put away**

guardar; (money) ahorrar. **put back** volver a poner; (clock) atrasar. **put down** bajar; (in writing) apuntar; (repress) reprimir; (kill) sacrificar. **put off** (postpone) aplazar; (disgust) censar; (revolt) asquear; disuadir. **put on** (clothes) ponerse; (a show) representar; (pretend) fingir. **put up** levantar; (hang) colgar; (resistance) oponer; (build) construir. **put up with** aguantar; conformarse con. **put upon** engañar.

putrid ['pjuːtrid] adj pútrido; podrido.

putt [pʌt] n put m. v tirar al hoyo. **putter** n putter m.

putty ['pʌti] n masilla f.

puzzle ['pʌzl] n enigma f; (game) rompecabezas m invar. v dejar perplejo. **puzzle out** resolver; descifrar. **puzzling** adj enigmático; misterioso.

pyjamas [pə'dʒɑːməz] pl n pijama m sing.

pylon ['pailən] n poste m.

pyramid ['pirəmid] n pirámide f.

python ['paiθən] n pitón m.

Q

quack¹ [kwak] n (duck) graznido m. v graznar.

quack² [kwak] n charlatán m.

quadrangle ['kwodraŋgl] n (courtyard) patio m; (math) cuadrángulo m.

quadrant ['kwodrənt] n cuadrante m.

quadrilateral [kwodrə'latərəl] nm, adj cuadrilátero.

quadruped ['kwodruped] nm, adj cuadrúpedo.

quadruple [kwod'ruːpl] adj cuádruple.

quadruplets [kwo'druːplits] pl n cuatrillizos, -as m, f pl.

quagmire ['kwagmaiə] n pantano m.

quail¹ [kweil] n (zool) codorniz f.

quail² [kweil] v acobardarse.

quaint [kweint] adj pintoresco; excéntrico.

quake [kweik] v estremecerse. n estremecimiento. **quake with fear** temblar de miedo.

qualify ['kwolifai] v (entitle) capacitar; calificar; modificar; limitar. **qualification** n reserva f; aptitud f; requisito m. **qualifications** pl n títulos m pl. **qualified** adj competente; capacitado; titulado; con reservas.

quality ['kwolɔti] n (*attribute*) cualidad *f*; calidad *f*.

qualm [kwaim] n escrúpulo *m*.

quandary ['kwondɔri] n incertidumbre *f*, dilema *m*.

quantify ['kwontifai] v determinar la cantidad de.

quantity ['kwontɔti] n cantidad *f*.

quarantine ['kworɔntiin] n cuarentena *f*. v someter a cuarentena.

quarrel ['kworɔl] n disputa *f*, pelea *f*. v disputar, pelear. **quarrelsome** *adj* peleador.

quarry[1] ['kwori] n (*stone, etc.*) cantera *f*. v explotar una cantera.

quarry[2] ['kwori] n presa *f*.

quarter ['kwoitɔ] n cuarto *m*; cuarta parte *f*; (*of year*) trimestre *m*; (*district*) barrio *m*. **quarter-final** n cuarto de final *m*. **quartermaster** n (*naut*) cabo de la marina *m*. **quarter past four** las cuatro y quince. **quarters** pl n (*mil*) cuartel *m* sing. **at close quarters** de cerca. **quarter to four** las cuatro menos cuarto. v dividir en cuatros; (*mil*) acuartelar. **quarterly** *adj* trimestral.

quartet [kwor'tet] n cuarteto *m*.

quartz [kwoits] n cuarzo *m*.

quash [kwoʃ] v amular; ahogar; (*rebellion*) reprimir.

quaver ['kweivɔ] n (*music*) corchea *f*; temblor *m*. v temblar.

quay [kii] n muelle *m*.

queasy ['kwiizi] *adj* (*sick*) mareado; (*upset*) delicado. **queasiness** n náuseas *f* pl.

queen [kwiim] n reina *f*; (*cards*) dama *f*. **Queen Mother** reina madre *f*.

queer [kwiɔ] *adj* raro; curioso; (*unwell*) indispuesto; (*slang: homosexual*) maricón. n (*slang*) maricón *m*, marica *f*.

quell [kwel] v reprimir.

quench [kwentʃ] v (*flames*) apagar; (*thirst*) aplacar; (*desire*) sofocar.

query ['kwiɔri] n pregunta *f*; duda *f*. v preguntar; dudar (de).

quest [kwest] n búsqueda *f*.

question ['kwestʃɔn] n pregunta *f*; cuestión *f*; problema *m*. **begging the question** petición de principio *f*. **beside the question** que no viene al caso. **out of the question** imposible. **question mark** signo de interrogación *m*. **without question** sin

duda. v preguntar; interrogar; poner en duda. **questionable** *adj* dudoso; discutible. **questioning** n interrogatorio *m*. **questionnaire** n cuestionario *m*.

queue [kjui] n cola *f*. v hacer cola.

quibble ['kwibl] n pega *f*; subterfugio *m*. v sutilizar; (*find fault*) ser quisquilloso.

quick [kwik] *adj* rápido; (*reply*) pronto; (*lively*) vivo; (*clever*) agudo; (*on feet*) ligero. **quicksand** n avena movediza *f*. **quick-tempered** *adj* irascible. **quick-witted** *adj* agudo. **quicken** v acelerar; estimular. **quickly** *adv* rápidamente.

quid [kwid] n (*coll*) libra *f*.

quiet ['kwaiɔt] *adj* silencioso; callado; (*step*) ligero; tranquilo; (*dress*) sobrio. n *also* **quietness** tranquilidad *f*; silencio *m*; reposo *m*. **quieten** v callar; calmar. **quietly** *adv* silenciosamente; tranquilamente.

quill [kwil] n (*feather*) pluma *f*; (*pen*) cálamo *m*; (*porcupine*) púa *f*.

quilt [kwilt] n colcha *f*; (*eiderdown*) edredón *m*. v acolchar.

quince [kwins] n membrillo *m*.

quinine [kwi'niin] n quinina *f*.

quinsy ['kwinzi] n angina *f*.

quintet [kwin'tet] n quinteto *m*.

quirk [kwɔik] n peculiaridad *f*.

quit [kwit] v (*job*) abandonar; (*place*) dejar; (*leave*) irse de.

quite [kwait] *adv* completamente, enteramente; exactamente; verdaderamente; (*fairly*) bastante.

quiver[1] ['kwivɔ] v tremblar; estremecerse. n temblor *m*; estremecimiento *m*.

quiver[2] ['kwivɔ] n (*for arrows*) aljaba *f*.

quiz [kwiz] n (*inquiry*) encuesta *f*; (*questioning*) interrogatorio *m*; examen *m*. v interrogar.

quizzical ['kwizikl] *adj* curioso; (*bantering*) burlón.

quota ['kwoutɔ] n cupo *m*; (*share*) cuota *f*.

quote [kwout] v citar; dar; (*comm*) cotizar. **quotation** n cita *f*; (*comm*) cotización *f*. **quotation marks** comillas *f* pl.

R

rabbi ['rabai] *n* rabino *m*.

rabbit ['rabit] *n* conejo *m*.

rabble ['rabl] *n* gentío *m*; (*derog*) populacho *m*.

rabies ['reibiːz] *n* rabia *f*. **rabid** *adj* rabioso.

race[1] [reis] *n* carrera *f*; (*yacht*) regata *f*. **racehorse** *n* caballo de carreras *m*. *v* (*person*) competir con; (*horse*) hacer correr; (*pulse*) latir a ritmo acelerado.

race[2] [reis] *n* raza *f*; familia *f*. **racial** *adj* racial. **racialism** *n also* **racism** racismo *m*. **racialist** *n*(*m*+*f*), *adj also* **racist** racista.

rack [rak] *n* (*shelf*) estante *m*; (*coats, etc.*) percha *f*; (*plates*) escurreplatos *m invar*; (*car roof*) baca *f*; (*torture*) potre *m*. *v* atormentar. **rack one's brains** devanarse los sesos.

racket[1] ['rakit] *n* (*sport*) raqueta *f*.

racket[2] ['rakit] *n* (*noise*) alboroto *m*, barullo *m*; (*coll: crime*) tráfico *m*; timo *m*.

radar ['reidaː] *n* radar *m*.

radial ['reidiəl] *adj* radial. **radial tyre** neumático radial *m*.

radiant ['reidiənt] *adj* resplandeciente. **radiance** *n* resplandor *m*.

radiate ['reidieit] *v* (*heat*) irradiar; (*rays*) emitir; (*spread*) difundir. **radiation** *n* radiación *f*. **radiator** *n* radiador *m*.

radical ['radikəl] *nm, adj* radical.

radio ['reidiou] *n* radio *f*. **radio beacon** radiofaro *m*. **radio contact** radiocomunicación *f*. **radio control** teledirección *f*. **radio station** emisora *f*. **radio wave** onda *f*. *v* transmitir por radio.

radioactive [reidiou'aktiv] *adj* radioactivo. **radioactivity** *n* radioactividad *f*.

radiography [reidi'ogrəfi] *n* radiografía *f*. **radiographer** *n* radiógrafo *m*.

radiology [reidi'olədʒi] *n* radiología *f*. **radiologist** *n* radiólogo *m*.

radiotherapy [reidiou'θerəpi] *n* radioterapia *f*.

radish ['radiʃ] *n* rábano *m*.

radium ['reidiəm] *n* radio *m*.

radius ['reidiəs] *n* radio *m*.

raffia ['rafiə] *n* rafia *f*.

raffle ['rafl] *n* rifa *f*. *v* rifar.

raft [raːft] *n* balsa *f*.

rafter ['raːftə] *n* viga *f*.

rag[1] [rag] *n* (*waste piece*) harapo *m*; (*cleaning*) trapo *m*; (*derog: newspaper*) periodicucho *m*. **ragamuffin** *n* golfo *m*.

ragged *adj* (*clothes*) hecho jirones; (*edge*) mellado.

rag[2] [rag] *v* (*coll*) tomar el pelo a. *n* payasadas *f pl*. **ragtime** *n* música sincopada *f*.

rage [reidʒ] *n* (*anger*) cólera *f*, rabia *f*; (*of elements*) furia *f*; (*fashion*) moda *f*. **be all the rage** hacer furor. *v* (*be angry*) estar furioso; (*wind, fire, beasts*) bramar; (*sea*) alborotarse. **raging** *adj* (*person*) furioso; (*pain*) muy fuerte; (*storm*) encrespado.

raid [reid] *n* (*mil*) correría *f*; (*aerial*) ataque *m*; (*police*) redada *f*; (*robbery*) asalto *m*. *v* hacer una redada; asaltar. **raider** *n* invasor *m*; (*thief*) ladrón *m*.

rail [reil] *n* (*stairs*) barandilla *f*; (*bridge*) antepecho *m*; (*balcony*) baranda *f*; (*bar*) barra *f*; (*fence*) cerco *m*; (*train, tram*) vía férrea *f*. **by rail** por ferrocarril. **railway** *or* US **railroad** *n* ferrocarril *m*.

railings ['reiliŋz] *pl n* barandilla *f sing*.

rain [rein] *n* lluvia *f*. **rainbow** *n* arco iris *m*. **raincoat** *n* impermeable *m*. **raindrop** *n* gota de lluvia *f*. **rainfall** *n* precipitación *f*; **rainwater** *n* agua de lluvia *f*. *v* llover. **rainy** *adj* lluvioso.

raise [reiz] *v* alzar, levantar; (*increase*) aumentar; provocar; (*problem*) plantar; (*animals*) criar.

raisin ['reizən] *n* pasa *f*.

rake [reik] *n* rastro *m*. *v* rastrillar. **rake together** reunir a duras penas.

rally ['rali] *n* reunión *f*; (*pol*) mitin político *m*; (*mot*) rallye *m*; (*tennis*) peloteo *m*. *v* reunir; (*recover*) recuperarse. **rally round** tomar el partido de.

ram [ram] *n* carnero *m*; (*battering ram*) ariete *m*. *v* (*earth, etc.*) apisonar; (*fist, head*) dar con; (*pack*) meter a la fuerza.

ramble ['rambl] *n* excursión *f*. *v* pasear; (*fig*) divagar.

ramp [ramp] *n* rampa *f*.

rampage ['rampeidʒ] *n* **be on the rampage** alborotar.

rampant ['rampənt] *adj* (*plant*) exuberante; (*heraldry*) rampante; (*aggressive*) violento. **be rampant** estar difundido.

rampart ['rampaɪt] *n* terraplén *m*, muralla *f*.

ramshackle ['ramʃakl] *adj* desvenajado.

ran [ran] *V* run.

ranch [raɪntʃ] *n* rancho *m*; hacienda *f*.

rancid ['ransid] *adj* rancio.

rancour ['raŋkə] *n* rencor *m*.

random ['randəm] *n* at random al azar. *adj* hecho al azar. random sample muestra cogida al azar *f*.

rang [raŋ] *V* ring.

range [reindʒ] *n* (*row*) fila *f*; (*mountains*) sierra *f*; (*area*) extensión *f*; (*distance*) alcance *m*; (*of an aircraft*) autonomía *f*; (*mil: firing*) campo de tiro *m*; (*voice*) registro *m*; (*colours, prices*) gama *f*; (*subjects*) variedad *f*; (*grazing land*) dehesa *f*; (*cooking stove*) cocina económica *f*. *v* (*place*) colocar; (*put in a row*) alinear; clasificar; (*wander*) recorrer.

rank¹ [raŋk] *n* fila *f*; grado *m*; categoría *f*. the rank and file la tropa *f*; (*ordinary people*) gente del montón *f*. *v* (*estimate*) situar, poner; figurar; (*mil*) alinear.

rank² [raŋk] *adj* lozano; rancio.

rankle ['raŋkl] *v* escocer.

ransack ['ransak] *v* saquear; (*search*) registrar.

ransom ['ransəm] *n* rescate *m*. hold to ransom exigir rescate. *v* rescatar.

rap [rap] *v* golpear. *n* golpecito *m*.

rape [reip] *n* violación *f*. *v* violar. rapist *n* violador *m*.

rapid ['rapid] *adj* rápido. rapids *pl n* rápidos *m pl*. rapidity *n* rapidez *f*.

rapier ['reipiə] *n* estoque *m*.

rapport [ra'pɔɪ] *n* relación *f*; armonía *f*.

rapture ['raptʃə] *n* éxtasis *m invar*. go into raptures over extasiarse por.

rare¹ ['reə] *adj* raro. rarity *n* rareza *f*.

rare² ['reə] *adj* (*cookery*) poco hecho.

rascal ['raɪskəl] *n* bribón *m*, pícaro *m*.

rash¹ [raʃ] *adj* temerario. rashness *n* temeridad *f*.

rash² [raʃ] *n* (*med*) erupción *f*.

rasher ['raʃə] *n* loncha *f*.

raspberry ['razbəri] *n* (*fruit*) frambuesa *f*; (*bush*) frambueso *m*.

rat [rat] *n* rata *f*. rat poison matarratas *m invar*. rat race competencia *f*.

rate [reit] *n* proporción *f*; índice *m*; velocidad *f*; ritmo *m*; precio; (*discount, interest*) tipo *m*; (*pulse*) frecuencia *f*. at any rate de todos modos. ratepayer *n* contribuyente *m, f*. rates *pl n* contribución municipal *f sing*. *v* valorar; considerar; clasificar; estimar. rateable *adj* valorable.

rather ['raɪðə] *adv* más bien; bastante; (*fairly*) algo. I would rather ... prefiero . . . .

ratify ['ratifai] *v* ratificar. ratification *n* ratificación *f*.

ratio ['reiʃiou] *n* razón *f*, relación *f*.

ration ['raʃən] *n* ración *f*. *v* racionar. rationing *n* racionamiento *m*.

rational ['raʃənl] *adj* racional; razonable; lógico. rationale *n* razón fundamental *f*. rationalize *v* racionalizar.

rattle ['ratl] *n* (*toy*) sonajero *m*; (*football fan's*) carraca *f*; ruido de sonajero; (*train noise*) traqueteo *m*; (*chains*) ruido metálico *m*; (*door, window*) golpe *m*; (*teeth*) castañeteo *m*; (*machine gun*) tableteo *m*; *v* hacer sonar; traquetear; hacer un ruido metálico; golpetear; castañetear; tabletear; (*put off*) desconcertar.

raucous ['rɔːkəs] *adj* ronco.

ravage ['ravidʒ] *n* estrago *m*. *v* asolar.

rave [reiv] *v* delirar, desvariar. rave over entusiasmarse por. raving *adj* delirante.

raven ['reivən] *n* cuervo *m*.

ravenous ['ravənəs] *adj* hambriento. be ravenous tener um hambre canina.

ravine [rə'viːn] *n* desfiladero *m*.

ravish ['raviʃ] *v* violar; raptar. ravishing *adj* encantador.

raw [rɔɪ] *adj* (*uncooked*) crudo; (*unrefined*) bruto; (*inexperienced*) novato; (*nerves*) a flor de piel; (*flesh*) vivo; (*weather*) frío y húmedo. raw deal (*coll*) injusticia *f*. raw materials materias primas *f pl*. rawness *n* crudeza *f*.

ray [rei] *n* rayo *m*; (*line, fish*) raya *f*.

rayon ['reion] *n* rayón *m*.

razor ['reizə] *n* navaja *f*; (*safety*) maquinilla de afeitar *f*; (*elec*) máquina de afeitar eléctrica *f*. razor blade hoja de afeitar *f*.

reach [riːtʃ] *v* (*arrive at*) llegar a; (*achieve*) lograr; (*stretch out*) extender; alcanzar. *n* alcance *m*; poder *m*; capacidad *f*. out of reach fuera del alcance. within reach al alcance.

react [ri'akt] *v* reaccionar. reaction *n* reacción *f*. reactionary *n, adj* reaccionario, -a. reactor *n* reactor *m*.

*read [riːd] *v* leer; estudiar; (*public address*) decir; (*riddle*) interpretar; (*meter, etc.*) marcar. reader *n* lector, -a *m, f*; (*university*) profesor, -a *m, f*; (*book*) libro de lectura *m*. reading *n* lectura *f*; estudio *m*; interpretación *f*. reading-glass *n* lente para leer *m*. reading-lamp lámpara de sobremesa *f*.

readjust [riːəˈdʒʌst] v reajustar. **readjustment** n reajuste m.

ready [ˈredi] adj listo; pronto; a mano. **get ready** prepararse. **ready cash** dinero contante m. **ready-made** adj hecho. **readily** adv fácilmente; en seguida. **readiness** n prontitud f; facilidad f.

real [riəl] adj real, verdadero. **realism** n realismo m. **realist** n realista m, f. **reality** n realidad f, verdad f. **really** adv realmente, en verdad. **really?** ¿de veras?

realize [ˈriəlaiz] v (understand) darse cuenta de; (achieve) llevar a cabo; (make real) realizar. **realization** n comprensión f; realización f.

realm [relm] n reino m; (fig) esfera f.

reap [riːp] v segar; (fig) cosechar. **reaping** n siega f; cosecha f. **reaping machine** segadora mecánica f.

reappear [riːəˈpiə] v reaparecer. **reappearance** n reaparición f.

rear[1] [riə] adj posterior, de atrás. **rear-admiral** n contraalmirante m. **rearguard** n retaguardia f. **rear-view mirror** retrovisor m. n parte posterior f, parte de atrás f; (of a column) cola f. **bring up the rear** cerrar la marcha.

rear[2] [riə] v (family) criar; (lift up) alzar, levantar; (horse, etc.) empinarse.

rearrange [riːəˈreindʒ] v arreglar de otra manera; volver a arreglar. **rearrangement** n nuevo arreglo m.

reason [ˈriːzn] n razón f. v razonar. **reasonable** adj razonable. **reasoning** n razonamiento m.

reassure [riːəˈʃuə] v asegurar de nuevo; confortar. **reassurance** n confianza restablecida f. **reassuring** adj tranquilizador.

rebate [ˈriːbeit] n rebaja f, descuento m.

rebel [ˈrebl] n(m+f). adj rebelde. v rebelarse. **rebellion** n rebelión f. **rebellious** adj rebelde.

rebound [riˈbaund; n ˈriːbaund] v rebotar. n rebote m.

rebuff [riˈbʌf] v rechazar. n desaire m.

***rebuild** [riːˈbild] v reedificar.

rebuke [riˈbjuːk] n censura f, reproche m. v censurar, reprochar.

recall [riˈkɔːl] v llamar; recordar. n llamada f; (dismissal) destitución f.

recant [riˈkant] v retractar.

recap [ˈriːkap] v (coll) recapitular. n recapitulación f.

recapture [riˈkaptʃə] v reconquistar; (recreate) hacer revivir. n reconquista f.

recede [riˈsiːd] v retroceder; (tide) descender.

receipt [rəˈsiːt] n (act of receiving) recepción f; (slip of paper) recibo m.

receive [rəˈsiːv] v recibir; aceptar. **receiver** n (of loot) recibidor, -a m, f; (law) síndico m; (phone) auricular m.

recent [ˈriːsnt] adj reciente. **recently** adv recientemente.

receptacle [rəˈseptəkl] n receptáculo m.

reception [rəˈsepʃən] n recepción f; acogida f. **receptionist** n recepcionista m, f. **receptive** adj receptivo.

recess [riˈses] n (hollow) hueco m; (niche) nicho m; (parliament) período de clausura m; (rest) descanso m.

recession [rəˈseʃən] n (comm) recesión f; (retreat) retroceso m.

recharge [riˈtʃɑːdʒ] v recargar.

recipe [ˈresəpi] n receta f.

recipient [rəˈsipiənt] n (receiver) receptor, -a m, f; (cheque, letter, etc.) destinatario, -a m, f.

reciprocate [rəˈsiprəkeit] v corresponder; intercambiar. **reciprocating engine** motor alternativo m. **reciprocal** adj recíproco.

recite [rəˈsait] v recitar. **recital** n (a relating) relato m; (music) recital m. **recitation** n relato m; recitación f.

reckless [ˈrekləs] adj temerario; audaz. **recklessness** n temeridad f; audacia f.

reckon [ˈrekən] v calcular; contar; considerar; (coll) creer. **reckoning** n cálculo m; cuenta f; (fig) retribución f.

reclaim [riˈkleim] v (land) ganar; (reform) reformar; (by-product) regenerar. **reclamation** n (claiming back) reclamación f; (moral) enmienda f; (land) aprovechamiento m; regeneración f.

recline [rəˈklain] v apoyar; recostar.

recluse [rəˈkluːs] n recluso, -a m, f.

recognize [ˈrekəgnaiz] v reconocer; confesar. **recognition** n reconocimiento m. **recognizable** adj identificable.

recoil [rəˈkoil; n ˈriːkoil] v echarse atrás; (gun) dar culatazo; (spring) aflojarse. n culatazo m; aflojamiento m; (repugnance) asco m.

recollect [rekəˈlekt] v acordarse de. **recollection** n recuerdo m.

recommence [rekəˈmens] v empezar de nuevo.

recommend [rekəˈmend] v recomendar; aconsejar. **recommendation** n recomendación f.

recompense ['rekəmpens] *n* recompensa *f*; (*law*) compensación *f*. *v* recompensar; compensar.

reconcile ['rekənsail] *v* (*dispute*) arreglar; (*individuals*) reconciliar; (*ideas*) conciliar. **reconcile oneself to** resignarse a. **reconciliation** *n* arreglo *m*; reconciliación *f*; conciliación *f*.

reconstruct [riːkən'strʌkt] *v* (*building*) reconstruir; (*crime*) reconstituir. **reconstruction** *n* reconstrucción *f*; reconstitución *f*.

record [rə'koid; *n* 'rekoid] *v* registrar; tomar nota de; (*sound*) grabar. *n* registro *m*; anotación *f*; grabación *f*; disco *m*; (*account*) relación *f*; (*minutes*) actas *f pl*; (*personal history*) historial *m*; (*sport*) récord *m*. **long-playing record** disco de larga duración *m*. **record-player** *n* tocadiscos *m invar*. **recorded** *adj* grabado; registrado. **recorded delivery** entrega registrada *f*. **recorder** *n* archivista *m*, *f*; (*music*) flauta *f*. **recording** *n* (*music*) grabación *f*.

recount [ri'kaunt; *n* 'riːkaunt] *v* contar. *n* recuento *m*.

recoup [ri'kuːp] *v* (*recover*) recuperar; (*compensate*) indemnizar.

recover [rə'kʌvə] *v* (*get back*) recuperar; (*get well*) recobrar; ganar; obtener. **recovery** *n* recuperación *f*; (*med*) restablecimiento *m*.

recreation [rekri'eiʃən] *n* recreación *f*; (*school break*) recreo *m*.

recrimination [rəkrimi'neiʃən] *n* recriminación *f*. **recriminate** *v* recriminar.

recruit [rə'kruːt] *n* recluta *m*. *v* reclutar. **recruitment** *n* reclutamiento *m*.

rectangle ['rektaŋgl] *n* rectángulo *m*. **rectangular** *adj* rectangular.

rectify ['rektifai] *v* rectificar.

rectum ['rektəm] *n* recto *m*.

recuperate [rə'kjuːpəreit] *v* recuperar; (*health*) recobrar. **recuperation** *n* recuperación *f*; (*health*) restablecimiento *m*.

recur [ri'kəː] *v* volver; repetirse. **recurrence** *n* vuelta *f*; repetición *f*; reaparición *f*. **recurrent** *adj also* **recurring** periódico; que vuelve; (*med*) recurrente.

red [red] *n* rojo *m*, colorado *m*. **in the red** deber dinero. *adj* rojo, colorado. **go red** ruborizarse. **Red Cross** Cruz Roja *f*. **redcurrant** grosella *f*. **red-handed** *adv* con las manos en la masa. **redhead** *n* pelirrojo, -a *m*, *f*. **red-hot** *adj* al rojo; ardiente. **red-letter day** día memorable

m. **red-light district** barrio de mala fama *m*. **red tape** (*coll*) papeleo *m*. **redness** *n* color rojo *m*.

redeem [rə'diːm] *v* (*promise*) cumplir; (*mortgage*) amortizar; (*pawn*) desempeñar; (*fault*) expiar; (*rescue*) rescatar. **redemption** *n* cumplimiento *m*; amortización *f*; desempeño *m*; expiación *f*; rescate *m*; (*rel*) redención *f*. **beyond redemption** sin redención, irremediable.

redirect [riːdai'rekt] *v* (*letter*, *etc.*) remitir al destinatario.

redress [rə'dres] *v* rectificar. *n* reparación *f*.

reduce [rə'djuːs] *v* reducir; rebajar; (*slim*) adelgazar. **reduction** *n* reducción *f*; (*length*) acortamiento *m*; (*width*) estrechamiento; (*weight*) adelgazamiento *m*; (*rank*) degradación *f*; (*prices*) disminución *f*; (*discount*) rebaja *f*; (*temperature*) baja *f*.

redundant [rə'dʌndənt] *adj* excesivo, superfluo. **be made redundant** perder su empleo. **redundancy** *n* desempleo *m*.

reed [riːd] *n* caña *f*; (*of wind instrument*) lengüeta *f*.

reef [riːf] *n* arrecife *m*.

reek [riːk] *v* apestar. *n* tufo *m*.

reel[1] [riːl] *n* (*cotton*) carrete *m*, bobina *f*; (*film*) cinta; (*fishing*) carretel *m*. **reel off** (*recite*) recitar de un tirón.

reel[2] [riːl] *v* (*sway*) hacer eses, dar vueltas.

refectory [rə'fektəri] *n* refectorio *m*.

refer [rə'fəː] *v* remitir; enviar; (*date*, *event*) situar; atribuir. **reference** *n* referencia *f*; alusión *f*; relación *f*; (*source of information*) fuente *f*; (*person*) fiador *m*. **reference book** libro de consulta *m*. **reference library** biblioteca de consulta *f*. **reference number** número de referencia *m*. **terms of reference** mandato *m*. **make reference to** referirse a. **without reference to** sin consultar. **with reference to** en cuanto a.

referee [refə'riː] *n* árbitro *m*; (*guarantor of character*) garante *m*. *v* arbitrar.

referendum [refə'rendəm] *n* referéndum *m*.

refill [riː'fil; *n* 'riːfil] *v* rellenar. *n* recambio *m*; carga *f*.

refine [rə'fain] *v* refinar; purificar; (*technique*) perfeccionar; (*style*) pulir. **refinement** *n* (*person*) refinamiento *m*; (*manners*) finura *f*; (*sugar*, *oil*) refinado *m*;

(*metal*) purificación *f*; (*technique*) perfeccionamiento *m*; (*style*) elegancia *f*. **refinery** *n* refinería *f*.

reflect [rə'flekt] *v* reflejar; (*think*) reflexionar. **reflection** *n* (*image*) reflejo *m*; (*act*) reflexión; meditación *f*; crítica *f*.

reflex ['rifleks] *nm, adj* reflejo. **reflexive** *adj* reflexivo.

reform [rə'fɔim] *v* reformar; formar de nuevo. *n* reforma *f*. **reformation** *n* reformación *f*. **reformed** *adj* reformado.

refract [rə'frakt] *v* refractar. **refraction** *n* refracción *f*.

refrain¹ [rə'frein] *v* abstenerse.

refrain² [rə'frein] *n* estribillo *m*.

refresh [rə'freʃ] *v* refrescar. **refresher course** cursillo de repaso *m*. **refreshing** *adj* refrescante. **refreshments** *pl n* refrescos *m pl*.

refrigerator [rə'fridʒəreitə] *n* refrigerador *m*, nevera *f*. **refrigerate** *v* refrigerar. **refrigeration** *n* refrigeración *f*.

refuel [ri:'fjuəl] *v* repostar(se).

refuge ['refjuidʒ] *n* refugio *m*; asilo *m*. **take refuge** refugiarse en. **refugee** *n* refugiado, -a *m, f*.

refund [ri'fʌnd; *n* 'ri:fʌnd] *v* reembolsar. *n* reembolso *m*.

refuse¹ [rə'fjuiz] *v* negar. **refusal** *n* negativa *f*; (*rejection*) rechazo *m*.

refuse² ['refjuis] *n* basura *f*, desecho *m*, desperdicios *m pl*.

refute [ri'fjuit] *v* refutar.

regain [ri'gein] *v* recobrar; (*return to*) volver a.

regal ['riigəl] *adj* real, regio.

regard [rə'gaid] *v* mirar; observar; considerar. **as regards** con respecto a. *n* mirada *f*; atención *f*; respeto *m*; aprecio *m*. **regards** *pl n* (*in a letter*) saludos *m pl*. **regarding** *prep* con respecto a. **regardless** *adv* a pesar de todo. **regardless of** sin tener en cuenta.

regatta [rə'gatə] *n* regata *f*.

regent ['riidʒənt] *n* regente *m, f*. **regency** *n* regencia *f*.

regime [rei'ʒiim] *n* régimen *m*.

regiment ['redʒimənt] *n* regimiento *m*. **regimental** *adj* del regimiento.

region ['riidʒən] *n* región *f*. **regional** *adj* regional.

register ['redʒistə] *n* registro *m*; lista *f*. *v* registrar; (*a complaint*) presentar; (*luggage*) facturar; (*letter*) certificar; (*birth*, death) declarar. **registrar** *n* registrador *m*; (*med*) doctor, -a *m, f*. **registration** *n* (*trademark*) registro *m*; inscripción *f*; declaración *f*; certificación *f*; facturación *f*; matrícula *f*. **registration number** número de matrícula *m*. **registration plate** placa de matrícula *f*. **registry office** registro civil *m*.

regress [ri'gres] *v* retroceder. **regression** *n* regresión *f*.

regret [rə'gret] *v* sentir, lamentar. *n* sentimiento *m*; pesar *m*; arrepentimiento *m*; excusas *f pl*. **regrettable** *adj* lamentable; doloroso.

regular ['regjulə] *adj* regular; normal; habituado. *n* (*mil*) regular; (*bar*) asiduo, -a *m, f*. **regularity** *n* regularidad *f*.

regulate ['regjuleit] *v* regular; ajustar.

regulation [regju'leiʃən] *n* regulación *f*; regla *f*. *adj* reglamentario.

rehabilitate [ri:hə'biliteit] *v* (*reputation*) rehabilitar; (*for work*) restaurar. **rehabilitation** *n* reconstrucción *f*; (*med*) reeducación *f*.

rehearse [rə'həis] *v* ensayar. **rehearsal** *n* ensayo *m*.

reign [rein] *n* reinado *m*; dominio *m*. *v* reinar.

reimburse [ri:im'bəis] *v* reembolsar. **reimbursement** *n* reembolso *m*.

rein [rein] *n* rienda *f*; (*fig*) riendas *f pl*.

reincarnation [ri:inkai'neiʃən] *n* reencarnación *f*.

reindeer ['reindiə] *n* reno *m*.

reinforce [ri:in'fɔis] *v* reforzar. **reinforcement** *n* refuerzo *m*. **reinforced concrete** hormigón armado *m*.

reinstate [ri:in'steit] *v* reinstalar; restablecer. **reinstatement** *n* reintegración *f*, restablecimiento *m*.

reinvest [ri:in'vest] *v* reinvertir. **reinvestment** *n* reinversión *f*.

reissue [ri:'iʃui] *v* (*book*) reeditar; (*shares, stamps*) volver a emitir.

reject [rə'dʒekt; *n* 'ri:dʒekt] *v* rechazar. *n* cosa defectuosa *f*. **rejection** *n* rechazamiento *m*; (*a reject*) cosa rechazada *f*.

rejoice [rə'dʒois] *v* alegrar, regocijar. **rejoicing** *n* alegría *f*, regocijo *m*.

rejoin [rə'dʒoin] *v* (*reply*) replicar; (*club, society, etc.*) reincorporarse a; (*friends*) reunirse con; (*two objects*) volver a unirse a.

rejuvenate [rə'dʒuːvəneit] v rejuvenecer. **rejuvenation** n rejuvenecimiento m.

relapse [rə'læps] n recaída f; (med) recidiva f. v recaer; reincidir.

relate [rə'leit] v (tell) contar; (be connected) relacionar. **related** adj (subjects) relacionado; (by birth or marriage) emparentado. **relating to** lo que tiene que ver con.

relation [rə'leiʃn] n (account) narración f; (relative) pariente, -a m, f; (connection) relación f. **relationship** n relación f; (kinship) parentesco m.

relative ['relətiv] adj relativo. n pariente, -a m, f. **relatively** adv relativamente. **relativity** n relatividad f.

relax [rə'læks] v relajar; (loosen) aflojar. **relaxation** n relajación f; descanso m; distracción f. **relaxing** adj relajante.

relay [ri'lei; n 'riːlei] v transmitir. n relevo m. **relay race** carrera de relevos f.

release [rə'liːs] n liberación f; (exemption) exención f; (film, record) salida f; (information) anuncio m; (gas, steam) escape m. v liberar; (film, record) estrenar; anunciar; (let go) soltar; (mechanism) disparar.

relegate ['religeit] v relegar. **relegation** n relegación f.

relent [rə'lent] v ceder; enternecerse. **relentless** adj inexorable.

relevant ['reləvənt] adj pertinente; relativo; aplicable. **relevance** n pertinencia f; aplicabilidad f.

reliable [ri'laiəbl] adj de confianza; seguro. **reliability** n seguridad f; formalidad f.

reliance [rə'laiəns] n dependencia f; (trust) confianza f.

relic ['relik] n reliquia f; vestigio m.

relief [rə'liːf] n alivio m; (aid) socorro m; (for the poor) auxilio m; (substitute worker) relevo m; (geog, art) relieve m. adj suplementario.

relieve [rə'liːv] v aliviar; liberar; (replace) relevar; (help) socorrer.

religion [rə'lidʒən] n religión f. **religious** adj religioso.

relinquish [rə'liŋkwiʃ] v renunciar.

relish ['reliʃ] v (food) saborear; (enjoy) disfrutar. n gusto m; atracción f; entusiasmo m; (food) condimento m.

relive [riː'liv] v volver a vivir, revivir.

reluctant [rə'lʌktənt] adj maldispuesto.

reluctance n resistencia f. **reluctantly** adv de mala gana.

rely [rə'lai] v **rely on** contar con, confiar en.

remain [rə'mein] v quedarse. **remainder** n residuo m; resto m. **remains** pl n restos m pl; ruinas f pl.

remand [rə'maind] v reencarcelar. n reencarcelamiento m. **be on remand** estar detenido.

remark [rə'maːk] n observación f; comentario m. v observar, notar; hacer una observación. **remarkable** adj notable.

remarry [riː'mari] v volver a casarse. **remarriage** n segundas nupcias f pl.

remedy ['remədi] n remedio m. v remediar. **remedial** adj remediador; reparador.

remember [ri'membə] v recordar, acordarse de. **remembrance** n recuerdo m.

remind [rə'maind] v recordar. **reminder** n advertencia f; (comm) notificación f.

reminiscence [remə'nisens] n reminiscencia f. **reminisce** v recordar el pasado. **reminiscent** adj evocador. **be reminiscent of** recordar.

remiss [rə'mis] adj descuidado.

remission [rə'miʃn] n remisión f, perdón m; exoneración f.

remit [rə'mit] v (send) remitir; (forgive) perdonar; (return to a lower court) devolver a un tribunal inferior. **remittance** n remesa f.

remnant ['remnənt] n resto m; (fabric) retal m.

remorse [rə'mois] n remordimiento m. **remorseful** adj arrepentido. **remorseless** adj sin remordimientos.

remote [rə'mout] adj (distant) lejano; (in time or space) remoto; (slight) ligero; (out-of-the-way) retirado; (stand-offish) distante. **remote control** mando a distancia m.

remove [rə'muːv] v quitar; sacar; separar; (move house) mudar. **removal** n mudanza f; (transfer) traslado m; (from office) despido m.

remunerate [rə'mjuːnəreit] v remunerar. **remuneration** n remuneración f. **remunerative** adj remunerador.

renaissance [rə'neisəns] n renacimiento m.

rename [riː'neim] v poner un nuevo nombre a.

render ['rendə] v (comm) rendir; dar; (a service) hacer; (assistance) prestar; interpretar; (fat) derretir. **rendering** n also **rendition** interpretación f.

rendezvous ['rondivur] n cita f. v reunir.

renegade ['renigeid] n, adj renegado, -a.

renew [rə'njur] v renovar; (extend) prorogar; (efforts) reanudar. **renewal** n renovación f; prórroga f; (continuation after interruption) reanudación f.

renounce [ri'nauns] v renunciar. **renunciation** n renunciación f.

renovate ['renəveit] v renovar; reformar. **renovation** n renovación f; reforma f.

renown [rə'naun] n renombre m, fama f. **renowned** adj renombrado, afamado.

rent [rent] n alquiler m. **rent-free** sin pagar alquiler. v alquilar. **rental** n alquiler m.

reopen [rir'oupən] v volver a abrir. **reopening** n reapertura f.

reorganize [rir'oɪgɔnaiz] v reorganizar. **reorganization** n reorganización f.

rep [rep] n (coll) viajante m.

repair [ri'peə] v reparar; componer. n reparación f; compostura f; arreglo m. **beyond repair** no tener arreglo. **closed for repairs** cerrado por reformas.

repartee [repar'tiɪ] n respuesta aguda f; (coll) dimes y diretes m pl.

repatriate [rir'patrieit] v repatriar. **repatriation** n repatriación f.

*repay [ri'pei] v (money) devolver; (debt) liquidar; (a person) compensar; (return) corresponder a. **repayment** n devolución f, pago m; (reward) recompensa f.

repeal [ri'piɪl] v revocar, abrogar. n revocación f, abrogación f.

repeat [rə'piɪt] v repitir; recitar. n repetición f.

repel [rə'pel] v repeler; rechazar. **repellent** adj repelente.

repent [rə'pent] v arrepentirse de. **repentance** n arrepentimiento m. **repentant** adj arrepentido.

repercussion [riɪpə'kʌʃən] n repercusión f.

repertoire ['repətwaɪ] n also **repertory** repertorio m.

repetition [repə'tiʃn] n repetición f. **repetitive** adj reiterativa.

replace [rə'pleis] v (substitute) sustituir; (put back) reponer. **replacement** n repuesto m; (person) sustituto, -a m, f.

replay [rir'plei] n 'rirplei] v (sport) volver a

jugar; (music) volver a tocar. n (sport) repetición de un partido f; (television) repetición f.

replenish [rə'pleniʃ] v rellenar. **replenishment** n relleno m.

replica ['replikə] n réplica f, copia f.

reply [rə'plai] v responder, contestar. n respuesta f, contestación f.

report [rə'poɪt] n (spoken account) relato m; (piece of news) noticia f; (official) informe m; (newspaper or broadcast story) reportaje m; (reputation) fama f; (school) boletín m; (explosion) estampido m. v relatar; (for a newspaper) hacer la crónica de; (message) repetir; (denounce) denunciar; presentar un informe. **reporter** n reportero m, periodista m, f.

repose [rə'pouz] n reposo m, descanso m. v reposar, descansar.

represent [reprə'zent] v representar. **representation** n representación f.

representative [reprə'zentətiv] adj representativo. n representante m, f.

repress [rə'pres] v reprimir. **repression** n represión f. **repressive** adj represivo.

reprieve [rə'priɪv] n (law) indulto m; (fig: relief) alivio m. v indultar; aliviar.

reprimand ['reprimaɪnd] n reprimenda f. v reprender.

reprint ['riɪprint; v rir'print] n reimpresión f. v reimprimir.

reprisal [rə'praizəl] n represalia f.

reproach [rə'proutʃ] v reprochar. n reproche m. **reproachful** adj reprensor, acusador.

reproduce [riɪprə'djuɪs] v reproducir. **reproduction** n reproducción f. **reproductive** adj reproductor.

reprove [rə'pruɪv] v reprobar, censurar. **reproof** n reprobación f, censura f.

reptile ['reptail] n reptil m.

republic [rə'pʌblik] n república f. **republican** n, adj republicano, -a.

repudiate [rə'pjuɪdieit] v (person) repudiar; (reject) rechazar; (contract) negarse a cumplir. **repudiation** n repudiación f; rechazo m; desconocimiento m.

repugnant [rə'pʌgnənt] adj repugnante. **repugnance** n repugnancia f.

repulsion [rə'pʌlʃn] n repulsión f. **repulsive** adj repulsivo. **repulsiveness** n carácter repulsivo m.

repute [rə'pjuɪt] n reputación f. **reputable** adj acreditado. **reputation** n reputación f. **reputed** adj supuesto.

request [ri'kwest] *n* ruego *m*; demanda *f*. at the request of a petición de. *v* rogar, pedir. **request stop** parada discrecional *f*.

requiem ['rekwiəm] *n* requiem *m*.

require [rə'kwaiə] *v* (*need*) requerir; (*demand*) exigir; (*desire*) desear. **requirement** *n* requisito *m*; necesidad *f*.

requisite ['rekwizit] *adj* necesario, indispensable.

requisition [,rekwi'ziʃən] *n* demanda *f*; pedido *m*. *v* requisar.

***reread** [ri:'ri:d] *v* releer.

re-route [ri:'ru:t] *v* cambiar el itinerario de.

***rerun** [ri:'rʌn; *n* 'ri:rʌn] *v* (*film*) reestrenar; (*race*) correr de nuevo. *n* reestreno *m*.

resale [ri:'seil] *n* reventa *f*.

rescue ['reskju:] *n* rescate *m*. **rescue operations** operaciones de salvamento *f pl*. **go to the rescue of** ir en auxilio de. *v* rescatar, salvar. **rescuer** *n* rescatador, -a *m*, *f*; salvador, -a *m*, *f*.

research [ri'sə:tʃ] *n* investigación *f*. *v* investigar. **researcher** *n* investigador, -a *m*, *f*.

***resell** [ri:'sel] *v* revender.

resemble [rə'zembl] *v* parecerse a. **resemblance** *n* parecido *m*.

resent [ri'zent] *v* tomar a mal; ofenderse por. **resentful** *adj* resentido; ofendido. **resentment** *n* resentimiento *m*.

reserve [rə'zə:v] *v* reservar. *n* reserva *f*; (*mil*) reservista *m*. **reservation** *n* reserva *f*. **reserved** *adj* reservado.

reservoir ['rezəvwa:] *n* represa *f*, embalse *m*.

reside [rə'zaid] *v* residir. **residence** *n* (*building*) residencia *f*; (*stay*) permanencia *f*. **resident** *n*(*m*+*f*), *adj* residente. **residential** *adj* residencial.

residue ['rezidju:] *n* residuo *m*. **residual** *adj* residual.

resign [rə'zain] *v* renunciar; (*hand over*) ceder. **resign oneself to** resignarse a. **resignation** *n* renuncia *f*; (*from a post*) dimisión *f*; resignación *f*. **resigned** *adj* resignado.

resilient [rə'ziliənt] *adj* elástico; (*human body*) resistente; (*person*) de carácter fuerte. **resilience** *n* elasticidad *f*; resistencia *f*; fuerza moral *f*.

resin ['rezin] *n* resina *f*.

resist [rə'zist] *v* resistir; (*bear*) aguantar;

(*impede*) impedir. **resistance** *n* resistencia *f*; aguante *f*. **resistant** *adj* resistente.

***resit** [ri:'sit] *v* (*exam*) representarse.

resolute ['rezəlu:t] *adj* resuelto.

resolve [rə'zolv] *v* resolverse. **resolution** *n* resolución *f*.

resonant ['rezənənt] *adj* resonante. **resonance** *n* resonancia *f*. **resonate** *v* resonar.

resort [rə'zo:t] *n* estación *f*; centro *m*; recurso *m*. **as a last resort** como último recurso. *v* **resort to** recurrir a.

resound [rə'zaund] *v* resonar; (*fig*) tener resonancias. **resounding** *adj* resonante; sonoro; (*fig*) tremendo.

resource [rə'zo:s] *n* recurso *m*; expediente *m*. **resourceful** *adj* ingenioso, inventivo. **resourcefulness** *n* ingenio *m*, inventiva *f*.

respect [rə'spekt] *n* respeto *m*; consideración *f*; (*aspect*) aspecto *m*. **pay one's respects to** presentar sus respetos a. **with respect to** con respecto a. *v* respetar. **respectable** *adj* respetable; decente. **respectful** *adj* respetuoso. **respective** *adj* respectivo.

respiration [respə'reiʃn] *n* respiración *f*.

respite ['respait] *n* respiro *m*.

respond [rə'spond] *v* contestar; responder; reaccionar. **response** *n* respuesta *f*. **responsive** *adj* sensible.

responsible [rə'sponsəbl] *adj* responsable. **responsibility** *n* responsabilidad *f*.

rest[1] [rest] *n* descanso *m*; reposo *m*; (*music*) pausa *f*; tranquilidad *f*; (*support*) apoyo *m*. *v* descansar; (*stop*) pararse; (*stay*) quedar; (*decision*) depender de; (*lean*) apoyar. **restful** *adj* descansado; tranquilo. **restive** *adj* inquieto. **restless** *adj* desasosegado.

rest[2] [rest] *n* (*remainder*) resto *m*. **the rest** lo demás.

restaurant ['restront] *n* restaurant(e) *m*, restorán *m*. **restaurant car** coche restaurante *m*.

restore [rə'sto:] *v* restaurar; establecer; (*return*) restituir; (*repair*) reformar; (*to former rank*) rehabilitar. **restoration** *n* restauración *f*; restablecimiento *m*; (*returning*) restituición *f*.

restrain [rə'strein] *v* impedir; limitar; (*repress*) contener. **restraint** *n* restricción *f*; limitación *f*; (*feelings*) represión *f*; moderación *f*.

restrict [rə'strikt] *v* restringir. **restricted** *adj* restringido; (*outlook*) estrecho.

restriction n restricción f. **restrictive** adj restrictivo.

result [rə'zʌlt] n resultado m. v resultar. **result from** derivarse de. **result in** tener por resultado. **resultant** adj resultante.

resume [rə'zjum] v reanudar. **resumption** n reanudación f.

résumé ['reizumei] n resumen m.

resurgence [ri'səidʒəns] n resurgimiento m.

resurrect [rezə'rekt] v resucitar. **resurrection** n resurrección f.

resuscitate [rə'sʌsəteit] v resucitar. **resuscitation** n resucitación f.

retail ['riteil] n venta al por menor. adj, adv al por menor. v vender al por menor; (relate) contar. **retailer** n vendedor al por menor.

retain [rə'tein] v (keep) quedarse con; conservar; retener.

retaliate [rə'talieit] v vengarse. **retaliation** n venganza f. **in retaliation** para vengarse.

retard [rə'taid] v retardar, retrasar. **retarded** adj atrasado.

reticent ['retisənt] adj reservado. **reticence** n reserva f.

retina ['retinə] n retina f.

retinue ['retinju] n comitiva f.

retire [rə'taiə] v (from work) jubilarse; (draw back) retirarse; (go to bed) cogerse. **retired** adj (trader, soldier) retirado; (civilian) jubilado. **retirement** n retiro m; jubilación f.

retort[1] [rə'tott] v replicar. n réplica f.

retort[2] [rə'tott] n (chem) retorta f.

retrace [ri'treis] v volver a trazar; repasar. **retrace one's steps** desandar lo andado.

retract [rə'trakt] v retractar. **retraction** n retractación f. retracción f.

retreat [rə'tritt] v retirarse; retroceder. n retirada f; (place) retiro m.

retrial [ri'traiəl] n nuevo juicio m.

retrieve [rə'triv] v recuperar; (from ruin) salvar; (hunting) cobrar. **retrieval** n recuperación f. **retriever** n (dog) perro cobrador m.

retrograde ['retrəgreid] adj a retrógrado.

retrospect ['retrəspekt] n **in retrospect** retrospectivamente. **retrospective** adj retrospectivo.

return [rə'tətn] v devolver; (refund) reembolsar; (lost or stolen property) restituir; (investment) dar; (elect) elegir; (come

back) volver. **return a call** devolver una visita. n vuelta f, retorno m; (reward) recompensa f; restitución f; (profit) ganancias f pl; (interest) interés m; (tax) declaración f; (ballot) resultados m pl. **many happy returns!** ¡feliz cumpleaños! **return ticket** billete de ida y vuelta m. **in return** en recompensa. **on sale or return** en depósito.

reunite [rijju'nait] v reunir. **reunion** n reunión f.

rev [rev] (mot) n revolución f. **rev counter** cuentarrevoluciones m invar. **rev up** acelerar.

reveal [rə'viil] v revelar, descubrir. **revealing** adj revelador. **revelation** n revelación f.

revel ['revl] v jaranear, ir de juerga. n jarana f, juerga f. **revelry** n jolgorio m.

revenge [rə'vendʒ] n venganza f. v vengar. **take revenge for** vengarse de.

revenue ['revinju] n (from taxes) rentas públicas f pl; (income) entrada f.

reverberate [rə'vəibəreit] v reverberar, reflejar. **reverberation** n reverberación f.

reverence ['revərəns] n reverencia f, veneración f. **revere** v reverenciar, venerar. **reverent** adj reverente, respetuoso.

reverse [rə'vəis] n lo contrario, reverso; (cloth) revés m; (coin) cruz f; (printed form) dorso m; (mot: gear) marcha atrás f. adj opuesto; contrario; inverso. v invertir; (turn the other way round) volver al revés; (decision) revocar; (car) dar marcha atrás. **reverse the charges** (phone) poner una conferencia a cobro revertido. **reversal** n inversión f. **reversible** adj reversible.

revert [rə'vəit] v volver; revertir.

review [rə'vju] n examen m; crítica f; (mil, theatre) revista f. v examinar; volver a examinar; hacer una crítica de. **reviewer** n crítico, -a m, f.

revise [rə'vaiz] v revisar; corregir. **revision** n repaso m; corrección f.

revive [rə'vaiv] v (med) reanimar, resucitar; (trade) reactivar; (play) reponer; (custom) restablecer; (interest) renovar; (hopes) despertar. **revival** n reanimación f; resucitación f; reactivación f; restablecimiento m; (interest) renacimiento m.

revoke [rə'vouk] v revocar; (withdraw) suspender.

revolt [rə'voult] n rebelión f. v (offend) dar asco a; rebelarse. revolting adj asqueroso.

revolution [revə'luːʃən] n revolución f. revolutionary n, adj revolucionario, -a. revolutionize v revolucionar.

revolve [rə'volv] v girar. revolver n revólver m. revolving door puerta giratoria f.

revue [rə'vjuː] n revista f.

revulsion [rə'vʌlʃən] n repulsión f.

reward [rə'wɔːd] n premio m, recompensa f. v premiar, recompensar.

*rewind [riː'waind] v (film, tape) rebobinar. rewinding n rebobinado m.

*rewrite [riː'rait] v volver a escribir; volver a redactar.

rhesus ['riːsəs] n macaco de la India m. rhesus factor factor Rhesus.

rhetoric ['retərik] n retórica f. rhetorical adj retórico.

rheumatism ['ruːmətizəm] n reumatismo m, reúma m. rheumatic adj reumático.

rhinoceros [rai'nosərəs] n rinoceronte m.

rhododendron [roudə'dendrən] n rododendro m.

rhubarb ['ruːbaːb] n ruibarbo m.

rhyme [raim] n rima f. v rimar.

rhythm ['riðəm] n ritmo m. rhythmic adj rítmico.

rib [rib] n costilla f; (umbrella) varilla f; (knitting) cordoncillo m.

ribbon ['ribən] n cinta f. in ribbons hecho jirones.

rice [rais] n arroz m.

rich [ritʃ] adj rico. riches pl n riqueza f sing. richness n abundancia f; fertilidad f.

rickety ['rikəti] adj tambaleante.

*rid [rid] v librar, desembarazar. get rid of deshacerse de. riddance n libramiento m. good riddance! ¡menudo alivio!

riddle¹ ['ridl] n enigma m; acertijo m.

riddle² ['ridl] v cribar.

*ride [raid] v montar; (horse) montar a caballo. ride a bicycle/motorbike montar en bicicleta/motocicleta. n vuelta f, paseo m; (journey) viaje m. rider n (horse) jinete m; (addition) cláusula adicional f. riding n equitación f.

ridge [ridʒ] n (hills) cadena f; (crest) cumbre f; (surface) ondulación f; (roof) caballete m.

ridicule ['ridikjuːl] n ridículo m. v ridiculizar. ridiculous adj ridículo.

rife [raif] adj abundante.

rifle¹ ['raifl] n fusil m. rifle range campo de tiro m.

rifle² ['raifl] v saquear.

rift [rift] n (fissure) grieta f; (in clouds) claro m; (fig) ruptura f.

rig [rig] n (naut) aparejo m. v (mast) enjarciar; preparar; arreglar; equipar; (election) amañar. rig out ataviar. rig up improvisar. rigging n aparejo m; montaje m; equipo m.

right [rait] adj (not left) derecho; bueno; bien; justo; correcto; exacto. be right tener razón. adv a la derecha; (straight) derecho; bien; correctamente; exactamente; inmediatamente. n bien m; justicia f; (divine, to the throne, etc.) derecho m; (right hand) derecha f. civil rights pl n derechos civiles m pl. right angle ángulo recto m. right-handed adj que usa la mano derecha. right-of-way n (public) servidumbre de paso m; (roads) prioridad f. right-wing adj (pol) derechista.

righteous ['raitʃəs] adj justo, honrado.

rightful ['raitfəl] adj legítimo.

rigid ['ridʒid] adj rígido; severo. rigidity n rigidez f; severidad f.

rigmarole ['rigməroul] n (coll) galimatías m invar.

rigour ['rigə] n rigor m; severidad f. rigorous adj riguroso; severo.

rim [rim] m (cup) borde m; (wheel) llanta f.

rind [raind] n (fruit) cáscara f; (cheese, bacon) corteza f.

ring¹ [riŋ] n (finger) anillo m, sortija f; círculo m; (napkin) aro m; (keys) llavero m. v formar círculo. ringleader n cabecilla m. ring road carretera de circunvalación f.

*ring² [riŋ] v (bell) sonar; llamar (por teléfono); (ears) zumbar. ring off (phone) colgar. ring up (phone) llamar (por teléfono); (curtain) subir. n (phone) llamada f; (sound) sonido m; (large bell) campaneo m; (electric bell) toque m; (alarm clock) timbre m; (laughter) cascabeleo m.

rink [riŋk] n (ice-skating) pista de hielo f; (roller-skating) pista de patinaje f.

rinse [rins] v aclarar. n aclarado m.

riot ['raiət] n revuelta f. run riot desmandarse. v alborotarse. rioter n alborotador, -a m, f. riotous adj alborotado.

rip [rip] v rasgar. **rip off** or **out** arrancar. n rasgón m, rasgadura f.
ripe [raip] adj maduro. **ripen** v madurar. **ripeness** n madurez f.
ripple ['ripl] n rizo m; (sound of water) chapoteo m; (conversation) murmullo m. v rizar.
*rise [raiz] v (get up) levantarse; (in the air) elevarse; (temperature, slope) subir; (in rank) ascender; salir; crecer; desarrollarse; (revolt) sublevarse. **rising** adj naciente; ascendente; creciente. n (sun, moon) salida f; (tide) flujo m; (water level) crecida f; (slope, temperature, curtain) subida f; (hill) elevación f; (development) desarrollo m; (prices, rate, pressure) aumento m. **give rise to** provocar.
risk [risk] n riesgo m, peligro m. **at risk** a riesgo. v arriesgar. **risky** adj arriesgado.
rissole ['risoul] n croqueta f.
rite [rait] n rito m.
ritual ['ritfuəl] nm, adj ritual.
rival ['raivəl] n(m+f), adj rival. v competir con. **rivalry** n rivalidad f, competencia f.
river ['rivə] n río m. **riverside** n ribera f. **River Plate** n Río de la Plata m.
rivet ['rivit] n remache m, roblón m. v (tech) remachar; (fig) fijar; (fig) cautivar. **rivetting** adj cautivador.
road [roud] n camino m; carretera f; (in town) calle f. **road-block** n barricada f. **road-side** n borde de la carretera m. **road sign** señal de tráfico f. **roadway** n calzada f. **roadworks** pl n obras f pl.
roam [roum] v rondar, vagar por.
roar [rɔ:] v (lion) rugir; (bull, sea, wind) bramar; (engine) zumbar; (shout) vociferar. **roar with anger** rugir de cólera. **roar with laughter** reírse a carcajadas. n rugido m; bramido m; zumbido m; (crowd) clamor m; vociferaciones f pl.
roast [roust] v (meat) asar; (coffee) tostar. nm, adj asado.
rob [rob] v robar, hurtar. **robber** n ladrón, -ona m, f. **robbery** n robo m, hurto m.
robe [roub] n (judge's) toga f; (dressing gown) bata f; (costume) traje m; (monk's) hábito m. v vestir.
robin ['robin] n petirrojo m.
robot ['roubot] n robot m.
robust [rə'bʌst] adj robusto, vigoroso.
rock¹ [rok] n roca f; (in the sea) peña f; (stone) piedra f; (sweet) pirulí m.
rock² [rok] v (cradle) mecer; (move)

balancear; (shake) sacudir. n (music) rock m. **rocking chair** mecedora f. **rocking-horse** n caballito de balancín m.
rocket ['rokit] n cohete m. v (prices) subir vertiginosamente.
rod [rod] n (pole) barra f; (fishing) caña f; (curtain) varilla f.
rode [roud] V ride.
rodent ['roudənt] n roedor m.
roe [rou] n (fish eggs) hueva f. **soft roe** lechas f pl.
rogue [roug] n granuja m, pícaro m. **roguish** adj pícaro, picaresco. **roguishness** n picardía f.
role [roul] n papel m.
roll [roul] n (paper, film, butter, tobacco) rollo m; (bread) panecillo m; (cloth) pieza f; (register) registro m; (list of names) nómina f; (thunder) fragor m; (drum) redoble m. **roll-call** n lista f. **roll of honour** lista de honor f. v hacer rodar; (cigarettes) liar; (waves) arrastrar. **roll along** rodar por. **roll over** dar una vuelta. **roller** n (lawn) rodillo m. **roller-coaster** n montaña rusa f. **roller-skate** n patín de ruedas m. **rolling-pin** n rodillo m.
romance [rou'mans] n (love) amores m pl; aventura amorosa f; (story) novela romántica f. adj (language) romance. v fantasear. **romantic** n, adj romántico, -a.
Rome [roum] n Roma. **Roman** n, adj romano, -a. **Roman Catholic** n, adj católico romano, católica romana. **Roman numeral** número romano m.
romp [romp] n retozo m. v retozar.
roof [ru:f] n, pl **roofs** (building) tejado m; (cave, car, etc.) techo m. **roof of the mouth** cielo de la boca m. **roof rack** baca f.
rook [ruk] n (bird) grajo m; (chess) torre f.
room [ru:m] n cuarto m; (public) sala f; (hotel) habitación de hotel f; (space) sitio m; (accommodation) alojamiento m. **double room** habitación de matrimonio f. **make room for** dejar sitio. **room and board** cama y comida f, pensión completa f. **room-mate** n compañero/compañera de habitación m, f. **room service** servicio de habitaciones m. **single room** habitación individual f. **roomy** adj espacioso.
roost [ru:st] n percha f; gallinero m. v posarse. **rooster** n gallo m.

root¹ [ruːt] *n* raíz *f*; origen *m*. *v* echar raíces; (*become fixed*) arraigar.

root² [ruːt] *v* (*pigs*) hozar.

rope [roup] *n* cuerda *f*; (*pearls*) sarta *f*. know the ropes estar al tanto. learn the ropes ponerse al tanto. *v* (*tie*) amarrar; (*lasso*) coger con lazo. rope off acordonar. ropy *adj* (*coll*) malo.

rosary ['rouzəri] *n* rosario *m*.

rose¹ [rouz] *n* rosa *f*. rose-bush *n* rosal *m*. rose garden rosaleda *f*. rosewood *n* palisandro *m*. rosy *adj* rosado.

rose² [rouz] *V* rise.

rosemary ['rouzməri] *n* romero *m*.

rosette [rou'zet] *n* escarapela *f*.

*rot [rot] *v* pudrirse. *n* putrefacción *f*; (*substance*) podredumbre *f*; (*coll: rubbish*) bobadas *f* pl. rotten *adj* podrido; (*coll: bad*) pésimo; (*coll: ill*) fatal.

rota ['routə] *n* lista *f*.

rotate [rou'teit] *v* (hacer) girar, (hacer) dar vueltas; (*crops*) alternar. rotary *adj* rotatorio, rotativo. rotation *n* giro *m*; revolución *f*.

rouge [ruːʒ] *n* colorete *m*.

rough [rʌf] *adj* (*surface*) áspero; (*coarse*) tosco; duro; brutal; (*draft*) aproximado. rough-and-ready *adj* improvisado. rough copy *or* draft borrador *m*. *v* rough it (*coll*) vivir sin comodidades. roughly *adv* más o menos. roughness *n* aspereza *f*; tosquedad *f*; brutalidad *f*; dureza *f*.

roulette [ruː'let] *n* ruleta *f*.

round [raund] *adj* redondo. *prep* alrededor de. *n* círculo *m*; esfera *f*; (*slice*) rodaja *f*; (*patrol, drinks*) ronda *f*; (*ammunition*) andanada *f*; (*applause*) salva *f*. *v* redondear; dar la vuelta; doblar. round off acabar. round up acorralar; reunir; (*figure*) redondear.

roundabout ['raundəbaut] *n* (*mot*) plaza circular *f*; (*fair*) tiovivo *m*. *adj* indirecto.

rouse [rauz] *v* despertar; animar.

route [ruːt] *n* ruta *f*, itinerario *m*.

routine [ruː'tiːn] *adj* rutinario. *n* rutina *f*.

rove [rouv] *v* vagar, errar.

row¹ [rou] *n* (*file*) fila *f*; (*knitting*) vuelta *f*.

row² [rou] *v* (*boat*) remar; (*a person*) llevar a remo. rowing *n* remo *m*. rowing boat *n* bote de remos *m*.

row³ [rau] *n* (*quarrel*) bronca *f*; (*fuss*) jaleo *m*; (*noise*) alboroto *m*. *v* reñir.

rowdy ['raudi] *n*(*m*+*f*), *adj* camorrista. rowdiness *n* alboroto *m*; ruido *m*.

royal ['roiəl] *adj* real, regio. royalist *n* monárquico, -a *m*, *f*. royalties *pl n* derechos de autor *m pl*. royalty *n* realeza *f*.

rub [rʌb] *n* frotamiento *m*. *v* frotar. rubbing *n* (*brass, etc.*) frotamiento *m*.

rubber ['rʌbə] *n* caucho *m*, goma *f*; (*eraser*) goma de borrar *f*. rubber band goma *f*. rubber stamp sello de goma *m*. rubber tree gomero *m*. rubbery *adj* parecido a la goma.

rubbish ['rʌbiʃ] *n* (*refuse*) basura *f*; (*waste*) desperdicios *m pl*; (*derog*) porquería *f*; (*nonsense*) tonterías *f pl*.

rubble ['rʌbl] *n* escombros *m pl*.

ruby ['ruːbi] *n* rubí *m*.

rucksack ['rʌksak] *n* mochila *f*.

rudder ['rʌdə] *n* timón *m*.

rude [ruːd] *adj* (*coarse*) grosero; (*impolite*) descortés; (*rough*) tosco; (*hard*) duro; (*painful*) penoso; (*health*) robusto. rudeness *n* grosería *f*; descortesía *f*; indecencia *f*.

rudiment ['ruːdimənt] *n* rudimento *m*. rudimentary *adj* rudimentario.

rueful ['ruːfəl] *adj* contrito; vergonzoso; triste. ruefully *adv* tristemente. ruefulness *n* tristeza *f*, aflicción *f*.

ruff [rʌf] *n* (*dress*) gorguera *f*; (*on animals*) collarín *m*.

ruffian ['rʌfiən] *n* rufián *m*.

ruffle ['rʌfl] *v* (*disturb*) agitar; (*hair*) desgreñar; (*feathers*) erizar; (*cloth*) fruncir; (*wrinkle*) arrugar; (*worry*) perturbar.

rug [rʌg] *n* (*carpet*) alfombra *f*; (*small carpet*) tapete *m*; (*blanket*) manta de viaje *f*.

rugged ['rʌgid] *adj* (*rock*) escarpado; (*ground*) accidentado; (*character*) desabrido; (*face*) duro; (*climate*) riguroso. ruggedness *n* lo escarpado; lo accidentado; desabrimiento *m*; dureza *f*.

ruin ['ruːin] *n* ruina *f*. *v* arruinar. ruinous *adj* ruinoso.

rule [ruːl] *n* regla *f*; mando *m*, gobierno *m*. as a rule por regla general. rule of the road reglamento del tráfico *m*. rules and regulations reglamento *m sing*. *v* mandar, gobernar; (*lines*) tirar (una línea). rule out excluir. ruler *n* gobernante *m*, *f*; soberano, -a *m*, *f*; (*measuring*) regla *f*. ruling *n* (*law*) decisión *f*.

rum [rʌm] *n* ron *m*.

rumble ['rʌmbl] *n* ruido sordo *m*; (*stomach*) borborigmo *m*. *v* retumbar; (*stomach*) sonar.

rummage ['rʌmidʒ] v revolver. **rummage sale** venta de prendas usadas f.

rumour ['ruːmə] n rumor m. **it is rumoured (that)** se rumorea (que).

rump [rʌmp] n (quadruped) ancas f pl; (person) trasero m; (cookery) cuarto trasero m.

***run** [rʌn] v correr; circular; (theatre) estar en cartel; (leak) salirse; (car) marchar; (machine) funcionar; (melt) derretirse; (colours) desteñirse; (road) pasar; (stockings) hacirse una carrerilla. n (race) carrera f; (short trip) paseo m; (of a train, etc.) trayecto m; (series) serie f; (ski) pista f; (print) tirada f. **in the long run** a la larga.

run away v escaparse. **runaway** nm, adj fugitivo.

run down v (knock over) atropellar; (criticize) poner por los suelos. **run-down** adj (exhausted) agotado. **rundown** n informe detallado m.

rung¹ [rʌŋ] V ring.

rung² [rʌŋ] n peldaño m.

run in v (mot) rodar; (arrest) detener.

runner ['rʌnə] n (athlete) corredor, -a m, f; (sledge) patín m. **runner bean** judía escarlata f. **runner-up** n subcampeón, -ona m, f.

run out v acabarse.

run over v (hit) pillar; (rehearse) volver a ensayar; (text) echar un vistazo a; (overflow) rebosar.

run up v (make quickly) hacer rápidamente; (flag) izar. **run up against** tropezar con.

runway ['rʌnwei] n pista f.

rupture ['rʌptʃə] n ruptura f; (med) hernia f. v romper.

rural ['ruərəl] adj rural, campestre.

ruse [ruːz] n ardid m.

rush¹ [rʌʃ] n ímpetu m; prisa f; carrera precipitada f. v hacer precipitadamente; meter prisa. **rush hour** hora punta f.

rush² [rʌʃ] n (bot) junco m.

rusk [rʌsk] n galleta dura f.

Russia ['rʌʃə] n Rusia f. **Russian** n, adj ruso, -a.

rust [rʌst] n orín m, herrumbre f. v oxidar. **rusty** adj oxidado.

rustic ['rʌstik] adj rústico.

rustle ['rʌsl] v (leaves) susurrar; (paper) crujir. n susurro m; crujido m.

rut [rʌt] n rodera f.

ruthless ['ruːθlis] adj despiadado, implacable.

rye [rai] n centeno m.

S

sabbatical [sə'batikəl] adj sabático. **sabbatical year** año de permiso m.

sable ['seibl] n cebellina f.

sabotage ['sabətaːʒ] n sabotaje m. v sabotear. **saboteur** n saboteador, -a m, f.

sabre ['seibə] n sable m.

saccharin ['sakərin] n sacarina f. adj sacarino.

sachet ['saʃei] n saquito m.

sack [sak] n saco m. **get the sack** (coll) recibir el pasaporte. v (coll) despedir.

sacrament ['sakrəmənt] n sacramento m.

sacred ['seikrid] adj sagrado.

sacrifice ['sakrifais] n sacrificio m. v sacrificar.

sacrilege ['sakrəlidʒ] n sacrilegio m. **sacrilegious** adj sacrílego.

sad [sad] adj triste. **sadden** v entristecer. **sadly** adv tristemente; (unfortunately) desgraciadamente. **sadness** n tristeza f.

saddle ['sadl] n (horse) silla f; (bicycle) sillín m. **saddle-bag** n (horse) alforja f; (bicycle) cartera f. **saddle with** cargar con. **saddler** n guarnicionero m. **saddlery** n guarnicones f pl.

sadism ['seidizəm] n sadismo m. **sadist** n sádico, -a m, f. **sadistic** adj sádico.

safari [sə'faːri] n safari m. **safari park** reserva f.

safe [seif] adj (unhurt) sano y salvo; (undamaged) intacto; (secure) seguro; (harmless) inofensivo; (trustworthy) de fiar. n caja de caudales f. **safekeeping** n custodia f. **be on the safe side** para mayor seguridad. **safely** adv a buen puerto; sin peligro. **safety** n seguridad f; salvamento m. **safety belt** cinturón de seguridad m. **safety pin** imperdible m.

safeguard ['seifgaːd] n salvaguardia f. v salvaguardar.

saffron ['safrən] n azafrán m. adj azafranado.

sag [sag] v doblegarse; flaquear. n hundimiento m; flexión f.

saga ['saɪgə] n saga f.
sage¹ [seidʒ] nm, adj sabio.
sage² [seidʒ] n (bot) salvia f.
Sagittarius [sadʒi'teəriəs] n Sagitario m.
said [sed] V say.
sail [seil] n vela f; (trip) paseo m; (windmill) brazo m. sailcloth n lona f. set sail hacerse a la mar. v (leave) salir; (cross) atravesar; (boat) navegar. sail through (coll) hacer muy fácilmente. sailing n (navigation) navegación f; (departure) salida f. sailing boat barco de vela m. sailor n marinero m.
saint [seint] n santo, -a m, f.
sake [seik] n for the sake of por; para; por amor de.
salad ['saləd] n ensalada f. salad cream mayonesa f. salad dressing vinagreta f.
salami [sə'laːmi] n salchichón m.
salary ['saləri] n sueldo m.
sale [seil] n venta f; (reductions) liquidación f. for or on sale en venta. sale-room n sala de subasta f. salesman n (shop) dependiente m; (rep) representante m. salesmanship n arte de vender m.
saline ['seilain] adj salino. salinity n salinidad f.
saliva [sə'laivə] n saliva f. salivary adj salival. salivate v salivar.
sallow ['salou] adj cetrino.
salmon ['samən] n salmón m.
salon ['salon] n salón m.
saloon [sə'luːn] n salón m; sala f. saloon bar salón interior m. saloon car coche salón m.
salt [soːlt] n sal f. salt-cellar n salero m. v salar. salty adj salado.
salute [sə'luːt] n saludo m; (gun) salva f. v saludar.
salvage ['salvidʒ] n salvamento m; objetos salvados m pl. v salvar.
salvation [sal'veifən] n salvación f.
same [seim] adj mismo; igual. pron el mismo, la misma. adv de la misma forma. all the same sin embargo. at the same time al mismo tiempo.
sample ['saːmpl] n muestra f; prueba f; ejemplo m. v probar; (drinks) catar.
sanatorium [sanə'toɪriəm] n sanatorio m.
sanctify ['saŋktifai] v santificar. sanctification n santificación f.
sanctimonious [saŋkti'mouniəs] adj santurrón.
sanction ['saŋkʃən] n sanción f. v sancionar; autorizar.

sanctity ['saŋktəti] n santidad f; inviolabilidad f.
sanctuary ['saŋktʃuəri] n santuario m; (refuge) refugio m; (animal) reserva f.
sand [sand] n arena f. sandbag n saco terrero m. sand dune duna f. sandpaper n papel de lija m. v (with sandpaper) lijar. sandy adj (beach) arenoso; (hair) rubio rojizo.
sandal ['sandl] n sandalia f.
sandwich ['sanwidʒ] n bocadillo m. v intercalar.
sane [sein] adj sano; razonable. sanity n juicio m; (sensibleness) sensatez f.
sang [saŋ] V sing.
sanitary ['sanitəri] adj sanitario; higiénico. sanitary towel paño higiénico m.
sank [saŋk] V sink.
sap [sap] n savia f.
sapphire ['safaiə] n zafiro m.
sarcasm ['saːkazəm] n sarcasmo m.
sardine [saɪ'diːn] n sardina f.
Sardinia [saɪ'dinjə] n Cerdeña f. Sardinian n, adj sardo, -a m, f.
sardonic [saɪ'donik] adj sardónico.
sash¹ [saʃ] n faja f; (chest ribbon) banda f; (waist) fajín m.
sash² [saʃ] n (frame) marco m. sash window ventana de guillotina f.
sat [sat] V sit.
Satan ['seitən] n Satán m, Satanás m. satanic adj satánico.
satchel ['satʃəl] n cartera f.
satellite ['satəlait] n satélite m.
satin ['satin] n raso m.
satire ['sataiə] n sátira f. satirical adj satírico. satirize v satirizar.
satisfy ['satisfai] v satisfacer; convencer. satisfaction n satisfacción f. satisfactory adj satisfactorio.
saturate ['satʃəreit] v saturar; (soak) empapar. saturation n saturación f. reach saturation point llegar al punto de saturación.
Saturday ['satədi] n sábado m.
sauce [soːs] n salsa f; (slang) insolencia f. saucy adj descarado; coquetón.
saucepan ['soːspən] n cacerola f.
saucer ['soːsə] n platillo m. flying saucer platillo volante m.
sauerkraut ['sauəkraut] n sauerkraut m.
sauna ['soːnə] n sauna f.
saunter ['soːntə] v pasearse. n paso lento m; paseo m.

sausage ['sɒsidʒ] *n* salchicha *f*. **sausage-meat** *n* carne de salchicha *f*. **sausage roll** empanadilla de salchicha *f*.

savage ['savidʒ] *adj* (*fierce*) feroz; (*primitive*) salvaje; cruel; violento. *n* salvaje *m*, *f*. *v* embestir. **savagery** *n* salvajada *f*; ferocidad *f*.

save[1] [seiv] *v* salvar; (*put aside*) ahorrar; (*keep till later*) quardar; (*protect*) proteger; (*goal*) parar. **savings** *pl n* ahorros *m pl*. **savings bank** caja de ahorros *f*.

save[2] [seiv] *prep* salvo, excepto. *conj* a no ser que.

saviour ['seivjə] *n* salvador, -a *m*, *f*.

savoir-faire [,savwɑr'feə] *n* desparpajo *m*; sentido común *m*.

savour ['seivə] *v* saborear; tener sabor de. *n* sabor *m*, gusto *m*. **savoury** *adj* sabroso; salado. *n* entremés salado *m*.

saw[1] [sɒi] *V* see.

*__saw__[2] [sɒi] *n* (*tool*) sierra *f*; (*proverb*) refrán *m*. **sawdust** *n* aserrín *m*. **sawmill** *n* aserradero *m*. *v* aserrar.

saxophone ['saksəfoun] *n* saxofón *m*.

*__say__ [sei] *v* decir; recitar. *n* have no say no tener ni voz ni voto. **saying** *n* (*act*) decir *m*; (*maxim*) refrán *m*.

scab [skab] *n* costra *f*, postilla *f*; (*derog: blackleg*) esquirol *m*.

scaffold ['skafəld] *n* (*platform*) tarima *f*; (*gallows*) cadalso *m*. **scaffolding** *n* andamio *m*.

scald [skɒld] *v* escaldar; (*instruments*) esterilizar. *n* escaldadura *f*. **scalding** *adj* hirviendo, hirviente.

scale[1] [skeil] *n* (*fish, etc.*) escama *f*; (*tartar*) sarro *m*. **scaly** *adj* escamoso; sarroso.

scale[2] [skeil] *n* (*music, measurement*) escala *f*; (*damage, etc.*) amplitud *f*. **scale drawing** dibujo hecho a escala *m*. *v* (*climb*) escalar. **scale down** reducir a escala.

scales [skeilz] *pl n* balanza *f sing*.

scallop ['skaləp] *n* (*zool*) venera *f*; (*cookery*) escalope *m*; (*sewing*) festón *m*. **scallop shell** concha *f*. *v* festonear.

scalp [skalp] *n* cuero cebelludo *m*. *v* escalpar.

scalpel ['skalpəl] *n* escalpelo *m*.

scamper ['skampə] *v* corretear.

scampi ['skampi] *n* gamba grande *f*.

scan [skan] *v* recorrer con la mirada; escrutar; (*tech*) explorar; (*poetry*) escandir.

scandal ['skandl] *n* escándalo *m*; (*gossip*)

chismorreo *m*; (*law*) difamación *f*. **scandalize** *v* escandalizar. **scandalous** *adj* escandaloso.

Scandinavia [,skandi'neivjə] *n* Escandinavia *f*. **Scandinavian** *n*, *adj* escandinavo, -a.

scant [skant] *adj also* **scanty** insuficiente. **scantily** *adv* muy ligeramente.

scapegoat ['skeipgout] *n* cabeza de turco *f*.

scar [skɑı] *n* cicatriz *f*. *v* cicatrizar; (*fig*) marcar.

scarce [skeəs] *adj* escaso; insuficiente; raro. **scarcely** *adv* apenas; casi. **scarcity** *n* escasez *f*.

scare [skeə] *n* susto *m*; alarma *f*. *v* asustar, espantar. **be scared** tener miedo. **scarecrow** *n* espantapájaros *m invar*.

scarf [skɑːf] *m* (*woollen*) bufanda *f*; (*light*) pañuelo *m*.

scarlet ['skɑːlit] *adj* escarlato. **scarlet fever** escarlatina *f*.

scathing ['skeiðiŋ] *adj* cáustico, mordaz.

scatter ['skatə] *v* esparcir; (*sprinkle*) salpicar; (*put to flight*) derrotar; dispersar; (*squander*) desparramar. **scatter-brained** *adj* atolondrado.

scavenge ['skavindʒ] *v* recoger; buscar entre. **scavenger** *n* barrendero *m*; animal que se alimenta de carroña *m*.

scene [siːn] *n* escena *f*; (*place*) lugar *m*; espectáculo *m*; vista *f*. **scenic** *adj* escénico; pintoresco.

scenery ['siːnəri] *n* (*landscape*) paisaje *m*; (*theatre*) decorado *m*.

scent [sent] *n* perfume *m*; (*smell*) olor *m*; (*track*) rastro *m*. *v* perfumar; (*smell*) oler.

sceptic ['skeptik] *n* escéptico, -a *m*, *f*. **sceptical** *adj* escéptico. **scepticism** *n* escepticismo *m*.

sceptre ['septə] *n* cetro *m*.

schedule ['ʃedjuːl] *n* programa *m*; (*time-table*) horario *m*. *v* programar; fijar.

scheme [skiːm] *n* plan *m*; proyecto *m*, esquema *m*; (*plot*) intriga *f*. *v* proyectar; intrigar, conspirar.

schizophrenia [,skitsə'friːniə] *n* esquizofrenia *f*. **schizophrenic** *n*, *adj* esquizofrénico, -a.

scholar ['skɒlə] *n* (*learned person*) erudito, -a *m*, *f*; (*schoolchild*) colegial, -a *m*, *f*, alumno, -a *m*, *f*; (*student*) estudiante *m*, *f*. **scholarly** *adj* erudito. **scholarship** *n* (*award*) beca *f*; erudición *f*.

scholastic [skə'lastik] *adj* escolar, escolástico.

school[1] [skuːl] *n* escuela *f*; *(private or secondary)* colegio *m*. **schoolboy** *n* alumno *m*, colegial *m*. **schoolgirl** *n* alumna *f*, colegiala *f*. **schooling** *n* educación *f*, enseñanza *f*. **schoolmaster** *n* *(primary)* maestro *m*; *(secondary)* profesor *m*. **schoolmistress** *n* maestra *f*; profesora *f*. **school-room** *n* clase *f*; sala de clase *f*.

school[2] [skuːl] *n* *(of fish)* banco *m*.

schooner ['skuːnə] *n* goleta *f*.

sciatica [sai'atikə] *n* ciática *f*. **sciatic** *adj* ciático.

science ['saiəns] *n* ciencia *f*. **science fiction** ciencia ficción *f*. **scientific** *adj* científico. **scientist** *n* científico, -a *m*, *f*.

scintillating ['sintileitiŋ] *adj* relumbrante; *(fig)* brillante.

scissors ['sizəz] *pl n* tijeras *f pl*.

scoff[1] [skof] *v* burlarse.

scoff[2] [skof] *v* *(coll: eat)* zamparse.

scold [skould] *v* reñir, reprender. *n* virago *f*. **scolding** *n* reprensión *f*.

scone [skon] *n* bollo *m*.

scoop [skuːp] *n* pala de mano *f*; *(press)* éxito periodístico *m*. *v* sacar con pala; *(dig)* excavar.

scooter ['skuːtə] *n* *(motor)* scooter *m*; *(child's)* patinete *m*.

scope [skoup] *n* *(range)* alcance *m*; *(opportunity)* libertad *f*; *(field of action)* esfera *f*.

scorch [skɔːtʃ] *n* quemadura *f*. *v* quemar; *(singe)* chamuscar.

score [skɔː] *n* *(number of points)* tanteo *m*; *(result)* resultado *m*; *(test marks)* calificación *f*; *(twenty)* veintena *f*; *(music)* partitura *f*; *(notch)* muesca *f*. **scoreboard** *n* marcador *m*. *v* *(point, goal)* marcar; orquestar; hacer una muesca en. **scorer** *n* *(scorekeeper)* tanteador *m*; *(football)* goleador *m*.

scorn [skɔːn] *n* desdén *m*, desprecio *m*. *v* desdeñar, despreciar. **scornful** *adj* desdeñoso, despreciativo.

Scorpio ['skɔːpiou] *n* Escorpión *m*.

scorpion ['skɔːpiən] *n* escorpión *m*.

Scotland ['skotlənd] *n* Escocia *f*. **Scot** *n* escocés, -esa *m*, *f*. **Scotch** *n* whisky escocés *m*. **Scots** *nm*, *adj* escocés. **Scottish** *adj* escocés.

scoundrel ['skaundrəl] *n* sinvergüenza *m*.

scour[1] [skauə] *v* *(clean)* fregar. **scourer** *n* *(pad)* estropajo *m*.

scour[2] [skauə] *v* *(search)* recorrer, batir.

scout [skaut] *n* explorador *m*. **scoutmaster** *n* jefe de exploradores *m*.

scowl [skaul] *v* fruncir el entrecejo. *n* ceño *m*.

scramble ['skrambl] *v* *(climb)* trepar; *(struggle)* pelearse; *(mix)* mezclar; *(eggs)* revolver. *n* lucha *f*, pelea *f*.

scrap [skrap] *n* *(piece)* trozo *m*; *(metal)* chatarra *f*; *(coll: fight)* pelea *f*. **scrapbook** *n* álbum de recortes *m*. papel para apuntes *m*. **scraps** *pl n* restos *m pl*, sobras *f pl*. *v* desechar; *(coll)*. pelear.

scrape [skreip] *n* *(noise)* chirrido *m*; *(act)* raspado *m*; *(mark)* arañazo *m*; *(graze)* rasguño *m*; *(coll: trouble)* apuro *m*. *v* raspar; *(graze)* arañar; *(drag)* arrastrar.

scratch [skratʃ] *n* arañazo *m*; raya *f*; rasguño *m*; cero *m*.

scrawl [skrɔːl] *v* garabatear. *n* garabato *m*.

scream [skriːm] *n* grito *m*, chillido *m*. *v* gritar, chillar.

screech [skriːtʃ] *v* chillar, gritar; *(brakes)* chirriar. *n* chillido *m*, grito *m*; chirrido *m*.

screen [skriːn] *n* *(TV, film)* pantalla *f*; *(folding)* biombo *m*; *(fig)* cortina *f*. **screen-play** *n* guión *m*. **screen test** prueba cinematográfica *f*. *v* *(film)* proyectar; *(shelter)* proteger; *(sift)* tamizar.

screw [skruː] *n* tornillo *m*; *(propeller)* hélice *f*. **screwdriver** *n* destornillador *m*. *v* atornillar. **screw up** *(paper)* arrugar.

scribble ['skribl] *v* garabatear. *n* garabato *m*.

script [skript] *n* *(film)* guión *m*; *(theatre)* argumento *m*; *(writing)* escritura *f*.

scripture ['skriptʃə] *n* *(school)* religión *f*; *(holy)* Sagrada Escritura *f*.

scroll [skroul] *n* rollo *m*; *(arch)* voluta *f*.

scrounge [skraundʒ] *(coll)* *v* sablear; gorronear. **scrounger** *n* sablista *m*, *f*; gorrón, -ona *m*, *f*.

scrub[1] [skrʌb] *n* fregado *m*; fricción *f*. *v* fregar; restregar; *(coll: cancel)* cancelar. **scrubbing brush** cepillo de fregar *m*.

scrub[2] [skrʌb] *n* matorral *m*; maleza *f*.

scruff [skrʌf] *n* by the scruff of the neck por el cogote.

scruffy ['skrʌfi] *adj* desaliñado. **scruffiness** *n* desaliño *m*.

scrum [skrʌm] *n* melée *f*.
scruple ['skruːpl] *n* escrúpulo *m*. **scrupulous** *adj* escrupuloso.
scrutiny ['skruːtəni] *n* escrutinio *m*. **scrutinize** *v* escudriñar.
scuffle ['skʌfl] *n* pelea *f*, refriega *f*. *v* pelear, reñir.
scull [skʌl] *n* remo *m*.
scullery ['skʌləri] *n* trascocina *f*.
sculpt [skʌlpt] *v* esculpir. **sculptor** *n* escultor, -a *m, f*. **sculpture** *n* escultura *f*.
scum [skʌm] *n* espuma *f*; (*derog*) escoria *f*.
scurf [skəːf] *n* caspa *f*.
scurvy ['skəːvi] *n* escorbuto *m*.
scuttle¹ ['skʌtl] *n* (*coal*) cubo del carbón *m*.
scuttle² ['skʌtl] *v* (*naut*) barrenar.
scuttle³ ['skʌtl] *v* escabullirse.
scythe [saið] *n* guadaña *f*. *v* guadañar.
sea [siː] *n* mar *m, f*.
sea-bed *n* fondo del mar *m*.
seaborne ['siːbɔːn] *adj* transportado por mar.
seafood ['siːfuːd] *n* mariscos *m pl*.
seafront ['siːfrʌnt] *n* paseo marítimo *m*.
seagoing ['siːgouiŋ] *adj* (*ship*) de alta mar; (*person*) marinero.
seagull ['siːgʌl] *n* gaviota *f*.
seahorse ['siːhɔːs] *n* caballo de mar *m*.
seal¹ [siːl] *n* sello *m*. *v* sellar; (*close*) cerrar; (*fate*) decidir. **sealing wax** lacre *m*.
seal² [siːl] *n* (*zool*) foca *f*. **sealskin** *n* piel de foca *f*.
sea-level *n* nivel del mar *m*.
sea-lion *n* león marino *m*.
seam [siːm] *n* (*sewing*) costura *f*; (*coal*) vena *f*; (*geol*) capa *f*. **seamy** *adj* (*fig*) sórdido.
seaman ['siːmən] *n pl* **seamen** marinero *m*.
séance ['seiãs] *n* sesión de espiritismo *f*.
sear [siə] *v* (*scorch*) abrasar; (*wither*) marchitar. **searing** *adj* (*pain*) punzante.
search [səːtʃ] *n* investigación *f*; (*to find something*) búsqueda *f*; (*house, car*) registro *m*. **searchlight** *n* reflector *m*. **search-party** *n* equipo de salvamento *m*. **search warrant** *n* mandamiento de registro *m*. *v* buscar; registrar; investigar. **searching** *adj* (*look*) penetrante; (*examination*) minucioso.
sea shell *n* concha marina *f*.
seashore ['siːʃɔː] *n* playa *f*; costa *f*.

seasick ['siːsik] *adj* be seasick marearse. **sea sickness** mareo *m*.
seaside ['siːsaid] *n* playa *f*; costa *f*. **seaside resort** estación balnearia *f*.
season ['siːzn] *n* estación *f*; temporada *f*; época *f*. **season ticket** abono *m*. *v* (*food*) sazonar; (*wood*) secar. **seasonal** *adj* estacional; (*work*) temporal. **seasoning** *n* condimento *m*.
seat [siːt] *n* asiento *m*; silla *f*; localidad *f*; centro *m*. **seat-belt** *n* cinturón de seguridad *m*. *v* sentar; colocar; tener cabida para.
seawater ['siːwɔːtə] *n* agua de mar *f*.
seaweed ['siːwiːd] *n* alga *f*.
seaworthy ['siːwəːði] *adj* marinero. **seaworthiness** *n* navegabilidad *f*.
secluded [siˈkluːdid] *adj* retirado; aislado. **seclusion** *n* reclusión *f*; soledad *f*.
second¹ ['sekənd] *n* (*time*) segundo *m*. **second hand** segundero *m*.
second² ['sekənd] *n* segundo, -a *m, f*. (*gear*) segunda *f*. **seconds** *pl n* artículos de segunda clase *m pl. adj* segundo. **on second thoughts** pensándolo bien. **second-class** *adj* de segunda clase. **travel second-class** viajar en segunda. **second-hand** *adj* de segunda mano, usado. **second-rate** *adj* de segunda categoría. *v* (*in debate*) apoyar. **secondly** *adv* en segundo lugar.
secondary ['sekəndəri] *adj* secundario. **secondary school** instituto de enseñanza media *m*.
secret ['siːkrit] *nm, adj* secreto. **secrecy** *n* secreto *m*. **secretive** *adj* reservado; callado. **secretly** *adv* en secreto.
secretary ['sekrətəri] *n* secretario, -a *m, f*. **secretarial** *adj* de secretario.
secrete [siˈkriːt] *v* (*hide*) esconder; (*med*) secretar. **secretion** *n* secreción *f*.
sect [sekt] *n* secta *f*. **sectarian** *adj* sectario.
section ['sekʃən] *n* sección *f*; parte *f*.
sector ['sektə] *n* sector *m*.
secular ['sekjulə] *adj* profano; secular; laico.
secure [siˈkjuə] *adj* seguro. *v* asegurar; cerrar firmemente; garantizar; conseguir; reservar; consolidar. **security** *n* seguridad *f*; (*for loan*) garantía *f*.
sedate [siˈdeit] *adj* sosegado; tranquilo. **sedation** *n* sedación *f*. **sedative** *nm, adj* sedante.

sediment ['sedimənt] *n* (*geol*) sedimento *m*; (*liquid*) poso *m*.

seduce [si'djuːs] *v* seducir. **seduction** *n* seducción *f*. **seductive** *adj* seductor.

see[1] [siː] *v* ver; comprender; mirar; visitar; recibir. **see off** ir a despedir. **see through** (*not be deceived*) calar. **see to** ocuparse de. **see you later!** ¡hasta luego!

see[2] [siː] *n* (*rel*) obispado *m*.

seed [siːd] *n* semilla *f*; (*fruit*) pepita *f*; (*sperm*) semen *m*. **seedless** *adj* sin semillas; sin pepitas. **seedling** *n* plantón *m*. **seedy** *adj* granado; (*coll*: *ill*) pachucho.

seek [siːk] *v* buscar; tratar; solicitar.

seem [siːm] *v* parecer. **seeming** *adj* aparente. **seemingly** *adv* al parecer, por lo visto.

seep [siːp] *v* rezumarse. **seepage** *n* filtración *f*.

seesaw ['siːsɔː] *n* columpio *m*, subibaja *m*. *v* columpiarse.

seethe [siːð] *v* borbotar. **seething** *adj* (*coll*) bufando de cólera.

segment ['segmənt] *n* segmento *m*; (*orange*, *etc.*) gajo *m*.

segregate ['segrigeit] *v* segregar. **segregation** *n* segregación *f*.

seize [siːz] *v* tomar; (*grab firmly*) agarrar; (*a person*) detener. **seize up** (*tech*) agarrotarse. **seizure** *n* asimiento *m*; detención *f*; (*property*) embargo *m*; (*in war*) toma *f*; (*med*) ataque *m*.

seldom ['seldəm] *adv* raramente.

select [sə'lekt] *v* escoger, elegir. *adj* escogido; (*exclusive*) selecto. **selection** *n* selección *f*. **selective** *adj* selectivo.

self [self] *n* sí mismo *m*, sí misma *f*; personalidad *f*.

self-addressed *adj* con su propia dirección.

self-adhesive *adj* autoadhesivo.

self-assured *adj* seguro de sí mismo. **self-assurance** *n* confianza en sí mismo *f*.

self-centred *adj* egocéntrico.

self-confident *adj* seguro de sí mismo. **self-confidence** *n* seguridad en sí mismo *f*.

self-conscious *adj* cohibido. **self-consciousness** *n* turbación *f*.

self-contained *adj* independiente.

self-control *n* dominio de sí mismo *m*. **self-controlled** *adj* sereno.

self-defence *n* (*technique*) autodefensa *f*; (*law*) legítima defensa *f*.

self-determination *n* autodeterminación *f*.

self-discipline *n* autodisciplina *f*.

self-educated *adj* autodidacto.

self-employed *adj* que trabaja por cuenta propia.

self-esteem *n* amor propio *m*.

self-evidence *adj* patente, manifiesto.

self-explanatory *adj* que se explica por sí mismo.

self-expression *n* expresión de la propia personalidad *f*.

self-interest *n* interés propio *m*.

selfish ['selfiʃ] *adj* egoísta. **selfishness** *n* egoísmo *m*.

selfless ['selflis] *adj* desinteresado.

self-made *adj* **self-made man** hijo de sus propias obras *m*.

self-opinionated *adj* obstinado.

self-pity *n* lástima de sí mismo *f*.

self-portrait *n* autorretrato *m*.

self-possessed *adj* seguro de sí mismo. **self-respect** *n* dignidad *f*.

self-righteous *adj* farisaico. **self-righteousness** *n* fariseísmo *m*.

self-rule *n* autonomía *f*.

self-sacrifice *n* sacrificio de sí mismo *m*.

selfsame ['selfseim] *adj* mismísimo *m*.

self-satisfied *adj* satisfecho de sí mismo.

self-service *n* autoservicio *m*.

self-sufficient *adj* independiente. **self-sufficiency** *n* independencia *f*.

self-willed *adj* obstinado.

self-winding *adj* de cuerda automática.

sell [sel] *v* vender(se); hacer vender. **sell off** liquidar. **seller** *n* vendedor, -a *m*, *f*; (*dealer*) comerciante *m*.

semantic [sə'mantik] *adj* semántico. **semantics** *n* semántica *f*.

semaphore ['seməfɔː] *n* semáforo *m*.

semblance ['sembləns] *n* apariencia *f*.

semen ['siːmən] *n* semen *m*.

semibreve ['semibriːv] *n* semibreve *f*.

semicircle ['semisəːkl] *n* semicírculo *m*. **semicircular** *adj* semicircular.

semicolon [,semi'koulən] *n* punto y coma *m*.

semiconscious [semi'konʃəs] *adj* semiconsciente.

semi-detached house *n* casa doble *f*.

semifinal [semi'fainl] *n* semifinal *f*.

seminar ['seminaɪ] *n* seminario *m*.

semi-precious *adj* fino; semiprecioso.

semiquaver ['semikweivə] *n* semicorchea *f*.

semitone ['semitoun] *n* semitono *m*.
semolina [ˌsemə'liːnə] *n* sémola *f*.
senate ['senit] *n* senado *m*. **senator** *n* senador *m*.
*send [send] *v* enviar, mandar; remitir; echar; transmitir. **send back** devolver. **send for** llamar a; (*mail-order*) escribir pidiendo.
senile ['siːnail] *adj* senil. **senility** *n* senilidad *f*.
senior ['siːnjə] *adj* (*age*) mayor; (*rank*) superior. *n* (*school*) mayor *m, f*. **seniority** *n* antigüedad *f*.
sensation [sen'seiʃən] *n* sensación *f*. **sensational** *adj* sensacional.
sense [sens] *n* sentido *m*; significado *m*; sensación *f*; sentimiento *m*; (*consensus*) sentir *m*. **senses** *pl n* (*reason*) juicio *m sing*; (*consciousness*) sentido *m*. *v* sentir. **senseless** *adj* (*unconscious*) sin sentido; (*silly*) insensato.
sensible ['sensəbl] *adj* sensato; razonable; (*clothes*) práctico.
sensitive ['sensitiv] *adj* sensible; (*easily hurt*) susceptible. **sensitivity** *n* sensibilidad *f*; susceptibilidad *f*.
sensual ['sensjuəl] *adj* sensual. **sensuality** *n* sensualidad *f*.
sensuous ['sensjuəs] *adj* sensual.
sent [sent] *V* send.
sentence ['sentəns] *n* (*gramm*) frase *f*; (*law*) sentencia *f*. *v* sentenciar, condenar.
sentiment ['sentimənt] *n* sentimiento *m*; (*sentimentality*) sentimentalismo *m*; opinión *f*. **sentimental** *adj* sentimental.
sentry ['sentri] *n* centinela *m*.
separate ['sepərət] *v* 'sepəreit] *adj* separado; distinto; independiente; (*room*) particular. *v* separar; dividir; distinguir entre. **separation** *n* separación *f*.
September [sep'tembə] *n* septiembre *m*, setiembre *m*.
septic ['septik] *adj* séptico.
sequel ['siːkwəl] *n* consecuencia *f*; secuela *f*.
sequence ['siːkwəns] *n* sucesión *f*; serie *f*; orden *m*.
sequin ['siːkwin] *n* lentejuela *f*.
serenade [serə'neid] *n* serenata *f*. *v* dar una serenata a.
serene [sə'riːn] *adj* sereno. **serenity** *n* serenidad *f*.
serf [səːf] *n* siervo, -a *m, f*.

sergeant ['saːdʒənt] *n* (*mil*) sargento *m*; (*police*) cabo *m*. **sergeant-major** *n* sargento mayor *m*.
serial ['siəriəl] *n* serial *m*. *adj* de serie; seriado. **serialize** *v* publicar por entregas.
series ['siəriz] *n* serie *f*.
serious ['siəriəs] *adj* serio; grave. **seriousness** *n* seriedad *f*; gravedad *f*.
sermon ['səːmən] *n* sermón *m*.
serpent ['səːpənt] *n* serpiente *f*.
serrated [sə'reitid] *adj* serrado; dentado.
servant ['səːvənt] *n* criado, -a *m, f*; sirviente, -a *m, f*; empleado, -a *m, f*; funcionario, -a *m, f*.
serve [səːv] *v* servir; atender. **it serves you right** te está bien empleado. *n* (*tennis*) saque *m*.
service ['səːvis] *n* servicio *m*; favor *m*; (*mot*) revisión *f*; (*tea*) juego *m*; (*tennis*) saque *m*. **service charge** servicio *m*. **serviceman** *n* militar *m*. **service station** (*mot*) estación de servicio *f*. *v* (*check*) revisar; (*maintain*) mantener. **serviceable** *adj* utilizable; práctico.
serviette [ˌsəːvi'et] *n* servilleta *f*.
servile ['səːvail] *adj* servil. **servility** *n* servilismo *m*.
session ['seʃən] *n* sesión *f*; junta *f*.
*set [set] *v* poner; colocar; fijar; (*clock*) regular; (*bones*) reducir; (*type*) componer; (*to music*) poner en música; (*sun*) ponerse. **set about** ponerse (a). **setback** *n* revés *m*; contratiempo *m*. **set off** (*leave*) partir; (*explode*) hacer estallar; (*cause*) hacer. **set out** partir; disponer. **set up** erigir; montar; establecer. *n* grupo *m*; (*tools, china, etc.*) juego *m*; (*kitchen implements*) batería *f*; (*books*) colección *f*; (*people*) clase *f*; (*clothes*) calda *f*; (*sun, etc.*) puesta *f*; (*radio, etc.*) aparato *m*; (*tennis*) set *m*; (*theatre*) decorado *m*. *adj* fijo; inmóvil; asignado; establecido. **setting** *n* (*adjustment*) ajuste *m*; (*theatre*) decorado *m*.
settee [se'tiː] *n* canapé *m*.
settle ['setl] *v* (*solve*) resolver; calmar; (*country*) colonizar. **settle down** instalarse; calmarse. **settle up** (*bill*) pagar. **settlement** *n* colonización *f*; arreglo *m*; liquidicación *f*; satisfacción *f*.
seven ['sevn] *nm, adj* siete. **seventh** *n, adj* séptimo, -a..
seventeen [sevn'tiːn] *nm, adj* diecisiete. **seventeenth** *n, adj* decimoséptimo, -a.

seventy ['sevntı] *nm. adj* setenta. **seventi-eth** *n. adj* septuagésimo, -a.

sever ['sevə] *v* cortar.

several ['sevrəl] *adj, pron* varios.

severe [sə'vıə] *adj* severo; duro; (*pain*) agudo; (*illness*) grave. **severity** *n* severidad *f*; gravedad *f*; (*weather*) inclemencia *f*.

***sew** [sou] *v* coser. **sewing** *n* costura *f*. **sewing machine** máquina de coser *f*.

sewage ['sjuidʒ] *n* aguas residuales *f pl*.

sewer ['sjuə] *n* alcantarilla *f*, albañal *m*.

sex [seks] *n* sexo *m*. **sexual** *adj* sexual. **sexual intercourse** relaciones sexuales *f pl*. **sexuality** *n* sexualidad *f*. **sexy** *adj* provocativo.

sextet [seks'tet] *n* sexteto *m*.

shabby ['ʃabı] *adj* andrajoso; (*behaviour*) mezquino.

shack [ʃak] *n* choza *f*.

shade [ʃeid] *n* sombra *f*; (*lamp*) pantalla *f*; (*colour*) tono *m*; (*meaning*) matiz *m*. *v* dar sombra; (*art*) sombrear. **shady** *adj* sombreado; (*person*) dudoso.

shadow ['ʃadou] *n* sombra *f*. **shadow cabinet** gabinete fantasma *m*. *v* (*follow*) seguir. **shadowy** *adj* indistinto; misterioso.

shaft [ʃaift] *n* (*handle*) mango *m*; (*lift*) hueco *m*; (*light*) rayo *m*; (*ventilation*) pozo de ventilación *m*; (*mine*) pozo *m*; (*spear*) asta *f*.

shaggy ['ʃagı] *adj* peludo.

***shake** [ʃeik] *v* sacudir; (*bottle*) agitar; (*head*) menear; (*brandish*) esgrimir. **shake hands** darse la mano. **shake off** librarse de. *n* sacudida *f*; meneo *m*; movimiento *m*; temblor *m*. **shaky** *adj* tembloroso; (*weak*) poco sólido.

shall [ʃal] *aux translated by future tense.*

shallot [ʃə'lot] *n* chalote *m*.

shallow ['ʃalou] *adj* poco profundo; superficial.

sham [ʃam] *adj* fingido, simulado; falso. *n* (*person*) impostor, -a *m, f*; (*object*) impostura *f*. *v* fingir, simular.

shame [ʃeim] *n* vergüenza *f*; deshonra *f*; pena *f*. *v* avergonzar; deshonrar. **shamefaced** *adj* avergonzado; tímido. **shameful** *adj* vergonzoso. **shameless** *adj* desvergonzado; sinvergüenza.

shampoo [ʃam'pu:] *n* champú *m*. *v* dar un champú a.

shamrock ['ʃamrok] *n* trébol *m*.

shandy ['ʃandı] *n* cerveza con gaseosa *f*.

shanty[1] ['ʃantı] *n* (*hut*) chabola *f*. **shanty town** barrio de las latas *m*.

shanty[2] ['ʃantı] *n* (*music*) saloma *f*.

shape [ʃeip] *n* forma *f*; figura *f*; aspecto *m*. *v* dar forma a; labrar; cortar; (*idea*) formular. **shapeless** *adj* informe. **shapely** *adj* bien proporcionado.

share [ʃeə] *n* parte *f*; (*comm*) acción *f*. **shareholder** *n* accionista *m, f*. *v* compartir.

shark [ʃaɪk] *n* tiburón *m*.

sharp [ʃaɪp] *adj* (*edge*) afilado; (*point*) punzante; (*bend*) brusco; (*phot*) nítido; (*outline*) definido; (*pain*) agudo; (*taste*) picante; (*clever*) vivo. *n* (*music*) sostenido *m*. **sharpen** *v* (*knife*) afilar; (*pencil*) sacar punta a. **sharpness** *n* lo afilado; agudeza *f*; (*clarity*) nitidez *f*.

shatter ['ʃatə] *v* destrozar; (*health*) quebrantar; (*fig*) echar por tierra. **shattered** *adj* destrozado; roto; quebrantado. **shattering** *adj* demoledor; fulgurante.

shave [ʃeiv] *v* afeitarse. **shaving** *n* (*of wood, metal*) viruta *f*. **shaving brush** brocha de afeitar *f*. **shaving cream** crema de afeitar *f*.

shawl [ʃo:l] *n* chal *m*.

she [ʃiː] *pron* ella. **she who** la que, aquella que, quien.

sheaf [ʃiːf] *n* (*corn*) gavilla *f*; (*arrows*) haz *m*; (*papers*) fajo *m*.

***shear** [ʃiə] *v* esquilar. **shears** *pl n* tijeras *f pl*.

sheath [ʃiːθ] *n* (*umbrella, knife, etc.*) funda *f*; (*sword*) vaina *f*. **sheathe** *v* envainar; cubrir.

***shed**[1] [ʃed] *v* (*drop*) deshacerse de.

shed[2] [ʃed] *n* cobertizo *m*; barraca *f*.

sheen [ʃiːn] *n* brillo *m*; (*silk*) viso *m*.

sheep [ʃiːp] *n* oveja *f*. **sheepdog** *n* perro pastor *m*. **sheepskin** *n* piel de carnero *f*. **sheepish** *adj* vergonzoso.

sheer[1] [ʃiə] *adj* completo; total; puro; (*cliff*) cortado a pico; (*stockings*) diáfano.

sheer[2] [ʃiə] *v* (*naut*) guiñar.

sheet [ʃiːt] *n* (*bed*) sábana *f*; (*paper, glass*) hoja *f*; (*ice*) capa *f*; (*metal*) chapa; (*water*) extensión *f*. **sheet lightning** fucilazo *m*. **sheet music** música en hojas sueltas *f*.

sheikh [ʃeik] *n* jeque *m*.

shelf [ʃelf] *n* estante *m*.

shell [ʃel] *n* concha *f*; (*crustacean*) caparazón *m*; (*egg, nut*) cáscara *f*; (*pea*) vaina *f*; (*cannon*) proyectil *m*. **shellfish** *pl*

n mariscos *m pl.* *v* (*mil*) bombardear;
(*peas, shrimps*) pelar; (*nuts*) descascarar.
shelter ['ʃeltə] *n* abrigo *m*; asilo *m*. *v*
abrigar; proteger; dar asilo.
shelve [ʃelv] *v* (*project*) dar carpetazo a.
shelving *n* estantería *f.*
shepherd ['ʃepəd] *n* pastor *m.*
sheriff ['ʃerif] *n* sheriff *m.*
sherry ['ʃeri] *n* jerez *m.*
shield [ʃiːld] *n* escudo *m*; (*fig*) defensa *f. v*
escudar; proteger.
shift [ʃift] *n* cambio *m*; movimiento *m*;
(*work*) turno *m.* **shift key** tecla de mayús-
culas *f.* **shift work** trabajo por turnos *m.*
v cambiar; mover. **shifty** *adj* furtivo.
shimmer ['ʃimə] *v* relucir. *n* luz trémula *f.*
shin [ʃin] *n* espinilla *f.*
*****shine** [ʃain] *v* brillar. *n* brillo *m*, lustre
m. **shiny** *adj* lustroso, brillante.
shingle ['ʃiŋgl] *n* (*pebbles*) guijarros *m pl.*
shingles *n* (*med*) herpes *m, f pl.*
ship [ʃip] *n* barco *m*, navío *m*, buque *m.*
shipshape *adj* en buen orden. **shipwreck**
n naufragio *m. v* embarcar; transportar;
(*send*) enviar. **shipment** *n* cargamento *m.*
shipping *n* barcos *m pl*, buques *m pl.*
shirk [ʃəːk] *v* esquivar. **shirker** *n* gandul,
-a *m, f.*
shirt [ʃəːt] *n* camisa *f.* **in one's shirt
sleeves** en mangas de camisá. **shirt-tail** *n*
faldón *m.*
shit [ʃit] *nf, interj* (*vulgar*) mierda. *v*
cagar.
shiver ['ʃivə] *v* temblar; estremecerse. *n*
temblor *m*; estremecimiento *m.*
shoal [ʃoul] *n* (*fish*) banco *m.*
shock [ʃok] *n* choque *m*; (*elec*) descarga *f.*
shock absorber amortiguador *m.* **shock-
proof** *adj* a prueba de choques. *v* conmocionar; escandalizar. **shocking** *adj*
escandaloso; espantoso; (*news*) aterrador.
shoddy ['ʃodi] *adj* inferior. **shoddiness** *n*
fabricación inferior *f.*
*****shoe** [ʃuː] *v* (*horse*) herrar. *n* zapato *m.*
shoelace *n* cordón *m.* **shoemaker** *n*
zapatero *m.* **shoe repairer's** zapatería de
viejo *f.* **shoe shop** zapatería *f.*
shone [ʃon] *V* shine.
shook [ʃuk] *V* shake.
*****shoot** [ʃuːt] *v* (*fire*) lanzar, tirar; (*kill*)
matar; (*wound*) herir; (*film*) filmar;
(*hunt*) cazar. *n* (*bot*) brote *m.* **shooting** *n*
tiro *m pl*; (*hunting*) caza *f.*
shop [ʃop] *n* tienda *f*; (*larger*) almacén *m.*

shop assistant *n* dependiente, -a *m, f.*
shopkeeper ['ʃopkiːpə] *n* comerciante *m,
f.*
shoplifter ['ʃopliftə] *n* ratero, -a *m, f.*
shoplifting *n* ratería *f.*
shopper ['ʃopə] *n* comprador, -a *m, f.*
shopping ['ʃopiŋ] *n* compras *f pl.* **go shopping** ir de compras. **shopping bag** bolsa
de la compra *f.* **shopping centre** centro
comercial *m.* **shopping trolley** carrito *m.*
shop steward *n* enlace sindical *m.*
shore [ʃoː] *n* (*beach*) playa *f*; (*edge of sea*)
orilla *f*; (*coast*) costa *f.*
short [ʃoːt] *adj* corto; pequeño; (*not tall*)
bajo; (*brusque*) seco; (*temper*) vivo. **in
short** en resumen. **shortage** *n* falta *f*,
escasez *f.* **shorten** *v* acortar; disminuir;
abreviar. **shortly** *adv* dentro de poco.
shortbread ['ʃoːtbred] *n* mantecada *f.*
short-circuit *n* cortocircuito. *v* ponerse en
cortocircuito.
shortcoming ['ʃoːtkʌmiŋ] *n* defecto *m.*
short cut *n* atajo *m.*
shorthand ['ʃoːthand] *n* taquigrafía *f.*
shorthand typist taquimecanógrafo, -a *m,
f.*
short list *n* lista de los posibles *f.*
short-lived *adj* efímero.
shorts [ʃoːts] *pl n* pantalones cortos *m pl.*
short-sighted *adj* miope.
short story *n* novela corta *f.*
short-tempered *adj* de mal genio.
short-term *adj* de corto plazo.
short wave *n* onda corta *f. adj* de onda
corta.
shot¹ [ʃot] *V* shoot.
shot² [ʃot] *n* bala *f*; tiro *m*; tirador, -a *m,
f*; (*sport*) peso *m*; (*med*) inyección *f.* **shotgun** *n* escopeta *f.*
should¹ [ʃud] *v* deber, tener que.
should² [ʃud] *aux translated by conditional
tense.*
shoulder ['ʃouldə] *n* hombro *m.* **shoulder-
blade** *n* omóplato *m*; (*animal*) paletilla *f.*
v llevar al hombro.
shout [ʃaut] *n* grito *m. v* gritar.
shove [ʃʌv] *n* empujón *m. v* empujar.
shovel ['ʃʌvl] *n* pala *f. v* traspalar.
*****show** [ʃou] *v* mostrar; descubrir; reve-
lar; exhibir; indicar; demostrar; probar.
n exposición *f*; espectáculo *m*; (*appearance*) apariencia *f*; (*ostentation*) pompa *f.*
show business *n* mundo del espectáculo
m.

shower ['ʃauə] n (rain) chubasco m; (bath) ducha f. v llover; ducharse; (pour) derramar.

show in v hacer pasar.

show jumping n concurso hípico m.

show off v (coll) darse pisto.

showpiece ['ʃoupiːs] n modelo m; obra maestra f.

showroom ['ʃourum] n sala de muestras f.

show up v (coll: arrive) aparecer; (embarrass) poner en evidencia.

showy ['ʃoui] adj ostentoso.

shrimp [ʃrimp] n camarón m.

shrine [ʃrain] n capilla f; santuario m; altar m.

*****shrink** [ʃriŋk] v (clothes) encoger. **shrink from** repugnarse de. **shrinkage** n encogimiento m.

shrivel ['ʃrivl] v secar, marchitar. **shrivel up** apergaminarse.

shroud [ʃraud] n sudario m, mortaja f; (fig) velo m. v amortajar; (fig) envolver.

Shrove Tuesday [ʃrouv] n martes de carnaval m.

shrub [ʃrʌb] n arbusto m. **shrubbery** n arbustos m pl, matorrales m pl.

shrug [ʃrʌg] v encogimiento de hombros m. v encogerse de hombros.

shudder ['ʃʌdə] n repeluzno m; (engine) vibración f. v estremecerse.

shuffle ['ʃʌfl] n arrastramiento de los pies m; (cards) barajada f. v arrastrar; barajar.

shun [ʃʌn] v evitar, rehuir.

shunt [ʃʌnt] v (trains) desviar.

*****shut** [ʃʌt] v cerrar. **shut in** encerrar. **shut out** no admitir. **shut up** (coll) callarse; hacer callar.

shutter ['ʃʌtə] n (window) postigo m; (phot) obturador m.

shuttle ['ʃʌtl] n lanzadera f. **shuttlecock** n volante m. **shuttle service** servicio regular de ida y vuelta m.

shy [ʃai] adj tímido. v (horse) espantarse. **shyness** n timidez f.

Siamese [ˌsaiə'miːz] adj (cat, twin) siamés. n siamés.

sick [sik] adj enfermo. **be sick** vomitar. **be sick of** (coll) estar harto de. **feel sick** tener náuseas. **sickbed** n lecho de enfermo m. **sick benefit** subidio de enfermedad m. **sicken** v poner enfermo. **sickening** adj nauseabundo; (distressing) deprimente. **sickly** adj (person) enfermizo; (taste) empalagoso. **sickness** n enfermedad f; (sea, air) mareo m.

sickle ['sikl] n hoz f.

side [said] n lado m; (edge) borde; (team) equipo m. **side with** ponerse de parte de. adj lateral; secundario; indirecto.

sideboard ['saidbɔːd] n aparador m.

sideburns ['saidbəːnz] pl n patillas f pl.

sidecar ['saidkaː] n sidecar m.

side effects pl n efectos secundarios m pl.

sidelight ['saidlait] n (mot) luz de posición f.

sideline ['saidlain] n negocio accesorio m; (sport) banquillo m.

sidelong ['saidlɔŋ] adj, adv de reojo.

side-splitting adj divertidísimo.

side-step v evitar.

side street n calle lateral f.

side-track v despistar.

sideways ['saidweiz] adv oblicuamente. adj de lado.

siding ['saidiŋ] n (rail) vía muerta f.

sidle ['saidl] v avanzar furtivamente. **sidle up** to acercarse furtivamente.

siege [siːdʒ] n sitio m, asedio m.

sieve [siv] n tamiz m, scolador m. v tamizar.

sift [sift] v tamizar; (sprinkle) espolvorear; (evidence) examinar cuidadosamente. **sift out** encontrar; seleccionar. **sifter** cedazo m.

sigh [sai] n suspiro m. v suspirar.

sight [sait] n vista f; espectáculo m. **sight-seeing** n turismo m. v avistar; (aim) apuntar.

sign [sain] n señal f; indicio m; (notice) anuncio m; muestra f. **signpost** n letrero m. v firmar.

signal ['signəl] n señal f. v hacer señales; indicar.

signature ['signətʃə] n firma f.

signify ['signifai] v significar. **significance** n significado m. **significant** adj significativo.

silence ['sailəns] n silencio m. v callar; hacer callar. **silencer** (mot, gun) n silenciador m. **silent** adj silencioso; callado.

silhouette [silu'et] n silueta f. **be silhouetted against** destacarse contra.

silk [silk] n seda f. **silkworm** n gusano de seda m. **silky** adj (fabric) sedoso; (voice, manner) suave.

sill [sil] n antepecho m, alféizar m.

silly ['sili] adj tonto, bobo. **silliness** n tontería f, bobería f.

silt [silt] *n* cieno *m*, limo *m*. **silt up** encenagar.

silver ['silvə] *n* plata *f*; (*coll*: *change*) suelto *m*. *adj* de plata; (*like silver*) plateado. **silver plate** baño de plata *m*. **silversmith** *n* platero *m*. *v* platear. **silvery** *adj* plateado; (*voice*) argentino.

similar ['similə] *adj* semejante, parecido. **similarity** *n* semejanza *f*.

simile ['siməli] *n* símil *m*.

simmer ['simə] *v* hervir a fuego lento; (*fig*) germinar. **simmer down** calmarse.

simple ['simpl] *adj* sencillo; natural; fácil; simple; puro; inocente; (*simple-minded*) necio. **simpleton** *n* simplón, -ona *m*, *f*. **simplicity** *n* sencillez *f*; simpleza *f*. **simplify** *v* simplificar. **simply** *adv* sencillamente; meramente.

simulate ['simjuleit] *v* similar. **simulation** *n* simulación *f*.

simultaneous [‚siməl'teinjəs] *adj* simultáneo.

sin [sin] *n* pecado *m*. *v* pecar. **sinful** *adj* (*person*) pecador; pecaminoso. **sinner** *n* pecador, -a *m*, *f*.

since [sins] *adv* desde entonces. *prep* desde. *conj* desde que; (*because*) ya que.

sincere [sin'siə] *adj* sincero. **sincerity** *n* sinceridad *f*.

sinew ['sinjuə] *n* tendón *m*.

****sing** [siŋ] *v* cantar. **singer** *n* cantor, -a *m*, *f*, cantante *m*, *f*. **singing** *n* canto *m*.

singe [sindʒ] *v* chamuscar. *n* chamusquina *f*.

single ['siŋgl] *adj* solo; único; (*copy*) suelto; (*not double*) individual; (*unmarried*) soltero. **single bed** cama individual *f*. **single file** fila de a uno *f*. **single-handed** *adv* sin ayuda. **single-minded** *adj* resuelto. **single room** habitación individual *f*. **single** (*ticket*) billete de ida *m*. **singles** *n* (*sport*) individual *m*. **single out** separar, distinguir.

singular ['siŋgulə] *nm*, *adj* singular.

sinister ['sinistə] *adj* siniestro.

****sink** [siŋk] *v* hundir, sumergir; (*mine*) cavar; (*voice*) bajar; (*collapse*) dejarse caer; (*go down*) descender. **sink in** (*idea*, *etc*.) darse cuenta de. *n* (*kitchen*) fregadero; (*bathroom*, *bedroom*) lavabo *m*.

sinuous ['sinjuəs] *adj* sinuoso.

sinus ['sainəs] *n* seno *m*. **sinusitis** *n* sinusitis *f*.

sip [sip] *n* sorbo *m*. *v* sorber, beber a sorbos.

siphon ['saifən] *n* sifón *m*. *v* trasegar con sifón. **siphon off** sacar con un sifón.

sir [sət] *n* señor *m*, caballero *m*.

siren ['saiərən] *n* sirena *f*.

sirloin ['sətloin] *n* solomillo *m*.

sister ['sistə] *n* hermana *f*; (*hospital*) enfermera *f*; (*nun*) monja *f*; (*religious title*) sor *f*. **sister-in-law** *n* cuñada *f*.

****sit** [sit] *v* sentar; (*exam*) presentarse a; (*committee*) ser miembro. **baby-sit** *v* cuidar niños. **sit down** sentarse. **sit up** incorporarse; (*stay up*) no acostarse. **sitting** *n* sentada *f*; sesión *f*; (*meal*) servicio *m*. **sittingroom** *n* sala de estar *f*.

site [sait] *n* lugar *m*, sitio *m*; (*building*) solar *m*; camping *m*.

situation [sitju'eifən] *n* situación *f*; (*job*) empleo *m*. **situate** *v* situar.

six [siks] *nm*, *adj* seis. **sixth** *n*, *adj* sexto, -a; (*date*) seis *m*.

sixteen [siks'tiːn] *nm*, *adj* dieciséis. **sixteenth** *n*, *adj* decimosexto, -a.

sixty ['siksti] *nm*, *adj* sesenta. **sixtieth** *n*, *adj* sexagésimo, -a.

size [saiz] *n* tamaño *m*; (*person*, *clothes*) talla *f*; (*gloves*, *shoes*) número *m*. **size up** evaluar, juzgar. **sizeable** *adj* grande; considerable.

sizzle ['sizl] *v* chisporrotear. *n* chisporroteo *m*.

skate[1] [skeit] *n* patín *m*. *v* patinar. **skateboard** *n* skateboard *m*. **skater** *n* patinador, -a *m*, *f*. **skating** *n* patinaje *m*. **skating-rink** *n* pista de patinaje *f*.

skate[2] [skeit] *n* (*fish*) raya *f*.

skeleton ['skelitn] *n* esqueleto *m*. *adj* (*staff*, *etc*.) muy reducido. **skeleton key** llave maestra *f*.

sketch [sketʃ] *n* dibujo *m*; (*rough*) croquis *m*; (*theatre*) sketch *m*. *v* dibujar; hacer un croquis de. **sketch-book** *n* bloc de dibujo *m*. **sketchy** *adj* incompleto; impreciso.

skewer ['skjuə] *n* brocheta *f*. *v* espetar.

ski [skiː] *n* esquí *m*. **ski-lift** telesquí *m*. *v* esquiar. **skier** *n* esquiador, -a *m*, *f*. **skiing** *n* esquí *m*.

skid [skid] *n* patinazo *m*. *v* patinar.

skill [skil] *n* habilidad *f*; destreza *f*. **skilful** *adj* hábil; diestro. **skilled** diestro; experto; (*worker*) cualificado.

skim [skim] *v* (*milk*) desnatar; (*surface*) rozar. **skim through** hojear.

skimp [skimp] v escatimar; chapucear. **skimpy** *adj* escaso; pequeño; corto.

skin [skin] *n* piel *f*; (*face*) cutis *m*; (*milk*) nata *f*. **skin-diving** *n* natación submarina *f*. **skin-tight** *adj* muy ajustado. v (*an animal*) despellejar. **skinny** *adj* flaco, descarnado.

skip [skip] *n* pequeño salto *m*, brinco *m*. v saltar, brincar; saltar a la comba; (*miss*) saltarse.

skipper ['skipə] *n* capitán *m*.

skirmish ['skəːmiʃ] *n* escaramuza *f*. v escaramuzar.

skirt [skəːt] *n* falda *f*. v dar la vuelta a. **skirting board** zócalo *m*.

skittle ['skitl] *n* bolo *m*. **skittles** *n* juego de bolos *m*.

skull [skʌl] *n* cráneo *m*. **skull and cross-bones** calavera *f*.

skunk [skʌŋk] *n* mofeta *f*.

sky [skai] *n* cielo *m*. **sky-blue** *nm, adj* azul celeste. **skylark** *n* alondra *f*. **skylight** *n* claraboya *f*. **skyline** *n* horizonte *m*. **sky-scraper** *n* rascacielos *m invar*.

slab [slab] *n* (*lump*) trozo *m*; (*cake*) porción *f*; (*block*) bloque *m*; (*stone*) losa *f*; (*metal*) plancha *f*; (*chocolate*) tableta *f*.

slack [slak] *adj* (*loose*) flojo; (*lazy*) perezoso; (*trade*) encalmado. **slacken** v aflojar; disminuir.

slacks [slaks] *pl n* pantalones *m pl*.

slag [slag] *n* escoria *f*. **slag heap** escorial *m*.

slam [slam] *n* golpe *m*; (*door*) portazo *m*; (*bridge*) slam *m*. v hacer golpear; cerrar de un golpe. **slam on the brakes** dar un frenazo.

slander ['slaːndə] *n* calumnia *f*; (*law*) difamación *f*. v calumniar; difamar. **slanderous** *adj* calumnioso; difamatorio.

slang [slaŋ] *n* germanía *f*, argot *m*; jerga *f*.

slant [slaːnt] *n* inclinación *f*, sesgo *m*. v inclinar. **slanting** *adj* inclinado, al sesgo.

slap [slap] *n* palmada *f*; (*on face*) bofetada *f*. v pegar con la mano; (*put*) poner violentamente. **slapdash** *adj* (*person*) descuidado; (*work*) chapucero. **slapstick** *n* payasada *f*.

slash [slaʃ] *n* (*knife*) cuchillada *f*; (*whip*) latigazo *m*. v acuchillar; dar latigazos a; (*coll: prices*) sacrificar.

slat [slat] *n* tablilla *f*.

slate [sleit] *n* pizarra *f*. v empizarrar.

slaughter ['slɔːtə] *n* matanza *f*. **slaughterhouse** *n* matadero *m*. v matar; exterminar.

slave [sleiv] *n* esclavo, -a *m, f*. v trabajar como un negro. **slavery** *n* esclavitud *f*.

sledge [sledʒ] *n* trineo *m*.

sledgehammer ['sledʒhamə] *n* almádena *f*.

sleek [sliːk] *adj* liso; pulcro.

*sleep [sliːp] v dormir; (*spend the night*) pasar la noche. *n* sueño *m*. **go to sleep** dormirse. **sleeper** (*rail*) traviesa *f*. **sleeping-bag** *n* saco de dormir *m*. **sleeping-pill** *n* somnífero *m*. **sleepless night** noche en blanco *f*. **sleepy** *adj* soñoliento.

sleet [sliːt] *n* aguanieve *f*. v caer aguanieve.

sleeve [sliːv] *n* manga *f*; (*record*) funda *f*. **sleeveless** *adj* sin manga.

sleigh [slei] *n* trineo *m*.

slender ['slendə] *adj* (*thin*) delgado, fino; (*light and graceful*) esbelto; (*resources*) escaso; (*excuse*) pobre; (*hopes*) ligero.

slice [slais] *n* tajada *f*; (*bread*) rebanada *f*; (*fruit*) raja *f*; (*implement*) pala *f*. v cortar; partir en tajadas/rebanadas/rajas.

slick [slik] *adj* (*derog*) astuto; resbaladizo. *n* (*oil*) capa de aceite *f*.

*slide [slaid] v deslizar; hacer resbalar. *n* (*children's*) tobogán *m*; (*act of sliding*) deslizamiento *m*; (*microscope*) portaobjeto *m*; (*phot*) diapositiva *f*. **slide-rule** *n* regla de cálculo *f*. **sliding** *adj* (*door*) corredera; (*roof*) corredizo; (*scale*) móvil.

slight [slait] *adj* pequeño; insignificante; (*person*) débil; frágil. v despreciar. *n* desprecio *m*. **slightest** *adj* lo más mínimo. **slightly** *adv* ligeramente.

slim [slim] *adj* delgado; esbelto. v adelgazar. **slimming** *adj* (*diet, etc.*) que no engorda, para adelgazar.

slime [slaim] *n* limo *m*; (*fig*) cieno *m*. **slimy** *adj* limoso; (*person*) rastrero.

*sling [sliŋ] v lanzar; suspender. *n* (*med*) cabestrillo *m*; (*weapon*) honda *f*.

*slink [sliŋk] v slink away escurrirse.

slip [slip] *n* (*error*) falta *f*; (*oversight*) inadvertencia *f*; (*skid*) patinazo *m*; (*stumble*) traspiés *m*; (*moral lapse*) desliz *m*; (*petticoat*) combinación *f*; (*pillow*) funda *f*; (*paper*) trozo *m*. **slip of the tongue or pen** lapsus *m*. v resbalar; pasar; poner; descorrer; escurrirse.

slipper ['slɪpə] n zapatilla f.

slippery ['slɪpəri] adj resbaladizo; (person) escurridizo.

*slit [slɪt] v cortar; rasgar. n cortadura f; resquicio m.

slither ['slɪðə] v resbalar; deslizarse.

slobber ['slɔbə] v babosear. n baba f.

sloe [slou] n endrina f.

slog [slɔg] n (coll) pesadez f. v (coll) sudar tinta.

slogan ['slougən] n slogan m.

slop [slɔp] v (splash) salpicar; (pour) derramar.

slope [sloup] n inclinación f; (hill) falda f. v inclinarse. **sloping** adj inclinado; (shoulders) caídos.

sloppy ['slɔpi] adj (food) aguoso; (garment) muy ancho; (careless) capucero; (sentimental) sensiblero. **sloppiness** n (sentiment) sensiblería f.

slot [slɔt] n ranura f, muesca f. v encajar; hacer una ranura.

slouch [slautʃ] v andar cabizbajo.

slovenly ['slʌvnli] adj desaliñado.

slow [slou] adj despacio; lento; (clock) atrasado; (stupid) tardo; (boring) aburrido. **in slow motion** a cámara lenta. **slow down** ir más despacio.

slug [slʌg] n (zool) babosa f; (bullet) posta f.

sluggish ['slʌgiʃ] adj perezoso; lento.

sluice [sluːs] n esclusa f. v regar; lavar.

slum [slʌm] n barrio bajo m. **the slums** tugurios m pl.

slumber ['slʌmbə] n sueño tranquilo m. v dormir tranquilo.

slump [slʌmp] n (fig) baja f; (comm) baja repentina f; depresión económica f. v desplomarse.

slung [slʌŋ] V sling.

slunk [slʌŋk] V slink.

slur [sləː] n baldón m; borrón m; (music) ligado m. v articular mal.

slush [slʌʃ] n nieve sucia y deshecha f.

slut [slʌt] n marrana f.

sly [slai] adj astuto; disimulado.

smack¹ [smak] n golpe m; bofetada f; (sound) chasquido m; v dar una bofetada; dar una palmada; pegar con la mano.

smack² [smak] v **smack of** saber a; (fig) oler a.

small [smɔːl] adj pequeño; poco; chico; escaso. **small change** dinero suelto m.

smallpox n viruela f. **small talk** charla f. **the small of the back** región lumbar f.

smart [smaːt] adj vivo; rápido; (clever) listo; de moda; majo. v picar. **smarten up** ponerse elegante. **smartness** n viveza f; elegancia f.

smash [smaʃ] n (sound) estrépito m; accidente m; (blow) puñetazo m; ruina f. v quebrar, romper; destruir; aplastar; chocar con. **smashing** adj (slang) estupendo.

smear [smiə] n mancha f; (med) frotis m; (fig) calumnia f. v manchar; (bread) untar; calumniar.

*smell [smel] v oler; tener olor. n olor m; (sense) olfato m. **smelly** adj maloliente.

smile [smail] n sonrisa f. v sonreír.

smirk [sməːk] n sonrisa afectada f. v sonreír afectadamente.

smock [smɔk] n blusa f.

smog [smɔg] n niebla espesa con humo f.

smoke [smouk] n humo m. **smoke-screen** n cortina de humo f. v humear; (tobacco) fumar. **smoker** n fumador, -a m, f. **no smoking** se prohíbe fumar. **smoky** adj que huele a humo.

smooth [smuːð] adj liso; suave; llano; uniforme; (person) suavón. v alisar; suavizar; suavizar. **smooth over** exculpar. **smoothly** adv lisamente; con suavidad.

smother ['smʌðə] v sofocar; apagar.

smoulder ['smouldə] v arder sin llama.

smudge [smʌdʒ] n mancha f; tiznón m. v manchar; tiznar.

smug [smʌg] adj pagado de sí mismo.

smuggle ['smʌgl] v pasar de contrabando; matutear. **smuggler** n contrabandista m, f. **smuggling** n contrabando m.

snack [snak] n bocado m, tentempié m. **snack bar** cafetería f.

snag [snag] n pega f, obstáculo m. v enganchar; estorbar.

snail [sneil] n caracol m.

snap [snap] n (fingers) castañeteo m; (bones, teeth, mouth) crujido m; (breaking wood) chasquido m; (bite) mordisco m; (phot) instantánea f. adj instantáneo; rápido. **snapdragon** n dragón m. **snapshot** n instantánea f. v (bones) romper; (branch) partir; (joints) hacer crujir; (dog) intentar morder; (person) regañar.

snare [sneə] n trampa f, lazo m. v atrapar.

snarl [snaːl] n gruñido m. v gruñir.

snatch [snatʃ] n fragmento m; (theft) robo m. v agarrar; tomar.

sneak [sniːk] v hacer furtivamente. sneak in/out entrar/salir furtivamente. n (slang) chivato, -a m, f.

sneer [sniə] v decir con desprecio. n desprecio m. sneering adj burlón.

sneeze [sniːz] n estornudo m. v estornudar.

sniff [snif] n aspiración f; inhalación f. v (smell) oler; aspirar.

snigger ['snigə] n risa disimulada f. reirse por lo bajo.

snip [snip] v cortar de un tijeretazo. n (coll: bargain) ganga f.

snipe [snaip] n agachadiza f. v snipe at (mil) tirotear. sniper n paco m.

snivel ['snivl] v lloriquear. snivelling adj llorón; mocoso.

snob [snob] n snob m, esnob m. snobbish adj snob, esnob.

snooker ['snuːkə] n snooker m.

snoop [snuːp] v fisgonear; entrometerse.

snooty ['snuːti] adj (coll) presumido.

snooze [snuːz] n siesta f; sueñecito m. v dormitar.

snore [snoː] n ronquido m. v roncar. snoring n ronquido m.

snorkel ['snoːkəl] n (swimmer's) tubo de respiración m; (submarine's) esnórquel m.

snort [snoːt] n resoplido m. v resoplar.

snout [snaut] n hocico m.

snow [snou] n nieve f. v nevar. be snowed under with estar abrumado de. snowy adj nevoso.

snowball ['snoubɔːl] n bola de nieve f. v tirar bolas de nieve; acumularse.

snowbound ['snoubaund] adj bloqueado por la nieve.

snowdrift ['snoudrift] n ventisquero m.

snowdrop ['snoudrop] n campanilla blanca f.

snowfall ['snoufɔːl] n nevada f.

snowflake ['snoufleik] n copo de nieve m.

snowstorm ['snoustɔːm] n tormenta de nieve f.

snub [snʌb] n repulsa f. v repulsar.

snuff [snʌf] n rapé m. snuff-box n tabaquera f. v (extinguish) despabilar.

snug [snʌg] adj cómodo; abrigadito.

snuggle ['snʌgl] v arrimarse; apretarse.

so [sou] adv así; tan; también; tanto; por lo tanto. conj así que, de modo que, de manera que. and so on y así sucesivamente. if so de ser así. is that so? ¿de veras? ... or so a poco más o menos ... . so as to de manera que. so-called adj llamado. so much or many tanto, tantos. so-so adj (coll) así así. so that para que. so what? ¿y qué?

soak [souk] v empapar. soak in penetrar en. soak up absorber. soaking n remojo m. soaking wet calado hasta los huesos.

soap [soup] n jabón m. soap dish jabonera f. soap powder jabón en polvo m. soapsuds pl n jabonaduras f pl. v jabonar. soapy adj jabonoso.

soar [soɪ] v remontarse; (fig) elevarse.

sob [sob] n sollozo m. v sollozar.

sober ['soubə] adj moderado; serio; (not drunk) sobrio. v sober up serenarse.

soccer ['sokə] n fútbol m.

sociable ['souʃəbl] adj sociable.

social ['souʃəl] adj social; (friendly) amistoso. social science sociología f. social security seguridad social f. socialism n socialismo m. socialist n(m+f), adj socialista. socialize v socializar.

society [sə'saiəti] n sociedad f.

sociology [sousi'olədʒi] n sociología f. sociological adj sociológico. sociologist n sociólogo, -a m, f.

sock [sok] n calcetín m.

socket ['sokit] n hueco m; (elec) enchufe m.

soda ['soudə] n (chem) sosa f; (water) agua de seltz f.

sodden ['sodn] adj empapado, saturado.

sofa ['soufə] n sofá m.

soft [soft] adj blando; suave; (low) bajo. soft-boiled adj (egg) pasado por agua. soften v ablandar; suavizar; bajar; softness n blandura f; suavidad f; dulzura f; debilidad f; estupidez f.

soggy ['sogi] adj empapado; (bread) pastoso.

soil[1] [soil] n tierra f.

soil[2] [soil] v ensuciar.

solar ['soulə] adj solar.

sold [sould] V sell.

solder ['soldə] n soldadura f. v soldar. soldering-iron n soldador m.

soldier ['souldʒə] n soldado m.

sole[1] [soul] adj solo, único.

sole[2] [soul] n (of shoe) suela f; (of foot) planta f. v solar.

sole[3] [soul] n (fish) lenguado m.

solemn ['soləm] *adj* solemne. **solemnity** *n* solemnidad *f*.

solicitor [sə'lisitə] *n* abogado, -a *m*, *f*.

solicitude [sə'lisitjuːd] *n* solicitud *f*.

solid ['solid] *adj* sólido; firme; continuo. *n* sólido *m*. **solids** *pl n* alimentos sólidos *m pl*. **solidarity** *n* solidaridad *f*. **solidify** *v* solidificarse; congelarse.

solitary ['solitəri] *adj* solitario; solo, único.

solitude ['solitjuːd] *n* soledad *f*.

solo ['soulou] *nm*, *adj* solo. **soloist** *n*. solista *m*, *f*.

solstice ['solstis] *n* solsticio *m*.

soluble ['soljubl] *adj* soluble.

solution [sə'luːʃən] *n* solución *f*.

solve [solv] *v* resolver; acertar.

solvent ['solvənt] *adj* (*finance*) solvente. *n* (*chem*) disolvente *m*. **solvency** *n* solvencia *f*.

sombre ['sombə] *adj* sombrío.

some [sʌm] *adj* algún, alguno, algunos; unos, varios. *pron* algunos; unos; un poco; parte. *adv* bestante; unos. **somebody** *or* **someone** *pron* alguien. **somehow** *adv* de algún modo; por alguna razón. **something** *pron* algo. **sometime** *adv* alguna vez, algún día. **sometimes** *adv* a veces, de vez en cuando. **somewhat** *adv* algo, algún tanto. **somewhere** *adv* en alguna parte. **somewhere else** en alguna otra parte.

somersault ['sʌməsoːlt] *n* salto mortal *m*. *v* dar un salto mortal.

son [sʌn] *n* hijo *m*. **son-in-law** *n* yerno *m*.

sonata [sə'naːtə] *n* sonata *f*.

song [soŋ] *n* (*art*) canto *m*; (*composition*) canción *f*.

sonic ['sonik] *adj* sónico.

sonnet ['sonit] *n* soneta *m*.

soon [suːn] *adv* pronto, dentro de poco; (*early*) temprano. **as soon as** tan pronto como. **sooner or later** tarde o temprano.

soot [sut] *n* hollín *m*.

soothe [suːð] *v* tranquilizar, calmar. **soothing** *adj* tranquilizador, calmante.

sophisticated [sə'fistikeitid] *adj* sofisticado; mundano; (*machinery*) complejo.

sopping ['sopiŋ] *adj* empapadísimo.

soprano [sə'praːnou] *n* soprano *m*, *f*.

sordid ['soːdid] *adj* sórdido.

sore [soː] *adj* malo; dolorido; (*fig*) doloroso. **sore point** tema delicado *m*. **sorely** *adv* (*bitterly*) profundamente; (*very*) muy. **soreness** *n* dolor *m*.

sorrow ['sorou] *n* pesar *m*; tristeza *f*. *v* afligirse. **sorrowful** *adj* afligido; triste.

sorry ['sori] *adj* afligido; triste; apenado; lastimoso. **feel sorry for** compadecer. *interj* ¡perdóneme! ¡disculpe!

sort [soːt] *n* clase *f*; especie *f*; tipo *m*; modo *m*; persona *f*. *v* separar de; clasificar. **sort out** apartar; (*problems*) arreglar. **sorting office** sala de batalla *f*.

soufflé ['suːflei] *n* soufflé *m*.

sought [soːt] *V* seek.

soul [soul] *n* alma *f*. **soulful** *adj* expresivo; conmovedor.

sound¹ [saund] *n* (*noise*) sonido *m*, ruido *m*. **sound barrier** barrera del sonido *f*. **sound effects** efectos sonoros *m pl*. **soundproof** *adj* insonoro. **sound-track** *n* pista sonora *f*. *v* sonar, resonar; (*seem*) parecer.

sound² [saund] *adj* sano; (*reasonable*) lógico; (*argument*) válido; (*policy*) prudente; (*investment*) seguro; (*comm*) solvente. **be sound asleep** estar profundamente dormido.

sound³ [saund] *v* (*depth*) sondar; (*opinion*) sondear.

soup [suːp] *n* sopa *f*. **clear soup** consomé *m*. **thick soup** puré *m*. **soup plate** plato sopero *m*. **soup spoon** cuchara sopera *f*.

sour [sauə] *adj* ácido, agrio. *v* agriar. **sourness** *n* acidez *f*; agrura *f*.

source [soːs] *n* fuente *f*; origen *m*.

south [sauθ] *n* sur *m*. *adj also* **southerly**, **southern** del sur. *adv* hacia el sur. **southbound** *adj* con rumbo al sur. **south-east** *nm*, *adj* sudeste. **south-west** *nm*, *adj* sudoeste.

South America *n* Sudamérica *f*, América del Sur *f*. **South American** sudamericano, -a *m*, *f*.

souvenir [suːvə'niə] *n* recuerdo *m*.

sovereign ['sovrin] *n*, *adj* soberano, -a.

***sow¹** [sou] *v* sembrar; esparcir.

sow² [sau] *n* cerda *f*, puerca *f*.

soya ['soiə] *n* soja *f*. **soya bean** soja *f*. **soy sauce** salsa picante de soja *f*.

spa [spaː] *n* balneario *m*; manantial mineral *m*.

space [speis] *n* espacio *m*; (*place*) sitio *m*; (*time*) temporada *f*. **spaceman** *n* astronauta *m*, cosmonauta *m*. **spaceship** *n* nave espacial *f*. *v* espaciar. **spacious** *adj* espacioso; amplio.

spade [speid] *n* pala *f*.
spades [speidz] *pl n* (*cards*) picos *m pl*;
(*Spanish cards*) espadas *f pl*.
spaghetti [spə'geti] *n* espaguetis *m pl*.
Spain [spein] *n* España *f*. Spaniard *n*
español. -a *m*, *f*. Spanish *nm*, *adj* español.
span [span] *n* (*time*) espacio *m*, duración
f; (*wings*) envergadura *f*; (*space*) distancia *f*; (*bridge*) tramo *m*. *v* atravesar;
medir.
spaniel ['spanjəl] *n* perro de aguas *m*;
(*cocker*) sabueso *m*.
spank [spaŋk] *v* dar una azotaina. spanking *n* azotaina *f*.
spanner ['spanə] *n* llave *f*.
spare [speə] *adj* de reserva; de sobra; disponible. spare part (*mot*) recambio *m*.
spare-ribs *pl n* (*cookery*) costillas de
cerdo *f pl*. spare room cuarto de los
invitados *m*. spare time ratos libres *m pl*.
spare tyre neumático de repuesto *m*. *v*
(*do without*) pasarse sin; (*avoid*) evitar;
(*expense*) escatimar. sparing *adj* (*words*)
parco; limitado; escaso; frugal.
spark [spaɪk] *n* chispa *f*. *v* chispear. spark
off provocar. sparking-plug *n* bujia *f*.
sparkle ['spaɪkl] *n* centelleo *m*; (*fig*) brillo
m. *v* centellear; (*fig*) brillar. sparkling *adj*
(*drink*) espumoso.
sparrow ['sparou] *n* gorrión *m*.
sparse [spaɪs] *adj* escaso, poco denso.
sparsely *adv* escasamente.
spasm ['spazəm] *n* espasmo *m*; (*fit*)
ataque *m*. spasmodic *adj* espasmódico.
spastic ['spastik] *n*, *adj* espástico, -a.
spat [spat] *V* spit.
spatial ['speiʃl] *adj* espacial.
spatula ['spatjulə] *n* espátula *f*.
spawn [spoɪn] *n* (*fish*) freza *f*, hueva *f*;
(*frog*) huevos *m pl*. *v* frezar; depositar.
*speak [spiɪk] *v* decir; hablar. speak up
hablar más fuerte. speak up for hablar en
'avor de. speaker *n* orador, -a *m*, *f*;
(*loudspeaker*) altavoz *m*.
spear [spiə] *n* lanza *f*. *v* traspasar. spearhead *n* vanguardia *f*.
special ['speʃəl] *adj* especial; particular;
extraordinario. specialist *n* especialista
m, *f*. speciality *n* especialidad *f*. specialize *v* especializar.
species ['spiɪʃiz] *n* especie *f*.
specify ['spesifai] *v* especificar. specific
adj específico. specification *n* especificación *f*; estipulación *f*; requisito *m*.

specimen ['spesimin] *n* (*biol*) espécimen
m; modelo *m*; (*sample*) muestra *f*;
(*example*) ejemplar *m*.
speck [spek] *n* manchita *f*; pizca *f*.
speckle *v* motear.
spectacle ['spektəkl] *n* espectáculo *m*.
spectacles *pl n* gafas *f pl*. spectacular *adj*
espectacular.
spectator [spek'teitə] *n* espectador, -a *m*,
f.
spectrum ['spektrəm] *n* espectro *m*.
speculate ['spekjuleit] *v* especular; conjeturar. speculation *n* especulación *f*;
conjetura *f*. speculative *adj* especulativo;
conjetural.
speech [spiɪtʃ] *n* (*address*) discurso *m*;
(*faculty*) habla *f*; (*lecture*) conferencia *f*;
conversación *f*; pronunciación *f*. speechless *adj* mudo.
*speed [spiɪd] *v* (*mot*) ir a toda velocidad.
speed along apresurarse. speed up acelerar. speeding *n* exces de velocidad *m*.
speedy *adj* veloz. *n* prisa *f*; velocidad *f*;
rapidez *f*. speedboat *n* lancha motora *f*.
speed limit velocidad máxima *f*. speedometer *n* velocímetro *m*.
*spell[1] [spel] *v* escribir; deletrear; significar. spelling *n* ortografía *f*.
spell[2] [spel] *n* (*magic*) hechizo *m*, encanto
m. spellbound *adj* encantado.
spell[3] [spel] *n* período *m*; turno *m*.
*spend [spend] *v* (*money*) gastar; (*time*)
pasar. spending *n* gasto *m*. spending
money dinero para gastos menudos *m*.
sperm [spəɪm] *n* esperma *f*.
spew [spjuɪ] *v* vomitar.
sphere [sfiə] *n* esfera *f*; (*province*) competencia *f*. spherical *adj* esférico.
spice [spais] *n* especia *f*. *v* especiar. spicy
adj especiado, picante; (*fig*) sabroso.
spider ['spaidə] *n* araña *f*. spider's web
telaraña *f*.
spike [spaik] *n* escarpia *f*.
*spill [spil] *v* derramar. *n* (*coll: fall*) caída
f.
*spin [spin] *v* girar, dar vueltas; dar
efecto a; (*cotton, silk, etc*.) hilar; (*web*)
tejer; (*fig: a yarn*) contar. spin-dryer *n*
secador centrífugo *m*. spin out prolongar.
spinning *n* hilado *m*. spinning wheel rueca *f*. *n* giro *m*.
spinach ['spinidʒ] *n* espinaca *f*.
spindle ['spindl] *n* (*axle, shaft*) eje *m*; (*of
a lathe*) mandril *m*; (*of a spinning wheel*)
huso *m*. spindly *adj* largirucho.

spine [spain] *n* (*anat*) espina dorsal *f*; (*zool*) púa *f*; (*book*) lomo *m*. **spinal** *adj* espinal. **spiny** *adj* espinoso.

spinster ['spinstə] *n* soltera *f*.

spiral ['spaiərəl] *adj* espiral. *n* espiral *f*. *v* dar vueltas en espiral.

spire ['spaiə] *n* aguja *f*.

spirit ['spirit] *n* espíritu *m*, alma *f*; (*ghost*) fantasma *m*; (*courage*) valor *m*; (*liveliness*) ánimo; (*mood*) humor *m*; alcohol *m*. **spirited** *adj* animado, vigoroso. **spirited** *adj* espiritual. **spiritualism** *n* espiritualismo *m*. **spiritualist** *n*(*m+f*), *adj* espiritualista.

*spit¹ [spit] *v* escupir. *n* saliva *f*, escupitajo *m*.

spit² [spit] *n* (*cookery*) espetón *m*, asador *m*; (*geog*) lengua de tierra *f*.

spite [spait] *n* rencor *m*, malevolencia *f*. **in spite of** a pesar de. *v* mortificar. **spiteful** *adj* rencoroso.

splash [splaʃ] *n* salpicadura *f*; (*sound*) chapoteo; (*mark*) mancha *f*. *v* salpicar.

spleen [spliːn] *n* (*anat*) bazo *m*; (*fig*) mal humor *m*.

splendid ['splendid] *adj* espléndido; excelente. **splendour** *n* resplandor *m*.

splice [splais] *v* empalmar; (*coll*: *marry*) unir, casar.

splint [splint] *n* férula *f*.

splinter ['splintə] *n* (*wood*) astilla *f*; (*bomb*) casco *m*; (*bone*) esquirla *f*; (*piece*) fragmento *m*. *v* astillar.

*split [split] *v* hender, partir; rajar; dividir; separar; (*atom*) desintegrar. *n* partido *m*, hendido *m*; división *f*; (*in cloth*) rasgón *m*; (*quarrel*) ruptura *f*. **split second** fracción de segundo *f*.

splutter ['splʌtə] *v* (*person*) farfullar; (*flame*) chisporrotear. *n* farfulla *f*; chisporroteo *m*.

*spoil [spoil] *v* estropear, echar a perder; (*child*) minar; (*damage*) dañar. **spoilsport** *n* aguafiestas *m*, *f invar*. **spoils** *pl n* botín *m sing*.

spoke¹ [spouk] *V* speak.

spoke² [spouk] *n* reyo *m*.

spokesman ['spouksmən] *n* portavoz *m*.

sponge [spʌndʒ] *n* esponja *f*; (*cake*) bizcocho esponjoso *m*. **sponge bag** esponjera *f*. *v* limpiar con esponja; (*coll*: *cadge*) sacar de gorra. **spongy** *adj* esponjoso.

sponsor ['sponsə] *n* (*for financial support*) patrocinador, -a *m*, *f*; (*warrantor*) fiador,

-a *m*, *f*; (*for club membership*) padrino, -a *m*, *f*. *v* patrocinar; fiar; apadrinar. **sponsorship** *n* patrocinio *m*.

spontaneous [spon'teinjəs] *adj* espontáneo. **spontaneity** *n* espontaneidad *f*.

spool [spuːl] *n* bobina *f*.

spoon [spuːn] *n* cuchara *f*. **spoonful** *n* cucharada *f*.

sporadic [spə'radik] *adj* esporádico.

sport [spoːt] *n* deporte *m*; (*plaything*) juguete *m*; (*amusement*) bula *f*. **sports car** coche deportivo *m*. **sports jacket** chaqueta de sport *f*. **sportsman/woman** *n* deportista *m*, *f*. *v* llevar; ostentar. **sporting** *adj* deportista; caballeroso. **sportive** *adj* juguetón; bromista.

spot [spot] *n* (*med*) grano *m*; espinilla *f*; (*mark*) mancha *f*; (*pattern*) lunar *m*; (*place*) sitio *m*; (*liquid*) gota *f*; parte *f*; punto *m*; (*coll*) poco *m*. **on the spot** en el momento; en el acto. **spot check** inspección repentina *f*. **spotlight** *n* foco *m*. *v* manchar; reconocer; notar. **spotless** *adj* inmaculado. **spotted** *adj* (*speckled*) moteado; con manchas; de lunares. **spotty** *adj* espinilloso.

spouse [spaus] *n* esposo, -a *m*, *f*.

spout [spaut] *n* (*teapot*) pitorro *m*; (*jug*) pico *m*; (*rainwater pipe*) caño *m*; (*jet*) chorro *m*; (*waterspout*) tromba *f*. *v* echar; (*coll*) soltar.

sprain [sprein] *n* torcedura *f*. *v* torcer.

sprawl [sproːl] *n* postura desgarbada *f*. *v* extender.

spray¹ [sprei] *n* (*water*) rociada *f*; (*sea*) espuma *f*; (*sprayer*) pulverizador *m*. *v* (*sprinkle*) rociar; pulverizar; (*crops*) fumigar; vaporizarse.

spray² [sprei] *n* (*flowers*) ramo *m*, ramillete *m*.

*spread [spred] *v* extender; (*on the ground*) exponer; (*marmalade, butter, etc.*) untar; propagar; difundir; (*wings*) desplegar. **spread out** esparcir. *n* propagación *f*, difusión *f*; (*town*) extensión *f*; (*span*) envergadura *f*; (*range*) gama *f*.

spree [spriː] *n* juerga *f*.

sprig [sprig] *n* ramito *m*.

sprightly ['spraitli] *adj* despierto, vivo.

*spring [spriŋ] *v* saltar. **spring up** brotar; surgir. *n* (*season*) primavera *f*; (*leap*) salto *m*, brinco *m*; (*water*) fuente *f*; (*coil*) muelle *m*. **springboard** *n* trampolín *m*. **spring-cleaning** *n* limpieza general *f*.

spring onion cebolleta *f.* **springy** *adj* elástico.

sprinkle ['spriŋkl] *v* (*water*) rociar; (*sugar, salt, etc.*) salpicar. **sprinkler** *n* regadera *f.* (*fire*) extintor *m.*

sprint [sprint] *n* sprint *m.* esprint *m.* *v* sprintar, esprintar.

sprout [spraut] *n* brote *m*, retoño *m.* **Brussels sprouts** coles de Bruselas *f pl.*

spruce [spruːs] *n* (*bot*) pícea *f.* *adj* elegante. **spruce up** acicalar.

spun [spʌn] *V* spin.

spur [spəː] *n* espuela *f.* (*fig*) estímulo *m.* **on the spur of the moment** sin pensarlo. *v* espolear. **spur on** estimular.

spurious ['spjuəriəs] *adj* espurio, falso.

spurn [spəːn] *v* desdeñar, rechazar.

spurt [spəːt] *n* (*water*) chorro *m.* (*energy*) gran esfuerzo *m.* *v* chorrear; hacer un gran esfuerzo; acelerar.

spy [spai] *n* espía *m*, *f.* *v* espiar; observar. **spying** *n* espionaje *m.*

squabble ['skwobl] *n* riña *f.* *v* disputar.

squad [skwod] *n* escuadra *f.* (*mil*) pelotón *m.*

squadron ['skwodrən] *n* (*mil*) escuadrón *m.* (*naut*) escuadra *f.* (*aero*) escuadrilla *f.*

squalid ['skwolid] *adj* mugriento; escuálido; miserable. **squalor** *n* mugre *f.* miseria *f.*

squall [skwoːl] *n* ráfaga *f.*

squander ['skwondə] *v* malgastar.

square [skweə] *n* (*shape*) cuadrado *m.* (*pattern*) cuadro *m.* (*chessboard*) casilla *f.* (*in a town*) plaza *f.* *adj* cuadrado; rectangular; (*coll: old-fashioned*) anticuado. *v* cuadrar; (*settle*) arreglar.

squash [skwoʃ] *n* (*sport*) juego de pelota *m.* (*drink*) limonada *f.* naranjada *f.* (*crushing*) aplastamiento *m.* *v* (*crush*) aplastar; (*squeeze*) apretar.

squat [skwot] *n* posición en cuchillas *f.* *adj* rechoncho. *v* agacharse. **squatter** *n* persona que ocupe ilegalmente un sitio *f.*

squawk [skwoːk] *n* graznido *m.* *v* graznar.

squeak [skwiːk] *n* (*mice, etc.*) chillido *m.* (*hinge*) chirrido *m.* *v* chillar; chirriar.

squeal [skwiːl] *n* chillido *m.* *v* chillar.

squeamish ['skwiːmiʃ] *adj* remilgado; delicado.

squeeze [skwiːz] *n* presión *f.* (*hug*) abrazo *m.* (*hand*) apretón *m.* (*crowd*) gentío *m.* *v* abrazar; apretar; (*extract*) exprimir.

squid [skwid] *n* calamar *m.*

squint [skwint] *n* (*med*) estrabismo *m.*

(*coll: glance*) ojeada *f.* *v* entrecerrar los ojos.

squirm [skwəːm] *v* retorcerse.

squirrel ['skwirəl] *n* ardilla *f.*

squirt [skwəːt] *n* chorro *m.* *v* lanzar; chorrear.

stab [stab] *n* puñalada. *v* apuñalar.

stabilize ['steibilaiz] *v* estabilizar. **stabilizer** *n* estabilizador *m.*

stable[1] ['steibl] *n* cuadra *f.*

stable[2] ['steibl] *adj* estable; fijo. **stability** *n* estabilidad *f.* firmeza *f.*

staccato [stə'kaːtou] *adv* staccato. *adj* (*voice, style, etc.*) entrecortado.

stack [stak] *n* (*hay, etc.*) almiar *m.* (*pile*) montón *m.* (*chimney*) cañón *m.* **stacks of** (*coll*) un montón de *m sing.* *v* hacinar; amontonar.

stadium ['steidiəm] *n* estadio *m.*

staff [staːf] *n* vara *f.* palo *m.* (*flag*) asta *f.* personal *m.* **staff-room** *n* (*school*) sala de profesores *f.* *v* proveer de personal.

stag [stag] *n* venado *m*, ciervo *m.* **stag party** reunión de hombres *f.*

stage [steidʒ] *n* (*theatre*) escenario *m.* (*platform*) estrado *m.* (*point*) etapa *f.* (*phase*) fase *f.* **stage manager** regidor de escena *m.* *v* representar; efectuar; organizar.

stagger ['stagə] *n* tambaleo *m.* *v* tambalearse; (*amaze*) asombrar; (*payments, etc.*) escalonar. **staggering** *adj* asombroso.

stagnant ['stagnənt] *adj* estancado. **stagnate** *v* estancarse. **stagnation** *n* estancamiento *m.*

staid [steid] *adj* serio; formal.

stain [stein] *n* mancha *f.* tinte *m.* **stain remover** quitamanchas *m invar.* *v* manchar; (*wood*) teñir. **stained-glass window** vidriera *f.*

stair [steə] *n* escalón *m.* **staircase** *n* also **stairs** *pl n* escalera *f sing.*

stake[1] [steik] *n* (*post*) poste *m.* estaca *f.* (*for plants*) rodrigón *m.* (*for execution*) hoguera *f.* *v* estacar.

stake[2] [steik] *n* (*bet*) apuesta *f.* (*investment*) intereses *m pl.* **at stake** en juego. *v* apostar.

stale [steil] *adj* (*bread*) duro; (*egg*) poco fresco; (*food*) rancio; (*air*) viciado. **staleness** *n* ranciedad *f.*

stalemate ['steilmeit] *n* (*chess*) ahogado *m.* (*fig*) punto muerto *m.*

stalk¹ [stɔːk] n (*stem*) tallo m.
stalk² [stɔːk] v acechar. **stalk in/out** entrar/salir con paso airado.
stall¹ [stɔːl] n (*market*) puesto m; (*theatre*) butaca f; (*exhibition*) caseta f. v (*engine*) parar.
stall² [stɔːl] v (*delay*) andar con rodeos. **stall off** dar largas a.
stallion ['staljən] n semental m.
stamina ['staminə] n vigor m; aguante m.
stammer ['stamə] n tartamudez f. v tartamudear.
stamp [stamp] n sello m, timbre m; marca f; impresión f; (*with foot*) zapatazo m. **stamp-collecting** n filatelia f. v estampar; sellar; imprimir; (*one's foot*) patear.
stampede [stam'piːd] n desbocamiento m; desbandada f. v provocar la desbandada de.
***stand** [stand] v (*on feet*) estar de pie; (*place*) poner; resistir; soportar; (*trial*) someterse a; (*remain*) permanecer; (*pay for*) sufragar. n posición f; plataforma f; (*coats, hats*) percha f; (*fig*) postura f. **stand for** significar; representar. **stand out** sobresalir. **standstill** n parada f. **come to a standstill** pararse. **stand up for** defender.
standard ['standəd] n (*weight, length, money*) patrón m; (*of living*) nivel m; modelo m; criterio m. adj normal; oficial; legal; (*comm*) standard. **standard lamp** lámpara de pie f. **standardize** v estandardizar; normalizar.
standing ['standiŋ] adj de pie; vertical; clásico; fijo. **standing order** (*bank*) pedido regular m. n posición f; situación f; reputación f; duración f.
stank [staŋk] V stink.
stanza ['stanzə] n estancia f, estrofa f.
staple¹ [steipl] n (*papers*) grapa f; (*of wool, cotton*) fibra f. v sujetar con una grapa.
staple² [steipl] adj básico; principal.
star [staː] n (*astron, cinema*) estrella f; asterisco m. **stars pl** n (*astrol*) astros m pl. **starfish** n estrella de mar f. v estrellar; ser protagonista. **stardom** n estrellato m. **starry** adj estrellado.
starboard ['staːbəd] n estribor m.
starch [staːtʃ] n almidón m. v almidonar. **starchy** adj almidonado.
stare [steə] n mirada fija f. v mirar fijamente.
stark [staːk] adj (*bleak*) desolado; (*stiff*) rígido; completo; puro; absoluto. **stark naked** completamente desnudo.
starling ['staːliŋ] n estornino m.
start [staːt] n comienzo m; (*of a race*) salida f; (*jump*) sobresalto m; (*fright*) susto m. v comenzar, empezar; (*clock*) poner en marcha; (*car*) arrancar; (*establish*) fundar; (*rumour*) lanzar; provocar; sobresaltar. **starter** n (*mot*) arranque m; (*meal*) entremés m.
startle ['staːtl] v asustar. **startling** adj sorprendente; alarmante.
state [steit] n estado m; condición f; (*luxury*) lujo m; gran pompa f. **statesman** n estadista m. v afirmar, declarar; dar; decir; consignar; exponer. **stately** adj majestuoso. **statement** n declaración f; informe m; comunicado m; (*bank*) balance mensual m.
static ['statik] adj estático. n (*radio*) parásitos m pl.
station ['steiʃən] n (*rail, radio*) estación f; (*position*) puesto m; (*place*) lugar m; (*social*) posición f. v apostar; estacionar.
stationary ['steiʃənəri] adj estacionario; inmóvil.
stationer ['steiʃənə] n papelero m. **stationer's** n papelería f. **stationery** n objetos de escritorio m pl; papel de escribir y sobres m.
statistics [stə'tistiks] n (*science*) estadística f. pl n (*data*) estadísticas f pl. **statistical** adj estadístico.
statue ['statjuː] n estatua f.
stature ['statʃə] n estatura f; (*fig*) talla f.
status ['steitəs] n (*standing*) categoría f; (*state*) condición f; (*social standing*) posición f.
statute ['statjuːt] n estatuo m. **statutory** adj establecido por la ley.
staunch¹ [stɔːntʃ] adj fiel; inquebrantable.
staunch² [stɔːntʃ] v restañar.
stay [stei] n estancia f; (*support*) apoyo m. v (*remain*) quedarse; (*postpone*) aplazar; (*endure*) resistir; (*support*) apoyar.
steadfast ['stedfaːst] adj constante; fijo.
steady ['stedi] adj constante; firme; regular; continuo. v estabilizar; calmar; sostener. **steadily** adv firmemente; regularmente; sin parar. **steadiness** n firmeza f; estabilidad f; uniformidad f; regularidad f.
steak [steik] n (*beefsteak*) bistec m; (*of other meat or fish*) filete m.

*steal [stiːl] v robar. stealing n robo m.
stealthy ['stelθi] adj furtivo.
steam [stiːm] n vapor m. let off steam
(coll) desahogarse. v echar vapor;
(cookery) cocinar al vapor.
steel [stiːl] n acero m. steel wool
estropajo m. steelworks pl n acería f sing.
steely adj acerado; inflexible.
steep¹ [stiːp] adj escarpado.
steep² [stiːp] v empapar.
steeple ['stiːpl] n aguja f. steeplechase n
carrera de obstáculos f. steeplejack n
reparador de chimeneas m.
steer [stiə] v (ship) gobernar; (vehicle)
dirigir; (bicycle) llevar; (course) seguir;
(car) manejar. steering n (naut) gobierno
m; (mot) conducción f. steering-wheel n
volante m.
stem¹ [stem] n tallo m; (glass) pie m.
stem from derivarse de.
stem² [stem] v (stop) detener, contener.
stench [stentʃ] n tufo m.
stencil ['stensl] n estarcido m. v (typing)
cliché de multicopista m.
step [step] n paso m; (stairs, ladder)
peldaño m; (doorway) umbral m;
(degree) escalón m; (measure) medida f.
stepladder n escalera de tijera f. v dar un
paso; ir. step up subir; aumentar.
stepbrother ['stepbrʌðə] n hermanastro
m.
stepdaughter ['stepdɔːtə] n hijastra f.
stepfather ['stepfɑːðə] n padrastro m.
stepmother ['stepmʌðə] n madrastra f.
stepsister ['stepsistə] n hermanastra f.
stepson ['stepsʌn] n hijastro m.
stereo ['steriou] nf, adj estéreo. stereophonic adj estereofónico.
stereotype ['steriətaip] n estereotipo m. v
estereotipar.
sterile ['sterail] adj estéril. sterility n
esterilidad f. sterilization esterilización f.
sterilize v esterilizar.
sterling ['stəːliŋ] n libra esterlina f. adj
(silver) plata de ley f; (character)
excelente.
stern¹ [stəːn] adj severo.
stern² [stəːn] n (naut) popa f.
stethoscope ['steθəskoup] n estetoscopio
m.
stew [stjuː] n estofado m. v (meat)
estofar; guisar; (fruit) cocer.
steward ['stjuəd] n camarero m; despen-
sero m. shop steward enlace sindical m.

stewardess n (ship) camarera f; (air)
azafata f.
stick¹ [stik] n madero m; estaca f; palo
m; (club) garrote m; (walking) bastón m.
*stick² [stik] v fijar; (thrust) clavar; (pene-
trate) pinchar; (glue) pegar; (stay)
quedarse. stick out sacar; sobresalir.
stick up for (coll) defender. sticky adj
pegajoso; (coll) difícil.
stickler ['stiklə] n be a stickler for dar
mucha importancia a.
stiff [stif] adj rígido; (manner) distante;
(person) severo. stiffen v atiesarse;
endurecerse. stiffness n rigidez f; frialdad
f; obstinación f.
stifle ['staifl] v ahogar, sofocar; (smile,
etc.) suprimir. stifling adj sofocante.
stigma ['stigmə] n estigma m.
stile [stail] n portilla con escalones f.
still¹ [stil] adv todavía, aún; (always)
siempre; (nevertheless) sin embargo; (sit,
stand) quieto. adj tranquilo; inmóvil;
silencioso. stillborn adj nacido muerto.
still life bodegón m. n calma f; (phot)
vista fija f.
still² [stil] n alambique m; destilería f.
stilt [stilt] n zanco m. stilted adj
campanudo.
stimulus ['stimjuləs] n, pl -li estímulo m;
incentivo m. stimulant nm, adj estimulante. stimulate v estimular. stimulation n
estímulo m.
*sting [stiŋ] v picar; herir; (coll: over-
charge) clavar. n (insect) aguijón m;
(wound) picadura f; (pain) escozor m.
*stink [stiŋk] v heder, oler mal. n hedor
m.
stint [stint] n sesión de trabajo f. v escatimar; limitar.
stipulate ['stipjuleit] v estipular. stipulation n estipulación f.
stir [stəː] n agitación f; sensación f; conmoción f. v (tea, etc.) revolver; mezclar;
(move) mover; excitar. stir up provocar;
fomentar.
stirrup ['stirəp] n estribo m.
stitch [stitʃ] n (sewing) puntada f; (knitting) punto m; (med) punto de sutura m;
(pain) dolor de costado m. v coser; (med)
suturar.
stoat [stout] n armiño m.
stock [stok] n (supply) reserva f; (farm)
ganado m; (cookery) caldo m; (lineage)
linaje m; (race) raza f; (tree) tronco m.
stockbroker n corredor de Bolsa m. stock

exchange Bolsa *f.* **stockpile** *n* reservas *f pl.* **stocktaking** *n* inventario *m.* *v* surtir, abastecer.

Stockholm ['stokhoum] *n* Estocolmo.

stocking ['stokiŋ] *n* media *f.*

stocky ['stoki] *adj* rechoncho.

stodge [stodʒ] *n* (*coll*) comida indigesta *f.* **stodgy** *adj* indigesto.

stoical ['stouikl] *adj* estoico.

stoke [stouk] *v* alimentar.

stole[1] [stoul] *V* steal.

stole[2] [stoul] *n* estola *f.*

stomach ['stʌmək] *n* estómago *m.* **stomach-ache** *n* dolor de estómago *m.* *v* soportar.

stone [stoun] *n* piedra *f.*; (*fruit*) hueso *m.*; (*med*) cálculo *m.* **stone-cold** *adj* helado. *v* (*throw*) apedrear. **stony** *adj* pedregoso.

stood [stud] *V* stand.

stool [stutl] *n* taburete *m.*

stoop [sturp] *n* espaldas encorvadas *f pl.* *v* encorvarse; agacharse. **stoop to** rebajarse a.

stop [stop] *n* parada *f.*; cesación *f.*; suspensión *f.*; (*stay*) estancia *f.*; (*gramm*) punto *m.* *v* parar; impedir; interrumpir; evitar; dejar de; (*a hole*) tapar; (*a gap*) rellenar; cesar. **stop-watch** *n* cronómetro *m.* **stoppage** *n* (*blockage*) obstrucción *f.*; (*strike*) huelga *f.* **stopper** *n* tapón *m.*

store [stot] *n* (*supply*) provisión *f.*; (*warehouse*) depósito *m.*; (*large shop*) almacén *m.*; (*smaller shop*) tienda *f.* *v* (*keep*) guardar; almacenar; (*supply*) suministrar. **storage** *n* almacenaje *m.*

storey ['stori] *n* piso *m.*

stork [stotk] *n* cigüeña *f.*

storm [stotm] *n* tempestad *f.*; (*thunderstorm*) tormenta *f.* *v* (*mil*) asaltar; (*wind*) ser tempestuoso; (*fig*) fabiar. **stormy** *adj* tempestuoso; violento.

story ['stori] *n* historia *f.*; cuento *m.*

stout [staut] *adj* fuerte; intrépido; gordo; grueso. *n* cerveza negra *f.*

stove [stouv] *n* (*cooker*) cocina *f.*; (*heater*) estufa *f.*

stow [stou] *v* colocar. meter. **stow away** guardar; esconder. **stowaway** *n* polizón *m.*

straddle ['stradl] *v* estar a caballo sobre; montar a horcajadas.

straggle ['stragl] *v* (*leg*) rezagarse; (*spread*) desparramarse. **straggler** *n* rezagado, -a *m, f.*

straight [streit] *adj* derecho; recto; en orden; (*hair*) lacio. *adv* derecho; directamente. **straight ahead** todo recto. **straight away** en seguida. **straightforward** *adj* sincero; (*simple*) sencillo. **straighten** *v* enderezar; arreglar.

strain[1] [strein] *n* tensión *f.*; esfuerzo *m.*; (*med*) torcedura *f.* *v* (*stretch*) estirar; forzar; (*sprain*) torcer; (*filter*) filtrar; (*cookery*) colar. **strainer** *n* colador *m.*

strain[2] [strein] *n* raza *f.*; tendencia *f.*

strait [streit] *n* estrecho *m.*

strand[1] [strand] *n* (*hair*) trenza *f.*; (*rope*) cabo *m.*; (*thread*) hebra *f.*

strand[2] [strand] *n* (*shore*) playa *f.*; (*river*) ribera *f.* *v* (*ship*) encallar. **be stranded** hallarse abandonado.

strange [streindʒ] *adj* extraño; raro; inesperado; (*unknown*) desconocido. **stranger** *n* desconocido, -a *m, f.*

strangle ['straŋgl] *v* estrangular. **stranglehold** *n* collar de fuerza *m.* **strangler** *n* estrangulador, -a *m, f.*

strap [strap] *n* correa *f.*; (*on garment*) tirante *m.* *v* atar con correa; (*med*) vendar. **strapping** *adj* robusto.

strategy ['stratədʒi] *n* estrategia *f.* **strategic** *adj* estratégico.

stratum ['straitəm] *n, pl* -ta estrato *m,* capa *f.*

straw [stroi] *n* paja *f.* **it's the last straw!** ¡es el colmo!

strawberry ['strotbəri] *n* (*plant and fruit*) fresa *f.*

stray [strei] *n* animal extraviado *m.* *adj* perdido; extraviado; aislado. *v* errar; desviarse; perderse.

streak [strik] *n* raya *f.*; vena *f.*; (*light*) rayo *m.* *v* rayar; ir como un rayo. **streaky** *adj* rayado.

stream [strim] *n* río *m.*; arroyo *m.*; corriente *f.* **streamlined** *adj* aerodinámico; (*mot*) carenado; (*efficient*) eficaz. *v* correr, fluir. **streamer** *n* serpentina *f.*

street [strit] *n* calle *f.*

strength [streŋθ] *n* fuerza *f.* **strengthen** *v* fortalecer; reforzar; confirmar.

strenuous ['strenjuəs] *adj* arduo; enérgico.

stress [stres] *n* tensión *f.*; presión *f.*; (*gramm*) acento tónico *m.* *v* (*emphasize*) subrayar; insistir en; acentuar.

stretch [stretʃ] *n* (*scope*) alcance *m.*; (*of arms, distance*) extensión *f.*; (*time*) período *m.*; (*of road*) trecho *m.* **home**

stretch última etapa *f. v* estirar; tender; extender. **stretcher** *n* camilla *f.*

stricken ['strikən] *adj* afligido.

strict [strikt] *adj* severo; exacto. **strictly** *adv* severamente; exactamente. **strictly speaking** en realidad. **strictness** *n* severidad *f*; exactitud *f.*

*****stride** [straid] *v* dar zancadas; andar a pasos largos. *n* zancada *f*; tranco *m.*

strident ['straidənt] *adj* estridente; llamativo.

strife [straif] *n* disputa *f*, lucha *f.*

*****strike** [straik] *n* (*industry*) huelga *f*; (*hit*) golpe *m*; (*oil, etc.*) descubrimiento *m. v* (*hit*) golpear; pegar; declararse en huelga; (*clock*) sonar; (*a bargain*) cerrar; descubrir; (*a match*) encender. **striker** *n* huelguista *m, f.* **striking** *adj* impresionante; en huelga.

*****string** [striŋ] *v* (*beads*) ensartar; (*hang*) enristrar. *n* cuerda *f*; (*of ears*) fila *f.* **string bean** judía verde *f.* **string quartet** cuarteto de cuerdas *m.* **stringy** *adj* fibroso.

stringent ['strindʒənt] *adj* estricto, riguroso.

strip[1] [strip] *v* quitar; (*undress*) desnudar; (*bed*) deshacer.

strip[2] [strip] *n* (*of land*) zona *f*; (*of wood*) listón *m*; (*tatter, scrap*) tira *f.*

stripe [straip] *n* raya *f*; azote *m.* **striped** *adj* con rayas.

*****strive** [straiv] *v* esforzarse (a).

strode [stroud] *V* **stride**.

stroke[1] [strouk] *n* golpe *m*, choque *m*; (*swimming*) braza *f*; (*clock*) campanada *f*; (*mark*) trazo *m*; (*med*) ataque *m*; (*lightning*) rayo *m.*

stroke[2] [strouk] *v* acariciar. *n* caricia *f.*

stroll [stroul] *n* vuelta *f*, paseo *m. v* dar un paseo, pasearse.

strong [stroŋ] *adj* fuerte; robusto. *adv* muy bien. **stronghold** *n* fortaleza *f*; (*fig*) baluarte *m.* **strong-minded** *adj* resuelto. **strong-room** *n* cámara acorazada *f.*

struck [strʌk] *V* **strike**.

structure ['strʌktʃə] *n* estructura *f*; construcción *f.* **structural** *adj* estructural; de construcción.

struggle ['strʌgl] *n* lucha *f. v* luchar; (*to escape*) forcejear. **struggle in/out** entrar/salir penosamente.

strum [strʌm] *v* (*guitar*) rasguear; (*other instruments*) rascar. *n* (*guitar*) rasgueo *m.*

strung [strʌŋ] *V* **string**.

strut[1] [strʌt] *v* pavonearse.

strut[2] [strʌt] *n* (*arch*) puntal *m*; (*aero*) montante *m.*

stub [stʌb] *n* (*tree*) tocón *m*; (*cigarette*) colilla *f*; (*cheque*) talón *m*; (*ticket*) resguardo *m*; (*pencil, candle*) cabo *m. v* (*toe*) tropezar con. **stub out** apagar.

stubble ['stʌbl] *n* rastrojo *m*; (*chin*) barba *f.*

stubborn ['stʌbən] *adj* terco; inflexible. **stubbornness** *n* terquedad *f*; tenacidad *f.*

stuck [stʌk] *V* **stick**.

stud[1] [stʌd] *n* (*collar*) botón de camisa *m*; (*boot*) taco *m*; (*nail, rivet*) tachón *m. v* tachonar. **studded with** sembrado de, lleno de.

stud[2] [stʌd] *n* (*place*) cuadra *f*; (*animal*) semental *m.* **stud horse** caballo padre *m.*

student ['stjuːdənt] *n* estudiante *m, f*; (*pupil*) alumno, -a *m, f.*

studio ['stjuːdiou] *n* estudio *m.*

study ['stʌdi] *n* estudio *m*; (*room*) gabinete *m. v* estudiar; examinar. **studious** *adj* estudioso; solícito.

stuff [stʌf] *n* material *m*, materia *f*; cosas *f pl*; (*cloth*) tejido *m. v* llenar; (*cram*) atestar; (*cookery*) rellenar. **stuffing** *n* (*furniture*) rehenchimiento *m*; (*cookery*) relleno *m*; (*padding*) paja *f.* **stuffy** *adj* mal ventilado; (*person*) pomposo.

stumble [stʌmbl] *v* tropezar.

stump [stʌmp] *n* (*tree*) tocón *m*; (*limb*) muñón *m*; (*pencil, etc.*) cabo *m*; (*cricket*) poste *m. v* (*fig*) dejar perplejo.

stun [stʌn] *v* aturdir; (*amaze*) pasmar. **stunning** *adj* aturdidor; (*coll*) fenomenal.

stung [stʌŋ] *V* **sting**.

stunk [stʌŋk] *V* **stink**.

stunt[1] [stʌnt] *v* impedir el crecimiento de. **stunted** *adj* atrofiado.

stunt[2] [stʌnt] *n* hazaña *f*; truco publicitario *m.* **stunt man** doble especial *m.*

stupid ['stjuːpid] *adj* estúpido. **stupidity** *n* estupidez *f.*

stupor ['stjuːpə] *n* estupor *m.*

sturdy ['stəːdi] *adj* robusto, vigoroso. **sturdiness** *n* robustez *f*; vigor *m.*

sturgeon ['stəːdʒən] *n* esturión *m.*

stutter ['stʌtə] *n* tartamudeo *m. v* tartamudear.

sty [stai] *n* (*pig*) pocilga *f*; (*med*) orzuelo *m.*

style [stail] *n* estilo *m*; (*kind*) tipo *m*; manera *f*; (*fashion*) moda *f*; (*clothes*) hechura *f*; (*hair*) peinado *m*. *v* (*design*) diseñar. **stylish** *adj* elegante.

stylus ['stailəs] *n* (*tool*) estilete *m*; (*record player*) aguja *f*.

suave [swɑːv] *adj* afable, urbano.

subconscious [sʌb'kɒnʃəs] *nm, adj* subconsciente.

subcontract [sʌbkən'trakt] *v* subcontratar. **subcontractor** *n* subcontratista *m*.

subdivide [sʌbdi'vaid] *v* subdividir(se). **subdivision** *n* subdivisión *f*.

subdue [səb'djuː] *v* (*riot, etc.*) sojuzgar; (*sound, light*) atenuar; (*voice*) bajar; (*pain*) aliviar; (*feelings*) contener. **subdued** *adj* sojuzgado; atenuado; bajo; aliviado; contenido.

subject ['sʌbdʒikt; *v* səb'dʒekt] *n* sujeto *m*; (*school*) asignatura *f*; (*theme*) tema *m*; motivo *m*; (*people*) súbdito, -a *m, f*. **subject to** sujeto a; propenso a. *v* sojuzgar; (*to an examination*) someter. **subjection** *n* sujeción *f*. **subjective** *adj* subjetivo.

subjunctive [səb'dʒʌŋktiv] *nm, adj* subjuntivo.

sublet [sʌb'let] *v* subarrendar.

sublime [sə'blaim] *adj* sublime. *n* lo sublime.

submarine ['sʌbməriːn] *n* submarino *m*.

submerge [səb'mɜːdʒ] *v* sumergir. *n* sumersión *f*.

submit [səb'mit] *v* someter. **submission** *n* sumisión *f*. **submissive** *adj* sumiso.

subnormal [sʌb'nɔːməl] *adj* subnormal.

subordinate [sə'bɔːdinət] *adj* (*gramm*) subordinado; subalterno. *n* subordinado, -a *m, f*; subalterno, -a *m, f*. *v* subordinar. **subordination** *n* subordinación *f*.

subscribe [səb'skraib] *v* **subscribe to** aprobar; (*newspaper*) subscribirse a. **subscriber** *n* suscriptor, -a *m, f*; abonado, -a *m, f*. **subscription** *n* suscripción *f*; abono *m*; (*membership fee*) cuota *f*.

subsequent ['sʌbsikwənt] *adj* subsiguiente; posterior.

subservient [səb'sɜːviənt] *adj* subordinado; servil.

subside [səb'said] *v* (*land*) hundirse; (*flood*) bajar; (*excitement*) calmarse; (*wind*) amainar. **subsidence** *n* hundimiento *m*.

subsidiary [səb'sidiəri] *adj* subsidiario; secundario; (*comm*) afiliado. *n* (*comm*) filial *f*.

subsidize ['sʌbsidaiz] *v* subvencionar. **subsidy** *n* subvención *f*.

subsist [səb'sist] *v* subsistir. **subsistence** *n* subsistencia *f*.

substance ['sʌbstəns] *n* sustancia *f*. **substantial** *adj* sustancial; sustancioso; importante.

substandard [sʌb'standəd] *adj* inferior.

substitute ['sʌbstitjuːt] *n* (*person*) sustituto, -a *m, f*. substituto, -a *m, f*; (*thing*) sucedáneo *m*. *v* sustituir, reemplazar. **substitution** *n* sustitución *f*.

subtitle ['sʌbtaitl] *n* subtítulo *m*. *v* subtitular.

subtle ['sʌtl] *adj* sutil; delicado. **subtlety** *n* sutileza *f*; delicadeza *f*.

subtract [səb'trakt] *v* restar, sustraer. **subtraction** *n* resta *f*, sustracción *f*.

suburb ['sʌbɜːb] *n* suburbio *m*. **the suburbs** las afueras *f pl*. **suburban** *adj* suburbano.

subvert [səb'vɜːt] *v* derribar; corromper. **subversion** *n* subversión *f*. **subversive** *adj* subversivo.

subway ['sʌbwei] *n* pasaje subterráneo *m*; (*US*) metro *m*.

succeed [sək'siːd] *v* triunfar; (*follow*) suceder; (*inherit*) heredar. **succeeding** *adj* sucesivo; venidero. **success** *n* éxito *m*; triunfo *m*. **successful** *adj* que tiene éxito; próspero. **successfully** *adv* con éxito. **succession** *n* sucesión *f*; herencia *f*. **successive** *adj* sucesivo. **successor** *n* sucesor, -a *m, f*.

succinct [sək'siŋkt] *adj* sucinto.

succulent ['sʌkjulənt] *adj* suculento; (*plant*) carnoso. *n* planta carnosa *f*.

succumb [sə'kʌm] *v* sucumbir.

such [sʌtʃ] *adj* tal; semejante, parecido; tan, tanto. **such as** como. *adv* tan, tanto. *pron* los que, las que; lo que; todo lo que; esto, éste, ésta. **as such** en sí.

suck [sʌk] *v* chupar; (*baby*) mamar. **suck up to** (*slang*) dar coba a.

sucker ['sʌkə] *n* (*bot*) chupón *m*; (*device*) émbolo *m*; (*slang: simpleton*) primo *m*.

suction ['sʌkʃən] *n* succión *f*.

sudden ['sʌdən] *adj* súbito; inesperado; repentino. **all of a sudden** de repente.

suds [sʌdz] *pl n* jabonaduras *f pl*.

sue [suː] *v* proceder contra.

suede [sweid] *n* ante *m*.

suet ['suit] *n* sebo *m*.

suffer ['sʌfə] *v* sufrir, padecer; tolerar; dejar; (*undergo*) aguantar. **suffering** *n* sufrimiento *m*, padecimiento *m*; dolor *m*.

sufficient [sə'fiʃənt] *adj* suficiente; bastante. **suffice** *v* ser suficiente. bastar. **sufficiently** *adv* suficientemente. bastante.

suffix ['sʌfiks] *n* sufijo *m*.

suffocate ['sʌfəkeit] *v* ahogar. sofocar. **suffocation** *n* ahogo *m*; asfixia *f*.

sugar ['ʃugə] *n* azúcar *m*. **sugar bowl** azucarero *m*. **sugar cane** caña de azúcar *f*. **sugar lump** terrón de azúcar *m*.

suggest [sə'dʒest] *v* sugerir; indicar. **suggestion** *n* sugerencia *f*; indicación *f*. **suggestive** *adj* sugestivo; evocador.

suicide ['suːisaid] *n* (*act*) suicidio *m*; (*person*) suicida *m, f*. **commit suicide** suicidarse. **suicidal** *adj* suicida.

suit [suːt] *n* traje *m*; (*woman's*) conjunto *m*; (*law*) pleito *m*; (*cards*) palo *m*. **suitcase** *n* maleta *f*. *v* convenir; venir bien a. **suitable** *adj* conveniente; apropiado.

suite [swiːt] *n* (*in hotel*) suite *f*; (*furniture*) juego *m*.

sulk [sʌlk] *v* enfurruñarse. *n* enfurruñamiento *m*. **sulky** *adj* enfurruñado.

sullen ['sʌlən] *adj* taciturno; malhumorado. **sullenness** *n* taciturnidad *f*; mal humor *m*.

sulphur ['sʌlfə] *n* azufre *m*. **sulphuric** *adj* sulfúrico.

sultan ['sʌltən] *n* sultán *m*.

sultana [sʌl'taɪnə] *n* pasa de Esmirna *f*.

sultry ['sʌltri] *adj* (*weather*) sofocante; (*person*) sensual.

sum [sʌm] *n* suma *f*; cantidad *f*; cálculo *m*. *v* **sum up** recapitular; resumir; (*person*) evaluar.

summarize ['sʌməraiz] *v* resumir. recapitular. **summary** *n* resumen *m*; *adj* sumario.

summer ['sʌmə] *n* verano *m*. **summer holidays** vacaciones de verano *f pl*. **summerhouse** *n* cenador *m*.

summit ['sʌmit] *n* cumbre *f*, cima *f*; (*fig*) apogeo *m*.

summon ['sʌmən] *v* llamar. convocar; mandar; hacer venir. **summon up** evocar.

summons ['sʌmənz] *pl n* llamamiento *m*; (*law*) citación f. *v* citar.

sumptuous ['sʌmptʃuəs] *adj* suntuoso.

sun [sʌn] *n* sol *m*. **sunny** *adj* bañado de sol.

sunbathe ['sʌnbeið] *v* tomar el sol. **sunbathing** *n* baños de sol *m pl*.

sunbeam ['sʌnbiːm] *n* rayo de sol *m*.

sunburn ['sʌnbəːn] *n* (*tan*) bronceado *m*;

(*pain*) quemadura del sol *f*. **sunburnt** *adj* bronceado; quemado por el sol.

Sunday ['sʌndi] *n* domingo *m*.

sundial ['sʌndaiəl] *n* reloj de sol *m*.

sundry ['sʌndri] *adj* varios. **all and sundry** todo el mundo. **sundries** *pl n* artículos diversos *m pl*.

sunflower ['sʌn.flauə] *n* girasol *m*.

sun-glasses ['sʌnglaɪsiz] *pl n* gafas de sol *f pl*.

sunk [sʌŋk] *V* sink.

sunlight ['sʌnlait] *n* luz del sol *f*.

sunrise ['sʌnraiz] *n* salida del sol *f*.

sunset ['sʌnset] *n* puesta del sol *f*.

sunshine ['sʌnʃain] *n* sol *m*.

sunstroke ['sʌnstrouk] *n* insolación *f*.

sun-tan ['sʌntan] *n* bronceado *m*. **sun-tan lotion** loción bronceadora *f*.

super ['suːpə] *adj* (*coll*) estupendo; formidable.

superannuation [.suːpəranju'eiʃən] *n* jubilación *f*.

superb [suː'pəːb] *adj* soberbio; magnífico.

supercilious [.suːpə'siliəs] *adj* altanero; desdeñoso.

superficial [.suːpə'fiʃəl] *adj* superficial.

superfluous [su'pəːfluəs] *adj* superfluo.

superhuman [suːpə'hjuːmən] *adj* sobrehumano.

superimpose [.suːpərim'pouz] *v* sobreponer. **superimposed** *adj* (*photo, etc.*) superpuesto.

superintendent [.suːpərin'tendənt] *n* superintendente *m, f*; director, -a *m, f*; (*police*) subjefe de la policía *m*.

superior [suː'piəriə] *n, adj* superior, -a. **superiority** *n* superioridad *f*.

superlative [suː'pəːlətiv] *adj* superlativo; supremo. (*gramm*) *nm, adj* superlativo.

supermarket ['suːpə.maːkit] *n* supermercado *m*.

supernatural [.suːpə'natʃərəl] *adj* sobrenatural. *n* lo sobrenatural.

supersede [.suːpə'siːd] *v* sustituir. reemplazar.

supersonic [.suːpə'sonik] *adj* supersónico.

superstition [suːpə'stiʃən] *n* superstición *f*. **superstitious** *adj* supersticioso.

supervise ['suːpəvaiz] *v* supervisar; vigilar. **supervision** *n* superintendencia *f*. **supervisor** *n* supervisor, -a *m, f*; director, -a *m, f*.

supper ['sʌpə] *n* cena *f*.

supple ['sʌpl] *adj* flexible, elástico. **suppleness** *n* flexibilidad *f*.

supplement ['sʌpləmənt] *n* suplemento *m*.
v suplir, complementar. **supplementary**
adj suplementario.

supply [sə'plai] *n* (*stock*) surtido *m*; provisión *f*; (*act of supplying*) suministro *m*.
supplies *pl n* material *m* sing; provisiones
f pl; (*stores*) víveres *m pl*. *v* alimentar;
proveer; abastecer; presentar.

support [sə'pott] *n* apoyo *m*; sostén *m*;
soporte *m*. *v* apoyar; sostener; defender;
(*financially*) mantener. **supporter** *n* partidario, -a *m*, *f*; (*sport*) aficionado, -a.

suppose [sə'pouz] *v* suponer. **supposed** *adj*
supuesto. **be supposed to** deber. **suppos-
edly** *adv* según se supone. **supposing** *conj*
si, suponiendo (que). **supposition** *n*
suposición *f*.

suppress [sə'pres] *v* suprimir; (*yawn,
laugh, etc.*) contener; (*passion*) dominar;
(*fact*) disimular; (*revolt*) sofocar; (*publication*) prohibir; (*news*) ocultar. **suppression** *n* supresión *f*; dominio *m*; represión
f; prohibición *f*; ocultación *f*.

supreme [su'priim] *adj* supremo.
supremacy *n* supremacía *f*.

surcharge ['sətfaidʒ] *n* sobrecarga *f*.

sure [ʃuə] *adj* seguro, cierto. **sure enough**
efectivamente. **sure-footed** *adj* de pie
firme. **surely** *adv* seguramente; sin duda.

surety ['ʃuərəti] *n* garantía *f*, fianza *f*.

surf [sətf] *n* resaca *f*; (*foam*) espuma *f*.
surf-board *n* tabla hawaiana *f*. **surfing** *n*
surf *m*.

surface ['sətfis] *n* superficie *f*. **on the surface** en apariencia. *v* (*road*) revestir;
(*swimmer*) salir a la superficie; (*submarine*) sacar a la superficie.

surfeit ['sətfit] *n* exceso *m*.

surge [sətdʒ] *n* oleada *f*; (*anger*) ola *f*. *v*
(*sea*) levantarse; (*crowd*) bullir.

surgeon ['sətdʒən] *n* cirujano *m*. **surgery**
n (*skill*) cirugía *f*; (*place*) consultorio *m*.
surgical *adj* quirúrgico.

surly ['sətli] *adj* malhumormado.

surmount [sə'maunt] *v* vencer, superar.

surname ['səneim] *n* apellido *m*.

surpass [sə'pais] *v* superar, sobrepasar.

surplus ['sətpləs] *n* excedente *m*. *adj*
sobrante.

surprise [sə'praiz] *n* sorpresa *f*. *adj* de
sorpresa. *v* sorprender.

surrealism [sə'riəlizəm] *n* surrealismo *m*.
surrealist *n*(*m + f*). *adj* surrealista. **surre-
alistic** *adj* surrealista.

surrender [sə'rendə] *v* rendir; (*give up*)
ceder; entregar. *n* rendición *f*; capitulación *f*.

surreptitious [ˌsʌrəp'tiʃəs] *adj* subrepticio.

surround [sə'raund] *v* cercar, rodear. *n*
borde *m*. **surrounding** *adj* circundante.
surroundings *pl n* (*environment*) medio
ambiente *m*; (*environs*) alrededores *m pl*.

survey ['sətvei; *v* sə'vei] *n* inspección *f*;
(*report*) informe *m*; (*of a question*) examen *m*; panorama *m*; (*land*) medición *f*.
v inspeccionar; estudiar; examinar; contemplar; medir. **surveying** *n* inspección *f*,
agrimensura *f*. **surveyor** *n* (*land*)
agrimensor *m*; (*house*) inspector *m*.

survive [sə'vaiv] *v* sobrevivir a. **survival** *n*
supervivencia *f*. **survivor** *n* sobreviviente
m, *f*.

susceptible [sə'septəbl] *adj* susceptible,
sensible.

suspect ['sʌspekt; *v* sə'spekt] *n*, *adj* sospechoso, -a. *v* sospechar.

suspend [sə'spend] *v* suspender. **suspender** *n* liga *f*. **suspense** *n* incertidumbre *f*;
(*book, film*) suspense *m*. **in suspense**
pendiente. **suspension** *n* suspensión *f*
suspension bridge puente colgante *m*.

suspicion [sə'spiʃən] *n* sospecha *f*. **suspicious** *adj* (*suspecting*) suspicaz; (*suspect-
ed*) sospechoso.

sustain [sə'stein] *v* sostener; mantener;
apoyar; (*suffer*) recibir.

swab [swob] *n* (*mop*) estropajo *m*; (*med*:
pad) tapón *m*. *v* fregar con estropajo;
limpiar con tapón.

swagger ['swagə] *n* pavoneo *m*. *v*
pavonearse; darse importancia.

swallow[1] ['swolou] *v* tragar. **swallow up**
tragarse. *n* trago *m*; (*amount*) bocado *m*.

swallow[2] ['swolou] *n* (*bird*) golondrina *f*.

swam [swam] *V* **swim**.

swamp [swomp] *n* pantano *m*, marisma *f*.
v sumergir; inundar. **swampy** *adj* pantanoso.

swan [swon] *n* cisne *m*.

swank [swaŋk] (*coll*) *n* fanfarronada *f*;
(*person*) fanfarrón, -ona *m*, *f*. *v* fanfarronear. **swanky** *adj* fanfarrón.

swap *or* **swop** [swop] *n* cambio *m*, trueque
m. *v* cambiar, trocar.

swarm [swotm] *n* (*bees*) enjambre *m*; (*fig*)
multitud *f*. *v* enjambrar; (*fig*) pulular.

swarthy ['swotði] *adj* moreno.

swat [swot] *v* aplastar.

sway [swei] n balanceo m; oscilación f; dominio m. v balancearse; oscilar; (influence) influir.

*swear [sweə] v jurar. **swear in** tomar juramento a. **swear-word** n palabrota f.

sweat [swet] n sudor m. v sudar.

sweater n suéter m.

swede [swiːd] n naba f.

Sweden ['swiːdn] n Suecia f. **Swede** n sueco, -a m, f. **Swedish** nm, adj sueco.

*sweep [swiːp] v deshollinar; barrer; explorar. **sweep in/out** entrar/salir rápidamente. **sweep through** difundirse. n (chimney) deshollinador m; (a cleaning) barrido m; (curve) curva f. **make a clean sweep** llevárselo todo. **sweeping** adj aplastante; demasiado general. **sweeping statement** declaración demasiado general f.

sweet [swiːt] adj (taste) dulce; (air, breath, etc.) fresco; (smell) bueno; (friendly) encantador; (kind) bondadoso. n (toffee) caramelo m; (dessert) postre m. **sweetbread** n mollejas f pl. **sweet corn** maíz tierno m. **sweetheart** n novio, -a m, f. **sweet potato** patata boniato f. **sweetshop** n confitería f. **sweeten** v azucarar, endulzar. **sweetly** adv dulcemente; (sound) melodiosamente. **sweetness** n dulzor m; (character) dulzura f.

*swell [swel] v hinchar; inflarse. n inflado m; hinchazón m; curvatura f. **swelling** n inflamiento m.

swelter ['sweltə] v sofocarse de calor. **sweltering** adj sofocante.

swerve [swəːv] v desviar; (vehicle) dar un viraje. n viraje m.

swift [swift] adj rápido; pronto. n (bird) vencejo m. **swiftness** rapidez f; prontitud f.

swill [swil] v lavar con mucho agua; (drink) beber a tragos. n (for pigs) bazofia f.

*swim [swim] v nadar. n baño m. **swimmer** n nadador, -a m, f. **swimming** n natación f. **swimming baths** or **pool** piscina f. **swimming costume** traje de baño m.

swindle ['swindl] n estafa f. v estafar. **swindler** n estafador, -a m, f.

swine [swain] n cerdo m, puerco m; (impol) canalla m, f.

*swing [swiŋ] v hacer girar; balancear; oscilar; virar. n (amusement) columpio m; oscilación f; impulso m; (pol) viraje m. **in full swing** a toda velocidad.

swipe [swaip] (coll) n golpetazo m. v golpear con fuerza; (steal) afanar.

swirl [swəːl] n remolino m. v arremolinarse.

swish [swiʃ] n silbo m; (of water) susurro m; (of garment) crujido m. v (cane) blandir; (tail) menear.

Swiss [swis] n, adj suizo, -a. **Swiss roll** brazo de gitano m.

switch [switʃ] n (elec) interruptor m, conmutador m; (change) paso m; (stick) varilla f. **switchboard** n centralita de teléfonos f. v (opinion, policy) cambiar de; (places) cambiar; (a train) desviar. **switch off** desconectar. **switch on** encender.

Switzerland ['switsələnd] n Suiza f.

swivel ['swivl] n pivote m. v girar sobre un eje; dar una vuelta.

swollen ['swoulən] V **swell.**

swoop [swuːp] n calada f; redada f. **at one fell swoop** de un solo golpe. v calarse, abatirse.

swop V **swap.**

sword [soːd] n espada f. **swordfish** n pez espada m.

sworn [swoːn] V **swear.**

swot [swot] (coll) n empollón, -ona m, f. v empollar. **swotting** n estudio m.

swum [swʌm] V **swim.**

swung [swʌŋ] V **swing.**

sycamore ['sikəmoː] n sicomoro m.

syllable ['siləbl] n sílaba f. **syllabic** adj silábico.

syllabus ['siləbəs] n programa m.

symbol ['simbl] n símbolo m, emblema m. **symbolic** adj simbólico. **symbolism** n simbolismo m. **symbolize** v simbolizar.

symmetry ['simitri] n simetría f. **symmetrical** adj simétrico.

sympathy ['simpəθi] n pésame m; compasión f. **sympathetic** adj compasivo; comprensivo; favorable. **sympathize with** compadecerse de.

symphony ['simfəni] n sinfonía f. **symphonic** adj sinfónico.

symposium [sim'pouziəm] n simposio m.

symptom ['simptəm] n síntoma m. **symptomatic** adj sintomático.

synagogue ['sinəgog] n sinagoga f.

synchromesh ['siŋkroumeʃ] n sincronizador.

synchronize ['siŋkrənaiz] v sincronizar. **synchronization** n sincronización f.

syncopate ['siŋkəpeit] *n* sincopar. **syncopation** *n* síncopa *f*.
syndicate ['sindikit] *n* sindicato *m*.
syndrome ['sindroum] *n* síndrome *m*.
synonym ['sinənim] *n* sinónimo *m*. **synonymous** *adj* sinónimo.
synopsis [si'nopsis] *n, pl* -ses sinopsis *f invar*.
syntax ['sintaks] *n* sintaxis *f*.
synthesis ['sinθisis] *n, pl* -ses síntesis *f invar*. **synthesize** *v* sintetizar.
syphilis ['sifilis] *n* sífilis *f*.
syringe [si'rindʒ] *n* jeringa *f*. *v* jeringar.
syrup ['sirəp] *n* (*med*) jarabe *m*; (*fruit*) almíbar *m*. **syrupy** *adj* almibarado.
system ['sistəm] *n* sistema *m*; método *m*. **systematic** *adj* sistemático.

T

tab [tab] *n* etiqueta *f*. **keep tabs on** (*coll*) tener controlado.
tabby ['tabi] *n* gato atigrador *m*.
table ['teibl] *n* mesa *f*. **table-cloth** *n* mantel *m*. **table-mat** *n* salvamanteleo *m invar*. **table-napkin** *n* servilleta *f*. **tablespoon** *n* cucharón *m*. **tablespoonful** cucharada *f*. **table tennis** tenis de mesa *m*. **clear the table** levantar la mesa. **set the table** poner la mesa.
table d'hôte [taːblə'dout] *n* menú *m*.
tablet ['tablit] *n* (*med, soap*) pastilla *f*; (*stone, chocolate*) tableta *f*; (*writing-paper*) bloc *m*.
taboo [ta'buː] *nm, adj* tabú.
tabulate ['tabjuleit] *v* tabular.
tacit ['tasit] *adj* tácito.
taciturn ['tasitəːn] *adj* taciturno.
tack [tak] *n* (*nail*) tachuela *f*; (*sewing*) hilván *m*; (*naut: change of direction*) virada *f*; (*distance sailed*) bordada *f*. *v* clavar con tachuelas; hilvanar; virar de bordo.
tackle ['takl] *n* (*ropes*) jarcias *f pl*; (*rigging*) aparejo *m*; (*equipment*) trastos *m pl*; (*sport*) placaje *m*. *v* placar; (*seize*) agarrar; (*fig*) abordar, emprender.
tact [takt] *n* tacto *m*. **tactful** *adj* con tacto, discreto. **tactless** *adj* falto de tacto, indiscreto.

tactics ['taktiks] *pl n* táctica *f sing*. **tactical** *adj* táctico.
tadpole ['tadpoul] *n* renacuajo *m*.
taffeta ['tafitə] *n* tafetán *m*.
tag [tag] *n* etiqueta *f*; (*shoelace*) herrete *m*; (*game*) pillapilla *m*. **tag along** (*coll*) seguir.
tail [teil] *n* cola *f*; rabo *m*; (*coat, shirt*) faldón *m*. **tail-end** *n* zaga *f*, rabera *f*. **tails** *pl n* (*coin*) cruz *f sing*. *v* (*coll*) seguir.
tailor ['teilə] *n* sastre *m*. *v* entallar; (*fig*) adaptar.
taint [teint] *v* (*stain*) manchar; (*food*) corromper; (*air*) viciar; (*fig*) mancillar. *n* mancha *f*; corrupción *f*; contaminación *f*.
***take** [teik] *v* tomar; llevarse; (*carry*) cargarse; (*phot*) sacar; (*shoe size*) calzar; (*occupy*) ocupar; (*responsibility*) asumir; (*bear*) aguantar; (*suppose*) suponer. **take after** parecerse a. **take along** llevarse. **take away** quitar; (*subtract*) restar. **take back** (*return*) devolver; (*retract*) retirar. **take down** (*pictures, curtains*) descolgar; (*from a shelf*) bajar; (*write*) apuntar. **take someone down a peg** (*coll*) bajarle los humos a alguien. **take in** acoger; (*situation*) entender; (*clothes*) achicar; (*coll: deceive*)|engañar. **take off** (*clothes*) quitarse; (*aero*) despegar. **take-off** *n* despegue *m*; (*coll*) imitamonos *m invar*. **take on** (*employ*) contratar; (*challenge*) competir con. **take-over** (*comm*) adquisición *f*.
talcum powder ['talkəm] *n* talco *m*.
tale [teil] *n* cuento *m*. **fairy tales** cuentos de hadas *m pl*. **tell tales** (*coll*) contar chismes.
talent ['talənt] *n* talento *m*. **talented** *adj* talentoso, talentudo.
talk [toːk] *n* conversación *f*; charla *f*; (*lecture*) conferencia *f*; (*speech*) discurso *m*. *v* decir; hablar. **talk back** replicar. **talk down to** ponerse al alcance de. **talk into** convencer para que. **talk over** discutir. **talkative** *adj* hablador. **talking** *n* conversación *f*. **talking point** tema de conversación *m*.
tall [toːl] *adj* alto; grande. **tallboy** *n* cómoda alta *f*. **tallness** *n* altura *f*; lo alto.
tally ['tali] *n* tarja *f*; cuenta *f*. *v* tarjar; cuadrar.
talon ['talən] *n* garra *f*.
tambourine [tambə'riːn] *n* pandereta *f*; pandero *m*.

tame [teim] *adj* manso; domesticado; (*not exciting*) aburrido. *v* domesticar; amansar.

tamper ['tampə] *v* **tamper with** (*text*) amañar; (*spoil*) estropear.

tampon ['tampon] *n* tapón *m*.

tan [tan] *n* bronceado *m*, color tostado *m*. *adj* bronceado, tostado. (*hide*) curtir; (*sun*) broncear, tostar.

tandem ['tandəm] *n* tándem *m*.

tangent ['tandʒənt] *nf, adj* tangente. **go off at a tangent** salirse por la tangente.

tangerine [tandʒə'riːn] *n* (*fruit*) mandarina *f*.

tangible ['tandʒəbl] *adj* tangible.

tangle ['taŋgl] *v* enmarañar; enredar. *n* maraña *f*; enredo *m*.

tank [taŋk] *n* tanque *m*, cisterna *f*, depósito *m*; (*mil*) tanque *m*. **tanker** *n* (*lorry*) camión cisterna *m*; (*ship*) petrolero *m*.

tankard ['taŋkəd] *n* jarro *m*.

tantalize ['tantəlaiz] *v* atormentar. **tantalizing** *adj* que atormenta.

tantamount ['tantəmaunt] *adj* **be tantamount to** ser equivalente a.

tantrum ['tantrəm] *n* berrinche *m*, rabieta *f*. **fly into a tantrum** coger una rabieta.

tap¹ [tap] *n* golpecito *m*. **tap-dance** *n* zapateado *m*. *v* golpear ligeramente.

tap² [tap] *n* (*water*) grifo *m*; (*barrel*) espita *f*. *v* poner una espita a; (*phone*) interceptar; (*fig: draw on*) utilizar.

tape [teip] *n* cinta *f*; (*recording*) cinta magnetofónica *f*. **tape-measure** *n* cinta métrica *f*. **tape-recorder** *n* magnetófono *m*. **tapeworm** *n* tenia *f*. *v* (*record*) grabar; (*fasten*) atar con cinta.

taper ['teipə] *n* (*candle*) vela *f*; (*narrowing*) estrachamiento *m*. *v* estrechar. **tapering** *adj* cónico.

tapestry ['tapəstri] *n* tapiz *m*.

tapioca [tapi'oukə] *n* tapioca *f*.

tar [taɪ] *n* alquitrán *m*. *v* alquitranar.

tarantula [tə'rantjulə] *n* tarántula *f*.

target ['taɪgit] *n* blanco *m*; (*fig*) objeto *m*.

tariff ['tarif] *n* tarifa *f*.

tarmac ['taɪmak] *n* superficie alquitranada *f*.

tarnish ['taɪniʃ] *v* deslustrar. *n* deslustre *m*.

tarpaulin [taɪ'poɪlin] *n* lona alquitranada *f*.

tarragon ['tarəgən] *n* estragón *m*.

tart¹ [taɪt] *adj* agrio; ácido.

tart² [taɪt] *n* tarta *f*; (*slang*) fulana *f*.

tartar ['taɪtə] *n* (*chem*) tártaro *m*; (*on teeth*) sarro *m*.

task [taɪsk] *n* tarea *f*. **taskmaster** *n* capataz *m*.

tassel ['tasəl] *n* borla *f*.

taste [teist] *n* (*sense*) gusto *m*; sabor *m*. *v* probar; saber. **taste of** saber a. **tasteful** *adj* de buen gusto. **tasteless** *adj* insípido; (*in bad taste*) de mal gusto. **tasty** *adj* sabroso.

tattered ['tatəd] *adj* andrajoso.

tattoo¹ [tə'tuɪ] *n* (*on skin*) tatuaje *m*. *v* tatuar.

tattoo² [tə'tuɪ] *n* (*mil*) desfile militar *m*; (*drumming*) repiqueteo *m*.

tatty ['tati] *adj* (*coll*) en mal estado.

taunt [toɪnt] *v* mofarse de. *n* mofa *f*. **taunting** *adj* burlón; provocante.

Taurus ['toɪrəs] *n* Tauro *m*.

taut [toɪt] *adj* tenso, tirante. **tautness** *n* tensión *f*, tirantez *f*.

tavern ['tavən] *n* (*bar*) taberna *f*; (*inn*) venta *f*.

tawny ['toɪni] *adj* leonado.

tax [taks] *n* impuesto *m*, contribución *f*. **tax-free** *adj* exento de impuestos. **tax evasion** evasión fiscal *f*. **tax haven** refugio fiscal *m*. **taxpayer** *n* contribuyente *m, f*. **tax return** declaración de renta *f*. *v* gravar con un impuesto; imponer contribuciones; (*try*) poner a prueba. **taxable** *adj* imponible. **taxation** *n* impuestos *m pl*; (*system*) sistema tributario *m*.

taxi ['taksi] *n* taxi *m*. **taxi-driver** *n* taxista *m, f*. **taximeter** *n* taxímetro *m*. **taxi rank** parada de taxis *f*. *v* (*aero*) rodar por la pista.

tea [tiɪ] *n* té *m*; (*snack*) merienda *f*. **teacup** *n* tasa de té *f*. **teapot** *n* tetera *f*. **teaspoon** *n* cucharilla *f*. **teaspoonful** *n* cucharadita *f*. **tea towel** trapo de cocina *m*.

*teach [tiɪtʃ] *v* enseñar. **teacher** *n* (*primary*) maestro, -a *m, f*; (*secondary*) profesor, -a *m, f*. **teaching** *n* enseñanza *f*.

teak [tiɪk] *n* teca *f*.

team [tiɪm] *n* (*yoked animals*) yunta *f*; (*horses*) tronco *m*; (*people*) equipo *m*. **team-mate** *n* compañero de equipo *m*. **team spirit** espíritu de equipo *m*. **teamwork** *n* trabajo de equipo *m*. *v* **team up** agruparse.

*tear¹ [teə] v desgarrar; (*snatch*) arrancar. **tear along/out** ir a toda velocidad. **tear down** demoler. **tear off** (*coupon*) cortar. n rasgón m.

tear² [tiə] n lágrima f. **tear gas** gas lacrimógeno m. **tear-jerker** (*coll*) n obra sentimental f. **tearful** adj lloroso.

tease [tiz] v provocar. n broma f; (*person*) bromista m, f. **teasing** n bromas f pl.

teat [tiit] n pezón m; (*animals*) teta f.

technique [tek'niːk] n técnica f. **technical** adj técnico. **technicality** n detalle técnico m. **technician** n técnico, -a m, f. **technological** adj tecnológico. **technology** n tecnología f.

teddy bear ['tedi̦beə] n osito de felpa m.

tedious ['tiːdiəs] adj latoso. **tediousness** n also **tedium** pesadez f, tedio m.

tee [tiː] n tee m. v **tee off** dar el primer golpe.

teem [tiːm] v pulular, hormiguear.

teenage ['tiːneidʒ] adj adolescente. **teenager** n adolescente m, f. **teens** pl n adolescencia f sing.

teeth [tiːθ] V **tooth**.

teethe [tiːð] v echar los dientes. **teething** n dentición f.

teetotaller [tiː'toutələ] n abstemio, -a m, f.

telecommunications [ˌtelikəmjuːniˈkeiʃənz] pl n telecomunicaciones f pl.

telegram ['teligram] n telegrama m.

telegraph ['teligrɑːf] n telégrafo m. **telegraph pole** poste telegráfico m. v telegrafiar. **telegraphic** adj telegráfico.

telepathy [tə'lepəθi] n telepatía f. **telepathic** adj telepático.

telephone ['telifoun] n teléfono m. **telephone box** or **kiosk** cabina telefónica f. **telephone call** llamada telefónica f. **telephone directory** guía de teléfonos f. **telephone exchange** central telefónica f. **telephone number** número de teléfono m. **telephone operator** or **telephonist** telefonista m, f. v telefonear a.

telescope ['teliskoup] n telescopio m. **telescopic** adj telescópico.

television ['teliviʒən] n televisión f. **television set** televisor m. **televise** v televisar.

telex ['teleks] n télex m.

*tell [tel] v decir; (*story*) contar; comunicar; mandar; (*identify*) reconocer; (*distinguish*) distinguir; (*deduce*) deducir;

(*observe*) notar. **tell against** perjudicar. **tell of** hablar de. **tell off** (*coll*) regañar. **tell on** afectar a. **telltale** adj revelador.

temper ['tempə] n (*anger*) cólera f; temperamento m; humor m. **lose one's temper** enfadarse. v templar.

temperament ['tempərəmənt] n temperamento m. **temperamental** adj caprichoso.

temperate ['tempərət] adj templado.

temperature ['temprətʃə] n temperatura f; (*med*) fiebre f.

tempestuous [tem'pestjuəs] adj tempestuoso.

temple¹ ['templ] n (*rel*) templo m.

temple² ['templ] n (*anat*) sien f.

tempo ['tempou] n (*music*) tiempo m; (*fig*) ritmo m.

temporary ['tempərəri] adj temporal, provisional. **temporary worker** temporario, -a m, f.

tempt [tempt] v tentar; seducir. **temptation** n tentación f.

ten [ten] nm, adj diez. **tenth** n, adj décimo, -a.

tenacious [tə'neiʃəs] adj tenaz. **tenaciousness** also **tenacity** n tenacidad f.

tenant ['tenənt] n habitante m, f. ocupante m, f. **tenancy** n alquiler m, arrendamiento m.

tend¹ [tend] v tender, tener tendencia a **tendency** n tendencia f.

tend² [tend] v (*look after*) cuidar; manejar.

tender¹ ['tendə] adj tierno; delicado, (*kind*) cariñoso; compasivo; (*sensitive*) sensible; (*painful*) dolorido. **tenderize** v ablandar. **tenderness** n (*affection*) ternura f; (*meat*) lo tierno.

tender² ['tendə] v ofertar, hacer una oferta. n oferta f. **legal tender** moneda corriente f.

tendon ['tendən] n tendón m.

tendril ['tendril] n zarcillo m.

tenement ['tenəmənt] n casa de vecindad f.

tennis ['tenis] n tenis m. **tennis ball** pelota de tenis f. **tennis court** campo de tenis m. **tennis player** tenista m, f. **tennis shoes** zapatos de tenis m pl.

tenor ['tenə] n (*music*) tenor m; (*sense*) significado m; (*course*) curso m.

tense¹ [tens] adj tenso; estirado. v tensar **tension** n tensión f.

tense² [tens] n tiempo m.

tent [tent] n tienda de campaña f. pitch a tent armar una tienda de campaña.

tentacle ['tentəkl] n tentáculo m.

tentative ['tentətiv] adj provisional; de tanteo; indeciso.

tenterhooks ['tentəhuks] pl n be on tenterhooks estar sobre ascuas.

tenuous ['tenjuəs] adj tenue; delgado.

tepid ['tepid] adj templaducho; (fig) tibio. tepidness n also tepidity tibieza f.

term [təːm] n período m; (comm) plazo m; (school) trimestre m; curso m; (end) término m. terms pl n condiciones f pl; (terminology) términos m pl; (comm) tarifa f sing; (relationship) relaciones f pl. come to terms with llegar a un acuerdo con. on good/bad terms with en buenas/malas relaciones con. terms of reference mandato m sing. v llamar, calificar.

terminal ['təːminəl] adj terminal, final. n final de línea m; (extremity) extremidad f; (elec) borne m.

terminate ['təːmineit] v terminar, concluir. termination n terminación f.

terminology [təːmi'nolədʒi] n terminología f.

terminus ['təːminəs] n término m.

terrace ['terəs] n terraza f; (houses) hilera de casas f.

terrain [tə'rein] n terreno m.

terrestrial [tə'restriəl] adj terrestre.

terrible ['terəbl] adj terrible; atroz; horrible. terribly adv terriblemente. terribly bad malísimo. terribly good buenísimo

terrier ['teriə] n terrier m.

terrify ['terifai] v aterrorizar. terrific adj (coll: excellent) estupendo; (coll: extreme) terrible; enorme.

territory ['teritəri] n territorio m. territorial adj territorial.

terror ['terə] n terror m. terrorism n terrorismo m. terrorist n(m+f), adj terrorista. terrorize v aterrorizar, aterrar.

terse [təːs] adj conciso.

terylene ® ['teriliːn] n terylene ® m.

test [test] n prueba f; examen m; (med) análisis m. test case (law) juicio que hace jurisprudencia m. test match partido internacional m. test paper examen m. test pilot piloto de pruebas m. test tube tubo de ensayo m. v probar; poner un examen a; analizar; (sight) graduar; (weight) comprobar.

testament ['testəmənt] n testamento m.

the New Testament el Nuevo Testamento m. the Old Testament el Antiguo Testamento m.

testicle ['testikl] n testículo m.

testify ['testifai] v testificar; dar testimonio.

testimony ['testiməni] n testimonio m. testimonial n testimonio m; recomendación f.

tetanus ['tetənəs] n tétanos m.

tether ['teðə] n traba f, atadura f. at the end of one's tether hartísimo. v trabar, atar.

text [tekst] n texto m. textbook n libro de texto m. textual adj textual.

textile ['tekstail] nm, adj textil.

texture ['tekstjuə] n textura f.

than [ðən] conj que; de; cuando; del que.

thank [θaŋk] v agradecer. thank you gracias. thanksgiving n acción de gracias f. thanks to gracias a. thankful adj agradecido. thankless adj desagradecido; ingrato.

that [ðat] adj ese, esa; aquel, aquella; el, la. pron ése, ésa; aquél, aquélla; (neuter) eso; (neuter: farther away) aquello; (before relative pron or of) el, la, lo; (who, which) que; el que, la que; quien; el cual, la cual; (neuter) lo que. adv así de; tan; tanto. conj que; de que; para que; porque.

thatch [θatʃ] n (straw) paja f; (roof) techo de paja m. v cubrir con un tejado de paja.

thaw [θɔː] n (ice) deshielo m; (snow) derretimento m. v deshelar; derretir.

the [ðə] art el, la (pl los, las); (neuter) lo.

theatre ['θiətə] n teatro m. theatrical adj teatral, de teatro.

theft [θeft] n hurto, robo.

their [ðeə] adj su, sus; suyo, suya.

theirs [ðeəz] pron el suyo, la suya.

them [ðem] pron ellos, ellas; (direct object) los, las; (indirect object) les.

theme [θiːm] n tema m. thematic adj temático.

themselves [ðəm'selvz] pl pron se; ellos mismos, ellas mismas; sí mismos, sí mismas. by themselves solos.

then [ðen] adv (that time) entonces; (afterwards) después, luego; (furthermore) además; (despite that) a pesar de eso; (consequently) por lo tanto. n entonces; ese momento. conj en ese caso; entonces.

theology [θi'olədʒi] n teología f. **theologian** n teólogo, -a m, f. **theological** adj teológico.

theorem ['θiərəm] n teorema m.

theory ['θiəri] n teoría f. **theoretical** adj teórico.

therapy ['θerəpi] n terapia f. **therapeutic** adj terapéutico. **therapist** n terapeuta m, f.

there [ðeə] adv ahí; allí; allá. *thereabouts* adv (place) por ahí, por allí; (degree) más o menos. **thereafter** adv después, más tarde. **thereby** adv por eso, por ello. **therefore** adv por lo tanto. **therein** adv allí dentro; en eso. **there is** or **are** hay. **thereof** adv de eso; su. **thereto** adv a eso, a ello. **thereupon** adv immediatamente después; sobre eso. **therewith** adv con eso. **there you are** eso es.

thermal ['θəɪməl] adj termal; (tech) térmico. n corriente de aire caliente que sube.

thermodynamics [θəɪmoudai'namiks] n termodinámica f.

thermometer [θə'momitə] n termómetro m.

thermonuclear [θəɪmou'njukliə] adj termonuclear.

Thermos ® ['θəɪməs] n termo ® m. **termos** ® m.

thermostat ['θəɪməstat] n termostato m. **thermostatic** adj termostático.

these [ðiɪz] pl adj estos, estas. pl pron éstos, éstas.

thesis ['θiɪsis] n, pl -ses tesis f invar.

they [ðei] pl pron ellos, ellas.

thick [θik] adj grueso; espeso; denso; (coll) torpe. **thick-skinned** adj (fig) insensible. **thicken** v espesar(se). **thickness** n espesor m.

thief [θiɪf] n ladrón, -ona m, f.

thigh [θai] n muslo m.

thimble ['θimbl] n dedal m.

thin [θin] adj (person) flaco; delgado; fino; (hair) ralo; (audience) escaso; (air) enrarecido; (beer) aguado; (voice) débil; (liquid) claro; (excuse) flojo. v adelgazar; (dilute) diluir. **thinness** n delgadez f. flaqueza f.

thing [θiŋ] n cosa f; objeto m; artículo m; (coll) chisme m. **things** pl n (affairs, belongings) cosas f pl.

*****think** [θiŋk] v pensar; meditar; imaginar. **I think so** creo que sí. **think about** pensar en. **think over** pensar bien.

third [θəɪd] adj tercero. n tercero, -a m, f; (fraction) tercio m; (music) tercera f. **third-party insurance** seguro contra tercera persona m. **third-rate** adj de poca calidad.

thirst [θəɪst] n sed f. v tener sed. **be thirsty** tener sed.

thirteen [θəɪ'tiɪn] nm, adj trece. **thirteenth** n, adj decimotercero, -a m, f.

thirty ['θəɪti] nm, adj treinta. **thirtieth** n, adj trigésimo, -a m, f.

this [ðis] adj este, esta. pron éste, ésta. adv tan; así de.

thistle ['θisl] n cardo m.

thong [θoŋ] n correa f.

thorn [θoɪn] n espina f. **thorny** adj espinoso.

thorough ['θʌrə] adj (search, etc.) minucioso; (person) concienzudo; a fondo; completo. **thoroughbred** n pura sangre m, f. **thoroughfare** n vía pública f. **thoroughly** adv a fondo; completamente. **thoroughness** n minuciosidad f.

those [ðouz] adj esos, esas; aquellos, aquellas. pron ésos, ésas; aquéllos, aquéllas.

though [ðou] conj aunque. adv sin embargo. **as though** como si.

thought [θoɪt] n pensamiento m; idea f; consideración f; intención f; opinión f. **thoughtful** adj pensativo; serio; (mindful) cuidadoso; (considerate) solícito. **thoughtless** adj irreflexivo; descuidado; desconsiderado.

thousand ['θauzənd] nm, adj mil. **thousandth** adj milésimo. n (fraction) milésima parte f; (position) número mil m.

thrash [θraʃ] v dar una paliza a. **thrash about** revolcarse. **thrash out** discutir a fondo. **thrashing** n paliza f.

thread [θred] n hilo m; (screw) rosca f. filete m. v ensartar, enhebrar. **threadbare** adj raído, gastado.

threat [θret] n amenaza f. **threaten** v amenazar.

three [θriɪ] nm, adj tres. **three-cornered** adj triangular. **three-dimensional** adj tridimensional. **threefold** adj triple. **three-legged** adj de tres patas. **three-piece suite** tresillo m. **three-ply** adj contrapachado. **three-quarter** adj tres cuartos.

thresh [θreʃ] v trillar. **threshing machine** n trilladora f.

threshold ['θreʃould] *n* umbral *m*.

threw [θruː] *V* throw.

thrift [θrift] *n* economía *f*. **thrifty** *adj* económico.

thrill [θril] *n* emoción *f*; (*quiver*) estremecimiento *m*. *v* estremecer. **thriller** *n* novela *or* película escalofriante *f*. **thrilling** *adj* emocionante; escalofriante.

thrive [θraiv] *v* crecer; desarrollarse; tener buena salud; prosperar. **thriving** *adj* lozano; próspero.

throat [θrout] *n* garganta *f*. **clear one's throat** aclararse la voz. **throaty** *adj* gutural.

throb [θrob] *n* (*heart*) latido *m*, palpitación *f*; (*engine*) zumbido *m*; (*pulse*) pulsación *f*; (*pain*) punzada *f*. *v* latir; pulsar; zumbar; dar punzadas.

thrombosis [θrom'bousis] *n* trombosis *f* invar.

throne [θroun] *n* trono *m*.

throng [θroŋ] *n* multitud *f*, muchedumbre *f*. *v* atestar; afluir.

throttle ['θrotl] *v* estrangular. . *n* (*tech*) regulador *m*; (*mot*) acelerador.

through [θruː] *adj* directo; continuo. *adv* de parte a parte; completamente. *prep* (*via*) por; (*time*) durante; (*place*) a través de. **no through road** calle sin salida *f*. **through traffic** tránsito *m*. **throughout** *prep* (*place*) por todo, en; (*time*) durante todo. *adv* hasta el final.

***throw** [θrou] *n* tiro *m*, lanzamiento *m*; (*wrestling*) tumbado *m*. *v* lanzar, tirar, arrojar; (*a blow*) dar; (*light*) proyectar. **throw away** tirar; (*get rid of*) desechar; (*money*) despilfarrar. **throw off** (*a habit*) renunciar a; (*the scent*) despistar. **throw out** expulsar, echar; rechazar. **throw up** (*job*) dejar; (*vomit*) devolver.

thrush [θrʌʃ] *n* tordo *m*.

***thrust** [θrʌst] *v* empujar; clavar; meter; poner. *n* empujón *m*; (*stab*) estocada *f*.

thud [θʌd] *n* ruido sordo *m*. *v* caer con un ruido sordo.

thumb [θʌm] *n* pulgar *m*. *v also* **thumb through** hojear. **thumb a lift** (*coll*) hacer autostop. **thumb index** uñeros *m pl*.

thump [θʌmp] *n* (*blow*) porrazo *m*; (*noise*) ruido sordo *m*. *v* (*strike*) golpear; (*heart*) latir con fuerza.

thunder ['θʌndə] *n* trueno *m*; (*fig*) estruendo *m*. **thunderstorm** *n* tormenta *f*. **thunderstruck** *adj* atónito. *v* tronar.

Thursday ['θəːzdi] *n* jueves *m*.

thus [ðʌs] *adv* así; de este modo.

thwart [θwoːt] *v* frustrar, impedir.

thyme [taim] *n* tomillo *m*.

thyroid ['θairoid] *n* tiroides *f invar. adj* tiroideo.

tiara [ti'aːrə] *n* tiara *f*.

tick¹ [tik] *n* (*mark*) marca *f*; (*sound*) tictac *m*. **tick off** (*coll*) reprender.

tick² [tik] *n* (*zool*) garrapata *f*.

ticket ['tikit] *n* (*price*) etiqueta *f*; (*entrance*) entrada *f*; (*transport*) billete *m*; (*permit*) pase *m*. **cloakroom ticket** número del guardarropa *m*. **complimentary ticket** entrada de favor *f*. **parking ticket** multa por aparcamiento indebido *f*. **return ticket** billete de ida y vuelta *m*. **single ticket** billete de ida *m*. **ticket agency** agencia de venta de billetes *f*. **ticket office** taquilla *f*.

tickle ['tikl] *v* hacer cosquillas a. *n* cosquilleo *m*. **ticklish** *adj* cosquilloso.

tide [taid] *n* marea *f*. **tide-mark** *n* línea de la marea alta *f*; (*coll*) lengua del aqua *f*. *v* **tide over** sacar de apuro.

tidy ['taidi] *adj* ordenado; (*appearance*) arreglado; (*clean*) limpio. *v* ordenar; limpiar. **tidily** *adv* bien; aseadamente. **tidiness** *n* orden *m*; aseo *m*.

tie [tai] *v* atar; (*lace*) lacear; (*knot*) hacer; (*unite*) unir; (*link*) ligar; (*sport*) empatar. *n* (*neck*) corbata *f*; (*knot*) nudo *m*; (*bond*) lazo *m*; (*sport*) empate *m*; (*fig*) atadura *f*.

tier [tiə] *n* grada *f*; (*row*) fila *f*; (*cake*) piso *m*.

tiger ['taigə] *n* tigre *m*.

tight [tait] *adj* (*bolt, knot, etc.*) apretado; (*clothes*) ajustado; (*taut*) tirante; (*control*) estricto; (*seal*) hermético; (*bend*) cerrado; (*coll: drunk*) borracho; (*coll: mean*) agarrado. **tight-fisted** *adj* tacaño. **tight-lipped** *adj* callado. **tightrope** *n* cuerda de volatinero *f*. *adv also* **tightly** bien; herméticamente. **hold tight!** ¡agárrense bien! **tighten** (*screw, etc.*) apretar; (*rope, etc.*) tensar; (*control*) estrechar. **tighten one's belt** (*coll*) apretarse el cinturón. **tights** *pl n* mallas *f pl*.

tile [tail] *n* (*roof*) teja *f*; (*floor*) baldosa *f*. *v* tejar; embaldosar.

till¹ [til] *V* until.

till² [til] *n* caja *f*.

till³ [til] *v* labrar, cultivar.

tiller ['tilə] *n* (*naut*) caña del timón *f.*

tilt [tilt] *n* inclinación *f.* **at full tilt** en toda mecha. *v* inclinar. **tilt at** arremeter contra.

timber ['timbə] *n* madera de construcción *f.* **timbered** (*house*) enmaderado.

time [taim] *n* tiempo *m,* momento *m;* época *f;* período *m;* (*season*) estación *f;* (*clock*) hora *f;* (*occasion*) vez *f;* (*fixed time period*) plazo *m;* (*music*) duración *f;* (*music: tempo*) compás *m;* (*sport*) final *m.* **a long time** mucho tiempo. **a short time** poco tiempo. **at the same time** al mismo tiempo. **from time to time** de vez en cuando. **in time** a tiempo. **on time** a la hora. **timeless** *adj* eternal. **timely** *adj* oportuno.

time exposure *n* exposición *f.*

time limit *n* límite de tiempo *m.*

timepiece ['taimpiːs] *n* reloj *m.*

timesaving ['taim,seiviŋ] *adj* que ahorra tiempo.

time signal *n* señal horaria *f.*

timetable ['taimteibl] *n* horario *m;* (*transport*) guía *f.*

time zone *n* huso horario *m.*

timid ['timid] *adj* tímido. **timidity** *n* timidez *f.*

tin [tin] *n* estaño *m;* (*tinplate*) hojalata *f;* (*can*) lata *f;* (*baking*) molde *m.* **tinfoil** *n* papel de estaño *m.* **tin-opener** *n* abrelatas *m invar.* **tinny** *adj* (*sound, taste*) metálico.

tinge [tindʒ] *n* tinte *m. v* teñir.

tingle ['tiŋgl] *v* sentir hormigueo. *n* hormigueo *m.*

tinker ['tiŋkə] *n* calderero *m. v* componer, arreglar. **tinker with** jugar con.

tinkle ['tiŋkl] *n* tintineo *m. v* hacer tintinear.

tinsel ['tinsəl] *n* oropel *m.*

tint [tint] *n* (*hair*) tinte *m;* tono *m;* matiz *m. v* teñir; matizar.

tiny ['taini] *adj* diminuto.

tip[1] [tip] *n* punta *f;* (*cigarette*) filtro *m.* **on tiptoe** de puntillas.

tip[2] [tip] *v* (*tilt*) inclinar; (*pour*) verter; (*upset*) volcar.

tip[3] [tip] *n* (*hint*) consejo *m,* información *f;* (*money*) propina *f. v* dar una propina a. **tip-off** *n* (*coll*) información *f.*

tipsy ['tipsi] *adj* (*coll*) achispado.

tire[1] ['taiə] *v* cansar(se). **tire out** agotar. **tired** *adj* cansado. **be tired of** estar harto de. **tiredness** *n* cansancio *m.* **tiresome** *adj* pesado.

tire[2] *V* tyre.

tissue ['tiʃuː] *n* (*anat*) tejido *m;* (*cloth*) tisú *m;* (*handkerchief*) pañuelo de papel *m.* **tissue paper** papel de seda *m.*

title ['taitl] *n* título *m;* derecho *m.* **title deed** título de propiedad *m.* **title page** portada *f. v* titular. **titled** *adj* con título de nobleza.

titter ['titə] *n* risita *f. v* reírse nerviosamente.

to [tu] *prep* a; (*direction*) hacia; (*as far as*) hasta; (*time*) menos; (*destination, purpose*) para; (*according to*) según; (*in juxtaposition*) contra; (*compared with*) en comparación con; (*in*) por; (*in memory of*) en honor a. **to-do** *n* (*coll*) follón *m.*

toad [toud] *n* sapo *m.* **toadstool** *n* hongo venenoso *m.*

toast [toust] *n* pan tostado *m;* (*speech*) brindis *m invar.* **toast-rack** *n* portatostadas *m invar. v* tostar. **toaster** *n* tostador *m.*

tobacco [tə'bakou] *n* tabaco *m.* **tobacconist's** *n* estanco *m.*

toboggan [tə'bogən] *n* tobogán *m. v* deslizarse en tobogán.

today [tə'dei] *nm, adj* hoy.

toddler ['todlə] *n* niño pequeño *m;* niña pequeña *f.*

toe [tou] *n* dedo del pie. **big toe** dedo gordo *m.* **toenail** *n* uña (del dedo del pie) *f.* **toe the line** (*coll*) conformarse.

toffee ['tofi] *n* caramelo *m.* **toffee-apple** *n* manzana garrapiñada *f.*

together [tə'geðə] *adv* juntos; (*at the same time*) a la vez; (*agreed*) de acuerdo. **togetherness** *n* solidaridad *f.*

toil [toil] *n* trabajo agotador *m. v* trabajar duro.

toilet ['toilit] *n* (*lavatory*) retrete *m;* (*washing, etc.*) arreglo *m.* **toilet paper** papel higiénico *m.* **toilet soap** jabón de tocador *m.* **toilet water** agua de Colonia *f.*

token ['toukən] *n* (*sign*) muestra *f,* prueba *f;* (*symbol*) símbolo *m;* (*keepsake*) recuerdo *m;* (*disc*) ficha *f;* (*book, record*) vale *m.* **as a token of** como prueba de. *adj* simbólico.

told [tould] *V* tell.

tolerate ['toləreit] *v* tolerar, soportar; admitir; respetar. **tolerable** *adj* tolerable; (*fair*) mediano. **tolerance** *n also* **toleration** tolerancia *f.* **tolerant** *adj* tolerante.

toll¹ [toul] *n* (*road*) peaje *m*; (*bridge*) pontaje *m*; (*victims*) bajas *f pl*. **toll-gate** *n* barrera de peaje *f*.

toll² [toul] *v* tocar. tañar.

tomato [tə'mattou] *n* tomate *m*.

tomb [tuːm] *n* tumba *f*. **tombstone** *n* piedra sepulcral *f*.

tomorrow [tə'morou] *nm, adv* mañana. **the day after tomorrow** pasado mañana *m*.

ton [tʌn] *n* tonelada *f*.

tone [toun] *n* tono *m*; estilo *m*. *v* (*colour*) matizar. **tone down** atenuarse.

tongs [toŋz] *pl n* (*coal*) tenazas *f pl*; (*sugar*) tenacillas *f pl*.

tongue [tʌŋ] *n* lengua *f*. **tongue-tied** *adj* mudo.

tonic ['tonik] *adj* tónico. *n* (*med*) tónico *m*; (*music*) tónica *f*.

tonight [tə'nait] *n, adv* esta noche.

tonsil ['tonsil] *n* amígdala *f*. **tonsillitis** *n* amigdalitis *f*.

too [tuː] *adv* demasiado; (*also*) también; (*moreover*) además.

took [tuk] *V* **take**.

tool [tuːl] *n* herramienta *f*; utensilio *m*. **toolshed** *n* cobertizo para herramientas *m*

tooth [tuːθ] *n, pl* **teeth** diente *m*; (*back tooth*) muela *f*. **toothache** *n* dolor de muelas *m*. **tooth-brush** *n* cepillo de dientes *m*. **toothpaste** *n* pasta dentífrica *f*. **toothpick** *n* palillo de dientes *m*. **toothless** *adj* desdentado.

top¹ [top] *n* parte de arriba *f*, lo alto *m*; (*of mountain*) cima *f*; (*of tin, pan, bottle, etc.*) tapa *f*; (*of page*) cabeza *f*; (*of the head*) coronilla *f*; (*surface*) superficie *f*. *adj* de arriba; (*best*) mejor; (*first*) primero. *v* (*cover*) cubrir; (*exceed*) superar. **top up** llenar completamente.

top² [top] *n* (*toy*) peón *m*, trompo *m*.

topaz ['toupaz] *n* topacio *m*.

topcoat ['topkout] *n* abrigo *m*.

topdressing ['top,dresiŋ] *n* abono *m*.

top hat *n* chistera *f*.

top-heavy *adj* inestable.

topic ['topik] *n* tema *m*, asunto *m*. **topical** *adj* de actualidad.

topography [tə'pogrəfi] *n* topografía *f*. **topographical** *adj* topográfico.

topple ['topl] *v* derribar, volcar, hacer caer.

top-secret *adj* confidencial.

topsoil ['topsoil] *n* tierra vegetal *f*.

topsy-turvy [topsi'təɪvi] *adj* revuelto.

torch [toɪtʃ] *n* (*electric*) linterna *f*; (*burning*) antorcha *f*.

tore [toɪ] *V* **tear**.

torment ['toɪment; *v* toɪ'ment] *n* tormento *m*, suplicio *m*. *v* atormentar.

tornado [toɪ'neidou] *n* tornado *m*.

torpedo [toɪ'piɪdou] *n* torpedo *m*. *v* torpedear.

torrent ['torənt] *n* torrente *m*. **torrential** *adj* torrencial.

torso ['toɪsou] *n* torso *m*.

tortoise ['toɪtəs] *n* tortuga *f*. **tortoise-shell** *n* carey *m*.

tortuous ['toɪtʃuəs] *adj* tortuoso.

torture ['toɪtʃə] *n* tortura *f*. *v* torturar. **torturer** *n* torcionario *m*.

toss [tos] *v* (*throw*) lanzamiento *m*; (*fall*) caída *f*; (*head*) sacudida *f*; (*coin*) sorteo a cara o cruz *m*; (*bull*) cogida *f*. *v* lanzar; sacudir; (*coin*) echar a cara o cruz; (*salad*) dar vueltas a.

tot¹ [tot] *n* (*child*) nene *m*; (*drink*) trago *m*.

tot² [tot] *v* **tot up** sumar.

total ['toutəl] *nm, adj* total. *v* (*add up*) sumar; (*add up to*) totalizar. **totalitarian** *n, adj* totalitario, -a.

totter ['totə] *v* bambolearse.

touch [tʌtʃ] *n* (*sense*) tacto *m*; (*contact*) contacto *m*; (*light stroke*) toque *m*; (*tap*) golpe ligero *m*; (*brush*) roce *m*. *v* tocar; rozar; (*reach*) alcanzar; (*affect*) afectar; (*move*) enternecer; (*food*) tomar. **touchy** *adj* susceptible.

tough [tʌf] *adj* (*hard*) duro; resistente; (*character*) tenaz; (*job*) difícil. **toughen** *v* endurecer. **toughness** *n* dureza *f*; resistencia *f*; dificultad *f*.

toupee ['tuɪpei] *n* tupé *m*.

tour [tuə] *n* excursión *f*; visita *f*; viaje *m*; (*theatre*) gira *f*. **package tour** viaje todo comprendido *m*. **tour of duty** turno de servicio *m*. *v* recorrer. **touring** *n* also **tourism** turismo *m*. **tourist** *n* turista *m, f*. **tourist agency** agencia de viajes *f*.

tournament ['tuənəmənt] *n* torneo *m*.

tousled ['tauzld] *adj* (*hair*) despeinado.

tow [tou] *n* remolque *m*. *v* remolcar; (*from towpath*) sirgar. **towpath** *n* camino de sirga *m*. **tow-rope** *n* remolque *m*.

towards [tə'woɪdz] *prep* hacia; (*for*) para; (*with*) con; (*with regard to*) con respecto a.

towel ['tauəl] n toalla f; (bath) toalla de baño f; (sanitary) paño higiénico m. **towel-rail** n toallero m. **towelling** n felpa f.

tower ['tauə] n torre f. **control tower** torre de control f. **tower over** dominar. **towering** adj sobresaliente.

town [taun] n (large) ciudad f; (small) pueblo m. **new town** pueblo nuevo m. **town hall** ayuntamiento m. **town planning** urbanismo m.

toxic ['toksik] adj tóxico.

toy [toi] n juguete m. adj de juguete. v toy with toquetear; (idea) acariciar.

trace [treis] n (trail) rastro m; (indication) indicio m; (a little) pizca f. v (plan) trazar; (through paper) calcar; (trail) rastrear; (find) encontrar. **tracing** n calco m. **tracing paper** papel de calcar m.

track [trak] n (of animals, people) huella f; (of things) rastro m; (path) sendero m; (rail) vía f; (course) curso m; (racing) pista f; (tank, tractor) oruga f. **tracksuit** n mono de entrenamiento m. v (hunt) rastrear; (pursue) seguir la pista de. **track down** acorralar. **tracker** n perseguidor m.

tract[1] [trakt] n (region) trecho m; (anat) aparato m.

tract[2] [trakt] n (pamphlet) folleto m.

tractor ['traktə] n tractor m.

trade [treid] n comercio m; (job) ramo m. **trademark** n marca de fábrica f. **tradesman** n comerciante m. **trade union** sindicato m. **trade unionist** sindicalista m, f. v comerciar; negociar; cambiar. **trade in** tomar como entrada. **trader** n comerciante m, f; negociante m, f.

tradition [trə'diʃən] n tradición f. **traditional** adj tradicional.

traffic ['trafik] n (mot) circulación f, tráfico m; (tourist) tránsito m; (trade) comercio m. **traffic jam** embotellamiento m. **traffic-light** n semáforo m. **traffic warden** guardián del tráfico m.

tragedy ['tradʒədi] n tragedia f. **tragic** adj trágico.

trail [treil] n (path) camino m, sendero; (person or animal) huellas f pl; (smoke) estela f; (blood) reguero m. v (drag) arrastrar; (chase) perseguir; (an animal) rastrear; (lag) ir detrás de; (hang down) colgar. **trailer** n (mot) remolque m; (film) trailer m.

train [trein] n (railway) tren m; (procession) desfile m; (series) serie f; (dress) cola f. v (teach) educar; (someone for a job) formar, capacitar; (animal) amaestrar; (horse) domar; (sport) entrenar. **trainee** n aprendiz. -a m, f. **trainer** n (sport) entrenador. -a m, f; (boxing) cuidador m; (animals) amaestrador. -a m, f; (horses) domador. -a m, f.

trait [treit] n rasgo m.

traitor ['treitə] n traidor. -a m, f.

tram [tram] n tranvía m.

tramp [tramp] n (person) vagabundo. -a m, f; (hike) caminata f; (sound) ruido de pasos m. v patear; vagabundear.

trample ['trampl] v pisotear, pisar.

trampoline ['trampəlin] n cama elástica f.

trance [trains] n trance m.

tranquil ['traŋkwil] adj tranquilo. **tranquillity** n tranquilidad f. **tranquillize** v tranquilizar. **tranquillizer** n tranquilizante m.

transact [tran'zakt] v (negotiate) tratar; (perform) llevar a cabo. **transaction** n (business) negociación f; (deal) transacción f.

transcend [tran'send] v exceder, superar. **transcendental** adj trascedental.

transcribe [tran'skraib] v transcribir. **transcription** n trascripción f.

transept ['transept] n transepto m.

transfer [trans'fəi; n 'transfəi] v trasladar; transferir. n traslado m; (law) cesión f; (picture) calcomanía f. **transferable** adj transferible. **not transferable** (right) inalienable; (ticket) intransferible.

transfix [trans'fiks] v traspasar.

transform [trans'foim] v transformar. **transformation** n transformación f. **transformer** n (elec) transformador m.

transfuse [trans'fjuiz] v transfundir. **transfusion** n transfusión f.

transient ['tranziənt] adj transitorio.

transistor [tran'zistə] n transistor m. **transistorize** v transistorizar.

transit ['transit] n tránsito m. **in transit de** tránsito.

transition [tran'ziʃən] n transición f. **transitional** adj transitorio.

transitive ['transitiv] adj transitivo.

transitory ['transitəri] adj transitorio.

translate [trans'leit] v traducir. **translation** n traducción f. **translator** n traductor. -a m, f.

translucent [trans'luisnt] adj translúcido. **translucence** n translucidez f.

transmit [tranz'mit] v transmitir, trasmitir. **transmission** n transmisión f. trasmisión f. **transmitter** n (*apparatus*) transmisor m; (*station*) emisora f.

transparent [trans'peərənt] adj transparente. **transparency** n transparencia f; (*phot*) transparente m.

transplant [trans'plaint; n 'transplaint] v trasplantar. n trasplante m.

transport ['transpoit; v trans'poit] n transporte m. v transportar. **transportation** n transporte m; (*convicts*) deportación f.

transpose [trans'pouz] v transponer; (*music*) transportar. **transposition** n transposición f. transporte m.

transverse ['tranzvəis] adj transverso.

transvestite [tranz'vestait] n travestido m.

trap [trap] n trampa f; (*mice, rats*) ratonera f; (*vehicle*) cabriolé m; (*tech*) sifón de depósito m; (*theatre*) escotillón m. **trapdoor** n trampa f. v coger; coger en una trampa; rodear; pillar; bloquear.

trapeze [trə'piɪz] n trapecio m. **trapeze artist** trapecista m, f.

trash [traʃ] n basura f; (*coll*) cachivaches m pl.

trauma ['trɔɪmə] n trauma f. **traumatic** adj traumático.

travel ['travl] v recorrer; viajar por. **travels** pl n viajes m pl. **travel agency** agencia de viajes f. **travel-sickness** n mareo m. **traveller** n viajero, -a m, f; (*comm*) viajante de comercio m. **traveller's cheque** cheque de viaje m.

travesty ['travəsti] n parodia f.

trawler ['trɔɪlə] n barco rastreador m. **trawling** n pesca a la rastrea f.

tray [trei] n bandeja f.

treachery ['tretʃəri] n traición f. **treacherous** adj (*person*) traidor; (*action*) traicionero.

treacle ['triɪkl] n melaza f.

*****tread** [tred] v pisar; (*walk*) andar por. **tread on** (*crush*) pisotear. n paso m; (*step of a staircase*) huella f; (*tyre*) banda de rodadura f.

treason ['triɪzn] n traición f.

treasure ['treʒə] n tesoro m. v valorar; guardar en la memoria. **treasurer** n tesorero, -a m, f. **treasury** n tesorería f.

treat [triɪt] v tratar; tomar; (*a patient*) atender; (*pay for*) invitar, comprar. n invitación f; placer m. **treatment** n trato m; (*med*) tratamiento m.

treatise ['triɪtiz] n tratado m.

treaty ['triɪti] n tratado m; acuerdo m.

treble ['trebl] n (*music*) tiple m, soprano m. adj triple; (*music*) de tiple. v triplicar. adv tres veces.

tree [triɪ] n árbol m.

trek [trek] v caminar trabajosamente. n expedición f; caminata f.

trellis ['trelis] n enrejado m; espaldera f. v poner un enrejado.

tremble ['trembl] v temblar. n temblor m.

tremendous [trə'mendəs] adj tremendo, enorme; extraordinario; (*coll: excellent*) formidable.

tremor ['tremə] n temblor m.

trench [trentʃ] n zanja f; (*mil*) trinchera f.

trend [trend] n tendencia f; dirección f; orientación f. **trendy** adj (*coll*) modernísimo.

trespass ['trespəs] n entrada ilegal f. v violar; abusar; invadir. **trespasser** n intruso, -a m, f. **trespassers will be prosecuted** prohibido el paso.

trestle ['tresl] n caballete m. **trestle table** mesa de caballete f.

trial ['traiəl] n (*law*) juicio m; (*experiment*) prueba f, ensayo m; (*annoyance*) molestia f; (*hardship*) dificultad f. adj de prueba.

triangle ['traiaŋgl] n triángulo m. **triangular** adj triangular.

tribe [traib] n tribu f. **tribal** adj tribal. **tribesman** n miembro de una tribu m.

tribunal [trai'bjuɪnl] n tribunal m.

tributary ['tribjutəri] n afluente m. adj tributario.

tribute ['tribjuɪt] n tributo m.

trick [trik] n (*stratagem*) truco m; (*ruse*) astucia f; (*practical joke*) broma f; (*cards*) baza f. **trick photography** trucaje m. **trick question** pega f. v engañar. **trickery** n engaño m; astucia f. **tricky** adj difícil; delicado.

trickle ['trikl] n hilo m, chorrito m. v verter poco a poco; gotear.

tricycle ['traisikl] n triciclo m.

trifle ['traifl] n nadería f. v **trifle with** jugar con. **trifling** adj insignificante.

trigger ['trigə] n gatillo m. v accionar. **trigger off** provocar.

trigonometry [trigə'nomətri] n trigonometría f.

trill [tril] n trino m. v trinar.

trim [trim] adj aseado; (*neat*) arreglado; elegante. v arreglar; (*reduce*) cercenar; (*hair*) entresacar; (*nails*) recortar; (*hedge*) podar; (*sails*) orientar. **trimmings** *pl n* recortes *m pl*; accesorios *m pl*.

trinket ['triŋkit] *n* dije *m*.

trio ['triːou] *n* trío *m*.

trip [trip] *n* (*voyage, effect of drugs*) viaje *m*; (*stumble*) tropezón *m*. *v* dar un traspié; tropezar; (*make someone fall*) echar la zancadilla.

tripe [traip] *n* callos *m pl*; (*coll*) bobadas *f pl*.

triple ['tripl] *nm, adj* triple. *v* triplicar. *adv* tres veces.

triplet ['triplit] *n* (*music*) tresillo *m*; (*poetry*) terceto *m*; (*person*) trillizo, -a *m, f*.

tripod ['traipod] *n* trípode *m*.

trite [trait] *adj* trillado, trivial. **triteness** *n* lo trillado; trivialidad *f*.

triumph ['traiʌmf] *n* triunfo *m*. *v* triunfar. **triumphant** *adj* triunfante. **triumphantly** *adv* triunfantemente.

trivial ['triviəl] *adj* trivial. **trivia** *pl n* also **trivialities** trivialidades *f pl*.

trod [trod] *V* **tread**.

trolley ['troli] *n* (*shopping*) carretilla *f*; (*tea*) carrito *m*; (*in mines*) vagoneta *f*.

trombone [trom'boun] *n* trombón *m*.

troop [truːp] *n* (*people*) banda *f*, grupo *m*; (*animals*) manada *f*. **troops** *pl n* (*mil*) tropas *f pl*. *v* **troop in/out** entrar/salir en tropel.

trophy ['troufi] *n* trofeo *m*.

tropic ['tropik] *n* trópico *m*. **Tropic of Cancer** Trópico de Cáncer. **Tropic of Capricorn** Trópico de Capricornio. **tropical** *adj* tropical.

trot [trot] *n* trote *m*. **on the trot** (*coll*) seguidos, seguidas. *v* trotar. **trotter** *n* mano *f*.

trouble ['trʌbl] *n* (*worry*) preocupación *f*; apuro *m*; pena *f*; (*misfortune*) desgracia *f*; problema *m*; disturbios *m pl*. **be in trouble** estar en un apuro. **look for trouble** buscar camorra. **what's the trouble?** ¿qué pasa? **troublemaker** *n* alborotador, -a *m, f*. **troublesome** *adj* molesto. *v* preocupar; perturbar; afectar; molestar.

trough [trof] *n* (*food*) pesebre *m*; (*drinking*) abrevadero *m*; (*depression*) depresión *f*.

trousers ['trauzəz] *pl n* pantalón *m sing*.

trout [traut] *n* trucha *f*.

trowel ['trauəl] *n* palustre *m*; (*gardening*) desplantador *m*.

truant ['truːənt] *n* **play truant** hacer novillos. **truancy** *n* rabona *f*.

truce [truːs] *n* tregua *f*. **call a truce** acordar una tregua.

truck [trʌk] *n* camión *m*; (*rail*) batea *f*. **truck driver** conductor de camión *m*.

trudge [trʌdʒ] *v* andar con dificultad.

true [truː] *adj* verdadero; (*faithful*) fiel; legítimo; (*real*) auténtico; (*accurate*) exacto. **true to life** conforme a la realidad. **truly** *adv* verdaderamente.

truffle ['trʌfl] *n* trufa *f*.

trump [trʌmp] *n* (*cards*) triunfo *m*. *v* fallar. **trump up** inventar.

trumpet ['trʌmpit] *n* trompeta *f*. *v* (*elephant*) barritar. **trumpeter** *n* trompetista *m, f*.

truncate [trʌŋ'keit] *v* truncar.

truncheon ['trʌntʃən] *n* matraca *f*; (*police*) porra *f*.

trunk [trʌŋk] *n* (*anat, bot*) tronco *m*; (*elephant*) trompa *f*; (*case*) baúl *m*. **trunk call** conferencia telefónica *f*. **trunk road** carretera principal *f*. **trunks** *pl n* calzoncillos cortos *m pl*.

truss [trʌs] *n* (*hay*) haz *m*; (*fruit*) racimo *m*; (*med*) braguero *m*. *v* atar.

trust [trʌst] *n* confianza *f*; (*law*) fideicomiso *m*; (*comm*) trust *m*; (*expectation*) esperanza *f*. **trustworthy** *adj* digno de confianza; fidedigno. *v* tener confianza en; confiar; esperar; creer. **trustee** *n* guardián *m*; (*law*) fideicomisario, -a *m, f*. **trusting** *adj* confiado. **trusty** *adj* leal, seguro.

truth [truːθ] *n* verdad *f*. **truthful** *adj* veraz; verdadero. **truthfulness** *n* veracidad *f*.

try [trai] *n* tentativa *f*, prueba *f*; (*rugby*) ensayo *m*. *v* probar; intentar; ensayar; (*law*) ver; (*strain*) poner a prueba; (*annoy*) molestar; (*tire*) cansar; (*afflict*) hacer sufrir. **try on** (*garment*) probarse. **try it on** (*coll*) intentar dar el pego. **trying** *adj* molesto.

tsar [zaː] *n* zar *m*.

T-shirt ['tiːʃəːt] *n* camiseta *f*.

tub [tʌb] *n* tina *f*; (*bath*) bañera *f*.

tuba ['tjuːbə] *n* tuba *f*.

tube [tjuːb] *n* tubo *m*; (*coll: underground*) metro *m*. **tubeless** *adj* (*tyre*) sin cámara.

tuber ['tjuːbə] *n* tubérculo *m*.

tuberculosis [tjubəːkju'lousis] *n* tuberculosis *f*.

tuck [tʌk] *n* (*sewing*) alforza *f*; (*food*) comida *f*; (*sweets*) cucherías *f pl*. *v* meter; (*sheets*) remeter; (*fold*) alforzar. **tuck up** (*in bed*) arropar.

Tuesday ['tjuːzdi] *n* martes *m*.
tuft [tʌft] *n* (*plants*) mata *f*; (*feathers*) penacho *m*; (*hair*) mechón *m*.
tug [tʌg] *n* tirón *m*; (*boat*) remolcador *m*. **tug-of-war** *n* juego de la cuerda *m*. *v* (*pull*) tirar; (*tow*) remolcar; (*drag*) arrastrar.
tuition [tjuˈiʃən] *n* enseñanza *f*.
tulip ['tjuːlip] *n* tulipán *m*.
tumble ['tʌmbl] *n* caída *f*; (*acrobatics*) voltereta *f*. *v* caerse; dar volteretas; (*knock over*) derribar. **tumbledown** *adj* ruinoso. **tumble-dryer** *n* secadora al aire caliente *f*. **tumbler** *n* (*glass*) vaso *m*; (*acrobat*) voltalinero, -a *m*, *f*.
tummy ['tʌmi] *n* (*coll*) barriga *f*.
tumour ['tjuːmə] *n* tumor *m*.
tumult ['tjuːmʌlt] *n* tumulto *m*. **tumultuous** *adj* tumultuoso.
tuna ['tjuːnə] *n* atún *m*.
tune [tjuːn] *n* aire *m*. **in tune** afinado. **out of tune** desafinado. *v* (*music*) afinar; (*mot*) poner a punto. **tune in to** (*radio*) sintonizar con. **tuneful** *adj* melodioso. **tuneless** *adj* discordante. **tuner** *n* (*person*) afinador *m*; (*radio*) sintonizador *m*. **tuning** afinación *f*; sintonización *f*; puesta a punto *f*. **tuning fork** diapasón *m*.
tunic ['tjuːnik] *n* túnica *f*.
tunnel ['tʌnl] *n* túnel *m*. *v* hacer un túnel en; (*dig*) cavar.
turban ['təːbən] *n* turbante *m*.
turbine ['təːbain] *n* turbina *f*.
turbot ['təːbət] *n* rodaballo *m*.
turbulent ['təːbjulənt] *adj* turbulento. **turbulence** *n* turbulencia *f*.
tureen [təˈriːn] *n* sopera *f*.
turf [təːf] *n* cesped *m*; (*sport*) turf *m*. *v* encespedar. **turf out** (*coll*) echar.
turkey ['təːki] *n* pavo *m*.
Turkish ['təːkiʃ] *nm*, *adj* turco. **Turkish bath** baño turco *m*.
turmeric ['təːmərik] *n* cúrcuma *f*.
turmoil ['təːmoil] *n* desorden *m*; agitación *f*; alboroto *m*.
turn [təːn] *n* vuelta *f*; (*road*) curva *f*; (*body*) movimiento *m*; (*opportunity*) turno *m*; (*change*) cambio *m*; (*change in situation*) viraje *m*; (*fright*) susto *m*. **take turns at** turnarse en. *v* dar vueltas; dar la vuelta a; (*body*) volver; (*corner*) doblar; (*page*) pasar; cambiar. **turn down** (*lower*) bajar; (*reject*) rechazar. **turn off** cerrar; (*light*) apagar; (*engine*) parar. **turn on**

(*light*, *radio*) encender; (*current*) conectar; (*coll: excite*) excitar. **turn out** (*end up*) resultar; (*light*) apagar. **turnover** *n* (*comm*) volumen de negocios *m*. **turnstile** *n* torniquete *m*. **turntable** *n* (*record-player*) plato giratorio *m*. **turn up** presentarse; (*appear*) aparecer. **turning** *n* vuelta *f*; curva *f*; (*side road*) bocacalle *f*. **turning point** momento crucial *m*.
turnip ['təːnip] *n* nabo *m*.
turpentine ['təːpəntain] *n* trementina *f*.
turquoise ['təːkwoiz] *n* (*stone*) turquesa *f*; (*colour*) azul turquesa *m*.
turret ['tʌrit] *n* torreón *m*; (*mil*) torreta *f*.
turtle ['təːtl] *n* tortuga de mar *f*. **turtle-neck** *n* (*jumper collar*) cuello que sube ligeramente *m*.
tusk [tʌsk] *n* defensa *f*.
tussle ['tʌsl] *n* pelea *f*; lucha *f*. *v* pelearse.
tutor ['tjuːtə] *n* (*private*) profesor particular *m*; (*university*) tutor *m*. *v* dar clases privadas.
tuxedo [tʌkˈsiːdou] *n* smoking *m*.
tweed [twiːd] *n* tweed *m*.
tweezers ['twiːzəz] *pl n* pinzas *f pl*.
twelve [twelv] *nm*, *adj* doce. **twelfth** *n*, *adj* duodécimo, -a.
twenty ['twenti] *nm*, *adj* veinte. **twentieth** *n*, *adj* vigésimo, -a.
twice [twais] *adv* dos veces.
twiddle ['twidl] *v* dar vueltas a. **twiddle one's thumbs** estar mano sobre mano.
twig [twig] *n* ramita *f*.
twilight ['twailait] *n* crepúsculo *m*.
twin [twin] *n*, *adj* gemelo, -a. **twin beds** camas gemelas *f pl*.
twine [twain] *n* bramante *m*. *v* (*twist*) retorcer; (*interlace*) trenzar; (*embrace*) rodear con.
twinge [twindʒ] *n* (*pain*) punzada *f*; (*fig*) arrebato *m*.
twinkle ['twiŋkl] *n* centelleo *m*; (*brightness*) brillo *m*. *v* centellear; (*eyes*) brillar.
twirl [twəːl] *v* dar vueltas a. *n* vuelta *f*.
twist [twist] *v* torcer; retorcer. *n* torcimiento *m*, torsión *f*; (*tobacco*) rollo *m*; vuelta *f*; deformación *f*; contorsión *f*; inclinación *f*; (*warp*) abarquillamiento *m*; (*ankle*) torcedura *f*; (*swindle*) trampa *f*.
twit [twit] *n* (*slang*) imbécil *m*, *f*.
twitch [twitʃ] *n* (*pull*) tirón *m*; (*med*) tic *m*. *v* tirar bruscamente de; (*nervously*) crispar.

twitter ['twitə] *v* gorjear. *n* gorjeo *m*.

two [tuː] *nm, adj* dos. **two-faced** *adj* falso. **two-legged** *adj* bípedo.

tycoon [taiˈkuːn] *n* magnate *m*.

type [taip] *n* (*sort*) tipo *m*, clase *f*; (*print*) carácter *m*, tipo *m*. **typesetting** *n* composición *f*. **typewriter** *n* máquina de escribir *f*. *v* escribir a máquina. **typical** *adj* típico. **typing** *n* mecanografía *f*. **typist** *n* mecanógrafo, -a *m, f*.

typhoid ['taifoid] *n* fiebre tifoidea *f*.

typhoon [taiˈfuːn] *n* tifón *m*.

tyrant ['tairənt] *n* tirano *m*. **tyrannical** *adj* tiránico. **tyranny** *n* tiranía *f*.

tyre *or US* **tire** ['taiə] *n* neumático *m*.

U

ubiquitous [juˈbikwitəs] *adj* ubicuo.

udder ['ʌdə] *n* ubre *f*.

ugly ['ʌgli] *adj* feo; repugnante. **ugliness** *n* fealdad *f*.

ulcer ['ʌlsə] *n* úlcera *f*.

ulterior [ʌlˈtiəriə] *adj* ulterior. **ulterior motive** segunda intención *f*.

ultimate ['ʌltimət] *adj* último; fundamental. **ultimately** *adv* por fin, al final; esencialmente. **ultimatum** *n* ultimátum *m*.

ultraviolet [ʌltrəˈvaiələt] *adj* ultravioleta.

umbilical [ʌmˈbilikəl] *adj* umbilical. **umbilical cord** cordón umbilical *m*.

umbrage ['ʌmbridʒ] *n* resentimiento *m*, enfado *m*. **take umbrage at** ofenderse por.

umbrella [ʌmˈbrelə] *n* paraguas *m invar*.

umpire ['ʌmpaiə] *n* árbitro *m*. *v* arbitrar.

umpteen [ʌmpˈtiːn] (*coll*) *adj* muchísimos. **umpteenth** *adj* enésimo.

unable [ʌnˈeibl] *adj* incapaz. **be unable to** (*physical*) ser incapaz de; (*due to circumstances*) no poder hacer.

unabridged [ʌnəˈbridʒd] *adj* íntegro.

unacceptable [ʌnəkˈseptəbl] *adj* inaceptable.

unaccompanied [ʌnəˈkʌmpənid] *adj* solo, sin compañía; (*music*) sin acompañamiento.

unaided [ʌnˈeidid] *adj* sin ayuda, solo.

unadulterated [ʌnəˈdʌltəreitid] *adj* no adulterado, sin mezcla.

unanimous [juˈnaniməs] *adj* unánime. **unanimity** *n* unanimidad *f*.

unarmed [ʌnˈaːmd] *adj* (*person*) sin armas; desarmado.

unattached [ʌnəˈtatʃt] *adj* (*loose*) suelto; libre; independiente.

unattractive [ʌnəˈtraktiv] *adj* poco atrayente, desagradable.

unauthorized [ʌnˈoːθəraizd] *adj* no autorizado.

unavoidable [ʌnəˈvoidəbl] *adj* inevitable.

unaware [ʌnəˈweə] *adj* inconsciente; ignorante. **be unaware of** ignorar. **unawares** *adv* sin querer; de improviso.

unbalanced [ʌnˈbalənst] *adj* desequilibrado; (*mentally*) trastornado.

unbearable [ʌnˈbeərəbl] *adj* insoportable, intolerable, insufrible.

unbelievable [ʌnbiˈliːvəbl] *adj* increíble.

*unbend [ʌnˈbend] *v* (*straighten*) desencorvar; (*fig*) relajar. **unbending** *adj* inflexible.

unbiased [ʌnˈbaiəst] *adj* imparcial.

unbreakable [ʌnˈbreikəbl] *adj* irrompible.

unbridled [ʌnˈbraidld] *adj* (*fig*) desenfrenado.

unbutton [ʌnˈbʌtn] *v* desabrochar; (*fig*) desahogarse.

uncalled-for [ʌnˈkoːldfoɪ] *adj* innecesario; injustificado; gratuito.

uncanny [ʌnˈkani] *adj* extraño; misterioso.

uncertain [ʌnˈsəːtn] *adj* incierto. **uncertainty** *n* incertidumbre *f*.

uncle ['ʌŋkl] *n* tío *m*.

uncomfortable [ʌnˈkʌmfətəbl] *adj* incómodo; (*anxious*) inquieto; (*awkward*) difícil.

uncommon [ʌnˈkomən] *adj* poco común, raro.

uncompromising [ʌnˈkomprəmaiziŋ] *adj* inflexible; irreconciliable.

unconditional [ʌnkənˈdiʃənl] *adj* incondicional.

unconscious [ʌnˈkonʃəs] *adj* (*med*) inconsciente; (*unaware*) ignorante.

unconventional [ʌnkənˈvenʃənl] *adj* poco convencional.

uncooked [ʌnˈkukt] *adj* no cocido, crudo.

uncouth [ʌnˈkuːθ] *adj* grosero.

uncover [ʌnˈkʌvə] *v* descubrir; (*reveal*) revelar; (*take the lid off*) destapar.

uncut [ʌnˈkʌt] *adj* no cortado.

undecided [ʌndi'saidid] *adj* indeciso; irresoluto.

undeniable [ʌndi'naiəbl] *adj* incontestable.

under ['ʌndə] *adv* debajo; abajo; más abajo; (*insufficient*) insuficiente; (*for less*) para menos. *prep* debajo de; bajo; por debajo de; menos de; (*age*) menor de; (*lower in rank*) por debajo de; (*repair, construction, etc.*) en; (*according to*) según; conforme a.

underarm ['ʌndəraɪm] *adj, adv* por debajo del brazo; sobacal.

undercharge [ʌndə'tʃaɪdʒ] *v* cobrar menos de lo debido.

underclothes ['ʌndəklouðz] *pl n* ropa interior *f sing*.

undercoat ['ʌndəkout] *n* (*paint*) primera capa *f*.

undercover [ʌndə'kʌvə] *adj* secreto; clandestino.

undercut [ʌndə'kʌt] *v* vender más barato que.

underdeveloped [ʌndədi'veləpt] *adj* de desarrollo atrasado; (*phot*) no revelado lo suficiente.

underdog ['ʌndədog] *n* desvalido *m*.

underdone [ʌndə'dʌn] *adj* (*meat*) poco hecho.

underestimate [ʌndə'estimeit] *v* tasar en menos; menospreciar. *n also* **underestimation** infravaloración *f*; menosprecio *m*.

underfoot [ʌndə'fut] *adv* debajo de los pies.

***undergo** [ʌndə'gou] *v* sufrir, pasar por.

undergraduate [ʌndə'gradjuət] *n* estudiante no licenciado, -a *m, f*.

underground ['ʌndəgraund; *adv* ʌndə'graund] *adj* subterráneo; oculto, secreto. *adv* bajo tierra; clandestinamente.

undergrowth ['ʌndəgrouθ] *n* maleza *f*.

underhand [ʌndə'hand] *adj* bajo mano; secreto.

***underlie** [ʌndə'lai] *v* estar debajo de; servir de base a. **underlying** *adj* básico; fundamental.

underline [ʌndə'lain] *v* subrayar. **underlining** *n* subrayado *m*.

undermine [ʌndə'main] *v* socavar, minar.

underneath [ʌndə'niːθ] *prep* bajo, debajo de. *adv* debajo, por debajo. *adj* inferior, de abajo.

underpaid [ʌndə'peid] *adj* mal pagado.

underpants ['ʌndəpants] *pl n* calzoncillos *m pl*.

underpass ['ʌndəpais] *n* paso subterráneo *m*.

underprivileged [ʌndə'privilidʒd] *adj* menesteroso.

underrate [ʌndə'reit] *v* subestimar.

underskirt ['ʌndəskəit] *n* enaguas *f pl*.

understaffed [ʌndə'staift] *adj* falto de personal.

***understand** [ʌndə'stand] *v* entender, comprender; (*believe*) creer. **understandable** *adj* comprensible. **understanding** *n* entendimiento *m*; comprensión *f*; (*reason*) razón *f*; interpretación *f*; (*knowledge*) conocimientos *m pl*; (*agreement*) acuerdo *m*.

understate *v* quitar importancia a. **make an understatement** describir sin énfasis. **that's an understatement!** ¡y usted que lo diga!

understudy ['ʌndəstʌdi] *n* suplente *m, f*. *v* suplir, doblar.

***undertake** [ʌndə'teik] *v* emprender; prometer. **undertaker** *n* empresario de pompas funebres *m*. **undertaking** *n* empresa *f*; compromiso *m*.

undertone ['ʌndətoun] *n* **in an undertone** en voz baja.

underwater [ʌndə'wɔitə] *adj* submarino.

underwear [ʌndəweə] *n* ropa interior *f*.

underweight [ʌndə'weit] *adj* de peso insuficiente.

underworld ['ʌndəwəild] *n* (*criminal*) hampa *f*; (*hell*) infierno *m*.

***underwrite** [ʌndə'rait] *v* (*sign, bonds*) subscribir; (*guarantee*) garantizar; (*insure*) asegurar.

undesirable [ʌndi'zaiərəbl] *adj* no deseable; pernicioso. *n* indeseable *m, f*.

***undo** [ʌn'duɪ] *v* (*open*) abrir; (*knot*) desatar; (*a tie*) desanudar; (*button*) desabrochar; (*parcel*) deshacer; (*zip*) bajar; (*ruin*) arruinar. **undoing** *n* ruina *f*. **come undone** desatarse.

undoubted [ʌn'dautid] *adj* indudable.

undress [ʌn'dres] *v* desnudar(se).

undue [ʌn'djuː] *adj* excesivo; impropio. **unduly** *adv* excesivamente; impropiamente.

undulate ['ʌndjuleit] *v* ondular. **undulating** *adj* ondulante. **undulation** *n* ondulación *f*.

unearth [ʌn'ɜːθ] v desenterrar; descubrir.
unearthly adj sobrenatural; misterioso; espantoso. **unearthly hour** (coll) hora intempestiva f.
uneasy [ʌn'iːzi] adj inquieto; molesto; agitado; preocupado.
uneducated [ʌn'edjukeitid] adj ineducado.
unemployed [ʌnem'ploid] adj parado, desempleado. **the unemployed** los parados m pl. **unemployment** n paro m, desempleo m.
unenthusiastic [ʌnenθjuːzi'astik] adj sin entusiasmo.
unequal [ʌn'iːkwəl] adj desigual; (inadequate) inadecuado; (med) irregular.
uneven [ʌn'iːvn] adj accidentado; (unequal) designal; (number) impar.
uneventful [ʌni'ventfəl] adj sin acontecimientos.
unexpected [ʌneks'pektid] adj inesperado.
unfailing [ʌn'feiliŋ] adj infalible; (inexhaustible) inagotable; (unceasing) constante.
unfair [ʌn'feə] adj injusto. **unfairness** n injusticia f.
unfaithful [ʌn'feiθfəl] adj infiel. **unfaithfulness** n infidelidad f.
unfamiliar [ʌnfə'miljə] adj desconocido; extraño.
unfasten [ʌn'faːsn] v (open) abrir; (dress, button) desabrochar; (knot) desatar; (set free) soltar; (loosen) aflojar.
unfavourable [ʌn'feivərəbl] adj desfavorable, adverso.
unfinished [ʌn'finiʃt] adj inacabado, no terminado.
unfit [ʌn'fit] adj incapaz; no apto; incompetente; impropio; (ill) enfermo, malo.
unfold [ʌn'fould] v desplegar; (plans) revelar; (thoughts) desarrollarse.
unforeseen [ʌnfɔː'siːn] adj imprevisto.
unforgivable [ʌnfə'givəbl] adj imperdonable.
unfortunate [ʌn'fɔːtʃənət] adj desafortunado; desgraciado.
unfounded [ʌn'faundid] adj infundado, sin fundamento.
unfriendly [ʌn'frendli] adj hostil; desfavorable.
unfurnished [ʌn'fɜːniʃd] adj desamueblado.
ungainly [ʌn'geinli] adj desgarbado.

ungrateful [ʌn'greitfəl] adj ingrato.
unhappy [ʌn'hapi] adj infeliz; triste. **unhappiness** n infelicidad f.
unhealthy [ʌn'helθi] adj (person) enfermo; (place) malsano.
unheard-of [ʌn'hɜːdɒv] adj inaudito; sin precedente.
unhoped-for [ʌn'houptfɔː] adj inesperado.
unhurt [ʌn'hɜːt] adj indemne, ileso.
unhygienic [ʌnhai'dʒiːnik] adj antihigiénico.
unicorn ['juːnikɔːn] n unicornio m.
unidentified flying object [ʌnai'dentifaid] n also **UFO** objeto volador no identificado m, OVNI m.
uniform ['juːnifɔːm] nm, adj uniforme. **uniformity** n uniformidad f.
unify ['juːnifai] v unificar. **unification** n unificación f.
unilateral [juːni'latərəl] adj unilateral.
unimaginative [ʌni'madʒinətiv] adj poco imaginativo.
unimportant [ʌnim'pɔːtnt] adj poco importante.
uninhabited [ʌnin'habitid] adj inhabitado.
uninhibited [ʌnin'hibitid] adj sin inhibición.
unintentional [ʌnin'tenʃənl] adj involuntario.
uninterested [ʌn'intristid] adj indiferente; desinteresado. **uninteresting** adj poco interesante.
union ['juːnjən] n unión f; (trade) sindicato m.
unique [juː'niːk] adj único.
unisex ['juːni,seks] adj (coll) unisexo invar.
unison ['juːnisn] n unisonancia. **in unison** al unísono.
unite [juː'nait] v unir; reunir; juntarse. **united** adj unido. **United Kingdom** Reino Unido m. **United Nations** Naciones Unidas f pl. **United States of America** Estados Unidos de América m pl.
unity ['juːniti] m unidad f.
universe ['juːnivɜːs] m universo m. **universal** adj universal.
university [juːni'vɜːsəti] n universidad f. adj universitario.
unjust [ʌn'dʒʌst] adj injusto.
unkempt [ʌn'kempt] adj descuidado; (hair) despeinado.
unkind [ʌn'kaind] adj poco amable; severo; cruel. **unkindness** n falta de amabilidad f; severidad f; crueldad f.

unknown [ʌn'noun] *n, adj* desconocido, -a.

unlawful [ʌn'lɔːfəl] *adj* ilegal; ilegítimo.

unless [ʌn'les] *conj* a no ser que, a menos que.

unlike [ʌn'laik] *adj* diferente, distinto. *prep* a diferencia de.

unlikely [ʌn'laikli] *adj* improbable; (*unexpected*) inverosímil.

unlimited [ʌn'limitid] *adj* ilimitado.

unload [ʌn'loud] *v* descargar; (*get rid of*) deshacerse de.

unlock [ʌn'lok] *v* abrir.

unlucky [ʌn'lʌki] *adj* desgraciado; (*day, number, etc.*) funesto.

unmarried [ʌn'marid] *adj* soltero.

unnatural [ʌn'natʃərəl] *adj* antinatural; anormal; artificial.

unnecessary [ʌn'nesəsəri] *adj* innecesario, inútil.

unnerving [ʌn'nɜːvɪŋ] *adj* desconcertante.

unnoticed [ʌn'noutist] *adv* inadvertido; desapercibido. **go** *or* **pass unnoticed** pasar desapercibido.

unobtainable [ʌnəb'teinəbl] *adj* que no se puede conseguir.

unobtrusive [ʌnəb'truːsiv] *adj* discreto, modesto.

unoccupied [ʌn'okjupaid] *adj* (*at leisure*) desocupado; (*untenanted*) deshabitado; (*seat*) libre.

unofficial [ʌnə'fiʃəl] *adj* no oficial.

unorthodox [ʌn'ɔːθədoks] *adj* poco ortodoxo.

unpack [ʌn'pak] *v* (*box*) desembalar; (*suitcase*) deshacer.

unpaid [ʌn'peid] *adj* impagado; (*bill*) por pagar; (*worker*) no retribuido.

unpleasant [ʌn'pleznt] *adj* (*weather*) desagradable; (*unfriendly*) antipático; (*annoying*) molesto.

unpopular [ʌn'popjulə] *adj* impopular.

unprecedented [ʌn'presidentid] *adj* sin precedentes.

unpredictable [ʌnprə'diktəbl] *adj* que no se puede prever; (*capricious*) antojadizo.

unqualified [ʌn'kwolifaid] *adj* sin título; (*without reservation*) sin reserva.

unravel [ʌn'ravəl] *v* (*wool*) deshacer; (*untangle*) desenredar; (*mystery*) desembrollar.

unreal [ʌn'riəl] *adj* irreal.

unreasonable [ʌn'riːzənəbl] *adj* irrazonable; extravagante; excesivo.

unrelenting [ʌnri'lentiŋ] *adj* implacable.

unreliable [ʌnri'laiəbl] *adj* (*character*) inconstante; (*person*) poco seguro; (*machine*) poco fiable; (*service*) dudoso.

unrest [ʌn'rest] *n* desasosiego *m*, agitación *f*.

unruly [ʌn'ruːli] *adj* ingobernable; rebelde.

unsafe [ʌn'seif] *adj* inseguro; peligroso.

unsatisfactory [ʌnsatis'faktəri] *adj* poco satisfactorio.

unscrew [ʌn'skruː] *v* destornillar.

unscrupulous [ʌn'skruːpjuləs] *adj* poco escrupuloso.

unselfish [ʌn'selfiʃ] *adj* desinteresado; generoso.

unsettle [ʌn'setl] *v* pertubar; (*mentally*) desequilibrar. **unsettled** *adj* perturbado; agitado; desequilibrado; (*weather*) incierto.

unsightly [ʌn'saitli] *adj* feo, repugnante.

unskilled [ʌn'skild] *adj* no cualificado; no especializado. **unskilled worker** obrero no cualificado *m*.

unsound [ʌn'saund] *adj* (*unhealthy*) enfermizo; (*mentally*) demente; (*morally*) corrompido; (*goods*) imperfecto; (*foundations*) poco sólido; (*business*) poco seguro; (*argument, opinion*) falso.

unspeakable [ʌn'spiːkəbl] *adj* indecible.

unspecified [ʌn'spesifaid] *adj* no especificado.

unstable [ʌn'steibl] *adj* inestable.

unsteady [ʌn'stedi] *adj* inestable; inconstante.

unstuck [ʌn'stʌk] *adj* **come unstuck** despegarse; (*hopes, plans*) fracasar.

unsuccessful [ʌnsək'sesfəl] *adj* sin éxito; (*person, attempt, etc.*) fracasado; (*candidate*) suspendido. **be unsuccessful** fracasar. **unsuccessfully** *adv* sin éxito; infructuosamente.

unsuitable [ʌn'suːtəbl] *adj* inapropiado; inconveniente; inoportuno.

untangle [ʌn'taŋgl] *v* desenmarañar.

untidy [ʌn'taidi] *adj* desarreglado; (*person*) desordenado. **untidiness** *n* desorden *m*.

untie [ʌn'tai] *v* desatar.

until [ən'til] *prep* hasta. *conj* hasta que.

untoward [ʌntə'woːd] *adj* insumiso; adverso; desafortunado.

untrue [ʌn'truː] *adj* falso, mentiroso; imaginario; infiel.

unusual [ʌn'juːʒuəl] *adj* desacostumbrado; extraño; excepcional.

unwanted [ʌn'wɒntɪd] *adj* no deseado; superfluo.

unwell [ʌn'wel] *adj* indispuesto, enfermo.

*unwind [ʌn'waɪnd] *v* desenrollar; (*relax*) descansar.

unwise [ʌn'waɪz] *adj* imprudente; indiscreto.

unworthy [ʌn'wəːði] *adj* indigno.

unwrap [ʌn'rap] *v* desenvolver; (*parcel*) deshacer.

up [ʌp] *adv* arriba; hacia arriba; al aire; en el aire; (*louder*) más fuerte; (*out of bed*) levantado; (*standing*) de pie, en pie. **be up to** ser capaz de. *prep* arriba; en; contra; en el fondo de. **walk up and down** pasearse a lo largo y a lo ancho. **ups and downs** los altibajos *m pl.* **up-and-coming** *adj* joven y prometedor.

upbringing ['ʌpbrɪŋɪŋ] *n* educación *f.*

update [ʌp'deɪt] *v* (*bring up to date*) poner al día; (*modernize*) modernizar.

upheaval [ʌp'hiːvl] *n* (*geol*) levantamiento *m*; (*fig*) agitación *f.*

uphill [ʌp'hil] *adj* ascendente; (*struggle*) arduo.

*uphold [ʌp'hould] *v* sostener; defender; confirmar.

upholster [ʌp'houlstə] *v* entapizar. **upholstery** *n* (*material*) tapicería *f*; (*filling*) relleno *m.*

upkeep ['ʌpkiːp] *n* mantenimiento *m.*

uplift [ʌp'lift] *n* (*geol*) elevación *f*; (*fig*) inspiración *f.*

upon [ə'pon] *prep* sobre, encima de.

upper ['ʌpə] *adj* alto; superior. **upperclass** *adj* de la clase alta. **upper hand** dominio *m.* **uppermost** *adj* más alto; predominante.

upright ['ʌpraɪt] *adj* vertical; derecho; (*fig*) recto. *adv* en posición vertical.

uprising ['ʌpraɪzɪŋ] *n* sublevación *f.*

uproar ['ʌprɔː] *n* alboroto *m*, tumulto *m.* **uproarious** *adj* tumultuoso; ruidoso.

uproot [ʌp'ruːt] *v* desarraigar; (*fig*) arrancar.

*upset [ʌp'set; *n* 'ʌpset] *v* (*knock over*) volcar; (*spill*) derramar; (*plans, etc.*) trastornar; desconcertar; (*displease*) enfadar. *adj* (*worried*) preocupado; (*ill*) indispuesto; (*nerves*) desquiciado; enfadado; (*stomach*) trastornado. *n* vuelco *m*; trastorno *m*; (*illness*) malestar *m*; dificultad *f*; (*trouble*) molestia *f.*

upshot ['ʌpʃot] *n* resultado *m.*

upside down [ʌpsaɪ'daun] *adv,* *adj* al revés.

upstairs [ʌp'steəz] *adv* arriba. **go upstairs** subir. *adj* de arriba.

upstream [ʌp'striːm] *adv* río arriba, aguas arriba; (*swim*) a contracorriente.

up-to-date *adj* moderno.

upward ['ʌpwəd] *adj* ascendente. **upwards** *adv* hacia arriba.

uranium [ju'reiniəm] *n* uranio *m.*

urban ['əːbən] *adj* urbano.

urchin ['əːtʃin] *n* pilluelo *m.*

urge [əːdʒ] *v* incitar; exhortar; requerir. *n* vivo deseo *m*; impulso *m.*

urgent ['əːdʒənt] *adj* urgente; insistente. **urgency** *n* urgencia *f*; insistencia *f.*

urine ['juːrin] *n* orina *f.* **urinate** *v* orinar.

urn [əːn] *n* urna *f.*

Uruguay ['juərəgwai] *n* Uruguay *m.* **Uruguayan** *n, adj* uruguayo, -a.

us [ʌs] *pron* nos; nosotros.

usage ['juːzidʒ] *n* (*custom*) usanza *f*; (*treatment*) tratos *m pl*; (*gramm*) uso *m.*

use [juːs; *v* juːz] *n* uso *m*; empleo *m*; (*tool*) manejo *m.* **it's no use** es inútil. **what's the use?** ¿para qué? *v* usar, emplear; consumir; tomar; utilizar. **use up** agotar. **used** de segunda mano. **be used for** servir para. **be used to** estar acostumbrado a. **get used to** habituarse a. **useful** *adj* útil. **useless** *adj* inútil. **user** *n* usuario, -a *m, f.*

usher ['ʌʃə] *n* (*law*) ujier *m*; (*theatre*) acomodador *m.* *v* **usher in** anunciar; hacer pasar. **usherette** *n* acomodadora *f.*

usual ['juːʒuəl] *adj* normal; habitual; acostumbrado. **as usual** como siempre. **usually** *adv* normalmente.

usurp [ju'zəːp] *v* usurpar.

utensil [ju'tensl] *n* utensilio *m.*

uterus ['juːtərəs] *n* útero *m.*

utility [ju'tiləti] *n* utilidad *f. adj* utilitario.

utilize ['juːtilaiz] *v* utilizar.

utmost ['ʌtmoust] *adj* mayor; supremo; extremo; más lejano. *n* máximo *m.* **do one's utmost** hacer todo lo posible.

utter¹ ['ʌtə] *v* decir; (*cries*) lanzar; (*sigh*) dar; (*sentiments*) expresar.

utter² ['ʌtə] *adj* absoluto; completo.

U-turn ['juːtəːn] *n* media vuelta *f.*

V

vacant *adj* (*empty*) vacío; deshabitado; (*free*) libre; (*absent-minded*) distraído; vago; estúpido. **vacancy** (*job*) vacante *f*; (*room*) habitación libre *f*. **no vacancies** completo.

vacate *v* dejar vacío.

vacation *n* vacaciones *f pl*.

vaccine *n* vacuna *f*. **vaccinate** *v* vacunar. **vaccination** *n* vacunación *f*.

vacillate *v* vacilar; oscilar. **vacillation** *n* vacilación *f*.

vacuum *n* vacío *m*. **vacuum cleaner** aspiradora *f*. **vacuum flask** termo *m*. *v* pasar la aspiradora en.

vagina *n* vagina *f*.

vagrant *n, adj* vagabundo, -a. **vagrancy** *n* vagabundeo *m*.

vague *adj* vago, indistinto; incierto.

vain *adj* vano, inútil; (*conceited*) vanidoso. **in vain** en vano.

valiant *adj* valeroso.

valid *adj* válido. **validity** *n* validez *f*.

valley *n* valle *m*.

value *n* valor *m*; precio *m*; importancia *f*. *v* (*appraise*) valorar, tasar; estimar; apreciar. **valuable** *adj* valioso; precioso; costoso. **valuables** *pl n* objetos de valor *m pl*. **valuation** *n* valuación *f*; estimación *f*.

valve *n* válvula *f*.

vampire *n* vampiro *m*.

van *n* (*road*) camión *m*; (*removal*) carro de mudanzas *m*; (*guard's*) furgón de equipajes *m*; (*leading section*) vanguardia *f*.

vandal *n* vándalo, -a *m, f*. **vandalism** *n* vandalismo *m*. **vandalize** *v* destrozar.

vanilla *n* vainilla *f*.

vanish *v* desaparecer.

vanity *n* vanidad *f*. **vanity case** neceser *m*.

vapour *n* vapor *m*. **vapourize** *v* vaporizar.

varicose veins *pl n* varices *f pl*.

variety *n* variedad *f*; diversidad *f*. **variety show** función de variedades *f*.

various *adj* diverso; vario.

varnish *n* barniz *m*. *v* barnizar.

vary *v* variar; cambiar; modificar. **vary from** diferenciarse de. **variable** *nf, adj* variable. **variant** *nf, adj* variante. **variation** *n* variación *f*.

vase *n* vaso *m*; jarrón *m*.

vasectomy *n* vasectomía *f*.

vast *adj* vasto. **vastness** *n* inmensidad *f*.

vat *n* tinaja *f*.

Vatican *n* Vaticano *m*. **Vatican City** Ciudad del Vaticano *f*.

vault[1] *n* (*cellar*) sótano *m*; (*arch*) bóveda *f*; (*tomb*) panteón *m*; (*bank*) cámara acorzada *f*.

vault[2] *v* saltar. *n* salto *m*. **vaulting horse** potro *m*.

veal *n* ternera *f*.

veer *v* (*wind*) girar; (*ship*) virar; (*fig*) cambiar.

vegetable *n* (*bot*) vegetal *m*; (*cookery*) verdura *f*, legumbre *f*. *adj* vegetal. **vegetable garden** huerto *m*, huerta *f*. **vegetarian** *n, adj* vegetariano, -a. **vegetation** *n* vegetación *f*.

vehement *adj* vehemente; violento. **vehemence** *n* vehemencia *f*; violencia *f*. **vehemently** *adj* con vehemencia.

vehicle *n* vehículo *m*.

veil *n* velo *m*. *v* velar.

vein *n* vena *f*.

velocity *n* velocidad *f*.

velvet *n* terciopelo *m*. *adj* de terciopelo. **velvety** *adj* aterciopelado.

vending machine *n* distribuidor automático *m*.

veneer *n* chapa *f*; (*fig: gloss*) barniz *m*. *v* chapear.

venerate *v* venerar. **venerable** *adj* venerable. **veneration** *n* veneración *f*.

venereal disease *n* enfermedad venérea *f*.

Venetian blind *n* persiana veneciana *f*.

Venezuela [‚veni'zweilə] *n* Venezuela *f*. **Venezuelan** *n, adj* venezolano, -a.

vengeance *n* venganza *f*. **with a vengeance** (*coll*) de verdad.

venison *n* venado *m*.

venom *n* veneno *m*. **venomous** *adj* venenoso.

vent *n* (*hole*) agujero *m*, abertura *f*; (*air-hole*) respiradero *m*; (*tube*) conducto de ventilación *m*. **give vent to** dar libre curso a. *v* desahogar.

ventilate *v* ventilar. **ventilation** *n* ventilación *f*.

ventriloquist *n* ventrílocuo, -a *m, f*. **ventriloquism** *n* ventriloquia *f*.

venture *n* aventura *f*, empresa arriesgada *f*. *v* aventurar; arriesgar.

venue *n* lugar de reunión *m*.

veranda n *also* **verandah** veranda f. galería f.

verb n verbo. **verbal** adj verbal.

verdict n veredicto m.

verge n margen m, borde m; (*lake*) orilla f. **on the verge of** (*fig*) a punto de, a dos dedos de. **v verge on** rayar en.

verify v verificar. **verification** n verificación f.

vermin n (*rats, mice, etc.*) bichos m pl; (*fleas, people*) sabandijas f pl. **verminous** adj (*lousy*) piojoso.

vermouth n vermut m.

vernacular adj vernáculo. n lenguaje vulgar m.

versatile adj de talentos variados; (*mind*) flexible. **versatility** n diversos talentos m pl; flexibilidad f.

verse n (*poetry*) poesía f; (*stanza*) estrofa f; (*Bible*) versículo m.

version n versión f.

versus prep contra.

vertebra n, pl -brae vértebra f. **vertebral** adj vertebral. **vertebrate** nm, adj vertebrado.

vertical nf, adj vertical.

vertigo n vértigo m.

very adv muy; mucho, mucha. **very much** mucho, muchísimo. adj mismo; propio; (*real*) verdadero; puro.

vessel n (*container*) vasija f; (*ship*) nave f.

vest n camiseta f.

vestibule n vestíbulo m.

vestige n vestigio m, rastro m.

vestry n vestuario m, sacristía f.

vet n (*coll*) veterinario m. v (*coll*) corregir; revisar.

veteran nm, adj veterano. **veteran troops** tropas aguerridas f pl.

veterinary surgeon n veterinario m.

veto n veto m. v vetar, poner el veto.

vex v molestar; enfadar. **vexation** n molestia f; disgusto m.

via prep por, por la vía de.

viable adj viable. **viability** n viabilidad f.

viaduct n viaducto m.

vibrate v vibrar. **vibration** n vibración f.

vicar n vicario m; (*of a parish*) cura m. **vicarage** n casa del cura f.

vicarious adj vicario.

vice¹ n (*evil*) vicio m; (*defect*) defecto m.

vice² n (*tool*) tornillo de banco m.

vice-chancellor n rector m.

vice-consul n vicecónsul m.

vice-president n vicepresidente m.

vice versa adv viceversa.

vicinity n vecindad f; (*nearness*) cercanía f.

vicious adj (*of vice*) vicioso; (*bad*) malo; (*depraved*) pervertido; (*taste*) corrompido; (*life*) disoluto; (*crime*) atroz. **vicious circle** círculo vicioso m. **viciousness** n lo vicioso; maldad f; perversidad f.

victim n víctima f. **victimize** v perseguir; tomar como víctima. **victimization** n persecución f.

victory n victoria f. **victorious** adj victorioso.

video-tape n cinta magnética video f. v grabar programas de televisión.

vie v competir, rivalizar.

Vienna n Viena f.

view n vista f; panorama m; inspección f; idea f. **viewfinder** n visor m. **viewpoint** punto de vista m. v mirar; visitar; considerar. **viewer** n (*TV*) telespectador, -a m, f; (*onlooker*) espectador, -a m, f; (*for slides*) visionadora f.

vigil n vela f, vigilia f. **vigilance** n vigilancia f. **vigilant** adj vigilante.

vigour n vigor m. **vigorous** adj vigoroso.

vile adj vil; horrible.

villa n chalet m; (*country house*) casa de campo f.

village n aldea f, pueblo m. **villager** n aldeano, -a m, f.

villain n canalla m. **villainy** n villanía f.

vindictive adj vengativo.

vine n vid f; parra f. **vineyard** n viña f.

vinegar n vinagre m.

vintage adj (*season*) vendimia f; (*crop*) cosecha f. **vintage wine** vino añejo m.

vinyl n vinilo m.

viola n (*music*) viola f.

violate v (*ravish*) violar; (*desecrate*) profanar; (*infringe*) contravenir. **violation** n violación f; profanación f; contravención f.

violence n violencia f. **violent** adj violente.

violet n (*flower, colour*) violeta f. adj violado.

violin n violín m. **violinist** n violinista m, f.

viper n víbora f.

virgin nf, adj virgen. **virginity** n virginidad f.

Virgo n Virgo m.
virile adj viril. virility n virilidad f.
virtually adv virtualmente; práctica-
mente.
virtue n virtud f; (advantage) ventaja f.
by virtue of debido a. virtuous adj virtuoso.
virus n virus m.
visa n visado m.
viscount n vizconde m. viscountess vizcondesa f.
visible adj visible. visibility n visibilidad f.
vision n (sight, apparition) visión f;
(capacity to see) vista f; (dream) sueño m.
visionary n, adj visionario, -a m, f.
visit n visita f. v (go to, call on) visitar;
(stay in) pasar una temporada en. visitor
n visitante m, f; visita f.
visor n visera f.
visual adj visual. visualize v imaginarse.
vital adj vital. vitality n vitalidad f. vitally
adv vitalmente.
vitamin n vitamina f.
vivacious adj vivo; vivaracho. vivacious-
ness n also vivacity viveza f, vivacidad f.
vivid adj vivo; (description) gráfico. vivid-
ness n (colour) viveza f, intensidad f;
(style) fuerza f.
vivisection n vivisección f.
vixen n zorra f, raposa f.
vocabulary n vocabulario m.
vocal adj vocal; (fig) ruidoso. vocalist n
cantante m, f.
vocation n vocación f. vocational adj
profesional.
vociferous adj ruidoso.
vodka n vodca m.
voice n voz f. v hablar; expresar.
void n vacío m. adj (empty) vacío; (job)
vacante; (law) nulo.
volatile adj (chem) volátil; (fig) voluble.
volcano n volcán m. volcanic adj volcánico.
volley n (bullets) andanada f; (arrows,
stones) lluvia f; (applause) salva f; (sport)
voleo m. v (missile) lanzar; (sport) volear.
volt n voltio m. voltage n voltaje m.
volume n (space, sound) volumen m;
(book) tomo m, volumen m. voluminous
adj voluminoso; abundante.
volunteer nm, adj voluntario. v ofrecer;
(remark) hacer; (information) dar.
voluptuous adj voluptuoso. voluptuousness n voluptuosidad f.
vomit n vómito m. v vomitar.

voodoo n vodú m.
voracious adj voraz. voraciousness n also
voracity voracidad f.
vote n voto m; (action) votación f. vote of
confidence voto de confianza f. vote of
thanks voto de gracias m. v votar; elegir;
proponer; declarar. voter n votante m, f;
elector, -a m, f.
vouch v vouch for (thing) responder de,
garantizar; (person) responder por.
voucher n (comm) bono m, vale m. lunch-
eon voucher vale de comida m.
vow n voto m; promesa solemne f. v
jurar; prometer.
vowel n vocal f.
voyage n viaje m. v viajar (por mar).
vulgar adj común; ordinario; grosero.
vulgarity n vulgaridad f; grosería f.
vulnerable adj vulnerable.
vulture n buitre m.

W

wad n (bung) tapón m; (notes) rollo m;
(cotton wool) bolita f. wadding n (cotton
wool) guata f; (filling) relleno m.
waddle v anadear. n anadeo m.
wade v vadear. wade through (book, etc.)
estudiar detenidamente.
wafer n (for ices) barquillo m. wafer-thin
adj finísimo.
waft v llevar por el aire; flotar. n ráfaga f.
wag v agitar; (tail) menear. n (tail)
coleada f; movimiento m; (joker)
bromista m, f.
wage n salario m, paga f. v wage war
hacer guerra.
wager n apuesta f. v apostar.
waggle v menear, agitar. n meneo m.
wagon n carro m; carreta f; (rail) vagón
m.
waif n niño abandonado m.
wail n lamento m, gemido. v lamentarse,
gemir.
waist n cintura f, talle m. waistband n
pretina f. waistcoat n chaleco m. waist-
line n cintura f.
wait n espera f. lie in wait for acechar. v
esperar; (at table) atender. waiter n mozo
m, camarero m. waiting n espera f;
servicio m. waiting-list n lista de espera f.

waiting-room n sala de espera f. **waitress** n camarera f.

waive v renunciar a; desitir de.

wake[1] n velatorio m.

***wake**[2] v also wake up despertar(se).

Wales n el País de Gales.

walk n paseo m; camino m; (*gait*) andar m; (*pace*) paso m. v (*go on foot*) recorrer a pie; (*distance*) hacer a pie; (*take out*) pasear; (*escort*) acompañar. **walkout** n huelga f. **walkover** n victoria fácil f. **walker** n paseante m, f. **walking** n andar m. **walking-stick** n bastón m.

wall n pared f; muro m. v murar; amurallar. **wallet** n cartera f.

wallflower n alhelí m. be a **wallflower** quedarse en el poyete.

wallop (*coll*) n golpazo m, trompazo m. v zurrar. **walloping** n paliza f.

wallow v revolcarse.

wallpaper n papel pintado m. v empapelar.

walnut n (*nut*) nuez f; (*tree, wood*) nogal m.

walrus n morsa f.

waltz n vals m. v valsar.

wan adj macilento.

wand n (*magic*) varita f; vara f.

wander v vagar por; (*stroll*) pasearse; (*mentally*) desvariar.

wane v (*moon*) menguar; (*fig*) decaer.

wangle v conseguir con trampas. (*coll*) n trampa f.

want n (*lack*) falta f; (*need*) necesidad f; (*poverty*) miseria f; (*wish*) deseo m; (*gap*) vacío m. for want of por falta de. v querer; desear; necesitar; (*ask*) pedir; (*look for*) buscar. **wanted** adj buscado (por la policía). **wanting** adj (*absent*) ausente; (*lacking*) deficiente.

wanton adj lascivo; (*promiscuous*) libertino; (*senseless*) sin sentido. **wantonness** n libertinaje f; crueldad f; exuberancia f; (*lack of moderation*) desenfreno m.

war n guerra f. be on the **warpath** (*coll*) estar buscando guerra. **warfare** n guerra f. **warhead** n cabeza de guerra f. **war memorial** monumento a los Caídos m. **War Office** Ministerio de la Guerra m. **warship** n buque de guerra m. **wartime** n tiempo de guerra m.

warble v gorjear, trinar. n gorjeo m, trino m.

ward n (*hospital*) sala f; (*pol*) distrito electoral m; (*law: guardianship*) custodia f; (*minor*) pupilo m. v ward off evitar.

warden n guarda m; vigilante m; director m.

warder n carcelero m; guardián m.

wardrobe n guardarropa m; (*theatre*) vestuario m.

warehouse n almacén m. v almacenar.

warm adj tibio; caliente; (*climate*) cálido; (*fire*) acogedor; (*welcome*) caluroso; (*kind*) cariñoso. v calentar; acalorar. warm up calentar; (*reheat*) recalentar. **warming-pan** n calentador de cama m. **warmth** n calor m; cordialidad f.

warn v advertir; aconsejar; (*rebuke*) amonestar. **warning** n advertencia f, aviso m; alarma f; ejemplo m; amonestación f. **warning light** lámpara indicadora f.

warp v (*wood*) alabear; (*yarn*) urdir; (*fig*) deformar. n alabeo m; urdimbre f; deformación f.

warrant n (*police*) orden f; (*law*) autorización f; justificación f; garantía f. v autorizar; justificar; garantizar. **warranty** n garantía f.

warren n (*rabbit*) conejal m; (*fig*) colmena f.

warrior n guerrero m.

Warsaw ['wɔːsɔː] n Varsovia.

wart [wɔːt] n verruga f.

wary ['weəri] adj cauto, precavido.

was [wɒz] V be.

wash [wɒʃ] v lavar; (*dishes*) fregar. wash away quitar. wash down (*swallow*) tragar. wash up fregar. **washable** adj lavable. **wash-and-wear** adj de lava y pon. **washbasin** n lavabo m. **washboard** n tabla de lavar f. **washer** n arandela f. **washing** n lavado m; colada f; fregado m. **washing machine** lavadora f. **washing powder** jabón en polvo m. **washing-up bowl** barreño m. **washout** n (*slang*) desastre m.

wasp [wɒsp] n avispa f.

waste [weist] n pérdida f; (*food*) desperdicios m pl; (*rubbish*) basura f. **waste disposal unit** vertedero de basuras m. **waste land** yermo m; erial m. **waste paper** papel usado m. **waste-paper basket** papelera f. v malgastar, despilfarrar; perder; (*use up*) consumir; (*by disuse*) desperdiciar. waste away consumirse. **wasteful** adj (*person*) despilfarrador, -a *m, f;* ruinoso. **waster** *n also* **wastrel** derrochador, -a *m, f.*

watch [wotʃ] *n (wrist)* reloj de la pulsera *m; (pocket)* reloj de bolsillo *m; (naut)* guardia *f;* vigilancia *f.* keep watch estar de guardia. **watch chain** cadena de reloj *f.* **watchdog** *n* perro guardián *m.* **watchmaker** *n* relojero *m.* **watchman** *n* vigilante *m.* **watch spring** muelle *m.* **watch strap** correa de reloj *f.* **watchword** *n* consigna *f.* *v* mirar, ver, observar; *(pay attention to)* fijarse en; *(keep an eye on)* vigilar. **watchful** *adj* atento; vigilante.

water ['wɔːtə] *n* agua *f. v (wet)* humedecer; *(soak)* mojar; *(plants)* regar; *(eyes)* llorar. **water down** moderar. **watery** *adj* acuoso; aguado, insípido.

water-biscuit *n* galleta de harina y agua *f.*

water-closet *n* retrete *m,* wáter *m.*

water-colour *n* acuarela *f.*

watercress ['wɔːtəkres] *n* berro *m.*

waterfall ['wɔːtəfɔːl] *n* cascada *f;* catarata *f.*

water-ice *n* sorbete *m.*

watering-can *n* regadera *f.*

water lily *n* nenúfar *m.*

waterline ['wɔːtəlain] *n* línea de flotación *f.*

waterlogged ['wɔːtəlogd] *adj (wood)* empapado; *(med)* inundado.

water main *n* cañería principal *f.*

watermark ['wɔːtəmɑːk] *n* filigrana *f; (tide)* marca del nivel de agua *f.*

watermelon ['wɔːtəmelən] *n* sandía *f.*

waterproof ['wɔːtəpruːf] *nm, adj* impermeable. *v* impermeabilizar.

watershed ['wɔːtəʃed] *n (fig)* momento decisivo *m; (geog)* línea divisoria de las aguas *f.*

water-ski *v* hacer esquí acuático. **water-skiing** *n* esquí acuático *m.*

water softener *n* ablandador del agua *m.*

watertight ['wɔːtətait] *adj* estanco; hermético; *(fig)* perfecto.

waterway ['wɔːtəwei] *n* vía navegable *f.*

waterworks ['wɔːtəwɜːks] *n* sistema de abastecimiento de agua *m.*

watt [wot] *n* vatio *m.*

wave [weiv] *n (sea)* ola *f; (hair)* ondulación *f; (physics, radio, etc.)*onda *f; (hand)* señal *f.* **permanent wave** permanente *f.* **waveband** *n* banda de ondas *f.* **wavelength** *n* longitud de onda *f. v* agitar; *(hair)* ondular. **wavy** *adj* ondulado.

waver ['weivə] *v* vacilar; *(falter)* flaquear; *(totter)* titubear. **wavering** *adj* vacilante; tembloroso.

wax[1] [waks] *n* cera *f.* **waxwork** *n* figura de cera *f.* **waxworks** *n* museo de figuras de cera *m. v* encerar. **waxy** *adj* ceroso.

wax[2] [waks] *v* crecer.

way [wei] *n* camino *m;* paso *m;* ruta *f;* senda *f;* dirección *f;* rumbo *m;* distancia *f; (journey)* viaje *m;* progreso *m;* modo *m,* manera *f; (means)* medio *m.* be in the way estar de por medio. by the way a propósito. give way ceder. on the way en camino. this way por aquí. under way en marcha; en preparación. way in entrada *f.* way out salida *f.*

***waylay** ['wei'lei] *v* abordar.

wayside ['weisaid] *n* borde del camino *m. adj* al borde del camino.

wayward ['weiwəd] *adj* voluntarioso; díscolo.

we [wiː] *pron* nosotros, -as.

weak [wiːk] *adj* débil; flaco; flojo. **weaken** *v* debilitar. **weakling** *n* persona débil *f;* cobarde *m.* **weakness** *n* debilidad *f; (point)* punto flaco *m.*

wealth [welθ] *n* riqueza *f;* abundancia *f.* **wealthy** *adj* rico.

wean [wiːn] *v (baby)* destetar. wean from apartar de.

weapon ['wepən] *n* arma *f.*

***wear** [weə] *v* llevar; poner; gastar. wear off pasar(se). wear out usarse, consumirse. *n* uso *m;* gasto *m;* deterioro *m.* wear and tear desgaste *m.*

weary ['wiəri] *adj* fatigado, cansado, aburrido. *v* fatigar, causar; aburrir. **wearily** *adv* cansadamente. **weariness** *n* fatiga *f.*

weasel ['wiːzl] *n* comadreja *f.*

weather ['weðə] *n* tiempo *m.* **weatherbeaten** *adj* curtido. **weather chart** mapa meteorológico *m.* **weathercock** *n* veleta *f.* **weather forecast** boletín meteorológico *m. v (survive)* superar.

***weave** [wiːv] *v* tejer; entrelazar; *(through traffic, etc.)* zigzaguear.

web [web] *n (spider)* tela de araña *f; (fabric)* tejido *m; (on feet)* membrana *f; (network)* red *f; (fig)* sarta *f.* **web-footed** *adj* palmípedo.

wed [wed] *v* casarse con; casar. **wedding** *n* boda *f,* casamiento *m.* **wedding dress** traje de novia *m.* **wedding ring** alianza *f.*

wedge [wedʒ] *n* cuña *f*, calzo *m*. *v* encajar; (*jam*) apretar.

Wednesday ['wenzdi] *n* miércoles *m*.

weed [wiːd] *n* mala hierba *f*. **weed-killer** *n* herbicida *m*. *v* desherbar. **weeding** *n* escarda *f*.

week [wiːk] *n* semana *f*. **a week today/tomorrow** hoy/mañana en ocho. **weekday** *n* día de trabajo *m*. **weekend** *n* fin de semana *m*. **weekly** *adj* semanal. **weekly** *n* semanario *m*.

***weep** [wiːp] *v* llorar, lamentar. **weeping willow** sauce llorón *m*.

weigh [wei] *v* pesar. **weigh down** doblar bajo un peso. **weight** *n* peso *m*. **pull one's weight** poner de su parte. **weightlifting** *n* halterofilia *f*. **weightlessness** *n* ingravidez *f*.

weird [wiəd] *adj* extraño; misterioso; fantástico. **weirdness** *n* misterio *m*; lo sobrenatural.

welcome ['welkəm] *adj* bienvenido; grato. **be welcome** ser oportuno. **you're welcome!** ¡eres el bienvenido!; (*after thanks*) ¡no hay de qué! **a bienvenida** *f*. *v* dar la bienvenida a; recibir; alegrarse por.

weld [weld] *v* soldar. **welder** *n* soldador *m*. **welding** *n* soldadura *f*.

welfare ['welfeə] *n* bienestar *m*, bien *m*. **welfare state** estado benefactor *m*.

well[1] [wel] *n* pozo *m*. **well up** brotar.

well[2] [wel] *adj*, *adv* bien. **as well** también.

well-advised *adj* juicioso.

well-behaved *adj* bien educado.

well-being *n* bienestar *m*.

well-born *adj* de buena familia.

well-bred *adj* (*person*) bien educado; (*animal*) de raza pura.

well-built *adj* bien hecho.

well-dressed *adj* bien vestido.

well-informed *adj* muy documentado.

wellington ['weliŋtən] *n* bota de agua *f*.

well-kept *adj* (*secret*) bien guardado; (*garden*) bien cuidado.

well-known *adj* bien conocido.

well-made *adj* bien hecho.

well-off *adj* rico.

well-paid *adj* bien pagado.

well-read *adj* leído.

well-spent *adj* (*time*) bien empleado.

well-spoken *adj* bienhablado.

well-timed *adj* oportuno.

well-to-do *adj* rico.

well-trodden *adj* trillado.

well-worn *adj* gastado.

Welsh [welʃ] *adj* galés. *n* (*language*) galés *m*; (*person*) galés, -esa *m*, *f*.

went [went] *V* go.

wept [wept] *V* weep.

were [wəː] *V* be.

west [west] *n* oeste *m*. **the West** el Mundo Occidental *m*. *adj* del oeste, occidental. *adv* al oeste, hacia el oeste. **westbound** *adj* con rumbo al oeste. **western** *adj* occidental, del oeste. *n* (*film*) western *m*. **westerly** del oeste, occidental. *adv* al oeste, hacia el oeste.

wet [wet] *adj* mojado; húmedo; (*weather*) lluvioso; (*paint*) fresco. **wet blanket** aguafiestas *m, f invar*. **wet suit** traje de buzo *m*. *n* lluvia *f*. *v* mojar; humedecer.

whack [wak] *n* golpe *m*. *v* golpear, pegar.

whale [weil] *n* ballena *f*.

wharf [wotf] *n* muelle *m*.

what [wot] *pron* lo que; (*interrog, interj*) qué, cuál, cómo, cuánto. *adj* el que, la que, lo que; qué.

whatever [wot'evə] *pron* todo lo que; lo que; cualquier cosa que. *adj* cualquiera. **nothing/whatever** nada en absoluto.

wheat [wiːt] *n* trigo *m*.

wheel [wiːl] *n* rueda *f*; (*steering*) volante *m*. **wheelbarrow** *n* carretilla *f*. **wheelchair** *n* sillón de ruedas *m*. *v* hacer rodar; empujar; dar una vuelta.

wheeze [wiz] *n* respiración dificultosa *f*. *v* respirar con dificultad. **wheezy** *adj* asmático.

whelk [welk] *n* buccino *m*.

when [wen] *adv* cuándo, a qué hora. *conj* cuando; en que; (*as soon as*) en cuanto. **whenever** *conj* cuando; cada vez que.

where [weə] *interrog adv* dónde; adónde; de dónde; por dónde; (*in what respect*) en qué. *relative adv* donde; en donde, en que, en el cual, en la cual; adonde, a donde, al que, al cual, a la cual. *conj* donde. **whereabouts** *adv* dónde, por dónde; *n* paradero *m*. **whereas** *conj* mientras, en tanto que. **whereupon** *adv* después de lo cual. **wherever** *conj* dondequiera que; a dondequiera que.

whether ['weðə] *conj* si.

which [witʃ] *interrog pron* cuál; qué. **relative pron** que; el cual, la cual, el que, la que; lo cual, lo que. *adj* qué; cuál; cuyo; cómo. **of which** del que, de la que; del cual; de la cual. **whichever** *pron* el que, la que; cualquiera que; *adj* cualquier.

whiff [wif] n soplo m; olorcillo m.

while [wail] conj mientras; (although) aunque. n rato m, tiempo m. while away pasar.

whim [wim] n capricho m.

whimper ['wimpə] n quejido m, gemido m. v quejarse, gemir.

whimsical ['wimzikl] adj caprichoso; fantástico.

whine [wain] n (animal) gañido m; (complaint) queja f; (pain) quejido m; (engine) zumbido m. v gañir; quejarse; zumbar.

whip [wip] n azote m; (riding) látigo m. whiplash n latigazo m. whip-round n (coll) colecta f. v azotar; (cookery) batir. whip up avivar. whipping n azotamiento m.

whippet ['wipit] n lebrel m.

whirl [wəil] n vuelta f, giro m; (fig) torbellino m. v dar vueltas, girar. whirlpool n remolino m.

whirr [wəi] n (wings) batir m; (engine) zumbido m. v girar; zumbar.

whisk [wisk] n (cookery) batidor. v batir.

whisker ['wiskə] n pelo del bigote m. whiskers pl n bigotes m pl.

whisky ['wiski] n whisky m.

whisper ['wispə] n cuchicheo m. v cuchichear.

whistle ['wisl] n pito m; (sound) silbido m; pitido m. v silbar.

white [wait] adj blanco. white elephant (fig) objeto costoso e inútil m. n blanco m; (person) blanco, -a m, f. whiten v blanquear. whiteness n blancura f.

whitewash ['waitwoʃ] n cal f. v encalar; (fig: cover up) encubrir.

whiting ['waitiŋ] n pescadilla f.

whittle ['witl] v tallar. whittle down reducir poco a poco.

whizz [wiz] n zumbido m. whizz-kid n (coll) promesa f. whizz past pasar como un rayo.

who [hui] relative pron quien, el quel la que; que, el cual, la cual; que, a quien. interrog pron quién. whoever pron quienquiera que, cualquiera que, el que, la que, quien.

whole [houl] adj todo, completo, entero, total; íntegro, intacto. n todo m, total m, totalidad f. on the whole en general. wholehearted adj sin reservas. wholeheartedly adv incondicionalmente. wholemeal adj integral. wholesome adj saludable.

wholesale ['houlseil] n venta al por mayor f. adj, adv al por mayor; en masa.

whom [huim] relative pron que, quien, a quien. interrog pron quién, a quién. of whom del cual, de la cual, de quien.

whooping cough ['huipiŋ] n tos ferina f.

whore [hoi] n (derog) puta f.

whose [huiz] relative pron cuyo, cuya. interrog pron de quién.

why [wai] adv (interrog) por qué; (on account of which) por el cual, por la cual, por lo cual. interj ¡vaya! ¡toma! ¡pues bien!

wick [wik] n mecha f.

wicked ['wikid] adj malo, perverso, malicioso. wickedness n maldad f, perversidad f.

wicker ['wikə] n mimbre m. wickerwork n cestería f.

wicket ['wikit] n (cricket) palos m pl.

wide [waid] adj ancho; vasto; grande. adv lejos; mucho. wide awake completamente despierto. widespread adj general. widely adv muy; mucho; generalmente.

widow ['widou] n viuda f. be widowed quedar viuda. widower n viudo m.

width [widθ] n anchura f.

wield [wiild] v (tool) manejar; (weapon) blandir; (power) ejercer.

wife [waif] n mujer f, esposa f.

wig [wig] n peluca f.

wiggle ['wigl] v menear. n meneo m. wiggly adj (line) ondulante.

wild [waild] adj (animal, person) salvaje; (plant) silvestre; (bull) bravo; (character) violento. like wildfire como un reguero de pólvora. wildlife n fauna f. wildly adv violentamente; locamente; frenéticamente; disolutamente.

wilderness ['wildənəs] n desierto m; soledad f.

wilful ['wilfəl] adj (stubborn) obstinado; (headstrong) voluntarioso; deliberado.

will[1] [wil] aux translated by future tense.

will[2] [wil] n voluntad f; testamento m. v disponer; desear; (bequeath) legar. against one's will de mal grado. willpower n fuerza de voluntad f. willing adj de buena voluntad; (obliging) complaciente. be willing to estar dispuesto a. willingly adv de buena gana. willingness n buena voluntad f.

willow ['wilou] n sauce m. willowy adj esbelto.

wilt [wilt] v marchitar(se); (*person*) languidecer.

wily ['waili] adj astuto, chuzón.

*****win** [win] n victoria f; (*amount won*) ganancia f. v ganar; conquistar; triunfar. **winner** n ganador, -a m, f; vencedor, -a m, f. **winning** adj ganador; (*smile, etc.*) encantador. **winnings** pl n ganancias f pl.

wince [wins] v hacer muecas. n mueca de dolar f.

winch [wintʃ] n torno m. v guindar.

wind[1] [wind] n viento m; (*breath*) aliento m; respiración f; (*med*) gases m pl. v dejar sin aliento. **windy** adj (*place*) expuesto al viento; (*day, night*) ventoso.

*****wind**[2] [waind] v devanar; envolver; enrollar; (*bend*) torcer; (*road*) serpentear; (*watch*) dar cuerda a. **wind up** terminar; (*comm*) liquidar. **winding** adj sinuoso; tortuoso.

wind-break n protección contra el viento f.

windfall ['windfɔːl] n fruta caída f; (*fig*) ganancia inesperada f.

wind instrument n instrumento de viento m.

windlass ['windləs] n torno m.

windmill ['wind,mil] n molino de viento m.

window ['windou] n ventana f; (*car*) ventanilla f; (*cashier's*) taquilla f; (*shop*) escaparate m. **window blind** persiana f. **window-box** n jardinera f. **window cleaner** limpiacristales m invar. **window-sill** n antepecho m. **window-shopping** n contemplación de escaparates f.

windpipe ['windpaip] n tráquea f.

windproof ['windpruːf] adj a prueba de viento.

windscreen ['windskriːn] n parabrisas m invar. **windscreen wiper** limpiaparabrisas m invar.

wind-sock n manga de aire f.

windswept ['windswept] adj (*hair*) despeinado.

wind tunnel n túnel aerodinámico m.

wine [wain] n vino m. **wineglass** n copa f. **wine list** lista de vinos f. **wine-taster** n catavinos m invar. **wine waiter** bodeguero m.

wing [wiŋ] n ala f. **wing chair** sillón de orejas m. **wing commander** teniente coronel m. **wing-mirror** n retrovisor m. **wing nut** palometa f. **wings** pl n (*theatre*) bastidores m pl. **wingspan** n envergadura f.

wink [wiŋk] n guiño m; (*light*) parpadeo m. v guiñar; (light) parpadear.

winkle ['wiŋkl] n bígaro m. v **winkle out** sacar con dificultad.

winter ['wintə] n invierno m. v invernar. **wintry** adj de invierno; (*fig*) frío.

wipe [waip] v limpiar; (*mop*) enjugar; (*dry*) secar. **wipe out** destruir. n limpieza f.

wire [waiə] n alambre m; (*elec*) cordón m, cable m; hilo m; (*piano*) cuerda f; telegrama m. **barbed wire** alambrada f. **wire-brush** n cepillo metálico m. **wire-cutters** pl n cortaalambres m invar. **wireless** n radio f. v telegrafiar; (*a house*) poner la instalación eléctrica de. **wiry** adj (*hair*) tieso; (*person*) enjuto y fuerte.

wise [waiz] adj sabio; juicioso; (*informed*) enterado. **wisdom** n sabiduría f; juicio m. **wisdom tooth** muela del juicio f.

wish [wiʃ] v querer; desear; gustar. n deseo m. **wishbone** n espoleta f. **wishful** adj deseroso. **wishful thinking** ilusiones f pl.

wisp [wisp] n (*straw*) manojo m; (*hair*) mechón m; (*smoke*) voluta f; (*trace*) vestigio m. **wispy** adj fino.

wistful ['wistfəl] adj triste; ansioso; pensativo. **wistfully** adv tristemente; con ansia.

wit [wit] n inteligencia f; agudeza f; (*humour*) gracia f; (*person*) persona aguda f. **be at one's wits' end** no saber qué hacer.

witch [witʃ] n bruja f. **witchcraft** n brujería f. **witch-doctor** n hechicero m. **witch-hunt** n persecución f.

with [wið] prep con; junto con; en manos de; más; en compañía de; (*because of*) de.

*****withdraw** [wið'drɔː] v quitar; apartar; retirar; sacar. **withdrawal** n retirada f; (*bank*) salida f; renuncia f; retractación f; abandono m. **withdrawn** adj ensimismado.

wither ['wiðə] v (*plant*) marchitar(se); (*weaken*) debilitar. **withered** adj marchito; seco. **withering** adj (*look*) fulminante; (*remark*) mordaz.

*****withhold** [wið'hould] v (*refuse*) negar; (*hold back*) retener; (*hide*) ocultar.

within [wi'ðin] adv dentro; (*at home*) en casa. prep dentro de; en; al alcance de; (*less than*) a menos de.

without [wi'ðaut] *prep* sin; *(outside)* fuera de. *adv* fuera.

*withstand [wið'stænd] *v* resistir, aguantar; oponerse a.

witness ['witnis] *n (person)* testigo *m*; *(evidence)* prueba *f*; *(testimony)* testimonio *m*. *v (be present at)* asistir a; *(document)* firmar como testigo. **witness to** atestiguar.

witty ['witi] *adj* salado, gracioso. **witticism** *n* rasgo de ingenio *m*, agudeza *f*.

wizard ['wizəd] *n* mago *m*.

wobble ['wobl] *v* tambalearse. *n* tambaleo *m*. **wobbly** *adj* tambaleante.

woke [wouk] *V* wake.

wolf [wulf] *n* lobo *m*. **wolfhound** *n* perro lobo *m*. **wolf-whistle** *n* silbido de admiración *m*. *v* **wolf down** *(coll)* zamparse.

woman ['wumən] *n, pl* **women** mujer *f*. **Women's Lib** *(coll)* Movimiento de la Liberación de la Mujer *m*. **womanhood** *n* mujeres *f pl*; femenidad *f*. **womanly** *adj* femenino.

womb [wuːm] *n* matriz *f*, útero *m*.

won [wʌn] *V* win.

wonder ['wʌndə] *n* maravilla *f*; milagro *m*; admiración *f*. **no wonder** no es de extrañar. *v* preguntarse; pensar; asombrarse. **wonderful** *adj* maravilloso; *(astonishing)* asombroso.

woo [wuː] *v* cortejar; *(fig)* solicitar. **wooing** *nm, adj* galanteo.

wood [wud] *n (forest)* bosque *m*; *(material)* madera *f*; *(stick)* palo *m*; *(firewood)* leña *f*. **wooden** *adj* de madera; *(stiff)* estirado. **woody** *adj* arbolado; *(stem)* leñoso.

woodcock ['wudkok] *n* chocha *f*, becada *f*.

woodcut ['wudkʌt] *n* grabado en madera *m*. **woodcutter** *n (forester)* leñador *m*.

woodland ['wudlənd] *n* bosque *m*.

woodpecker ['wudpekə] *n* pájaro carpintero *m*.

wood-pigeon *n* paloma torcaz *f*.

woodshed ['wudʃed] *n* leñera *f*.

woodwind ['wudwind] *n (music)* instrumentos de viento de madera *m pl*.

woodwork ['wudwəːk] *n* carpintería *f*.

woodworm ['wudwəːm] *n* carcoma *f*.

wool [wul] *n* lana *f*. **woollen** *adj* de lana. **woolly** *adj* lanoso; de lana; *(ideas)* borroso.

word [wəːd] *n* palabra *f*; *(gramm)* vocablo *m*. **in other words** en otras palabras; es

decir. *v* expresar; redactar. **wording** *n* redacción *f*; términos *m pl*. **wordy** *adj* verboso.

wore [woː] *V* wear.

work [wəːk] *n* trabajo *m*, obra *f*. **men at work** obras *f pl*. **out of work** parado, -a. *v* trabajar. **work out** resolver. **workable** *adj (plan)* realizable.

worker ['wəːkə] *n* trabajador, -a *m, f*; obrero, -a *m, f*.

work-force *n* mano de obra *f*.

working ['wəːkiŋ] *n* trabajo *m*; funcionamiento *m*; manejo *m*; cultivo *m*. **working-class** *adj* de la clase obrera. **workings** *pl n* excavaciones *f pl*.

workman ['wəːkmən] *n* trabajador *m*; obrero *m*. **workmanship** *n (skill)* artesanía *f*; ejecución *f*.

work permit *n* permiso de trabajo *m*.

workshop ['wəːkʃop] *n* taller *m*.

work-to-rule *n* trabajo a ritmo lento *m*.

world [wəːld] *n* mundo *m*. **world-wide** *adj* mundial. **worldly** *adj* mundano; material.

worm [wəːm] *n* guzano *m*; *(earthworm)* lombriz *f*.

worn [woːn] *V* wear.

worry ['wʌri] *n* preocupación *f*. *v* preocupar(se); molestar. **don't worry!** ¡no te ocupes! **worried** *adj* preocupado.

worse [wəːs] *adj, adv* peor. **get worse** or **worsen** empeorar. **to make matters worse** para empeorar las cosas. *n* lo peor.

worship ['wəːʃip] *n* culto *m*; *(fig)* adoración *f*. *v* venerar; *(fig)* adorar.

worst [wəːst] *adj, adv* peor. *n* el peor *m*, la peor *f*, lo peor. **at worst** en el peor de los casos.

worsted ['wustid] *n* estambre *m*.

worth [wəːθ] *n* valor *m*; mérito *m*; valía *f*; fortuna *f*. **be worth** valer. **be worth it** merecer la pena. **worthless** *adj* sin valor; inútil. **worthwhile** *adj* que vale la pena; útil.

would [wud] *aux translated by conditional or imperfect tense*.

wound¹ [waund] *V* wind².

wound² [wuːnd] *n* herida *f*. *v* herir.

wove [wouv] *V* weave.

wrangle ['ræŋgl] *n* disputa *f*. *v* discutir.

wrap [ræp] *v* envolver; cubrir. **wrap up** abrigarse. *n (shawl)* chal *m*. **wrapper** *n* envoltura *f*; *(book)* sobrecubierta *f*. **wrapping** *n* envoltura *f*. **wrapping-paper** *n* papel de envolver *m*.

wreath [riːθ] *n* guirnalda *f*; (*funeral*) corona *f*. **wreathe** *v* enguirnaldar; (*wind*) enroscar.

wreck [rek] *n* (*ship*) naufragio *m*; (*train, car, plane*) restos *m pl*; (*accident*) accidente *m*; (*person*) ruina *f*. *v* (*ship*) hundir; (*building*) destruir; destrozar; (*hopes*) estropear. **wreckage** *n* restos *m pl*; (*building*) escombros *m pl*.

wren [ren] *n* reyezuelo *m*.

wrench [rentʃ] *n* (*tool*) llave inglesa *f*; (*pull*) tirón *m*; (*emotional*) dolor *m*. *v* arrancar; (*med*) torcer.

wrestle ['resl] *v* luchar con *or* contra. **wrestler** *n* luchador, -a *m, f*. **wrestling** *n* lucha *f*.

wretch [retʃ] *n* desgraciado, -a *m, f*; miserable *m, f*. **wretched** *adj* desgraciado; (*weather*) miserable; horrible.

wriggle ['rigl] *v* menear; agitar; (*fish*) colear. *n* meneo *m*; serpenteo *m*.

*****wring** [riŋ] *v* retorcer. **wringer** *n* escurridor *m*. **wringing wet** chorreando.

wrinkle ['riŋkl] *n* arruga *f*. *v* arrugar.

wrist [rist] *n* muñeca *f*.

writ [rit] *n* (*law*) orden *f*, mandato *m*. **issue a writ against someone** demandar a alguien en juicio.

*****write** [rait] *v* escribir; redactar. **writer** *n* escritor, -a *m, f*; autor, -a *m, f*. **writing** *n* el escribir *m*; (*handwriting*) escritura *f*; (*something written*) escrito *m*. **in writing** por escrito. **writing-pad** *n* bloc de papel de escribir *m*. **writing-paper** *n* papel de escribir *m*.

writhe [raið] *v* retorcerse; angustiarse.

wrong [roŋ] *adj* malo; mal; (*incorrect*) equivocado; impropio; falso; erróneo. **be wrong** tener la culpa; (*mistaken*) estar equivocado. *adv* mal. *n* mal *m*; error *m*; daño *m*; injusticia *f*. **wrongful** *adj* injusto; ilegal.

wrote [rout] *V* write.

wrought iron [ˌrɔːt'aiən] *n* hierro forjado *m*.

wry [rai] *adj* torcido; doblado; (*smile*) forzado.

X

xenophobia *n* xenofobia *f*. **xenophobic** *adj* xenófobo.

Xerox ® *n* (*machine*) Xérox ® *m*, fotocopiadora *f*; (*copy*) xerografía *f*. *v* fotocopiar.

Xmas *V* Christmas.

X-ray *n* (*photo*) radiografía *f*. **X-rays** *pl n* rayos X *m pl*. *v* radiografiar.

xylophone *n* xilófono *m*.

Y

yacht *n* yate *m*. **yachting** *n* navegación a vela *f*.

yank *n* tirón *m*. *v* dar un tirón.

yap *n* ladrido *m*. *v* ladrar.

yard *n* patio *m*; (*site*) depósito *m*; (*repair*) taller *m*; (*rail*) estación *f*.

yarn *n* hilo *m*; (*tale*) cuento *m*.

yawn *v* bostezar; (*hole*) abrirse. *n* bostezo *m*.

year *n* año *m*. **yearbook** *n* anuario *m*. **yearly** *adj* anual.

yearn *v* anhelar, ansiar. **yearning** *n* anhelo *m*, ansia *f*.

yeast *n* levadura *f*; (*fig*) fermento *m*.

yell *n* grito *m*. *v* gritar.

yellow *nm, adj* amarillo. *v* volver amarillo.

yelp *n* gañido *m*. *v* gañir.

yes *nm, adv* sí.

yesterday *nm, adv* ayer. **the day before yesterday** anteayer.

yet *adv* todavía, aún; (*already*) ya. *conj* sin embargo, no obstante; (*but*) pero.

yew *n* tejo *m*.

yield *v* producir; entregar; dar; ceder; (*interest*) devengar. *n* producción *f*; (*crop*) cosecha *f*; (*interest*) rédito *m*.

yodel *n* canción tirolesa *f*. *v* cantar a la tirolesa.

yoga *n* yoga *m*.

yoghurt *n* yogur *m*.

yoke *n* (*animals*) yugo *m*; (*oxen*) yunta *f*; (*dress*) canesú *m*. *v* **yoke together** trabajar juntos.

yolk *n* yema *f*.

yonder *adv* allá, a lo lejos.

you *pron* (*subject: fam*) tú *sing*; (*subject: fam*) vosotros, vosotras *pl*; (*after prep*) ti; (*direct and indirect object*) te *sing*; (*direct and indirect object*) os *pl*; (*subject and after prep: polite*) usted, ustedes; (*direct object*) le, la; (*indirect object*) le; (*indirect object with direct object pron*) se *sing. pl.*

young *adj* joven. *pl n* (*people*) los jóvenes *m pl*; (*of an animal*) cría *f sing*. **youngster** *n* joven *m, f*.

your *adj* (*fam*) tu *sing*, vuestro *pl*; (*polite*) su, sus, de usted, de ustedes. **yours** *pron* (*fam*) el tuyo, la tuya, los tuyos, las tuyas, el vuestro, la vuestra, los vuestros, las vuestras; (*polite*) el suyo, la suya, el de usted, la de usted.

yourself *pron* (*fam*) tú mismo *m*, tú misma *f*; (*after prep*) ti *m, f*; (*polite*) usted mismo *m*, usted misma *f*. **by yourself** tú solo, usted solo. **yourselves** *pl pron* (*fam*) vosotros mismos *m pl*; vosotras mismas *f pl*; (*polite*) ustedes mismos *m pl*, ustedes mismas *f pl*.

youth *n* juventud *f*; (*boy*) joven *m*. **youth hostel** albergue de juventud *m*.

Yugogslavia [ju:gə'sla:rviə] *n* Yugoslavia *f*.

Yugoslav *n, adj* yugoslavo, -a. **Yugoslavian** *n, adj* yugoslavo, -a.

Z

zany *adj* (*coll*) estrafalario.

zeal *n* celo *m*. **zealous** *adj* celoso.

zebra *n* cebra *f*. **zebra crossing** paso de peatones *m*.

zero *n* cero *m*. **zero hour** hora H *f*. momento decisivo *m*.

zest *n* ánimo *m*; brío *m*; sabor *m*. **zestful** *adj* animado; sabroso.

zigzag *n* zigzag *m*. *v* zigzaguear.

zinc *n* cinc *m*, zinc *m*.

zip *n* cremallera *f*. **zip code** (*US*) código postal *m*. *v* **zip up** subir la cremallera de.

zodiac *n* zodiaco *m*.

zone *n* zona *f*. *v* dividir en zonas.

zoo *n* zoo *m*, parque zoológico *m*.

zoology *n* zoología *f*. **zoological** *adj* zoológico. **zoologist** *n* zoólogo, -a *m, f*.

zoom *n* zumbido *m*. **zoom lens** zoom *m*. *v* zumbar. **zoom past** (*coll*) pasar zumbando.

Spanish—Inglés

A

a [a] *prep* to, at; on, in; by, by means of.

abacero [aβa'θero] *sm* grocer. **abacería** *sf* grocery.

abad [a'βað] *sm* abbot. **abadesa** *sf* abbess. **abadía** *sf* abbey.

abadejo [aβa'ðexo] *sm* codfish.

abajo [a'βaxo] *adv* underneath, below, down. ¡abajo . . . ! *interj* down with . . . ! de abajo *adj* lower.

abalanzar [aβalan'θar] *v* balance; hurl. **abalanzarse a** rush at.

abandonar [aβando'nar] *v* abandon; leave. **abandonarse** *v* give way; lose heart. **abandonado** *adj* abandoned; slovenly. **abandono** *sm* abandonment; neglect.

abanicar [aβani'kar] *v* fan. **abanico** *sm* fan.

abarcar [aβar'kar] *v* take in; comprise; undertake.

abarrotar [aβarro'tar] *v* stow; fill up; overload.

***abastecer** [aβaste'θer] *v* supply, provide with. **abastecimiento** *sm* supply. **abasto** *sm* supply of provisions.

abatir [aβa'tir] *v* knock down; kill; humble. **abatido** *adj* dejected; depressed; dismayed. **abatimiento** *sm* depression; discouragement.

abdicar [aβði'kar] *v* abdicate. **abdicación** *sf* abdication.

abdomen [aβ'ðomen] *sm* abdomen.

abedul [aβe'ðul] *sm* birch-tree.

abeja [a'βexa] *sf* bee. **abeja machiega** honey bee.

aberración [aβerra'θjon] *sf* aberration.

abertura [aβer'tura] *sf* aperture, opening; gap.

abeto [a'βeto] *sm* fir.

abierto [a'βjerto] *adj* open; candid.

abigarrar [aβigar'rar] *v* variegate; fleck. **abigarrado** *adj* flecked; mottled; variegated.

abismo [a'βismo] *sm* abyss. **abismal** *adj* abysmal.

abjurar [aβxu'rar] *v* abjure, forswear. **abjuración** *sf* abjuration.

ablandar [aβlan'dar] *v* soften. **ablandarse** *v* mellow; relent.

***abnegarse** [aβne'garse] *v* deny oneself; renounce.

abobado [aβo'βaðo] *adj* stupid, silly; stupefied.

abocarse [aβo'karse] *v* approach; meet by appointment.

abochornar [aβotʃor'nar] *v* overheat; (*fig*) shame. **abochornarse** *v* blush.

abofetear [aβofete'ar] *v* slap.

abogar [aβo'gar] *v* plead; advocate.

abolengo [aβo'lengo] *sm* ancestry; inheritance.

abolir [aβo'lir] *v* abolish.

abollar [aβo'ʎar] *v* dent. **abolladura** *sf* dent. **abollonar** *v* emboss.

abominar [aβomi'nar] *v* abominate. **abominable** *adj* abominable. **abominación** *sf* abomination.

abonar [aβo'nar] *v* guarantee; stand surety for; subscribe to; improve; (*agr*) manure. **abonado** *adj* safe; sure; trustworthy. *sm* subscriber; season-ticket holder. **abono** *sm* guarantee; subscription; fertilizer.

abordar [aβor'ðar] *v* approach; (*mar*) board ship; (*mar*) put into port.

aborigen [aβo'rixen] *s(m+f)*, *adj* aborigine, aboriginal.

***aborrecer** [aβorre'θer] *v* hate. **aborrecimiento** *sm* hatred.

abortar [aβor'tar] *v* abort. **aborto** *sm* (*med*) abortion; (*fig*) failure.

abotonar [aβoto'nar] v button up.

abovedado [aβoβe'ðaðo] adj arched. abovedar v arch.

abrasar [aβra'sar] v burn; dry up. abrasarse (de, en) v (de, en amor) burn with. abrasivo adj abrasive.

abrazar [aβra'θar] v embrace, hug. abrazo sm embrace.

abrelatas [aβre'latas] sm invar tin-opener.

abreviar [aβre'βjar] v abbreviate; speed up. abreviatura sf abbreviation.

abrigar [aβri'gar] v shelter; wrap up. abrigo sm shelter; overcoat.

abril [a'βril] sm April.

abrir [a'βrir] v open; extend; unfold; reveal.

abrochar [aβro'tʃar] v fasten; button.

abrogar [aβro'gar] v repeal. abrogación sf repeal.

abrumar [aβru'mar] v oppress; weigh down; overwhelm; annoy. abrumarse v become foggy. abrumador adj overwhelming; annoying.

abrupto [a'βrupto] adj rugged; steep; abrupt.

absceso [aβs'θeso] sm abscess.

ábside ['aβsiðe] sm apse.

absolución [aβsolu'θjon] sf (rel) absolution; (jur) acquittal.

absoluto [aβso'luto] adj absolute; complete; (fig) overbearing. en absoluto absolutely.

*absolver [aβsol'βer] v absolve; acquit.

absorber [aβsor'βer] v absorb. absorbente adj absorbent. absorción sf absorption. absorto adj absorbed; amazed.

abstemio [aβs'temjo] adj abstemious.

*abstenerse [aβste'nerse] v abstain. abstinencia sf abstinence.

abstracto [aβs'trakto] adj abstract. abstracción sf abstraction. *abstraer v abstract; refrain from; become thoughtful. abstraer de exclude; do without. abstraído adj retired; preoccupied; absent-minded.

absurdo [aβ'surðo] adj absurd.

abuelo [a'βuelo] sm grandfather. abuela sf grandmother.

abultar [aβul'tar] v enlarge; increase; be bulky. abultado adj bulky; exaggerated. abultamiento sm bulkiness; exaggeration.

abundar [aβun'dar] v abound. abundancia sf abundance. abundante adj abundant.

aburrir [aβur'rir] v bore; (fam) spend time/money; grow bored; grow weary.

aburrido adj boring; weary. aburrimiento sm boredom; wearisomeness.

abusar [aβu'sar] v abuse; impose upon; go too far. abuso sm abuse; misuse.

abyecto [a'βjecto] adj abject. abyección sf degradation; misery.

acá [a'ka] adv here; now. acá y allá here and there.

acabar [aka'βar] v end; complete; kill; be destroyed. acabar de have just. acabarse v run out. acabado adj finished; perfect. sm finish.

academia [aka'ðemja] sf academy. académico adj academic.

*acaecer [akae'θer] v happen. acaecimiento sm happening.

acalorar [akalo'rar] v make warm; (fig) excite. acalorarse v become heated. acalorado adj hot.

acallar [aka'ʎar] v quieten; silence; (fig) ease.

acampar [akam'par] v camp.

acantilado [akanti'laðo] adj steep; rocky. sm cliff.

acaparar [akapa'rar] v monopolize; hoard. acaparador adj monopolistic; (fig) acquisitive.

acariciar [akari'θjar] v caress, fondle, stroke; (fig) cherish. acariciador adj caressing.

acarrear [akarre'ar] v transport; carry; (fig) cause; bring about.

acaso [a'kaso] sm chance. adv perhaps. por si acaso just in case.

acatar [aka'tar] v respect; heed; observe. acatable adj worthy of respect. acatador adj respectful. acatamiento sm respect.

acaudalar [akauða'lar] v accumulate, hoard. acaudalado adj wealthy.

acaudillar [akauði'ʎar] v lead, command. acaudillamiento sm leadership.

acceder [akθe'ðer] v accede, consent. acceder a agree to. accesión sf agreement.

acceso [ak'θeso] sm access; (med) fit.

accidente [akθi'ðente] sm accident. accidental adj accidental.

acción [ak'θjon] sf action. acciones s pl shares pl. stock sing. accionar v work, actuate. accionista s(m+f) shareholder.

acebo [a'θeβo] sm holly.

acechar [aθe'tʃar] v spy on; watch; ambush; stalk. acecho sm observation; lying in wait.

aceite [a'θeite] *sm* oil. **aceite de motor** engine oil. **aceitoso** *adj* oily. **aceituna** *sf* olive.

acelerar [aθele'rar] *v* accelerate; quicken. **acelerarse** *v* hurry. **acelerador** *sm* accelerator.

acendrar [aθen'drar] *v* (*metales*) refine; (*fig*) purify.

acentuar [aθen'twar] *v* accentuate; stress. **acento** *sm* accent; stress.

aceptar [aθep'tar] *v* accept. **aceptable** *adj* acceptable, passable. **aceptación** *sf* acceptance.

acequia [a'θekja] *sf* irrigation ditch; drain.

acera [a'θera] *sf* pavement.

acerbo [a'θerβo] *adj* harsh; sharp; sour; (*fig*) severe.

acerar [aθe'rar] *v* harden with steel; strengthen; (*fig*) fortify.

acerca de [a'θerka ðe] *adv* about.

acercar [aθer'kar] *v* approach; bring near. **acercarse** *v* approach, draw near. **acercamiento** *sm* approach; approximation; reconciliation.

acero [a'θero] *sm* steel.

acérrimo [a'θerrimo] *adj* very strong; extremely tenacious; stalwart.

*****acertar** [aθer'tar] *v* (*el blanco*) hit; guess; be right; find; succeed. **acertado** *adj* correct; apt.

acertijo [aθer'tixo] *sm* riddle.

aciago [a'θjago] *adj* unlucky; ill-fated.

acicalar [aθika'lar] *v* polish; bedeck, groom; (*fam*) spruce oneself up. **acicalado** *adj* spruce; dapper; polished. **acicaladura** *sf also* **acicalamiento** *sm* polishing; grooming; dressing up.

ácido ['aθiðo] *sm, adj* acid.

acierto [a'θjerto] *sm* success; good idea, skill.

aclamar [akla'mar] *v* acclaim; applaud. **aclamación** *sf* acclamation.

aclarar [akla'rar] *v* explain, clarify; (*color*) lighten; thin out; (*dudas*) remove; (*la ropa*) rinse. **aclaración** *sf* explanation. **aclarado** *sm* rinse.

aclimatizar [aklimati'θar] *v* acclimatize.

acné [ak'ne] *sm* acne.

acobardar [akoβar'ðar] *v* frighten; discourage.

acoger [ako'xer] *v* welcome; receive; shelter; accept. **acogerse** *v* take refuge. **acogedor** *adj* (*persona*) welcoming; (*ambiente*) friendly. **acogida** *sf* welcome.

acolchar [akol'tʃar] *v* pad; upholster; (*fig*) muffle. **acolchado** *adj* padded.

acólito [a'kolito] *sm* acolyte.

acometer [akome'ter] *v* attack; undertake; fill; occur to. **acometida** *sf* attack.

acomodar [akomo'ðar] *v* arrange; settle; accommodate; adjust; adapt; prepare; (*fig*) reconcile. **acomodación** *sf* arrangement; preparation. **acomodamente** *adv* conveniently; easily. **acomodadizo** *adj* accommodating; adaptable. **acomodado** *adj* convenient; prepared; well-to-do. **acomodador** *sm* usher. **acomodamiento** *sm* convenience; arrangement; preparation.

acompañar [akompa'ɲar] *v* accompany; escort. **acompañamiento** *sm* accompaniment; escort; (*cortejo*) funeral procession.

acondicionar [akondiθjo'nar] *v* set up; fix; prepare; improve. **acondicionarse** *v* condition oneself. **acondicionado** *adj* equipped. **aire acondicionado** air-conditioning.

acongojar [akongo'xar] *v* sadden; distress.

aconsejar [akonse'xar] *v* advise. **aconsejarse** *v* seek advice.

*****acontecer** [akonte'θer] *v* happen. **acontecimiento** *sm* event.

acopiar [ako'pjar] *v* store; collect. **acopiamiento** *sm* stock.

acoplar [ako'plar] *v* fit; connect; couple; (*animales*) mate. **acoplarse** *v* become friends again. **acoplado** *adj* well-matched. **acoplamiento** *sm* connection; coordination.

acorazar [akora'θar] *v* armour. **acorazado** *adj* armoured; (*fig*) hardened.

*****acordar** [akor'ðar] *v* agree; decide; remind. **acordarse** *v* remember; agree. **acordado** *adj* agreed to; wise.

acordeón [akorðe'on] *sm* accordion.

acordonar [akorðo'nar] *v* cordon off; (*los zapatos*) lace. **acordonado** *adj* cordoned off; ribbed.

acorralar [akorra'lar] *v* enclose; corner; round up.

acortar [akor'tar] *v* shorten; reduce. **acortarse** *v* become shorter; (*intimidarse*) be shy. **acortamiento** *sm* shortening; reduction.

acosar [ako'sar] *v* hound; pursue, harass; pester **acoso** *sm* pursuit.

acostar [akos'tar] v lay down; put to bed. **acostarse** v lie down; go to bed.

acostumbrar [akostum'brar] v accustom; be in the habit of. **acostumbrarse a** v become used to. **acostumbrado** adj usual.

acotar [ako'tar] v (terreno) demarcate; enclose; delimit; outline; accept. **acotado** adj enclosed. **acotamiento** sm demarcation; boundary mark; outline.

acre[1] ['akre] adj acrid; bitter.

acre[2] ['akre] sm acre.

acrecentar [akreθen'tar] v increase. **acrecentamiento** sm increase; growth.

acreditar [akreði'tar] v accredit; prove; vouch for; authorize; (com) credit. **acreditado** adj reputable.

acreedor [akree'ðor] s(m+f) creditor. adj worthy.

acribillar [akriβi'ʎar] v riddle with holes.

acróbata [a'kroβata] s(m+f) acrobat.

acta ['akta] sf minutes of a meeting; official document.

actitud [akti'tuð] sf posture, attitude.

activar [akti'βar] v speed up; stimulate; (quim) activate. **actividad** sf activity.

activo [ak'tiβo] adj active. sm (com) assets pl.

acto ['akto] n act, deed; ceremony; (teatro) act. **salón de actos** sm assembly hall. **actor** sm actor. **actriz** sf actress. **actual** adj present; topical; of this month. **actualmente** adv at present; nowadays.

actuar [ak'twar] v act; perform; behave. **actuación** sf action; performance; conduct. **actuario** sm (jur) clerk of the court.

acuarela [akwa'rela] sf watercolour.

acuario [a'kwario] sm aquarium.

acuático [a'kwatiko] adj aquatic.

acuciar [aku'θjar] v urge; pester; (anhelar) long for. **acucioso** adj urgent; diligent; desirous.

acuclillarse [akukli'ʎarse] v crouch, squat.

acuchillar [akutʃi'ʎar] v knife, stab, hack. **acuchillado** adj knifed; (fig) experienced.

acudir [aku'ðir] v come; go; (a una cita) keep; answer; attend; help; (al médico) consult.

acueducto [akwe'ðukto] sm aqueduct.

acuerdo [a'kwerðo] sm agreement. **¡de acuerdo!** O.K.! **ponerse de acuerdo** come to an agreement.

acumular [akumu'lar] v accumulate; pile; store. **acumulación** sf accumulation.

acuñar [aku'ɲar] v (monedas) mint; (poner cuñas) wedge.

acuoso [aku'oso] adj watery. **acuosidad** sf wateriness.

acurrucarse [akurru'karse] v curl up.

acusar [aku'sar] v (jur) accuse; charge; blame; denounce; reveal; (com) acknowledge. **acusación** sf accusation. **acusado** sm (jur) defendant.

acústico [a'kustiko] adj acoustic. **acústica** sf acoustics.

achacar [atʃa'kar] v attribute.

achatar [atʃa'tar] v flatten.

achicar [atʃi'kar] v reduce; (mar) bale; (fig) humiliate. **achicado** adj childish.

achicoria [atʃi'korja] sf chicory.

achicharrar [atʃitʃar'rar] v burn; (molestar) annoy. **achicharradero** sm furnace.

achispado [atʃis'paðo] adj tipsy. **achispar** v make tipsy.

adalid [aða'lið] sm leader.

adaptar [aðap'tar] v adapt; adjust. **adaptabilidad** sf adaptability. **adaptable** adj adaptable. **adaptación** sf adaptation; (tecn) fitting.

adecuado [aðe'kwaðo] adj adequate; suitable.

adefesio [aðe'fesjo] (fam) sm nonsense; (traje) ridiculous garment; (persona) ridiculously dressed person.

adelantar [aðelan'tar] v advance; (reloj) put forward; speed up; gain; (auto) overtake. **prohibido adelantar** no overtaking. **adelantarse** v go forward. **adelantado** adj advanced. **adelantamiento** sm also **adelanto** advance. **adelante** adv ahead, forward. **¡adelante!** come in! **de hoy en adelante** in future.

adelgazar [aðelga'θar] v make thin; slim. **adelgazador** adj slimming. **adelgazamiento** sm slimming. **régimen de adelgazamiento** diet.

ademán [aðe'man] sm expression; gesture. **ademanes** s pl manners.

además [aðe'mas] adv besides, furthermore. **además de** as well as.

adentro [a'ðentro] adv within, inside. **¡adentro!** come in! **mar adentro** out to sea. **tierra adentro** inland.

adepto [a'ðepto] s(m+f) adept; supporter.

adestrar V **adiestrar**.

aderezar [aðere'θar] v adorn; (culin) prepare; guide. **aderezo** sm adornment; cooking; seasoning; (de ensalada) dressing.

adeudar [aðeu'ðar] *v* owe; (*com*) charge; run into debt. **adeudado** *adj* owing; (*persona*) in debt. **adeudo** *sm* (*deuda*) debt; (*com*) charge.

***adherir** [aðe'rir] *v* adhere, stick. **adherirse** adhere to. **adherencia** *sf* (*acción de pegar*) adherence. **adhesión** *sf* adhesion; (*apoyo*) support. **adhesivo** *sm, adj* adhesive.

adición [aði'θyon] *sf* addition. **adicional** *adj* additional. **adicionar** *v* add.

adicto [a'ðikto] *adj* devoted. *s(m+f)* supporter; addict.

adiestrar [aðjes'trar] *v* train, teach. **adiestrador, -a** *sm, sf* trainer. **adiestramiento** *sm* training.

adinerado [aðine'raðo] *adj* wealthy. **adinerado, -a** *sm, sf* rich person. **adinerarse** *v* (*fam*) make one's fortune.

adiós [a'ðjos] *interj, sm* goodbye.

adivinar [aðiβi'nar] *v* foretell; guess; (*el pensamiento*) read. **adivinable** *adj* foreseeable. **adivinación** *sf also* **adivinamiento** *sm* divination; guessing. **adivinador, -a** *sm, sf* fortune-teller.

adjetivo [aðxe'tiβo] *sm* adjective.

adjudicar [aðxuði'kar] *v* award; adjudicate.

adjuntar [aðxun'tar] *v* attach; enclose; give.

adjunto [að'xunto] *adj* attached; enclosed. *sm* assistant.

administrar [aðminis'trar] *v* administer, control; (*fam*) hand out. **administración** *sf* administration. **administrativo** *adj* administrative.

admirar [aðmi'rar] *v* admire. **admirarse** *v* surprise, astonish. **admirable** *adj* admirable. **admiración** *sf* admiration.

admirador, -a [aðmi'raðor], -a *sm, sf* admirer. *adj* admiring.

admitir [aðmi'tir] *v* admit; accept; allow; acknowledge. **admisible** *adj* admissible. acceptable. **admisión** *sf* admission; acceptance.

adobar [aðo'βar] *v* pickle; season; cook.

***adolecer** [aðole'θer] *v* fall ill. **adolecer de** suffer from.

adolescencia [aðoles'θenθja] *sf* adolescence. **adolescente** *s(m+f), adj* adolescent.

adonde ['aðonde] *adv* where. ¿**adónde?** where?

adoptar [aðop'tar] *v* adopt; assume. **adopción** *sf* adoption. **adoptivo** *adj* adoptive.

adoquín [aðo'kin] *sm* paving-stone; (*fam*) dunce. **adoquinar** *v* pave.

adorar [aðo'rar] *v* adore; worship; pray. **adorable** *adj* adorable. **adoración** *sf* adoration; worship.

***adormecer** [aðorme'θer] *v* make sleepy. **adormecerse** fall asleep. **adormecerse en** give oneself up to.

adormidera [aðormi'ðera] *sf* poppy.

adornar [aðor'nar] *v* adorn, decorate; (*trajes*) trim; (*coc*) garnish; (*fig*) embellish. **adornarse** *v* dress up. **adorno** *sm* decoration; trimming; garnish.

***adquirir** [aðki'rir] *v* acquire, obtain. **adquisición** *sf* acquisition; (*compra*) purchase. **adquisitivo** *adj* acquisitive.

adrede [a'ðrede] *adv* on purpose.

adscribir [aðskri'βir] *v* attribute, ascribe; assign. **adscripción** *sf* attribution; assignment. **adscripto** *adj* attributed; assigned.

aduana [a'ðwana] *sf* customs *pl*. **derechos de aduana** *sm pl* customs duty *sing*. **aduanero** *sm* customs officer.

***aducir** [aðu'θir] *v* (*razones*) allege; (*un texto*) quote; (*pruebas*) offer as proof.

adueñarse [aðwe'parse] *v* appropriate.

adular [aðu'lar] *v* flatter. **adulación** *sf* flattery.

adulterar [aðulte'rar] *v* adulterate; commit adultery. **adulterio** *sm* adultery. **adúltero, -a** *sm, sf* adulterer, adulteress.

adulto [a'ðulto], -a *s, adj* adult.

adusto [a'ðusto] *adj* very hot; (*fig*) harsh.

advenedizo [aðβene'ðiθo], -a *s, adj* upstart.

advenimiento [aðβeni'mjento] *sm* advent; coming.

adverbio [að'βerβjo] *sm* adverb.

adversario [aðβer'sarjo] *sm* adversary. **adversidad** *sf* adversity. **adverso** *adj* adverse; opposing.

***advertir** [aðβer'tir] *v* warn; recommend; (*señalar*) point out; tell; (*comprender*) realize. **advertido** *adj* informed; experienced. **advertencia** *sf also* **advertimiento** *sm* warning.

adyacente [aðja'θente] *adj* adjacent.

aéreo [a'ereo] *adj* aerial.

aerodinámica [aeroði'namika] *sf* aerodynamics. **aerodinámico** *adj* aerodynamic.

aeronáutica [aero'nautika] *sf* aeronautics. **aeronáutico** *adj* aeronautical.

aeroplano [aero'plano] *sm* aeroplane.

aeropuerto [aero'pwerto] *sm* airport.

aerosol [aero'sol] *sm* aerosol.

afable [a'faβle] *adj* pleasant; genial. **afabilidad** *sf* affability.

afamado [afa'maðo] *adj* famous.

afán [a'fan] *sm* (*trabajo penoso*) toil; (*deseo*) desire; (*entusiasmo*) zeal; (*preocupación*) anxiety. **afanador** *adj* enthusiastic. **afanar** *v* work hard; (*fig: robar*) steal. **afanarse** *v* exert oneself. **afanoso** *adj* laborious; hectic.

afección [afek'θjon] *sf* (*cariño*) affection; (*med*) complaint. **afeccionarse** *v* grow fond.

afectar [afek'tar] *v* affect; pretend; adopt; (*atañer*) concern; (*dañar*) damage. **afectado** *adj* spoiled; unnatural; upset. **afecto** [a'fekto] *adj* dear. **afecto a** fond of. *sm* affection.

afeitar [afei'tar] *v* shave. **afeitarse** *v* shave; make up one's face. **afeite** *sm* make-up, cosmetics *pl*.

afeminado [afemi'naðo] *adj* effeminate. *sm* effeminate person.

aferrar [afer'rar] v seize; (*mar*) moor. **aferrarse *v* cling.

afianzar [afjan'θar] *v* reinforce; establish; restore; guarantee; seize; support. **afianzarse** *v* steady oneself; become strong. **afianzamiento** *sm* surety; guarantee; establishment.

afición [afi'θjon] *sf* inclination; fondness; (*interés*) hobby. **la afición** *sf* the fans *pl*. **aficionado, -a** *sm*, *sf* fan. *adj* amateur; keen.

afilar [afi'lar] *v* sharpen; grind. **afilado** *adj* sharp. **afilador** *sm* (*persona*) knife-grinder; (*correa*) strop. **afilamiento** *sm* (*la nariz*) pointedness; (*los dedos*) slenderness.

afiliar [afi'ljar] *v* affiliate. **afiliación** *sf* affiliation.

afín [a'fin] *adj* adjacent; similar; related. **afinidad** *sf* similarity, affinity.

afinar [afi'nar] *v* polish; perfect; (*música*) tune. **afinarse** *v* become slimmer. **afinadura** *sf also* **afinamiento** *sm* tuning; (*fig*) refinement.

afirmar [afir'mar] *v* affirm; strengthen. **afirmarse** *v* steady oneself. **afirmación** *sf* statement; strengthening. **afirmativo** *adj* affirmative.

aflicción [aflik'θjon] *sf* affliction, grief. **afligido** *adj* distressed; (*por una muerte*) bereaved. **afligir** *v* grieve; distress; afflict.

aflojar [aflo'xar] *v* loosen, slacken; relax; (*fiebre*) abate; (*fam*) fork out, cough up. **aflojamiento** *sm* loosening, slackening; abatement; relaxation.

afluencia [aflu'enθja] *sf* crowd; (*tropel*) rush; influx; abundance.

**afluir [aflu'ir] v flow.

afónico [a'foniko] *adj* hoarse, voiceless. **afonía** *sf* loss of voice.

aforar [afo'rar] v gauge, measure; appraise. **aforo *sm* measurement; appraisal.

aforrar [afor'rar] *v* (*ropa, etc.*) line. **aforrarse** *v* wrap oneself up.

afortunado [afortu'naðo] *adj* fortunate; happy.

afrenta [a'frenta] *sf* insult; disgrace. **afrentar** *v* insult. **afrentarse** *v* be ashamed. **afrentador** *adj also* **afrentoso** insulting; offensive.

África ['afrika] *sf* Africa. **africano, -a** *s, adj* African.

afrontar [afron'tar] *v* confront; bring face to face. **afrontamiento** *sm* confrontation.

afuera [a'fwera] *adv* out, outside. ¡afuera! get out! **afueras** *s pl* suburbs *pl*.

agachar [aga'tʃar] *v* lower, bend. **agacharse** *v* bend over; crouch; (*para evitar algo*) duck. **agachada** *sf* (*fam*) trick.

agalla [a'gaʎa] *sf* gill; (*fam*) pluck. **agallas** *s pl* tonsils *pl*.

agarrar [agar'rar] *v* seize, clutch; (*comprender*) grasp; get; take; win; (*fam*) stick. **agarro** *sm* hold, grasp. **agarradero** *sm* handle.

agarrotar [agarro'tar] *v* tighten; strangle. **agarrotarse** *v* (*motor*) seize up; (*músculo*) go numb. **agarrotado** *adj* bound; stiff; seized up.

agasajar [agasa'xar] *v* welcome warmly; entertain. **agasajo** *sm* gift; welcome. **agasajos** *sm pl* hospitality *sing*.

agazapar [agaθa'par] *v* (*fam*) nab, catch. **agazaparse** *v* crouch; duck.

agencia [a'xenθja] *sf* agency; office. **agencia de prensa** news agency. **agencia de turismo** *or* **viajes** travel agency. **agenciar** *v* get; (*fam*) wangle. **agente** *sm* agent; policeman. **agente de bolsa** stockbroker. **agente inmobiliario** estate agent.

agenda [a'xenda] *sf* diary.

ágil ['axil] *adj* agile. **agilidad** *sf* agility.

agitar [axi'tar] *v* wave; shake; upset; stir up. **agitarse** *v* sway; fidget. **agitación** *sf* waving; shaking; movement; excitement.

agitado adj agitated; rough. **agitador, -a** sm, sf agitator.

aglomerar [aglome'rar] v form a crowd; amass. **aglomeración** sf mass. **aglomeración de tráfico** traffic jam.

agobiar [ago'βjar] v weigh down; overwhelm; humiliate; depress. **agobiado** v bent down; overwhelmed; exhausted. **agobio** sm burden.

agolparse [agol'parse] v crowd together; amass. **agolpamiento** sm crowd; (cosas) pile.

agonía [ago'nia] sf (muerte) death; desire; agony. **agonizar** v be dying; suffer; annoy.

*__agorar__ [ago'rar] v predict. **agorero, -a** sm, sf fortune-teller.

agosto [a'gosto] sm August.

agotar [ago'tar] v drain; exhaust. **agotador** adj exhausting. **agotamiento** sm exhaustion.

agraciar [agra'θjar] v adorn; award; pardon. **agraciado** adj pretty; graceful.

agradar [agra'ðar] v please. **agradable** adj pleasant.

*__agradecer__ [agraðe'θer] v thank; be grateful for; be welcome. **agradecido** adj grateful. **¡muy agradecido!** much obliged! **agradecimiento** sm gratitude.

agrado [agra'ðo] sm pleasure; liking.

agrandar [agran'ðar] v make larger; exaggerate. **agrandamiento** sm enlargement.

agravar [agra'βar] v aggravate; worsen. **agravación** sf also **agravamiento** sm aggravation. **agravante** adj aggravating.

agraviar [agra'βjar] v offend; insult; wrong; take offence. **agravio** sm insult; affront; wrong.

*__agredir__ [agre'ðir] v assault.

agregado [agre'gaðo] sm aggregate; assistant; attaché; addition. **agregar** join; incorporate. **agregarse** v be added; be incorporated.

agricultura [agrikul'tura] sf agriculture. **agrícola** adj agricultural.

agrietar [agrje'tar] v crack; chap.

agrio ['agrjo] adj sour; (carácter) bitter. sm (sabor) sourness.

agrupar [agru'par] v group; gather together. **agruparse** v come together.

agua [a'gwa] sf water. **agua abajo/arriba** down-/upstream. **agua dulce** fresh water. **entre dos aguas** sitting on the fence. **hacer agua** leak. **irse al agua** fall through.

aguacate [agwa'kate] sm avocado pear.

aguacero [agwa'θero] sm shower, downpour.

aguantar [agwan'tar] v tolerate, bear; (sostener) support; (esperar) wait, await; (durar) last. **aguante** sm patience; endurance.

aguar [a'gwar] v dilute; spoil. **aguarse** be ruined. **aguado** adj watered down.

aguardar [agwar'ðar] v wait for.

aguardiente [agwar'ðjente] sm liquor.

aguarrás [agwar'ras] sm turpentine.

aguazal [agwa'θal] sm mire.

agudeza [agu'deθa] sf (de los sentidos) sharpness; (del dolor) acuteness; (ingenio) wit. **agudizar** v sharpen; worsen. **agudo** adj sharp; acute; witty.

agüero [a'gwero] sm omen. **de buen agüero** lucky.

aguijar [agi'xar] v goad; hurry. **aguijón** sm (de un insecto) sting; stimulus. **aguijonada** sf sting; prick. **aguijonear** v goad; spur on.

águila ['agila] sf eagle. **águila ratonera** buzzard.

aguinaldo [agi'naldo] sm Christmas present.

aguja [a'guxa] sf needle; (reloj) hand; (arq) spire. **agujas** s pl points pl.

agujero [agu'xero] sm hole; (alfiletero) pincushion.

agujetas [agu'xetas] sf pl stiffness sing. **lleno de agujetas** stiff all over.

aguzar [agu'θar] v sharpen; (estimular) encourage; (el apetito) whet. **aguzado** adj sharp; sharpened. **aguzador** adj sharpening.

ahí [a'i] adv there. **de ahí** thus, so. **por ahí** that way; thereabouts. **¡ahí es nada!** fancy that!

ahijada [ai'xaða] sf goddaughter; protégée. **ahijado** sm godson; protégé.

ahincar [ain'kar] v urge. **ahincarse** v hurry. **ahincadamente** adv tenaciously. **ahincado** adj insistent; eager. **ahínco** sm effort.

ahogar [ao'gar] v drown; flood; stifle; overwhelm. **ahogarse** v drown. be drowned. **ahogadero** sm Turkish bath. **ahogado** adj drowned; (por el gas) asphyxiated; strangled; (grito) muffled. **ahogador** adj suffocating. **ahogo** sm breathlessness; (angustia) distress.

ahora [a'ora] adv now. conj now, now then. **ahora bien** come now. **ahora mismo** right away.

ahorcar [aor'kar] v hang. **ahorcarse** v hang oneself. **ahorcadura** sf hanging.

ahorrar [aor'rar] v save; free; avoid. **ahorrador** adj thrifty. **ahorro** sm saving; thrift.

ahuecar [awe'kar] v hollow. ¡**ahueca**! (fam) scram!

ahumar [au'mar] v (culin) smoke; (llenar de humo) fill with smoke. **ahumarse** v taste smoky; (fam: emborracharse) become tipsy. **ahumado** adj smoky; smoked; (fam) tipsy.

ahuyentar [aujen'tar] v frighten off; keep at bay; (fig) dismiss. **ahuyentarse** v flee.

airado [ai'raðo] adj vexed; immoral.

aire ['aire] sm air; (parecido) likeness; (aspecto) appearance; (porte) bearing; (música) time; (auto: estrangulador) choke. **hace aire** it's windy. **aire acondicionado** air conditioning. **aireación** sf ventilation. **airear** v ventilate. **airoso** adj ventilated; windy; (fig) graceful.

aislar [ais'lar] v isolate; (elec) insulate. **aislado** adj alone; remote; insulated. **aislador** adj insulating. **cinta aisladora** sf insulating tape. **aislamiento** sm isolation; insulation.

ajar [a'xar] v crumple; wrinkle; fade; (fig) age.

ajedrez [axe'ðreθ] sm chess.

ajeno [a'xeno] adj of other people; alien; free; detached; irrelevant.

ajetreo [axe'treo] sm rush; activity; bustle; exhaustion. **ajetreado** adj busy. **ajetrearse** v be busy; rush; exhaust oneself.

ajo ['axo] sm garlic. **ajo cebollino** chive. **ajo porro** leek. **diente de ajo** clove of garlic. **soltar ajos** swear.

ajuar [a'xwar] sm (de novia) trousseau; (de casa) furnishings pl.

ajustar [axus'tar] v adjust; arrange; tighten. **ajuste** sm adjustment; fitting.

ajusticiar [axusti'θjar] v execute.

al [al] contraction of **a el**.

ala ['ala] sf wing; hat brim.

alabar [ala'ßar] v praise. **alabarse** v (jactarse) boast. **alabanza** sf praise.

alabastro [ala'ßastro] sm alabaster.

alacena [ala'θena] sf larder; cupboard.

alacrán [ala'kran] sm scorpion.

alambicar [alambi'kar] v distil; complicate; (precio) minimize. **alambicado** adj elaborate; (estilo) subtle; affected; minimized. **alambique** sm still. **pasar algo por el alambique** examine something very carefully.

alambre [a'lambre] sm wire. **alambrada** sf (de la guerra) barbed wire; (reja) wire netting.

alameda [ala'meða] sf (avenida) tree-lined walk; (de álamos) poplar grove.

álamo ['alamo] sm poplar. **álamo temblón** aspen.

alano [a'lano] sm mastiff.

alarde [a'larðe] sm parade; display. **alardear** v boast. **alardeo** sm boasting.

alargar [alar'gar] v lengthen, increase, enlarge; (posponer) defer; (dar) reach, hand; (la mano) stretch. **alargarse** v get longer. **alargado** adj elongated. **alargamiento** sm lengthening; extension.

alarido [ala'riðo] sm yell, shriek.

alarmar [alar'mar] v alarm; alert. **alarmarse** v be frightened. **alarma** sf alarm.

alba ['alßa] sf dawn.

albañil [alßa'nil] sm bricklayer.

albaricoque [alßari'koke] sm apricot.

albatros [alßa'tros] sm albatross.

albedrío [alße'ðrio] sm will; (capricho) whim; custom. **libre albedrío** free will.

albergar [alßer'gar] v shelter; accommodate; (fig) cherish. **albergue** sm lodgings pl; (refugio) shelter; (posada) hostel.

albóndiga [al'ßonðiga] sf rissole.

albor [al'ßor] sm dawn; (blancura) whiteness.

albornoz [alßor'noθ] sm bathrobe.

alborotar [alßoro'tar] v make a noise; disturb. **alborotarse** v (perturbarse) become upset; get excited; (una muchedumbre) riot. **alborotado** adj excited; (fig) eventful. **alborotador** adj noisy; rebellious. **alboroto** sm disturbance, uproar.

alborozar [alßoro'θar] v gladden; produce laughter. **alborozarse** v rejoice. **alborozado** adj overjoyed.

álbum ['alßum] sm album.

alcachofa [alka'tʃofa] sf artichoke.

alcahuete [alka'wete] sm pimp; (chismoso) gossip. **alcahueta** sf procuress; gossip.

alcalde [al'kalðe] sm mayor. **alcaldesa** sf mayoress. **alcaldía** sf mayorship; (oficina) mayor's office.

alcance [al'kanθe] sm reach; (sonido, arma de fuego, etc.) range; scope; importance. **al alcance** within reach. **dar alcance** a catch up with. **alcanzar** v reach; catch up; understand; hit; affect; succeed; be enough; (*durar*) last.

alcantarilla [alkanta'riʎa] *sf* sewer; drain.

alcázar [al'kaθar] *sm* palace; fortress; (*mar*) quarterdeck.

alcoba [al'koβa] *sf* bedroom.

alcohol [alko'ol] *sm* alcohol. **alcohólico, -a** *s. adj* alcoholic.

alcornoque [alkor'noke] *sm* cork tree; (*fig*) nitwit.

aldaba [al'ðaβa] *sf* door knocker; (*pestillo*) latch, bolt. **tener buenas aldabas** (*fam*) have influential friends.

aldea [al'ðea] *sf* village.

aleación [alea'θjon] *sf* alloy.

alegar [ale'ɣar] *v* allege; state; emphasize; quote; (*jur*) plead, claim. **alegato** *sm* declaration; plea.

alegoría [aleɣo'ria] *sf* allegory. **alegórico** *adj* allegorical.

alegrar [ale'ɣrar] *v* gladden; make merry; be pleasing to; excite. **alegrarse** *v* be happy; (*fam*) become tipsy. **alegre** *adj* happy; bright; good; (*fam*) tipsy; (*atrevido*) daring. **alegría** *sf* joy; happiness. **¡qué alegría!** great!

alejar [ale'xar] *v* move away; keep away; avert. **alejarse** *v* go away. **alejado** *adj* far away; aloof. **alejamiento** *sm* removal; absence.

Alemania [ale'manja] *sf* Germany. **alemán, -ana** *sm, sf* German (person). **alemán** *sm* (*idioma*) German (language).

*****alentar** [alen'tar] *v* breathe; (*fig*) glow; (*animar*) encourage. **alentado** *adj* encouraged; (*orgulloso*) proud; (*valiente*) brave. **alentador** *adj* encouraging.

alerce [a'lerθe] *sm* larch.

alergia [a'lerxja] *sf* allergy. **alérgico** *adj* allergic.

alero [a'lero] *sm* eaves *pl*. **estar en el alero** hang in the balance.

alerta [a'lerta] *sm* alert. *adv* on the alert. **¡alerta!** look out! **alertar** *v* alert, warn. **alerto** *adj* alert.

aleta [a'leta] *sf* (*peces*) fin; (*foca*) flipper.

aleve [a'leβe] *adj also* **alevoso** treacherous. **alevosía** *sf* treachery. **alevoso, -a** *sm, sf* traitor.

alfabeto [alfa'βeto] *sm* alphabet. **alfabético** *adj* alphabetical. **por orden alfabético** in alphabetical order. **alfabetizado** *adj* literate.

alfarero [alfa'rero] *sm* potter. **alfarería** *sf* pottery (art and workshop).

alférez [al'fereθ] *sm* (*mil*) second lieutenant.

alfil [al'fil] *sm* (*ajedrez*) bishop.

alfiler [alfi'ler] *sm* pin; brooch. **alfiler de la ropa** clothes-peg. **alfilerar** *v* pin. **alfilerazo** *sm* pinprick.

alfombra [al'fombra] *sf* carpet; rug. **alfombrar** *v* carpet.

alforja [al'forxa] *sf* rucksack.

alga ['alga] *sf* seaweed.

algarabía [alɣara'βia] *sf* Arabic; (*fig*) gibberish; (*ruido*) noise, row.

algazara [alɣa'θara] *sf* hubbub, uproar.

álgebra ['alxebra] *sf* algebra. **algebráico** *adj also* **algébrico** algebraic.

álgido [ˈalxiðo] *adj* icy cold; (*fig*) decisive.

algo ['algo] *pron* something; anything. *adv* rather, quite. *sm* something; (*comida*) snack.

algodón [algo'ðon] *sm* cotton. **algodón hidrófilo** cotton wool.

alguacil [algwa'θil] *sm* sheriff; city governor.

alguien ['algjen] *pron* someone, somebody; (*interrog*) anybody.

algún [al'gun] *adj* some, any. **algún tanto** a little.

alguno [al'guno] *adj* some, any. *pron* one; some; someone. **algunos** *ms pl* some, a few.

alhaja [al'axa] *sf* jewel; treasure.

albelí [ale'li] *sm, pl* **-líes** wallflower.

alheña [a'leɲa] *sf* privet; blight, mildew. **alheñar** *v* (*secarse*) wither; become mildewed.

alhucema [alu'θema] *sf* lavender.

aliaga [ali'aga] *sf* gorse.

aliar [ali'ar] *v* ally. **aliado, -a** *sm, sf* ally. **alianza** *sf* alliance.

alicaído [alika'iðo] *adj* depressed; weak.

alicates [ali'kates] *sm pl* pliers, pincers *pl*.

aliciente [ali'θjente] *sm* lure; interest; encouragement.

alienar [alje'nar] *v* alienate. **alienación** *sf* alienation. **alienado** *adj* insane.

aliento [a'ljento] *sm* breath; (*fig*) courage. **cobrar aliento** catch one's breath.

aligerar [alixe'rar] *v* lighten; shorten; alleviate. **aligerarse** *v* get a move on.

alimentar [alimen'tar] *v* feed; supply; (*promover*) foster. **alimentación** *sf* food; feeding. **alimenticio** *adj* nourishing. **alimento** *sm* food.

alinear [aline'ar] *v* line up. **alinearse en** join. **alineación** *sf also* **alineamiento** *sm* alignment.

aliñar [ali'nar] *v* adorn; (*culin*) season; prepare. **aliño** *sm* adornment; seasoning; preparation.

alisar [ali'sar] *v* smooth; polish; level. **alisaduras** *sf pl* shavings *pl*.

alistar [alis'tar] *v* list; recruit; prepare. **alistado** *adj* enlisted. **alistamiento** *sm* enlistment.

aliviar [ali'βjar] *v* lighten; alleviate; help; console. **aliviarse** *v* feel better, recover. **alivio** *sm* lightening; relief. **... de alivio** (*fam*) a hell of a ....

alma ['alma] *sf* soul; spirit; person. **con el alma en la boca** at death's door.

almacén [alma'θen] *sm* warehouse; department store. **almacenaje** *sm* storage. **almacenero** *sm* storekeeper.

almanaque [alma'nake] *sm* almanac; diary.

almeja [al'mexa] *sf* clam.

almendra [al'mendra] *sf* almond. **almendro** *sm* almond tree.

almiar [al'mjar] *sm* haystack.

almíbar [al'miβar] *sm* syrup.

almidón [almi'ðon] *sm* starch.

almirante [almi'rante] *sm* admiral. **almirantazgo** *sm* admiralty.

almohada [almo'aða] *sf* pillow; cushion; (*funda*) pillowslip.

almoneda [almo'neða] *sf* auction; (*a bajo precio*) clearance sale.

almorranas [almor'ranas] *sf pl* haemorrhoids *pl*, piles *pl*.

*almorzar [almor'θar] *v* lunch. **almuerzo** *sm* lunch.

alojar [alo'xar] *v* lodge, accommodate. **alojarse** *v* put up, stay. **alojamiento** *sm* accommodation, lodgings *pl*.

alondra [a'londra] *sf* lark.

alpargata [alpar'gata] *sf* rope-soled shoe. **alpargatería** *sf* shoe factory *or* shop.

Alpes [alpes] *sm pl* Alps *pl*.

alpinismo [alpi'nismo] *sm* mountaineering. **alpinista** *s(m+f)* climber.

alpiste [al'piste] *sm* canary seed; (*fam*) drink; (*fam*) money.

alquería [alke'ria] *sf* farm; (*aldea*) village.

alquilar [alki'lar] *v* rent; hire; charter. **alquilarse** *v* be for hire; to be let. **se alquila** (*casa*) to let; (*coche*) for hire. **alquiler** *sm* renting; letting; hiring.

alquileres *sm pl* rent *sing*. **exento de alquiler** rent-free.

alquimia [al'kimja] *sf* alchemy.

alquitrán [alki'tran] *sm* tar. **alquitranado** *adj* tarred.

alrededor [alreðe'ðor] *adv* round, around. **alrededor de** about, around. **alrededores** *sm pl* environs *pl*, outskirts *pl*.

alta ['alta] *sf* (*del hospital*) discharge; (*ingreso*) enrolment. **dar de alta** pass as fit. **darse de alta** enrol.

altanero [alta'nero] *adj* haughty, arrogant.

altar [al'tar] *sm* altar.

altavoz [alta'βoθ] *sm* loudspeaker.

alterar [alte'rar] *v* change, alter; disturb; (*estropear*) spoil. **alterarse** *v* go sour; change; be disturbed; get excited. **alteración** *sf* alteration; (*altercado*) quarrel.

altercar [alter'kar] *v* argue, quarrel. **altercación** *sf* argument, quarrel.

alternar [alter'nar] *v* alternate; be sociable. **alterno** *adj* alternating; alternate.

alternativa [alterna'tiβa] *sf* alternative choice; (*trabajo*) shift-work; (*rotación de cosechas*) rotation. **tomar la alternativa** qualify as a bullfighter.

alto¹ ['alto] *adj* tall; high; upper; (*fuerte*) loud; advanced; noble. **lo alto** the top. *adv* high; high up; out loud. *sm* (*elevación*) hill; (*altura*) height. **alteza** *sf* height; (*título*) highness; grandeur. **altitud** *sf* altitude; (*geog*) elevation.

alto² *sm, interj* halt. **hacer alto** stop.

alubia [a'luβja] *sf* French bean.

alucinación [aluθina'θjon] *sf* hallucination.

alud [a'luð] *sm* avalanche.

aludir [alu'ðir] *v* allude, mention. **aludido** *adj* in question. **no darse por aludido** turn a deaf ear.

alumbrar [alum'brar] *v* light; illuminate; give light; (*descubrir*) find; (*parir*) give birth; (*brillar*) shine. **alumbrarse** *v* (*fam*) become tipsy. **alumbramiento** *sm* lighting; illumination. **alumbrante** *adj* illuminating; (*fig*) enlightening.

aluminio [alu'minjo] *sm* aluminium.

alumno [a'lumno] *sm* pupil, student.

alzar [al'θar] *v* raise; lift. **alzarse** *v* rise; stand out. **alza** *sf* raise. **¡alza!** bravo! **alzamiento** *sm* increase; uprising.

allá [a'ʎa] *adv* there; long ago. **más allá** farther on. **vamos allá** let's go.

allanar [aʎa'nar] *v* level, flatten, smooth. **allanar el terreno** clear the way.

allegar [aʎe'gar] v collect, reap; add; unite. **allegar fondos** raise funds. **allegarse** v arrive; approach. **allegarse a** become attached to.

allegado [aʎe'gaðo], **-a** sm, sf relative; close friend. adj related, close. **allegamiento** sm collection; gathering; union; friendship; relationship.

allende [a'ʎende] adv beyond; besides. **allende el mar** overseas.

allí [a'ʎi] adv there; then. **aquí y allí** here and there. **por allí** over there.

ama ['ama] sf mistress of the house; (patrona) landlady.

amable [a'maβle] adj kind. **amabilidad** sf kindness.

amaestrar [amaes'trar] v train.

amagar [ama'gar] v threaten; show signs of. **amagarse** v (fam) hide.

amainar [amai'nar] v lessen; moderate. **amainarse** v yield.

amalgamar [amalga'mar] v amalgamate. **amalgamación** sf amalgamation.

amamantar [amaman'tar] v suckle, nurse. **amamantador** adj suckling. **amamantamiento** sm suckling.

***amanecer** [amane'θer] v dawn; arrive at break of day. sm dawn, daybreak.

amansar [aman'sar] v break in; tame; (fig: dolor) ease.

amante [a'mante] sm, sf lover. adj fond.

amañado [ama'ɲaðo] adj skilful; (falso) fake. **amañar** v fix; fake.

amapola [ama'pola] sf poppy.

amar [a'mar] v love.

amargar [amar'gar] v embitter; be or taste bitter. **amargo** adj bitter. **amargor** sm also **amargura** sf bitterness.

amarillo [ama'riʎo] adj yellow.

amarrar [amar'rar] v fasten; tie; moor. **amarradero** sm moorings pl. **amarro** sm fastening.

amartelar [amarte'lar] v (enamorar) make lovesick; (dar celos) make jealous. **amartelarse de** (fam) get a crush on.

amartillar [amarti'ʎar] v hammer.

amasar [ama'sar] v knead; mix; prepare; (med) massage; (fam) cook up; (fig) amass. **amasijo** sm (harina) dough; (fam) mixture, hotchpotch; plot.

amatista [ama'tista] sf amethyst.

ámbar ['ambar] sm amber.

ambición [ambi'θjon] sf ambition. **ambicioso** adj ambitious.

ambiente [am'bjente] sm atmosphere; environment. adj surrounding.

ambiguo [am'bigwo] adj ambiguous. **ambigüedad** sf ambiguity.

ámbito ['ambito] sm (recinto) enclosure; (alcance) scope; sphere; (extensión) expanse.

ambos ['ambos] adj, pron both.

ambulancia [ambu'lanθja] sf ambulance.

ambulante [ambu'lante] adj travelling; walking.

amedrentar [ameðren'tar] v frighten.

amenazar [amena'θar] v threaten. **amenaza** sf threat. **amenazador** adj threatening.

amenguar [amen'gwar] v lessen; (deshonrar) dishonour.

amenizar [ameni'θar] v make pleasant. **amenidad** sf pleasantness; amenity. **ameno** adj pleasant, delightful.

América [a'merika] sf America. **América del Norte/Sur** North/South America. **América Latina** Latin America. **americano, -a** s, adj American.

ametralladora [ametraʎa'ðora] sf machine gun.

amianto [a'mjanto] sm asbestos.

amígdala [a'migðala] sf tonsil. **amigdalitis** sf tonsillitis.

amigo [a'migo] sm friend; boyfriend. **amiga** sf friend; girlfriend; mistress. **amigo por correspondencia** pen friend. **amigo** adj friendly.

amilanar [amila'nar] v frighten, terrify. **amilanarse** v become terrified.

aminorar [amino'rar] v lessen, reduce. **aminoración** sf lessening.

amistad [amis'taθ] sf friendship. **amistades** sf pl friends pl. **hacer las amistades** make up. **amistar** v reconcile. **amistoso** adj friendly.

amnesia [am'nesja] sf amnesia.

amnistía [amnis'tia] sf amnesty. **amnistiar** v grant an amnesty to.

amo ['amo] sm master; overseer; employer; proprietor; (fam) boss.

amodorrarse [amoðor'rarse] v become drowsy. **amodorrado** adj drowsy.

amohinar [amoi'nar] v irritate; fret. **amohinarse** v become irritated or peevish.

***amolar** [amo'lar] v (cuchillo) grind, sharpen; (fam: fastidiar) annoy.

amoldar [amol'ðar] v mould; fit; shape. **amoldarse** v adapt oneself.

amonestar [amones'tar] *v* warn; advise; admonish; *(anuncio de bodas)* publish the banns of. **amonestación** *sf* warning, admonition. **correr las amonestaciones** publish the banns.

amontonar [amonto'nar] *v* pile up; accumulate **amontonarse** *v* crowd together; heap up; *(fam)* become angry.

amor [a'mor] *sm* love; devotion. **amor interesado** love of money. **amor propio** self-esteem. **amoroso** *adj* affectionate.

amoratar [amora'tar] *v* *(frío)* make purple; *(golpes)* bruise. **amoratado** *adj* purple; black and blue.

amordazar [amorða'θar] *v* gag; *(un perro)* muzzle; *(fig)* gag, silence.

amorfo [a'morfo] *adj* amorphous.

amortiguar [amorti'gwar] *v* *(luz)* dim; *(ruido)* deaden; *(fuego)* damp; *(golpe)* cushion; *(fig)* mitigate. **amortiguación** *sf also* **amortiguamiento** *sm* dimming; deadening; mitigation.

amortiguador [amortigwa'ðor] *sm* *(auto)* shock absorber. *adj* dimming; deadening; mitigating.

amortizar [amorti'θar] *v* amortize; *(una máquina)* depreciate.

amotinar [amoti'nar] *v* incite to revolt; *(fig)* disturb. **amotinarse** *v* mutiny. **amotinado** *adj also* **amotinador** mutinous, rebellious. **amotinamiento** *sm* mutiny.

amparar [ampa'rar] *v* shelter; protect, *(ayudar)* help. **ampararse** *v* seek help *or* protection. **amparo** *sm* aid; protection; refuge.

ampliar [am'pljar] *v* enlarge; lengthen; expand; increase. **amplio** *adj* wide, full; spacious. **amplitud** *sf* width; fullness; spaciousness; extent.

amplificar [amplifi'kar] *v* amplify. **amplificación** *sf* amplification. **amplificador** *sm* amplifier; *adj* amplifying.

ampolla [am'poʎa] *sf* blister; *(redoma)* phial; *(frasco)* flask. **ampollar** *v* blister.

amputar [ampu'tar] *v* amputate. **amputación** *sf* amputation.

amueblar [amwe'βlar] *v* furnish.

amuleto [amu'leto] *sm* amulet.

anacronismo [anakro'nismo] *sm* anachronism.

anales [a'nales] *sm pl* annals *pl*. **analista** *s(m+f)* annalist.

analfabeto [analfa'βeto], **-a** *s, adj* illiterate.

análisis [a'nalisis] *sm invar* analysis. **analista** *s(m+f)* analyst. **analítico** *adj* analytical. **analizar** *v* analyse.

analogía [analo'xia] *sf* analogy. **análogo** *adj* analogous, similar.

ananás [ana'nas] *sm* pineapple.

anaquel [ana'kel] *sm* shelf. **anaquelería** *sf* shelving.

anarquía [anar'kia] *sf* anarchy. **anarquismo** *sm* anarchism. **anarquista** *s(m+f)*, *adj* anarchist.

anatomía [anato'mia] *sf* anatomy. **anatómico** *adj* anatomical.

anca ['anka] *sf* haunch; rump. **ancas** *sf pl* *(fam)* bottom *sing*.

anciano [an'θjano] *adj* old. *sm* old man. **ancianidad** *sf* old age.

ancla ['ankla] *sf* anchor. **anclar** *v also* **echar anclas** anchor.

ancho ['antʃo] *adj* wide, broad; thick; *(fig)* relieved. *sm* width. **a sus anchas** at ease. **anchura** *sf* width; fullness; *(media)* measurement; *(fig: frescura)* cheek.

anchoa [an'tʃoa] *sf* anchovy.

Andalucía [andalu'θia] *sf* Andalusia. **andaluz, -a** *s, adj* Andalusian.

andamio [an'damjo] *sm* scaffold; platform. **andamios** *sm pl* scaffolding *sing*.

*****andar** [an'dar] *v* walk; go; come; *(máquina)* work; *(correr)* run. **¡anda!** go on! **andar en** be engaged in; rummage in. *sm* walk, gait.

andas ['andas] *sf pl* *(para una imagen)* portable platform *sing*; *(féretro)* bier *sing*; *(para enfermo)* stretcher *sing*.

andén [an'den] *sm* station platform; *(de autopista)* hard shoulder.

Andorra [an'dorra] *sf* Andorra. **andorrano, -a** *s, adj* Andorran.

andrajo [an'draxo] *sm* rag. **estar hecho un andrajo** be in rags. **andrajoso** *adj* ragged, tattered.

anécdota [a'nekðota] *sf* anecdote. **anecdótico** *adj* anecdotal.

anegar [ane'gar] *v* flood; drown. **anegación** *sf* drowning; flooding.

anejo [a'nexo] *adj* joined, attached. *sm* annexe.

anemia [a'nemja] *sf* anaemia. **anémico** *adj* anaemic.

anestésico [anes'tesiko] *sm, adj* anaesthetic. **anestesista** *s(m+f)* anaesthetist.

anexar [anek'sar] *v* annex. **anexión** *sf* annexation

anfibio [an'fiβjo] *sm* amphibian. *adj* amphibious.

anfiteatro [anfite'atro] *sm* amphitheatre; (*universidad*) lecture theatre; (*teatro*) gallery.

anfitrión [anfitri'on], **-ona** *sm, sf* host, hostess.

ángel ['anxel] *sm* angel. **tener ángel** be charming. **angelical** *adj also* **angélico** angelic. **angelito** *sm* cherub.

angina [an'xina] *sf* angina.

anglicano [angli'kano], **-a** *s. adj* Anglican.

angosto [an'gosto] *adj* narrow. **angostura** *sf* narrowness.

anguila [an'gila] *sf* eel.

ángulo ['angulo] *sm* angle; bend. **anguloso** *adj* angular.

angustiar [angus'tjar] *v* distress; worry. **angustia** *sf* anguish. **angustiado** *adj* distressed; miserable. **angustioso** *adj* distressing; anguished.

anhelar [ane'lar] *v* pant, gasp; (*desear*) yearn for, crave. **anhelo** *sm* panting; desire.

anidar [ani'ðar] *v* nest; (*fig*) shelter.

anillo [a'niʎo] *sm* ring. **anillo de boda** wedding ring. **anillo de compromiso** *or* **pedida** engagement ring. **anillar** *v* ring.

ánima ['anima] *sf* soul.

animal [ani'mal] *sm* animal, beast. *adj* animal. **animalada** *sf* stupid thing to do *or* say; (*grosería*) bad language.

animar [ani'mar] *v* animate; entertain; encourage; comfort. **animarse** *v* cheer up. **animación** *sf* animation. **animado** *adj* lively. **animador**, **-a** *sm, sf* entertainer; master of ceremonies; *adj* entertaining; encouraging.

ánimo ['animo] *sm* soul; spirit; mind; courage; intention. **¡ánimo!** come on! **animoso** *adj* spirited; courageous.

aniquilar [aniki'lar] *v* annihilate.

anís [a'nis] *sm* aniseed.

aniversario [aniβer'sarjo] *sm* anniversary.

ano ['ano] *sm* anus.

anoche [a'notʃe] *adv* last night.

*****anochecer** [anotʃe'θer] *v* grow dark. *sm* nightfall.

anomalía [anoma'lia] *sf* anomaly. **anómalo** *adj* anomalous.

anónimo [a'nonimo] *adj* anonymous. *sm* anonymous person.

anormal [anor'mal] *adj* abnormal. **anormalidad** *sf* abnormality.

anotar [ano'tar] *v* note, jot down. **anotación** *sf* note.

ansiar [an'sjar] *v* long for. **ansia** *sf* longing; (*pena*) anguish; (*fervor*) eagerness. **ansias** *sf pl* retching *sing*. **ansiedad** *sf* longing; anxiety; eagerness. **ansioso** *adj* anxious; eager; longing.

antagonismo [antago'nismo] *sm* antagonism. **antagonista** *adj* antagonistic. **antagonizar** *v* antagonize.

antaño [an'taɲo] *adv* last year; formerly.

antártico [an'tartiko] *adj* antarctic. *sm* the Antarctic. **Antártica** *sf* Antarctica.

ante¹ ['ante] *prep* before; in the presence of; with regard to. **ante todo** to begin with.

ante² ['ante] *sm* suede.

anteanoche [antea'notʃe] *adv* the night before last.

anteayer [antea'jer] *adv* the day before yesterday.

antecedente [anteθe'ðente] *sm* antecedent. *adj* previous. **antecedencia** *sf* lineage. **anteceder** *v* precede.

antecesor [anteθe'sor], **-a** *sm, sf* predecessor; ancestor. *adj* antecedent.

antelación [antela'θjon] *sf* preference. **con antelación** in advance.

antemano [ante'mano] *adv* **de antemano** beforehand.

antena [an'tena] *sf* (*radio*) aerial; (*insecto*) antenna.

antenatal [antena'tal] *adj* antenatal.

anteojo [ante'oxo] *sm* small telescope. **anteojos** *sm pl* spectacles *pl*.

antepasado [antepa'saðo] *adj* previous. *sm* ancestor.

antepecho [ante'petʃo] *sm* (*de escalera*) handrail; (*de ventana*) window sill.

*****anteponer** [antepo'ner] *v* prefer. **anteponerse** *v* push forward.

anterior [ante'rjor] *adj* preceding, former; front.

antes ['antes] *adv* before, formerly; first; rather. **antes de** before. **antes que** rather than. **cuanto antes** as soon as possible.

antiaéreo [antja'ereo] *adj* anti-aircraft.

antibiótico [anti'bjotiko] *sm, adj* antibiotic.

anticiclón [antiθi'klon] *sm* anticyclone.

anticipar [antiθi'par] *v* anticipate; advance. **anticiparse a** (*con infinitivo*) to ... before. **anticipación** *sf* anticipation. **con anticipación** in advance. **anticipado**

adj early, premature. **anticipo** *sm* advance payment; foretaste.

anticoncepcional [antikonθepθjo'nal] *sm*, *adj* contraceptive. **anticonceptivo** *adj* contraceptive.

anticuado [anti'kwaðo] *adj* out of date; old-fashioned.

anticuario [anti'kwarjo], **-a** *sm*, *sf* antiquarian.

antídoto [an'tiðoto] *sm* antidote.

antieconómico [antieko'nomiko] *adj* uneconomic.

antiguo [an'tigwo] *adj* ancient, antique; senior; former. **de antiguo** of old. **antigualla** *sf* antique; (*persona*) old fogey; (*noticia*) stale news. **antiguamente** *adv* formerly. **antigüedad** *sf* antiquity; seniority.

antílope [an'tilope] *sm* antelope.

Antillas [an'tiʎas] *sf pl* West Indies.

antipatía [antipa'tia] *sf* antipathy; dislike; unfriendliness. **antipático** *adj* disagreeable; unfriendly; nasty.

antisemítico [antise'mitiko] *adj* anti-Semitic. **antisemitismo** *sm* anti-Semitism.

antiséptico [anti'septiko] *sm*, *adj* antiseptic.

antisocial [antiso'θjal] *adj* antisocial.

antítesis [an'titesis] *sf* antithesis.

antojarse [anto'xarse] *v* seem; imagine; fancy; take a fancy to. **antojársele a uno** take it into one's head to.

antojo [an'toxo] *sm* whim; (*lunar*) birthmark. **antojos** *sm pl* craving *sing*. **antojadizo** *adj* capricious.

antología [antolo'xia] *sf* anthology.

antorcha [an'tortʃa] *sf* torch.

antro ['antro] *sm* cave, den; (*fam*: *tasca*) low dive.

antropófago [antro'pofago], **-a** *sm*, *sf* cannibal. *adj* cannibalistic. **antropofagia** *sf* cannibalism.

antropología [antropolo'xia] *sf* anthropology. **antropológico** *adj* anthropological. **antropólogo**, **-a** *sm*, *sf* anthropologist.

anual [a'nwal] *adj* annual. **anualidad** *sf* annuity. **anuario** *sm* yearbook.

anublar [anu'βlar] *v* cloud over, obscure. **anublarse** *v* become cloudy; fade away.

anudar [anu'ðar] *v* knot; join; tie; (*empezar*) begin. **anudarse** become knotted; (*plantas*) wither. **anudadura** *sf* also **anudamiento** *sm* knotting; withering.

anular [anu'lar] *v* (*cheque*) cancel; (*ley*) repeal; (*fig*: *dominar*) overshadow. **anularse** *v* (*fig*: *renunciar*) give up everything. **anulación** *sf* cancellation; abrogation; repeal. **anulador** *adj* repealing.

anunciar [anun'θjar] *v* announce, proclaim; notify; (*hacer publicidad*) advertise; (*predecir*) foretell. **anunciador**, **-a** *sm*, *sf* announcer; advertiser; *adj* announcing; advertising. **anuncio** *sm* announcement; advertisement; omen; sign.

anzuelo [an'θwelo] *sm* fish-hook; (*fig*: *aliciente*) lure.

añadir [apa'ðir] *v* add; increase. **añadido** *sm* addition. **añadidura** *sf* addition; extra. **por añadidura** furthermore, besides.

añejo [a'pexo] *adj* mature; (*carne*) cured; very old.

añicos [a'pikos] *sm pl* pieces, bits. **hacerse añicos** wear oneself out.

añil [a'pil] *sm* indigo plant; indigo dye.

año ['apo] *sm* year. **al año** yearly. **tener ... años** be ... years old. **todos los años** every year.

añorar [apo'rar] *v* long for; be homesick. **añoranza** *sf* homesickness; nostalgia; yearning.

*****apacentar** [apaθen'tar] *v* graze. **apacentadero** *sm* pasture. **apacentador**, **-a** *sm*, *sf* herdsman/woman.

apacible [apa'θiβle] *adj* mild; gentle; peaceful. **apacibilidad** *sf* mildness; peacefulness.

apaciguar [apaθi'gwar] *v* pacify; appease. **apaciguarse** *v* calm down. **apaciguador**, **-a** *sm*, *sf* peace-maker. **apaciguamiento** *sm* pacification; appeasement.

apagar [apa'gar] *v* (*fuego*) extinguish; switch off; muffle; (*sed*) quench; (*dolor*) soothe; (*disturbio*) calm down. **apagado** *adj* extinguished; dull; lifeless; muffled. **apagaincendios** *sm invar* fire-extinguisher.

apalear [apale'ar] *v* beat; (*grano*) thresh; (*maltratar*) thrash. **apaleo** *sm* beating; winnowing; thrashing.

apañar [apa'par] *v* fix; arrange; repair; (*ataviar*) dress up; (*coger*) grab; (*fam*: *robar*) swipe; (*fam*: *preparar*) get ready. **apañado** *adj* handy; dressed up.

aparador [apara'ðor] *sm* sideboard; (*escaparate*) shop window.

aparato [apa'rato] *sm* apparatus; machine; ceremony.

*aparecer [apare'θer] v appear. aparecido sm ghost.

aparejar [apare'xar] v prepare; (caballos) harness, saddle; (cuadro) prime. aparejador sm quantity surveyor. aparejo sm preparation; equipment; harness.

aparentar [aparen'tar] v pretend; feign.

aparente [apa'rente] adj apparent; evident; (adecuado) suitable.

aparición [apari'θjon] sf appearance; (visión) apparition; publication.

apariencia [apari'enθja] sf appearance; aspect; probability.

apartamento [aparta'mento] sm flat.

apartar [apar'tar] v separate; (quitar) remove; (clasificar) sort; (poner a un lado) put aside. apartarse v turn aside; (irse) leave. apartado adj separated; distant; sm paragraph; (habitación) spare room. apartado de correos post-office box. apartamiento sm separation; remoteness. aparte adv apart (from); aside.

apasionar [apasjo'nar] v rouse, stir. apasionarse v become excited. apasionado adj madly in love; passionate; (ardiente) fervent. apasionamiento sm passion.

apatía [apa'tia] sf apathy. apático adj apathetic.

apear [ape'ar] v get down, dismount. apearse v alight, get off.

apedrear [apeðre'ar] v stone. apedrearse v hail. apedreo sm stoning.

apelar [ape'lar] v appeal. apelar a appeal to. apelar de appeal against.

apellido [ape'ʎiðo] sm surname; (apodo) nickname. apellido de soltera maiden name.

apenar [ape'nar] v grieve.

apenas [a'penas] adv scarcely; no sooner than.

apéndice [a'penðiθe] sm appendix; supplement. apendicitis sf appendicitis.

apercibir [aperθi'βir] v prepare; (proveer) equip; (advertir) warn. apercibirse de equip oneself with. apercibimiento sm preparation; advice; (jur) summons.

aperitivo [aperi'tiβo] sm appetizer; aperitif. adj appetizing.

apero [a'pero] sm equipment; tools pl.

apertura [aper'tura] sf opening.

apesadumbrar [apesadum'brar] v grieve, afflict. apesadumbrarse v be upset.

apestar [apes'tar] v infect; (fig) vex; (fam) stink. apestado adj (olor) foul; (que tiene peste) plague-ridden; infested.

*apetecer [apete'θer] v have a hankering for, fancy; (bienvenido) be welcome. apetecible adj desirable, tempting. apetencia sf desire; appetite.

apetito [ape'tito] sm appetite.

apiadarse [apja'ðarse] v have pity on.

ápice ['apiθe] sm apex; jot, iota.

apiñar [api'nar] v squeeze together. apiñarse v crowd, throng. apiñadura sf also apiñamiento sm congestion; throng.

apio ['apjo] sm celery.

apisonadora [apisona'ðora] sf steam roller. apisonar v flatten. apisonamiento sm flattening.

aplacar [apla'kar] v appease; calm. aplacable adj appeasable. aplacamiento sm appeasement. aplacador adj appeasing.

aplanar [apla'nar] v level, flatten; (fam) make dejected. aplanador adj levelling. aplanadora sf leveller. aplanamiento sm levelling, flattening; (fam) dejection.

aplastar [aplas'tar] v crush, flatten.

aplaudir [aplau'ðir] v applaud. aplauso sm applause.

aplazar [apla'θar] v postpone; (convocar) summon. aplazamiento sm postponement; summons.

aplicar [apli'kar] v apply; attach; (recursos, dinero) assign. aplicarse v apply oneself; be applicable. aplicación sf application. aplicado adj studious.

aplomo [a'plomo] sm aplomb, self-confidence. aplomado adj self-assured.

apocar [apo'kar] v lessen; belittle. apocarse v become cowed. apocado adj spineless, timid. apocamiento sm timidity.

apodar [apo'ðar] v nickname. apodo sm nickname.

apoderar [apoðe'rar] v authorize. apoderarse de take possession of. apoderado sm agent; sports manager.

apogeo [apo'xeo] sm climax; summit.

apolillarse [apoli'ʎarse] v become motheaten. apolilladura sf moth-hole.

apoplejía [apople'xia] sf apoplexy. apoplético, -a s, adj apoplectic.

aportar [apor'tar] v bring, contribute; arrive. aportación sf contribution.

aposentar [aposen'tar] v lodge; give lodging to. aposentarse v take lodgings. aposentamiento sm lodging. aposento sm room; lodging.

*apostar [apos'tar] *v* bet. **apostarse** *v* bet; take up one's post. **apostador, -a** *sm, sf* punter.

apóstol [a'postol] *sm* apostle. **apostólico** *adj* apostolic.

apóstrofo [a'postrofo] *sm* (*gram*) apostrophe.

apoyar [apo'jar] *v* support; back up; lean; rest. **apoyar en** lean against. **apoyarse en** lean on. **apoyo** *sm* support.

apreciar [apre'θjar] *v* appreciate; value. **apreciar en mucho** value highly. **apreciable** *adj* appreciable; estimable; (*ruido*) audible. **apreciación** *sf* appreciation; (*valoración*) appraisal. **apreciativo** *adj* appreciative. **aprecio** *sm* appraisal; esteem.

aprehender [apreen'der] *v* seize; understand. **aprehensible** *adj* understandable. **aprehensión** *sf* capture, arrest; understanding.

apremiar [apre'mjar] *v* press, urge; (*obligar*) force; (*dar prisa*) hurry. **apremiador** *adj* urgent. **apremio** *sm* urgency; compulsion.

aprender [apren'der] *v* learn. **aprendiz, -a** *sm, sf* apprentice. **aprendizaje** *sm* apprenticeship.

aprensión [apren'sjon] *sf* apprehension, fear. **aprensivo** *adj* apprehensive.

apresar [apre'sar] *v* seize, arrest. **apresamiento** *sm* seizure.

aprestar [apres'tar] *v* prepare; (*telas*) size. **aprestarse** *v* get ready. **apresto** *sm* preparation.

apresurar [apresu'rar] *v* hurry, quicken. **apresuradamente** *adv* hastily. **apresurado** *adj* hurried. **apresuramiento** *sm* haste.

*apretar [apre'tar] *v* squeeze; grip; tighten; (*botón*) press; (*la mano*) shake; (*dolor*) get worse; (*comprimir*) press down. **apretarse** *v* crowd together; huddle together. **apretado** *adj* tight; (*colchón*) hard; cramped; cluttered; difficult; (*tacaño*) miserly. **apretón** *sm* squeeze; (*fam: aprieto*) tight spot; (*fam: accesidad natural*) call of nature. **aprieto** *sm* awkward situation.

aprisa [a'prisa] *adv* quickly.

aprisionar [aprisjon'ar] *v* imprison.

*aprobar [apro'βar] *v* approve; approve of; (*examen*) pass. **aprobación** *sf* approval; pass. **aprobado** *adj* approved. *sm* pass.

apropiar [apro'pjar] *v* appropriate; adapt.

apropiarse de algo appropriate something. **apropiado** *adj* appropriate, suitable.

aprovechar [aproβe'tʃar] *v* profit by; be useful; make progress. **aprovecharse de** take advantage of. **aprovechado** *adj* thrifty; (*apañado*) resourceful; studious; (*egoísta*) selfish. **aprovechamiento** *sm* profit; exploitation; benefit.

aproximar [aproksi'mar] *v* bring nearer. **aproximarse** *v* approach. **aproximación** *sf* approximation; nearness. **aproximado** *adj* approximate.

aptitud [apti'tuð] *sf* aptitude; capacity. **apto** *adj* apt; suitable.

apuesta [a'pwesta] *sf* bet.

apuesto [a'pwesto] *adj* smart, spruce.

apuntar [apun'tar] *v* (*señalar*) point at; (*arma*) aim; (*sugerir*) point out; (*anotar*) make a note of; (*demostrar*) display; (*sacar punta*) sharpen; (*jugar*) bet; (*teatro*) prompt. **apuntarse** *v* put one's name down; (*fam*) enrol. **apuntado** *adj* pointed. **apunte** *sm* (*nota*) note; (*puesta*) stake; prompter; (*teatro*) cue; (*dibujo*) sketch.

apuñalar [apuɲa'lar] *v* stab.

apurar [apu'rar] *v* purify; (*acabar*) exhaust; (*vaciar*) drain; examine in detail; (*dar prisa*) rush, hurry. **apurarse** *v* (*preocuparse*) worry; hurry up. **apuradamente** *adv* with difficulty; (*ser indigente*) in want; (*fam*) exactly. **apurado** *adj* (*pobre*) hard up; (*agotado*) worn out; (*avergonzado*) embarrassed. **apuro** *sm* (*dificultad*) tight spot; embarrassment.

aquejar [ake'xar] *v* afflict. **aquejoso** *adj* afflicted.

aquel, aquella [a'kel, a'keʎa] *adj* that. **aquellos, aquellas** *pl* those. **aquél, aquélla** *pron* that; the one; the former.

aquí [a'ki] *adv* here. **de aquí en adelante** from now on. **heme aquí** here I am. **por aquí** this way.

aquietar [akje'tar] *v* quieten.

aquilatar [akila'tar] *v* test, examine closely.

Arabia [a'raβja] *sf* Arabia. **árabe** *adj* Arab, Arabian, Arabic; *sm, sf* Arab, Arabian; *sm* (*lengua*) Arabic. **arábico** *adj* also **arábigo** Arabic.

arancel [aran'θel] *sm* tariff, duty.

araña [a'raɲa] *sf* spider; (*luz*) chandelier. **arañar** [ara'ɲar] *v* scratch. **arañada** *sf* scratch. **arañador** *adj* scratching, scraping. **arañazo** *sm* scratch.

arar [a'rar] v plough. **arado** sm plough.

arbitrar [arβi'trar] v arbitrate; referee.
arbitraje sm arbitration. **arbitrario** adj
arbitrary. **árbitro** sm referee, umpire.

arbitrio [ar'βitrjo] sm (voluntad) will;
(recurso) means; (jur) judgment. **arbitrios**
sm pl taxes pl.

árbol ['arβol] sm tree; (tecn) shaft; (palo)
mast. **árbol de Navidad** Christmas tree.
arboleda sf wood, spinney.

arbusto [ar'βusto] sm bush.

arca ['arka] sf box, chest. **arca de agua**
reservoir.

arcada [ar'kaða] sf arcade. **arcadas** sf pl
nausea sing.

arcaico [ar'kaiko] adj archaic. **arcaísmo**
sm archaism.

arce ['arθe] sm maple.

arcilla [ar'θiʎa] sf clay.

arco ['arko] sm arc; arch; (arma, música)
bow. **arco iris** rainbow.

archiduque [artʃi'ðuke] sm archduke.
archiduquesa sf archduchess.

archipiélago [artʃi'pjelago] sm archipelago.

archivo [ar'tʃiβo] sm file; archives pl.
archivador sm filing cabinet. **archivar** v
file. **archivero, -a** sm, sf also **archivista**
s(m+f) archivist.

arder [ar'ðer] v burn; (estiércol) rot; (fig)
seethe. **arderse** v burn up. **ardiente** adj
ardent, burning; feverish.

ardid [ar'ðið] sm trick, ruse.

ardilla [ar'ðiʎa] sf squirrel.

ardor [ar'ðor] sm ardour; (quemazón)
burn; (fig) enthusiasm. **ardorosamente**
adv ardently. **ardoroso** adj burning;
feverish; fervent.

arduo ['arðuo] adj arduous, difficult.

área ['area] sf area.

arena [a'rena] sf sand; (en el circo) arena;
(ruedo) bullring. **arena movediza** quicksand. **arenal** sm stretch of sand. **arenar** v
sand.

arengar [aren'gar] v harangue. **arenga** sf
harangue.

arenque [a'renke] sm herring.

argamasa [arga'masa] sf mortar.
argamasar v mortar.

Argentina [arxen'tina] sf Argentina.
argentino adj (de plata) silvery; Argentinian. **argentino, -a** sm, sf Argentine,
Argentinian.

argolla [ar'goʎa] sf large metal ring;
hoop.

argucia [ar'guθja] sf fallacy; subtlety.

***argüir** [ar'gwir] v (alegar) argue; indi-
cate; demonstrate; (delatar) accuse;
infer.

aria ['arja] sf aria.

argumento [argu'mento] sm argument;
(cuento) plot. **argumentador** adj argumentative.

aridez [ari'ðeθ] sf dryness. **aridecer** v dry
up. **aridecerse** v become dry. **árido** adj
arid. **medida de áridos** sf dry measure.

arisco [a'risko] adj (tímido) shy; (huraño)
unfriendly; (animales) wild.

aristocracia [aristo'kraθja] sf aristocracy.
aristócrata s(m+f) aristocrat. **aristocrático** adj aristocratic.

aritmética [arit'metika] sf arithmetic.
aritmético adj arithmetic, arithmetical.

armada [ar'maða] sf navy, fleet.

armar [ar'mar] v arm; prepare; reinforce;
(proveer) provide; organize. **armarse** v
arm oneself; prepare oneself; (estallar)
break out. **arma** sf weapon. **armado** adj
armed. **armadura** sf armour; framework.
armamento sm armament.

armario [ar'marjo] sm cupboard; (para
ropa) wardrobe.

armazón [arma'θon] sm (anat) skeleton. sf
(conjunto de piezas) framework.

armería [arme'ria] sf gunsmiths; (heráldica) heraldry.

armisticio [armis'tiθjo] sm armistice.

armonía [armo'nia] sf harmony. **armónico**
adj also **armonioso** harmonious.
armónica [ar'monika] sf harmonica.

aro ['aro] sm (argolla) iron ring; (de tonel)
hoop.

aroma [a'roma] sm aroma. **aromático** adj
aromatic, fragrant. **aromatizante** adj
flavouring. **aromatizar** v flavour.

arpa ['arpa] sf harp. **arpista** s(m+f) harpist.

arpón [ar'pon] sm harpoon.

arquear [arke'ar] v arch, curve. **arqueo** sm
arching.

arqueología [arkeolo'xia] sf archaeology.
arqueológico adj archaeological. **arqueólogo** sm archaeologist.

arquero [ar'kero] sm archer; (com) cashier.

arquitectura [arkitek'tura] sf architecture.
arquitecto sm architect.

arrabal [arra'βal] sm suburb. **arrabales** sm
pl outskirts pl.

arraigar [arrai'gar] v take root. **arraigarse** v settle down. **arraigado** adj deep-rooted. **arraigo** sm roots pl; influence.

arrancar [arran'kar] v root up, tear out, force out; (las flemas) expectorate; (suspiro) heave; (agarrar) snatch; (auto) start. **arrancarse** v begin. **arrancada** sf sudden start; jerk. **arrancado** adj uprooted; (fam) broke. **arrancadura** sf pulling; uprooting; (dientes) extraction. **arranque** sm (auto) starting; (carretera) beginning; (energía) burst; origin.

arrasar [arra'sar] v (llenar) fill to the brim; (edificio) demolish; (allanar) level. **arrasarse** v clear up. **arrasadura** sf levelling. **arrasamiento** sm levelling; demolition.

arrastrar [arras'trar] v pull, haul, drag; (viento) blow away; (provocar) give rise to; attract. **arrastrarse** v crawl, creep. **arrastre** sm dragging; haulage. **ser de mucho arrastre** be highly influential.

arrebatar [arreβa'tar] v snatch; (viento) blow away; carry away; (arrancar) rip off; enrage; captivate. **arrebatarse** v get overcooked. **arrebatadamente** adv hurriedly. **arrebatadizo** adj short-tempered. **arrebatamiento** sm seizure; (éxtasis) rapture. **arrebato** sm (furor) rage; rapture.

arrebujarse [arreβu'xarse] v wrap oneself up.

arreciar [arre'θjar] v grow worse or stronger; increase in intensity.

arrecife [arre'θife] sm reef.

arreglar [arre'glar] v organize, regulate; (poner en orden) tidy; (disponer) arrange; (componer) mend; get ready; (rectificar) put right. **arreglarse** v be content; (vestirse) dress; (ponerse de acuerdo) agree; (ir tirando) get by. **arreglado** adj regulated; tidy; (bien vestido) smart; reasonable; (conducta) good. **arreglo** sm agreement; arrangement; repair.

arremeter [arreme'ter] v attack. **arremetida** sf assault.

*__arrendar__ [arren'dar] v let; (alquilar) rent. **arrendador** sm landlord; (que toma en alquiler) tenant. **arrendadora** sf landlady; tenant. **arrendamiento** sm letting; rent.

arreo [ar'reo] sm adornment. **arreos** sm pl harness sing.

*__arrepentirse__ [arrepen'tirse] v repent. **arrepentimiento** sm repentance.

arrestar [arres'tar] v arrest. **arrestarse** v rush boldly. **arrestado** adj imprisoned; (audaz) bold. **arresto** sm arrest; imprisonment. **arrestos** sm pl boldness sing.

arriar [ar'rjar] v (vela, bandera) strike, lower; (cable) slacken. **arriarse** v (inundarse) be flooded.

arriba [ar'riβa] adv up; upstairs; above. **de arriba abajo** from head to foot. ¡**mano arriba**! hands up! **arriba** prep above.

arribar [arri'βar] v arrive. **arribar a** reach. **arribada** sf arrival.

arriendo [ar'rjendo] sm letting; renting; hiring.

arriesgar [arrjes'gar] v risk. **arriesgarse** v take a risk. **arriesgarse en** venture on. **arriesgado** adj dangerous.

arrimar [arri'mar] v (acercar) get near or close; put away. **arrimarse** v draw up; gather together; live together.

arrinconar [arrinko'nar] v corner; (desechar) discard; (fam: vivir solo) live in isolation. **arrinconado** adj (olvidado) forgotten; (abandonado) forsaken.

arroba [ar'roβa] sf weight of 11.5 kg.

arrobar [arro'βar] v entrance. **arrobado** adj in ecstasy. **arrobador** adj bewitching. **arrobamiento** sm also **arrobo** ecstasy, rapture.

arrodillarse [arroðiʎ'Aarse] v kneel. **arrodillamiento** sm kneeling.

arrogancia [arro'ganθja] sf arrogance. **arrogante** adj arrogant.

arrojar [arro'xar] v throw, hurl; emit. **arrojarse** v hurl oneself. **arrojado** adj bold. **arrojo** sm boldness, daring.

arrollar [arro'ʎar] v (enrollar) roll up; (llevarse) sweep away; (atropellar) run over; (aniquilar) crush.

arropar [arro'par] v (abrigarse) wrap up; (en una cama) tuck up; cover.

arrostrar [arros'trar] v face up to, confront.

arroyo [ar'roʎo] sm stream; (calle) gutter.

arroz [ar'roθ] sm rice.

arrugar [arru'gar] v wrinkle; (ropa) crease. **arruga** sf wrinkle; crease.

arruinar [arrui'nar] v ruin; destroy.

arrullar [arru'ʎar] v lull to sleep; (paloma) coo. **arrullo** sm cooing.

arrumbar [arrum'bar] v discard; (fig) ignore.

arrurruz [arrur'ruθ] sm arrowroot.

arsenal [arse'nal] sm arsenal; (astillero) shipyard.

arsénico [ar'seniko] *sm* arsenic.

arte ['arte] *sm*, *sf* art; *(hechura)* workmanship; *(astucia)* cunning. **no tener arte ni parte en** have nothing to do with. **por buenas o malas artes** by fair means or foul.

artefacto [arte'fakto] *sm* device, appliance.

artejo [ar'texo] *sm* knuckle.

arteria [ar'terja] *sf* artery.

artesano [arte'sano] *sm* craftsman. **artesanía** *sf* craftsmanship.

ártico ['artiko] *adj* arctic. **Ártico** *sm* the Arctic. **Círculo Polar Ártico** *sm* Arctic Circle.

articular [artiku'lar] *v* articulate, join together. **articulación** *sf* articulation.

artículo [ar'tikulo] *sm* article; item; *(dictionary)* entry. **artículos** *sm pl* goods *pl*.

artificial [artifi'θjal] *adj* artificial.

artificio [arti'fiθjo] *sm* device; skill; *(truco)* trick.

artillería [artiʎe'ria] *sf* artillery. **artillero** *sm* gunner.

artimaña [arti'maɲa] *sf (trampa)* trap; *(astucia)* trick.

artista [ar'tista] *s(m+f)* artist; actor, actress. **artístico** *adj* artistic.

artritis [ar'tritis] *sf* arthritis.

arzobispo [arθo'βispo] *sm* archbishop.

as [as] *sm* ace.

asa ['asa] *sf* handle.

asado [a'saðo] *sm (culin)* roast (meat). *adj* roast, roasted. **asador** *sm* spit. **asar** *v* roast; *(fam)* pester.

asalariado [asala'rjaðo], **-a** *sm*, *sf* wage-earner. *adj* paid, wage-earning.

asaltar [asal'tar] *v* assault, attack; *(banco)* raid; *(fig: idea)* cross one's mind. **asalto** *sm* attack; *(boxeo)* round.

asamblea [asam'blea] *sf* assembly, meeting.

asbesto [as'βesto] *sm* asbestos.

ascendencia [asθen'ðenθja] *sf* ancestry; origin; *(predominio)* influence.

*ascender [asθen'der] *v* ascend; *(subir a)* add up; *(empleo)* be promoted; promote. **ascendiente** *sm* influence. **ascendientes** *sm pl* ancestors *pl*, ancestry *sing*. **ascension** *sf* ascent; promotion. **ascensor** *sm* lift. **ascensorista** *s(m+f)* lift attendant.

asco ['asko] *sm* disgust, loathing. **dar asco** disgust. **hacer asco** turn one's nose up.

ascua ['askwa] *sf* ember. **estar sobre ascuas** be on tenterhooks.

asear [ase'ar] *v* clean; wash; decorate; *(arreglar)* tidy up. **asearse** *v* have a wash; spruce oneself up. **aseado** *adj* clean; tidy. **aseo** *sm* cleanliness; tidiness.

asechar [ase'tʃar] *v* ambush. **asecho** *sm* trap.

asediar [ase'ðjar] *v* besiege; *(fig)* bother. **asedio** *sm* siege.

asegurar [asegu'rar] *v* secure; safeguard; *(consolidar)* strengthen; *(confortar)* reassure; insure; assure. **asegurarse** *v* make sure. **asegurado** *adj* insured; assured. **asegurador** *sm* underwriter. **aseguramiento** *sm* securing; insurance; assurance.

asemejarse [aseme'xarse] *v* resemble, be alike.

*asentar [asen'tar] *v* place; seat; *(cimientos)* lay; *(polvo)* settle; *(campamento)* pitch; *(establecer)* found; *(afilar)* sharpen; *(convenir)* agree; *(acalmar)* calm down; *(ir bien)* be suitable. **asentarse** *v* sit down; settle down.

*asentir [asen'tir] *v* agree, assent. **asentimiento** *sm* assent.

asequible [ase'kiβle] *adj* reasonable; *(alcanzable)* obtainable; affable.

*aserrar [aser'rar] *v* saw. **aserradero** *sm* sawmill. **aserrado** *adj* serrated. **aserrín** *sm* sawdust.

aserto [a'serto] *sm* assertion.

asesinar [asesi'nar] *v* murder; assassinate. **asesinato** *sm* murder; assassination. **asesino** *adj* murderous.

asesorar [aseso'rar] *v* advise; take advice. **asesoramiento** *sm* advising; opinion.

asestar [ases'tar] *v (arma)* aim; *(golpe)* strike. **asestadura** *sf* aiming.

asfalto [as'falto] *sm* asphalt. **asfaltado** *adj* covered with asphalt. **asfaltar** *v* asphalt.

asfixiar [asfik'sjar] *v* suffocate. **asfixia** *sf* suffocation.

así [a'si] *adv* so, thus, in this way, in that way. **así así** so-so. **así como** just as; as well as. **así que** as soon as; therefore. **así sea** so be it.

Asia ['asja] *sf* Asia. **asiático, -a** *s, adj* Asiatic, Asian.

asidero [asi'ðero] *sm* handle; *(fig)* excuse.

asiduo [a'siðwo] *adj* assiduous, hard-working; frequent.

asiento [a'sjento] *sm* seat, chair; place; *(de botellas, etc.)* base, bottom; *(tratado)* treaty; note; stability; *(sentido común)* common sense. **asientos** *sm pl* seat *sing*.

bottom *sing.* **asiento de estómago** attack of indigestion. **tomar asiento** sit down.

asignar [asig'nar] *v* assign; attribute; allocate. **asignación** *sf* (*atribución*) allocation; (*cita*) appointment; (*subsidio*) grant; (*sueldo*) wages.

asignatura [asigna'tura] *sf* (scholastic) subject.

asilo [a'silo] *sm* asylum; refuge; home; shelter.

asimilar [asimi'lar] *v* assimilate; compare. **asimilarse** *v* be assimilated; (*asemejarse*) resemble. **asimilación** *sf* assimilation; comparison.

asimismo [asi'mismo] *adv* in like manner, in the same way.

asir [a'sir] *v* grasp; grip; (*plantas*) take root. **asirse de** hang on to.

asistir [asis'tir] *v* help; attend; be present; (*testigo*) witness. **asistencia** *sf* assistance; attendance; (*teatro, etc.*) audience; (*muchedumbre*) crowd; (*médica*) care; presence. **asistencias** *sf pl* maintenance *sing.* **asistenta** *sf* charlady; (*hotel*) chambermaid. **asistente** *sm* assistant; (*mil*) orderly; member of an audience.

asma ['asma] *sf* asthma.

asno ['asno] *sm* donkey, ass; (*fig*) idiot.

asociar [aso'θjar] *v* associate; (*com*) enter into partnership. **asociarse** *v* associate oneself; share. **asociación** *sf* association; (*com*) partnership. **asociado** *sm* member.

asolar [aso'lar] *v* destroy; (*arrasar*) flatten; (*calor*) parch. **asolador** *adj* devastating. **asolamiento** *sm* devastation.

asolear [asole'ar] *v* put in the sun. **asolearse** *v* sunbathe.

asomar [aso'mar] *v* show, appear. **asomarse** *v* lean out; (*fam: archisparse*) become tipsy. **asomada** *sf* brief appearance. **asomo** *sm* appearance; (*sombra*) shadow; (*indicio*) hint.

asombrar [asom'brar] *v* astonish; (*dar sombra*) shade; (*color*) darken. **asombrador** *adj* astonishing. **asombramiento** *sm also* **asombro** *sm* astonishment; (*fam: aparecido*) ghost. **asombroso** *adj* astonishing; stupefying.

aspecto [as'pekto] *sm* aspect; appearance. **áspero** [as'pero] *adj* (*tosco*) rough; (*agrio*) sour; (*persona*) gruff; (*voz*) harsh; (*clima*) hard; (*terreno*) rugged. **aspereza** *sf* roughness; sourness; harshness.

aspersión [asper'sjon] *sf* sprinkling; spraying. **asperjar** *v* sprinkle.

aspirar [aspi'rar] *v* inhale; (*fig*) aspire. **aspiración** *sf* inhalation; aspiration. **aspiradora** *sf* vacuum cleaner.

aspirina [aspi'rina] *sf* aspirin.

asqueroso [aske'roso] *adj* disgusting; vile; dirty; repulsive. **asquerosidad** *sf* filth; obscenity.

asta ['asta] *sf* (*arma*) spear; (*palo*) shaft; (*de la bandera*) staff; (*cuerno*) horn. **a media asta** at half mast.

asterisco [aste'risko] *sm* asterisk.

astil [as'til] *sm* handle; (*pluma*) quill.

astillar [asti'ʎar] *v* splinter; smash. **astillero** [asti'ʎero] *sm* shipyard.

astringir [astrin'xir] *v* constrict; (*sujetar*) blind. **astringente** *sm, adj* astringent.

astro ['astro] *sm* star.

astrología [astrolo'xia] *sf* astrology. **astrólogo** *sm* astrologer.

astronauta [astro'nauta] *s(m+f)* astronaut. **astronáutica** *sf* astronautics.

astronomía [astrono'mia] *sf* astronomy. **astronómico** *adj* astronomical. **astrónomo** *sm* astronomer.

astucia [as'tuθja] *sf* (*habilidad*) cleverness; (*ingenio*) cunning. **astuto** *adj* clever; cunning.

asumir [asu'mir] *v* assume.

asunto [a'sunto] *sm* (*tema*) subject; (*cosa*) affair; (*negocio*) business; (*caso*) fact; (*cuestión*) matter. **asuntos a tratar** *pl* agenda *sing.* **asuntos exteriores** foreign affairs.

asustar [asus'tar] *v* frighten.

atacar [ata'kar] *v* attack; (*recalcar*) stuff; (*un botón*) fasten. **atacador, -a** *sm, sf* assailant. **ataque** *sm* attack; (*med*) fit. **ataque cardíaco** heart attack. **ataque fulminante** (*med*) stroke.

atado [a'tado] *sm* bundle. *adj* shy.

atajar [ata'xar] *v* intercept; (*detener*) check; (*impedir*) obstruct; (*tomar el camino más corto*) take a short cut. **atajador, -a** *sm, sf* interceptor. **atajo** *sm* short cut.

atar [a'tar] *v* tie; lace; bind. **loco de atar** raving mad. **atarse** *v* become confused. **atador** *adj* binding. **atadura** *sf* binding; (*cuerda*) rope; (*fig: vínculo*) bond.

atardecer [atarðe'θer] *v* get late; grow dark. *sm* dusk.

atareado [atare'aðo] *adj* very busy. **atarear** *v* load with work.

atascar [atas'kar] *v* plug, stop (a leak); obstruct. **atascadero** *sm* mire; (*fig*) stumbling-block. **atasco** *sm* obstruction.

ataúd [ata'uð] *sm* coffin.

ataviar [ata'βjar] *v* dress up, adorn. **ataviarse en** *or* **de dress** oneself up in. **atavío** *sm* attire.

ateísmo [ate'ismo] *sm* atheism. **ateísta** *s*(*m*+*f*) atheist. **ateo, -a** *sm*, *sf* atheist.

atemorizar [atemori'θar] *v* frighten.

atención [aten'θjon] *sf* attention; courtesy; interest; (*cariño*) kindness. **prestar atención** pay attention. **atenciones** *sf pl* business affairs. **atento** *adj* attentive; kind; careful; special; (*consciente*) aware.

*atender [aten'der] *v* attend to; (*cuidar*) look after; serve; (*una máquina*) service; (*un aviso*) listen to.

*atenerse [ate'nerse] *v* abide, adhere; (*a una persona*) rely on.

atentar [aten'tar] *v* attempt; offend.

atenuar [ate'nwar] *v* attenuate; lessen; (*la luz*) dim. **atenuación** *sf* attenuation.

*aterrar¹ [ater'rar] *v* demolish.

aterrar² [ater'rar] *v* frighten, terrify. **aterrador** *adj* terrifying.

aterrizar [aterri'θar] *v* (*aviac*) land. **aterrizaje** *sm* landing.

aterrorizar [aterrori'θar] *v* terrify; terrorize. **aterrorizador** *adj* terrifying.

atesorar [ateso'rar] *v* hoard; (*fig*) possess. **atesoramiento** *sm* hoarding.

*atestar [ates'tar] *v* (*llenar*) stuff; (*un tren*) crowd, pack; (*desordenar*) clutter up. **atestado** *adj* full up; packed.

atestiguar [atesti'gwar] *v* testify.

ático ['atiko] *sm* attic.

atisbar [atis'βar] *v* (*mirar*) spy on; (*vislumbrar*) distinguish; (*vigilar*) watch for. **atisbo** *sm* spying; (*fig*) hint.

atizar [ati'θar] *v* (*el fuego*) poke, stir; (*fig*) stir up, incite. **atizador** *sm* poker.

Atlántico [at'lantiko] *sm* Atlantic. **atlántico** *adj* Atlantic.

atlas ['atlas] *sm* atlas.

atleta [at'leta] *s*(*m*+*f*) athlete. **atlético** *adj* athletic. **atletismo** *sm* athletics.

atmósfera [at'mosfera] *sf* atmosphere. **mala atmósfera** atmospherics *pl*. **atmosférico** *adj* atmospheric.

atolondrar [atolon'drar] *v* confuse; (*aturdir*) stun. **atolondrarse** *v* lose one's head. **atolondradamente** *adv* recklessly. **atolondramiento** *sm* recklessness; confusion.

atolladero [atoʎa'ðero] *sm* bog; (*fig*) impasse. **atollarse** *v* get bogged down.

átomo ['atomo] *sm* atom. **atómico** *adj* atomic.

atónito [a'tonito] *adj* astonished.

atontar [aton'tar] *v* (*golpe*) stun, daze; (*dejar sin habla*) dumbfound; (*embrutecer*) deaden; (*drogas*) make stupid. **atontado** *adj* stunned; bewildered; dumbfounded; stupid.

atormentar [atormen'tar] *v* torment; torture. **atormentador** *sm* tormentor; torturer.

atornillar [atorni'ʎar] *v* screw in/on/down.

atosigar [atosi'gar] *v* poison; (*molestar*) pester. **atosigarse** *v* toil. **atosigador** *adj* poisoning; pestering. **atosigamiento** *sm* poisoning; pestering.

atracar [atra'kar] *v* (*robar*) hold up; moor; (*fam*) gorge. **atracarse** *v* gorge oneself. **atracada** *sf* docking; (*pelea*) scuffle. **atracador** *sm* bandit.

atracción [atrak'θjon] *sf* attraction. **atracciones** *sf pl* entertainment *sing*. **atractivo** *adj* attractive.

*atraer [atra'er] *v* attract. **atracción** *sf* attraction. **atracciones** *sf pl* entertainment *sing*.

atrancar [atran'kar] *v* (*puerta*) bar; block up. **atrancarse** *v* become blocked/stuck/jammed.

atrapar [atra'par] *v* catch, trap.

atrás [a'tras] *adv* behind; in the rear; back; backwards; previously. **¡atrás!** get back! **atrasado** *adj* late; behind; in arrears; (*reloj*) slow; backward; in debt. **atrasar** *v* (*diferir*) postpone; put back; slow down; lose (time). **atrasarse** lag behind; be late; be slow. **atraso** *sm* delay; backwardness; slowness.

*atravesar [atraβe'sar] *v* (*poner*) place *or* put across; (*traspasar*) pierce; penetrate; cross; (*apostar*) bet. **atravesarse** *v* stand *or* lie across; get stuck; interfere; quarrel. **atravesado** *adj* lying across; pierced; (*fig*) wicked.

atreverse [atre'βerse] *v* dare; venture; be insolent. **atrevido, -a** *sm*, *sf* daredevil; cheeky person. **atrevimiento** *sm* boldness; effrontery.

*atribuir [atriβu'ir] *v* attribute. **atribución** *sf* attribution. **atributo** *sm* attribute.

atrocidad [atroθi'ðað] *sf* atrocity. **atroz** *adj* atrocious. **atrozmente** *adv* atrociously.

atrófia [a'trofja] *sf* atrophy. **atrofiar** *v* atrophy.

atropellar [atrope'ʎar] *v* knock down; *(pisotear)* trample on; *(ultrajar)* offend; *(agraviar)* bully; *(trabajo)* rush. **atropellar por** ignore. **atropellarse** *v* hurry. **atropelladamente** *adv* hurriedly. **atropellado** *adj* hasty. **atropellador** *adj* precipitate. **atropello** *sm* jostling, pushing; accident; outrage.

atún [a'tun] *sm* tunny, tuna.

aturdir [atur'ðir] *v* stun, daze; *(marear)* make dizzy; bewilder. **aturdido** *adj* dazed; *(imprudente)* thoughtless. **aturdidor** *adj* deafening. **aturdimiento** *sm* daze; giddiness; amazement.

aturrullar [aturru'ʎar] *v* confuse, bewilder. **aturrullarse** *v* become confused; panic.

atusar [atu'sar] *v* *(cortar)* trim; *(alisar)* smooth; *(acariciar)* stroke. **atusarse** *v* spruce oneself up.

audacia [au'ðaθja] *sf* audacity. **audaz** *adj* audacious.

audible [au'ðiβle] *adj* audible. **audibilidad** *sf* audibility.

audición [auði'θjon] *sf* hearing; *(prueba)* audition.

audiencia [au'ðjenθja] *sf* audience; hearing; *(tribunal)* court.

audífono [au'ðifono] *sm* hearing aid.

audiovisual [auðjoβi'swal] *adj* audiovisual.

auge ['auxe] *sm* peak; progress.

augurar [augu'rar] *v* predict. **augurio** *sm* augury, omen.

aula ['aula] *sf* lecture hall; *(escuela)* classroom. **aula magna** assembly hall.

aullar [au'ʎar] *v* howl. **aullido** *sm* howl.

aumentar [aumen'tar] *v* increase; *(sueldo)* raise; magnify; *(mejorar)* get better; *(empeorar)* get worse. **aumento** *sm* increase; rise; magnification.

aun [a'un] *adv* even. **aun así** even so. **aun cuando** although. **aún** *adv* still, yet. **aún no** not yet.

aunque [a'unke] *conj* even though, although.

áureo ['aureo] *adj* gold(en).

aureola [aure'ola] *sf* halo.

auricular [auriku'lar] *adj* of the ear, aural.

sm *(dedo)* little finger; *(teléfono)* telephone receiver. **auriculares** *sm pl* headphones *pl*.

aurora [au'rora] *sf* dawn.

ausencia [au'senθja] *sf* absence. **ausente** *adj* absent; missing.

auspicio [aus'piθjo] *sm* auspice, omen; *(patrocinio)* patronage.

austero [aus'tero] *adj* austere. **austeridad** *sf* austerity.

austral [aus'tral] *adj* southern.

Australia [aus'tralja] *sf* Australia. **australiano, -a** *s, adj* Australian.

Austria ['austrja] *sf* Austria. **austriaco, -a** *s, adj* Austrian.

auténtico [au'tentiko] *adj* authentic. **autenticar** *v* authenticate. **autenticidad** *sf* authenticity.

autístico [au'tistiko] *adj* autistic.

auto¹ ['auto] *sm* *(fam)* car. **auto de choque** dodgem car.

auto² *sm* *(jur)* sentence; *(de un pleito)* judgment. **autos** *sm pl* proceedings *pl*.

autobiografía [autoβjogra'fia] *sf* autobiography. **autobiográfico** *adj* autobiographical.

autobús [auto'βus] *sm* bus.

autocar [auto'kar] *sm* motor coach.

autodominio [autoðo'minjo] *sm* self-control.

autoescuela [autoes'kwela] *sf* driving school.

autoexpresión [autoekspre'sjon] *sf* self-expression.

autógrafo [au'tografo] *sm, adj* autograph.

automata [au'tomata] *sm* robot.

automático [auto'matiko] *adj* automatic. **automización** *sf* automation.

automóvil [auto'moβil] *sm* motorcar. **automovilista** *s(m+f)* motorist.

autonomía [autono'mia] *sf* autonomy. **autónomo** *adj* autonomous.

autopista [auto'pista] *sf* motorway.

autopsia [au'topsja] *sf* autopsy, post-mortem.

autor [au'tor], **-a** *sm, sf* author; creator.

autorizar [autori'θar] *v* authorize; approve. **autoridad** *sf* authority. **autoritario** *adj* authoritarian. **autorización** *sf* authorization. **autorizado** *adj* authorized, official; *(seguro)* reliable.

autorretrato [autorre'trato] *sm* self-portrait.

autoservicio [autoser'βiθjo] *sm* self-service restaurant; supermarket.

autostop [auto'stop] *sm* hitchhiking.
hacer el autostop hitchhike. **autostopista**
s(m+f) hitchhiker.
auxiliar [auksi'ljar] *v* help; attend. *sm, adj*
assistant; auxiliary.
avalancha [aβa'lantʃa] *sf* avalanche.
avalorar [aβalo'rar] *v* (*realzar*) enhance;
(*fig*) inspire.
avaluar [aβalu'ar] *v* value, appraise.
avanzar [aβan'θar] *v* advance, progress.
avance *sm* advance; (*com*) balance.
avanzada *sf* (*mil*) outpost.
avaricia [aβa'riθja] *sf* avarice. **avaricioso**
adj greedy; miserly. **avaro** *adj* miserly,
mean.
avasallar [aβasa'ʎar] *v* subjugate; dominate. **avasallarse** *v* submit.
ave ['aβe] *sf* bird. **aves de corral** *pl* poultry *sing*.
avecinarse [aβeθi'narse] *v* approach.
avellana [aβe'ʎana] *sf* hazelnut.
avena [a'βena] *sf sing* oats *pl*.
avenencia [aβe'nenθja] *sf* agreement;
(*arreglo*) compromise.
avenida [aβe'niða] *sf* avenue.
***avenir** [aβe'nir] *v* reconcile, bring
together; (*suceder*) happen. **avenirse** *v*
agree; adapt; correspond to. **avenimiento**
sm agreement.
aventajar [aβenta'xar] *v* lead; come in
front of; (*sobresalir*) surpass; prefer.
aventajado *adj* outstanding; favourable.
aventura [aβen'tura] *sf* adventure; (*riesgo*) risk; (*amor*) affair. **aventurado** *adj*
risky. **aventurar** *v* risk; venture. **aventurero** *adj* adventurous.
***avergonzar** [aβergon'θar] *v* shame;
(*poner en un apuro*) embarrass.
avergonzarse *v* be ashamed. **avergonzado**
adj ashamed; embarrassed.
avería¹ [aβe'ria] *sf* aviary.
avería² [aβe'ria] *sf* (*coche*) breakdown;
(*daño*) damage. **averiar** *v* damage; break
down.
averiguar [aβeri'gwar] *v* investigate;
(*examinar*) verify. **averiguación** *sf* investigation; verification. **averiguador** *adj*
investigating; inquiring.
aversión [aβer'sjon] *sf* aversion.
avestruz [aβes'truθ] *sm* ostrich.
aviación [aβja'θjon] *sf* aviation; air force.
aviador, -a *sm, sf* aviator.
ávido ['aβiðo] avid; (*con ganas*) eager.
avidez *sf* avidity; eagerness.

avinagrar [aβina'grar] *v* sour, make bitter.
avinagrado *adj* sour; (*fam*) peevish.
avión¹ [a'βjon] *sm* aircraft. **avión a reacción** jet plane. **por avión** by airmail.
avión² *sm* swift; martin.
avisar [aβi'sar] *v* inform; advise; admonish. **avisado** *adj* prudent. **mal avisado**
rash. **avisador**, -a *sm, sf* adviser; informer; messenger. **aviso** *sm* notice;
announcement; advice; (*advertencia*)
warning; prudence.
avispa [a'βispa] *sf* wasp.
avivar [aβi'βar] *v* enliven; (*acelerar*) hast-
en; revive. **avivador** *adj* hastening; enliv-
ening.
ay ['ai] *interj* alas!
aya ['aja] *sf* governess!
ayer [a'jer] *adv* yesterday; (*fig*) formerly,
lately. *sm* the recent past. **de ayer acá**
since yesterday.
ayo ['ajo] *sm* tutor.
ayudar [aju'ðar] *v* help. **ayudarse** *v* help
each other; make use of. **ayuda** *sf* help.
ayudante, -a *sm, sf* assistant.
ayunar [aju'nar] *v* fast. **ayuno** *sm* fast,
fasting.
ayuntamiento [ajunta'mjento] *sm* union;
joint; (*cópula*) copulation; (*institución*)
town council; (*edificio*) town hall.
azada [a'θaða] *sf* hoe; spade.
azafata [aθa'fata] *sf* air hostess.
azafrán [aθa'fran] *sm* saffron.
azahar [aθa'ar] *sm* orange blossom; lemon blossom.
azar [a'θar] *sm* chance, accident;
(*desgracia*) misfortune. **al azar** at random.
azogue [a'θoge] *sm* mercury.
azorar [aθo'rar] *v* upset, embarrass.
azorarse *v* become flustered. **azoramiento**
sm embarrassment; (*miedo*) fear.
azotar [aθo'tar] *v* beat; (*a un niño*) spank;
(*látigo*) whip. **azote** *sm* whip; spanking;
(*fig: verdugo*) scourge.
azotea [aθo'tea] *sf* flat roof.
azúcar [a'θukar] *sm or sf* sugar. **azúcar en
terrón** lump sugar. **azúcar extra fina** cast-
or sugar. **azúcar morena** brown sugar.
azucarado *adj* sugary. **azucarero**, -a *sm, sf*
sugar bowl.
azucena [aθu'θena] *sf* white lily.
azufre [a'θufre] *sm* sulphur.
azul [a'θul] *sm, adj* blue. **azul marino** navy
blue. **azulado** *adj* blue, bluish.

azulejo [aθu'lexo] *sm* tile.
azuzar [aθu'θar] *v* (*fig*) incite; urge; cause trouble. azuzador, -a *sm. sf* trouble-maker.

B

baba ['baβa] *sf* saliva. spit. babero *sm* bib.
Babia ['baβja] *sf* estar en Babia have one's head in the clouds.
babor [ba'βor] *sm* (*mar*) port side.
babosa [ba'βosa] *sf* slug.
bacalao [baka'lao] *sm* cod.
bacía [ba'θia] *sf* (*de barbero*) shaving-bowl; (*recipiente*) metal basin.
bacteria [bak'teria] *sf* germ. bacterias *sf pl* bacteria *pl*.
bache ['batʃe] *sm* pothole.
bachiller [batʃi'ʎer] *s*(*m*+*f*) holder of a school-leaving certificate; (*universidad*) holder of a bachelor's degree. bachillerato *sm* school-leaving certificate; bachelor's degree.
bagaje [ba'gaxe] *sm* (*mil*) baggage; (*animal*) beast of burden.
bahía [ba'ia] *sf* bay.
bailar [bai'lar] *v* dance. bailarín, -ina *sm. sf* ballet dancer. baile *sm* dancing; dance; ball. baile de disfraces *or* trajes fancy-dress ball.
bajamar [baxa'mar] *sf* low tide.
bajar [ba'xar] *v* get down; lower; let down; take *or* bring down. baja *sf* fall. drop. bajada *sf* (*caída*) drop; (*pendiente*) slope; (*descendimiento*) descent.
bajo ['baxo] *adj* (*estatura*) short; low; lowered; (*sonido*) soft; (*conducta*) disgraceful. *adv* low; below; quietly, softly. *prep* under. bajeza *sf* base act; lowness.
bajón [ba'xon] *sm* (*música*) bassoon; (*bajada*) fall.
bala ['bala] *sf* (*proyectil*) bullet; (*algodón*) bale. balazo *sm* (*tiro*) shot; (*herida*) wound.
balada [ba'laða] *sf* ballad.
baladí [bala'ði] *adj* trivial, unimportant.
baladrón [bala'ðron], -ona *sm. sf* boaster. braggart. *adj* boastful.
balancear [balanθe'ar] *v* balance; (*barco*)

roll; (*vacilar*) hesitate. balancearse *v* roll; (*en un columpio*) swing. balance *sm* (*com*) balance sheet; (*inventario*) stocktaking. balanceo *sm* balancing; (*oscilación*) swaying. balanza *sf* scales *pl*.
balar [ba'lar] *v* bleat.
balaustrada [balau'straða] *sf* balustrade.
balbucear [balβuθe'ar] *v* stammer, stutter. balbuceo *sm* stammer.
balcón [bal'kon] *sm* balcony.
baldar [bal'ðar] *v* cripple; (*naipes*) trump; (*molestar*) inconvenience. baldarse *v* wear oneself out. baldado, -a *sm. sf* cripple. baldadura *sf* infirmity.
balde[1] [bal'ðe] *sm* bucket.
balde[2] *adv* de balde free of charge. en balde in vain.
baldío [bal'ðio] *sm* wasteland. *adj* uncultivated; (*fig*) useless.
baldón [bal'ðon] *sm* (*afrenta*) affront; (*deshonra*) disgrace.
baldosa [bal'ðosa] *sf* paving tile.
balneario [balne'arjo] *sm* spa.
balón [ba'lon] *sm* ball, football; (*com*) bale. baloncesto *sm* basketball. balonvolea *sm* volleyball.
balsa[1] ['balsa] *sf* balsa.
balsa[2] *sf* raft.
balsa[3] *sf* (*agua*) pond.
bálsamo ['balsamo] *sm* balsam; (*fig*) balm.
Báltico ['baltiko] *sm* Baltic Sea. báltico *adj* Baltic.
ballena [ba'ʎena] *sf* whale.
ballesta [ba'ʎesta] *sf* crossbow. ballestero *sm* archer.
ballet [ba'le] *sm* ballet.
bambolear [bambole'ar] *v* sway.
bambolla [bam'boʎa] *sf* show, ostentation. darse bambolla show off.
bambú [bam'bu] *sm* bamboo.
banana [ba'nana] *sf* banana. banano *sm* banana tree.
banasta [ba'nasta] *sf* large basket.
banca ['banka] *sf* (*asiento*) bench; (*com*) banking.
bancarrota [bankar'rota] *sf* bankruptcy. hacer bancarrota go bankrupt.
banco ['banko] *sm* bench; (*iglesia*) pew; (*colegio*) desk; (*com*) bank.
banda ['banda] *sf* group; (*pandilla*) gang; (*faja*) sash; (*cinta*) ribbon; (*lado*) side; (*orilla*) river bank. bandada *sf* flock.
bandeja [ban'dexa] *sf* tray.

bandera [ban'dera] *sf* flag, banner. **a banderas desplegadas** openly. **banderilla** *sf* bullfighter's dart. **banderillero** *sm* one who thrusts banderillas into the bull.

bandido [ban'diðo] *sm* bandit.

bando ['bando] *sm* proclamation; (*facción*) faction; party; (*pez*) shoal (of fish).

bandolero [bando'lero], -a *sm, sf* bandit.

banjo ['banxo] *sm* banjo.

banquete [ban'kete] *sm* banquet, feast.

bañar [ba'par] *v* bathe. **bañarse** *v* (*en la bañera*) have a bath; (*en el mar*) bathe. **bañera** *sf* bathtub. **bañero** *sm* lifeguard. **bañista** *s(m+f)* bather. **baño** *sm* bath; (*en el agua*) dip, swim; (*cubierta*) coating. **cuarto de baño** bathroom.

baquetear [bakete'ar] *v* (*incomodar*) bother; (*maltratar*) treat harshly. **baquetazo** *sm* blow, knock. **baqueteo** *sm* (*traqueteo*) jolting; (*molestia*) bother.

bar [bar] *sm* bar.

baraja [ba'raxa] *sf* pack of cards. **barajar** *v* (*confusión*) shuffle.

barandilla [baran'diʎa] *sf* rail, railing.

barato [ba'rato] *adj* cheap. **dar de barato** take for granted. **baratear** *v* undersell. **baratija** *sf* trinket. **baratijas** *sf pl* junk *sing*. **baratura** *sf* cheapness.

baraúnda [bara'unda] *sf* (*alboroto*) uproar; (*confusión*) chaos.

barba ['barβa] *sf* beard. **barba a barba** face to face. **barbado** *adj* bearded. **barbería** *sf* barber's shop. **barbero** *sm* barber. **barbudo** *adj* having a full beard.

bárbaro ['barβaro], -a *sm, sf* barbarian; (*fig*) lout. *adj* barbarous, barbaric; (*bruto*) rough; (*fam*) fantastic. **barbaridad** *sf* barbarity; (*ultraje*) outrage. **¡qué barbaridad!** fancy that! how terrible!

barbecho [bar'βetʃo] *sm* fallow land. **barbechar** *v* leave fallow.

barbilla [bar'βiʎa] *sf* chin.

barca ['barka] *sf* boat. **barca de pasaje** ferry boat.

barco ['barko] *sm* ship, boat. **ir en barco** go by boat.

barnizar [barni'θar] *v* (*madera*) varnish; (*cerámica*) glaze. **barniz** *sm* varnish; glaze.

barómetro [ba'rometro] *sm* barometer. **barométrico** *adj* barometric.

barón [ba'ron] *sm* baron. **baronesa** *sf* baroness. **baronet** *sm* baronet.

barquillo [bar'kiʎo] *sm* thin sweet wafer.

barra ['barra] *sf* (*metal, madera, chocolate, jabón, etc.*) bar; (*vara*) rod; (*joya*) pin; (*palanca*) lever; (*pan*) loaf; (*jur*) dock; (*mar*) tiller.

barraca [bar'raka] *sf* cabin, hut; (*feria*) stall.

barranco [bar'ranko] *sm* ravine, gully; (*fig*) obstacle.

barrenar [barre'nar] *v* drill, bore; (*leyes*) violate; (*una empresa*) foil. **barrena** *sf* drill.

barrer [bar'rer] *v* sweep.

barrera [bar'rera] *sf* barrier; obstacle; gate. **barrera de peaje** tollgate.

barricada [barri'kada] *sf* barricade.

barriga [bar'riga] *sf* belly.

barril [bar'ril] *sm* barrel.

barrio ['barrjo] *sm* district, quarter.

barro ['barro] *sm* mud. **barroso** *adj* muddy.

barroco [bar'roko] *sm* baroque period. *adj* baroque.

barruntar [barrun'tar] *v* have a feeling; (*suponer*) suppose. **barruntador** *adj* prophetic. **barrunte** *or* **barrunto** *sm* feeling; supposition; (*indicio*) sign.

bártulos ['bartulos] *sm pl* belongings, odds and ends. **liar los bártulos** pack one's bags.

barullo [ba'ruʎo] *sm* confusion; (*alboroto*) row. **a barullo** galore.

basar [ba'sar] *v* found; base. **basarse en** be based on. **base** *sf* base, basis. **a base de** by. **alimento base** staple food. **básico** *adj* basic, essential.

bastante [bas'tante] *adj* enough. *adv* enough, sufficiently; (*algo*) rather, fairly. **bastar** *v* suffice. **¡basta!** that's enough!

bastardo [bas'tardo], -a *s, adj* bastard. **bastardear** *v* degenerate. **bastardilla** *sf* italics *pl*. **bastardillo** *adj* italic.

bastidor [basti'ðor] *sm* frame; (*ventana*) sash. **entre bastidores** behind the scenes.

basto[1] ['basto] *adj* coarse, crude.

basto[2] *sm* (*arnés*) pack-saddle.

basto[3] *sm* (*naipes*) ace of clubs. **bastos** *pl* clubs.

bastón [bas'ton] *sm* cane, stick.

basura [ba'sura] *sf* rubbish, litter. **basurero** *sm* dustman.

bata ['bata] *sm* (*de cama*) dressing gown; (*de médico, etc.*) overall.

batalla [ba'taʎa] *sf* battle. **campo de batalla** battlefield.

batata [ba'tata] *sf* sweet potato.

batea [ba'tea] *sf* (*barco*) punt; (*bandeja*) tray; (*vagón*) open wagon.

batería [bate'ria] *sf* battery; (*teatro*) footlights; (*música*) percussion. **batería de cocina** kitchen utensils *pl*.

batir [ba'tir] *v* (*huevos*) beat; (*las manos*) clap; (*vencer*) defeat; (*derribar*) knock down; (*culin*) whisk. **batirse** *v* fight. **batido** *sm* (*leche*) milk shake; (*culin*) batter. **batidor** *sm* whisk.

batuta [ba'tuta] *sf* (*música*) baton. **llevar la batuta** rule the roost.

baúl [ba'ul] *sm* trunk.

bautizar [bauti'θar] *v* baptize, christen; (*fam*: *vino*, *etc*.) water down. **bautismo** *sm* baptism, christening. **bautista** *sm* Baptist.

baya ['baja] *sf* berry.

bayeta [ba'jeta] *sf* baize; floorcloth; rag.

bayoneta [bajo'neta] *sf* bayonet.

baza ['baθa] *sf* (*naipes*) trick. **meter baza** intervene.

bazar [ba'θar] *sm* bazaar.

bazo ['baθo] *sm* spleen. *adj* brownish yellow.

beato [be'ato] *adj* pious; blessed; (*fam*) sanctimonious.

beber [be'βer] *v* drink. **beberse** *v* drink up. **bebida** *sf* drink.

beca ['beka] *sf* grant; scholarship.

becerro [be'θerro] *sm* yearling calf.

bedel [be'ðel] *sm* porter; beadle.

befar [be'far] *v* mock, taunt. **befa** *sf* jeer, taunt.

béisbol ['beisβol] *sm* baseball.

Belén [be'len] *s* Bethlehem. **belén** *sm* Nativity scene; (*fam*) bedlam.

Bélgica ['belxika] *sf* Belgium. **belga** *s(m+f)*, *adj* Belgian.

bélico ['beliko] *adj* warlike. **belicosidad** *sf* bellicosity. **belicoso** *adj* bellicose.

beligerante [belixe'rante] *s(m+f)*, *adj* belligerent. **beligerancia** *sf* belligerence.

bellaco [be'ʎako], **-a** *sm*, *sf* rogue. *adj* cunning; wicked.

belleza [be'ʎeθa] *sf* beauty. **bellísimo** *adj* gorgeous. **bello** *adj* beautiful; noble.

bellota [be'ʎota] *sf* acorn.

bemol [be'mol] *sm*, *adj* (*música*) flat.

bencina [ben'θina] *sf* benzine.

***bendecir** [benðe'θir] *v* bless; praise. **bendición** *sf* benediction; grace. **bendito** *adj* blessed; saintly; (*fam*) wretched.

beneficiar [benefi'θjar] *v* benefit; profit. **benefactor, -a** *sm*, *sf also* **beneficiador, -a** benefactor. **beneficencia** *sf* charity; welfare. **beneficiado, -a** *sm*, *sf also* **beneficiario, -a** beneficiary. **beneficio** *sm* benefit; gain. **beneficioso** *adj* beneficial.

benemérito [bene'merito] *adj* worthy, well-deserving.

beneplácito [bene'plaθito] *sm* consent, approval.

benevolencia [benevo'lenθja] *sf* benevolence. **benevolente** *or* **benévolo** *adj* benevolent.

benignidad [benigni'ðað] *sf* kindness; (*clima*) mildness. **benigno** *adj* kind; mild.

beodo [be'oðo], **-a** *sm*, *sf* drunkard. *adj* drunk.

berberecho [berβe'retʃo] *sm* cockle.

berenjena [beren'xena] *sf* aubergine.

bermejo [ber'mexo] *adj* vermilion; (*cabellos*) ginger.

bermellón [berme'ʎon] *sm* vermilion.

berrear [berre'ar] *v* bellow; yell. **berrearse** *v* (*fam*) spill the beans. **berrido** *sm* bellow; yell.

berrinche [ber'rintʃe] *sm* (*fam*) tantrum.

berro ['berro] *sm* watercress.

berza ['berθa] *sf* cabbage.

besar [be'sar] *v* kiss. **beso** *sm* kiss.

bestia ['bestja] *sf* beast, animal. *sm*, *sf* (*persona*) beast; idiot. **bestial** *adj* bestial; beastly; (*fam*) smashing; enormous. **bestialidad** *sf* bestiality; beastliness.

betún [be'tun] *sm* shoe polish; bitumen.

biblia ['biβlia] *sf* Bible. **bíblico** *adj* biblical.

bibliografía [biβliogra'fia] *sf* bibliography. **bibliográfico** *adj* bibliographic(al). **bibliógrafo, -a** *sm*, *sf* bibliographer.

biblioteca [biβlio'teka] *sf* library. **bibliotecario, -a** *sm*, *sf* librarian.

biceps ['biθeps] *sm invar* biceps.

bicicleta [biθi'kleta] *sf* bicycle.

bicho ['bitʃo] *sm* small animal; insect; (*fam*) odd character; (*fam*) ugly person.

bieldo ['bjelðo] *sm* pitchfork.

bien [bjen] *adv* well; right; properly; very; fully; easily; gladly. **ahora bien** nevertheless. **o bien** or else. **¿y bien?** so what? *sm* good; welfare; advantage; gain; darling. **bien que** *conj also* **si bien** although. **no bien** no sooner. **bienes** *sm pl* property *sing*, riches. **bienes inmuebles** real estate *sing*.

bienal [bje'nal] *sf, adj* biennial.
bienaventurado [bjenaβentu'raðo] *adj* happy; blessed; (*fig*) naïve.
bienestar [bjenes'tar] *sm* well-being; comfort.
bienhechor [bjene'tʃor], **-a** *sm, sf* benefactor.
bienio ['bjenjo] *sm* period of two years.
bienvenida [bjenβe'niða] *sf* welcome. **dar la bienvenida a** welcome.
biftec [bif'tek] *sm* steak.
bifurcarse [bifur'karse] *v* fork; branch off. **bifurcación** *sf* fork; junction.
bigamia [bi'gamja] *sf* bigamy. **bígamo, -a** *sm, sf* bigamist.
bigote [bi'gote] *sm* moustache.
bilingüe [bi'lingwe] *adj* bilingual.
bilis ['bilis] *sf* bile; (*fig*) bad temper.
billar [bi'ʎar] *sm* billiards. **billar ruso** snooker.
billete [bi'ʎete] *sm* ticket; (*dinero*) banknote; (*carta*) letter. **billete de abono** season ticket. **billete de ida** single ticket. **billete de ida y vuelta** return ticket. **sacar un billete** buy a ticket.
billón [bi'ʎon] *sm* billion.
binóculo [bi'nokulo] *sm* binoculars *pl*.
biografía [biogra'fia] *sf* biography. **biográfico** *adj* biographical. **biógrafo, -a** *sm, sf* biographer.
biología [biolo'xia] *sf* biology. **biológico** *adj* biological. **biólogo** *sm* biologist.
biombo ['bjombo] *sm* folding screen.
bióxido [bi'oksido] *sm* dioxide. **bióxido de carbono** carbon dioxide.
biplano [bi'plano] *sm* biplane.
birlar [bir'lar] *v* (*fam: robar*) pinch, swipe; (*fam: matar*) bump off.
bisabuela [bisa'βwela] *sf* great-grandmother. **bisabuelo** *sm* great-grandfather.
bisagra [bi'sagra] *sf* hinge.
bisiesto [bi'sjesto] *adj* **año bisiesto** leap year.
bisoño [bi'soɲo], **-a** *sm, sf* greenhorn, novice; (*mil*) rookie.
bizarría [biθar'ria] *sf* (*valor*) bravery; generosity.
bizcar [biθ'kar] *v* squint. **bizco** *adj* cross-eyed. **dejar bizco** (*fam*) dumbfound.
bizcocho [biθ'kotʃo] *sm* sponge cake. **bizcocho borracho** rum baba.
bizma [biθma] *sf* poultice.
blanco ['blanko], **-a** *adj* white; blank; (*fam*) cowardly. *sm, sf* white man/woman; white colour; *sm* (*de tiro*)

target. **blanca** *sf* (*música*) minim. **no tener blanca** be completely broke. **blancura** *sf* whiteness. **dar en el blanco** be on target. **quedarse en blanco** be disappointed. **blanquear** *v* whiten; whitewash. **blanquecer** *v* whitewash; bleach.
blandir [blan'dir] *v* flourish, brandish.
blando ['blando] *adj* soft; mild; gentle. *adv* softly; gently. **blandura** *sf* softness; tenderness; (*carácter*) weakness.
blasfemar [blasfe'mar] *v* blaspheme; (*fig*) curse. **blasfemia** *sf* blasphemy; curse. **blasfemo, -a** *sm, sf* blasphemer.
blasón [bla'son] *sm* heraldry; (*escudo*) coat of arms. **hacer blasón de** boast about.
blindaje [blin'daxe] *sm* armour. **blindado** *adj* armoured; armour-plated.
bloquear [bloke'ar] *v* block; obstruct; (*mil*) blockade. **bloque** *sm* block; bloc. **bloqueo** *sm* blockade.
blusa ['blusa] *sf* blouse; (*guardapolvo*) overall.
boa ['boa] *sf* boa constrictor.
boato [bo'ato] *sm* pomp; show.
bobada [bo'baða] *sf* nonsense; foolish thing. **bobería** *sf* stupidity. **bobo, -a** *sm, sf* fool, idiot.
bobina [bo'bina] *sf* reel, spool.
boca ['boka] *sf* mouth; opening. **a boca de jarro** point-blank. **a boca de noche** at dusk. **boca abajo/arriba** face down/up. **¡punto en boca!** mum's the word!
bocacalle [boka'kaʎe] *sf* intersection.
bocadillo [boka'ðiʎo] *sm* sandwich; snack. **bocado** *sm* mouthful; bite.
boceto [bo'θeto] *sm* (*dibujo*) sketch; (*escrito*) draft.
bocina [bo'θina] *sf* trumpet; (*aut*) horn, hooter.
bochorno [bo'tʃorno] *sm* sultry weather; (*vergüenza*) embarrassment; (*mareo*) giddiness. **sufrir un bochorno** feel embarrassed. **bochornoso** *adj* sultry; thundery; embarrassing.
boda ['boða] *sf* wedding, marriage.
bodega [bo'ðega] *sf* wine cellar; wine shop; bar.
bofetada [bofe'taða] *sf* slap; blow.
boga ['boga] *sf* (*mar*) rowing; (*fig*) vogue. **estar en boga** be in fashion. **bogador, -a** *sm, sf* rower.
bohemio [bo'emjo], **-a** *s, adj* Bohemian; (*gitano*) gipsy.

boicotear [boikote'ar] v boycott. **boicot** or **boicoteo** sm boycott.

boina ['boina] sf beret.

bola ['bola] sf ball; (*canica*) marble; (*betún*) shoe polish; (*del mundo*) globe; (*fig*) fib. **bola de naftalina** mothball. **bolear** v fib; throw.

boleta [bo'leta] sf ticket; pass; (*vale*) voucher; (*votación*) ballot paper.

boleto [bo'leto] sm lottery ticket; betting slip; (*fam*) fib. **boletín** sm bulletin. **boletín de noticias** news bulletin. **boletín de precios** price list. **boletín meteorológico** weather forecast.

bolígrafo [bo'ligrafo] sm ballpoint pen.

Bolivia [bo'liβja] sf Bolivia. **boliviano, -a** s, adj Bolivian.

bolsa ['bolsa] sf bag; purse. **bolsillo** sm pocket.

bollo ['boλo] sm roll, bun, small loaf.

bomba ['bomba] sf pump, bomb. **bomba de gasolina** petrol pump.

bombardear [bombarðe'ar] v bombard.

bombilla [bom'biλa] sf (*elec*) light bulb; (*tecn*) small pump; glass tube.

bombo ['bombo] sm big drum; great praise. adj surprised.

bombón [bom'bon] sm sweet, chocolate.

bonachón [bona'tʃon] adj (*fam*) genial.

bondad [bon'dað] sf goodness; kindness. **tenga la bondad de ... please ... . bondadoso** adj warm-hearted; good.

bonete [bo'nete] sm academic cap. **gran bonete** important person.

bonito [bo'nito] adj pretty, nice, graceful.

bono ['bono] sm voucher; certificate; bond. **bono postal** money-order.

boquear [boke'ar] v gasp; utter; be dying. **boqueada** sf gasp.

boquerón [boke'ron] sm large opening; anchovy; whitebait. **boquete** sm small hole; gap.

boquiabierto [bokja'βjerto] adj open-mouthed; gaping.

boquilla [bo'kiλa] sf mouthpiece; nozzle; pipe stem.

borboll(e)ar [borβo'λar] v bubble. **borbolleo** sm bubbling. **borbollón** sm bubble.

borbotar [borβo'tar] v bubble; boil; gush. **borbotón** sm bubbling; boiling.

bordar [bor'ðar] v embroider. **bordado** sm embroidery.

borde [bor'ðe] sm border, edge; rim. **bordear** v skirt, edge round.

bordillo [bor'ðiλo] sm kerb.

bordo ['borðo] sm (*mar*) side of a ship; tack. **a bordo** on board. **de alto bordo** ocean-going.

boreal [bore'al] adj northern.

bornear [borne'ar] v bend, turn, twist; warp.

borra ['borra] sf coarse wool; nap; waste; (*fam*) idle chatter.

borracho [bor'ratʃo] adj drunk; (*fam*) crazy. **borrachera** or **borrachería** sf drunkenness; drunken spree.

borrador [borra'ðor] sm rough copy; blotter; scribbling pad.

borrar [bor'rar] v cross out; erase; blot. **goma de borrar** rubber. **borrable** adj erasable.

borrasca [bor'raska] sf storm; squall. **borrascoso** adj stormy; squally; (*fig*) boisterous.

borrico [bor'riko] sm ass. **puesto en el borrico** hellbent.

borrón [bor'ron] sm blot, smudge; blemish; stain. **borronear** v scribble (on). **borroso** adj blurred; smudged; stained; illegible.

bosque ['boske] sm forest, wood.

bosquejar [boske'xar] v make a rough sketch of. **bosquejo** sm outline; sketch.

bostezar [boste'θar] v yawn. **bostezo** sm yawn.

bota¹ ['bota] sf boot. **ponerse las botas a** do justice to (something).

bota² sf wineskin.

botánica [bo'tanika] sf botany. **botánico** adj botanical. **botanista** s(m+f) botanist.

botar [bo'tar] v throw, fling; launch.

bote¹ ['bote] sm thrust; blow; jump; bounce.

bote² sm jar; can.

bote³ sm boat. **bote salvavidas** lifeboat.

botella [bo'teλa] sf bottle.

botica [bo'tika] sf chemist's shop; medicine chest; medicines pl; shop, store. **hay de todo como en botica** there is everything under the sun. **boticario** sm chemist.

botija [bo'tixa] sf earthenware pot. **botijo** sm earthenware jug.

botín [bo'tin] sm booty, loot.

botón [bo'ton] sm button; (*flor*) bud; (*puerta*) knob. **botonar** v bud.

bóveda ['boβeða] sf vault. **bóveda de jardín** bower.

bovino [bo'βino] *adj* bovine.

boxear [bokse'ar] *v* box. **boxeador** *sm* boxer. **boxeo** *sm* boxing.

boya ['boja] *sf* buoy. **boyante** *adj* buoyant.

bozal [bo'θal] *sm* muzzle. *s(m+f)* (*fam*) greenhorn. *adj* (*fam*) stupid; foolish; untamed.

bracero [bra'θero], -a *sm, sf* hired hand; labourer.

braga ['braga] *sf* (*cuerda*) guy-rope; (*de mujer*) knickers *pl*; (*de niño*) nappy. **calzarse las bragas** wear the trousers.

bramar [bra'mar] *v* roar, bellow. **bramido** *sm* roar, bellow.

brasa ['brasa] *sf* live coal. **estar en brasas** be on edge. **brasero** *sm* brazier.

Brasil [bra'sil] *sm* Brazil. **brasileño**, -a *s, adj* Brazilian.

bravío [bra'βio] *adj* wild; fierce. *sm* fierceness.

bravo ['braβo] *adj* brave; fierce; (*fam*) rough; (*fam*) rude; (*fam*) luxurious. **mar bravo** rough sea. **¡bravo!** *interj* bravo! well done! **bravura** *sf* ferocity; courage; manliness.

brazada [bra'θaða] *sf* arm movement; stroke. **brazado** *sm* armful.

brazalete [braθa'lete] *sm* bracelet.

brazo ['braθo] *sm* arm; branch; (*fig*) strength, power. **brazo a brazo** hand to hand. **a brazo partido** with bare fists. **brazo derecho** right-hand man. **tener brazo** be tough.

brea ['brea] *sf* pitch, tar.

brebaje [bre'βaxe] *sm* concoction, potion.

brecol ['brekol] *sm* broccoli.

brecha ['bretʃa] *sf* breach, opening.

bregar¹ [bre'gar] *v* struggle; fight. **brega** *sf* struggle; quarrel. **andar a la brega** (*fig*) slog away.

bregar² *v* (*amasar*) knead.

Bretaña [bre'taɲa] *sf* Britain; Brittany. **Gran Bretaña** Great Britain. **bretón**, -ona *s, adj* Breton.

breve ['breβe] *adj* brief, short. **en breve** before long. *sf* (*música*) breve. **brevedad** *sf* brevity.

brezal [bre'θal] *sm* heath. **brezo** *sm* heather.

bribón [bri'βon], -ona *sm, sf* rascal; rogue; vagabond. *adj* rascally.

brida ['briða] *sf* bridle; rein; horsemanship. **a toda brida** hell for leather.

brigada [bri'gaða] *sf* brigade; gang; squad. *sm* sergeant-major.

brillar [bri'ʎar] *v* shine; sparkle; gleam. **brillante** *adj* brilliant; shining; glossy. **brillo** *sm* brilliance; brightness; glitter.

brincar [brin'kar] *v* bounce; jump; hop. **brinco** *sm* jump; hop; skip; bounce.

brindar [brin'ðar] *v* offer; drink someone's health. **brindis** *sm invar* toast.

brío ['brio] *sm* spirit; vigour; determination. **brioso** *adj* spirited; vigorous; determined; elegant.

brisa ['brisa] *sf* breeze.

británico [bri'taniko], -a *sm, sf* Briton. *adj* British. **los británicos** the British.

brocha ['brotʃa] *sf* paintbrush; (*afeitar*) shaving brush.

broche ['brotʃe] *sm* brooch; clasp, clip. **broche de oro** finishing touch.

broma ['broma] *sf* joke; fun; trick. **broma pesada** practical joke. **en broma** as a joke. **sin broma** joking apart. **bromear** *v* joke. **bromista** *s(m+f)* practical joker; funny person.

bromuro [bro'muro] *sm* bromide.

bronca ['bronka] *sf* (*fam*) row; brawl; ticking off. **echar una bronca** tick off.

bronce ['bronθe] *sm* bronze. **bronceado** *adj* bronzed; sun-tanned.

bronco ['bronko] *adj* rough; brittle; (*voz*) harsh; (*carácter*) hard, rude.

bronquial [bronki'al] *adj* bronchial. **bronquitis** *sf* bronchitis.

brotar [bro'tar] *v* grow; bud; germinate; spring forth. **brote** *sm* bud; shoot; (*agua*) gushing; (*fiebre*) rise; (*fig*) outbreak.

bruja ['bruxa] *sf* witch. **brujo** *sm* sorcerer.

brújula ['bruxula] *sf* compass. **perder la brújula** lose one's grip.

bruma ['bruma] *sf* mist. **brumoso** *adj* misty.

bruno ['bruno] *adj* dark brown.

bruñir [bru'ɲir] *v* polish. **bruñido** *sm* shine, polish. **bruñidor** *sm* polisher.

brusco ['brusko] *adj* brusque; abrupt; rough.

Bruselas [bru'selas] *sf* Brussels.

bruto ['bruto] *adj* coarse; brutish; rough; gross. *sm* brute; beast. **en bruto** gross; rough; uncut. **brutal** *adj* brutal; savage. **brutalidad** *sf* brutality; brutishness.

bucear [buθe'ar] *v* dive; swim underwater. **buceo** *sm* dive; diving; skin diving.

bucle ['bukle] *sm* curl; ringlet.

buche ['butʃe] *sm* craw; crop; stomach; (*fam*) belly; (*fam*) bosom, breast.

budismo [bu'ðismo] *sm* Buddhism. **budista** *s*(*m*+*f*). *adj* Buddhist.

buenaventura [bwenaβen'tura] *sf* good luck, fortune.

bueno ['bweno] *adj also* **buen** good; right; sound; fine; (*fam*) funny; (*fam*) amazing. *interj, conj* well; all right. **a buenas** of one's own accord. **buena voluntad** goodwill. **de buena gana** willingly. **¡buenas!** hello! **buenas noches** good night. **buenas tardes** good afternoon; good evening. **buenos días** good morning. **de buenas a primeras** without warning; at first sight; straight away. **estar de buenas** be in a good mood.

buey [bwej] *sm* ox. **a paso de buey** at a snail's pace.

búfalo ['bufalo] *sm* buffalo.

bufanda [bu'fanda] *sf* scarf, muffler.

bufar [bu'far] *v* spit; snort; puff and blow.

bufete [bu'fete] *sm* (*mesa*) writing-desk; (*despacho*) solicitor's office; clientele.

buhardilla [bwar'ðiʎa] *sf* attic, garret; skylight.

búho ['buo] *sm* owl; (*fam*) recluse.

buhonero [bwo'nero] *sm* pedlar, hawker. **buhonería** *sf* hawking, peddling.

buitre ['bwitre] *sm* vulture.

bujía [bu'xia] *sf* candle; candlepower; (*aut*) sparking-plug.

bulbo ['bulβo] *sm* (*bot*) bulb. **bulboso** *adj* bulbous.

Bulgaria [bul'garja] *sf* Bulgaria. **búlgaro, -a** *s, adj* Bulgarian.

bulto ['bulto] *sm* bulk, size; shape, form; bale, package; piece of luggage; (*med*) lump, swelling. **a bulto** approximately. **de bulto** obvious. **escoger a bulto** pick at random.

bulla ['buʎa] *sf* noise; bustle. **meter bulla** kick up a racket.

bullir [bu'ʎir] *v* boil; swarm; stir; bustle; abound; itch. **bullicio** *sm* bustle; uproar. **bullicioso** *adj* lively; noisy; bustling.

buñuelo [bu'nwelo] *sm* fritter; doughnut; (*fam*) mess.

buque ['buke] *sm* ship, vessel. **buque de guerra** warship. **buque cargero** freighter.

burbujear [burβuxe'ar] *v* bubble. **burbuja** *sf* bubble.

burdel [bur'ðel] *sm* brothel.

burdo [bur'ðo] *adj* clumsy; coarse; crude.

burgués [bur'ges] *adj* bourgeois, middle-class. **burguesía** *sf* bourgeoisie, middle class.

burla ['burla] *sf* hoax; joke; trick; taunt. **burlar** *v* hoax; trick; mock. **burlarse de** make fun of. **burlería** *sf* fun; artifice; deceit; ridicule.

burocracia [buro'kraθja] *sf* bureaucracy. **burócrata** *s*(*m*+*f*) bureaucrat. **burocrático** *adj* bureaucratic.

burro ['burro] *sm* donkey; (*fam*) fool. **burro cargado de letras** pompous ass.

buscar [bus'kar] *v* search for, look for. **busca** *sf* search. **en busca de** in search of. **buscador, -a** *sm, sf* seeker. **búsqueda** *sf* search.

busto ['busto] *sm* bust.

butaca [bu'taka] *sf* theatre seat; armchair.

buzo ['buðo] *sm* diver. **campana de buzo** diving-bell.

buzón [bu'θon] *sm* pillar box, letter box; plug, bung.

C

cabal [ka'βal] *adj* exact; complete; perfect. *adv* exactly; perfectly.

cábala ['kaβala] *sf* (*fig*) intrigue; divination.

cabalgar [kaβal'gar] *v* ride. **cabalgada** *sf* raid; cavalcade. **cabalgador** *sm* horseman.

caballa [ka'βaʎa] *sf* mackerel.

caballero [kaβa'ʎero] *sm* horseman; gentleman; knight. **caballeresco** *adj* chivalrous. **caballería** *sf* cavalry.

caballete [kaβa'ʎete] *sm* ridge; trestle; easel; bridge of the nose.

caballo [ka'βaʎo] *sm* horse; (*ajedrez*) knight; (*naipes*) queen. **a caballo** on horseback. **caballo de vapor** horsepower. **caballo entero** stallion. **caballito** *sm* pony.

cabaña [ka'βana] *sf* cabin; herd, flock.

cabaret [kaβa're] *sm* cabaret; nightclub.

cabecear [kaβeθe'ar] *v* nod; shake one's head. **cabecera** *sf* (*de mesa, cama, etc.*) head; river's source.

cabello [ka'βeʎo] *sm* hair. **traído por los cabellos** far-fetched. **cabelludo** *adj* hairy; shaggy; downy.

calcio

*caber [ka'βer] v fit, find room; befall; be possible. **no cabe duda** there is no doubt.

cabestro [ka'βestro] sm halter; leading ox. **llevar del cabestro** lead by the nose. **cabestrillo** sm arm sling.

cabeza [ka'βeθa] sf head; chief; summit; capital. **cabeza de turco** scapegoat. **cabeza torcida** hypocrite. **cabezudo** adj big-headed.

cabida [ka'βiða] sf capacity, space. **dar cabida a** make room for. **tener cabida** be appropriate.

cabildo [ka'βilðo] sm town council; (rel) chapter.

cabina [ka'βina] sf cabin; telephone kiosk.

cabizbajo [kaβiθ'βaxo] adj downcast.

cable ['kaβle] sm cable, rope; cable(gram). **cablegrafiar** v cable. **cablegrama** sm cable(gram).

cabo ['kaβo] sm cape, headland; end; stump; handle; rope; corporal; bit, piece. **al cabo de** at the end of. **llevar a cabo** carry out.

cabotaje [kaβo'taxe] sm coastal navigation.

cabra ['kaβra] sf goat.

cabria ['kaβrja] sf crane, hoist.

cabriola [ka'βrjola] sf gambol; hop; jump. **cabriolar** v jump; caper.

cacahuete [kaka'wete] sm peanut.

cacao [ka'kao] sm cocoa; cacao.

cacarear [kakare'ar] v crow, cackle; boast. **cacareo** sm crowing, cackling; boasting.

cacería [kaθe'ria] sf hunting; hunt.

cacerola [kaθe'rola] sf saucepan.

cacique [ka'θike] sm political boss; tyrant.

caco ['kako] sm pickpocket; thief; (fam) coward.

cacto ['kakto] sm cactus.

cacharrería [katʃarre'ria] sf crockery. **cacharro** sm earthenware vessel; thing; piece of junk. **lavar los cacharros** do the washing-up.

cachemir [katʃe'mir] sm cashmere.

cachete [ka'tʃete] sm blow, slap; cheek; swollen cheek. **cachetear** v slap.

cachivache [katʃi'βatʃe] sm pot; thing; utensil; bauble.

cacho ['katʃo] sm piece, chunk, slice.

cachorro [ka'tʃorro], -a sm, sf pup; cub; kitten.

cada ['kaða] adj invar each, every. **cada vez más** more and more.

cadáver [ka'ðaβer] sm corpse.

cadena [ka'ðena] sf chain. **cadena perpetua** life imprisonment. **estar en cadena** be in prison.

cadencia [ka'ðenθja] sf cadence, rhythm.

cadera [ka'ðera] sf hip.

cadete [ka'ðete] sm cadet.

caducar [kaðu'kar] v expire, lapse; become senile. **caduco** adj senile; in decline.

*caer [ka'er] v fall, drop, tumble; decline; fall due; fade; fit, suit; realize, understand; be located, lie. **caer en** or **sobre** fall upon. **caer en la cuenta** understand. **caer en saco roto** fall on deaf ears. **caída** sf fall; downfall; lapse.

café [ka'fe] sm coffee; café. **café con leche** white coffee. **café solo** black coffee. **cafeína** sf caffeine. **cafetera** sf coffee pot. **cafetería** sf coffee bar.

caimán [kai'man] sm alligator.

caja ['kaxa] sf box, case; safe; coffin; frame; hole, slot; cash box; cashier's office; cash; (música) drum; (auto) body. **caja de ahorros** savings bank. **cajero**, -a sm, sf cashier. **cajetilla** sf packet; small box. **cajón** sm large box; crate, chest; drawer; coffin.

cal [kal] sf lime.

calabaza [kala'βaθa] sf pumpkin; gourd; (fam) fool. **dar calabazas a** (examen) fail; jilt. **llevar calabazas** be jilted. **calabazada** sf (fam) blow on the head.

calabozo [kala'βoθo] sm prison cell; pruning knife.

calamar [kala'mar] sm squid.

calambre [ka'lambre] sm cramp.

calamidad [kalami'ðað] sf calamity.

calar [ka'lar] v soak; perforate; slice; size up; (fam) pick pockets. **calarse hasta los huesos** get soaked to the skin.

calavera [kala'βera] sf skull. **calaverada** sf wild escapade, tomfoolery. **calaverear** v act recklessly; live it up.

calcar [kal'kar] v trace; copy; trample upon. **calco** sm tracing; copy.

calce ['kalθe] sm (de rueda) rim; wedge.

calceta [kal'θeta] sf stocking; fetter. **hacer calceta** knit. **calcetero**, -a sm, sf hosier. **calcetín** sm sock.

calcinar [kalθi'nar] v burn, blacken.

calcio ['kalθjo] sm calcium.

calcular [kalku'lar] v calculate. **calculación** sf calculation. **calculadora** sf calculating machine. **cálculo** sm calculation; estimate; (med) gallstone.

calda ['kalða] sf heating. **caldas** sf pl thermal springs pl.

caldera [kal'ðera] sf cauldron, boiling pan. **calderilla** sf small change.

caldo ['kalðo] sm broth; soup; salad dressing. **caldos** sm pl liquid foodstuffs pl; wines pl.

calefacción [kalefak'θjon] sf heating. **calefacción central** central heating.

calendario [kalen'darjo] sm calendar.

*****calentar** [kalen'tar] v heat, warm; (fam) thrash. **calentarse** v warm oneself; become excited. **calentador** sm heater. **calentura** sf fever. **caliente** adj hot, warm.

caletre [ka'letre] sm (fam) good sense, sound judgment.

calibrar [kali'βrar] v calibrate; gauge, measure. **calibre** sm calibre; gauge; (fig) importance.

calidad [kali'ðað] sf quality; (med) fever. **calidades** sf pl conditions pl; rules pl. **a calidad de que** on condition that. **en calidad de** in the capacity of.

cálido ['kaliðo] adj hot, warm.

calificar [kalifi'kar] v qualify; judge; distinguish; prove worthy. **calificarse** v give proof of nobility. **calificación** sf appreciation; distinction; judgment. **calificado** adj distinguished; suitable.

calina [ka'lina] sf mist, fog.

cáliz ['kaliθ] sm chalice, cup.

calmante [kal'mante] adj soothing. sm sedative.

calmar [kal'mar] v calm; be calm. **calmarse** v quieten down. **calma** sf calm, lull. **calmoso** adj calm.

calor [ka'lor] sm heat, warmth; fervour; fever. **hacer calor** (temperatura) be hot. **tener calor** (persona) be hot. **caluroso** adj hot, warm; (fig) ardent.

caloría [kalo'ria] sf calorie.

calvo ['kalβo] adj bald; bare; threadbare. **calvez** sf also **calvicie** baldness.

calzar [kal'θar] v put shoes on; wear (shoes, gloves, spurs); wedge. **calza** sf chock; (fam) stocking. **calzada** sf roadway.

calzón [kal'θon] sm trousers pl; safety belt. **calzones** sm pl trousers pl. **calzoncillos** sm pl underpants pl.

callar [ka'ʎar] v be silent; shut up. **callado** adj silent; reserved; secret. **de callado** quietly.

calle ['kaʎe] sf street, road. **dejar en la calle** leave penniless. **hacer calle** clear the way. **callejón** sm alley. **callejón sin salida** cul-de-sac. **callejuela** sf back street; (fig) loophole.

callo ['kaʎo] sm (med) corn, callus. **callos** sm pl tripe sing. **calloso** adj hard, callous.

cama ['kama] sf bed; litter; floor. **caer en cama** fall ill. **cama de campaña/matrimonio/soltero** camp/double/single bed.

camafeo [kama'feo] sm cameo.

camaleón [kamale'on] sm chameleon.

camandulero [kamandu'lero] adj (fam) sly; hypocritical.

cámara ['kamara] sf room; loft; chamber; cine or TV camera; inner tube. **ayuda de cámara** sf valet. **música de cámara** sf chamber music.

camarada [kama'raða] sm comrade; colleague.

camarero [kama'rero] sm waiter; steward. **camarera** sf waitress; stewardess; chambermaid.

camarilla [kama'riʎa] sf clique; parliamentary lobby.

camarón [kama'ron] sm shrimp.

camarote [kama'rote] sm cabin.

cambiar [kam'bjar] v change; exchange. **cambiante** sm moneychanger. **cambio** sm change; alteration; small change. **a cambio de** in exchange for. **en cambio** on the other hand.

camelar [kame'lar] v (fam) flatter; woo. **cameleo** sm (fam) flattery.

camello [ka'meʎo] sm camel.

camilla [ka'miʎa] sf stretcher; litter; couch.

caminar [kami'nar] v walk; travel; move along. **caminante** s(m+f) traveller. **camino** sm path; road; route; way. **abrirse camino** make one's way. **camino adelante** straight on. **ponerse en camino** set out.

camión [ka'mjon] sm lorry. **camión de bomberos** fire engine.

camisa [ka'misa] sf shirt; fruit skin; casing; lining; dust jacket; paper wrapper. **camisa de dormir** nightdress. **camisa de fuerza** straightjacket. **dejar sin camisa** ruin (someone). **camiseta** sf vest. **camisón** sm nightdress; nightshirt.

camorra [ka'morra] *sf* (*fam*) quarrel, fight. **buscar camorra** look for trouble.

campamento [kampa'mento] *sm* camp. **campar** *v* camp; excel.

campana [kam'pana] *sf* bell; mantelpiece; parish (church); curfew.

campante [kam'pante] *adj* proud; pleased; (*fam*) relaxed, cool.

campaña [kam'paɲa] *sf* plain; campaign.

campechano [kampe'tʃano] *adj* (*fam*) genial; frank. **campechanía** *sf* good nature; frankness.

campeón [kampe'on], **-ona** *sm, sf* champion. **campeón de venta** bestseller. **campeonato** *sm* championship. **de campeonato** (*fig, fam*) fantastic.

campo ['kampo] *sm* field; countryside; camp; pitch; background. **campo de aviación** airfield. **campo raso** open country. **campesino, -a** *s, adj* peasant, rustic.

can [kan] *sm* dog; trigger.

cana ['kana] *sf* white *or* grey hair. **peinar canas** be getting old.

Canadá [kana'ða] *sm* Canada. **canadiense** *s*(*m*+*f*), *adj* Canadian.

canal [ka'nal] *sm* canal; channel; ditch; tube. *sf* carcass. **canalón** *sm* drainpipe; gutter.

canalla [ka'naʎa] *sf* rabble, mob. *sm* swine, scoundrel.

canapé [kana'pe] *sm* couch, sofa; (*culin*) canapé.

Canarias [ka'narjas] *sf pl* Canary Islands *pl*. **canario, -a** *sm, sf* inhabitant of the Canary Islands.

canario [ka'narjo] *sm* canary.

canasta [ka'nasta] *sf* basket.

cancelar [kanθe'lar] *v* cancel, annul. **cancelación** *sf* cancellation.

cáncer ['kanθer] *sm* (*med*) cancer. **Cáncer** *sm* (*astron*) Cancer.

canciller [kanθi'ʎer] *sm* chancellor.

canción [kan'θjon] *sf* song; tune; rhyme. **mudar de canción** change one's tune. **cancionero** *sm* song-book.

cancha ['kantʃa] *sf* football ground; tennis court; racecourse.

candado [kan'daðo] *sm* padlock.

candela [kan'dela] *sf* candle; candlestick; fire; blossom; (*fam*) light. **candelero** *sm* candlestick; oil lamp. **poner en el candelero** make popular.

candente [kan'dente] *adj* red-hot, burning.

candidato [kandi'ðato] *sm* candidate. **candidatura** *sf* candidature.

cándido ['kandiðo] *adj* innocent, pure; gullible; candid. **candidez** *sf* candour; gullibility; stupid remark.

candil [kan'ðil] *sm* oil lamp.

candor [kan'dor] *sm* innocence; candour; simplicity. **candoroso** *adj* ingenuous; innocent; frank.

canela [ka'nela] *sf* cinnamon.

canelón [kane'lon] *sm* gutter; spout; icicle.

cangrejo [kan'grexo] *sm* crab.

canguro [kan'guro] *sm* kangaroo.

caníbal [ka'niβal] *s*(*m*+*f*), *adj* cannibal. **canibalismo** *sm* cannibalism.

canilla [ka'niʎa] *sf* (*tecn*) bobbin, spool; (*med*) shinbone; tap, spout.

canino [ka'nino] *adj* canine. **hambre canina** ravenous hunger.

canjear [kanxe'ar] *v* exchange. **canje** *sm* exchange.

cano ['kano] *adj* white-haired, grey-haired; (*fig*) ancient.

canoa [ka'noa] *sf* canoe.

canon ['kanon] *sm* rule; levy; perfect example; (*rel, música*) canon.

canónigo [ka'noniɣo] *sm* (*rel*) canon. **canónico** *adj* canonical. **canonización** *sf* canonization. **canonizar** *v* canonize.

cansar [kan'sar] *v* tire, fatigue. **cansado** *adj* tired, weary; tiresome. **vista cansada** weak eyesight. **cansancio** *sm* weariness, fatigue.

cantar [kan'tar] *v* sing; chant; praise; (*fam*) squeal, confess. *sm* song; tune; poem. **cantante** *s*(*m*+*f*) singer.

cántara ['kantara] *sf* pitcher; liquid measure.

cántaro ['kantaro] *sm* pitcher. **llover a cántaros** rain cats and dogs.

cantera [kan'tera] *sf* quarry; (*fig*) breeding ground, source. **cantería** *sf* masonry; building made of hewn stone. **cantero** *sm* stonemason; crust of bread; strip of land.

cantidad [kanti'ðað] *sf* quantity, amount.

cantimplora [kantim'plora] *sf* siphon; water bottle.

cantina [kan'tina] *sf* buffet; canteen; wine cellar; picnic basket.

canto[1] ['kanto] *sm* song; singing. **cantor, -a** *sm, sf* singer.

canto[2] *sm* edge; border; crust; corner.

pebble. **al canto** (*fam*) in support. **de canto** edgeways.

caña ['kaɲa] *sf* cane; reed; walking stick; beer glass; shin bone. **caña de azúcar** sugar-cane. **caña de pescar** fishing-rod.

cañada [ka'ɲaða] *sf* glen, ravine.

cáñamo ['kaɲamo] *sm* hemp.

caño ['kaɲo] *sm* pipe; sewer. **cañería** *sf* drain; piping.

cañón [ka'ɲon] *sm* canyon; cannon, gun; gun barrel; pipe, tube.

caoba [ka'oβa] *sf* mahogany.

caos ['kaos] *sm* chaos. **caótico** *adj* chaotic.

capa ['kapa] *sf* cloak; cape; covering; lid.

capacidad [kapaθi'ðað] *sf* capacity; ability; opportunity.

capacha [ka'patʃa] *sf also* **capacho** *sm* shopping basket.

capar [ka'par] *v* castrate; (*fam*) reduce.

capataz [kapa'taθ] *sm* foreman; overseer.

capaz [ka'paθ] *adj* capable; able; spacious.

capellán [kape'ʎan] *sm* chaplain.

capilar [kapi'lar] *sm*, *adj* capillary.

capilla [ka'piʎa] *sf* chapel; choir; hood. **estar en capilla** (*fam*) be in suspense.

capital [kapi'tal] *sm* (*com*) capital. *sf* capital city. *adj* principal.

capitán [kapi'tan] *sm* captain, leader. **capitanear** *v* command; lead.

capitular [kapitu'lar] *v* capitulate; make an agreement. **capitulación** *sf* capitulation; agreement.

capítulo [ka'pitulo] *sm* (*libro*) chapter; town council meeting; (*rel*) chapter.

capón [ka'pon] *sm* capon; eunuch; gelding; bundle of sticks.

capote [ka'pote] *sm* cape; greatcoat. **capotear** *v* (*fig*, *fam*) shirk.

capricho [ka'pritʃo] *sm* caprice, whim. **caprichoso** *adj* capricious.

cápsula ['kapsula] *sf* capsule; cartridge case; metal cap.

captar [kap'tar] *v* win over; gain; grasp.

capturar [kaptu'rar] *v* capture; arrest. **captura** *sf* capture.

capucha [ka'putʃa] *sf* hood; circumflex accent.

capuchina [kapu'tʃina] *sf* nasturtium.

capullo [ka'puʎo] *sm* cocoon; bud. **en capullo** in embryo.

cara ['kara] *sf* face; appearance; surface. **cara adelante/atrás** forwards/backwards. **cara o cruz** heads or tails. **dar la cara** face the music. **hacer cara a** face up to. **tener cara de** look like.

carabina [kara'βina] *sf* carbine; rifle. **carabinero** *sm* rifleman.

caracol [kara'kol] *sm* snail; spiral.

carácter [ka'rakter] *sm* character; nature; condition; sign, mark. **característica** *sf* characteristic. **característico** *adj* characteristic. **caracterización** *sf* characterization; (*teatro*) make-up. **caracterizar** *v* characterize; confer an honour on; (*teatro*) make up.

¡caramba! [ka'ramba] *interj* damn it!

caramelo [kara'melo] *sm* sweet, toffee; caramel.

carapacho [kara'patʃo] *sm* shell, carapace.

carátula [ka'ratula] *sf* mask; (*fam*) theatre, stage.

caravana [kara'βana] *sf* caravan; group, crowd.

carbohidrato [karβoi'ðrato] *sm* carbohydrate.

carbón [kar'βon] *sm* coal; charcoal; carbon; carbon paper. **carbonera** *sf* coal cellar; coal scuttle; charcoal burner. **carbonería** *sf* coalyard. **carbono** *sm* carbon.

carbunclo [kar'βunklo] *sm also* **carbunco** (*med*) carbuncle.

carburador [karβura'ðor] *sm* carburettor.

carcajada [karka'xaða] *sf* burst of laughter.

cárcel ['karθel] *sf* prison. **carcelero, -a** *sm*, *sf* jailer, warder.

carcomer [karko'mer] *v* corrode, eat away; undermine.

cardar [kar'ðar] *v* (*tecn*) card, comb. **carda** *sf* (*tecn*) card, carding; (*fam*) reprimand.

cardenal [karðe'nal] *sm* cardinal; bruise.

cardíaco [kar'ðiako] *adj* cardiac.

cardinal [karði'nal] *adj* principal; cardinal.

cardo ['karðo] *sm* thistle.

carear [kare'ar] *v* confront; compare; come face to face. **carearse** *v* meet.

*carecer [kare'θer] *v* lack, need. **carencia** *sf* lack, shortage; deficiency.

carestía [kares'tia] *sf* shortage, scarcity; high price.

careta [ka'reta] *sf* mask. **careta antigás** gasmask.

carey [ka'rej] *sm* turtle; tortoiseshell.

cargar [kar'gar] *v* load; burden; charge; tax; blame; attack; (*fam*) vex; lean, incline. **cargarse de** become full; be overburdened; (*fam*) be fed up; (*cielo*) become dark. **carga** *sf* load, burden; charge; tax; pressure. **cargadero** *sm* loading bay. **cargador** *sm* freighter; loader; carrier. **cargamento** *sm* cargo, load.

cargo ['kargo] *sm* post; accusation; responsibility; (*com*) charge; freighter. **cuenta a cargo** *sf* charge account.

cariarse [ka'rjarse] *v* decay. **caries** *sf invar* caries.

caribe [ka'riβe] *s(m+f)*, *adj* Caribbean. **Mar Caribe** *sm* Caribbean Sea.

caricatura [karika'tura] *sf* caricature.

caricia [ka'riθja] *sf* caress. **caricioso** *adj* caressing.

caridad [kari'ðað] *sf* charity. **caritativo** *adj* charitable.

cariño [ka'riɲo] *sm* love, affection. **cariñoso** *adj* affectionate, loving.

cariz [ka'riθ] *sm* appearance, aspect.

carmesí [karme'si] *sm*, *adj* crimson.

carmín [kar'min] *sm*, *adj* carmine.

carnada [kar'naða] *sf* bait.

carnaval [karna'βal] *sm* carnival.

carne ['karne] *sf* meat, flesh. **carne magra** lean meat. **carnal** *adj* carnal. **carnicería** *sf* butcher's shop. **carnicero** *sm* butcher.

carnero [kar'nero] *sm* sheep; ram; mutton; cemetery.

carpa ['karpa] *sf* carp.

caro ['karo] *adj* expensive, dear, beloved.

carpeta [kar'peta] *sf* folder, file; portfolio; briefcase; tablecloth. **dar carpetazo a** shelve.

carpintería [karpinte'ria] *sf* carpentry; carpenter's shop. **carpintero** *sm* carpenter, joiner.

carrera [kar'rera] *sf* race; road; career; course; line; (*media*) ladder. **de carrera** swiftly. **hacer carrera** succeed.

carreta [kar'reta] *sf* cart, wagon. **carretear** *v* cart, haul.

carrete [kar'rete] *sm* reel, spool, bobbin.

carretera [karre'tera] *sf* road, highway. **carretera de circunvalación** by-pass.

carril [kar'ril] *sm* furrow, rut; narrow road; rail.

carro ['karro] *sm* cart; car; typewriter carriage. **carro blindado** armoured car. **carro de mudanzas** removal van.

carroña [kar'roɲa] *sf* carrion.

carroza [kar'roθa] *sf* carriage; state coach; float

carta ['karta] *sf* letter; chart; map; playing card; charter, document **carta certificada** registered letter. **carta de venta** bill of sale. **tomar cartas en** (*fam*) take part in.

cartel [kar'tel] *sm* placard, poster **cartelera** *sf* hoarding.

cartera [kar'tera] *sf* wallet; purse; briefcase; notebook; portfolio; office of a cabinet minister.

cartero [kar'tero] *sm* postman.

cartílago [kar'tilago] *sm* cartilage.

cartón [kar'ton] *sm* cardboard; carton; cartoon.

cartucho [kar'tutʃo] *sm* cartridge; paper cone.

casa ['kasa] *sf* house, home; household; business; building; flat. **casa de empeños** pawnshop. **casa de huéspedes** boarding-house. **casa pública** brothel. **casa y comida** board and lodging. **en casa** at home. **un amigo de casa** a friend of the family.

casar [ka'sar] *v* give in marriage; join. **casarse con** marry, get married. **casamiento** *sm* marriage.

cascabel [kaska'βel] *sm* small bell. **serpiente de cascabel** *sf* rattlesnake. **cascabelada** *sf* (*fam*) foolish action.

cascada [kas'kaða] *sf* waterfall.

cascar [kas'kar] *v* crack; burst; split; break; (*fam*) beat up; (*fam*) cough up; (*fam*) chatter; (*fam*) kick the bucket.

cáscara ['kaskara] *sf* shell; peel; rind; husk; bark.

cascarón [kaska'ron] *sm* egg-shell.

casco ['kasko] *sm* skull; helmet; skin, segment; shrapnel **cascotes** *sm pl* rubble *sing*.

caserío [kase'rio] *sm* group of houses; settlement; country house.

casero [ka'sero] *adj* home-made, familiar; informal; (*fam*) domestic. *sm* landlord; tenant; caretaker.

casi ['kasi] *adv* nearly, almost

casilla [ka'siʎa] *sf* hut, cabin; lodge; pigeonhole; section.

caso ['kaso] *sm* case, matter; event; chance; occasion. **el caso es** the fact is **en tal caso** in such a case **en todo caso** in any case. **hacer caso a** pay attention to.

caspa ['kaspa] *sf* dandruff.

casta ['kasta] *sf* caste; breed; class.

castaño [kas'taɲo] *sm* chestnut-tree;

chestnut brown. *adj* chestnut. **castaña** *sf* chestnut; hair bun.

castañuela [kasta'ɲwela] *sf* castanet.

castellano [kaste'ʎano], **-a** *s, adj* Castilian. *sm (lengua)* Castilian.

castidad [kasti'ðað] *sf* chastity.

castigar [kasti'gar] *v* punish, chastise. **castigo** *sm* punishment.

Castilla [kas'tiʎa] *sf* Castile.

castillo [kas'tiʎo] *sm* castle.

castizo [kas'tiθo] *adj* pure; pure-blooded; traditional.

casto ['kasto] *adj* chaste, pure.

castor [kas'tor] *sm* beaver.

castrar [kas'trar] *v* castrate; (*agr*) prune. **castrado** *sm* eunuch.

castrense [kas'trense] *adj* military.

casual [ka'swal] *adj* chance, coincidental. **casualidad** *sf* chance; coincidence; accident. **por casualidad** by chance.

casucha [ka'sutʃa] *sf also* **casuca** hovel.

cataclismo [kata'klismo] *sm* cataclysm.

catacumbas [kata'cumbas] *sf pl* catacombs *pl*.

catadura[1] [kata'ðura] *sf* tasting. **catador** *sm* taster, sampler. **catar** *v* taste, sample.

catadura[2] *sf (fam)* expression, look.

catalejo [kata'lexo] *sm* telescope.

catálogo [ka'talogo] *sm* catalogue. **catalogar** *v* catalogue; classify.

Cataluña [kata'luɲa] *sf* Catalonia.

cataplasma [kata'plasma] *sf* poultice.

catarata [kata'rata] *sf* waterfall; (*med*) cataract.

catarro [ka'tarro] *sm* catarrh, common cold. **catarro pradial** hay fever. **coger un catarro** catch cold.

catástrofe [ka'tastrofe] *sf* catastrophe. **catastrófico** *adj* catastrophic.

catecismo [kate'θismo] *sm* catechism.

cátedra ['kateðra] *sf* lecture room; senior teaching post; (*puesto*) chair.

catedral [kate'ðral] *sf* cathedral.

categoría [katego'ria] *sf* category; class; rank. **categórico** *adj* categorical; strict.

caterva [ka'terβa] *sf* crowd; heap.

cátodo ['katoðo] *sm* cathode.

católico [ka'toliko], **-a** *s, adj* (Roman) Catholic. **catolicismo** *sm* (Roman) Catholicism.

catorce [ka'torθe] *sm, adj* fourteen. **catorceno** *adj* fourteenth.

catre ['katre] *sm* camp-bed; cot.

cauce ['kauθe] *sm* river bed; ditch.

caución [kau'θjon] *sf* caution; pledge; bail.

caucho ['kautʃo] *sm* rubber.

caudal [kau'ðal] *sm* wealth; abundance.

caudillo [kau'ðiʎo] *sm* leader, chief.

causar [kau'sar] *v* cause, create, occasion. **causa** *sf* cause, reason, motive; (*jur*) trial. **a causa de** owing to. **causa pública** public welfare.

cáustico ['kaustiko] *adj* caustic, burning; scathing.

cautela [kau'tela] *sf* care, caution; cunning. **cauteloso** *adj* cautious; cunning. **cauto** *adj* cautious, wary.

cautivar [kauti'βar] *v* capture; captivate; charm. **cautividad** *sf* captivity. **cautivo, -a** *sm, sf* captive.

cavar [ka'βar] *v* dig; excavate; (*agr*) dress; ponder. **cava** *sf* cultivation. **cavadura** *sf* digging; dressing.

caverna [ka'βerna] *sf* cavern, cave. **cavernoso** *adj* cavernous; (*fig*) deep.

cavidad [kaβi'ðað] *sf* cavity.

cavilar [kaβi'lar] *v* think deeply, meditate. **caviloso** *adj* pensive; worried.

cayado [ka'jaðo] *sm* shepherd's crook; walking-stick.

cazar [ka'θar] *v* hunt; chase; shoot; catch. **caza** *sf* hunt; chase; game. **cazador, -a** *sm, sf* hunter.

cazo ['kaθo] *sm* ladle; saucepan; gluepot. **cazo eléctrico** electric kettle.

cazoleta [kaθo'leta] *sf* small pan; pipe bowl.

cazuela [ka'θwela] *sf* casserole; (*teatro*) the gods.

cebada [θe'βaða] *sf* barley. **cebadar** *v* feed (animals).

cebar [θe'βar] *v* feed, fatten up; prime, charge; penetrate; long for. **cebarse en** vent one's rage on; gloat over.

cebolla [θe'βoʎa] *sf* onion; flower bulb. **cebollana** *sf* chive. **cebolleta** *sf* leek.

cebra ['θeβra] *sf* zebra. **paso de cebra** *sm* zebra crossing.

cecear [θeθe'ar] *v* lisp. **ceceo** *sm* lisp. **ceceoso** *adj* lisping.

ceder [θe'ðer] *v* give up; yield; sag.

cedro ['θeðro] *sm* cedar.

cédula ['θeðula] *sf* charter; certificate; form; patent.

*****cegar** [θe'gar] *v* blind; go blind; block up; cover. **cegador** *adj* blinding. **cegarra** *adj* (*fam*) short-sighted. **cegarrita** *adj* (*fam*) peering. **ceguedad** *or* **ceguera** *sf* blindness.

ceja ['θexa] *sf* eyebrow; mountain top; rim; cloud-cap. **fruncir las cejas** knit one's brows. **quemarse las cejas** burn the midnight oil. **tener entre ceja y ceja** (*fam*) concentrate on.

celada [θe'laða] *sf* helmet; trick; ambush.

celar [θe'lar] *v* check on; watch; conceal; protect. **celador** *sm* watchman.

celda ['θelða] *sf* cell.

celebrar [θele'βrar] *v* celebrate; praise; acclaim; conduct; (*rel*) say mass. **celebrarse** *v* take place. **celebración** *sf* celebration; acclamation. **celebrante** *sm* celebrant priest. **célebre** *adj* famous. **celebridad** *sf* fame; celebration.

celeridad [θeleri'ðað] *sf* speed.

celeste [θe'leste] *adj* heavenly.

celibato [θeli'βato] *sm* celibacy; (*fam*) bachelor. **célibe** *s(m+f)* single person; bachelor; spinster.

celo ['θelo] *sm* zeal; heat, rut. **celos** *sm pl* jealousy *sing*. **dar celos** a make jealous. **tener celos** be jealous. **celosía** *sf* window lattice; venetian blind; jealousy. **celoso** *adj* zealous; jealous.

celta ['θelta] *s(m+f)* Celt. *sm* (*lengua*) Celtic.

célula ['θelula] *sf* cell.

celuloide [θelu'loiðe] *sm* celluloid.

celulosa [θelu'losa] *sf* cellulose.

cementerio [θemen'terjo] *sm* cemetery.

cemento [θe'mento] *sm* cement. **cemento armado** reinforced concrete.

cenagal [θena'gal] *sm* marsh, swamp; (*fam*) tight spot, mess.

cenar [θe'nar] *v* dine on, have for supper/dinner. **cena** *sf* evening meal, supper, dinner.

cenefa [θe'nefa] *sf* border; edging; frieze.

ceniza [θe'niθa] *sf* ash, cinder. **convertir en cenizas** reduce to ashes. **cenicero** *sm* ashtray.

censo ['θenso] *sm* census; tax; annuity; pension; ground rent; (*fig*) burden. **censar** *v* take a census of. **censor** *sm* censor; auditor.

censurar [θensu'rar] *v* censor; censure; condemn. **censura** *sf* censoring; censorship. **censurable** *adj* blameworthy. **censurador** *sm* censor. **censurista** *s(m+f)* critic; fault-finder.

centellear [θenteʎe'ar] *v also* **centellar**

sparkle; flash; twinkle; flicker. **centella** *sf* flash; spark. **centelleo** *sm* gleam; glitter; sparkle.

centavo [θen'taβo] *sm* cent.

centena [θen'tena] *sf* hundred. **centenada** *sf also* **centenar** *sm* hundred. **a** *or* **por centenares** by the hundred. **centenario** *sm* centenary.

centeno¹ [θen'teno] *sm* rye.

centeno² *adj* hundred.

centésimo [θen'tesimo] *adj* hundredth. *sm* cent.

centígrado [θen'tigraðo] *adj* centigrade.

centímetro [θen'timetro] *sm* centimetre.

céntimo ['θentimo] *adj* hundredth. *sm* cent.

centinela [θenti'nela] *s(m+f)* guard, sentry.

centrar [θen'trar] *v* centre. **central** *adj* central. **central** *sf* head office; headquarters; power station; switchboard. **centro** *sm* centre, middle; aim, goal, objective.

centrífugo [θen'trifugo] *adj* centrifugal.

centroamérica [θentroa'merika] *sf* Central America. **centroamericano** *adj* Central American.

centuria [θen'turja] *sf* century.

*****ceñir** [θe'nir] *v* gird, surround, encircle; crown; frame; shorten, take in; be a tight fit for. **ceñirse** *v* limit; adapt oneself to; cling. **ceñido** *adj* tight-fitting. **ceñidor** *sm* belt.

ceño ['θeno] *sm* frown. **fruncir el ceño** frown. **ceñudo** *adj* frowning.

cepa ['θepa] *sf* tree stump; stock; root; origin.

cepillar [θepi'ʎar] *v* brush; plane. **cepillarse** *v* (*fam*) fail an exam; (*fam*) polish off. **cepillo** *sm* brush; plane.

cepo ['θepo] *sm* branch; stocks *pl*; collecting box; (*tecn*) clamp, socket.

cera ['θera] *sf* wax.

cerámico [θe'ramiko] *adj* ceramic. **cerámica** *sf* ceramics; pottery.

cerca ['θerka] *adv* near, close, nearby. **cerca de** close by; almost; about. **de cerca** closely. **cercanía** *sf* nearness. **cercanías** *sf pl* vicinity *sing*, neighbourhood *sing*. **cercano** *adj* near, close.

cercar [θer'kar] *v* enclose; fence; surround. **cerca** *sf* enclosure, wall, fence. **cercado** *sm* enclosure.

cerco ['θerko] *sm* ring; circle; enclosure; frame; siege.

cerda [ˈθerda] sf (zool) sow; bristle.
cerdear v (animales) be lame, limp. cerdo
sm pig; pork. cerdoso adj bristly.

Cerdeña [θerˈðeɲa] sf Sardinia.

cereal [θereˈal] sm, adj cereal.

cerebro [θeˈreβro] sm brain. cerebral adj
cerebral.

ceremonia [θereˈmonja] sf ceremony. ceremonial adj ceremonial. ceremonioso adj
ceremonious.

cereza [θeˈreθa] sf cherry. cerezo sm cherry tree.

cerilla [θeˈriʎa] sf match.

*cerner [θerˈner] v sift; sieve; examine
carefully; drizzle. cernerse v sway; waddle; hover; threaten.

cero [ˈθero] sm zero, nothing.

*cerrar [θerˈrar] v shut, close. cerrarse v
close up; stand firm; heal; cloud over.
cerrar con llave lock. cerrar la boca shut
up. cerrar la marcha bring up the rear.
cerrado adj closed; secretive; obtuse;
overcast. cerradura sf lock; locking up.
cerraje sm lock.

cerril [θerˈril] adj rough, rocky; wild; ill-
bred.

cerro [ˈθerro] sm hill, ridge; animal's
neck.

cerrojo [θerˈroxo] sm bolt.

certeza [θerˈteθa] sf also certidumbre certainty.

certificar [θertifiˈkar] v certify; register;
guarantee. certificado sm certificate; registered letter.

cervato [θerˈβato] sm (zool) fawn.

cerveza [θerˈβeθa] sf beer.

cerviz [θerˈβiθ] sf nape of the neck, cer-
vix. bajar la cerviz bow one's head.

cesar [θeˈsar] v cease, stop; leave one's
job. cesación sf cessation, stoppage.
cesante adj out of office, unemployed.
cesantía sf suspension from office.

cesión [θeˈsjon] sf transfer; assignment;
conveyance; resignation.

césped [ˈθespeð] sf turf, lawn. césped
inglés lawn.

cesta [ˈθesta] sf basket, hamper. cestería
sf basketwork, wickerwork. cesto sm
basket.

cetro [ˈθetro] sm sceptre; (fig) power.

cía [ˈθia] sf hip-bone.

cianuro [θjaˈnuro] sm cyanide.

ciática [ˈθiˈatika] sf sciatica. ciático adj sciatic.

cicatería [θikateˈria] sf stinginess.

cicatriz [θikaˈtriθ] sf scar.

ciclismo [θiˈklismo] sm cycling. ciclista
s(m+f) cyclist.

ciclo [ˈθiklo] sm cycle. cíclico adj cyclical.

ciclón [θiˈklon] sm cyclone.

cidra [ˈθiðra] sf citron. cidro sm citron
tree.

ciego [ˈθjego], -a sm, sf blind person. adj
blind.

cielo [ˈθjelo] sm sky; heaven; ceiling; climate. ¡cielos! good heavens!

ciempiés [θjemˈpjes] sm invar centipede.

ciénaga [ˈθjenaga] sf bog, marsh, swamp.

ciencia [ˈθjenθja] sf science; knowledge,
learning. ciencia ficción science fiction.

científico [θjenˈtifiko], -a sm, sf scientist.
adj scientific.

cieno [ˈθjeno] sm mud. cienoso adj muddy.

ciento [ˈθjento] sm, adj also cien hundred.

cierre [ˈθjerre] sm closing; fastening; lock.

cierto [ˈθjerto] adj certain. adv certainly.
de cierto certainly. por cierto of course.

ciervo [ˈθjerβo] sm deer; stag. cierva sf
hind.

cierzo [ˈθjerθo] sm north wind.

cifra [ˈθifra] sf number, figure; cipher;
code; abbreviation. en cifra in short.
cifrar v summarize; cipher; enclose.
cifrar las esperanzas en set one's hopes
on.

cigarro [θiˈgarro] sm cigar. cigarillo sm
cigarette.

cigüeña [θiˈgweɲa] sf stork.

cilindro [θiˈlindro] sm cylinder. cilíndrico
adj cylindrical.

cima [ˈθima] sf top; summit. dar cima a
finish off. por cima at the top; superficially.

címbalo [ˈθimbalo] sm cymbal.

cimbrar [θimˈbrar] v also cimbrear
vibrate; bend; sway.

*cimentar [θimenˈtar] v found; establish.
cimiento sm foundation.

cinc [θink] sm zinc.

cincel [θinˈθel] sm chisel. cincelador sm
engraver; stonecutter.

cinco [ˈθinko] sm, adj five.

cincuenta [θinˈkwenta] sm, adj fifty.

cinchar [θinˈtʃar] v girth; fasten with
hoops. cincha sf girth, cinch. cincho sm
belt; hoop.

cine [ˈθine] sm cinema.

cínico ['θiniko], **-a** *sm. sf* cynic. *adj* cynical; shameless. **cinismo** *sm* cynicism.

cínife ['θinife] *sm* mosquito.

cinta ['θinta] *sf* ribbon; strip; tape; tape-measure. **cinteado** *adj* beribboned.

cintura [θin'tura] *sf* waist; belt. **meter a uno en cintura** make someone behave. **cinturón** *sm* belt; zone; circle. **cinturón de seguridad** safety belt.

ciprés [θi'pres] *sm* cypress.

circo ['θirko] *sm* circus.

circuito [θir'kwito] *sm* circuit.

circular [θirku'lar] *v* circulate; circularize; move. *adj* round, circular. **circulación** *sf* circulation; traffic.

circuncidar [θirkunθi'ðar] *v* circumcise. **circuncisión** *sf* circumcision. **circunciso** *adj* circumcised.

circundar [θirkun'dar] *v* surround, encircle.

circunferencia [θirkunfe'renθja] *sf* circumference.

circunflejo [θirkun'flexo] *sm* circumflex.

circunscribir [θirkunskri'βir] *v* circumscribe.

circunspecto [θirkun'spekto] *adj* circumspect. **circunspección** *sf* circumspection.

circunstancia [θirkun'stanθja] *sf* circumstance; condition; incident. **circunstancial** *adj* circumstantial. **circunstante** *adj* surrounding; present.

circunvecino [θirkunβe'θino] *adj* neighbouring.

ciruela [θi'rwela] *sf* plum. **ciruelo** *sm* plum-tree.

cirugía [θiru'xia] *sf* surgery. **cirujano** *sm* surgeon.

cisco ['θisko] *sm* coal dust; (*fam*) hubbub.

cisma ['θisma] *sm* schism; discord.

cisne ['θisne] *sm* swan.

cisterna [θis'terna] *sf* cistern, water tank.

cita ['θita] *sf* citation; appointment; quotation. **citar** *v* make an appointment; quote; (*jur*) summons.

ciudad [θju'ðað] *sf* city. **ciudadanía** *sf* citizenship. **ciudadano, -a** *sm, sf* citizen. **ciudadela** *sf* citadel.

cívico ['θiβiko] *adj* civic; patriotic.

civilizar [θiβili'θar] *v* civilize. **civil** *adj* civil. **civilización** *sf* civilization.

cizalla [θi'θaʎa] *sf* shears *pl*; metal shavings *pl*.

clamar [kla'mar] *v* cry out; beseech.

clamor [kla'mor] *sm* shout; cry. **clamorear** *v* cry out for; beseech. **clamoroso** *adj* noisy.

clandestino [klandes'tino] *adj* secret.

clara ['klara] *sf* white of egg; bald patch

claraboya [klara'βoja] *sf* skylight.

clarear [klare'ar] *v* clear; dawn; grow light; be transparent; (*fam*) reveal secrets.

clarete [kla'rete] *sm* claret.

clarificar [klarifi'kar] *v* clarify. **clarificación** *sf* clarification.

clarín [kla'rin] *sm* bugle.

clarinete [klari'nete] *sm* clarinet.

claro ['klaro] *adj* light; clear; distinct *adv* clearly. *sm* opening; space; clearing. **claro que** of course. **claro que sí** certainly **claridad** *sf* clarity; light; brightness.

clase ['klase] *sf* class, type; lesson; classroom. **clase media** middle class. **clase particular** private lesson.

clásico ['klasiko] *adj* classic(al). *sm* classic.

clasificar [klasifi'kar] *v* classify **clasificación** *sf* classification.

claudicar [klauði'kar] *v* limp; (*fam*) yield; (*fig*) shirk; (*fig*) falter. **claudicación** *sf* limping; yielding; shirking.

claustro ['klaustro] *sm* cloister, teaching staff. **claustral** *adj* cloistered.

claustrofobia [klaustro'foβja] *sf* claustrophobia.

cláusula ['klausula] *sf* clause.

clavar [kla'βar] *v* nail; fasten, fix; (*fam*) cheat. **clava** *sf* club, cudgel. **clavado en la cama** bed-ridden. **clavija** *sf* peg, pin **clavo** *sm* nail; spike.

clave ['klaβe] *sf* key; clue; clef. *sm* harpsichord.

clavel [kla'βel] *sm* carnation.

clavícula [kla'βikula] *sf* collar bone.

clemencia [kle'menθja] *sf* mercy **clemente** *adj* merciful.

clérigo ['klerigo] *sm* clergyman, priest **clerical** *adj* clerical. **clericato** *sm* also **clero** clergy.

cliente ['kljente], **-a** *sm, sf* client, customer; patient. **clientela** *sf* clients *pl*, customers *pl*; practice.

clima ['klima] *sm* climate. **climático** *adj* climatic.

clínica ['klinika] *sf* clinic. **clínico** *adj* clinical.

clisé [kli'se] *sm* (*foto*) negative; (*fig*) cliché.

cloaca [klo'aka] *sf* sewer. drain.

cloro ['kloro] *sm* chlorine.

clorofila [kloro'fila] *sf* chlorophyll.

cloroformo [kloro'formo] *sm* chloroform. **clorofornar** *v* chloroform.

club [kluβ] *sm* club. **club de noche** night-club.

coacción [koak'θjon] *sf* coercion. **coactivo** *adj* coercive.

coagular [koagu'lar] *v* coagulate; curdle; clot. **coagulación** *sf* coagulation; clotting.

coalición [koali'θjon] *sf* coalition.

coartada [koar'taða] *sf* alibi.

coartar [koar'tar] *v* hinder; prevent; limit; restrict.

cobarde [ko'βarðe] *s(m+f)* coward. *adj* cowardly. **cobardía** *sf* cowardice.

cobertizo [koβer'tiθo] *sm* garage; shed. **cobertura** [koβer'tura] *sf* covering.

cobijar [koβi'xar] *v* cover, shelter. **cobijo** *sm* shelter.

cobrar [ko'βrar] *v* charge; earn; gain. **cobrarse** *v* (*med*) recover. **cobradero** *adj* recoverable. **cobrador, -a** *sm, sf* collector; conductor; receiver. **cobranza** *sf* collection; receipt.

cobre ['koβre] *sm* copper. **batirse el cobre** (*fam*) get on with it. **cobres** *sm pl* (*música*) brass.

*cocer [ko'θer] *v* cook. **cocido** *sm* stew.

cocinar [koθi'nar] *v* cook. **cocina** *sf* kitchen; cookery. **cocinero, -a** *sm, sf* cook.

coco ['koko] *sm* coconut; coconut palm; grub, larva; (*fam*) face; (*fam*) head. **hacer cocos** make faces.

cocodrilo [koko'ðrilo] *sm* crocodile.

cóctel ['koktel] *sm* cocktail.

coche ['kotʃe] *sm* car; coach; carriage. **coche cama** sleeper. **coche de alquiler** self-drive car. **coche fúnebre** hearse.

cochino [ko'tʃino], **-a** *sm, sf* pig, swine. *adj* (*fam*) rotten; filthy; disgusting. **cochinada** *sf* filth; filthy thing. **cochinera** *sf* pigsty.

codear [koðe'ar] *v* nudge, elbow. **codearse** *v* rub shoulders with. **codazo** *sm* nudge. **codo** *sm* elbow; bend.

codeína [koðe'ina] *sf* codeine.

codelincuente [koðelin'kwente] *s(m+f)* accomplice. **codelincuencia** *sf* complicity.

códice ['koðiθe] *sm* codex.

codiciar [koði'θjar] *v* covet. **codicia** *sf* greed. **codicioso** *adj* greedy.

codificar [koðifi'kar] *v* codify. **codificación** *sf* codification

código ['koðigo] *sm* code. **código de carreteras** highway code.

codillo [ko'ðiʎo] *sm* forearm; (*culin*) shoulder.

codorniz [koðor'niθ] *sf* quail.

coercer [koer'θer] *v* coerce. **coerción** *sf* coercion.

coexistir [koeksis'tir] *v* coexist. **coexistencia** *sf* coexistence.

cofia ['kofja] *sf* coif; hair-net.

cofradía [kofra'ðia] *sf* fraternity; society. **cofre** ['kofre] *sm* chest.

coger [ko'xer] *v* get; take; catch; seize; fit; collect. **cogida** *sf* gathering; (*tauromaquia*) goring. **cogido** *sm* fold, pleat.

cogote [ko'gote] *sm* nape of the neck. **ser tieso de cogote** be stiff-necked.

cohete [ko'ete] *sm* rocket.

cohibir [koi'βir] *v* inhibit; embarrass. **cohibidor** *adj* inhibiting. **cohibición** *sf* inhibition. **cohibido** *adj* restricted.

cohombrillo [koom'briʎo] *sm* gherkin. **cohombro** *sm* cucumber.

coincidencia [koinθi'ðenθja] *sf* coincidence. **coincidente** *adj* coincidental.

cojear [koxe'ar] *v* limp; hobble; (*fig*) waver; (*fig*) lapse. **cojera** *sf* lameness. **cojo** *adj* lame; lopsided.

cojín [ko'xin] *sm* cushion. **cojinete** *sm* small pillow; pad; (*tecn*) bearing. **cojinete de bolas** ball-bearing.

cok [kok] *sm* coke.

col [kol] *sf* cabbage. **coles de Bruselas** Brussels sprouts *pl*.

cola ['kola] *sf* tail; end; (*vestido*) train; queue; glue. **hacer cola** form a queue.

colaborar [kolaβo'rar] *v* collaborate. **colaboración** *sf* collaboration. **colaborador, -a** *sm, sf* collaborator.

colapso [ko'lapso] *sm* collapse, breakdown.

*colar [ko'lar] *v* strain; filter; wash; confer; (*fig, fam*) slip through. **colarse** *v* slip; gatecrash; jump the queue; err. **colada** *sf* washing. **coladero** *sm* colander, sieve.

colcha ['koltʃa] *sf* bedspread.

colchón [kol'tʃon] *sm* mattress.

colear [kole'ar] *v* wag the tail.

colección [kolek'θjon] *sf* collection. **colectivo** *adj* collective. **colectividad** *sf* collectivity; community.

colega [ko'lega] *sm* colleague.

colegio [ko'lexjo] *sm* college, school. **colegial** *sm* schoolboy.

colegir [kole'xir] *v* infer, conclude.

cólera ['kolera] *sf* anger. *sm* cholera. **colérico** *adj* angry.

coleta [ko'leta] *sf* pigtail; postscript.

*colgar [kol'gar] *v* hang, hang up, hang out. **colgadero** *sm* hook; peg; hanger. **puente colgante** *sm* suspension bridge.

coliflor [koli'flor] *sf* cauliflower.

colilla [ko'liʎa] *sf* cigarette stub.

colina [ko'lina] *sf* hill.

colindar [kolin'dar] *v* adjoin. **colindante** *adj* adjacent.

colisión [koli'sjon] *sf* collision.

colmar [kol'mar] *v* fill to overflowing. **colmado** *adj* plentiful.

colmena [kol'mena] *sf* beehive.

colmillo [kol'miʎo] *sm* tooth; fang; tusk. **enseñar los colmillos** (*fam*) threaten.

colmo ['kolmo] *sm* highest point; limit.

colocar [kolo'kar] *v* place; put in position; arrange; find employment for. **colocarse** *v* get a job. **colocación** *sf* employment; position; investment.

Colombia [ko'lombja] *sf* Colombia. **colombiano, -a** *s, adj* Colombian.

colonia [ko'lonja] *sf* colony. **colonial** *adj* colonial; imported. **colonialismo** *sm* colonialism. **colonización** *sf* colonization. **colonizar** *v* colonize. **colono** *sm* colonist, colonial.

coloquio [ko'lokjo] *sm* conversation.

color [ko'lor] *sm* colour; dye; paint; complexion. **colorado** *sm, adj* coloured; red. **ponerse colorado** blush. **colorar** *v* colour, dye. **colorear** *v* colour, dye; grow red; ripen. **colorete** *sm* rouge. **colorido** *sm* colour, colouring. **colorín** *sm* goldfinch; (*fam*) measles.

colosal [kolo'sal] *adj* colossal.

columbrar [kolum'brar] *v* glimpse; (*fig*) suspect.

columna [ko'lumna] *sf* column, pillar.

columpiar [kolum'pjar] *v* swing. **columpiarse** *v* sway; (*fam*) waddle; blunder. **columpio** *sm* swing.

collado [ko'ʎaðo] *sm* hill; fell.

collar [ko'ʎar] *sm* necklace; collar.

coma[1] ['koma] *sf* (*gram*) comma.

coma[2] *sm* (*med*) coma.

comadre [ko'maðre] *sf* midwife; godmother; (*fam*) neighbour, friend. **comadrear** *v* gossip. **comadreo** *sm* gossip.

comadreja [koma'ðrexa] *sf* weasel.

comadrona [koma'ðrona] *sf* midwife.

comandante [koman'dante] *sm* commander. **comandar** *v* command.

comandita [koman'dita] *sf* sleeping partnership. **socio comanditario** *sm* sleeping partner.

comarca [ko'marka] *sf* region, district.

comba ['komba] *sf* bend, curve; camber; sag. **combadura** *sf* curvature; camber.

combatir [komba'tir] *v* combat, fight. **combate** . *sm* combat, battle, struggle. **combatiente** *sm* fighter; soldier.

combinar [kombi'nar] *v* combine; plan, arrange. **combinación** *sf* combination; project; permutation. **combinatorio** *adj* combining.

combustible [kombus'tiβle] *adj* combustible. *sm* fuel.

comedero [kome'ðero] *adj* edible. *sm* dining-room; feeding-trough.

comedia [ko'meðja] *sf* play; comedy; theatre. **comediante, -a** *sm, sf* actor/actress.

comediar [kome'ðjar] *v* divide into equal shares.

comedido [kome'ðiðo] *adj* polite, courteous; moderate. **comedir** *v* prepare. **comedirse** *v* restrain oneself.

comedor [kome'ðor] *sm* dining-room.

comensal [komen'sal] *sm* table companion.

comentar [komen'tar] *v* comment on; discuss. **comentario** *sm* commentary. **comentarista** *s(m+f)* commentator. **comento** *sm* comment.

*comenzar [komen'θar] *v* commence. **comienzo** *sm* beginning.

comer [ko'mer] *v* eat; corrode; erode. **no tener qué comer** have nothing to eat. **ser de buen comer** have a good appetite. **comerse** *v* swallow; eat up. **comestible** *adj* edible. **comestibles** *sm pl* food *sing*; groceries *pl*. **comida** *sf* food; meal; lunch.

comercio [ko'merθjo] *sm* commerce; trade; shop. **comercio al por mayor/menor** wholesale/retail trade. **comerciante** *sm* shopkeeper; merchant; tradesman. **comerciar** *v* trade.

cometa [ko'meta] *sf* kite. *sm* comet.

cometer [kome'ter] *v* commit. **cometido** *sm* task; assignment; mission.

comezón [kome'θon] *sf* itch; itching.

cómico ['komiko] *adj* comic(al). *sm* comedian.

comilón [komi'lon], **-ona** *sm, sf* glutton. *adj* gluttonous. *sf* feast.

comillas [ko'miʎas] *sf pl* inverted commas *pl.*

comisaría [komisa'ria] *sf* police station. **comisario** *sm* commissary; commissioner; police inspector.

comisión [komi'sjon] *sf* commission; mission; committee.

comiso [ko'miso] *sm* (*jur*) confiscation.

comité [komi'te] *sm* committee.

comitiva [komi'tiβa] *sf* retinue.

como ['komo] *adv* how; as; as if; why; when; so that; about, approximately. *conj* as, since, because; if, **así como** as soon as; in the same way that. **como quiera que sea** in one way or another. **tan pronto como** as soon as. **¿cómo?** *adv* how? why? in what way? **¡cómo!** *interj* what! why! eh! **el cómo y el porqué** the how and the why.

cómoda ['komoða] *sf* chest of drawers.

cómodo ['komoðo] *adj* convenient; comfortable. **comodidad** *sf* convenience. comfort. **a su comodidad** at your earliest convenience.

compacto [kom'pakto] *adj* compact, close.

*****compadecer** [kompaðe'θer] *v* pity. **compadecerse** *v* sympathize; agree.

compadre [kom'paðre] *sm* godfather; pal, crony.

compaginar [kompaxi'nar] *v* arrange; combine; join; match; agree.

compañero [kompa'ɲero], **-a** *sm, sf* companion, partner; one of a pair. **compañerismo** *sm* fellowship. **compañía** *sf* company, society.

comparar [kompa'rar] *v* compare. **comparación** *sf* comparison. **comparativo** *adj* comparative.

*****comparecer** [kompare'θer] *v* appear in court. **orden de comparecer** *sm* summons.

compartimiento [komparti'mjento] *sm* compartment; section; division. **compartir** *v* divide; share.

compás [kom'pas] *sm* (*mar*) compass; (*mat*) pair of compasses; rhythm; pattern, standard. **llevar el compás** beat time. **compasado** *adj* orderly, moderate. **compasar** *v* measure; regulate.

compasión [kompa'sjon] *sf* compassion. **compasivo** *adj* compassionate.

compatible [kompa'tiβle] *adj* compatible. **compatibilidad** *sf* compatibility.

compatriota [kompa'trjota] *s(m+f)* compatriot.

compeler [kompe'ler] *v* compel.

compendio [kom'pendjo] *sm* compendium; summary, précis. **en compendio** briefly. **compendir** *v* summarize.

compensar [kompen'sar] *v* compensate; offset; make amends. **compensación** *sf* compensation. **compensatorio** *adj* compensatory.

*****competir** [kompe'tir] *v* compete; contest. **competencia** *sf* competition; concern; competence. **competente** *adj* competent; able. **competición** *sf* competition. **competidor, -a** *sm, sf* competitor.

compilar [kompi'lar] *v* compile. **compilación** *sf* compilation.

compinche [kom'pintʃe] *s(m+f)* pal, chum; accomplice.

*****complacer** [kompla'θer] *v* please; oblige; humour. **complacerse** *v* be pleased, be glad (to). **complacencia** *sf* pleasure; indulgence. **complaciente** *adj* helpful; obliging.

complejo [kom'plexo] *adj, sm* complex. **complejidad** *sf* complexity.

complementario [komplemen'tarjo] *adj* complementary. **complemento** *sm* complement.

completar [komple'tar] *v* complete. **completo** *adj* complete.

complicar [kompli'kar] *v* complicate; be complicated *or* confused. **complicarse** *v* become confused *or* complicated. **complicación** *sf* complication. **complicado** *adj* complicated.

cómplice ['kompliθe] *s(m+f)* accomplice. **complicidad** *sf* complicity.

complot [kom'plot] *sm* plot; intrigue; (*fam*) understanding.

*****componer** [kompo'ner] *v* compose; form; repair; adjust; write. **componerse** *v* compose oneself; tidy oneself up; dress up; agree. **componerse de** consist of. **componedor, -a** *sm, sf* compositor; repairer; arbitrator. **componente** *sm* component; ingredient. **componible** *adj* adjustable.

comportar [kompor'tar] *v* tolerate; involve. **comportarse** *v* behave. **comportamiento** *sm* behaviour. **comporte** *sm* behaviour; bearing.

composición [komposi'θjon] *sf* composition; mixture; agreement; settlement. **compositor, -a** *sm, sf* composer.

compostura [kompos'tura] *sf* composition, structure; repair; neatness; adornment; agreement; composure; adjustment.

compota [kom'pota] *sf* (*culin*) compote.

comprar [kom'prar] *v* buy; bribe. **compra** *sf* purchase. **comprador, -a** *sm*, *sf* shopper.

comprender [kompren'der] *v* understand; include. **comprensibilidad** *sf* intelligibility. **comprensible** *adj* understandable. **comprensión** *sf* understanding; inclusion. **comprensivo** *adj* understanding; comprising.

comprimir [kompri'mir] *v* squeeze, compress. **comprimirse** *v* control oneself. **compresa** *sf* compress; sanitary towel. **compresión** *sf* compression.

*comprobar [kompro'βar] *v* verify, check. **comprobación** *sf* verification. **comprobante** *adj* verifying. *sm* voucher; receipt.

comprometer [komprome'ter] *v* risk; compromise; commit. **comprometido** *adj* embarrassing; committed; implicated. **compromiso** *sm* commitment; agreement; compromise.

compuesto [kom'pwesto] *sm* compound. *adj* compound; repaired; dressed-up.

compunción [kompun'θjon] *sf* compunction; contrition.

computar [kompu'tar] *v* compute, calculate. **computadora** *sf* computer.

comulgar [komul'gar] *v* give/take communion; (*fig*) share.

común [ko'mun] *adj* common; ordinary; vulgar. *sm* community, public toilet. **por lo común** generally. **comunal** *adj* communal.

comunicar [komuni'kar] *v* communicate; convey; transmit; (*dos cuartos*) connect. **comunicarse** *v* spread; keep in touch with; exchange. **comunicación** *sf* communication; message. **comunicativo** *adj* talkative; catching.

comunidad [komuni'ðað] *sf* community.

comunión [komu'njon] *sf* communion.

comunismo [komu'nismo] *sm* communism. **comunista** *s(m + f)*, *adj* communist.

con [kon] *prep* with; by; in spite of; to, towards. **con que** *conj* whereupon; and so. **con tal que** provided that.

cóncavo ['konkaβo] *adj* concave. **concavidad** *sf* hollow, cavity.

*concebir [konθe'βir] *v* conceive; imagine; understand; take; (*med*) conceive.

concebible *adj* conceivable, imaginable. **concepción** *sf* conception, idea; (*med*) conception. **concepto** *sm* concept; idea; opinion; witticism.

conceder [konθe'ðer] *v* concede, grant; allow; spare; award. **concesión** *sf* concession; grant.

concejo [kon'θexo] *sm* council. **concejal** *sm* councillor. **concejil** *adj* municipal.

concentrar [konθen'trar] *v* concentrate. **concentración** *sf* concentration.

concerniente [konθer'njente] *adj* concerning, regarding. **concernir** *v* concern.

*concertar [konθer'tar] *v* harmonize; agree; adjust; compare. **concertado** *adj* concerted.

conciencia [kon'θjenθja] *sf* conscience; consciousness; mind; conscientiousness. **concienzudo** *adj* conscientious.

concierto [kon'θjerto] *sm* concert; concerto; agreement; (*fig*) harmony. **de concierto** in agreement.

conciliar [konθi'ljar] *v* conciliate; reconcile; gain. *adj* of a council. *sm* councillor. **concilio** *sm* councillor; council.

conciso [kon'θiso] *adj* concise.

concitar [konθi'tar] *v* stir up.

*concluir [konklu'ir] *v* conclude; deduce; settle; convince. **conclusión** *sf* conclusion.

*concordar [konkor'ðar] *v* agree. **concordancia** *sf* agreement. **concorde** *adj* in agreement. **concordia** *sf* harmony.

concretar [konkre'tar] *v* bring together; limit; specify; state explicitly. **concretarse** *v* confine oneself; be definite; keep; take shape. **concreto** *adj* concrete, specific. **en concreto** in brief.

concubina [konku'βina] *sf* concubine.

concurrir [konkur'rir] *v* meet; attend; go; coincide; contribute; concur; compete. **concurrido** *adj* popular; crowded. **concurso** *sm* meeting; cooperation; help; competition.

concusión [konku'sjon] *sf* concussion.

concha ['kontʃa] *sf* shell.

condado [kon'daðo] *sm* earldom; county. **conde** *sm* earl. **condesa** *sf* countess.

condecorar [kondeko'rar] *v* (*persona*) decorate. **condecoración** *sf* medal, decoration.

condenar [konde'nar] *v* condemn; sentence; block up. **condena** *sf* sentence; conviction. **cumplir condena** serve a sentence. **condenación** *sf* condemnation;

damnation. **condenado, -a** *sm, sf* condemned person; wretch.

condensar [konden'sar] *v* condense. **condensación** *sf* condensation. **condensador** *sm* condenser.

*****condescender** [kondesθen'der] *v* condescend; yield; comply. **condescendencia** *sf* condescension; compliance. **condescendiente** *adj* condescending; obliging.

condicionar [kondiθjo'nar] *v* condition; determine. **condición** *sf* condition; quality; temperament.

condimentar [kondimen'tar] *v* season. **condimento** *sm* seasoning, condiment.

condolerse [kondo'lerse] *v* condole, sympathize. **condolencia** *sf* condolence.

condonar [kondo'nar] *v* pardon, condone; (*deuda*) cancel. **condonación** *sf* pardon.

*****conducir** [kondu'θir] *v* conduct; transport; guide; manage; (*auto*) drive; be suitable. **conducirse** *v* behave. **conducción** *sf* transport; guidance; direction, management. **conducción a izquierda** left-hand drive. **permiso de conducción** *sm* driving licence. **conducta** *sf* transport; conduct; direction; behaviour.

conducto [kon'dukto] *sm* conduit; pipe. **conductor** *sm* (*tecn*) conductor.

conectar [konek'tar] *v* connect; switch on. **conectador** *sm* connector. **conexión** *sf* connection.

conejo [ko'nexo] *sm* rabbit.

confabularse [konfaβu'larse] *v* plot. **confabulación** *sf* conspiracy.

confeccionar [konfekθjon'ar] *v* make, make up. **confección** *sf* making; tailoring; clothing. **confeccionado** *adj* ready-made, ready-to-wear.

confederar [konfeðe'rar] *v* confederate. **confederación** *sf* confederation, confederacy.

conferenciar [konferen'θjar] *v* talk, discuss. **conferencia** *sf* conference; lecture; telephone call. **conferencia a cobro revertido** reverse-charge call. **conferencia en la cumbre** summit conference. **conferencia interurbana** trunk call.

*****conferir** [konfe'rir] *v* confer, consult; award, grant.

*****confesar** [konfe'sar] *v* confess, admit **confesar de plano** own up. **confesión** *sf* confession.

confeti [kon'feti] *sm pl* confetti *sing*.

confiar [kon'fjar] *v* entrust; trust; rely. **confiable** *adj* trustworthy. **confiado** *adj* confident; trusting. **confianza** *sf* confidence; reliability; informality.

confidencia [konfi'ðenθja] *sf* secret; confidence. **confidencial** *adj* confidential. **confidente** *adj* faithful.

confinar [konfi'nar] *v* confine; banish. **confinar con** border on. **confín** *sm* border, limit.

confirmar [konfir'mar] *v* confirm. **confirmarse** *v* be confirmed. **confirmación** *sf* confirmation.

confiscar [konfis'kar] *v* confiscate. **confiscación** *sf* confiscation.

confitar [konfi'tar] *v* coat with sugar; preserve in syrup. **confite** *sm* sweet. **confitería** *sf* sweet-shop. **confitura** *sf* candied fruit.

conflicto [kon'flikto] *sm* conflict.

*****confluir** [konflu'ir] *v* converge. meet.

conformar [konfor'mar] *v* conform. **conformarse** *v* resign oneself. **conforme** *adj* in agreement; alike; according. **conforme a** in accordance with. **según y conforme** it all depends.

confortar [konfor'tar] *v* comfort; encourage. **confortable** *adj* comfortable. **conforte** *sm* solace, comfort.

confrontar [konfron'tar] *v* confront; compare. **confrontar con** border on; confront. **confrontación** *sf* confrontation.

confundir [konfun'dir] *v* confuse; mistake. **confusión** *sf* confusion. **confuso** *adj* confused; embarrassed.

congelar [konxe'lar] *v* freeze; congeal. **congelación** *sf* freezing. **congelación de salarios** wage freeze. **congelador** *sm* freezer.

congénito [kon'xenito] *adj* congenital.

congestionar [konxestjo'nar] *v* congest. **congestión** *sf* congestion.

conglomerarse [konglome'rarse] *v* conglomerate. **conglomeración** *sf* conglomeration.

congoja [kon'goxa] *sf* agony; distress.

congratular [kongratu'lar] *v* congratulate **congratularse** *v* be delighted. **congratulación** *sf* congratulation; delight.

congregar [kongre'gar] *v* congregate. **congregación** *sf* congregation.

congreso [kon'greso] *sm* congress; assembly; conference.

congrio ['kongrjo] *sm* conger eel.

congruente [kongru'ente] *adj* congruent; suitable. **congruencia** *sf* congruence; suitability.

cónico ['koniko] *adj* conical.

conífero [ko'nifero] *adj* coniferous. **conífera** *sf* conifer.

conjeturar [konxetu'rar] *v* conjecture, guess. **conjetura** *sf* conjecture, guess.

conjugar [konxu'gar] *v* combine; (*gram*) conjugate. **conjugación** *sf* conjugation.

conjunto [kon'xunto] *sm* whole. *adj* joint. **en conjunto** as a whole. **conjunción** *sf* (*gram*) conjunction.

conjurar [konxu'rar] *v* bind by oath; implore; ward off; conspire; exorcise. **cónjura** *sf also* **conjuración** conspiracy. **conjurador** *sm* exorcist. **conjuro** *sm* exorcism; entreaty.

conmemorar [konmemo'rar] *v* commemorate. **conmemoración** *sf* commemoration. **conmemorativo** *adj* commemorative.

conmigo [kon'migo] *pron* with me, with myself.

conminar [konmi'nar] *v* threaten; warn. **conminativo** *adj* threatening; compulsory.

conmiseración [konmisera'θjon] *sf* commiseration.

conmoción [konmo'θjon] *sf* commotion; upheaval; shock. **conmoción cerebral** concussion.

conmover [konmo'βer] *v* disturb; touch. **conmoverse** *v* be moved. **conmovedor** *adj* moving, touching.

conmutar [konmu'tar] *v* exchange. **conmutador** *sm* switch.

connivencia [konni'βenθja] *sf* connivance.

connotar [konno'tar] *v* imply. **connotación** *sf* connotation.

cono ['kono] *sm* cone.

*conocer [kono'θer] *v* know; understand; recognize. **conocer de** know about. **conocer de** *or* **en** (*jur*) try (a case). **conocer de nombre** know by name. **conocerse** *v* meet; be acquainted with. **se conoce que** it is clear that. **conocedor, -a** *s, adj* expert. **conocido, -a** *sm, sf* acquaintance. **conocimiento** *sm* knowledge; good sense; consciousness; (*com*) bill of lading; proof of identity. **perder el conocimiento** lose consciousness.

conque ['konke] *conj* so. *sm* (*fam*) condition. **conqué** *sm* (*fam*) means.

conquistar [konkis'tar] *v* conquer; win; win over. **conquista** *sf* conquest. **conquistador, -a** *sm, sf* conqueror.

consabido [konsa'βiðo] *adj* traditional; well known; aforementioned.

consagrar [konsa'grar] *v* consecrate; dedicate. **consagración** *sf* consecration; dedication.

consanguíneo [konsan'gineo] *adj* related by blood. **consanguinidad** *sf* blood relationship.

consciente [kons'θjente] *adj* conscious.

consecuencia [konse'kwenθja] *sf* consequence; outcome; consistency. **en** *or* **por consecuencia** consequently. **ser de consecuencia** be of importance. **traer como consecuencia** result in. **consecuente** *adj* consequent; consistent.

consecutivo [konseku'tiβo] *adj* consecutive.

*conseguir [konse'gir] *v* get; attain; procure; bring about; manage. **dar por conseguido** take for granted.

consejo [kon'sexo] *sm* advice; counsel; council. **consejo de guerra** court-martial. **entrar en consejo** begin consultation. **consejero** *sm* adviser; member of board of directors.

*consentir [konsen'tir] *v* allow; believe; tolerate; spoil; agree. **consentir en** consent to. **consentirse** *v* begin to crack; come loose. **consentido** *adj* pampered.

conserje [kon'serxe] *sm* porter, doorkeeper.

conservar [konser'βar] *v* conserve; preserve. **conservarse** *v* last, wear well. **conserva** *sf* preserved food; jam; pickles *pl*. **conservación** *sf* conservation; preserving. **conservador, -a** *sm, sf* (*pol*) Conservative; (*museo*) curator.

considerar [konsiðe'rar] *v* consider. **considerable** *adj* considerable; substantial. **consideración** *sf* consideration. **por consideración a** out of respect for. **ser de consideración** be important. **tener** *or* **guardar consideraciones** show consideration.

consignar [konsig'nar] *v* consign; assign; deposit; send. **consignación** *sf* consignment. **consigna** *sf* left-luggage office; password; slogan.

consigo [kon'sigo] *pron* with him/her/you/one.

consiguiente [konsi'gjente] *adj* consequent.

consistir [konsis'tir] *v* consist. **consistir en** consist of. **consistencia** *sf* consistency. **consistente** *adj* consistent.

*****consolar** [konso'lar] *v* console. **consolación** *sf* consolation.

consolidar [konsoli'ðar] *v* consolidate; strengthen. **consolidación** *sf* consolidation.

consonante [konso'nante] *sm* consonant. *adj* rhyming; harmonious. **consonancia** *sf* rhyme; harmony. **consonar** *v* rhyme; harmonize.

consorte [kon'sorte] *s(m+f)* consort; accomplice; companion. **consorcio** *sm* association; fellowship; consortium.

conspicuo [kons'pikwo] *adj* conspicuous.

conspirar [konspi'rar] *v* conspire, plot. **conspiración** *sf* conspiracy, plot.

constante [kons'tante] *adj* constant. **constancia** *sf* constancy.

constar [kons'tar] *v* be clear; be evident; be on record. **constar de** consist of. **constar en** appear; be recorded.

constelación [konstela'θjon] *sf* constellation; climate.

consternarse [konster'narse] *v* be dismayed. **consternación** *sf* consternation, dismay.

constiparse [konsti'parse] *v* catch a cold. **constipación** *sf* cold. **estar constipado** have a cold.

*****constituir** [konstitu'ir] *v* constitute; establish; compose. **constitución** *sf* constitution.

constreñir [konstre'ɲir] *v* constrain; force; constipate. **constreñimiento** *sm* constraint. **constricción** *sf* constriction.

*****construir** [konstru'ir] *v* construct. **construcción** *sf* construction. **constructor, -a** *sm, sf* builder, constructor.

consuelo [kon'swelo] *sm* consolation.

cónsul ['konsul] *sm* consul. **consulado** *sm* consulate.

consultar [konsul'tar] *v* consult. **consulta** *sf* consultation.

consumado [konsu'maðo] *adj* consummate; accomplished. **consumación** *sf* consummation; completion. **consumar** *v* accomplish; complete.

consumir [konsu'mir] *v* consume. **consumirse** *v* languish; be uneasy. **consumido** *adj* consumed; (*fam*) lean; (*fam*) timid. **consumo** *sm* consumption.

contabilidad [kontaβili'ðað] *sf* accounting; bookkeeping. **contable** *sm* bookkeeper; accountant.

contacto [kon'takto] *sm* contact.

contagiar [konta'xjar] *v* infect, contaminate; corrupt. **contagio** *sm* contagion. **contagioso** *adj* contagious.

contaminar [kontami'nar] *v* contaminate. **contaminación** *sf* contamination.

*****contar** [kon'tar] *v* count; relate. **contar con** count on; expect; possess. **contado** *adj* counted, limited. **al contado** cash down. **de contado** immediately. **por de contado** certainly. **contador** *sm* counter; cashier; (*tecn*) meter. **contador de aparcamiento** parking meter.

contemplar [kontem'plar] *v* contemplate. **contemplación** *sf* contemplation. **contemplativo** *adj* contemplative.

contemporáneo [kontempo'raneo], **-a** *s, adj* contemporary.

*****contender** [konten'der] *v* contend; struggle; argue. **contención** *sf* contention. **contencioso** *adj* contentious. **contendedor** *sm* contender, antagonist. **contendiente** *s(m+f)* litigant. **contienda** *sf* contest; dispute.

*****contener** [konte'ner] *v* contain; control; suppress; stop.

contenido [konte'niðo] *adj* reserved; moderate; contained. *sm* contents *pl*.

contentar [konten'tar] *v* satisfy, content. **contentarse** *v* be pleased. **contentamiento** *sm* contentment. **contento** *adj* content, satisfied.

contestar [kontes'tar] *v* answer; confirm; agree. **contestable** *adj* questionable. **contestación** *sf* reply; dispute.

contexto [kon'teksto] *sm* context.

contigo [kon'tigo] *pron* (*fam*) with you.

contiguo [kon'tigwo] *adj* contiguous; adjoining. **contigüidad** *sf* contiguity.

continente [konti'nente] *sm* continent; bearing; container. *adj* containing; continent. **continencia** *sf* continence. **continental** *adj* continental.

contingente [kontin'xente] *adj* contingent, accidental. *sm* contingent. **contingencia** *sf* contingency.

continuar [konti'nwar] *v* continue; remain; endure. **continuación** *sf* continuation. **a continuación de** following. **continuo** *adj* continuous.

contorno [kon'torno] *sm* contour, outline.

contornos *sm pl* environs *pl.* **en contorno** round about.

contra ['kontra] *prep* against; opposite; facing. **el pro y el contra** the pros and cons. **en contra** in opposition to.

contrabajo [kontra'βaxo] *sm* double bass.

contrabando [kontra'βando] *sm* contraband; smuggling.

contracción [kontrak'θjon] *sf* contraction.

***contradecir** [kontraðe'θir] *v* contradict. **contradicción** *sf* contradiction.

***contraer** [kontra'er] *v* contract; enter into; be infected with. **contraer matrimonio con** marry.

contrafuerte [kontra'fwerte] *sm* buttress.

***contrahacer** [kontraa'θer] *v* counterfeit; copy. **contrahacerse** *v* feign.

contrahecho [kontra'etʃo] *adj* deformed.

contramaestre [kontrama'estre] *sm* foreman; (*mar*) boatswain.

contramandar [kontraman'dar] *v* countermand.

contrapelo [kontra'pelo] *adv* **a contrapelo** against the grain.

contrapesar [kontrape'sar] *v* counterpoise, counterbalance; offset. **contrapeso** *sm* counterpoise.

contraponer [kontrapo'ner] *v* set against; oppose; contrast.

contrapunto [kontra'punto] *sm* counterpoint.

contrariar [kontra'rjar] *v* oppose. **contrariedad** *sf* opposition; setback; annoyance.

contrario [kon'trarjo], -a *sm, sf* opponent. **al contrario** on the contrary. **de lo contrario** otherwise. *adj* contrary, opposite.

contrarrestar [kontrarres'tar] *v* counteract; oppose; resist; (*la pelota*) return.

contrarrevolución [kontrarreβolu'θjon] *sf* counter-revolution. **contrarrevolucionario**, -a *s, adj* counter-revolutionary.

contrasentido [kontrasen'tiðo] *sm* contradiction; nonsense; mistranslation; misinterpretation.

contraseña [kontra'seɲa] *sf* countersign; password.

contrastar [kontras'tar] *v* contrast; resist; inspect. **contraste** *sm* contrast; opposition; hallmark; inspector. **en contraste con** in contrast to.

contrato [kon'trato] *sm* contract; covenant.

contraveneno [kontraβe'neno] *sm* antidote.

***contravenir** [kontraβe'nir] *v* contravene. **contravención** *sf* contravention.

***contribuir** [kontri'βwir] *v* contribute; pay tax. **contribución** *sf* contribution; tax. **contribuyente** *s(m+f)* tax-payer.

contrición [kontri'θjon] *sf* contrition.

contrincante [kontrin'kante] *sm* competitor; rival.

controversia [kontro'βersja] *sf* controversy. **controvertible** *adj* controversial. **controvertir** *v* dispute, argue.

contumacia [kontu'maθja] *sf* stubbornness, obstinacy; (*jur*) contempt of court. **contumaz** *adj* stubborn; perverse.

conturbar [kontur'βar] *v* perturb; disturb. **conturbación** *sf* perturbation.

contusión [kontu'sjon] *sf* contusion, bruise. **contusionar** *v* bruise.

***convalecer** [konβale'θer] *v* convalesce. **convalecencia** *sf* convalescence.

convecino [konβe'θino] *adj* neighbouring.

convencer [konβen'θer] *v* convince. **convencedor** *adj* convincing. **convencimiento** *sm* conviction.

***convenir** [konβe'nir] *v* agree, be agreed; arrange; be convenient; be advisable. **me conviene** it suits me. **convención** *sf* convention; agreement; assembly. **convencional** *adj* conventional. **convenible** *adj* docile. **conveniencia** *sf* convenience; conformity; usefulness; advantage. **conveniente** *adj* convenient; expedient; proper. **convenio** *sm* agreement; compact.

convento [kon'βento] *sm* convent.

converger [konβer'xer] *v also* **convergir** converge; (*fig*) agree. **convergencia** *sf* convergence. **convergente** *adj* convergent.

conversar [konβer'sar] *v* converse. **conversar con** talk to. **conversar sobre** talk about. **conversador** *adj* sociable. **conversación** *sf* conversation.

***convertir** [konβer'tir] *v* convert. **convertirse** *v* become, turn into. **conversión** *sf* conversion. **convertible** *adj* convertible.

convexo [kon'βekso] *adj* convex. **convexidad** *sf* convexity.

convicción [konβik'θjon] *sf* conviction. **convicto** *adj* convicted.

convidar [konβi'ðar] *v* invite. **convidarse** *v* offer one's services. **convidada** *sf* (*fam*) invitation to a drink. **pagar la convidada** (*fam*) treat to a drink. **convidado**, -a *sm.*

sf guest. **convidador, -a** *sm, sf* host/hostess.

convincente [konβin'θente] *adj* convincing.

convivir [konβi'βir] *v* coexist. **convivencia** *sf* coexistence.

convocar [konβo'kar] *v* convoke. **convocación** *sf* convocation. **convocador, -a** *sm, sf* convener. **convocatoria** *sf* summons.

convoy [kon'βoj] *sm* convoy. **convoyar** *v* convoy.

convulsión [konβul'sjon] *sf* convulsion. **convulsivo** *adj* convulsive.

conyugal [konju'gal] *adj* conjugal. **cónyuge** *s(m + f)* spouse.

coñac [ko'nak] *sm* cognac, brandy.

cooperar [koope'rar] *v* cooperate. **cooperación** *sf* cooperation. **cooperativa** *sf* cooperative.

coordinar [koorδi'nar] *v* coordinate. **coordinación** *sf* coordination.

copa ['kopa] *sf* glass; cup; goblet. **sombrero de copa** top-hat. **tomar una copa** have a drink. **copas** *sf pl* (*naipes*) hearts. **copado** *adj* (*árbol*) bushy. **copera** *sf* cupboard; sideboard.

Copenhague kope'nage] *sf* Copenhagen.

copete [ko'pete] *sm* tuft of hair; bun; (*pájaro*) crest; summit; (*fig*) haughtiness. **de alto copete** aristocratic.

copiar [ko'pjar] *v* copy; record. **copia** *sf* copy; duplicate; image; abundance. **copiador, -a** *sm, sf* copier. **copiante** *s(m + f)* copyist.

copla ['kopla] *sf* verse; song; ballad. **coplas de ciego** doggerel.

copo ['kopo] *sm* flake; ball of wool; clot; lump.

coque ['koke] *sm* coke.

coquetear [kokete'ar] *v* flirt. **coqueta** *sf* flirt. **coqueteo** *sm* flirtation. **coquetón** *sm* (*fam*) philanderer.

coraje [ko'raxe] *sm* courage; anger. **corajinoso** *adj* irate.

coral [ko'ral] *sm* coral. *adj* choral.

coraza [ko'raθa] *sf* armour.

corazón [kora'θon] *sm* heart. **de corazón** sincerely.

corbata [kor'βata] *sf* necktie.

corcovado [korko'βaδo], **-a** *sm, sf* hunchback. *adj* hunchbacked.

corchea [kor'tʃea] *sf* (*música*) quaver.

corchete [kor'tʃete] *sm* clasp.

corcho ['kortʃo] *sm* cork.

cordel [kor'δel] *sm* thin rope, line. **a cordel** in a straight line.

cordero [kor'δero] *sm* lamb.

cordial [kor'δjal] *adj* invigorating, stimulating; cordial, friendly. **dedo cordial** *sm* middle finger. **cordialidad** *sf* cordiality.

cordillera [korδi'ʎera] *sf* mountain range.

cordón [kor'δon] *sm* string; cord; braid.

cordura [kor'δura] *sf* prudence; discretion.

coreografía [koreogra'fia] *sf* choreography.

cornada [kor'nada] *sf* goring. **cornear** *v* gore.

corneja [kor'nexa] *sf* crow.

corneta [kor'neta] *sf* bugle; hunting horn. **corneta de llaves** cornet.

cornudo [kor'nuδo] *adj* horned; cuckolded. *sm* cuckold.

coro ['koro] *sm* chorus.

coronar [koro'nar] *v* crown. **corona** *sf* crown. **coronación** *sf* coronation.

coronel [koro'nel] *sm* colonel.

coronilla [koro'niʎa] *sf* crown of the head.

corporal [korpo'ral] *adj* corporal. **corporación** *sf* corporation. **corpóreo** *adj* corporeal. **corpulencia** *sf* corpulence. **corpulento** *adj* corpulent.

corpúsculo [kor'pusculo] *sm* corpuscle.

corral [kor'ral] *sm* yard; courtyard; corral; enclosure.

correa [kor'rea] *sf* leather strap; belt. **correa de ventilador** fan belt.

corredor [korre'δor] *sm* corridor; runner; (*com*) broker.

*corregir** [korre'xir] *v* correct. **corregirse** *v* reform oneself. **corrección** *sf* correction; punishment. **correccional** *adj* reformatory. **correctivo** *sm, adj* corrective. **correcto** *adj* correct; well-bred.

correo [kor'reo] *sm* mail, post; post office; courier. **correo certificado** registered post. **a vuelta de correo** by return of post.

correr [kor'rer] *v* run; flow; pass; sail; cover; travel over. **correrse** *v* move; (*fam*) talk too much.

corresponder [korrespon'der] *v* correspond; concern; reply; repay; be grateful; belong to; match; suit; fit. **a quien corresponda** to whom it may concern. **corresponderse** *v* correspond; agree; like each other. **correspondencia** *sf* correspondence, letters *pl*; agreement; reciprocation. **corresponsal** *s(m+f)* newspaper correspondent.

corrida [kor'riða] *sf* sprint. **corrida de toros** bullfight.

corrido [kor'riðo] ¹ *adj* abashed; experienced; over the specified weight.

corriente [kor'rjente] *sf* current, flow. *adj* current; running; everyday; standard; fluent. **agua corriente** running water. **al corriente** informed, up-to-date. **corriente alterna/continua** alternating/direct current. **corriente de aire** draught.

corroborar [korroβo'rar] *v* corroborate; strengthen. **corroboración** *sf* corroboration.

****corroer** [korro'er] *v* corrode. **corrosión** *sf* corrosion.

corromper [korrom'per] *v* corrupt; ruin; bribe. **corromperse** *v* putrefy; be corrupted. **corrupción** *sf* corruption; stink; bribery.

corsé [kor'se] *sm* corset.

cortabolsas [korta'bolsas] *sm invar* (*fam*) pickpocket.

cortaplumas [korta'plumas] *sm invar* penknife.

cortar [kor'tar] *v* cut; cut short; break in on; stop; switch off. **cortarse** *v* cut oneself; become embarrassed. **cortante** *adj* cutting; sharp. **corte** *sm* cut; cutting edge.

corte ['korte] *sf* (royal) court.

cortejar [korte'xar] *v* court; accompany. **cortejo** *sm* courtship; accompaniment; homage.

cortesía [korte'sia] *sf* courtesy. **cortés** *adj* courteous.

corteza [kor'teθa] *sf* bark; rind; crust.

cortijo [kor'tixo] *sm* farmhouse and farm.

cortina [kor'tina] *sf* curtain; screen; dregs *pl*. **cortina de hierro** iron curtain. **cortina de humo** smokescreen.

corto ['korto] *adj* short; defective; stupid; timid. **corto circuito** *sm* short circuit. **corto de vista** short-sighted.

corvo ['korβo] *adj* curved; bent; crooked.

cosa ['kosa] *sf* thing; something; affair. **cosa de oír/ver** something worth listening to/seeing. **no sea cosa que** lest.

cosecha [ko'setʃa] *sf* harvest. **cosechar** *v* reap, harvest.

coser [ko'ser] *v* sew; stitch; join. **coserse la boca** (*fam*) keep mum.

cosquillas [kos'kiʎas] *sf* tickling; ticklishness. **hacer cosquillas a** tickle. **cosquillear** *v* tickle. **cosquilloso** *adj* ticklish.

costa¹ ['kosta] *sf* coast. **costear** *v* sail along the coast. **costera** *sf* slope, hill. **costero** *adj* coastal.

costa² *sf* cost; expense. **a toda costa** at all costs. **costar** *v* cost; cause. **coste** *sm* cost, price.

costado [kos'taðo] *sm* side. **costados** *sm pl* lineage *sing*.

costilla [kos'tiʎa] *sf* rib; chop, cutlet. **costillas** *sf pl* shoulders *pl*.

costra ['kostra] *sf* scab; crust; (*fam*) filthiness.

costumbre [kos'tumbre] *sf* custom. **de costumbre** usual; usually.

costura [kos'tura] *sf* sewing; seam; dressmaking. **costurera** *sf* seamstress.

cotejar [kote'xar] *v* compare. **cotejo** *sm* comparison.

cotidiano [koti'ðjano] *adj* daily.

coto ['koto] *sm* enclosure; reserve; limit. **coto de caza** hunting reserve.

cotorra [ko'torra] *sf* parrot; magpie; (*fam*) chatterbox.

coyuntura [konjun'tura] *sf* joint; opportunity.

coz [koθ] *sf* recoil; kick.

cráneo ['kraneo] *sm* skull.

cráter ['krater] *sm* crater.

crear [kre'ar] *v* create; make; invent; found. **creación** *sf* creation. **creador, -a** *sm, sf* creator; inventor. **creativo** *adj* also **creador** creative.

****crecer** [kre'θer] *v* grow. **crecerse** *v* become conceited; take courage. **creces** *sf pl* increase *sing*. **con creces** amply, with interest. **crecido** *adj* grown; high; large; in flood. **crecimiento** *sm* growth; increase; flooding.

credenciales [kreðen'θjales] *sf pl* credentials *pl*.

crédito ['kreðito] *sm* credit; credence; reputation. **carta de crédito** *sf* credit card.

credo ['kreðo] *sm* creed.

crédulo ['kreðulo] *adj* credulous.

****creer** [kre'er] *v* believe; think. ¡**créamelo**! believe me! ¡**ya lo creo**! of course! **creíble** *adj* credible.

crema ['krema] *sf* cream; custard.

cremación [krema'θjon] *sf* cremation.

cremallera [krema'ʎera] *sf* zip-fastener.
crepúsculo [kre'puskulo] *sm* twilight.
crespo ['krespo] *adj* crispy; fuzzy; crinkled; (*fig*) obscure; (*fig*) angry.
cresta ['kresta] *sf* crest, comb; tuft.
creta ['kreta] *sf* chalk.
criar [kri'ar] *v* breed; create; beget. criarse *v* grow up; be raised *or* reared. cria *sf* act of breeding; litter; brood; young. criada *sf* maid. criadero *sm* (*plants*) nursery. criado *sm* manservant. crianza *sf* breeding; nursing. buena/mala crianza good/bad upbringing. criatura *sf* creature; infant.
cribar [kri'βar] *v* sieve; sift. criba *sf* sieve; screen.
crimen ['krimen] *sm* crime. criminal *sm*, *adj* criminal.
criollo [kri'oʎo], -a *s*, *adj* Creole.
cripta ['kripta] *sf* crypt.
crisálida [kri'saliða] *sf* chrysalis.
crisantemo [krisan'temo] *sm* chrysanthemum.
crisis ['krisis] *sf invar* crisis (*pl* -ses).
crisol [kri'sol] *sm* crucible.
crispar [kris'par] *v* cause to contract *or* twitch; contort; irritate. crisparse *v* twitch.
cristal [kirs'tal] *sm* crystal; glass; window; mirror. cristal de contacto contact lens. cristal tallado cut glass. cristal trasero (*auto*) rear window. cristalería *sf* glassworks; glassware. cristalero, -a *sm*, *sf* glazier; glassblower. cristalino *adj* crystalline; (*fig*) limpid.
Cristo ['kristo] *sm* Christ. cristiandad *sf* Christianity. cristianismo *sm* Christianity. cristiano, -a *s*, *adj* Christian.
criterio [kri'terjo] *sm* criterion (*pl* -a); point of view; opinion.
criticar [kriti'kar] *v* criticize. crítica *sf* criticism; review.
crítico ['kritiko] *sm* critic. *adj* critical.
cromo ['kromo] *sm* chromium, chrome; picture card.
crónica ['kronika] *sf* chronicle; report. cronista *sm* chronicler; correspondent.
crónico ['kroniko] *adj* chronic.
cronología [kronolo'xia] *sf* chronology. cronológico *adj* chronological.
cronómetro [kro'nometro] *sm* chronometer; stopwatch.
croqueta [kro'keta] *sf* croquette.
croquis ['krokis] *sm invar* sketch, rough draft.

crucero [kru'θero] *sm* cruiser; cruise; crossroads *pl*.
crucificar [kruθifi'kar] *v* crucify. crucifijo *sm* crucifix. crucifixión *sf* crucifixion.
crucigrama [kruθi'grama] *sm* crossword puzzle.
crudo ['kruðo] *adj* crude; raw; immature; (*fam*) boastful.
cruel [kru'el] *adj* cruel. crueldad *sf* cruelty.
cruento [kru'ento] *adj* bloody.
crujir [kru'xir] *v* creak; rustle; crackle. crujido *sm* creak; rustle; crackle.
crustáceo [krus'taθeo] *sm*, *adj* crustacean.
cruz [kruθ] *sf* cross. en cruz crosswise. cruzada *sf* crusade; crossroads *pl*. cruzado *sm* crusader; knight. cruzar *v* cross; cross oneself; pass *or* place across; dub. cruzarse *v* pass each other; exchange.
cuaderno [kwa'ðerno] *sm* notebook; exercise book; (*fam*) pack of cards.
cuadra ['kwaðra] *sf* stable; hut; large hall; hospital ward.
cuadragésimo [kwaðra'xesimo] *adj* fortieth.
cuadrante [kwa'ðrante] *adj* squaring. *sm* quadrant.
cuadrar [kwa'ðrar] *v* square. cuadrado *adj* square; stocky; perfect.
cuadrilla [kwa'ðriʎa] *sf* gang. cuadrillero *sm* foreman.
cuadro ['kwaðro] *sm* square; picture; sight, scene. en cuadro in a square.
cuadrúpedo [kwa'ðrupeðo] *sm*, *adj* quadruped.
cuajar [kwa'xar] *v* coagulate; congeal; clot; settle; fill with; (*fam*) catch on. cuajado *adj* curdled; congealed; (*fig*) dumbfounded. cuajadura *sf* curdling; congealing; coagulation.
cual [kwal] *pron* which; who. *adv* such as. a cual más equally. ¿cuál? *pron interrog* which? what?
cualidad [kwali'ðað] *sf* quality.
cualquier [kwal'kjer] *adj* (*con sustantivo*) any. cualquiera *pron*, *pl* cualesquiera any; anyone; anybody.
cuan [kwan] *adv* how; as.
cuando ['kwando] *adv* when. de vez en cuando from time to time. hasta cuando until. ¿cuándo? *adv interrog* when?
cuantía [kwan'tia] *sf* quantity.
cuanto ['kwanto] *adj* as much as; all; whatever. *adv* en cuanto as soon as. en

cuanto a as to. **¿cuánto?** *pron interrog* how much? how long?

cuarenta [kwa'renta] *sm, adj* forty.

cuaresma [kwa'resma] *sf* Lent.

cuartear [kwarte'ar] *v* quarter; cut into joints. **cuartearse** *v* crack.

cuartel [kwar'tel] *sm* quarter; barracks.

cuarto ['kwarto] *adj* fourth. *sm* quarter; room. **cuarto de baño** bathroom. **cuarto de estar** livingroom.

cuarzo ['kwarθo] *sm* quartz.

cuatro ['kwatro] *sm, adj* four.

cuba ['kuba] *sf* barrel; tub; drunkard. **estar como una cuba** (*fam*) be drunk.

Cuba *sf* Cuba. **cubano, -a** *s, adj* Cuban.

cúbico ['kuβiko] *adj* cubic. **raíz cubica** *sf* cube root.

cubículo [ku'βikulo] *sm* cubicle.

cubo ['kuβo] *sm* bucket.

cubrir [ku'βrir] *v* cover; drown; repay. **cubrirse** *v* cover oneself; put on one's hat; cloud over. **cubierta** *sf* cover; roof; tyre; bedspread; (*mar*) deck. **cubierto** *sm* cover; place-setting; menu. **bajo cubierto** under cover. **precio del cubierto** *sm* cover charge.

cucaracha [kuka'ratʃa] *sf* cockroach.

cuclillas [ku'kliʎas] *adv* **en cuclillas** squatting, on one's haunches.

cuclillo [ku'kliʎo] *sm* cuckoo; cuckold.

cuchara [ku'tʃara] *sf* spoon; ladle; trowel. **cucharada** *sf* spoonful. **cucharadita** *sf* teaspoonful. **cucharita** *sf* teaspoon; coffeespoon. **cucharón** *sm* ladle; scoop.

cuchichear [kutʃitʃe'ar] *v* whisper. **cuchicheo** *sm* whisper; whispering.

cuchilla [ku'tʃiʎa] *sf* kitchen knife; chopper; razor blade; range of mountains. **patines de cuchilla** *sm pl* ice skates *pl*. **cuchillada** *sf* slash; stab; knifing. **andar a cuchilladas** be at daggers drawn. **cuchillería** *sf* cutlery; cutlery shop. **cuchillo** *sm* knife.

cuello ['kweʎo] *sm* collar; neck; throat. **cuello de pico** V-neck. **cuello vuelto** polo neck.

cuenca ['kwenka] *sf* wooden bowl; eye socket; (*geog*) basin.

cuenta ['kwenta] *sf* account; bill; count; report. **a cuenta** on account. **¿a cuenta de qué?** why? **tener en cuenta** bear in mind.

cuento ['kwento] *sm* tale; fib; fuss. **cuento chino** nonsense.

cuerda ['kwerða] *sf* cord; rope; string;

chain; (*anat*) chord. **cuerdas vocales** vocal chords *pl*.

cuerdo ['kwerðo], **-a** *sm, sf* sane person. *adj* sane.

cuerno ['kwerno] *sm* horn; antler; feeler.

cuero ['kwero] *sm* skin; hide; leather.

cuerpo ['kwerpo] *sm* body; piece, section; stage; corps. **cuerpo de casa** housework. **cuerpo entero** full-length. **cuerpo muerto** (*mar*) mooring buoy.

cuervo ['kwerβo] *sm* raven.

cuesta ['kwesta] *sf* slope; hill. **a cuestas** on one's back. **cuesta abajo/arriba** down/uphill.

cuestión [kwes'tjon] *sf* question, issue; dispute. **cuestionar** *v* question; argue.

cueva ['kweβa] *sf* cave; cellar; den.

cuidar [kwi'ðar] *v* take care of; pay attention to. **cuidar de que** take care that. **no cuidarse de** take no notice of. **cuidado** *sm* care; carefulness; affair; worry. **¡cuidado!** beware! **cuidador** *adj* careful.

cuita ['kwita] *sf* worry; sorrow. **cuitado** *adj* worried; bashful.

culebra [ku'leβra] *sf* snake; (*fam*) practical joke. **culebrear** *v* wriggle; zigzag.

culinario [kuli'narjo] *adj* culinary.

culminar [kulmi'nar] *v* culminate. **culminación** *sf* culmination. **culminante** *adj* culminating.

culo ['kulo] *sm* (*fam*) bottom, arse. **ir de culo** go downhill.

culpar [kul'par] *v* blame. **culparse** *v* take the blame. **culpa** *sm* blame; fault; guilt. **echar la culpa a** lay the blame on. **culpabilidad** *sf* culpability. **culpable** *adj* guilty.

cultivar [kulti'βar] *v* cultivate; grow; develop. **cultivador, -a** *sm, sf* farmer; grower; *sf* (*máquina*) cultivator. **cultivación** *sf* cultivation; culture. **cultivo** *sm* cultivation; culture.

culto ['kulto] *adj* cultivated; cultured; civilized. *sm* worship; cult. **rendir culto a** worship. **cultura** *sf* culture, learning.

cumbre ['kumbre] *sf* peak, summit.

cumpleaños [kumple'aɲos] *sm invar* birthday. **feliz cumpleaños** happy birthday.

cumplir [kum'plir] *v* fulfil; reach; end; do one's duty. **cumplirse** *v* be realized. **cumplir años** have a birthday. **por cumplir** as a matter of form. **cumplido** *adj* plentiful;

faultless; polite. **cumplimentar** *v* compliment; fulfil. **cumplimentero** *adj* excessively formal. **cumplimiento** *sm* compliment; fulfilment; politeness.

cúmulo ['kumulo] *sm* heap; large amount; (*nube*) cumulus.

cuna ['kuna] *sf* cradle; (*fig*) origin; birthplace.

cundir [kun'dir] *v* spread; increase; grow.

cuneta [ku'neta] *sf* ditch; gutter; hard shoulder.

cuña ['kuɲa] *sf* wedge; chock. **tener cuña** (*fam*) have friends at court.

cuñado [ku'ɲado] *sm* brother-in-law.

cuño ['kuɲo] *sm* die; die-stamp; (*fig*) impression.

cuota ['kwota] *sf* quota; contribution; dues *pl*.

cupón [ku'pon] *sm* coupon; ticket.

cúpula ['kupula] *sf* dome.

cura¹ ['kura] *sm* priest. **cura párroco** parish priest.

cura² *sf* cure; healing; remedy; treatment; dressing. **primera cura** first aid. **curación** *sf* cure. **curador, -a** *sm, sf* guardian; tutor; curator. **curativo** *adj* healing.

curioso [ku'rjoso] *adj* curious; neat; attentive. *sm* bystander. **curiosidad** *sf* curiosity.

cursar [kur'sar] *v* attend; study; frequent. **cursado** *adj* skilled. **cursante** *s*(*m*+*f*) student.

cursi ['kursi] *adj* pretentious; affected; vulgar. *s*(*m*+*f*) pretentious person; snob.

curso ['kurso] *sm* course; direction; school year. **curso acelerado** crash course.

curtir [kur'tir] *v* tan; harden. **curtirse** *v* become tanned; become hardened; accustom oneself. **curtidor** *sm* tanner. **curtiduría** *sf* tannery. **curtimiento** *sm* tanning.

curva ['kurβa] *sf* curve; bend. **curvar** *v* curve; bend. **curvatura** *sf* curvature. **curvo** *adj* curved; bent.

cúspide ['kuspiðe] *sf* peak; summit.

custodiar [kusto'ðjar] *v* take care of; guard; defend. **custodia** *sf* custody. **custodio** *sm* custodian.

cutis ['kutis] *sm invar* skin; complexion.

cuyo ['kujo] *pron* whose; of which; of whom.

CH

chabacano [tʃaβa'kano] *adj* vulgar, common. **chabacanería** *sf* vulgarity; vulgar remark.

chacal [tʃa'kal] *sm* jackal.

chafar [sʃa'far] *v* flatten; crush; crease; (*en una discusión*) stump.

chal [tʃal] *sm* shawl.

chalado [tʃa'laðo] *adj* (*fam*) crazy, dotty.

chalán [tʃa'lan] *sm* horse dealer; shady businessman.

chaleco [tʃa'leko] *sm* waistcoat.

chalupa [tʃa'lupa] *sf* canoe; launch.

chambelán [tʃambe'lan] *sm* chamberlain.

champaña [tʃam'paɲa] *sm* champagne.

champú [tʃam'pu] *sm* shampoo.

chamuscar [tʃamus'kar] *v* singe, scorch.

chancear [tʃanθe'ar] *v* joke. **chancearse** *v* make fun of. **chanza** *sf* joke.

chanchullo [tʃan'tʃuʎo] *sm* (*fam*) crooked deal.

chantaje [tʃan'taxe] *sm* blackmail. **chantajista** *s*(*m*+*f*) blackmailer.

chapa ['tʃapa] *sf* metal sheet; rouge; (*fam*) common sense.

chaparro [tʃa'parro] *adj* (*fam*) tubby.

chaparrón [tʃapar'ron] *sm* downpour, cloudburst.

chapón [tʃa'pon] *sm* ink blot.

chapotear [tʃapote'ar] *v* sponge; moisten; splash. **chapoteo** *sm* sponging; moistening; splashing.

chapucero [tʃapu'θero], **-a** *sm, sf* bungler; liar. *adj* crude, clumsy. **chapucear** *v* botch, bungle.

chapuzar [tʃapu'θar] *v* duck, plunge into water.

chaqueta [tʃa'keta] *sf* jacket.

charca ['tʃarka] *sf* pool.

charco ['tʃarko] *sm* puddle.

charlar [tʃar'lar] *v* (*fam*) chat, chatter; gossip. **charla** *sf* (*fam*) chatter, talk. **charlador, -a** *sm, sf also* **charlatán, -ana** *sm, sf* chatterbox. **charladuría** *sf* chatter; gossip.

charol [tʃa'rol] *sm* varnish; patent leather. **darse charol** boast. **charolar** *v* varnish.

charro ['tʃarro] *adj* (*fam*) churlish; illbred; tawdry. **charrada** *sf* boorishness.

chasquear [tʃaske'ar] v trick; disappoint. **chasco** sm trick; disappointment.

chato ['tʃato] adj flat-nosed; flat. sm small glass.

chaval [tʃa'βal] sm (fam) lad; kid. **chavala** sf (fam) lass; girl.

Checoslovaquia [tʃekoslo'βakja] sf Czechoslovakia. **checoslovaco, -a** s, adj Czechoslovak(ian).

cheque ['tʃeke] sm cheque. **cheque de viajero** traveller's cheque.

chicle ['tʃikle] sm chewing gum.

chico ['tʃiko] adj small. sm boy. **chica** sf girl.

chichón [tʃi'tʃon] sm lump, bump.

chiflar [tʃi'flar] v whistle; hiss; (fam) swig. **chiflarse por** be crazy about. **chifla** sf whistle; hissing. **chiflado, -a** sm, sf (fam) crackpot; (fam: aficionado) fan; adj (fam) crazy.

chile ['tʃile] sm chili, chilli.

Chile ['tʃile] sm Chile. **chileno, -a** s, adj Chilean.

chillar [tʃi'ʎar] v scream; howl; squeak; blare. **chillador** adj screaming; shrieking. **chillería** sf screaming; scolding. **chillido** sm scream; howl; squeak.

chimenea [tʃime'nea] sf chimney; fireplace.

chimpancé [tʃimpan'θe] sm chimpanzee.

china ['tʃina] sf porcelain; china.

China sf China. **chino, -a** s, adj Chinese.

chinche ['tʃintʃe] sf bedbug.

chingar [tʃin'gar] v (fam) drink; (fam) pester.

Chipre ['tʃipre] sm Cyprus. **chipriota** s(m+f), adj Cypriot.

chiripa [tʃi'ripa] sf fluke, lucky accident.

chirriar [tʃirri'ar] v creak; squeak; chatter. **chirrido** sm creaking; squeaking; chattering.

chisme ['tʃisme] sm gadget; contrivance; knick-knack. **chismes** sm pl gossip sing. **chismear** v gossip. **chismería** sf tittle-tattle. **chismoso** adj gossiping.

chispear [tʃispe'ar] v spark; sparkle; drizzle. **chispa** sf spark; little bit. **chispeante** adj sparkling.

chisporrotear [tʃisporrote'ar] v spark; sizzle. **chisporroteo** sm sparking; sizzling.

chistar [tʃis'tar] v speak; open one's lips. **no chistar** say not a word. ¡**chite!** interj hush!

chiste ['tʃiste] sf joke. **tener chiste** be funny. **chistoso** adj funny; joking.

chivo ['tʃiβo], -a sm, sf (zool) kid.

chocar [tʃo'kar] v surprise; shock; collide. **choque** sm shock; jolt; crash; dispute.

chocolate [tʃoko'late] sm chocolate. **chocolatería** chocolate shop.

chochear [tʃotʃe'ar] v be in one's dotage. **chochera** sf dotage. **chocho** adj doddering.

chofer ['tʃofer] sm chauffeur.

chorizo [tʃo'riθo] sm spicy sausage.

chorrear [tʃorre'ar] v gush; spout; drip. **chorreo** sm gushing; spouting; dripping. **chorro** sm jet; gush; flow; stream.

choza ['tʃoθa] sf hut, hovel.

chubasco [tʃu'βasko] sm shower; squall; (fig) setback.

chuleta [tʃu'leta] sf chop, cutlet; (fam) slap.

chulo ['tʃulo] sm pimp; (fam) ruffian; (fam) spiv. adj cheeky; flashy; insolent. **chulada** sf cheek; vulgar thing; funny thing. **chulear** v get cheeky with.

chungar [tʃun'gar] v (fam) tease; tell jokes. **chunga** sf banter, fun.

chupar [tʃu'par] v suck; absorb. **chuparse** v become worn to a shadow. **chupada** sf suck, sucking. **chupadero, -a** sm, sf chupador adj sucking; absorbent. **chupete** sm (para niños) dummy. **chupetear** v suck at.

churro ['tʃurro] sm deep-fried batter; (fam) dead loss.

chusco ['tʃusko], -a sm, sf wag, wit. adj funny.

chusma ['tʃusma] sf rabble, riffraff.

chuzo ['tʃuθo] sm (arma) pike. **llover a chuzos** pour down.

D

dactilógrafo [dakti'lografo], -a sm, sf typist. **dactilografía** sf typing.

dádiva ['daðiβa] sf gift. **dadivoso** adj generous.

dado ['daðo] sm die (pl dice).

daga ['daga] sf dagger.

dama ['dama] sf lady; mistress; (ajedrez) queen; (juego de damas) king. **damas** sf pl draughts.

damasco [da'masko] sm damask.

damnificar [damnifi'kar] *v* injure, harm.

danés [da'nes], **-esa** *sm, sf* Dane. *sm* (*lengua*) Danish. *adj* Danish.

danzar [dan'θar] *v* dance. **danza** *sf* dance, dancing. **danzante, -a** *sm, sf* dancer.

dañar [da'ɲar] *v* harm; damage; spoil. **dañino** *adj* destructive. **daño** *sm* injury; damage; loss.

*****dar** [dar] *v* give; grant; yield; (*reloj*) strike; (*naipes*) deal. **dar a** face; overlook. **dar como** *or* **por** declare; consider. **dar con** meet. **lo mismo da** it makes no difference. **darse** *v* regard oneself; devote oneself; matter; occur. **darse cuenta** realize.

dardo ['darðo] *sm* dart.

dársena ['darsena] *sm* dock.

dátil ['datil] *sm* (*fruto*) date.

dato ['dato] *sm* fact; piece of information.

de [de] *prep* of; from.

debajo [de'βaxo] *adv* underneath. **debajo de** *prep* under, beneath, below.

debatir [deβa'tir] *v* debate, discuss. **debate** *sm* debate.

deber [de'βer] *v* owe; must; ought. *sm* duty; debt. **debidamente** *adv* fittingly. **debido** *adj* fitting; just. **debido a** due to. **débito** *sm* debt.

debilitar [deβili'tar] *v* weaken. **débil** *adj* weak. **debilidad** *sf* weakness.

*****decaer** [deka'er] *v* decline; decay. **decadencia** *sf* decadence; decline. **decadente** *adj* decadent.

decano [de'kano] *sm* dean.

decapitar [dekapi'tar] *v* decapitate. **decapitación** *sf* decapitation.

decena [de'θena] *sf* unit of ten.

decencia [de'θenθja] *sf* decency; modesty; cleanliness. **decente** *adj* decent; modest; clean.

decenio [de'θenjo] *sm* decade.

decepción [deθep'θjon] *sf* disappointment.

decidir [deθi'ðir] *v* decide. **decidirse** *v* make up one's mind. **decisión** *sf* decision. **decisivo** *adj* decisive.

décima ['deθima] *sf* tenth; tithe. **decimal** *adj* decimal. **décimo** *adj* tenth. **decimoctavo** *adj* eighteenth. **decimocuarto** *adj* fourteenth. **decimonono** *or* **decimonoveno** *adj* nineteenth. **decimoquinto** *adj* fifteenth. **decimoséptimo** *adj* seventeenth. **decimosexto** *adj* sixteenth. **decimotercio** *adj* thirteenth.

*****decir** [de'θir] *v* say; tell; speak; call. **¿diga?** (*teléfono*) hello!

declamar [dekla'mar] *v* declaim; speak out; recite. **declamación** *sf* declamation; oration. **declamador, -a** *sm, sf* orator.

declarar [dekla'rar] *v* declare; state; explain. **declararse** *v* declare oneself; (*fuego, etc.*) break out; (*amor*) propose. **declaración** *sf* declaration.

declinar [dekli'nar] *v* decay; fade; depart; (*gram*) decline. **declinación** *sf* decline; (*gram*) declension.

declive [de'kliβe] *sm* slope; (*com*) slump.

decorar [deko'rar] *v* decorate. **decoración** *sf* decoration. **decorador, -a** *sm, sf* decorator. **decorativo** *adj* decorative.

decoro [de'koro] *sm* decorum; dignity; respect.

*****decrecer** [dekre'θer] *v* decrease. **decremento** *sm* diminution.

decrépito [de'krepito] *adj* decrepit.

decretar [dekre'tar] *v* decree. **decreto** *sm* decree.

dedal [de'ðal] *sm* thimble.

dédalo [de'ðalo] *sm* maze.

dedicar [deði'kar] *v* dedicate, devote. **dedicación** *sf* dedication. **dedicatoria** *sf* (*libro*) dedication.

dedillo [de'ðiʎo] *sm* **al dedillo** at one's fingertips.

dedo ['deðo] *sm* finger; toe. **dedo del corazón** middle finger. **dedo índice** forefinger. **dedo meñique** little finger. **dedo pulgar** thumb.

*****deducir** [deðu'θir] *v* deduce; allege; deduct. **deducción** *sf* deduction. **deductivo** *adj* deductive.

defectible [defek'tiβle] *adj* fallible; defective. **defecto** *sm* defect. **defectuoso** *adj* defective.

*****defender** [defen'der] *v* defend; prohibit; oppose. **defendible** *adj* defensible. **defendido, -a** *sm, sf* (*jur*) defendant. **defensa** *sf* defence; shelter. **defensa pasiva civil** defence. **defensivo** *adj* defensive. **defensor, -a** *sm, sf* protector; counsel.

deferencia [defe'renθja] *sf* deference. **deferente** *adj* deferential.

*****deferir** [defe'rir] *v* defer; delegate.

deficiencia [defi'θjenθja] *sf* deficiency. **deficiente** *adj* deficient.

definir [defi'nir] *v* define. **definición** *sf* definition. **definido** *adj* definite. **definitivo** *adj* definitive. **en definitiva** in short.

deformar [defor'mar] v deform; disfigure. **deformación** sf deformation; distortion. **deforme** adj deformed; abnormal. **deformidad** sf deformity; (fig) perversion.

defraudar [defrau'dar] v defraud; evade; disappoint; frustrate. **defraudar al fisco** evade taxes. **defraudación** sf fraud; deceit. **defraudador, -a** sm, sf tax evader; swindler.

defuncion [defun'θjon] sf decease.

degenerar [dexene'rar] v degenerate. **degeneración** sf degeneration.

deglutir [deglu'tir] v swallow. **deglución** sf swallowing.

***degollar** [dego'ʎar] v cut the throat of; behead; (fig) ruin. **degollación** sf throat-cutting; decapitation. **degolladero** sm slaughter-house; scaffold. **degollador, -a** sm, sf executioner.

degradar [degra'ðar] v degrade. **degradación** sf degradation.

degustación [degusta'θion] sf tasting; sampling.

dehesa [de'esa] sf pasture.

deificar [deifi'kar] v deify. **deidad** sf deity. **deificación** sf deification.

dejar [de'xar] v leave; yield; drop; let, allow. **dejar de** leave off, stop; fail to. **dejarse** v neglect oneself. **dejarse vencer** give in to. **dejarse de** cease to.

del [del] contraction of de el.

delantal [delan'tal] sm apron.

delante [de'lante] adv before, in front, ahead. **delante de** before, in front of. **delantera** sf front; advantage; lead. **delantero** adj front; foremost.

delatar [dela'tar] v denounce; betray. **delator, -a** sm, sf informer.

delegar [dele'gar] v delegate. **delegación** sf delegation. **delegado** adj delegated.

deleitar [delei'tar] v delight; please. **deleitarse** v take delight. **deleite** sm delight; pleasure. **deleitoso** adj delightful.

deletrear [deletre'ar] v spell out; interpret. **deletreo** sm spelling out; decipherment.

deleznable [deleθ'naβle] adj brittle; fragile; frail.

delfín [del'fin] sm dolphin.

delgado [del'gaðo] adj thin; delicate; ingenious. **delgadez** sf thinness.

deliberar [deliβe'rar] v deliberate, consider. **deliberación** sf deliberation. **deliberado** adj deliberate.

delicado [deli'kaðo] adj delicate; tender; touchy. **delicadez** sf delicacy; tenderness; touchiness; frailty; squeamishness.

delicioso [deli'θjoso] adj delicious; delightful. **delicia** sf delight.

delimitar [delimi'tar] v delimit. **delimitación** sf delimitation.

delincuencia [delin'kwenθja] sf delinquency. **delincuente** s(m+f) delinquent; criminal.

delinear [deline'ar] v delineate; outline; sketch. **delineación** sf delineation. **delineante** sm draughtsman.

delirar [deli'rar] v be delirious; rave. **delirio** sm delirium.

delito [de'lito] sm crime.

delta ['delta] sm delta.

demacrarse [dema'krarse] v waste away. **demacración** sf emaciation. **demacrado** adj emaciated.

demagogia [dema'goxja] sf demagogy. **demagogo** sm demagogue.

demandar [deman'dar] v request; desire; (jur) sue. **demanda** sf demand; appeal; petition; question. **demandado, -a** sm, sf (jur) defendant. **demandante** s(m+f) (jur) plaintiff.

demarcar [demar'kar] v demarcate. **demarcación** sf demarcation.

demás [de'mas] adj other; rest; remaining. **los demás, las demás** the others. **estar demás** be unwanted. **y demás** etcetera. **demasía** sf excess; outrage; insolence. **demasiado** adj, adv too much.

demencia [de'menθja] sf insanity. **demente** adj insane.

democracia [demo'kraθja] sf democracy. **demócrata** adj democratic. s(m+f) democrat. **democrático** adj democratic.

***demoler** [demo'ler] v demolish. **demolición** sf demolition.

demonio [de'monjo] sm demon. **demoniaco** adj demoniac.

demorar [demo'rar] v delay; remain. **demora** sf delay.

***demostrar** [demos'trar] v demonstrate; prove. **demostrable** adj demonstrable. **demostración** sf demonstration. **demostrativo** adj demonstrative.

***denegar** [dene'gar] v deny, refuse. **denegación** sf denial, refusal.

denigrar [deni'grar] v denigrate; slander; insult. **denigración** sf denigration; disgrace.

denominar [denomi'nar] v name.
denominación sf denomination.

denotar [deno'tar] v denote; indicate.

denso ['denso] adj dense. **densidad** sf density.

dentado [den'taðo] adj toothed; jagged; (tecn) cogged. **dentadura** sf set of teeth.

dental adj dental. **dentar** v furnish with teeth; cut one's teeth. **dentellar** v (dientes) chatter. **dentellear** v bite. **dentífrico** sm toothpaste. **dentista** s(m + f) dentist.

dentro ['dentro] adv inside, within. **dentro de poco** shortly.

denudar [denu'ðar] v denude.

denunciar [denun'θjar] v denounce; inform; accuse. **denuncia** sf denunciation; accusation.

departamento [departa'mento] sm department.

depender [depen'der] v depend. **dependencia** sf dependence; reliance. **dependiente, -a** sm, sf shop assistant. **dependiente de** dependent on.

deplorar [deplo'rar] v deplore; regret. **deplorable** adj deplorable.

*deponer [depo'ner] v lay down; lay aside; remove from office; depose; (jur) give evidence; defecate. **deponente** s(m + f) witness.

deportar [depor'tar] v deport. **deportación** sf deportation.

deporte [de'porte] sm sport. **deportismo** sm sport; enthusiasm for sport. **deportista** s(m + f) sportsman/woman. **coche deportivo** sports car.

depositar [deposi'tar] v deposit. **depósito** sm deposit; store; tank; tip.

depravar [depra'βar] v deprave; corrupt. **depravación** sf depravity. **depravado** adj depraved.

depreciar [depre'θjar] v depreciate, lessen in value. **depreciación** sf depreciation.

deprimir [depri'mir] v depress. **depresión** sf depression. **depresivo** adj depressing.

depurar [depu'rar] v purify. **depuración** sf purification.

derecha [de'retʃa] sf right; right hand. **a la derecha** on the right. **derecho** sm law; adj right; straight; upright.

derivar [deri'βar] v derive. **derivación** sf derivation.

derogar [dero'gar] v repeal; abolish; cancel. **derogación** sf repeal; abolition.

derramar [derra'mar] v spill; overflow; scatter; spread. **derramarse** v be scattered; overflow. **derrame** sm spilling; leakage; overflow; slope.

*derretir [derre'tir] v melt; dissipate. **derretirse** v be deeply in love; (fam) be impatient. **derretimiento** sm melting; (fam) consuming passion.

derribar [derri'βar] v tear down; knock down; throw down. **derribarse** v fall down. **derribo** sm demolition. **derribos** sm pl rubble sing.

derrocar [derro'kar] v hurl down; ruin.

derrochar [derro'tʃar] v squander. **derrochador, -a** s, adj prodigal; spendthrift.

derrotar [derro'tar] v defeat; ruin; put to flight. **derrota** sf defeat; failure. **derrotado** adj defeated; shabby.

derrumbar [derrum'bar] v knock down, hurl down, pull down. **derrumbarse** v collapse. **derrumbo** sm collapse; overthrow; demolition.

desabotonar [desaβoto'nar] v unbutton; blossom. **desabotonarse** v come undone.

desabrigar [desaβri'gar] v uncover; leave without shelter; take off clothing. **desabrigado** adj uncovered; unprotected; exposed. **desabrigo** sm uncovering; exposure.

desabrochar [desaβro'tʃar] v unfasten; undo. **desabrocharse** v come undone.

desacatar [desaka'tar] v be disrespectful; disobey. **desacato** sm disrespect; contempt.

*desacertar [desaθer'tar] v be wrong; act foolishly. **desacertado** adj mistaken; ill-advised; unsuccessful; unfortunate; clumsy. **desacierto** sm mistake, blunder.

desacomodar [desakomo'ðar] v inconvenience; dismiss. **desacomodarse** v lose one's job. **desacomodado** adj poor; inconvenient; unemployed. **desacomodamiento** sm also **desacomodo** sm discomfort; inconvenience.

desaconsejado [desakonse'xaðo] adj ill-advised. **desaconsejar** v advise against.

*desacordar [desakor'ðar] v put out of tune. **desacordarse** v get out of tune; be forgetful. **desacordado** adj discordant.

desacostumbrar [desakostum'brar] v break a habit. **desacostumbrado** adj unusual.

desacreditar [desakreði'tar] v discredit.

desacuerdo [desa'kwerðo] sm discord; disagreement; unconsciousness.

desafecto [desa'fekto] *adj* disaffected; indifferent; adverse.

desafinar [desafi'nar] *v* be out of tune; *(fig)* speak out of turn.

desafio [desa'fio] *sm* challenge.

desagradar [desagra'ðar] *v* displease; be unpleasant. **desagradable** *adj* unpleasant.

desagradecido [desagraðe'θiðo], -a *sm, sf* ingrate. *adj* ungrateful.

desagraviar [desagra'βjar] *v* make amends for. **desagravio** *sm* indemnity; compensation.

desaguar [desa'gwar] *v* drain. **desaguadero** *sm* drain; channel. **desagüe** *sm* drainage; outlet.

desahogar [desao'gar] *v* ease; console. **desahogarse** *v* recover; free oneself; speak one's mind; get out of debt. **desahogado** *adj* impudent; well-off; spacious; uncluttered. **desahogo** *sm* ease; comfort; relief.

desahuciar [desau'θjar] *v* evict; despair of. **desahucio** *sm* eviction.

desairar [desai'rar] *v* disregard; snub. **desairado** *adj* spurned; unattractive; awkward. **desaire** *sm* snub; rebuff; gracelessness.

desajustar [desaxus'tar] *v* disarrange. **desajustarse** *v* break down. **desajuste** *sm* breakdown.

desalado [desa'laðo] *adj* impatient; hasty; unsalted.

*****desalentar** [desalen'tar] *v* make breathless; discourage. **desalentarse** *v* lose heart.

desaliñar [desali'ɲar] *v* disturb; ruffle. **desaliñado** *adj* slovenly. **desaliño** *sm* slovenliness; uncleanness; negligence.

desalojar [desalo'xar] *v* remove; eject. **desalojarse** *v* move out. **desalojamiento** *sm* ejection.

desalquilado [desalki'laðo] *adj* vacant. **desalquilar** *v* vacate.

desamor [desa'mor] *sm* indifference; ingratitude.

desamparar [desampa'rar] *v* abandon. **desamparo** *sm* abandonment; helplessness.

desangrar [desan'grar] *v* bleed; impoverish. **desangrarse** *v* lose much blood.

desanimar [desani'mar] *v* discourage. **desanimarse** *v* become discouraged. **desánimo** *sm* discouragement.

desanudar [desanu'ðar] *v* untie; disentangle.

desapacible [desapa'θiβle] *adj* disagreeable. **desapacibilidad** *sf* unpleasantness.

*****desaparecer** [desapare'θer] *v* disappear; hide; wear off. **desaparecido** *adj* missing. **desaparecimiento** *sm* disappearance.

desapegarse [desape'garse] *v* lose interest in. **desapego** *sm* lack of interest; coldness.

desapercibido [desaperθi'βiðo] *adj* unnoticed. **coger desapercibido** catch unawares.

desapoderar [desapoðe'rar] *v* dispossess; dismiss.

*****desapretar** [desapre'tar] *v* loosen.

*****desaprobar** [desapro'βar] *v* disapprove of. **desaprobación** *sf* disapproval.

desaprovechar [desaproβe'tʃar] *v* waste; lose ground. **desaprovechado** *adj* unprofitable; backward. **desaprovechamiento** *sm* waste; misuse.

desapuntar [desapun'tar] *v* unstitch.

desarmar [desar'mar] *v* disarm; disband; dismantle; calm. **desarme** *sm* disarmament.

desarraigar [desarrai'gar] *v* uproot. **desarraigado** *adj* uprooted; rootless.

desarreglar [desarre'glar] *v* upset; disarrange. **desarreglado** *adj* slovenly; faulty. **desarreglo** *sm* disorder; untidiness; trouble.

desarrollar [desarro'ʎar] *v* unfold; develop. **desarrollo** *sm* development.

desarrugar [desarru'gar] *v* smooth out.

desasear [desase'ar] *v* soil; disarrange. **desaseo** *sm* dirtiness; disorder.

*****desasir** [desa'sir] *v* loosen, undo. **desasirse de** get rid of.

*****desasosegar** [desasose'gar] *v* disturb. **desasosiego** *sm* disquiet; restlessness.

desastre [de'sastre] *sm* disaster. **desastrado** *adj* unlucky; dirty; disorderly. **desastroso** *adj* disastrous.

desatar [desa'tar] *v* undo; unravel. **desatarse** *v* break out; lose all reserve. **desatadura** *sf* untying.

*****desatender** [desaten'der] *v* ignore; slight. **desatención** *sf* inattention; discourtesy. **desatentado** *adj* absent-minded. **desatento** *adj* discourteous.

desatinar [desati'nar] *v* bewilder; rave; blunder. **desatinado** *adj* silly; rash. **desatino** *sm* absurdity; blunder; tactlessness.

*****desavenir** [desaβe'nir] *v* cause to quarrel. **desavenirse** *v* quarrel. **desavenido** *adj* incompatible.

desaventajado [desaβenta'xaðo] *adj* unfavourable; inferior.

desaviar [desa'βjar] *v* lead astray; deprive of necessities; inconvenience. **desavío** *sm* inconvenience; lack of means.

desayunar [desaju'nar] *v* breakfast. **desayuno** *sm* breakfast.

desazonar [desaθo'nar] *v* render tasteless; displease. **desazón** *sm* insipidity; displeasure. **desazonado** *adj* tasteless; displeased.

desbandarse [desβan'darse] *v* disband; disperse.

desbarajustar [desβaraxus'tar] *v* confuse. **desbarajuste** *sm* confusion.

desbaratar [desβara'tar] *v* ruin; spoil; waste; talk rubbish. **desbaratarse** *v* fall apart; get carried away. **desbaratado** *adj* wrecked; dissipated. **desbaratamiento** *sm* waste; disorder; wrecking.

desbordar [desβor'ðar] *v* flood; overflow; (*fig*) lose one's self-control. **desbordamiento** *sm* overflow.

descabezar [deskaβe'θar] *v* behead. **descabezarse** *v* rack one's brains. **descabezado** *adj* headless; rash.

descalabrar [deskala'βrar] *v* wound (in the head); maltreat; defeat. **descalabro** *sm* setback; defeat.

descalificar [deskalifi'kar] *v* disqualify. **descalificación** *sf* disqualification.

descalzar [deskal'θar] *v* take off one's shoes. **descalzo** *adj* barefoot.

descamisado [deskami'saðo] *adj* destitute. *sm* tramp.

descansar [deskan'sar] *v* rest; sleep; lean; depend. **descansado** *adj* rested. **descanso** *sm* rest; repose.

descarado [deska'raðo] *adj* brazen; cheeky; blatant.

descargar [deskar'gar] *v* unload; discharge; free; absolve. **descarga** *sf* discharge; unloading. **descargado** *adj* (*batería*) flat. **descargo** *sm* unloading; discharge of debt. **descargue** *sm* unloading of goods.

descartar [deskar'tar] *v* discard; leave out. **descartarse** *v* get out of. **descarte** *sm* discarding; rejection.

*****descender** [desθen'der] *v* descend; flow; lower. **descendencia** *sf* lineage. **descendiente** *s(m+f)* descendant. **descenso** *sm* descent; fall; decline.

descentralizar [desθentrali'θar] *v* decentralize.

descifrar [desθi'frar] *v* decipher. **descifrable** *adj* decipherable.

*****descolgar** [deskol'gar] *v* lower; (*teléfono*) pick up; take down. **descolgarse** *v* come down; slip; drop; surprise.

descolorar [deskolo'rar] *v* discolour. **descolorido** *adj* discoloured.

descomedido [deskome'ðiðo] *adj* immoderate; disproportionate; rude. **descomedirse** *v* go too far.

*****descomponer** [deskompo'ner] *v* decompose; disturb. **descomponerse** *v* rot; become upset. **descomposición** *sf* decomposition. **descompuesto** *adj* broken; faulty; insolent.

*****desconcertar** [deskonθer'tar] *v* disconcert; damage. **desconcierto** *sm* disorder; confusion.

desconectar [deskonek'tar] *v* disconnect.

desconfiar [deskon'fjar] *v* lack confidence. **desconfiar de** distrust. **desconfiado** *adj* distrustful. **desconfianza** *sf* mistrust, suspicion.

desconformar [deskonfor'mar] *v* disagree, dissent.

*****desconocer** [deskono'θer] *v* fail to recognize; ignore; deny; disown. **desconocido** *adj* unknown; unrecognized; ungrateful. **desconocimiento** *sm* ignorance; ingratitude; repudiation.

desconsiderado [deskonside'raðo] *adj* inconsiderate.

*****desconsolar** [deskonso'lar] *v* grieve, distress. **desconsolado** *adj* disconsolate. **desconsuelo** *sm* grief; affliction.

*****descontar** [deskon'tar] *v* discount; deduct; take for granted.

descontento [deskon'tento] *adj* dissatisfied.

descontinuar [deskontinu'ar] *v* discontinue.

descorazonar [deskorazo'nar] *v* discourage.

descorchar [deskor't∫ar] *v* uncork. **descorchador** *sm* corkscrew.

descortés [deskor'tes] *adj* discourteous. **descortesía** *sf* discourtesy.

descreer [deskre'er] *v* disbelieve; discredit. **descrédito** *sm* discredit.

describir [deskri'βir] *v* describe. **descripción** *sf* description. **descriptivo** *adj* descriptive.

descuajar [deskwa'xar] *v* liquefy; uproot; dishearten.

descubrir [desku'βrir] *v* discover; uncover; publish. **descubierto** *adj* exposed; manifest; hatless. **descubridor, -a** *sm, sf* discoverer. **descubrimiento** *sm* discovery.

descuento [des'kwento] *sm* discount.

descuidar [deskwi'ðar] *v* neglect; release; distract. **descuidar de** forget to. **¡descuida!** don't worry! **descuidarse** *v* be careless; neglect one's health. **descuidado** *adj* neglectful; careless; casual. **descuido** *sm* negligence; carelessness; thoughtlessness.

desde ['desðe] *prep* from; since; after. **desde luego** of course; immediately.

***desdecir** [desðe'θir] *v* gainsay; be unworthy of. **desdecirse** *v* retract.

desdeñar [desðe'nar] *v* disdain; scorn. **desdén** *sm* disdain; scorn. **al desdén** nonchalantly. **desdeñoso** *adj* disdainful.

desdicha [des'ðitʃa] *sf* misfortune; misery. **desdichado** *adj* unfortunate; wretched.

desdoblar [desðo'βlar] *v* unfold; split.

desdorar [desðo'rar] *v* tarnish. **desdoro** *sm* stain; dishonour.

desear [dese'ar] *v* wish, desire. **deseable** *adj* desirable. **deseo** *sm* desire. **deseoso** *adj* desirous.

desecar [dese'kar] *v* dry up.

desechar [dese'tʃar] *v* refuse; reject. **desecho** *sm* residue; rubbish; contempt.

desembalar [desemba'lar] *v* unpack.

desembarazar [desembara'θar] *v* clear; extricate; vacate. **desembarazarse** *v* get rid of. **desembarazo** *sm* freedom; naturalness.

desembarcar [desembar'kar] *v* unload; disembark. **desembarcadero** *sm* landing-stage. **desembarco** *sm* disembarkation; landing.

desembocar [desembo'kar] *v* flow; empty. **desembocadura** *sf* mouth; outlet; opening.

desembolsar [desembol'sar] *v* pay out. **desembolso** *sm* payment. **desembolsos** *sm pl* expenses *pl*.

desembragar [desembra'gar] *v* disengage; release; (*auto*) declutch. **desembrague** *sm* disengaging; (*auto*) declutching; (*auto*) clutch pedal.

desembrollar [desembro'ʎar] *v* disentangle; sort out.

desempate [desem'pate] *sm* (*fútbol*) play-off.

desempeñar [desempe'nar] *v* (*teatro*) play

a role; release from debt. **desempeño** *sm* redemption of a pledge; freedom from an obligation.

desempleado [desemple'aðo] *adj* unemployed. **desempleo** *sm* unemployment.

desencantar [desenkan'tar] *v* disillusion. **desencanto** *sm* disillusionment.

desenfadar [desenfa'ðar] *v* appease. **desenfadarse** *v* calm down. **desenfadado** *adj* free, unencumbered. **desenfado** *sm* freedom; naturalness.

desenfrenar [desenfre'nar] *v* unbridle. **desenfrenarse** *v* give way to passion. **desenfrenado** *adj* unbridled. **desenfreno** *sm* licentiousness.

desenganchar [desengan'tʃar] *v* unfasten, unhook.

desengañar [desenga'nar] *v* disabuse, disillusion. **desengaño** *sm* disillusionment.

desenlace [desen'laθe] *sm* dénouement; outcome.

desenredar [desenre'ðar] *v* disentangle; straighten out. **desenredo** *sm* disentanglement.

desenrollar [desenro'ʎar] *v* unroll; unwind.

***desentenderse** [desenten'derse] *v* pretend to be ignorant (of); take no part in.

***desenterrar** [desenter'rar] *v* disinter; unearth; recall. **desenterramiento** *sm* disinterment; recollection.

desentonar [desento'nar] *v* be out of tune; humiliate; behave badly. **desentono** *sm* discord; bad behaviour.

desentrañar [desentra'nar] *v* disembowel; (*fig*) unravel.

desenvainar [desenβai'nar] *v* unsheath; (*fig*) bring into the open.

***desenvolver** [desenβol'βer] *v* unwrap; unwind; develop; expand. **desenvolverse** *v* become unwrapped; fend for oneself; prosper. **desenvoltura** *sf* naturalness; cheerfulness; eloquence.

deseo [de'seo] *V* **desear**.

desequilibrar [desekili'βrar] *v* unbalance. **desequilibrado** *adj* off balance; mentally unbalanced. **desequilibrio** *sm* imbalance.

desertar [deser'tar] *v* desert. **desertor, -a** *sm, sf* deserter.

desesperar [desespe'rar] *v* (cause to) despair; exasperate. **desesperación** *sf* desperation; despair; anger. **desesperado** *adj* desperate; hopeless. **desesperanza** *sf* despair.

desestimar [desesti'mar] v undervalue;
reject. **desestima** sf lack of esteem.

desfachatado [desfatʃa'taðo] adj brazen;
shameless. **desfachatez** sf brazenness;
impudence.

desfalcar [desfal'kar] v embezzle. **desfalco**
sm embezzlement.

*desfallecer [desfaʎe'θer] v faint; weaken.
desfallecido adj faint; weak. **desfal-
lecimiento** sm weakness; faintness.

desfavorable [desfaβo'raβle] adj
unfavourable.

desfigurar [desfigu'rar] v disfigure; disguise; distort. **desfiguramiento** sm disfigurement; distortion.

desfilar [desfi'lar] v parade. **desfiladero** sm
gorge, defile. **desfile** sm parade. **desfile de
modas** fashion show.

desgajar [desga'xar] v tear off; break off.

desganar [desga'nar] v spoil the appetite
of. **desganarse** v lose one's appetite.
desgana sf loss of appetite; reluctance.
desganado adj lacking appetite; reluctant.

desgarbado [degar'βaðo] adj gawky;
ungainly.

desgarrar [degar'rar] v rend; tear; (fig:
corazón) break. **desgarrado** adj dissolute.
desgarro sm tear; impudence.

desgastar [desgas'tar] v wear away; corrode; ruin. **desgaste** sm wear; corrosion;
ruin.

desgraciar [desgra'θjar] v displease; prevent; spoil. **desgraciarse** v fail; lose
favour. **desgracia** sf misfortune; accident; grief; disgrace; unfriendliness. **por
desgracia** unfortunately. **desgraciado** adj
unlucky; unhappy; in disgrace.

deshabitado [desaβi'taðo] adj uninhabited.

*deshacer [desa'θer] v undo; cancel;
destroy; frustrate. **deshacerse** v get rid
of; break; go to pieces. **deshacerse por
strive to.

*deshelar [dese'lar] v thaw; melt. **deshe-
lamiento** sm de-icing. **deshielo** sm thawing; melting.

desheredar [desere'ðar] v disinherit.
desheredado adj disinherited; underprivileged. **desheredamiento** sm disinheritance.

deshidratar [desiðra'tar] v dehydrate.
deshidratación sf dehydration.

deshilar [desi'lar] v unravel. **deshilado** adj
unravelled; frayed.

deshilvanado [desilβa'naðo] adj (fig: discurso) disjointed; disconnected.

deshinchar [desin'tʃar] v deflate; give
vent to. **deshincharse** v go down; go flat;
(fig) come off one's high horse.
deshinchado adj flat; deflated.
deshinchadura sf deflation.

deshojar [deso'xar] v defoliate.

deshollinar [desoʎi'nar] v sweep chim-
neys. **deshollinador** sm chimney-sweep.

deshonesto [deso'nesto] adj dishonest;
indecent.

deshonrar [deson'rar] v dishonour.
deshonra sf dishonour; affront.
deshonroso adj shameful, disgraceful.

deshora [des'ora] adv **a deshora** at an
inconvenient time.

deshuesar [deswe'sar] v (carne) bone;
(fruta) stone.

desidia [de'siðja] sf carelessness; inertia.
desidioso adj lazy.

desierto [de'sjerto] sm desert. adj desert-
ed.

designar [desig'nar] v designate. **designación** sf designation. **designio** sm intention, idea.

desigual [desi'gwal] adj unequal; uneven;
changeable; different. **desigualdad** sf inequality.

desilusionar [desilusjo'nar] v disillusion.
desilución sf disillusionment.

desinfectar [desinfek'tar] v disinfect.
desinfección sf disinfection. **desinfectante**
sm, adj disinfectant.

desinflar [desin'flar] v deflate.

desinterés [desinte'res] sm disinterest.
desinteresado adj disinterested.

desistir [desis'tir] v desist.

desleal [desle'al] adj disloyal. **deslealdad**
sf disloyalty.

deslenguado [deslen'gwado] adj foulmouthed; shameless. **deslenguarse** v
(fam) use foul language.

desligar [desli'gar] v loosen; untie; (fig)
absolve. **desligarse** v break away.

deslindar [deslin'dar] v define the limits
of. **deslinde** sm delimitation.

deslizar [desli'θar] v slip; glide; slide.
desliz sm skid; (fig) indiscretion.
deslizadero sm slippery place.

*deslucir [deslu'θir] v tarnish.

deslumbrar [deslum'βrar] v dazzle; (fig)
bewilder. **deslumbrador** adj dazzling.
deslumbramiento sm dazzle; glare.

desmán [des'man] *sm* excess; misconduct; outrage.

desmandar [desman'dar] *v* countermand. **desmandarse** *v* stray; get out of hand.

desmantelar [desmante'lar] *v* dismantle.

desmayar [desma'jar] *v* falter; discourage. **desmayarse** *v* faint. **desmayado** *adj* faint, fainting. **desmayo** *sm* swoon.

***desmedirse** [desme'ðirse] *v* forget oneself; lose self-control. **desmedido** *adj* excessive.

desmejorar [desmexo'rar] *v* weaken; impair. **desmejorarse** *v* deteriorate.

***desmembrar** [desmem'brar] *v* dismember; divide. **desmembración** *sf* dismemberment.

***desmentir** [desmen'tir] *v* contradict; deny; belie. **desmentirse** *v* go back on one's word.

desmenuzar [desmenu'θar] *v* crumble; sift.

desmerecer [desmere'θer] *v* be unworthy of; be inferior. **desmerecimiento** *sm* demerit.

desmesurado [desmesu'raðo] *adj* disproportionate; excessive. **desmesurarse** *v* go too far.

desmontar [desmon'tar] *v* clear; level; (*árbol*) fell; dismantle.

desmoralizar [desmorali'θar] *v* demoralize. **desmoralización** *sf* demoralization.

desmoronar [desmoro'nar] *v* cause to crumble away. **desmoronarse** *v* crumble.

desnatar [desna'tar] *v* (*leche*) skim; (*fig*) take the best of.

desnivel [desni'βel] *sm* unevenness; gradient; difference of level.

desnudar [desnu'ðar] *v* strip, denude. **desnudez** *sf* nakedness. **desnudo** *adj* naked.

***desobedecer** [desoβeðe'θer] *v* disobey. **desobediencia** *sf* disobedience. **desobediente** *adj* disobedient.

desocupar [desoku'par] *v* vacate. **desocuparse** *v* leave work; retire. **desocupación** *sf* leisure; unemployment. **desocupado** *adj* idle; unemployed; free.

desolar [deso'lar] *v* lay waste; afflict. **desolarse** *v* grieve. **desolación** *sf* desolation. **desolado** *adj* desolate; disconsolate.

desodorante [desoðo'rante] *sm, adj* deodorant.

desorden [des'orden] *sm* disorder. **desordenado** *adj* disordered.

desorganizar [desorgani'θar] *v* disorganize. **desorganización** *sf* disorganization.

desorientar [desorjen'tar] *v* mislead; (*fig*) confuse. **desorientarse** *v* lose one's bearings. **desorientación** *sf* disorientation; perplexity.

despabilado [despaβi'laðo] *adj* wide awake; alert. **despabilarse** *v* wake up.

despacio [des'paθjo] *adv* slowly; gradually.

despachar [despa'tʃar] *v* dispatch; attend to; dismiss. **despacharse** *v* get rid of; finish; hurry. **despacho** *sm* dispatch; customs clearance; study; office; warrant; telegram.

despachurrar [despatʃur'rar] *v* (*fam*) crush; squash; (*fig*) make a mess of.

desparpajo [despar'paxo] *sm* self-assurance; nonchalance. **desparpajado** *adj* self-assured. **desparpajar** *v* disarrange; (*fam*) prattle.

desparramar [desparra'mar] *v* scatter; squander.

despavorido [despaβori'ðo] *adj* terrified.

despectivo [despek'tiβo] *adj* contemptuous, scornful.

despechar [despe'tʃar] *v* drive to despair; slight; enrage; (*fam*) wean. **despecharse** *v* despair. **despecho** *sm* despair. **a despecho de** in spite of.

despedazar [despeða'θar] *v* tear to pieces; smash.

***despedir** [despe'ðir] *v* dismiss; see off; give off; escort. **despedirse** *v* say goodbye. **despedida** *sf* dismissal; farewell.

despegar [despe'gar] *v* unstick. **despegarse** *v* become detached; become indifferent. **despegado** *adj* unstuck; (*fig*) cold.

despeinar [despei'nar] *v* disarrange the hair.

despejar [despe'xar] *v* free from obstructions. **despejarse** *v* be free and easy. **despejado** *adj* bright; clear. **despejo** *sm* brightness; self-confidence.

despellejar [despeʎe'xar] *v* skin, flay.

despensa [des'pensa] *sf* pantry; store of food.

despeñadero [despeɲa'ðero] *sm* precipice; (*fam*) risk. **despeñadizo** *adj* steep. **despeñar** *v* precipitate. **despeño** *sm* fall.

desperdiciar [desperði'θjar] *v* waste. **desperdiciador, -a** *sm, sf* squanderer.

desperezarse [despere'θarse] *v* stretch oneself; rouse oneself.

*despertar [desper'tar] *v* awaken.
despertarse *v* wake up. **despertador** *sm*
alarm clock; warning. **despertamiento** *sm*
awakening. **despierto** *adj* awake; watchful.

despiadado [despja'ðaðo] *adj* cruel, pitiless.

despilfarrar [despilfar'rar] *v* squander.
despilfarrado *adj* wasteful; shabby.
despilfarro *sm* waste; slovenliness.

despintar [despin'tar] *v* take paint off;
fade.

despistar [despis'tar] *v* throw off the
scent. **despistarse** *v* get lost. **despiste** *sm*
absent-mindedness.

*desplegar [desple'gar] *v* unfold; reveal;
display. **desplegadura** *sf* unfolding.

desplomarse [desplo'marse] *v* tilt; collapse; drop. **desplomo** *sm* (*pared, etc.*)
bulge.

despojar [despo'xar] *v* deprive; dispossess. **despojarse** *v* divest oneself. **despojo**
sm plunder. **despojos** *sm pl* scraps *pl*,
leavings *pl*.

desposado [despo'saðo] *adj* newly-wed.
desposanda *sf* bride. **desposando** *sm*
bridegroom. **desposar** *v* marry.
desposarse *v* become engaged; get married.

desposeer [despose'er] *v* dispossess.

déspota ['despota] *sm* despot. **despótico**
adj despotic. **despotismo** *sm* despotism.

despreciar [despre'θjar] *v* reject; ignore;
despise. **despreciarse de** not deign to.
despreciable *adj* despicable. **desprecio** *sm*
scorn; contempt; snub.

desprender [despren'der] *v* separate,
remove; give off. **desprenderse** *v* withdraw; renounce; be deduced.
desprendimiento *sm* disinterestedness;
generosity; separation. **desprendimiento
de tierras** landslide.

desprevenido [despreβe'niðo] *adj* unpre-
pared. **desprevención** *sf* lack of foresight.

desproporción [despropor'θjon] *sf* dispro-
portion. **desproporcionado** *adj* disproportionate.

después [des'pwes] *adv* afterwards, after,
next, later; since. **después de** after.
después que after.

desquiciar [deski'θjar] *v* unhinge; disconnect. **desquiciarse** *v* lose control.
desquiciado *adj* off balance; (*fam*) crazy.

desquitar [deski'tar] *v* compensate.

desquitarse *v* recoup; get one's revenge.
desquite *sm* compensation; revenge.

destacar [desta'kar] *v* (*mil*) detach; stand
out. **destacarse** *v* be conspicuous. **destacado** *adj* outstanding.

destajo [des'taxo] *sm* piecework. **destajar**
v settle the terms for a job.

destapar [desta'par] *v* uncover. **destaparse**
v reveal oneself.

destartalado [destarta'laðo] *adj* (*casa*)
tumbledown; rambling.

destello [des'teλo] *sm* sparkling. **destellar**
v sparkle.

destemplar [destem'plar] *v* disconcert.
destemplarse *v* get out of tune; lose one's
temper. **destemplado** *adj* out of tune;
inharmonious.

*desteñir [deste'ɲir] *v* discolour; fade.

*desterrar [dester'rar] *v* banish; (*fig*) discard. **desterrarse** *v* go into exile. **destierro** *sm* exile.

destilar [desti'lar] *v* distil; filter; ooze.
destilación *sf* distillation. **destilador** *sm*
still.

destinar [desti'nar] *v* destine; assign.
destino *sm* destiny; destination; job. **con
destino a** bound for. **destinario** *sm*
addressee.

*destituir [desti'twir] *v* dismiss; deprive
of. **destitución** *sf* removal; dismissal.

destornillar [destorni'λar] *v* unscrew.
destornillarse *v* (*fam*) go crazy. **destornillador** *sm* screwdriver.

destreza [des'treθa] *sf* skill, dexterity.

destronar [destro'nar] *v* dethrone;
depose. **destronamiento** *sm* dethrone-
ment.

destrozar [destro'θar] *v* destroy; squander. **destrozo** *sm* destruction.

*destruir [destru'ir] *v* destroy. **destruirse** *v*
(*mat*) cancel out. **destrucción** *sf* destruction. **destructivo** *adj* destructive. **destructor** *adj* destructive.

desunir [desu'nir] *v* separate; disunite.
desunión *sf* separation.

desusar [desu'sar] *v* be unaccustomed to.
desusarse *v* become obsolete. **desusado**
adj obsolete. **desuso** *sm* disuse.

desvalido [desβa'liðo] *adj* helpless; destitute.

desvalijar [desβali'xar] *v* rifle; rob.

desván [des'βan] *sm* attic.

*desvanecer [desβane'θer] *v* make disappear; remove. **desvanecerse** *v* evaporate;
disappear; faint. **desvanecido** *adj* smug;

vain; (*med*) faint. **desvanecimiento** *sm* disappearance; smugness; faint.

desvariar [desβa'rjar] *v* rave. **desvarío** *sm* delirium.

desvelar [desβe'lar] *v* stop from sleeping. **desvelarse** *v* stay awake; (*fig*) dedicate oneself. **desvelo** *sm* insomnia; effort; devotion. **gracias a mis desvelos** thanks to my efforts.

desventaja [desβen'taxa] *sf* disadvantage. **desventajoso** *adj* disadvantageous.

desventura [desβen'tura] *sf* misfortune. **desventurado** *adj* unfortunate; faint-hearted.

desvergonzado [desβergon'θaðo], -a *sm*, *sf* shameless person. *adj* shameless.

desviar [des'βjar] *v* deviate; turn aside. **desviarse** *v* branch off. **desvío** *sm* detour; deviation.

desvirtuar [desβir'twar] *v* impair; decrease in strength *or* merit.

desvivirse [desβi'βirse] *v* long for; go out of one's way to.

detallar [deta'ʎar] *v* (*com*) retail; tell in detail. **detalle** *sm* detail; nice gesture. **vender al detalle** sell retail. **detalladamente** *adv* in detail. **detallista** *s(m+f)* retailer.

detective [detek'tiβe] *s(m+f)* detective.

***detener** [dete'ner] *v* detain. **detenerse** *v* linger. **detención** *sf* arrest; delay; thoroughness. **detenido** *adj* under arrest; careful.

detergente [deter'xente] *sm*, *adj* detergent.

deteriorar [deterjo'rar] *v* deteriorate; damage. **deterioración** *sf also* **deterioro** *sm* deterioration.

determinar [determi'nar] *v* determine. **determinarse** *v* make up one's mind. **determinación** *sf* determination; decision. **determinado** *adj* determined; decided; definite.

detestar [detes'tar] *v* detest. **detestable** *adj* detestable. **detestación** *sf* detestation.

detonar [deto'nar] *v* detonate. **detonación** *sf* detonation.

***detractar** [detrak'tar] *v* defame. **detracción** *sf* defamation.

***detraer** [detra'er] *v* denigrate; withdraw.

detrás [de'tras] *adv* behind. **detrás de** *prep* behind. **por detrás de uno** behind someone's back.

detrimento [detri'mento] *sm* detriment; damage. **en detrimento de** to the detriment of.

deuda ['deuða] *sf* debt; trespass. **deudor**, -a *sm*, *sf* debtor.

deudo ['deuðo], -a *sm*, *sf* relative. *sm* relationship.

devanar [deβa'nar] *v* wind, coil. **devanarse los sesos** (*fam*) rack one's brains.

devanear [deβane'ar] *v* rave. **devaneo** *sm* delirium; flirtation.

devastar [deβas'tar] *v* devastate. **devastación** *sf* devastation.

devengar [deβen'gar] *v* have due; (*intereses*) yield.

devoción [deβo'θjon] *sf* devotion. **devocionario** *sm* prayer book.

***devolver** [deβol'βer] *v* return. **devolución** *sf* return; refund.

devorar [deβo'rar] *v* devour.

devoto [de'βoto], -a *sm*, *sf* devotee. *adj* devout; devoted.

día ['dia] *sm* day. **¡buenos días!** good morning! **del día** fresh. **ocho días a week. todos los días** every day.

diablo ['djaβlo] *sm* devil. **diabólico** *adj* diabolical.

diafragma [dja'fragma] *sm* diaphragm.

diagnosticar [diagnosti'kar] *v* diagnose. **diagnosis** *sf invar* diagnosis. **diagnóstico** *adj* diagnostic.

diagonal [diago'nal] *sf*, *adj* diagonal.

diagrama [dia'grama] *sm* diagram.

dialecto [dia'lekto] *sm* dialect.

diálogo [di'alogo] *sm* dialogue.

diamante [dia'mante] *sm* diamond.

diámetro [di'ametro] *sm* diameter. **diametral** *adj* diametric.

diario [di'arjo] *sm* daily newspaper; diary. **diario hablado** news bulletin. *adj* daily. **de diario** for everyday use.

diarrea [diar'rea] *sf* diarrhoea.

dibujar [diβu'xar] *v* draw. **dibujante** *s(m+f)* artist; designer; cartoonist; draughtsman. **dibujo** *sm* drawing; sketch; design.

dicción [dik'θjon] *sf* diction; word.

diccionario [dikθjo'narjo] *sm* dictionary.

diciembre [di'θjembre] *sm* December.

dictado [dik'taðo] *sm* dictation; title. **dictados** *sm pl* dictates *pl*. **dictador** *sm* dictator. **dictadura** *sf* dictatorship. **dictar** *v* dictate.

dictamen [dik'tamen] *sm* opinion; advice; report.

dicha ['ditʃa] sf happiness; good luck. por dicha luckily. dichoso adj happy; lucky; (fam) boring.

dicho ['ditʃo] V decir. sm saying; remark; proverb. dicho y hecho no sooner said than done.

diente ['djente] sm tooth.

diestra ['djestra] sf right hand. diestro adj right; skilful; sly.

dieta ['djeta] sf diet.

diez [djeθ] sm, adj ten. diecinueve sm, adj nineteen. dieciocho sm, adj eighteen. dieciséis sm, adj sixteen. diecisiete sm, adj seventeen. diezmar v decimate.

difamar [difa'mar] v defame, slander. difamación sf defamation. difamatorio adj defamatory.

diferencia [dife'renθja] sf difference. a diferencia de unlike. diferenciar v differentiate; differ. diferenciarse be different. diferente adj different.

*diferir [dife'rir] v defer; differ.

difícil [di'fiθil] adj difficult. dificultad sf difficulty. dificultar v make difficult; hinder.

difidente [difi'ðente] adj mistrustful. difidencia sf mistrust.

difundir [difun'dir] v diffuse; broadcast; divulge; spread. difusión sf spread; broadcast; diffusion.

difunto [di'funto] adj dead. sm deceased person.

*digerir [dixe'rir] v digest; (fig) endure. digestible adj digestible. digestión sf digestion.

dignarse [dig'narse] v deign, condescend.

dignidad [digni'ðað] sf dignity; rank. dignitario sm dignitary. digno adj worthy.

digresión [digre'sjon] sf digression.

dilación [dila'θjon] sf delay.

dilatar [dila'tar] v dilate; expand; delay. dilatarse v speak at great length. dilatación sf extension; delay. dilatado adj numerous; long-winded. dilatorio adj dilatory.

dilema [di'lema] sm dilemma.

diligencia [dili'xenθja] sf diligence; (fam) job.

dilucidar [diluθi'ðar] v elucidate; solve.

diluir [dilu'ir] v dilute. dilución sf dilution.

diluvio [di'luβjo] sm deluge.

dimanar [dima'nar] v arise from; flow.

dimensión [dimen'sjon] sf dimension.

diminutivo [diminu'tiβo] adj diminutive. diminuto adj tiny.

dimitir [dimi'tir] v resign. dimisión sf resignation.

Dinamarca [dina'marka] sf Denmark. dinamarqués, -esa sm, sf Dane; adj Danish.

dinamita [dina'mita] sf dynamite.

dínamo ['dinamo] sm dynamo. dinámico adj dynamic.

dinastía [dinas'tia] sf dynasty.

dinero [di'nero] sm money. de dinero rich. dinero suelto loose change. estar mal de dinero be hard up.

dintel [din'tel] sm lintel.

dio [djo] V dar.

diócesi(s) [di'oθesi(s)] sf invar diocese.

dios [djos] sm god, idol. diosa sf goddess.

diploma [di'ploma] sf diploma.

diplomacia [diplo'maθja] sf diplomacy. diplomático sm diplomat; adj diplomatic.

diputado [dipu'taðo] sm deputy, delegate, representative.

dique ['dike] sm dike; dam; dry dock.

dirigir [diri'xir] v direct; govern; steer; regulate. dirigirse v go; speak; write. dirección sf direction; directorship; management; postal address. directivo adj directive; guiding. directo adj direct; straight. director, -a sm, sf director; editor. directorio sm directory.

*discernir [disθer'nir] v discern. discernimiento sm discernment.

disciplina [disθip'lina] sf discipline; doctrine; obedience. disciplinar v discipline; train.

discípulo [dis'θipulo], -a sm, sf disciple; pupil.

disco ['disko] sm disc; record; discus.

disconforme [diskon'forme] adj in disagreement. disconformidad sf disagreement.

discontinuar [disconti'nwar] *v* discontinue. **discontinuación** *sf* discontinuation. **discontinuo** *adj* discontinuous.

discordia [dis'korðja] *sf* discord. **discordante** *adj also* **discorde** discordant.

discoteca [disko'teka] *sf* disco; record library.

discreción [diskre'θjon] *sf* discretion. **a discreción** optional, at will.

discrepancia [diskre'panθja] *sf* discrepancy.

discreto [dis'kreto] *adj* discreet; moderate; sober; witty.

disculpar [diskul'par] *v* excuse; forgive. *v* apologize. **disculpa** *sf* excuse; apology.

discurrir [disku'rrir] *v* ponder; speak; roam; invent.

discurso [dis'kurso] *sm* discourse; reasoning; passage of time. **discursivo** *adj* discursive.

discutir [disku'tir] *v* discuss; debate. **discusión** *sf* discussion; argument. **discutido** *adj* controversial.

disecar [dise'kar] *v* dissect. **disección** *sf* dissection.

diseminar [disemi'nar] *v* scatter. **diseminarse** *v* spread. **diseminación** *sf* dissemination.

disentería [disente'ria] *sf* dysentery.

***disentir** [disen'tir] *v* dissent; differ. **disensión** *sf* dissent; disagreement; quarrel.

diseñar [dise'ɲar] *v* sketch; design. **diseñador, -a** *sm, sf* designer. **diseño** *sm* sketch; design.

disfrazar [disfra'θar] *v* disguise. **disfraz** *sm* disguise; fancy dress.

disfrutar [disfru'tar] *v* possess; enjoy; receive. **disfrute** *sm* enjoyment.

disgregar [disgre'gar] *v* disintegrate; separate. **disgregación** *sf* disintegration; separation.

disgustar [disgus'tar] *v* upset; displease. **disgustarse** *v* become angry. **disgustado** *adj* annoyed; displeased; disappointed. **disgusto** *sm* annoyance; displeasure; repugnance; trouble.

disidente [disi'ðente] *s(m + f)*, *adj* dissident. **disidir** *v* dissent.

disimular [disimu'lar] *v* pretend; dissemble; hide; tolerate. **disimulable** *adj* excusable. **disimulo** *sm* concealment; indulgence.

disipar [disi'par] *v* dissipate. **disiparse** *v* disperse; vanish; clear up. **disipación** *sf* dissipation. **disipado** *adj* dissipated.

dislocar [dislo'kar] *v* dislocate. **dislocación** *sf* dislocation.

***disminuir** [disminu'ir] *v* diminish. **diminución** *sf* decrease; reduction.

disociar [diso'θjar] *v* dissociate. **disociación** *sf* dissociation.

***disolver** [disol'ßer] *v* dissolve. **disoluble** *adj* dissoluble. **disolución** *sf* dissolution; (*fig*) dissoluteness. **disoluto** *adj* dissolute.

***disonar** [diso'nar] *v* disagree; be inharmonious. **disonancia** *sf* discord. **disonante** *adj* discordant.

disparar [dispa'rar] *v* fire; shoot; throw. **dispararse** *v* explode; fly off; race. **disparadamente** *adv* hurriedly; foolishly. **disparo** *sm* firing; shot; attack.

disparatado [dispara'taðo] *adj* absurd. **disparatar** *v* talk nonsense; act foolishly. **disparate** *sm* absurdity.

disparidad [dispari'ðað] *sf* disparity.

dispensar [dispen'sar] *v* dispense; pardon. **dispense usted** forgive me. **dispensa** *sf* dispensation; exemption. **dispensable** *adj* dispensable. **dispensario** *sm* dispensary.

dispersar [disper'sar] *v* disperse. **dispersión** *sf* dispersal. **disperso** *adj* dispersed, scattered.

***disponer** [dispo'ner] *v* dispose; arrange; decide; prepare. **disponer de** dispose of; have. **disponerse** *a* get ready. **disponible** *adj* disposable; available. **disposición** *sf* disposition; instruction; inclination; determination. **tomar disposiciones** take steps. **ultima disposición** last will and testament. **dispuesto** *adj* arranged; disposed; ready; willing.

disputar [dispu'tar] *v* dispute; debate. **disputa** *sf* dispute, argument.

distancia [dis'tanθja] *sf* distance. **distante** *adj* distant.

distinguir [distin'gir] *v* distinguish; esteem. **distinción** *sf* distinction; politeness. **distinguido** *adj* distinguished. **distintivo** *adj* distinctive. **distinto** *adj* distinct; different.

***distraer** [distra'er] *v* distract; entertain. **distracción** *sf* distraction. **distraído** *adj* absent-minded; entertaining.

***distribuir** [distrißu'ir] *v* distribute; deliver; allot. **distribución** *sf* distribution. **cuadro de distribución** *sm* switchboard. **distribuidor** *sm* (*auto*) distributor; agent. **distribuidor automático** slot machine.

distrito [dis'trito] *sm* district.

disturbar [distur'βar] *v* disturb. **disturbio** *sm* disturbance.

disuadir [diswa'ðir] *v* dissuade.

diurno [di'urno] *adj* daily.

divagar [diβa'gar] *v* digress; roam. **divagación** *sf* digression.

diván [di'βan] *sm* divan.

divergir [diβer'xir] *v* diverge; disagree. **divergencia** *sf* divergence. **divergente** *adj* divergent.

diverso [di'βerso] *adj* diverse. **diversos** *adj pl* various; many. **diversidad** *sf* diversity.

*****divertir** [diβer'tir] *v* entertain; divert. **divertido** *adj* amusing; entertaining.

dividir [diβi'ðir] *v* divide; split. **división** *sf* division; (*gram*) hyphen, dash. **divisor** *sm* divider. **divisorio** *adj* dividing.

divino [di'βino] *adj* divine. **divinidad** *sf* divinity.

divisa [di'βisa] *sf* emblem; (*com*) currency. **divisas** *sf pl* (*com*) foreign exchange *sing*. **control de divisas** (*com*) exchange control.

divisar [diβi'sar] *v* distinguish, discern.

divorciar [diβor'θjar] *v* divorce. **divorciarse** *v* get divorced. **divorciado, -a** *sm, sf* divorcee. **divorcio** *sm* divorce.

divulgar [diβul'gar] *v* divulge; circulate; spread. **divulgarse** *v* come out. **divulgación** *sf* disclosure.

doblar [do'βlar] *v* double; fold; bend; (*fig*) persuade; (*fig*) submit. **doblarse** *v* fold; buckle; yield. **dobladillo** *sm* hem; trouser turn-up. **dobladura** *sf* crease, fold. **doble** *adj also* **doblado** double; dual; stocky; deceitful. **el doble** twice as much.

doce [d ce] *sm, adj* twelve. **docena** *sf* dozen.

docente [do'θente] *adj* educational. **personal docente** teaching staff.

dócil [do'θil] *adj* docile; obedient. **docilidad** *sf* docility.

doctor [dok'tor], **-a** *sm, sf* doctor. **docto** *adj* learned. **doctorado** *sm* doctorate.

doctrina [dok'trina] *sf* doctrine. **doctrinal** *adj* doctrinal.

documentar [dokumen'tar] *v* document. **documentación** *sf* documentation; identity papers *pl*.

dogal [do'gal] *sm* halter.

dogma ['dogma] *sm* dogma. **dogmático** *adj* dogmatic. **dogmatismo** *sm* dogmatism.

dogo ['dogo] *sm* bulldog.

*****doler** [do'ler] *v* hurt; ache; grieve. **dolerse de** feel the effects of; regret; pity. **dolor** *sm* pain; grief; repentance. **dolorido** *adj* in pain; grief-stricken. **doloroso** *adj* painful; pitiful; sorrowful.

domar [do'mar] *v* tame; train. **doma** *sf* training.

doméstico [do'mestiko], **-a** *sm, sf* servant. *adj* domestic. **domesticar** *v* domesticate. **domesticidad** *sf* domesticity.

domiciliar [domiθi'ljar] *v* domicile. **domiciliarse** *v* take up residence. **domiciliado** *adj* resident. **domicilio** *sm* home.

dominar [domi'nar] *v* dominate; master. **dominación** *sf* domination; authority. **dominador** *adj* dominating. **dominante** *adj* dominating; dominant. **dominio** *sm* dominion; authority; supremacy.

domingo [do'mingo] *sm* Sunday. **hacer domingo** take a day off.

dominó [domi'no] *sm* (*juego*) dominoes *pl*.

don¹ [don] *sm* (*con nombre de pila*) Mr.

don² *sm* gift; talent. **donación** *sf* donation. **donador, -a** *sm, sf* donor. **donar** *v* give, bestow. **donativo** *sm* offering.

donaire [do'naire] *sm* charm, grace; wit. **donairoso** *adj* graceful; witty.

donde ['donðe] *adv* where. **dondequiera** *adv* wherever. **¿dónde?** where? **¿por dónde?** which way?

doña ['doɲa] *sf* (*con el nombre de pila de una señora o una viuda*) Mrs.

dorar [do'rar] *v* gild; (*culin*) brown. **dorado** *adj* gilt; golden.

*****dormir** [dor'mir] *v* sleep. **dormirse** *v* go to sleep. **dormilón, -ona** *sm, sf* sleepyhead. **dormitorio** *sm* dormitory.

dorso ['dorso] *sm* back. **dorsal** *adj* dorsal.

dos [dos] *sm, adj* two. **dos veces** twice. **las dos** two o'clock. **los dos** both.

dosis ['dosis] *sf invar* dose. **dosificación** *sf* dosage. **dosificar** *v* dose.

dotar [do'tar] *v* endow; equip; staff. **dotación** *sf* endowment; foundation; personnel. **dotado** *adj* endowed; gifted. **dotador, -a** *sm, sf* donor. **dote** *sf* dowry. **dotes** *sf pl* endowments *pl*, talents *pl*.

draga ['draga] *sf* dredge. **dragado** *sm* dredging. **dragar** *v* dredge; (*minas*) sweep.

dragón [dra'gon] *sm* dragon.

drama ['drama] *sm* drama. **dramática** *sf* dramatic art. **dramático** *adj* dramatic. **dramatizar** *v* dramatize. **dramaturgo, -a** *sm, sf* playwright.

drenaje [dre'naxe] *sm* drainage. **drenar** *v* drain.

droga ['droga] *sf* drug. *(fam, fig)* trick, practical joke, fib. **drogadicto, -a** *s, adj* drug addict. **drogar** *v* drug, dope.

dual [dwal] *adj* dual. **dualidad** *sf* duality. **dualismo** *sm* dualism.

ducado [du'kaðo] *sm* duchy.

dúctil ['duktil] *adj* ductile; malleable.

ducha ['dutʃa] *sf* shower. **ducharse** *v* have or take a shower.

dudar [du'ðar] *v* doubt. **duda** *sf* doubt. **sin duda** doubtless. **dudoso** *adj* doubtful; dubious.

duelo¹ ['dwelo] *sm* sorrow; mourning.

duelo² *sm* duel.

duende ['dwende] *sm* imp; goblin; elf.

dueño ['dweɲo], **-a** *sm, sf* owner; master/mistress; landlord/landlady.

dulce ['dulθe] *sm* sweet. *adj* sweet; mild; gentle; soft; *(agua)* fresh. **dulcería** *sf* confectionery. **dulzura** *sf* sweetness; mildness.

dúo ['duo] *sm* duet.

duodécimo [duo'ðeθimo] *sm, adj* twelfth.

duplicar [dupli'kar] *v* duplicate. **duplicarse** *v* double. **duplicación** *sf* duplication; doubling. **duplicado** *sm, adj* duplicate. **duplicador** *sm* duplicator.

duplicidad [dupliθi'ðað] *sf* duplicity.

duque ['duke] *sm* duke. **duquesa** *sf* duchess.

durar [du'rar] *v* last, endure. **durable** *adj* durable. **duración** *sf* duration. **durante** *adv* during.

durazno [du'raθno] *sm* peach; peach tree.

durmiente [dur'mjente] *adj* sleeping.

duro ['duro] *adj* hard; firm. **dureza** *sf* hardness; severity.

E

e [e] *conj* and.

ébano ['eβano] *sm* ebony.

ebrio ['eβrjo] *adj* drunk.

eclesiástico [ekle'sjastiko] *adj, sm* ecclesiastic.

eclipse [e'klipse] *sm* eclipse. **eclipsar** *v* eclipse.

eco ['eko] *sm* echo.

economía [ekono'mia] *sf* economy. **económico** *adj* economical. **economista** *s(m+f)* economist. **economizar** *v* economize.

ecuador [ekwa'ðor] *sm* equator.

ecuestre [e'kwestre] *adj* equestrian.

echar [e'tʃar] *v* throw; emit; *(naipes)* deal/pour out; dismiss; begin; perform. **echar a** start to. **echar abajo** demolish. **echar a perder** spoil. **echar de ver** notice. **echarse** *v* lie down.

edad [e'ðað] *sf* age. **edad madura** middle age.

edicto [e'ðikto] *sm* edict.

edificar [eðifi'kar] *v* build; *(fig)* edify. **edificio** *sm* edifice.

editar [eði'tar] *v* publish. **edición** *sf* edition. **editor, -a** *sm, sf* publisher.

edredón [eðre'ðon] *sm* eiderdown.

educar [eðu'kar] *v* educate; bring up; train. **educación** *sf* education; upbringing. **educado** *adj* educated; well-mannered.

efectivo [efek'tiβo] *adj* effective; real. **dinero efectivo** *sm* cash. **efecto** *sm* effect; result; *(com)* document. **efectos** *sm pl* effects *pl*, assets *pl*. **efectos en cartera** holdings *pl*. **efectuar** *v* carry out.

efervescencia [eferβes'θenθja] *sf* effervescence. **efervescente** *adj* effervescent.

eficacia [efi'kaθja] *sf* efficacy; efficiency. **eficaz** *adj* efficacious; efficient. **eficiencia** *sf* efficiency. **eficiente** *adj* efficient.

efigie [e'fixje] *sf* effigy.

efímero [e'fimero] *adj* ephemeral.

efusión [efu'sjon] *sf* effusion.

Egipto [e'xipto] *sm* Egypt. **egipcio, -a s, adj** Egyptian.

egoísmo [ego'ismo] *sm* egoism. **egoísta** *s(m+f)* egoist. **egotismo** *sm* egotism. **egotista** *s(m+f)* egotist.

egregio [e'grexjo] *adj* eminent.

eje ['exe] *sm* axis; axle; *(fig)* core, hub. **eje del mundo** earth's axis.

ejecutar [exeku'tar] *v* execute; put to death; seize; perform. **ejecución** *sf* execution. **ejecutivo** *sm, adj* executive. **ejecutor, -a** *sm, sf* executor; executioner.

ejemplar [exem'plar] *sm* copy; model;

specimen; example. *adj* exemplary. **ejem-
plificar** *v* exemplify. **ejemplo** *sm* example.
dar ejemplo set an example. **sin ejemplo**
unprecedented.

ejercer [exer'θer] *v* practise; exercise.
ejercicio *sm* exercise.

ejército [e'xerθito] *sm* army.

el [el] *art m* the.

él [el] *pron* he, it.

elaborar [elaβo'rar] *v* elaborate; make;
manufacture. **elaboración** *sf* elaboration.
elaborado *adj* elaborate.

elástico [e'lastiko] *sm, adj* elastic. **elasticidad** *sf* elasticity.

elección [elek'θjon] *sf* election; choice;
selection. **elector, -a** *sm, sf* elector.
electorado *sm* electorate. **electoral** *adj*
electoral.

eléctrico [e'lektriko] *adj* electric(al). **electricidad** *sf* electricity. **electrizar** *v* electrify. **electrocutar** *v* electrocute. **electrodo**
sm electrode. **electrónico** *adj* electronic.

elefante [ele'fante] *sm* elephant.

elegancia [ele'ganθja] *sf* elegance. **elegante** *adj* elegant.

*****elegir** [ele'xir] *v* elect, choose. **elegible**
adj eligible.

elemental [elemen'tal] *adj* elementary.
elemento *sm* element. **elementos** *sm pl*
elements; rudiments.

elevar [ele'βar] *v* elevate, lift, raise.
elevarse *v* rise; soar; be elated. **elevación**
sf elevation; rapture; pride. **elevado** *adj*
lofty; sublime.

eliminar [elimi'nar] *v* eliminate. **eliminación** *sf* elimination.

elocución [eloku'θjon] *sf* elocution.
elocuencia *sf* eloquence. **elocuente** *adj*
eloquent.

elogiar [elo'xjar] *v* praise. **elogio** *sm*
praise. **elogioso** *adj* laudatory.

elucidar [eluθi'ðar] *v* elucidate. **elucida-
ción** *sf* elucidation.

eludir [elu'ðir] *v* elude.

ella ['eʎa] *pron* she, it.

ello ['eʎo] *pron* it.

emanar [ema'nar] *v* emanate. **emanación**
sf emanation.

emancipar [emanθi'par] *v* emancipate.
emancipación *sf* emancipation.

embajada [emba'xaða] *sf* embassy; (*fig*)
errand. **embajador** *sm* ambassador.

embalar [emba'lar] *v* pack, bale. **embalaje**
sm packing; bale.

embarazar [embara'θar] *v* embarrass;
hinder; make pregnant. **embarazarse** *v*
become pregnant. **embarazada** *adj* pregnant. **embarazo** *sm* embarrassment;
obstacle; pregnancy. **embarazoso** *adj*
embarrassing; awkward.

embarcar [embar'kar] *v* embark; ship;
(*fam*) involve. **embarcarse** *v* go on board.
embarcación *sf* boat; embarkation; voyage. **embarcadero** *sm* landing-stage.
embarco *sm* embarkation.

embargar [embar'gar] *v* (*jur*) seize; (*fig*)
overcome; blunt. **embargo** *sm* embargo.
sin embargo nevertheless.

embarque [em'barke] *sm* shipment.

embarrar [embar'rar] *v* smear; cover with
mud. **embarrarse** *v* get dirty.

embeber [embe'βer] *v* absorb, soak up;
shrink. **embebecerse** *v* (*fig*) immerse oneself.

*****embellecer** [embeʎe'θer] *v* embellish.

*****embestir** [embes'tir] *v* attack; charge.
embestida *sf* onslaught; charge.

emblema [em'blema] *sm* emblem.
emblemático *adj* emblematic.

embobar [embo'βar] *v* stupefy; fascinate.

embocar [embo'kar] *v* put in the mouth;
enter; (*fig*) swallow. **embocadura** *sf*
mouth of a river; (*vino*) taste; (*caballo*)
bit.

embolsar [embol'sar] *v* pocket.

emborrachar [emborra'tʃar] *v* intoxicate.
emborracharse *v* get drunk.

emboscar [embos'kar] *v* ambush. **embos-
carse** *v* lie in ambush. **emboscada** *sf*
ambush.

embotar [embo'tar] *v* blunt, dull; pack in
a jar. **embotarse** *v* become enervated.
embotadura *sf also* embotamiento *sm*
bluntness, dullness.

embotellar [embote'ʎar] *v* bottle.
embotellarse *v* learn by heart. **embote-
llado** *adj* bottled; jammed. **embotellamiento** *sm* bottling; traffic jam.

embozar [embo'θar] *v* muffle; wrap up.
embozadamente *adv* secretly. **embozo** *sm*
fold; (*fig*) disguise. **quitarse el embozo**
bare one's face.

embragar [embra'gar] *v* (*auto*) engage the
clutch. **embrague** *sm* (*auto*) clutch.

embriagarse [embrja'garse] *v* get drunk.
embriagado *adj* drunk.

embrión [em'brjon] *sm* embryo. **embrio-
logía** *sf* embryology.

embrollar [embro'ʎar] v muddle, confuse. **embrollarse** v get mixed up. **embrollo** sm confusion.

embrujar [embru'xar] v bewitch.

*****embrutecer** [embrute'θer] v brutalize; stupefy.

embudo [em'buðo] sm funnel; crater; (fig) trick.

embuste [em'buste] sm lie; trick. **embustear** v lie; cheat. **embustería** sf deceit; imposture. **embustero, -a** sm, sf liar; cheat; adj lying; deceitful.

embutir [embu'tir] v stuff; cram; (tecn) inlay. **embutido** sm sausage.

emergencia [emer'xenθja] sf emergence; emergency. **emergente** adj emergent; resultant. **emerger** v emerge.

emigrar [emi'grar] v emigrate; migrate. **emigración** sf emigration; migration. **emigrado, -a** sm, sf emigrant. **emigrante** s(m+f), adj emigrant.

eminencia [emi'nenθja] sf eminence; height. **eminente** adj eminent.

emisario [emi'sarjo], **-a** sm, sf emissary.

emitir [emi'tir] v emit; broadcast; transmit. **emisión** sf emission; broadcast; programme. **emisor** sm transmitter. **emisora** sf radio station.

emoción [emo'θjon] sf emotion; thrill. **emocionante** adj moving; exciting.

empachar [empa'tʃar] v satiate; give indigestion; sicken; conceal; (fig) hinder. **empacharse** v have indigestion; become confused; get fed up. **empachado** adj clumsy; sick; fed up. **empacho** sm indigestion; (fig) embarrassment.

empadronar [empaðro'nar] v register. **empadronamiento** sm census.

empalagar [empala'gar] v cloy; vex. **empalagarse** v get fed up. **empalagoso** adj cloying.

empalar [empa'lar] v impale.

empalizada [empali'θaða] sf stockade. **empalizar** v fence.

empalmar [empal'mar] v splice; couple, join. **empalme** sm joint; junction.

empanada [empa'naða] sf meat pie.

empañar [empa'ɲar] v tarnish; swathe; obscure. **empañarse** v cloud over. **empañado** adj misty.

empapar [empa'par] v soak; drench. **empapamiento** sm soaking.

empapelar [empape'lar] v paper; wrap in paper.

empaquetar [empake'tar] v pack, package. **empaque** sm packing.

emparejar [empare'xar] v match; pair; draw level; catch up. **emparejadura** sf matching; levelling.

empastar [empas'tar] v paste; fill. **empastado** adj filled; (libro) clothbound.

empatar [empa'tar] v (juegos) tie, draw. **empate** sm tie, draw.

*****empedernir** [empeðer'nir] v harden. **empedernido** adj hardened; inveterate.

*****empedrar** [empe'ðrar] v pave. **empedrado** adj paved; cobbled.

empeine [em'peine] sm groin; instep; (med) impetigo.

empeñar [empe'ɲar] v pawn, pledge; commit; get involved. **empeñarse** v start; strive; get into debt. **empeñado** adj insistent. **empeño** sm pledge; contract; insistence; yearning. **casa de empeño** sf pawnshop. **en empeño** in pawn.

empeorar [empeo'rar] v make worse; worsen. **empeoramiento** sm deterioration.

*****empequeñecer** [empekeɲe'θer] v dwarf; belittle.

emperador [empera'ðor] sm emperor. **emperatriz** sf empress.

*****empezar** [empe'θar] v begin.

empinar [empi'nar] v straighten; exalt. **empinarse** v rear up; stand on tiptoe; tower. **empinado** adj erect; on tiptoe; haughty.

empírico [em'piriko] adj empirical. **empirismo** sm empiricism.

emplazar [empla'θar] v summon; locate. **emplazamiento** sm (jur) summons.

emplear [emple'ar] v employ; use; invest; spend. **empleado, -a** sm, sf employee. **empleador, -a** sm, sf employer. **empleo** sm employment; job; use.

*****empobrecer** [empoβre'θer] v impoverish. **empobrecimiento** sm impoverishment.

empollar [empo'ʎar] v hatch; (fam) swot, mug up.

emponzoñar [emponθo'ɲar] v poison. **emponzoñamiento** sm poisoning.

empotrar [empo'trar] v embed. **empotramiento** sm embedding.

emprender [empren'der] v undertake; start; attack. **emprender con** accost. **emprendedor** adj enterprising.

empresa [em'presa] sf enterprise; (com) company; management. **empresario, -a** sm, sf impresario; contractor.

empréstito [em'prestito] *sm* loan.

empujar [empu'xar] *v* push; press; (*fig*) urge. **empuje** *sm* push; enterprise. a **empujes** by fits and starts.

empuñar [empu'ɲar] *v* seize; take up. **empuñadura** *sf* hilt.

emular [emu'lar] *v* emulate.

emulsión [emul'sjon] *sf* emulsion. **emulsionar** *v* emulsify.

en [en] *prep* on; in; into; onto. **en casa** at home. **en donde** where. **en tren** by train.

enaguas [e'nagwas] *sf pl* petticoat *sing*.

enajenar [enaxe'nar] *v* alienate; transfer; drive mad; enrapture. **enajenarse** *v* lose one's self-control. **enajenación** *sf also* **enajenamiento** *sm* alienation; absent-mindedness; rapture; panic.

enamorar [enamo'rar] *v* court; win the love of. **enamorarse** *v* fall in love. **enamorado, -a** *sm, sf* sweetheart.

enano [e'nano], **-a** *sm, sf* dwarf.

enarbolar [enarβo'lar] *v* hoist. **enarbolarse** *v* rear; lose one's temper.

*****enardecer** [enarðe'θer] *v* inflame. **enardecerse** *v* become excited.

encabestrar [enkaβes'trar] *v* put a halter on.

encabezar [enkaβe'θar] *v* lead; head; take a census of; put a title to. **encabezamiento** *sm* headline; heading; census.

encadenar [enkaðe'nar] *v* chain, shackle. **encadenamiento** *sm* chaining; (*fig*) linking.

encajar [enka'xar] *v* fit; join; bear; pocket; drop; land. **encajarse** *v* get stuck; squeeze in. **encajadura** *sf* (*hueso*) setting; socket. **encaje** *sm* joint; setting; socket; lace.

encallar [enka'ʎar] *v* run aground. **encallarse** *v* harden. **encalladero** *sm* sandbank; reef.

encaminar [enkami'nar] *v* direct; guide. **encaminarse** *v* set out for.

encandilar [enkandi'lar] *v* dazzle; stimulate. **encandilarse** *v* (*ojos*) sparkle.

encantar [enkan'tar] *v* enchant; charm. **encantado** *adj* charmed; haunted. **¡encantado!** pleased to meet you! **encantador** *adj* charming. **encanto** *sm* charm; delight.

encapotar [enkapo'tar] *v* cover with a cloak. **encapotarse** *v* cloak oneself; look sullen; cloud over. **encapotado** *adj* overcast.

encapricharse [enkapri'tʃarse] *v* set one's mind on. **encapricharse por** *or* **con** become infatuated with.

encarar [enka'rar] *v* face up to; aim; confront. **encaramiento** *sm* encounter.

encarcelar [enkarθe'lar] *v* imprison. **encarcelamiento** *sm* imprisonment.

*****encarecer** [enkare'θer] *v* raise the price of; praise; urge. **encarecidamente** *adv* earnestly. **encarecido** *adj* highly recommended. **encarecimiento** *sm* price increase; emphasis; recommendation.

encargar [enkar'gar] *v* (*com*) order; commission; entrust; charge; advise. **encargarse de** take charge of. **encargado** *sm* agent. **encargo** *sm* errand; job; order.

encarnar [enkar'nar] *v* personify; heal; pierce the flesh; bait. **encarnarse** *v* mix, join in. **encarnación** *sf* incarnation. **encarnado** *adj* incarnate; red; (*uña*) ingrowing.

encarnizar [enkarni'θar] *v* infuriate. **encarnizarse** *v* devour. **encarnizado** *adj* inflamed; bloody.

encasillar [enkasi'ʎar] *v* classify.

encauzar [enkau'θar] *v* channel; direct. **encauzamiento** *sm* channelling; (*fig*) guidance.

*****encender** [enθen'der] *v* light; set on fire; turn on; arouse. **encendedor** *sm* lighter. **encendido** *adj* lit; burning; flushed. **encendimiento** *sm* burning; ardour.

*****encerrar** [enθe'rrar] *v* shut up; enclose; contain. **encerrarse** *v* live in seclusion. **encerramiento** *sm* enclosure; lock-up. **encierro** *sm* enclosure; prison.

encía [en'θia] *sf* (*anat*) gum.

enciclopedia [enθiklo'peðja] *sf* encyclopaedia. **enciclopédico** *adj* encyclopaedic.

encima [en'θima] *adv* above; overhead. **por encima** over; quickly; superficially. **encima de** on top of.

encina [en'θina] *sf* ilex, holm oak.

encinta [en'θinta] *adj* pregnant.

enclavar [enkla'βar] *v* locate; nail; pierce. **enclave** *sm* enclave; situation.

enclenque [en'klenke] *adj* sickly; feeble; skinny.

encoger [enko'xer] *v* shrink. **encogerse de hombros** shrug one's shoulders. **encogido** *adj* shrunk; (*fig*) timid. **encogimiento** *sm* shrinkage; shyness.

encolar [enko'lar] *v* glue. **encolamiento** *sm* gluing.

*encomendar [enkomen'ðar] v entrust. **encomendarse** v commend oneself. **encomienda** sf assignment; tribute; land concession.

encomiar [enko'mjar] v praise. **encomiador** adj laudatory.

enconar [enko'nar] v inflame; infect. **enconarse** v become inflamed; become infected; get angry.

encontrar [enkon'trar] v find; meet. **encontrarse** v find oneself; quarrel. **encontrado** adj opposed.

encopetado [enkope'taðo] adj of noble birth; aristocratic; presumptuous.

encorvar [enkor'βar] v curve. **encorvarse** v become bent; (caballo) buck. **encorvado** adj bent; stooped. **encorvamiento** sm bend; stoop.

encrespar [enkres'par] v curl; make rough; excite; irritate. **encresparse** v curl; become rough; become entangled.

encrucijada [enkruθi'xaða] sf crossroads pl.

encuadernar [enkwaðer'nar] v (libro) bind. **encuadernación** sf bookbinding.

encuadrar [enkwa'ðrar] v frame; insert. **encuadre** sm frame.

*encubrir [enku'βrir] v conceal; (jur) receive stolen goods. **encubierto** adj concealed. **encubrimiento** sm concealment.

encuentro [en'kwentro] sm encounter; collision.

encumbrar [enkum'brar] v raise; ascend; exalt. **encumbrado** adj high, lofty. **encumbramiento** sm height; praise.

enchufar [entʃu'far] v plug in; connect. **enchufado, -a** sm, sf (fam) wirepuller. **enchufe** sm electric plug; joint; (fam) cushy job. **enchufismo** sm (fam) wirepulling.

endeble [en'deβle] adj frail. **endeblez** sf frailty.

endémico [en'demiko] adj endemic.

enderezar [endere'θar] v straighten; guide; put right. **enderezarse** v stand up straight. **enderezado** adj favourable.

endeudarse [endeu'ðarse] v get into debt.

endiablado [endja'βlaðo] adj devilish. **endiablar** v bedevil.

endiosar [endjo'sar] v deify. **endiosarse** v be conceited. **endiosado** adj deified; conceited.

endosar [endo'sar] v also **endorsar** endorse. **endoso** sm also **endorso** sm endorsement.

endulzar [endul'θar] v sweeten. **endulzadura** sf sweetening.

*endurecer [endure'θer] v harden. **endurecido** adj hardened. **endurecimiento** sm hardening.

enebro [e'neβro] sm juniper.

enemigo [ene'miɣo], **-a** sm, sf enemy. adj hostile. **enemistar** v make an enemy of.

energía [ener'xia] sf energy. **enérgico** adj energetic; vigorous; drastic.

enero [e'nero] sm January.

enfadar [enfa'ðar] v anger. **enfado** sm anger; annoyance. **enfadoso** adj annoying.

énfasis ['enfasis] s(m or f) emphasis. **enfático** adj emphatic.

enfermar [enfer'mar] v make ill; fall ill. **enfermedad** sf illness. **enfermedad profesional** occupational disease. **enfermería** sf infirmary. **enfermera, -o** sf, sm nurse. **enfermo** adj ill.

enfilar [enfi'lar] v line up.

*enflaquecer [enflake'θer] v weaken; make thin; grow thin. **enflaquecimiento** sm weakening; emaciation.

enfocar [enfo'kar] v focus; approach, tackle. **enfoque** sm focus; approach.

enfrascar [enfras'kar] v bottle. **enfrascarse** v become involved; become engrossed.

enfrentar [enfren'tar] v confront; face; resist. **enfrentarse** v face up to. **enfrente** adv opposite. **enfrente de** prep opposite.

enfriar [enfri'ar] v cool. **enfriarse** v cool down. **enfriadero** sm coldroom. **enfriamiento** sm cooling.

*enfurecer [enfure'θer] v infuriate. **enfurecerse** v rage. **enfurecimiento** sm fury.

enganchar [engan'tʃar] v hook; hitch; hang up; harness. **enganche** sm hook; coupling; harnessing; enlistment.

engañar [enga'ɲar] v deceive. **engaño** sm deceit. **engañoso** adj deceitful.

engatusar [engatu'sar] v coax; flatter. **engatusamiento** sm coaxing.

engendrar [enxen'drar] v engender; breed. **engendrador** adj generating. **engendramiento** sm generating. **engendro** sm foetus; abortion; monster; brainchild.

englobar [englo'βar] v include; embrace.

engordar [engor'ðar] v fatten; gain weight. **engorde** sm (animales) fattening up.

engorro [en'gorro] *sm* nuisance. engorroso *adj* troublesome.

engranar [engra'nar] *v* put in gear, mesh, interlock. engranaje *sm* gear; cogs; connection.

*engrandecer [engrande'θer] *v* enlarge; exaggerate; promote. engrandecimiento *sm* enlargement; increase; exaggeration.

engrasar [engra'sar] *v* grease. engrase *sm* greasing.

engreído [engre'iðo] *adj* conceited. engreimiento *sm* conceit. engreir *v* make conceited.

*engrosar [engro'sar] *v* fatten; thicken; increase. engrosarse *v* enlarge. engrosamiento *sm* fattening; thickening.

*engullir [engu'ʎir] *v* gobble; gulp down.

enhiesto [e'njesto] *adj* erect; upright. enhestar *v* erect. enhestarse *v* rise; straighten oneself up.

enhorabuena [enora'βwena] *sf* congratulations *pl*. dar la enhorabuena congratulate. enhoramala *adv* inopportunely.

enigma [e'nigma] *sm* enigma. enigmático *adj* enigmatic.

enjabonar [enxaβo'nar] *v* soap. enjabonadura *sf* lathering.

enjambre [en'xambre] *sm* swarm. enjambrar *v* swarm.

enjaular [enxau'lar] *v* cage.

enjuagar [enxwa'gar] *v* rinse. enjuague *sm* rinse, rinsing; (*fig*) plot.

enjugar [enxu'gar] *v* dry; wipe; cancel. enjugador *sm* clothes-drier.

enjuiciar [enxwi'θjar] *v* (*jur*) sue; try; prosecute; judge. enjuiciamiento *sm* trial; lawsuit; judgment.

enlace [en'laθe] *sm* link; connection; liaison; marriage. enlazar *v* join; connect; relate. enlazarse *v* marry.

*enloquecer [enloke'θer] *v* madden. enloquecido *adj* mad. enloquecimiento *sm* madness.

enlosar [enlo'sar] *v* tile; pave. enlosado *sm* tiling; paving.

*enlucir [enlu'θir] *v* plaster; polish. enlucido *sm* plaster. enlucimiento *sm* plastering; polishing.

enlutar [enlu'tar] *v* dress in mourning. (*fig*) sadden. enlutado *adj* in mourning.

enmarañar [enmara'nar] *v* entangle; muddle; confuse. enmarañamiento *sm* tangle; confusion.

enmascarar [enmaska'rar] *v* mask. enmascararse *v* go in disguise. enmascaramiento *sm* camouflage.

*enmendar [enmen'dar] *v* amend; correct; reform. enmendadura *sf* correction. enmienda *sf* rectification; repair; amendment.

*enmohecer [enmoe'θer] *v* rust; make mouldy. enmohecerse *v* get rusty; grow mouldy. enmohecimiento *sm* rusting; mouldering.

*enmudecer [enmuðe'θer] *v* silence. enmudecerse *v* fall silent; become dumb.

ennoblecer [ennoβle'θer] *v* ennoble; do honour to. ennoblecimiento *sm* ennobling.

enojar [eno'xar] *v* annoy; offend. enojarse *v* get cross. enojado *adj* angry. enojo *sm* annoyance; anger.

*enorgullecer [enorguʎe'θer] *v* make proud. enorgullecerse *v* grow proud. enorgullecerse de pride oneself on. enorgullecimiento *sm* pride.

enorme [e'norme] *adj* enormous. enormidad *sf* hugeness; enormity.

*enrarecer [enrare'θer] *v* make rare; rarefy. enrarecerse *v* become scarce. enrarecido *adj* rarefied. enrarecimiento *sm* scarcity.

enredar [enre'ðar] *v* catch; entangle; compromise; involve. enredarse *v* become involved. planta enredadera *sf* climbing plant. enredador *adj* mischievous. enredo *sm* tangle; mess; love affair. enredoso *adj* complicated; mischievous.

enrevesado [enreβe'saðo] *adj* complicated, involved.

*enriquecer [enrike'θer] *v* enrich.

*enrojecer [enroxe'θer] *v* redden; cause to blush. enrojecerse *v* blush. enrojecimiento *sm* glowing; blush.

enrollar [enro'ʎar] *v* coil up. enrollamiento *sm* rolling up; coiling.

*enronquecer [enronke'θer] *v* make hoarse. enronquecimiento *sm* hoarseness.

enroscar [enros'kar] *v* twist, curl. enroscarse *v* curl up. enroscadura *sf* twisting, curling.

ensalada [ensa'laða] *sf* salad.

ensalmar [ensal'mar] *v* (*huesos*) set; cure. ensalmador, -a *sm, sf* quack; bonesetter. ensalmo *sm* quack remedy.

ensalzar [ensal'θar] *v* praise. ensalzarse *v* boast. ensalzamiento *sm* praise.

ensamblar [ensam'blar] *v* assemble; join.

ensamblado *sm* joint. ensamblador *sm* joiner. ensamblaje *sm* joining; joint.

ensanchar [ensan'tʃar] *v* grow broader; enlarge; stretch. ensancharse *v* put on airs. ensanche *sm* enlargement; extension; new suburb.

ensañar [ensa'ɲar] *v* infuriate. ensañarse *v* be merciless.

ensayar [ensa'jar] *v* test; try; rehearse. ensayarse *v* practise; rehearse. ensayo *sm* test; trial; essay; rehearsal. ensayo general dress rehearsal.

ensenada [ense'naða] *sf* cove; inlet.

enseñar [ense'ɲar] *v* show; teach. bien/mal enseñado well/ill-bred. enseñanza *sf* teaching; education.

enseres [en'seres] *sm pl* goods and chattels; equipment *sing*.

ensillar [ensi'ʎar] *v* saddle.

ensimismarse [ensimis'marse] *v* become lost in thought. ensimismado *adj* lost in thought. ensimismamiento *sm* pensiveness.

*ensordecer [ensorðe'θer] *v* deafen. ensordecerse *v* grow deaf. ensordecedor *adj* deafening. ensordecimiento *sm* deafness.

ensuciar [ensu'θjar] *v* dirty. ensuciador *adj* dirtying. ensuciamiento *sm* dirtiness, dirt.

ensueño [en'sweɲo] *sm* dream; fantasy. ¡ni por ensueño! not likely!

entablar [enta'βlar] *v* begin; open; establish; board up; put in a splint; (*juegos*) set up. entablado *sm* planking; wooden floor.

entallar [enta'ʎar] *v* carve; notch; engrave; fit to the body. entalladura *sf* notch; mortise; carving.

ente ['ente] *sm* entity; (*fam*) fellow.

*entender [enten'der] *v* understand; believe; mean. entenderse *v* make oneself understood. entendedor, -a *sm, sf* expert. entendidamente *adv* cleverly. entendido *adj* understood; well informed; clever. ¡entendido! O.K.!

enterar [ente'rar] *v* inform; instruct. enterarse *v* become aware. enterado *adj* aware.

*enternecer [enterne'θer] *v* soften. enternecerse *v* be moved; relent.

entero [en'tero] *adj* entire, whole; perfect; pure; strong. por entero completely. enteramente *adv* entirely.

*enterrar [enter'rar] *v* bury. entarrador *sm* gravedigger. entierro *sm* burial; funeral.

entidad [enti'ðað] *sf* society; company; significance; entity.

entonar [ento'nar] *v* tune; intone; sing in tune. entonación *sf* intonation. entonado *adj* in tune; haughty.

entonces [en'tonθes] *adv* then; in that case; and so.

entornar [entor'nar] *v* (*ojos, puerta*) half close; tilt.

*entorpecer [entorpe'θer] *v* benumb; obstruct. entorpecimiento *sm* numbness; sluggishness; obstruction.

entrada [en'traða] *sf* entrance; doorway; admission; (*deporte*) gate; ticket; income; takings *pl*. derechos de entrada *sm pl* import duty *sing*. de entrada to begin with. entrar *v* enter; flow into; fit; join; introduce; invade. el año que entra the coming year.

entrambos [en'trambos] *pl adj* both.

entraña [en'traɲa] *sf* essence; core; disposition. entrañas *sf pl* entrails, bowels. no tener entrañas be heartless. entrañable *adj* dear, beloved. entrañar *v* bury deep; involve. entrañarse *v* penetrate to the core.

entre ['entre] *prep* between; among. entre semana on weekdays. entretanto *adv* meanwhile.

entreabierto [entrea'βjerto] *adj* half-open.

entrecejo [entre'θexo] *sm* frown.

entregar [entre'gar] *v* deliver; surrender. entrega *sf* delivery; (*fascículo*) instalment.

entrelazar [entrela'θar] *v* entwine.

entremés [entre'mes] *sm* (*culin*) hors d'oeuvre; (*teatro*) short farce.

entremeter [entreme'ter] *v* also entrometer mix; insert. entremeterse also entrometerse *v* interfere. entremetido, -a *sm, sf* also entrometido, -a busybody.

entrenar [entre'nar] *v* train; coach. entrenador, -a *sm, sf* trainer; coach. entrenamiento *sm* training; coaching.

entresacar [entresa'kar] *v* select; prune; thin out.

entresuelo [entre'swelo] *sm* mezzanine.

entretejer [entrete'xer] *v* interweave.

*entretener [entrete'ner] *v* entertain; delay; maintain. entretenerse *v* pass the time. entretenido *adj* entertaining; busy. entretenimiento *sm* entertainment; pastime; delaying.

*entrever [entre'βer] *v* make out; foresee.
entrevista [entre'βista] *sf* interview.
entrevistar *v* interview. **entrevistarse** *v*
hold an interview.
*entristecer [entriste'θer] *v* sadden.
entristecerse *v* grow sad. **entristecimiento**
sm sadness.
*entumecer [entume'θer] *v* numb.
entumecerse *v* go numb; (*mar*) surge.
entumecido *adj* numb. **entumecimiento**
sm numbness.
enturbiar [entur'βjar] *v* make cloudy;
muddy. **enturbiarse** *v* be in disorder.
entusiasmar [entusjas'mar] *v* fill with
enthusiasm. **entusiasmarse** *v* be very
keen. **entusiasmo** *sm* enthusiasm. **entusiasta** *s(m+f)* enthusiast; *adj* enthusiastic. **entusiástico** *adj* enthusiastic.
enumerar [enume'rar] *v* enumerate.
enumeración *sf* enumeration.
'enunciar [enun'θjar] *v* enunciate, state.
enunciación *sf* statement, enunciation.
envainar [enβai'nar] *v* sheathe.
*envanecer [enβane'θer] *v* make vain.
envanecimiento *sm* vanity.
envasar [enβa'sar] *v* pack; wrap; bottle.
envasador *sm* packer; large funnel.
envase *sm* packing; bottling; container.
*envejecer [enβexe'θer] *v* age.
envejecerse *v* grow old. **envejecido** *adj*
aged. **envejecimiento** *sm* ageing.
envenenar [enβene'nar] *v* poison.
envenenador *adj* poisonous.
envenenamiento *sm* poisoning; pollution.
envergadura [enβerga'ðura] *sf* wingspan;
(*fig*) scope.
enviar [en'βjar] *v* send. **enviado, -a** *sm, sf*
messenger; representative; envoy.
envidiar [enβi'ðjar] *v* envy. **envidia** *sf*
envy. **envidioso** *adj* envious.
*envilecer [enβile'θer] *v* debase.
envilecimiento *sm* debasement; degradation.
envío [en'βio] *sm* dispatch; shipment;
remittance.
*envolver [enβol'βer] *v* envelop; wrap
up; involve; imply; (*mil*) encircle. **envoltura** *sf* wrapping; envelope.
enzarzar [enθar'θar] *v* cover with brambles; set at odds. **enzarzarse** *v* get caught
up in brambles; (*fig*) squabble.
enzima [en'θima] *sf* enzyme.
épico ['epiko] *adj* epic.
epidemia [epi'ðemja] *sf* epidemic.
epidémico *adj* epidemic.

epígrafe [e'pigrafe] *sm* epigraph.
epílogo [e'pilogo] *sm* epilogue.
episcopado [episko'paðo] *sm* bishopric;
episcopate. **episcopal** *adj* episcopal.
episodio [epi'soðjo] *sm* episode.
epitafio [epi'tafjo] *sm* epitaph.
época ['epoka] *sf* epoch.
equidad [eki'ðað] *sf* equity; fairness.
equilibrar [ekili'βrar] *v* balance. **equilibrio**
sm equilibrium; balance; poise. **equilib-
rismo** *sm* acrobatics. **equilibrista** *s(m+f)*
acrobat.
equinoccio [eki'nokθjo] *sm* equinox. **equinoccial** *adj* equinoctial.
equipar [eki'par] *v* equip. **equipaje** *sm* luggage; equipment. **equipo** *sm* team;
equipment; trousseau.
equitación [ekita'θjon] *sf* riding; horsemanship.
equitativo [ekita'tiβo] *adj* fair, equitable.
equivalencia [ekiβa'lenθja] *sf* equivalence.
equivalente *adj* equivalent. **equivaler** *v* be
equivalent.
equivocar [ekiβo'kar] *v* mistake. **equivocarse** *v* be mistaken. **equivocación** *sf* mistake. **equívoco** *adj* ambiguous.
era[1] ['era] *sf* era.
era[2] ['era] *V* ser.
eremita [ere'mita] *sm* also **ermitaño** *sm*
hermit.
eres ['eres] *V* ser.
*erguir [er'gir] *v* raise, erect. **erguirse** *v*
straighten up. **erguimiento** *sm* raising.
erigir [eri'xir] *v* erect; build; establish.
erigirse *v* set oneself up. **erección** *sf* erection; establishment. **erecto** *adj* erect.
erizar [eri'θar] *v* bristle. **erizarse** *v* bristle;
(*pelo*) stand on end. **erizado** *adj* bristly.
erizo [e'riβo] *sm* hedgehog.
erradicar [erraði'kar] *v* eradicate; uproot.
erradicación *sf* eradication.
*errar [er'rar] *v* miss; fail; wander.
errarse *v* be mistaken. **erradizo** *adj* wandering. **errado** *adj* mistaken. **errante** *adj*
wandering; nomadic. **erróneo** *adj* errone-
ous, mistaken. **error** *sm* error.
eructar [eruk'tar] *v* belch. **eructo** *sm*
belch.
erudición [eruði'θjon] *sf* erudition.
erudito, -a *sm, sf* scholar; *adj* erudite.
erupción [erup'θjon] *sf* eruption; (*med*)
rash. **eruptivo** *adj* eruptive.
esbelto [es'βelto] *adj* slim. **esbeltez** *sf*
slimness.

esbozar [esβo'θar] v sketch. **esbozo** sm
sketch.

escabechar [eskaβe'tʃar] v (culin) pickle;
(fam) fail an exam; (fam) bump off.
escabeche sm pickle.

escabroso [eska'βroso] adj rough; crude;
harsh; (fig) difficult. **escabro** sm (med)
scab. **escabrosidad** sf roughness; crudity;
harshness.

***escabullirse** [eskaβu'ʎirse] v sneak away
or out.

escala [es'kala] sf ladder; scale; port of
call. **en gran escala** on a large scale.
escala franca free port. **hacer escala en**
put in at. **escalar** v climb; escalate.
escalamiento sm escalation.

escaldar [eskal'dar] v scald; make red
hot. **escaldado** adj scalded; cautious.

escalera [eska'lera] sf stairs pl. **escalera
móvie** escalator.

escalfar [eskal'far] v (culin) poach.
escalfado adj poached. **escalfador** sm
poacher.

escalofrío [eskalo'frio] sm shiver. **escalofriante** adj bloodcurdling.

escalón [eska'lon] sm rung; step.
escalonar v space; stagger. **escalonado**
adj spread out; staggered.
escalonamiento sm spacing; staggering.

escalonia [eska'lonja] sf also **escaloña**
shallot.

escalpelo [eskal'pelo] sm scalpel.

escama [es'kama] sf (jabón) flake;
(animal) scale. **escamado** adj (fam) suspicious. **escamar** v scale; (fam) make suspicious. **escamarse** v (fam) become suspicious. **escamoso** adj scaly; (fam) suspicious.

escamot(e)ar [eskamo't(j)ar] v make disappear; shirk. **escamoteo** sm (fam) swindle. **escamoteador**, -a sm, sf conjurer;
(fam) swindler.

escampar [eskam'par] v clear out; stop
raining. **escampada** sf clear spell.

escándalo [es'kandalo] sm scandal;
uproar; viciousness. **dar un escándalo**
make a scene. **escandalizar** v scandalize.
escandalizarse v be shocked. **escandaloso**
adj scandalous; turbulent.

escaño [es'kaɲo] sm bench; seat in Parliament.

escapar [eska'par] v escape. **escaparse** v
escape; leak. **escapada** sf escape; escapade. **escape** sm escape; leakage. **a**

escape at full speed. **tubo de escape**
exhaust pipe.

escaparate [eskapa'rate] sm shop window.

escarabajo [eskara'βaxo] sm beetle; (fam)
dwarf.

escaramuza [eskara'muθa] sf skirmish.
escaramucear v skirmish.

escarbar [eskar'βar] v scratch; scrape;
pry into. **escarbo** sm scraping; scratching.

escarcha [es'kartʃa] sf frost.

escarlata [eskar'lata] sf, adj scarlet.

***escarmentar** [eskarmen'tar] v punish;
learn from experience; be warned.
escarmiento sm punishment; warning.

***escarnecer** [eskarne'θer] v mock.
escarnecimiento sm scorn; derision.

escarola [eska'rola] sf endive.

escarpa [es'karpa] sf slope.

escasear [eskase'ar] v skimp; be scarce.
escasamente adv scantily. **escasez** sf scarcity. **escaso** adj scarce; skimpy.

escena [es'θena] sf scene; stage. **poner en
escena** stage. **escénico** adj scenic.

escéptico [es'θeptiko] s, adj sceptic(al).
esceptisismo sm scepticism.

***esclarecer** [esklare'θer] v brighten; clear;
dawn. **esclarecido** adj illustrious.
esclarecimiento sm illumination; splendour; dawn.

esclavitud [esklaβi'tuð] sf slavery.
esclavizar v enslave. **esclavo**, -a sm, sf
slave.

esclusa [es'klusa] sf lock; floodgate.
esclusa de aire airlock.

escoba [es'koβa] sf broom, brush. **escobar**
v sweep, brush.

***escocer** [esko'θer] v smart, sting.
escocerse v chafe. **escocedor** adj painful.
escocedura sf sting.

escoger [esko'xer] v choose. **escogido** adj
chosen, choice. **escogimiento** sm choice,
selection.

escolar [esko'lar] s(m + f) schoolboy/girl.
adj scholastic. **escolástica** sf scholasti-
cism. **escolástico** adj scholastic.

escolta [es'kolta] sf escort. **escoltar** v
escort.

escollo [es'koʎo] sm reef; difficulty; danger.

escombro [es'kombro] sm mackerel; déb-
ris; rubbish.

esconder [eskon'der] v hide. **esconderse** v
conceal oneself. **escondidamente** adv

secretly. **escondite** *sm* hiding place; (*juego*) hide-and-seek.

escopeta [esko'peta] *sf* shotgun; rifle. **escopeta de aire comprimido** airgun.

escoplo [es'koplo] *sm* chisel. **escoplear** *v* chisel; gouge.

escoria [es'korja] *sf* slag; dross; (*fig*) scum. **escorial** *sm* slag heap.

escorpión [eskor'pjon] *sf* scorpion.

escotado [esko'taðo] *adj* (*vestido*) low-cut. **escotar** *v* lower the neckline; scoop out.

escotilla [esko'tiʎa] *sf* (*mar*) hatch.

escribano [eskri'βano] *sm* clerk; notary.

*escribir [eskri'βir] *v* write. **escribir a máquina** type. **escribirse** *v* spell. **escribido** *adj* (*fam*) well read. **escribiente** *s*(*m*+*f*) clerk. **escrito a mano** handwritten. *sm* writing; document; letter. **escritor,-a** *sm, sf* writer. **escritorio** *sm* bureau; office. **escritura** *sf* writing; script; (*jur*) deed.

escrúpulo [es'krupulo] *sm* scruple; conscientiousness. **escrupuloso** *adj* scrupulous.

escrutinio [eskru'tinjo] *sm* scrutiny. **escrutar** *v* scrutinize.

escuadra [es'kwaðra] *sf* carpenter's square; (*mil*) squad; (*mil*) corporal; (*mar*) squadron; (*fig*) gang. **a escuadra** at right angles. **escuadrar** *v* square.

escuálido [es'kwaliðo] *adj* squalid; weak; skinny. **escualidez** *sf* squalor; weakness; emaciation.

escuchar [esku'tʃar] *v* listen to; hear. **escucharse** *v* pay too much attention to oneself. **escucha** *sf* listening; sentry; chaperone. **a la escucha** on the alert. **escuchador,-a** *sm, sf* listener.

escudero [esku'ðero] *sm* squire; page. **escudar** *v* shield. **escudo** *sm* shield.

escudriñar [eskuðri'nar] *v* scrutinize. **escudriñador** *adj* examining; curious. **escudriñamiento** *sm* investigation; search.

escuela [es'kwela] *sf* school.

esculpir [eskul'pir] *v* sculpture; engrave. **escultor,-a** *sm, sf* sculptor. **escultura** *sf* sculpture.

escupir [esku'pir] *v* spit. **escupidura** *sf* spittle.

escurrir [esku'rrir] *v* drain; wring out; drip; slip; ooze. **escurrirse** *v* drain; sneak off. **escurridizo** *adj* slippery. **escurridor** *sm* plate rack; colander; draining board; wringer. **escurriduras** *sf pl* dregs *pl*. **escurrimiento** *sm* draining; dripping.

ese ['ese] *adj also* **esa** that.

ése ['ese] *pron also* **ésa** that one; the former.

esencia [e'senθja] *sf* essence. **esencial** *adj* essential.

esfera [es'fera] *sf* sphere. **esférico** *adj* spherical.

esfinge [es'finxe] *sf* sphinx.

*esforzar [esfor'θar] *v* invigorate; strengthen; encourage. **esforzarse** *v* make an effort. **esforzado** *adj* vigorous. **esfuerzo** *sm* effort.

esgrimir [esgri'mir] *v* brandish; fence. **esgrima** *sf* fencing. **esgrimidor,-a** *sm, sf* fencer.

eslabón [esla'βon] *sm* link. **eslabonamiento** *sm* linking. **eslabonar** *v* link.

esmaltar [esmal'tar] *v* enamel; (*las uñas*) varnish. **esmalte** *sm* varnish.

esmerado [esme'raðo] *adj* careful; painstaking. **esmerar** *v* polish; take great pains.

esmeralda [esme'ralða] *sf* emerald.

esnórquel [es'norkel] *sm* snorkel.

eso ['eso] *pron* that, that thing. **en eso** at that moment. **eso es** that's right. **eso mismo** just so. **por eso** because of that. **esos** *adj pl also* **esas** those. **ésos** *pron pl also* **ésas** those; the former.

espabilar [espaβi'lar] *v* (*vela*) snuff. **espabilarse** *v* (*fam*) look sharp.

espaciar [espa'θjar] *v* space out; spread. **espaciarse** *v* expatiate; enjoy oneself. **espacial** *adj* space. **nave espacial** spaceship. **espaciamiento** *sm* spacing. **espacio** *sm* space. **espacioso** *adj* spacious.

espada [es'paða] *sf* sword; swordsman. *sm* matador. **pez espada** swordfish.

espalda [es'palða] *sf* shoulder; back. **a espaldas** behind someone's back. **volver las espaldas** turn tail.

espantapájaros [espanta'paxaros] *sm invar* scarecrow.

espantar [espan'tar] *v* scare. **espantarse** *v* take fright. **espanto** *sm* fright; terror. **espantoso** *adj* frightful; amazing.

España [es'pana] *sf* Spain.

español [espa'nol], **-a** *sm, sf* Spaniard. *sm* (*lengua*) Spanish. *adj* Spanish.

*esparcir [espar'θir] *v* scatter; spread. **esparcirse** *v* amuse oneself. **esparcidamente** *adv* separately. **esparcido** *adj* cheerful; amusing; scattered. **esparcimiento** *sm* scattering; pastime.

espárrago [es'parrago] *sm* asparagus.

espasmo [es'pasmo] *sm* spasm. espasmódico *adj* spasmodic.

especia [es'peθja] *sf* spice.

especial [espe'θjal] *adj* special; particular. en especial especially. especialidad *sf* speciality. especialista *s(m+f)*, *adj* specialist. especializarse *v* specialize.

especie [es'peθje] *sf* species; kind; affair; appearance.

específico [espe'θifiko] *adj* specific. *sm* (*med*) patent medicine. especificación *sf* specification. especificación normalizada standard specification. especificar *v* specify.

espectáculo [espek'takulo] *sm* spectacle; entertainment. espectacular *adj* spectacular. espectador, -a *sm*, *sf* spectator.

espectro [es'pektro] *sm* spectre.

espejo [es'pexo] *sm* mirror. espejo retrovisor (*auto*) rear-view mirror. espejismo *sm* mirage.

esperar [espe'rar] *v* hope; expect; await. esperar a que wait until. espera *sf* waiting; expectation; delay. sala de espera waiting room. esperanza *sf* hope. esperanzador *adj* encouraging.

esperpento [esper'pento] *sm* fright; grotesqueness; absurdity.

espesar [espe'sar] *v* thicken; tighten. espeso *adj* thick; greasy. espesamiento *sm* thickening.

espetar [espe'tar] *v* (*culin*) skewer; pierce. espetarse *v* be pompous.

espía [es'pia] *s(m+f)* spy. espiar *v* spy upon. espionaje *sm* espionage.

espiga [es'piga] *sf* (*bot*) ear, spike. espigado *adj* gone to seed. espigar *v* glean.

espín [es'pin] *sm* porcupine.

espina [es'pina] *sf* thorn; spine; splinter; fishbone. espina dorsal backbone.

espinaca [espi'naka] *sf* spinach.

espiral [espi'ral] *sf*, *adj* spiral.

espíritu [es'piritu] *sm* spirit; soul; ghost; wit; breathing. espiritado *adj* possessed; (*fam*) skinny. espiritismo *sm* spiritualism. espiritista *s(m+f)* spiritualist. espiritoso *adj* spirited. espiritual *adj* spiritual. espiritualidad *sf* spirituality.

espléndido [es'plendiðo] *adj* splendid; magnificent. esplendor *sm* splendour.

espliego [es'pljego] *sm* lavender.

esplín [es'plin] *sm* spleen.

espolear [espole'ar] *v* spur, spur on. espoleo *sm* spurring.

esponja [es'ponxa] *sf* sponge. esponjar *v* make spongy; puff up. esponjarse *v* become spongy; (*fig*) become puffed up with pride; glow with health.

esponsales [espon'sales] *sm pl* betrothal sing.

espontáneo [espon'taneo] *adj* spontaneous. espontaneidad *sf* spontaneity.

esporádico [espo'raðiko] *adj* sporadic.

esposa [es'posa] *sf* wife. esposas *sf pl* handcuffs. esposado *adj* newly married; handcuffed.

espuela [es'pwela] *sf* spur. echar la espuela have one for the road.

espuma [es'puma] *sf* foam; froth; lather. espumadera *sf* strainer. espumajear *v* foam at the mouth. espumajoso *adj* foaming; frothy. espumar *v* skim; froth; lather; sparkle. espumoso *adj* frothy; sparkling.

esquela [es'kela] *sf* note; short letter; obituary.

esqueleto [eske'leto] *sm* skeleton.

esquema [es'kema] *sm* scheme. esquemático *adj* schematic.

esquí [es'ki] *sm*, *pl* esquíes *or* esquís ski. esquiador, -a *sm*, *sf* skier. esquiar *v* ski.

esquilar [eski'lar] *v* shear, clip. sin esquilar unshorn.

esquimal [eski'mal] *sm*, *adj* Eskimo.

esquina [es'kina] *sf* (*afuera*) corner. doblar la esquina turn the corner. esquinar *v* form a corner with.

esquirol [eski'rol] *sm* (*fam*) strike-breaker, blackleg.

esquivar [eski'βar] *v* avoid, shun; disappear. esquivarse *v* shy away. esquivo *adj* unsociable.

estabilidad [estaβili'ðað] *sf* stability. estabilizar *v* stabilize. estable *adj* stable.

*estabelcer [estaβle'θer] *v* establish. establecerse *v* settle down; set up. establecido *adj* established. establecimiento *sm* establishment.

establo [es'taβlo] *sm* cowshed.

estaca [es'taka] *sf* stake, post. estacada *sf* fence; stockade. estacar *v* fence; stake out.

estación [esta'θjon] *sf* station; season. estacionamiento *sm* parking. estacionar *v* park.

estadio [es'taðjo] *sm* stadium; (*med*) phase.

estado [es'taðo] *sm* state; status; order; estate; statement. **estado de ánimo** state of mind. **estar en estado** be pregnant. **hombre de estado** statesman.

Estados Unidos [es'taðos u'niðos] *sm pl* United States (of America). **estadounidense** *s(m+f)*, *adj* American.

estafa [es'tafa] *sf* swindle. **estafador, -a** *sm, sf* swindler. **estafar** *v* swindle.

estafeta [esta'feta] *sf* courier; sub-post office.

estallar [esta'ʎar] *v* explode; burst; erupt. **estallido** *sm* explosion; crash.

estampar [estam'par] *v* stamp; print; imprint. **estampa** *sf* print; engraving; impression; footprint.

estampida [estam'piða] *sf* stampede; explosion, bang. **estampido** *sm* explosion, bang.

estancar [estan'kar] *v* stem; block; delay; monopolize. **estancarse** *v* stagnate. **estancación** *sf* stagnation. **estancado** *adj* stagnant; blocked. **estanco** *sm* monopoly; state tobacco shop. **estanquero, -a** *sm, sf* tobacconist.

estandarte [estan'darte] *sm* banner.

estanque [es'tanke] *sm* reservoir; ornamental pond.

estante [es'tante] *sm* shelf. **estantería** *sf* shelving; bookcase.

estaño [es'taɲo] *sm* tin. **estañar** *v* solder.

*****estar** [es'tar] *v* be. **está bien** (it's) all right. **estar para** be about to. **no está he** *or* she is not at home. **ya que estamos** while we're at it.

estático [es'tatiko] *adj* static.

estatua [es'tatwa] *sf* statue.

estatura [esta'tura] *sf* stature, height.

estatuto [esta'tuto] *sm* statute. **estatuario** *adj* statutory.

este[1] ['este] *adj* also **esta** this; the latter.

este[2] *sm, adj* east.

éste ['este] *pron* also **ésta** this.

estela [es'tela] *sf* (*mar*) wake; trail.

estelar [este'lar] *adj* stellar.

estepa [es'tepa] *sf* steppe.

estera [es'tera] *sf* matting.

estereofónico [estereo'foniko] *adj* stereophonic.

estereotipo [estereo'tipo] *sm* stereotype.

estéril [es'teril] *adj* sterile; pointless. **esterelizar** *v* sterilize.

esterlina [ester'lina] *adj* sterling. **libra esterlina** pound sterling.

estético [es'tetiko] *adj* aesthetic. **estética** *sf* aesthetics.

estetoscopio [esteto'skopjo] *sm* stethoscope.

estiércol [es'tjerkol] *sm* manure.

estigma [es'tigma] *sm* stigma. **estigmatizar** *v* stigmatize.

estilar [esti'lar] *v* be accustomed; (*documento*) draw up; be in use; be in fashion. **estilístico** *adj* stylistic. **estilizado** *adj* stylized. **estilo** *sm* style; type; fashion.

estimar [esti'mar] *v* esteem; estimate. **estima** *sf* esteem. **estimable** *adj* estimable. **estimación** *sf* estimate; estimation.

estimular [estimu'lar] *v* stimulate. **estimulante** *adj* stimulating; *sm* (*med*) stimulant. **estímulo** *sm* stimulus.

estipular [estipu'lar] *v* stipulate. **estipulación** *sf* stipulation.

estirar [esti'rar] *v* stretch; extend. **estirado** *adj* affected; miserly. **estirón** *sm* jerk.

estirpe [es'tirpe] *sf* lineage; stock.

esto ['esto] *pron* this. **en esto** whereupon.

estofa [es'tofa] *sf* (*fig*) quality; class; brocade. **estofado** *adj* quilted; (*culin*) stewed. **estofar** *v* quilt; stew.

estoico [es'toiko], **-a** *s*, *adj* stoic. **estoicismo** *sm* stoicism.

estómago [es'tomago] *sm* stomach. **estomagar** *v* give indigestion.

estorbar [estor'βar] *v* hinder; be in the way. **estorbo** *sm* hindrance; obstruction.

estornino [estor'nino] *sm* starling.

estornudar [estornu'ðar] *v* sneeze. **estornudo** *sm* sneeze.

estoy [es'toi] *V* estar.

estrafalario [estrafa'larjo] *adj* outlandish; extravagant; slovenly.

estrada [es'traða] *sf* road, highway.

estragar [estra'gar] *v* corrupt; destroy. **estrago** *sm* ruin, havoc. **hacer estragos** wreak havoc.

estrangular [estrangu'lar] *v* strangle. **estrangulación** *sf* strangulation. **estrangulador** *sm* strangler; (*auto*) choke.

estratagema [estrata'xema] *sf* stratagem. **estrategia** *sf* strategy. **estratégico** *adj* strategic.

estrechar [estre'tʃar] *v* make smaller; tighten; bring closer together. **estrecharse** *v* become narrower; squeeze together; shake hands; make economies. **estrechamente** *adv* narrowly. **estrechamiento** *sm* narrowing; taking-in;

tightening; handshake. **estrecho** adj narrow; cramped; tight; strict.

estrella [es'treʎa] sf star. **estrellado** adj starry.

estrellar [estre'ʎar] v smash (to pieces).

*estremecer [estreme'θer] v shake; startle. **estremecerse** v shudder; tremble. **estremecimiento** sm shake; shudder; tremble.

estrenar [estre'nar] v wear for the first time; (teatro) perform for the first time. **estreno** sm inauguration; first night; dress rehearsal.

estrenuo [es'trenwo] adj strong; courageous.

estreñido [estre'ɲiðo] adj constipated. **estreñimiento** sm constipation.

estrépito [es'trepito] sm noise, din; fuss. **estrepitoso** adj noisy; resounding.

estribo [es'triβo] sm stirrup; step; running-board. **perder los estribos** lose one's head.

estribor [estri'βor] sm (mar) starboard.

estricto [es'trikto] adj strict.

estridente [estri'ðente] adj strident.

estropajo [estro'paxo] sm scourer; rubbish. **estropajoso** adj thick; stringy; slovenly.

estropear [estrope'ar] v spoil; break; maim; age.

estructura [estruk'tura] sf structure; framework. **estructural** adj structural. **estructurar** v organize; construct.

estruendo [estru'endo] sm din; uproar; bustle; pomp. **estruendoso** adj noisy.

estrujar [estru'xar] v squeeze; crush. **estrujadura** sf pressure. **estrujón** sm squeeze.

estuario [es'twarjo] sm estuary.

estuche [es'tutʃe] sm box; case; casket; sheath.

estudiar [estu'ðjar] v study. **estudiante** s(m + f) student. **estudio** sm study; research; studio. **estudioso** adj studious.

estufa [es'tufa] sf stove; fire; hothouse.

estupefacto [estupe'fakto] adj stupefied; astonished. **estupefacción** sf stupefaction; astonishment.

estupefaciente [estupefa'θjente] adj stupefying; astonishing. sm (med) narcotic.

estupendo [estu'pendo] adj stupendous.

estúpido [es'tupiðo] adj stupid. **estupidez** sf stupidity. **estupor** sm stupor.

esturión [estu'rjon] sm sturgeon.

etapa [e'tapa] sf (de un viaje) stage; period.

éter ['eter] sm ether. **etereo** adj ethereal.

eternidad [eterni'ðað] sf eternity. **eternal** adj eternal. **eternizar** v perpetuate.

ética ['etika] sf ethics. **ético** adj ethical.

etimología [etimolo'xia] sf etymology. **etimológico** adj etymological.

etiqueta [eti'keta] sf etiquette; label; tag. **etiquetero** adj formal.

eucalipto [euka'lipto] sm eucalyptus.

eufemismo [eufe'mismo] sm euphemism. **eufemístico** adj euphemistic.

eunuco [eu'nuko] sm eunuch.

Europa [eu'ropa] sf Europe. **europeo, -a** s. adj European.

eutanasia [euta'nasja] sf euthanasia.

evacuar [eβa'kwar] v evacuate; fulfil. **evacuación** sf evacuation. **evacuado, -a** sm, sf evacuee.

evadir [eβa'ðir] v evade. **evadirse** v escape. **evadido, -a** sm, sf fugitive. **evasión** sf escape; flight. **evasivo** adj evasive.

evaluar [eβa'lwar] v evaluate; value. **evaluación** sf evaluation.

evangélico [eβan'xeliko] adj evangelical. **evangelio** sm gospel. **evangelista** sm evangelist.

evaporar [evapo'rar] v evaporate. **evaporación** sf evaporation.

evento [e'βento] sm (unforeseen) event.

eventual [even'twal] adj temporary; possible; accidental. **eventualidad** sf contingency.

evidencia [evi'ðenθja] sf certainty; proof; evidence. **evidenciar** v make evident. **evidente** adj evident.

evitar [eβi'tar] v avoid. **evitable** adj avoidable.

evocar [evo'kar] v evoke. **evocación** sf evocation. **evocativo** adj evocative.

evolución [evolu'θjon] sf evolution. **evolucionar** v evolve. **evolutivo** adj evolutionary.

exacerbar [eksaθer'βar] v exacerbate; exasperate. **exacerbación** sf exacerbation.

exactitud [eksakti'tuð] sf exactitude; accuracy. **exacto** adj exact; correct.

exagerar [eksaxe'rar] v exaggerate. **exagerado** adj exaggerated. **exageración** sf exaggeration.

exaltar [eksal'tar] v exalt; raise; praise. **exaltarse** v get worked up; get heated. **exaltación** sf exaltation. **exaltado** adj hotheaded.

examinar [eksami'nar] *v* examine;
inspect; test. **examinarse** *v* take an examination. **examen** *sm* examination;
inquiry; investigation. **examen de conductor** driving test. **examinador, -a** *sm, sf*
examiner.

exangüe [ek'sangwe] *adj* bloodless; weak.

exánime [ek'sanime] *adj* lifeless; unconscious; weak. **caer exánime** fall in a
faint.

exasperar [eksaspe'rar] *v* exasperate; vex.
exasperarse *v* become annoyed. **exasperación** *sf* exasperation. **exasperante** *adj*
exasperating.

excavar [ekska'βar] *v* excavate; dig.
excavación *sf* excavation.

exceder [eksθe'ðer] *v* exceed. **excederse** *v*
forget oneself. **excedente** *adj* exceeding;
excessive.

excelencia [eksθe'lenθja] *sf* excellence.
excelente *adj* excellent; first-rate.

excéntrico [eks'θentriko] *adj, sm* eccentric. **excentricidad** *sf* eccentricity.

excepción [eksθep'θjon] *sf* exception. **a
excepción de** with the exception of.
estado de excepción state of emergency.
excepcional *adj* exceptional. **excepto** *prep*
excepting.

excerpta [ek'θerpta] *sf* excerpt.

excesivo [eksθe'siβo] *adj* excessive.
exceso *sm* excess; surplus. **exceso de
equipaje** excess luggage.

excitar [eksθi'tar] *v* excite; stir up.
excitabilidad *sf* excitability. **excitable** *adj*
excitable. **excitante** *adj* exciting.

exclamar [ekskla'mar] *v* exclaim.
exclamarse contra protest against.
exclamación *sf* exclamation. **exclamativo**
adj exclamatory.

*****excluir** [eksklu'ir] *v* exclude. **exclusivo**
adj exclusive. **exclusión** *sf* exclusion.

excomulgar [ekskomul'gar] *v* excommunicate. **excomulgación** *sf* excommunication. **excomulgado** *adj* excommunicated;
(*fam*) accused.

excreción [ekskre'θjon] *sf* excretion.
excremento *sm* excrement. **excretar** *v*
excrete.

excursión [ekskur'sjon] *sf* excursion.
excursión a pie hike. **ir de excursión** go
on an outing. **excursionista** *s(m+f)* trip-
per; hiker.

excusar [eksku'sar] *v* excuse; avoid;
exempt. **excusarse** *v* apologize. **excusa** *sf*

excuse; apology. **excusable** *adj* pardonable. **excusadamente** *adv* unnecessarily.
excusado *adj* excused; unnecessary;
exempt; concealed; private. **excusado es
decir** needless to say. **excusado** *sm* toilet.

exentar [eksen'tar] *v* exempt. **exención** *sf*
exemption. **exento** *adj* exempt.

exequias [ek'sekjas] *sf pl* funeral rites.

exhalar [eksa'lar] *v* exhale; emit; utter.
exhalación *sf* exhalation; vapour; shooting star; lightning flash.

exhausto [ek'sausto] *adj* exhausted.
exhaustivo *adj* exhaustive.

exhibir [eksi'βir] *v* exhibit. **exhibición** *sf*
exhibition. **exhibicionismo** *sm* exhibition-
ism. **exhibicionista** *s(m+f)* exhibitionist.

exhortar [eksor'tar] *v* exhort. **exhortación**
sf exhortation.

exigir [eksi'xir] *v* demand. **exigencia** *sf*
demand; requirement. **exigente** *adj*
exacting.

exiguo [ek'sigwo] *adj* scanty. **exigüidad** *sf*
scantiness.

eximir [eksi'mir] *v* exempt; excuse. **exi-
mente** *adj* exempting.

existir [eksis'tir] *v* exist. **existencia** *sf* existence. **en existencia** in stock. **existente**
adj existent; extant; in stock.

éxito ['eksito] *sm* success; result. **tener
éxito** be successful.

éxodo ['eksoðo] *sm* exodus, emigration.

exonerar [eksone'rar] *v* exonerate;
relieve; dismiss. **exoneración** *sf* exoneration; relief.

exorbitante [eksorβi'tante] *adj* exorbitant, excessive.

exorcizar [eksorθi'θar] *v* exorcize.
exorcismo *sm* exorcism. **exorcista** *sm*
exorcist.

exótico [ek'sotiko] *adj* exotic.

expansión [ekspan'sjon] *sf* expansion;
recreation. **expansionarse** *v* give vent to
one's feelings. **expansivo** *adj* expansive.

expatriar [ekspatri'ar] *v* exile. **expatriación** *sf* banishment.

expectación [ekspekta'θjon] *sf* expectation. **expectante** *adj* expectant.

expedición [ekspeði'θjon] *sf* expedition;
party; shipment; dispatch; speed.

*****expedir** [ekspe'ðir] *v* send, dispatch;
issue. **expediente** *sm* (*jur*) proceedings *pl*;
dossier; inquiry; record. **expediente** *adj*
expedient.

expendedor [ekspenðe'ðor], **-a** *sm, sf*

dealer; retailer; ticket agent. *adj* spending.

experiencia [ekspe'rjenθja] *sf* experience; experiment.

experimentar [eksperimen'tar] *v* experiment; test; feel. **experimentado** *adj* experienced. **experimental** *adj* experimental. **experimento** *sm* experiment.

experto [eks'perto] *sm, adj* expert.

expiar [eks'pjar] *v* atone for. **expiación** *sf* atonement.

expirar [ekspi'rar] *v* expire; die; die down. **expiración** *sf* expiration.

explanar [ekspla'nar] *v* level; (*fig*) explain. **explanación** *sf* levelling; (*fig*) explanation.

explicar [ekspli'kar] *v* explain; justify; lecture. **explicarse** *v* speak plainly; understand. **explicación** *sf* explanation. **explicativo** *adj* explanatory.

explícito [eks'pliθito] *adj* explicit.

explorar [eksplo'rar] *v* explore, investigate. **exploración** *sf* exploration. **explorador** *sm* explorer; (*mil*) scout; boy scout; *adj* exploratory.

explosión [eksplo'sjon] *sf* explosion. **explosivo** *sm, adj* explosive.

explotar [eksplo'tar] *v* exploit; develop; cultivate; explode. **explotación** *sf* exploitation; operation; development; cultivation.

***exponer** [ekspo'ner] *v* expose; set out; explain. **exponerse** *v* lay oneself open. **exponente** *s(m+f)* exponent; example; proof.

exportar [ekspor'tar] *v* export. **exportación** *sf* export. **exportador, -a** *sm, sf* exporter.

exposición [exposi'θjon] *sf* exhibition; display; statement; explanation; risk; (*foto*) exposure. **sala de exposición** showroom.

exprés [eks'pres] *sm* (*tren*) express; (*café*) espresso.

expresar [ekspre'sar] *v* express, convey. **expresarse** *v* express oneself; state. **expresamente** *adv* specifically; explicitly. **expresión** *sf* expression. **expresiones** *sf pl* greetings; regards. **expresivamente** *adv* expressively; affectionately. **expresivo** *adj* expressive; affectionate. **expreso** *adj* expressed; express.

exprimir [ekspri'mir] *v* squeeze; exploit. **exprimidor** *sm* squeezer.

expuesto [eks'pwesto] *adj* on display; exposed; explained.

expulsar [ekspul'sar] *v* expel, throw out.

exquisito [ekski'sito] *adj* exquisite; delightful; refined.

éxtasis ['ekstasis] *sm invar* ecstasy.

***extender** [eksten'der] *v* extend; spread. **extenderse** *v* spread; range; enlarge. **extendido** *adj* extended; widespread; outstretched. **extensamente** *adv* at length. **extensible** *adj* extending. **extensión** *sf* extension; expanse; extent; area. **extensivo** *adj* extendible. **extenso** *adj* extensive; large; widespread; full.

extenuar [ekste'nwar] *v* weaken; exhaust. **extenuación** *sf* emaciation; extenuation.

exterior [ekste'rjor] *adj* exterior; external; foreign. **asuntos exteriores** *sm pl* foreign affairs. *sm* outside; exterior; appearance. **al exterior** outside. **del exterior** from abroad.

exterminar [ekstermi'nar] *v* exterminate. **exterminación** *sf* extermination. **exterminador, -a** *sm, sf* exterminator.

externo [eks'terno], **-a** *sm, sf* day pupil. *adj* external; outward. **externado** *sm* day school.

extinguir [ekstin'gir] *v* extinguish; wipe out; put down. **extinguirse** *v* die out. **extinción** *sf* extinction. **extinto** *adj* extinct. **extintor** *sm* fire extinguisher.

extirpar [ekstir'par] *v* uproot; remove. **extirpación** *sf* uprooting; extraction.

extra ['ekstra] *adj invar* extra; best-quality. *sm* (*cine, teatro*) extra.

***extraer** [ekstra'er] *v* extract; release. **extracción** *sf* extraction; birth. **extracto** *sm* extract; excerpt; abstract.

extranjero [ekstran'xero], **-a** *sm, sf* foreigner; foreign countries *pl*. *adj* foreign.

extrañar [ekstra'par] *v* be surprised; surprise; be shy; banish. **extrañarse** *v* go into exile. **extrañamiento** *sm* surprise; banishment. **extrañeza** *sf* strangeness; surprise. **extraño, -a** *sm, sf* stranger. **extraño** *adj* strange; peculiar; foreign.

extraordinario [ekstraorði'narjo] *adj* extraordinary. *sm* (*diario*) special edition.

extravagancia [ekstraβa'ganθja] *sf* extravagance; strangeness. **extravagante** *adj* extravagant; eccentric.

extraviar [ekstra'βjar] *v* lose; mislay; mislead. **extraviarse** *v* get lost; be missing; go astray.

extremar [ekstre'mar] *v* take to extremes. **extremarse** *v* do one's best.

extremo [ek'stremo] *adj* extreme, last. **en caso extremo** as a last resort. *sm* extreme; end; point. **al extremo de** to the point of. **de extremo a extremo** from end to end. **Extremo Oriente** Far East. **extremidad** *sf* extremity; end; limit.

exuberancia [eksuβe'ranθja] *sf* exuberance; abundance. **exuberante** *adj* exuberant.

exudar [eksu'ðar] *v* exude. **exudación** *sf* exudation.

exultar [eksul'tar] *v* exult. **exultación** *sf* exultation.

F

fábrica ['faβrika] *sf* factory; manufacture. **fabricación** *sf* manufacture. **de fabricación casera** home-made. **fabricación en serie** mass production. **fabricante** *s(m+f)* manufacturer. **fabricar** *v* manufacture; make; build.

fábula [fa'βula] *sf* fable; story; gossip. **fabuloso** *adj* fabulous; incredible.

facción [fak'θjon] *sf* faction; gang. **facciones** *sf pl* features.

faceta [fa'θeta] *sf* facet.

facial [fa'θjal] *adj* facial.

fácil ['faθil] *adj* easy; simple; likely; well-behaved. **facilidad** *sf* facility; ease; fluency; gift. **facilitar** *v* facilitate; supply; provide; arrange. **fácilmente** *adv* easily.

facsímil [fak'simil] *sm, adj also* **facsímile** facsimile.

factible [fak'tiβle] *adj* feasible.

factor [fak'tor] *sm* factor; agent.

facturar [faktu'rar] *v* invoice; (*ferrocarril*) register luggage. **factura** *sf* invoice. **facturación** *sf* invoicing.

facultad [fakul'taθ] *sf* faculty; authority; school. **facultar** *v* commission; authorize. **facultativo** *adj* optional.

facha ['fatʃa] *sf* (*fam*) appearance, looks; (*fam*) mess.

fachada [fa'tʃaða] *sf* façade.

faena [fa'ena] *sf* task; (*fam*) dirty trick. **estar de faena** be at work. **faenas domésticas** housework.

fagot [fa'got] *sm* bassoon.

faisán [fai'san] *sm* pheasant.

faja ['faxa] *sf* bandage; sash; belt; wrapper; strip of land. **fajar** *v* wrap; bandage.

falaz [fa'laθ] *adj* fallacious; deceitful.

falda ['falda] *sf* skirt; side of a hill; hat brim; lap.

falsear [false'ar] *v* falsify. **falseador, -a** *sm, sf* forger; counterfeiter. **falseamiento** *sm* misrepresentation. **falsedad** *sf* falsity. **falseo** *sm* bevelling. **falso** *adj* false; treacherous; sham.

falsificar [falsifi'kar] *v* falsify; forge; adulterate. **falsificación** *sf* falsification; adulteration.

falta ['falta] *sf* lack, want, need; shortage; failure; (*deporte*) foul. **faltar** *v* be lacking; fail; be absent; be untrue. **falto** *sm* shortage; deficiency; fault. **falto** *adj* short; deficient; incomplete.

fallar [fa'ʎar] *v* (*jur*) judge; sentence; fail; (*naipes*) trump. **no falla** it's always the same. **sin falla** without fail.

*****fallecer** [faʎe'θer] *v* die. **fallecido** *adj* deceased. **fallecimiento** *sm* death.

fallido [fa'ʎiðo] *sm* bankrupt. *adj* bankrupt; unsuccessful. **fallo** *sm* (*jur*) sentence, judgment; failure; fault; (*naipes*) trump.

fama ['fama] *sf* fame; reputation. **es fama que** it is rumoured that. **famoso** *adj* famous.

familia [fa'milja] *sf* family; household. **familiar** *adj* family; familiar; simple. **familiar** *sm* friend; relative. **familiaridad** *sf* familiarity. **familiarizar** *v* familiarize.

fanático [fa'natiko] *adj, sm* fanatic(al). **fanatismo** *sm* fanaticism.

fanfarrón [fanfar'ron], **-ona** *sm, sf* bully; braggart. *adj* boastful. **fanfarronear** *v* brag.

fango ['fango] *sm* mire, mud. **fangal** *sm* quagmire. **fangoso** *adj* muddy.

fantasía [fanta'sia] *sf* fantasy; fancy; whim. **joyas de fantasía** imitation jewellery.

fantasma [fan'tasma] *sm* ghost. **fantasmal** *adj* ghostly.

fantástico [fan'tastiko] *adj* fantastic; wonderful; vain.

fantoche [fan'totʃe] *sm* puppet; foolish figure.

fardo [far'ðo] *sm* bundle, pack; burden.

fariseo [fari'seo] *sm* Pharisee; (*fam*) hypocrite. **farisaico** *adj* (*fam*) hypocritical.

fiado

farmacia [far'maθja] *sf* chemist's shop. **farmacia de guardia** all-night chemist's. **farmacéutico** *adj* pharmaceutical.

faro ['faro] *sm* lighthouse; beacon; (*auto*) headlamp.

farol [fa'rol] *sm* lantern; lamp; street lamp; (*fam*) swank.

farsa ['farsa] *sf* farce; humbug. **farsante** *sm* charlatan.

fas [fas] *adv* (*fam*) **por fas o por nefas** rightly or wrongly; by hook or by crook.

fascinar [fasθi'nar] *v* fascinate. **fascinación** *sf* fascination. **fascinador** *adj* fascinating.

fascismo [fas'θismo] *sm* fascism. **fascista** *s, adj* fascist.

fase ['fase] *sf* phase.

fastidiar [fasti'ðjar] *v* annoy; bore; upset. **¡no fastidies!** don't talk rot! **fastidio** *sm* annoyance; nuisance. **fastidioso** *adj* annoying; tedious.

fastuoso [fas'twoso] *adj* magnificent, grand, splendid.

fatal [fa'tal] *adj* fatal; inevitable; (*fam*) awful. **fatalidad** *sf* fatality; bad luck; destiny; disaster. **fatalista** *s*(*m+f*) fatalist. **fatalismo** *sm* fatalism.

fatigar [fati'gar] *v* weary; annoy. **fatigarse** *v* get tired. **fatiga** *sf* fatigue. **fatigas** *sf pl* troubles. **fatigoso** *adj* tiring; tiresome; laboured.

fatuidad [fatwi'ðað] *sf* fatuity; vanity.

fausto ['fausto] *adj* lucky; happy. *sm* display; pomp.

favor [fa'βor] *sm* favour; gift; grace; help. **a favor de** in favour of. **de favor** complimentary. **hacer el favor de** be so kind as to. **por favor** please. **favorable** *adj* favourable. **favorecer** *v* favour; help. **favoritismo** *sm* favouritism. **favorito, -a** *s, adj* favourite.

faz [faθ] *sf* face; obverse.

fe [fe] *sf* faith; faithfulness; trust; witness; certificate. **a fe de** on the word of. **dar fe de** certify. **prestar fe a** believe in.

fealdad [feal'ðað] *sf* ugliness.

febrero [fe'βrero] *sm* February.

febril [fe'βril] *adj* feverish; (*fig*) anxious.

fecundar [fekun'dar] *v* fertilize. **fecundación** *sf* fertilization. **fecundidad** *sf* fertility; fruitfulness. **fecundizar** *v* fertilize. **fecundo** *adj* fertile; fruitful; prolific. **fecundo** en full of.

fecha ['fetʃa] *sf* date. **hasta la fecha** to date. **fechar** *v* date.

federación [feðera'θjon] *sf* federation.

federal *adj* federal. **federalismo** *sm* federalism. **federar** *v* federate. **federativo** *adj* federative.

fehaciente [fea'θjente] *adj* (*jur*) authentic; irrefutable; reliable.

felicidad [feliθi'ðað] *sf* happiness; success. **¡felicidades!** congratulations! **feliz** *adj* happy; fortunate.

felicitar [feliθi'tar] *v* congratulate. **felicitación** *sf* congratulation; compliment.

feligrés [feli'gres], -esa *sm, sf* parishioner. **feligresía** *sf* parish.

felino [fe'lino] *sm, adj* feline.

felpa ['felpa] *sf* plush; towelling; (*fam*) beating. **felpar** *v* cover with plush. **felpudo** *adj* plushy.

femenino [feme'nino] *adj* feminine; female. **feminismo** *sm* feminism. **feminista** *s, adj* feminist.

***fenecer** [fene'θer] *v* die; end. **fenecimiento** *sm* death; end.

fenómeno [fe'nomeno] *sm* phenomenon; freak. *adj* fantastic.

feo ['feo] *adj* ugly.

féretro ['feretro] *sm* coffin; bier.

feria ['ferja] *sf* fair; show; festival; holiday. **feria de muestras** trade fair.

fermentar [fermen'tar] *v* ferment; agitate. **fermentación** *sf* fermentation.

ferocidad [feroθi'ðað] *sf* ferocity; fury. **feroz** *adj* savage; wild; fierce.

férreo ['ferreo] *adj* iron; ferrous; (*fig*) stern. **ferretería** *sf* ironmonger's shop; hardware shop. **ferretero** *sm* ironmonger.

ferrocarril [ferrokar'ril] *sm* railway. **ferroviario** *adj* railway.

fértil ['fertil] *adj* fertile; abundant. **fertilidad** *sf* fertility. **fertilizante** *sm* fertilizer. **fertilizar** *v* fertilize.

ferviente [fer'βjente] *adj* fervent. **fervor** *sm* fervour. **fervoroso** *adj* fervid, ardent.

festejar [feste'xar] *v* entertain; feast; celebrate; woo. **festejo** *sm* entertainment; celebration; courtship.

festival [festi'βal] *sm* festival. *adj* festive. **festividad** *sf* festivity. **festivo** *adj* festive.

fétido ['fetiðo] *adj* fetid, stinking.

feto ['feto] *sm* foetus. **fetal** *adj* foetal.

feudal [feu'ðal] *adj* feudal. **feudalismo** *sm* feudalism.

fiado ['fjaðo] *sm* trust. **comprar al fiado** buy on credit. **fiador, -a** *sm, sf* guarantor. **fiador** *sm* press stud; pin; bracket; tumbler; safety catch. **salir fiador de** go bail for. **fianza** *sf* deposit; guarantor; surety.

libertad bajo fianza release on bail. **fiar** *v* guarantee; go bail for; sell on credit; trust. **no se fía** no credit given.

fiambre ['fjambre] *sm* cold cooked meat; (*coll*) corpse.

fiasco [fi'asko] *sm* fiasco; flop.

fibra ['fiβra] *sf* fibre; (*fig*) vigour. **fibra de vidrio** fibreglass.

ficción [fik'θjon] *sf* fiction; invention. **ficticio** *adj* fictitious.

ficha ['fitʃa] *sf* counter, chip; (*juegos*) piece; filing card.

fidedigno [fiðe'ðigno] *adj* trustworthy. **fidelidad** *sf* loyalty, fidelity. **alta fidelidad** hi-fi.

fideos [fi'ðeos] *sm pl* noodles.

fiebre ['fjeβre] *sf* fever. **tener fiebre** be feverish.

fiel [fjel] *adj* faithful; true; accurate; reliable; honourable. *sm* good Christian; inspector; scale pointer.

fieltro ['fjeltro] *sm* felt; (*tejido*) felt hat.

fiera ['fjera] *sf* wild beast; (*persona*) brute. **casa de fieras** menagerie. **fiero** *adj* wild.

fiesta ['fjesta] *sf* feast day; holiday; party. **estar de fiesta** be in high spirits. **hacer fiestas a uno** make a fuss over someone.

figurar [figu'rar] *v* shape; adorn; figure; pretend. **figurarse** *v* imagine, seem. **figura** *sf* shape; figure; face; (*música*) note; (*naipes*) court card; (*fig*) personality; (*fam*) unpleasant person. **figurado** *adj also* figurative.

fijar [fi'xar] *v* fasten; fix; stick; secure; draw up. **fijarse** *v* settle; take notice; look. **¡fíjate!** just think! **¡fijamos en esto!** that's settled! **fijación** *sf* setting; fixing; sticking. **fijador** *sm* fixative. **fijeza** *sf* fixity; certainty; firmness. **fijo** *adj* fixed; permanent; steady.

fila ['fila] *sf* row; line; file; column. **en fila india** in single file.

filantropía [filantro'pia] *sf* philanthropy. **filantrópico** *adj* philanthropic. **filántropo, -a** *sm, sf* philanthropist.

filete [fi'lete] *sm* sirloin; fillet; (*ropa*) edging; (*tecn*) screw thread.

filiación [filja'θjon] *sf* filiation; relationship; association; personal description. **filial** [fi'ljal] *adj* filial. *sf* subsidiary.

filigrana [fili'grana] *sf* filigree work; watermark; delicate object.

filo ['filo] *sm* cutting edge; dividing line. **dar un filo a** sharpen. **por filo** exactly.

filón [fi'lon] *sm* (*mineral*) vein, seam; (*fam*) cushy job.

filosofía [filoso'fia] *sf* philosophy. **filosofar** *v* philosophize. **filósofo, -a** *sm, sf* philosopher. **filósofe** *adj* philosophic(al).

filtrar [fil'trar] *v* filter; strain. **filtrarse** *v* seep through. **filtración** *sf* filtration; (*fig*) leak. **filtrador** *sm* filter. **filtro** *sm* filter; strainer; love potion.

fin [fin] *sm* end; death; aim. **a fin de** in order to. **a fines de** at the end of. **al fin y al cabo** when all is said and done. **por fin** at last.

final [fi'nal] *adj* final. *sm* end. **al final de** at the end of. **finalidad** *sf* aim; purpose; finality. **finalizar** *v* finalize.

financiar [finan'θjar] *v* finance. **financiero** *sm* financier. **financiero** *adj* financial. **finanzas** *sf pl* finances.

finca ['finka] *sf* property; estate; farm.

fineza [fi'neθa] *sf* refinement; kindness; gift.

fingir [fin'xir] *v* pretend; sham. **fingirse** *v* pretend to be. **fingimiento** *sm* pretence; deceit.

Finlandia [fin'landja] *sf* Finland. **finlandés, -esa** *s, adj* Finn(ish).

fino ['fino] *adj* fine; refined; delicate; sharp; shrewd; elegant; precious; select; pure.

firmar [fir'mar] *v* sign. **firma** *sf* signature; (*negocio*) firm.

firme ['firme] *adj* firm; steady; rigid; hard; settled. *sm* firm ground; foundation; roadbed. **de firme** steadily. **oferta en firme** firm offer. **¡firmes!** (*mil*) attention! **firmeza** *sf* firmness; steadfastness.

fiscal [fis'kal] *adj* fiscal; tax. *sm* treasury official; (*jur*) public prosecutor. **fiscalizar** *v* control; criticize; pry into. **fisco** *sm* exchequer.

física ['fisika] *sf* physics. **físico** *sm* physician; physique. **físico** *adj* physical. **físico, -a** *sm, sf* physicist.

fisiología [fisjolo'xia] *sf* physiology. **fisiológico** *adj* physiological. **fisiólogo, -a** *sm, sf* physiologist.

fisionomía [fisjono'mia] *sf* physiognomy.

fisioterapia [fisjote'rapja] *sf* physiotherapy. **fisioterapeuta** *s(m+f)* physiotherapist.

flaco ['flako] *adj* thin; weak; (*memoria*) short. *sm* weak point. **flaquear** *v* weaken; slacken; flag; fail. **flaqueza** *sf* thinness; frailty.

flagrante [fla'grante] *adj* flagrant, blatant. **en flagrante** in the act.

flamante [fla'mante] *adj* blazing; brand-new.

flamenco[1] [fla'menko] *adj* Flemish; gypsy; flamenco.

flamenco[2] *sm* flamingo.

flanco ['flanko] *sm* flank. **coger por el flanco** catch unawares.

flauta ['flauta] *sf* flute. **flautista** *s(m+f)* flautist.

fleco ['fleko] *sm* fringe.

flecha ['fletʃa] *sf* arrow. **flecha de dirección** traffic indicator. **flecha de mar** squid. **subir en flecha** shoot up. **flechar** *v* shoot with an arrow; *(fam)* inspire love at first sight; *(fam)* rush. **flechero** *sm* archer.

fletar [fle'tar] *v* charter; hire. **fletamento** *also* **fletamiento** *sm* charter. **flete** *sm* freight.

flexible [flek'siβle] *adj* flexible. *sm* flex. **flexibilidad** *sf* flexibility. **flexión** *sf* flexing; *(gram)* inflexion.

flojo ['floxo] *adj* loose; weak; meagre; lazy. **flojear** *v* slacken; grow weak. **flojedad** *sf* slackness; weakness; carelessness.

flor [flor] *sf* flower. **a flor de tierra** at ground level. **echar flores** flatter. **en flor** in bloom. **flor de lis** lily. **floral** *adj* floral. **florar** *v* flower. **florecer** *v* flourish; flower. **florescencia** *v* mildew. **florería** *sf* florist's shop. **florero** *sm* vase. **florido** *adj* flowery; florid. **florista** *s(m+f)* florist.

flotar [flo'tar] *v* float; flutter; stream. **flota** *sf* fleet. **flotable** *adj* buoyant. **flotación** *sf* floatation; fluttering. **flotante** *adj* floating; flowing. **flote** *sm* floatation. **a flote** afloat.

fluctuar [fluk'twar] *v* fluctuate. **fluctuación** *sf* fluctuation.

*****fluir** [flu'ir] *v* flow. **fluente** *adj* fluid; flowing. **fluidez** *sf* fluidity; fluency. **fluído** *sm*, *adj* fluid. **flujo** *sm* stream; flow; rising tide. **flujo de vientre** diarrhoea.

fluorescencia [fluores'θenθja] *sf* fluorescence. **fluorescente** *adj* fluorescent.

fluoruro [flwo'ruro] *sm* fluoride.

fobia ['foβja] *sf* phobia.

foca ['foka] *sf* *(zool)* seal.

foco ['foko] *sm* focus; centre; source. **focal** *adj* focal.

fogata [fo'gata] *sf* blaze; bonfire.

fogón [fo'gon] *sm* fireplace; stove.

fogoso [fo'goso] *adj* fiery; impetuous.

follaje [fo'ʎaxe] *sm* foliage; excessive decoration.

folletín [foʎe'tin] *sm* serial story; newspaper article. **folleto** *sm* pamphlet. **folletista** *s(m+f)* pamphleteer.

follón [fo'ʎon] *adj* lazy; arrogant; blustering; cowardly. **follón, -ona** *sm, sf* good-for-nothing; coward; loafer.*

fomentar [fomen'tar] *v* foment; warm; incubate; *(fig)* encourage.

fonda ['fonda] *sf* inn, boarding house.

fondear [fonde'ar] *v* anchor; sound; search.

fondo ['fondo] *sm* bottom; depth; essence; capital; fund; character; disposition. **a fondo** thoroughly. **artículo de fondo** leading article. **en el fondo** at heart. **estar en fondos** be well off.

fontanero [fonta'nero] *sm* plumber. **fontanar** *sm* spring. **fontanería** *sf* plumbing.

forajido [fora'xiðo], **-a** *sm, sf* outlaw; fugitive.

forastero [foras'tero], **-a** *sm, sf* stranger; alien. *adj* strange.

forcejear [forθexe'ar] *v* struggle, strive. **forcej(e)o** *sm* struggle.

forense [fo'rense] *adj* forensic; strange.

forjar [for'xar] *v* forge; beat into shape; invent. **forja** *sf* forge; forging.

formal [for'mal] *adj* formal; regular; methodical; serious; steady; reliable. **formalidad** *sf* formality; seriousness; orderliness; propriety. **formalismo** *sm* formalism. **formalizar** *v* formulate; legalize. **formalizarse** *v* take seriously.

formar [for'mar] *v* form; educate; train. **formarse** *v* be trained; develop. **forma** *sf* form; shape; manner; convention; mould. **de forma que** so that. **tener buenas formas** be polite.

formidable [formi'ðaβle] *adj* formidable; tremendous. **¡formidable!** great!

fórmula ['formula] *sf* formula; *(med)* prescription.

fornicar [forni'kar] *v* fornicate. **fornicación** *sf* fornication. **fornicador, -a** *sm, sf* fornicator.

fornido [for'niðo] *adj* robust, husky.

foro ['foro] *sm* forum; legal profession; leasehold; *(teatro)* back.

forraje [fo'rraxe] *sm* fodder; forage; *(fam)* hodgepodge. **forajeador** *sm* forager. **forrajear** *v* forage.

forrar [for'rar] v line; pad; put a cover on. **forrarse** v line one's pockets. **forro** sm lining; cover.

*fortalecer [fortale'θer] v strengthen; encourage. **fortalecimiento** sm fortification; strengthening. **fortaleza** sf fortress; fortitude; vigour. **fortificación** sf fortification. **fortificar** v fortify; strengthen. **fortificarse** v gain strength.

fortuito [for'twito] adj fortuitous; accidental.

fortuna [for'tuna] sf fortune, wealth; good luck; happiness; fate. **por fortuna** luckily. **probar fortuna** try one's luck.

*forzar [for'θar] v force; rape. **forzadamente** adv forcibly. **forzado** adj forced; hard; far-fetched. **forzosamente** adv unavoidably. **forzoso** adj unavoidable; necessary.

fosa ['fosa] sf grave; (anat) cavity.

fosfato [fos'fato] sm phosphate. **fosforescencia** sf phosphorescence. **fosforescente** adj phosphorescent. **fósforo** sm phosphorus; match.

fósil ['fosil] sm fossil. **fosilizarse** v fossilize.

foso ['foso] sm hole; ditch; (teatro) pit; (mil) trench.

fotocopiar [fotoko'pjar] v photocopy. **fotocopia** sf photocopy. **fotocopiadora** sf copier.

fotografía [fotogra'fia] sf photography; photograph. **fotografiar** v photograph. **fotográfico** adj photographic. **fotógrafo, -a** sm, sf photographer.

frac [frak] sm dress coat, tails pl.

fracasar [fraka'sar] v fail. **fracaso** sm failure.

fracción [frak'θjon] sf (mat) fraction; portion; fragment. **fraccionamiento** sm breaking-up. **fraccionar** v break up; divide.

fractura [frak'tura] sf (med) fracture. **robo con fractura** sm burglary. **fracturar** v fracture.

fragancia [fra'ganθja] sf fragrance. **fragante** adj fragrant; flagrant.

fragata [fra'gata] sf frigate.

frágil ['fraxil] adj fragile; weak. **fragilidad** sf fragility; weakness.

fragmento [frag'mento] sm fragment. **fragmentar** v fragment. **fragmentario** adj fragmentary.

fragor [fra'gor] sm row, noise. **fragoroso** adj deafening.

fraguar [fra'gwar] v (hierro) forge; concoct; (cemento) harden. **fragua** sf forge. **fraguador, -a** sm, sf schemer, plotter.

fraile ['fraile] sm friar, monk.

frambuesa [fram'bwesa] sf raspberry. **frambueso** sm raspberry bush.

Francia ['franθja] sf France. **francés, -esa** sm, sf Frenchman/woman. **francés** sm, adj French.

francmasón [frankma'son] sm freemason. **francmasonería** sf freemasonry.

franco ['franko] adj frank, open; generous; free; (com) post or duty free.

franela [fra'nela] sf flannel.

franja ['franxa] sf fringe; border. **franjar** v fringe, trim.

franquear [franke'ar] v free; clear; exempt; grant. **franquearse** v open one's heart. **franqueo** sm franking, stamping; postage.

franqueza [fran'keθa] sf frankness; generosity; freedom.

frasco ['frasko] sm flask.

frase ['frase] sf (gram) sentence; phrase; expression. **frase hecha** cliché. **fraseología** sf phraseology.

fraternal [frater'nal] adj fraternal. **fraternidad** sf fraternity. **fraternizar** v fraternize. **fraterno** adj fraternal.

fraude ['frauðe] sm fraud; deception. **fraudulencia** sf dishonesty. **fraudulento** adj fraudulent.

fray [fraj] sm (rel) friar, brother.

frecuencia [fre'kwenθja] sf frequency. **con frecuencia** often. **frecuentar** v frequent. **frecuente** adj frequent.

*fregar [fre'gar] v rub; scrub; wash up. **fregadero** sm sink. **fregado** sm rubbing; scrubbing; washing; (fam) intrigue. **fregador, -a** sm, sf dishwasher; sm sink, dishcloth.

*freír [fre'ir] v fry; (fam) bother. **freidura** sf frying. **freiduría** sf fish shop.

fréjol ['frexol] sm kidney bean.

frenar [fre'nar] v brake; check. **freno** sm brake; bridle. **freno de mano** handbrake. **poner/soltar el freno** apply/release the brake.

frenesí [frene'si] sm frenzy.

frente ['frente] sm front; face; façade. **al frente** at the head. **de frente** forward. **en frente** opposite. sf forehead; head. **frente a frente** face to face.

fresa ['fresa] sf strawberry.

fresco ['fresko] adj cool; fresh; new; calm. frescura sf coolness; freshness; fertility; calmness; indifference; (fam) insolence.

fresno ['fresno] sm (bot) ash.

fricción [frik'θjon] sf friction; (med) massage. friccionar v rub; massage.

frígidez [frixi'ðeθ] sf frigidity. frígido adj frigid. frigorífico sm refrigerating; refrigerator.

frijón [fri'xon] sm bean.

frío ['frio] adj cold; cool; indifferent. sm cold. coger frío catch cold. tener frío be cold. frialdad sf coldness; indifference; impotence.

friolera [frjo'lera] sf triviality, trifle.

frisar [fri'sar] v frizz, curl. frisar en (edad) border on.

frito ['frito] V freír. adj fried. estar frito be fed up. patatas fritas chips. quedarse frito (fam) nod off.

frívolo ['friβolo] adj frivolous. frivolidad sf frivolity.

frondoso [fron'doso] adj leafy; lush. frondosidad sf leafiness; lushness.

frontera [fron'tera] sf frontier.

frotar [fro'tar] v rub; (cerilla) strike. frotación sf rubbing; friction. frote sm rub.

fructífero [fruk'tifero] adj fruit-bearing; fruitful.

frugal [fru'gal] adj frugal. frugalidad sf frugality.

fruncir [frun'θir] v wrinkle; gather; pleat. fruncir el ceño frown. fruncido adj gathered; wrinkled. fruncimiento sm gathering; wrinkling.

frustrar [frus'trar] v frustrate. frustrarse v fail.

fruta ['fruta] sf fruit. fruta de sartén fritter. frutal adj fruit. frutería sf fruiterer's. frutero, -a sm, sf fruiterer. fruto sm fruit; product; result; offspring; profit. frutos civiles (jur) unearned income.

fue¹ ['fue] V ir.

fue² ['fue] V ser.

fuego ['fwego] sm fire; light; burner; heat; rash; passion; zeal. apagar el fuego put out the fire. arma de fuego firearm. cocer a fuego lento/vivo cook slowly/quickly. fuegos artificiales fireworks. prender fuego a set fire to.

fuelle ['fweʎe] sm bellows.

fuente ['fwente] sf fountain; spring; source; serving dish.

fuera ['fwera] adv outside; out; abroad. aquí/allí fuera out here/there. estar fuera be away. ¡fuera! get out! ir fuera go outside. por fuera on the outside.

fuero ['fwero] sm law; code of laws; jurisdiction.

fuerte ['fwerte] adj strong; large; heavy; concentrated. precio fuerte full price. sm (mil) fort; stronghold. fuerza sf strength; loudness; power; effort; electric current. fuerza pública police force.

fugarse [fu'garse] v run away; escape. fuga sf escape; elopement; (gas, etc.) leak; (música) fugue. ponerse en fuga take flight. fugaz adj fleeting. fugitivo, -a s, adj fugitive.

fulano [fu'lano] sm so-and-so, what's-his-name. fulana sf whore.

fulcro ['fulkro] sm fulcrum.

fulgor [ful'gor] sm glow; sparkle; brilliance. fulgente also fúlgido adj brilliant. fulgir v shine. fulgurante adj shining; glowing. fulgurar v flash; shine; glow.

fulminante [fulmi'nante] adj explosive; thundering; (med) grave; (med) mortal. fulminar v strike (by lightning); thunder; explode.

fumar [fu'mar] v smoke. prohibido fumar no smoking. fumarse v squander. fumada sf (de humo) puff.

fumigar [fumi'gar] v fumigate. fumigación sf fumigation. fumigador sm fumigator.

funcionar [funθjo'nar] v function, work, go. no funciona out of order. función sf function; performance; party; duty. funcional adj functional. funcionamiento sm functioning; operation; performance. funcionario, -a sm, sf public official.

funda ['funda] sf case, cover. funda de almohada pillowcase.

fundar [fun'dar] v found; establish; base. fundarse v be based. fundación sf foundation. fundado adj founded; justified. fundamental adj fundamental. fundamento sm foundation; basis; reason; reliability.

fundir [fun'dir] v cast; smelt; melt; merge. fundición sf melting; smelting; foundry.

fúnebre ['funeβre] adj funeral; mournful. coche fúnebre hearse.

funesto [fu'nesto] adj ill-fated; disastrous; fatal.

furgón [fur'gon] *sm* wagon; truck; van. **furgón de cola** guard's van. **furgoneta** *sf* van. **furgoneta familiar** station wagon.

furia ['furja] *sf* fury; violence; frenzy. **furioso** *adj* furious; raging; enormous. **furor** *sm* fury; passion; fever. **con furor** furiously. **hacer furor** be all the rage.

furtivo [fur'tiβo] *adj* furtive; sly.

furúnculo [fu'runkulo] *sm* (*med*) boil.

fusible [fu'siβle] *adj* fusible. *sm* fuse.

fusil [fu'sil] *sm* rifle.

fusión [fu'sjon] *sf* fusion; melting; thawing. **fusionar** *v* fuse; merge. **fusionamiento** *sm* merger.

fuste ['fuste] *sm* wood; (*fig*) importance. **gente de fuste** people of consequence.

fútbol ['futβol] *sm* football. **futbolista** *sm* footballer.

fútil ['futil] *adj* futile, trivial. **futilidad** *sf* futility; triviality.

futuro [fu'turo] *sm, adj* future. **futurista** *adj* futuristic.

G

gabán [ga'βan] *sm* overcoat.

gabardina [gaβar'ðina] *sf* raincoat.

gabinete [gaβi'nete] *sm* (*pol*) cabinet; study; studio.

gacela [ga'θela] *sf* gazelle.

gaceta [ga'θeta] *sf* gazette; journal. **gacetero** *sm* journalist; **gacetilla** *sf* gossip column.

gachas ['gatʃas] *sf pl* porridge *sing*; slops *pl*.

gacho ['gatʃo] *adj* drooping.

gafas ['gafas] *sf pl* spectacles. **gafas de sol** sunglasses.

gajo ['gaxo] *sm* (*de horcas*) prong; (*de naranja*) segment; (*de frutas*) cluster.

gala ['gala] *sf* full dress; pomp; elegance. **de gala** in full dress. **hacer gala de** show off. **tener a gala** pride oneself in.

galán [ga'lan] *sm* gallant; suitor; handsome man; (*teatro*) leading man. **galante** *adj* gallant; flirtatious. **galantear** *v* woo; flirt; flatter. **galanteo** *sm* flirtation; courting; flattery. **galantería** *sf* gallantry; elegance.

galardón [galar'ðon] *sm* reward. **galardonar** *v* reward.

galeón [gale'on] *sm* galleon.

galera [ga'lera] *sf* (*mar*) galley; wagon.

galería [gale'ria] *sf* gallery.

Gales ['gales] *sm* Wales. **galés, -esa** *sm, sf* Welshman/woman. **galés** *sm* (*lengua*) Welsh.

galgo ['galgo] *sm* greyhound.

galón¹ [ga'lon] *sm* braid; (*mil*) stripe. **quitar los galones** demote.

galón² *sm* gallon.

galopar [galo'par] *v* gallop. **galope** *sm* gallop. **a medio galope** at a canter.

galvanizar [galβani'θar] *v* galvanize.

gallardo [ga'ʎarðo] *adj* elegant; gallant. **gallardía** *sf* elegance; charm. **gallardear** *v* behave gracefully.

galleta [ga'ʎeta] *sf* biscuit.

gallina [ga'ʎina] *sf* hen, chicken. **gallo** *sm* cock, rooster.

gamuza [ga'muθa] *sf* chamois; (*trapo*) duster.

gana ['gana] *sf* desire; wish; appetite. **de buena/mala gana** willingly/unwillingly. **tener ganas de** want to.

ganadería [ganaðe'ria] *sf* cattle-raising; cattle farm; cattle; breed. **ganadero, -a** *sm, sf* cattle-raiser; stockbreeder. **ganado** *sm* cattle; livestock.

ganar [ga'nar] *v* gain, get; earn; take; surpass. **ganar en peso** put on weight. **ganancia** *sf* profit. **ganancias** *sf pl* earnings; winnings.

gancho ['gantʃo] *sm* hook; (*fam*) decoy; (*fam*) pimp; (*fam*) sex appeal.

ganga ['ganga] *sf* (*fam*) bargain; (*fam*) cushy job.

gangrena [gan'grena] *sf* gangrene. **gangrenoso** *adj* gangrenous.

ganso ['ganso] *sm* goose, gander; (*fam*) boor. **gansada** *sf* (*fam*) stupid thing.

garabatear [garaβate'ar] *v* scribble; (*fam*) beat about the bush. **garabateo** *sm* scribbling. **garabato** *sm* scribble.

garaje [ga'raxe] *sm* garage.

garantizar [garanti'θar] *v* guarantee. **garantía** *sf* guarantee.

garbanzo [gar'βanθo] *sm* chickpea.

garbo [gar'βo] *sm* grace; generosity; jauntiness. **garboso** *adj* graceful; generous; jaunty.

garganta [gar'ganta] *sf* throat. **tener buena garganta** have a good voice. **gargantear** *v* warble.

gargarizar [gargari'θar] *v* gargle. **gárgara** *sf* gargle.

gárgola ['gargola] *sf* gargoyle.

garita [ga'rita] *sf* sentry box; lavatory; porter's lodge. **garita de señales** signal-box.

garra ['garra] *sf* claw.

garrafa [ga'rrafa] *sf* decanter.

garrapata [garra'pata] *sf* (*zool*) tick.

garrote [ga'rrote] *sm* stick, club; garotte; (*med*) tourniquet. **dar garrote a** execute.

garza [gar'θa] *sf* heron.

gas [gas] *sm* gas. **a todo gas** flat out.

gasa ['gasa] *sf* gauze.

gaseosa [gase'osa] *sf* lemonade.

gasolina [gaso'lina] *sf* petrol. **gasolinera** *sf* petrol pump.

gastar [gas'tar] *v* spend; waste; wear out or away. **gasto** *sm* expense; outlay. **gastos** *sm pl* expenses; costs. **gastos generales** overheads.

gatillo [ga'tiʎo] *sm* trigger; dentist's forceps; (*tecn*) jack.

gato ['gato] *sm* cat; (*tecn*) jack; (*fam*) hoard. **a gatas** on all fours. **gatear** *v* clamber; (*fam*) crawl. **gatearse** *v* scratch.

gavilán [gaβi'lan] *sm* hawk; (*pluma*) nib; (*bot*) thistle.

gavilla [ga'βiʎa] *sf* sheaf; bundle; (*fam*) gang.

gaviota [ga'βjota] *sf* seagull.

gazapo [ga'θapo] *sm* young rabbit; slip of the tongue; blunder; misprint.

gazpacho [gaθ'patʃo] *sm* cold vegetable soup.

gelatina [xela'tina] *sf* gelatine.

gelignita [xelig'nita] *sf* gelignite.

gemelo [xe'melo] *sm, adj* twin. *sm pl* cufflinks; opera glasses.

*****gemir** [xe'mir] *v* groan. **gemido** *sm* groan; wail.

genealogía [xenealo'xia] *sf* genealogy. **genealógico** *adj* genealogical. **árbol genealógico** family tree.

generación [xenera'θjon] *sf* generation. **generador** *sm* (*tecn*) generator. **generar** *v* generate.

generalizar [xenerali'θar] *v* generalize. **general** *adj* general. **general** *sm* (*mil*) general. **generalidad** *sf* majority. **generalización** *sf* generalization.

genérico [xe'neriko] *adj* generic. **género** *sm* race; kind; style; material; article; gender. **géneros** *sm pl* goods, merchandise *sing*.

generoso [xene'roso] *adj* generous. **generosidad** *sf* generosity.

genética [xe'netika] *sf* genetics. **genético** *adj* genetic.

genial [xe'njal] *adj* brilliant; outstanding; pleasant. **genio** *sm* genius; character. **estar de mal genio** be in a bad temper.

genital [xeni'tal] *adj* genital. **genitales** *sm pl* genitals.

gente ['xente] *sf* people. **gente baja** lower classes. **gente menuda** children.

gentil [xen'til] *adj* charming; genteel; civil; gentile; heathen. *sm* gentile; heathen; pagan. **gentileza** *sf* grace; elegance; gentility; civility.

gentío [xen'tio] *sm* crowd.

genuino [xe'nwino] *adj* genuine.

geografía [xeogra'fia] *sf* geography. **geográfico** *adj* geographic(al). **geógrafo** *sm* geographer.

geología [xeolo'xia] *sf* geology. **geológico** *adj* geological. **geólogo** *sm* geologist.

geometría [xeome'tria] *sf* geometry. **geométrico** *adj* geometric.

geranio [xe'ranjo] *sm* geranium.

gerencia [xe'renθja] *sf* management. **gerente** *sm* manager.

germinar [xermi'nar] *v* germinate. **germen** *sm* germ.

gesticular [xestiku'lar] *v* gesticulate. **gesticulación** *sf* gesticulation; grimace.

gestión [xes'tjon] *sf* arrangement; measure; management. **gestionar** *v* negotiate; get hold of.

gesto ['xesto] *sm* expression; countenance; gesture.

geyser ['xejser] *sm* geyser.

gigante [xi'gante] *sm* giant. *adj* gigantic.

gimnasia [xim'nasja] *sf* gymnastics. **gimnasio** *sm* gymnasium. **gimnasta** *s(m+f)* gymnast.

ginebra [xi'neβra] *sf* gin.

ginecología [xinekolo'xia] *sf* gynaecology. **ginecólogo, -a** *sm, sf* gynaecologist.

gira ['xira] *sf* tour; excursion; picnic.

giralda [xi'ralða] *sf* weathercock.

girar [xi'rar] *v* turn; swivel; send; (*com*) draw. **girar dinero** remit money. **giratorio** *adj* gyratory. **puerta giratoria** revolving door. **giro** *sm* turn; (*com*) draft. **giro postal** *sm* postal order; money order.

girasol [xira'sol] *sm* sunflower.

gitano [xi'tano], -a *s, adj* gypsy.

glacial [gla'θjal] *adj* freezing.
glaciar [gla'θjar] *sm* glacier.
gladio ['glaðjo] *sm* (*bot*) gladiolus.
glándula ['glandula] *sf* gland. **glandular** *adj* glandular.
glicerina [gliθe'rina] *sf* glycerine.
global [glo'βal] *adj* global; comprehensive; total. **globo** *sm* globe, sphere. **en globo** all in all. **globo ocular** eyeball. **globular** *adj* globular. **glóbulo** *sm* globule.
gloriarse [glo'rjarse] *v* boast; glory. **gloria** *sf* glory; (*culin*) custard tart. **glorificación** *sf* glorification. **glorificar** *v* glorify. **glorioso** *adj* glorious; conceited.
glosar [glo'sar] *v* annotate. **glosa** *sf* annotation. **glosario** *sm* glossary.
glotón [glo'ton], **-ona** *sm, sf* glutton. *adj* gluttonous.
glucosa [glu'kosa] *sf* glucose.
***gobernar** [goβer'nar] *v* govern; control; manage. **gobernación** *sf* government. **gobernador** *sm* governor. **gobierno** *sm* (*pol*) government; guidance.
goce [ˈgoθe] *sm* enjoyment.
gol [gol] *sm* (*deporte*) goal. **golear** *v* score a goal.
golfo ['golfo] *sm* gulf; (*geog*) bay; guttersnipe.
golondrina [golon'drina] *sf* (*zool*) swallow.
golosina [golo'sina] *sf* sweet; delicacy; (*fig*) desire; (*fig*) greed. **goloso** *adj* sweet-toothed; appetizing; greedy.
golpe [golpe'ar] *v* strike, hit. **golpe** *sm* blow; coup; large amount; attack. **golpe de estado** coup d'état. **golpe de gracia** coup de grâce.
goma ['goma] *sf* rubber; gum; rubber band; elastic. **goma de borrar** eraser. **goma espuma** foam rubber.
gordo ['gorðo] *sm, adj* fat. **gordura** *sf* fatness, obesity.
gorila [go'rila] *sf* gorilla.
gorjear [gorxe'ar] *v* chirp, trill; twitter. **gorjeo** *sm* chirping; trilling; twittering.
gorra ['gorra] *sf* peaked cap; bonnet; (*fam*) sponger. **de gorra** free. **vivir de gorra** sponge.
gorrión [gor'rjon] *sf* sparrow.
gorro ['gorro] *sm* cap.
gotear [gote'ar] *v* drip; trickle; leak. **gota** *sf* drop. **gotera** *sf* leak; gutter. **goteras** *sf pl* (*fig*) aches and pains.
gótico ['gotiko] *adj* Gothic.

gozar [go'θar] *v* enjoy; possess. **gozarse** *v* rejoice. **gozo** *sm* joy. **gozoso** *adj* joyful.
gozne ['goθne] *sm* hinge.
grabar [gra'βar] *v* engrave; carve; imprint; record. **grabado** *sm* engraving; picture; recording. **grabador de cinta** *sm* tape recorder.
gracia ['graθja] *sf* grace; favour; charm; joke. **me hace gracia** it amuses me. **tener gracia** be amusing.
gracias ['graθjas] *sf pl* thanks. **acción de gracias** thanksgiving. **dar gracias** thank. **muchas gracias** many thanks.
gracioso [gra'θjoso] *adj* graceful; amusing; gracious. *sm* (*teatro*) buffoon.
grada ['graða] *sf* step; stair. **gradería** *sf* flight of steps; row of seats.
grado ['graðo] *sm* grade; degree; rank; pleasure. **de grado** willingly. **graduación** *sf* graduation. **gradual** *adj* gradual. **graduando, -a** *sm, sf* undergraduate. **graduar** *v* graduate; award a degree to. **graduarse** *v* gain a degree.
gráfico ['grafiko] *adj* graphic. *sm* graph; diagram.
grajo ['graxo] *sm* (*zool*) rook.
gramática [gra'matika] *sf* grammar. **gramático** *adj* grammatical.
gramo ['gramo] *sm* gramme.
gramófono [gra'mofono] *sm* gramophone.
gran [gran] *V* **grande**.
grana[1] ['grana] *sf* small seed; seeding time.
grana[2] *sf, adj* scarlet.
granada [gra'naða] *sf* pomegranate.
grande ['grande] *adj also* **gran** large, big, great. **grandeza** *sf* greatness; size. **grandioso** *adj* grandiose; grand.
granel [gra'nel] *adv* **a granel** in bulk.
granero [gra'nero] *sm* granary.
granito [gra'nito] *sm* granite.
granizar [grani'θar] *v* hail. **granizo** *sm* hail.
granja ['granxa] *sf* farm. **granja avícola** poultry farm. **granjero, -a** *sm, sf* farmer.
grano ['grano] *sm* grain; bean; pimple. **ir al grano** come to the point. **granoso** *adj* granular.
grapa ['grapa] *sf* clamp; staple; dowel.
grasa ['grasa] *sf* grease; fat. **grasera** *sf* dripping pan. **graslento** *adj* greasy; oily; filthy. **graso** *adj* fatty.
gratificar [gratifi'kar] *v* gratify; reward; tip. **gratificación** *sf* reward; gratuity; bonus; gratification.

gratis ['gratis] *adv* free.

gratitud [grati'tuð] *sf* gratitude.

grato ['grato] *adj* pleasing; pleasant; welcome. **me es grato ...** I am pleased ....

gratuito [gra'twito] *adj* free; gratuitous.

gravamen [gra'βamen] *sm* charge; obligation; burden; tax. **gravar** *v* burden; oppress. **gravar impuestos a** *or* **sobre** tax.

grave [gra'βe] *adj* grave, serious; weighty. **ponerse grave** become gravely ill. **gravedad** *sf* gravity, seriousness.

gravitar [graβi'tar] *v* gravitate. **gravitación** *sf* gravitation, gravity.

graznar [graθ'nar] *v* croak; cackle. **graznido** *sm* croak; cackle.

Grecia ['greθja] *sf* Greece. **griego** s, *adj* Greek. **griego** *sm* (*idioma*) Greek; (*fam*) gibberish.

greda ['greða] *sf* clay. **gredoso** *adj* clayey.

gregario [gre'garjo] *adj* gregarious.

gremio ['gremjo] *sm* guild; fraternity; union. **gremio obrero** trade union.

greña ['grenja] *sf* tangled hair. **andar a la greña** (*fam*) squabble.

grey [grej] *sf* congregation; flock, herd.

grieta ['grjeta] *sf* crack.

grifo ['grifo] *sm* tap. **al grifo** on draught.

grillo ['griʎo] *sm* (*zool*) cricket. **grillos** *sm pl* shackles, fetters.

gringo ['gringo] *, -a sm, sf* (*fam*) foreigner.

gripe ['gripe] *sf* (*med*) influenza, flu.

gris [gris] *adj* grey.

gritar [gri'tar] *v* shout, scream, yell. **grito** *sm* shout, scream, yell. **el último grito** the latest fashion.

grosella [gro'seʎa] *sf* currant. **grosella espinosa/negra/roja** gooseberry/ blackcurrant/redcurrant.

grosería [grose'ria] *sf* vulgarity. **grosero** *adj* vulgar.

grotesco [gro'tesko] *adj* grotesque; absurd.

grúa ['grua] *sf* (*tecn*) crane.

grueso [gru'eso] *adj* thick; large; heavy; dull; slow; coarse. *sm* thickness; heaviness. **gruesa** *sf* (*número*) gross.

grulla ['gruʎa] *sf* (*zool*) crane.

grumete [gru'mete] *sm* cabin boy.

*****gruñir** [gru'nir] *v* growl. **gruñido** *sm* growl.

grupo ['grupo] *sm* group. **grupo sanguíneo** blood group.

gruta ['gruta] *sf* grotto; cave.

guadaña [gwa'ðaɲa] *sf* scythe.

guante ['gwante] *sm* glove. **guantear** *v* slap.

guapo ['gwapo] *adj* handsome; pretty; flashy. *sm* boaster; bully; (*fam*) lover.

guardar [gwar'ðar] *v* guard; keep; protect; respect. **guarda** *s(m+f)* guard; keeper. **guarda** *sf* custody; protection. **guardacostas** *sm invar* coastguard. **guardafuego** *sm* hearth fender. **guardapolvo** *sm* dust-cover. **guardarropa** *sm* wardrobe; cloakroom. **guardia** *sf* guard; police force. **guardia civil** Civil Guard.

guardián [gwar'ðjan] *, -a sm, sf* guardian; keeper; caretaker.

guardilla [gwar'ðiʎa] *sf* attic.

guarida [gwa'riða] *sf* den, lair; haunt; shelter.

*****guarnecer** [gwarne'θer] *v* equip; provide; furnish; adorn; garnish; plaster. **guarnición** *sf* adornment; provision; (*mil*) garrison. **guarnicionar** *v* garrison.

guasa ['gwasa] *sf* joke. **sin guasa** seriously. **guasearse** *v* (*fam*) joke; tease. **guaseo** *sm* leg-pull.

gubernamental [guβernamen'tal] *adj* governmental.

guerra ['gerra] *sf* war. **guerra mundial** world war. **guerrear** *v* wage war. **guerrero, -a sm, sf** warrior. **guerrilla** *sf* guerrilla band; guerrilla warfare. **guerrillero** *sm* guerrilla fighter.

guiar [gi'ar] *v* guide; steer; drive. **guía** *sm* (*persona*) guide. **guía** *sf* (*libro*) guide, guidebook. **guía sonora** soundtrack.

guija ['gixa] *sf* pebble.

guillotina [giʎo'tina] *sf* guillotine. **guillotinar** *v* guillotine.

guiñar [gi'nar] *v* wink. **guiño** *sm* wink.

guión [gi'on] *sm* hyphen; film script; outline; subtitle.

guisa ['gisa] *sf* way, manner. **a guisa de** like. **de tal guisa** in such a manner.

guisado [gi'saðo] *sm* stew. **guisar** *v* cook; prepare. **guiso** *sm* cooked dish; stew.

guisante [gi'sante] *sm* pea. **guisante de olor** sweet pea.

guitarra [gi'tarra] *sf* guitar. **guitarrista** *s(m+f)* guitarist.

gula ['gula] *sf* greed.

gusano [gu'sano] *sm* worm; maggot; caterpillar. **gusano de seda** silkworm.

gustar [gus'tar] *v* please; like; taste; try. **gustar de** enjoy. **¡así me gusta!** that's what I like! **gusto** *sm* pleasure; fancy;

style; taste; flavour. **de buen/mal gusto**
in good/bad taste. **con mucho gusto** with
great pleasure. **¡mucho gusto!** how do
you do? **gustoso** *adj* tasty; pleasant.
gutural [gutu'ral] *adj* guttural.

H

haba ['aβa] *sf* broad bean; swelling;
bruise.
***haber** [a'βer] *v* have. **haber de** have to.
hay que one must. **no hay de que** don't
mention it. **haberes** *sm pl* assets; property *sing*; income *sing*.
habichuela [aβi'tʃwela] *sf* bean. **habichuela verde** French bean.
hábil ['aβil] *adj* clever; able. **habilidad** *sf*
cleverness; ability.
habilitar [aβili'tar] *v* qualify; enable.
habilitación *sf* qualification.
habitar [aβi'tar] *v* inhabit. **habitable** *adj*
habitable. **habitación** *sf* habitation;
room; lodgings *pl*. **habitante** *s(m + f)*
inhabitant.
hábito ['aβito] *sm* habit; attire. **habitual**
adj habitual. **habituar** *v* accustom.
habituarse *v* become accustomed to.
hablar [a'βlar] *v* speak, talk. **¿quién
habla?** (*al teléfono*) who's speaking? **se
habla español** Spanish spoken. **habla** *sf*
language; speech. **hablador, -a** *sm, sf*
chatterbox. **hablilla** *sf* rumour; gossip.
hacedero [aθe'ðero] *adj* feasible. **hacedor,
-a** *sm, sf* creator.
hacendado [aθen'daðo] *sm* landowner.
***hacer** [a'θer] *v* do; make; perform; pro-
duce. **hacer calor/frío** be hot/cold. **hacer
fiesta** take a holiday. **hace mucho tiempo
que** it is a long time since. **hacer para**
make an effort to. **hacerse** *v* become.
hacia ['aθja] *prep* towards; about. **hacia
atrás** backwards.
hacienda [a'θjenda] *sf* estate; ranch.
hacina [a'θina] *sf* stack, rick. **hacinar** *v*
stack; amass.
hacha ['atʃa] *sf* axe.
hada ['aða] *sf* fairy. **hada madrina** fairy
godmother. **cuento de hadas** *sm* fairy
tale.
hado ['aðo] *sm* fate.

halagar [ala'gar] *v* flatter. **halago** *sm*
flattery. **halagüeño** *adj* flattering.
halcón [al'kon] *sm* falcon. **halconería** *sf*
falconry.
hálito ['alito] *sm* breath.
hallar [a'ʎar] *v* find; find out. **hallarse** *v*
be situated. **hallarse bien con** be pleased
with. **hallazgo** *sm* discovery.
hamaca [a'maka] *sf* hammock.
hambre ['ambre] *sf* hunger; starvation.
pasar hambre go hungry. **tener hambre**
be hungry. **hambriento** *adj* hungry.
hamburguesa [ambur'gesa] *sf* hamburger.
haragán [ara'gan] *adj* lazy. **haraganear** *v*
idle.
harapiento [ara'pjento] *adj* ragged.
harapo *sm* rag.
harina [a'rina] *sf* flour. **harinero** *adj also*
harinoso floury.
hartar [ar'tar] *v* stuff; gorge; weary; bore.
harto *adj* satiated. **hartura** *sf* satiety.
hasta ['asta] *prep* until; up to; as much
as; as far as. *adv* even. **hasta ahora** up to
now. **hasta aquí** so far. **hasta luego**
(*interj*) so long, good-bye. **hasta que**
until.
hastío [as'tio] *sm* disgust; weariness. **has-
tiar** *v* disgust; bore.
hato ['ato] *sm* herd; flock; gang.
hay [aj] there is; there are. **hay que** one
must.
haya ['aja] *sf* beech.
haz¹ [aθ] *sm* bunch; bundle; sheaf.
haz² *sf* face; surface. **a sobre haz** on the
surface.
hazaña [a'θaɲa] *sf* deed; feat; exploit.
hazmerreír [aθmerre'ir] *sm* laughing-
stock.
hebilla [e'βiʎa] *sf* buckle; clasp.
hebra ['eβra] *sf* fibre; thread; (*de madera*)
grain.
hebreo [e'βreo] *s, adj* Hebrew. *sm*
(*lengua*) Hebrew.
hechicero [etʃi'θero] *sm* sorcerer; wizard.
hechicera *sf* sorceress; witch. **hechicería**
sf witchcraft; sorcery; enchantment.
hechizar *v* bewitch. **hechizo** *sm* magic
spell.
hecho ['etʃo] *V* **hacer**. *adj* mature;
finished; cooked. **hecho y derecho** in
every sense of the word. **muy/poco
hecho** overdone/underdone. *sm* fact;
deed; feat; matter; event. **de hecho** in
fact. **hechura** *sf* making; making-up;
shape; workmanship.

hediondo [e'ðjondo] *adj* stinking; repulsive. **heder** *v* stink; vex. **hedor** *sm* stink.

***helar** [e'lar] *v* freeze. **helada** *sf* frost. **helado** *sm* ice cream.

helecho [e'letʃo] *sm* fern.

hélice ['eliθe] *sf* helix; spiral; propeller.

helicóptero [eli'koptero] *sm* helicopter.

hembra ['embra] *sf* female; clasp; socket; (*de tornillo*) nut.

hemisferio [emis'ferjo] *sm* hemisphere. **hemisférico** *adj* hemispheric, hemispherical.

hemorragia [emor'raxja] *sf* haemorrhage. **hemorroides** [emor'rojðes] *sf pl* haemorrhoids.

***henchirse** [en'tʃirse] *v* swell up; stuff oneself. **henchidura** *sf* filling.

***hender** [en'der] *v* split. **hendidura** *sf* split; crack.

heno ['eno] *sm* hay.

heraldo [e'raldo] *sm* herald. **heráldica** *sf* heraldry. *adj* heraldic.

herbaje [er'βaxe] *sm* pasture. **herbario** *adj* herbal. **herbicida** *sm* weedkiller. **herbívoro, -a** *sm, sf* herbivore. **herbívoro** *adj* herbivorous. **herbolario** *sm* herbalist. **herboso** *adj* grassy.

heredar [ere'ðar] *v* inherit. **heredad** *sf* estate. **heredero, -a** *sm, sf* heir/heiress. **hereditario** *adj* hereditary.

hereje [e'rexe] *s(m+f)* heretic. **herejía** *sf* heresy. **herético** *adj* heretic.

herencia [e'renθja] *sf* inheritance; heredity.

***herir** [e'rir] *v* wound. **herida** *sf* wound. **herido** *sm* casualty.

hermano [er'mano] *sm* brother. **hermana** *sf* sister. **hermandad** *sf* brotherhood. **hermanastro, -a** *sm, sf* stepbrother/stepsister.

hermético [er'metiko] *adj* hermetic.

hermoso [er'moso] *adj* beautiful; handsome. **hermosura** *sf* beauty; handsomeness.

héroe ['eroe] *sm* hero. **heroico** *adj* heroic. **heroína** *sf* heroine. **heroísmo** *sm* heroism.

heroína [ero'ina] *sf* heroin.

herramienta [erra'mjenta] *sf* tool; implement.

***herrar** [er'rar] *v* (*caballo*) shoe. **herradura** *sf* horseshoe. **camino de herradura** bridle path. **herrería** *sf* smithy, forge. **herrero** *sm* blacksmith.

herrumbre [er'rumbre] *sf* rust. **herrumbrar** *v* rust. **herrumbroso** *adj* rusty.

***hervir** [er'βir] *v* boil. **hervidero** *sm* boiling; bubbling; (*fig*) swarm, crowd; hotbed. **hervidor** *sm* kettle. **hervor** *sm* boiling; fervour.

hesitar [esi'tar] *v* hesitate. **hesitación** *sf* hesitation.

hez [eθ] *sf, pl* **heces** dregs *pl*; scum.

hibernar [iβer'nar] *v* hibernate. **hibernación** *sf* hibernation.

híbrido ['iβriðo] *sm, adj* hybrid. **hibridación** *sf* hybridization. **hibridizar** *v* hybridize.

hidalgo [i'ðalgo] *sm* nobleman. *adj* noble. **hidalguía** *sf* nobility.

hidráulico [i'ðrauliko] *adj* hydraulic. **freno hidráulico** *sm* hydraulic brake.

hidroala [iðro'ala] *sf* hovercraft.

hidroavión [iðroa'βjon] *sm* seaplane.

hidroeléctrico [iðroe'lektriko] *adj* hydroelectric.

hidrofobia [iðro'foβja] *sf* hydrophobia.

hidrógeno [i'ðroxeno] *sm* hydrogen.

hidropesía [iðrope'sia] *sf* dropsy.

hiedra ['jeðra] *sf* ivy.

hielo ['jelo] *sm* ice.

hiena ['jena] *sf* hyena.

hierba ['jerβa] *sf* grass; herb. **mala hierba** weed.

hierbabuena [jerβa'βwena] *sf* mint.

hierro ['jerro] *sm* iron. **hierro colado** cast iron. **hierro forjado** wrought iron.

hígado ['igaðo] *sm* liver.

higiene [i'xjene] *sf* hygiene. **higiénico** *adj* hygienic. **paños higiénicos** *sm pl* sanitary towels.

higo ['igo] *sm* fig. **higuera** *sf* fig-tree.

hijo ['ixo] *sm* son. **hijos** *sm pl* children. **hija** *sf* daughter. **hijo/hija político, -a** son/daughter-in-law.

hilar [i'lar] *v* spin; infer. **hiladora** *sf* spinning wheel. **hilandería** *sf* spinning. **hilandero, -a** *sm, sf* (*persona*) spinner.

hilarante [ila'rante] *adj* hilarious. **hilaridad** *sf* hilarity.

hilera [i'lera] *sf* row; rank; file.

hilo ['ilo] *sm* thread; yarn; wire. **hilo de coser** sewing thread. **hilo de perlas** string of pearls. **telegrafía sin hilos** *sf* wireless telegraphy.

himno ['imno] *sm* hymn; anthem. **himno nacional** national anthem. **himnario** *sm* hymn book.

hincapié [inka'pje] *sm* foothold; emphasis. **hacer hincapié en** insist on.

hincar [in'kar] v drive in; sink; plunge. **hincarse de rodillas** kneel down.

hinchar [in'tʃar] v inflate; swell. **hincharse** v puff up; (fam) become bigheaded. **hinchazón** sm (med) swelling; arrogance.

hinojo [i'noxo] sm fennel. **hinojos** sm pl knees.

hípico ['ipiko] adj equine. **hipismo** sm show-jumping. **hipódromo** sm race course.

hipnosis [ip'nosis] sm hypnosis. **hipnótico** adj hypnotic. **hipnotismo** sm hypnotism. **hipnotizador, -a** sm, sf hypnotist. **hipnotizar** v hypnotize.

hipo ['ipo] sm hiccup; longing; grudge. **tener hipo** have the hiccups.

hipocondría [ipokon'dria] sf hypochondria. **hipocondríaco, -a** sm, sf hypochondriac.

hipocresía [ipokre'sia] sf hypocrisy. **hipócrita** adj hypocritical. **hipócrita** s(m+f) hypocrite.

hipodérmico [ipo'ðermiko] adj hypodermic.

hipopótamo [ipo'potamo] sm hippopotamus.

hipotecar [ipote'kar] v mortgage. **hipoteca** sf mortgage.

hipótesis [i'potesis] sf hypothesis. **hipotético** adj hypothetical.

hirsuto [ir'suto] adj hairy.

hirviente [ir'βjente] adj boiling.

hispánico [is'paniko] adj Hispanic.

hispanoamericano [ispanoameri'kano] s, adj Spanish American.

histerectomía [isterekto'mia] sf hysterectomy.

histeria [i'sterja] sf hysteria. **histérico** adj hysterical.

historia [is'torja] sf history; story; fib; gossip; trouble. **armar historias** (fam) make trouble. **historiador, -a** sm, sf historian. **histórico** adj historical; historic.

hogar [o'gar] sm hearth; home.

hoguera [o'gera] sf bonfire.

hoja ['oxa] sf leaf; petal; sheet; layer; flake; blade; newspaper; (formulario) form. **hoja de afeitar** razor blade. **hoja de paga** payroll.

hojalata [oxa'lata] sf tinplate; tin.

hojear [oxe'ar] v leaf through.

Holanda [o'landa] sf Holland. **holandés** adj Dutch. **holandés** sm Dutchman; (lengua) Dutch. **holandesa** sf Dutchwoman.

*__holgar__ [ol'gar] v rest; be idle; be unnecessary. **holgarse** v enjoy oneself. **holgazán** adj idle. **holgazanear** v idle. **holgura** sf roominess; comfort.

*__hollar__ [o'ʎar] v tread; trample down.

hollín [o'ʎin] sm soot. **hollimiento** adj sooty.

hombre ['ombre] sm man. **hombre bueno** arbiter. **hombre de negocios** businessman. **¡hombre!** good heavens, man! **hombrear** v act the man.

hombro ['ombro] sm (anat) shoulder. **echarse al hombro** shoulder.

homenaje [ome'naxe] sm homage. **homenajear** v pay homage to.

homeópata [ome'opata] s(m+f) homeopath. adj homeopathic. **homeopatía** sf homeopathy.

homicida [omi'θiða] s(m+f) murderer. adj homicidal. **homicidio** sm murder.

homogéneo [omo'xeneo] adj homogeneous. **homogeneidad** sf homogeneity; homogeneousness.

homólogo [o'mologo] adj corresponding; synonymous.

honda ['onda] sf catapult; sling.

hondo ['ondo] adj deep. sm bottom. **hondonada** sf depression; hollow. **hondura** sf depth.

honesto [o'nesto] adj honest; modest; chaste. **honestidad** sf honesty; modesty; chastity.

hongo ['ongo] sm mushroom; bowler hat.

honor [o'nor] sm honour. **honorable** adj honourable. **honorario** adj honorary. **honorario** sm honorarium. **honra** sf honour; reputation; dignity; respect. **tener a mucha honra** be very proud of. **honradez** sf honesty; uprightness. **honrado** adj honest; upright. **honrar** v honour; be a credit to. **honrarse** v be honoured. **honroso** adj honourable.

hora ['ora] sf hour. **pedir hora** make an appointment. **¿qué hora es?** what time is it? **horario** adj hour. **horario** sm hours of work; timetable.

horca ['orka] sf gallows pl; pitchfork. **horcado** adj forked.

horda ['orða] sf horde.

horizonte [ori'θonte] sm horizon. **horizontal** adj horizontal.

hormiga [or'miga] sf ant; itch. **hormigoso** adj ant-eaten; itchy. **hormiguear** v swarm; creep; itch. **hormigueo** sm itching; swarming. **hormiguero** *sm* ant-hill; swarm.

hormigón [ormi'gon] *sm* concrete. **hormigón armado** reinforced concrete.

hormona [or'mona] *sf* hormone.

hornero [or'nero], **-a** *sm*, *sf* baker. **hornear** *v* bake. **hornería** *sf* baking.

horno [orno] *sm* oven; furnace. **bornillo** *sm* stove, cooker; gas or electric ring.

horóscopo [o'roskopo] *sm* horoscope.

horquilla [or'kiʎa] *sf* pitchfork; hairpin; rowlock.

horrible [or'riβle] *adj* horrible.

horror [or'ror] *sm* horror. **borrendo** *adj* hideous; horrible. **horrífico** *adj* horrific, horrifying. **horrorizar** *v* horrify. **horroroso** *adj* horrid, horrible.

hortaliza [orta'liθa] *sf* green vegetable. **hortelano**, **-a** *sm*, *sf* gardener. **hortelano** *adj* market-gardening.

horticultura [ortikul'tura] *sf* horticulture. **horticula** *adj* horticultural.

hosco ['osko] *adj* grim; surly; gloomy. **hoscoso** *adj* bristly.

hospedar [ospe'ðar] *v* lodge, put up. **hospedarse** *v* have lodgings. **hospedaje** *sf* lodging. **bospedería** *sf* inn, hostelry.

hospicio [os'piθjo] *sm* orphanage; poor-house.

hospital [ospi'tal] *sm* hospital. **hospitalario** *adj* hospitable. **hospitalidad** *sf* hospitality. **hospitalización** *sf* hospitalization. **hospitalizar** *v* hospitalize.

hostelero [oste'lero], **-a** *sm*, *sf* innkeeper. **hostería** *sf* inn.

hostia ['ostja] *sf* (*rel*) wafer; (*fam*) bashing.

hostigar [osti'gar] *v* whip; harass; molest. **hostigamiento** *sm* harassing; molesting; lashing. **hostigo** *sm* lash.

hostil [os'til] *adj* hostile. **hostilidad** *sf* hostility.

hotel [o'tel] *sm* hotel; villa. **hotelería** *sf* hotel-keeping. **hotelero**, **-a** *sm*, *sf* hotel-keeper.

hoy [oj] *adv* today; now. **de hoy en adelante** from now on. **hoy en día** nowadays. **hoy por hoy** for the time being.

hoya ['oja] *sf* hole; valley.

hoyo ['ojo] *sm* pit; hole; dent; grave. **hoyuelo** *sm* small hole; dimple.

hoz [oθ] *sf* sickle; ravine.

hueco ['weko] *adj* hollow; empty; vain; resonant. *sm* hollow; gap; cavity; vacancy.

huelga ['welga] *sf* (*de obreros*) strike. **huelgista** *s(m+f)* striker.

huelgo ['welgo] *sm* breath; (*tecn*) play.

huella ['weʎa] *sf* footprint; tread; impression. **huella digital** fingerprint. **huella de sonido** soundtrack.

huérfano ['werfano], **-a** *sm*, *sf* orphan.

huerta ['werta] *sf* vegetable garden; orchard; irrigated land. **huerto** *sm* orchard; kitchen garden.

hueso ['weso] *sm* bone; stone; pip. (*fam*) drudgery. **dar con sus huesos** end up. **estar en los huesos** be very thin. **huesudo** *adj* bony.

huésped ['wespeð], **-a** *sm*, *sf* guest; lodger. **casa de huéspedes** boarding house.

hueva ['weβa] *sf* roe. **huevas** *sf pl* spawn.

huevo ['weβo] *sm* egg. **huevo de Pascua** Easter egg. **huevo duro** hard-boiled egg. **huevo escalfado** poached egg. **huevo frito** fried egg. **huevo pasado por agua** soft-boiled egg. **huevo revuelto** scrambled egg.

*****huir** [wir] *v* flee. **huida** *sf* flight; escape.

hule[1] ['ule] *sm* oilskin; rubber.

hule[2] *sm* (*cornada*) goring.

hulla ['uʎa] *sf* coal.

humano [u'mano] *adj* human; humane. *sm* human being. **humanar** *v* humanize. **humanidad** *sf* humanity. **humanismo** *sm* humanism. **humanista** *s(m+f)* humanist. **humanitario**, **-a** *s*, *adj* humanitarian.

húmedo ['umeðo] *adj* humid, damp, moist. **humedad** *sf* humidity. dampness. **humedecer** *v* dampen, moisten.

humillar [umi'ʎar] *v* humiliate; shame. **humildad** *sf* humility. **humilde** *adj* humble. **humillación** *sf* humiliation.

humo ['umo] *sm* smoke; fumes *pl*. **vender humos** boast. **humear** *v* smoke. **humoso** *adj* smoky.

humor [u'mor] *sm* humour; temper; mood. **buen/mal humor** good/bad temper. **humorada** *sf* witticism. **humorista** *s(m+f)* humorist. **humorístico** *adj* humorous.

hundir [un'dir] *v* sink; drive in; crush. **hundirse** *v* go under; collapse. **hundimiento** *sm* sinking; collapse.

Hungría [un'gria] *sf* Hungary. **húngaro** *s*, *adj* Hungarian.

huracán [ura'kan] *sm* hurricane.

hurgar [ur'gar] *v* poke; stir; pick. **hurgón** *sm* poker.

hurón [u'ron] *sm* ferret. huronear *v* hunt with a ferret; (*fam*) pry.

hurtadillas [urta'ðiʎas] *adv* a hurtadillas slyly, stealthily.

hurtar [ur'tar] *v* steal; remove; cheat. hurtar el cuerpo dodge. hurtador, -a *sm, sf* thief. hurto *sm* theft; thing stolen.

husmear [usme'ar] *v* scent; track; (*fam*) pry; (*fam*: carne) smell high. husmeo *sm* scenting; smelling; prying.

huso ['uso] *sm* spindle; (*avión*) fuselage.

I

íbice ['iβiθe] *sm* ibex.

ictericia [ikte'riθja] *sf* jaundice.

ida ['iða] *sf* departure; journey. idas y venidas coming and going.

idea [i'ðea] *sf* idea; intention. tener idea de intend to. ideal *adj* ideal; imaginary. idealismo *sm* idealism. idealista *s, adj* idealist. idealizar *v* idealize. idear *v* imagine; plan.

idéntico [i'ðentiko] *adj* identical. identidad *sf* identity. identificación *sf* identification. identificar *v* identify.

ideología [iðeolo'xia] *sf* ideology. ideológico *adj* ideological.

idilio [i'ðiljo] *sm* idyll. idílico *adj* idyllic.

idioma [i'ðjoma] *sm* language. idiomático *adj* idiomatic; linguistic.

idiosincrasia [iðjosin'krasja] *sf* idiosyncrasy. idiosincrásico *adj* idiosyncratic.

idiota [i'ðjota] *s(m+f)* idiot. *adj* idiotic. idiotez *sf* idiocy. idiótico *adj* idiotic.

ídolo [i'ðolo] *sm* idol. idólatra *s(m+f)* idolater. idólatra *adj* idolatrous. idolatrar *v* idolize. idolatría *sf* idolatry.

idóneo [i'ðoneo] *adj* apt, fit. idoneidad *sf* aptness, fitness.

iglesia [i'glesja] *sf* church.

ignición [igni'θjon] *sf* ignition. ignito *adj* ignited.

ignominia [igno'minja] *sf* ignominy. ignominioso *adj* ignominious.

ignorar [igno'rar] *v* be unaware of; refuse to know. ignorancia *sf* ignorance. ignorante *adj* ignorant.

igual [i'gwal] *adj* same; equal; even. por igual evenly. es igual it makes no difference. igualar *v* equalize. igualación *sf* equalization. igualdad *sf* equality.

ijada [i'xaða] *sf* flank. ijadear *v* pant.

ilegal [ile'gal] *adj* illegal. ilegalidad *sf* illegality.

ilegible [ile'xiβle] *adj* illegible.

ilegítimo [ile'xitimo] *adj* illegitimate. ilegitimidad *sf* illegitimacy.

ileso [i'leso] *adj* unharmed.

ilícito [i'liθito] *adj* illicit.

ilógico [i'loxiko] *adj* illogical.

iluminar [ilumi'nar] *v* illuminate. iluminación *sf* illumination.

ilusión [ilu'sjon] *sf* illusion; delusion; expectation. ilusionado *adj* eager. ilusionar *v* fascinate. ilusionarse *v* delude oneself; build up hopes. ilusionismo *sm* conjuring trick. ilusionista *s(m+f)* conjurer. iluso *adj* deceived; deluded. ilusorio *adj* illusory.

ilustrar [ilu'strar] *v* illustrate. ilustración *sf* illustration; enlightenment. ilustrador, -a *sm, sf* illustrator.

imaginar [imaxi'nar] *v* imagine. imagen *sf* image. imaginación *sf* imagination. imaginario *adj* imaginary. imaginativo *adj* imaginative.

imán [i'man] *sm* magnet. imanar *v also* imantar magnetize. imantación *sf* magnetization.

imbécil [im'beθil] *adj* imbecile. imbecilidad *sf* imbecility.

imborrable [imbor'raβle] *adj* unforgettable.

*imbuir [imbu'ir] *v* imbue.

imitar [imi'tar] *v* imitate, copy. imitable *adj* imitable. imitación *sf* imitation. imitador, -a *sm, sf* imitator. imitativo *adj* imitative.

impaciente [impa'θjente] *adj* impatient. impaciencia *sf* impatience. impacientarse *v* become impatient.

impacto [im'pakto] *sm* impact.

impar [im'par] *adj* (*mat*) odd. número impar odd number.

imparcial [impar'θjal] *adj* impartial. imparcialidad *sf* impartiality.

impartir [impar'tir] *v* impart.

impasible [impa'siβle] *adj* impassive. impasibilidad *sf* impassivity.

impávido [im'paβiðo] *adj* fearless, dauntless. impavidez *sf* fearlessness, dauntlessness.

impecable [impe'kaβle] *adj* impeccable. **impecabilidad** *sf* impeccability.

*****impedir** [impe'ðir] *v* impede; prevent. **impediente** *adj* obstructing. **impedimento** *sm* impediment.

impeler [impe'ler] *v* impel; drive; propel.

impenetrable [impene'traβle] *adj* impenetrable.

impenitente [impeni'tente] *adj* impenitent.

imperar [impe'rar] *v* rule; prevail. **imperativo** *adj* imperative; commanding.

imperceptible [imperθep'tiβle] *adj* imperceptible.

imperdible [imper'ðiβle] *sm* safety pin.

imperdonable [imperðo'naβle] *adj* unforgivable.

imperfecto [imper'fekto] *adj* imperfect. **imperfección** *sf* imperfection.

imperio [im'perjo] *sm* empire. **imperial** *adj* imperial. **imperialismo** *sm* imperialism. **imperialista** *s*, *adj* imperialist.

impermeable [imperme'aβle] *adj* waterproof. *sm* mackintosh.

impersonal [imperso'nal] *adj* impersonal.

impertinente [imperti'nente] *adj* impertinent. **impertinencia** *sf* impertinence.

imperturbable [impertur'βaβle] *adj* imperturbable. **imperturbabilidad** *sf* imperturbability.

impetu ['impetu] *sm* impetus. **impetuosidad** *sf* impetuosity.

impío [im'pio] *adj* godless, impious. **impiedad** *sf* impiety.

implacable [impla'kaβle] *adj* implacable. **implacabilidad** *sf* implacability.

implantar [implan'tar] *v* implant.

implicar [impli'kar] *v* imply; implicate; entail. **implicación** *sf* implication; contradiction. **implicatorio** *adj* contradictory.

implícito [im'pliθito] *adj* implicit.

implorar [implo'rar] *v* implore, beg. **imploración** *sf* entreaty.

*****imponer** [impo'ner] *v* impose; inflict; acquaint; inspire; deposit; impute falsely. **imponerse** *v* dominate. **imponente** *adj* imposing; striking; (*fam*) sensational, smashing.

impopular [impopu'lar] *adj* unpopular. **impopularidad** *sf* unpopularity.

importante [impor'tante] *adj* important. **importancia** *sf* importance. **importar** *v* matter, concern. **no importa** it doesn't matter.

importunar [importu'nar] *v* importune,

pester. **importunidad** *sf* importunity. **importuno** *adj* importunate, pestering.

imposible [impo'siβle] *adj* impossible. **imposibilidad** *sf* impossibility. **imposibilitar** *v* make impossible.

imposición [imposi'θjon] *sf* imposition; tax.

impostor [impos'tor], -**a** *sm*, *sf* impostor.

impotente [impo'tente] *adj* impotent; powerless. **impotencia** *sf* impotence.

impracticable [imprakti'kaβle] *adj* impracticable.

imprecar [impre'kar] *v* curse. **imprecación** *sf* curse. **imprecatorio** *adj* abusive.

impreciso [impre'θiso] *adj* imprecise. **imprecisión** *sf* imprecision.

impregnar [impreg'nar] *v* impregnate; saturate. **impregnable** *adj* absorbent. **impregnación** *sf* impregnation.

imprescindible [impresθin'diβle] *adj* indispensable.

impreso [im'preso] *adj* printed. **imprenta** *sf* press; printing. **impresión** *sf* impression; imprint; stamp; print; printing; edition. **impresionable** *adj* impressionable. **impresionar** *v* impress; shock. **impresionarse** *v* be deeply moved. **impresionismo** *sm* impressionism. **impresionista** *s(m + f)* impressionist. **impresor** *sm* printer.

imprevisto [impre'βisto] *adj* unexpected.

imprimir [impri'mir] *v* print; implant.

improbable [impro'βaβle] *adj* improbable. **improbabilidad** *sf* improbability.

improbo ['improβo] *adj* wicked; arduous. **improbidad** *sf* dishonesty.

improcedente [improθe'ðente] *adj* improper; inappropriate; (*jur*) inadmissible. **improcedencia** *sf* impropriety; inappropriateness; (*jur*) inadmissibility.

improductivo [improduk'tiβo] *adj* unproductive.

impropio [im'propjo] *adj* improper; unbecoming. **impropiedad** *sf* impropriety.

impróvido [im'proβiðo] *adj* improvident. **improvidencia** *sf* improvidence.

improvisar [improβi'sar] *v* improvise. **improvisación** *sf* improvisation.

improvisto [impro'βisto] *adj* unforeseen. **a la improvista** without warning.

imprudente [impru'ðente] *adj* imprudent. **imprudencia** *sf* imprudence.

impúdico [im'puðiko] *adj* shameless, immodest.

impuesto [im'pwesto] *sm* tax; duty.

impugnar [impug'nar] *v* impugn; oppose; refute.

impulsar [impul'sar] *v* impel; drive; move. **impulsión** *sf* impulse; impetus. **impulso** *sm* impulse; drive; momentum.

impune [im'pune] *adj* unpunished. **impunidad** *sf* impunity.

impuro [im'puro] *adj* impure; lewd. **impureza** *sf* impurity; lewdness. **impurificación** *sf* defilement. **impurificar** *v* defile.

imputar [impu'tar] *v* impute; ascribe. **imputable** *adj* chargeable. **imputación** *sf* imputation; accusation.

inacabable [inaka'βaβle] *adj* endless.

inaccesible [inakθe'siβle] *adj* inaccessible. **inaccesibilidad** *sf* inaccessibility.

inaceptable [inaθep'taβle] *adj* unacceptable.

inacostumbrado [inakostum'braðo] *adj* unaccustomed.

inactivo [inak'tiβo] *adj* inactive. **inactividad** *sf* inactivity.

inadecuado [inaðe'kwaðo] *adj* inadequate. **inadecuación** *sf* inadequacy.

inadmisible [inaðmi'siβle] *adj* inadmissible.

inadvertido [inaðβer'tiðo] *adj* inadvertent. **inadvertencia** *sf* inadvertence, carelessness.

inagotable [inago'taβle] *adj* inexhaustible.

inaguantable [inagwan'taβle] *adj* unbearable.

inajenable [inaxe'naβle] *adj* inalienable.

inalterable [inalte'raβle] *adj* unalterable; imperturbable. **inalterabilidad** *sf* immutability; imperturbability. **inalterado** *adj* unchanged.

inanición [inani'θjon] *sf* starvation; weakness; exhaustion.

inanimado [inani'maðo] *adj* inanimate, lifeless.

inapagable [inapa'gaβle] *adj* unquenchable.

inaplicable [inapli'kaβle] *adj* inapplicable. **inaplicado** *adj* indolent.

inapreciable [inapre'θjaβle] *adj* priceless; invaluable.

inapto [in'apto] *adj* unsuitable; incapable.

inasequible [inase'kiβle] *adj* unattainable.

inaudible [inau'ðiβle] *adj* inaudible.

inaudito [inau'ðito] *adj* unheard of; outrageous.

inaugurar [inaugu'rar] *v* inaugurate. **inauguración** *sf* inauguration.

incalculable [inkalku'laβle] *adj* incalculable.

incandescente [inkandes'θente] *adj* incandescent. **incandescencia** *sf* incandescence.

incansable [inkan'saβle] *adj* indefatigable, untiring.

incapacitar [inkapaθi'tar] *v* incapacitate; disable; disqualify. **incapacidad** *sf* incapacity; incompetence; disability. **incapaz** *adj* unfit; incompetent.

incautarse [inkau'tarse] *v* (*jur*) confiscate. **incautación** *sf* confiscation.

incauto [in'kauto] *adj* incautious; gullible.

incendiar [inθen'djar] *v* set on fire. **incendiarse** *v* catch fire. **incendiario, -a** *sm, sf* arsonist. **incendiario** *adj* incendiary. **incendio** *sm* fire. **incendio provocado** arson.

incentivo [inθen'tiβo] *sm* incentive. **incentivar** *v* incite.

incertidumbre [inθerti'ðumbre] *sf* uncertainty.

incesante [inθe'sante] *adj* incessant.

incesto [in'θesto] *sm* incest. **incestuoso** *adj* incestuous.

incidente [inθi'ðente] *sm* incident. *adj* incidental. **incidencia** *sf* incident; incidence. **incidental** *adj* incidental.

incienso [in'θjenso] *sm* incense.

incierto [in'θjerto] *adj* uncertain; untrue.

incinerar [inθine'rar] *v* incinerate; cremate. **incineración** *sf* incineration; cremation.

incipiente [inθi'pjente] *adj* incipient.

incisivo [inθi'siβo] *adj* incisive; cutting. *sm* (*diente*) incisor. **incisión** *sf* incision, cut. **inciso** *adj* cut.

incitar [inθi'tar] *v* incite; instigate. **incitación** *sf* incitement; enticement. **incitador, -a** *sm, sf* instigator.

incivil [inθi'βil] *adj* uncivil, impolite.

inclemente [inkle'mente] *adj* inclement; harsh. **inclemencia** *sf* inclemency; harshness.

inclinar [inkli'nar] *v* incline; lean; influence; induce; lower. **inclinarse** *v* feel disposed; bow; stoop. **inclinación** *sf* inclination; leaning; slope; dip. **inclinado** *adj* inclined; sloping.

*incluir [inklu'ir] *v* include. **inclusión** *sf* inclusion. **inclusivo** *adj* inclusive. **incluso** *adj* included; enclosed. **incluso** *adv* even.

incógnito [in'kognito] *adj* unknown. **de
incógnito** incognito.
incoherente [inkoe'rente] *adj* incoherent.
incoherencia *sf* incoherence.
incoloro [inko'loro] *adj* colourless.
incombustible [inkombus'tiβle] *adj*
incombustible, fireproof.
incomodar [inkomo'ðar] *v* disturb, annoy,
molest. **incomodidad** *sf* inconvenience;
discomfort. **incómodo** *adj* uncomfortable; annoying.
incomparable [inkompa'raβle] *adj* incomparable.
incompatible [inkompa'tiβle] *adj* incompatible. **incompatibilidad** *sf* incompatibility.
incompetente [inkompe'tente] *adj* incompetent. **incompetencia** *sf* incompetence.
incompleto [inkom'pleto] *adj* incomplete.
incompletamente *adv* incompletely.
incomprensible [inkompren'siβle] *adj*
incomprehensible. **incomprensibilidad** *sf*
incomprehensibility. **incomprensión** *sf*
lack of understanding.
incomunicado [inkomuni'kaðo] *adj* isolated. **incomunicable** *adj* incommunicable.
incomunicación *sf* isolation. **incomunicar**
v isolate.
inconcebible [inkonθe'βiβle] *adj* inconceivable.
inconcluso [inkon'kluso] *adj* unfinished;
inconclusive.
incondicional [inkondiθjo'nal] *adj* unconditional. *s(m+f)* staunch supporter.
inconfundible [inkonfun'diβle] *adj* unmistakable.
incongruente [inkongru'ente] *adj* incongruous; incongruent. **incongruencia** *sf*
incongruousness; incongruity.
inconmensurable [inkonmensu'raβle] *adj*
immeasurable.
inconmovible [inkonmo'βiβle] *adj*
unshakable; firm.
inconsciente [inkons'θjente] *adj* unconscious; unaware; thoughtless. **incon-
sciencia** *sf* unconsciousness; unaware-
ness; thoughtlessness.
inconsecuente [inkonse'kwente] *adj*
inconsequential; inconsistent. **inconsecuencia** *sf* inconsistency.
inconsiderado [inkonsiðe'raðo] *adj* ill-
considered. **inconsideración** *sf* inconsid-
erateness.
inconstante [inkon'stante] *adj* inconstant,

fickle. **inconstancia** *sf* inconstancy, fickleness.
incontable [inkon'taβle] *adj* innumerable.
incontestable [inkontes'taβle] *adj* incontestable, indisputable.
incontinente [inkonti'nente] *adj* incontinent. **incontinencia** *sf* incontinence.
inconveniente [inkonβe'njente] *adj* inconvenient, impolite. *sm* objection; trouble;
obstacle. **inconveniencia** *sf* inconvenience; impropriety; unsuitability.
incorporar [inkorpo'rar] *v* incorporate.
incorporarse *v* sit up; become a member.
incorporación *sf* incorporation.
incorporado *adj* incorporated.
incorrecto [inkor'rekto] *adj* incorrect.
incorrección *sf* inaccuracy. **incor-
regibilidad** *sf* incorrigibility. **incorregible**
adj incorrigible.
incorrupto [inkor'rupto] *adj* incorrupt,
pure. **incorruptible** *adj* incorruptible.
incrédulo [in'kreðulo] *adj* incredulous,
sceptical. **incredulidad** *sf* incredulity,
scepticism. **increíble** *adj* incredible.
incremento [inkre'mento] *sm* increase.
increpar [inkre'par] *v* reproach; rebuke.
increpación *sf* rebuke.
incriminar [inkrimi'nar] *v* incriminate;
exaggerate. **incriminación** *sf* incrimina-
tion.
incrustar [inkrus'tar] *v* encrust. **incrustación** *sf* encrustation.
incubar [inku'βar] *v* incubate; (*med*) be
sickening for. **incubación** *sf* incubation.
incubadora *sf* incubator.
inculcar [inkul'kar] *v* inculcate. **inculcarse**
v be obstinate. **inculcación** *sf* inculcation.
inculpable [inkul'paβle] *adj* blameless.
inculpabilidad *sf* blamelessness.
inculto [in'kulto] *adj* uncouth; uneducated. **incultura** *sf* lack of culture.
incumbencia [inkum'benθja] *sf* responsibility, duty. **incumbir** *v* be incumbent
upon.
incurable [inku'raβle] *adj* incurable.
incurrir [inkur'rir] *v* incur; fall; commit.
incursión [inkur'sjon] *sf* incursion, raid.
indagar [inda'gar] *v* investigate. **indaga-
ción** *sf* investigation. **indagador, -a** *sm, sf*
investigator.
indebido [inde'βiðo] *adj* unjust; improper.
indecente [inde'θente] *adj* indecent; foul;
wretched. **indecencia** *sf* indecency;
obscenity.

indecible [inde'θiβle] *adj* indescribable; unspeakable.

indecifrable [indeθi'fraβle] *adj* indecipherable.

indecisión [inde'θisjon] *sf* indecision. **indeciso** *adj* indecisive.

indecoroso [indeco'roso] *adj* indecorous. **indecoro** *sm* lack of propriety.

indefectible [indefek'tiβle] *adj* unfailing.

indefenso [inde'fenso] *adj* defenceless. **indefendible** *adj* indefensible.

indefinible [indefi'niβle] *adj* indefinable. **indefinido** *adj* indefinite.

indeleble [inde'leβle] *adj* indelible.

indelicado [indeli'kaðo] *adj* indelicate. **indelicadeza** *sf* indelicacy.

indemne [in'demne] *adj* unhurt. **indemnidad** *sf* indemnity. **indemnización** *sf* compensation. **indemnizar** *v* indemnify, compensate.

independencia [indepen'denθja] *sf* independence. **independiente** *adj* independent.

indescriptible [indescrip'tiβle] *adj* indescribable.

indeseable [indese'aβle] *adj* undesirable.

indestructible [indestruk'tiβle] *adj* indestructible. **indestructibilidad** *sf* indestructibility.

indeterminado [indetermi'naðo] *adj* indeterminate; undetermined.

India ['indja] *sf* India. **indio, -a** *s, adj* Indian.

indicar [indi'kar] *v* indicate; show; suggest. **indicación** *sf* indication. **indicado** *adj* suitable; recommended. **indicador** *sm* pointer; gauge. **indicativo** *adj* indicative. *sm* (*gram*) indicative.

índice ['indiθe] *sm* index.

indicio [in'diθjo] *sm* sign; trace. **indicios** *sm pl* (*jur*) evidence *sing*.

indiferencia [indife'renθja] *sf* indifference. **indiferente** *adj* indifferent.

indígena [in'dixena] *s(m+f)*, *adj* native.

indigestión [indixes'tjon] *sf* indigestion. **indigestible** *adj* indigestible.

indignar [indig'nar] *v* anger, annoy. **indignarse** *v* become indignant. **indignación** *sf* indignation. **indignidad** *sf* indignity. **indigno** *adj* unworthy; disgraceful.

indirecta [indi'rekta] *sf* innuendo. **indirecto** *adj* indirect.

indisciplina [indisθi'plina] *sf* indiscipline. **indisciplinado** *adj* undisciplined.

indiscreción [indiskre'θjon] *sf* indiscretion. **indiscreto** *adj* indiscreet.

indisculpable [indiskul'paβle] *adj* inexcusable.

indiscutible [indisku'tiβle] *adj* unquestionable.

indisoluble [indiso'luβle] *adj* indissoluble.

indispensable [indispen'saβle] *adj* indispensable.

*indisponer [indispo'ner] *v* upset; render unfit. **indisponerse** *v* become ill. **indisposición** *sf* indisposition. **indispuesto** *adj* indisposed, poorly.

indisputable [indispu'taβle] *adj* indisputable.

indistinto [indis'tinto] *adj* indistinct; vague.

individual [indiβi'ðwal] *adj* individual. **individualidad** *sf* individuality. **individualismo** *sm* individualism. **individualista** *s(m+f)* individualist. **individualizar** *v* individualize. **individuo, -a** *sm*, *sf* individual.

indivisible [indiβi'siβle] *adj* indivisible. **indiviso** *adj* undivided.

índole ['indole] *sf* nature.

indolente [indo'lente] *adj* indolent; painless. **indolencia** *sf* indolence; painlessness.

indómito [in'domito] *adj* untamed; indomitable.

indubitable [induβi'taβle] *adj* indubitable.

*inducir [indu'θir] *v* persuade; lead; infer. **inducción** *sf* induction. **inducimiento** *sm* inducement.

indudable [indu'ðaβle] *adj* unquestionable.

indulgente [indul'xente] *adj* indulgent. **indulgencia** *sf* indulgence.

indultar [indul'tar] *v* pardon; excuse. **indulto** *sm* mercy; reprieve; exemption.

indumento [indu'mento] *sm* apparel.

industria [in'dustrja] *sf* industry; business; ingenuity. **de industria** on purpose. **industrial** *adj* industrial. **industrial** *sm* industrialist. **industrialismo** *sm* industrialism. **industrializar** *v* industrialize. **industrioso** *adj* industrious.

inédito [i'neðito] *adj* unpublished.

inefable [ine'faβle] *adj* ineffable.

ineficaz [inefi'kaθ] *adj* inefficient. **ineficacia** *sf* inefficiency.

ineludible [inelu'ðiβle] *adj* inevitable.

inepto [i'nepto] *adj* inept. **ineptitud** *sf* ineptitude.

inequívoco [ine'kiβoko] *adj* unmistakable.
inercia [i'nerθja] *sf* inertia; lifelessness.
inerme [i'nerme] *adj* unarmed.
inerte [i'nerte] *adj* inert.
inesperado [inespe'raðo] *adj* unexpected, unforeseen.
inestable [ines'taβle] *adj* unstable.
inestabilidad *sf* instability.
inestimable [inesti'maβle] *adj* invaluable.
inevitable [ineβi'taβle] *adj* inevitable.
inexacto [inek'sakto] *adj* inaccurate. **inexactitud** *sf* inaccuracy.
inexcusable [ineksku'saβle] *adj* inexcusable; essential.
inexorable [inekso'raβle] *adj* inexorable.
inexperto [ineks'perto] *adj* inexperienced.
inexplicable [inekspli'kaβle] *adj* inexplicable.
infalible [infa'liβle] *adj* infallible. **infalibilidad** *sf* infallibility.
infamar [infa'mar] *v* dishonour. **infamación** *sf* defamation. **infame** *adj* infamous. **infamia** *sf* infamy.
infante [in'fante] *sm, adj* infant. *sm* prince. **infancia** *sf* infancy. **infantil** *adj* infantile.
infantería [infante'ria] *sf* infantry.
infatigable [infati'gaβle] *adj* indefatigable.
infausto [in'fausto] *adj* ill-omened; ill-famed.
infectar [infek'tar] *v* infect. **infección** *sf* infection. **infeccioso** *adj* infectious.
infeliz [infe'liθ] *adj* unhappy. *s(m+f)* luckless person.
inferior [infe'rjor] *adj* inferior; lower. *sm* inferior. **inferioridad** *sf* inferiority.
***inferir** [infe'rir] *v* infer; inflict. **inferirse** *v* follow.
infernal [infer'nal] *adj* infernal.
infestar [infes'tar] *v* infest; overrun. **infestación** *sf* infestation.
infiel [in'fjel] *adj* unfaithful. *s(m+f)* infidel.
infierno [in'fjerno] *sm* hell.
ínfimo ['infimo] *adj* lowest; vilest.
infinito [infi'nito] *adj* infinite. **infinidad** *sf* infinity. **infinitivo** *sm* (*gram*) infinitive.
inflamar [infla'mar] *v* inflame. **inflamable** *adj* inflammable. **inflamación** *sf* inflammation.
inflar [in'flar] *v* inflate. **inflación** *sf* inflation; swelling.
inflexible [inflek'siβle] *adj* inflexible. **inflexibilidad** *sf* inflexibility.
infligir [infli'xir] *v* inflict.

***influir** [influ'ir] *v* influence; affect. **influencia** *sf* influence; authority. **influente** *adj* also **influyente** influential. **influjo** *sm* influence; flood.
informal [infor'mal] *adj* informal; unreliable. **informalidad** *sf* informality; unreliability.
informar [infor'mar] *v* inform; notify. **informarse** *v* find out. **información** *sf* information; judicial inquiry. **informador, -a** *sm, sf* informant. **informe** *sm* report; testimonial. **informe** *adj* shapeless.
infortunio [infor'tunjo] *sm* misfortune. **infortunado** *adj* unfortunate.
infracción [infrak'θjon] *sf* breach; infringement. **infractor, -a** *sm, sf* transgressor.
infranqueable [infranke'aβle] *adj* impassable; insurmountable.
infringir [infrin'xir] *v* infringe; violate.
infructuoso [infruk'twoso] *adj* fruitless.
infundado [infun'daðo] *adj* unfounded.
infundir [infun'dir] *v* instil. **infusión** *sf* inspiration.
ingeniería [inxenje'ria] *sf* engineering. **ingeniero** *sm* engineer.
ingenio [in'xenjo] *sm* talent; wit; ingenuity; device. **ingeniosidad** *sf* ingenuity. **ingenioso** *adj* ingenious.
ingenuo [in'xenwo] *adj* naïve; frank; simple. **ingenuidad** *sf* frankness; credulity.
***ingerir** [inxe'rir] *v* (*comida*) consume. **ingerirse** *v* meddle. **ingerencia** *sf* interference.
Inglaterra [ingla'terra] *sf* England. **inglés** *adj* English; *sm* Englishman; (*idioma*) English. **inglesa** *sf* Englishwoman.
ingrato [in'grato] *adj* ungrateful; unpleasant. **ingratitud** *sf* ingratitude.
ingrediente [ingre'ðjente] *sm* ingredient.
ingresar [ingre'sar] *v* enter; join; (*hospital*) be admitted; (*dinero*) deposit. **ingreso** *sm* entrance; (*com*) deposit; admission. **derecho de ingreso** *sm* entrance fee.
inhábil [i'naβil] *adj* incompetent; tactless. **día inhábil** non-working day. **inhabilidad** *sf* incompetence; inability. **inhabilitar** *v* disqualify; disable.
inhabitable [inaβi'taβle] *adj* uninhabitable. **inhabitado** *adj* uninhabited.
inhalar [ina'lar] *v* inhale. **inhalación** *sf* inhalation.

inherente [ine'rente] *adj* inherent. **inher-
encia** *sf* inherence.
inhibir [ini'βir] *v* inhibit. **inhibirse** *v*
refrain. **inhibición** *sf* inhibition. **inhib-
itorio** *adj* inhibitive.
inhospitalario [inospita'larjo] *adj* inhospi-
table. **inhospitalidad** *sf* inhospitableness.
inhumano [inu'mano] *adj* inhuman.
inhumanidad *sf* inhumanity.
inhumar [inu'mar] *v* bury.
inicial [ini'θjal] *adj, sf* initial. **iniciación** *sf*
initiation. **iniciado, -a** *sm, sf* initiate.
iniciador, -a *sm, sf* initiator. **iniciar** *v* initiate. **iniciativa** *sf* initiative.
inicuo [i'nikwo] *adj* wicked. **iniquidad** *sf*
iniquity.
injertar [inxer'tar] *v* graft. **injerto** *sm*
graft, grafting.
injuriar [inxuri'ar] *v* insult; damage;
injure. **injuria** *sf* offence; harm.
injuriador *adj* offensive. **injurioso** *adj*
insulting.
injusticia [inxus'tiθja] *sf* injustice. **injusto**
adj unjust.
inmediato [inme'δjato] *adj* immediate. **de
inmediato** immediately.
inmejorable [inmexo'raβle] *adj*
unsurpassable.
inmemorial [inmemo'rjal] *adj* immemori-
al.
inmenso [in'menso] *adj* immense.
inmerecido [inmere'θiδo] *adj* undeserved.
inmigrar [inmi'grar] *v* immigrate. **inmigración** *sf* immigration. **inmigrante** *s(m+f)*,
adj immigrant.
inminente [inmi'nente] *adj* imminent.
inminencia *sf* imminence.
inmoderado [inmoδe'raδo] *adj* excessive.
inmoderación *sf* excess.
inmodestia [inmodes'tia] *sf* immodesty.
inmodesto *adj* immodest.
inmolar [inmo'lar] *v* sacrifice. **inmolación**
sf sacrifice.
inmoral [inmo'ral] *adj* immoral.
inmoralidad *sf* immorality.
inmortal [inmor'tal] *adj, s(m+f)* immortal. **inmortalidad** *sf* immortality.
inmortalizar *v* immortalize.
inmóvil [in'moβil] *adj* motionless.
inmovible *adj* immovable. **inmovilidad** *sf*
immobility. **inmovilizar** *v* immobilize.
inmueble [in'mweβle] *sm* property; real
estate.
inmundo [in'mundo] *adj* filthy; impure.
inmundicia *sf* filth; impurity.

inmune [in'mune] *adj* immune; exempt.
inmunidad *sf* immunity; exemption.
inmunización *sf* immunization. **inmunizar**
v immunize.
inmutar [inmu'tar] *v* change. **inmutarse** *v*
change one's expression. **inmutabilidad** *sf*
immutability. **inmutable** *adj* immutable.
innato [in'nato] *adj* innate.
innecesario [inneθe'sarjo] *adj* unnecessary.
innegable [in'negaβle] *adj* undeniable.
innoble [in'noβle] *adj* ignoble.
innocuo [in'nokwo] *adj also* inocuo innocuous.
innovar [inno'βar] *v* innovate. **innovación**
sf innovation. **innovador, -a** *sm, sf* inno-
vator. **innovador** *adj* innovative.
innovamiento *sm* innovation.
innumerable [innume'raβle] *adj* innumerable.
inobediente [inoβe'δjente] *adj* disobedient. **inobediencia** *sf* disobedience.
inocente [ino'θente] *adj* innocent.
inocencia *sf* innocence.
inocular [inoku'lar] *v* inoculate; contaminate. **inoculación** *sf* inoculation.
inodoro [ino'δoro] *adj* odourless.
inofensivo [inofen'siβo] *adj* harmless.
inolvidable [inolβi'δaβle] *adj* unforgettable.
inoperable [inope'raβle] *adj* inoperable.
inopinado [inopi'naδo] *adj* unexpected.
inoportuno [inopor'tuno] *adj* inopportune.
inoxidable [inoksi'δaβle] *adj* rustless;
stainless. **acero inoxidable** *sm* stainless
steel.
inquebrantable [inkeβran'taβle] *adj*
unbreakable; unyielding.
inquietar [inkje'tar] *v* disturb; disquiet.
inquietador *adj* disquieting. **inquietante**
adj disquieting. **inquieto** *adj* restless.
inquietud *sf* restlessness.
inquilino [inki'lino], **-a** *sm, sf* tenant.
inquilinato *sm* lease.
*****inquirir** [inki'rir] *v* investigate; examine.
inquiridor, -a *sm, sf* inquirer. **inquisición**
sf inquisition; inquiry. **inquisidor** *sm*
inquisitor. **inquisitivo** *adj* inquisitive.
insaciable [insa'θjaβle] *adj* insatiable.
insalubre [insa'luβre] *adj* unhealthy.
insalubridad *sf* unhealthiness.
insanable [insa'naβle] *adj* incurable.

insano [in'sano] *adj* insane; unhealthy. **insania** *sf* insanity.

inscribir [inskri'βir] *v* inscribe; register. **inscripción** *sf* inscription; registration.

insecto [in'sekto] *sm* insect. **insecticida** *sm* insecticide. **insectólogo, -a** *sm, sf* entomologist.

inseguro [inse'guro] *adj* insecure; unsafe; uncertain. **inseguridad** *sf* insecurity; uncertainty.

insensato [insen'sato] *adj* senseless; wild. **insensatez** *sf* folly.

insensible [insen'siβle] *adj* insensible; insensitive; imperceptible. **insensibilidad** *sf* insensibility; insensitiveness.

insertar [inser'tar] *v* insert. **inserto** *sm* insertion.

inservible [inser'βiβle] *adj* useless.

insidioso [insi'ðjoso] *adj* insidious.

insigne [in'signe] *adj* illustrious, distinguished.

insignia [in'signja] *sf* badge; banner. **insignias** *sf pl* insignia.

insignificante [insignifi'kante] *adj* insignificant. **insignificancia** *sf* insignificance.

insincero [insin'θero] *adj* insincere. **insinceridad** *sf* insincerity.

insinuar [insinu'ar] *v* insinuate, suggest. **insinuarse** *v* work one's way (into); make advances. **insinuación** *sf* insinuation; suggestiveness. **insinuante** *adj* insinuating; suggestive.

insípido [in'sipiðo] *adj* insipid, tasteless. **insipidez** *sf* tastelessness.

insistir [insis'tir] *v* insist; persist. **insistencia** *sf* insistence; persistence. **insistente** *adj* insistent; persistent.

insociable [inso'θjaβle] *adj* unsociable. **insociabilidad** *sf* unsociability, unsociableness.

insolación [insola'θjon] *sf* sunstroke. **insolar** *v* expose to the sun. **insolarse** *v* get sunstroke.

insolente [inso'lente] *adj* insolent. **insolencia** *sf* insolence.

insólito [in'solito] *adj* unusual.

insolvente [insol'βente] *adj* insolvent, penniless. **insoluble** *adj* insoluble. **insolvencia** *sf* insolvency.

insomne [in'somne] *s(m+f), adj* insomniac. **insomnio** *sm* insomnia.

insondable [inson'daβle] *adj* unfathomable.

insoportable [insopor'taβle] *adj* intolerable.

inspeccionar [inspekθjo'nar] *v* inspect. **inspección** *sf* inspection. **inspector, -a** *sm, sf* inspector.

inspirar [inspi'rar] *v* inhale; inspire. **inspiración** *sf* inhalation; inspiration. **inspirador** *adj* inspirational.

instable [in'staβle] *adj* unstable. **instabilidad** *sf* instability.

instalar [insta'lar] *v* install; establish. **instalación** *sf* installation; (*fábrica*) plant. **instalador** *sm* fitter.

instancia [instan'θja] *sf* petition; application form.

instante [in'stante] *sm* instant; moment. *adj* insistent. **instantánea** *sf* snapshot. **instantáneo** *adj* instantaneous. **instantemente** *adv* insistently.

instaurar [instau'rar] *v* set up; restore. **instauración** *sf* restoration. **instaurativo** *adj* restorative.

instigar [insti'gar] *v* instigate; incite. **instigación** *sf* instigation. **instigador, -a** *sm, sf* instigator.

instintivo [instin'tiβo] *adj* instinctive. **instinto** *sm* instinct.

*****instituir** [institu'ir] *v* institute. **institución** *sf* institution. **instituto** *sm* institute; state secondary school.

*****instruir** [instru'ir] *v* instruct. **instrucción** *sf* instruction; education; knowledge. **instructivo** *adj* instructive. **instructor, -a** *sm, sf* instructor. **instruido** *adj* educated.

instrumento [instru'mento] *sm* instrument. **instrumentación** *sf* orchestration. **instrumental** *adj* instrumental. **instrumentar** *v* orchestrate. **instrumentista** *s(m+f)* instrumentalist; instrument-maker.

insubordinar [insuβorði'nar] *v* incite to rebellion. **insubordinarse** *v* rebel. **insubordinación** *sf* insubordination. **insubordinado** *adj* insubordinate.

insubstancial [insuβstan'θjal] *adj* insubstantial.

insuficiente [insufi'θjente] *adj* insufficient; inadequate. **insuficiencia** *sf* insufficiency; inadequacy.

insufrible [insu'friβle] *adj* insufferable.

insular [insu'lar] *adj* insular.

insulso [in'sulso] *adj* dull; tasteless. **insulsez** *sf* tastelessness.

insultar [insul'tar] *v* insult. **insultador** *adj* also **insultante** insulting. **insulto** *sm* insult.

insuperable [insupe'raβle] *adj* insuperable.

insurgente [insur'xente] *s(m+f)* rebel. *adj* rebellious. insurrección *sf* rebellion. insurreccionarse *v* rebel. insurrecto, -a *s, adj* insurgent.

intacto [in'takto] *adj* intact.

intachable [inta'tʃaβle] *adj* irreproachable.

intangible [intan'xiβle] *adj* intangible. intangibilidad *sf* intangibility.

integrar [inte'grar] *v* integrate; compose; complete; repay. integración *sf* integration. integral *adj* integral. pan integral *sm* wholemeal bread. integrante *adj* integral. integridad *sf* integrity. integro *adj* entire, whole.

intelecto [inte'lekto] *sm* intellect. intelectual *s(m+f), adj* intellectual. intelectualidad *sf* intelligentsia. intelectualismo *sm* intellectualism.

inteligente [inteli'xente] *adj* intelligent. inteligencia *sf* intelligence; knowledge; comprehension. inteligibilidad *sf* intelligibility. inteligible *adj* intelligible.

intemperante [intempe'rante] *adj* intemperate. intemperancia *sf* intemperance.

intemperie [intem'perje] *sf* bad weather. estar a la intemperie be out in the open.

intempestivo [intempes'tiβo] *adj* inopportune.

intención [inten'θjon] *sf* intention. primera intención frankness. segunda intención duplicity. intencionadamente *adv* deliberately. intencionado *adj* deliberate. intencional *adj* intentional.

intenso [in'tenso] *adj* intense. intensidad *sf* intensity. intensificar *v* intensify. intensión *sf* intensity. intensivo *adj* intensive.

intentar [inten'tar] *v* try. intento *sm* attempt.

intercalar [interka'lar] *v* insert.

intercambio [inter'kambjo] *sm* interchange. intercambiar *v* interchange, exchange. intercambiable *adj* interchangeable.

interceder [interθe'ðer] *v* intercede. intercesión *sf* intercession.

interceptar [interθep'tar] *v* intercept; block. interceptación *sf* interception.

interdecir [interðe'θir] *v* prohibit. interdicción *sf also* interdicto *sm* prohibition.

interesar [intere'sar] *v* interest. interés *sm* interest. llevar interés bear interest. interesante *adj* interesting.

*interferir [interfe'rir] *v* interfere. interferencia *sf* interference.

interin ['interin] *sm* interim. interino *adj* provisional; acting.

interior [inte'rjor] *adj* interior; internal; inner; home. *sm* interior; inside; inland.

interjección [interxek'θjon] *sf* interjection.

intermedio [inter'meðjo] *sm* interval; interlude. *adj* intermediate. intermediar *v* mediate. intermediario, -a *s, adj* intermediary.

interminable [intermi'naβle] *adj* interminable.

intermisión [intermi'sjon] *sf* intermission. intermitente [intermi'tente] *adj* intermittent.

internacional [internaθjo'nal] *adj* international. internacionalismo *sm* internationalism. internacionalista *s(m+f)* internationalist.

internar [inter'nar] *v* intern; confine. internarse *v* penetrate; intrude. internamiento *sm* internment. interno *adj* internal; domestic. escuela interna *sf* boarding school.

interpelar [interpe'lar] *v* appeal to, implore. interpelación *sf* appeal.

*interponer [interpo'ner] *v* interpose. interponerse *v* intervene. interposición *sf* intervention; (*jur*) lodging of an appeal.

interpretar [interpre'tar] *v* interpret. interpretación *sf* interpretation. intérprete *s(m+f)* interpreter.

interrogar [interro'gar] *v* question. interrogación *sf* question; question mark. interrogativo *adj* interrogative. interrogatorio *sm* interrogation.

interrumpir [interrum'pir] *v* interrupt. interrupción *sf* interruption. interruptor *sm* electrical switch.

intervalo [inter'βalo] *sm* interval; gap.

*intervenir [interβe'nir] *v* intervene; interfere; participate; happen; control; (*med*) operate on; (*com*) audit. intervención *sf* intervention; control; operation; audit. interventor *sm* auditor; inspector; supervisor.

intestado [intes'taðo] *adj* intestate.

intestino [intes'tino] *adj* internal. *sm* intestine. intestinal *adj* intestinal.

intimar [inti'mar] *v* intimate; become close friends. intimación *sf* declaration.

intimidad *sf* intimacy. en la intimidad privately. íntimo *adj* intimate.

intimidar [intimi'ðar] *v* intimidate. intimidación *sf* intimidation.

intolerable [intole'raβle] *adj* intolerable. intolerancia *sf* intolerance. intolerante *adj* intolerant.

intoxicar [intoksi'kar] *v* poison. intoxicación *sf* poisoning.

intraducible [intraðu'θiβle] *adj* untranslatable.

intranquilo [intran'kilo] *adj* restless. intranquilidad *sf* restlessness.

intransigente [intransi'xente] *adj* intransigent. intransigencia *sf* intransigence.

intransitable [intransi'taβle] *adj* impassable.

intransitivo [intransi'tiβo] *adj* (*gram*) intransitive.

intratable [intra'taβle] *adj* intractable; unsociable.

intrépido [in'trepiðo] *adj* brave. intrepidez *sf* valour.

intrigar [intri'gar] *v* intrigue. intriga *sf* intrigue. intrigante *adj* intriguing.

intrincado [intrin'kaðo] *adj* intricate; entangled.

intrínseco [in'trinseko] *adj* intrinsic.

*introducir [introðu'θir] *v* introduce. introducción *sf* introduction. introductor *adj* introductory.

intruso [in'truso], -a *sm, sf* intruder. *adj* intrusive. intrusarse *v* intrude. intrusión *sf* intrusion.

intuición [intwi'θjon] *sf* intuition. intuir *v* feel; sense. intuitivo *adj* intuitive.

inundar [inun'dar] *v* flood. inundación *sf* flood. inundante *adj* flooding.

inusitado [inusi'taðo] *adj* unusual.

inútil [i'nutil] *adj* useless. inutilidad *sf* uselessness. inutilizar *v* render useless.

invadir [inβa'ðir] *v* invade. invasión *sf* invasion. invasor, -a *sm, sf* invader.

invalidar [inβali'ðar] *v* invalidate. invalidación *sf* invalidity. inválido, -a *sm, sf* invalid. *adj* invalid, void.

invariable [inva'rjaβle] *adj* invariable.

invencible [inβen'θiβle] *adj* invincible. invencibilidad *sf* invincibility.

inventar [inβen'tar] *v* invent. invención *sf* invention. inventivo *adj* inventive. invento *sm* invention. inventor, -a *sm, sf* inventor.

inventario [inβen'tarjo] *sm* inventory.

invernáculo [inβer'nakulo] *sm* also invernadero greenhouse, hothouse.

*invernar [inβer'nar] *v* winter; hibernate. invernada *sf* winter; hibernation. invernal *adj* wintry.

inverosímil [inβero'simil] *adj* improbable. inverosimilitud *sf* improbability.

invertebrado [inβerte'βraðo] *sm, adj* invertebrate.

*invertir [inβer'tir] *v* invert; (*com*) invest. inversión *sf* inversion; investment. inverso *adj* inverse, inverted. por la inversa the other way round.

investigar [inβesti'gar] *v* investigate. investigación *sf* investigation. investigador, -a *sm, sf* investigator; researcher.

*investir [inβes'tir] *v* invest; confer upon. investidura *sf* investiture.

inveterado [inβete'raðo] *adj* inveterate, confirmed.

invicto [in'βikto] *adj* undefeated.

invierno [in'βjerno] *sm* winter.

inviolable [inβjo'laβle] *adj* inviolable. inviolado *adj* inviolate.

invisible [inβi'siβle] *adj* invisible. invisibilidad *sf* invisibility.

invitar [inβi'tar] *v* invite; call on. invitar a una copa stand a drink. invitación *sf* invitation. invitado, -a *sm, sf* guest.

invocar [inβo'kar] *v* invoke. invocación *sf* invocation.

involuntario [inβolun'tarjo] *adj* involuntary.

invulnerable [inβulne'raβle] *adj* invulnerable. invulnerabilidad *sf* invulnerability.

inyectar [injek'tar] *v* inject. inyección *sf* injection. inyectado *adj* congested.

*ir [ir] *v* go; walk; come; suit. irse *v* go away. ir a medias go halves. ir tirando get by.

ira ['ira] *sf* anger. iracundia *sf* wrath. iracundo *adj* wrathful.

iris ['iris] *sm* (*anat*) iris. arco iris *sm* rainbow.

Irlanda [ir'landa] *sf* Ireland. irlandés *adj* Irish. *sm* Irishman; (*idioma*) Irish. irlandesa *sf* Irishwoman.

ironía [iro'nia] *sf* irony. irónico *adj* ironic(al).

irracional [irraθjo'nal] *adj* irrational. irracionalidad *sf* irrationality.

irradiar [irra'ðjar] *v* irradiate, radiate. irradiación *sf* irradiation.

irrazonable [irraθo'naβle] *adj* unreasonable.

irreal [irre'al] *adj* unreal. **irrealidad** *sf* unreality.

irreconciliable [irrekonθi'ljaβle] *adj* irreconcilable.

irrecuperable [irrekupe'raβle] *adj* irretrievable.

irreemplazable [irreempla'θaβle] *adj* irreplaceable.

irreflexión [irreflek'sjon] *sf* hastiness; thoughtlessness. **irreflexivo** hasty; thoughtless.

irrefrenable [irrefre'naβle] *adj* uncontrollable.

irrefutable [irrefu'taβle] *adj* irrefutable.

irregular [irregu'lar] *adj* irregular. **irregularidad** *sf* irregularity.

irreligioso [irreli'xjoso] *adj* irreligious.

irremediable [irreme'ðjaβle] *adj* incurable.

irreprimible [irrepri'miβle] *adj* irrepressible.

irresistible [irresis'tiβle] *adj* irresistible.

irresoluto [irreso'luto] *adj* irresolute. **irresoluble** *adj* unsolvable. **irresolución** *sf* irresolution, indecision.

irrespetuoso [irrespe'twoso] *adj* disrespectful.

irresponsable [irrespon'saβle] *adj* irresponsible. **irresponsabilidad** *sf* irresponsibility.

irrigar [irri'gar] *v* irrigate. **irrigación** *sf* irrigation. **irrigador** *sm* sprinkler.

irritable [irri'taβle] *adj* irritable. **irritabilidad** *sf* irritability. **irritación** *sf* irritation. **irritante** *sm, adj* irritant. **irritar** *v* irritate.

isla ['isla] *sf* island. **en isla** isolated. **isleño, -a** *sm, sf* islander.

Islandia [is'landja] *sf* Iceland. **islandés, -esa** *sm, sf* Icelander; *sm* (*idioma*) Icelandic. **islandés** *adj* Icelandic.

istmo ['istmo] *sm* isthmus.

Italia [i'talja] *sf* Italy. **italiano, -a** *s, adj* Italian.

itinerario [itine'rarjo] *sm* itinerary.

izar [i'θar] *v* hoist.

izquierda [iθ'kjerða] *sf* left; left hand; left wing. **mantenerse a la izquierda** keep left. **izquierdo** *adj* left; left-handed.

J

jabalí [xaβa'li] *sm* wild boar.

jabalina [xaβa'lina] *sf* javelin; (*zool*) wild sow.

jabón [xa'βon] *sm* soap. **jabón de tocador** toilet soap. **jabonar** *v* soap. **jabonera** *sf* soap-dish. **jabonoso** *adj* soapy.

jaca ['xaka] *sf* pony.

jacinto [xa'θinto] *sm* hyacinth.

jactarse [xak'tarse] *v* boast. **jactancia** *sf* boasting. **jactancioso** *adj* boastful.

jadear [xaðe'ar] *v* pant. **jadeante** *adj* panting. **jadeo** *sm* pant; panting.

jalear [xale'ar] *v* urge on. **jaleo** *sm* row, din. **armar un jaleo** start a row.

jamás [xa'mas] *adv* never. **nunca jamás** never ever.

jamón [xa'mon] *sm* ham. **jamón serrano** cured ham.

Japón [xa'pon] *sm* Japan. **japonés** *s(m+f), adj* Japanese.

jaque ['xake] *sm* (*ajedrez*) check.

jaqueca [xa'keka] *sf* migraine. **dar jaqueca a** (*fam*) pester.

jarabe [xa'raβe] *sm* syrup.

jarana [xa'rana] *sf* spree; rumpus; trick. **dar jarabe a uno** (*fam*) butter someone up.

jardín [xar'ðin] *sm* garden. **jardinería** *sf* gardening. **jardinero, -a** *sm, sf* gardener.

jarra ['xarra] *sf* jug, pitcher. **jarro** *sm* jug; jar. **jarrón** *sm* vase.

jaula ['xaula] *sf* cage; crate; playpen.

jazmín [xaθ'min] *sm* jasmine.

jefe ['xefe] *sm* chief; head; leader. **jefa** *sf* head; manageress. **jefatura** *sf* leadership; managership; chieftaincy. **jefatura de policía** police headquarters.

jengibre [xen'xiβre] *sm* ginger.

jeque ['xeke] *sm* sheikh.

jerarquía [xerar'kia] *sf* hierarchy. **jerárquico** *adj* hierarchical.

jerez [xe'reθ] *sm* sherry.

jerga ['xerga] *sf also* **jerigonza** jargon.

jeringa [xe'ringa] *sf* syringe. **jeringar** *v* syringe; (*fam*) annoy.

jeroglífico [xero'glifiko] *s, adj* hieroglyphic.

jersey [xer'sei] *sm* jersey.

jesuita [xesu'ita] *sm, adj* Jesuit. **jesuítico** *adj* jesuitical.

jeta ['xeta] *sf* snout; thick lips; (*fam*) face, mug. **poner jeta** pull a face.

jilguero [xil'gero] *sm* goldfinch.

jinete [xi'nete] *sm* horseman; saddle horse; thoroughbred horse. **jinetear** *v* ride on horseback.

jirafa [xi'rafa] *sf* giraffe.

jocoso [xo'koso] *adj* amusing. **jocosidad** *sf* humour.

jofaina [xo'faina] *sf* washbowl.

jornada [xor'nada] *sf* journey; working day; session; expedition; (*teatro*) act. **al fin de la jornada** at the end of the day. **jornal** *sm* day's wage. **jornalero** *sm* day labourer.

joroba [xo'roβa] *sf* hump; (*fam*) pest. **jorobado, -a** *s, adj* hunchback.

jota ['xota] *sf* letter *j*; jot; Spanish dance.

joven ['xoβen] *adj* young. **jovenes** *s(m+f) pl* youth.

joya ['xoja] *sf* jewel. **joyería** *sf* jewellery. **joyero** *sm* jeweller.

jubilar [xuβi'lar] *v* retire; pension off. **jubilarse** *v* retire; rejoice. **jubilación** *sf* pension; retirement; jubilation.

jubileo [xuβi'leo] *sm* jubilee; comings and goings *pl*.

júbilo ['xuβilo] *sm* jubilation, rejoicing. **jubiloso** *adj* jubilant.

judía [xu'ðia] *sf* bean. **judía blanca** haricot bean. **judía escarlata** runner bean. **judía verde** French bean.

judicial [xuði'θjal] *adj* judicial. **judicatura** *sf* judicature.

judío [xu'ðio], **-a** *sm, sf* Jew. *adj* Jewish. **judaico** *adj* Jewish. **judaismo** *sm* Judaism.

juego ['xwego] *sm* game; sport; gambling; play; (*platos, tazas, etc.*) set; service.

juerga ['xwerga] *sf* (*fam*) spree, binge. **juergista** *s(m+f)* reveller.

jueves ['xweβes] *sm* Thursday.

juez [xweθ] *sm* judge, justice. **juez de hecho** juror.

***jugar** [xu'gar] *v* play; bet; gamble. **jugarse** *v* bet; risk. **jugada** move; throw; stroke; shot; play. **mala jugada** dirty trick. **jugador, -a** *sm, sf* player; gambler.

juglar [xu'glar], **-a** *sm, sf* minstrel.

jugo ['xugo] *sm* juice; sap. **jugoso** *adj* juicy.

juguete [xu'gete] *sm* toy; plaything. **juguetear** *v* frolic. **jugueteo** *sm* frolicking. **juguetería** *sf* toyshop.

juicio ['xwiθjo] *sm* (*jur*) trial; judgment; opinion; sense. **a juicio de** in the opinion of. **perder el juicio** lose one's mind. **juicioso** *adj* judicious.

julio ['xuljo] *sm* July.

jumento [xu'mento] *sm* ass.

junco[1] ['xunko] *sm* (*bot*) reed.

junco[2] *sm* (*mar*) junk.

jungla ['xungla] *sf* jungle.

junio ['xunjo] *sm* June.

junquera [xun'kera] *sf* (*bot*) rush.

junquillo [xun'kiʎo] *sm* (*bot*) jonquil.

juntar [xun'tar] *v* join; assemble; unite; collect. **juntarse** *v* meet; join; gather; live together. **junta** *sf* meeting; session; board; council; junta. **junto** *adj* joined, united, together. *adv* **junto a** near. **muy junto** very close.

juramentar [xuramen'tar] *v* swear in. **juramentarse** *v* take an oath. **jura** *sf* oath; swearing. **jurado** *adj* sworn; *sm* jury. **jurado de cuentas** chartered accountant. **juramento** *sm* oath; curse. **juramento falso** perjury. **jurar** *v* swear. **jurar al cargo** take the oath of office.

jurídico [xu'riðiko] *adj* juridical, legal.

jurisconsulto [xuriskon'sulto] *sm* legal expert. **jurisdicción** *sf* jurisdiction. **jurisprudencia** *sf* jurisprudence. **jurista** *sm* jurist, lawyer.

justa ['xusta] *sf* joust; contest.

justificar [xustifi'kar] *v* justify. **justificarse** *v* clear oneself. **justamente** *adv* justly; exactly. **¡justamente!** precisely! **justicia** *sf* justice; execution. **justiciable** *adj* actionable. **justiciero** *adj* just. **justificable** *adj* justifiable. **justificación** *sf* justification. **justificado** *adj* justified.

justo ['xusto] *adj* just; lawful; precise. *adv* exactly; tightly.

juvenil [xuβe'nil] *adj* youthful. *s(m+f)* junior. **juventud** *sf* youth.

juzgar [xuθ'gar] *v* judge; consider. **juzgar mal** misjudge. **juzgado** *sm* court.

K

kaki ['kaki] *sm, adj* khaki.

kilo ['kilo] *sm* kilo.

kilogramo [kilo'gramo] *sm* kilogramme.

kilolitro [kilo'litro] *sm* kilolitre.

kilómetro [ki'lometro] *sm* kilometre.
kilométrico *adj* kilometric.
kilovatio [kilo'βatjo] *sm* kilowatt.
kiosco ['kjosko] *sm* kiosk.

L

la [la] *art f* the. *pron* her, it.
laberinto [laβe'rinto] *sm* labyrinth; maze.
labio ['laβjo] *sm* lip. **labial** *adj* labial.
labor [la'βor] *sf* work; labour. **laborador** *sm* worker; farmer. **laborar** *v* work; till. **laborear** *v* work; till; mine. **laboreo** *sm* working; tilling; mining. **laborioso** *adj* industrious; laborious. **laborismo** *sm* (*pol*) Labour party. **laborista** *s(m+f)* Labour-party member.
laboratorio [laβora'torjo] *sm* laboratory.
labrar [la'βrar] *v* fashion; carve; work; cultivate; build; bring about. **labradero** *adj* workable; arable. **labrador, -a** *sm, sf* peasant. **labranza** *sf* farming; farmland. **labriego** *sm* peasant; farmhand.
laburno [la'βurno] *sm* laburnum.
laca ['laka] *sf* lacquer, varnish.
lacayo [la'kajo] *sm* lackey.
lacerar [laθe'rar] *v* lacerate; harm; (*fruta*) damage. **laceración** *sf* laceration; damage.
lacio ['laθjo] *adj* limp; lank; withered.
lacónico [la'koniko] *adj* laconic.
lacrar[1] [la'krar] *v* infect; damage. **lacra** *sf* blemish.
lacrar[2] *v* seal. **lacre** *sm* sealing wax.
lacrimoso [lakri'moso] *adj* tearful.
lácteo ['lakteo] *adj* milky. **vía láctea** *sf* Milky Way. **productos lácteos** *sm pl* dairy products. **lactante** *adj* suckling; nursling. **lactar** *v* suckle.
ladear [laðe'ar] *v* tip, tilt, overturn; deviate; skirt. **ladeo** *sm* tipping, tilting.
ladera [la'ðera] *sf* slope; hillside.
ladino [la'ðino] *adj* multilingual; crafty.
lado ['laðo] *sm* side; way; space; direction; protection. **al lado** close. **al lado de** beside. **por el lado de** in the direction of.
ladrar [la'ðrar] *v* bark. **ladrido** *sm* bark; barking.
ladrillo [la'ðiʎo] *sm* brick, tile.
ladrón [la'ðron], **-a** *sm, sf* thief, robber. *sm* sluice gate; multiple socket.

lagarto [la'garto] *sm* lizard.
lago ['lago] *sm* lake.
lágrima ['lagrima] *sf* tear; drop. **verter lágrimas** shed tears. **lagrimoso** *adj* tearful.
laguna [la'guna] *sf* lagoon; pond; gap.
laico ['laiko] *adj* lay, secular.
lamentar [lamen'tar] *v* lament; regret; grieve. **lamentarse** *v* complain. **lamentable** *adj* deplorable. **lamentación** *sf* lamentation, lament. **lamento** *sm* lament; mourning. **lamentoso** *adj* lamentable, mournful.
lamer [la'mer] *v* lick.
lámina ['lamina] *sf* metal sheet; picture; engraving. **laminar** *v* laminate.
lámpara ['lampara] *sf* lamp; light; valve.
lana ['lana] *sf* wool; fleece. **lana de vidrio** fibreglass. **lanudo** *adj* woolly; shaggy.
lance ['lanθe] *sm* throw; event; move; stroke. **lance de fortuna** chance. **de lance** second-hand.
lanceta [lan'θeta] *sf* lancet.
lancha ['lantʃa] *sf* launch; flagstone. **lancha salvavidas** lifeboat. **lanchero** *sm* boatman.
langosta [lan'gosta] *sf* lobster; locust.
***languidecer** [langiðe'θer] *v* languish. **languidez** *sf* languor. **lánguido** *adj* languid.
lanza ['lanθa] *sf* spear; lance; pike; nozzle.
lanzar [lan'θar] *v* throw; fling; evict. **lanzarse** *v* spring. **lanzamiento** *sm* launching.
lápida ['lapiða] *sf* stone slab; tablet.
lápiz ['lapiθ] *sm* pencil. **lapicero** *sm* pencil-holder.
lapso ['lapso] *sm* lapse.
lar [lar] *sm* hearth; home.
largar [lar'gar] *v* loosen; free. **largarse** *v* go away.
largo ['largo] *adj* long; (*fam*) generous. *sm* length. **a lo largo de** the length of. **dar largas** a delay. **largueza** *sf* length; generosity.
laringe [la'rinxe] *sf* larynx.
larva ['larβa] *sf* larva.
lascivo [las'θiβo] *adj* lascivious. **lascivia** *sf* lasciviousness.
laso ['laso] *adj* weary. **lasitud** *sf* lassitude.
lástima ['lastima] *sf* pity; complaint. **¡qué lástima!** what a pity! **lastimar** *v* hurt. **lastimarse** *v* pity; complain. **lastimoso** *adj* pitiable, pitiful.

lastre ['lastre] *sm* ballast.

lata ['lata] *sf* tin, can; (*fam*) nuisance. **dar la lata** (*fam*) pester.

latente [la'tente] *adj* latent.

lateral [late'ral] *adj* lateral, side.

látigo ['latiɣo] *sm* whip. **latigazo** *sm* whiplash.

latín [la'tin] *sm* Latin. **latinoamericano, -a** *s, adj* Latin American.

latir [la'tir] *v* beat; throb. **latido** *sm* heartbeat; throb.

latitud [lati'tuð] *sf* latitude; breadth. **lato** *adj* broad.

latón [la'ton] *sm* brass.

latoso [la'toso] *adj* (*fam*) annoying; boring.

latrocinio [latro'θinjo] *sm* theft.

laúd [la'uð] *sm* lute.

laudable [lau'ðaβle] *adj* praiseworthy.

laurel [lau'rel] *sm* laurel; laurel wreath. **laureado** *adj* laureate. **laurear** *v* honour; reward. **lauro** *sm* (*fig*) glory.

lava ['laβa] *sf* lava.

lavar [la'βar] *v* wash. **lavable** *adj* washable. **lavabo** *sm* wash-basin. **lavación** *sf* lotion; wash. **lavadero** *sm* washing-place. **lavado** *sm* wash; washing. **lavadora** *sf* washing machine. **lavandería** *sf* laundry.

laxante [lak'sante] *sm* laxative. **laxidad** *sf* laxity.

lazo ['laθo] *sm* lasso; loop; bow; knot; snare; link.

leal [le'al] *adj* loyal. **lealdad** *sf* loyalty.

lebrel [le'βrel] *sm* greyhound.

lección [lek'θjon] *sf* lesson. **lector, -a** *sm, sf* reader; lecturer. **lectura** *sf* reading matter.

leche ['letʃe] *sf* milk. **lechería** *sf* dairy. **lechero** *sm* milkman.

lecho ['letʃo] *sm* bed; layer.

lechuga [le'tʃuɣa] *sf* lettuce.

lechuza [le'tʃuθa] *sf* owl.

*leer [le'er] *v* read.

legación [leɣa'θjon] *sf* legation. **legado** *sm* legacy; ambassador.

legal [le'ɣal] *adj* legal; lawful. **legalidad** *sf* legality. **legalización** *sf* legalization. **legalizar** *v* legalize.

legar [le'ɣar] *v* bequeath; depute.

legendario [lexen'darjo] *adj* legendary.

legible [le'xiβle] *adj* legible.

legión [le'xjon] *sf* legion.

legislar [lexis'lar] *v* legislate. **legislación** *sf* legislation. **legislador, -a** *sm, sf* legislator.

legislativo *adj* legislative. **legislatura** *sf* legislature.

legitimar [lexiti'mar] *v* prove; justify. **legitimidad** *sf* legitimacy. **legítimo** *adj* legitimate.

lego ['leɣo] *adj* lay. *sm* layman.

legua ['leɣwa] *sf* league.

legumbre [le'ɣumbre] *sf* vegetable.

lejía [le'xia] *sf* bleach.

lejos ['lexos] *adv* far away. **a lo lejos** in the distance. *sm* perspective; background. **lejanía** *sf* distance. **lejano** *adj* far-away.

lema ['lema] *sf* motto.

lencería [lenθe'ria] *sf* linen goods; lingerie.

lengua ['lengwa] *sf* tongue; language. **trabarse la lengua** become tongue-tied. **lenguaje** *sm* language; speech; style. **lenguado** [len'gwaðo] *sm* (*zool*) sole. **lengüeta** [len'gweta] *sf* (*de zapato*) tongue.

lenidad [leni'ðað] *sf* lenience; mildness.

lente ['lente] *s*(*m+f*) lens. **lente de aumento** magnifying glass. **lentes** *pl* glasses, spectacles. **lentes de contacto** contact lenses.

lenteja [len'texa] *sf* lentil.

lento ['lento] *adj* slow. **lentitud** *sf* slowness.

leña ['leɲa] *sf* firewood.

león [le'on] *sm* lion. **leona** *sf* lioness. **leonino** *adj* leonine.

lepra ['lepra] *sf* leprosy. **leproso** *adj* leprous.

lesión [le'sjon] *sf* injury. **lesionar** *v* injure. **lesivo** *adj* injurious.

letanía [leta'nia] *sf* litany; long list.

letargo [le'tarɣo] *sm* lethargy. **letárgico** *adj* lethargic.

letra ['letra] *sf* letter; handwriting; lyric; (*com*) draft. **Letras** *sf pl* literature; Arts. **letra mayúscula** capital letter. **letra minúscula** lower-case letter. **letrado** *sm* lawyer. **letrero** *sm* label; sign.

leva ['leβa] *sf* (*tecn*) cam; lever. **árbol de levas** camshaft.

levadizo [leβa'ðiθo] *adj* that can be lifted. **puente levadizo** *sm* drawbridge.

levadura [leβa'ðura] *sf* leaven, yeast.

levantar [leβan'tar] *v* lift; raise; erect. **levantarse** *v* rise, get up. **levantamiento** *sm* raising; insurrection. **levantado** *adj* raised; lofty.

leve ['leβe] *adj* slight; trifling. **levedad** *sf* lightness; slightness.

léxico ['leksiko] *adj* lexical. *sm* dictionary; vocabulary.

ley [lej] *sf* law; loyalty; standard. **a toda ley** according to rule. **tener ley a** be very fond of.

leyenda [le'jenda] *sf* legend.

liar [ljar] *v* bind; tie up; (*fam*) involve. **liarlas** *v* (*fam*) clear off. **liarse** *v* (*fam*) join; start an affair; get involved.

libélula [li'βelula] *sf* dragonfly.

liberal [liβe'ral] *adj* generous. **liberalidad** *sf* generosity.

libertar [liβer'tar] *v also* **liberar** liberate, free. **libertad** *sf* freedom; independence. **libertador, -a** *sm, sf* liberator.

libertinaje [liβerti'naxe] *sm* licentiousness. **libertino, -a** *s, adj* libertine.

libra ['liβra] *sf* (*peso*) pound. **libra esterlina** pound sterling.

librar [li'βrar] *v* free; exempt; deliver; despatch; expedite; (*com*) draw; pass sentence. **librador, -a** *sm, sf* liberator. **libramiento** *sm* delivery; rescue; (*com*) draft. **libranza** *sf* (*com*) draft. **libre** *adj* free; vacant; isolated; loose.

librería [liβre'ria] *sf* bookshop; bookselling; bookcase. **librero, -a** *sm, sf* bookseller.

libreta [li'βreta] *sf* notebook; cashbook; one-pound loaf.

libro ['liβro] *sm* book. **libro diario** journal. **libro mayor** ledger.

licenciar [liθen'θjar] *v* license. **licenciarse** *v* graduate. **licencia** *sf* licence; degree; (*mil*) leave. **licenciado, -a** *sm, sf* graduate; *sm* lawyer; discharged soldier. **licenciatura** *sf* Bachelor's degree.

licencioso [liθen'θjoso] *adj* licentious.

liceo [li'θeo] *sm* lyceum; secondary school.

licitar [liθi'tar] *v* (*subasta*) bid. **licitación** *sf* bid. **licitador, -a** *sm, sf* bidder.

lícito ['liθito] *adj* authorized.

licor [li'kor] *sm* liquor; liqueur.

líder [li'δer] *sm* leader.

lidiar [li'δjar] *v* (*toros*) fight. **lidia** *sf* bullfight. **lidiador** *sm* bullfighter.

liebre ['ljeβre] *sf* hare. **coger una liebre** (*fam*) come a cropper.

lienzo ['ljenθo] *sm* canvas; linen.

liga ['liga] *sf* garter; league; alloy. **ligadura** *sf* ligature; bond. **ligamento** *sm* ligament; bond. **ligar** *v* bind; tie; unite; alloy. **ligarse** *v* join; band together.

ligero [li'xero] *adj* light; swift; frivolous.

ligereza *sf* lightness; swiftness; frivolousness.

lija ['lixa] *sf* sandpaper; (*zool*) dogfish. **lijar** *v* sandpaper.

lila ['lila] *sf* (*bot*) lilac. *sm* (*color*) lilac. *adj* (*fam*) foolish.

lima¹ ['lima] *sf* file; polish. **limar** *v* file; polish; undermine. **limadura** *sf* filing.

lima² *sf* lime; lime tree.

limaza [li'maθa] *sf* slug.

limitar [limi'tar] *v* limit. **limitación** *sf* limitation. **límite** *sm* limit; boundary.

limón [li'mon] *sm* lemon; lemon tree. **limonada** *sf* lemonade. **limonero** *sm* lemon tree.

limosna [li'mosna] *sf* alms *pl*.

limpiabotas [limpja'βotas] *sm invar* bootblack.

limpiadera [limpja'δera] *sf* clothes brush.

limpiadientes [limpja'δjentes] *sm invar* toothpick.

limpiar [lim'pjar] *v* clean; clear; wipe; prune; weed. **limpiador, -a** *sm, sf* cleaner. **limpiadura** *sf* cleaning. **limpieza** *sf* cleanness. **limpio** *adj* clean; clear; pure. **jugar limpio** play fair. **poner en limpio** copy out.

linaje [li'naxe] *sm* lineage. **linaje humano** mankind.

linaza [li'naθa] *sf* linseed.

lince ['linθe] *sm* lynx.

linchar [lin't∫ar] *v* lynch. **linchamiento** *sm* lynching.

lindar [lin'dar] *v* **lindar con** border; adjoin. **linde** *sf* boundary. **lindero** *sm* limit.

lindo ['lindo] *adj* pretty; handsome; nice. **de lo lindo** a great deal. **lindeza** *sf* beauty; niceness. **lindura** *sf* prettiness.

línea ['linea] *sf* line; boundary; class. **línea aérea** airline. **lineal** *adj* linear.

lingüista [lin'gwista] *s(m+f)* linguist. **lingüística** *sf* linguistics. **lingüístico** *adj* linguistic.

linimento [lini'mento] *sm* liniment.

lino ['lino] *sm* linen.

linóleo [li'noleo] *sm* linoleum.

linterna [lin'terna] *sf* lantern; lamp; torch; lighthouse.

lío ['lio] *sm* parcel; trouble; mess. **armar un lío** raise a rumpus.

liquidar [liki'δar] *v* liquefy; liquidate, settle up. **liquidez** *sf* fluidity. **líquido** *sm, adj* liquid; (*com*) net. **líquido imponible** net taxable amount.

lira ['lira] sf lyre; inspiration.

lírica ['lirika] sf lyric poetry. lírico adj lyric.

lirio ['lirjo] sm lily.

lirón [li'ron] sm dormouse. dormir como un lirón sleep like a log.

lisiar [li'sjar] v cripple. lisiado adj crippled.

liso ['liso] adj smooth.

lisonjear [lisonxe'ar] v flatter. lisonja sf flattery. lisonjero adj flattering.

lista ['lista] sf list; stripe; band. a listas striped. lista de correos poste restante. lista de platos menu.

listo ['listo] adj ready; finished; clever.

litera [li'tera] sf berth; bunk; (cama) litter.

literato [lite'rato], -a sm, sf literary person. adj literary. literatura sf literature.

litigar [liti'gar] v go to law, litigate. litigación sf litigation. litigio sm lawsuit. litigioso adj contentious.

litografía [lito'grafja] sf lithograph; lithography. litográfico adj lithographic.

litoral [lito'ral] adj coastal. sm shore.

litro ['litro] sm litre.

liturgia [litur'xia] sf liturgy. litúrgico adj liturgical.

liviano [li'βjano] adj light; trivial; lewd. liviandad sf lightness; triviality; lewdness.

lívido ['liβiðo] adj livid.

lo [lo] art m him, it; that, what.

loable [lo'aβle] adj praiseworthy. loa sf praise. loador adj praising. loar v praise.

lobo ['loβo] sm wolf. lobo marino seal. lobero adj wolfish.

lóbrego ['loβrego] adj gloomy, murky. lobreguecer v darken; grow dark. lobreguez sf gloom; murk.

lóbulo ['loβulo] sm lobe.

local [lo'kal] adj local. sm place. localidad sf locality; (teatro) seat. sacar localidades get tickets. localizar v localize.

loción [lo'θjon] sf lotion.

loco ['loko], -a adj mad; excessive. sm, sf mad person. volverse loco go mad. locura sf madness; folly. hacer locuras act madly.

locomoción [lokomo'θjon] sf locomotion. locomotora sf locomotive.

locuaz [lo'kwaθ] adj talkative. locuacidad sf talkativeness.

locutor [loku'tor], -a sm, sf radio announcer; commentator.

lodo ['loðo] sm mud. lodoso adj muddy.

lógica ['loxika] sf logic. lógico adj logical. lógicamente adv logically; naturally. logística sf logistics.

lograr [lo'grar] v get; achieve. lograrse v succeed. logrería sf profiteering. logro sm success; profit; usury.

loma ['loma] sf hill; slope.

lombriz [lom'briθ] sf worm; earthworm. lombriz solitaria tapeworm.

lomo ['lomo] sm (carne) loin; (animal) back; (libro) spine.

lona ['lona] sf canvas.

Londres ['londres] sm London.

longaniza [longa'niθa] sf pork sausage.

longevidad [lonxeβi'ðað] sf longevity.

longitud [lonxi'tuθ] sf longitude. longitudinal adj longitudinal.

lonja ['lonxa] sf (de carne) slice; grocer's shop; strap; church porch.

loro ['loro] sm parrot.

losa ['losa] sf stone slab; tile.

lote ['lote] sm (com) lot; share; prize.

loza ['loθa] sf crockery; pottery.

lozano [lo'θano] adj luxuriant; lush; robust; sprightly. lozanía sf luxuriance.

lubrificar [luβrifi'kar] v also lubricar lubricate. lubricación sf also lubrificación lubrication. lubricante sm, adj also lubrificante lubricant.

lúcido ['luθiðo] adj lucid; shining. lucidez sf lucidity; brilliance.

luciérnaga [lu'θjernaga] sf glow-worm.

*lucir [lu'θir] v shine; gleam; excel; show off. lucirse v be successful; dress up.

lucro ['lukro] sm profit, gain. lucros y daños profit and loss.

luchar [lu'tʃar] v fight, struggle. lucha sf fight, struggle. lucha libre all-in wrestling. luchador, -a sm, sf fighter.

luego ['lwego] adv then; next; later; presently. conj as; therefore. luego que as soon as. desde luego of course. hasta luego so long.

lugar [lu'gar] sm place; occasion; chance; opportunity. en lugar de instead of. tener lugar take place.

lugarteniente [lugarte'njente] sm lieutenant.

lúgubre ['luguβre] adj lugubrious.

lujo ['luxo] sm luxury. de lujo de luxe. lujoso adj luxurious.

lujuria [lu'xurja] sf lust; lechery. lujuriar v lust. lujurioso adj lustful; lecherous.

lumbago [lum'bago] *sm* lumbago.

lumbre ['lumbre] *sf* fire; brightness; light; skylight. echar lumbres spark. lumbrera *sf* luminary; skylight; air vent; (*fig*) leading light.

luminoso [lumi'noso] *adj* bright; luminous.

luna ['luna] *sf* moon. luna de miel honeymoon. lunar *adj* lunar. lunático, -a *s, adj* lunatic.

lunar [lu'nar] *sm* mole; beauty spot; blemish.

lunes ['lunes] *sm* Monday.

lupa ['lupa] *sf* magnifying glass.

lupanar [lupa'nar] *sm* brothel.

lustrar [lus'trar] *v* polish; purify. lustre *sm* lustre; gloss; splendour.

luto ['luto] *sm* mourning; bereavement. ir de luto be in mourning.

Luxemburgo [luksem'burgo] *sm* Luxembourg.

luz [luθ] *sf* light; daylight; window. a todas luces clearly. dar la luz put the light on.

LL

llaga ['ʎaga] *sf* ulcer; sore; wound. llagar *v* ulcerate; wound.

llama¹ ['ʎama] *sf* (*fuego*) flame. estar en llamas burst into flames. llamear *v* blaze.

llama² *sf* (*pantano*) swamp.

llama² *sf* (*zool*) llama.

llamar [ʎa'mar] *v* call; appeal to; name; attract. llamarse *v* be called. ¿cómo se llama? what is your name? llamado *adj* so-called. llamada *sf* call; summons. llamador, -a *sm, sf* caller; messenger.

llana ['ʎana] *sf* trowel.

llano ['ʎano] *adj* flat; plain; straightforward. número llano Roman numeral. *sm* plain; flatness. llanura *sf* evenness; flat land.

llanta ['ʎanta] *sf* iron hoop; rim.

llanto ['ʎanto] *sm* lament; crying.

llave ['ʎaβe] *sf* key; spanner. llave maestra skeleton key. llave inglesa adjustable spanner.

llegar [ʎe'gar] *v* arrive; reach; suffice;

happen. llegarse *v* come *or* go round. llegar a end up at. llegar a ser become. llegada *sf* arrival. a la llegada on arrival.

llenar [ʎe'nar] *v* fill; be satisfied. lleno *adj* full; covered; complete. de lleno completely. llenura *sf* abundance.

llevar [ʎe'βar] *v* take; carry; wear; deal with; sever; charge; manage; (*tiempo*) spend. llevar a cabo carry out. llevarse *v* take away. llevarse bien con get on well with.

llorar [ʎo'rar] *v* weep, cry; mourn. llorón, -ona *adj* weepy. lloroso *adj* tearful.

llover [ʎo'βer] *v* rain. llover a cántaros pour down. lloverse *v* (*tejado*) leak. lloviznar *v* drizzle. llovizna *sf* drizzle.

lluvia *sf* rain. lluvioso *adj* rainy.

M

macabro [ma'kaβro] *adj* macabre.

macarrón [makar'ron] *sm* macaroon. macarrones *sm pl* macaroni *sing*.

macanudo [maka'nuðo] *adj* (*fam*) terrific.

maceta [ma'θeta] *sf* flowerpot.

macilento [maθi'lento] *adj* lean; wan.

macizo [ma'θiθo] *adj* solid. *sm* mass; flowerbed. macizar *v* fill up.

mácula ['makula] *sf* spot, stain. macular *v* spot, stain.

machacar [matʃa'kar] *v* pound; crush; bombard; (*fig*) harp on. machacón, -ona *sm, sf* bore; swot. machaconería *sf* tiresomeness. machaqueo *sm* pounding; crushing; harping.

machete [ma'tʃete] *sm* machete; hunting-knife.

macho ['matʃo] *adj* male; masculine; virile. *sm* (*fam*) he-man; sledgehammer; he-mule. machismo *sm* virility.

machucar [matʃu'kar] *v* beat; pound; bruise.

madeja [ma'ðexa] *sf* skein; mop of hair.

madera [ma'ðera] *sf* wood, timber; horn. tener madera de have the makings of. maderería *sf* timber yard. madero *sm* beam; log.

madrastra [ma'ðrastra] *sf* stepmother.

madre ['maðre] *sf* mother. madre política mother-in-law.

madreselva [maðre'selβa] *sf* honeysuckle.

madriguera [maðri'gera] *sf* den; warren.

madrina [ma'ðrina] *sf* godmother; patroness. **madrina de boda** bridesmaid.

madrugar [maðru'gar] *v* rise early. **madrugada** *sf* early morning. **madrugador, -a** *sm, sf* early riser.

madurar [maðu'rar] *v* mature, ripen. **madurez** *sf* maturity; wisdom. **maduro** *adj* ripe; middle-aged.

maestría [maes'tria] *sf* mastery. **maestrar** *v* direct; conduct; domineer. **maestra** *sf* mistress; schoolmistress. **maestro** *sm* master; teacher; *adj* master, main, chief. **magistral** *adj* masterly.

magia ['maxja] *sf* magic. **mágico** *adj* magic(al). **mágico** *sm* magician.

magistrado [maxi'straðo] *sm* magistrate. **magistratura** *sf* judicature.

magnánimo [mag'nanimo] *adj* magnanimous. **magnanimidad** *sf* magnanimity.

magnético [mag'netiko] *adj* magnetic. **magnetismo** *sm* magnetism. **magnetizar** *v* magnetize.

magnetofón [magneto'fon] *sm* also **magnetófono** tape recorder. **cinta magnetofónica** recording tape.

magnífico [mag'nifiko] *adj* magnificent. **magnificencia** *sf* magnificence.

magnitud [magni'tuð] *sf* size, magnitude.

mago ['mago] *sm* magician, wizard.

magro ['magro] *adj* thin, lean. *sm* lean meat.

magullar [magu'ʎar] *v* bruise. **magulladura** *sf* bruise.

maíz [ma'iθ] *sm* maize. **harina de maíz** cornflour.

majadero [maxa'ðero] *adj* silly; boring. *sm* pestle. **majadería** *sf* nonsense. **majadura** *sf* crushing, pounding. **majar** *v* crush, pound.

majestad [maxes'taθ] *sf* majesty; royalty; grandeur. **majestuoso** *adj* majestic; stately; solemn.

majo ['maxo], **-a** *sm, sf* dandy. *adj* sporty; swaggering; genial.

mal [mal] *adj* V **malo**. *adv* badly; poorly; wrongly. *sm* wrong; evil; illness; harm. **de mal en peor** from bad to worse. **echar a mal** despise; waste. **llevar a mal** take offence at. **mal que bien** somehow or other.

malaconsejado [malakonse'xaðo] *adj* ill-advised.

malacostumbrado [malakostum'braðo] *adj* spoiled.

malaventura [malaβen'tura] *sf* misfortune. **malaventurado** *adj* unlucky.

malbaratar [malβara'tar] *v* squander; undersell.

malcontento [malkon'tento], **-a** *sm, sf* malcontent. *adj* discontented.

malcriado [malkri'aðo] *adj* ill-bred. **malcriar** *v* spoil.

maldad [mal'ðaθ] *sf* wickedness.

*** maldecir** [malðe'θir] *v* curse. **maldecir de** speak ill of. **maldición** *sf* curse. **maldito** *adj* accursed.

maleable [male'aβle] *adj* malleable. **maleabilidad** *sf* malleability.

malear [male'ar] *v* damage; spoil. **malearse** *v* go wrong.

maleficio [male'fiθjo] *sm* injury; witchcraft. **maleficiar** *v* hurt; bewitch.

malestar [males'tar] *sm* uneasiness.

maleta [ma'leta] *sf* suitcase; (*auto*) boot. **hacer la maleta** pack up.

malévolo [ma'leβolo] *adj* malevolent. **malevolencia** *sf* malevolence.

maleza [ma'leθa] *sf* thicket; weeds *pl*.

malgastar [malgas'tar] *v* squander, waste. **malgastador, -a** *s, adj* spendthrift.

malhablado [mala'βlaðo] *adj* foulmouthed.

malhechor [male'tʃor], **-a** *sm, sf* wrongdoer. **malhecho** *sm* misdeed.

malhumorado [malumo'raðo] *adj* ill-tempered.

malicia [ma'liθja] *sf* malice; slyness; mischievousness. **maliciable** *adj* suspicious. **maliciarse** *v* go bad. **malicioso** *adj* malicious; shrewd; sly.

maligno [ma'ligno] *adj* malignant; malicious. **malignidad** *sf* malignity; malice.

malintencionado [malintenθjo'naðo] *adj* ill-disposed.

malo ['malo] *adj* also **mal** bad; evil; wrong; poor; difficult; sick. **estar malo** be ill. **mala fama** ill fame. **venir de malas** have bad intentions.

malograr [malo'grar] *v* waste; miss. **malograrse** *v* fail; fall through. **malogrado** *adj* abortive. **malogro** *sm* failure.

*** malquerer** [malke'rer] *v* hate. **malquerencia** *sf* ill-will; hatred.

malsano [mal'sano] *adj* unhealthy; sick; insanitary.

malta ['malta] *sf* malt.

Malta ['malta] *sf* Malta. **maltés, -esa** *s, adj* Maltese; *sm* (*idioma*) Maltese.

maltratar [maltra'tar] *v* ill-treat. **maltraer** *v* hurt; abuse. **maltrato** *sm* ill-treatment.

malva ['mal βa] *sf* mallow. **malva real** hollyhock.

malvado [mal'βaðo], **-a** *sm, sf* evildoer. *adj* wicked.

malla ['maʎa] *sf* mesh; network; (*de metal*) mail. **mallas** *sf pl* tights.

mallo ['maʎo] *sm* mallet.

mamá [ma'ma] *sf also* **mama** mum(my), mother.

mamar [ma'mar] *v* suck; acquire. **mamarse** *v* get drunk; fiddle, wangle. **mamoso** *adj* sucking.

mamífero [ma'mifero] *sm* mammal.

mampostería [mamposte'ria] *sf* masonry. **mampuesto** *sm* rubble.

manada [ma'naða] *sf* herd, flock; crowd. **manadero** *sm* herdsman; shepherd.

manantial [manan'tjal] *sm* spring; source, origin. **manar** *v* flow; issue.

mancebo [man'θeβo] *sm* youth; shop assistant; bachelor.

manco ['manko] *adj* one-handed; one-armed; crippled; faulty. **mancar** *v* cripple.

mancomunar [mankomu'nar] *v* join, unite. **mancomún** *adv* jointly. **mancomunarse** *v* merge. **mancomunidad** *sf* association, confederation.

manchar [man'tʃar] *v* stain; mark. **mancha** *sf* stain; mark; dishonour.

mandar [man'dar] *v* order; command; send; bequeath. **mandarse** *v* manage by oneself. **mandadero, -a** *sm, sf* messenger. **mandado** *sm* order; errand. **mandamiento** *sm* commandment, order.

mandatario [manda'tarjo] *sm* attorney; agent; mandatary. **mandato** *sm* commandment; mandate. **mandato judicial** writ.

mandíbula [man'diβula] *sf* jawbone.

mando ['mando] *sm* command; power; authority.

manejar [mane'xar] *v* operate; handle; manage. **manejable** *adj* manageable. **manejo** *sm* operation; handling; control; stratagem.

manera [ma'nera] *sf* manner; mode; way; fashion. **a manera de** by way of. **de ninguna manera** by no means. **de todas maneras** by all means. **manera de ver** outlook.

manga ['manga] *sf* sleeve; hosepipe; waterspout. **manga de agua** shower. **manga de viento** whirlwind. **manguera** *sf* garden hose.

mango[1] ['mango] *sm* (*bot*) mango.

mango[2] *sm* handle; stock.

manía [ma'nia] *sf* mania, craze. **maníaco** *adj, sm* maniac.

maniatar [manja'tar] *v* manacle.

manicomio [mani'komjo] *sm* lunatic asylum.

*****manifestar** [manifes'tar] *v* show; declare; manifest. **manifestación** *sf* manifestation. **manifestante** *s(m+f)* demonstrator. **manifiesto** *adj* clear, evident. **manifiesto** *sm* manifesto.

maniobrar [manjo'βrar] *v* manoeuvre; operate; manipulate; plot. **maniobra** *sf* manoeuvre; stratagem; handling.

manipular [manipu'lar] *v* manipulate. **manipulación** *sf* manipulation. **manipulador, -a** *sm, sf* manipulator.

maniquí [mani'ki] *sm* tailor's dummy; puppet. *sf* mannequin; model.

manivela [mani'βela] *sf* (*auto*) crank.

mano ['mano] *sf* hand; paw; (*pintura*) coat; (*juego*) hand, round, turn. **a mano** by hand. **a mano salva** without risk. **de segunda mano** secondhand. **darse las manos** shake hands. **mano a mano** in a friendly way. **manojo** *sm* handful.

manosear [manose'ar] *v* handle; paw; fondle. **manoseado** *adj* hackneyed.

mansión [man'sjon] *sf* mansion.

manso ['manso] *adj* tame; gentle; meek. **mansedumbre** *sf* tameness; meekness.

manta ['manta] *sf* blanket; rug; (*fam*) thrashing.

manteca [man'teka] *sf* grease; lard; butter; cream. **mantecada** *sf* slice of bread and butter.

mantecado [mante'kaðo] *sm* ice-cream; bun.

mantel ['mantel] *sm* tablecloth.

*****mantener** [mante'ner] *v* maintain; hold; defend; feed; sustain. **mantenimiento** *sm* maintenance.

mantequilla [mante'kiʎa] *sf* butter. **mantequera** *sf* churn; butter-dish. **mantequería** *sf* dairy.

mantilla [man'tiʎa] *sf* mantilla, shawl.

manto ['manto] *sm* cloak. **mantón** *sm* shawl.

manual [ma'nwal] *sm* handbook. *adj* manual.

manubrio [manu'βrio] *sm* handle; crank.

manufactura [manufak'tura] *sf* manufacture; factory. **manufacturado** *adj* manufactured. **manufacturar** *v* manufacture.

manuscrito [manu'skrito] *sm* manuscript.

manzana [man'θana] *sf* apple; block of flats. **manzano** *sm* apple tree.

maña ['maɲa] *sf* skill; bad habit; cunning. **mañoso** *adj* clever; crafty.

mañana [ma'ɲana] *sf* morning. *sm, adv* tomorrow. **de mañana** early. **hasta mañana** see you tomorrow. **pasado mañana** the day after tomorrow.

mapa ['mapa] *sm* map; chart.

máquina ['makina] *sf* machine; locomotive; engine; car; bicycle. **a toda máquina** at full speed. **máquina de coser** sewing machine. **máquina de escribir** typewriter. **máquina registradora** cash register.

maquinación [makina'θjon] *sf* machination; plotting. **maquinal** *adj* automatic; mechanical. **maquinar** *v* plot.

mar [mar] *s(m+f)* sea. **alta mar** high seas. **baja mar** low tide.

maraña [ma'raɲa] *sf* thicket; tangle; perplexity. **marañar** *v* tangle. **marañoso** *adj* entangling.

maravillar [maraβi'ʎar] *v* wonder; amaze. **maravilla** *sf* marvel; wonder. **maravilloso** *adj* wonderful.

marcar [mar'kar] *v* mark; brand; show; dial; score. **marca** *sf* mark; make; gauge; label. **marca registrada** registered trademark.

marcial [mar'θjal] *adj* martial; warlike.

marco ['marko] *sm* frame; setting; *(moneda)* mark.

marchar [mar'tʃar] *v* march; go; run; work; depart. **marcharse** *v* go away. **marcha** *sf* march; course; movement; departure. **poner en marcha** set in motion.

marchitar [martʃi'tar] *v* fade; wither; shrivel. **marchitable** *adj* perishable. **marchito** *adj* faded.

marea [ma'rea] *sf* tide; light breeze; dew. **marea creciente/menguante** flood/ebb tide.

marearse [mare'arse] *v* feel (sea) sick. **mareado** *adj* (sea) sick; dizzy. **mareo** *sm* sickness; *(fam)* nuisance.

marfil [mar'fil] *sm* ivory.

margarina [marga'rina] *sf* margarine.

margarita [marga'rita] *sf* daisy; pearl.

margen [mar'xen] *sm* border; margin; verge; shoulder; fringe. **al margen de** in addition to. *sf* river bank; seashore.

marica [ma'rika] *sf* magpie. *sm (fam)* sissy. **maricón** *sm* homosexual.

marido [ma'riðo] *sm* husband.

mariguana [mari'gwana] *sf also* **marihuana** marijuana.

marina [ma'rina] *sf* navy; shore; seamanship. **marinero** *sm* sailor. **marinero** *adj* seafaring; seaworthy. **marino** *sm* sailor. **marino** *adj* marine.

mariposa [mari'posa] *sf* butterfly.

mariquita [mari'kita] *sf* ladybird.

mariscal [maris'kal] *sm* marshal. **mariscal de campo** field marshal.

marisco [ma'risko] *sm* seafood; shellfish.

marítimo [ma'ritimo] *adj* maritime.

marmita [mar'mita] *sf* stewpot.

mármol ['marmol] *sm* marble. **marmóreo** *adj* marble.

marqués [mar'kes] *sm* marquis. **marquesa** *sf* marchioness.

marrano [ma'rrano] *sm* pig. *adj* filthy.

marrón [ma'rron] *adj* brown; maroon. *sm (color)* chestnut.

marsopa [mar'sopa] *sf* porpoise.

martes ['martes] *sm invar* Tuesday.

martillar [marti'ʎar] *v* hammer. **martillo** *sm* hammer.

martín pescador [mar'tin peska'ðor] *sm* kingfisher.

mártir ['martir] *s(m+f)* martyr. **martirio** *sm* martyrdom.

marxista [mark'sista] *s(m+f)* Marxist. **marxismo** *sm* Marxism.

marzo ['marθo] *sm* March.

mas [mas] *conj* but; yet. **mas que** although.

más [mas] *adv* more; most. **nada más** nothing else. **es más** moreover. **más bien** rather. **por más que** however much. *sm* plus.

masa ['masa] *sf* mass; volume; dough; mortar.

masaje [ma'saxe] *sm* massage. **masajista** *s(m+f)* masseur; masseuse.

mascar [mas'kar] *v* chew; *(fam)* mumble. **mascadura** *sf* chewing.

máscara ['maskara] *sf* mask. **mascarada** *sf* masquerade.

masculino [masku'lino] *adj* masculine; male. *sm (gram)* masculine. **masculinidad** *sf* masculinity.

masón [ma'son] *sm* freemason. **masonería** *sf* freemasonry.

masoquismo [maso'kismo] *sm* masochism. **masoquista** *s(m+f)* masochist. masoquista *adj* masochistic.

masticar [masti'kar] *v* chew. **masticación** *sf* mastication.

mástil ['mastil] *sm* (*mar*) mast; pole; post.

mastín [mas'tin] *sm* mastiff. **mastín danés** Great Dane.

masturbación [mastur βa'θjon] *sf* masturbation. **masturbarse** *v* masturbate.

mata ['mata] *sf* bush; shrub; grove; mop of hair.

matafuego [mata'fwego] *sm* fire extinguisher.

matar [ma'tar] *v* kill, slaughter; tire out; put out. **matadero** *sm* slaughterhouse. **matador** *sm* bullfighter. **matanza** *sf* slaughter.

matamoscas [mata'moskas] *sm invar* flyswatter.

matarratas [matar'ratas] *sm invar* rat poison.

mate¹ ['mate] *sm* (check)mate.

mate² *adj* mat, dull.

matemáticas [mate'matikas] *sf* mathematics. **matemático, -a** *sm*, *sf* mathematician. matemático *adj* mathematical.

materia [ma'terja] *sf* matter; stuff; subject. **materia prima** raw material. **en materia de** as regards. **material** *adj* material. **material** *sm* stuff, material. **materiales de derribo** rubble *sing*. **materialismo** *sm* materialism. **materialista** *s(m+f)* materialist. **materialista** *adj* materialistic. **materializar** *v* materialize.

maternal [mater'nal] *adj* maternal. **maternidad** *sf* maternity. **casa de maternidad** maternity hospital. **materno** *adj* maternal.

matinal [mati'nal] *adj* morning.

matiz ['matiθ] *sm* tint; hue; shade; shade of meaning. **matizado** *adj* variegated. **matizar** *v* blend; shade.

matorral [mator'ral] *sm* bush; thicket; scrubland.

matricular [matriku'lar] *v* enrol; register; matriculate. **matricularse** *v* register; (*contienda*) enter. **matrícula** *sf* register; enrolment; matriculation; (*auto*) licence plate.

matrimonio [matri'monjo] *sm* matrimony, marriage; (*fam*) married couple.

matriz [ma'triθ] *sf* matrix; womb. *adj* mother; chief. **casa matriz** headquarters.

matrona [ma'trona] *sf* matron; midwife.

matute [ma'tute] *sm* smuggling; contraband. **matutear** *v* smuggle. **matutero, -a** *sm*, *sf* smuggler.

matutino [matu'tino] *adj also* **matutinal** morning.

maullar [mau'ʎar] *v* mew. **maullido** *sm* mewing.

mausoleo [mauso'leo] *sm* mausoleum.

máxima ['maksima] *sf* maxim.

máxime ['maksime] *adv* especially; principally. **máximo** *adj*, *sm* maximum.

maya ['maja] *sf* daisy.

mayo ['majo] *sm* May; maypole.

mayonesa [majo'nesa] *sf* mayonnaise.

mayor [ma'jor] *sm* head, chief. *adj* older, elder; major, main; larger; adult. **calle mayor** high street. **al por mayor** wholesale. **mayoral** *sm* foreman; farm manager.

mayorazgo [majo'raθgo] *sm* primogeniture; first born son; entailed estate.

mayordomo [major'ðomo] *sm* butler; steward.

mayoría [majo'ria] *sf* majority; coming of age.

mayorista [majo'rista] *sm* wholesaler. *adj* wholesale.

mayúscula [ma'juskula] *sf* capital letter.

maza ['maθa] *sf* mace; club; butt. **mazada** *sf* blow with a club.

mazapán [maθa'pan] *sm* marzipan.

mazmorra [maθ'morra] *sf* dungeon.

me [me] *pron* me, myself.

mear [me'ar] *v* (*vulgar*) piss. **mearse** *v* wet oneself. **meadero** *sm* urinal.

mecánica [me'kanika] *sf* mechanics; machinery. **mecánico** *sm* mechanic; driver. **mecanismo** *sm* mechanism. **mecanizar** *v* mechanize.

mecanógrafo [meka'nografo], **-a** *sm*, *sf* typist. **mecanografía** *sf* typewriting. **mecanografiar** *v* type.

mecer [me'θer] *v* rock; swing; shake; stir. **mecedor** *sm* swing. **mecedora** *sf* rocking-chair.

mecha ['metʃa] *sf* wick; fuse; match.

mechera [me'tʃera] *sf* (*fam*) shoplifter.

mechero [me'tʃero] *sm* cigarette lighter; gas burner.

medalla [me'ðaʎa] *sf* medal.

media ['meðja] *sf* stocking.

mediado [me'ðjaðo] *adj* half-full; halfway through; half-finished. **a mediados de** in *or* about the middle of.

mediano [me'ðjano] *adj* medium; average; mediocre. **medianero** *adj* intermediate; interceding.

medianoche [meðja'notʃe] *sf* midnight.

mediante [me'ðjante] *adj* intervening. *prep* by means of. **mediar** *v* intervene; mediate; elapse.

medicina [meði'θina] *sf* medicine. **medicación** *sf* medication. **medicamento** *sm* medicament. **medicar** *v* medicate. **medicinal** *adj* medicinal. **médico** *sm* doctor. **médico** *adj* medical.

medio ['meðjo] *sm* middle; half; medium; way. **de medio a medio** completely. **medios** *sm pl* means, resources. *adv* half; partly. **medidas a medias** half-measures. *adj* half; middle; average; medium. **de medio cuerpo** half-length.

mediocre [me'ðjokre] *adj* mediocre. **mediocridad** *sf* mediocrity.

mediodía [meðjo'ðia] *sm* midday, noon; south.

medioeval [meðjoe'βal] *adj* medieval.

***medir** [me'ðir] *v* measure; scan. **medirse** *v* act prudently. **medida** *sf* measure(ment); step; moderation. **a medida que** according as.

meditar [meði'tar] *v* meditate (on). **meditabundo** *adj* pensive. **meditación** *sf* meditation.

mediterráneo [meðiter'raneo] *adj* Mediterranean.

medrar [me'ðrar] *v* prosper, thrive; grow. **medra** *sf* prosperity; growth. **medro** *sm* progress; improvement.

medroso [me'ðroso] *adj* fearful; timid; frightening.

médula ['meðula] *sf also* medula marrow; (*fig*) essence.

medusa [me'ðusa] *sf* jellyfish.

megáfono [me'gafono] *sm* megaphone.

megalómano [mega'lomano], **-a** *sm, sf* megalomaniac. **megalomanía** *sf* megalomania.

mejilla [me'xiʎa] *sf* cheek.

mejor [me'xor] *adj* better; best. *adv* better; best; rather. **a lo mejor** probably. **mejor que mejor** better still. **tanto mejor** so much the better. **mejora** *sf* improvement. **mejorar** *v* improve; surpass. **mejorarse** *v* get better.

melancólico [melan'koliko] *adj* melancholy. **melancolía** *sf* melancholy.

melandro [me'landro] *sm* badger.

melaza [me'laθa] *sf* molasses; treacle.

melena [me'lena] *sf* mane; long hair.

melindroso [melin'droso] *adj* finicky; squeamish.

melocotón [meloko'ton] *sm* peach; peach tree.

melodía [melo'ðia] *sf* melody; tune. **melodioso** *adj* melodious.

melodrama [melo'ðrama] *sm* melodrama. **melodramático** *adj* melodramatic.

melón [me'lon] *sm* melon.

meloso [me'loso] *adj* honeyed; mild; sickly.

mella ['meʎa] *sf* notch; dent; impression. **hacer mella a** make a deep impression on.

mellizo [me'ʎiθo]. **-a** *s, adj* twin.

membrana [mem'brana] *sf* membrane.

membrillo [mem'briʎo] *sm* quince; quince tree.

memorable [memo'raβle] *adj* memorable. **memorar** *v* remember. **memoria** *sf* memory; record. **de memoria** by heart. **memorial** *sm* memorial; petition.

mencionar [menθjo'nar] *v* mention, name. **mención** *sf* mention.

mendigar [mendi'gar] *v* beg. **mendicación** *sf* begging. **mendicante** *adj* begging. **mendigante** *sm* beggar. **mendigo, -a** *sm, sf* beggar.

menear [mene'ar] *v* stir; shake; sway; manage; run. **meneo** *sm* wag; shake; rearranging.

menester [menes'ter] *sm* need; want; occupation. **ser menester** be necessary. **menesteroso** *adj* needy.

menguar [men'gwar] *v* lessen; decline. **mengua** *sf* lessening; decline. **menguado** *adj* impaired; diminished; wretched.

menopausia [meno'pausja] *sf* menopause.

menor [me'nor] *adj* minor; lesser; least; younger; youngest; smaller; smallest. **al por menor** retail.

menos ['menos] *adj* less, fewer. *adv* less; minus; except. **al, a lo** *or* **por lo menos** at least. **echar de menos** miss.

menoscabar [menoska'βar] *v* lessen; impair; discredit. **menoscabo** *sm* reduction; impairment.

menospreciar [menospre'θjar] *v* underrate; despise. **menospreciable** contemptible. **menosprecio** *sm* contempt; scorn; disrespect; undervaluation.

mensaje [men'saxe] *sm* message. **mensajero, -a** *sm, sf* messenger.

menstruar [menstru'ar] v menstruate. **menstruación** sf menstruation. **menstrual** adj menstrual.

mensual [men'swal] adj monthly. **mensualidad** sf monthly salary.

mensurar [mensu'rar] v measure. **mensura** sf measure. **mensural** adj measuring.

menta ['menta] sf mint; peppermint.

mental [men'tal] adj mental; intellectual. **mentalidad** sf mentality. **mente** sf mind. **irse de la mente** slip one's mind.

mentecato [mente'kato], -a sm, sf simpleton. adj foolish; half-witted.

***mentir** [men'tir] v lie. **mentir con disagree. mentira** sf lie; error. **parece mentira** it's hard to believe.

menudear [menuðe'ar] v repeat frequently; happen often. **menudencia** sf detail; minuteness; pettiness. **menudencias** sf pl or **menudas** sm pl offal sing. **menudo** adj small, tiny; petty. **a menudo** often.

meñique [me'pike] sm little finger. adj tiny.

meollo [me'oʎo] sm (anat) marrow; brains pl; (fig) essence.

meple ['meple] sm maple.

mercado [mer'kaðo] sm market. **Mercado Común** Common Market. **mercadear** v trade. **mercader** sm merchant. **mercadería** sf merchandise. **mercancía** sf goods pl. **mercante** adj merchant. **mercantil** adj mercantile.

merced [mer'θeð] sf mercy; favour. **merced a** thanks to.

mercenario [merθe'narjo], -a s, adj mercenary.

mercero [mer'θero], -a sm, sf haberdasher. **mercería** sf haberdashery.

mercurio [mer'kurjo] sm mercury. **mercurial** adj mercurial.

***merecer** [mere'θer] v deserve; be worthy of. **merecer la pena** be worthwhile. **merecimiento** sm merit.

***merendar** [meren'dar] v take afternoon tea; have an afternoon snack. **merendarse a** get the better of. **merendero** sm open-air café. **merienda** sf afternoon snack.

merengue [me'renge] sm meringue.

meridiano [meri'ðjano] sm, adj meridian. **meridiana** sf couch. **meridional** adj southern.

mérito ['merito] sm merit; value. **hacer mérito de** mention. **meritorio** adj meritorious.

merla ['merla] sf blackbird.

merluza [mer'luθa] sf hake.

mermar [mer'mar] v decrease, reduce. **merma** sf reduction; wastage; loss.

mermelada [merme'laða] sf marmalade; jam.

mero ['mero] adj mere, pure.

merodear [meroðe'ar] v maraud. **merodeador**, -a sm, sf marauder.

mes [mes] sm month. **al mes** per month.

mesa ['mesa] sf table; desk. **mesa de cambios** bank. **alzar la mesa** clear the table.

meseta [me'seta] sf plateau; staircase landing.

mesón [me'son] sm inn, hostelry. **mesonero**, -a sm, sf innkeeper.

mestizo [mes'tiθo], -a s, adj half-caste.

mesura [me'sura] sf dignity; politeness; moderation.

meta ['meta] sf goal; aim; destination. **guardameta** sm goalkeeper.

metabolismo [metabo'lismo] sm metabolism.

metafísica [meta'fiska] sf metaphysics. **metafísico** adj metaphysical.

metáfora [me'tafora] sf metaphor. **metafórico** adj metaphorical.

metal [me'tal] sm metal; (música) brass; (voz) timbre. **metálico** adj metallic. **metalurgia** sf metallurgy.

meteoro [mete'oro] sm meteor. **meteórico** adj meteoric. **meteorito** sm meteorite. **meteorología** sf meteorology.

meter [me'ter] v insert, put in; smuggle; produce; reduce. **meterse** v interfere; intervene. **meterse a** turn to. **meterse con** quarrel with. **metido** adj compressed.

meticuloso [metiku'loso] adj meticulous.

metodista [meto'ðista] s(m+f), adj Methodist. **metodismo** sm Methodism.

método ['metoðo] sm method, manner. **metódico** adj methodical.

métrico [me'triko] adj metric(al). **metro** sm metre; underground railway.

metrónomo [me'tronomo] sm metronome.

metrópoli [me'tropoli] sf metropolis. **metropolitano** adj metropolitan.

mezclar [meθ'klar] v mix; blend. **mezclarse** v mingle; intermarry. **mezcla** sf mixture, medley. **mezcladora** sf mixer, blender. **mezcolanza** sf hotchpotch.

mezquino [meθ'kino] *adj* mean. **mezquindad** *sf* meanness.

mezquita [meθ'kita] *sf* mosque.

mi [mi] *adj* my. **mí** *pron* me.

miaja ['mjaxa] *sf* crumb; bit.

mico ['miko] *sm* monkey.

microbio [mi'kroβjo] *sm* microbe. **microbiología** *sf* microbiology.

micrófono [mi'krofono] *sm* microphone.

microscopio [mikro'skopjo] *sm* microscope. **microscópico** *adj* microscopic.

miedo [mi'eðo] *sm* fear. **dar miedo a** frighten. **tener miedo** be afraid. **miedoso** *adj* frightened.

miel [mi'el] *sf* honey. **miel de caña** molasses.

miembro ['mjembro] *sm* member; limb.

miente ['mjente] *sf* mind; thought. **caer en mientes** come to mind. **¡ni por mientes!** not on your life! **parar mientes en** consider.

mientras ['mjentras] *adv*, *conj* while; meanwhile; so long as. **mientras tanto** meanwhile.

miércoles [mi'erkoles] *sm* Wednesday. **miércoles de ceniza** Ash Wednesday.

mierda [mi'erða] *sf* (*fam*) shit; muck. **¡váyase a la mierda!** go to hell!

mies [mjes] *sf* corn. **mieses** *sf pl* cornfield.

miga ['miga] *sf* crumb; substance. **hacer buenas migas con** get on well with.

migración [migra'θjon] *sf* migration. **migratorio** *adj* migratory.

migraña [mi'graɲa] *sf* migraine.

mil [mil] *sm*, *adj* thousand. **milésimo** *adj* thousandth. **miles de** masses of.

milagro [mi'lagro] *sm* miracle; wonder. **milagroso** *adj* miraculous.

milano [mi'lano] *sm* (*ave*) kite.

mildeu [mil'deu] *sm* mildew.

milicia [mi'liθja] *sf* militia; military service. **militar** *adj* military. *sm* soldier.

miligramo [mili'gramo] *sm* milligramme.

milla ['miʎa] *sf* mile.

millar [mi'ʎar] *sm* thousand. **a millares** in thousands.

millón [mi'ʎon] *sm* million. **millonésimo** *adj* millionth. **millonario, -a** *sm*, *sf* millionaire.

mimar [mi'mar] *v* spoil; pamper.

mimbre ['mimbre] *s(m+f)* wicker.

minar [mi'nar] *y* mine. **mina** *sf* mine; store; pencil lead. **minador** *sm* miner; (*mar*) minelayer. **minero** *sm* miner; mine-owner.

minarete [mina'rete] *sm* minaret.

mineral [mine'ral] *sm*, *adj* mineral. **mineralogía** *sf* mineralogy.

miniatura [minja'tura] *sf* miniature.

mínimo ['minimo] *sm*, *adj* minimum.

ministerio [mini'sterjo] *sm* ministry; office. **ministerial** *adj* ministerial. **ministrador** *sm* administrator. **ministrar** *v* minister; administer. **ministro** *sm* minister; judge. **primer ministro** prime minister.

minoría [mino'ria] *sf* minority. **minorar** *v* diminish.

minucioso [minu'θjoso] *adj* meticulous; minute.

minué [minu'e] *sm* minuet.

minúscula [mi'nuskula] *sf* small letter.

minuta [mi'nuta] *sf* memo; menu; list. **minutar** *v* make notes on.

minutía [minu'tia] *sf* carnation.

minuto [mi'nuto] *sm* minute.

mío ['mio] *adj*, *pron pers* mine.

miope [mi'ope] *adj* shortsighted. **miopía** *sf* myopia.

miosotis [mjo'sotis] *sm* forget-me-not.

mirar [mi'rar] *v* look; consider.. **mira** *sf* sight. **estar a la mira** be on the lookout. **con miras a** with a view to. **mirada** *sf* look; glance. **miradero** *sm* centre of attention; vantage point. **mirado** *adj* circumspect. **mirador** *sm* bay window. **miramiento** *sm* look; consideration; respect.

mirasol [mira'sol] *sm* sunflower.

mirlo ['mirlo] *sm* blackbird.

mirra ['mirra] *sf* myrrh.

mirto ['mirto] *sf* mass. **misal** *sm* missal.

miserable [mise'raβle] *adj* wretched, miserable. **miseria** *sf* misery; poverty. **misericordia** *sf* mercy; compassion. **misericordioso** *adj* merciful; compassionate. **mísero** *adj* wretched.

misión [misi'on] *sf* mission.

mismo ['mismo] *adj* same; own; very; just; right. **aquí mismo** right here. **lo mismo con** the same goes for. **yo mismo** I myself.

misterio [mis'terjo] *sm* mystery. **misterioso** *adj* mysterious. **misticismo** *sm* mysticism. **místico, -a** *s*, *adj* mystic. **mistificación** *sf* falsification; trick. **mistificar** *v* falsify; deceive.

mitad [mi'tað] *sf* half; middle.

mítico ['mitiko] *adj* mythical. **mito** *m* myth. **mitología** *sf* mythology. **mitológico** *adj* mythological.

mitigar [miti'gar] v mitigate; relieve. mitigación sf mitigation. mitigante adj mitigating.

mitin ['mitin] sm political rally.

mitón [mi'ton] sm mitten.

mitra ['mitra] sf mitre.

mixto ['miksto] adj mixed. sm compound. mixtura sf mixture. mixturar v mix.

mobiliario [moβili'arjo] sm furniture.

mocasín [moka'sin] sm moccasin.

mocero [mo'θero] adj sensual. mocear v act like a youngster. mocedad sf youth; youthful prank.

moción [mo'θjon] sf motion.

moco ['moko] sm mucus. mocoso adj mucous.

mochila [mo'tʃila] sf rucksack.

mocho ['motʃo] adj shorn; lopped; (sin cuernos) hornless.

moda ['moða] sf fashion. de moda in fashion. pasado de moda old-fashioned.

modales [mo'ðales] sm pl manners.

modelo [mo'ðelo] sm, adj model. modela sf fashion model. modelar v model.

moderar [moðe'rar] v moderate; restrain. moderación sf moderation. moderado adj moderate. moderador, -a sm, sf moderator. moderativo adj moderating.

moderno [mo'ðerno] adj modern. modernidad sf modernity. modernizar v modernize. modernizarse v get up-to-date.

modesto [mo'ðesto] adj modest. modestía sf modesty.

módico ['moðiko] adj moderate. modicidad sf moderateness.

modificar [moðifi'kar] v modify. modificación sf modification.

modismo [mo'ðismo] sm idiom.

modista [mo'ðista] sf dressmaker.

modo ['moðo] sm mode; manner; method. de modo que so that. de todos modos in any case.

modorra [mo'ðorra] sf drowsiness. modorro adj drowsy.

modular [moðu'lar] v modulate. modulación sf modulation.

mofar [mo'far] v scoff; mock. mofarse de jeer at. mofa sf mockery. mofador adj mocking.

mohín [mo'in] sm grimace. mohino adj sulky.

moho ['moo] sm mould; rust. mohoso adj mouldy; rusty. ponerse mohoso go mouldy; rust.

mojar [mo'xar] v wet; moisten; soak. mojado adj wet; damp.

mojigato [moxi'gato], -a sm, sf hypocrite; prude. adj hypocritical; prudish.

mojón [mo'xon] sm landmark.

moldar [mol'ðar] v also moldear mould. molde sm mould. moldura sf moulding.

molécula [mo'lekula] sf molecule. molecular adj molecular.

*moler [mo'ler] v grind; crush; (fig) bore, weary. moledura sf grinding; milling; exhaustion.

molestar [moles'tar] v annoy; bother; disturb. molestarse v worry. no se moleste don't bother. molestía sf trouble. molesto adj tiresome; embarrassing.

molinero [moli'nero] sm miller. molino sm mill.

molusco [mo'lusko] sm mollusc.

mollera [mo'ʎera] sf crown of the head; (fig) brains. cerrado de mollera dense; obstinate.

momentáneo [momen'taneo] adj momentary. momento sm moment; momentum. al momento immediately.

momia ['momja] sf (cadáver) mummy. momificación sf mummification. momificar v mummify.

monada [mo'naða] sf kindness; flattery, dirty trick. ¡qué monada! how lovely!

monarca [mo'narka] sm monarch. monarquía sf monarchy. monárquico adj monarchic(al).

monasterio [monas'terjo] sm monastery. monástico adj monastic.

mondar [mon'dar] v clean; prune; strip; trim; peel. monda sf pruning; trimming; cleaning. mondadientes m invar toothpick. mondador, -a sm, sf pruner; peeler; cleaner. mondo adj pure; bare; clean.

moneda [mo'neða] sf money; coin. monedero sm purse. monedero falso counterfeiter.

monitor ['monitor], -a sm, sf monitor.

monja ['monxa] sf nun. monje sm monk.

mono[1] ['mono] sm monkey; ape.

mono[2] adj lovely; cute.

monólogo [mo'nologo] sm monologue.

monopolizar [monopoli'θar] v monopolize. monopolio sm monopoly.

monosílabo [mono'silaβo] sm monosyllable.

monótono [mo'notono] adj monotonous. monotonía sf monotony.

monstruo ['monstruo] *sm* monster. **mon-struosidad** *sf* monstrosity. **monstruoso** *adj* monstrous.

monta ['monta] *sf* mounting; amount. **montacargas** *sm invar* service lift. **montaje** *sm* mounting.

montaña [mon'taɲa] *sf* mountain. **montañés** *adj* of mountains. **montañismo** *sm* mountaineering. **montañoso** *adj* mountainous. **monte** *sm* mountain; mount.

montar [mon'tar] *v* mount; ride; assemble; establish. **montura** *sf* mount; saddle; frame; mounting.

montera [mon'tera] *sf* cloth cap; bullfighter's hat; skylight. **montero** *sm* hunter.

montón [mon'ton] *sm* heap, pile. **a montones** lots of.

monumento [monu'mento] *sm* monument; memorial. **monumental** *adj* monumental.

moño ['moɲo] *sm* bun, topknot. **ponerse moños** put on airs.

mora¹ ['mora] *sf* blackberry; mulberry.

mora² *sf* delay.

morada [mo'raða] *sf* abode; sojourn. **morar** *v* dwell.

morado [mo'raðo] *adj* purple; violet. **ponerse morado** stuff oneself.

moral [mo'ral] *adj* moral. **morales** *sf pl* morals. **moraleja** *sf (de un cuento)* moral. **moralidad** *sf* morality. **moralista** *s(m+f)* moralist. **moralizar** *v* moralize.

mórbido ['morβiðo] *adj* morbid; delicate. **morbidez** *sf* tenderness. **morbilidad** *sf* morbidity. **morboso** *adj* morbid; diseased.

morcilla [mor'θiʎa] *sf* black pudding.

mordaz [mor'ðaθ] *adj* mordant; pungent.

mordaza [mor'ðaθa] *sf (en la boca)* gag.

*****morder** [mor'ðer] *v* bite. **mordedura** *sf* bite. **mordiente** *adj* biting. **mordiscar** *v* nibble. **mordiscón** *sm* nibble; mouthful.

moreno [mo'reno] *adj* brown; tanned; dark.

morera [mo'rera] *sf* mulberry tree.

morfina [mor'fina] *sf* morphine.

moribundo [mori'βundo] *adj* moribund.

*****morir** [mo'rir] *v* die; end; fade. **morirse por** crave.

mormón [mor'mon], **-a** *sm*, *sf* Mormon. **mormonismo** *sm* Mormonism.

moro ['moro], **-a** *sm*, *sf* Moor. *adj* Moorish.

moroso [mo'roso] *adj* slow; sluggish; late. **morosidad** *sf* slowness; inactivity.

morralla [mor'raʎa] *sf* rubbish; *(fig)* rabble.

morriña [mor'riɲa] *sf* nostalgia; homesickness.

mortaja [mor'taxa] *sf* shroud.

mortal [mor'tal] *adj* mortal; lethal; awful. *s(m+f)* mortal. **mortalidad** *sf* mortality.

mortero [mor'tero] *sm* mortar.

mortífero [mor'tifero] *adj* deadly, fatal.

mortificar [mortifi'kar] *v* mortify. **mortificación** *sf* mortification.

mosca ['moska] *sf* fly. **papar moscas** gape. **moscarda** *sf* bluebottle. **moscardón** *sm* blowfly; hornet.

mosquete [mos'kete] *sm* musket. **mosquetero** *sm* musketeer.

mosquito [mos'kito] *sm* mosquito; gnat. **mosquitero** *sm* mosquito net.

mostaza [mos'taθa] *sf* mustard.

*****mostrar** [mos'trar] *v* show; exhibit; point out. **mostrable** *adj* demonstrable. **mostrador** *sm (reloj)* dial; *(tienda)* counter.

mote ['mote] *sm* nickname. **motejar** *v* label; name.

motín [mo'tin] *sm* uprising; mutiny.

motivar [moti'βar] *v* cause, give rise to; justify; explain. **motivación** *sf* motivation. **motivo** *sm* motive; grounds *pl.* **con motivo de** owing to.

motocicleta [motoθi'kleta] *sf* motor cycle. **motociclista** *s(m+f)* motor-cyclist.

motor ['motor] *sm* motor; engine. **motorista** *s(m+f)* motor-cyclist. **motorizar** *v* motorize.

motriz [mo'triθ] *adj* motive.

mover [mo'βer] *v* move; shake; stir; incite. **moverse** *v* get a move on. **movedizo** *adj* movable; inconstant. **movible** *adj* mobile. **móvil** *adj* mobile; fickle. **movilidad** *sf* mobility. **movilizar** *v* mobilize. **movilización** *sf* mobilization. **movimiento** *sm* movement; motion; activity.

mozo ['moθo] *sm* youth, lad; waiter. **moza** *sf* girl; servant.

mucoso [mu'koso] *adj* mucous. **mucosidad** *sf* mucus.

muchacho [mu'tʃatʃo] *sm* boy; chap. **muchacha** *sf* girl; servant.

muchedumbre [mutʃe'ðumbre] *sf* crowd; *(fig)* a lot.

mucho ['mutʃo] *adj* a lot of; much; great; many. *pron* many; a lot. *adv* much; a lot; a long time. **con mucho** by far. **por mucho que** however much.

mudar [mu'ðar] *v* change; remove; shed. **mudarse** *v* move house; change one's clothes. **muda** *sf* change; moulting. **mudable** *adj* changeable; variable. **mudanza** *sf* change; removal. **camión de mudanzas** *sm* removal van.

mudo ['muðo] *adj* dumb; mute. **mudez** *sf* dumbness.

mueble ['mweβle] *sm* piece of furniture. **muebles** *sm pl* furniture *sing*.

mueca ['mweka] *sf* grimace.

muela ['mwela] *sf* molar. **muela del juicio** wisdom tooth.

muelle ['mweʎe] *adj* soft; luxurious. *sm* wharf; embankment; spring.

muérdago [mu'erðago] *sm* mistletoe.

muerte ['mwerte] *sf* death; murder. **de mala muerte** (*fam*) rotten, lousy.

muerto ['mwerto] *V* **morir**. *adj* dead. *sm* corpse.

muestra ['mwestra] *sf* sample, example; specimen; sign.

mugir [mu'xir] *v* roar; bellow; low. **mugido** *sm* roar; bellow; lowing.

mujer [mu'xer] *sf* woman; wife.

muleta [mu'leta] *sf* crutch; bullfighter's cape.

mulo ['mulo] *sm* mule.

multar [mul'tar] *v* fine. **multa** *sf* fine.

múltiple ['multiple] *adj* multiple; many. **multiplicación** *sf* multiplication. **multiplicar** *v* multiply, increase.

multitud [multi'tuð] *sf* multitude, crowd.

*mullir [mu'ʎir] *v* beat; break up; loosen. **mullido** *adj* soft; fluffy.

mundo ['mundo] *sm* world; (*fam*) crowd. **todo el mundo** everybody. **mundanal** *adj* worldly. **mundanería** *sf* worldliness. **mundial** *adj* world; worldwide. **mundovisión** *sm* broadcasting by satellite.

municipal [muniθi'pal] *adj* municipal. *sm* policeman. **municipalidad** *sf* municipality. **municipio** *sm* town council.

munífico [mu'nifiko] *adj* munificent; liberal. **munificencia** *sf* munificence; liberality.

muñeca [mu'ɲeka] *sf* doll; dressmaker's dummy; wrist.

muralla [mu'raʎa] *sf* wall; rampart. **mural** *adj*, *sm* mural. **murar** *v* wall. **muro** *sm* wall.

murciélago [murθi'elago] *sm* (*zool*) bat.

murmullo [mur'muʎo] *sm* murmur; whisper; rustle.

murmurar [murmu'rar] *v* murmur; whisper; mutter; gossip. **murmuración** *sf* gossiping. **murmurio** *sm* murmuring.

músculo ['muskulo] *sm* muscle. **muscular** *adj* muscular.

muselina [muse'lina] *sf* muslin.

museo [mu'seo] *sm* museum; art gallery.

musgo ['musgo] *sm* moss.

música ['musika] *sf* music. **musical** *adj* musical. **músico**, **-a** *sm*, *sf* musician. **musicología** *sf* musicology.

muslo ['muslo] *sm* thigh.

mustio ['mustjo] *adj* withered; sad. **mustiarse** *v* wither.

mutación [muta'θjon] *sf* mutation; change. **mutabilidad** *sf* mutability. **mutante** *sm*, *adj* mutant.

mutilar [muti'lar] *v* mutilate; cripple. **mutilación** *sf* mutilation. **mutilado**, **-a** *sm*, *sf* cripple.

mutual ['mutwal] *adj* mutual. **mutuo** *adj* mutual; joint.

muy [mwi] *adv* very; quite; too; much. **muy señor mío** (*carta*) Dear Sir.

N

nabo ['naβo] *sm* turnip.

nácar ['nakar] *sm* mother-of-pearl.

*nacer [na'θer] *v* be born; originate. **nacido** *adj* born. **naciente** *adj* growing. **nacimiento** *sm* birth; origin.

nación [na'θjon] *sf* nation. **nacional** *adj* national. *s(m + f)* national; native. **nacionalidad** *sf* nationality. **nacionalismo** *sm* nationalism. **nacionalizar** *v* nationalize.

nada ['naða] *sf* nothing. *adv* by no means. **de nada** don't mention it. **nada más** only.

nadar [na'ðar] *v* swim. **nadador**, **-a** *sm*, *sf* swimmer.

nadie ['naðje] *pron* nobody, no one.

naipe ['naipe] *sm* playing-card.

nalga ['nalga] *sf* buttock.

naranja [na'ranxa] *sf* orange. **naranjada** *sf* orangeade. **naranjo** *sm* orange tree.

narciso [nar'θiso] *sm* narcissus. **narcisismo** *sm* narcissism.

narcótico [nar'kotiko] *sm*, *adj* narcotic.

nariz [na'riθ] *sf*, *pl* **narices** nose.

narrar [nar'rar] *v* narrate. **narración** *sf* narration. **narrador.** -a *sm*, *sf* narrator. **narrativa** *sf* narrative.

nasal [na'sal] *adj* nasal.

nata ['nata] *sf* cream; curd; (*fig*) the best. **natillas** *sf pl* custard *sing*.

natación [nata'θjon] *sf* swimming.

natal [na'tal] *adj* natal; native. *sm* birth; birthday. **natalidad** *sf* birthrate.

nativo [na'tiβo], -a *s*, *adj* native. **natividad** *sf* nativity. **nato** *adj* born.

natural [natu'ral] *s(m+f)* native; citizen. *sm* nature. *adj* natural. **naturaleza** *sf* nature; nationality. **naturalidad** *sf* naturalness; citizenship.

naufragar [naufra'gar] *v* sink; be shipwrecked. **naufragio** *sm* shipwreck. **náufrago** *adj* shipwrecked.

náusea ['nausea] *sf* nausea. **nauseabundo** *adj* nauseous; nauseating.

náutico ['nautiko] *adj* nautical. **náutica** *sf* navigation.

navaja [na'βaxa] *sf* penknife; razor. **navajada** *sf* stab; gash.

naval [na'βal] *adj* naval. **nave** *sf* or **navio** *sm* ship. **navegable** *adj* navigable. **navegación** *sf* navigation; sailing. **navegante** *sm* navigator.

neblina [ne'βlina] *sf* mist, fog. **nebulosidad** *sf* nebulosity; haziness. **nebuloso** *adj* nebulous.

necedad [neθe'ðað] *sf* foolishness; nonsense. **necio** *adj* foolish.

necesario [neθe'sarjo] *adj* necessary. **necesidad** *sf* necessity; poverty. **necesitado** *adj* needy. **necesitar** *v* need.

néctar ['nektar] *sm* nectar.

nefario [ne'farjo] *adj* nefarious.

nefasto [ne'fasto] *adj* ill-omened; unlucky.

***negar** [ne'gar] *v* deny; refuse. **negarse** *v* decline. **negación** *sf* negation. **negativa** *sm* (*foto*) negative; *sf* refusal.

negligencia [negli'xenθja] *sf* negligence. **negligente** *adj* negligent.

negociar [nego'θjar] *v* trade; negotiate. **negociable** *adj* negotiable. **negociación** *sf* transaction; negotiation. **negociado** *sm* bureau; divison. **negociador,** -a *sm*, *sf*

negotiator; agent. **negociante** *sm* businessman; merchant. **negocio** *sm* business; trade; negotiation.

negro ['negro], -a *s*, *adj* black. **negrura** *sf* blackness.

nene ['nene], -a *sm*, *sf* baby.

nenúfar [ne'nufar] *sm* waterlily.

neón [ne'on] *sm* neon.

nepotismo [nepo'tismo] *sm* nepotism.

nervio ['nerβjo] *sm* nerve; (*de una hoja*) rib; sinew. **crisparle los nervios a uno** get on someone's nerves. **tener los nervios en punta** be on edge. **nerviosidad** *sf* nervousness. **nervioso** *adj* nervous. **crisis nerviosa** *sf* nervous breakdown.

neto ['neto] *adj* pure; clear; (*com*) net.

neumático [neu'matiko] *sm* tyre. *adj* pneumatic.

neumonía [neumo'nia] *sf* pneumonia.

neuralgia [neu'ralxja] *sf* neuralgia. **neurálgico** *adj* neuralgic.

neurótico [neu'rotiko] *adj* neurotic. **neurosis** *sf* neurosis.

neutro ['neutro] *adj* neutral; (*gram*) neuter. **neutral** *s(m+f)*, *adj* neutral. **neutralidad** *sf* neutrality. **neutralizar** *v* neutralize.

***nevar** [ne'βar] *v* snow. **nevada** *sf* snow storm. **nevasca** *sf* snowfall. **nevera** *sf* refrigerator. **nevisca** *sf* light snowfall. **neviscar** *v* snow lightly. **nevoso** *adj* snowy.

nexo ['nekso] *sm* link, tie.

ni [ni] *conj* neither; nor; or; not even. **ni uno ni otro** neither one nor the other.

nicotina [niko'tina] *sf* nicotine.

nicho ['nitʃo] *sm* niche.

nido ['niðo] *sm* nest. **cunas de nido** pull-out beds. **nidada** *sf* brood; clutch. **nidal** *sm* nest; nest egg.

niebla [ni'eβla] *sf* fog; mist; mildew.

nieto [ni'eto] *sm* grandson. **nieta** *sf* granddaughter.

nieve [ni'eβe] *sf* snow.

nilón [ni'lon] *sm* nylon.

ninfa ['ninfa] *sf* nymph.

ninguno [nin'guno] *adj* also **ningún** no; not one. **de ninguna manera** in no way. *pron* nobody.

niña ['nina] *sf* little girl; (*del ojo*) pupil. **niñada** *sf* childishness. **niñera** *sf* nanny. **niñez** *sf* childhood. **niño** *sm* little boy; child. **desde niño** from childhood.

níquel ['nikel] *sm* nickel. **niquelar** *v* nickel-plate.

níspero ['nispero] *sm* medlar tree. níspola *sf* medlar.

nítido ['nitiðo] *adj* clear; bright. nitidez *sf* brightness; neatness.

nitrógeno [ni'troxeno] *sm* nitrogen. nitrato *sm* nitrate. nítrico *adj* nitric. nitro *sm* nitre; saltpetre. nitroso *adj* nitrous.

nivelar [niβe'lar] *v* level; balance. nivelarse *v* become level. nivelarse con get even with. nivel *sm* level; standard. nivel de aire spirit-level. nivel de vida standard of living. paso a nivel level-crossing. nivelación *sf* levelling.

no [no] *adv* no; not. no bien no sooner. no más only. no obtante in spite of. que no if only.

noble ['noβle] *adj* noble. *sm* nobleman. nobleza *sf* nobility.

noción [no'θjon] *sf* notion; idea. nociones *sf pl* smattering *sing*; rudiments.

nocivo [no'θiβo] *adj* noxious; harmful.

nocturno [nok'turno] *adj* nocturnal; night. noctámbulo, -a *sm*, *sf* sleepwalker.

noche ['notʃe] *sf* night; evening. por la noche at night. Nochebuena *sf* Christmas Eve.

nódulo ['noðulo] *sm* nodule.

nogal [no'gal] *sm also* noguera *sf* walnut tree.

nómada ['nomaða] *s(m+f)* nomad. *adj* nomadic.

nombrar [nom'brar] *v* name; nominate; mention. nombradía *sf* reputation. nombramiento *sm* naming; nomination. nombre *sm* name; title. nombre de pila Christian name. nomenclatura *sf* nomenclature; terminology; catalogue. nómina *sf* list; payroll. nominación *sf* nomination. nominal *adj* nominal. nominativo *sm* (*gram*) nominative.

non [non] *adj* (*mat*) odd. *sm* odd number.

nonagésimo [nona'xesimo] *adj* ninetieth. nonagenario, -a *s*, *adj* nonagenarian.

norabuena [nora'βwena] *sf* congratulations *pl*. *adv* by good fortune. noramala *adv* unfortunately.

nordeste [nor'ðeste] *sm* north-east; (*viento*) northeaster. *adj* north-east.

noria [no'ria] *sf* waterwheel.

norma ['norma] *sf* norm; rule. normal *adj* normal. normalidad *sf* normality. normalizar *v* normalize.

noroeste [noro'este] *sm* north-west; (*viento*) northwesterly. *adj* north-west.

norte ['norte] *sm*, *adj* north. perder el norte lose one's bearings. norteño *adj* northern.

Noruega [nor'wega] *sf* Norway. noruego, -a *sm*, *sf* (*persona*) Norwegian; *sm* (*idioma*) Norwegian.

nos [nos] *pron* us, ourselves.

nosotros [no'sotros] *pron* we; us, ourselves.

nostalgia [nos'talxja] *sf* nostalgia. nostálgico *adj* nostalgic; homesick.

notar [no'tar] *v* note; notice; note down. nota *sf* (*música, etc.*) note; mark; report; repute. notabilidad *sf* notability. notable *adj* notable. notación *sf* notation.

notario [no'tarjo] *sm* notary. notaría *sf* notary's office.

noticiar [noti'θjar] *v* notify. noticia(s) *sf* (*pl*) news *sing*. noticiario *sm* news bulletin. noticiero, -a *sm*, *sf* reporter. notición *sm* (*fam*) big news. noticioso *adj* well-informed. notificación *sf* notification.

notorio [no'torjo] *adj* notorious. notoriedad *sf* notoriety.

novato [no'βato], -a *s*, *adj* novice.

novecientos [noβe'θjentos] *adj*, *s* nine hundred.

novedad [nove'ðað] *sf* novelty; change. novedades *sf pl* latest models.

novela [no'βela] *sf* novel. novelista *s(m+f)* novelist.

noveno [no'βeno] *adj* ninth. noventa *adj* ninety.

novia [no'βja] *sf* girlfriend; fiancée; bride. traje de novia wedding dress. novio *sm* boyfriend; fiancé; bridegroom.

novicio [no'βiθjo] *sm* beginner; apprentice. noviciado *sm* novitiate; apprenticeship.

noviembre [no'βjembre] *sm* November.

novilla [no'βiʎa] *sf* heifer. novillada *sf* bullfight with young bulls. novillero *sm* novice bullfighter. novillo *sm* young bull. hacer novillos play truant.

nube ['nuβe] *sf* cloud. estar por las nubes (*precios*) be sky-high. poner por las nubes praise to the skies. nublado *adj* overcast. nublar *v* cloud over. nubloso *adj* cloudy; ill-fated.

núcleo ['nukleo] *sm* nucleus; core; (*bot*) stone. nuclear *adj* nuclear.

nudillo [nu'ðiʎo] *sm* knuckle.

nudo[1] [nu'ðo] *sm* knot; bond; tumour.

nudo[2] *adj* nude.

nuera ['nwera] *sf* daughter-in-law.
nuestro ['nwestro] *adj* our.` *pron* ours.
nueva ['nweβa] *sf* news. **nuevo** *adj* new.
de **nuevo** again. **nuevo flamante** brand
new.
nueve ['nweβe] *adj, sm* nine.
nuez [nweθ] *sf* nut; walnut. **nuez de la
garganta** Adam's apple.
nulo ['nulo] *adj* null; void; *(fig)* hopeless.
numerar [nume'rar] *v* number. **numeral**
sm, adj numeral. **numérico** *adj* numerical. **número** *sm* number; size; quantity.
numeroso *adj* numerous.
nunca ['nunka] *adv* never; ever. **casi nunca** hardly ever.
nuncio ['nunθjo] *sm* nuncio; *(fig)* omen.
nupcial [nup'θjal] *adj* nuptial. **nupcias** *sf
pl* nuptials.
nutria [nu'tria] *sf also* **nutra** *sf* otter.
nutrir [nu'trir] *v* nourish. **nutrición** *sf*
nutrition. **nutrimento** *sm* nutriment.

Ñ

ñaque ['nake] *sm* odds and ends.
ñoño ['noɲo] *adj* insipid; prudish; fussy.
ñoñería *sf also* **ñoñez** *sf* insipidity; prud-
ery; fussiness.
ñu [nu] *sm* gnu.

O

o [o] *conj* or. **o . . . o** either . . . or. **o sea**
in other words.
obcecar [oβθe'kar] *v* blind; deceive. **obce-
carse** *v* become blind; be dazzled. **obce-
cado** *adj* blind; obdurate.
obduración [oβðura'θjon] *sf* obduracy;
obstinacy.
*****obedecer** [oβeðe'θer] *v* obey. **obediencia**
sf obedience. **obediente** *adj* obedient.
obertura [oβer'tura] *sf (música)* overture.
obesidad [oβesi'ðað] *sf* obesity. **obeso** *adj*
obese.
obispo [o'βispo] *sm* bishop. **obispado** *sm*
bishopric.
obituario [oβi'twarjo] *sm* obituary.

objetar [oβxe'tar] *v* object (to). **objeción**
sf objection. **objetivo** *sm* objective. **objeto**
sm object.
oblicuo [o'βlikwo] *adj* oblique. **oblicuar** *v*
slant.
obligar [oβli'gar] *v* oblige; force. **verse
obligado a** be forced to. **obligación** *sf*
obligation. **obligado** *adj* essential. **obligatorio** *adj* compulsory.
obliterar [oβlite'rar] *v* obliterate;
obstruct.
oblongo [o'βlongo] *adj* oblong.
obrar [o'βrar] *v* work; operate; make;
build; behave. **obra** *sf* work. **obra maestra** masterpiece. **obrero, -a** *sm, sf* worker.
obsceno [oβs'θeno] *adj* obscene.
obscenidad *sf* obscenity.
*****obscurecer** [oβskure'θer] *v also*
oscurecer obscure, darken. **obscuridad** *sf*
obscurity. **obscuro** *adj* obscure.
obsequiar [oβseki'ar] *v* entertain; treat;
present. **obsequio** *sm* courtesy; gift. **obse-
quioso** *adj* obsequious; attentive.
observar [oβser'var] *v* observe. **observación** *sf* observation. **observador, -a** *sm, sf*
observer. **observancia** *sf* observance.
observante *adj* observant. **observatorio**
sm observatory.
obsesión [oβse'sjon] *sf* obsession. **obsesionante** *adj* obsessive. **obseso** *adj*
obsessed.
obsoleto [oβso'leto] *adj* obsolete.
obstáculo [oβ'stakulo] *sm* obstacle.
obstante [oβ'stante] *prep* in spite of. *adv*
no **obstante** notwithstanding; nevertheless. **obstar** *v* hinder; oppose.
obstetricia [oβste'triθja] *sf* obstetrics.
obstétrico *adj* obstetric.
obstinarse [oβsti'narse] *v* be obstinate;
persist. **obstinación** *sf* obstinacy.
obstinado *adj* obstinate.
*****obstruir** [oβstru'ir] *v* obstruct. **obstruc-
ción** *sf* obstruction. **obstructivo** *adj*
obstructive.
*****obtener** [oβte'ner] *v* obtain. **obtención** *sf*
attainment.
obturar [obtu'rar] *v* stop up, plug. **obturación** *sf* plugging; sealing. **velocidad de
obturación** *(foto)* shutter speed.
obturador *sm* plug; *(foto)* shutter.
obtuso [oβ'tuso] *adj* obtuse.
obús [o'βus] *sm* howitzer.
obvio ['oββjo] *adj* obvious. **obviar** *v* obvi-
ate.

oca ['oka] *sf* goose.

ocasión [oka'sjon] *sf* occasion; opportunity; reason. **ocasional** *adj* occasional; chance. **ocasionalmente** *adv* occasionally; accidentally. **ocasionar** *v* cause.

ocaso [o'kaso] *sm* sunset; decline; west.

occidental [okθiðen'tal] *adj* western, occidental. **occidente** *sm* west.

océano [o'θeano] *sm* ocean.

ocio ['oθjo] *sm* leisure; idleness. **ociosidad** *sf* idleness. **ocioso** *adj* idle.

ocre ['okre] *sm* ochre.

octágono [ok'tagono] *adj* octagonal. *sm* octagon.

octava [ok'taβa] *sf* octave. **octavo** *adj* eighth. **octogenario, -a** *sm, sf* octogenarian. **octogésimo** *adj* eightieth.

octubre [ok'tuβre] *sm* October.

ocular [oku'lar] *adj* ocular. **testigo ocular** eyewitness. *sm* eyepiece. **oculista** *s(m+f)* oculist.

ocultar [okul'tar] *v* hide. **ocultación** *sf* concealment; dissimulation. **oculto** *adj* secret; hidden; occult.

ocupar [oku'par] *v* occupy; employ; take over. **ocuparse (de)** look after; do; employ. **ocupación** *sf* occupation. **ocupado** *adj* occupied; taken; engaged. **ocupante** *s(m+f)* occupant.

occurrir [okur'rir] *v* occur. **ocurrencia** *sf* occurrence; (*fig*) witticism; idea. **ocurrente** *adj* witty.

ochenta [o'tʃenta] *sm, adj* eighty. **ocho** *sm, adj* eight.

oda ['oða] *sf* ode.

odiar [o'ðjar] *v* hate. **odio** *sm* hate, hatred. **tener odio a uno** hate someone. **odiosidad** *sf* hatefulness; odiousness. **odioso** *adj* odious; hateful.

odorífero [oðo'rifero] *adj* odoriferous, fragrant.

oeste [o'este] *sm* west.

ofender [ofen'der] *v* offend; insult. **ofenderse** *v* resent. **ofensa** *sf* offence; insult. **ofensiva** *sf* attack. **ofensivo** *adj* offensive; insulting. **ofensor, -a** *sm, sf* offender.

oferta [o'ferta] *sf* offer; bid; tender; gift. **ley de la oferta y la demanda** law of supply and demand.

oficial [ofi'θjal] *adj, sm* official. **oficialía** *sf* clerkship. **oficina** *sf* office; agency; laboratory. **oficio** *sm* job; appointment; calling. **oficioso** *adj* diligent; meddlesome.

*ofrecer [ofre'θer] *v* offer. **ofrecerse** *v* volunteer. **¿qué se le ofrece a usted?** may I help you? **ofrecimiento** *sm* offer. **ofrendar** *v* contribute. **ofrenda** *sf* offer.

ofuscar [ofus'kar] *v* bewilder; dazzle.

ogro ['ogro] *sm* ogre.

oigo [o'igo] *V* **oír**.

*oír [o'ir] *v* hear; listen to. **oírse** *v* be heard. **oír decir que** hear that. **oída** *sf* hearing. **oíble** *adj* audible. **oído** *sm* hearing; ear. **dolor de oídos** earache.

ojal [o'xal] *sm* buttonhole.

ojalá [oxa'la] *interj* let's hope so! would to God! *conj* if only.

ojear[1] [oxe'ar] *v* look at. **ojeada** *sf* glance.

ojear[2] *v* (*en la caza*) start game; (*espantar*) scare off.

ojo ['oxo] *sm* eye; opening; hole; keyhole; (*puente*) span. **¡ojo!** look out!

ola ['ola] *sf* wave. **ola de calor** heatwave.

olé [o'le] *interj* bravo!

oleandro [ole'andro] *sm* oleander.

óleo ['oleo] *sm* oil. **pintura al óleo** *sf* oil painting. **oleoducto** *sm* pipeline. **oleosidad** *sf* oiliness. **oleoso** *adj* oily.

*oler [o'ler] *v* smell. **oler bien/mal** smell good/bad. **olfatear** *v* smell; sniff; sniff out. **olfato** *sm* sense of smell. **olfatorio** *adj* olfactory. **oliente** *adj* smelling. **olor** *sm* smell. **oloroso** *adj* fragrant.

oligarquía [oligar'kia] *sf* oligarchy.

olímpico [o'limpiko] *adj* Olympic. **juegos olímpicos** Olympic games.

oliva [o'liβa] *sf* olive; olive tree. **olivar** *sm* olive grove. **olivo** *sm* olive tree.

olmo ['olmo] *sm* elm tree. **olmeda** *sf* elm grove.

olvidar [olβi'ðar] *v* forget. **olvidadizo** *adj* forgetful. **olvido** *sm* forgetfulness.

olla ['oʎa] *sf* pot; kettle; stew; (*remolino*) eddy. **olla exprés** pressure cooker. **olla podrida** hotpot.

ombligo [om'bligo] *sm* navel; (*fig*) core.

ominoso [omi'noso] *adj* ominous.

omitir [omi'tir] *v* omit; neglect. **omisión** *sf* omission. **omiso** *adj* careless. **hacer caso omiso de** ignore; overlook.

ómnibus [om'niβus] *sm* omnibus.

omnipotencia [omnipo'tenθja] *sf* omnipotence. **omnipotente** *adj* omnipotent.

omnisciencia [omni'sθjenθja] *sf* omniscience. **omniscio** *adj* omniscient.

omnívoro [om'niβoro] *adj* omnivorous.

once ['onθe] *sm, adj* eleven.

onda ['onda] *sf* wave; ripple. **onda corta/larga/media** short/long/medium wave. **onda luminosa** light wave. **onda sonora** sound wave. **ondear** *v* wave. **ondearse** *v* swing. **ondulación** *sf* undulation. **ondulado** *adj* wavy. **ondulante** *adj* undulating. **ondular** *v* undulate; wriggle.

oneroso [one'roso] *adj* onerous.

ónice ['oniθe] *sm also* **ónique**, **ónix** onyx.

onza ['onθa] *sf* (*peso y animal*) ounce.

opaco [o'pako] *adj* opaque; dull. **opacidad** *sf* opacity.

opción [op'θjon] *sf* option. **opcional** *adj* optional.

ópera ['opera] *sf* opera.

operar [ope'rar] *v* operate. **operación** *sf* operation. **operador**, **-a** *sm*, *sf* operator; surgeon; projectionist. **operante** *adj* operative. **operario**, **-a** *sm*, *sf* operative, worker. **operativo** *adj* operative.

opinar [opi'nar] *v* think; judge. **opinión** *sf* opinion.

opio ['opjo] *sm* opium.

*oponer [opo'ner] *v* oppose; hinder; contradict. **oponerse a** compete for. **oposición** *sf* opposition. **opositor**, **-a** *sm*, *sf* opponent; competitor.

oportunidad [oportuni'ðað] *sf* opportunity. **oportunista** *adj* opportunist. **oportuno** *adj* opportune.

oprimir [opri'mir] *v* oppress; depress. **opresión** *sf* oppression. **opresivo** *adj* oppressive. **opresor**, **-a** *sm*, *sf* oppressor.

oprobio [o'proβjo] *sm* opprobium, disgrace. **oprobioso** *adj* disgraceful.

optar [op'tar] *v* opt, choose.

óptico ['optiko] *adj* optic, optical. *sm* optician.

optimismo [opti'mismo] *sm* optimism. **optimista** *s*(*m* + *f*) optimist.

óptimo ['optimo] *adj* optimum, best.

opuesto [o'pwesto] *adj* opposed; against.

opulento [opu'lento] *adj* opulent. **opulencia** *sf* opulence.

oquedad [oke'ðað] *sf* hole; hollow.

ora ['ora] *conj* now.

oráculo [o'rakulo] *sm* oracle.

orangután [orangu'tan] *sm* orangutan.

orar [o'rar] *v* pray; plead; make a speech. **oración** *sf* oration; prayer. **partes de la oración** parts of speech. **orador**, **-a** *sm*, *sf* orator. **orador sagrado** preacher. **oral** *adj* oral.

orbe ['orβe] *sm* orb, globe.

órbita ['orβita] *sf* orbit. **orbitar** *v* orbit.

ordenar [orðe'nar] *v* order, command; tidy; direct; ordain. **ordenarse** *v* become ordained. **orden** *sm* order, sequence. **por su orden** successively. **ordenación** *sf* arrangement; ordination. **ordenanza** *sf* arrangement; ordinance.

ordeñar [orðe'nar] *v* milk.

ordinal [orði'nal] *adj* ordinal.

ordinario [orði'narjo] *adj* ordinary; common. **de ordinario** usually.

orear [ore'ar] *v* air, ventilate. **orearse** *v* get a breath of fresh air.

oreja [o'rexa] *sf* ear. **bajar las orejas** knuckle under.

orfebre [or'feβre] *sm* goldsmith; silversmith. **orfebrería** *sf* goldwork; silverwork.

orfeón [orfe'on] *sm* choral society.

orgánico [or'ganiko] *adj* organic. **organismo** *sm* organism. **organista** *s*(*m* + *f*) organist. **organización** *sf* organization. **organizador**, **-a** *sm*, *sf* organizer. **organo** *sm* organ.

orgasmo [or'gasmo] *sm* orgasm.

orgía [or'xia] *sf* orgy.

orgulloso [orgu'loso] *adj* proud. *sm* pride.

orientarse [orjen'tarse] *v* find one's bearings. **orientación** *sf* orientation. **oriental** *adj* oriental, eastern. **oriente** *sm* orient, east. **Extremo Oriente** Far East. **Oriente Medio** Middle East.

orificio [ori'fiθjo] *sm* orifice, hole.

origen [o'rixen] *sm* origin; native country. **original** *adj* original. **originalidad** *sf* originality. **originar** *v* originate. **originarse** *v* arise.

orilla [o'riʎa] *sf* edge; bank; shore. **a orillas de** on the banks of.

orín [o'rin] *sm* rust.

orina [o'rina] *sf* urine. **orinal** *sm* chamber pot. **orinar** *v* urinate.

oriundo [o'rjundo] *adj* native of.

orlar [or'lar] *v* border, edge. **orla** *sf* border, trimming.

ornamentar [ornamen'tar] *v* adorn, decorate. **ornamentación** *sf* ornamentation. **ornamental** *adj* ornamental. **ornamento** *sm* ornament. **ornar** *v* adorn. **ornato** *sm* adornment.

ornitología [ornitolo'xia] *sf* ornithology. **ornitólogo** *sm* ornithologist.

oro ['oro] *sm* gold. **oro batido** gold leaf. **oro en bruto** bullion. **oropel** *sm* tinsel.

orquesta [or'kesta] sf orchestra. orquestación sf orchestration. orquestar v orchestrate.

orquidea [or'kiðea] sf orchid.

ortega [or'tega] sf grouse.

ortodoxo [orto'ðokso] adj orthodox.
ortodoxia sf orthodoxy.

ortografía [ortogra'fia] sf orthography,
spelling.

ortopédico [orto'peðiko], -a sm, sf ortho-
pedist. adj orthopedic.

oruga [o'ruga] sf caterpillar.

os [os] pron pl you.

osa ['osa] sf she-bear. oso bear. oso blanco polar bear.

osar [o'sar] v dare. osadía sf daring. osado
adj daring.

oscilar [osθi'lar] v oscillate, swing. oscilación sf oscillation.

oscuro [os'kuro] adj dark, obscure.
oscurecer v darken; confuse. oscuridad sf
obscurity.

ostensible [osten'siβle] adj ostensible;
apparent. ostentación sf ostentation.
ostentar v show off. ostentativo adj also
ostentoso ostentatious.

ostra ['ostra] sf oyster.

otear [ote'ar] v make out; watch; scan.

otoño [o'tono] sm autumn. otoñada sf
autumn season. otoñal adj autumnal.
otoñarse v be seasoned.

otorgar [otor'gar] v grant; award; confer.
otorgamiento sm granting; authorization.

otro ['otro] adj other; another. otra vez
again. otro tanto the same (again). pron
another. algún otro some other.

ovación [oβa'θjon] sf ovation. ovacionar v
give an ovation to.

óvalo ['oβalo] sm oval; ellipse. oval adj
oval.

ovario [o'βarjo] sm ovary.

oveja [o'βexa] sf ewe; sheep.

ovillo [o'βiʎo] sm (de lana) ball; heap.

oxidar [oksi'ðar] v oxidize. óxido sm
oxide. oxígeno sm oxygen.

oye ['oje] V oir.

oyente [o'jente] adj hearing. s(m+f) listener.

ozono [o'θono] sm ozone.

P

pabellón [paβe'ʎon] sm pavilion; bell
tent; summerhouse; hospital block; flag.

*pacer [pa'θer] v graze, pasture.

paciencia [pa'θjenθja] sf patience.
paciente s(m+f), adj patient. pacienzudo
adj long-suffering.

pacificar [paθifi'kar] v pacify. pacificación
sf pacification. pacificador adj pacifying.
pacífico adj pacific, peaceful. Oceano
Pacífico Pacific Ocean. pacifismo sm pacifism. pacifista s(m+f) pacifist.

pacotilla [pako'tiʎa] sf inferior goods pl.
de pacotilla shoddy.

pactar [pak'tar] v make a pact, agree.
pacto sm pact, agreement.

pachorra [pa'tʃorra] sf sluggishness; indolence.

*padecer [paðe'θer] v suffer; endure.
padecer de suffer from. padecimiento sm
suffering; ailment.

padre ['paðre] sm father. padres sm pl
parents. padrastro sm stepfather. Padre
Nuestro Lord's Prayer. padrino sm godfather; second; sponsor. padrino de boda
best man.

padrón [pa'ðron] sm census; pattern;
memorial; (fam) indulgent father.

pagano [pa'gano], -a sm, sf, adj pagan.

pagar [pa'gar] v pay. pagarse de take a
liking to. paga sf payment; salary.
pagadero adj payable. pagador, -a sm, sf
payer. pagaduría sf pay office. pagaré sm
IOU. pago sm payment; reward.

página ['paxina] sf page.

país [pa'is] sm country. paisaje sm landscape; countryside. paisanaje sm peas-
antry. paisano, -na sm, sf compatriot;
peasant.

Países Bajos [pa'ises'βaxos] sm pl The
Netherlands.

paja ['paxa] sf straw. echar pajas draw
lots. pajita sf drinking straw.

pájaro ['paxaro] sm bird. pajarera sf birdcage.

paje ['paxe] sm (niño) page.

pala ['pala] sf shovel; spade; scoop; dustpan; bat. palazo sm blow with a stick.

palabra [pa'laβra] sf word. de palabra by
word of mouth. faltar a la palabra break
one's word. palabreo sm verbiage.

palabrista *s(m+f)* chatterbox. **palabrota** *sf* swear word.

palacio [pa'laθjo] *sm* palace; mansion. **en palacio** at court.

paladar [pala'ðar] *sm* palate. **paladear** *v* taste, relish.

palanca [pa'lanka] *sf* crowbar; lever; (*fam*) influence.

palangana [palan'gana] *sf* washbasin.

palco ['palko] *sm* (*teatro*) box.

paleta [pa'leta] *sf* shovel; trowel; (*de pintor*) palette; (*de hélice*) blade; (*anat*) shoulder blade.

paliar [pali'ar] *v* alleviate. **paliativo** *adj* palliative.

*****palidecer** [paliðe'θer] *v* become pale. **palidez** paleness. **pálido** *adj* pale.

palillo [pa'liλo] *sm* toothpick; small stick.

paliza [pa'liθa] *sf* beating, hiding.

palma ['palma] *sf* palm tree; (*anat*) palm. **palmada** *sf* slap; applause. **palmar** *adj* clear, obvious. **palmatoria** *sf* candlestick; cane. **palmear** *v* clap hands. **palmera** *sf* palm tree.

palmo ['palmo] *sm* (*medida*) span, handbreadth. **palmotear** *v* applaud. **palmoteo** *sm* applause.

palo ['palo] *sm* stick; pole; handle; blow with a stick; mast. **dar de palos** thrash.

paloma [pa'loma] *sf* dove; pigeon. **palomar** *sm* dovecote. **palomino** *sm* young pigeon.

palpable [pal'paβle] *adj* palpable.

palpar [pal'par] *v* feel, touch. **palparse** *v* grope.

palpitar [palpi'tar] *v* palpitate, throb. **palpitación** *sf* palpitation. **palpitante** *adj* palpitating, throbbing.

paludismo [palu'ðismo] *sm* malaria.

palurdo [pa'lurðo] *sm, adj* rustic.

palustre[1] [pa'lustre] *adj* marshy.

palustre[2] *sm* trowel.

pan [pan] *sm* bread; loaf; dough. **pan ácimo** unleavened bread. **panadería** *sf* bread shop. **panadero, -a** *sm, sf* baker.

pana ['pana] *sf* corduroy. **pana lisa** velvet.

panal [pa'nal] *sm* honeycomb.

panamá [pana'ma] *sm* Panama hat.

panamericano [panameri'kano] *adj* panAmerican.

pancarta [pan'karta] *sf* placard.

pandereta [pande'reta] *sf* tambourine.

pandilla [pan'diλa] *sf* gang; clique.

panfleto [pan'fleto] *sm* pamphlet. **panfletista** *s(m+f)* pamphleteer.

pánico ['paniko] *sm, adj* panic.

pantalón [panta'lon] *sm also* **pantalones** trousers.

pantalla [pan'taλa] *sf* lampshade; screen.

pantano [pan'tano] *sm* marsh; bog. **pantanal** *sm* marshland. **pantanoso** *adj* swampy.

panteísta [pante'ista] *s(m+f)* pantheist. **panteísmo** *sm* pantheism.

pantera [pan'tera] *sf* panther.

pantomima [panto'mima] *sf* pantomime.

pantorrilla [panto'riλa] *sf* (*anat*) calf.

pantufla [pan'tufla] *sf or* **pantuflo** *sm* slipper.

panza ['panθa] *sf* belly. **panzada** *sf* bellyful.

pañal [pa'nal] *sm* nappy.

pañería [pane'ria] *sf* drapery. **pañero** *sm* draper. **pañete** *sm* light cloth. **paño** *sm* cloth. **paños menores** underclothes. **pañuelo** *sm* handkerchief.

papa[1] ['papa] *sm* pope. **papado** *sm* papacy. **papal** *adj* papal.

papa[2] *sf* potato.

papá [pa'pa] *sm* daddy.

papada [pa'paða] *sf* double chin.

papagayo [papa'gajo] *sm* parrot.

papar [pa'par] *v* eat; gulp. **papamoscas** *m invar* flycatcher; (*fig*) simpleton. **papar moscas** gape.

papel [pa'pel] *sm* paper. **papel de forrar** brown paper. **papel de fumar** cigarette paper. **papeleo** *sm* paper work; (*fam*) red tape. **papelera** *sf* wastepaper basket. **papelería** *sf* stationer's.

papera [pa'pera] *sf* goitre. **paperas** *sf pl* mumps *sing*.

papiro [pa'piro] *sm* papyrus.

paquete [pa'kete] *sm* packet.

par [par] *sm* pair. *adj* equal. **sin par** matchless.

para ['para] *prep* for; towards. **para mañana** by tomorrow. **¿para qué?** why?

parábola [pa'raβola] *sf* parable; parabola.

parabrisas [para'βrisas] *sm invar* windscreen.

paracaídas [paraka'iðas] *sm invar* parachute. **paracaidista** *s(m+f)* parachutist.

parachoques [para'ʃtokes] *sm invar* (*auto*) bumper.

parada [pa'raða] *sf* stop; stopping; (*taxi*) rank; pause; parade; dam. **paradero** *sm* whereabouts; destination; home. **parado** *adj* motionless; unemployed.

paradoja [para'ðoxa] *sf* paradox.
paradójico *adj* paradoxical.

parador [para'ðor] *sm* tourist hotel.

parafina [para'fina] *sf* paraffin.

paráfrasis [pa'rafrasis] *sf invar* paraphrase. **parafrasear** *v* paraphrase.

paraguas [pa'ragwas] *sm invar* umbrella.

paraíso [para'iso] *sm* paradise; *(teatro)* gallery.

paralela [para'lela] *sf* parallel. **paralelas** *sf pl* parallel bars. **paralelo** *sm, adj* parallel.

parálisis [pa'ralisis] *sf* paralysis. **paralítico** *sm, adj* paralytic. **paralizar** *v* paralyse.

páramo ['paramo] *sm* wilderness; bleak plateau. **paramera** *sf* desert.

parangón [paran'gon] *sm* comparison. **parangonar** *v* compare.

parapeto [para'peto] *sm* parapet; railing.

parar [pa'rar] *v* stop; check. **pararse** *v* stay; end up. **parar en mal** come to a bad end.

pararrayos [parar'rajos] *sm invar* lightning conductor.

parásito [pa'rasito] *sm* parasite. *adj* parasitic.

parasol [para'sol] *sm* parasol.

parcela [par'θela] *sf (de tierra)* plot. **parcelar** *v* parcel out.

parcial [par'θjal] *adj* partial. **parcialidad** *sf* partiality.

parco ['parko] *adj* frugal; mean; sparing.

parche ['partʃe] *sm* plaster; patch; drumhead.

pardo ['parðo] *adj* dark; brown.

parear [pare'ar] *v* match, pair.

***parecer** [para'θer] *v* seem; appear. **parecerse** *v* resemble. **parecido** *adj* similar. **bien parecido** good-looking.

pared [pa'reð] *sf* wall. **paredón** *sm* large wall.

pareja [pa'rexa] *sf* pair; couple. **parejo** *adj* even; equal.

parentela [paren'tela] *sf* kindred. **parentesco** *sm* kinship.

paréntesis [pa'rentesis] *sm* parenthesis; bracket.

paridad [pari'ðað] *sf* comparison; parity.

pariente [pa'rjente] *sm* relation.

parir [pa'rir] *v* give birth to.

París [pa'ris] *s* Paris.

parla ['parla] *sf* gossip; chatter. **parlador**, **-a** *sm, sf* talker. **parlanchín** *adj* talkative.

parlante *adj* chattering. **parlar** *v* chatter.

parleta *sf* small talk.

parlamento [parla'mento] *sm* parliament. **parlamentario** *adj* parliamentary.

paro ['paro] *sm* stoppage; unemployment.

parodiar [paro'ðjar] *v* parody. **parodia** *sf* parody.

paroxismo [parok'sismo] *sm* paroxysm.

parpadear [parpaðe'ar] *v* blink; wink. **parpadeo** *sm* blinking; winking. **párpado** *sm* eyelid.

parque ['parke] *sm* park.

parra ['parra] *sf* vine. **hoja de parra** figleaf. **parra virgen** Virginia creeper.

párrafo ['parrafo] *sm* paragraph.

parricida [parri'θiða] *s(m+f) (criminal)* parricide. **parricidio** *sm (crimen)* parricide.

parrilla [par'riʎa] *sf* grill; gridiron; grate; grillroom.

párroco ['parroko] *sm* parish priest. **parroquia** *sf* parish; parish church. **parroquial** *adj* parochial. **parroquiano**, **-a** *sm, sf* parishioner; regular customer.

parsimonia [parsi'monja] *sf* parsimony; frugality; calmness.

parte ['parte] *sf* part; share; point; side; way; party; role; actor. **en otra parte** elsewhere. **por todas partes** everywhere. **por una parte y por otra** on the one hand and on the other.

partera [par'tera] *sf* midwife.

partición [parti'θjon] *sf* partition; division. **partible** *adj* divisible.

participar [partiθi'par] *v* participate; partake; invest; inform; announce. **participación** *sf* participation; share; announcement. **participante** *s(m+f)* participant; informant; competitor. **partícipe** *s(m+f)* participant.

participio [parti'θipjo] *sm (gram)* participle.

partícula [par'tikula] *sf* particle.

particular [partiku'lar] *adj* particular; peculiar; individual; personal. **casa particular** private house. *sm* matter; individual; civilian. **particularidad** *sf* peculiarity. **particularizar** *v* specify; distinguish; prefer. **particularizarse** *v* stand out. **particularamente** *adv* in particular.

partida [par'tiða] *sf* departure; certificate; *(com)* entry; item; party; game. **partida de campo** picnic. **partida doble** double entry. **partidario**, **-a** *sm, sf* follower; partisan.

partido [par'tiðo] *sm (deporte)* match;

(*pol*) party. *adj* divided. **darse a partido** give in. **sacar partido** benefit from.
partir [par'tir] *v* leave, depart; divide; share. **a partir de hoy** from today on. **partirse** *v* differ in opinion; depart. **partidor** *sm* distributor.
partitura [parti'tura] *sf* (*música*) score.
parto ['parto] *sm* childbirth; delivery; (*fig*) brainchild.
parvo ['parβo] *adj* little. **párvulo** *adj* very small.
pasa ['pasa] *sf* raisin. **pasa de Corinto** currant.
pasada [pa'saða] *sf* passage; (*aves*) flight. **de pasada** in passing. **mala pasada** dirty trick. **pasadero** *adj* tolerable.
pasado [pa'saðo] *sm, adj* past. **lo pasado, pasado** let bygones be bygones. **pasado mañana** the day after tomorrow.
pasador [pasa'ðor], -a *sm, sf* smuggler. *sm* filter; colander; bolt; pin; fastener. **pasadores** *sm pl* cufflinks *pl*.
pasaje [pa'saxe] *sm* passage; fare; ticket; voyage; passengers *pl*. **pasajero**, -a *sm, sf* passenger.
pasamano [pasa'mano] *sm* bannister; handrail.
pasapasa [pasa'pasa] *sm* sleight-of-hand.
pasaporte [pasa'porte] *sm* passport.
pasar [pa'sar] *v* pass; give; spend; take; send; run; cross; penetrate. **pasar de moda** be out of fashion. **pasarlo bien/mal** have a good/bad time. **pasar por** be considered. **pasar por alto** overlook. **¿qué pasa?** what's up? **pasarse** pass off; be over; miss. **pasarse de** be too. **pasarse por** call in at.
pasarela [pasa'rela] *sf* footbridge; gangway.
pasatiempo [pasa'tjempo] *sm* pastime; amusement.
pascua ['paskwa] *sf* (*rel*) feast; Christmas; Easter; Epiphany; Passover. **¡felices pascuas y próspero año nuevo!** merry Christmas and a happy New Year!
pase ['pase] *sm* invitation; permission; (*autorización*) pass.
pasear [pase'ar] *v* go for a walk; take for a walk; go for a ride. **paseo** *sm* walk; drive; ride.
pasillo [pa'siλo] *sm* corridor, passage.
pasión [pasi'on] *sf* passion. **pasional** *adj* passionate.
pasivo [pa'siβo] *adj* passive. *sm* (*com*) liabilities *pl*. **pasividad** *sf* passivity.

pasmar [pas'mar] *v* chill; stun; amaze. **pasmo** *sm* amazement; convulsion. **pasmoso** *adj* wonderful.
paso ['paso] *sm* step; pace; walk; passage; situation. **paso a nivel** level-crossing. **paso a paso** step by step. **salir del paso** get out of a difficulty.
pasta ['pasta] *sf* pasta; dough; paste. **pastas** *sf pl* noodles.
pastar [pas'tar] *v* graze, pasture.
pastel [pas'tel] *sm* cake, pastry; (*color*) pastel. **pastel de carne** meat pie. **pastelería** *sf* cake shop; cakes *pl*; confectionery. **pastelero**, -a *sm, sf* pastrycook.
pastilla [pas'tiλa] *sf* bar; piece; tablet.
pastinaca [pasti'naka] *sf* (*bot*) turnip; (*zool*) stingray.
pasto ['pasto] *sm* grass; pasture. **a pasto** galore. **pastor** *sm* shepherd; pastor. **pastoral** *adj* pastoral. **pastorear** *v* pasture.
pastura [pas'tura] *sf* pasture; fodder.
pata ['pata] *sf* (*de animal*) foot; leg; paw. **meter la pata** (*fam*) put one's foot in it. **tener mala pata** (*fam*) be unlucky. **patada** *sf* kick; stamp. **patalear** *v* stamp; kick about. **pataleo** *sm* kicking.
patán [pa'tan] *sm* lout. *adj* churlish. **patanería** *sf* boorishness.
patata [pa'tata] *sf* potato. **patatas fritas** chips.
patear [pate'ar] *v* kick; stamp.
patente [pa'tente] *sm* (*com*) patent. *adj* obvious.
paternal [pater'nal] *adj* paternal. **paternidad** *sf* paternity. **paterno** *adj* paternal.
patético [pa'tetiko] *adj* pathetic.
patíbulo [pa'tiβulo] *sm* gallows *pl*.
patillas [pa'tiλas] *sf pl* whiskers *pl*, sideboards *pl*.
patín [pa'tin] *sm* skate. **patín de ruedas** roller skate. **patinadero** *sm* skating rink. **patinador**, -a *sm, sf* skater. **patinaje** *sm* skating. **patinar** *v* skate; skid. **patinazo** *sm* skid; (*fam*) blunder. **patinete** *sm* child's scooter.
patio ['patjo] *sm* patio; yard.
pato ['pato] *sm* duck. **pagar el pato** (*fam*) carry the can.
patochada [pato'tʃaða] *sf* blunder.
patología [patolo'xia] *sf* pathology. **patológico** *adj* pathological. **patólogo** *sm* pathologist.

patraña [pa'traɲa] *sf* cock-and-bull story; fib.

patria ['patrja] *sf* native land. **patriota** *s(m+f)* patriot. **patriótico** *adj* patriotic. **patriotismo** *sm* patriotism.

patriarca [pa'trjarka] *sm* patriarch. **patriarcal** *adj* patriarchal.

patricio [pa'triθjo], **-a** *sm, sf, adj* patrician.

patrimonio [patri'monjo] *sm* patrimony, birthright. **patrimonial** *adj* patrimonial.

patrocinar [patroθi'nar] *v* patronize; sponsor. **patrocinador**, **-a** *sm, sf* patron; sponsor. **patrocinio** *sm* patronage; sponsorship.

patrón [pa'tron] *sm* patron; owner; landlord; pattern. **patronato** *sm* patronage; board of trustees; society.

patrono [pa'trono] *sm* boss; patron saint; owner.

patrulla [pa'truʎa] *sf* patrol. **patrullar** *v* patrol.

paulatino [paula'tino] *adj* slow, gradual. **paulatinamente** *adj* gradually; little by little.

pausa ['pausa] *sf* pause; (*música*) rest. **pausado** *adj* slow; deliberate. **pausar** *v* pause; interrupt.

pauta ['pauta] *sf* rule; model; lines *pl*. **pautar** *v* rule; give instructions. **papel pautado** ruled paper.

pávido ['paβiðo] *adj* timid.

pavimentar [paβimen'tar] *v* pave; surface. **pavimento** *sm* pavement.

pavo ['paβo] *sm* turkey. **pavo real** peacock. **pavonear** *v* show off.

pavor [pa'βor] *sm* terror; dread. **pavorido** *adj* terror-stricken. **pavoroso** *adj* dreadful; awful. **pavura** *sf* fear; dread.

payaso [pa'jaso] *sm* clown. **payasada** *sf* clowning.

paz [paθ] *sf* peace. **hacer las paces** make it up. **¡paz!** hush!

peaje [pe'axe] *sm* toll. **peajero** *sm* tollcollector.

peatón [pea'ton] *sm* pedestrian.

peca ['peka] *sf* spot; freckle. **pecoso** *adj* freckled.

pecar [pe'kar] *v* sin. **pecado** *sm* sin. **pecador**, **-a** *sm, sf* sinner. **pecaminoso** *adj* sinful.

pécora ['pekora] *sf* sheep; (*fam*) slut.

peculiar [peku'ljar] *adj* peculiar; special. **peculiaridad** *sf* peculiarity. **peculiarmente** peculiarly.

pechera [pe'tʃera] *sf* bib; shirt-front.

pecho ['petʃo] *sm* chest; bosom; breast; courage; tax. **dar el pecho** suckle. **enfermo del pecho** consumptive. **pechuga** *sf* (*de ave*) breast.

pedagogía [peðago'xia] *sf* pedagogy. **pedagógico** *adj* teaching. **pedagogo** *sm* teacher.

pedal [pe'ðal] *sm* pedal. **pedalear** *v* pedal.

pedante [pe'ðante] *s(m+f)* pedant. *adj* pedantic. **pedantería** *sf* pedantry.

pedazo [pe'ðaθo] *sm* piece. **hacerse pedazos** be smashed to bits.

pedernal [peðer'nal] *sm* flint.

pedestal [peðe'stal] *sm* pedestal.

pedestre [pe'ðestre] *adj* pedestrian.

pediatría [peðja'tria] *sf* paediatrics. **pediatra** or **pediatra** *sm* paediatrician.

pedicuro [peði'kuro], **-a** *sm, sf* chiropodist. *sf* chiropody.

*****pedir** [pe'ðir] *v* ask; ask for; order. **pedir limosna** beg. **pedir prestado** borrow. **pedido** *sm* demand; (*com*) order. **pedimento** *sm* petition.

pedo ['peðo] *sm* (*vulgar*) fart.

pedregal [peðre'gal] *sm* stony ground. **pedrea** *sf* stoning; hailstorm. **pedregoso** *adj* stony. **pedrería** *sf* jewels *pl*. **pedrero** *sm* stone-cutter. **pedrisco** *sm* hailstorm.

pegar [pe'gar] *v* hit; glue; (*med*) infect; take effect; give; let out; fire; sew on. **pegar fuego** a set fire to. **pegar un tiro** fire a shot. **pega** *sf* difficulty; hoax; snag. **poner pegas a** find fault with. **pegajoso** *adj* sticky; infectious.

peinar [pei'nar] *v* comb. **peinado** *sm* coiffure. **peinador**, **-a** *sm, sf* hairdresser; *sm* bathrobe. **peine** *sm* comb.

pelar [pe'lar] *v* cut; peel; shear; skin; shell. **pelar la pava** woo. **pelado** *adj* shorn; peeled; bare. **pelaje** *sm* fur. **pelambre** *sm* (*de animales*) hair. **pelambrera** *sf* fleece.

peldaño [pel'ðaɲo] *sm* stair; step.

pelear [pele'ar] *v* fight. **pelearse con alguien** fight somebody. **pelea** *sf* fight. **peleador** *sm* fight.

pelele [pe'lele] *sm* puppet; dummy.

peliagudo [pelja'guðo] *adj* (*fig*) difficult, tough.

pelícano [pe'likano] *sm* pelican.

película [pe'likula] *sf* film.

peligro [pe'ligro] *sm* danger. **peligrarse** *v* be in danger. **peligroso** *adj* dangerous.

pelmazo [pel'maθo] *sm also* **pelma** *sf* bore; crushed mass.

pelo ['pelo] *sm* hair; (*en madera*) grain; nap. **de medio pelo** low-class. **soltarse el pelo** show one's true colours. **pelón** *adj* bald.

pelota [pe'lota] *sf* ball. **echarse la pelota** pass the buck. **en pelota** naked.

pelotón [pelo'ton] *sm* platoon; squad.

peltre ['peltre] *sm* pewter.

peluca [pe'luka] *sf* wig.

peludo [pe'luðo] *adj* hairy.

peluquero [pelu'kero], **-a** *sm, sf* hairdresser. **peluquería** *sf* hairdresser's.

pelusa [pe'lusa] *sf* down; fuzz; (*fam*) jealousy.

pelleja [pe'ʎexa] *sf also* **pellejo** *sm* hide, skin. **jugarse el pellejo** risk one's neck.

pellizcar [peʎiθ'kar] *v* nip, pinch. **pellizco** *sm* nip, pinch.

pello ['peʎo] *sm* fur jacket.

pena ['pena] *sf* pain; grief; hardship; penalty; effort. **pena capital** capital punishment. **¡qué pena!** what a shame! **penable** *adj* punishable. **penado** *adj* painful. **penal** *adj* penal. **penalidad** *sf* penalty. **penar** *v* punish; suffer. **penarse** *v* grieve.

pender [pen'der] *v* hang; (*jur*) be pending. **pendiente** *adj* hanging; pending. **estar pendiente de** depend on.

péndulo ['pendulo] *sm* pendulum.

pene ['pene] *sm* penis.

penetrar [pene'trar] *v* penetrate; comprehend. **penetrarse** *v* become aware of; imbibe. **penetrable** *adj* penetrable. **penetración** *sf* penetration. **penetrante** *adj* penetrating.

penicilina [peniθi'lina] *sf* penicillin.

península [pe'ninsula] *sf* peninsula. **peninsular** *adj* peninsular.

penique [pe'nike] *sm* penny.

penitencia [peni'tenθja] *sf* penitence. **hacer penitencia** (*fam*) take pot-luck. **penitencial** *adj* penitential. **penitenciaria** *sf* penitentiary. **penitente** *adj* penitent.

penoso [pe'noso] *adj* painful; difficult.

*pensar [pen'sar] *v* think; think over; intend. **pensar en** think about. **pensado** *adj* deliberate. **de pensado** on purpose. **pensador**, **-a** *sm, sf* thinker. **pensamiento** *sm* thought. **pensativo** *adj* thoughtful.

pensión [pensi'on] *sf* pension; boarding house; hardship. **pensionado**, **-a** *sm, sf* pensioner. **pensionar** *v* pension. **pensionista** *s*(*m* + *f*) pensioner; boarder.

pentágono [pen'tagono] *sm* pentagon.

penúltimo [pe'nultimo] *adj* penultimate.

penumbra [pe'numβra] *sf* half-light.

penuria [pe'nurja] *sf* penury; shortage.

peña ['peɲa] *sf* crag; rock; cliff; group of friends. **peñasco** *sm* large rock. **peñascoso** *adj* rocky. **peñón** *sm* rocky mountain. **el Peñón de Gibraltar** the Rock of Gibraltar.

peón [pe'on] *sm* unskilled labourer; pedestrian; foot-soldier; (*ajedrez*) pawn.

peonía [peo'nia] *sf* peony.

peor [pe'or] *adj*, *adv* worse; worst. **peoría** *sf* worsening.

pepino [pe'pino] *sm* cucumber. **no valer un pepino** not be worth a damn. **pepinillo** *sm* gherkin.

pepita [pe'pita] *sf* seed, pip; (*oro*) nugget.

pequeño [pe'keɲo] *adj* small; humble. **pequeñez** *sf* smallness; pettiness.

pera ['pera] *sf* pear; light-switch; (*barba*) goatee; sinecure. **peral** *sm* pear tree.

perca ['perka] *sf* (*zool*) perch.

percance [per'kanθe] *sm* mishap; profit.

percatarse [perka'tarse] *v* notice.

percibir [perθi'βir] *v* perceive; collect. **percepción** *sf* perception; collection. **perceptible** *adj* perceptible. **perceptivo** *adj* perceptive. **perceptor**, **-a** *sm, sf* perceiver. **percibo** *sm* collecting.

percusión [perku'sjon] *sf* percussion.

percha ['pertʃa] *sf* perch; pole; hat-stand; coat-rack.

*perder [per'ðer] *v* lose; spoil; waste. **perderse por** be inordinately fond of. **perdición** *sf* loss; perdition. **pérdida** *sf* damage; waste. **perdido** *adj* lost; dissolute.

perdiz [per'ðiθ] *sf* partridge.

perdonar [perðo'nar] *v* pardon; excuse. **perdón** *sm* pardon; mercy. **con perdón** by your leave. **perdonable** *adj* pardonable. **perdonavidas** *m invar* (*fam*) bully.

perdurar [perðu'rar] *v* endure. **perdurable** *adj* everlasting.

*perecer [pere'θer] *v* perish. **perecerse por** crave. **perecedero** *adj* perishable.

peregrinar [peregri'nar] *v* travel; go on a pilgrimage. **peregrinación** *sf* pilgrimage. **peregrino**, **-a** *sm, sf* pilgrim.

perejil [pere'xil] *sm* parsley.

perenne [pe'renne] *adj* perennial.

perentorio [peren'torjo] *adj* peremptory; urgent.

perezoso [pere'θoso] *adj* lazy. **pereza** *sf* laziness.

perfecto [per'fekto] *adj* perfect. **perfección** *sf* perfection. **perfeccionamiento** *sm* improvement; perfection. **perfeccionar** *v* perfect; improve.

pérfido ['perfiðo] *adj* perfidious. **perfidia** *sf* perfidy.

perfilar [perfi'lar] *v* outline. **perfil** *sm* profile; outline.

perforar [perfo'rar] *v* perforate; drill; puncture. **perforación** *sf* perforation. **perforadora** *sf* drill.

perfumar [perfu'mar] *v* perfume. **perfume** *sm* perfume. **perfumería** *sf* perfume shop.

perfunctorio [perfunk'torjo] *adj* perfunctory.

pericial [peri'θjal] *adj* expert. **pericia** *sf* skill.

perico [pe'riko] *sm* parakeet; toupee.

periferia [peri'ferja] *sf* periphery.

perímetro [pe'rimetro] *sm* perimeter.

periódico [peri'oðiko] *sm* periodical; newspaper. *adj* periodic. **periodicidad** *sf* recurrence. **periodismo** *sm* journalism. **periodista** *s(m+f)* journalist. **periodístico** *adj* journalistic. **período** *or* **periodo** *sm* period. **período de prácticas** probationary period.

peripecia [peri'peθja] *sf* vicissitude; incident; adventure.

periscopio [peris'kopjo] *sm* periscope.

perjudicar [perxuði'kar] *v* prejudice; harm. **perjudicial** *adj* harmful. **perjuicio** *sm* prejudice; damage.

perjurar [perxu'rar] *v* perjure oneself. **perjurio** *sm* perjury. **perjuro, -a** *sm, sf* perjurer.

perla ['perla] *sf* pearl. **de perlas** perfectly.

*****permanecer** [permane'θer] *v* stay, remain. **permanencia** *sf* stay; permanence. **permanente** *adj* permanent.

permitir [permi'tir] *v* permit. **¿me permite?** may I? **permisible** *adj* permissible. **permisivo** *adj* permissive. **permiso** *sm* permission; permit; leave; licence. **con permiso** if I may.

permutar [permu'tar] *v* permute; exchange. **permuta** *sf* exchange; permutation. **permutación** *sf* permutation.

perniabierto [pernia'βjerto] *adj* bandy-legged.

pernicioso [perni'θjoso] *adj* pernicious.

pernoctar [pernok'tar] *v* spend the night.

pero[1] ['pero] *conj* but; yet. **¡pero bueno!** why!

pero[2] *sm* pear tree.

perogrullada [perogru'ʎaða] *sf* platitude.

perorar [pero'rar] *v* make a speech. **peroración** *sf* peroration.

peróxido [per'oksiðo] *sm* peroxide.

perpendicular [perpendiku'lar] *sf, adj* perpendicular.

perpetrar [perpe'trar] *v* perpetrate. **perpetración** *sf* perpetration.

perpetuar [perpe'twar] *v* perpetuate. **perpetuación** *sf* perpetuation. **perpetuidad** *sf* perpetuity. **perpetuo** *adj* perpetual.

perplejo [per'plexo] *adj* perplexed; perplexing. **perplejidad** *sf* perplexity.

perro ['perro] *sm* dog; (*fam*) penny. **perra** *sf* bitch. **perrera** *sf* kennel; dog pound; dogcatcher's wagon. **perrero** *sm* dogcatcher.

*****perseguir** [perse'gir] *v* pursue; persecute. **persecución** *sf* pursuit; persecution. **perseguidor, -a** *sm, sf* pursuer; persecutor.

perseverar [perseβe'rar] *v* persevere. **perseverancia** *sf* perseverance. **perseverante** *adj* persevering.

persiana [per'sjana] *sf* slatted shutter. **persiana veneciana** venetian blind.

persistir [persis'tir] *v* persist. **persistencia** *sf* persistence. **persistente** *adj* persistent.

persona [per'sona] *sf* person. **persona a persona** man to man. **personaje** *sm* personage; (*teatro*) character. **personal** *adj* personal. **personalidad** *sf* personality. **personalismo** *sm* partiality. **personalizar** *v* personalize. **personarse** *v* appear in person. **personificar** *v* personify.

perspectiva [perspek'tiβa] *sf* perspective; outlook.

perspicaz [perspi'kaθ] *adj* perspicacious. **perspicacia** *sf* perspicacity.

persuadir [perswa'ðir] *v* persuade. **persuasión** *sf* persuasion. **persuasivo** *adj* persuasive.

*****pertenecer** [pertene'θer] *v* belong. **perteneciente** *adj* belonging. **pertenencia** *sf* ownership; property; membership.

pértiga ['pertiga] *sf* pole. **salto de pértiga** pole vault.

pertiguero [perti'gero] *sm* verger.

pertinaz [perti'naθ] *adj* pertinacious. **pertinacia** *sf* pertinacity.

pertinente [perti'nente] *adj* pertinent. **pertinencia** *sf* pertinence.

pertrechar [pertre't∫ar] *v* supply; equip. **pertrechos** *sm pl* equipment *sing*; munitions *pl*.

perturbar [pertur'βar] *v* perturb. **perturbación** *sf* perturbation. **perturbador** *adj* perturbing.

*****pervertir** [perβer'tir] *v* pervert. **perversidad** *sf* perversity. **perversión** *sf* perversion. **perverso** *adj* perverse.

pesa ['pesa] *sf* weight. **pesas y medidas** weights and measures. **pesadez** *sf* heaviness; drowsiness; hardship.

pesadilla [pesa'ðiʎa] *sf* nightmare.

pesado [pe'saðo] *adj* heavy; sluggish. *sm* bore. **pesadumbre** *sf* grief.

pésame ['pesame] *sm* condolence.

pesar [pe'sar] *v* weigh. **a pesar de** in spite of. **me pesa mucho** I'm very sorry.

pescar [pes'kar] *v* fish. **pesca** *sf* fishing. **pescada** *sf* hake. **pescadería** *sf* fish shop; fish market. **pescadero** *sm* fishmonger. **pescado** *sm* fish. **pescador** *sm* fisherman. **pescador de caña** angler.

pescuezo [pes'kweθo] *sm* neck.

pesebre [pe'seβre] *sm* crib; manger.

pesimista [pesi'mista] *s(m+f)* pessimist. *adj* pessimistic. **pesimismo** *sm* pessimism.

pésimo ['pesimo] *adj* worthless.

peso ['peso] *sm* weight; balance; scales *pl*; peso. **en peso** bodily. **peso específico** specific gravity.

pesquisa [pes'kisa] *sf* inquiry.

pestañear [pestaɲe'ar] *v* blink. **pestaña** *sf* eyelash; fringe; hem. **pestañeo** *sm* blink.

peste ['peste] *sf* plague; corruption; poison. **echar pestes** curse. **pesticida** *sf* pesticide. **pestilencia** *sf* pestilence. **pestilente** *adj* pestilent; stinking.

pestillo [pes'tiʎo] *sm* bolt; latch.

petaca [pe'taka] *sf* tobacco pouch; cigarette case.

pétalo ['petalo] *sm* petal.

petardo [pe'tarðo] *sm* firework; (*fam*) swindle.

petición [peti'θjon] *sf* petition; plea. **peticionario, -a** *sm, sf* petitioner.

petirrojo [petir'roxo] *sm* robin.

peto ['peto] *sm* bib; breastplate.

petrificar [petrifi'kar] *v* petrify. **pétreo** *adj* stony.

petróleo [pe'troleo] *sm* petroleum. **petrolero** *sm* oil-tanker.

petulante [petu'lante] *adj* petulant; insolent. **petulancia** *sf* petulance; insolence.

peyorativo [pejora'tiβo] *adj* pejorative.

pez [peθ] *sm* fish. *sf* pitch, tar.

pezón [pe'θon] *sm* (*bot*) stalk; (*anat*) nipple.

pezuña [pe'θuɲa] *sf* hoof.

piadoso [pja'ðoso] *adj* pious; merciful.

piano ['pjano] *sm* piano. **pianista** *s(m+f)* pianist.

piar [pjar] *v* chirp.

piara ['pjara] *sf* herd.

pica ['pika] *sf* lance, pike; goad; pick; magpie.

picadillo [pika'ðiʎo] *sm* minced meat.

picante [pi'kante] *adj* hot; spicy; pungent; biting.

picaporte [pika'porte] *sm* door handle; latch; knocker; latch-key.

picar [pi'kar] *v* prick, pierce; sting; burn; punch; bite, eat; chop up. **picado** *adj* bitten; stung; minced; sour; bad. **picadura** *sf* bite; sting; peck.

picardear [pikar'ðjar] *v* corrupt; get up to mischief. **picardía** *sf* dirty trick; craftiness; mischief. **picaresco** *adj* roguish. **pícaro, -a** *sm, sf* rogue.

pico ['piko] *sm* beak; peak; pickaxe. **darse el pico** kiss. **pico carpintero** woodpecker. **son las cuatro y pico** it is just after four.

picotear [pikote'ar] *v* peck; chatter. **picotearse** *v* wrangle. **picotada** *sf also* **picotazo** *sm* peck. **picotero, -a** *sm, sf* chatterbox.

pichón [pi't∫on] *sm* pigeon. **pichona** *sf* (*fam*) darling.

pie [pje] *sm* foot; base; stem. **a cuatro pies** on all fours. **dar pie a** give cause for. **de pies a cabeza** from head to foot.

piedad [pje'ðað] *sf* piety; pity.

piedra ['pjeðra] *sf* stone.

piel [pjel] *sf* skin.

pienso ['pjenso] *sm* fodder. **ni por pienso** not likely.

pierna ['pjerna] *sf* leg.

pieza ['pjeθa] *sf* piece; part; room. **dejar de una pieza** leave speechless.

pífano ['pifano] *sm* fife.

pigmento [pig'mento] *sm* pigment.

pigmeo [pig'meo] **-a** *s, adj* pygmy.

pijama [pi'xama] *sm* pyjamas *pl*.

pila¹ ['pila] *sf* heap; battery.

pila² *sf* basin; trough; font. **nombre de pila** Christian name.

pilar [pi'lar] *sm* pillar; pier; milestone; basin.

píldora ['pilðora] *sf* pill.

pilón [pi'lon] *sm* basin; trough; mortar; pylon.

piloto [pi'loto] *sm* pilot; (*auto*) rear light, parking light.

piltrafa [pil'trafa] *sf* gristly meat. **piltrafas** *sf pl* scraps *pl*.

pillar [pi'ʎar] *v* pillage; get; run over; (*fam*) catch. **pillaje** *sm* pillage.

pillo [pi'ʎo], **-a** *sm*, *sf* scoundrel. *adj* villainous. **pillastre** *sm or* **pillastron** *sm* rogue. **pillería** *sf* gang of villains; knavery.

pimienta [pi'mjenta] *sf* pepper. **pimiento** *sm* (*planta*) pepper. **pimentón** *sm* paprika.

pimpollo [pim'poʎo] *sm* sprout; sapling; (*fam*) handsome boy, pretty girl.

pináculo [pi'nakulo] *sm* pinnacle.

pinar [pi'nar] *sm* pine forest.

pincel [pin'θel] *sm* paintbrush. **pincelada** *sf* brush-stroke. **pincelar** *v* paint.

pinchar [pin'tʃar] *v* puncture. **pincharse** *v* have a puncture. **pinchazo** *sm* puncture. **pincho** *sm* point; prickle; spine.

pingo ['pingo] *sm* rag; devil. **pingos** *sm pl* (*fam*) togs.

pingüe ['pingwe] *adj* fatty; abundant.

pingüino [pin'gwino] *sm* penguin.

pino ['pino] *sm* pine tree. **pinocha** *sf* pine needle.

pintar [pin'tar] *v* paint. **pintarse** *v* make oneself up. **pinta** *sf* spot. **tener buena/mala pinta** look good/bad. **pintor**, **-a** *sm*, *sf* painter. **pintoresco** *adj* picturesque. **pintorrear** *v* (*fam*) daub. **pintura** *sf* painting; picture.

pinzas ['pinθas] *sf pl* tweezers; pincers; forceps; tongs; clothes pegs.

pinzón [pin'θon] *sm* finch.

piña ['piɲa] *sf* pineapple; pine cone.

piñón [pi'ɲon] *sm* pinion.

pío¹ ['pio] *sm* chirp.

pío² *adj* pious; merciful.

piojo ['pjoxo] *sm* louse. **piojoso** *adj* lousy.

pipa ['pipa] *sf* pipe; pip.

pique ['pike] *sm* pique; resentment, **echar a pique** sink; ruin.

piqueta [pi'keta] *sf* pickaxe.

piquete [pi'kete] *sm* picket; squad; sting; hole.

piragua [pi'ragwa] *sf* canoe.

pirámide [pi'ramiðe] *sf* pyramid. **piramidal** *adj* pyramidal.

pirata [pi'rata] *sm*, *adj* pirate.

Pirineos [piri'neos] *sm pl* Pyrenees *pl*.

piropear [pirope'ar] *v* (*fam*) compliment. **piropo** *sm* compliment.

pirotecnia [piro'teknja] *sf* fireworks *pl*.

pirueta [pi'rweta] *sf* pirouette. **piruetear** *v* pirouette.

pisar [pi'sar] *v* tread; trample. **pisada** *sf* footprint; step. **pisapapeles** *sm invar* paperweight.

piscina [pis'θina] *sf* swimming pool.

piscolabis [pisko'laβis] *sm invar* (*fam*) snack.

piso ['piso] *sm* floor; storey; flat. **piso bajo** ground floor.

pisotear [pisote'ar] *v* trample. **pisoteo** *sm* trampling.

pista ['pista] *sf* track; trail; runway; court; ring; rink. **pista de baile** dance floor.

pistola [pis'tola] *sf* pistol. **pistolera** *sf* holster. **pistolero** *sm* gunman.

pistón [pis'ton] *sm* piston.

pitar [pi'tar] *v* whistle at; blow a whistle; boo, hiss. **pitada** *sf* whistle.

pitón [pi'ton] *sm* python.

pizarra [pi'θarra] *sf* blackboard; slate.

pizca ['piθka] *sf* (*fam*) crumb; drop; pinch.

placa ['plaka] *sf* plate; badge; plaque. **placa de matrícula** (*auto*) number plate.

*placer [pla'θer] *v* please. *sm* pleasure. **a placer** at one's leisure.

plácido ['plaθiðo] *adj* placid; pleasant.

plagar [pla'gar] *v* plague. **plaga** *sf* plague.

plagiar [pla'xjar] *v* plagiarize. **plagio** *sm* plagiarism.

plan [plan] *sm* plan; project.

plana ['plana] *sf* (*imprenta*) page; (*llanura*) plain.

planchar [plan'tʃar] *v* iron, press. **mesa de planchar** *sf* ironing board. **plancha** *sf* iron. **planchado** *sm* ironing.

planear [plane'ar] *v* plan; glide. **planeo** *sm* gliding.

planeta [pla'neta] *sf* planet. **planetario** *sm* planetarium.

planicie [pla'niθje] *sf* plain; plateau.

planificar [planifi'kar] *v* plan. **planificación** *sf* planning.

plano ['plano] *adj* flat; level; smooth. *sm* map; plan; plane. **de plano** directly. **plano acotado** contour map. **primer plano** close-up.

plantar [plan'tar] *v* plant; erect. **plantarse** *v* stop; settle; stand firm. **planta** *sf* plant; (*pie*) sole; plan; floor. **plantación** *sf* plantation. **plante** *sm* strike; mutiny. **plantío** *sm* field; vegetable plot. **plantón** *sm* seedling.

plantear [plante'ar] *v* expound; create; institute; introduce. **planteamiento** *sm* exposition; introduction; layout.

plantel [plan'tel] *sm* (*bot*) nursery.

plantilla [plan'tiʎa] *sf* model, pattern; sole (of shoe); (*com*) payroll.

plasma ['plasma] *sm* plasma.

plasmar [plas'mar] *v* mould. **plasmarse** *v* materialize.

plástico ['plastiko] *sm*, *adj* plastic. **plasticidad** *sf* plasticity.

plata ['plata] *sf* silver; (*fig*) money. **hablar en plata** speak frankly.

plataforma [plata'forma] *sf* platform; flatcar; oilrig. **plataforma de lanzamiento** launching pad.

plátano ['platano] *sm* banana; banana tree; plane tree.

platea [pla'tea] *sf* (*teatro*) stalls *pl*.

platear [plate'ar] *v* silverplate. **platero** *sm* silversmith.

plática ['platika] *sf* chat; sermon.

platija [pla'tixa] *sf* plaice.

platillo [pla'tiʎo] *sm* saucer. **platillo volante** flying saucer.

platino [pla'tino] *sm* platinum.

plato ['plato] *sm* plate; course; dish. **hacer plato** serve a meal.

platónico [pla'toniko] *adj* platonic.

plausible [plau'siβle] *adj* plausible; praiseworthy. **plausibilidad** *sf* plausibility; praiseworthiness.

playa ['plaja] *sf* beach; seaside.

plaza [pla'θa] *sf* town square; market; town; position. **¡plaza!** make way!

plazo ['plaθo] *sm* time limit; instalment. **comprar a plazos** buy on hire-purchase.

pleamar [plea'mar] *sf* high tide.

plebe ['pleβe] *sf* common people *pl*. **plebeye** *adj* plebeian.

plebiscito [pleβis'θito] *sm* plebiscite.

*plegar [ple'gar] *v* fold; bend; pleat. **plegable** *adj* folding; collapsible; pliable. **plegadera** *sf* paper-knife. **pliegue** *sm* crease; tuck; pleat.

pleitear [pleite'ar] *v* litigate; plead. **pleito** *sm* lawsuit.

pleno ['pleno] *adj* complete; full. **plenamente** *adv* fully. **plenitud** *sf* fullness; abundance.

pliego ['pljego] *sm* sheet of paper; sealed letter. **pliego de condiciones** specifications *pl*.

plomo ['plomo] *sm* lead; fuse. **a plomo** straight down. **plomada** *sf* lead pencil; plumb line. **plomería** *sf* plumbing. **plomero** *sm* plumber.

pluma ['pluma] *sf* feather; pen. **pluma estilográfica** fountain pen. **plumaje** *sm* plumage.

plural [plu'ral] *sm*, *adj* plural. **pluralidad** *sf* majority.

plus [plus] *sm* bonus. **plus de carestía de vida** cost-of-living bonus.

pluscuamperfecto [pluskwamper'fekto] *sm* pluperfect.

plusmarca [plus'marka] (*deporte*) *sm* record. **plusmarquista** *s*(*m*+*f*) record-holder.

*poblar [po'βlar] *v* populate, inhabit; stock; colonize; plant. **poblarse** *v* bud; leaf. **población** *sf* population; town. **poblado** *sm* town; village. **poblador, -a** *sm*, *sf* settler.

pobre ['poβre] *adj* poor. *sm* pauper. **¡pobre de tí!** you poor thing! **pobrete** *adj* wretched. **pobretón** *adj* very poor. **pobreza** *sf* poverty.

pocilga [po'θilga] *sf* pigsty.

poción [po'θjon] *sf* potion.

poco ['poko] *adj* (*cantidad*) little; small. *adv* little; not very; not long. **un poco a** little. **pocos** *adj pl* few. **poco antes** shortly before. **poco a poco** little by little. **por poco** nearly.

podar [po'ðar] *v* prune. **poda** *sf* pruning. **podadera** *sf* pruning shears.

podenco [po'ðenko] *sm* hound.

*poder[1] [po'ðer] *v* can, be able to; be possible. **hasta más no poder** as much as one can. **no poder más** be exhausted. **puede ser** perhaps.

poder[2] *sm* power; capacity; possession. **casarse por poderes** marry by proxy. **hacer un poder** make an effort. **poder disuasivo** deterrent. **poderío** *sm* authority; wealth. **poderoso** *adj* powerful.

poema [po'ema] *sm* poem. **poesía** *sf* poetry. **poeta** *sm* poet. **poético** *adj* poetic. **poetisa** *sf* poetess.

*podrir *V* pudrir.

polaco [po'lako] *adj* Polish. *sm* Pole; (*idioma*) Polish.

polar [po'lar] *adj* polar. **polaridad** *sf* polarity. **polarizar** *v* polarize.

polea [po'lea] *sf* pulley.

polémica [po'lemika] *sf* polemic; polemics *pl*. **polémico** *adj* polemical.

polen [po'len] *sm* pollen.

policía [po'liθja] *sf* police force. *sm* policeman. **policiaco** *adj* police. **novela policiaca** detective novel.

poligamia [poli'gamja] *sf* polygamy. **polígamo** *adj* polygamous.

polígono [po'ligno] *sm* polygon. **polígono industrial** industrial estate. **poligonal** *adj* polygonal.

polilla [po'liʎa] *sf* moth.

pólipo [po'lipo] *sm* polyp.

política [po'litika] *sf* politics; policy. **político** *sm* politician. **padre político** father-in-law.

póliza [po'liθa] *sf* policy; contract; stamp. **póliza de seguros** insurance policy.

polizón [poli'θon] *sm* stowaway.

polo [po'lo] *sm* (*geog*) pole; (*tecn*) terminal; (*deporte*) polo; ice lolly. **polo acuático** water polo. **Polo Norte/Sur** North/South Pole.

Polonia [po'lonja] *sf* Poland. **polonesa** *sf* polonaise.

poltrona [pol'trona] *sf* easy chair. **poltrón** *adj* lazy.

polvo [pol'βo] *sm* powder; dust. **café en polvo** instant coffee. **polvos** *sm pl* powder *sing*. **polvos de talco** talcum powder. **polvareda** *sf* dust cloud; (*fig*) to-do. **polver.** *sf* powder compact. **pólvora** *sf* gunpowder.

polla [po'ʎa] *sf* pullet. **pollo** *sm* chicken. **polluelo** *sm* chick.

pómez [po'meθ] *sf* pumice.

pomo [po'mo] *sm* pommel; doorknob.

pompa [pom'pa] *sf* pomp; bubble; display. **pomposidad** *sf* pomposity. **pomposo** *adj* pompous.

pómpulo [po'mpulo] *sm* cheekbone.

ponche [pon'tʃe] *sm* (*bebida*) punch.

poncho [pon'tʃo] *sm* poncho. *adj* listless.

ponderar [ponde'rar] *v* weigh up; praise highly. **ponderable** *adj* praiseworthy. **ponderación** *sf* weighing up; exaggerated praise. **ponderado** *adj* measured; prudent. **ponderativo** *adj* excessive; deliberative.

ponente [po'nente] *sm* reporter. **ponencia** *sf* report.

***poner** [po'ner] *v* put; set. **poner al día** bring up to date. **poner casa** move (house). **poner de comer** feed. **ponerse** *v* turn oneself; dress; get down to; arrive. **ponerse bueno** recover. **ponerse guapo** smarten oneself up.

poniente [po'njente] *sm* west.

pontificado [pontifi'kaðo] *sm* papacy. **pontifical** *adj* pontifical. **pontífice** *sm* pope.

pontón [pon'ton] *sm* (*puente*) pontoon.

ponzoña [pon'θoɲa] *sf* poison. **ponzoñoso** *adj* poisonous.

popa [po'pa] *sf* stern. **a popa** astern.

popelina [pope'lina] *sf* poplin.

populacho [popu'latʃo] *sm* rabble.

popular [popu'lar] *adj* popular. **popularidad** *sf* popularity. **popularizar** *v* popularize.

por [por] *prep* for; by; through; during; in exchange for. **por ciento** per cent. **por más que** however. **por si acaso** in case. **por supuesto** of course.

porcelana [porθe'lana] *sf* porcelain.

porcentaje [porθen'taxe] *sm* percentage.

porción [por'θjon] *sf* portion.

porche [por'tʃe] *sm* porch.

pordiosero [porðjo'sero], -a *sm, sf* beggar.

porfiar [por'fjar] *v* insist; persist; argue. **porfía** *sf* insistence. **porfiado** *adj* stubborn.

pormenor [porme'nor] *sm* detail. **al pormenor** retail.

pornografía [pornogra'fia] *sf* pornography.

poro [po'ro] *sm* pore. **poroso** *adj* porous.

porque [por'ke] *conj* because.

porqué [por'ke] *sm* reason.

porquería [porke'ria] *sf* disgusting mess; muck.

porra [po'rra] *sf* club; truncheon. **porrazo** *sm* blow.

porro [po'rro] *sm* leek.

porrón [po'rron] *adj* dull, stupid. **a porrones** (*fam*) galore.

portador [porta'ðor] *sm* (*com*) bearer. **portar** *v* bear, carry. **portarse** *v* behave oneself. **portátil** *adj* portable.

portal [por'tal] *sm* entrance hall, portal.

portamonedas [portamo'neðas] *sm invar* wallet.

portavoz [porta'βoθ] *sm* megaphone; spokesman.

portazgo [por'taθgo] *sm* toll.
portazo [por'taθo] *sm* slam. **dar un portazo** slam the door.
porte ['porte] *sm* transport; carriage; conduct.
portento [por'tento] *sm* marvel. **portentoso** *adj* marvellous.
portería [porte'ria] *sf* porter's lodge. **portero, -a** *sm, sf* porter.
portezuela [porte'θwela] *sf* (*auto*) door.
pórtico ['portiko] *sm* portico.
portilla [por'tiʎa] *sf* porthole.
Portugal [portu'gal] *sm* Portugal. **portugués, -esa** *s, adj* Portuguese; *sm* (*idioma*) Portuguese.
porvenir [porβe'nir] *sm* future. **sin porvenir** without prospects.
pos [pos] *adj* **en pos de** behind.
posada [po'saða] *sf* inn; lodging. **posadero, -a** *sm, sf* innkeeper.
posar [po'sar] *v* alight; pose; lodge; lay down. **posarse** *v* settle; land.
***poseer** [pose'er] *v* possess; hold; master. **posesión** *sf* possession. **posesiones** *sf pl* property *sing*.
posible [po'siβle] *adj* possible. **posibilidad** *sf* possibility. **posibilitar** *v* facilitate.
posición [posi'θjon] *sf* position.
positivo [posi'tiβo] *adj, sm* positive.
***posponer** [pospo'ner] *v* postpone; value less.
postal [pos'tal] *adj* postal. *sf* postcard. **giro postal** *sm* money order; postal order.
postdata [post'ðata] *sf* postscript.
poste ['poste] *sm* pole; pillar; post. **poste indicador** signpost.
postergar [poster'gar] *v* pass over; postpone; adjourn. **postergación** *sf* postponement; adjournment.
posteridad [posteri'ðað] *sf* posterity. **posterior** *adj* posterior; subsequent; later.
postizo [pos'tiθo] *adj* false; artificial; assumed. *sm* hairpiece. **pierna postiza** *sf* artificial leg.
postrar [pos'trar] *v* prostrate. **postrarse** *v* kneel down; weaken. **postración** *sf* prostration. **postrado** *adj* prostrate.
postre ['postre] *sm* dessert.
postremo [pos'tremo] *adj* last. **postrimería** *sf* end, death.
postular [postu'lar] *v* postulate; request; apply for; collect. **postulación** *sf* collection. **postulado** *sm* postulate. **postulante, -a** *sm, sf* collector; applicant.

póstumo ['postumo] *adj* posthumous.
postura [pos'tura] *sf* posture; attitude.
potable [po'taβle] *adj* drinkable.
potaje [po'taxe] *sm* stew; soup.
potasio [po'tasjo] *sm* potassium.
pote ['pote] *sm* jar; jug.
potencia [po'tenθja] *sf* power; ability; potential. **potencial** *adj* potential. **potentado** *sm* potentate. **potente** *adj* powerful.
potestad [potes'tað] *sf* authority; power.
potro ['potro] *sm* colt; instrument of torture.
pozo ['poθo] *sm* hole; well; shaft; bilge.
práctica ['praktika] *sf* practice; method. **practicabilidad** *sf* practicability. **practicable** *adj* practicable. **practicante** *s(m + f)* nurse; practitioner. **practicar** *v* practise; play; perform. **práctico** *adj* practical; experienced.
pradera [pra'ðera] *sf* meadow; prairie. **prado** *sm* field, meadow.
pragmático [prag'matiko] *adj* pragmatic. **pragmatismo** *sm* pragmatism.
preámbulo [pre'ambulo] *sm* preamble.
precario [pre'karjo] *adj* precarious. **precariedad** *sf* precariousness.
precaución [prekau'θjon] *sf* precaution. **con precaución** cautiously. **precaver** *v* forestall. **precaverse** *v* be on one's guard (against).
preceder [preθe'ðer] *v* precede. **precedencia** *sf* precedence; preference. **precedente** *sm* precedent.
precepto [pre'θepto] *sm* precept; regulation. **preceptivo** *adj* compulsory.
preciar [pre'θjar] *v* value. **preciarse** *v* boast. **preciado** *adj* prized; boastful. **precio** *sm* price; esteem. **preciosidad** *sf* excellence. **precioso** *adj* precious; witty.
precipicio [preθi'piθjo] *sm* precipice.
precipitar [preθipi'tar] *v* precipitate. **precipitarse** *v* rush. **precipitación** *sf* precipitation; haste. **precipitado** *adj* also **precipitoso** hasty, rash.
precisar [preθi'sar] *v* need; be necessary; define; fix. **precisamente** *adv* precisely; necessarily. **precisión** *sf* precision; necessity. **preciso** *adj* precise; necessary.
***preconcebir** [prekonθe'βir] *v* preconceive. **preconcebido** *adj* preconceived.
preconizar [prekoni'θar] *v* praise; recommend; suggest. **preconización** *sf* recommendation; praise.

precoz [pre'koθ] *adj* precocious.
precocidad *sf* precocity.
precursor [prekur'sor] *sm* forerunner.
predecesor [preðeθe'sor], -a *sm, sf* predecessor.
***predecir** [preðe'θir] *v* predict. **predicción**
sf prediction.
predestinar [preðesti'nar] *v* predestine.
predestinación *sf* predestination.
prédica ['preðika] *sf* sermon; preaching.
predicación *sf* preaching. **predicaderas** *sf
pl (fam)* eloquence *sing.* predicador, -a
sm, sf preacher. **predicar** *v* preach.
predicado [preði'kaðo] *sm (gram)* predicate.
predicamento [preðika'mento] *sm* predicament; prestige.
predilección [preðilek'θjon] *sf* predilec-
tion.
***predisponer** [preðispo'ner] *v* predispose.
predisponer contra prejudice against.
predisposición *sf* predisposition.
predominar [preðomi'nar] *v* predominate.
predominancia *sf* predominance.
predominante *adj* predominant.
preeminente [preemi'nente] *adj* pre-eminent. **preeminencia** *sf* pre-eminence.
prefabricar [prefaβri'kar] *v* prefabricate.
prefabricación *sf* prefabrication.
prefacio [pre'faθjo] *sm* preface.
prefecto [pre'fekto] *sm* prefect. **prefectura**
sf prefecture.
***preferir** [prefe'rir] *v* prefer. **preferencia** *sf*
preference. **preferente** *adj* preferential;
preferable. **preferible** *adj* preferable.
preferido *adj* favourite.
prefigurar [prefigu'rar] *v* prefigure, foreshadow. **prefiguración** *sf* prefiguration.
prefijo [pre'fixo] *adj* prefixed. *sm* prefix.
prefijar *v* prefix; prearrange.
pregonar [prego'nar] *v* proclaim,
announce. **pregón** *sm* proclamation.
pregonero *sm* town crier.
preguntar [pregun'tar] *v* ask; query;
inquire. **preguntarse** *v* wonder. **pregunta**
sf question. **preguntador**, -a *sm, sf* ques-
tioner.
prehistórico [preis'toriko] *adj* prehistoric.
prejuicio [pre'xwiθjo] *sm* prejudice.
prejuzgar *v* prejudge.
prelado [pre'laðo] *sm* prelate.
preliminar [prelimi'nar] *adj, sm* preliminary. **preliminarios** *sm pl* preliminaries
pl.
preludio [pre'luðjo] *sm* prelude.

prematuro [prema'turo] *adj* premature.
premeditar [premeði'tar] *v* premeditate.
premeditación *sf* premeditation.
premiar [pre'mjar] *v* reward. **premio** *sm*
reward; prize; *(com)* premium. **premio
gordo** first prize.
premisa [pre'misa] *sf* premise, assumption.
premonición [premoni'θjon] *sf* premonition.
premura [pre'mura] *sf* urgency; tightness.
prenda ['prenda] *sf* pledge; *(com)* security; garment; darling. **en prenda** as a
token of. **prendar** *v* pledge; pawn; please.
prendarse de fall in love with. **prendería**
sf second-hand shop. **prendero**, -a *sm, sf*
second-hand dealer; pawnbroker.
prensa ['prensa] *sf* press; printing press.
dar a la prensa publish. **prensar** *v* press.
prensil [pren'sil] *adj* prehensile.
preñado [pre'ñaðo] *adj* pregnant; bulging; full. **preñar** *v* become pregnant;
impregnate. **preñez** *sf* pregnancy.
preocupar [preoku'par] *v* preoccupy; worry; get worried. ¡no se preocupe! don't
worry! **preocupación** *sf* preoccupation;
prejudice; worry. **preocupado** *adj* preoccupied; worried.
preparar [prepa'rar] *v* prepare. **preparación** *sf* preparation. **preparativo** *adj also*
preparatorio preparatory.
preponderar [preponde'rar] *v* preponder-
ate, prevail. **preponderancia** *sf* prepon-
derance. **preponderante** *adj* preponder-
ant.
preposición [preposi'θjon] *sf (gram)* preposition.
prerrogativa [prerroga'tiβa] *sf* prerogative.
presa¹ ['presa] *sf* capture; prey; victim;
quarry; seizure. **presas** *sf pl* fangs *pl*; tal-
ons' *pl.* **ave de presa** *sf* bird of prey.
presa² *sf* dam; weir. **presa de contención**
reservoir.
presagiar [presa'xjar] *v* presage. **presagio**
sm omen.
présbita ['presβita] *adj also* **présbite** long-
sighted. **presbicia** *sf* longsightedness.
presbítero [pres'βitero] *sm* priest.
presbiterado *sm* priesthood.
prescindir [presθin'dir] *v* do without.
prescindible *adj* dispensable.
prescribir [preskri'βir] *v* prescribe; determine. **prescripción** *sf* prescription.
prescrito *adj* prescribed.

presenciar [presen'θjar] *v* attend; witness.

presencia *sf* presence; appearance. **presencia de ánimo** presence of mind.

presentar [presen'tar] *v* present; introduce; submit; propose; tender. **le presento a** may I introduce you to. **presentarse** *v* present oneself; arise; turn up; report; apply. **presentable** *adj* presentable. **presentación** *sf* presentation; introduction. **presente** *adj* present. **mejorando lo presente** present company excepted.

*presentir [presen'tir] *v* have forebodings of. **presentimiento** *sm* presentiment.

preservar [preser'βar] *v* preserve; protect. **preservación** *sf* preservation; protection. **preservador** *adj* preservative. **preservativo** *sm* condom.

presidencia [presi'ðenθja] *sf* presidency. **presidente** *sm* president.

presidiario [presi'ðjarjo] *sm* convict. **presidio** *sm* prison; penal servitude.

presidir [presi'ðir] *v* preside over; dominate.

presilla [pre'siʎa] *sf* loop; fastener.

presión [pre'sjon] *sf* pressure.

preso ['preso] *sm* prisoner. *adj* captured.

prestar [pres'tar] *v* lend. **prestación** *sf* lending. **prestado** *adj* loaned. **dar/pedir prestado** lend/borrow. **prestador, -a** *sm, sf* lender. **prestamista** *s(m+f)* moneylender. **préstamo** *sm* loan. **prestario, -a** *sm, sf* borrower.

presteza [pres'teθa] *sf* promptness.

prestidigitador [prestiðixita'ðor] *sm* conjurer; magician. **prestidigitación** *sf* conjuring; magic.

prestigio [pres'tixjo] *sm* prestige; trick. **prestigiado** *adj* also **prestigioso** prestigious.

presto ['presto] *adj* prompt; ready. *adv* promptly.

presumir [presu'mir] *v* presume, assume. **según cabe presumir** presumably. **presumirse** *v* swank; be presumptuous. **presumible** *adj* presumable. **presunción** *sf* assumption; presumptuousness. **presunto** *adj* presumed. **presuntuosidad** *sf* conceit. **presuntuoso** *adj* conceited.

*presuponer [presupo'ner] *v* presuppose; budget. **presupuesto** *sm* budget; reason; supposition.

presura [pre'sura] *sf* promptness; persistence. **presuroso** *adj* prompt; hasty.

pretender [preten'der] *v* claim; aspire to; seek; want; apply for; allege; pretend. **pretendiente** *sm* pretender; claimant; suitor. **pretensión** *sf* pretension; claim.

pretérito [pre'terito] *sm* (*gram*) past.

pretexto [pre'teksto] *sm* pretext.

*prevalecer [preβale'θer] *v* prevail. **prevaleciente** *adj* prevailing.

prevaricar [preβari'kar] *v* prevaricate. **prevaricación** *sf* prevarication; breach of trust. **prevaricador, -a** *sm, sf* prevaricator.

*prevenir [preβe'nir] *v* prevent; warn; prepare; foresee. **prevención** *sf* prevention; warning; preparation; prejudice; police station. **prevenido** *adj* prepared; forewarned. **bien prevenido** full. **preventivo** *adj* preventive.

*prever [pre'βer] *v* foresee; anticipate. **previsión** *sf* foresight; forecast. **caja de previsión** *sf* social security.

previo ['preβjo] *adj* previous. **previo pago** after payment.

prieto ['prjeto] *adj* dark; mean.

prima ['prima] *sf* premium; bonus.

primado [pri'maðo] *sm* (*rel*) primate.

primario [pri'marjo] *adj* primary.

primavera [prima'βera] *sf* spring.

primer [pri'mer] *adj* first. **primeramente** *adv* first; mainly. **primero** *adj* first; best; principal. **de primera** first-class.

primitivo [primi'tiβo] *adj* primitive; original.

primo ['primo] *adj* prime. *sm* cousin.

primogénito [primo'xenito] *adj* first-born.

primor [pri'mor] *sm* beauty; delicacy; skill. **primoroso** *adj* exquisite; skilful.

princesa [prin'θesa] *sf* princess.

principal [prinθi'pal] *adj, sm* principal.

príncipe ['prinθipe] *sm* prince.

principiar [prinθi'pjar] *v* start. **principiante** *s(m+f)* novice. **principio** *sm* beginning.

pringar [prin'gar] *v* stain with grease; wound; involve; slander. **pringarse** *v* embezzle. **pringón** *adj* greasy. **pringoso** *adj* fatty, greasy. **pringue** *s(m+f)* grease stain; dripping.

prior [pri'or] *sm* (*rel*) prior. *adj* prior. **priora** *sf* prioress. **priorato** *sm* priory. **prioridad** *sf* priority.

prisa ['prisa] *sf* hurry. **darse prisa** hurry. **tener prisa** be in a hurry.

prisión [pri'sjon] *sf* prison; imprisonment. **prisionero, -a** *sm, sf* prisoner.

prisma ['prisma] *sm* prism. **prismático** *adj* prismatic.

privar¹ [pri'βar] *v* deprive; prohibit. **privación** *sf* deprivation. **privado** *adj* private.

privar² *v* be in favour; be popular.

privilegiar [priβile'xjar] *v* grant a favour to. **privilegio** *sm* privilege.

pro [pro] *sm* benefit, profit. **en pro de** on behalf of. **hombre de pro** *sm* honest man.

proa ['proa] *sf* (*mar*) prow, bow, bows *pl*. **mascarón de proa** *sm* figurehead.

probable [pro'βaβle] *adj* probable. **probabilidad** *sf* probability.

*probar [pro'βar] *v* test; try; taste; prove. **probarse** *v* try on. **probador** *sm* fitting-room. **probanza** *sf* proof. **probeta** *sf* test tube.

probidad [proβi'ðað] *sf* probity, integrity.

problema [pro'βlema] *sm* problem.

proceder [proθe'ðer] *v* proceed; behave; originate. **procedencia** *sf* origin; port of departure. **procedente** *adj* originating; reasonable; proper. **procedimiento** *sm* process.

procesar [proθe'sar] *v* prosecute. **procesado, -a** *sm, sf* accused. **procesal** *adj* procedural. **procesamiento** *sm* prosecution.

procesión [proθe'sjon] *sf* procession.

proclamar [prokla'mar] *v* proclaim. **proclama** *sf also* **proclamación** proclamation.

procrear [prokre'ar] *v* procreate. **procreación** *sf* procreation. **procreador, -a** *sm, sf* procreator.

procurar [proku'rar] *v* cause; attempt; obtain; succeed; give. **procura** *sf* power of attorney. **procurador, -a** *sm, sf* lawyer.

prodigar [proði'gar] *v* squander; lavish. **prodigalidad** *sf* prodigality.

prodigio [pro'ðixjo] *sm* prodigy. **prodigioso** *adj* prodigious.

pródigo ['proðigo] *adj* prodigal; wasteful.

*producir [proðu'θir] *v* produce. **producirse** *v* happen. **producción** *sf* production. **productivo** *adj* productive. **producto** *sm* product. **productor, -a** *sm, sf* producer.

proeza [pro'eθa] *sf* deed; feat.

profanar [profa'nar] *v* profane. **profanación** *sf* profanation. **profano** *adj* profane.

profecía [profe'θia] *sf* prophecy. **profeta** *sm* prophet. **profético** *adj* prophetic. **profetisa** *sf* prophetess. **profetizar** *v* prophesy.

*proferir [profe'rir] *v* utter.

profesar [profe'sar] *v* profess; manifest; practise a profession. **profesión** *sf* profession. **profesional** *adj* professional. **profesor, -a** *sm, sf* professor, teacher. **profesorado** *sm* professorship; teaching staff.

prófugo ['profugo], **-a** *s, adj* fugitive.

profundizar [profundi'θar] *v* deepen. **profundidad** *sf* depth. **profundo** *adj* deep.

profusión [profu'sjon] *sf* profusion. **profuso** *adj* profuse.

progenie [pro'xenje] *sf* progeny. **progenitor** *sm* progenitor. **progenitores** *sm pl* ancestors *pl*; parents *pl*. **progenitura** *sf* offspring.

programa [pro'grama] *sm* programme.

progresar [progre'sar] *v* progress. **progresión** *sf* progression. **progresivo** *adj* progressive. **progreso** *sm* progress.

prohibir [proi'βir] *v* prohibit. **se prohibe fumar** no smoking. **prohibición** *sf* prohibition. **prohibitivo** *adj* prohibitive.

prohijar [proi'xar] *v* adopt. **prohijamiento** *sm* adoption.

prójimo ['proximo] *sm* fellow man; neighbour; (*fam*) bloke.

prole ['prole] *sf* offspring.

prolapso [pro'lapso] *sm* prolapse.

proletario [prole'tarjo], **-a** *s, adj* proletarian.

prolífico [pro'lifiko] *adj* prolific.

prolijo [pro'lixo] *adj* tedious; long-winded. **prolijidad** *sf* long-windedness.

prólogo ['prologo] *sm* prologue.

prolongar [prolon'gar] *v* prolong. **prolongación** *sf* prolongation. **prolongado** *adj* prolonged.

promediar [prome'ðjar] *v* bisect; average out; mediate. **promedio** *sm* middle; average.

promesa [pro'mesa] *sf* promise. **prometer** *v* promise. **prometerse** *v* expect; become engaged. **prometérselas felices** have high hopes. **prometida** *sf* fiancée. **prometido** *sm* fiancé.

prominencia [promi'nenθja] *sf* prominence; projection; bulge. **prominente** *adj* prominent.

promiscuo [pro'miskwo] *adj* promiscuous; ambiguous.

promontorio [promon'torjo] *sm* promontory.

*promover [promo'βer] *v* promote. **promoción** *sf* promotion. **promotor, -a** *sm, sf* promoter.

promulgar [promul'gar] v promulgate. promulgación sf promulgation.

pronombre [pro'nombre] sm pronoun.

pronosticar [pronosti'kar] v prognosticate. pronosticación sf prognostication, forecast. pronóstico sm prediction.

prontitud [pronti'tuð] sf promptness. pronto adv quickly, at once. ¡hasta pronto! see you soon!

pronunciar [pronun'θjar] v pronounce. pronunciarse v rebel. pronunciación sf pronunciation. pronunciamiento sm rising; (jur) pronouncement.

propagar [propa'gar] v propagate. propagación sf propagation. propaganda sf propaganda.

propalar [propa'lar] v publish; divulge.

propenso [pro'penso] adj prone. propender v incline. propensión sf inclination.

propicio [pro'piθjo] adj propitious. propiciación sf propitiation. propiciar v propitiate.

propiedad [propje'ðað] sf property; ownership; propriety; resemblance. propietario, -a sm, sf landlord/lady.

propina [pro'pina] sf (dinero) tip.

propio ['propjo] adj proper; own; particular. nombre propio sm proper noun. ser propio de be typical of. sus propias palabras his very words. propiamente adv properly.

*proponer [propo'ner] v propose. proponente s(m+f) proposer. proposición sf proposition; proposal.

proporción [propor'θjon] sf proportion. proporcionado adj proportionate. bien proporcionado well proportioned. proporcional adj proportional. proporcionar v supply; cause; adapt.

propósito [pro'posito] sm purpose; intention. a propósito by the way. a propósito de with regard to. de propósito on purpose.

propuesta [pro'pwesta] sf proposal.

propulsar [propul'sar] v propel. propulsión sf propulsion. propulsor sm propeller.

prorrata [pro'rrata] sf quota. a prorrata pro rata.

prórroga ['prorroga] sf prorogation, extension. prorrogar v prorogue, adjourn.

prorrumpir [prorrum'pir] v break out.

prosa ['prosa] sf prose. prosaico adj prosaic.

proscribir [proskri'βir] v proscribe, ban. proscripción sf proscription, prohibition. proscrito adj outlawed, banished.

prosecución [proseku'θjon] sf pursuit; continuation. proseguir v pursue; continue.

prosélito [pro'selito] sm proselyte.

prospecto [pros'pekto] sm prospectus.

prosperar [prospe'rar] v prosper. prosperidad sf prosperity. próspero adj prosperous.

prosternarse [proster'narse] v prostrate oneself.

prostituir [prostitu'ir] v prostitute. prostíbulo sm brothel. prostitución sf prostitution. prostituta sf prostitute.

protagonista [protago'nista] s(m+f) protagonist.

proteger [prote'xer] v protect. protección sf protection. protector adj protective. protegido sm protégé.

proteína [prote'ina] sf protein.

protestar [protes'tar] v protest. protesta sf protest. protestación sf protestation. protestante s(m+f), adj Protestant. protestantismo sm Protestantism.

protocolo [proto'kolo] sm protocol.

prototipo [proto'tipo] sm prototype.

protuberancia [protuβe'ranθja] sf protuberance. protuberante adj protuberant.

provecho [pro'βetʃo] sm advantage; profit. de provecho useful. sacar provecho de benefit from. provechoso adj profitable.

proveer [proβe'er] v provide; deal with; decide; fill. proveedor, -a sm, sf supplier.

*provenir [proβe'nir] v originate. proveniente adj originating.

proverbio [pro'βerβjo] sm proverb. proverbial adj proverbial.

providencia [proβi'ðenθja] sf providence; foresight. providencial adj providential. providente adj provident.

provincia [pro'βinθja] sf province. provincial adj provincial. provincialismo sm provincialism.

provisión [proβisi'on] sf provision. provisional adj provisional. provisionalmente adv provisionally. provisor sm purveyer. provisto adj supplied.

provocar [proβo'kar] v provoke; cause. provocación sf provocation. provocador adj provocative. provocante adj provoking.

próximo ['proksimo] *adj* next; neighbouring. la semana próxima next week. proximamente *adv* closely; soon. proximidad *sf* proximity.

proyectar [projek'tar] *v* project; plan; throw. proyección *sf* projection. proyectil *sm* projectile. proyecto *sm* project. proyector *sm* projector; searchlight; spotlight.

prudencia [pru'ðenθja] *sf* prudence. prudencial *adj* (*fam*) moderate. prudente *adj* prudent.

prueba ['prweßa] *sf* test; proof; tasting; (*deporte*) event. a prueba on trial. a prueba de proof against.

prurito [pru'rito] *sm* itch; urge.

psicoanálisis [psikoa'nalisis] *sm invar* psychoanalysis. psicoanalista *s(m+f)* psychoanalyst. psicoanalizar *v* psychoanalyse.

psicología [psikolo'xia] *sf* psychology. psicológico *adj* psychological. psicólogo, -a *sm, sf* psychologist.

psiquiatría [psikja'tria] *sf* psychiatry. psiquiatra *s(m+f)* psychiatrist. psiquiátrico *adj* psychiatric.

púa ['pua] *sf* prong; barb; thorn; sharp point.

pubertad [pußer'tað] *sf* puberty.

publicar [pußli'kar] *v* publish. publicación *sf* publication. publicidad *sf* publicity; advertising. público *sm, adj* public. dar al público publish.

puchero [pu'tʃero] *sm* stew; cooking-pot. ganarse el puchero earn one's daily bread.

pucho ['putʃo] *sm* cigarette *or* cigar end; fag-end.

púdico ['puðiko] *adj* chaste; modest. pudicia *sf* chastity; modesty.

pudiente [pu'ðjente] *adj* rich.

pudín [pu'ðin] *sm* pudding.

pudor [pu'ðor] *sm* modesty; shame. pudoroso *adj* modest.

*pudrir [pu'ðrir] *v* rot, decay. pudrición *sf* putrefaction. pudrimiento *sm* rotting.

pueblo ['pweßlo] *sm* people; town; village. de pueblos from the country.

puente ['pwente] *sm* bridge. puente colgante suspension bridge.

puerco ['pwerko] *sm* pig. *adj* filthy. puerca *sf* sow. puerco espín porcupine.

pueril [pue'ril] *adj* childish. puerilidad *sf* childishness.

puerro ['pwerro] *sm* leek.

puerta ['pwerta] *sf* door; entrance. puerta principal front door. puerta trasera back door.

puerto ['pwerto] *sm* port; harbour; mountain pass.

pues [pwes] *adv, conj* then; since; because; well; so; yes. pues bien OK. ¡pues claro! of course! ¿pues qué? so what?

puesta ['pwesta] *sf* (*del sol*) setting; bet; putting. puesta en escena staging.

puesto ['pwesto] *sm* small shop; place; stall; job. puesto de periódicos newspaper stand.

pugnar [pug'nar] *v* fight; struggle. pugna *sf* fight. pugnaz *adj* pugnacious.

pujar [pu'xar] *v* strain; strive; outbid. pujante *adj* strong. pujanza *sf* strength.

pulcritud [pulkri'tuð] *sf* neatness; care. pulcro *adj* neat, tidy.

pulga ['pulga] *sf* flea. pulgoso *adj* flea-ridden.

pulgada [pul'gaða] *sf* inch. pulgar *sm* thumb.

pulir [pu'lir] *v* polish; adorn. pulidez *sf* polish; neatness. pulido *adj* polished; smooth; neat. pulidor *sm* polisher. pulimentar *v* polish. pulimento *sm* polish, shine.

pulmón [pul'mon] *sm* lung. pulmonía *sf* pneumonia.

pulpa ['pulpa] *sf* pulp.

púlpito ['pulpito] *sm* pulpit.

pulpo ['pulpo] *sm* octopus.

pulsar [pul'sar] *v* pulsate. pulso *sm* pulse; wrist; steady hand.

pulsera [pul'sera] *sf* bracelet; watch strap. reloj de pulsera *sm* wristwatch.

pulverizar [pulßeri'θar] *v* pulverize; spray. pulverización *sf* pulverization. pulverizador *sm* spray; atomizer.

pulla ['puʎa] *sf* taunt; obscenity.

punción [pun'θjon] *sf* (*med*) puncture.

punición [puni'θjon] *sf* punishment. punible *adj* punishable. punitivo *adj* punitive.

punta ['punta] *sf* point; tip; head; end; nail. horas punta *sf pl* rush hours *pl*. sacar punta a sharpen. velocidad punta *sf* top speed.

puntada [pun'taða] *sf* stitch.

puntapié [punta'pje] *sm* kick. echar a puntapiés kick out.

puntear [punte'ar] v stitch; tick off; perforate. **punteado** sm (música) plucking.

puntería [punte'ria] sf aim; marksmanship. **puntero** adj outstanding.

puntilla [pun'tiʎa] sf tack; nib; fine lace. **de puntillas** on tiptoe.

punto ['punto] sm point; full stop; stitch; mark; honour; matter; item. **al punto** at once. **dos puntos** colon. **en punto on the dot. ¡punto en boca!** mum's the word!

puntual [puntu'al] adj punctual; reliable. **puntualidad** sf punctuality; reliability.

puntualizar [puntwali'θar] v arrange; determine; perfect; settle.

puntuar [pun'twar] v punctuate. **puntuación** sf punctuation. **signos de puntuación** sm pl punctuation marks pl.

punzar [pun'θar] v pierce. **punzada** sf prick; twinge. **punzante** adj sharp. **punzón** sm awl, punch.

puñado [pu'naðo] sm handful. **puñada** sf also **puñetazo** sm blow, clout. **puño** sm fist; cuff. **de propio puño** in one's own handwriting.

puñal [pu'nal] sm dagger. **puñalada** sf stab.

pupila [pu'pila] sf (anat) pupil.

pupilaje [pupi'laxe] sm boarding-house; tutelage.

pupitre [pu'pitre] sm desk.

puré [pu're] sm purée. **puré de patatas** mashed potatoes pl.

pureza [pu'reθa] sf purity. **purificación** sf purification. **purificar** v purify. **purista** s(m+f) purist. **puro** adj pure; simple.

purgar [pur'gar] v purge; purify. **purgante** sm purgative. **purgativo** adj purgative. **purgatorio** sm purgatory.

puritano [puri'tano], **-a** s, adj puritan. **puritanismo** sm puritanism.

púrpura ['purpura] sf purple.

pus [pus] sm pus, matter.

pusilánime [pusi'lanime] adj cowardly. **pusilanimidad** sf cowardliness.

pústula ['pustula] sf (med) pustule, pimple.

puta ['puta] sf (fam) whore, prostitute. **puto** sm (fam) bugger.

putrefacción [putrefak'θjon] sf putrefaction. **putrefacto** adj rotten. **pútrido** adj putrid.

puya ['puja] sf goad; (fig) gibe.

Q

que [ke] pron who; whom; that; which. conj that; because; than. **que sí** of course. **más que** more than.

qué [ke] pron, adj what. **¿qué pasa?** what's going on? **¡qué miedo!** what a fright! **¡qué raro!** how extraordinary!

*****quebrar** [ke'βrar] v break; go bankrupt. **quebrado** adj broken; bankrupt. **quebradura** sf crack; gap. **quebrantar** v shatter. **quebranto** sm exhaustion.

queda ['keða] sf curfew.

quedar [ke'ðar] v stay; remain; sojourn. **quedarse** v stay behind. **quedar en nada** come to nothing.

quedo ['keðo] adj quiet; still. adv quietly.

quehaceres [kea'θeres] sm pl chores; duties.

quejarse [ke'xarse] v complain; moan. **queja** sf complaint. **quejido** sm groan. **quejoso** adj plaintive; complaining.

quemar [ke'mar] v burn; scorch. **quema** sf burning; fire. **quemadura** sf burn; scald. **quemante** adj burning. **quemazón** sf burning; burn.

querella [ke'reʎa] sf quarrel; (jur) complaint. **querellarse** v lodge a complaint.

*****querer** [ke'rer] v love; want; try; determine. sm affection. **querido** adj dear.

queso ['keso] sm cheese. **queso rallado** grated cheese.

quiá [ki'a] interj never! surely not!

quicio ['kiθjo] sm hinge. **fuera de quicio** out of order.

quiebra [ki'eβra] sf bankruptcy; slump; fissure.

quien [ki'en] pron who; whom; whoever. **quién** pron interrog who. **¿quién sabe?** who knows? **quienquiera** pron whoever, whosoever.

quieto [ki'eto] adj still, quiet. **quietud** sf stillness.

quijote [ki'xote] sm quixotic person; idealist.

quilate [ki'late] sm carat.

quilla ['kiʎa] sf keel.

quimera [ki'mera] sf hallucination; quarrel. **quimérico** adj fantastic.

química ['kimika] sf chemistry.

quincalla [kin'kaʎa] sf hardware; ironmongery. **quincallero, -a** sm, sf ironmonger.

quince ['kinθe] *sm, adj* fifteen. **quincena** *sf* fortnight. **quincuagésima** *adj* fiftieth. **quinientos** *adj invar* five hundred.

quinta ['kinta] *sf* country house; conscription; (*música*) fifth.

quintal [kin'tal] *sm* hundredweight.

quinto ['kinto] *adj* fifth.

quiosco [ki'osko] *sm* kiosk.

quirúrgico [ki'rurxiko] *adj* surgical.

quisquilla [kis'kiʎa] *sf* quibble; trifle; (*zool*) shrimp.

quiste ['kiste] *sm* (*med*) cyst.

quitamanchas [kita'mantʃas] *sm invar* stain-remover.

quitar [ki'tar] *v* remove; take off; take away. **quitarse** *v* get rid of; withdraw; abstain. **de quita y pon** easily detachable.

quitasol [kita'sol] *sm* parasol, sunshade.

quizá(s) [ki'θa(s)] *adv* perhaps, maybe.

R

rábano ['raβano] *sm* radish.

rabiar [ra'βjar] *v* rave, rage. **rabiar por** long for. **rabia** *sf* rage, fury; (*med*) rabies. **rabioso** *adj* rabid.

rabino [ra'βino] *sm* rabbi.

rabo ['raβo] *sm* tail; stalk. **hacer rabona** play truant.

racial [ra'θjal] *adj* racial.

racimo [ra'θimo] *sm* bunch; cluster.

raciocinar [raθoθi'nar] *v also* **racionar** ration. **ración** *sf* portion, ration.

racional [raθjo'nal] *adj* rational. **racionalidad** *sf* rationality. **racionalista** *adj* rationalist.

racista [ra'θista] *s(m+f)* racist.

racha ['ratʃa] *sf* gust of wind; streak of luck; split.

radiactivo [raðjak'tiβo] *adj* radioactive. **radioactividad** *sf* radioactivity.

radiar [ra'ðjar] *v* radiate; broadcast. **radiación** *sf* radiation; broadcasting. **radiador** *sm* radiator. **radiante** *adj* radiant.

radicar [raði'kar] *v* take root; settle. **radicación** *sf* taking root.

radical [raði'kal] *adj* radical, fundamental. **radicalismo** *sm* radicalism.

radio¹ ['raðjo] *sm* radius.

radio² *sm* radium.

radio³ *sf* radio. **radiodifusión** *sf* broadcasting. **radiomisora** *sf* radio station. **radioyente** *s(m+f)* listener.

*raer [ra'er] *v* scrape; erase.

raíz [ra'iθ] *sf* root. **bienes raíces** real estate *sing*.

rajar [ra'xar] *v* slit; crack; slice. **raja** *sf* crack; slice.

ralea [ra'lea] *sf* sort; breed.

rallar [ra'ʎar] *v* grate. **rallador** *sm* grater. **rallo** *sm* rasp.

rama ['rama] *sf* (*bot*) branch, bough.

rambla ['rambla] *sf* avenue; gully.

ramificarse [ramifi'karse] *v* branch out. **ramificación** *sf* ramification.

ramillete [rami'ʎete] *sm* bunch of flowers, posy; cluster.

ramo ['ramo] *sm* (*bot*) branch; cluster; bouquet.

rampa ['rampa] *sf* ramp.

ramplón [ram'plon] *adj* coarse, vulgar.

rana ['rana] *sf* frog.

rancio ['ranθjo] *adj* rancid, rank, stale.

rancho ['rantʃo] *sm* (*comida*) mess; farm; ranch. **ranchero** *sm* rancher.

rango ['rango] *sm* class, rank.

ranura [ra'nura] *sf* groove.

rapaz [ra'paθ] *adj* rapacious. **rapacidad** *sf* rapacity.

rapé [ra'pe] *sm* snuff.

rápido [ra'piðo] *adj* rapid. **rapidez** *sf* speed.

rapiña [ra'piɲa] *sf* robbery with violence.

rapsodia [rap'soðja] *sf* rhapsody.

raptar [rap'tar] *v* carry off, abduct; kidnap. **rapto** *sm* abduction. **raptor, -a** *sm, sf* kidnapper.

raquero [ra'kero] *sm* beachcomber.

raqueta [ra'keta] *sf* racket.

raro ['raro] *adj* rare. **rareza** *sf* rarity.

ras [ras] *sm* level. **a ras de tierra** at ground level.

rascacielos [raska'θjelos] *sm invar* skyscraper.

rascar [ras'kar] *v* scratch; scrape. **rascadura** *sf* scratching.

rasgar [ras'gar] *v* tear; rip; slash.

rasgo ['rasgo] *sm* feature; feat; (*de pluma*) stroke.

raso ['raso] *adj* flat; level; smooth.

raspar [ras'par] *v* rasp; slash. **raspa** *sf* rasp. **raspadura** *sf* rasping.

rastra ['rastra] *sf* trail; trace; sledge.

rastrear [rastre'ar] v trace; track; rake.
rastrillar [rastri'ʎar] v rake. **rastrillo** sm rake.
rastro ['rastro] sm track; trail.
rastrojo [ras'troxo] sm stubble.
rasurar [rasu'rar] v shave. **rasura** sf shaving.
rata ['rata] sf rat.
ratería [rate'ria] sf larceny, petty thieving. **ratero, -a** sm, sf petty thief.
ratificar [ratifi'kar] v ratify. **ratificación** sf ratification.
rato ['rato] sm a little while, short period of time. **al poco rato** shortly after.
ratón [ra'ton] sm mouse. **ratonera** sf mousetrap.
rayar [ra'jar] v rule; draw lines on; underline. **raya** sf line; stripe; limit. **a raya** within bounds. **rayado** adj lined; striped.
rayo ['rajo] sm beam, ray of light; flash of lightning.
raza ['raθa] sf race; lineage; breed.
razón [ra'θon] sf reason; rationale. **tener razón** be right. **razonable** adj reasonable. **razonar** v reason; justify.
reacción [reak'θjon] sf reaction. **reaccionar** v react. **reaccionario** s(m+f) reactionary. **reactor** sm reactor.
reacio [re'aθjo] adj obstinate.
real¹ [re'al] adj real.
real² adj royal.
realce [re'alθe] sm (arte) relief; highlight; importance.
realizar [reali'θar] v realize; make; perform.
realzar [real'θar] v raise; emboss; dignify.
reanimar [reani'mar] v revive; encourage.
reanudar [reanu'ðar] v renew. **reanudarse** v start again.
***reaparecer** [reapare'θer] v reappear. **reaparición** sf reappearance.
rebajar [reβa'xar] v lessen, reduce; lower; allow discount; (bebida) weaken. **rebaja** sf reduction.
rebanada [reβa'naða] sf slice. **rebanar** v slice.
rebaño [re'βaɲo] sm flock; herd.
rebasar [reβa'sar] v go beyond, exceed; overtake; overflow.
rebatir [reβa'tir] v rebut, refute; repel. **reboto** sm (mil) alarm, call to arms; surprise attack.
rebeca [re'βeka] sf cardigan.

rebelarse [reβe'larse] v rebel. **rebelde** adj rebellious. **rebeldía** sf rebelliousness. **rebelión** sf rebellion.
rebosar [reβo'sar] v overflow. **rebosadura** sf overflowing.
rebotar [reβo'tar] v bend back; rebound; bounce. **rebotación** sf bouncing. **rebote** sm bounce.
rebozar [reβo'θar] v muffle. **rebozo** sm muffler. **sin rebozo** openly.
rebuscar [reβus'kar] v search for. **rebusca** sf search. **rebuscado** adj elaborate.
rebuznar [reβuθ'nar] v bray. **rebuzno** sm bray.
recado [re'kaðo] sm errand; message. **recadista** s(m+f) messenger.
***recaer** [reka'er] v relapse. **recaída** sf relapse.
recalcar [rekal'kar] v cram; pack; stress. **recalcadura** sf pressing; packing.
recalcitrante [rekalθi'trante] adj recalcitrant.
***recalentar** [rekalen'tar] v reheat; rekindle. **recalentarse** v overheat.
recambio [re'kambjo] sm re-exchange. **piezas de recambio** sf pl spare parts.
recargar [rekar'gar] v reload; overload; increase; recharge. **recarga** sf refill. **recargable** adj refillable. **recargo** sm additional load; surcharge.
recatarse [reka'tarse] v be cautious. **recatar** v cover up. **recatado** adj prudent. **recato** sm prudence.
recaudar [rekau'ðar] v collect. **recaudación** sf collection. **recaudador** sm tax collector. **a buen recaudo** in safe keeping.
recelar [reθe'lar] v suspect; fear. **recelo** sm mistrust. **receloso** adj suspicious.
recepción [reθep'θjon] sf reception; receipt; admission.
receptáculo [reθep'takulo] sm receptacle.
receptor [reθep'tor] sm recipient, receiver.
recesión [reθe'sjon] sf recession.
receta [re'θeta] sf formula; recipe; prescription.
recibir [reθi'βir] v receive. **recibidor, -a** sm, sf receiver. **recibo** sm reception; (com) receipt. **acusar recibo** (com) acknowledge receipt.
recién [re'θjen] adv recently, lately, just. **recién llegado** sm newcomer. **reciente** adj recent, new.
recinto [re'θinto] sm enclosure; precinct, district.

recio ['reθjo] *adj* tough, strong. *adv* loud-ly.

recipiente [reθi'pjente] *sm* receptacle; recipient.

reciprocar [reθipro'kar] *v* reciprocate. **recíproco** *adj* reciprocal.

recitar [reθi'tar] *v* recite. *sm* recital. **recitación** *sf* recitation.

reclamar [rekla'mar] *v* claim; demand; appeal. **reclamación** *sf* claim; protest. **reclamo** *sm* call; advertisement.

reclinar [rekli'nar] *v* lean, recline. **reclinación** *sf* leaning.

reclusión [reklu'sjon] *sf* seclusion; imprisonment. **recluso, -a** *sm, sf* recluse; convict.

recluta [re'kluta] *sm* recruit; conscript. **reclutamiento** *sm* recruitment. **reclutar** *v* recruit; conscript.

recobrar [reko'βrar] *v* recover; recuperate; regain. **recobro** *sm* recovery.

recoger [reko'xer] *v* pick up; gather; collect; confiscate; take in; shrink. **recogerse** *v* withdraw within oneself. **recogida** *sf* collection; harvest; withdrawal. **recogido** *adj* short; small; secluded. **recogimiento** *sm* withdrawal.

recolección [rekolek'θjon] *sf* gathering; harvest; recollection; compilation. **recolectar** *v* harvest.

*recomendar** [rekomen'dar] *v* recommend; commend. **recomendación** *sf* recommendation. **recomendado, -a** *sm, sf* protégé/protégée.

recompensar [rekompen'sar] *v* recompense, reward. **recompenso** *sf* compensation; recompense.

reconciliarse [rekonθi'ljarse] *v* reconcile oneself. **reconciliación** *sf* reconciliation.

recóndito [re'kondito] *adj* secret; obscure.

*reconocer** [rekono'θer] *v* recognize; acknowledge; examine closely. **reconocible** *adj* recognizable. **recononcimiento** *sm* recognition; acknowledgement; examination.

reconquista [rekon'kista] *sf* reconquest. **reconquistar** *v* reconquer.

reconsiderar [rekonsiδe'rar] *v* reconsider.

*reconstituir** [rekonstitu'ir] *v* reconstitute. **reconstitución** *sf* reconstitution.

*reconstruir** [rekonstru'ir] *v* reconstruct.

*reconvenir** [rekonβe'nir] *v* reproach; rebuke. **reconvención** *sf* reproach.

recopilar [rekopi'lar] *v* compile; summarize. **recopilación** *sf* compilation; summary. **recopilador** *sm* compiler.

*recordar** [rekor'δar] *v* remember; commemorate; remind. **recordarse** *v* wake up. **para recordar** in memory. **recordable** *adj* memorable. **recordativo** *adj* reminiscent.

recorrer [reko'rrer] *v* go over; traverse; examine; survey; repair. **recorrido** *sm* journey; run; revision.

recortar [rekor'tar] *v* cut out; cut down; clip; trim; stand out. **recorte** *sm* cutting; outline.

recoveco [reko'βeko] *sm* bend; nook; recess.

recrearse [rekre'arse] *v* amuse oneself. **recreación** *sf* recreation. **recreo** *sm* recreation; amusement.

recriminar [rekrimi'nar] *v* recriminate. **recriminación** *sf* recrimination.

*recrudecer** [rekruδe'θer] *v* recur; break out again.

rectángulo [rek'tangulo] *sm* rectangle. **rectangular** *adj* rectangular.

rectificar [rektifi'kar] *v* rectify; correct. **rectificación** *sf* rectification.

rectitud [rekti'tuδ] *sf* rectitude; rightness. **recto** *adj* right; just; straight.

rector [rek'tor] *sm* rector; principal; governor. **rectoría** *sf* rectory.

recua ['rekwa] *sf* drove, herd; (*fig*) gang.

recuento [re'kwento] *sm* recount; calculation; inventory.

recuerdo [re'kwerδo] *sm* recollection; memory. **recuerdos** *sm pl* regards *pl*.

recular [reku'lar] *v* recoil. **reculada** *sf* recoil.

recuperar [rekupe'rar] *v* recuperate. **recuperación** *sf* recovery.

recurrir [reku'rrir] *v* revert; resort (to). **recurrir a** have recourse to. **recurso** *sm* recourse; appeal.

recusar [reku'sar] *v* refuse; reject. **recusación** *sf* refusal; rejection.

rechazar [retʃa'θar] *v* repel; deny. **rechazamiento** *sm* repulsion. **rechazo** *sm* rebound; rejection.

rechinar [retʃi'nar] *v* creak; squeak; (*los dientes*) gnash. **rechinamiento** *sm* creaking; squeaking.

rechoncho [re'tʃontʃo] *adj* squat; chubby.

red [reδ] *sf* net; grid; grille; grating; snare. **caer en la red** fall into the trap. **red ferroviaria** railway system.

redactar [reðak'tar] *v* edit. **redacción** *sf* editing; journalism. **redactor, -a** *sm, sf* editor; writer.

redención [reðen'θjon] *sf* redemption; help; salvation. **redentor, -a** *sm, sf* redeemer.

redimir [reði'mir] *v* redeem; ransom. **redimible** *adj* redeemable.

rédito ['reðito] *sm* income. **rédito imponible** taxable income.

redoblar [reðo'βlar] *v* double; redouble; repeat. **redobladura** *sf* redoubling.

redondear [reðonde'ar] *v* round; round off. **redondo** *adj* round; spherical. **negocio redondo** *sm* square deal.

*reducir [reðu'θir] *v* reduce; lessen; compress; scale down **reducción** *sf* reduction. **reducido** *adj* reduced; abridged.

redundar [reðun'dar] *v* redound; overflow.

reembolsar [reembol'sar] *v* reimburse, repay. **reembolso** *sm* reimbursement; refund. **contra reembolso** cash on delivery.

reemplazar [reempla'θar] *v* replace. **reemplazable** *adj* replaceable. **reemplazo** *sm* replacement.

referencia [refe'renθja] *sf* reference; account; allusion. **referente** *adj* referring. **referido** *adj* aforementioned; in question.

referéndum [refe'rendum] *sm* referendum.

*referir [refe'rir] *v* refer; narrate; describe.

refinar [refi'nar] *v* refine; polish; perfect. **refinación** *sf* refinement. **refinado** *adj* refined; slick. **refinadura** *sf* refinement. **refinería** *sf* refinery.

reflectar [reflek'tar] *v* reflect. **reflector** *sm* reflector; searchlight.

reflejar [refle'xar] *v* reflect; show. **refleja** *sf* reflection. **reflejo** *sm* reflection; reflex; glare.

reflexión [reflek'sjon] *sf* reflection. **reflexionar** *v* reflect. **reflexivo** *adj* (*gram*) reflexive.

reflujo [re'fluxo] *sm* ebb.

reformar [refor'mar] *v* reform; amend; remake; improve; repair. **reforma** *sf* reform, reformation. **reformación** *sf* reformation. **reformador, -a** *sm, sf* reformer. **reformativo** *adj* reformative. **reformatorio** *sm* reformatory.

*reforzar [refor'θar] *v* reinforce; strengthen; encourage; boost. **reforzado** *adj* reinforced.

refractario [refrak'tarjo] *adj* refractory. **refracción** *sf* refraction. **refractar** *v* refract.

refrán [re'fran] *sm* proverb, saying.

*refregar [refre'gar] *v* rub; scour; scold. **refregadura** *sf* rubbing, friction.

refrenar [refre'nar] *v* curb, control. **refrenamiento** *sm* restraint.

refrescar [refres'kar] *v* refresh; cool; repeat; revise. **refrescadura** *sf* refreshing. **refrescante** *adj* refreshing; cooling. **refresco** *sm* refreshment; cold drink.

refuerzo [re'fwerθo] *sm* reinforcement; backing; help.

refugiarse [refu'xjarse] *v* shelter. **refugio** *sm* refuge. **refugio de peatones** traffic island. **refugiado, -a** *sm, sf* refugee.

refulgir [reful'xir] *v* shine, gleam. **refulgencia** *sf* brilliance. **refulgente** *adj* brilliant.

refundir [refun'dir] *v* recast; adapt; refurbish. **refundición** *sf* recasting; adaptation.

refunfuñar [refunfu'ɲar] *v* grumble, grouse. **refunfuñadura** *sf also* **refunfuño** *sm* grumbling.

refutar [refu'tar] *v* refute. **refutable** *adj* refutable. **refutación** *sf* refutation.

regadera [rega'ðera] *sf* watering-can; channel; irrigation ditch. **regadero** *sm* irrigation ditch. **regadío** *sm* irrigated land. **regadizo** *adj* irrigable. **regadura** *sf* irrigation. **regar** *v* water; irrigate; sprinkle.

regalar [rega'lar] *v* give; treat; regale; entertain. **regalador, -a** *sm, sf* entertainer. **regalo** *sm* gift; pleasure; treat; entertainment.

regaliz [rega'liθ] *sm* liquorice.

regañar [rega'ɲar] *v* scold; quarrel; growl; grumble. **regaño** *sm* scolding; quarrel; growl; grumble.

regata [re'gata] *sf* regatta.

regatear [regate'ar] *v* haggle; bargain; retail; begrudge; dodge. **regate** *sm* dodge. **regateo** *sm* haggling. **regatería** *sf* retail. **regatero, -a** *sm, sf* retailer.

regazo [re'gaθo] *sm* lap.

regencia [re'xenθja] *sf* regency.

regenerar [rexene'rar] *v* regenerate. **regeneración** *sf* regeneration. **regenerativo** *adj* regenerative.

regentar [rexen'tar] *v* manage; govern; boss. **regente** *sm* regent; director; professor. **regentear** *v* domineer.

régimen ['reximen] *sm* regime; system; rate; diet; performance.

regimiento [rexi'mjento] *sm* regiment; administration; government; town council. **regimentación** *sf* regimentation. **regimental** *adj* regimental. **regimentar** *v* regiment.

región [re'xjon] *sf* region; territory; area; space. **regional** *adj* regional.

***regir** [re'xir] *v* govern; manage; control; obtain; prevail; steer.

registrar [rexis'trar] *v* register; inspect; record; search; show. **registración** *sf* registration. **registrado** *adj* registered; examined. **registrador** *sm* registrar; inspector. **registradora** *sf* cash register. **registro** *sm* register; registry; inspection.

reglar [re'glar] *v* rule; regulate; control. **reglarse** *v* conform; reform. **regla** *sf* rule; method; discipline; menstruation. **a regla** by rule. **regla de cálculo** slide rule. **regladamente** *adv* regularly. **reglado** *adj* regular; regulated; temperate. **reglamentación** *sf* regulation. **reglamentar** *v* regulate. **reglamentario** *adj* statutory. **reglamento** *sm* statute; rules and regulations *pl*.

regocijar [regoθi'xar] *v* rejoice; gladden. **regocijarse** *v* rejoice; exult. **regocijador** *adj* cheering. **regocijo** *sm* joy, gladness.

regresar [regre'sar] *v* return.

regular [regu'lar] *adj* regular; average; ordinary. **por lo regular** as a rule. *v* regulate; control; adjust. **regulación** *adj* regulation; control. **regulación a distancia** remote control. **regulado** *adj* regulated; regular. **regulador** *sm* regulator; throttle. **regulador de volumen** volume control. **regularidad** *sf* regularity; ordinariness. **regularización** *sf* regularization. **regularizar** *v* regularize.

rehabilitar [reaβili'tar] *v* rehabilitate. **rehabilitación** *sf* rehabilitation.

***rehacer** [rea'θer] *v* remake; recover; renovate; repair. **rehacerse** *v* recuperate. **rehecho** *adj* remade; squat.

rehén [re'en] *sm* hostage.

***rehuir** [re'wir] *v* flee; shrink from; avoid; shirk. **rehuida** *sf* flight.

rehusar [reu'sar] *v* refuse; reject.

reimprimir [reimpri'mir] *v* reprint. **reimpresión** *sf* reprint. **reimpreso** *adj* reprinted.

reinar [rei'nar] *v* reign; prevail. **reina** *sf* queen. **reinante** *adj* reigning. **reinado** *sm* reign. **reino** *sm* kingdom, reign. **reino animal** animal kingdom.

reincidir [reinθi'ðir] *v* backslide; relapse into; reiterate. **reincidencia** *sf* backsliding; reiteration. **reincidente** *adj* backsliding; relapsing; reiterating.

reintegrar [reinte'grar] *v* reintegrate; reimburse; recover. **reintegrarse** *v* recoup oneself. **reintegrable** *adj* reimbursable. **reintegración** *sf* reintegration; restoration. **reintegro** *sm* recovery; reimbursement.

***reír** [re'ir] *v* laugh. **reírse de** make fun of.

reiterar [reite'rar] *v* reiterate. **reiteración** *sf* reiteration.

reivindicar [reiβindi'kar] *v* reclaim; claim; rehabilitate. **reivindicación** *sf* claim; recovery.

reja ['rexa] *sf* grating; grille; ploughshare; lattice. **rejado** *sm* grating; railing. **rejería** *sf* ornamental ironwork. **rejilla** *sf* small grating; (*tren*) luggage rack.

***rejuvenecer** [rexuβene'θer] *v* rejuvenate. **rejuvenecimiento** *sm* rejuvenation.

relación [rela'θjon] *sf* relation; connection; report; narrative; intercourse; relationship. **relaciones** *sf pl* courtship *sing*; engagement *sing*. **relacionado** *adj* related. **relacionar** *v* relate; report; connect. **relacionarse** *v* be related; be connected.

relajar [rela'xar] *v* relax; remit; loosen; debauch. **relajación** *sf* relaxation; loosening; laxity; rupture. **relajadamente** *adv* loosely, dissolutely. **relajado** *adj* lax; ruptured. **relajador** *adj* relaxing.

relámpago [re'lampago] *sm* lightning. **relámpago difuso** sheet lightning.

relatar [rela'tar] *v* report; relate; tell. **relatador, -a** *sm, sf* narrator.

relatividad [relatiβi'ðað] *sf* relativity.

relevar [rele'βar] *v* relieve; absolve; replace; free; emboss. **relevación** *sf* relief; liberation; remission. **relevante** *adj* outstanding. **relevo** *sm* relay race. **relieve** *sm* relief; prominence. **en relieve** embossed.

relicario [reli'karjo] *sm* reliquary, shrine; locket.

religión [reli'xjon] *sf* religion; faith; creed.

religioso [reli'xjoso] *sm* friar, monk; religious person. *adj* religious.

reliquia [re'likja] *sf* relic; memento; ailment. **reliquia de familia** heirloom.

reloj [re'lox] *sm* clock; watch. **reloj de caja** grandfather clock. **reloj de cuclillo** cuckoo clock. **reloj despertador** alarm clock. **reloj pulsera** wristwatch. **relojería** *sf* watchmaker's shop. **relojero** *sm* watchmaker.

*****relucir** [relu'θir] *v* shine; excel. **sacar a relucir** show off. **reluciente** *adj* gleaming.

reluctante [reluk'tante] *adj* reluctant.

relumbrar [relum'brar] *v* dazzle; glare. **relumbrante** *adj* dazzling. **relumbre** *sm* sparkle; flash. **relumbrón** *sm* glare; tinsel. **relumbroso** *adj* dazzling.

rellenar [reʎe'nar] *v* refill; fill; stuff; cram. **rellenable** *adj* refillable. **relleno** *sm* filling; stuffing; packing.

remachar [rema'tʃar] *v* rivet; stress. **remachado** *adj* riveted; (*fam*) quiet. **remache** *sm* rivet.

remanente [rema'nente] *sm* remains *pl*.

remanso [re'manso] *sm* backwater; sluggishness.

remar [re'mar] *v* row; toil.

rematar [rema'tar] *v* finish; kill; knock down at auction. **rematado** *adj* completely ruined. **rematante** *sm* highest bidder. **remate** *sm* end; finishing touch; highest bid.

remediar [reme'ðjar] *v* remedy; help; prevent. **remediable** *adj* remediable. **remedio** *sm* remedy. **no hay remedio** it can't be helped.

*****remendar** [remen'dar] *v* repair; patch; darn. **remendado** *adj* spotty; patched. **remendón, -ona** *sm, sf* mender; repairer. **remiendo** *sm* repair; patch. **echar un remiendo a** put a patch on.

remero [re'mero] *sm* oarsman.

remesa [re'mesa] *sf* remittance; consignment; shipment. **remesar** *v* remit; ship.

remilgado [remil'gaðo] *adj* mincing; prim; squeamish. **remilgarse** *v* simper. **remilgo** *sm* smirk; primness.

reminiscencia [remini'sθenθja] *sf* reminiscence.

remirado [remi'raðo] *adj* considerate; cautious; discreet. **remirar** *v* review. **remirarse** *v* take great pains; enjoy looking over.

remisión [remi'sjon] *sf* remission; pardon; reference. **remisible** *adj* pardonable. **remiso** *adj* remiss.

remitir [remi'tir] *v* send; pardon; adjourn; abate. **remitirse a** quote from. **remitido** *sm* dispatch.

remo ['remo] *sm* oar; paddle; rowing. **remos** *sm pl* limbs *pl*.

remojar [remo'xar] *v* soak; steep. **remojo** *sm* soaking; steeping.

remolcha [remo'latʃa] *sf* beetroot.

remolcar [remol'kar] *v* tow; haul. **remolcador** *sm* tug.

remolino [remo'lino] *sm* whirlwind; whirlpool; (*fig*) throng. **remolinar** *v* eddy.

remontar [remon'tar] *v* remount; mend; go back in time; raise; frighten. **remonte** *sm* repair; remounting; rising.

remordimiento [remorði'mjento] *sm* remorse.

remoto [re'moto] *adj* remote; improbable.

*****remover** [remo'βer] *v* remove; move; stir; discharge. **removimiento** *sm* removal.

remunerar [remune'rar] *v* remunerate. **remuneración** *sf* remuneration. **remunerativo** *adj* remunerative.

*****renacer** [rena'θer] *v* be reborn; recover. **renacimiento** *sm* rebirth; renaissance.

renacuajo [rena'kwaxo] *sm* tadpole.

rencilla [ren'θiʎa] *sf* squabble; feud. **rencilloso** *adj* quarrelsome.

rencor [ren'kor] *sm* rancour. **rencoroso** *adj* rancorous.

*****rendir** [ren'dir] *v* conquer; yield; surrender. **rendirse** *v* wear oneself out. **rendición** *sf* surrender; (*com*) profit. **rendido** *adj* submissive. **rendimiento** *sm* humility; weariness; output.

*****renegar** [rene'gar] *v* disown; detest; curse. **renegado, -a** *sm, sf* renegade. **renegador, -a** *sm, sf* blasphemer.

renglón [ren'glon] *sm* written or printed line. **leer entre renglones** read between the lines.

reno ['reno] *sm* reindeer.

renombre [re'nombre] *sm* renown; surname. **renombrado** *adj* renowned.

*****renovar** [reno'βar] *v* renovate; renew. **renovable** *adj* renewable. **renovación** *sf* renovation; renewal. **renuevo** *sm* renewal; sprout.

rentar [ren'tar] *v* yield an income or profit. **renta** *sf* income; profit. **rentero, -a** *sm,* *sf* tenant farmer. **rentista** *s(m+f)* stockholder. **rentístico** *adj* financial.

renunciar [renun'θjar] *v* renounce; resign. **renuncia** *sf* renunciation; resignation.

*reñir [re'ɲir] *v* scold; quarrel. **reñido** *adj* on bad terms. **reñidor** *adj* quarrelsome.

reo ['reo]. **-a** *sm, sf* defendant. *adj* guilty.

reojo [re'oxo] *sm* **mirar de reojo** look askance.

reorganizar [reorgani'θar] *v* reorganize. **reorganización** *sf* reorganization.

reparar [repa'rar] *v* repair; restore; correct; make amends for; observe; parry. **reparable** *adj* noteworthy. **reparador**, **-a** *sm, sf* repairer; faultfinder. **reparo** *sm* repair; remedy; observation; protection.

repartir [repar'tir] *v* share; distribute. **repartición** *sf* distribution. **repartidor**, **-a** *sm, sf* distributor. **reparto** *sm* distribution; *(teatro)* cast.

repasar [repa'sar] *v* revise; review; retrace. **repaso** *sm* review; *(fam)* reprimand.

repatriar [repa'trjar] *v* repatriate. **repatriación** *sf* repatriation. **repatriado**, **-a** *sm, sf* repatriate.

repeler [repe'ler] *v* repel. **repelente** *adj* repellent.

repente [re'pente] *sm* sudden impulse. **de repente** suddenly.

repercutir [reperku'tir] *v* re-echo; rebound. **repercusión** *sf* repercussion; reverberation.

repertorio [reper'torjo] *sm* repertory; repertoire.

*repetir [repe'tir] *v* repeat; recite. **repetición** *sf* repetition; recital.

repisa [re'pisa] *sf* shelf; ledge; bracket. **repisa de chimenea** mantelpiece. **repisa de ventana** window sill.

*replegar [reple'gar] *v* refold; *(mil)* retreat. **replegable** *adj* folding. **repliegue** *sm* fold, crease; retreat.

repleto [re'pleto] *adj* replete; plump.

réplica ['replika] *sf* answer; replica. **replicar** *v* argue; answer back. **replicato** *sm* argument; answer.

repoblación [repoβla'θjon] *sf* repopulation; restocking; reforestation. **repoblar** *v* repopulate; restock; reforest.

repollo [re'poʎo] *sm* cabbage.

*reponer [repo'ner] *v* replace; restore. **reponerse** *v* recover.

reportar [repor'tar] *v* restrain; obtain; bring. **reportarse** *v* contain oneself. **reportamiento** *sm* restraint.

reposar [repo'sar] *v* rest; lie down; settle; lie buried. **reposo** *sm* repose.

repostería [reposte'ria] *sf* pastry shop; pantry. **repostero**, **-a** *sm, sf* pastrycook; confectioner.

reprender [repren'der] *v* reprimand. **reprensible** *adj* reprehensible. **reprensor** *adj* reproachful.

represalia [repre'salja] *sf* reprisal.

representar [represen'tar] *v* represent; signify; describe; express; perform; appear to have. **representarse** *v* imagine. **representable** *adj* representable; performable. **representación** *sf* representation; performance. **representante** *s(m+f)* representative; actor, actress. **representativo** *adj* representative.

represión [repre'sjon] *sm* repression; control. **represivo** *adj* repressive.

reprimenda [repri'menda] *sf* reprimand.

reprimir [repri'mir] *v* repress; suppress. **reprimible** *adj* repressible.

*reprobar [repro'βar] *v* reprove; condemn; *(examen)* fail. **reprobable** *adj* reprehensible. **reprobación** *sf* reproof; failure. **reprobado**, **-a** *sm, sf* also **réprobo**, **-a** *sm, sf* reprobate.

reprochar [repro'tʃar] *v* reproach; challenge. **reprochable** *adj* reproachable; reproachful. **reprochador**, **-a** *sm, sf* reproacher.

*reproducir [reproðu'θir] *v* reproduce. **reproducible** *adj* reproducible. **reproducción** *sf* reproduction. **reproductor**, **-a** *sm, sf* breeder.

reptil [rep'til] *sm* reptile.

república [re'puβlika] *sf* republic. **republicanismo** *sm* republicanism. **republicano**, **-a** *sm, sf* republican.

repudiar [repu'ðjar] *v* repudiate. **repudiación** *sf* repudiation.

repuesto [re'pwesto] *sm* supply; store; sideboard. **de repuesto** spare, extra. *adj* replaced; secluded; recovered.

repugnar [repug'nar] *v* contradict; object to; be repugnant. **repugnarse** *v* conflict. **repugnacia** *sf* repugnance; opposition. **repugnante** *adj* repugnant.

repulsivo [repul'siβo] *adj* repulsive. **repulsa** *sf* refusal; rebuke. **repulsar** *v* reject; refuse. **repulsión** *sf* rejection; refusal.

reputar [repu'tar] *v* repute; consider; esteem. **reputación** *sf* reputation. **reputado** *adj* reputed.

*****requebrar** [reke'βrar] *v* woo; flatter; flirt with. **requebrador, -a** *sm, sf* flirt.

requemar [reke'mar] *v* scorch; inflame; overcook. **requemarse** *v* smoulder; become tanned. **requemado** *adj* burnt; tanned. **requemamiento** *sm* bite; sting. **requemante** *adj* burning; stinging.

*****requerir** [reke'rir] *v* request; require; urge; notify; summon; examine. **requeriente** *adj* requiring. **requerimiento** *sm* requisition; summons; notification; request.

requesón [reke'son] *sm* curd; cottage cheese.

requisar [reki'sar] *v* requisition. **requisa** *sf* tour of inspection; requisition. **requisición** *sf* requisition. **requisito** *adj* requisite.

res [res] *sf* head of cattle; animal.

resabio [re'saβjo] *sm* bad habit; unpleasant aftertaste. **resabiado** *adj* crafty; wicked; spoiled. **resabiar** *v* pervert; become vicious. **resabiarse** *v* become annoyed.

resaca [re'saka] *sf* undertow; surf; surge.

resaltar [resal'tar] *v* rebound, stand out. **resalte** *sm* projection. **resalto** *sm* rebound.

resarcir [resar'θir] *v* compensate. **resarcirse de** make up for. **resarcimiento** *sm* compensation.

resbalar [resβa'lar] *v* slide; skid; slip. **resbaladero** *also* **resbaladizo, resbalante** *adj* slippery. **resbalador** *adj* sliding. **resbaladura** *sf* skid mark. **resbalón** *sm* slide; slip; skid.

rescatar [reska'tar] *v* rescue; recover; save; ransom; make up for. **rescate** *sm* redemption; rescue; ransom.

rescindir [resθin'dir] *v* rescind. **rescisión** *sf* annulment.

rescoldo [res'kolðo] *sm* misgiving; embers *pl.*

resecar [rese'kar] *v* dry thoroughly. **reseco** *adj* desiccated.

*****resentirse** [resen'tirse] *v* feel the effects; be weakened.

reseñar [rese'ɲar] *v* review; outline. **reseña** *sf* review; outline.

reservar [reser'βar] *v* reserve; preserve; conceal. **reserva** *sf* reserve; reservation. **a reserva de** with the intention of. **reserva de asiento** reservation. **sin reserva** frankly. **reservado** *adj* reserved; discreet.

resfriar [resfri'ar] *v* cool; turn cold. **resfriarse** *v* catch cold. **resfriado** *m* (*med*) cold.

resguardar [resgwar'ðar] *v* defend; preserve. **resguardarse** *v* protect oneself. **resguardo** *sm* defence; protection; guarantee. **reguardo de correos** postal receipt.

residencia [resi'ðenθja] *sf* residence; boarding house. **residencial** *adj* residential. **residente** *s*(*m+f*) resident. **residir** *v* reside.

residuo [re'siðwo] *sm* residue. **residuos** *sm pl* refuse. *sing.* **residual** *adj* residual.

resignar [resig'nar] *v* resign; renounce. **resignarse** *v* resign oneself. **resigna** *sf* renunciation. **resignación** *sf* resignation.

resina [re'sina] *sf* resin.

resistir [resis'tir] *v* resist; refuse. **resistencia** *sf* resistance; stamina. **resistente** *adj* resistant.

resolución [resolu'θjon] *sf* resolution; decision. **resoluto** *adj* resolute; skilled.

*****resolver** [resol'βer] *v* resolve; decide; analyse. **resolverse** *v* make up one's mind.

*****resollar** [reso'ʎar] *v* pant; puff; snort.

*****resonar** [reso'nar] *v* resound. **resonancia** *sf* resonance. **resonante** *adj* resonant.

resoplar [reso'plar] *v* snort; puff. **resoplido** *sm* snort; puff.

resorte [re'sorte] *sm* resort; means; motive; (*mec*) spring; elasticity.

respaldar [respal'ðar] *v* back; support; endorse. **respaldarse** *v* lean. **respaldo** *sm* chair back; support.

respecto [res'pekto] *sm* respect. **con respecto a** with regard to.

respetar [respe'tar] *v* respect. **respetabilidad** *sf* respectability. **respetable** *adj* respectable. **respetador** *adj* respectful. **respeto** *sm* respect. **respetuoso** *adj* respectful.

respirar [respi'rar] *v* breathe. **respiración** *sf* respiration; breath. **respiro** *sm* breathing. **respiradero** *sm* ventilator.

*****resplandecer** [resplanðe'θer] *v* glitter. **resplandeciente** *adj* glittering. **resplandor** *sm* glitter.

responder [respon'der] *v* respond. **responder por** vouch for. **respondón** *adj* saucy. **responsivo** *adj* responsive. **respuesta** *sf* reply; refutation.

responsable [respon'saβle] *adj* responsible. **responsabilidad** *sf* responsibility.

*resquebrajar [reskeβra'xar] *v also*
resquebrar split; crack. **resquebra(ja)dura**
sf crack.

resquemar [reske'mar] *v* sting the tongue.
sm sting in the mouth; remorse; resentment.

resquicio [res'kiθjo] *sm* crack; chink; (*fig*)
slight chance.

*restablecer [restaβle'θer] *v* re-establish.
restablecerse *v* recover from illness. **restablecimiento** *sm* re-establishment; recovery.

restallar [resta'ʎar] *v* crack; crackle.

restante [res'tante] *adj* remaining. *sm*
remainder.

restar [res'tar] *v* subtract; remain.

restaurante [restau'rante] *sm* restaurant.
restauración *sf* restoration. **restaurar** *v*
restore; recover; repair.

*restituir [restitu'ir] *v* restore; pay back.
restituirse *v* return. **restituición** *sf* restitu-
tion.

resto ['resto] *sm* rest, remainder.

*restregar [restre'gar] *v* rub; scrub; wipe.
restregón *sm* rubbing; scrubbing; wip-
ing.

restricción [restrik'θjon] *sf* restriction.
restrictivo *adj* restrictive.

restringir [restrin'xir] *v* restrict.

resucitar [resuθi'tar] *v* resuscitate.
resucitación *sf* resuscitation.

resuello [re'sweʎo] *sm* breathing.

resuelto [re'swelto] *adj* resolute; resolved;
firm.

resultar [resul'tar] *v* result; happen; turn
out; go. **resulta** *sf* result, effect. **resultado**
sm result. **resultante** *adj* resultant.

resumir [resu'mir] *v* summarize; abbreviate. **resumen** *sm* summary. **en resumen**
in brief. **resumido** *adj* summarized.

retablo [re'taβlo] *sm* altarpiece.

retaguardia [reta'gwarδja] *sf* rearguard.

retal [re'tal] *sm* remnant.

retama [re'tama] *sf* (*bot*) broom.

retardar [retar'δar] *v* retard, delay; (*reloj*)
put back. **retardación** *sf* delay. **retardo**
sm delay.

retén [re'ten] *sm* spare, reserve.

*retener [rete'ner] *v* retain; deduct;
detain; arrest. **retención** *sf* retention;
deduction; detention. **retentiva** *sf* memory. **retentivo** *adj* retentive.

retina [re'tina] *sf* retina.

retintín [retin'tin] *sm* jingle.

retirar [reti'rar] *v* withdraw. **retirarse** *v* go

into seclusion. **retirada** *sf* retreat.
retirado *adj* retired; remote. **retiro** *sm*
retirement; retreat.

reto ['reto] *sm* challenge.

retocar [reto'kar] *v* retouch. **retoque** *sm*
retouching.

*retorcer [retor'θer] *v* twist; distort.
retorcerse *v* writhe. **retorcimiento** *sm*
contortion.

retórica [re'torika] *sf* rhetoric. **retórico** *adj*
rhetorical.

retornar [retor'nar] *v* return. **retorno** *sm*
return; remuneration.

retractar [retrak'tar] *v* retract. **retracción**
sf retraction. **retractable** *adj also* **retráctil**
retractable.

*retraer [retra'er] *v* dissuade; bring again.
retraerse *v* shelter; retreat. **retraído** *adj*
retiring; unsociable. **retraimiento** *sm*
retirement; retreat.

retrasar [retra'sar] *v* delay; put back;
(*reloj*) be slow. **retrasarse** *v* be late.
retraso *sm* delay; lateness.

retratar [retra'tar] *v* portray. **retratista**
s(m + f) portrait painter. **retrato** *sm* portrait.

retrete [re'trete] *sm* lavatory.

*retribuir [retriβu'ir] *v* recompense;
repay. **retribuición** *sf* retribution; recompense.

retroceder [retroθe'δer] *v* recede; fall
back. **retroceso** *sm* retreat; (*com*) slump.
retrogresión *sf* retrogression.

retruécano [retru'ekano] *sm* pun.

retumbar [retum'bar] *v* resound.
retumbante *adj* resounding. **retumbo** *sm*
rumble.

reuma ['reuma] *sm* rheumatism. **reumático** *adj* rheumatic. **reumatismo** *sm* rheumatism.

reunir [reu'nir] *v* reunite; unite; gather;
reconcile. **reunión** *sf* meeting.

revalidar [reβali'δar] *v* ratify; confirm.
revalidación *sf* ratification.

revancha [re'βantʃa] *sf* revenge.

revelar [reβe'lar] *v* reveal; (*foto*) develop.
revelación *sf* revelation. **revelador** *adj*
revealing.

revendedor [reβende'δor], **-a** *sm, sf* retailer. **revender** *v* retail.

*reventar [reβen'tar] *v* burst. **reventarse** *v*
blow up. **reventón** *sm* burst; blowout.

reverberar [reβerβe'rar] *v* reverberate.
reverberación *sf* reverberation. **reverbero**
sm reverberation; reflector.

*reverdecer [reβerðe'θer] *v* grow green again; revive.

reverenciar [reβeren'θjar] *v* reverence, venerate. **reverencia** *sf* reverence. **reverendo** *adj* reverend. **reverente** *adj* reverent.

reversión [reβer'sjon] *sf* reversion. **reversible** *adj* revertible. **reverso** *adj* reverse.

revés [re'βes] *sm* reverse; back; setback. **al revés** upside down; inside out; back to front. **revesado** *adj* complicated; unruly.

revisar [reβi'sar] *v* revise; review. **revisión** *sf* revision; review; (*com*) audit. **revista** *sf* review; journal.

revivir [reβi'βir] *v* revive. **revivicar** *v* revive.

revocar [reβo'kar] *v* revoke; dissuade.

*revolcar [reβol'kar] *v* knock down; defeat; (*fam*) fail an exam. **revolcarse** *v* wallow.

revoltillo [reβol'tiʎo] *sm also* **revoltijo** jumble; mess.

revoltoso [reβol'toso] *adj* mischievous; unruly.

revolución [reβolu'θjon] *sf* revolution. **revolucionario, -a** *sm, sf* revolutionary.

*revolver [reβol'βer] *v* revolve; stir; disturb. **revolverse** *v* turn round.

revólver [re'βolβer] *sm* revolver.

revoque [re'βoke] *sm* plaster; stucco; whitewash.

revuelta [re'βwelta] *sf* revolt; turn; bend; change. **revuelto** *adj* difficult; unruly; upside down; disturbed.

rey [rej] *sm* king.

reyerta [re'jerta] *sf* quarrel; brawl.

rezagar [reθa'gar] *v* defer; postpone; leave behind. **rezagarse** *v* straggle. **rezagado** *sm* (*mil*) straggler. **rezago** *sm* remainder.

rezar [re'θar] *v* pray, pray for. **rezo** *sm* prayer; prayers *pl*.

rezumarse [reθu'marse] *v* ooze, drip; leak out.

riachuelo [rja'tʃwelo] *sm* brook. **ría** *sf* estuary.

ribera [ri'βera] *sf* river bank; shore.

ribete [ri'βete] *sm* (*de ropa*) border, edging; trimmings *pl*. **ribetear** *v* border; edge.

ricino [ri'θino] *sm* castor-oil plant. **aceite de ricino** *sm* castor oil.

rico [‘riko], -a *sm, sf* rich person. *adj* rich; handsome; tasty.

ridiculizar [riðikuli'θar] *v* ridicule. **ridículo** *adj* ridiculous.

riego [‘rjego] *sm* irrigation.

riel [rjel] *sm* ingot; (*ferro*) rail.

rienda [‘rjenda] *sf* rein. **a rienda suelta** at full speed. **llevar las riendas** be in control.

riesgo [‘rjesgo] *sm* risk.

rifar [ri'far] *v* raffle. **rifa** *sf* raffle.

rifle [‘rifle] *sm* rifle.

rígido [‘rixiðo] *adj* rigid. **rigidez** *sf* rigidity.

rigor [ri'gor] *sm* severity; rigour. **rigorismo** *sm* austerity. **riguroso** *adj* rigorous.

rimar [ri'mar] *v* rhyme. **rima** *sf* rhyme.

rimbombante [rimbom'bante] *adj* grandiloquent; bombastic. **rimbombancia** *sf* grandiloquence.

rincón [rin'kon] *sm* corner. **rinconada** *sf* corner table.

rinoceronte [rinoθe'ronte] *sm* rhinoceros.

riña [‘riɲa] *sf* brawl; fight; quarrel.

riñón [ri'ɲon] *sm* kidney.

río [‘rio] *sm* river. **río arriba** upstream.

ripio [‘ripjo] *sm* rubble; refuse; residue. **no perder ripio** not to miss a trick.

riqueza [ri'keθa] *sf* wealth.

risa [‘risa] *sf* laughter; laugh. **riseño** *adj* smiling; happy.

ristre [‘ristre] *sm* **en ristre** at the ready.

ritmo [‘ritmo] *sm* rhythm. **rítmico** *adj* rhythmic.

rito [‘rito] *sm* rite. **ritual** *sm* ritual. **ritualismo** *sm* ritualism. **ritualista** *adj* ritualistic.

rival [ri'βal] *s(m+f)*, *adj* rival. **rivalidad** *sf* rivalry. **rivalizar** *v* vie. **rivalizar con** rival.

rizar [ri'θar] *v* (*pelo*) curl. **rizado** *sm* curling. **rizador** *sm* curling-iron. **rizo** *adj* curly.

robar [ro'βar] *v* rob, steal; kidnap. **robo** *sm* robbery.

roble [‘roβle] *sm* oak.

*robustecer [roβuste'θer] *v* strengthen. **robustecerse** *v* gain strength. **robustecimiento** *sm* strengthening. **robustez** *sf* robustness. **robusto** *adj* robust.

roca [‘roka] *sf* rock.

roce [‘roθe] *sm* friction; rubbing; chafing.

rociar [ro'θjar] *v* sprinkle; spray; strew; moisten. **rociada** *sf* sprinkling; spraying; dew. **rociadera** *sf* watering can. **rociador** *sm* sprinkler.

rocín [ro'θin] *sm* nag; hack.

rodapié [roða'pje] *sm* skirting-board.

***rodar** [ro'ðar] *v* roll; revolve; rotate. **rodado** *adj (auto)* run-in. **tránsito rodado** *sm* road traffic. **rodaja** *sf* small wheel. **rodaje** *sm* wheels *pl*.

rodear [roðe'ar] *v* encircle; enclose; go round. **rodearse** *v* surround oneself. **rodeo** *sm* detour; evasion; rodeo.

rodezno [ro'ðeθno] *sm* waterwheel; cogwheel.

rodilla [ro'ðiʎa] *sf* knee. **de rodillas** kneeling.

rodillo [ro'ðiʎo] *sm* rolling pin; roller; mangle.

***roer** [ro'er] *v* gnaw; nibble. **roerse** *v* bite. **roedor** *adj* gnawing.

***rogar** [ro'gar] *v* beg; pray. **rogación** *sf* petition. **rogativa** *sf* supplication.

rojo ['roxo] *adj* red. *sm* red; rouge. **rojear** *v* redden. **rojizo** *adj* reddish.

rollizo [ro'ʎiθo] *adj* chubby; plump.

rollo ['roʎo] *sm* roll; cylinder; *(foto)* film.

romance [ro'manθe] *sm, adj* romance. *sm* ballad. **romancero** *sm* ballad collection; ballad singer. **romántico** *adj* romantic.

romería [rome'ria] *sf* pilgrimage. **romero, -a** *sm, sf* pilgrim; *sm* rosemary.

romo ['romo] *adj* snub-nosed; blunt; dull.

rompecabezas [rompeka'βeθas] *sm invar* puzzle; jigsaw; riddle.

rompeolas [rompe'olas] *sm invar* breakwater.

romper [rom'per] *v* break; fracture; break out. **rompimiento** *sm* break; breach.

ron [ron] *sm* rum.

roncar [ron'kar] *v* snore; roar; boast. **ronca** *sf* bellow. **ronquido** *sm* snore.

ronco ['ronko] *adj* hoarse. **ronquedad** *sf* hoarseness.

rondar [ron'dar] *v* patrol; go round; pursue; haunt; serenade. **rondador** *sm* patrolman. **ronda** *sf* patrol; round of drinks.

ronronear [ronrone'ar] *v* purr.

ronzal [ron'θal] *sm* halter.

roña ['roɲa] *sf* filth; mange; rust; *(fam)* meanness. *adj* stingy. **roñoso** *adj* mangy; filthy; stingy.

ropa ['ropa] *sf* clothes *pl*, clothing. **ropa de cama** bed linen. **ropa interior** underclothes. **ropero** *sm* wardrobe.

roque ['roke] *sm (ajedrez)* rook.

rosa ['rosa] *sf* rose. **novela rosa** *sf* romantic novel. **rosado** *adj* rose-coloured. **rosal** *sm* rosebush.

rosario [ro'sarjo] *sm* rosary.

rosca ['roska] *sf* thread of a screw; doughnut; bread roll.

rostro ['rostro] *sm* countenance, face. **hacer rostro a** face.

rotación [rota'θjon] *sf* rotation. **rotativo** *adj* rotary.

roto ['roto] *adj* broken; torn. *sm* hole.

rotular [rotu'lar] *v* label. **rótula** *sf* label; placard.

rotundo [ro'tundo] *adj* round; *(fig)* emphatic. **rotundidad** *sf* roundness.

roturar [rotu'rar] *v (tierra)* break up. **rotura** *sf* breaking.

rozar [ro'θar] *v* graze; scrape. **rozarse** *v* be tongue-tied; trip over one's feet. **rozamiento** *sm* rubbing, friction.

rubí [ru'βi] *sm, pl* **rubíes** ruby.

rubio [ru'βjo] *sm, adj* blond. **rubia** *sf* blonde.

rubor [ru'βor] *sm* blush. **ruborizarse** *v* blush. **ruboroso** *adj* blushing.

rúbrica ['ruβrika] *sf* rubric; heading; flourish after a signature. **rubricar** *v* sign with a flourish.

rudeza [ru'ðeθa] *sf* roughness, rudeness. **rudo** *adj* rough; coarse; crude.

rudimento [ruði'mento] *sm* rudiment.

rueca [ru'eka] *sf* distaff.

rueda [ru'eða] *sf* wheel. **rueda de recambio** spare wheel.

ruedo [ru'eðo] *sm* edge; hem; round mat.

ruego [ru'ego] *sm* request; supplication.

rugir [ru'xir] *v* roar; bellow; howl. **rugido** *sm* roar; bellow; howl.

rugoso [ru'goso] *adj* wrinkled.

ruibarbo [rui'βarβo] *sm* rhubarb.

ruido [ru'iðo] *sm* noise; rumour. **meter ruido** make a noise. **ruidoso** *adj* noisy.

ruin [ru'in] *adj* mean; foul; puny. **ruindad** *sf* meanness; villainy.

ruina [ru'ina] *sf* ruin; ruins *pl*. **ruinoso** *adj* ruinous.

ruiseñor [ruise'ɲor] *sm* nightingale.

rumbo ['rumbo] *sm* course; direction; *(fam)* pomp. **hacer rumbo** set a course. **rumboso** *adj* splendid; lavish.

rumiar [ru'mjar] *v* ruminate; chew; grumble. **rumiante** *sm* ruminant.

rumor [ru'mor] *sm* rumour; noise; murmur. **rumorear** *v* rumour. **rumoroso** *adj* murmuring.

ruptura [rup'tura] *sf* rupture; break.
rural [ru'ral] *adj* rural.
Rusia ['rusja] *sf* Russia. **ruso, -a** *sm, sf* Russian.
rústico ['rustiko] *adj* rustic.
ruta ['ruta] *sf* route; road.
rutina [ru'tina] *sf* routine. **rutinario** *adj* routine; unimaginative.

S

sábado ['saβaðo] *sm* Saturday.
sabana [sa'βana] *sf* savannah.
sábana ['saβana] *sf* sheet.
sabanilla [saβa'niʎa] *sf* small cloth, napkin.
sabañón [saβa'ɲon] *sm* chilblain.
*** saber** [sa'βer] *v* know; know how to; be aware of. **a saber** namely. **sabedor** *adj* well-informed. **sabidillo, -a** *sm, sf* (*fam*) know-all. **sabido** *adj* known; learned. **sabiduría** *sf* knowledge; wisdom. **sabio** *adj* wise.
sabor [sa'βor] *sm* taste; flavour. **saborear** *v* taste; savour. **saborearse** *v* smack one's lips. **saboroso** *adj* tasty; savoury.
sabotear [saβote'ar] *v* sabotage. **saboteador, -a** *sm, sf* saboteur. **sabotaje** *sm* sabotage.
sabroso [sa'βroso] *adj* delicious; tasty; pleasant; racy.
sabueso [sa'βweso] *sm* bloodhound.
sacabocados [sakaβo'kaðos] *sm invar* (*tecn*) punch.
sacacorchos [saka'kortʃos] *sm invar* corkscrew.
sacamanchas [saka'mantʃas] *sm invar* stain-remover.
sacar [sa'kar] *v* get out; put out; draw; publish; take out; buy tickets; (*tenis*) serve. **saca** *sf* extraction; exportation.
sacarina [saka'rina] *sf* saccharine.
sacerdote [saker'ðote] *sm* priest. **sacerdocio** *sm* priesthood. **sacerdotal** *adj* priestly. **sacerdotisa** *sf* priestess.
saciar [sa'θjar] *v* satiate. **saciedad** *sf* satiety.
saco ['sako] *sm* sack; bag; plunder. **entrar a saco** plunder.
sacramento [sakra'mento] *sm* sacrament. **sacramental** *adj* sacramental.

sacrificar [sakrifi'kar] *v* sacrifice. **sacrificadero** *sm* slaughterhouse. **sacrificio** *sm* sacrifice; slaughter.
sacrilegio [sakri'lexjo] *sm* sacrilege. **sacrílego** *adj* sacrilegious.
sacro ['sakro] *adj* sacred. **sacrosanto** *adj* sacrosanct.
sacudir [saku'ðir] *v* shake, jolt. **sacudirse** *v* shake off; repel. **sacudida** *sf* shake, jolt.
sádico ['saðiko] *adj* sadistic. **sadismo** *sm* sadism. **sadista** *s(m+f)* sadist.
saeta [sa'eta] *sf* arrow; watch *or* clock hand. **saetada** *sf* arrow wound. **saetera** *sf* loophole. **saetero** *sm* bowman.
sagacidad [sagaθi'ðað] *sf* shrewdness. **sagaz** *adj* shrewd, wise.
sagrado [sa'graðo] *adj* sacred, holy. *sm* sanctuary.
sajón [sa'xon], **-ona** *s, adj* Saxon.
sal [sal] *sf* salt; wit; charm. **salero** *sm* salt cellar; wit; charm. **saleroso** *adj* (*fam*) witty; charming.
sala ['sala] *sf* hall; drawing-room; (*med*) ward; (*teatro*) house. **sala de conferencias** lecture hall. **sala de espera** waiting-room.
salacidad [salaθi'ðað] *sf* lechery.
salar [sa'lar] *v* salt. **salado** *adj* salty; witty.
salario [sa'larjo] *sm* salary, pay.
salchicha [sal'tʃitʃa] *sf* sausage. **salchichón** *sm* salami.
saldar [sal'ðar] *v* settle; liquidate; pay off. **saldo** *sm* payment; balance; bargain sale.
salida [sa'liða] *sf* departure; exit; start; outskirts *pl*; pretext; (*del sol*) rising; outcome; projection; witticism. **calle sin salida** *sf* cul-de-sac. **dar salida a** sell. **tener buenas salidas** be full of witty remarks. **saliente** *adj* projecting.
salina [sa'lina] *sm* salt mine. **salino** *adj* saline.
*** salir** [sa'lir] *v* leave; emerge; (*astron*) rise; happen. **salir para** leave for. **salir por alguien** vouch for someone. **salirse** *v* leak; overflow; escape.
saliva [sa'liβa] *sf* saliva. **salivar** *v* salivate.
salmo ['salmo] *sm* psalm. **salmista** *s(m+f)* psalmist. **salmodia** *sf* psalmody.
salmón [sal'mon] *sm* salmon.
salmuera [sal'mwera] *sf* brine.
salón [sa'lon] *sm* large hall; drawing-room.
salpicar [salpi'kar] *v* splash; sprinkle. **salpicadura** *sf* splash; spatter.
salpimentar [salpimen'tar] *v* season with salt and pepper.

salpullido [salpu'ʎiðo] *sm* (*med*) rash.

salsa ['salsa] *sf* sauce, gravy.

saltamontes [salta'montes] *sm invar* grasshopper.

saltar [sal'tar] *v* jump; skip; break; explode. **salto** *sm* jump; hop; chasm. **salto de agua** waterfall. **salto de altura** high jump. **salto con garrocha** pole vault. **salto mortal** somersault.

saltear [salte'ar] *v* rob; assault. **salteador** *sm* highwayman. **salteamiento** *sm* highway robbery.

salubre [sa'luβre] *adj* salubrious, healthy. **salubridad** *sf* wholesomeness. **salud** *sf* health. ¡**salud**! cheers! **saludable** *adj* salutary. **saludador** *sm* quack doctor.

salvaguardar [salβagwar'ðar] *v* safeguard. **salvaguardia** *sf* safeguard.

saludar [salu'ðar] *v* salute; greet. **le saluda atentamente** yours faithfully. **saludo** *sm* greeting; salute. **saludos** *sm pl* regards *pl*, best wishes *pl*. **salutación** *sf* greeting.

salvaje [sal'βaxe] *adj* wild; uncultivated; savage. **salvajada** *sf* barbarity. **salvajería** *sf* savagery.

salvamanteles [salβaman'teles] *sm invar* table mat.

salvar [sal'βar] *v* save, rescue; except; cross; overcome. **salvarse** *v* escape. **salvamento** *sm* salvation; salvage. **salvador** *adj* healing; saving.

salvavidas [salβa'βiðas] *sm invar* lifebelt; life buoy; lifeboat.

salvedad [salβe'ðað] *sf* proviso; reservation; distinction.

salvia ['salβja] *sf* sage.

salvo ['salβo] *adv* except, saving. *adj* safe. **a salvo** safe. **poner a salvo** rescue. **salvo que** unless.

salvoconducto [salβokòn'dukto] *sm* safeconduct.

san [san] *adj* saint; noly. *V* santo.

sanar [sa'nar] *v* heal; cure; get better. **sanable** *adj* curable. **sanatorio** *sm* sanatorium.

sanción [san'θjon] *sf* sanction. **sancionar** *v* sanction.

sandalia [san'dalja] *sf* sandal.

sandía [san'dia] *sf* watermelon.

sanear [sane'ar] *v* guarantee; drain; repair. **saneado** *adj* unencumbered; nett. **saneamiento** *sm* surety; drainage.

sangrar [san'grar] *v* bleed; drain off. **sangradera** *sf* lancet. **sangre** *sf* blood. **a sangre fría** in cold blood. **sangriento** *adj*
bloody. **sanguinario** *adj* bloodthirsty. **sanguinolento** *adj* bloody.

sangría [san'gria] *sf* bleeding; drink made of fruit and red wine.

sanguijuela [sangi'xwela] *sf* leech.

sanidad [sani'ðað] *sf* health; sanitation. **sanitario** *adj* sanitary. **sano** *adj* healthy; wholesome; sound; good.

santiamén [santja'men] *sm* instant. **en un santiamén** in a jiffy.

santificar [santifi'kar] *v* sanctify, consecrate. **santificación** *sf* sanctification.

santiguar [santi'gwar] *v* bless. **santiguarse** *v* cross oneself.

santo ['santo], **-a** *sm*, *sf* saint. *adj* sacred; saintly; holy. **santo y bueno** all well and good.

santuario [san'twarjo] *sm* sanctuary, shrine.

saña ['sana] *sf* rage; cruelty. **sañoso** *adj* furious; cruel.

sapo ['sapo] *sm* toad.

saquear [sake'ar] *v* plunder. **saqueo** *sm* plunder. **saqueador, -a** *sm*, *sf* looter.

sarampión [saram'pjon] *sm* measles.

sarcasmo [sar'kasmo] *sm* sarcasm. **sarcástico** *adj* sarcastic.

sarcófago [sar'kofago] *sm* sarcophagus.

sardina [sar'ðina] *sf* sardine.

sardónico [sar'ðoniko] *adj* sardonic.

sargento [sar'xento] *sm* sergeant.

sarna ['sarna] *sf* scabies; itch. **sarnoso** *adj* mangy.

sartén [sar'ten] *sf* frying pan.

sastre ['sastre] *sm* tailor. **sastrería** *sf* tailoring; tailor's shop.

satélite [sa'telite] *sm* satellite.

sátira ['satira] *sf* satire. **satírico** *adj* satirical. **satirizar** *v* satirize.

*****satisfacer** [satisfa'θer] *v* satisfy; please. **satisfacerse** *v* satisfy oneself; take revenge. **satisfacción** *sf* satisfaction. **satisfactorio** *adj* satisfactory. **satisfecho** *adj* satisfied.

saturar [satu'rar] *v* saturate. **saturación** *sf* saturation.

sauce ['sauθe] *sm* willow.

saúco [sa'uko] *sm* (*bot*) elder.

savia ['saβja] *sf* sap.

saxófono [sak'sofono] *sm* saxophone.

saya ['saja] *sf* skirt, petticoat. **sayo** *sm* smock.

sazonar [saθo'nar] *v* (*culin*) season; ripen.

sazón *sf* season; (*culin*) flavour; mellowness. **a la sazón** at the time. **sazonado** *adj* tasty; well seasoned.

se [se] *pron* himself; herself; yourself; oneself; itself; themselves; yourselves; one another; each other. **se dice** they say. **se habla inglés** English is spoken.

sebo ['seβo] *sm* grease. **seboso** *adj* greasy.

secar [se'kar] *v* dry. **secarse** *v* dry oneself; dry up. **seca** *sf* drought; sandbank. **secador** *sm* hair-dryer. **secadora** *sf* clothes-dryer. **secano** *sm* dry land. **secante** *sm* blotting paper. **seco** *adj* dry; lean; hoarse. **en seco** high and dry.

sección [sek'θjon] *sf* section.

secretario [sekre'tarjo], **-a** *sm, sf* secretary. **secretaría** *sf* secretariat.

secreto [se'kreto] *adj* secret; private; hidden. *sm* secrecy, secret knowledge. **secreto a voces** open secret. **secreteo** *sm* private conversation.

secta ['sekta] *sf* sect. **sectario, -a** *sm, sf* sectarian.

secuaz [se'kwaθ] *sm* follower, supporter.

secuestrar [sekwes'trar] *v* kidnap; hijack. **secuestrado, -a** *sm, sf* kidnapper; hijacker. **secuestro** *sm* kidnap; hijack.

secular [seku'lar] *adj* secular. **secularizar** *v* secularize.

secundar [sekun'dar] *v* second, support.

sed [seð] *sf* thirst. **tener sed** be thirsty. **sediento** *adj* thirsty.

seda ['seða] *sf* silk. **sedoso** *adj* silky.

sedante [se'ðante] *sm* sedative. *adj* calming.

sede ['seðe] *sf* (*rel*) see; (*de gobierno*) seat. **Santa Sede** Holy See.

sedentario [seðen'tarjo] *adj* sedentary.

sedería [seðe'ria] *sf* silk trade; drapery.

sedición [seði'θjon] *sf* sedition. **sedicioso** *adj* seditious.

sedimento [seði'mento] *sm* sediment. **sedimentar** *v* deposit.

*****seducir** [seðu'θir] *v* seduce; attract. **seducción** *sf* seduction. **seductivo** *adj* seductive. **seductor, -a** *sm, sf* seducer.

*****segar** [se'gar] *v* reap; mow. **segadora** *sf* mower; reaper.

seglar [se'glar] *sm* layman. *adj* secular.

segmento [seg'mento] *sm* segment.

segregar [segre'gar] *v* segregate. **segregación** *sf* segregation.

*****seguir** [se'gir] *v* follow; pursue; continue. **seguida** *sf* continuation. **en seguida** at once. **seguido** *adj* successive; straight. **cuatro días seguidos** four days running. **seguimiento** *sm* pursuit; following.

según [se'gun] *prep* according to. *adv* it all depends. *conj* as.

segundo [se'gundo] *adj, sm* second.

segundón [segun'don] *sm* second son.

seguro [se'guro] *adj* sure; safe. *sm* safety catch; insurance. **seguridad** *sf* safety; certainty.

seis ['seis] *sm, adj* six.

selección [selek'θjon] *sf* selection. **seleccionar** *v* select. **selectivo** *adj* selective. **selecto** *adj* select.

selva ['selβa] *sf* forest; jungle. **selvoso** *adj* wooded, forested.

sello ['seʎo] *sm* stamp; seal. **selladura** *sf* sealing. **sellar** *v* stamp; seal.

semáforo [se'maforo] *sm* semaphore; traffic lights *pl*.

semana [se'mana] *sf* week. **semanal** *adj* weekly. **semanario** *sm* weekly publication.

semblante [sem'blante] *sm* face; appearance.

*****sembrar** [sem'brar] *v* sow; scatter. **sembradera** *sf* seed-drill. **sembrador, -a** *sm, sf* sower.

semejar [seme'xar] *v* resemble. **semejante** *adj* similar. **semejanza** *sf* similarity.

semen ['semen] *sm* semen. **semental** *sm* sire. **sementera** *sf* sowing; seed-time.

semestre [se'mestre] *sm* semester. **semestral** *adj* half-yearly.

semicírculo [semi'θirkulo] *sm* semicircle. **semicircular** *adj* semicircular.

semilla [se'miʎa] *sf* seed. **semillero** *sm* seedbed.

seminario [semi'narjo] *sm* seminary; seminar; seedbed.

senado [se'naðo] *sm* senate. **senador** *sm* senator.

sencillo [sen'θiʎo] *adj* simple; easy. **sencillez** *sf* simplicity.

senda ['senda] *sf* path. **sendero** *sm* path.

sendos ['sendos] *adj pl* each.

senectud [senek'tuð] *sf* old age.

senil [se'nil] *adj* senile. **senilidad** *sf* senility.

seno ['seno] *sm* bosom, breast; haven, refuge.

sensación [sensa'θjon] *sf* sensation. **sensacional** *adj* sensational.

sensatez [sensa'teθ] *sf* good sense. **sensato** *adj* sensible.

sensibilidad [sensiβili'ðað] *sf* sensibility; sensitivity. **sensible** *adj* sensitive; sensible; considerable.

sensiblería [sensiβle'ria] *sf* sentimentality. **sensiblero** *adj* sentimental.

sensitivo [sensi'tiβo] *adj* relating to the senses; sensitive.

sensual [sen'swal] *adj* sensual. **sensualidad** *sf* sensuality.

***sentar** [sen'tar] *v* seat; place; locate; establish; press; suit; fit. **sentarse** *v* sit down; settle. **sentada** *sf* sit-in. **sentado** *adj* seated; established.

sentencia [sen'tenθja] *sf* (*jur*) sentence. **sentenciar** *v* (*jur*) sentence. **sentencioso** *adj* sententious.

sentido [sen'tiðo] *sm* sense; meaning; direction; feeling. **sin sentido** meaningless. **tener sentido** make sense. *adj* heartfelt; moving; sincere.

sentimiento [senti'mjento] *sm* feeling; emotion; sentiment; grief. **sentimental** *adj* sentimental.

***sentir** [sen'tir] *v* feel; hear; regret. **lo siento mucho** I am very sorry. **sentirse** *v* feel; suffer from. **sentirse enfermo** feel ill. **sentirse obligado** a feel obliged to.

seña ['sepa] *sf* mark; sign; signal; password. **señas** *sf pl* address *sing*.

señal [se'pal] *sf* signal; sign; mark. **en señal de** in proof of. **señaladamente** *adv* signally. **señalado** *adj* famous. **señalar** *v* mark; signal; point out; denote. **señalarse** *v* distinguish oneself.

señor [se'por] *sm* mister; gentleman; lord; master. **El Señor** the Lord. **señora** *sf* lady; wife; mistress; madam. **la señora de García** Mrs García. **señorear** *v* domineer. **señorearse** *v* take possession. **señoría** *sf* lordship. **señorío** *sm* dominion; stateliness. **señorita** *sf* miss; young lady.

separar [sepa'rar] *v* separate; divide; discharge. **separable** *adj* separable. **separación** *sf* separation; dismissal. **separado** *adj* separate. **por separado** separately.

septentrional [septentrjo'nal] *adj* northern.

séptico ['septiko] *adj* septic.

septiembre [sep'tjembre] *sm* September.

séptimo ['septimo] *adj* seventh.

septuagésimo [septwa'xesimo] *adj* seventieth.

sepulcro [se'pulkro] *sm* tomb, grave.

sepultar [sepul'tar] *v* bury. **sepultura** *sf* grave; burial. **sepulturero** *sm* gravedigger.

sequedad [seke'ðað] *sf* dryness; curtness. **sequía** *sf* drought.

séquito ['sekito] *sm* entourage, followers *pl*.

***ser** [ser] *v* be; exist; occur. **a no ser por** but for. **sea lo que sea** come what may. **si no es que** unless.

seráfico [se'rafiko] *adj* seraphic. **serafín** *sm* seraph.

serenar [sere'nar] *v* calm; settle. **sereno** *adj* serene; calm. **serenidad** *sf* serenity; calmness.

serenata [sere'nata] *sf* serenade.

serie ['serje] *sf* series. **fabricación en serie** *sf* mass production.

serio ['serjo] *adj* serious. **tomar en serio** take seriously. **seriedad** *sf* seriousness; sincerity.

sermón [ser'mon] *sm* sermon.

serpiente [ser'pjente] *sf* serpent. **serpiente de cascabel** rattlesnake. **serpentear** *v* wriggle. **serpentino** *adj* serpentine.

serrano [se'rrano] *adj* of the mountains. *sm* highlander. **serranía** *sf* mountainous country.

***serrar** [se'rrar] *v* saw. **serrado** *adj* serrated. **serrín** *sm* sawdust.

servicio [ser'βiθjo] *sm* service; attendance. **estar de servicio** be on duty. **servicios** *sm pl* toilet *sing*. **servible** *adj* serviceable. **servidor, -a** *sm*, *sf* servant. **su seguro servidor** yours faithfully. **servidumbre** *sf* household staff; servitude. **servil** *adj* servile. **servilismo** *sm* servility.

servilleta [serβi'ʎeta] *sf* napkin.

***servir** [ser'βir] *v* serve. **para servir a usted** at your service. **servir de** act as. **servirse** *v* help oneself. **servirse de** make use of.

sesenta [se'senta] *sm*, *adj* sixty.

sesgar [ses'gar] *v* slant; twist. **sesgo** *sm* slant; twist.

sesión [se'sjon] *sf* session; conference.

seso ['seso] *sm* brain; sense, understanding, wisdom. **perder el seso** go mad.

seta ['seta] *sf* mushroom.

setenta [se'tenta] *sm*, *adj* seventy.

setiembre *V* septiembre.

seto ['seto] *sm* fence.

seudónimo [seu'ðonimo] *sm* pseudonym. **seudo** *adj* (*fam*) pseudo.

severo [se'βero] *adj* severe; harsh. **severidad** *sf* severity.

sexagésimo [seksa'xesimo] *adj* sixtieth. **sexagenario, -a** *sm, sf* sexagenarian.

sexo ['sekso] *sm* sex. **sexual** *adj* sexual. **sexualidad** *sf* sexuality.

sexto ['seksto] *adj* sixth. **sexteto** *sm* sextet.

si [si] *conj* if; whether. **si bien** although.

sí[1] [si] *adv* yes; indeed. **eso sí que es yes**, that's it. *sm* consent. **dar el sí** agree.

sí[2] *pron* himself; herself; itself; yourself; oneself; themselves; yourselves. **de por sí** in itself. **entre sí** among themselves. **metido en sí** pensive.

sibilante [siβi'lante] *adj* sibilant.

siderurgia [siðe'rurxja] *sf* iron and steel industry.

sidra ['siðra] *sf* cider.

siega ['sjega] *sf* reaping, harvesting.

siembra ['sjembra] *sf* sowing.

siempre ['sjempre] *adv* always. **siempre jamás** for ever and ever. **siempre que** whenever; provided that.

sien [sjen] *sf* (*anat*) temple.

sierra ['sjerra] *sf* saw; mountain range.

siervo ['sjerβo] *sm* slave; servant.

siesta ['sjesta] *sf* siesta.

siete ['sjete] *adj, sm* seven.

sífilis ['sifilis] *sm* syphilis. **sifilítico, -a** *s, adj* syphilitic.

sifón [si'fon] *sm* soda water; syphon.

sigilar [sixi'lar] *v* conceal. **sigilo** *sm* secrecy. **sigiloso** *adj* secretive.

siglo ['siglo] *sm* century. **siglo de oro** golden age.

signar [sig'nar] *v* sign, seal. **signarse** *v* cross oneself. **signatura** *sf* signature.

significar [signifi'kar] *v* signify; notify. **significado** *sm* meaning; significance. **significativo** *adj* significant.

signo ['signo] *sm* sign; symbol.

siguiente [si'gjente] *adj* following, next.

sílaba ['silaβa] *sf* syllable.

silbar [sil'βar] *v* whistle; hiss. **silbido** *sm* whistle, hiss.

silencio [si'lenθjo] *sm* silence. **silenciador** *sm* (*de arma*) silencer. **silenciar** *v* silence. **silencioso** *adj* silent.

silueta [si'lweta] *sf* silhouette, outline.

silvestre [sil'βestre] *adj* wild. **silvicultura** *sf* forestry.

silla ['siʎa] *sf* chair; seat; saddle. **silla de tijera** deck chair. **sillón** *sm* armchair.

sima ['sima] *sf* abyss.

símbolo ['simbolo] *sm* symbol. **simbólico** *adj* symbolic. **simbolismo** *sm* symbolism. **simbolizar** *v* symbolize.

simetría [sime'tria] *sf* symmetry. **simétrico** *adj* symmetrical.

simiente [si'mjente] *sf* seed.

símil ['simil] *adj* similar. *sm* comparison; simile. **similar** *adj* similar. **similitud** *sf* similarity.

simpatía [simpa'tia] *sf* affection; sympathy; friendliness; charm. **simpático** *adj* charming; friendly; nice. **simpatizar** *v* sympathize; get on.

simple ['simple] *adj* simple; pure; naïve. **simplemente** *adv* merely. **simpleza** *sf* simplicity; simpleness; silly thing. **simplicidad** *sf* simplicity. **simplificar** *v* simplify. **simplón, -ona** *sm, sf* simpleton.

simulacro [simu'lakro] *sm* image; semblance.

simular [simu'lar] *v* simulate. **simulación** *sf* pretence. **simulado** *adj* sham.

simultáneo [simul'taneo] *adj* simultaneous. **simultaneidad** *sf* simultaneousness.

sin [sin] *prep* without; but for; apart from. **sin embargo** nevertheless. **sin falta** without fail. **sin que** without.

sinagoga [sina'goga] *sf* synagogue.

sincero [sin'θero] *adj* sincere. **sinceridad** *sf* sincerity.

síncopa ['sinkopa] *sf* syncopation. **sincopar** *v* syncopate.

sindicato [sindi'kato] *sm* trade union; syndicate. **sindical** *adj* trade-union. **sindicalismo** *sm* trade-unionism. **síndico** *sm* trustee.

sinfín [sin'fin] *sm* endless number.

sinfonía [sinfo'nia] *sf* symphony. **sinfónico** *adj* symphonic.

singular [singu'lar] *adj* singular; exceptional; unique; excellent. **singularidad** *sf* singularity; excellence. **singularizar** *v* single out. **singularizarse** *v* distinguish oneself.

siniestro [si'njestro] *adj* (*dirección*) left; sinister. *sm* catastrophe. **siniestrado, -a** *sm, sf* victim of an accident.

sinnúmero [sin'numero] *sm* endless number.

sino[1] ['sino] *conj* but, except. **no sólo ... sino ...** not only ... but also ... .

sino[2] *sm* fate.

sinónimo [si'nonimo] *sm* synonym. *adj* synonymous.

sinopsis [si'nopsis] *sf* synopsis (*pl* -ses).

sinrazón [sinra'θon] *sf* injustice.

sinsabor [sinsa'βor] *sm* trouble.

sintaxis [sin'taksis] *sf* syntax. **sintáctico** *adj* syntactic.

síntesis ['sintesis] *sf* synthesis (*pl* -ses). **sintético** *adj* synthetic.

síntoma ['sintoma] *sm* symptom. **sintomático** *adj* symptomatic.

sintonizar [sintoni'θar] *v* (*radio*) tune in. **sintonía** *sf* signature tune.

sinvergüenza [sinβer'gwenθa] *adj* shameless. *s*(*m+f*) cad.

siquiera [si'kjera] *adv* at least; even; just. **ni siquiera** not at all. *conj* even if; even though. **siquiera ... siquiera ...** whether ... or whether ....

sirena [si'rena] *sf* (*ninfa*) siren. mermaid; (*tecn*) siren, fog-horn.

sirviente [sir'βjente] *sm* servant.

sisar [si'sar] *v* pilfer; cheat. **sisa** *sf* theft, pilfering.

sísmico ['sismiko] *adj* seismic. **sismógrafo** *sm* seismograph.

sistema [sis'tema] *sm* system, method. **sistemático** *adj* systematic.

sitiar [si'tjar] *sm* besiege; surround.

sitio ['sitjo] *sm* place; room, space; siege. **no hay sitio** there is no room.

situar [si'twar] *v* situate; put. **situación** *sf* situation.

so [so] *prep* under. **so pena de** under penalty of.

sobaco [so'βako] *sm* armpit.

sobado [so'βaðo] *adj* kneaded; (*fam*) shabby, well-worn. **sobar** *v* knead; thrash; crumple; fondle.

soberanía [soβera'nia] *sf* sovereignty. **soberano, -a** *i, adj* sovereign.

soberbia [so'βerβja] *sf* pride; magnificence, pomp. **soberbio** *adj* proud; superb.

sobornar [soβor'nar] *v* bribe. **soborno** *sm* bribe; bribery.

sobrar [so'βrar] *sf* surplus. **de sobra** in excess. **sobras** *sf pl* remains *pl*. **sobradamente** *adv* excessively. **sobrado** *adj* abundant; superfluous. **sobrancero** *adj* unemployed. **sobrante** *adj* spare.

sobre¹ ['soβre] *prep* on; upon; over; above; about. **sobre las diez** about ten o'clock. **sobre todo** above all.

sobre² *sm* envelope.

sobrecama [soβre'kama] *sm* bedspread.

sobrecargar [soβrekar'gar] *v* overload. **sobrecarga** *sf* extra burden. **sobrecargo** *sm* purser.

sobrecejo [soβre'θexo] *sm* frown.

sobrecoger [soβreko'xer] *v* surprise, take aback. **sobrecogerse** *v* be startled.

sobredicho [soβre'ðitʃo] *adj* aforesaid.

sobrehumano [soβreu'mano] *adj* superhuman.

sobremanera [soβrema'nera] *adv* exceedingly.

sobremesa [soβre'mesa] *sf* dessert; table cover; after-dinner chat.

sobrenatural [soβrenatu'ral] *adj* supernatural.

sobrepasar [soβrepa'sar] *v* surpass.

*sobreponer [soβrepo'ner] *v* superimpose. **sobreponerse a** overcome. **sobrepuesto** *adj* superimposed.

sobreprecio [soβre'preθjo] *sm* surcharge.

*sobresalir [soβresa'lir] *v* excel. **sobresaliente** *adj* outstanding.

sobresaltar [soβresal'tar] *v* attack; frighten. **sobresalto** *sm* sudden attack; shock. **de sobresalto** suddenly.

sobrescrito [soβre'skrito] *sm* (*en un sobre*) address.

sobretodo [soβre'toðo] *sm* overcoat.

*sobrevenir [soβreβe'nir] *v* happen suddenly.

sobrevivir [soβreβi'βir] *v* survive. **sobreviviente** *s*(*m+f*) survivor.

sobriedad [soβrie'ðað] *sf* sobriety. **sobrio** *adj* sober, moderate.

sobrino [so'βrino] *sm* nephew. **sobrina** *sf* niece.

socarrón [sokar'ron] *adj* sarcastic; sly. **socarronería** *sf* sarcasm; slyness.

socavar [soka'βar] *v* undermine. **socavón** *sm* excavation.

sociable [so'θjaβle] *adj* sociable. **sociabilidad** *sf* sociability.

social [so'θjal] *adj* social. **socializar** *v* socialize. **socialismo** *sm* socialism. **socialista** *s*(*m+f*) socialist.

sociedad [soθje'ðað] *sf* society. **socio, -a** *sm, sf* associate.

sociología [soθjolo'xia] *sf* sociology. **sociólogo, -a** *sm, sf* sociologist.

socorrer [sokor'rer] *v* help. **socorrido** *adj* helpful; handy. **socorro** *sm* succour; relief. **¡socorro!** help!

soda ['soða] *sf* soda-water.

soez [so'eθ] *adj* obscene; vulgar.

sofá [so'fa] sf sofa, settee.

sofocar [sofo'kar] v suffocate. sofocación sf suffocation. sofocado adj breathless. sofoco sm suffocation.

soga ['soga] sf rope, cord. hacer soga lag behind.

soja ['soxa] sf soya.

sojuzgar [soxuθ'gar] v subdue.

sol [sol] sm sun; sunlight. hace sol it's sunny. tomar el sol sunbathe.

solamente [sola'mente] adv only. no solamente not only.

solapa [so'lapa] sf flap; lapel; (fig) pretext. solapado adj sly. solapar v overlap; (fig) cover up, hide.

*solar [so'lar] adj solar. sm lot; plot; building site.

solaz [so'laθ] sm recreation; solace. a solaz with pleasure. solazar v distract; amuse; solace.

soldado [sol'ðaðo] sm soldier.

*soldar [sol'ðar] v solder; weld; (huesos) knit. soldador sm soldering iron. soldadura sf welding.

soledad [sole'ðað] sf loneliness, solitude.

solemne [so'lemne] adj solemn. solemnidad sf solemnity. solemnizar v solemnize.

*soler [so'ler] v be in the habit of; usually be or do. suele comer mucho he usually eats a lot.

solera [so'lera] sf prop; stone pavement; tradition; strong old wine.

solicitar [soliθi'tar] v request; pursue; canvass. solicitación sf solicitation; application. solicitador, -a sm, sf or solicitante sm petitioner; applicant. solícito adj solicitous. solicitud sf solicitude.

solidaridad [soliðari'ðað] sf solidarity. solidar v consolidate. solidario adj mutual. solidez sf solidity. solidificar v solidify. sólido adj solid.

solitario [soli'tarjo], -a sm, sf hermit, recluse. adj lonely; solitary; alone; single.

solo ['solo] adj alone; single; unique; only; (música) solo. sm (música) solo.

sólo ['solo] adv only, merely.

*soltar [sol'tar] v release; free; loosen; break; shed. soltarse v break loose; become unscrewed; lose one's inhibitions.

soltero [sol'tero] sm bachelor. adj single. soltera sf spinster. soltería sf celibacy. solterona sf old maid.

soltura [sol'tura] sf looseness; agility; fluency. con soltura fluently.

soluble [so'luβle] adj soluble. solubilidad sf solubility. solución sf solution. solucionar v solve.

solvencia [sol'βenθja] sf solvency; settlement. solvente adj solvent.

sollo ['soʎo] sm sturgeon.

sollozar [soʎo'θar] v sob. sollozo sm sob.

sombra ['sombra] sf shadow; shade. dar sombra a shade.

sombrero [som'brero] sm hat.

sombrilla [som'briʎa] sf parasol.

sombrío [som'brio] sm shady spot. adj shady; gloomy. sombroso adj shady.

somero [so'mero] adj superficial.

someter [some'ter] v submit; subdue. sometimiento sm submission.

somnífero [som'nifero] sm sleeping pill.

somnolencia [somno'lenθja] sf sleepiness. somnámbulo, -a sm, sf sleepwalker. somnolente adj sleepy.

son [son] sm sound; rumour; manner. por este son by this means.

*sonar [so'nar] v sound; ring; chime. sonarse v blow one's nose. sonante adj sounding; ringing.

sondear [sonde'ar] v fathom; sound out.

soneto [so'neto] sm sonnet.

sonido [so'niðo] sm sound.

sonoro [so'noro] adj sonorous; resonant. sonoridad sf sonority.

*sonreír [sonre'ir] v smile. sonriente adj smiling. sonrisa sf smile.

sonrojar [sonro'xar] v blush; flush. sonrojo sm blush.

*soñar [so'nar] v dream. soñador, -a sm, sf dreamer. soñera sf drowsiness. soñoliento adj drowsy.

sopa ['sopa] sf soup. como una sopa soaked to the skin. sopero sm soup plate.

sopapo [so'papo] sm (fam) blow, punch. sopapear v chuck under the chin; punch.

soplar [so'plar] v blow; blow out; blow away; prompt. sopladura sf blowing. soplillo sm fan; blower. soplo sm blowing; puff of wind. soplón, -ona sm, sf informer.

sopor [so'por] sm drowsiness.

soportar [sopor'tar] v support; tolerate; endure. soporte sm support; stand.

sor [sor] sf (rel) sister.

sorber [sor'βer] v sip; suck; soak up. sorbete sm sherbet; water ice. sorbetón *sm* large draught. **sorbo** *sm* sip; swallow; gulp.

sordera [sor'ðera] *sf* deafness. **sordo** *adj* deaf; muffled.

sórdido ['sorðiðo] *adj* squalid. **sordidez** *sf* squalor.

sordomudo [sorðo'muðo]. **-a** *sm, sf* deaf-mute. *adj* deaf and dumb.

sorprender [sorpren'der] *v* surprise. **sorprendente** *adj* surprising. **sorpresa** *sf* surprise.

sortear [sorte'ar] *v* cast lots for; avoid, get round. **sorteable** *adj* avoidable. **sorteo** *sm* raffle; casting of lots; dodging.

sortija [sor'tixa] *sf* ring; (*de pelo*) curl.

sortilegio [sorti'lexjo] *sm* sorcery; charm. **sortilega** *sf* sorceress. **sortilego** *sm* sorcerer.

sosegar [sose'gar] *v* calm, quieten. **sosiego** *sm* calm, quiet.

soslayar [sosla'jar] *v* place obliquely; dodge; avoid. **soslayo** *adj* oblique.

soso ['soso] *adj* tasteless; dull.

sospechar [sospe't∫ar] *v* suspect. **sospecha** *sf* suspicion. **sospechoso** *adj* suspicious, suspect.

sostener [soste'ner] *v* support; sustain. **sostén** *sm* support; brassière. **sostenedor, -a** *sm, sf* supporter. **sostenido** *adj* sustained; constant.

sota ['sota] *sf* (*deporte*) jack; (*fam*) hussy.

sotana [so'tana] *sf* cassock.

sótano ['sotano] *sm* basement, cellar.

soto ['soto] *sm* thicket, copse.

soviet [so'βjet] *sm* Soviet. **soviético** *adj* Soviet.

spaghettis [spa'getis] *sm pl* spaghetti *sing*.

su [su] *adj* his; her; its; your; their; one's.

suave ['swaβe] *adj* smooth; soft; mild. **suavidad** *sf* smoothness; softness. **suavizar** *v* soften; smooth; strop.

subarrendar [suβarren'dar] *v* sublet, sublease. **subarriendo** *sm* subletting.

subasta [su'βasta] *sf* auction. **subastar** *v* auction.

subcampeón [subkam'pjon], **-ona** *sm, sf* runner-up.

subconsciencia [subkons'θjenθja] *sf* subconscious. **subconsciente** *adj* subconscious.

subdesarrollado [suβðesarro'ʎaðo] *adj* underdeveloped. **subdesarrollo** *sm* under-development.

súbdito ['suβðito] *sm* subject, citizen.

subdividir [suβðiβi'ðir] *v* subdivide. **subdivisión** *sf* subdivision.

subir [su'βir] *v* climb; go up; rise; lift; promote. **subir al coche** get into the car. **subirse** *v* rise; become conceited. **subida** *sf* ascent. **subido** *adj* (*color*) bright.

súbito ['suβito] *adj* sudden. *adv* suddenly.

subjuntivo [subxun'tiβo] *sm* (*gram*) subjunctive.

sublevar [suβle'βar] *v* incite to rebellion. **sublevarse** *v* rebel. **sublevación** *sf* rebellion.

sublime [su'βlime] *adj* sublime, lofty. **sublimación** *sf* sublimation. **sublimidad** *sf* sublimity.

submarino [suβma'rino] *adj* underwater. *sm* submarine.

subordinado [suβorði'naðo] *adj* subordinate. **subordinar** *v* subordinate.

subproducto [suβpro'ðukto] *sm* by-product.

subrayar [suβra'jar] *v* underline, underscore; emphasize. **subrayado** *sm* underlining; emphasis.

subsanar [suβsa'nar] *v* excuse; redeem.

subscribir [suβskri'βir] *v* subscribe; sign. **subscripción** *sf* subscription.

subseguir [suβse'gir] *v* follow. **subsiguiente** *adj* subsequent.

subsidiario [suβsi'ðjarjo] *adj* subsidiary.

subsidio [suβ'siðjo] *sm* subsidy, grant, allowance.

subsistir [suβsis'tir] *v* subsist; exist. **subsistencia** *sf* permanence; subsistence. **subsistente** *adj* subsisting.

substancia [suβ'stanθja] *sf* substance. **en substancia** briefly. **substancial** *adj* substantial. **substanciar** *v* summarize; substantiate. **substancioso** *adj* substantial.

substituir [suβstitu'ir] *v* substitute. **substitución** *sf* substitution. **substitutivo** *adj* substitute.

substraer [suβstra'er] *v* subtract; remove; steal. **substraerse** *v* evade; withdraw. **substracción** *sf* subtraction; stealing.

subterfugio [suβter'fuxjo] *sm* subterfuge.

subterráneo [suβter'raneo] *adj* subterranean.

subtítulo [suβ'titulo] *sm* subtitle.

suburbio [suβ'urβjo] *sm* outskirts *pl*; slum. **suburbano** *adj* suburban.

subvención [suββen'θjon] *sf* subsidy. **subvencionar** *v* subsidize.

subvertir [suββer'tir] v subvert. subversión sf subversion. subversivo adj subversive.

subyugar [suβju'gar] v subjugate. subyugación sf subjugation.

suceder [suθe'ðer] v succeed; follow; happen. sucedido sm event. sucediente adj following. sucesión sf succession; offspring. sucesivamente adv successively. sucesivo adj successive. en lo sucesivo hereafter. suceso sm event; outcome.

suciedad [suθje'ðað] sf dirt, dirtiness. sucio adj dirty; vile, mean.

sucinto [su'θinto] adj succinct, brief.

sucumbir [sukum'bir] v succumb.

sucursal [sukur'sal] sm branch.

sud [suð] sm south.

sudamericano [suðameri'kano], -a s, adj South American.

sudar [su'ðar] v sweat. sudar tinta (fam) sweat blood. sudor sm sweat. sudoroso adj sweaty.

sudeste [su'ðeste] adj, sm south-east.

sudoeste [suðo'este] sm, adj south-west.

Suecia ['sweθja] sf Sweden.

sueco ['sweko], -a sm, sf Swede. sm (idioma) Swedish. adj Swedish.

suegro ['swegro] sm father-in-law.

suela ['swela] sf (de zapato) sole. suelas sf pl sandals pl.

sueldo ['sweldo] sm salary; wage; pay. a sueldo paid.

suelo ['swelo] sm ground; soil; floor. echar al suelo demolish.

suelto ['swelto] adj free; loose; separate; agile.

sueño ['sweɲo] sm dream; sleep. tener sueño be sleepy.

suero ['swero] sm serum; whey.

suerte ['swerte] sf luck; fate; chance; kind; manner; quality. ¡buena suerte! good luck! de otra suerte otherwise. de tal suerte que in such a way that.

suéter ['sweter] sm sweater.

suficiencia [sufi'θjenθja] sf sufficiency; ability; self-importance. suficiente adj sufficient; capable.

sufragar [sufra'gar] v help; finance. sufragar por vote for. sufragio sm suffrage.

sufrir [suf'rir] v suffer; endure. sufrido adj long-suffering. sufrimiento sm suffering; patience.

*sugerir [suxe'rir] v suggest, hint. sugerencia sf suggestion. sugerente adj suggestive. sugestión sf suggestion. sugestionable adj suggestible. sugestionar v influence. sugestivo adj suggestive; stimulating.

suicidarse [swiθi'ðarse] v commit suicide. suicida s(m+f) (persona) suicide. suicidio sm suicide.

Suiza ['swiθa] sf Switzerland. suizo, -a s, adj Swiss.

sujetar [suxe'tar] v secure; hold; fasten; seize; tie; restrain; subordinate. sujetarse v hang on; hold up; subject oneself to; abide by. sujerción sf subjection; control. sujetapapeles sm invar paperclip. sujeto sm subject; individual.

sumar [su'mar] v add, add up. sumarse v join in. suma sf sum; summary; essence. en suma in short. sumadora sf adding machine. sumamente adv extremely. sumaria sf (jur) indictment. sumario sm summary.

sumergir [sumer'xir] v submerge, plunge. sumersión sf submersion.

suministrar [suminis'trar] v supply, provide. suministro sm supply. suministros sm pl supplies pl, provisions pl.

sumir [su'mir] v submerge; sink.

sumisión [sumi'sjon] sf submission. sumiso adj submissive.

sumo ['sumo] adj greatest; supreme. tribunal supremo sm supreme court.

suntuoso [sun'twoso] adj sumptuous. suntuosidad sf sumptuousness.

supeditar [supeði'tar] v subdue, subordinate. supeditación sf subjection.

superar [supe'rar] v surpass; overcome. superable adj surmountable. superación sf overcoming.

superávit [supe'raβit] sm surplus.

superchería [supertʃe'ria] sf fraud; swindle.

superficial [superfi'θjal] adj superficial. superficie sf surface; area.

superfluo [super'fluo] adj superfluous. superfluidad sf superfluity.

superior [supe'rjor] adj better; superior. sm superior.

superlativo [superla'tiβo] adj superlative.

supermercado [supermer'kaðo] sm supermarket.

supersecreto [superse'kreto] adj top secret.

superstición [supersti'θjon] *sf* superstition. **supersticioso** *adj* superstitious.

supervivencia [superβi'βenθja] *sf* survival. **superviviente** *s(m+f)* survivor.

supino [su'pino] *adj* supine.

suplantar [suplan'tar] *v* supplant; forge.

suplemento [suple'mento] *sm* supplement. **suplementario** *adj* supplementary; extra. **horas suplementarias** *sf pl* overtime *sing*.

suplente [su'plente] *s, adj* substitute.

súplica ['suplika] *sf* supplication; petition. **suplicación** *sf* supplication; wafer biscuit. **suplicante** *s(m+f)* supplicant. **suplicar** *v* implore; beseech.

suplicio [su'pliθjo] *sm* torture.

suplir [su'plir] *v* make up for; substitute.

***suponer** [supo'ner] *v* suppose; believe; mean; guess. **suposición** *sf* supposition; slander.

supremo [su'premo] *adj* supreme. **supremacía** *sf* supremacy.

suprimir [supri'mir] *v* suppress; delete; omit; eliminate. **supresión** *sf* suppression; deletion.

supuesto [su'pwesto] *adj* supposed; so-called; hypothetical; feigned. **¡por supuesto!** of course! **supuesto que** since; if. *sm* hypothesis (*pl* -ses).

sur [sur] *adj* southern. *sm* south.

surcar [sur'kar] *v* plough; cleave.

surgir [sur'xir] *v* rise; spring forth; appear; anchor. **surgidero** *sm* anchorage.

surrealista [surreal'ista] *s(m+f)* surrealist. **surrealismo** *sm* surrealism.

surtido [sur'tiðo] *adj* assorted. **bien surtido** well stocked. *sm* stock; range; assortment. **surtidor** *sm* jet; fountain; petrol pump. **surtir** *v* supply. **surtir un pedido** fill an order.

susceptibilidad [susθeptiβili'ðað] *sf* susceptibility. **susceptible** *adj* susceptible.

suscitar [susθi'tar] *v* agitate, stir up. **suscitar interés** arouse interest.

suscribir *V* subscribir.

susodicho [suso'ðitʃo] *adj* aforementioned.

suspender [suspen'der] *v* suspend; adjourn; hang; fail; interrupt. **suspensión** *sf* suspension. **suspenso** *sm* (*examen*) failure.

suspicacia [suspi'kaθja] *sf* suspicion; misgiving. **suspicaz** *adj* suspicious.

suspirar [suspi'rar] *v* sigh. **suspirado** *adj* longed for, wished for. **suspiro** *sm* sigh.

sustancia *V* substancia.

sustentar [susten'tar] *v* sustain; maintain. **sustentamiento** *sm* sustenance; maintenance. **sustento** *sm* sustenance.

***sustituir** *V* substituir.

susto ['susto] *sm* fright. **dar susto a** frighten.

susurrar [susur'rar] *v* whisper; murmur. **susurrarse** *v* be rumoured. **susurrante** *adj* whispering. **susurro** *sm* whisper; murmur.

sutil [su'til] *adj* subtle; sharp; slender; delicate. **sutileza** *sf* subtlety; thinness; sharpness. **sutilizar** *v* thin down; polish; sharpen.

sutura [su'tura] *sf* suture.

suyo ['sujo] *adj* of his; of hers; of yours; of theirs. *pron* his; hers; yours; its; theirs. **lo suyo** one's share. **muy suyo** typical of one.

T

tabaco [ta'βako] *sm* tobacco. **tabacalero, -a** *sm, sf* tobacconist.

tábano ['taβano] *sm* horsefly.

taberna [ta'βerna] *sf* tavern; public house.

tabique [ta'βike] *sm* partition; dividing wall. **tabicar** *v* wall up.

tabla ['taβla] *sf* board, plank; tablet; slab; index; vegetable plot. **tablas** *sf pl* (*teatro*) stage *sing*. **pisar las tablas** go on the stage. **tablado** *sm* wooden platform; bedstead; gallows. **tablaje** *sm* boards *pl*. **tablajería** *sf* gambling. **tablear** *vb* saw into planks. **tablero** *sm* planking; blackboard; gambling den. **tableta** *sf* tablet. **tablilla** *sf* notice-board. **tablón** *sm* beam.

tabú [ta'βu] *sm* taboo.

tabular [tabu'lar] *adj* tabular. *v* tabulate.

taburete [taβu'rete] *sm* stool.

tacaño [ta'kaɲo] *adj* mean, stingy. **tacañería** *sf* meanness.

tácito [ta'θito] *adj* tacit. **taciturnidad** *sf* taciturnity. **taciturno** *adj* taciturn.

taco ['tako] *sm* wad; plug; billiard cue; draught; oath. **soltar un taco** utter an oath.

tacón [ta'kon] *sm* heel, **taconazo** *sm* blow *or* tap with the heel.

tacto ['takto] *sm* touch; sense of touch; tact.

tachar [ta'tʃar] *v* accuse; erase. **tacha** *sf* fault; tack, small nail. **poner tacha** find fault. **tachón** *sm* (*carpintería*) stud. **tachonado** *adj* studded. **tachonar** *v* stud. **tachoso** *adj* defective. **tachuela** *sf* small tack.

tahona [ta'ona] *sf* bakery.

taimado [tai'maðo] *adj* sly, crafty; sullen.

tajar [ta'xar] *v* cut; hew; cleave. **taja** *sf* incision. **tajada** *sf* slice. **sacar tajada** profit. **tajadero** *sm* chopping-block. **tajador** *sm* chopper.

tal [tal] *adj* such; such a. **el tal** that fellow. **tal como** such as. **tal vez** perhaps. *pron* someone; such a person *or* thing. **como tal** as such. *adv* so; as though.

taladrar [tala'ðrar] *v* bore, drill. **taladro** *sm* bore, drill.

talante [ta'lante] *sm* mood; look; grace. **de buen/mal talante** in a good/bad mood.

talar[1] [ta'lar] *v* cut down, fell.

talar[2] *adj* full-length.

talco ['talko] *sm* tinsel; talcum powder.

talega [ta'lega] *sf* money bag; nappy.

talento [ta'lento] *sm* talent. **talentoso** *adj* talented. **talentudo** *adj* over-talented.

talón [ta'lon] *sm* heel; counterfoil; voucher; coupon.

talud [ta'luð] *sm* slope.

tallar [ta'ʎar] *v* carve; appraise; deal cards.

tallarín [taʎa'rin] *sm* noodle.

talle ['taʎe] *sm* figure; waist.

taller [ta'ʎer] *sm* workshop; studio.

tallo ['taʎo] *sm* stem, stalk.

tamaño [ta'maɲo] *sm* size. **de tamaño natural** life-size.

tambalearse [tambale'arse] *v* stagger; wobble; sway.

también [tam'bjen] *adv* also, too.

tambor [tam'bor] *sm* drum. **tambor-mayor** drum major.

Támesis ['tamesis] *sm* Thames.

tamiz [ta'miθ] *sm* sieve. **pasar por tamiz** sift.

tampoco [tam'poko] *adv* neither.

tan [tan] *adv* so. **tan siquiera** even if only.

tanda ['tanda] *sf* turn; shift; relay; gang.

tangente [tan'xente] *sm*, *adj* tangent.

tangerina [tanxe'rina] *sf* tangerine.

tangible [tan'xiβle] *adj* tangible.

tanque ['tanke] *sm* tank.

tantear [tante'ar] *v* try; test; sound; keep score. **tantearse** *v* think carefully. **tanteo** *sm* calculation; score.

tanto ['tanto] *adj* as much; so much; as great; so great. *adv* so much; as much; so; thus. **tanto como** as much as. **por lo tanto** therefore. *sm* amount; sum. **otro tanto** as much again.

***tañer** [ta'ɲer] *v* (*música*) play. **tañido** *sm* tune; twanging.

tapacubo [tapa'kuβo] *sm* hub-cap.

tapar [ta'par] *v* cover up; plug; cap; cork. **tapa** *sf* lid; cover. **tapadero** *sm* stopper. **taparrabo** *sm* loincloth. **tapón** *sm* cork; stopper.

tapia ['tapja] *sf* garden wall. **tapiar** *v* wall up.

tapicería [tapiθe'ria] *sf* tapestry; upholstery. **tapicero**, -**a** *sm*, *sf* upholsterer. **tapiz** *sm* tapestry. **tapizar** *v* hang with tapestry; upholster.

taquigrafía [takigra'fia] *sf* shorthand. **taquígrafo**, -**a** *sm*, *sf* stenographer.

taquilla [ta'kiʎa] *sf* box office; till.

tararear [tarare'ar] *v* hum.

tardar [tar'ðar] *v* delay; take a long time. **tardanza** *sf* slowness.

tarde ['tarðe] *sf* afternoon; evening. *adv* late. **se hace tarde** it's getting late. **tardecer** *v* grow late.

tarea [ta'rea] *sf* task; homework.

tarifa [ta'rifa] *sf* tariff; price list; rate.

tarima [ta'rima] *sf* stand; platform.

tarjeta [tar'xeta] *sf* card. **tarjeta postal** postcard.

tarro ['tarro] *sm* jar.

tarta ['tarta] *sf* cake, tart.

tartamudear [tartamuðe'ar] *v* stammer, stutter. **tartamudeo** *sm* stammer, stutter. **tartamudo**, -**a** *sm*, *sf* stutterer.

tasar [ta'sar] *v* appraise; value. **tasa** *sf* rate; valuation. **sin tasa** without limit. **tasación** *sf* valuation.

tatarabuelo [tatara'βwelo] *sm* great-great-grandfather. **tatarabuela** *sf* great-great-grandmother.

tatuaje [ta'twaxe] *sm* tattoo. **tatuar** *v* tattoo.

tauromaquia [tauro'makja] *sf* bullfighting.

taxidermia [taksi'ðermja] *sf* taxidermy. **taxidermista** *s*(*m*+*f*) taxidermist.

taxi ['taksi] sm taxi. taxímetro sm taximeter. taxista s(m+f) taxi-driver.

taza ['taθa] sf cup.

te [te] pron you; to you; yourself; to yourself.

té [te] sm tea.

teatro [te'atro] sm theatre. teátrico adj theatrical. teatrero, -a sm, sf theatregoer.

tecla ['tekla] sf key. teclado sm keyboard. teclear v strum; try.

técnica ['teknika] sf technique. técnico, -a sm, sf technician. tecnología sf technology. tecnólogo, -a sm, sf technologist.

techado [te'tʃaðo] sm roof; ceiling. bajo techado under cover. techar v put a roof on. techo sm roof; ceiling.

tedio ['teðjo] sm tedium. tedioso adj tedious.

teja ['texa] sf tile. tejado sm tiled roof. tejar v tile. tejaroz sm eaves pl.

tejer [te'xer] v knit; weave. tejedor, -a sm, sf weaver. tejedura sf texture; weaving.

tejón [te'xon] sm (zool) badger.

tela ['tela] sf cloth; material. tela de araña spider's web. telar sm loom.

telaraña [tela'raɲa] sf cobweb.

telefonear [telefone'ar] v telephone. teléfono sm telephone.

telegrafiar [telegra'fjar] v telegraph. telegrafía sf telegraphy. telégrafo sm telegraph.

telegrama [tele'grama] sm telegram.

telemando [tele'mando] sm remote control.

telepatía [telepa'tia] sf telepathy. telepático adj telepathic.

telescopio [tele'skopjo] sm telescope. telescópico adj telescopic.

telestudio [tele'stuðjo] sm television studio.

televisión [teleβi'sjon] sf television. televisar v televise. televisor sm television set.

telina [te'lina] sf clam.

telón [te'lon] sm curtain. telón de acero Iron Curtain.

tema ['tema] sm theme. temático adj thematic.

*temblar [tem'blar] v tremble, shiver, shake. temblor sm shudder. temblor de tierra earthquake. tembloroso adj trembling, shuddering.

temer [te'mer] v fear, be afraid. temeridad

sf temerity. temeroso adj fearful. temor sm fear.

temperamento [tempera'mento] sm temperament, nature. temperancia sf temperance. temperar v temper.

temperatura [tempera'tura] sf temperature.

tempestad [tempes'tað] sf storm. tempestuoso adj stormy.

templar [tem'plar] v temper; moderate. templado adj temperate.

temple ['temple] sm temperature; mood; distemper. pintura al temple sf painting in distemper.

templo ['templo] sm temple.

temporada [tempo'raða] sf space of time, season, period.

temporal [tempo'ral] adj also temporáneo temporary; temporal, worldly, secular. sm bad weather.

temprano [tem'prano] adj, adv early.

tenaz [te'naθ] adj tenacious. tenacidad sf tenacity. tenazas sf pl pincers pl.

tendedero [tende'ðero] sm clothes line; place for drying clothes.

tendencia [ten'denθja] sf tendency.

*tender [ten'der] v spread out; extend; hang up; lay; set.

tendero [ten'dero], -a sm, sf shopkeeper.

tendón [ten'don] sm (anat) tendon.

tenebroso [tene'βroso] adj dark, gloomy. tenebrosidad sf gloom.

tenedor [tene'ðor] sm fork; holder. tenedor de libros bookkeeper. teneduría sf bookkeeping.

tenencia [te'nenθja] sf tenancy, occupancy; tenure.

*tener [te'ner] v have; possess; hold; spend. tener en mucho esteem. tener para sí think. tener puesto wear.

tenería [tene'ria] sf tannery.

tenia ['tenja] sf tapeworm.

teniente [te'njente] sm lieutenant. teniente coronel sm lieutenant-colonel.

tenis ['tenis] sm tennis.

tenor¹ ['tenor] sm tenor.

tenor² sm meaning, purport.

tenso ['tenso] adj tense, taut. tensión sf tension. tensión arterial blood pressure.

*tentar [ten'tar] v tempt; feel; attempt; examine. tentación sf temptation. tentador sm tempter. tentadora sf temptress. tentativa sf attempt. tentativo adj tentative.

tentáculo [ten'takulo] *sm* tentacle.
tentempié [tentempi'e] *sm* (*fam*) snack.
tenue ['tenwe] *adj* tenuous; faint; subdued. **tenuidad** *sf* slightness.
***teñir** [te'nir] *v*, dye, stain, colour. **teñidura** *sf* dyeing.
teología [teolo'xia] *sf* theology. **teólogo** *sm* theologian.
teorema [teo'rema] *sf* theorem.
teoría [teo'ria] *sf* theory. **teórico** *adj* theoretical. **teorizar** *v* theorize.
teosofía [teoso'fia] *sf* theosophy.
tercero [ter'θero] *adj*. *sm* third.
terapéutico [tera'peutiko] *adj* therapeutic. **teurapéutica** *sf* therapeutics.
terciar [ter'θjar] *v* tilt sideways; divide into three; mediate. **tercio** *adj* third.
terciopelo [terθjo'pelo] *sm* velvet. **terciopelado** *adj* velvety.
terco ['terko] *adj* stubborn.
tergiversar [terxiβer'sar] *v* misrepresent; distort. **tergiversación** *sf* distortion.
terminar [termi'nar] *v* finish, end; complete. **terminación** *sf* end. **terminal** *adj* terminal. **terminante** *adj* decisive. **terminología** *sf* terminology.
término ['termino] *sm* end. **dar termino a** bring to an end. **termino medio** average. **termita** [ter'mita] *sf also* **termite** *sm* termite.
termo ['termo] *sm* vacuum flask.
termodinámica [termoδi'namika] *sf* thermodynamics.
termómetro [ter'mometro] *sm* thermometer.
termonuclear [termonukle'ar] *adj* thermonuclear.
termostato [termo'stato] *sm* thermostat.
ternero [ter'nero] *sm* calf; veal.
terneza [ter'neθa] *sf* tenderness; endearment.
ternilla [ter'niʎa] *sf* gristle.
terquedad [terke'δaδ] *sf* stubbornness, obstinacy.
terraplén [terra'plen] *sm* terrace; embankment.
terraza [ter'raθa] *sf* terrace.
terremoto [terre'moto] *sm* earthquake.
terreno [ter'reno] *sm* terrain; land. **ceder terreno** give ground.
terrestre [ter'restre] *adj* terrestrial.
terrible [ter'riβle] *adj* terrible. **terrífico** *adj* terrifying.
territorial [territo'rjal] *adj* territorial. **territorio** *sm* territory.

terrón [ter'ron] *sm* lump of sugar; clod of earth.
terror [ter'ror] *sm* terror. **terrorismo** *sm* terrorism. **terrorista** *s*(*m*+*f*) terrorist.
terso ['terso] *adj* smooth; glossy; polished. **tersar** *v* smooth. **tersura** *sf* smoothness.
tertulia [ter'tulja] *sf* social gathering; company.
tesis ['tesis] *sf invar* thesis.
tesón [te'son] *sm* tenacity; persistence; inflexibility. **tesonería** *sf* doggedness.
tesoro [te'soro] *sm* treasure. **tesorería** *sf* treasury. **tesorero**, **-a** *sm*, *sf* treasurer.
testa ['testa] *sf* head.
testar [tes'tar] *v* make a will. **testamento** *sm* will, testament.
testarudo [testa'ruδo] *adj* stubborn, obstinate. **testarudez** *sf* obstinacy.
testificar [testifi'kar] *v* testify; witness. **testigo** *sm* witness. **testimonial** *adj* bearing witness. **testimoniar** *v* bear witness to. **testimonio** *sm* witness; testimony.
testículo [tes'tikulo] *sm* testicle.
teta ['teta] *sf* teat, nipple; mammary gland; udder.
tetera [te'tera] *sf* teapot.
tétrico ['tetriko] *adj* gloomy; grave; sullen.
textil [teks'til] *sm*, *adj* textile.
texto ['teksto] *sm* text; textbook.
textura [teks'tura] *sf* texture.
tez [teθ] *sf* complexion, skin.
ti [ti] *pron* (*fam*) you. **de ti para mí** between you and me.
tía ['tia] *sf* aunt; old mother; (*fam*) tart. **no hay tu tía** nothing doing.
tibio ['tiβjo] *adj* lukewarm. **tibieza** *sf* tepidity.
tiburón [tiβu'ron] *sm* shark.
tiempo ['tjempo] *sm* time; weather; (*gram*) tense. **al poco tiempo** soon after. **tiempo atrás** some time ago. **tiempo de perros** filthy weather.
tienda ['tjenda] *sf* shop, store; tent. **tienda de modas** boutique.
tienta ['tjenta] *sf* probe. **andar a tientas** feel one's way.
tiento ['tjento] *sm* feel, tough; tact. **a tiento** by touch.
tierno ['tjerno] *adj* tender; fresh. **pan tierno** fresh bread.
tierra ['tjerra] *sf* earth; land; country; ground. **echar por tierra** wreck. **tierra vegetal** topsoil.

tieso ['tjeso] *adj* stiff; firm. **adv** strongly. **tiesura** *sf* stiffness.

tiesto ['tjesto] *sm* flower pot.

tifo ['tifo] *sm* typhus.

tifoideo [tifoi'ðeo] *adj* typhoid. **fiebre tifoidea** *sf* typhoid fever.

tifón [ti'fon] *sm* typhoon.

tigre ['tigre] *sm* tiger.

tijeras [ti'xeras] *sf pl* scissors; shears.

tilín [ti'lin] *sm* ting-a-ling. **en un tilín** in a flash.

tilo ['tilo] *sm* lime, linden tree.

timar [ti'mar] *v* cheat. **timador** *sm* swindler.

timbrar [tim'brar] *v* stamp; seal. **timbre** *sm* bell; postage stamp.

tímido ['timiðo] *adj* timid. **timidez** *sf* timidity.

timo ['timo] *sm* cheat; swindle.

timón [ti'mon] *sm* helm; rudder. **timonear** *v* (*mar*) steer. **timonero** *sm* helmsman.

tímpano ['timpano] *sm* (*anat*) eardrum; (*música*) kettledrum.

tina ['tina] *sf* tub. **tinaja** *sf* large earthen jar.

tinglado [tin'glaðo] *sm* shed; platform.

tinieblas [ti'njeβlas] *sf pl* darkness *sing*; (*fig*) confusion *sing*.

tino ['tino] *sm* tact; moderation; skill. **sin tino** stupidly.

tinta ['tinta] *sf* ink; hue, colour. **tinte** *sm* dye; stain; shade. **tintero** *sm* inkstand, inkwell. **tintorería** *sf* dyeing; dry-cleaning. **tintorero, -a** *sm*, *sf* dyer; dry-cleaner. **tintura** dye; rouge.

tintín [tin'tin] *sm* tinkle. **tintinear** *v* tinkle.

tinto ['tinto] *adj* dyed. **vino tinto** *sm* red wine.

tiña ['tiɲa] *sf* ringworm.

tío ['tio] *sm* uncle.

tiovivo [tjo'βiβo] *sm* merry-go-round.

típico ['tipiko] *adj* typical; characteristic.

tiple ['tiple] *sm* (*música*) treble. *sf* soprano.

tipo ['tipo] *sm* type, pattern; model; standard; (*fam*) fellow. **tipo de cambio** rate of exchange.

tipografía [tipogra'fia] *sf* printing. **tipógrafo** *sm* printer.

tira ['tira] *sf* long strip, band.

tirada [ti'raða] *sf* throw; stretch; circulation. **tirador** *sm* marksman; handle.

tirado [ti'raðo] *adj* streamlined; (*fam*) dead easy; (*fam*) dirt cheap.

tiranía [tira'nia] *sf* tyranny. **tirano, -a** *sm*, *sf* tyrant. **tiranizar** *v* tyrannize.

tirante [ti'rante] *adj* taut. **tirantez** *sf* tautness.

tirar [ti'rar] *v* throw, fling; pull. **tirar por una calle** turn down a street.

tiritar [tiri'tar] *v* shiver. **tiritón** *sm* shiver.

tiro ['tiro] *sm* throw; shot; discharge; report; blow; practical joke. **tiro al blanco** target practice.

tiroides [ti'rojðes] *sm* thyroid.

tirón [ti'ron] *sm* haul, jerk; cramp; tyro, beginner. **de un tirón** straight off.

tiroteo [tiro'teo] *sm* firing, crossfire. **tirotear** *v* snipe at.

tisis ['tisis] *sf* tuberculosis.

títere ['titere] *sm* puppet; marionette.

titubear [tituβe'ar] *v* vacillate; totter, stagger; stammer. **titubeo** *sm* staggering; hesitation.

título ['titulo] *sm* title; license, diploma; degree. **titular** *adj* titular.

tiza ['tiθa] *sf* chalk.

tiznar [tiθ'nar] *v* stain, tarnish. **tiznado** *adj* stained, grimy. **tiznajo** *sm* smudge.

toalla [to'aʎa] *sf* towel. **toalla de baño** bathtowel. **toallero** *sm* towel-rail.

tobillo [to'βiʎo] *sm* ankle.

tobogán [toβa'gan] *sm* slide; chute.

tocadiscos [toka'ðiskos] *sm invar* record-player.

tocado [to'kaðo] *sm* coiffure.

tocador [toka'ðor] *sm* dressing-table.

tocar [to'kar] *v* touch; feel; (*música*) play; belong; concern; border on; be one's turn. **tocarse** *v* put on one's hat.

tocino [to'θino] *sm* bacon; salt pork.

todavía [toða'βia] *adv* yet, still; nevertheless. **todavía más** even more.

todo ['toðo] *adj* all; entire; every; each. **todo el mundo** everybody. **todo o nada** all or nothing.

toldo ['tolðo] *sm* awning.

tolerar [tole'rar] *v* tolerate; bear. **tolerable** *adj* tolerable. **tolerancia** *sf* tolerance. **tolerante** *adj* tolerant.

tomar [to'mar] *v* take; hold; get; gather. **tomarse** *v* get rusty. **tomada** *sf* capture. **tomadura** *sf* taking.

tomate [to'mate] *sm* tomato. **tomatera** *sf* tomato plant.

tomillo [to'miʎo] *sm* thyme.

tomo ['tomo] *sm* tome, volume; bulk.

ton [ton] *sm* motive; occasion. **sin ton ni son** without rhyme or reason.

tonada [to'naða] *sf* song. **tonalidad** *sf* tonality.

tonel [to'nel] *sm* cask, barrel.

tonelada [tone'laða] *sf* ton. **tonelaje** *sm* tonnage.

tónico ['toniko] *sm, adj* (*música*) tonic. **tonificar** *v* (*med*) tone up.

tono ['tono] *sm* (*música*) pitch; tone; manner. **darse tono** put on airs.

tontería [tonte'ria] *sf* foolishness, nonsense. **tonto** *adj* foolish, silly; stupid; ignorant.

topacio [to'paθjo] *sm* topaz.

topar [to'par] *v* collide with; strike against; encounter; meet by chance.

tope ['tope] *sm* top, summit; end. **al tope** end to end.

tópico ['topiko] *sm* topic. *adj* topical.

topo ['topo] *sm* mole. **topera** *sf* molehill.

topografía [topogra'fia] *sf* topography. **topográfico** *adj* topographical.

toque ['toke] *sm* touch; peal of bells; test, trial.

tórax ['toraks] *sm* thorax.

torbellino [torβe'ʎino] *sm* whirlwind; whirlpool.

***torcer** [tor'θer] *v* twist; turn; wrench; bend. **torcedura** *sf* twisting; sprain. **torcido** *adj* twisted; bent. **torcimiento** *sm* distortion.

tordo ['torðo] *sm* thrush.

torear [tore'ar] *v* fight the bull. **torero** *sm* bullfighter.

tormenta [tor'menta] *sf* storm. **tormentoso** *adj* stormy.

tormentar [tormen'tar] *v* torment. **tormento** *sm* torment; affliction; pain.

tornar [tor'nar] *v* turn; return; do again. **torna** *sf* return. **tornarse** *v* become.

tornasol [torna'sol] *sm* (*bot*) sunflower; litmus.

torneo [tor'neo] *sm* tournament.

tornillo [tor'niʎo] *sm* screw.

torniquete [torni'kete] *sm* tourniquet; turnstile.

toro ['toro] *sm* bull. **toros** *sm pl* bullfight.

toronja [to'ronxa] *sf* grapefruit.

torpe ['torpe] *adj* clumsy; indecent. **torpeza** *sf* clumsiness; indecency.

torpedo [tor'peðo] *sm* torpedo. **torpedero** *sm* torpedo-boat.

tórpido ['torpiðo] *adj* torpid. **torpor** *sm* torpor.

torre ['torre] *sf* tower.

torrente [tor'rente] *sm* torrent. **torrencial** *adj* torrential.

tórrido ['torriðo] *adj* torrid.

torta ['torta] *sf* cake; pie. **tortada** *sf* meat pie. **tortera** *sf* pie dish.

tortilla [tor'tiʎa] *sf* omelette.

tortuga [tor'tuga] *sf* tortoise; turtle.

tortura [tor'tura] *sf* torture. **tortuoso** *adj* tortuous.

tos [tos] *sf* cough. **tos ferina** whooping-cough. **toser** *v* cough.

tosco ['tosko] *adj* coarse; crude; clumsy. **tosquedad** *sf* roughness; crudeness.

***tostar** [tos'tar] *v* toast; roast; tan. **tostada** *sf* piece of toast.

total [to'tal] *sm* total. **totalidad** *sf* totality. **totalitario** *adj* totalitarian. **totalizar** *v* total.

tóxico ['toksiko] *sm* poison. *adj* poisonous. **toxicar** *v* poison.

toxicómano [toksi'komano], **-a** *sm, sf* drug-addict. **toxicomanía** *sf* drug-addiction.

tozudo [to'θuðo] *adj* stubborn.

traba ['traβa] *sf* link; fetter; hindrance. **poner trabas** hinder. **trabadura** *sf* bond. **trabamiento** *sm* joining. **trabar** *v* join; fetter; strike up. **trabar amistad** become friends. **trabón** *sm* fetter.

trabajar [traβa'xar] *v* work; work on; elaborate; trouble; deal in. **trabajado** *adj* elaborate. **trabajador, -a** *sm, sf* worker. **trabajo** *sm* work; toil; exertion; hardship. **trabajoso** *adj* laborious.

trabalenguas [traβa'lengwas] *sm invar* tongue-twister.

tracción [trak'θjon] *sf* traction. **tractor** *sm* tractor.

tradición [traði'θjon] *sf* tradition. **tradicional** *adj* traditional.

***traducir** [traðu'θir] *v* translate; interpret. **traducción** *sf* translation. **traductor, -a** *sm, sf* translator.

***traer** [tra'er] *v* bring; carry; fetch; result in; wear. **traer a mal traer** treat roughly. **traer a cuento** mention. **traerse** *v* be dressed; behave.

traficar [trafi'kar] *v* trade; travel. **traficante** *s(m+f)* dealer. **tráfico** *sm* trade; traffic.

tragaluz [traga'luθ] *sf* skylight.

tragar [tra'gar] *v* swallow. **no puedo tragarle** I can't stand him. **tragadero** *sm* gullet. **trago** *sm* swallow; gulp.

tragedia [tra'xeðia] *sf* tragedy. **tragico** *adj* tragic.

traicionar [traiθjo'nar] *v* betray. **traición** *sf* treason; treachery. **traicionero** *adj* treacherous. **traidor, -a** *sm, sf* traitor.

traje ['traxe] *sm* dress; suit; costume. **traje de etiqueta** evening dress. **baile de trajes** *sm* fancy-dress ball.

trajín [tra'xin] *sm* haulage; coming and going. **trajinante** *sm* (*com*) carrier.

tramar [tra'mar] *v* weave; plan, plot. **trama** *sf* weft; plot.

tramitar [trami'tar] *v* negotiate, arrange. **tramitación** *sf* arrangements *pl*. **trámite** *sm* procedure; formality.

tramo ['tramo] *sm* (*puente*) span; (*escaleras*) flight; (*terreno*) strip.

trampa ['trampa] *sf* trap; trapdoor; fraud. **tramposo** *adj* deceitful.

trampear [trampe'ar] *v* defraud; scrape by. **trampeador, -a** *sm, sf* swindler.

trampolín [trampo'lin] *sm* ski jump; springboard.

trancar [tran'kar] *v* (*puerta*) bar; stride. **tranca** *sf* stick; club; (*fam*) drunkenness. **tranco** *sm* stride.

trance ['tranθe] *sm* trance; critical situation. **a todo trance** at all costs.

tranquilizar [trankili'θar] *v* tranquillize. **tranquilidad** *sf* tranquillity. **tranquilo** *adj* tranquil.

transacción [transak'θjon] *sf* transaction. **transatlántico** [transat'lantiko] *adj* transatlantic. *sm* (*mar*) liner.

transbordar [transβor'ðar] *v* transfer. **transbordo** *sm* transfer.

transcribir [transkri'βir] *v* transcribe. **transcripción** *sf* transcription.

transcurrir [transkur'rir] *v* elapse, pass. **transcurso** *sm* course or lapse of time.

transeúnte [transe'unte] *adj* transitory, transient. *s(m+f)* transient, passer-by.

***transferir** [transfe'rir] *v* transfer. **transferible** *adj* transferable.

transfigurar [transfigu'rar] *v* transfigure. **transfiguración** *sf* transfiguration.

transformar [transfor'mar] *v* transform. **transformación** *sf* transformation.

tránsfuga ['transfuga] *sm* deserter.

***transgredir** [transgre'ðir] *v* transgress, violate. **transgresión** *sf* transgression. **transgresor, -a** *sm, sf* transgressor.

transición [transi'θjon] *sf* transition.

transido [tran'siðo] *adj* overwhelmed; stricken.

transigir [transi'xir] *v* compromise. **transigencia** *sf* tolerance. **transigente** *adj* tolerant.

transistor [transis'tor] *sm* transistor.

transitar [transi'tar] *v* travel; pass. **transitivo** *adj* (*gram*) transitive. **tránsito** *sm* transit; passage; transition. **transitorio** *adj* transitory.

transmitir [transmi'tir] *v* transmit. **transmisión** *sf* transmission. **transmisor** *sm* transmitter.

transparencia [transpa'renθja] *sf* transparency. **transparente** *adj* transparent.

transpirar [transpi'rar] *v* perspire; transpire. **transpiración** *sf* perspiration.

***transponer** [transpo'ner] *v* transpose; transplant. **transponerse** *v* get down; get sleepy.

transportar [transpor'tar] *v* transport; (*música*) transpose. **transportarse** get carried away. **transporte** *sm* transport. **transposición** *sf* transposition.

tranvía [tran'βia] *sm* tramway; tram.

trapaza [tra'paθa] *sf* swindle, fraud; trick. **trapacear** *v* defraud. **trapacista** *s(m+f)* swindler.

trapecio [tra'peθjo] *sm* trapeze.

trapo ['trapo] *sm* rag. *pl* old clothes.

traquetear [trakete'ar] *v* shake up; rattle. **traqueteo** *sm* rattling; jolting.

tras [tras] *prep* after; behind; beyond. **tras de** in addition to.

***trascender** [trasθen'der] *v* transcend; leak out; spread. **trascendencia** *sf* transcendence. **trascendental** *adj* momentous. **trascendente** *adj* transcendent.

***trasegar** [trase'gar] *v* decant; upset.

trasero [tra'sero] *adj* rear. *sm* behind. **trasera** *sf* back; rear.

trasladar [trasla'ðar] *v* transfer; translate; postpone. **trasladarse** *v* go; move. **traslación** *sf* transfer; translation. **traslado** *sm* copy; transfer.

***traslucirse** [traslu'θirse] *v* shine; show through. **traslúcido** *adj* translucent.

traslumbrar [traslum'brar] *v* dazzle.

trasmutar [trasmu'tar] *v* transmute. **trasmutación** *sf* transmutation.

trasnochar [trasno'tʃar] *v* be up all *or* most of the night.

traspasar [traspa'sar] *v* transfer; transfix; transgress. **traspasador, -a** *sm, sf* transgressor. **traspaso** *sm* transfer; transgression.

traspié [tras'pje] *sm* stumble.

trasplantar [trasplan'tar] *v* transplant. **trasplantarse** *v* migrate. **trasplante** *sm* transplant.

trasquilar [traski'lar] *v* shear, snip, clip. **trasquilado** *adj* sheared; cropped.

traste ['traste] *sm* (*música*) fret. **ir al traste** fall through, fail.

trasto ['trasto] *sm* tool; weapon; equipment; piece of furniture.

trastornar [trastor'nar] *v* upset; turn upside down. **trastornado** *adj* unbalanced. **trastorno** *sm* upheaval; inconvenience.

trasunto [tra'sunto] *sm* copy, reproduction; likeness. **trasuntar** *v* copy.

tratar [tra'tar] *v* treat; deal with; handle. **tratable** *adj* manageable. **tratamiento** *sm* treatment. **trato** *sm* treatment; behaviour; bargain. **mal trato** ill-treatment.

través [tra'βes] *sm* slant; bias; reverse. **a través de** across.

travesero [traβe'sero] *adj* transverse. **travesía** *sf* crossroad.

travesura [traβe'sura] *sf* trick, prank.

traviesa [tra'βjesa] *sf* (*ferrocarril*) sleeper; (*arq*) rafter; bet.

travieso [tra'βjeso] *adj* transverse, cross; lively; mischievous. **a campo traviesa** cross-country.

trayecto [tra'jekto] *sm* route; fare stage; distance; way; itinerary. **trayectoria** *sf* trajectory.

trazar [tra'θar] *v* draw; plot; trace; design. **traza** *sf* sketch. **bien/mal trazado** good/bad looking. **trazador, -a** *sm, sf* designer.

trébol ['treβol] *sm* clover.

trece ['treθe] *adj, sm* thirteen.

trecho ['tretʃo] *sm* space; distance; lapse; stretch.

tregua ['tregwa] *sf* truce; respite.

treinta ['treinta] *adj, sm* thirty.

tremendo [tre'mendo] *adj* tremendous.

trémulo ['tremulo] *adj* tremulous.

tren [tren] *sm* train. **tren botijo** excursion train.

trenzar [tren'θar] *v* braid. **trenza** *sf* plait, braid.

trementina [tremen'tina] *sf* turpentine.

trepar [tre'par] *v* climb. **trepa** *sf* climbing. **trepadoras** *sf pl* climbing plants.

trepidar [trepi'ðar] *v* shake, tremble. **trepidación** *sf* tremor.

tres [tres] *adj, sm* three.

triángulo [tri'angulo] *sm* triangle. **triangular** *adj* triangular.

tribu ['triβu] *sf* tribe.

tribuna [tri'βuna] *sf* tribune; gallery; grandstand. **tribunal** *sm* tribunal.

tributar [triβu'tar] *v* pay. **tributable** *adj* tributary. **tributación** *sf* tax. **tributante** *s(m+f)* taxpayer. **tributo** *sm* tribute; tax.

triciclo [tri'θiklo] *sm* tricycle.

tricotar [triko'tar] *v* knit.

trigo ['trigo] *sm* wheat. **trigal** *sm* wheatfield.

trigésimo [tri'xesimo] *adj* thirtieth.

trigonometría [trigonome'tria] *sf* trigonometry.

trillar [tri'ʎar] *v* thresh; beat. **trilla** *sf* threshing. **trillador, -a** *sm, sf* threshing machine.

trimestre [tri'mestre] *sm* three-month term. **trimestral** *adj* quarterly.

trinar [tri'nar] *v* trill. **trinado** *sm* trill.

trincar [trin'kar] *v* break; bind; hold down.

trinchar [trin'tʃar] *v* carve. **trinchante** *sm* carving-knife. **trinchero** *adj* carving.

trinchera [trin'tʃera] *sf* trench.

trineo [tri'neo] *sm* sledge, sled, sleigh.

trinidad [trini'ðað] *sf* trinity.

trinitaria [trini'tarja] *sf* pansy.

tripa ['tripa] *sf* intestine. **tener malas tripas** be cruel.

triple ['triple] *adj* triple.

trípode ['tripoðe] *sm* tripod.

tripulación [tripula'θjon] *sf* crew. **tripulante** *sm* member of the crew.

triscar [tris'kar] *v* mingle; stamp; frisk. **trisca** *sf* crunch.

triste ['triste] *adj* sad, mournful, gloomy. **tristeza** *sf* sadness.

triturar [tritu'rar] *v* grind, crush. **trituración** *sf* grinding.

triunfar [triun'far] *v* triumph. **triunfador, -a** *sm, sf* victor. **triunfal** *adj* triumphal. **triunfante** *adj* triumphant. **triunfo** *sm* triumph.

trivial [tri'βjal] *adj* trivial. **trivialidad** *sf* triviality.

triza ['triθa] *sf* shred; particle, fragment.

trocar [tro'kar] *v* exchange. **trocarse** *v* change into. **trocamiento** *sm* exchange.

trochemoche [trotʃe'motʃe] *adv* higgledy-piggledy.

trofeo [tro'feo] *sm* trophy.

trole ['trole] *sm* trolley.

tromba ['tromba] *sf* waterspout.

trombón [trom'bon] *sm* trombone.

trompa ['trompa] *sf* hunting horn; (*elefante*) trunk; proboscis.

trompada [trom'paða] *sf* bump; thump.

trompeta [trom'peta] *sf* trumpet. **trompetero** *sm* trumpeter.

***tronar** [tro'nar] *v* thunder. **tronada** *sf* thunderstorm. **tronante** *adj* thunderous. **tronido** *sm* thunderclap.

tronco ['tronko] *sm* tree trunk; stalk; stern.

tronchar [tron'tʃar] *v* bring down; break up.

trono ['trono] *sm* throne.

tropa ['tropa] *sf* troop.

tropel [tro'pel] *sm* crowd. **en tropel** in a rush. **tropelía** *sf* rush, hurry.

***tropezar** [trope'θar] *v* stumble; run into. **tropiezo** *sm* stumble.

trópico ['tropiko] *sm* tropic. **tropical** *adj* tropical.

trotar [tro'tar] *v* trot. **trote** *sm* trot.

trozo ['troθo] *sm* piece, fragment, bit.

truco ['truko] *sm* trick.

trucha ['trutʃa] *sf* trout; (*mec*) crane.

trueno [tru'eno] *sm* thunder.

trueque [tru'eke] *sm* exchange, barter.

trufa ['trufa] *sf* truffle.

truncar [trun'kar] *v* truncate, abridge. **truncado** *adj* truncated.

tu [tu] *adj* (*fam*) your.

tú [tu] *pron* (*fam*) you.

tubérculo [tu'βerkulo] *sm* tubercle; tuber. **tuberculosis** *sf* tuberculosis. **tuberculoso** *adj* tubercular.

tubo ['tuβo] *sm* tube, pipe. **tubería** *sf* tubing. **tubular** *adj* tubular.

tuerca ['twerka] *sf* (*mec*) nut. **tuerca a mariposa** wing nut.

tuerto ['twerto], -a *sm*, *sf* one-eyed person. *adj* one-eyed.

tuétano [tu'etano] *sm* (*anat*) marrow.

tufo ['tufo] *sm* vapour; fume; stench. **tufarada** *sf* whiff.

tul [tul] *sm* tulle.

tulipán [tuli'pan] *sm* tulip.

tullido [tu'ʎiðo] *adj* cripple. **tullirse** *v* be crippled.

tumba¹ ['tumba] *sf* tomb.

tumba² *sf* tumble. **tumbar** *v* knock down; tumble.

tumor [tu'mor] *sm* tumour.

tumulto [tu'multo] *sm* tumult. **tumultuoso** *adj* tumultuous.

tunante [tu'nante] *s(m+f)* rascal, crook. *adj* rascally. **tunantería** *sf* crookedness.

túnel ['tunel] *sm* tunnel.

túnica ['tunika] *sf* tunic.

tuno ['tuno] *sm* rogue.

tupé [tu'pe] *sm* toupee.

tupido [tu'piðo] *adj* thick; dense.

turba ['turβa] *sf* crowd; heap; peat. **turbal** *sm* peat bog.

turbante [tur'βante] *sm* turban.

turbar [tur'βar] *v* disturb. **turbarse** *v* be embarrassed.

turbina [tur'βina] *sf* turbine.

turbulento [turβu'lento] *adj* turbulent, disorderly. **turbulencia** *sf* turbulence.

turismo [tu'rismo] *sm* tourism. **turista** *s(m+f)* tourist.

turnar [tur'nar] *v* alternate, take turns. **turno** *sm* turn, shift. **por turno** in turn.

turón [tu'ron] *sm* polecat.

turquesa [tur'kesa] *sf* turquoise.

turrón [tur'ron] *sm* nougat.

tutear [tute'ar] *v* address as *tú*.

tutela [tu'tela] *sf* protection; tutelage. **tutelar** *adj* guardian.

tutor [tu'tor] *sm* tutor; guardian. **tutoría** *sf* guardianship.

tuyo ['tujo] *pron* (*fam*) yours; of yours.

U

u [u] *conj* or (before words beginning with *o* or *ho*).

ubicar [uβi'kar] *v* be situated; (*auto*) park. **ubicarse** *v* place oneself. **ubicuidad** *sf* ubiquity. **ubicuo** *adj* ubiquitous.

ubre ['uβre] *sf* udder.

ufanarse [ufa'narse] *v* boast. **ufano** *adj* proud, conceited. **ufanía** *sf* pride, arrogance.

ujier [u'xjer] *sm* usher.

úlcera ['ulθera] *sf* ulcer. **ulcerado** *adj* ulcerated.

ulterior [ulte'rjor] *adj* further, farther; ulterior. **ulteriormente** *adj* later.

ultimar [ulti'mar] *v* conclude, finish. **ultimación** *sf* conclusion. **últimamente**

adv finally; recently. **ultimátum** *sm* ultimatum. **último** *adj* last; latest. **por último** finally.

ultrajar [ultra'xar] *v* outrage; insult. **ultraje** *sm* outrage. **ultrajoso** *adj* outrageous.

ultramarino [ultrama'rino] *adj* overseas. **ultramar** *sm* overseas countries *pl*. **ir a ultramar** go abroad.

ultranza [ul'tranθa] *adv* **a ultranza** to the death; at all costs.

umbral [um'bral] *sm* threshold. **pisar los umbrales** cross the threshold.

umbrío [um'brio] *adj also* **umbroso** shady.

un [un] *art also* **una** a; one. *adj* one.

unánime [u'nanime] *adj* unanimous. **unanimidad** *sf* unanimity.

unción [un'θjon] *sf* anointing, unction. **extremaunción** *sf* (*rel*) extreme unction.

uncir [un'θir] *v* yoke.

undécimo [un'deθimo], **-a** *s*, *adj* eleventh.

undoso [un'doso] *adj* wavy. **undulación** *sf* undulation. **undulante** *adj* undulating. **undular** *v* undulate.

ungir [un'xir] *v* anoint. **ungimiento** *sm* unction. **ungüento** *sm* ointment.

único ['uniko] *adj* only, sole, single; unique. **únicamente** *adv* only, solely.

unicornio [uni'kornjo] *sm* unicorn.

unidad [uni'ðað] *sf* unity; union; unit. **unido** *adj* united. **unificación** *sf* unification. **unificar** *v* unify.

uniformar [unifor'mar] *v* make uniform; standardize. **uniforme** *adj*, *sm* uniform. **uniformidad** *sf* uniformity.

unión [u'njon] *sf* union; unity; marriage. **unir** *v* join; mix. **unirse** *v* join; mingle.

Unión Soviética [u'njon so'βjetika] *sf* Soviet Union.

unísono [u'nisono] *adj* harmonious. **al unísono** in unison; unanimously.

universidad [uniβersi'ðað] *sf* university. **universitario** *adj* of a university.

universo [uni'βerso] *sm* universe. **universal** *adj* universal. **universalidad** *sf* universality.

uno ['uno] *adj* one; only. *pron* one; someone. **unos** *pron pl* some; a few. **unos y otros** all.

untar [un'tar] *v* grease; smear; stain; spread. **unto** *sm* grease; ointment.

uña ['uɲa] *sf* (*anat*) nail; talon, claw; hoof. **esconder las uñas** hide one's feelings. **uñero** *sm* ingrowing toenail.

uranio [u'ranjo] *sm* uranium.

urbano [ur'βano] *adj* urban; urbane. **urbanidad** *sf* urbanity. **urbanístico** *adj* urban. **urbanización** *sf* town planning. **urbe** *sf* large city.

urdir [ur'ðir] *v* warp; (*fig*) plot, scheme.

urgencia [ur'xenθja] *sf* urgency; emergency. **urgente** *adj* urgent. **urgir** *v* be urgent; urge. **me urge el tiempo** I am pressed for time.

urinario [uri'narjo] *sm* urinal.

urna ['urna] *sf* urn; ballot box.

urogallo [uro'gaʎo] *sm* (*zool*) grouse.

urraca [u'rraka] *sf* magpie.

usar [u'sar] *v* use; employ; be accustomed. **usado** *adj* used; worn. **usanza** *sf* custom; usage. **uso** *sm* use; wear; custom; enjoyment; fashion. **al uso de** in the style of.

usted [u'steð] *pron also* **Vd** you. **¡a usted!** thank you!

usual [u'swal] *adj* usual.

usufructo [u'sufrukto] *sm* use; enjoyment.

usura [u'sura] *sf* usury. **usurero, -a** *sm*, *sf* usurer.

usurpar [usur'par] *v* usurp. **usurpación** *sf* usurpation. **usurpador, -a** *sm*, *sf* usurper.

utensilio [uten'siljo] *sm* utensil; implement, tool.

útero ['utero] *sm* uterus. **uterino** *adj* uterine.

útil ['util] *sm* tool. *adj* useful; fit. **utilidad** *sf* utility, usefulness. **utilitario** *adj* utilitarian. **utilizar** *v* utilize, use.

uva ['uβa] *sf* grape. **uva pasa** raisin.

V

vaca ['baka] *sf* cow; beef.

vacaciones [βaka'θjones] *sf pl* vacation *sing*; holidays *pl*. **irse de vacaciones** go on holiday.

vacante [βa'kante] *adj* vacant. *sf* vacancy. **vacar** *v* fall vacant.

vacilar [βaθi'lar] *v* hesitate. **vacilante** *adj* unstable, unsteady. **vacilación** *sf* vacillation.

vacío [βa'θio] *adj* empty. *sm* void; vacuum. **vaciar** *v* empty; pour out. **vacuo** *adj* empty; vacuous.

vacunar [βaku'nar] v vaccinate. **vacunación** sf vaccination.

vadear [βaðe'ar] v wade; surmount, overcome. **vadeable** adj fordable.

vagar [βa'gar] v wander, move about. sm leisure; ease. **vagabundo, -a** sm, sf vagabond. **vagante** adj vagrant.

vago ['βago] adj vague; indolent. sm tramp; loafer. **vaguedad** sf vagueness.

vagón [βa'gon] sm railway carriage; wagon. **vagón restaurante** dining-car. **vagoneta** sf small truck.

vahear [βae'ar] v steam. **vaho** sm vapour.

vahído [βa'iðo] sm vertigo, dizziness.

vaina ['βaina] sf sheath; scabbard; pod. **vainilla** [βai'niʎa] sf vanilla.

vaivén [βai'βen] sm fluctuation; sway; swinging movement.

vajilla [βa'xiʎa] sf tableware, dishes pl.

vale ['βale] sm voucher; receipt; IOU. **valedero** [βale'ðero] adj valid.

valentía [βalen'tia] sf valour, courage; brave or courageous act; bragging. **valentón, -ona** sm, sf braggart.

*valer [βa'ler] v be worth; cost; be equal to. **vale la pena** be worthwhile. **válgame la frase** if you don't mind my saying so. **valerse** v make use of. **valía** sf value, worth.

valeroso [βale'roso] adj brave; valuable.

validar [βali'ðar] v validate; make binding. **validación** sf validation; ratification. **válido** adj valid. **validez** sf validity.

valiente [βa'ljente] adj valiant, courageous; strong; first-rate.

valija [βa'lixa] sf valise; case; mail bag.

valimiento [βali'mjento] sm value; good will; protection; favour.

valor [βa'lor] sm value, worth; price; valour, courage. adj valuable. **valoración** sf valuation. **valorar** v value, appraise.

valsar [βal'sar] v waltz. **vals** sm waltz.

valuar [βalu'ar] v value, appraise, assess. **valuacción** sf valuation.

válvula ['βalβula] sf valve.

vallar [βa'ʎar] v fence in, enclose. **valla** sf fence. **vallado** sm enclosure.

valle ['βaʎe] sm valley.

vampiro [βam'piro] sm vampire.

vanagloriarse [βanaglo'rjarse] v boast. **vanagloria** sf boasting, vainglory.

vándalo ['βandalo] sm, adj vandal. **vandalismo** sm vandalism.

vanguardia [βan'gwarðja] sf vanguard; avant-garde.

vano ['βano] adj vain; idle. **en vano** in vain. **vanidad** sf vanity. **vanidoso** adj vain.

vapor [βa'por] sm vapour; steam; (mar) steamer. **vaporización** sf evaporation. **vaporizar** v evaporate.

vaquero [βa'kero] sm cowboy. **vaquería** sf herd of cows.

vaqueta [βa'keta] sf cowhide.

vara ['βara] sf rod, pole, staff; (medida) yard. **tener vara alta** have the upper hand.

varar [βa'rar] v launch; run aground.

variar [βa'rjar] v vary, change. **variable** adj variable. **variación** sf variation. **variado** adj varied. **variante** sf variant; version.

varice [βa'riθe], sf also **várice** varicose vein.

varilla [βa'riʎa] sf small stick; jawbone; curtain rail.

vario ['βarjo] adj varied, diverse. **varios** adj several.

varón [βa'ron] sm, adj male. **varonil** adj manly, virile.

vaselina ® [βase'lina] sf Vaseline ®.

vasija [βa'sixa] sf vessel; bowl; dish. **vaso** sm glass, tumbler.

vástago ['βastago] sm stem, shoot, sprout; scion, offspring.

vasto ['βasto] adj vast. **vastedad** sf vastness.

vaticinar [βatiθi'nar] v predict, foretell. **vaticinador, -a** sm, sf prophet, seer. **vaticinio** sm divination; prophecy.

vatio ['βatjo] sm (elec) watt.

vecino [βe'θino], -a sm, sf neighbour. **vecinal** adj local. **vecindad** sf neighbourhood.

vedar [βe'ðar] v veto; prohibit; hinder. **veda** sf prohibition. **vedado** sm game preserve.

vega ['βega] sf plain; tract of fertile ground.

vegetación [βexeta'θjon] sf vegetation. **vegetal** adj vegetable. **vegetar** v grow; (fig) vegetate. **vegetariano, -a** sm, sf vegetarian.

vehemencia [βee'menθja] sf vehemence. **vehemente** adj vehement.

vehículo [βe'ikulo] sm vehicle.

veinte ['βeinte] sm, adj twenty.

vejar [βe'xar] v vex, harass, annoy. **vejación** sf vexation. **vejatorio** adj vexatious.

vejez [βe'xeθ] *sf* old age.

vejiga [βe'xiɣa] *sf* blister; bladder.

vela ['βela] *sf* vigil, watch; candle; sail.
velar *v* keep watch; stay awake.

veleidad [βelei'ðað] *sf* whim; fickleness.
veleidoso *adj* fickle.

velero [βe'lero] *sm* sailing ship; glider.

velo ['βelo] *sm* veil.

velocidad [βeloθi'ðað] *sf* velocity.
velocímetro *sm* speedometer. veloz *adj*
fast, quick.

vello ['βeʎo] *sm* soft hair, down; fluff.
velloso *adj* dowry.

vena ['βena] *sf* vein; scan. trabajar por
venas work in fits and starts.

venablo [βe'naβlo] *sm* javelin.

venado [βe'naðo] *sm* deer; (*culin*) venison.

venal [βe'nal] *adj* venal.

vencer [βen'θer] *v* defeat; win; (*com*) fall
due. vencerse *v* control oneself. vencible
adj beatable. los vencidos the losers.
vencimiento *sm* victory; (*com*) expiration, falling due.

vendar [βen'dar] *v* bandage. venda *sf* also
vendaje *sm* bandage.

vendaval [βenda'βal] *sm* gale.

vender [βen'der] *v* sell. vendedor *sm* seller, vendor; salesperson. vendible *adj*
saleable.

vendimia [βen'ðimja] *sf* grape harvest;
vintage.

veneno [βe'neno] *sm* venom, poison.
venenoso *adj* poisonous.

venerar [βene'rar] *v* venerate. venerable
adj venerable. veneración *sf* veneration.

venéreo [βe'nereo] *adj* venereal.

venero [βe'nero] *sm* spring of water;
source, origin, root.

vengar [βen'gar] *v* avenge. vengador, -a
sm, sf avenger. venganza *sf* vengeance.
vengativo *adj* vindictive.

venia ['βenja] *sf* forgiveness, pardon; permission, leave.

*venir [βe'nir] *v* come. venir bien be suitable *or* convenient. venirse *v* come *or* go
back. venida *sf* arrival, coming; return.
venidero *adj* coming, future.

venta ['βenta] *sf* sale, market; inn. venta
a plazos hire purchase. ventero, -a *sm, sf*
innkeeper.

ventaja [βen'taxa] *sf* advantage. ventajoso
adj advantageous.

ventana [βen'tana] *sf* window.

ventilar [βenti'lar] *v* ventilate. ventilación

sf ventilation. ventilador *sm* ventilator;
fan.

ventosa [βen'tosa] *sf* vent.

ventoso [βen'toso] *sf* vent.

ventoso [βen'toso] *adj* windy. ventosidad
sf flatulence.

ventrílocuo [βen'trilokwo] *sm* ventriloquist. ventriloquia *sf* ventriloquism.

ventura [βen'tura] *sf* joy, happiness; good
luck. mala ventura ill luck. venturado,
venturero *or* venturoso *adj* lucky; happy.

*ver [βer] *v* see. *sm* view; aspect; opinion; looks *pl*, appearance. echar de ver
notice. estar viendo have a feeling. vamos
a ver let's see.

vera ['βera] *sf* border, edge.

verano [βe'rano] *sm* summer. veranear *v*
spend the summer. veraneo *sm* summer
holiday.

veras ['βeras] *sf pl* truth *sing*. de veras
indeed, really. veracidad *sf* veracity. veraz *adj* truthful.

verbo ['βerβo] *sm* verb. verbosidad *sf* ver-
bosity. verboso *adj* verbose.

verdad [βer'ðað] *sf* truth. verdadero *adj*
true; real, authentic; sincere; truthful.

verde ['βerðe] *adj* green; immature; fresh;
young; immodest, obscene. darse un
verde amuse oneself.

verdugo [βer'ðugo] *sm* executioner; hangman; scourge. verdugón *sm* weal (from
whiplash).

verdulero [βerðu'lero] *sm* greengrocer.
verdulería *sf* greengrocer's. verdura *sf*
greenness. verduras *sf pl* vegetables.

veredicto [βere'ðikto] *sm* verdict.

vergüenza [βer'gwenθa] *sf* shame;
affront; disgrace; shyness, timidity. sin
vergüenza shameless. vergonzoso *adj*
shy; shameful.

verídico [βe'riðiko] *adj* truthful.

verificar [βerifi'kar] *v* verify; examine,
inspect; check. verificarse *v* prove true;
be verified. verificación *sf* verification.
verificativo *adj* corroborative.

verosímil [βero'simil] *adj* likely, probable.
verosimilitud *sf* probability.

verruga [βer'ruga] *sf* wart.

versado [βer'saðo] *adj* versed, experienced; skilful.

versar [βer'sar] *v* go round; spin. versar
sobre to treat of, deal with.

versátil [βer'satil] *adj* versatile; variable;
inconstant. versatilidad *sf* versatility;
changeableness.

versículo [βer'sikulo] sm verse. **versificar** v versify. **verso** sm verse. **verso suelto** blank verse.

versión [βer'sjon] sf version.

vértebra ['βerteβra] sf vertebra. **vertebrado** sm, adj vertebrate.

***verter** [βer'ter] v spill, empty; pour; interpret, translate. **vertedero** sm drain. **vertedor** sm sewer.

vertical [βerti'kal] adj vertical.

vértice ['βertiθe] sm apex.

vértigo [βertigo] sm vertigo. **vertiginoso** adj giddy.

vesícula [βe'sikula] sf (anat) vesicle; blister.

vestíbulo [βes'tiβulo] sm vestibule, entrance hall; lobby.

vestigio [βes'tixjo] sm vestige; footstep; trace.

***vestir** [βes'tir] v dress; clothe. **vestirse** get dressed. **vestido** sm dress.

veta ['βeta] sf vein of ore, etc.; grain in wood; streak.

veterano [βete'rano] sm, adj veteran.

veterinaria [βeteri'narja] sf veterinary science. **veterinario** sm vet.

veto ['βeto] sm veto.

vez [βeθ] sf turn; time; occasion. **a la vez** at once. **a veces** sometimes. **otra vez** once more. **tal vez** perhaps.

vía ['βia] sf road; way; track. **vía aérea** air mail. **en vías de** in the process of. **Vía Láctea** Milky Way.

viable ['βjaβle] adj viable.

viaducto [βja'ðukto] sm viaduct.

viajar [βja'xar] v travel. **viajante** s(m+f) traveller. **viaje** sm trip, journey. **viajero, -a** sm, sf traveller; passenger.

víbora ['βiβora] sf viper.

vibrar [βi'βrar] v vibrate, shake. **vibración** sf vibration. **vibrador** sm vibrator. **vibrante** adj vibrating; vibrant.

vicario [βi'karjo] sm vicar.

viciar [βi'θjar] v vitiate; corrupt. **vicio** sm vice; defect. **de vicio** for no reason at all. **vicioso** adj vicious.

vicisitud [βiθisi'tuð] sf vicissitude, mishap.

víctima ['βiktima] sf victim; sacrifice.

victoria [βik'torja] sf victory. **victorioso** adj victorious.

vid [βið] sf vine.

vida ['βiða] sf life. **en mi vida** never in my life. **nivel de vida** sm standard of living.

vidriar [βi'ðrjar] v glaze. **vidriera** sf stained glass. **vidrio** sm glass. **vidrioso** adj glassy.

viejo ['βjexo] adj old. sm old man. **vieja** sf old woman.

viento ['βjento] sm wind.

vientre ['βjentre] sm abdomen, belly; womb; bowels pl.

viernes ['βjernes] sm Friday. **Viernes Santo** Good Friday.

viga ['βiga] sf beam; timber.

vigente [βi'xente] adj (jur) in force, valid. **vigencia** sf validity. **en vigencia** in effect; in force.

vigésimo [βi'xesimo] adj twentieth.

vigilar [βixi'lar] v watch over. **vigilancia** sf vigilance. **vigilante** adj vigilant. **vigilia** sf watchfulness; vigil.

vigor [βi'gor] sm vigour. **vigoroso** adj vigorous.

vil [βil] adj vile. **vileza** sf vileness.

vilo ['βilo] adv **en vilo** aloft; suspended; (fig) on tenterhooks.

villa ['βiʎa] sf villa; town.

villancico [βiʎan'θiko] sm Christmas carol.

villanía [βiʎa'nia] sf villainy; coarse expression.

vinagre [βi'nagre] sm vinegar. **vinagroso** adj vinegary.

vínculo ['βinkulo] sm link; chain; tie.

vindicar [βindi'kar] v vindicate. **vindicación** sf vindication.

vino¹ ['βino] sm wine. **vino tinto** red wine. **vino de solera** vintage wine. **vinícola** adj relating to wine or wine production. **viña** sf vineyard.

viñeta [βi'neta] sf vignette.

violar [βjo'lar] v violate; rape. **violación** sf violation; rape. **violador** sm rapist.

violencia [βjo'lenθja] sf violence. **violentar** v force, open by force; violate; do violence to.

violeta [βjo'leta] adj, sf violet.

violín [βjo'lin] sm violin. **violinista** s(m+f) violinist. **violón** sm double-bass.

virar [βi'rar] v veer; change direction; (mar) tack.

virgen [βir'xen] adj, sf virgin. **virginidad** sf virginity.

viril [βi'ril] adj virile. **virilidad** sf virility.

virtual [βir'twal] adj virtual; potential.

virtud [βir'tuð] sf virtue. **virtuoso** adj virtuous. **virtuosidad** sf virtuosity.

viruela [βi'rwela] *sf* smallpox.

virulencia [βiru'lenθja] *sf* virulence. **virulento** *adj* virulent.

visado [βi'saðo] *sm* visa.

visaje [βi'saxe] *sm* smirk, grimace. **visajero** *adj* grimacing.

vísceras ['βisθeras] *sf pl* viscera *pl*.

viscoso [βis'koso] *adj* viscous. **viscosidad** *sf* viscosity.

visera [βi'sera] *sf* visor.

visible [βi'siβle] *adj* visible. **visibilidad** *sf* visibility.

visión [βi'sjon] *sf* vision, eyesight; dream, fantasy; view. **visionario, -a** *sm, sf* visionary.

visitar [βisi'tar] *v* visit; inspect. **visita** *sf* visit; visitor. **hacer una visita** pay a visit.

vislumbrar [βislum'brar] *v* catch a glimpse of. **vislumbre** *sf* glimpse; glimmer.

viso ['βiso] *sm* aspect, appearance; gleam.

víspera ['βispera] *sf* eve; (*fig*) approach. **en vísperas de** on the eve of.

vista ['βista] *sf* view; eyesight; appearance, look; gaze. **a primera vista** at first sight. **con vistas de** with a view to. **¡hasta la vista!** good-bye!

visto ['βisto] *adj* seen; obvious. **bien visto** approved of. **visto bueno** authorized. **visto que** seeing that.

vistoso [βis'toso] *adj* showy; (*fam*) loud.

visual [βi'swal] *adj* visual.

vital [βi'tal] *adj* vital. **vitalidad** *sf* vitality.

vitamina [βita'mina] *sf* vitamin.

vitela [βi'tela] *sf* vellum.

vitorear [βitore'ar] *v* shout, cheer, acclaim. **¡vítor!** bravo!

vítreo [βi'treo] *adj* vitreous. **vitrina** *sf* showcase.

vitriólico [βi'trjoliko] *adv* vitriolic. **vitriolo** *sm* vitriol.

vituperar [βitupe'rar] *v* vituperate; abuse; insult. **vituperación** *sf* blame.

viuda ['βjuða] *sf* widow. **viudo** *sm* widower. **viudez** *sf* widowhood.

vivaz [βi'βaθ] *adj* vivacious. **vivacidad** *sf* vivacity.

víveres ['βiβeres] *sm pl* provisions *pl*.

vivero [βi'βero] *sm* fishpond.

viveza [βi'βeθa] *sf* gaiety, liveliness.

vivienda [βi'βjenda] *sf* housing; dwelling, lodgings *pl*. **vividero** *adj* habitable.

vivificar [βiβifi'kar] *v* animate, bring to life.

vivir [βi'βir] *v* live. **¿quién vive?** who goes there? *sm* way of life.

vivisección [βiβisek'θjon] *sf* vivisection.

vivo ['βiβo] *adj* living, alive; vivid. **al vivo** to the life.

vizconde [βiθ'konde] *sm* viscount. **vizcondesa** *sf* viscountess.

vocablo [βo'kaβlo] *sm* word. **vocabulario** *sm* vocabulary.

vocación [βoka'θjon] *sf* vocation.

vocal [βo'kal] *adj* vocal. *sm* voter. *sf* vowel.

vocear [βoθe'ar] *v* bawl. **vocerío** *sm* bawling. **vocero** *sm* spokesman.

vociferar [βoθife'rar] *v* bawl; shout.

vocinglero [βoθin'glero] *adj* vociferous; loud-mouthed; talkative. **vocinglería** *sf* clamour, uproar.

volante [βo'lante] *adj* flying. *sm* steering-wheel; shuttlecock.

***volar** [βo'lar] *v* fly; blow up, explode. **volarse** *v* become furious.

volátil [βo'latil] *adj* volatile.

volcán [βol'kan] *sm* volcano. **volcánico** *adj* volcanic.

***volcar** [βol'kar] *v* upset; capsize. **volcarse** *v* fall over; bend over backwards.

volear [βole'ar] *v* volley. **voleo** *sm* volley.

volición [βoli'θjon] *sf* volition.

voltaje [βol'taxe] *sm* voltage. **voltio** *sm* volt.

voltear [βolte'ar] *v* overturn; revolve; tumble. **volteador, -a** *sm, sf* tumbler. **volteo** *sm* somersault.

voluble [βo'luβle] *adj* changeable. **volubilidad** *sf* changeable.

volumen [βolu'men] *sm* volume. **voluminoso** *adj* voluminous.

voluntad [βolun'taθ] *sf* volition; affection. **a voluntad** at will. **buena voluntad** goodwill.

voluntario [βolun'tarjo] *adj* voluntary. **voluntariedad** *sf* free will.

voluptuoso [βolup'twoso] *adj* voluptuous. **voluptuosidad** *sf* voluptuousness.

***volver** [βol'βer] *v* return; turn; turn over. **volver sobre sí** pull oneself together. **volverse** *v* become; go back. **volverse loco** go mad.

vomitar [βomi'tar] *v* vomit. **vómito** *sm* vomit.

voraz [βo'raθ] *adj* voracious. **voracidad** *sf* voracity.

vórtice ['βortiθe] *sm* vortex.

vosotros [βo'sotros] *pron pl* (*fam*) you.

votar [βo'tar] *v* vote. **votante** *s*(*m*+*f*) voter. **voto** *sm* vote; vow.

voz [βoθ] *sf* voice; shout; report. **a media voz** in a whisper. **dar voces** call out.

vuelco ['βwelko] *sm* upset; overturning.

vuelo ['βwelo] *sm* flight; flying; wing. **al vuelo** in flight. **en un vuelo** in a jiffy.

vuelta ['βwelta] *sf* turn; return; bend; reverse; recompense. **dar una vuelta** take a stroll. **estar de vuelta** be back.

vuestro ['βwestro] *pron* yours. *adj* your.

vulcanizar [βulkani'θar] *v* vulcanize.

vulgar [βul'gar] *adj* common; ordinary; vulgar. **el hombre vulgar** the common man.

vulnerar [βulne'rar] *v* wound. **vulnerabilidad** *sf* vulnerability. **vulnerable** *adj* vulnerable.

X

xilófono [ksi'lofono] *sm* xylophone.

Y

y [i] *conj* and.

ya [ja] *adv* already; now; yet; later. **ya que** since. **ya voy** I'm just coming.

yacimiento [jaθi'mjento] *sm* (*minerales*) bed. **yacente** *adj* recumbent.

yanqui [jan'ki] *adj, sm* (*fam*) Yankee.

yarda ['jarða] *sf* yard.

yate ['jate] *sm* yacht.

yedra ['jeðra] *sf* ivy.

yegua ['jegwa] *sf* mare.

yelmo ['jelmo] *sm* helmet.

yema ['jema] *sf* yolk; bud; button. **yema del dedo** tip of the finger.

yerba ['jerβa] *sf* grass; herb.

yermo ['jermo] *sm* waste land. *adj* barren; desert.

yerno ['jerno] *sm* son-in-law.

yerro ['jerro] *sm* error; mistake.

yeso ['jeso] *sm* gypsum; plaster; plaster cast.

yo [jo] *pron* I; myself; me; ego.

yodo ['joðo] *sm* iodine.

yogur [jo'gur] *sm* yoghurt.

yugo ['jugo] *sm* yoke.

yugular [jugu'lar] *adj* jugular.

yunque ['junke] *sm* anvil.

yunta ['junta] *sf* couple, pair; (*de bueys*) yoke.

yute ['jute] *sm* jute.

***yuxtaponer** [jukstapo'ner] *v* juxtapose. **yuxtaposición** *sf* juxtaposition. **yuxtapuesto** *adj* juxtaposed.

Z

zafar [θa'far] *v* loosen; free; clear; lighten. **zafarse** *v* run away.

zafio ['θafjo] *adj* uncouth.

zafiro [θa'firo] *sm* sapphire.

zaga ['θaga] *sf* rear; back.

zaguán [θa'gwan] *sm* entrance hall.

***zaherir** [θae'rir] *v* censure; mock; reproach.

zahurda [θa'urða] *sf* pigsty.

zalamería [θalame'ria] *sf* flattery. **zalamero, -a** *sm, sf* flatterer.

zamarra [θa'marra] *sf* sheepskin jacket.

zambo ['θambo] *adj* knock-kneed. *sm* half-breed; monkey.

***zambullir** [θambu'ʎir] *v* dive. **zambullida** *sf* dive.

zampar [θam'par] *v* polish off; shove in; devour. **zamparse** *v* rush.

zanahoria [θana'orja] *sf* carrot.

zancada [θan'kaða] *sf* long stride. **en dos zancadas** in a trice. **zancadilla** *sf* trip; trap. **echar la zancadilla** trip up.

zanco ['θanko] *sm* stilt.

zancudo [θan'kuðo] *adj* long-legged.

zángano ['θangano] *sm* (*insecto*) drone; (*fig*) loafer; fool.

zangolotear [θangolote'ar] *v* shake; fidget; rattle. **zangoloteo** *sm* shaking; rattling.

zanja ['θanxa] *sf* ditch; trench. **abrir las zanjas** lay the foundations.

zapa ['θapa] *sf* spade; trench. **zapapico** *sm* pickaxe. **zapar** *v* undermine.

zapatear [θapate'ar] *v* kick; ill-treat; tap-dance. **zapateado** *sm* Andalusian dance. **zapatería** *sf* shoe shop; shoe factory.

zapatero, -a *sm, sf* shoemaker. zapatilla *sf*
slipper. zapato *sm* shoe.
zar [θar] *sm* tsar.
zarandear [θarande'ar] *v* sift; winnow;
shake. zaranda *sf* sieve.
zaraza [θa'raθa] *sf* chintz.
zarcillo [θar'θiʎo] *sm* hoe; barrel hoop;
vine tendril; ear-ring.
zarco [θarko] *adj* (*ojos*) light blue.
zarpa ['θarpa] *v* claw; paw. echar la zarpa
grab hold. zarpar *v* weigh anchor.
zarpazo *sm* whack.
zarza ['θarθa] *sf* bramble, blackberry
bush. zarzamora *sf* (*fruto*) blackberry.
zarzo [θarθo] *sm* hurdle.
zarzuela [θar'θwela] *sf* light *or* comic
opera.
zeta ['θeta] *sf* letter *z*.
zigzaguear [θigθage'ar] *v* zigzag. zigzag
sm zigzag.
zinc [θink] *sm* zinc.
zócalo ['θokalo] *sm* plinth; skirting
board.
zodiaco [θo'ðjako] *sm* zodiac.
zona ['θona] *sf* zone; area. zona edificada
built-up area. zonas verdes green belt
sing.
zoología [θoolo'xia] *sf* zoology. zoológico

adj zoological. parque zoológico *sm* zoological gardens *pl*, zoo. zoólogo, -a *sm, sf*
zoologist.
zoquete [θo'kete] *sm* chunk of wood;
piece of stale bread; (*fam*) blockhead.
zorro [θorro] *sm* fox. zorra *sf* vixen. zor-
rera *sf* foxhole.
zozobrar [θoθo'βrar] *v* wreck; capsize;
founder; (*fig*) worry. zozobra *sf* founder-
ing; worry.
zueco ['θweko] *sm* clog; galosh.
zumbar [θum'bar] *v* buzz; hum; strike;
whack. zumbarse de make fun of.
zumbido *sm* humming; buzzing.
zumbón [θum'bon], -a *sm, sf* jester; tease.
adj waggish.
zumo ['θumo] *sm* juice. zumoso *adj* juicy.
zurcir [θur'θir] *v* darn. zurcido *sm* darn;
stitch. zurcidura *sf* darning.
zurdo ['θurðo], -a *sm, sf* left-handed person. *adj* left-handed.
zurrar [θur'rar] *v* thrash; (*cuero*) dress;
curry. zurra *sf* tanning; thrashing. zur-
rador *sm* tanner.
zurrón [θur'ron] *sm* leather bag; husk.
zutano ['θu'tano], -a *sm, sf* so-and-so. fulano, zutano y mengano Tom, Dick, and
Harry.